Human Neuroanatomy

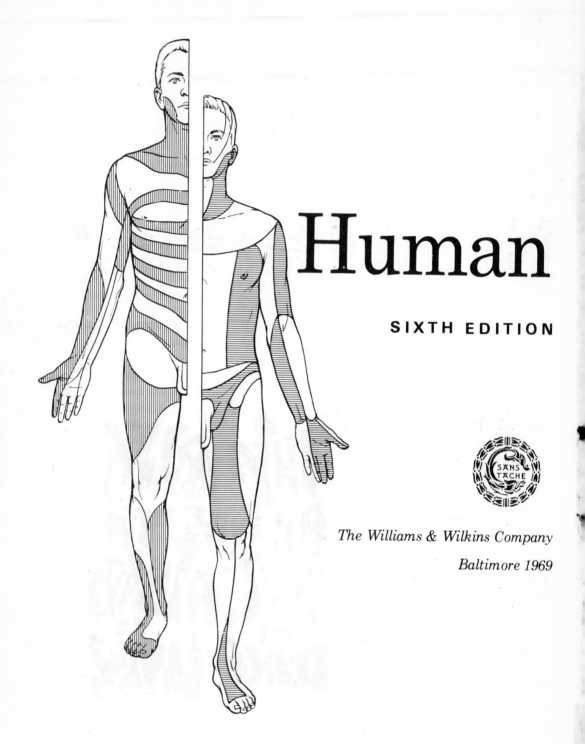

Human

SIXTH EDITION

The Williams & Wilkins Company

Baltimore 1969

Neuroanatomy

(FORMERLY STRONG AND ELWYN'S HUMAN NEUROANATOMY)

RAYMOND C. TRUEX, A.B., M.S., Ph.D.

Professor of Anatomy, Temple University, School of Medicine

MALCOLM B. CARPENTER, A.B., M.D.

Professor of Anatomy, College of Physicians and Surgeons, Columbia University

Published May, 1943
Reprinted December, 1943
Reprinted December, 1945
Reprinted December, 1946
Second Edition, 1948
Reprinted June, 1951
Third Edition, 1953
Fourth Edition, 1959
Reprinted October, 1960
Reprinted August, 1962
Fifth Edition, 1964
Reprinted July, 1965
Sixth Edition, 1969
Reprinted April, 1970

Copyright © , 1969
The Williams & Wilkins Company
428 East Preston Street
Baltimore, Maryland 21202 U.S.A.

Made in the United States of America

Library of Congress Catalog Card Number 69-16601

Composed and Printed at
Waverly Press, Inc.
Mount Royal and Guilford Avenues
Baltimore, Maryland 21202 U.S.A.

Preface to the Sixth Edition

This edition comes at a time when most American medical schools are evaluating, proposing, or initiating new curricula. Curricular innovations are designed to provide future physicians with both a more integrated program in broad aspects of medicine, and specialized training and experience in a field of the student's choice. While the basic medical sciences will continue to form the foundation of medical education, as they have in the past, they will be taught in closer relationship with the clinical disciplines. This relationship will extend not only throughout the medical school years, but probably into residency training programs. Considerable thought will be given to the selection of core material in the basic medical sciences. Since few courses dealing with the structure and function of the nervous system will be identical, and a variety of new elective courses will be offered to students, there will be a need for a reasonably comprehensive student textbook. The authors have attempted to provide the student with a textbook of neuroanatomy that might be expected to meet these requirements.

The sixth edition has undergone extensive revision and reorganization. The chapter sequence has been revised so that the gross anatomy of the nervous system is introduced earlier, and all material dealing with the blood supply of the central nervous system has been incorporated within a single chapter. The development and the histogenesis of the nervous system have been consolidated into one chapter. The chapter on the autonomic nervous system now precedes chapters dealing with the detailed study of the central nervous system. The longest and most difficult chapter for students (The Diencephalon and Corpus Striatum) has been divided into three chapters of more reasonable length. The atlas section has been enlarged and now consists of 24 full color plates of transverse sections stained by the Klüver and Barrera ('53) technic, and photographs of 8 sagittal sections stained by the Weigert technic. Over one hundred and sixty new and revised illustrations have been added in various chapters, many of them in color.

Extensive revision and rewriting were done in all chapters. The authors have continued to use the Paris Nomina Anatomica (PNA) in its amended form as adopted by the International Anatomical Nomenclature Committee (1965). Responsibility for editorial revision of different chapters was divided as in the fifth edition. Professor Truex edited chapters 1 to 3, and 5 through 12. Professor Carpenter edited chapters 4, and 13 through 22. Additions to the atlas section were drawn by Marjorie Stodgell, Head of the Medical Art Department of Hahnemann Medical College, under the guidance of Professor Truex. New and revised illustrations in the chapters edited by Professor Truex were prepared by Marjorie Stodgell and

Crystel Lazo; new and revised illustrations in the chapters edited by Professor Carpenter were done by Robert J. Demarest of the Department of Anatomy, College of Physicians and Surgeons, Columbia University. The authors acknowledge with deep appreciation the skills of the medical artists whose talents have contributed so much to the concepts presented in the text. The photographic assistance of Mr. Jack Taylor, Temple University School of Medicine and of Mr. Antonio B. Pereira of Columbia University is gratefully acknowledged.

We also are indebted to our colleagues at our respective medical schools for the valuable suggestions, criticisms and materials used in the preparation of this text: At Temple University, School of Medicine, Drs. R. J. Troyer, S. S. Philips, N. B. Bates, Mrs. M. Q. Smythe and Mrs. M. J. Taylor; at the College of Physicians and Surgeons, Columbia University, Drs. M. B. Bunge, R. P. Bunge, E. W. Dempsey, S. A. Luse, F. A. Mettler, C. R. Noback, J. E. Shriver, and Mrs. Greta Katzauer. We are grateful to Dr. J. B. Angevine of the University of Arizona, Dr. C. A. Fox of Wayne State University, Dr. O. Hassler of the University of Umeå (Sweden), Dr. William R. Kennedy, University of Minnesota, Dr. Henry J. Ralston, III, of Stanford University, and Dr. Joseph G. Wood, University of Texas at San Antonio, for illustrations used in the text. The cooperation of the C. V. Mosby Company, Rockefeller University Press, Oxford University Press, Elsevier Publishing Company, American Physiological Society and the Wistar Institute of Anatomy and Biology in granting permission to use certain illustrations is acknowledged with gratitude. Special acknowledgment must go to Mrs. Ruth Gutmann for secretarial and editorial assistance, and for the meticulous supervision of the bibliography and index.

The authors are deeply indebted to the publishers for their continued confidence, encouragement, and many courtesies extending over a considerable period of time.

Raymond C. Truex
Malcolm B. Carpenter

Preface to First Edition

Neurology, more perhaps than any other branch of medicine, is dependent on an accurate knowledge of anatomy as a basis for the intelligent diagnosis and localization of neural disturbances. This book, the result of many years of neuroanatomical teaching, is intended to supply this basic anatomical need, to give the student and physician a thorough and clear presentation of the structural mechanisms of the human nervous system together with some understanding of their functional and clinical significance. It is an attempt to link structure and function into a dynamic pattern without sacrificing anatomical detail.

The book is a human neuroanatomy sufficiently rich in content to obviate the necessity of constantly consulting larger anatomical texts. It may be conveniently divided into two parts. The first part (Chapters I–VIII) is concerned with the general organization and meaning of the nervous system, its embryology and histological structure, and with some fundamental neurological problems as they apply to man. This is followed by a discussion of the organization and segmental distribution of the peripheral nerve elements, including an analysis of the functional components of the spinal nerves and of the various receptors and effectors. If these earlier chapters are perhaps more extensive than in most other texts, it is due to the conviction that the book should be complete in itself, and also that a knowledge of these preliminaries is essential for an understanding of the complex machinery of the spinal cord and brain.

The second and larger part (Chapters IX–XX) is devoted to the architectonics of the central nervous system and may be regarded as "applied neuroanatomy." Special features of this part are the many fine photographs, both gross and microscopic, of the human brain and spinal cord, the great wealth of anatomical detail, and the discussion of the structural mechanisms in the light of clinical experience. While the individual portions of the nervous system are treated separately, an attempt has been made to achieve organic structural continuity by judicious repetition and overlapping and by constant reference to related topics already familiar to the student from previous chapters. The plan of exposition is substantially the same for each topic. The gross structure and relationships are concisely but thoroughly reviewed with the aid of clear and graphic illustrations. The internal structure is then presented in detail, usually based on a carefully graded series of fine and clearly labeled microphotographs of human material. At each level the student is familiarized with the exact location, extent and relationships of the various structures seen in the section. Finally the anatomical features of each part are reviewed more comprehensively as three-dimensional structural mechanisms, with a full discussion of their connections and clinical significance. We believe that this treatment will make the complicated structural details alive and interesting to the student. The illustrations are not segregated in the back of the book in the form of an atlas but are scattered in the text, in proper relation to the levels studied.

Besides the many original illustrations, a number of others selected from various and duly acknowledged sources have been completely redrawn and relabeled for the sake of clarity and simplicity. All the illustrations, whether original or borrowed, have been executed by Frances H. Elwyn to whose skill and patience the authors are deeply indebted. We are also indebted to Dr. H. Alsop Riley for the use of several microphotographs; to Drs. R. C. Truex and Benjamin Salzer for the reading of several chapters; and especially to Dr. Otto Marburg for his many stimulating discussions and suggestions and for his critical reading of the chapters on the mesencephalon, diencephalon, and cerebral hemispheres. Thanks are also due to Rosette Spoerri for her competent help in preparing the manuscript and bibliography.

The authors cannot express too strongly their obligation to the publishers for their continuous courtesy and cooperation in all matters, and for their infinite patience in waiting for a manuscript long overdue.

Adolph Elwyn
Oliver S. Strong

Contents

Chapter 5

Development and Histogenesis of the Nervous System   **89**

Chapter 6

The Neuron   **107**

Chapter 7

Neuroglia, Ependyma and Choroid Plexus   **148**

Chapter 8

Peripheral Nerves and Their Ganglia   **164**

Chapter 9

Peripheral Terminations of Afferent and Efferent Nerve Fibers   **173**

CHAPTER 1

Origin And Composition Of The Nervous System

In the never ending history of life, the human nervous system represents man's greatest heritage from the ancient past, and the culmination of innumerable evolutionary changes. Through a continuous series of adaptations to environment and increased functional needs, organisms developed more efficient nervous systems capable of interpreting and responding to a variety of physical and chemical stimuli. Man, possessing the ability to reason, has evolved the most elaborate neural mechanism of any living creature. The human system consists of a *central nervous system*, the brain and spinal cord; a *peripheral nervous system*, which includes the cranial and spinal nerves; and an *autonomic* or involuntary system. A brief survey of some representative lower animals will emphasize their kinship to the mammals and provide a keener appreciation of this extraordinary system in man.

Microscopic unicellular animals are unique in that the protoplasm performs all the necessary life activities, including irritability, motility, and adaptation of behavior to the surrounding environment. It is well known that Paramecium can avoid mechanical obstacles, excessive temperatures, and irritating chemicals by virtue of the rhythmic movement of surface cilia. The control center for the coordinated beating of the cilia is located near the gullet, and if this region is destroyed the animal loses control of all movements. Although the protozoa manifest the basic properties of the higher forms, they possess no specialized sensory or motor cells. It will be recalled that nerve cells (neurons) are the structural and functional units of all nervous systems. Each neuron has a nucleated cell body (perikaryon) and one or many processes. The processes include an axon and one or more dendrites. (Fig. 6-1). The processes are cytoplasmic extensions of the cell body and may terminate near or at some distance from the cell body. Details of neuron structure are presented in Chapter 6.

PRIMITIVE NEURAL MECHANISMS

It is in the aquatic coelenterates that a primitive neural mechanism is first observed. As examples, the hydra, jelly fish, and sea anemone have a layer of modified external cells (ectoderm) and an internal layer (endoderm) that lines a hollow digestive cavity (Fig. 1–1A). Slender sensory cells are found between the columnar epithelial cells, and the latter have fine contractile fibrils in their bases. In the jelly-like stratum between the two cell layers of the hydra are nerve cells whose processes communicate with the surface sensory cells and also send

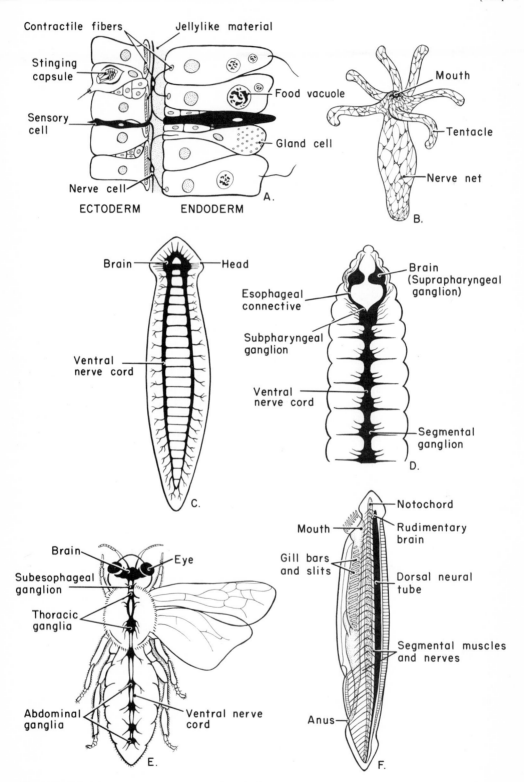

Fig. 1–1. Primitive nervous systems. *A* and *B*, hydra; *C*, planaria; *D*, earthworm; *E*, bee; *F*, amphioxus (modified from Buchsbaum, '48, courtesy of the University of Chicago Press).

fibrils to the contractile bases of the epithelial cells. Thus a network of nerve cells extends throughout the entire animal. The *nerve net* (Fig. 1-1*B*) is thought to consist of separate neural units, so that a nerve impulse must pass across definite breaks at the junction of two nerve cells. Such junctions or *synapses* between two nerve cells are characteristic of more highly developed nervous systems. Synapses of higher forms are polarized, and so constituted that a nerve impulse can pass across them in only one direction. However, in the nerve net of the hydra it is possible for impulses to cross the synapses in either direction and there are no discrete pathways. Impulses travel slowly and in a diffuse manner over this primitive nervous network, for there is little evidence of a "control center" or ganglionic brain.

Centralization. Representing further development, the flat worms are characterized by body symmetry, a head with photosensitive spots and other sense organs, the appearance of mesoderm with true muscle cells, and a more refined organization of tissues into organ systems. Planaria is an ideal example of this lowly phylum, for in the head the nervous tissue is concentrated into a bilobed mass called the brain, or head ganglion (Fig. 1-1*C*). Two strands or cords of nerve cells and fibers extend backward from the brain beneath the gastrovascular cavity, near the ventral surface of the animal. The brain and ladder-type nerve cords mark the first appearance of a central nervous system, although the nerve net of lower forms still persists. The brain is chiefly a sensory relay center that transmits impulses from the eyes and sense organs of the head region. The brain is not necessary for coordinated muscular activity, for a planaria deprived of its brain can still move along in a coordinated fashion. Because of its eyes, numerous sense organs, and centralized nervous system, this little animal manifests more rapid responses, independent locomotion, and a more varied behavior than does the hydra.

Segmentation. In adaptation to its subterranean life, the common earthworm has lost the prominent sense organ and eyes of the head region. At the same time the body segments have become streamlined as in other burrowing animals (Fig. 1-1*D*). The brain, or suprapharyngeal ganglion, remains essentially a sensory relay center for microscopic surface cells that are sensitive to light, touch, and probably chemicals. A worm deprived of this head ganglion shows little change in behavior and movement. A smaller subpharyngeal ganglion is interposed between the brain above and a ventrally placed double nerve cord that extends to the posterior end of the animal. If the lower subpharyngeal ganglion is removed, a worm no longer eats and fails to burrow in a normal fashion. In the earthworm, each segmental ganglion of the nerve cord serves as a center which receives afferent impulses from sensory cells in the skin. Each ganglion also sends efferent impulses that coordinate the alternate contractions of well developed circular and longitudinal muscle layers. The intricate segmental neural apparatus of the earthworm presumably possesses all the components of a *simple reflex arc*, namely, the ability to respond *segmentally* and *involuntarily* to an appropriate stimulus. Larger nerve fibers within the ventral nerve cord extend over many segments and provide collateral branches to each of the segmental ganglia. Such giant fibers permit the longitudinal layers of muscle in all segments of the worm to contract simultaneously. This sudden contraction of the whole body is a stereotyped response that can be elicited by strong stimulation of any region. In such emergencies the simple reflexes of each segment become incorporated into a *mass response*, so that *intersegmental reflexes* take precedence over the local *segmental reflexes*. The coordination between cranial and caudal body segments also is evident to all who have observed the locomotion of an earthworm. The appearance and interplay of segmental and intersegmental reflexes in a centralized nervous system is of the utmost importance, for such simple reflexes form the neural basis of spinal cord activity in man. Of special significance is the nervous control of definitive muscle layers. Once this intimate relationship is established, it becomes more elaborate and refined in higher forms.

The honey bee is included here as an illustrious example of the arthropod body plan (Fig. 1–1E). The individual body segments of lower forms are here incorporated into body regions—a head, a thorax, and an abdomen. The head now has movable mouth parts, simple and compound eyes capable of discerning light and movement, and a pair of jointed antennae sensitive to touch and chemical odors. The thorax provides attachment for two pairs of wings and three pairs of jointed legs. The appearance of the head and thorax necessitated alterations in both muscular and nervous systems, namely, splitting of muscle layers into discrete muscle bundles and consolidation of neural elements into larger nerve ganglia adjacent to the major muscle masses (Fig. 1–1E). Synchronous wing movements and locomotion of jointed appendages are both attained by many of the insects through this refined *neuromuscular mechanism*. The brain has ceased to be a mere sensory relay center. Now a greater number of response patterns have been added, and the bee has a measure of social and adaptive behavior as an integral part of instinctive behavior. All of the "specializations" in the organ systems attain their highest invertebrate development in the lowly arthropods, which represent the peak of invertebrate evolution. A voluminous amount of very basic information has been gleaned from a variety of fascinating studies on the neural mechanisms of the invertebrates. Recently these studies have been comprehensively reviewed by Bullock and Horridge ('65).

Neural Tube. At this point it is desirable to recall the morphology of the primitive chordates. These unusual animals occupy a unique position midway between the invertebrates and the vertebrates. They all have, at some time in their life history, a cartilage-like bar, the *notochord;* a *tubular nervous system* located dorsal to the digestive tract; and pharyngeal gill bars and gill slits. Of the three subgroups (amphioxi, tunicates, and acorn worms), the amphioxus is perhaps the best known and the most like higher vertebrates (Fig. 1–1F). Although of questionable ancestry, this animal is included because it illustrates advanced (vertebrate) and regressive (invertebrate) structural changes simultaneously. Hence it possesses a hollow, dorsally placed neural tube with segmented musculature, but no definitive brain, eyes, or special sense organs, and it has a very primitive digestive tract. The amphioxus also has more gill slits and gill bars than fish of higher forms, yet it has no cranial nerves or paired fins.

Thus by a gradual process of centralization, a spinal cord has evolved from the primitive nerve net. This spinal cord in higher animals constitutes the primitive and most caudal portion of the central nervous system. The fact that the spinal cord developed anatomically in conjunction with, and assumed functional control over, the segmental muscles of the trunk is again emphasized.

Spinal Nerves. In the lower vertebrates (e.g., lamprey eel), the sensory fibers are collected into separate bundles that course between the myotomes to enter the posterior surface of the spinal cord (Fig. 1–2A). Motor nerve cells located in the gray matter of the spinal cord send their processes (*axons*) out through the anterior surface of the spinal cord as ventral motor nerves. Each motor nerve enters the medial surface of the corresponding myotome and immediately breaks up into smaller branches. In this way the *dorsal sensory* and *ventral motor* nerves alternate with each other as they enter and leave the spinal cord. In all higher vertebrates the sensory and motor fibers are consolidated into a single nerve trunk, serving each segment of the cord.

The bipolar sensory nerve cells of the invertebrate are scattered in the periphery near the receptor endings (Figs. 1–1A; 1–3, A and C). This arrangement still persists in some cranial nerves of the vertebrates (Fig. 1–3, B and D). However, the *sensory* cells of all spinal nerves have migrated toward the spinal cord in most vertebrates and man (Fig. 1–3E).

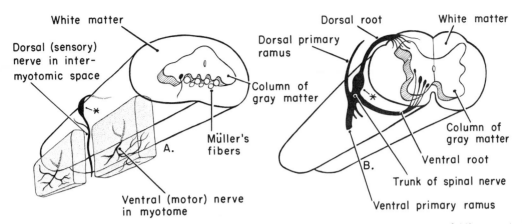

Fig. 1-2. Diagram of spinal nerves and spinal cord. In the amphioxus and the lamprey eel (*A*), separate dorsal and ventral roots alternate as they arise from the spinal cord. In most higher vertebrates (*B*) and in all mammals, the dorsal (sensory) and ventral (motor) roots are combined to form a single trunk. An *asterisk* (*) indicates the dorsal root ganglion in both diagrams.

The bipolar sensory cells have become unipolar neurons (Figs. 5-4, 5-5, and 6-1*A*), and these assembled masses of nerve cells outside the central nervous system form the dorsal root ganglia of the spinal nerves (Fig. 1-2*B*).

VERTEBRATE NERVOUS SYSTEM

The simple relationship between myotome and ventral motor nerve is continued in the vertebrates. Each spinal nerve divides into a *dorsal primary ramus*, which provides sensory and motor fibers to the integument and muscles of the back, and a larger *ventral primary ramus*, which provides like fibers to the skin and muscles of the anterolateral trunk (Figs. 1-2*B* and 8-1). The "cord segment-spinal nerve-myotome" distribution is repeated bilaterally for each segment of the body, proceeding from the cranial to the caudal end of the spinal cord. Some animals have only a few paired spinal nerves and body segments; others have many (e.g., frog, 10; man, 31; dog, 36; cat, 38; horse, 42).

Plexus Formation. In vertebrates with fins or appendages the simple arrangement of the ventral primary ramus becomes more complex in the regions where the limb buds develop. Muscles and connective tissue derived from each myotome retain nerve fibers from the original segmental spinal nerve. In a similar manner, the skin overlying the appendage also keeps its segmental sensory nerve fibers (Figs. 10-1 and 10-2). As a result, the ventral primary rami of several spinal nerves unite with each other to form a "plexus" in the region of a limb bud or appendage (e.g., Figs. 10-6 and 10-9). The large muscle mass in an appendage attract a greater number of sensory and motor nerves. As a result, both the spinal nerves and the segments of the spinal cord are considerably enlarged in the regions of the limb plexuses (e.g., cervical and lumbar enlargements in man, Fig. 3-1).

The branches of each plexus (*peripheral nerves*) then distribute sensory fibers to the original segment of skin (*dermatome*) and motor fibers to the original segment of muscle mesoderm (*myotome*). Two, three, or more myotomes usually contribute mesoderm to a single muscle in mammals. This fusion of segmental mesoderm explains why most limb muscles in man receive motor nerve fibers from two, three, or even more segmental nerves (Figs. 10-4 and 10-5).

Cephalization. Soon after the spinal cord was evolved, a large number of nerve cells accumulated on its cephalic end. Hypothetically, this diffuse network of cells and fibers might be considered

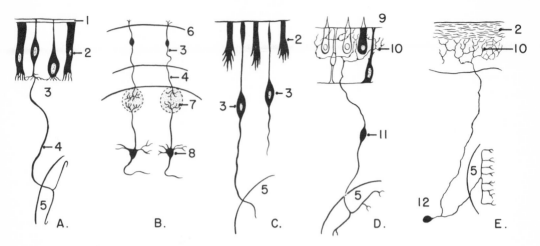

Fig. 1–3. Location and shape of sensory neurons in different animals (modified from Retzius, 1892): *A*, earthworm (Lumbricus); *B*, man; *C*, mollusks (Limax); *D*, man; *E*, vertebrates. The neurosensory cells of lower forms (*A* and *C*) are compared with similar neural structures of man (*B*, *D*, and *E*.) *1*, Cuticula; *2*, surface epithelial cells; *3*, neurosensory cell; *4*, axon or central process of sensory cell; *5*, central nervous system; *6*, olfactory mucous membrane; *7*, glomerulus near periphery of olfactory bulb; *8*, mitral cell; *9*, hair cells in macula; *10*, peripheral nerve terminals of sensory neuron; *11*, bipolar sensory neuron in vestibular ganglion (of Scarpa); *12*, unipolar sensory neuron of dorsal root ganglion.

analogous to the *"reticular formation."* These nerve cells regulated the activity of spinal motor neurons, which in turn controlled groups of segmental muscles. A modified reticular substrate is present in the nervous system of all higher vertebrates. In man this diffuse system exists throughout all levels of the *brain stem*, and functionally it is capable of modifying the reflex activity of the spinal motor neurons. Additional groups of nerve cells evolved within the reticular formation very early in vertebrate evolution. Some of the new clusters of cells function either as relay *nuclei* or end stations for incoming sensory fibers of taste, touch, vision, hearing, and equilibrium. Other central nerve cells related to cranial nerves were concerned with reflex control of visceral motor activity in the circulatory, digestive, and respiratory systems. Another new group of larger motor neurons appeared in the brain stem to assume control of the skeletal muscles of the eyes and the tongue. Other motor neurons supplied the striated muscles derived from the mesoderm of the branchial arches.

Brain. All of these nerve cell and fiber additions to the cephalic end of the spinal cord contribute to the formation of a brain stem, which in mammals is subdivided for purposes of description into four parts. The *myelencephalon* or *medulla oblongata*, the most caudal segment of the brain stem, is continuous with the spinal cord. A second portion, the *metencephalon*, is composed of the *pons* and *cerebellum*. The third segment is designated as the *mesencephalon* or midbrain, while the fourth and most cranial portion of the brain stem is the *diencephalon*. The *telencephalon*, which is *not* a part of the brain stem, expands to cover most of the brain stem structures. The telencephalon is composed of the cerebral hemispheres and the basal ganglia. Each of these units of the brain have special anatomical features, subdivisions, and neural functions. The relative sizes of these brain subdivisions and some of their specific functions are indicated in Figure 1–5.

The action of each portion of the brain stem is integrated with the functional activity of the more cranial brain segments by *ascending fiber pathways*. Through these pathways each of the brain segments contributes information to all higher levels. In a similar manner, higher regions of the brain stem are connected to more caudally placed segments by means of *descending fiber pathways*. Such descending tracts subject each of the lower segments to a measure of modified activity (inhibition and facilitation). For example, the cerebral cortex represents the highest level of sensory and motor integration. Normally it regulates neural activities within the brain stem and spinal cord. The pons and medulla, acting alone, exercise some control over neural activity in the spinal cord. If isolated from all higher portions of the brain stem, the spinal cord can maintain a measure of segmental reflex activity.

Generally speaking, there is a correlation between the size of a particular part of an animal's brain and its importance in the life of that animal. Six representative brains are illustrated in Figure 1–4. When examined as a series, they demonstrate clearly that the vertebrate brain has evolved by a gradual "cephalic shift" of function from the lower brain stem (fish) to the higher cerebral cortex (man). It also is evident that certain neural structures attain considerable size and obvious functional importance in lower forms, but become proportionately smaller and therefore less conspicuous in higher forms (e.g., olfactory bulb, optic lobe). However, once a neural structure becomes incorporated into the vertebrate brain, it usually remains in higher animals even though reduced in size and functional significance (e.g., olfactory mechanism and epiphysis of man).

The primitive cerebellum developed in conjunction with the lateral line system, semicircular canals, and maculae of the vestibular system. It assumes significance as a center for the reflex regulation of muscle tonus and muscular coordination. One can better appreciate the need for a highly developed cerebellar apparatus in fish and birds if one recalls that these animals move in three dimensions and must balance their bodies in a fluid or gaseous environment. Reptiles and most land-dwelling mammals, on the other hand, move primarily in two dimensions, but they still require a cerebellum for muscular coordination (synergy).

The size of the optic nerve and lobe (Fig. 1–4) show that visual stimuli play an important role in the life of most vertebrates, particularly birds and mammals. In man the optic relay centers and visual cortex cannot be seen in a lateral view of the brain.

Smell is probably the most important sense in some lower vertebrates (fish, frog, alligator). Some mammals, however, still have a very acute sense of smell (rat, cat, dog, ungulates), and in these animals the olfactory areas of the brain are more prominent. In birds and man the sense of smell is poorly developed and this area of the brain is very small.

Masses of nerve cells buried deep in the cerebral hemispheres comprise the basal ganglia, which are subcortical telencephalic structures. Since they are adjacent to the diencephalon, they likewise become overlayed by the expanding cerebral hemispheres in the brains of higher vertebrates. Both the diencephalon and the basal ganglia therefore are hidden in higher forms and cannot be identified in surface views of the brain. However, the basal ganglia are quite prominent internal features in brains of lower vertebrates (fish, birds). Most of the bird cerebrum (goose, Fig. 1–4) is composed of these basal ganglia covered by thin layers of white matter and cortex. The thalamus (part of the diencephalon) of fish and birds serves as a center for sensory integration. The adjacent subcortical telencephalic masses of gray matter are the precursors of the mammalian basal ganglia. The cells of the avian entopeduncular nucleus (homologue of the medial segment of the globus pallidus) serve as connections between the primitive forebrain and the diffuse descending motor pathways of the midbrain (Kappers et al. '36, Fox et al. '66). This diffuse motor system dominates and varies the level of responses of the more caudal motor centers in the brain stem and spinal cord.

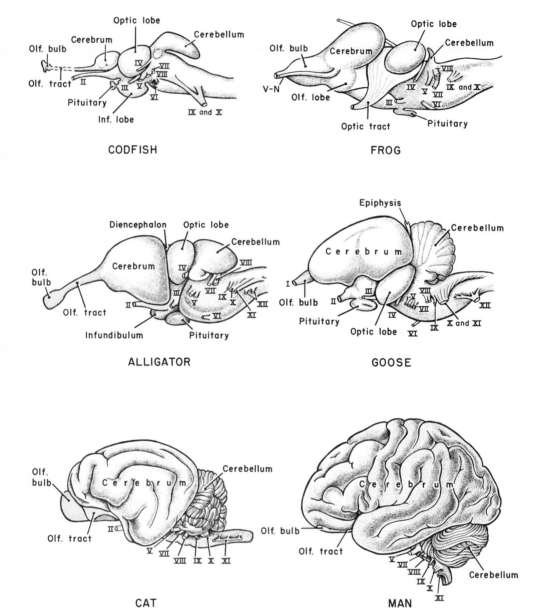

FIG. 1-4. A representative series of vertebrate brains

Through such circuits, the primitive globus pallidus is able to initiate and maintain the automatic, stereotyped basic movements of swimming and flying so essential to the fish and bird. This old motor system still functions in man but new neural circuits have been added. However, it still participates in the smooth blending of movement patterns, particularly the semiautomatic, synchronized group actions of muscles (Fig. 1-5).

Cerebral Cortex. As the olfactory areas of the cerebral cortex (*paleopallium*) diminished in reptiles, birds, and man (Fig. 1-4), an extensive new cortex was elaborated (*neocortex, neopallium*). As the cerebrum increased in size, it became necessary to enlarge the surface area, yet keep the brain volume within reasonable limits. This was accomplished by the formation of folds or convolutions. In the lower mammals convolutions are

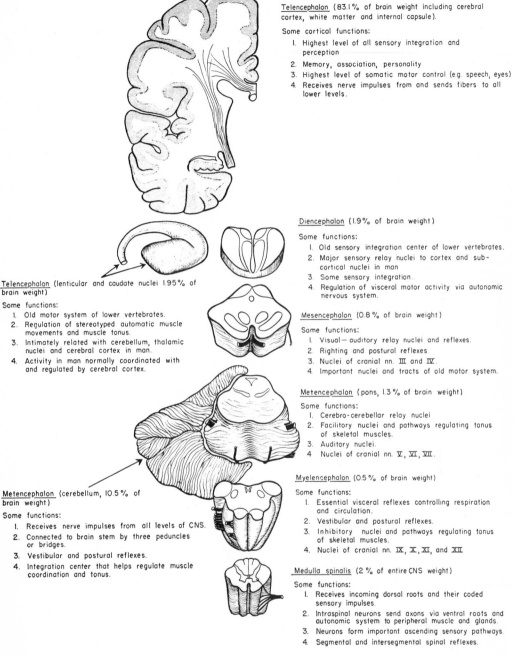

Telencephalon (83.1% of brain weight including cerebral cortex, white matter and internal capsule).

Some cortical functions:
1. Highest level of all sensory integration and perception
2. Memory, association, personality
3. Highest level of somatic motor control (e.g. speech, eyes)
4. Receives nerve impulses from and sends fibers to all lower levels.

Telencephalon (lenticular and caudate nuclei 1.95% of brain weight)

Some functions:
1. Old motor system of lower vertebrates.
2. Regulation of stereotyped automatic muscle movements and muscle tonus.
3. Intimately related with cerebellum, thalamic nuclei and cerebral cortex in man.
4. Activity in man normally coordinated with and regulated by cerebral cortex.

Diencephalon (1.9% of brain weight)

Some functions:
1. Old sensory integration center of lower vertebrates.
2. Major sensory relay nuclei to cortex and sub-cortical nuclei in man.
3. Some sensory integration.
4. Regulation of visceral motor activity via autonomic nervous system.

Mesencephalon (0.8% of brain weight)

Some functions:
1. Visual — auditory relay nuclei and reflexes.
2. Righting and postural reflexes
3. Nuclei of cranial nn. III and IV.
4. Important nuclei and tracts of old motor system.

Metencephalon (pons, 1.3% of brain weight)

Some functions:
1. Cerebro-cerebellar relay nuclei
2. Facilitory nuclei and pathways regulating tonus of skeletal muscles.
3. Auditory nuclei.
4. Nuclei of cranial nn. V, VI, VII.

Metencephalon (cerebellum, 10.5% of brain weight)

Some functions:
1. Receives nerve impulses from all levels of CNS.
2. Connected to brain stem by three peduncles or bridges.
3. Vestibular and postural reflexes.
4. Integration center that helps regulate muscle coordination and tonus.

Myelencephalon (0.5% of brain weight)

Some functions:
1. Essential visceral reflexes controlling respiration and circulation.
2. Vestibular and postural reflexes.
3. Inhibitory nuclei and pathways regulating tonus of skeletal muscles.
4. Nuclei of cranial nn. IX, X, XI, and XII

Medulla spinalis (2% of entire CNS weight)

Some functions:
1. Receives incoming dorsal roots and their coded sensory impulses.
2. Intraspinal neurons send axons via ventral roots and autonomic system to peripheral muscle and glands.
3. Neurons form important ascending sensory pathways.
4. Segmental and intersegmental spinal reflexes.

FIG. 1–5. Schema showing subdivisions, weights, and some functions of the human nervous system. (Weight of each subdivision based on data of Jenkins and Truex, '63.)

few, but in the human and cetacean brain they reach a prodigious number.

This elaborate convoluted mantle of layered gray matter assumed control over the more caudal sensory and motor systems of the thalamus and basal ganglia. Specialized areas were promptly differentiated within the neocortex, and the thalamus then projected its sensory messages (nerve impulses) from lower levels to a new sensory (*somesthetic*) area of the cortex. In a similar manner other thalamic fibers relayed visual and auditory impulses to special areas of the cerebral cortex. Ascending fibers within the diffuse reticular formation of the brain stem also relay impulses to the overlying cortex.

Of necessity, a new motor area developed in the cerebral cortex. The new motor pathways (*corticobulbar* and *corticospinal tracts*) established intimate neural connections with the older pallidal motor system and sent descending fibers to all the cranial and spinal motor nerve cells. By the integration, control, and use of pre-existing neural mechanisms of the basal ganglia, cerebellum, and reticular formation, this new motor system provided for smooth voluntary muscle movements. Both individual muscles and groups of muscles could thus be controlled to produce fine isolated movement, as well as the more complicated muscle actions common in the daily life of man. Although these intricate muscle actions are initiated and controlled by the motor neurons of the new motor system, one must remember that each of the older motor systems is contributing an essential component that is often hidden or masked.

In addition to the specialized projection and reception areas, the neocortex of higher mammals has perfected neural mechanisms for the more complex correlation and discrimination of sensory impulses. There is also greater storage and utilization of previous sensory and motor reactions. This sensory neural agency may be termed *associative memory* and the motor responses *mnemonic* (memory) *reactions*.

The receptors of the nose, eye, and ear were of primary importance in the development of mnemonic reactions. The centers for these three great senses are already indicated by the three primary expansions of the developing brain: the forebrain expansion for the nose; diencephalon and midbrain expansions for the eye and the ear; and the hindbrain enlargement or cerebellum for the vestibular part of the ear (Fig. 5-9). These three cephalic segments continue to en-

large and become highly differentiated in man. They receive stimuli from other parts of the body and become important coordinating areas within the brain. Cortex, basal ganglia, thalamus, midbrain, cerebellum, and reticular formation are often called *suprasegmental* in contrast to the segmental (spinal cord) part of the central nervous system. The spinal segments are more intimately related to the peripheral nerves and contain the simpler and more fundamental neural mechanisms.

Each of the old and new sensory and motor units thus were blended into the remarkable nervous system found in man (Fig. 1-5). The primate nervous system is a composite of ascending *integrated levels*, with vital nerve pathways connecting them together (e.g., spinal cord level; medulla-pons-cerebellum level; mesencephalon; diencephalon-basal ganglia level; cortical level). The normal interplay between these neural levels may be disrupted by injury to one or more parts resulting in abnormal function and behavior. Signs and symptoms may appear which represent an irritative lesion or discharging locus, or actual *deficits* due to loss of essential nerve cells and fibers at a higher level. *Release phenomena* also may appear. They represent a return to poorly controlled nervous activity in the older motor systems due to complete or partial destruction of suprasegmental motor centers.

Peripheral Nervous System. Visceral motor centers are present in the spinal cord, brain stem, and higher levels of most vertebrates. Such nerve cells within the central nervous system and in outlying ganglia form a two-neuron visceral motor pathway for the reflex control of all smooth muscle, cardiac muscle, and glandular epithelium of the body. This diffuse involuntary neural mechanism is designated the *autonomic nervous system* (Fig. 11-1). The cranial and spinal nerves, including elements of the autonomic, comprise the *peripheral nervous system*. Through peripheral nerves, the brain and spinal cord receive all incoming sensory information and transmit all outgoing motor commands. Special attention is focused on those motor cells of the brain stem and spinal cord whose *axons* travel in either the cranial or spinal nerves. These efferent nerve cells and their axons constitute the last neural link or *final common pathway* between the central nervous system and the skeletal muscles and visceral structures of the body.

Although we are primarily concerned here with the nervous system of man, we should be ever mindful that this system evolved through a series of increasingly complex modifications imposed upon the simpler nervous systems of our remote forebears. During embryonic development, the human nervous system repeats many of these ancestral stages. Indeed, the older systems appear first, and many of the more recent neural acquisitions are not functionally mature in man and other mammals even at the time of birth (Kaes, '07; Truex et al., '55; Yakovlev and Lecours, '67; Parmelee et al. '67).

In studying neuroanatomy, one of the major objectives is to provide a clear understanding of the major pathways between these integrated levels of the human nervous system. The anatomical approach affords a firm foundation for the comprehension of both normal and abnormal function of this intricate and fascinating system in man.

CHAPTER 2

The Meninges And Cerebrospinal Fluid

The fresh brain and spinal cord are soft and of semigelatinous consistency. Within their bony encasement, these vital soft organs are protected, supported, and nourished by three membranous coverings or meninges. The most external connective tissue envelope or *dura mater* (*pachymeninx*) is tough, tenacious, and poorly extensible (Fig. 2-2). A thin, cobweb-like middle layer formed of delicate interlacing reticular fibers constitutes the *arachnoid*. The most internal layer of connective tissue fibers is the *pia mater*. It closely invests and follows the contours of the entire brain and spinal cord. The pia mater and arachnoid have a similar structure, and it is probable that they are developed from the same embryonic layer. For these reasons the pia and arachnoid are often regarded as a single structure, the *leptomeninx* or *leptomeninges*. The terms pia mater and arachnoid have been retained in the following account to designate, respectively, the inner vascular and outer membranous layers of the pia-arachnoid.

Dura Mater. The *spinal dura* corresponds to the inner layer of the cerebral dura, the vertebrae having their own separate periosteum. Both inner and outer surfaces of the spinal dura are covered by a single layer of flat cells, and it is separated from the periosteum by the narrow *epidural space*, in which are found anas-tomosing venous channels lying in areolar tissue rich in fat (Fig. 2-1). It is maintained by some that the spinal dura contains lymphatics which open on both of its surfaces. Between the dura and the arachnoid is the capillary *subdural space* moistened by fluid and believed to communicate by clefts with the tissue spaces in the sheaths of nerves and through them with the deep lymphatic vessels of the neck and groin. The subdural space has no direct communication with the subarachnoid space. The spinal dura is attached to the outer surface of the arachnoid by threadlike trabeculae.

As the nerve roots penetrate the dura mater, they receive a dural investment which is continuous with the relatively thin epineurium of the peripheral nerve.

The spinal dura extends as a closed, tough sac from the margins of the foramen magnum above (Fig. 2-5) to the level of the second sacral vertebra below. Opposite the second sacral vertebra, the dura forms an investment about the filum terminale to form a thin fibrous cord, the *coccygeal ligament*. The latter extends caudally to the dorsal surface of the coccyx, where it blends with the periosteum and posterior longitudinal ligament of the vertebral column. The spinal cord usually terminates at the lower border of the first lumbar vertebra, and the lower portion of

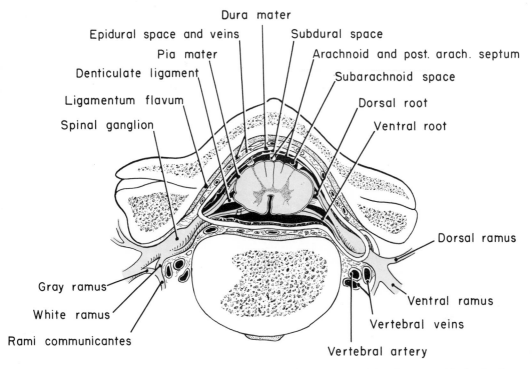

FIG. 2-1. Spinal cord and its meningeal coverings. Note the continuity of the pia mater with the denticulate ligament and of the dura mater with the epineurium of the spinal nerves. (modified from Corning, '22.)

the dural cul-de-sac is occupied by the filum terminale and cauda equina (Fig. 3-1). This region is therefore most suitable for tapping the cerebrospinal fluid (lumbar puncture), since there is no likelihood of injury to the spinal cord.

The *cerebral dura* serves both as an investing sheath for the brain and as periosteum for the inner surface of the cranium (Fig. 2-4). It consists of two layers: (1) a thin inner layer of dense fibrous tissue lined on its internal surface with a single layer of flat cells; and (2) an outer layer much richer in blood vessels and nerves, which forms the periosteum. Between the two layers are the large venous sinuses of the brain (Fig. 2-8). The cerebral dura gives off several reduplications or septa which divide the cranial cavity into incomplete compartments. The *falx cerebri* is a sickle-shaped, median septum extending from the crista galli to the internal occipital protuberance, which separates the two hemispheres. The *tentorium cerebelli* is a transverse, arched septum

placed between the occipital lobes and the cerebellum. Its free anterior border forms the tentorial incisure through which the brain stem passes (Fig. 4-4). From the midline of its undersurface, a small sagittal septum, the *falx cerebelli*, incompletely separates the hemispheres of the cerebellum. The *diaphragma sellae* forms the fibrous roof of the pituitary fossa (sella turcica) and is perforated by the infundibulum (Fig. 4-4).

The dura mater receives its major blood supply through the middle meningeal artery, a branch of the maxillary artery which enters the skull through the foramen spinosum. Additional dural vessels are provided by the anterior meningeal branches of the ophthalmic artery and the posterior meningeal branches of the occipital and vertebral arteries. Laceration and injury of these vessels can rapidly produce a space-occupying epidural hemorrhage or hematoma—an emergency that requires surgical intervention. The sensory innervation of the supratentorial portion

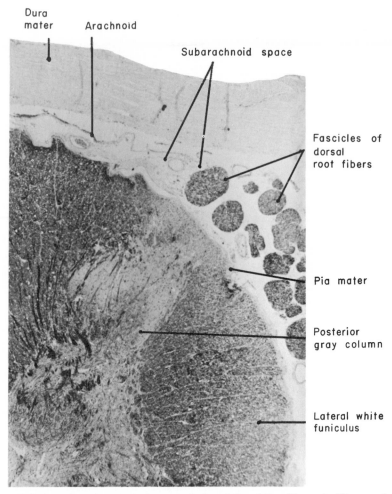

Fig. 2-2. Relations of meninges to the human spinal cord. Luxol-Fast Blue stain. Photograph. ×28.

of the dura is derived from the branches of the trigeminal nerve (Penfield and McNaughton, '40). Recent studies of human fetal specimens indicate that the sensory and vasomotor innervations of the dura mater on the walls of the posterior cranial fossa are all derived from ascending branches of the three upper cervical spinal nerves, the vagus nerve, and the superior cervical sympathetic ganglion (Kimmel, '59, '61).

Pia Mater. This investing vascular membrane is composed of two layers. An inner, more membranous layer (*intima pia* of Key and Retzius, 1875) is composed of a closely felted network of fine reticular and elastic fibers. It is the intima pia which is adherent to the underlying nervous tissue and sends fibrous septa into the spinal cord (Fig. 2-2). At the points where blood vessels enter or leave the central nervous system, the intima pia is invaginated to form the outer wall of a perivascular space (Fig. 2-9). Like the arachnoid, the intima pia is avascular and derives its nutrition by diffusion from the cerebrospinal fluid and underlying nervous tissue (Millen and Woollam, '61, '62). The more superficial layer of *epipial* tissue is formed by a loose meshwork of collagenous fiber bundles continuous with the arachnoid trabeculae (Figs. 2-3 and 2-8). This layer is well developed about the spinal cord; however, there is little epipial tissue over the lateral surfaces of the brain. The blood vessels of the spinal cord, including central branches of the anterior spinal artery, lie within this layer. In contrast, the cere-

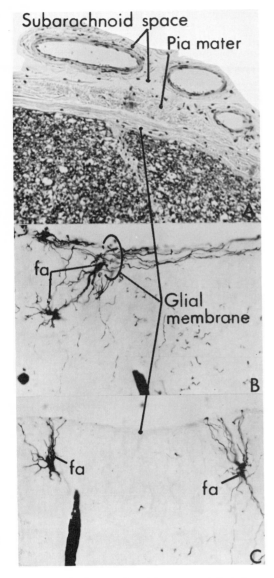

Subarachnoid space

Pia mater

fa

Glial
membrane

A

B

fa

fa

C

FIG. 2-3. Photographs of human cord that demonstrate the structure and relations of pia mater and external glial membrane. These layers form the covering of the spinal cord. **A.** Note glial membrane is closely adherent to inner surface of pia mater. Luxol-Fast Blue-cresyl violet. ×143. In **B** and **C** the processes and terminal enlargements of fibrous astrocytes (fa) are identified as they enter into the formation of the glial membrane. Golgi Stain. ×263.

bral arteries and veins in their cortical distribution lie upon the surface of the intima pia within the subarachnoid space. In the interstices of the epipial layer are irregular spaces filled with cerebrospinal fluid which communicate superficially with

the subarachnoid space and, more deeply, with the perivascular spaces of the nervous tissue (Fig. 2-9).

The spinal cord is anchored to the dura mater by two lateral series of flattened collagenous bands of epipial tissue called *denticulate ligaments* (Figs. 2-1 and 2-5). Each ligament is attached medially to the lateral aspect of the cord, midway between the dorsal and ventral roots, along the whole length of the spinal cord from the medulla (Fig. 2-5) to the conus medullaris. The lateral border presents a series of pointed processes which are firmly attached to the arachnoid and inner surface of the dura mater. The pointed dural attachments of the denticulate ligaments alternate with the dural evaginations which mark the exits of the cervical, thoracic, and first lumbar spinal nerves (Fig. 2-5).

On each lateral surface of the spinal cord there may be as many as 24, or as few as 18, processes anchoring the spinal cord to the dura. The epipial tissue continues as a narrow seam to the tip of the conus medullaris, where it fuses with the opposite seam and continues caudally as the covering of the filum terminale.

Certain regions of the pia mater deserve special attention. The epipial layer surrounding the brain and spinal cord is interrupted at the filamentous attachments of the cranial and spinal nerves. As the individual nerve fibers enter or leave the brain and spinal cord they pierce the intima pia from which they derive an investment of squamous cells and fine reticular fibers (Fig. 2-2). The more fibrous intima pia is firmly anchored to the surface of the spinal cord by a thin but distinct *superficial glial membrane* (Fig. 2-3). The latter is composed of many fine processes of more deeply located fibrous astrocytes. Cell bodies of astrocytes can be observed in the glial membrane and many of the glial fibers possess bulbous expansions. The glial fibers and astrocytes are particularly prominent in the regions where the dorsal and ventral spinal roots penetrate the pia mater. In the region of the posterior intermediate sulcus such glial elements constitute a barrier to the regenerating nerve fibers of avulsed or injured dorsal roots.

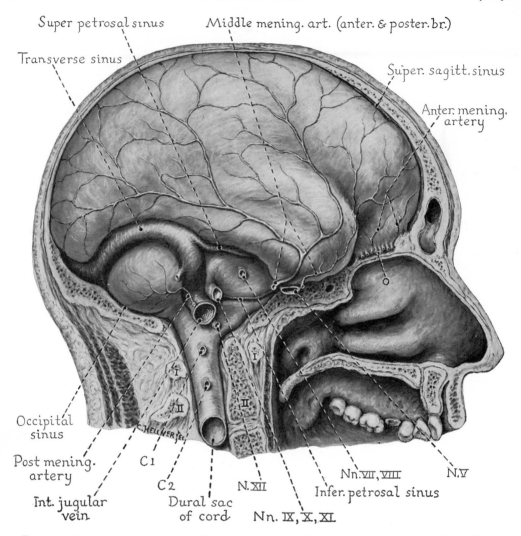

Super petrosal sinus   Middle mening. art. (anter. & poster. br.)

Transverse sinus

Super. sagitt. sinus

Anter. mening. artery

Occipital sinus

Post mening. artery   C1

Int. jugular vein   C2   N. XII

Dural sac of cord

Nn. IX, X, XI

Nn. VII, VIII   N. V

Infer. petrosal sinus

Fig. 2–4. External view of dural sac of brain and upper cervical cord. *I*, Atlas; *II*, axis; *C1* and *C2*, dural sheaths of first and second cervical nerves; *Nn. V–XII*, dural sheaths of corresponding cranial nerves; *O*, dural sheaths of fila olfactoria.

In the region of the ventricles the brain wall is formed by a single layer of ependymal cells, the outer surface of which is firmly adherent to the pia mater. Thus in the roof of the third ventricle, in the lower part of the roof of the fourth ventricle, and on the medial wall of the lateral ventricle (choroid fissure), the intima pia blends with the ependymal layer to form the *tela choroidea* (Fig. 7–11). The tela choroidea provides areas for the anchorage of the choroid plexuses in the ventricles. It has a triangular shape in the roof of the third and fourth ventricles,

while the tela choroidea of the lateral ventricle (Figs. 3–13 and 3–22) is horseshoe-shaped as it follows the choroidal fissure. The two layers of the pia mater in the transverse cerebral fissure, below the splenium of the corpus callosum and above the pineal body, are sometimes called the *velum interpositum* (Fig. 3–13B). Between these two layers lie the internal cerebral veins, branches of the posterior cerebral artery, and arteries to the choroid plexuses of the third and lateral ventricles.

Arachnoid. The arachnoid or outer

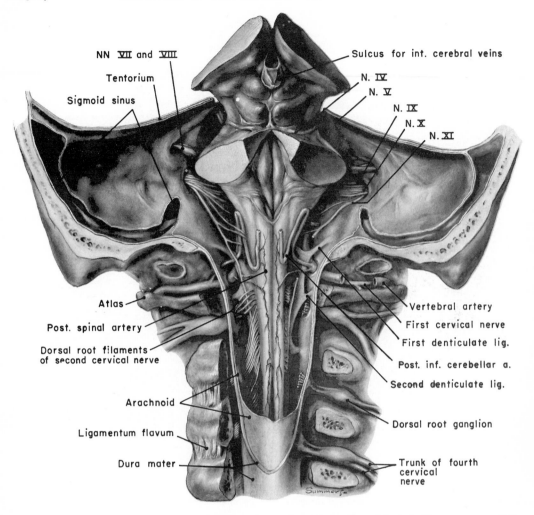

NN VII and VIII

Tentorium

Sigmoid sinus

Sulcus for int. cerebral veins

N. IV

N. V

N. IX

N. X

N. XI

Atlas

Post. spinal artery

Dorsal root filaments
of second cervical nerve

Arachnoid

Ligamentum flavum

Dura mater

Vertebral artery

First cervical nerve

First denticulate lig.

Post. inf. cerebellar a.

Second denticulate lig.

Dorsal root ganglion

Trunk of fourth
cervical
nerve

FIG. 2–5. Posterior spinal view of cord, brain stem, and meninges (from Mettler's *Neuroanatomy*, 1948; courtesy of C. V. Mosby Company).

portion of the pia-arachnoid is a delicate nonvascular membrane which passes over the sulci without dipping into them and extends as perineural epithelium along the roots of the cerebrospinal nerves and along the optic nerve (Shanthaveerappa and Bourne, '64, '66). It is partly separated from the pia by fluid spaces and by trabeculae which pass from pia to arachnoid (Figs. 2–2 and 2–8). Collectively these spaces constitute the *subarachnoid space* and may be regarded as dilations of pial spaces by which the embryologically single leptomeninx is transformed into the double, incompletely separated pia-arachnoid of the adult. In the spinal regions

the arachnoid trabeculae are few and usually concentrated into several subarachnoid septa; hence the subarachnoid space is a more continuous cavity and the arachnoid a more distinct membrane (Figs. 2–1 and 2–2). The arachnoid, trabeculae, and epipial surface are all covered with a single layer of flattened cells with large pale oval nuclei. When certain substances are injected in the subarachnoid space, these cells may swell and participate in phagocytic activity by ingesting particles of the foreign material. They may even become detached and form free macrophages.

The subarachnoid space is filled with

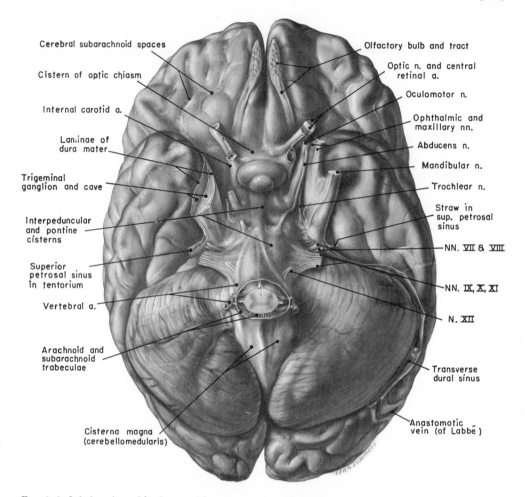

Cerebral subarachnoid spaces

Cistern of optic chiasm

Internal carotid a.

Laminae of dura mater

Trigeminal ganglion and cave

Interpeduncular and pontine cisterns

Superior petrosal sinus in tentorium

Vertebral a.

Arachnoid and subarachnoid trabeculae

Cisterna magna (cerebellomedularis)

Olfactory bulb and tract

Optic n. and central retinal a.

Oculomotor n.

Ophthalmic and maxillary nn.

Abducens n.

Mandibular n.

Trochlear n.

Straw in sup. petrosal sinus

NN. VII & VIII

NN. IX, X, XI

N. XII

Transverse dural sinus

Anastomotic vein (of Labbé)

FIG. 2–6. Inferior view of brain, cranial nerves, and meninges showing locations of subarachnoid cisterns (from Mettler's *Neuroanatomy*, 1948; courtesy of C. V. Mosby Company).

cerebrospinal fluid and is in direct communication with the fourth ventricle of the brain by means of three apertures—one median and two lateral. The median aperture, or *foramen of Magendie*, is located in the caudal part of the thin ventricular roof; the lateral apertures, or *foramina of Luschka*, open into the pontine subarachnoid cistern posterior to the emerging fibers of the ninth cranial nerve (Fig. 2–6).

In the cranial cavity the extent of the subarachnoid space shows many local variations due to the irregular contour of the brain surface. Over the convex surfaces of the convolutions, the pia and arachnoid are close to each other with

only a narrow space between them. When passing over sulci, the pia dips in while the arachnoid bridges over; hence the subarachnoid spaces are deeper in these sites (Fig. 2–8). At the base of the brain and its transition to the spinal cord, the arachnoid becomes widely separated from the pia in certain places, giving rise to the *subarachnoid cisterns* (Figs. 2–6 and 2–7). The whole medulla is surrounded by a rather wide subarachnoid space, which is most extensive posteriorly, where the arachnoid passes from the posterior surface of the medulla to the inferior surface of the cerebellum. This is the large *cisterna cerebellomedullaris* (magna) into which the foramen of Magendie opens. An-

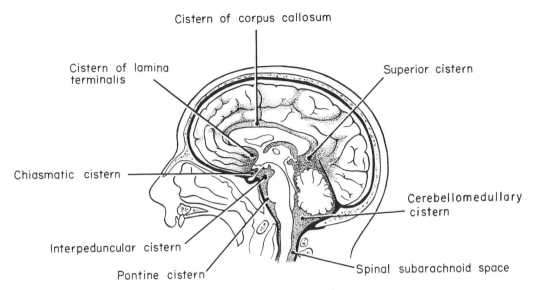

Fig. 2-7. Median view of subarachnoid cisterns

teriorly the medullary subarachnoid space widens into the *cisterna pontis*. The midbrain is completely surrounded by cisterns —posteriorly by the *cisterna superior* and anteriorly by the *cisterna interpeduncularis*, which extends laterally over the stem of the lateral sulcus. In front of the interpeduncular cistern is the *cisterna chiasmatica*, followed anteriorly and superiorly by cisterns along the lamina terminalis and the superior convex surface of the corpus callosum (Fig. 2-7). The subarachnoid space surrounding the posterior, superior and lateral surfaces of the midbrain is often referred to clinically as the *cisterna ambiens* (Davidoff and Dyke, '51; Taveras and Wood, '64) while others use the term cisterna venae magnae cerebri to indicate the combined area of the cisterna superior and cisterna ambiens. Important structures included within the cisterna ambiens are the great vein of Galen, posterior cerebral and superior cerebellar arteries and the trochlear nerves.

Arachnoid granulations (Pacchionian bodies). In places, the cerebral pia-arachnoid sends tufted prolongations through the inner layer of the dura, which protrude into a venous sinus or venous lacuna. Such granulations are visible to the naked eye, and histologically each granulation demonstrates numerous tufts or villi. In the parasagittal region, adjacent to the superior sagittal sinus, the pia-arachnoid becomes more compact and a well defined subarachnoid space is not present. Arachnoid granulations are simple prolongations of pia-arachnoid tissue. The villi show a thin, outer limiting membrane, deep to which are bundles of collagenous and elastic fibers (Figs. 2-8 and 2-9). The internal fibrous mesh may be wavy or have a coiled appearance. Scattered among the fibers are numerous cells similar to those observed in the pia-arachnoid. Many villi exhibit a surface aggregation of small, pale, oval cells which appear to form an "epithelial cell cap." Strands of such cells also may be seen extending into the substance of the villus. The structure of a small granulation within a lateral lacuna of the superior sagittal sinus is shown in Figure 2-9. They are most numerous along the interhemispheric fissure, in relation to the superior longitudinal sinus, but are found also along the other venous sinuses within the skull. Arachnoid villi also have been described in the spinal arachnoid (Elman, '23), and along the optic nerve (Shanthaveerappa and Bourne, '64). In both the spinal and cerebral arachnoid, cell clusters are sometimes formed which become attached to the dura. These growths may become calcified or, under

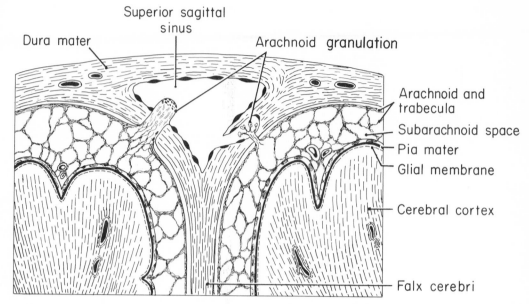

FIG. 2–8. Diagram of meningeal-cortical relationships. Arachnoid granulations may penetrate dural sinus or terminate in lateral lacuna of sinus. The pia is firmly anchored to cortex by the glial membrane.

abnormal conditions, form the sites of neoplastic tumors. Arachnoid granulations more frequently occur with advancing age.

Such granulations are the major site of fluid transfer from the subarachnoid space to the venous system. The dural sinuses cannot collapse and the pressure within them is negative in the upright position. Venous pressure is therefore less than the hydrostatic pressure of the cerebrospinal fluid so that fluid moves from the subarachnoid space to the venous dural sinuses. Arachnoid granulations appear to function as passive, pressure dependent, one-way-flow-valves whose membranes are readily permeable to metabolites, Prussian blue reagents, and even large molecular-weight substances. For example, if plasma proteins, serum albumin or inulin are injected into the subarachnoid space they rapidly appear in the venous blood (see Davson, '60 and Tschirgi, '60).

Cerebrospinal Fluid. The cerebrospinal fluid (CSF) system normally contains 125 ml. and it is estimated that 45 to 130 ml. or more are formed per day in man—hence the daily turnover of fluid is ap-

preciable. It is a clear, colorless fluid with a specific gravity of 1.004 to 1.007. It contains small amounts of protein and glucose, larger amounts of potassium and sodium chloride, and only traces of sulfate, phosphate, calcium and uric acid. The CSF has no cellular components although 1–5 cells per cubic millimeter are considered to be within normal limits. The CSF acts as a protective layer that cushions and buffers the delicate neural tissues against trauma. It also provides a fluid pathway for chemical substances to reach the intercellular spaces of the brain, as well as pathways for neural metabolites to be returned to the venous system (Fig. 2–12). It should be remembered that the brain is nearly incompressible within the rigid confines of the cranium. Hence the combined volume of brain tissue, cerebrospinal fluid and intracranial blood must be maintained at a nearly constant level. Therefore, the volume of any one of the three components can be increased only at the expense of one or both of the others. The ingenious regulation of fluid volumes with their respective hydrostatic and osmotic pressures normally maintains the

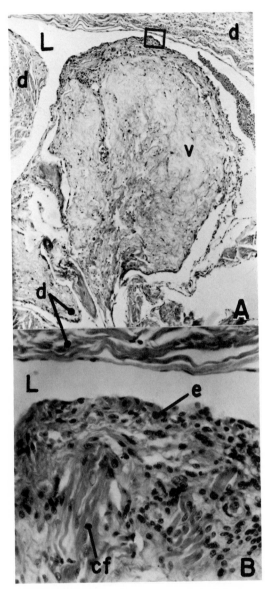

Fig. 2-9. *A*. Section of a human arachnoid granulation (**V**) in lateral lacuna of dural sinus (**L**). Relations of the dura (*d*) and area of enlargement are identified. ×28. *B*. Magnified area to demonstrate epithelial cap (*e*) and connective tissue fibers (*cf*) of granulation. Luxol-Fast Blue-cresyl violet stain. Photograph, ×270.

intracranial pressure within narrow limits and thereby insures replenishment of glucose, oxygen, and ions so essential to brain metabolism. In the recumbent position, the CSF pressure in the lumbar region of

man is 100–150 mm H_2O. In the sitting position the CSF pressure rises to 200–300 mm H_2O. An excessive amount of CSF fluid elevates these pressures above normal limits (hydrocephalus) which are injurious to nerve tissue and may cause changes in the configuration of the ventricles. Such increased fluid may result from an overproduction, an obstruction to flow, or inadequate absorption. The bulk of the cerebrospinal fluid is formed as a secretory process involving the expenditure of metabolic energy. This occurs by the active transport of Na^+ and Cl^- across the epithelial cells of the choroid plexus and into the ventricle; water then follows passively to maintain osmotic equilibrium. Smaller amounts of cerebrospinal fluid are derived from the ependyma and subjacent glial elements, as well as the capillary beds that supply the pia-arachnoid. The CSF is drained from the lateral and third ventricles by the cerebral aqueduct which opens into the fourth ventricle (Fig. 3-12). Through the medial and lateral apertures of the fourth ventricle, the fluid circulates in the cisterns and subarachnoid spaces surrounding the brain and spinal cord. As noted earlier the bulk of the CSF is passively returned to the venous system through the arachnoid villi. Lesser amounts of fluid may be taken up by the ependyma, arachnoidal capillaries and lymphatics of the meninges and perivascular tissues.

Barriers related to the brain. The functional capacity of all neurons of the brain and spinal cord are dependent upon the nature of the chemical milieu which surrounds them. To maintain an adequate ionic and oxygen atmosphere within the narrow limits of neuron survival requires the existence of a most unique physiochemical system. Such a system, albeit ill-defined, does exist to regulate the transport of chemical substances between arterial blood, cerebrospinal fluid and the brain tissues. There is a striking difference in the concentration of various substances in the CSF in comparison to the plasma. There are also differences in the rate of transfer of these substances from the

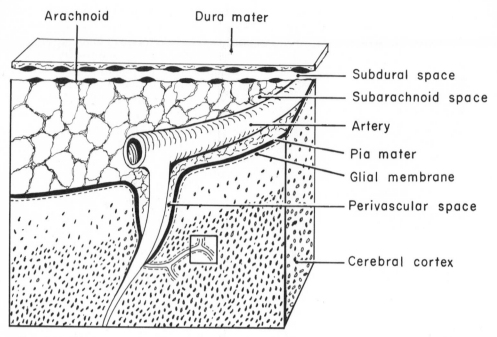

Fig. 2-10. Diagram of subarachnoid and perivascular spaces. Rectangular area in lower right is shown in Fig. 2-11.

plasma to the CSF, and to the nerve cells. Some substances do not penetrate the cerebral capillary walls to reach the brain tissue, others do so only very slowly. These differential chemical pathways to the central nervous system neurons have been investigated extensively in laboratory animals and man. Microchemical assay, localization of isotopes, fluorescent dyes and electron microscopic methods, among others, have been utilized to elucidate some of the gaps in our knowledge concerning the structure and function of these pathways. Such barriers constitute regions where there is restricted diffusion of molecules across interfaces as compared to their rate of passage across other tissues (e.g. brain, skeletal muscle, liver, etc.). Blood-brain barrier, blood-CSF barrier and brain-CSF barrier are useful terms only if they are defined in terms of rate constants for diffusion across these tissue interfaces, or equated with the volume that a given substance occupies in the brain (Woodbury, '65). Evidence has been presented that the barriers develop at the

time when blood vessels invade the brain (Grazer and Clemente '57). Additional evidence suggests that the adult barriers react differently to the electric charge of various vital dyes (Friedmann and Elkeles, '32; and Bakay, '52, '56). According to these authors the blood-brain barrier is more permeable to basic (positively charged) dyes, whereas the blood-CSF barrier is more permeable to acid (negatively charged) dyes. Such interfaces are both structural and functional entities which dynamically control the transfer of chemical substances into and out of the three fluid compartments of the brain (i.e. intercellular, intracellular and CSF). The relative importance of each of the components of the barriers shown in Figure 2-12 remains to be determined. For extensive presentations on this subject the student is referred to the excellent review articles by Rodriguez ('55, '57), Davson ('60), Schmidt ('60), Sokoloff ('60), Tower ('60), Tschirgi ('60), Millen and Woollam ('62).

Blood-Brain Barrier. Arteries of the

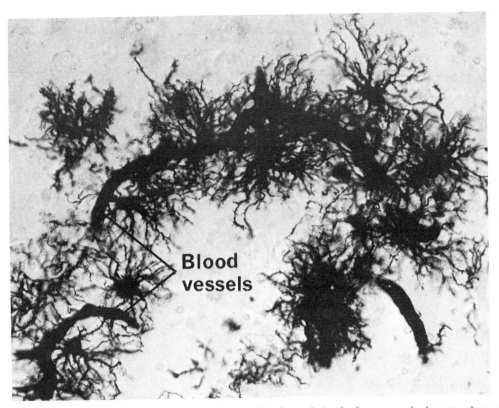

Fig. 2–11. Astrocytes and perivascular processes on blood vessels in the human cerebral cortex. Area of this photograph is indicated by insert in Figure 2–10. Golgi stain. ×450.

brain and spinal cord are invested with connective tissue of the pia-arachnoid as they lie in the subarachnoid space (Fig. 2–10). The pia and subjacent glial membrane blend with the vessel wall before it penetrates into the substance of the brain or spinal cord. The smaller branches of the arterial tree, within the nervous tissue, have only thin neuroglial membrane investments which persist down to the capillary level. The capillary endothelium, its continuous and homogeneous basement membrane, and the numerous processes of the astrocytes are all that separate the plasma in the vessel from the intercellular spaces within the central nervous system. These are the structures that have been equated by one or more investigators with the blood-brain barrier. Large numbers of astrocytes with perivascular feet are always present along the course of vessels in brain tissues stained by the Golgi technic (Fig. 2–11). Maynard et al. ('57) observed that the expanded astrocytic processes form but a single incomplete layer around capillaries with only limited overlap. They estimate from electron micrographs that such astrocytic feet cover about 85 per cent of total capillary surface. These authors also noted that the capillary endothelial cells of the central nervous system form a completely continuous layer without any suggestion of fenestrations such as those seen in the capillaries of the kidney. One or more of the components of the blood-brain barrier are stained after the intravenous injection of either aminoacridine dye proflavine HCl or the semicolloidal dye trypan blue—yet these dyes do not stain the adjacent neural tissue. However, several special structures within the central nervous system of adult animals do become stained after the intravenous injection of such vital dyes or

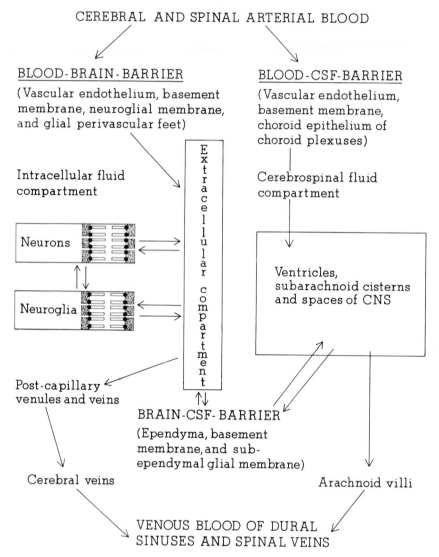

CEREBRAL AND SPINAL ARTERIAL BLOOD

BLOOD-BRAIN-BARRIER
(Vascular endothelium, basement membrane, neuroglial membrane, and glial perivascular feet)

BLOOD-CSF-BARRIER
(Vascular endothelium, basement membrane, choroid epithelium of choroid plexuses)

Intracellular fluid compartment

Extracellular compartment

Cerebrospinal fluid compartment

Neurons

Neuroglia

Ventricles, subarachnoid cisterns and spaces of CNS

Post-capillary venules and veins

BRAIN-CSF-BARRIER
(Ependyma, basement membrane, and sub-ependymal glial membrane)

Cerebral veins

Arachnoid villi

VENOUS BLOOD OF DURAL SINUSES AND SPINAL VEINS

Fig. 2–12. Diagram of the structural and functional relationships between the blood supply, cerebrospinal fluid and brain structures. Tissue elements that may participate in the formation of the so-called "barriers" are indicated in parentheses. Intercellular substances entering the neurons and neuroglial cells (i.e., intracellular compartment) must pass through the cell membrane, which is shown schematically as a protein-lipoid structure. Solid arrows indicate direction of fluid flow under normal, and experimental conditions.

they accumulate blood-borne radiotracers (e.g. P^{32}). These areas, presumably devoid of a blood-brain barrier, include the pineal body, pituitary gland, area postrema, subfornical organ, supraoptic crest and choroid plexus. All of these regions are highly vascular, and many are known or suspected to have a secretory function. Thus the blood-brain barrier, except in the special regions noted above, functions as a differential filter that permits the exchange of many substances from blood to the *extracellular compartment* (i.e. intercellular or interstitial fluid). It appears to be impermeable to other substances (e.g. vital dyes).

It will be noted in Figure 2–12 that the neurons and neuroglial cells comprise the *intracellular fluid compartment* of the brain. Passage of substances into, and out of, glial and neuronal cells takes place from the extracellular space and through cell membranes—not by direct entrance from the plasma. Estimates of the total extracellular space between neurons, neuroglia and capillaries of the brain vary widely with the different methods that have been used. Electron micrographic studies do not support the concept of widespread extracellular spaces in the CNS. Neurons, neuroglial cells and their processes take up essentially all the available room except for a fairly constant space of only 200 Å between adjacent elements (Schultz et al, '57; Farquhar and Hartmann, '57; Dempsey and Luse, '58). Neurochemical studies, on the other hand, assumed that the chloride ion is essentially distributed in the extracellular fluid and have used brain chloride as a measure of the extent of the extracellular volume in the brain. Such values for brain extracellular space range between 25 per cent (Woodbury, '58) and 40 per cent (Elliott and Jasper, '49). Though the total extracellular space of the brain may be somewhat larger than the 4 per cent determined from electron micrographs it is probably less than 25 per cent.

The narrow interstitial channels observed in electron micrographs can transport solutes between the plasma, interstitial fluid and cellular elements. There is evidence also that the interstitial fluid is not formed by an inward bulk movement of cerebrospinal fluid, but rather, that the subarachnoid CSF is formed in part, by a centrifugal flow of interstitial fluid out of the central nervous system (Davson, '60). The inflow and outflow of the interstitial fluids from the extracellular compartment are indicated by the arrows in Figure 2–12.

Blood-Cerebrospinal Fluid Barrier. The epithelium and adnexa of the choroid plexuses of the lateral, third and fourth ventricles are responsible for the actively secreted CSF as noted above (Fig. 2–12). Evidence that it is an effective barrier is attested to by the relatively higher concentration of sodium and chloride ions in CSF than in the plasma. In composition the CSF is the same as that of the interstitial tissue of the brain. It is interesting to note that P^{32} as inorganic phosphate when injected intravenously traversed the choroid plexus and then the CSF to reach the cerebral cortex (Bakay, '56). Thus the blood-CSF barrier is an effective one-way entry into the CSF fluid compartment of the brain, while the major drainage route is the arachnoid villus.

Brain-CSF Barrier. The ependyma and subjacent glial tissues constitute a potential barrier between the CSF and interstitial fluid of the brain. They are indeed structural entities, but the bulk of experimental evidence indicates that these elements pose little obstruction to the passage of fluids between the CSF and extracellular compartments. As noted above, the ependyma contributes to the CSF, while vital dyes, fluorescent dyes, and isotopes injected into the CSF can gain access to the interstitial fluid and thence to the neuroglia and neurons of the brain. The path of such experimentally injected material is indicated schematically by the arrows in Figure 2–12. Attention is again called to the similarity in ionic composition of the CSF and interstitial fluids, for they play an important role in the maintenance and variation of membrane potentials in the central nervous system.

We have briefly reviewed some of the unique interrelations of the meninges, blood vessels and fluids of the brain. Before undertaking the developmental aspects of the nervous system it would be desirable at this point to know more about the gross subdivisions and blood supply of the brain and spinal cord.

CHAPTER 3

Gross Consideration Of The Central Nervous System

The examination of the spinal cord and brain *in situ* is a prerequisite for a student beginning a course in neuroanatomy. It will clarify many of the meningeal relationships discussed in the preceding chapter and will also permit a lasting visual impression of the bones, ligaments, and meninges that house, support, and protect the central nervous system and attached nerves. Although the brain and spinal cord observed in the laboratory have been hardened by fixatives or embalming, it should be remembered that during life these structures are quite soft and in a semigelatinous state.

A familiarity with the gross appearance of the fixed brain and spinal cord is an equally valuable experience, for one can form clearer concepts of internal microscopic structure if he possesses a thorough knowledge of macroscopic surface appearance. One should not be overwhelmed with the number of named structures to be identified in the central nervous system. Illustrations occupy more than half of the space in this chapter, and the structures will be encountered again and again in subsequent chapters. The relationships of the structures will become more familiar, and their functions more meaningful, as study of the nervous system progresses. For this reason the gross topography of the spinal cord, brain stem, and cerebral hemisphere is now presented.

THE SPINAL CORD

The spinal cord surrounded by its coverings lies loosely in the vertebral canal, extending from the foramen magnum, where it is continuous with the medulla oblongata (Fig. 2–5), to the lower border of the first lumbar vertebra (Fig. 3–2). During early development, the spinal cord extends to the lower end of the sacrum, but from the fourth month on, the vertebral column elongates more rapidly than the cord. The latter, anchored above to the medulla oblongata, is pulled upward in the spinal canal, its caudal tip reaching the third lumbar vertebra at birth and the lower border of the first lumbar in the adult. Variations have been found, the spinal cord terminating as high as the twelfth thoracic, or as low as the third lumbar vertebra. It is said to be slightly lower in women.

The spinal cord is cylindrical in shape and somewhat flattened anteroposteriorly, especially in the cervical portion. It shows two spindle-shaped swellings, the *cervical* and *lumbar* enlargements, comprising those portions of the cord which innervate, respectively, the upper and lower extremities (Fig. 3–1). In animals without typical limbs there are no enlargements, the spinal cord having a uniform diameter which gradually narrows in its caudal portions. Below the lumbar enlargement the cord rapidly narrows to a cone-shaped

termination, the *conus medullaris*. From
the conus a slender non-nervous filament,
the *filum terminale*, extends downward to
the fundus of the dural sac, at the level
of the second sacral vertebra. There it
penetrates the dura and, invested by a
dural process, continues as the coccygeal
ligament to the posterior surface of the
coccyx and passes into the periosteum of
the latter. A prolongation of the central
canal of the spinal cord continues into
the upper portion of the filum terminale,
which is otherwise composed mainly of
pial connective tissue.

Though the spinal cord is intrinsically
a continuous and unsegmented structure,
the 31 pairs of nerves which arise from it
produce an appearance of external segmentation. Each segment is that portion
of the cord which furnishes dorsal and
ventral root filaments to a single pair of
nerves. On this basis there are 31 segments corresponding to the nerve pairs;
8 cervical, 12 thoracic, 5 lumbar, 5 sacral,
and usually 1 coccygeal (Figs. 3–1 and
3–2). The first cervical nerve emerges
between the atlas and the occipital bone.

During early development, the "segments" of the spinal cord correspond
closely to the respective embryonal vertebrae, and the spinal nerves pass laterally
to their intervertebral foramina. Later, as
the vertebral column grows more rapidly
than the cord, the latter is pulled upward,
and the interval between the spinal origin
of a nerve and its vertebral exit gradually
increases in length. Hence the lumbar and
sacral nerves have long roots which descend in the dural sac to reach their respective intervertebral foramina (Figs.
3–1 and 3–2). This bundle of descending
roots surrounding the filum terminale resembles a horse's tail and hence is known
as the *cauda equina*. The exact relations
of the spinal cord segments to the vertebral bodies and processes are shown in
Fig. 3–2.

The length of the spinal cord from its
upper limit to the tip of the conus medullaris is about 45 cm. in the male and 43
cm. in the female, contrasted to a length
of about 70 cm. for the vertebral column.
Its weight is about 35 grams. In the mid-

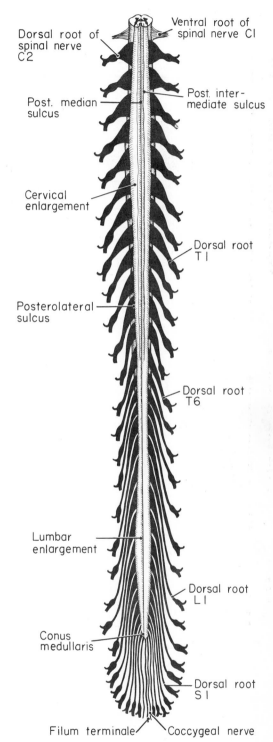

FIG. 3–1. Posterior view of spinal cord showing
attached dorsal root filaments and spinal ganglia.
Letters and *numbers* indicate corresponding spinal
nerves.

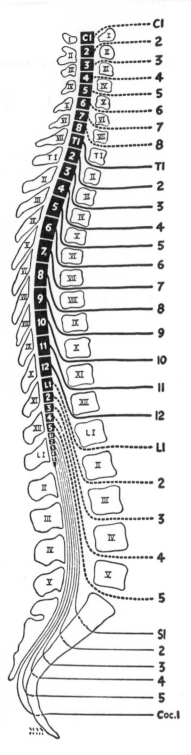

thoracic region, the transverse and sagittal diameters are about 10 mm. and 8 mm., respectively; in the cervical enlargement (sixth cervical), 13 to 14 mm. and 9 mm.; in the lumbar enlargement (third lumbar), about 12 mm. and 8.5 mm. (see Fig. 12–3).

General Topography. When freed from its meninges, the surface of the cord shows a number of longitudinal furrows (Figs. 3–1 and 3–3). On the anterior side is the deep *anterior median fissure*, which penetrates into the cord for a depth of some 3 mm. and into which extends a fold of the epipia containing blood vessels. On the posterior surface is the shallow *posterior median sulcus*. This sulcus is continuous with a delicate glial partition, the *posterior median septum*, which extends into the cord to a depth of 5 mm. and reaches the deep-lying gray. More laterally are the *posterolateral* and *anterolateral sulci*. The former is a fairly distinct furrow into which the filaments of the dorsal roots enter in a rectilinear manner (Fig. 3–1). The anterolateral sulcus marks the exit of the ventral root fibers and is hardly distinguishable, since the ventral roots emerge in groups of irregular filaments occupying an area of about 2 mm. in transverse diameter. In the cervical and upper thoracic cord another furrow, the *posterior intermediate sulcus*, extends internally between the median and posterolateral sulci. The anterior median fissure and posterior median septum divide the cord into two incompletely separated halves connected by a narrow median bridge, or commissure, composed of gray and white matter.

In a transverse section the cord is seen to consist of a centrally placed gray substance surrounded everywhere by a mantle of white (Figs. 3–3 and 12–3). The latter is composed mainly of closely packed myelinated fibers and hence appears glistening white in the fresh condition. The central substance appears pinkish-gray, for it contains numerous unmyelinated nerve fibers, cell bodies, dendrites and terminal arborizations, and has a much richer blood supply. The gray substance forms a continuous deeply notched column extending the entire length of the cord (Fig. 3–3), which in section shows the

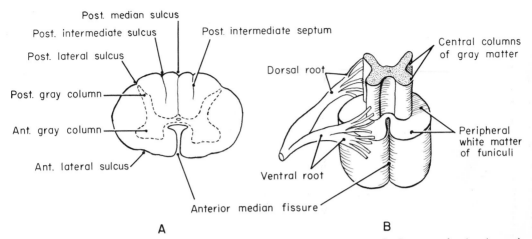

FIG. 3–3. *A*, External and internal topography of cervical spinal cord. *B*, Diagram showing internal arrangement of gray and white matter of the spinal cord.

form of a butterfly, or of the letter H. The odd-shaped vertical bars form the gray columns of the lateral halves of the cord, and the cross bar constitutes the gray commissure containing the central canal. In each half the gray substance extending posterior to the gray commissure is called the *posterior column* or *horn*, that extending anteriorly is the *anterior column* or *horn*. The portion connecting the two and from which the gray commissure extends is known as the intermediate gray. In the thoracic cord a slender lateral protrusion constitutes the *lateral* or *intermediolateral column* or *horn* (Figs. 12–1 and 12–8). In the concavity between posterior and anterior horn, small processes of gray extend into the white, where they become intimately interlaced with longitudinally running fibers, forming the *reticular process* or *reticular formation*, which is developed most extensively in the cervical portion of the cord (Fig. 12–1).

The gray commissure is divided by the central canal into posterior and anterior gray commissures. Immediately surrounding the central canal is a light granular area composed mainly of neuroglia and known as the central gelatinous substance (substantia gliosa).

The mantle of white is divided by the entering dorsal and the emerging ventral roots into three main regions: a *posterior funiculus* lying between the posterior median septum and dorsal roots; a *lateral*

funiculus between the dorsal and ventral roots; and an *anterior funiculus* between the anterior median fissure and the ventral roots. Since the posterior gray horn extends almost to the periphery of the cord, the posterior funiculus is delimited from the rest of the white. There is, however, no clear boundary between the other two funiculi, the two together really constituting a single U-shaped anterolateral funiculus. Just anterior to the anterior gray commissure is a bundle of transverse fibers, the *anterior white commissure*, composed of crossing fibers from various nerve cells to be described later (Fig. 12–1).

Before the gross topography of the brain is undertaken, the student should examine the course of the vertebral and internal carotid arteries and their intracranial branches. A familiarity with the vascular pattern and its branches (Figs. 2–5, 4–3, and 4–4) is essential at this stage, for many of the arteries and veins are destroyed when the pia-arachnoid layers are removed to expose the surface of the brain.

THE BRAIN STEM

The lateral and posterior surfaces of the brain stem are largely hidden from view in an intact brain by the cerebral hemispheres and cerebellum (Fig. 3–4). Inspection of the inferior surface of such a specimen reveals the anterior surface of the medulla, the pons, the midbrain, the structures forming the floor of the hypo-

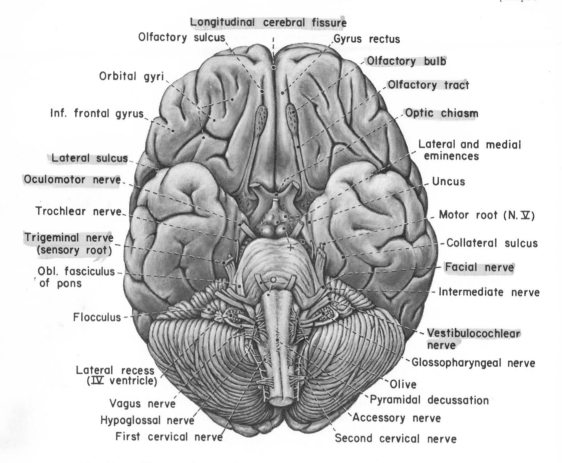

Longitudinal cerebral fissure
Olfactory sulcus
Gyrus rectus
Olfactory bulb
Orbital gyri
Olfactory tract
Inf. frontal gyrus
Optic chiasm
Lateral and medial eminences
Lateral sulcus
Oculomotor nerve
Uncus
Trochlear nerve
Motor root (N. V)
Trigeminal nerve (sensory root)
Collateral sulcus
Obl. fasciculus of pons
Facial nerve
Intermediate nerve
Flocculus
Vestibulocochlear nerve
Glossopharyngeal nerve
Lateral recess (IV ventricle)
Olive
Vagus nerve
Pyramidal decussation
Hypoglossal nerve
Accessory nerve
First cervical nerve
Second cervical nerve

+ = Mammillary body; cerebral peduncle

O = Abducens nerve; pyramid of medulla

FIG. 3–4. Inferior surface of the brain with attached cranial nerves. (Truex and Kellner, *Detailed Atlas of the Head and Neck*, 1958; courtesy of Oxford University Press).

thalamus, and the attachments of the cranial nerves. The major portions of the diencephalon also are buried from view. Removal of the cerebral hemispheres and cerebellum permits the exposure of all surfaces of the *brain stem*, which is composed of the four caudal subdivisions of the brain (i.e., medulla, pons, midbrain, diencephalon). The exposed anterior, posterior, and lateral surfaces of the dissected brain stem are shown in Figures 3–5, 3–6 and 3–7. The major surface structures are identified in each of these illustrations.

In such specimens the cut surfaces of the fiber bundles, which connect the brain stem with the detached portions, can be seen. The massive fiber bundle at the rostral end is the *internal capsule*. It

is literally a "turnpike" of fibers connecting the cerebral hemispheres above with all the segments of the brain stem and spinal cord below (Figs. 3–5 and 3–19). The three smaller bundles are the cerebellar peduncles: the *inferior cerebellar peduncle* (*restiform body*), the *middle cerebellar peduncle* (*brachium pontis*), and the *superior cerebellar peduncle* (*brachium conjunctivum*). The inferior connects the medulla with the cerebellum, while the middle is a large bridge between the pons and the cerebellum (Figs. 3–5 and 3–6). The smaller superior peduncle extends upward to connect the cerebellum and midbrain (Figs. 3–7 and 3–19).

Further examination of the isolated brain stem will reveal several striking

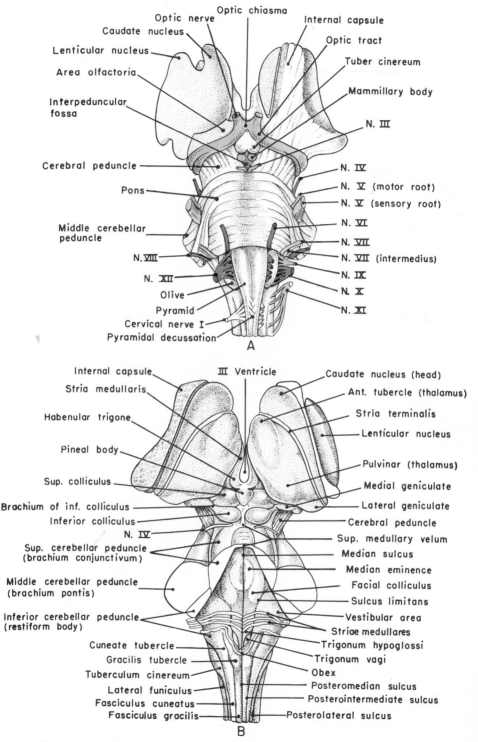

FIG. 3–5. Topography of the human brain stem and relationships of attached cranial nerves. *A*, Anterior view; *B*, posterior view.

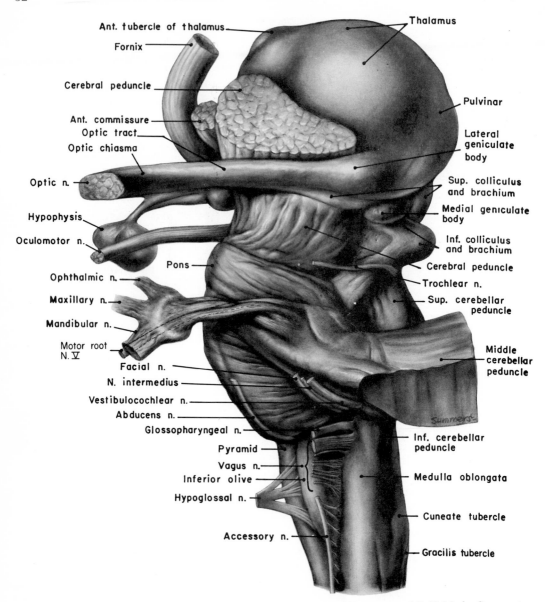

Ant. tubercle of thalamus
Fornix
Cerebral peduncle
Ant. commissure
Optic tract
Optic chiasma
Optic n.
Hypophysis
Oculomotor n.
Ophthalmic n.
Maxillary n.
Mandibular n.
Motor root N. V
Facial n.
N. intermedius
Vestibulocochlear n.
Abducens n.
Glossopharyngeal n.
Pyramid
Vagus n.
Inferior olive
Hypoglossal n.
Accessory n.
Pons

Thalamus
Pulvinar
Lateral geniculate body
Sup. colliculus and brachium
Medial geniculate body
Inf. colliculus and brachium
Cerebral peduncle
Trochlear n.
Sup. cerebellar peduncle
Middle cerebellar peduncle
Inf. cerebellar peduncle
Medulla oblongata
Cuneate tubercle
Gracilis tubercle

Fig. 3–6. Lateral view of the brain stem (Mettler, *Neuroanatomy*, 1948; courtesy of C. V. Mosby Company)

changes when it is compared to the spinal cord. It becomes progressively larger, proceeding from the medulla to the diencephalon (Fig. 3–6). The increase in size is the result of two factors: first, the need for visceral and somatic nuclei to receive information from, and extend motor control over, all the structures supplied by the cranial nerves; and second, the development of extensive coordinating mechanisms as each higher segment of the brain stem becomes integrated with existing

lower levels. The pons and medulla are further distorted by the expansion of the central canal of the spinal cord to form the broad, but shallow, fourth ventricle.

The Cranial Nerves. The origin and arrangement of the twelve pairs of cranial nerves stand out in sharp contrast to the serial attachments of the dorsal and ventral roots of the spinal nerves (Figs. 3–1 and 3–4). Each segmental spinal nerve has four functional types of nerve fibers (Fig. 12–17), and each type occupies a

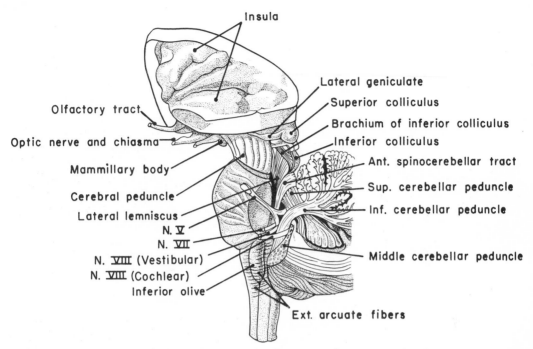

FIG. 3–7. Lateral view of the brain stem, partially dissected to show some of the fiber tracts (modified from Elze, '32).

localized region in both the embryonic and adult spinal cord (Fig. 5–3A). The same four functional types of nerve fibers are present in some of the cranial nerves. Three new "special" types of fibers are added. Two new sensory categories transmit specialized nerve impulses: those from the taste buds are designated *special visceral afferent* (SVA); olfactory nerve fibers also are considered by some to be in this category. Nerve fibers conveying visual impulses from the retina, and auditory impulses from the cochlea, are designated *special somatic afferent* (SSA). A third functional category, *special visceral efferent* (SVE), is used to designate the motor fibers that supply skeletal muscles of the head and neck which were derived from mesoderm of the embryonic branchial arches. Such muscles often are spoken of as "branchiomeric muscles"; they receive their special motor fibers via cranial nerves V, VII, IX, X, and XI.

The addition of special nuclei and of larger visceral nuclei, expansion of the fourth ventricle, development of the cerebellum, and formation of new pathways all play a part in altering the location of these functional neurons within the brain stem. (Compare Figs. 5–3A and 14–3). The location of the functional components observed in the spinal cord has shifted within the medulla to a posterior position, and the nuclei of the special neurons lie in a posterolateral position (Fig. 14–3). New cell groups and large fiber pathways also are added to the ventral and lateral surfaces of the medulla (e.g., pyramid and olive). As a result of these internal changes, the older ascending sensory and descending motor systems come to lie in a more posterior position in the brain stem, while the newer descending tracts and integrating pathways occupy the anterior and lateral areas.

This internal rearrangement of cell groups and fiber pathways accounts for the size and surface topography of the brain stem and for the altered arrangement of the cranial nerves (Fig. 3–4). The individual cranial nerves vary widely in the composition of their functional components. Some are entirely sensory, some are mainly motor, and some resemble mixed spinal nerves in having both afferent and efferent fibers.

In the following paragraphs, only the gross aspects of the brain are presented briefly. Special emphasis is given to those structures that will help the student orient and better interpret microscopic sections made from different levels. Each major subdivision of the brain will be presented in more detail in subsequent chapters.

The Medulla (Myelencephalon). This conically expanded continuation of the cervical spinal cord extends from the foramen magnum to the caudal border of the pons. It has a transverse diameter of 9 to 12 mm. at the foramen magnum, attains a diameter of 24 mm. near the pons, and is approximately 28 mm. in length.

The sulci observed on the surfaces of the spinal cord (Fig. 3–3) continue upward into the medulla (Fig. 3–5). Above the medulla, only the posterior median sulcus and sulcus limitans are present and of use in orientation. The *anterior median fissure* is partially obliterated in the lower medulla by the obliquely crossing fiber bundles of the pyramidal decussation. Above the decussation the sulcus deepens as it ascends, and on either side it is flanked by a tapering longitudinal prominence, the *pyramid* (Fig. 3–5A). The *anterolateral* (*preolivary*) *sulcus* extends upward as a prominent furrow to separate the pyramid and *inferior olive* on each side. The hypoglossal (XII) nerve and, lower down, the first cervical nerve emerge through this sulcus. At the junction of pons and medulla, the abducens (VI) nerve also emerges from this sulcus. A more lateral and deeper *postolivary sulcus* separates the inferior olive from the *tuberculum cinereum* (trigeminal eminence) and *inferior cerebellar peduncle*. Emerging from this sulcus are the roots of the facial (VII), glossopharyngeal (IX), and vagus (X) nerves (Figs. 3–5 and 3–6). Below the level of the olive, but in line with the above nerves, are the rootlets of the accessory (XI) nerve, which arise in part from the lower medulla and in part from the upper four or five segments of the cervical spinal cord. The vestibulocochlear nerve (VIII) enters the caudal border of the pons, immediately lateral to the roots of the facial nerve (Fig. 3–4). The vestibu-

lar division enters the medulla-pons junction by passing medial to the inferior cerebellar peduncle (Fig. 3–7).

On the lateral and posterior surfaces of the medulla, one can easily identify the inferior cerebellar peduncle and the cuneate and gracilis tubercles. The latter two eminences are formed by the *nucleus cuneatus* and *nucleus gracilis*, respectively.

The Fourth Ventricle. The fourth ventricle is the broad, but shallow, cavity of the hindbrain, extending from the middle of the medulla, where it is continuous with the central canal, to the cerebral aqueduct of the midbrain. Its floor is formed by the posterior surface of the medulla and the pontine tegmentum; its roof by the superior medullary velum, a portion of the cerebellum, the inferior medullary velum, and the tela choroidea (Fig. 3–10). At its widest portion just behind the brachium pontis, it is continued on each side into a tubular *lateral recess*. The recess curves laterally over the inferior cerebellar peduncle to open as the lateral aperture of the fourth ventricle on the lateral aspect of the upper medulla (Figs. 3–4 and 4–3).

The white substance of the cerebellum, which forms part of the roof, splits at an acute angle into two thin white laminae, enclosing between them a peaklike roof recess of the fourth ventricle (Fig. 3–10). One lamina, the *superior medullary velum*, extends rostrally to the midbrain and forms the roof of the superior, or pontine, portion of the ventricle. The other layer, the *inferior medullary velum*, passes caudally for a short distance and then becomes continuous with the *tela choroidea*, which forms the roof of the lower, or medullary portion of the ventricle. From the tela the *choroid plexus* projects into the ventricle. This is composed of irregular nodular evaginations of the tela choroidea containing vascular loops covered by a modified ependymal epithelium (Fig. 7–11). These vascular tufts are evaginated in the form of two longitudinal ridges placed near the midline and extending from the most caudal portion of the ventricle to the inferior medullary velum to which the tela is attached. From each of these ridges another strip of choroid plexus extends practically at right angles through the whole length of the lateral recess. At its distal end, each recess opens into the subarachnoid space by a small lateral aperture (*foramen of Luschka*) through which protrudes a portion of the choroid plexus, which elsewhere is always limited to the ventricular cavities of the brain (Fig. 3–4). A similar but medially placed aperture (*foramen of Magendie*) is found in the most caudal part of the ventricular roof. Through these three openings, the cerebrospinal fluid produced, in part, by the choroid plexuses of the brain ventricles escapes into the subarachnoid spaces.

The rhomboid or diamond-shaped floor of the fourth ventricle is known as the *rhomboid fossa* (Figs. 3–5*B* and 14–2). It is widest at its lateral angles, where the fossa is continued into the lateral recesses. The apex of its rostral angle is directed toward the midbrain, and that of the caudal angle toward the central canal. The pointed caudal end of the fossa, because of its resemblance to a pen, is called the *calamus scriptorius*. The upper, larger triangular area belongs to the pons, and the lateral walls and lateral portions of the roof of the rhomboid fossa are formed by the *superior cerebellar peduncles*. These two fiber bundles emerge from the cerebellum above the lateral recess and extend to the midbrain, approaching each other as they proceed rostrally. The roof of this part of the ventricle is completed by the superior medullary velum, which is attached to the medial borders of the two superior cerebellar peduncles (Fig. 3–5*B*). The lower triangular area belongs to the medulla and is bounded laterally by the gracilis and cuneate tubercles and the inferior cerebellar peduncle.

The rhomboid fossa is divided into two symmetrical halves by the *median sulcus*, which extends the whole length of the ventricular floor. The *sulcus limitans* divides each half into a medial longitudinal ridge (*median eminence*) and a lateral triangular region (*area vestibularis*) Figs. 14–2 and 14–3). Beneath the latter lie the terminal nuclei of the vestibular nerve (Fig. 3–5*B*). From the region of the lateral recess, a varying number of whitish strands may be seen running transversely or obliquely toward the midline, where they disappear in the median sulcus. These are the *striae medullares*, whose significance will be discussed later. The region traversed by the striae medullares in the floor of the fossa is sometimes called the intermediate portion of the rhomboid fossa and is continuous on each side with the lateral recess.

The median eminence, produced largely by subjacent motor nuclei of the cranial nerves, is narrow in the lower part of the fossa but widens in a rostral direction. The tapering caudal portion is called the *trigonum hypoglossi* because of the underlying nucleus of the hypoglossal nerve (Fig. 3–5). Above the striae medullares it expands into a rounded eminence, the *facial colliculus*, caused by the underlying nucleus of the sixth nerve and the root fibers of the seventh nerve, which here pass dorsally over the abducens nucleus. The deepened portion of the sulcus limitans, lateral to the facial colliculus, is the *superior fovea*.

Lateral to the hypoglossal trigone is another oval area, the *trigonum vagi*, beneath which lie the dorsal nuclei of the vagus nerve. The deepening of the sulcus limitans in this region is often known as the *inferior fovea*. A white strip, the *funiculus separans*, composed of neuroglial tissue, separates the trigonum vagi from the *area postrema*, a narrow zone bordering on the lateral wall of the ventricle (Fig. 14–16).

With these large anterior and posterior landmarks of the medulla in mind, it is not too difficult to recognize them when they appear in stained microscopic sections. For example, Fig. 14–8 (page 307) is a transverse section cut at the level of the pyramidal decussation, while Figure 14–11 (page 309) is a section through a slightly higher level. Can you recognize the prominent features in Figure 14–11 of the pyramid, cuneate tubercle, and gracilis tubercle (clava)? A stained section of the medulla cut higher in the region of the lateral recess of the fourth ventricle, in-

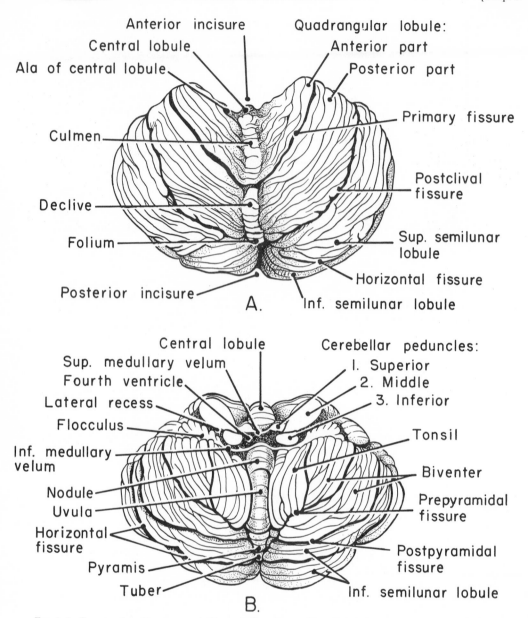

Fig. 3–8. Topography of human cerebellum. *A*, Superior surface; *B*, inferior surface (after Jacob, '28)

ferior cerebellar peduncle, and inferior olive would be similar to Figure 14–21.

The Pons (Metencephalon). This segment of the brain stem appears anteriorly as a bulging mass of transverse fibers, and it is separated from the cerebellum posteriorly by the fourth ventricle (Figs. 3–5 and 3–6). The pons is delimited from the cerebral peduncles of the midbrain by the superior pontine sulcus, and from the anterior surface of the medulla by the inferior pontine sulcus. The distance between these two sulci is 20 to 30 mm., and the width of the pons varies from 30 to 36 mm.

The most prominent external feature of the pons anteriorly is the broad band of predominantly transverse fibers. Laterally the fibers are collected into a large bundle, the *middle cerebellar peduncle*

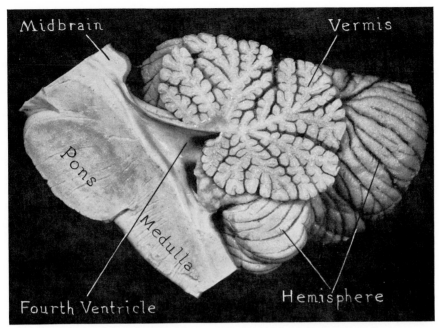

FIG. 3-9. Median longitudinal section through cerebellum (photograph)

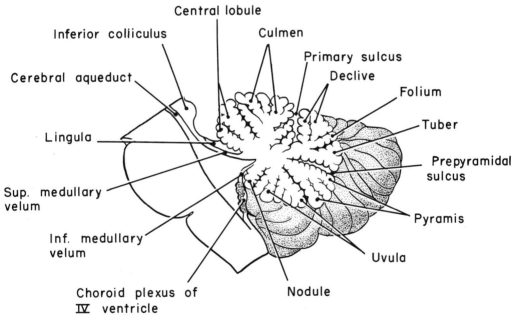

FIG. 3-10. Median section through cerebellum corresponding to structures shown in Fig. 3-9

(*brachium pontis*). This bridge of fibers passes posteriorly and somewhat caudally to fan out and end within the cerebellar hemispheres (Fig. 3-7). An anterior median depression, the *basilar sulcus*, indicates the position of the basilar artery, while laterally the trigeminal (V) nerve emerges midway between the superior and inferior pontine sulci.

The structure of the pons can be better appreciated when viewed in transverse section, for then one can visualize its two main portions (Figs. 15-1 and A-8). The dorsal or *tegmental portion* represents the cranial continuation of the reticular formation of the medulla. Within this tegmental portion are the motor and sensory nuclei of cranial nerves (i.e., V, VI, VII, VIII), ascending sensory and older descending motor pathways, and several integrating pathways. Within the larger anterior, or *ventral portion*, of the pons are the transverse pontine fibers, the pontine nuclei, and the descending fiber bundles of the corticobulbar and corticospinal tracts. The latter are assembled into a compact bundle on each side at the lower end of the pons and form the pyramid of the medulla (Figs. 3-5 and 3-19).

The Cerebellum. The cerebellum lies posterior to the medulla oblongata and pons, beyond which it extends laterally for a considerable distance. Two surfaces may be distinguished: a superior somewha flattened surface covered by the tentorium (Figs. 2-7 and 4-4), and a strongly convex inferior surface which fills the cerebellar fossae of the occipital bone. The superior margin of the cerebellum is notched by the shallow *anterior cerebellar incisure* (Fig. 3-8), and the inferior margin by the deeper and narrower *posterior cerebellar incisure*, which contains a fold of the dura mater, the falx cerebelli.

The human cerebellum consists of a median portion, the *vermis*, connecting two lateral lobes or *hemispheres*. The superior portion of the vermis is poorly delimited from the hemispheres, but on the inferior surface, two deep sulci separate the vermis from the lateral portions. The convex inferior surface is divided into two halves by a deep median fossa continuous with the posterior incisure. This is the *vallecula cerebelli*, whose floor is formed by the inferior vermis and in which is lodged the medulla oblongata.

Structurally the cerebellum consists of a superficial mantle of gray matter, the cerebellar cortex, enclosing an internal mass of white, the corpus medullare. Within the latter are found four pairs of nuclear masses: the fastigial, globose, emboliform, and dentate nuclei (Fig. 17-11). The surface of the cerebellum receives its characteristic appearance from numerous transversely running sulci and fissures of varying depth, which separate a large number of narrow leaflike lamina, the cerebellar *folia* or *gyri*. These lamina are in turn folded into secondary and tertiary folia, each composed of a medullary core capped by a superficial layer of cortex. In median sections this complex branching of the corpus medullare and its cortical covering presents a treelike appearance to which the name *arbor vitae* has been given (Figs. 3-9 and 3-10).

The more prominent transverse fissures, some of which nearly reach the roof of the fourth ventricle, divide the cerebellum into a number of lobules, each with a medial portion belonging to the vermis and two winglike extensions belonging to the hemispheres (Figs. 3-8 and 3-10). These lobules are still encumbered with peculiar and meaningless morphological names given to them by the older anatomists. Thus the superior vermis consists of the *lingula;* the *lobulus centralis;* the *monticulus*, which is divided into the *culmen* and the *declive;* and the *folium vermis*. On the under surface, the inferior vermis includes the *tuber*, the *pyramis*, the *uvula*, and the *nodulus*. Each of these lobules has corresponding lateral continuations in the hemispheres (Fig. 17-1). The central lobule is continued into the *alae lobuli centralis*, and the monticulus into the *quadrangular lobule*, whose anterior portion belongs to the culmen and posterior portion to the declive. The folium vermis extends laterally into the *superior semilunar lobule*, separated from the *inferior semilunar lobule*, which belongs to the tuber, by the horizontal cerebellar fissure, which roughly marks the boundary between the superior and inferior surfaces. The remaining hemispheral portions are the *biventer lobules* for the pyramis, the *tonsils* for the uvula, and the *flocculi* for the nodulus. The flocculi lie on the inferior surface of the middle cerebellar peduncle and are connected with the nodule by the peduncles of the flocculi and the inferior medullary velum (Fig. 3-8B).

The Midbrain (Mesencephalon). The midbrain is the smallest and least differentiated of the five brain divisions. It has a length of 15 to 20 mm. Its caudal part is overlapped anteriorly by the cephalic portion of the pons. Externally the posterior surface extends from the exit of the fourth cranial nerve to the root of the pineal body, and the anterior surface, from the rostral border of the pons to the mammillary bodies (Figs. 3–5 and 3–6).

The midbrain consists of a posterior part, the *quadrigeminal plate* or *tectum*, and a more massive *anterolateral* portion known as the *cerebral peduncles*. Its narrow channel or cavity, extending from the fourth to the third ventricle, is the *cerebral aqueduct*. In section each cerebral peduncle shows a division into a posterior part, the *tegmentum*, continuous with that of the pons, and an anterior part, the *crus cerebri*, separated from each other by a broad pigmented plate of gray matter, the *substantia nigra*.

Viewed from the anterior surface, the crus cerebri appear as two massive fiber bundles extending from the rostral border of the pons to the optic tracts, where they disappear into the deep substance of the forebrain. On emerging from the pons the crus cerebri diverge laterally, enclosing between them a deep triangular groove, the *interpeduncular fossa*, bounded rostrally by the mammillary bodies (Fig. 3–5 A). When freed from the pia, the floor of this fossa shows a number of fine perforations serving for the passage of blood vessels and hence is known as the *posterior perforated substance*.

On the posterior surface the quadrigeminal plate or tectum shows two pairs of eminences, the *superior* and *inferior colliculi*. The colliculi of the two sides are separated by a median longitudinal groove in the rostral portion of which lies the pineal body, tucked in between the superior colliculi (Figs. 3–5B, A25 and A26). A narrow band extending from the superior medullary velum and known as the *frenulum veli* is attached to the caudal part of the sulcus.

Each colliculus is connected with the thalamus by a superficially placed fiber bundle, which arises from the lateral margin of the colliculus and constitutes its arm or *brachium*. The *inferior collicular brachium* is a short flat band which runs from the inferior colliculus to the medial geniculate body, one of the caudal thalamic nuclei lying closely apposed to the lateral surface of the midbrain (Figs. 3–5 and 3–6). The *superior collicular brachium* is a longer, narrower strand extending from the superior colliculus to the lateral geniculate body of the thalamus. Some fibers of the optic tract bypass the lateral geniculate body and go directly to the superior colliculus (Fig. 3–6).

The midbrain contains the principal segmental mechanisms for ocular reflexes, eye movements, and higher postural reflex centers related especially to the "righting reactions" from abnormal to normal positions. This segment also contains various paths to and from the cerebellum, cerebral cortex, striatum, and other forebrain structures. The motor nuclei of cranial nerves III and IV also lie in the midbrain (Figs. A10 and A11).

Diencephalon. The superior surface of the diencephalon forms part of the floor of the lateral ventricle and the lateral walls of the third ventricle (Figs. 3–11, 3–12 and 3–13). Thus the lateral ventricle, corpus callosum, fornix, and velum interpositum (Fig. 3–13) all form the superior boundary of the diencephalon. The internal capsule and optic tract constitute the lateral boundary of the diencephalon (Fig. 3–13B). Caudally the diencephalon becomes continuous with the tegmentum of the midbrain, while the internal capsule fibers enter the crus cerebri (Figs. A-19 and A-30).

The diencephalon, which encloses the third ventricle, has four major parts, each composed of one or more structures: (1) epithalamus, (2) thalamus and metathalamus, (3) hypothalamus, and (4) subthalamus.

In median and superior views the structures of the *epithalamus* that can be identified grossly (Figs. 3–5, 3–12 and A-25) include the pineal body, habenular trigone, stria medullaris, tenia thalami, and the posterior commissure. The posterior commissure is a histologic landmark that indicates the junctional zone between the

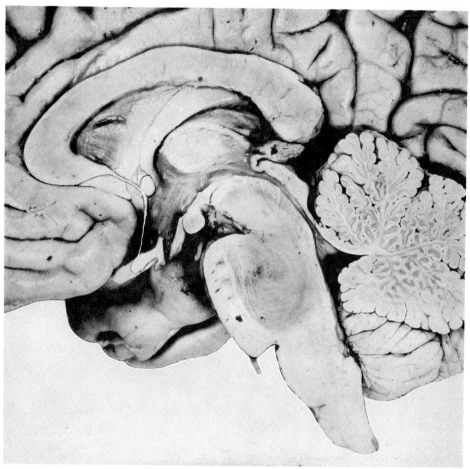

FIG. 3–11. Median sagittal section of human brain stem (photograph). For identification of structures see Figure 3–12.

diencephalon and mesencephalon. (Figs. 18–4 and A-26).

The *thalamus* forms the great bulk of the diencephalon and appears as an egg-shaped, nuclear mass (Fig. 3–6) lying obliquely across the cranial end of the brain stem. It has a small *anterior tubercle* and a larger posterior swelling, the *pulvinar*, on its superior surface (Fig. 3–5B). The extent and internal structure of the thalamus are best appreciated when viewed in frontal section (Figs. 3–13 and A-19). The free superior surface is covered by a thin layer of fibers (*stratum zonale*) which gives it a white appearance. A narrower lateral strip of the superior surface forms part of the floor of the lateral ventricle and is covered by a layer of ependymal cells, the *lamina affixa*. To the medial

border of this lamina is attached the tenia of the choroid plexus of the lateral ventricle (Fig. 3–13A). At the junction of the medial and superior surfaces, a white strip of fibers (*stria medullaris*) extends along the roof of the third ventricle to end caudally in the habenular trigone. Laterally the thalamus is bounded by a thin layer of nerve fibers (*external medullary lamina*) and scattered nerve cells which separate the thalamus and internal capsule. An *internal medullary lamina*, composed of fine fibers, divides the internal thalamus into anterior, medial, central, and lateral nuclear masses. The medial surface of the thalamus extends from the stria medullaris to the hypothalamic sulcus. This surface forms part of the lateral wall of the third ventricle, and in approximately 80% of

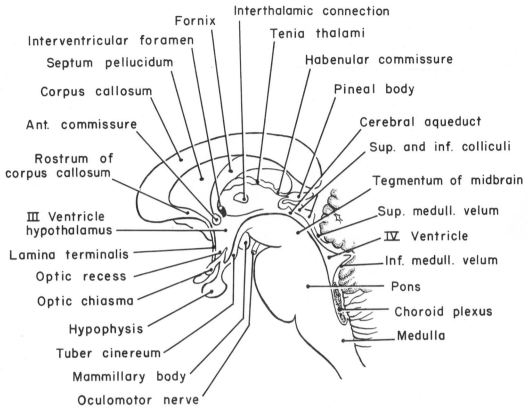

FIG. 3–12. Median section of brain stem corresponding to structures shown in Figure 3–11

human brains an *interthalamic adhesion* (massa intermedia) of gray matter spans the ventricle to connect the two thalami (Figs. 3–12 and 3–13).

The *hypothalamus* is a small but important wedge-shaped area which forms the inferior lateral wall and floor of the third ventricle (Fig. 3–13B). Several small hypothalamic nuclear groups form the walls of the ventricle (Fig. 19–16). The floor is formed by grossly visible hypothalamic structures, which include the *optic chiasm, infundibulum, tuber cinereum, mammillary bodies,* and the *neurohypophysis* (Fig. 3–12).

The *subthalamus* is a compact transition zone between the thalamus above and the tegmentum of the midbrain below. It is bounded by the thalamus superiorly, the hypothalamus medially, and the internal capsule laterally (Fig. 3–13B). Like the medulla oblongata, it is small in size, but is an area of great functional significance. The subthalamic nucleus and zona incerta

are within this region, and the red nucleus and substantia nigra also extend into it. All the ascending sensory pathways from lower levels traverse the subthalamus en route to the thalamus, as well as numerous fasciculi to and from the corpus striatum (Fig. A-28).

The *metathalamus* is composed of the two ovoid geniculate bodies located on the posterolateral surface of the brain stem inferior to the pulvinar (Figs. 3–5 and 3–6). The smaller *medial geniculate body* is an auditory relay nucleus connected to the inferior colliculus by the brachium of the inferior colliculus. The larger *lateral geniculate body* is an enlargement on the distal end of the optic tract. It is connected with the superior colliculus through a thickened band of fibers, the brachium of the superior colliculus (Fig. 3–6). Axons from the cells of the lateral geniculate body form the *optic radiation* (geniculocalcarine tract). This body serves

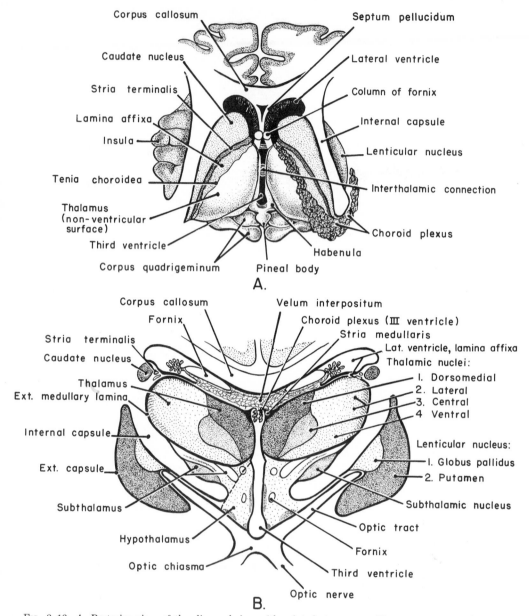

FIG. 3–13. *A*, Posterior view of the diencephalon with related structures. All gray matter is *stippled*. *B*, Schematic frontal section through the diencephalon and related structures. Nuclei and gray matter are *stippled*.

as a relay nucleus for visual nerve impulses (Figs. 3–15 and 3–19).

Basal Ganglia. This term often is used to designate several gray masses which develop in, and belong to, the telencephalon. These include the caudate, lenticular, and amygdaloid nuclei and a thin strip of detached insular cortex called the claus-

trum (Figs. 3–13, 3–23, 3–26 and 3–27). The caudate and lenticular nuclei constitute the *corpus striatum*. They have a striated appearance when observed in frontal and transverse sections (Figs. 3–26, 3–27 and 20–10).

The diencephalon and corpus striatum arise near each other, become closely as-

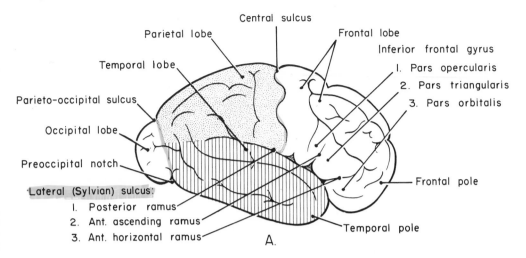

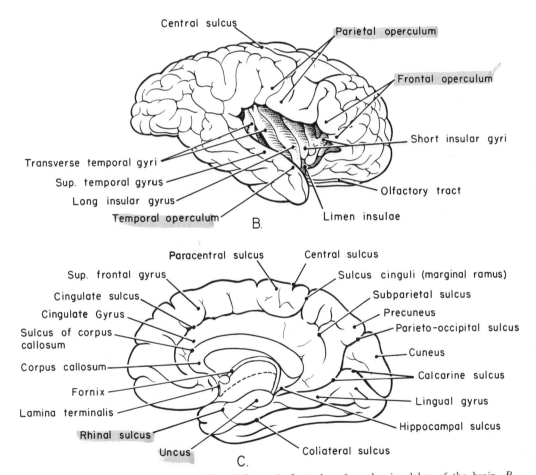

Central sulcus

Parietal lobe

Temporal lobe

Parieto-occipital sulcus

Occipital lobe

Preoccipital notch

Lateral (Sylvian) sulcus:
   1. Posterior ramus
   2. Ant. ascending ramus
   3. Ant. horizontal ramus

Frontal lobe

Inferior frontal gyrus
   1. Pars opercularis
   2. Pars triangularis
   3. Pars orbitalis

Frontal pole

Temporal pole

A.

Central sulcus

Parietal operculum

Frontal operculum

Short insular gyri

Transverse temporal gyri

Sup. temporal gyrus

Long insular gyrus

Temporal operculum

Olfactory tract

Limen insulae

B.

Paracentral sulcus

Sup. frontal gyrus

Cingulate sulcus

Cingulate Gyrus

Sulcus of corpus callosum

Corpus callosum

Fornix

Lamina terminalis

Rhinal sulcus

Uncus

Central sulcus

Sulcus cinguli (marginal ramus)

Subparietal sulcus

Precuneus

Parieto-occipital sulcus

Cuneus

Calcarine sulcus

Lingual gyrus

Hippocampal sulcus

Coliateral sulcus

C.

Fig. 3-14. Diagrams of right cerebral hemisphere. *A*, Lateral surface showing lobes of the brain. *B*, Lateral surface with the lips (*opercula*) of the lateral sulcus drawn apart to expose the insula. *C*, Medial surface showing principal gyri and sulci.

sociated anatomically, and soon become buried together by the expansion of the cerebral hemispheres. The corpus striatum develops as a thickening in the hemispheric wall at the point of evagination (i.e., adjacent to the interventricular foramen and diencephalon). As the corpus striatum and thalamic nuclei increase in thickness, they approach each other and finally fuse. The line of junction on the superior lateral surface of the diencephalon is marked by a groove, the *terminal sulcus*. In this sulcus is found a small fiber bundle (*stria terminalis*) and the *terminal vein* (Figs. 3–5 and 3–13*B*). The internal capsule fibers partially subdivide the corpus striatum, so that most of the caudate nucleus lies medially with the diencephalon (Figs. 3–13 and 3–26), while the lenticular nucleus is lateral to the internal capsule. The relations of these buried gray masses are best visualized in isolated brain stem preparations (Figs. 3–5 and 3–6), in frontal and transverse sections of the brain (Figs. 3–26 and 3–27), or by staged brain dissections as shown in Figures 3–18 to 3–23.

THE CEREBRAL HEMISPHERES

External Topography

By means of the sulci and fissures the brain is subdivided into a number of lobes, named in accordance with their topographical relations to the skull. This subdivision is largely a convenient one, and some of the lobar boundaries have to be arbitrarily determined. Furthermore each lobe consists of several histologically and functionally distinct cortical areas, some of which may overlap the anatomical boundaries of the lobe. In general, five lobes usually are recognized: *frontal*, *parietal*, *occipital*, *temporal*, and *insular* (Fig. 3–14). The olfactory portions are not included in the above named lobes, but are regarded as constituting a separate anatomical entity, the *rhinencephalon*. Parts of more than one lobe may be included when the brain is considered from a functional standpoint. For example the cingulate gyrus, hippocampus, and adjacent cortex often collectively are called the "limbic lobe," as indicated diagram-

matically in Figure 21–12. Further details on the structure and function of the rhinencephalon are presented in Chapter 21.

Each hemisphere consists of the pallium and the deep-lying basal ganglia, whose structure and connections will be discussed in Chapter 20. The pallium or cerebral mantle is composed of an internal fibrous mass, the white or medullary substance, that is everywhere covered superficially by a layer of gray matter, the cerebral cortex.

The cerebral hemispheres are separated from each other by the deep vertical *longitudinal fissure* containing the falx cerebri. In front and behind, the separation is complete, but in the middle portion the fissure extends only to the corpus callosum, a broad band of commissural fibers uniting the two hemispheres. Posteriorly the hemispheres overlap the thalamus, midbrain, and cerebellum. They are separated from these structures by the *transverse fissure*, which is occupied posteriorly by the tentorium cerebelli. In each hemisphere three surfaces may be distinguished: lateral, medial, and inferior. A rounded border intervenes between the convex lateral and the flat vertical medial surfaces, and an inferior rounded border separates the lateral and inferior surfaces (Figs. 3–14 and 3–15). The latter surface is more complex in shape, closely moulded in front to the base of the skull. Its anterior portion occupies the anterior and middle cranial fossa, and its posterior portion rests on the tentorium cerebelli (Figs. 3–4 and 4–4).

The Lateral Surface (Figs. 3–14 and 3–16). The most striking furrows on the convex surface are the *lateral sulcus* and the *central sulcus*. The *lateral sulcus* starts on the inferior surface as a deep cleft, the Sylvian fossa, separating the frontal and temporal lobes, then extends to the lateral surface, where it divides into three branches. The short anterior horizontal and anterior ascending branches incise the inferior gyrus of the frontal lobe. The long posterior branch passes backward almost horizontally and then curves upward to terminate in the parietal lobe (Fig. 3–14).

The *central sulcus (of Rolando)* is a deep

and usually continuous furrow running downward and slightly forward from the middle of the superior border of the hemisphere to the lateral sulcus without quite reaching the latter. The sulcus shows two kneelike bends and usually incises the superior border to reach the medial surface (Figs. 3–16 and 3–20).

The **frontal lobe** comprises about one-third of the hemispheric surface. It extends from the frontal pole to the central sulcus and is limited below by the lateral sulcus. On the convex surface, four main convolutions may be distinguished (Fig. 3–16). The vertical *precentral gyrus* runs parallel to the central sulcus and is limited in front by the *precentral sulcus*, which is sometimes broken up into superior and inferior segments. This gyrus comprises the motor, and a considerable part of the premotor, area and is the site of origin of a part of the corticospinal and corticobulbar tracts. The rest of the frontal lobe is composed of three horizontal convolutions, the *superior, middle,* and *inferior frontal gyri,* separated from each other by the *superior* and *inferior frontal sulci.* Often a shallower middle frontal sulcus divides the broad middle gyrus into an upper and lower tier. The inferior frontal gyrus, which forms the frontal operculum of the insula, is subdivided by the anterior branches of the lateral fissure into orbital, triangular, and opercular portions (Fig. 3–14*A*). In the left or dominant hemisphere, the triangular and opercular portions are known as Broca's area, which is regarded as the cortical center for the motor formulation of speech.

The smaller **parietal lobe** is more difficult to delimit on the convex surface. Bounded sharply in front by the central sulcus, its posterior part merges imperceptibly with the occipital lobe behind and the temporal lobe below. Its occipital boundary is arbitrarily established by a vertical line drawn from the upper end of the parieto-occipital sulcus to a shallow depression on the inferior hemispheric border about 4 cm. from the occipital pole, known as the preoccipital notch (Fig. 3–14). Its temporal boundary is similarly established by an imaginary line extending the posterior ramus of the lateral sulcus to the occipitoparietal line determined above.

The sulci on the convex surface of the parietal lobe vary considerably in different individuals. As a rule two main sulci are distinguished, though these may be continuous with each other and form a single sulcus of complicated form (Fig. 3–16). The *postcentral sulcus* is usually broken up into superior and inferior segments. It runs parallel to the central sulcus and forms the caudal boundary of the vertical *postcentral gyrus,* which represents the sensory area of the cerebral cortex. The *intraparietal sulcus,* which is usually a direct continuation of the inferior postcentral, arches backward to the occipital lobe. Here it often ends as the transverse occipital sulcus beneath the lateral margin of the parieto-occipital sulcus. The sulcus divides the rest of the parietal lobe into a *superior parietal lobule* lying above it and an *inferior parietal lobule* below (Fig. 3–16). The inferior lobule is primarily represented by the *supramarginal gyrus,* which curves around the terminal ascending portion of the lateral sulcus, and the *angular gyrus,* which similarly surrounds the ascending terminal part of the superior temporal sulcus. The inferior portions of the precentral, postcentral, and supramarginal gyri constitute the parietal operculum of the insula (Fig. 3–14).

The large **temporal lobe,** whose anterior tip is known as the temporal pole, shows three horizontal convolutions, the *superior, middle,* and *inferior temporal gyri,* separated by similarly named sulci. The deep and constant superior temporal sulcus begins at the temporal pole and runs parallel to the lateral sulcus, and its ascending terminal portion is surrounded by the angular gyrus. The posterior portions of the irregular and segmented middle temporal sulcus are related to small gyri in the posterior parietal area. The inferior temporal sulcus can only be seen on the inferior surface. The superior temporal gyrus forms the temporal operculum, and its broad superior surface, which faces the lateral sulcus, is marked in its caudal portion by several short, obliquely running convolutions, the *transverse tem-*

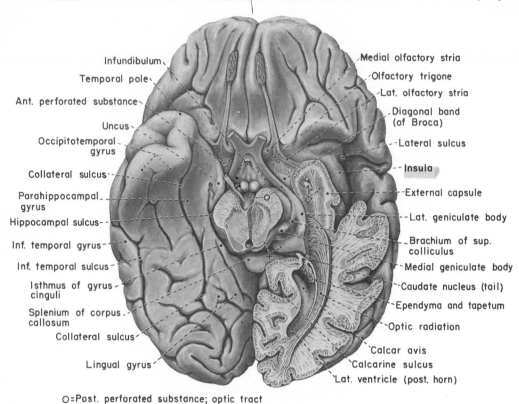

Infundibulum

Temporal pole

Ant. perforated substance

Uncus

Occipitotemporal gyrus

Collateral sulcus

Parahippocampal gyrus

Hippocampal sulcus

Inf. temporal gyrus

Inf. temporal sulcus

Isthmus of gyrus cinguli

Splenium of corpus callosum

Collateral sulcus

Lingual gyrus

Medial olfactory stria

Olfactory trigone

Lat. olfactory stria

Diagonal band (of Broca)

Lateral sulcus

Insula

External capsule

Lat. geniculate body

Brachium of sup. colliculus

Medial geniculate body

Caudate nucleus (tail)

Ependyma and tapetum

Optic radiation

Calcar avis

Calcarine sulcus

Lat. ventricle (post. horn)

O=Post. perforated substance; optic tract

◊=Ant. commissure; lenticular nucleus

+=Pulvinar of thalamus; brachium of inferior colliculus

FIG. 3–15. Inferior surface of the brain showing principal gyri and sulci. The left hemisphere has been partially dissected to demonstrate the visual pathways and relation of the optic radiation to the lateral ventricle. See relations in Figure 3–24. (Truex and Kellner, *Detailed Atlas of Head and Neck*, 1948; courtesy of Oxford University Press).

poràl gyri (of Heschl). The most anterior gyrus represents the auditory projection area of the cortex (Fig. 3–14).

The small **occipital lobe,** whose rounded apex constitutes the occipital pole, occupies only a restricted portion on the convex surface of the hemisphere. It is composed of a number of irregular and variable *lateral occipital gyri*, which are usually separated into a superior and an inferior group by the more definite and constant *lateral occipital sulcus* (Fig. 3–16).

The **insula (island of Reil)** lies buried in the lateral sulcus and can only be seen when the lips of that sulcus are drawn apart or the opercular portions removed (Fig. 3–14*B*). It then appears as a large conical or triangular elevation, the apex of which is directed forward and down-

ward to the floor of the lateral fossa. This point is known as the *limen* or threshold of the insula. The surface of the insula curves over to the inferior surface of the hemisphere and comes into relation with the olfactory area. The base of the insula is surrounded by the *circular sulcus*, really triangular in shape, which separates it from the frontal, parietal, and temporal opercula. Except for the limen, the surface of the insula is covered by sulci and gyri. A deep oblique furrow, the *longitudinal sulcus*, running parallel to the central sulcus, divides the insula into a larger anterior and a smaller posterior part. The former is composed of a number of short convolutions, the *gyri breves*. The posterior part consists of a single long convolution, the *gyrus longus*, which often shows an incomplete bifurcation.

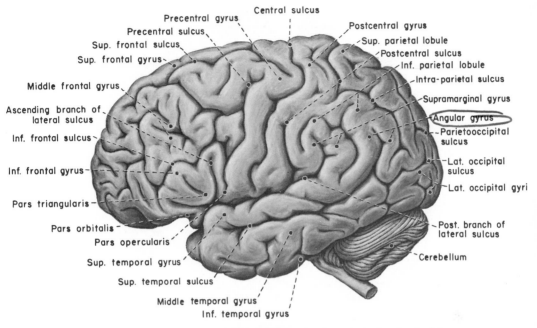

Precentral gyrus
Central sulcus
Precentral sulcus
Sup. frontal sulcus
Sup. frontal gyrus
Middle frontal gyrus
Ascending branch of lateral sulcus
Inf. frontal sulcus
Inf. frontal gyrus
Pars triangularis
Pars orbitalis
Pars opercularis
Sup. temporal gyrus
Sup. temporal sulcus
Middle temporal gyrus
Inf. temporal gyrus

Postcentral gyrus
Sup. parietal lobule
Postcentral sulcus
Inf. parietal lobule
Intra-parietal sulcus
Supramarginal gyrus
Angular gyrus
Parietooccipital sulcus
Lat. occipital sulcus
Lat. occipital gyri
Post. branch of lateral sulcus
Cerebellum

FIG. 3–16. Lateral surface of left hemisphere showing principal gyri and sulci

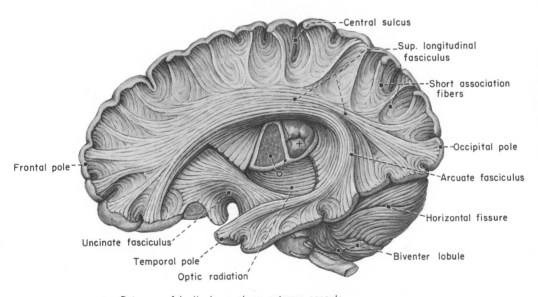

Central sulcus
Sup. longitudinal fasciculus
Short association fibers
Occipital pole
Arcuate fasciculus
Horizontal fissure
Biventer lobule

Frontal pole
Uncinate fasciculus
Temporal pole
Optic radiation

O = Putamen of lenticular nucleus; extreme capsule
+ = Cortex of insula

FIG. 3–17. Same specimen partially dissected to display underlying long and short association fibers. (Truex and Kellner, *Detailed Atlas of the Head and Neck*, 1948; courtesy of Oxford University Press).

The Medial Surface. This surface is exposed in its entirety only after the brain has been divided in the midsagittal plane and the brain stem removed posterior to the thalamus (Figs. 3–14*C* and 3–20). The cut surface of the corpus callosum appears as a white, broadly arched band whose thickened caudal end or *splenium* overhangs the pineal body and midbrain. The rostral margin turns abruptly downward

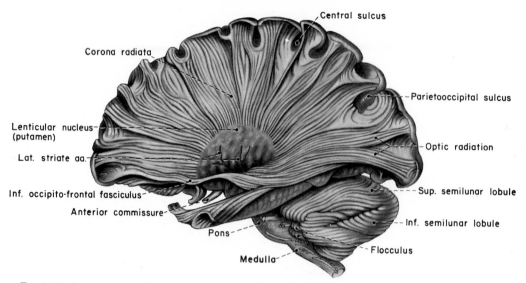

Fig. 3–18. Same specimen shown in Figures 3–16 and 3–17. Association fibers, external capsule, and insula have been removed to expose the relations of the lenticular nucleus and optic radiation.

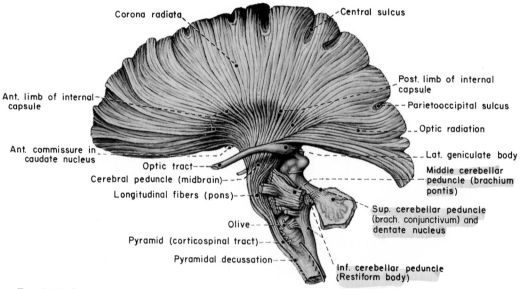

Fig. 3–19. Same specimen as shown above. Deeper dissection has been completed to demonstrate the continuity and relations of the internal capsule and cerebellar penduncles. (Truex and Kellner, *Detailed Atlas of the Head and Neck*, 1948; courtesy of Oxford University Press).

to form the *genu* and then tapers downward and backward as the *rostrum* of the corpus callosum (Fig. 3–20). The rostrum becomes attenuated into a thin membrane which extends to the anterior commissure and there becomes continuous with the lamina terminalis (Figs. 3–12 and 3–14C). Another white band, the *fornix*, emerges from the inferior side of the splenium,

arches forward over the thalamus, and enters the substance of the hypothalamus immediately in front of the interventricular foramen (Figs. 3–20 and A–26). The triangular area between fornix and corpus callosum is occupied by the membranous *septum pellucidum*.

The convolutions on the medial surface are somewhat flatter than on the convex

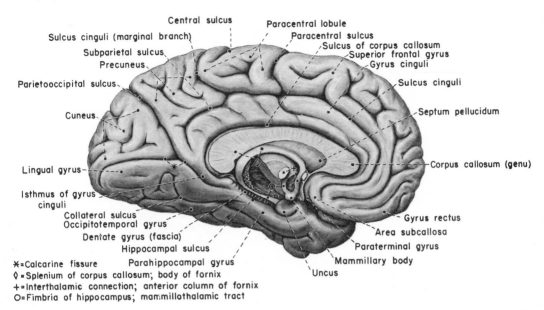

Central sulcus
Sulcus cinguli (marginal branch)
Subparietal sulcus
Precuneus
Parietooccipital sulcus
Cuneus
Lingual gyrus
Isthmus of gyrus cinguli
Collateral sulcus
Occipitotemporal gyrus
Dentate gyrus (fascia)
Hippocampal sulcus
Parahippocampal gyrus

Paracentral lobule
Paracentral sulcus
Sulcus of corpus callosum
Superior frontal gyrus
Gyrus cinguli
Sulcus cinguli
Septum pellucidum
Corpus callosum (genu)
Gyrus rectus
Area subcallosa
Paraterminal gyrus
Mammillary body
Uncus

✱=Calcarine fissure
◊ =Splenium of corpus callosum; body of fornix
+=Interthalamic connection; anterior column of fornix
O=Fimbria of hippocampus; mammillothalamic tract

FIG. 3-20. Medial surface of left hemisphere showing principal gyri and sulci. The ependyma and part of the thalamic nuclei were removed to expose the relations of the anterior column of the fornix and the mammillothalamic tract.

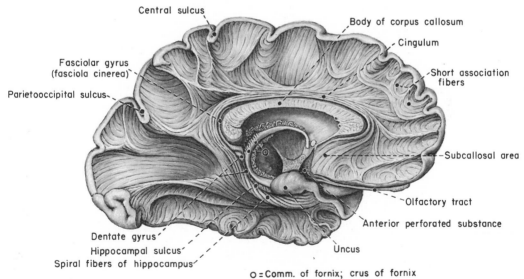

Central sulcus
Fasciolar gyrus (fasciola cinerea)
Parietooccipital sulcus
Dentate gyrus
Hippocampal sulcus
Spiral fibers of hippocampus

Body of corpus callosum
Cingulum
Short association fibers
Subcallosal area
Olfactory tract
Anterior perforated substance
Uncus

O = Comm. of fornix; crus of fornix

FIG. 3-21. Same specimen partially dissected to display underlying long and short association fibers. (Truex and Kellner, *Detailed Atlas of the Head and Neck*, 1948; courtesy of Oxford University Press).

surface, and here it is even more difficult to determine the boundaries of individual lobes. Many convolutions continue uninterruptedly from one lobe to another. Only the superior half of the occipital lobe is sharply separated from the parietal by the deep parieto-occipital sulcus. A sur-

vey of the principal sulci will facilitate an understanding of the convolutional pattern and the allocation of the various parts to the respective lobes.

The corpus callosum is separated from the gyrus overlying it by the *callosal sulcus*. Beginning at the genu, the sulcus follows the superior surface of the corpus callosum and curves around the splenium to be continued as the *hippocampal sulcus*, which extends to the anterior portion of the temporal lobe (Figs. 3–14C and 3–20). The *sulcus cinguli* runs parallel with the callosal sulcus to about the region of the splenium, where it turns upward as the *marginal sulcus* and reaches the superior border a short distance behind the central sulcus. Another furrow, the *subparietal sulcus*, which is usually regarded as a direct prolongation of the sulcus cinguli, though often discontinuous with it, passes backward around the splenium. The sulcus cinguli gives off a number of ascending branches, one of which, the *paracentral sulcus*, may reach the superior border at a point corresponding roughly to the position of the precentral sulcus (Fig. 3–20).

Thus the whole medial surface in front of and above the corpus callosum is divided by the cingular (and subparietal) sulcus into two tiers, an outer or marginal tier and an inner one, the *gyrus cinguli*, encircling the corpus callosum. The whole anterior portion of the outer tier up to the paracentral sulcus belongs to the frontal lobe and is the medial extension of the superior frontal gyrus. The paracentral lobule, between the paracentral and marginal sulci, is notched by the central sulcus. This area represents the medial continuation of both precentral and postcentral gyri, which here become continuous. The larger anterior portion belongs to the frontal, the small posterior portion to the parietal lobe. Behind the marginal ramus is the *precuneus* or *quadrate lobule*, belonging entirely to the parietal lobe and sharply marked off behind from the occipital lobe by the deep parieto-occipital sulcus (Fig. 3–20).

Closely related to the rostrum of the corpus callosum are two small cortical fields belonging to the rhinencephalon. The *paraterminal gyrus* is closely applied to the rostral lamina, and more anterior is the *area subcallosa* (Broca). The latter is continuous in front with the superior frontal gyrus and above with the gyrus cinguli (Fig. 3–20).

The *calcarine sulcus* is a deeply arched cleft extending from the midtemporal region to the occipital pole, its anterior portion producing an elevation (*calcar avis*) in the wall of the lateral ventricle (Fig. 3–15). Beginning near the hippocampal fissure, it runs horizontally backward and, near its middle, is joined at acute angles by the *parieto-occipital sulcus*, which extends obliquely downward and forward from the superior border. Then the calcarine fissure arches inferiorly and usually terminates near the occipital pole, occasionally rounding the pole and extending a short distance on the lateral surface. Inferior to the calcarine fissure is the deep *collateral sulcus*, which likewise produces an impression in the ventricular wall (Fig. 3–22). It runs forward from the region of the occipital pole and, in the anterior portion of the temporal lobe, usually becomes continuous with the shallow *rhinal sulcus*, a phylogenetically old furrow separating the terminal paleopallial portion of the parahippocampal gyrus from the rest of the temporal lobe (Fig. 3–14C). Below and parallel to the collateral sulcus is the inferior temporal sulcus, practically at the margin of transition between the inferior and lateral surfaces.

The above named sulci enclose the following convolutions of the occipital and temporal lobes. The occipital lobe is divided by the *calcarine sulcus* into the superior wedge-shaped *cuneus*, which is limited above by the parieto-occipital sulcus, and the ventral tongue-shaped *lingual gyrus*, which is bounded below by the collateral sulcus (Fig. 3–20). The cuneus belongs entirely to the occipital lobe, but the lingual gyrus extends into the temporal lobe. The lips of the calcarine sulcus constitute the primary visual area of the cortex. Anteriorly the lingual gyrus overlaps the caudal part of the *parahippocampal gyrus*, the most medial convolution of the temporal lobe. It is bounded inferiorly by the rhinal and collateral sulci and superiorly by the hippocampal sulcus. The rostral portion of the parahippocampal gyrus hooks around the front end of the *hippocampal sulcus* to form a short recurrent convolution, the *uncus*.

The parahippocampal gyrus is directly continuous with the gyrus cinguli by a narrow strip of cortex known as the *isthmus of the gyrus cinguli*. Inferior to the parahippocampal and lingual gyri and forming part of the inferior surface is the long *occipitotemporal gyrus*, which is bounded above by the collateral sulcus and below by the inferior temporal sulcus. The larger anterior part of the gyrus cinguli (anterior to the region of the central sulcus) belongs to the frontal lobe, and the smaller posterior portion to the parietal. The parahippocampal gyrus and uncus are included in the temporal lobe.

The **inferior** surface is divided into two parts. The larger posterior portion belonging to the temporal and occipital lobes rests on the tentorium cerebelli and middle cranial fossa (Fig. 3–15). Its gyri and sulci, visible on the medial surface, have been descibed in the preceding paragraphs. The smaller anterior part forms the orbital surface of the frontal lobe. It is divided by the deep straight *olfactory sulcus* into a narrow medial convolution, the *gyrus rectus*, and a larger lateral area composed of a number of irregular and variable *orbital gyri* (Fig. 3–4). The irregular sulci which separate the orbital convolutions form patterns of various shapes. Sometimes they have the form of a Maltese cross or an H, dividing the orbital area into four portions: lateral, medial, anterior, and posterior. Laterally the orbital area is continuous with the inferior frontal gyrus.

On the orbital surface are seen also a number of structures belonging to the olfactory lobe (Figs. 3–4, 3–15 and 4–3). The *olfactory bulb*, resting on the cribriform plate of the ethmoid bone, is a flattened ovoid body, continuous caudally with a slender band, the *olfactory tract*. Both these structures are lodged in the olfactory sulcus. Posteriorly the olfactory tract bifurcates into the *lateral* and *medial olfactory striae*, the bifurcation enclosing a triangular area, the *olfactory trigone*. Immediately behind the trigone is an irregular rhomboid area limited caudally by the optic tract. This area, especially in its anterior portion, is studded with numerous apertures which serve for the passage of blood vessels; hence it is known as the *anterior perforated substance* (Figs. 3–15 and A-23). All these structures belong to the olfactory lobe and will be discussed more fully with the rhinencephalon.

The Medullary Substance

The white substance, especially in man, forms a large portion of the hemisphere. It fills in all the space between cortex, ventricle, and basal ganglia and forms the medullary core of the various convolutions. It is composed of three types of fibers: (1) *projection fibers* connecting the cortex with lower levels of the nervous system; (2) *association fibers* connecting the various cortical areas of the same hemisphere; and (3) *commissural fibers,* which establish connections between areas of similar structure and function in the two hemispheres.

Many of the fiber pathways which form this seemingly homogeneous mass of white matter can be exposed by careful dissection of previously hardened or boiled specimens (Jenkins and Truex, '63). Detailed relations of the thalamus, basal ganglia, and brain stem are also revealed by dissections which begin on either the lateral (Figs. 3–16 to 3–19) or medial (Figs. 3–20 to 3–23) brain surfaces.

The intact relations of both the superficial and deep structures of the brain are shown in the series of frontal and transverse sections that follow (Figs. 3–26, 3–27, and A-14 to A-24). A key figure indicates the plane of section for each illustration. These illustrations will help explain text material and serve as a guide for dissection.

Projection Fibers. Afferent and efferent projection fibers arise from the whole extent of the cortex and enter the white substance, where they form a radiating mass of fibers, the *corona radiata*, converging toward the brain stem (Figs. 3–18 and 3–19). On reaching the latter, they form a broad compact fiber band, the **internal capsule,** flanked medially by the thalamus and caudate nucleus and laterally by the lenticular nucleus (Figs. 3–

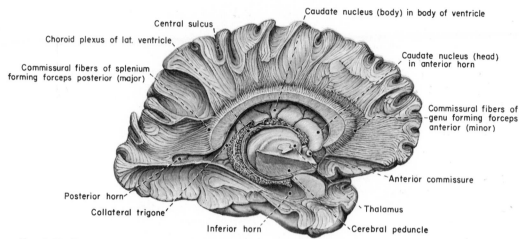

Fig. 3-22. Same specimen as shown in Figures 3-20 and 3-21. Deeper dissection has exposed the relations of the corpus callosum, lateral ventricle, and choroid plexus.

13*B* and *A*-15). The afferent fibers comprise the thalamocortical radiations in the internal capsule. The larger efferent bundles include: (1) the corticospinal and corticobulbar tracts; (2) the frontopontine tract from the prefrontal and precentral cortex; (3) the temporoparietopontine tract from the temporal and parietal lobes; and (4) corticothalamic fibers from most parts of the cortex, which are usually distributed with the corresponding thalamocortical fibers. Smaller efferent bundles arising from all areas of the cortex, especially from the premotor cortex, go to the corpus striatum. Additional efferent cortical fibers go to the hypothalamus, substantia nigra, red nucleus, and midbrain tegmentum. This conspicuous bundle of ascending and descending fibers has a fan-shaped superior telencephalic portion (corona radiata) and a curved portion at diencephalic levels (internal capsule), and it forms the crus cerebri in the midbrain. It is thus a continuous fiber bundle (Fig. 3-19). When horizontal sections are made through the curved portion at the diencephalon level, the fibers of the internal capsule have a broad V-shaped appearance pointed medially (Figs. 3-26 and 19-11). An *anterior limb* only partially separates the head of the caudate nucleus and the lenticular nucleus, for the putamen and head of the caudate nuclei remain continuous inferiorly (Figs. 3-23 and 21-4). The apex of

the V, or *genu*, separates the head of the caudate nucleus and the thalamus, while the two parts of the lenticular nucleus (putamen and globus pallidus) fill the V laterally. The *posterior limb* separates the thalamus and lenticular nucleus. The auditory radiations form part of the posterior limb before they pass below the lenticular nucleus en route to the temporal cortex (Fig. 19-11).

The most posterior component of the internal capsule is the large and well-defined *optic radiation* (Figs. 3-18, 3-23 and 3-26). It is composed of fibers going to (geniculocalcarine), and coming from (occipitogeniculate and occipitomesencephalic), the occipital cortex. As the fibers of the optic radiation enter and leave the lateral geniculate body and adjacent thalamus, they pass deep to the posterior portion of the lenticular nucleus (Fig. 3-18). Some of the fibers sweep forward in a broad loop (Figs. 3-17 and 3-23) as they curve laterally to form part of the roof and lateral wall of the posterior horn (Figs. 3-15, 3-23 and 3-24). The fibers of the radiation are separated from the lumen by two structures: a thin band of callosal fibers called the *tapetum* (Fig. 3-24) and the ependymal lining of the ventricle.

Association Fibers. The association fibers are tremendously developed in man. They may run either within the cortex itself or in the medullary substance and are hence designated as *intracortical* and

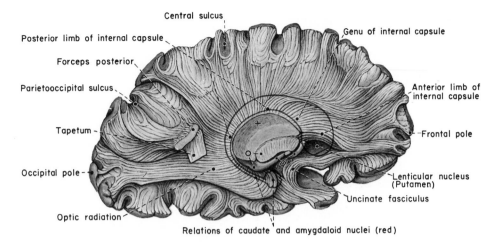

Central sulcus

Posterior limb of internal capsule

Forceps posterior

Parietooccipital sulcus

Tapetum

Occipital pole

Optic radiation

Genu of internal capsule

Anterior limb of internal capsule

Frontal pole

Lenticular nucleus (Putamen)

Uncinate fasciculus

Relations of caudate and amygdaloid nuclei (red)

+ = Thalamus
O = Lat. geniculate body; cerebral peduncle
◊ = Optic tract; anterior commissure

FIG. 3–23. Same specimen as shown above. Most of the corpus callosum, the choroid plexus, and the caudate nucleus were removed to display the medial surfaces of the optic radiation and internal capsule. See the relations of optic radiation in Figures 3–15 and 3–24. (Truex and Kellner, *Detailed Atlas of the Head and Neck*, 1948; courtesy of Oxford University Press).

subcortical. The latter, which are discussed here, may be grouped into short and long association fibers. The short ones, known as arcuate fibers, curve around the floor of each sulcus, thus connecting adjacent convolutions (Figs. 3–17 and 3–21). Such fibers are found in every part of the neopallium and always run transversely to the long axis of the sulcus. Short subcortical fibers which run lengthwise are unknown; hence diffusion of neural impulses along a single convolution must be mediated entirely by intracortical fibers. Besides the short arcuate fibers, there are longer ones which may bridge two or even three sulci.

The **long association fibers,** which interconnect parts of different lobes within the same hemisphere, lie more deeply in the medullary substance. The majority are organized into more or less distinct, longitudinally running bundles which have an arched course conforming to the shape of the hemisphere. The most prominent of these are the uncinate fasciculus, arcuate fasciculus, and cingulum. The *uncinate fasciculus*, lying immediately below the limen insulae, is a compact bundle in its middle portion but spreads out

fanlike at either end (Figs. 3–17, 3–23, and A-24). The most inferior fibers loop sharply around the lateral fossa, connecting the posterior orbital gyri with the tip of the parahippocampal gyrus. The looping superior fibers gradually flatten out, and finally, becoming straight, run obliquely downward from the frontal to the temporal lobe. The bundle connects the orbital gyri and rostral portions of the middle and inferior frontal convolutions with the anterior portion of the temporal lobe. The most deeply placed part of the fascicle is designated as the *inferior occipitofrontal fasciculus*, which is believed to connect the frontal and occipital lobes (Fig. 3–18).

Lying more superiorly is a similar bundle, the *arcuate fasciculus*, which sweeps around the insula parallel to the circular sulcus. It likewise has a compact middle portion with radiating fan-shaped ends (Fig. 3–17). In its inferior portion, the fibers are strongly arched and connect the superior and middle frontal convolutions with the temporal lobe, some fibers reaching the temporal pole. The superior part, also known as the *superior longitudinal fasciculus*, connects the upper

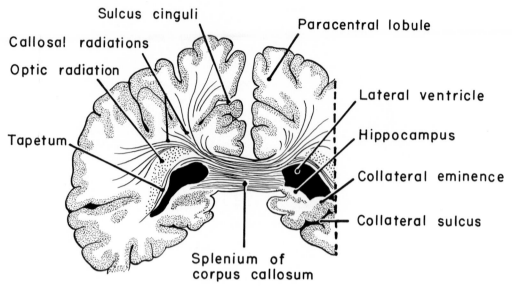

Fig. 3–24. Diagram of frontal section of brain passing though splenium of corpus callosum. Dissections of the optic radiation are shown in Figures 3–15 and 3–18.

and caudal portions of the frontal lobe, including the precentral gyrus, with the occipital and parietal lobes.

The medial surfaces of the frontal, parietal, and temporal lobes are likewise interconnected by a system of long association fibers which run longitudinally in the underlying medullary substance. Many of these fibers are organized diffusely but the basal portion of this system forms a well-marked, arched bundle, the *cingulum*. It is placed in the medullary substance of the gyrus cinguli, immediately above the corpus callosum (Fig. 3–21). The bundle follows the contour of the gyrus cinguli, extending from beneath the rostrum of the corpus callosum (subcallosal area) to the splenium where it is continued as a greatly diminished strand into the parahippocampal gyrus and uncus. The cingulum contains fibers of varying length, the longest and most curved ones connecting the frontal lobe with the parahippocampal and adjacent temporal regions.

Running along the lateral walls of the posterior and inferior horns of the lateral ventricle is a longitudinal band of fibers which extends from the occipital to the temporal pole and was formerly thought

to be an occipitotemporal association tract. It has been designated by some as the *inferior longitudinal fasciculus*, and by others as the *external sagittal stratum*. When the bundle is exposed from the medial surface, however, it becomes obvious that it consists mainly of fibers of the geniculocalcarine tract (optic radiation), which run forward into the temporal lobe and then loop backward to go to the calcarine region (Figs. 3–18, 3–23 and 3–24). Afferent projection fibers from the pulvinar to the occipital cortex and efferent temporopontine fibers likewise contribute to the bundle. It seems certain that the external sagittal stratum constitutes primarily a mixed fiber system of which the geniculocalcarine tract forms by far the largest component.

Vertical association fibers running in the medullary substance of the convex surface are also found, but in relatively few numbers. The *vertical occipital fasciculus* runs in the front part of the occipital lobe and apparently connects the inferior parietal lobule with the more caudal portions of the temporal gyri. Other vertical fibers connect the more superior regions of the frontal lobe with the orbital gyri.

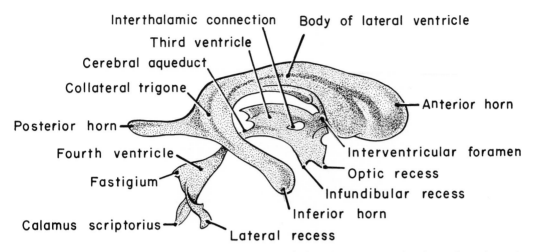

FIG. 3–25. Cast of the brain ventricles. Compare with lateral ventricle of left hemisphere shown in Figure 3–22.

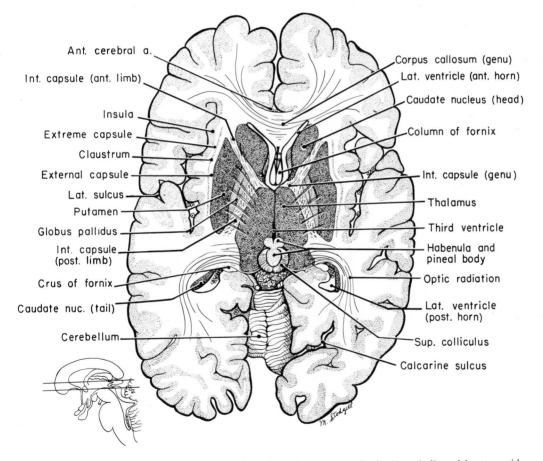

FIG. 3–26. Diagram of a horizontal section through the long axis of the brain as indicated by *top quide line in small key diagram*. Note relations of internal capsule to thalamus, caudate and lenticular nuclei.

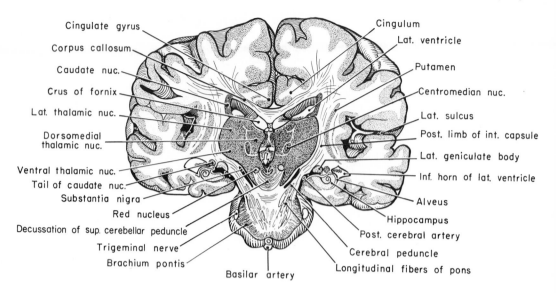

FIG. 3–27. Diagram of a frontal section of brain through junction of thalamus and midbrain rostral to the posterior commissure. The *arrow* indicates the ostium of the cerebral aqueduct.

The *fornix* forms a distinct white band of fibers which can be seen partially on the medial brain surface. It extends from the anterior commissure anteriorly to the hippocampus inferiorly (Figs. 3–20 and 3–21). Fibers of the *anterior columns* of the fornix split to pass anterior and posterior to the anterior commissure. Most of the fibers pass behind the commissure, sink beneath the ependyma of the third ventricle, and descend to form a white covering on the mammillary body (Fig. 3–20). The anterior columns become approximated as they arch upward over the thalamus to form the *body* of the fornix. The body divides posteriorly to form two large *crura*, which curve laterally and inferiorly to form a thin white fascicle, the *fimbria* of the fornix (Figs. 21–4 and 21–6). The two diverging crura are connected posteriorly by the small flattened *commissure of the fornix* (Fig. 3–21). Owing to the length and curved course of the fornix, its cut fibers may appear twice in some transverse sections (e.g., Figs. 3–26 and *A*-17).

Another small white bundle that can be dissected from the substance of the thalamus is the *mammillothalamic* tract. It extends upwards from the mammillary body to the anterior nuclear group of the thalamus. This bundle is a diencephalic fiber bundle, however, and is not a cortical association pathway.

The external and extreme capsules are shown in Figures 3–17, 3–26 and 20–1. These two thin layers of white matter that enclose the claustrum are composed primarily of association fibers.

Commissural Fibers. The crossed commissural fibers are primarily represented by the massive *corpus callosum*, which reciprocally interconnects the neopallial cortex of the two hemispheres. In its middle portions, the commissure is a broad thick plate of densely packed transverse fibers in the floor of the interhemispheric fissure which forms most of the roof of the lateral ventricles (Fig. 3–22). Laterally it spreads out on either side into a mass of radiating fibers, the callosal radiations, which are distributed to practically all parts of the cortex. Since the rostral and caudal ends of the corpus callosum are placed at a considerable distance from the frontal and occipital poles respectively, the fibers distributed to these regions of the two hemispheres form U-shaped bundles known as the *anterior* and the *posterior forceps*. The former loops forward from the genu toward the frontal pole (Fig. 3–26); the larger posterior forcep loops backward toward the occipital pole. The genu supplies the larger anterior part of the frontal lobe; the whole parietal lobe and the caudal portion of the frontal lobe receive fibers from the body of the commissure. The fibers which connect the temporal and occipital lobes traverse the splenium and posterior part of the trunk. These fibers are split by the optic radiations which run in a more horizontal course through this portion of the medullary substance (Fig. 3–24). The superior fibers supply the lateral portions of the temporal and occipital lobes. The inferior fibers pass medial to the sagittal strata and form a thin medullary plate, the *tapetum*, which sweeps around the ependymal lining of the roof and lateral wall of the inferior and posterior horn (Fig. 3–24). The tapetum is distributed to the medial and inferior surfaces of the temporal and occipital lobes.

The exact distribution of the callosal fibers has not been fully ascertained. For the most part they connect identical portions of the two hemispheres, but fibers connecting morphologically dissimilar areas also are present. The fibers are difficult to follow beyond the lateral ventricles, where they become intermingled with association and projection fibers.

The *anterior commissure* is a large bundle of white fibers crossing the median plane through the lamina terminalis (Figs. 3–12, 3–18 and 3–23). Its fibers connect the olfactory bulb, and portions of the temporal lobe of the two hemispheres (Brodal, '48). Experimental studies in the monkey have shown that some of these commissural fibers traverse the external capsule to reach the cortex of the middle temporal gyrus as well (Fox et al., '48). In its horizontal course, the anterior commissure can be traced through the most ventral part of the lenticular nucleus (Figs. 3–15 and 3–23). It is also a prominent landmark in gross and microscopic sections that cut through this area (Figs. A-16, A-17, A-18 and A-25).

The Third Ventricle

Although chiefly surrounded by structures of the diencephalon, the third ventricle is a vital channel interposed between the lateral ventricles and the more caudally placed cerebral aqueduct and fourth ventricle (Fig. 3–25). The two thalami form its lateral walls, while its anterior wall is composed of the lamina terminalis and anterior commissure (Figs. 3–11 and 3–13). Hypothalamic structures form the floor. These are the optic chiasm, infundibulum, tuber cinereum, and mammillary bodies. The roof is formed by the thin layer of ependyma, which is attached to the striae medullares thalami. On the outer surface of the ependymal roof is a fold of pia mater, loose connective tissue, and blood vessels (velum interpositum). Vascular pial folds invaginate the ependymal layer, and together they form the choroid plexuses (Fig 3–13). Two plexuses extend the entire length of the roof, between the interventricular foramen, and the habenular trigone.

Small outpocketings are produced along the margins of the third ventricle by diencephalic structures. These small *recesses* (optic, infundibular, and pineal) often are visualized during air studies of the ventricles and thus provide valuable radiological landmarks (Fig. 3–25). Likewise, shadows of the interthalamic connection and anterior commissure, as well as a calcified pineal body, can be identified in many films.

The Lateral Ventricles

These ependyma-lined cavities have an arched shape corresponding to the form of the hemispheres. They communicate with the rostral part of the third ventricle by two short channels, the *interventricular foramina* (Figs. 3–12 and 3–25). The ventricles vary considerably in width, in some cases being narrow and cleftlike, in other cases becoming relatively wide spaces. Normally they contain variable amounts of cerebrospinal fluid. Pathological enlargement of the ventricles, and a corresponding increase in their fluid content, constitutes the condition known as internal hydrocephalus.

Each ventricle consists of a *central portion* or *body* from which three prolongations or horns extend, respectively, into the frontal, temporal, and occipital lobes (Figs. 3–22 and 3–25). The **anterior** or **frontal horn** extends forward from the interventricular foramen and in frontal section has a triangular shape (Fig. A-24). Its roof and rostral wall are formed by the corpus callosum, while medially it is separated from the horn of the opposite side by the thin vertical laminae of the septum pellucidum. The slanting floor and lateral wall are formed by the head of the caudate nucleus, whose surface bulges convexly into the cavity of the anterior horn (Figs. 3–22 and A-24).

The **central portion** is a relatively shallow cavity extending from the interventricular foramen to the splenium, where it enlarges into the *collateral trigone* formed by the junction of posterior and inferior horns (Fig. 3–22). Its roof is formed by the corpus callosum. The floor is formed by a number of structures (Figs. 3–13 and A-19). Most laterally is the caudate nucleus, forming a bulge in the ventricular cavity. Proceeding medially are the stria terminalis, a part of the thalamic surface (lamina affixa), the choroid plexus, and the fornix.

The **posterior** or **occipital horn** extends a variable distance into the occipital lobe. It may be quite short and taper rapidly to a point, or it may form a longer, more tubular prolongation. Its roof and lateral wall are formed by the tapetal fibers of the corpus callosum (Figs. 3–15 and 3–24), its floor by the medullary substance of the occipital lobe. The medial wall shows a longitudinal prominence, the *calcar avis*, produced by the deep penetration of the calcarine fissure (Fig. 3–15).

The **inferior** or **temporal horn** begins at the collateral trigone, curves inferiorly around the posterior portion of the thalamus, and extends rostrally into the medial part of the temporal lobe, ending about 1 inch from the temporal pole (Fig.

3–22). Its floor, directly continuous with that of the posterior horn, is marked by a more or less distinct prominence, the *collateral eminence*, caused by the deep collateral fissure (Fig. 3–24). The roof and lateral wall are formed largely by the tapetum and optic radiation. In the medial region of the roof a small part is furnished by the tail of the caudate nucleus and the accompanying stria terminalis (Figs. 3–13 and A-19).

The most remarkable feature of the inferior horn is the *hippocampus* (*horn of Ammon*), which is produced by the infolding of the pallium along the hippocampal sulcus (Figs. 3–21, 3–27 and 21–8). The hippocampus is a prominent sickle-shaped ridge on the medial wall of the horn, extending from the region of the splenium to the temporal tip of the ventricle, where it is continuous with the ventricular surface of the uncus. Running along the superior and medial surfaces of the hippocampus is a flattened white band, the *fimbria*, which extends from the region of the uncus toward the splenium and is directly continued into the crus of the fornix (Figs. 3–20, 3–27 and 21–7). Hippocampus and fimbria are in part overlapped by the inferior portion of the choroid plexus, which extends from the interventricular foramen to the tip of the inferior horn (Figs. 3–13 and 3–22).

It will be shown that the cerebral vesicle during development expanded first anteriorly, then superiorly (see Fig. 5–10A). Later, it expanded in a posterior and inferior direction. This embryonic pattern of growth accounts for the C-shaped configuration of several structures observed in the adult cerebral hemisphere (e.g., lateral ventricle, caudate nucleus, choroid plexus, and fornix). The curvature of these adult structures also accounts for their appearance twice in one plane of section (Figs. 3–26, 3–27 and A-15). Likewise, embryonic development of the cerebral vesicle (page 101) and the enlargement of the corpus callosum (Fig. 5–13) help explain the pattern and relations of the cerebral blood vessels, which are considered next.

CHAPTER 4

Blood Supply Of The Central Nervous System

Metabolically the brain is one of the most active organs of the body. Its metabolism depends almost entirely upon the aerobic combustion of glucose. Since there is little storage of glucose or oxygen in the brain, brief interference with cerebral circulation can produce profound disturbances of neurological and mental functions. The duration of consciousness after complete cessation of brain circulation is less than 10 seconds. Estimates of cerebral blood flow based on the nitrous oxide method of Kety and Schmidt ('48) indicate a normal blood flow of about 50 ml per 100 gm of brain tissue per minute. Thus, a brain of average weight has a normal blood flow of about 750 ml per minute. The mean oxygen consumption in the normal conscious individual is about 3.3 ml per 100 gm. of brain tissue, or about 46 ml per minute for the entire brain. Thus the brain, constituting about 2 percent of the body weight, requires about 17 percent of the normal cardiac output and consumes about 20 percent of the oxygen utilized by the entire body. Since the brain is not a homogeneous organ, the metabolic activity and nutritive requirements of various regions differ greatly.

If adequate circulation is not maintained to local regions of the brain or spinal cord, the neural tissue deprived of its blood supply undergoes necrosis with subsequent softening and degeneration. Neural lesions resulting from local, or regional, impairment of blood supply constitute the most common type of focal or generalized injury to the central nervous system. Most commonly, vascular lesions result from disease of the cerebral vessels (arteriosclerosis) which leads to thrombosis of particular vessels. Occlusions of cerebral vessels due to embolism may result from fragments of blood clots, fat, tumors or in some instances, from air bubbles. Hemorrhage into the brain or meninges may result from pathological changes in cerebral vessels. One of the most common causes of spontaneous hemorrhage into the brain and the subarachnoid space is rupture of abnormal sacculations (aneurysms), most of which are of congenital origin. Localized neural lesions resulting from interruptions of blood supply often can be correlated with specific sensory and motor changes which are characteristic for different cerebral vessels.

BLOOD SUPPLY OF THE SPINAL CORD

The arterial supply of the spinal cord is derived from two principal sources: (1) the *vertebral arteries*, and (2) the *radicular arteries* derived from segmental vessels (i.e., deep cervical, intercostal,

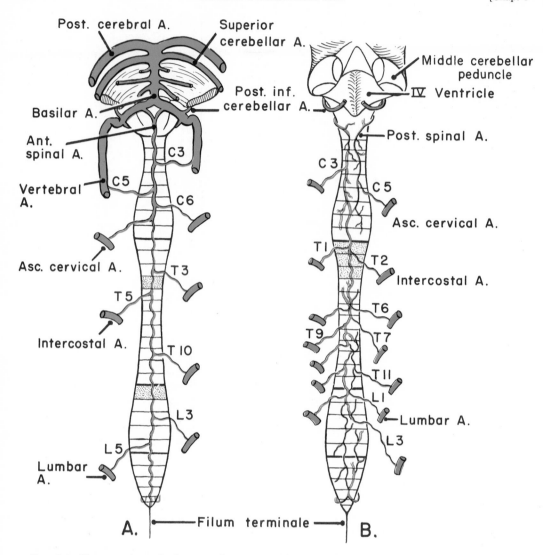

FIG. 4–1. Diagram of vessels that contribute arterial blood to the spinal cord. *A*, Anterior surface and arteries; *B*, posterior surface and arteries. Vulnerable segments of the spinal cord are *stippled*. *Letters* and *numbers* indicate most important radicular arteries. (Based on the work of Bolton, '39; Suh and Alexander, '39; and Zülch, '54.)

lumbar and sacral arteries). Virtually the entire cervical spinal cord is supplied by small branches of the two vertebral arteries (Fig. 4–1). Radicular arteries course along the spinal nerves, pass through the intervertebral foramina and divide into smaller *anterior* and larger *posterior radicular arteries*.

Each vertebral artery gives off two small, but highly important, arteries as it ascends along the anterolateral surface of the medulla. The first, or most inferior

branch, the *posterior spinal artery*, turns dorsally and descends as a discrete vessel on the posterior surface of the spinal cord (Fig. 4–1*B*). As the two posterior spinal arteries descend, they receive a variable number of contributions (from 5 to 8) from the posterior radicular arteries. The second, or more superior branch, is the anterior spinal artery. These two vessels unite anterior to the pyramids to form a single descending *anterior spinal artery* (Fig. 4–1*A*). This vessel provides

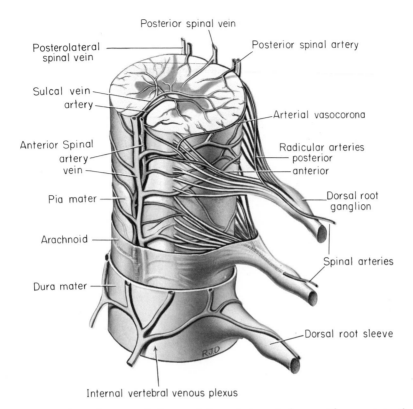

FIG. 4–2. Blood supply and venous drainage of the spinal cord shown with respect to the meninges and internal structure.

midline rami to the lower medulla, and caudally gives off sulcal arteries that enter the anterior median fissure to supply the spinal cord. The single anterior spinal artery varies in size as it descends. According to Suh and Alexander ('39), the continuity of this artery is dependent upon the anastomosing vessels it receives from the anterior radicular arteries (6 to 8). A plexus of smaller arteries within the pia mater, the *arterial vasocorona*, interconnects the larger arterial vessels on the anterior and posterior surfaces of the spinal cord (Fig. 4–2).

The blood supply of the spinal cord may be jeopardized in certain transitional regions where its arterial supply is derived from two different sources. For example, the cervical segments are supplied primarily by branches of the vertebral artery and to a lesser extent by small branches of the ascending cervical artery. The upper segments of the thoracic spinal cord, on the other hand, are dependent upon the radicular branches of the intercostal arteries. If one or more of the parent intercostal vessels are compromised by injury or ligature, segments of the spinal cord T1–4 could not be adequately maintained by the small sulcal branches of the anterior spinal artery (Fig. 4–1A). For this reason, thoracic segments T1–4, particularly T4, are considered vulnerable areas in the distribution of the anterior spinal artery (Zülch, '54). Spinal cord segment L1 is an equally vulnerable region. The posterior surface of the cord most susceptible to vascular insult is also in segments T1–4 (Fig. 4–1B). Such vascular injuries may result in necrosis of an entire segment and produce neurological symptoms comparable to complete cord transection (page 295).

The anterior spinal artery gives off a number of *sulcal* (sulcocommissural) branches which enter the anterior median fissure of the cord and pass alternately to the right and left (Gillilan, '58). Only in the lumbar and sacral segments does an occasional single sulcal artery penetrate into the fissure and divide into left and right branches. The anterior sulcal arteries are most numerous in the lumbar region and least numerous in the thoracic region, where the segmental blood supply is poorest. In the thoracic region only one sulcal artery may enter an entire segment (Herren and Alexander, '39).

The anterior spinal artery, through its sulcal branches, supplies the anterior and lateral horns, the central gray, and the base of the posterior horn (Fig. 4–2). It also supplies the anterior and lateral funiculi, including the lateral pyramidal tract. To a lesser degree, the lateral funiculus also is supplied by branches from the arterial vasocorona. The posterior spinal arteries nourish the posterior gray horn and posterior funiculus.

The venous distribution is in the main similar to that of the arteries (Fig. 4–2). There are 6 to 11 anterior and 5 to 10 posterior radicular veins, one of which, situated in the lumbar region, is of considerably greater caliber and is known as the *vena radicularis magna* (Suh and Alexander, '39). The posterior radicular veins form a more or less distinct posterior median spinal vein, or trunk, along the whole extent of the cord, as well as smaller paired posterolateral trunks. Similarly, an anterior median vein, and paired anterolateral venous trunks, are formed from the anterior radicular veins. As in the case of the arteries, a meningeal plexus of veins, the vasocorona, connects the longitudinal trunks. From the anterior spinal vein, sulcal branches pass into the anterior median fissure and enter the cord, each sulcal vessel as a rule receiving venous blood from both sides of the cord.

The posterior radicular veins (and posterior trunks) drain the posterior funiculus, the posterior horn, including its base, and a narrow strip of lateral funiculus immediately adjacent to the posterior horn (Fig. 4–2). The anterior spinal vein, through the sulcal vessels, drains the sulcomarginal white matter and the medial portion of the anterior horn. The lateral portions of the anterior horn, the lateral horn, and the anterior and lateral funiculi are drained by branches of the venous vasocorona (Fig. 4–2).

THE BLOOD SUPPLY OF THE BRAIN

The entire brain is supplied by two pairs of arterial trunks, the internal carotid arteries and the vertebral arteries. On the left the common carotid artery arises directly from the aortic arch; the right common carotid is one of the two branches which arises from the bifurcation of the brachiocephalic artery. The common carotid artery bifurcates at the upper level of the thyroid cartilage forming the internal and external carotid arteries.

The Internal Carotid Artery can be divided into four segments: cervical, intrapetrosal, intracavernous and supraclinoid. The *cervical segment*, which has no branches, extends from the bifurcation of the common carotid to the point where the vessel enters the carotid canal in the petrous bone. The *intrapetrosal segment* of this vessel is surrounded by dense bone. The *intracavernous segment* of the internal carotid artery lies close to the medial wall of the cavernous sinus, courses nearly horizontally, and bears important relationships to cranial nerves III, IV, V and VI which are within this sinus. The *supraclinoid segment* of the internal carotid begins as the artery emerges from the cavernous sinus and passes medial to the anterior clinoid process. This portion of the artery usually extends upward and backward toward its bifurcation, but variations are common. The intracavernous and supraclinoid portions of the internal carotid artery are referred to as the "carotid siphon" by neuroradiologists (Taveras and Wood, '64). Although all major branches of the internal carotid artery arise from the supraclinoid portion of this vessel, numerous small branches are given off from the intrapetrosal and intracavernous portions. These include branches to the tympanic cavity (caroticotympanic), the cavernous and inferior petrosal sinuses, the trigeminal ganglion, and the meninges of the middle fossa.

Major branches of the internal carotid artery, originating from the supraclinoid portion, are the ophthalmic, posterior communicating, and anterior choroidal arteries (Fig. 4–3 and 4–4). The *ophthalmic artery* enters the orbit through the optic foramen, ventral and lateral to the optic nerve. The *posterior communicating artery* arises from the dorsal aspect of the carotid siphon and passes posteriorly and medially to join the posterior cerebral artery. The *anterior choroidal artery* usually arises from the internal carotid artery distal to the posterior communicating artery, and passes backward across the optic tract and then laterally to enter the choroidal fissure in the temporal lobe. Lateral to the optic chiasm the internal carotid artery divides into its two terminal branches: the smaller *anterior cerebral artery* and the larger *middle cerebral artery*, which is regarded as the direct continuation of the internal carotid artery.

Most of the arterial blood within the internal carotid artery is distributed by the more mobile branches of the anterior and middle cerebral arteries. The rostral parts of the brain normally supplied by these two arteries, are the anterior half of the thalamus, the corpus striatum, the corpus callosum, most of the internal capsule, the medial and lateral surfaces of the frontal and parietal lobes, and the lateral surface of the temporal lobe (Figs. 4–3, 4–5, 4–6, and 4–10).

The Vertebral Artery originates as the first branch of the subclavian artery on each side, enters the foramen transversarium of the 6th cervical vertebra and ascends in the foramina transversaria in all higher cervical vertebrae. This artery curves posteriorly around the superior articular process of the atlas, passes forward and medially to pierce the atlanto-occipital membrane and dura, and enters the posterior fossa through the foramen magnum. The cervical part of the vertebral artery gives rise to spinal and muscular branches. Thin radicular branches of the vertebral artery pass through the intervertebral foramina to supply the meninges and spinal cord (Fig. 4–1). The relationships of the two vertebral ar-

teries to the anterior and posterior surfaces of the caudal brain stem are shown in Figures 2–5, 2–6, 4–1 and 4–3. The two vertebral arteries unite at the caudal border of the pons to form the basilar artery. Branches of these three arteries normally provide the sole arterial blood supply to the caudal structures of the brain, including the cervical spinal cord, medulla, pons, midbrain, cerebellum, posterior portion of the thalamus, occipital lobe, and medioinferior surfaces of the temporal lobe (Fig. 4–3). The slender labyrinthine branch of the basilar artery follows the course of the vestibulocochlear nerve and thus nourishes internal ear structures through its vestibular and cochlear rami.

The Cerebral Arterial Circle (of Willis) is a circular, or heptagonal, arterial wreath surrounding the optic chiasm, tuber cinereum and interpeduncular region, formed by the anastomosing branches of the internal carotid arteries and the basilar artery. This arterial circle is formed by anterior and posterior communicating arteries and proximal portions of the anterior, middle, and posterior cerebral arteries. The *anterior cerebral arteries* run medially and rostrally toward the interhemispheric fissure; in the region in front of the optic chiasm these two arteries are joined by a short connecting vessel, the *anterior communicating artery*. At the rostral border of the pons the basilar artery bifurcates forming the two *posterior cerebral arteries*. The *posterior communicating arteries* arise from the internal carotid arteries and anastomose with proximal portions of the posterior cerebral arteries. The posterior cerebral arteries give rise to numerous small branches that enter the interpeduncular fossa and hypothalamus, while the main vessels pass laterally, rostral to the root fibers of the oculomotor nerve, and encircle part of the mesencephalon before passing above the tentorium cerebelli (Figs. 4–3 and 4–4). The cerebral arterial circle formed by the anastomoses of these vessels is said to equalize blood flow to various parts of the brain, but normally there is little ex-

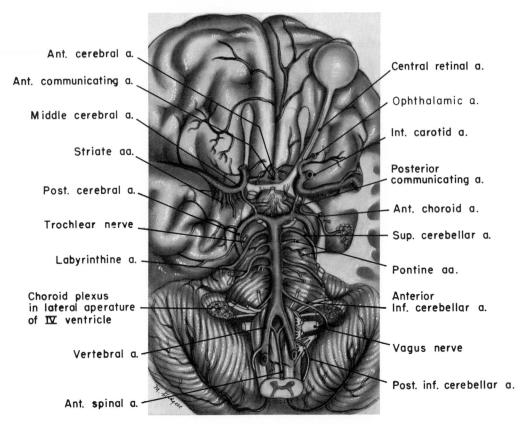

Ant. cerebral a.

Ant. communicating a.

Middle cerebral a.

Striate aa.

Post. cerebral a.

Trochlear nerve

Labyrinthine a.

Choroid plexus
in lateral aperature
of IV ventricle

Vertebral a.

Ant. spinal a.

Central retinal a.

Ophthalamic a.

Int. carotid a.

Posterior
communicating a.

Ant. choroid a.

Sup. cerebellar a.

Pontine aa.

Anterior
Inf. cerebellar a.

Vagus nerve

Post. inf. cerebellar a.

FIG. 4–3. Formation and branches of the arterial circle on the inferior surface of the brain. The relationships of the arterial circle to structures on the base of the skull are shown in Figure 4–4.

change of blood between the right and left halves of the arterial circle, because of the equality of blood pressure. Alterations of blood flow in the arterial circle undoubtedly occur following occlusion of one or more of the arteries contributing to the circle. However, the communicating arteries of the arterial circle often form functionally inadequate anastomoses which account for the high incidence of serious disturbances in blood flow following unilateral occlusion or compression of the internal carotid artery, especially in elderly individuals.

Relationships of the arterial circle and its branches to the inferior surface of the brain and the origins of the respective cranial nerves are shown in Figure 4–3. The *in situ* surgical relationships of the arterial circle to the base of the skull following removal of the brain can be appreciated by comparing Figure 4–4 with the relationships illustrated in Figure 4–3.

From the arterial circle and the main cerebral arteries (anterior, middle, and posterior) arise two types of branches: the *central* or *ganglionic*, and the *circumferential* or *cortical*. The central and cortical arteries form two distinct systems. The *central* arteries arise from the circle of Willis and the proximal portions of the three cerebral arteries, dip perpendicularly into the brain substance, and supply the diencephalon, corpus striatum, and internal capsule. For a long time these penetrating vessels have been referred to as terminal or end-arteries. Studies by Scharrer ('44) indicate that the vast majority of arteries in the brains of lower animals are end-arteries but that in the human brain there are no end-arteries. Precapillary anastomoses have been observed in man and animals, but these

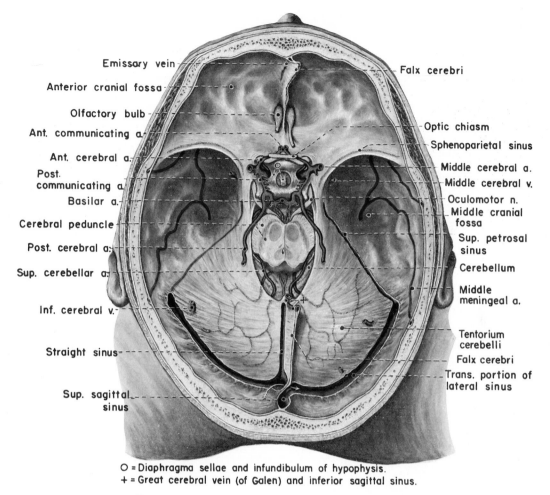

O = Diaphragma sellae and infundibulum of hypophysis.
+ = Great cerebral vein (of Galen) and inferior sagittal sinus.

FIG. 4–4. Cranial cavity after brain was removed to demonstrate relationships of the cerebral arterial circle, adjacent neural structures, and reflections of the dura mater. (Truex and Kellner, *Detailed Atlas of the Head and Neck*, 1948; courtesy of Oxford University Press.)

anastomoses usually are not sufficient to maintain adequate circulation if a major vessel is occluded suddenly. Thus, occlusion of one of these arteries produces a softening in the area deprived of an adequate blood supply. The anterior and posterior choroidal arteries, respectively branches of the internal carotid and posterior cerebral arteries, may be included in this group.

The larger *cortical* branches of each cerebral artery enter the pia mater, where they form a superficial plexus of more or less freely anastomosing vessels, which in some places may be continuous with the plexuses derived from the other main arteries. From these plexuses arise the smaller terminal arteries which enter the brain substance at right angles and run for variable distances. The shorter ones arborize in the cortex, while the longer ones supply the more deeply placed medullary substance of the hemispheres. Owing to the anastomoses of the larger cortical branches, the occlusion of one of these vessels is compensated to a variable extent by the blood supply from neighboring branches, though such collateral circulation is rarely sufficient to prevent brain damage. The great majority of vascular occlusions occur in the cerebral vessels before they enter the substance of the brain. Areas of the cerebral cortex, internal capsule, or basal ganglia

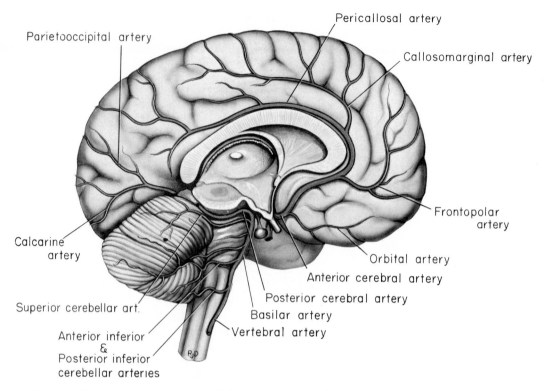

Fig. 4-5. Principal arteries on the medial surface of the cerebrum shown together with the arteries of the brain stem and cerebellum.

which lie between the territorial distributions of two primary arteries are the sites most severely involved after vascular injury (Mettler et al., '54). The degree of brain damage is variable and depends upon several factors (e.g., site of injury, amount of vascular overlap and confluence, and the rapidity with which an occlusion develops).

The Cortical Branches

The Anterior Cerebral Artery, originating at the bifurcation of the internal carotid artery, passes medially and forward dorsal to the optic nerve and approaches the corresponding artery of the opposite side with which it connects via the anterior communicating artery (Fig. 4-3). The artery then enters the interhemispheric fissure and passes forward and upward on the medial surface of the hemisphere (Fig. 4-5). In its course the artery curves around the genu of the corpus callosum and continues posteriorly along the superior surface of that commissure as the *pericallosal artery*. Branches of the pericallosal artery, which may be considered the terminal part of the anterior cerebral artery, anastomose with branches of the posterior cerebral artery. The first portion of the anterior cerebral artery gives off many small branches which supply the rostrum of the corpus callosum, the head of the caudate nucleus and the septum pellucidum. The *medial striate artery* (recurrent artery of Heubner) arises from this segment proximal to, but near, the anterior communicating artery. This vessel then courses backwards and laterally, and enters the anterior perforated substance together with the more medial lenticulostriate arteries (Figs. 4-8 and 4-10). It supplies the anteromedial part of the head of the caudate nucleus, adjacent parts of the internal capsule and putamen, and parts of the septal nuclei. The medial striate artery is said to

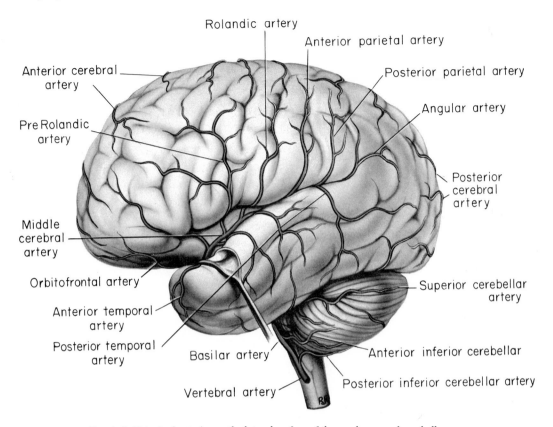

Rolandic artery

Anterior parietal artery

Posterior parietal artery

Anterior cerebral artery

Angular artery

Pre Rolandic artery

Posterior cerebral artery

Middle cerebral artery

Orbitofrontal artery

Superior cerebellar artery

Anterior temporal artery

Posterior temporal artery

Basilar artery

Anterior inferior cerebellar

Vertebral artery

Posterior inferior cerebellar artery

Fig. 4–6. Principal arteries on the lateral surface of the cerebrum and cerebellum.

anastomose with the lenticulostriate arteries and surface branches of the anterior and middle cerebral arteries (Kaplan, '58).

Orbital branches of the anterior cerebral artery arise from the ascending portion of this vessel just below the corpus callosum. These branches extend forward to supply the orbital and medial surfaces of the frontal lobe (Fig. 4–3). A *frontopolar branch* of the anterior cerebral artery is given off as the anterior cerebral artery curves around the genu of the corpus callosum. Two or three branches of the frontopolar artery supply medial parts of the frontal lobe and extend laterally on reaching the convexity of the hemisphere. A major branch of the anterior cerebral artery, the *callosomarginal artery*, arises distal to the frontopolar artery and passes backward and upward in the callosomarginal sulcus, dorsal to the cingulate gyrus (Fig. 4–5). Branches of this artery

supply the paracentral lobule and parts of the cingulate gyrus. The *pericallosal artery* is the terminal branch of the anterior cerebral artery and continues caudally along the dorsal surface of the corpus callosum; its terminal branches supply the precuneus.

The Middle Cerebral Artery, the continuation of the internal carotid artery, passes laterally over the anterior perforated substance to the lateral cerebral fossa between the temporal lobe and the insula (Fig. 4–6). This artery divides into a number of large branches in the insular region which course upward and backward; as these arteries reach the uppermost portions of the insula, they reverse their course abruptly and pass downward to the lower margin of the lateral sulcus. Branches of the middle cerebral artery emerge from the lateral sulcus and are distributed in a "fan-like" fashion over the lateral convexity of the hemisphere. These cortical branches supply lateral portions of the orbital gyri, the inferior and middle frontal gyri, large parts of the precentral and postcentral gyri, the superior and inferior parietal lobules, and the superior and middle temporal gyri, including the temporal pole. In many instances the territory of the middle cerebral artery is extended caudally to supply most of the lateral gyri of the occipital lobe.

The first branches to arise from the middle cerebral artery are the *lenticulostriate arteries* which enter the anterior perforated substance (Fig. 4–8). These vessels will be considered with the central or ganglionic branches (p. 71). The next branches to arise from the middle cerebral artery are the anterior temporal artery and the orbitofrontal artery (Fig. 4–6). The *anterior temporal artery* frequently anastomoses with temporal branches of the posterior cerebral artery, while the *orbitofrontal artery* may anastomose with the frontopolar branch of the anterior cerebral artery. Ascending branches of the middle cerebral artery, given off more distally, include *pre-Rolandic branches*, a *Rolandic branch*, an *anterior parietal* (or post-Rolandic) *branch* and a *posterior parietal branch*. A *posterior temporal branch* extends backwards to supply lateral portions of the occipital lobe. The angular branches supplying the angular gyrus constitute the terminal part of the middle cerebral artery.

Thus the extensive and important territory nourished by the middle cerebral artery includes the motor and premotor areas, the somesthetic and auditory projection areas, and the higher receptive association areas. Occlusion of the middle cerebral artery near the origin of its cortical branches, when not fatal, produces a contralateral hemiplegia most marked in the upper extremity and face, and a contralateral sensory loss of the cortical type, in which there may be astereognosis and inability to distinguish between different intensities of stimuli. When the left or dominant hemisphere is involved, there are also severe aphasic disturbances both in the (motor) formulation of speech (verbal aphasia) and the comprehension of spoken or written words (page 586).

The Posterior Cerebral Arteries are formed by the bifurcation of the basilar artery. These vessels pass laterally and backward over the crus cerebri and receive anastomoses from the posterior communicating artery (Figs. 4–3, 4–4 and 4–5). These vessels continue along the lateral aspect of the midbrain following the medial margins of the tentorium, and then pass dorsal to the tentorium to course on the under surface of the temporal lobe.

The posterior cerebral artery divides into two main branches, the posterior temporal (temporo-occipital) and the internal occipital arteries. The *posterior temporal artery* gives off an anterior temporal branch which supplies anterior portions of the inferior surface of the temporal lobe and frequently anastomoses with branches of the anterior temporal artery derived from the middle cerebral artery (Fig. 4–5 and 4–7). More posterior branches of this vessel supply the occipito-temporal and lingual gyri. The *internal occipital artery* divides into the *parieto-occipital artery* and the *calcarine artery* both of which supply different regions on the medial aspect of the occipital lobe. Thus the cortical branches of the posterior cerebral artery supply the medial and inferior surfaces of the occipital lobe and the inferior surface of the temporal lobe, except for the temporal pole (Figs. 4–5 and 4–7). Branches of these arteries extend onto the lateral surface of the brain and supply the inferior temporal gyrus, and variable portions of the lateral occipital region; some of the branches from the medial surface supply a considerable part of the superior parietal lobule. In these regions branches of the posterior cerebral artery anastomose with marginal branches of the anterior and middle cerebral arteries. The calcarine branch of the posterior cerebral artery is of major importance because it supplies the primary visual cortex. The extensive anastomoses mentioned above appear to explain why occlusion of the posterior cerebral artery rarely produces softening (encephalomalacia) in the total distribution of this vessel. Occlusion of the posterior cerebral artery produces a contralateral homonymous hemianopsia, frequently with sparing of macular vision. Anastomoses between branches of the middle and posterior cerebral arteries in the region of the occipital pole probably account for the preservation of macular vision.

The introduction of cerebral angiography as a diagnostic technic in clinical neurology (Moniz, '31, '34) has emphasized the great importance of the anatomical distribution, course, and variations of individual cerebral vessels. This technic is based upon the injection of radiopaque solutions into the internal carotid or vertebral arteries, and the taking of rapid serial roentgenograms showing various phases of the passage of the radiopaque solution through cerebral vessels. Cerebral angiography is particularly useful in localizing aneurysms and vascular malformations, and often it provides specific information concerning occlusive vascular disease and space-occupying intracranial masses. Cerebral aneurysms are mostly of congenital origin and appear to arise frequently from vessels on the inferior surface of the brain. Although it has been stated that aneurysms arise only at the point of bifurcation of an artery, Dandy ('47) found that many were not associated with arterial branching. Vascular malformations are of many types; arteriovenous malformations are characterized by an abnormal nest of blood vessels in which there are direct anastomoses of arteries and veins. Cerebral angiography is of importance in diagnosing occlusive vascular disease in the internal carotid (both cervical and intracranial portions) and in the vertebral and the basilar arteries, as well as in the trunk of the middle cerebral artery. It is more difficult to ascertain the presence of vascular occlusions in the distal branches of the anterior, middle, and posterior cerebral arteries (Taveras, '61) because of direct end-to-end anastomoses between branches of these vessels on the surface

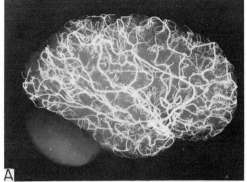

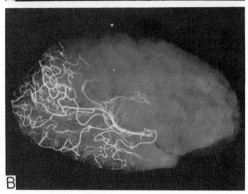

Fig. 4–7. Roentgenograms of fresh cadaver brains in which cerebral vessels have been injected with radiopaque material. A. Injections of the anterior, middle and posterior cerebral arteries. B. Injection of the posterior cerebral artery. Note the filling of the thalamoperforating branches. (Courtesy of Dr. Harry A. Kaplan.)

of the brain. While intracerebral hemorrhage cannot be distinguished angiographically from cerebral edema or other avascular space-occupying lesions, intracranial hemorrhage sometimes can be localized on the basis of occlusion of certain vessels and displacement of others (Bull, '61). Space-occupying intracranial lesions, including tumor, often can be localized on the basis of displacement of cerebral vessels. Certain highly vascular brain tumors may produce what is called a "tumor stain" in the cerebral angiogram.

While cerebral angiography provides invaluable diagnostic information, it is unusual for the contrast medium to permeate the very small terminal arteries. Injection of the internal carotid artery

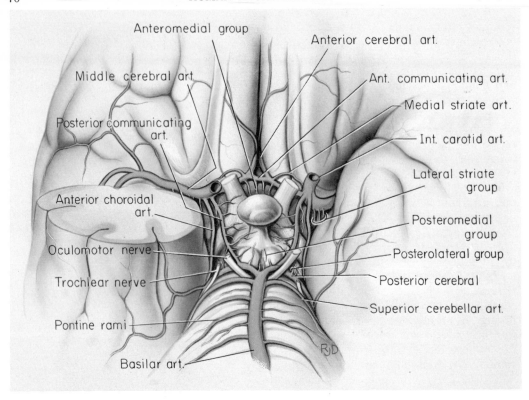

Anteromedial group

Anterior cerebral art.

Middle cerebral art.

Ant. communicating art.

Medial striate art.

Posterior communicating art.

Int. carotid art.

Lateral striate group

Anterior choroidal art.

Posteromedial group

Oculomotor nerve

Posterolateral group

Trochlear nerve

Posterior cerebral

Superior cerebellar art.

Pontine rami

RJD

Basilar art.

FIG. 4–8. The cerebral arterial circle (Willis) at the base of the brain showing the distribution of the ganglionic branches. These vessels form anteromedial, posteromedial, posterolateral and lateral striate groups. The medial striate and anterior choroidal arteries also are shown.

usually permits visualization of the main branches of the anterior and middle cerebral arteries on the side of the injection. A radiographic technic for studying individual cerebral vessels and their branches in fresh cadaver brains has been developed by Kaplan ('56, '58, '61). The exquisite detail which can be brought out by this method is demonstrated in Figures 4–7 and 4–9.

The Central Branches

The **central or ganglionic arteries** which supply the diencephalon, corpus striatum, and internal capsule are arranged in four general groups: anteromedial, anterolateral, posteromedial, and posterolateral (Fig. 4–8).

The *anteromedial arteries* arise from the domain of the anterior cerebral and anterior communicating arteries, but some twigs come directly from the terminal portion of the internal carotid (Fig. 4–8). They enter the most medial portion of the anterior perforated space and are distributed to the anterior hypothalamus, including the preoptic and suprachiasmatic regions.

The *posteromedial arteries* which enter the tuber cinereum, mammillary bodies, and interpeduncular fossa are derived from the most proximal portion of the posterior cerebral, and from the whole extent of the posterior communicating arteries. Some twigs come directly from the internal carotid artery just before its bifurcation. A rostral and caudal group may be distinguished. The rostral group supplies the hypophysis, infundibulum, and tuberal regions of the hypothalamus. A number of vessels, the *thalamoperforating arteries*, penetrate more deeply and are distributed to the anterior and medial portions of the thalamus. The caudal group supplies the mammillary region of the hypothalamus, the subthalamic region,

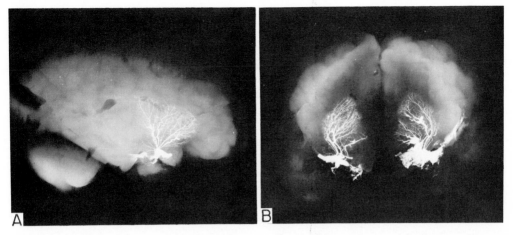

Fig. 4–9. Roentgenograms of fresh cadaver brains in which individual arteries have been injected with radiopaque material. *A* and *B* show lateral and frontal views, respectively, of the deep ganglionic branches of the middle cerebral artery that penetrate the brain in the anterior perforated substance. (Courtesy of Dr. Harry A. Kaplan.)

and sends small branches to the medial nuclei of the thalamus. Other vessels from the caudal group are distributed in the midbrain to the rapheal region of the tegmentum, the red nucleus, and medial portions of the crus cerebri.

The *posterolateral* (*thalamogeniculate*) *arteries* arise more laterally from the posterior cerebral arteries (Figs. 4–8 and 4–10). They penetrate the lateral geniculate body and supply the larger caudal half of the thalamus, including the geniculate bodies, the pulvinar, and most of the lateral nuclear mass.

The *anterolateral* (*striate*) *arteries*, which pierce the anterior perforated substance, arise mainly from the initial portion of the middle cerebral artery and, to a lesser extent, from the anterior cerebral (Figs. 4–3 and 4–8). As a rule, those from the anterior cerebral artery supply the rostroventral portion of the head of the caudate nucleus and adjacent portions of the putamen and internal capsule. The rest of the putamen, caudate nucleus, and anterior limb of the internal capsule are supplied by branches from the middle cerebral artery, excepting only the most caudal tip of the putamen and the recurving portion of the caudate tail (Fig. 4–10). These branches also nourish lateral parts of the globus pallidus and dorsal portions of the posterior limb of the

internal capsule. In some instances all the striate arteries may be derived from the middle cerebral artery. One of the striate arteries, described as the cerebral vessel most prone to rupture, has been called the "artery of cerebral hemorrhage" (Charcot). Such an artery usually cannot be distinguished anatomically. While it appears doubtful that the striate arteries supply parts of the thalamus, vessels, referred to as lenticulo-optic arteries, have been described. The central perforating branches arising from the middle cerebral artery are shown radiographically in injected specimens in Figure 4–9.

Choroidal Arteries. The anterior and posterior choroidal arteries may be regarded as distinctive central branches. The *anterior choroidal artery* usually arises from the internal carotid artery distal to the origin of the posterior communicating artery, but it may arise from the middle cerebral artery, or the posterior communicating artery (Carpenter et al., '54). This artery passes backward across the optic tract, to which it usually gives a few small branches, and then courses laterally towards the medial surface of the rostral part of the temporal lobe (Figs. 4–8 and 4–10). The vessel passes into the inferior horn of the lateral ventricle through the choroidal fissure where it supplies the choroid plexus. In addition

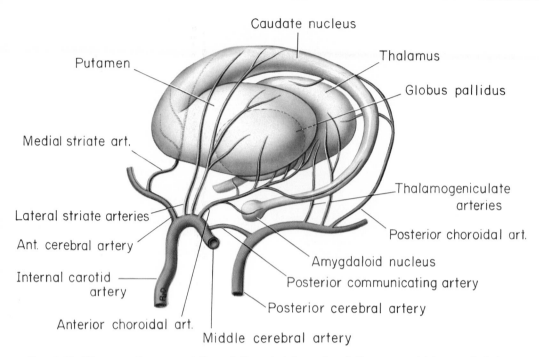

Fig. 4-10. Diagrammatic representation of the arterial supply of the corpus striatum and thalamus (modified from Aitken, '09).

the anterior choroidal artery supplies the hippocampal formation, portions of both segments of the globus pallidus (i.e., lateral parts of the medial pallidal segment and medial parts of the lateral pallidal segment), a large ventral part of the posterior limb of the internal capsule, and the entire retrolenticular portion of the internal capsule (Fig. 4-11). Smaller branches of this vessel supply parts of the amygdaloid nuclear complex, ventral portions of the tail of the caudate nucleus, and extreme posterior parts of the putamen. A few branches of this artery enter lateral portions of the thalamus (Kaplan and Ford, '66). Alexander ('42) considered the anterior choroidal artery as a vessel highly susceptible to thrombosis because of its long subarachnoid course and its relatively small caliber. It appears significant that the globus pallidus and hippocampal formation, two of the most vulnerable structures of the brain, are both supplied by this artery.

The *posterior choroidal arteries* arising from the posterior cerebral artery (Fig. 4-10) consist of one medial posterior

choroidal artery and at least two lateral posterior choroidal arteries (Galloway and Greitz, '60). The medial posterior choroidal artery arises from the proximal part of the posterior cerebral artery, curves around the midbrain and reaches the region lateral to the pineal body. This vessel gives off branches to the tectum, the choroid plexus of the third ventricle, and the superior and medial surfaces of the thalamus. The lateral posterior choroidal arteries arise from the posterior cerebral artery as this vessel encircles the brain stem. These vessels penetrate the choroidal fissure where they anastomose with branches of the anterior choroidal artery (Carpenter et al., '54).

The *arterial supply of the basal ganglia, internal capsule and diencephalon* can be summarized briefly. The striatum (caudate nucleus and putamen) is supplied mainly by striate arteries derived from the middle cerebral artery. The anteromedial part of the head of the caudate nucleus is supplied by the medial striate branch of of the anterior cerebral artery, while the recurving tail of the caudate nucleus, and

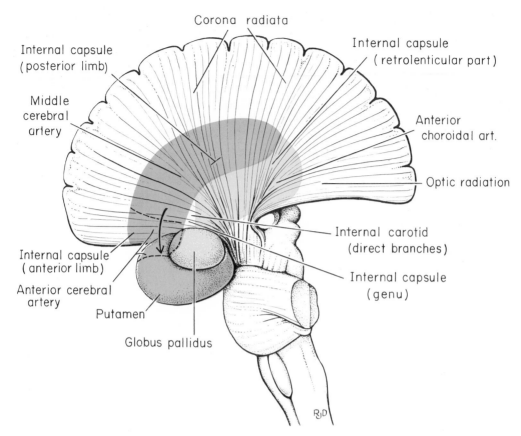

Fig. 4-11. Diagram of the blood supply of the internal capsule and corpus striatum. The putamen and globus pallidus are shown rotated ventrally away from their normal position adjacent to the internal capsule. Regions supplied by branches of the middle and anterior cerebral arteries are shown in *red*; portions of the internal capsule and corpus striatum supplied by the anterior choroidal artery are in *yellow*. Direct branches of the internal carotid artery supply the genu of the internal capsule (Alexander, '42).

the extreme posterior part of the putamen are nourished by branches of the anterior choroidal artery (Fig. 4–10). The lateral segment of the globus pallidus appears to have a variable blood supply. It receives branches from both the striate arteries (Mettler et al., '56) and the anterior choroidal artery (Fig. 4–11). The lateral part of the medial pallidal segment and the medial part of the lateral pallidal segment are supplied by the anterior choroidal artery. Branches from the posterior communicating artery nourish medial portions of the medial pallidal segment.

The *anterior* and *posterior limbs of the internal capsule* are supplied primarily by the striate branches of the middle cerebral artery (Fig. 4-11). The medial striate artery supplies a medial part of the anterior limb of the internal capsule. As a rule, the genu of the internal capsule receives one or more direct branches from the internal carotid (Alexander, '42). Ventral parts of the posterior limb of the internal capsule, and its retrolenticular portion are supplied by branches of the anterior choroidal artery.

The *thalamus* is nourished mainly by the posterolateral (thalamogeniculate) and posteromedial (thalamoperforating) arteries (Figs. 4-7, 4-8 and 4-10). The posterolateral arteries supply the caudal and lateral regions, and the posteromedial arteries supply the anterior and medial regions. The medial posterior choroidal artery contributes branches which supply superior and medial portions of the thalamus. The anterior *hypothalamus* and preoptic region receive their blood supply from the anteromedian ganglionic arteries. Remaining portions of the hypothalamus and the subthalamic region are supplied by branches of the posteromedian group derived from the posterior cerebral and posterior communicating arteries.

Vertebral Basilar System

With the exception of the most rostral portions of the crus cerebri, the entire blood supply of the medulla, pons, mesencephalon, and cerebellum is derived from the vertebral basilar system. The intracranial part of each **vertebral artery,** as it passes over the anterior surface of the medulla, gives rise to: (1) a *posterior spinal artery*, (2) an *anterior spinal artery*, (3) a large *posterior inferior cerebellar artery*, and (4) a *posterior meningeal artery*. The two vertebral arteries unite to form the basilar artery at the lower border of the pons. This large vessel passes rostrally in the basilar sulcus and bifurcates at the upper border of the pons, forming the posterior cerebral arteries. The **basilar artery** gives rise to: (1) the *anterior inferior cerebellar arteries*, (2) the *labyrinthine arteries*, (3) *numerous paramedian* and *circumferential pontine rami*, and (4) the *superior cerebellar arteries*. The *posterior cerebral arteries*, representing the terminal branches of the basilar artery, furnish the main blood supply to the midbrain via branches which arise from proximal portions of these vessels. The labyrinthine arteries do not supply the brain stem, but pass laterally through the internal auditory meati.

The Medulla and Pons are supplied by the anterior and posterior spinal arteries, and by branches of the vertebral, basilar and the posterior inferior cerebellar arteries. Minor contributions also may be made by the *superior* and the *anterior inferior cerebellar arteries*. There is great variation in the extent of the areas

supplied by each vessel, as well as considerable overlapping of adjacent fields. These variations are due in part to the different levels of origin of the anterior spinal arteries, and to the equally varying level of fusion of the two vertebrals into the basilar artery. Not uncommonly one or another artery may be missing altogether and its place taken by the vessel supplying the adjacent territory. Thus the area of the posterior spinal artery may be taken over by the posterior inferior cerebellar artery, or the latter may be replaced by branches from the vertebral artery. Since the vascular supply of this region has considerable clinical importance, the main structures normally supplied by the various arteries are summarized briefly (Figs. 4–12 and 4–13).

The *anterior spinal artery* supplies the medial structures of the medulla, including the pyramids and pyramidal decussation, medial lemniscus, medial longitudinal fasciculus, predorsal bundle, and hypoglossal nucleus, except its most cephalic portion. In addition the artery supplies the medial accessory olive, the most caudal portions of the solitary nucleus and fasciculus, and the dorsal motor nucleus of the vagus. In the upper medulla the distribution of the anterior spinal artery is reduced gradually, and it is replaced by branches of the vertebral and basilar arteries. (Fig. 4–12).

The *bulbar branches of the vertebral artery* normally supply the pyramids at the lower border of the pons, the most cephalic part of the hypoglossal nucleus, and most of the inferior olive, including the dorsal accessory olive. The artery also supplies olivocerebellar fibers traversing the reticular formation, portions of the dorsal motor nucleus of the vagus, and the solitary nucleus and fasciculus in the region of the calamus scriptorius. At the level of the pyramidal decussation the most caudal branches are distributed to practically the whole lateral region of the medulla lying between the anterior horn and the fasciculus cuneatus.

The *posterior inferior cerebellar artery* supplies the retro-olivary region, which contains the spinothalamic and rubro-spinal tracts, the spinal trigeminal nucleus and tract, the nucleus ambiguus, the dorsal motor nucleus of the vagus, and the emerging fibers of these nuclei, as well as ventral parts of the inferior cerebellar peduncle. Descending central autonomic tracts also are found in this area.

The *posterior spinal artery* supplies the gracile and cuneate fasciculi and their nuclei, and the caudal and dorsal portions of the inferior cerebellar peduncle (Fig. 4-1). When missing, its territory is taken over by the posterior inferior cerebellar artery.

The ventral portion of the pons receives arterial blood from three series of branches, all derived from the *basilar artery* (Fig. 4-12). The first series is that of the paramedian arteries, which leave the dorsal surface of the parent vessel to supply the most medial pontine area, including the pontine nuclei and the corticopontine, corticospinal, and corticobulbar tracts. Smaller arterial twigs also penetrate dorsally to supply the most ventral part of the pontine tegmentum, including a portion of the medial lemniscus. Obstruction of the paramedian arteries usually is followed by hemiplegia (at times a quadriplegia); pseudobulbar palsy, including dysarthria and dysphagia; transitory hemianesthesia; paresis of conjugate eye movements with deviation of the eyes to the side opposite the lesion (Frantzen and Olivarius, '57); or bilateral ophthalmoplegia (Masucci, '65). A second group of *short circumferential arteries* supply a wedge of tissue along the anterolateral pontine surface. Neural structures in this intermediate area of the pons include a variable number of fibers of the corticospinal tract and medial lemniscus, pontine nuclei and pontocerebellar fibers, and part of the nuclei and fibers of the trigeminal and facial nerves. Some of the circumferential branches may ascend to supply part of the superior cerebral peduncle. Obstruction of the short circumferential arteries on one side, therefore, may result in ipsilateral cerebellar

symptoms, contralateral hemianesthesia, and visceral disturbances of the sympathetic system, including an ipsilateral Horner's syndrome (see page 232).

The third series, or *long circumferential arteries*, pass laterally on the anterior surface of the pons to anastomose with smaller branches of the anterior inferior cerebellar and superior cerebellar arteries (Fig. 4-12). The long circumferential and *anterior inferior cerebellar arteries* supply most of the tegmentum in the caudal portion of the pons, whereas the long circumferential and *superior cerebellar arteries* supply a similar area in the more rostral levels of the pons. Important neural structures within this area of vascular distribution are the nuclei of cranial nerves III to VIII, the spinal trigeminal nucleus and tract, the medial longitudinal fasciculus, the medial lemniscus, the spinothalamic and spinocerebellar tracts, the superior cerebellar peduncle, and the reticular formation. Obstruction of these vessels may produce nuclear injury and paresis of one or more of the cranial nerves mentioned, paresis of conjugate eye movements, contralateral hemianesthesia, ipsilateral cerebellar symptoms, nystagmus, and sympathetic disturbances. Alterations in the individual's sensorium may increase until coma supervenes owing to anoxia or hemorrhage into the pontine tegmentum.

Complete or partial thrombosis of the basilar artery may occur suddenly and is accompanied by severe headache, vomiting, and a precipitous loss of consciousness. Complete thrombosis is generally fatal, although recoveries have been observed after partial occlusion (Haugsted, '56). Thrombosis of the basilar artery was once considered of purely academic interest. Today it is of great practical importance as well, for it can be recognized during life and aids in the differential diagnosis and case prognosis. The symptoms of basilar artery occlusion (usually bilateral) are due to massive pontine damage and include a deep comatose state, generalized loss of muscular tone (flaccidity of limbs), dilated or pin-

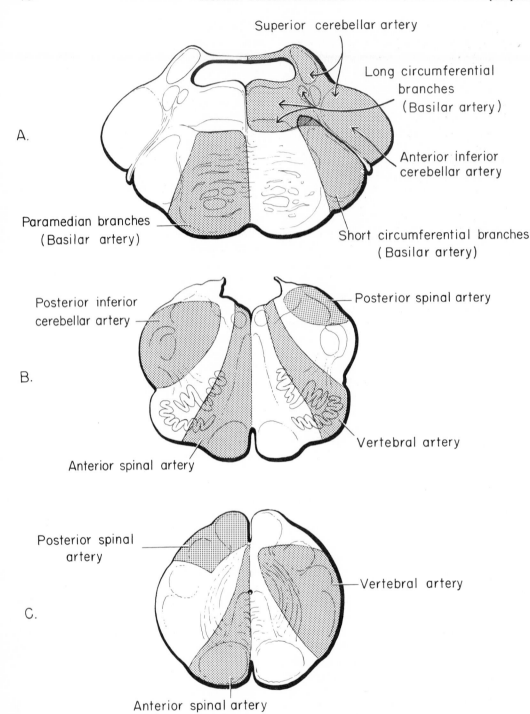

Fig. 4–12. Diagrams showing the arterial supply of the medulla and pons. Medullary levels shown are through the posterior column nuclei and the inferior olivary nuclear complex (based on Stopford, '15, '16). The pons is supplied by paramedian and circumferential branches of the basilar artery (Frantzen and Olivarius, '57).

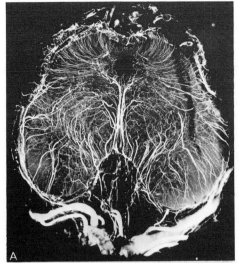

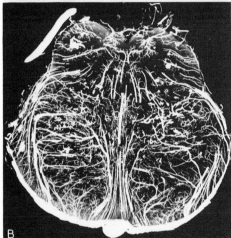

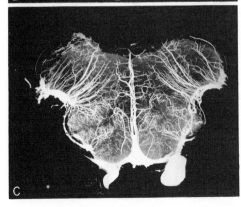

point pupils that do not react to light, and loss of superficial abdominal reflexes. Increased muscle tone and Babinski responses may be present within a variable period of time after such vascular accidents. There is often an intermingling of symptoms, depending upon the level, branches, and degree of arterial occlusion. For example, thrombosis of the rostral part of the basilar artery, near its bifurcation into the two posterior cerebral arteries, may result only in visual defects (bilateral homonymous hemianopsia, page 481).

The venous drainage of the hindbrain has been demonstrated recently by stereomicroangiography (Hassler, '67). The paramedian veins which run near the midline to the ventral surface of the brain stem are inclined caudally in the upper pons, but are nearly perpendicular to the axis of the brain stem in more caudal regions. At the junction of pons and medulla a conspicuously large vein consistently drains the floor of the fourth ventricle. Veins draining ventral portions of the pons usually empty into paired longitudinal venous plexuses several millimeters lateral to the basilar artery. However, in some instances these veins enter a single unpaired vein situated between the basilar artery and the brain stem parenchyma. In the lower medulla posterior veins are larger than the anterior veins and penetrate deeper regions. Although the veins of the hindbrain seldom accompany the arterial branches in the same vascular sheath, the intraparenchymatous venous angioarchitecture resembles the arterial pattern. Anastomoses between intraparenchymatous veins occur mainly at the capillary level. Large

FIG. 4–13. Microangiograms of the blood supply of the midbrain, pons and medulla made from 4 mm thick injected specimens. In the midbrain (A) the tegmentum is supplied mainly by branches of the posterior cerebral and superior cerebellar arteries, but it also receives contributions from the paramedian and both long and short circumferential arteries. The upper pons (B) receives paramedian and circumferential branches from the basilar artery, as well as branches of the superior cerebellar artery distributed to dorsal regions. The vascular pattern in the upper medulla (C) should be compared with the diagram of Fig. 4–12. (Courtesy of Dr. O. Hassler, '67.)

FIG. 4–14. Microangiogram of a 4 mm mid-sagittal section of the midbrain, pons and medulla made from an injected specimen. Paramedian arteries form different angles with the basilar artery at different levels. In the caudal midbrain and upper pons, they are inclined caudally; in the upper medulla and caudal pons these vessels are inclined rostrally. (Courtesy of Dr. O. Hassler, '67.)

veins draining the choroid plexus of ventricle IV, most of the pons, and the upper medulla, empty into the sigmoid sinus, or the superior or inferior petrosal sinuses. Veins draining caudal parts of the medulla empty into the anterior and posterior spinal veins (Hassler, '67).

The Mesencephalon receives its blood supply principally from branches of the basilar artery, although branches of the internal carotid also contribute. The main vessels supplying this portion of the brain stem include: (1) the *posterior cerebral artery*, (2) the *superior cerebellar artery*, (3) branches of the *posterior communicating artery*, and (4) branches of the *anterior choroidal artery*. Branches from these arteries may be grouped, as in the case of the pons, into: (1) *paramedian arteries* which enter medially and nourish structures on both sides of the midline, and (2) *circumferential arteries*, both long and short, which wind laterally around the crus cerebri and supply lateral and dorsal regions of the midbrain. Paramedian branches are derived from the posterior communicating artery, from the basilar bifurcation, and from proximal portions of the posterior cerebral arteries. These vessels form an extensive plexus in the interpeduncular fossa, and enter the brain stem in the posterior perforated substance. They supply the rapheal region, the oculomotor complex, the medial longitudinal fasciculus, the red nucleus, and medial parts of the substantia nigra and crus cerebri. Branches of the anterior choroidal artery supply similar vessels which enter rostral portions of the interpeduncular fossa.

Short circumferential branches arise in part from the interpeduncular plexus and in part from proximal portions of the posterior cerebral and superior cerebellar arteries. These arteries supply central and lateral parts of the crus cerebri, the substantia nigra, and lateral portions of the midbrain tegmentum. In the rostral mesencephalon some branches of the anterior choroidal artery are distributed to the interpeduncular fossa. Long circumferential arteries arise primarily from the posterior cerebral artery. The most important of these is the *quadrigeminal artery* which encircles the lateral surface of the midbrain and provides the main blood supply to the superior and inferior colliculi. Other vessels contributing to the blood supply of the tectum are branches of the medial posterior choroidal artery and the superior cerebellar artery.

Angiographic studies (Hassler, '67a) of the arterial pattern of the human brain stem clearly demonstrate the distribution of paramedian and circumferential arteries in the upper pons and midbrain (Fig. 4-13 and 4-14). Sagittal sections show that paramedian arteries entering the brain stem at various levels do so at different angles. At the junction of pons and medulla, these vessels are directed forward at an oblique angle, while at rostral pontine levels these vessels course obliquely in a caudal direction.

Numerous veins of the mesencephalon arise from capillaries and, in general, run near the arteries, but not directly with them. These veins form an extensive peripheral plexus in the pia and are collected by the basal veins which drain into either the great cerebral vein (Galen) or the internal cerebral veins.

Cerebellum. Each half of the cerebellum is supplied by one superior and two inferior cerebellar arteries passing respectively to the superior and inferior surfaces of the cerebellum (Figs. 4-5 and 4-6). The *posterior inferior cerebellar artery* arises from the vertebral artery, courses rostrolaterally along the surface of the medulla and then curves upward onto the inferior surface of the cerebellum. This vessel supplies the inferior vermis, especially the uvula and nodulus, as well as the cerebellar tonsil and the inferolateral surface of the cerebellar hemisphere. Medial branches of this artery supply portions of the choroid plexus of the fourth ventricle. The *anterior inferior cerebellar artery* is usually the most caudal large vessel arising from the basilar artery, but it is highly variable both in its origin and area of distribution (Kaplan and Ford, '66). This vessel passes caudally and laterally to reach the inferior surface of the cerebellum where it supplies the pyramis, tuber, flocculus and portions of the inferior surface of the cerebellar hemisphere. It also sends branches to the deep portion of the corpus medullare and the dentate nucleus. In some cases, the flocculus and portions of the tonsil and biventer lobule may be supplied by an inconstant middle inferior cerebellar artery. The *superior cerebellar artery* arises from the rostral part of the basilar artery. On reaching the cerebellum, it divides into two main branches, a median one for the superior vermis and adjacent lateral portions, and a lateral one for the remaining hemispheral portions of the superior surface. From these arteries numerous branches extend deeply into the cerebellum to go to the superior medullary velum, middle and superior peduncles, deep portion of the corpus medullare, and the intrinsic cerebellar nuclei, including parts of the dentate nucleus. Twigs also are given to the choroid plexus of the fourth ventricle.

The veins have a course generally similar to that of the arteries. A superior and an inferior median vein drain the respective portions of the vermis, adjacent paravermal regions and the deep cerebellar nuclei. The superior vein terminates in the *great cerebral vein (Galen)*, while the inferior vein drains into the straight and lateral sinuses. Superior and inferior lateral veins drain blood from the hemispheres and flocculi to the lateral, and, in part, to the superior and petrosal sinuses.

Arteries of the Dura. The cranial dura mater is supplied by a number of meningeal arteries derived from several sources. The largest and most important is the *middle meningeal artery*, which supplies most of the dura and practically its entire calvarial portion. It is a branch of the maxillary artery which enters the cranial cavity through the foramen spinosum and then divides into an anterior and a posterior branch (Figs. 2-4 and 4-4). Each of the branches runs outward and upward and extends toward the superior sagittal sinus, giving off numerous subsidiary branches which run forward and backward. A small *accessory meningeal artery*, which may arise from the maxillary artery or from the middle meningeal artery, enters the middle fossa through the oval foramen. This vessel supplies the dura of the middle fossa and the trigeminal ganglion. Meningeal branches from the intracavernous portion of the internal carotid artery also supply the dura of the middle fossa.

In addition, the dura of the anterior and the posterior fossae receives a number of

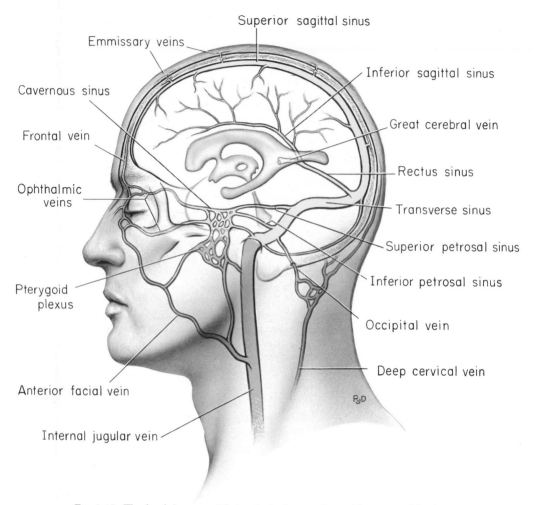

Superior sagittal sinus

Emmissary veins

Inferior sagittal sinus

Cavernous sinus

Great cerebral vein

Frontal vein

Rectus sinus

Ophthalmic veins

Transverse sinus

Superior petrosal sinus

Inferior petrosal sinus

Pterygoid plexus

Occipital vein

Deep cervical vein

Anterior facial vein

Internal jugular vein

FIG. 4–15. The dural sinuses and their principal connections with extracranial veins.

arteries, known respectively as the *anterior* and *posterior meningeal rami* or *arteries*. The anterior meningeal rami, usually two in number, are branches of the anterior and posterior ethmoidal arteries. The dura of the posterior fossa is supplied mainly by a variable number of posterior meningeal arteries. These include: (1) one or more meningeal branches from the occipital artery entering through the jugular and hypoglossal foramina, (2) meningeal branches of the vertebral artery reaching the posterior fossa through the foramen magnum, and (3) several branches of the ascending pharyngeal artery entering through the foramen lacerum and hypoglossal canal.

CEREBRAL VEINS AND VENOUS SINUSES

The cerebral veins of the brain do not run together with the arteries. Emerging as fine branches from the substance of the brain, they form a pial plexus from which arise the larger venous channels or cerebral veins. These veins run in the pia for a variable distance, pass through the subarachnoid space, and empty into a system of intercommunicating endothelium-lined channels, the *sinuses of the dura mater*, located between the meningeal and periosteal layers of the dura (Fig. 4–4). The walls of these sinuses, unlike those of other veins, are composed of the tough fibrous tissue of the dura; hence,

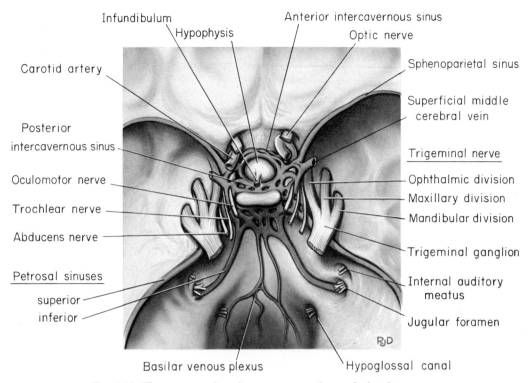

FIG. 4–16. The cavernous sinus, its venous connections and related structures.

they exhibit a greater tautness and do not collapse when sectioned. The various venous sinuses converge at the internal occipital protuberance into two transversely running sinuses, one for each side, which enter the jugular foramen to form the internal jugular vein. Besides draining the blood from the brain, the venous sinuses communicate with the superficial veins of the head by a number of small vessels which perforate the skull as *emissary veins* (Fig. 4–15).

The *superior sagittal sinus* extends from the foramen cecum to the internal occipital protuberance, lying along the attached border of the falx cerebri, and constantly increases in caliber as it proceeds caudally. In its middle portion it gives off a number of lateral diverticula, the *venous lacunae*, into which the arachnoid villi protrude. The narrower and shorter *inferior sagittal sinus* extends caudally along the free border of the falx. On reaching the anterior border of the tentorium, it is joined by the *great cerebral vein* (*Galen*), which drains the deep structures of the brain, and the two veins form the *sinus rectus*. The latter runs backwards and downwards along the line of attachment of the falx and tentorium and joins the superior sagittal sinus near the internal occipital protuberance (Fig. 4–4). From this place the two *transverse sinuses* arise, each of which passes laterally and forward in the transverse groove of the occipital bone. On reaching the occipitopetrosal junction, each curves sharply caudally and, as the *sigmoid sinus*, leaves the skull through the jugular foramen. The point of union of the superior sagittal, straight, and transverse sinuses is known as the *sinus confluens*; it also receives the small unpaired *occipital sinus* coming from the region of the foramen magnum and ascending in the falx cerebelli. The *confluens* is asymmetrical and shows many individual variations (*arrow* in Fig. 4–4). In relatively few cases is there an actual union of the four sinuses. Most often the superior sagittal sinus turns to the right to become continuous

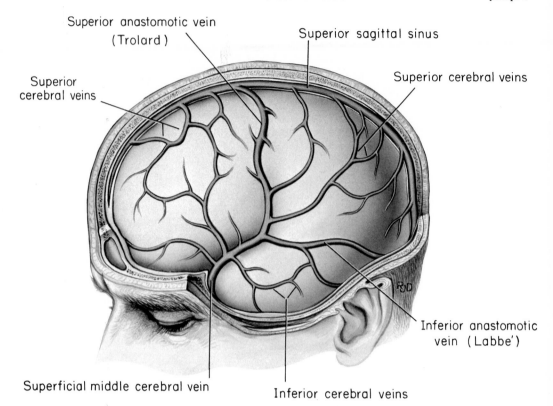

Superior anastomotic vein
(Trolard)

Superior sagittal sinus

Superior
cerebral veins

Superior cerebral veins

Inferior anastomotic
vein (Labbe')

Superficial middle cerebral vein

Inferior cerebral veins

FIG. 4–17. The external cerebral veins on the convexity of the hemisphere.

with the right transverse sinus, while the straight sinus bends to the left as the left transverse sinus. In general, the venous blood of the superior cerebral veins and the superior sagittal, right transverse, and right sigmoid sinuses is drained by the right internal jugular vein. Most of the venous blood of the Galenic vein, the straight sinus, left transverse, and left sigmoid sinuses usually is drained by the left internal jugular vein.

The important *cavernous sinus* is a large irregular space located on the side of the sphenoid bone, lateral to the sella turcica. It is a network of intercommunicating cavernous channels enclosing the internal carotid artery, the oculomotor, trochlear, and abducens nerves, and the ophthalmic division of the trigeminal nerve. The cavernous sinus of each side is connected with the other by venous channels which pass anterior and posterior to the hypophysis and by the *basilar venous plexus*.

The latter venous plexus extends along the basilar portion of the occipital bone as far caudally as the foramen magnum where it communicates with the venous plexuses of the vertebral canal (Fig. 4–16). The venous ring, surrounding the hypophysis and composed of the two cavernous sinuses and their connecting channels, often is designated as the *circular sinus*. Each cavernous sinus likewise may be regarded as a confluens sinuum. Rostrally it receives the two ophthalmic veins through the orbital fissure and the small *sphenoparietal sinus*, which runs along the under surface of the lesser wing of the sphenoid (Figs. 4–4 and 4–16). Posteriorly it empties into the superior and inferior petrosal sinuses, through which it is connected, respectively, with the transverse sinus and the bulb of the internal jugular vein.

As already stated, the dural sinuses communicate with extracranial veins by a

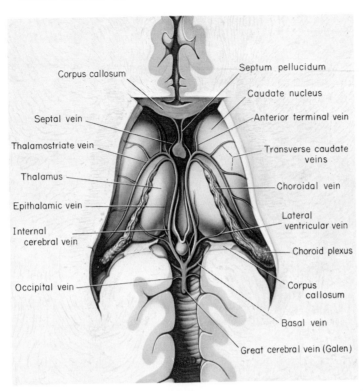

Corpus callosum
Septum pellucidum
Caudate nucleus
Septal vein
Anterior terminal vein
Thalamostriate vein
Transverse caudate veins
Thalamus
Choroidal vein
Epithalamic vein
Lateral ventricular vein
Internal cerebral vein
Choroid plexus
Occipital vein
Corpus callosum
Basal vein
Great cerebral vein (Galen)

FIG. 4–18. The internal cerebral veins and their tributaries (modified from Schwartz and Fink, '26).

number of emissaries (Fig. 4–15). Thus the superior sagittal sinus is connected with the frontal and nasal veins through the frontal diploic veins and the emissaries of the foramen cecum (Fig. 4–4). It also sends a *parietal emissary* to the superficial temporal vein. The confluens sinuum usually gives off an *occipital emissary* to the occipital vein, which is connected also with the transverse sinus by the larger *mastoid emissary*. Smaller emissaries from the sigmoid sinus pass through the condyloid and hypoglossal foramina and communicate with vertebral and deep cervical veins. The cavernous sinus, besides receiving the ophthalmic veins, is connected with the internal jugular vein and with the pterygoid and pharyngeal plexuses by fine venous nets which pass through the oval, spinous, lacerated, carotid, and jugular foramina.

The Cerebral Veins. The cerebral veins which, like the dural sinuses, are devoid of valves, usually are divided into superficial and deep groups. The superficial cerebral veins drain the blood from the cortex and subcortical medullary substance and empty into the superior sagittal sinus or into the several basal sinuses (cavernous, petrosal, and transverse). The deep veins, draining the deep medullary substance, the basal ganglia, and dorsal portions of the diencephalon, ultimately terminate in the internal and great cerebral veins (Figs. 4–18 and 4–19). While the two groups of veins are anatomically distinct, they are interconnected by numerous anastomotic channels, both intracerebral and extracerebral. Thus large surface areas can be drained through the great cerebral vein (Galen). Conversely territories supplied by deep cerebral veins may be handled when necessity arises by surface vessels. This anastomotic venous arrangement facilitates the drainage of capillary beds by shifting the blood from one area to another and readily equalizes regional increases in pressure due to occlusion or other factors. As a result, the occlusion of even a large vein, if not too

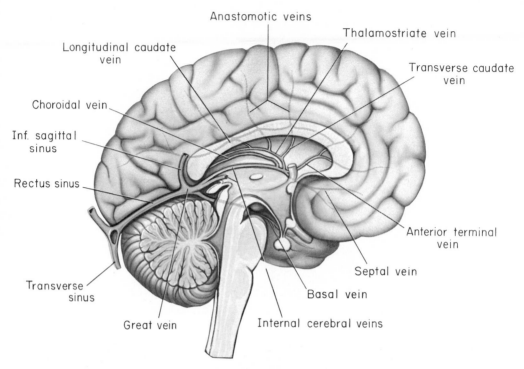

Fig. 4-19. Mid-sagittal view of the internal cerebral veins showing the relationship of the great vein to the rectus sinus (Schlesinger, '39).

rapid, will produce slight and transitory effects. When occlusion or increase in pressure occurs suddenly, there will be marked hyperemia and more or less extensive hemorrhages, as in birth injuries and occasionally in cases of adult thrombosis (Schwartz and Fink, '26; Schlesinger, '39).

The Superficial Cerebral Veins arise from the cortex and subcortical medullary substance, anastomose freely in the pia, and form a number of larger vessels which empty into the various sinuses. They include the superior and inferior cerebral veins and the superficial middle cerebral vein. The *superior cerebral veins*, about 10 to 15 in number, collect blood from the convex and medial surfaces of the brain and open into the superior sagittal sinus, or its venous lacunae (Fig. 4-17). Many of them, especially the larger posterior ones, run obliquely forward through the subarachnoid space and enter the sinus in a direction opposed to that of the blood flow, often after a short

intradural course parallel to the sinus. Some of the veins from the medial surface of the brain drain into the inferior sagittal sinus. The *inferior cerebral veins* drain the basal surface of the hemisphere and the lower portion of its lateral surface. Those on the lateral surface usually empty into the *superficial middle cerebral vein*, which runs along the lateral sulcus and terminates in the cavernous or sphenoparietal sinus (Figs. 4-4, 4-16, and 4-17). The middle vein receives many anastomotic branches from the superior cerebral veins, and in many cases two of these channels become quite prominent. These are the *great anastomotic vein (Trolard)* and the *posterior anastomotic vein (Labbé)*, which connect the superficial middle cerebral vein respectively with tributaries of the superior sagittal and the transverse sinuses. On the inferior surface, the small inferior cerebral veins arising from extensive pial plexuses drain in part into the basal sinuses. Those from the tentorial surface

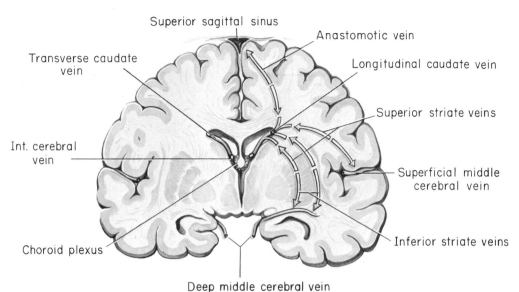

Fig. 4–20. Transverse section through the brain of the rhesus monkey showing diagrammatically the connections between deep and superficial veins (Schlesinger, '39).

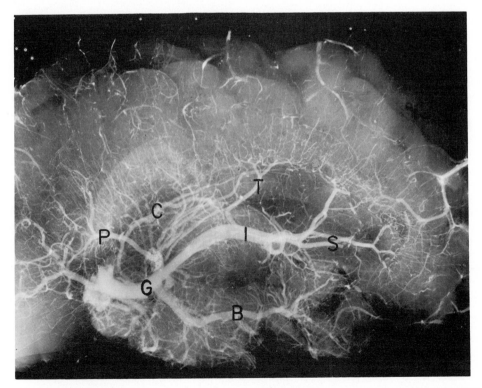

Fig. 4–21. Angiographic appearance of the deep venous system in one intact cerebral hemisphere. Letters indicate the following: S, septal vein; T, thalamostriate vein; I, internal cerebral vein; B, basal vein; C, choroidal vein; G, great cerebral vein (Galen); and P, occipital vein (vein of the posterior horn). (Courtesy of Dr. O. Hassler, '66.)

of the brain empty into the transverse and superior petrosal sinuses (Fig. 4–4). Those from the anterior temporal lobe and from the interpeduncular regions drain partly into the cavernous and sphenoparietal sinuses, while some veins from the orbital region join the superior or the inferior sagittal sinus.

In addition, large cortical areas, especially on the inferior and medial surfaces, are drained by a number of vessels which empty into the great cerebral vein before the latter bifurcates into the two internal cerebral veins (Figs. 4–18 and 4–19). These are anastomotic veins which connect the superficial and deep systems. The more important ones include the occipital vein, the basal vein (Rosenthal), and the posterior callosal vein. Veins of this group are best considered in relation to the deep cerebral veins.

The Deep Cerebral Veins of major importance are: (1) the internal cerebral veins, (2) the basal vein (Rosenthal), and (3) the great vein (Galen).

The *internal cerebral veins* consist of two paired veins, situated just lateral to the midline in the tela choroidea of the roof of the third ventricle (velum interpositum; Figs. 4–18 and 4–19). The veins begin in the region of the interventricular foramina and extend caudally over the superior and medial surface of the thalamus. Caudally the veins enter the upper part of the quadrigeminal cistern where they join to form the great vein (Galen). Veins draining into the internal cerebral vein of each side include: (1) the thalamostriate vein (terminal vein), (2) the choroidal vein, (3) the septal vein, (4) the epithalamic vein, and (5) the lateral ventricular vein.

The *thalamostriate vein* runs forward in the terminal sulcus at the junction of the thalamus and caudate nucleus. This vein receives the *anterior terminal vein* which drains the ventricular surface of the head of the caudate nucleus. Numerous *transverse caudate veins* join the thalamostriate throughout its course. Distally the transverse caudate veins extend over the caudate nucleus to the lateral angle of the ventricle where they

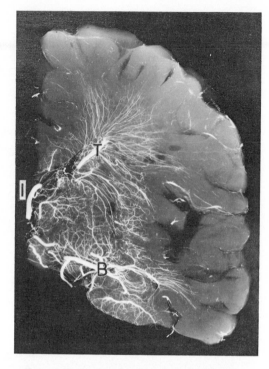

Fig. 4–22. Angioarchitecture of the deep cerebral venous system as shown in 1 cm thick coronal section. Anastomoses between deep and superficial veins are evident. Letters indicate the following: T, terminal vein: B, basal vein; I, internal cerebral vein. Compare with Fig. 4–20. (Courtesy of Dr. O. Hassler, '66.)

enter the adjacent white matter. In this area the smaller tributaries form the *longitudinal caudate veins*. The latter veins divide at acute angles into a number of branches which fan out into the white matter, as a rule following the fibers of the corpus callosum (Figs. 4–19 and 4–20). Some of the shorter branches drain the deep capillary plexuses of the white matter. Other longer branches, extending almost to the cortex, may be regarded as intracerebral anastomotic channels connecting ventricular and surface veins. In addition the transverse and longitudinal caudate veins give rise to another group of branches known as the *superior striate veins*. These veins pass ventrally through and around the caudate nucleus, perforate the internal capsule, and break up into a number of smaller vessels which drain the dense capillary plexus of the lenticular nucleus (Fig. 4–20). This capillary plexus is drained from below by the *inferior striate veins* which converge upon the anterior perforated substance and enter the deep middle vein.

The *choroidal vein* runs along the lateral border of the choroid plexus and distally extends into the inferior horn of the lateral ventricle. This tortuous vessel drains portions of the choroid plexus and adjacent hippocampal regions. The choroid plexus also is drained by the choroidal branch of the basal vein and, to a lesser extent, through the lateral ventricular vein.

The *septal vein* drains the septum pellucidum and rostral portions of the corpus callosum. Distally branches of this vein extend beneath the head of the caudate nucleus into the medullary substance at the base of the frontal lobe (Figs. 4–18 and 4–19). The septal vein joins the internal cerebral vein in the region of the interventricular foramen.

The *epithalamic vein* is a small vessel which drains the dorsal part of the diencephalon. This vein enters the internal cerebral vein, or the great cerebral vein, near their point of junction. Blood from ventral portions of the thalamus and from the hypothalamus is drained by vessels which pass ventrally into the pial venous plexus of the interpeduncular fossa. From this plexus venous blood is conveyed into the cavernous or sphenoparietal sinuses or into tributaries of the basal vein.

The *lateral ventricular vein* courses over the superior caudal surface of the thalamus (Fig. 4–18) and enters the internal cerebral vein as this vessel joins the great cerebral vein. Occasionally this vein terminates directly in the great cerebral vein. Distally the lateral ventricular vein extends over the surface of the thalamus and the tail of the caudate nucleus and enters the medullary substance at the angle of the lateral ventricle. Small branches of this vein arise from the choroid plexus, and from the white matter of the parahippocampal gyrus.

The *great cerebral vein* (Galen) receives the two internal cerebral veins, the two basal veins, the two occipital veins

and the posterior callosal vein (Figs. 4–18, 4–19 and 4–21). This very short vein extends posteriorly beneath the splenium of the corpus callosum and empties into the anterior part of the rectus sinus. The walls of this vein are delicate and easily torn, even in the adult.

The *basal vein* (Rosenthal) arises near the medial aspect of the anterior part of the temporal lobe where it receives tributaries from the medial surface and temporal horn (Figs. 4–19 and 4–21). This vein receives the anterior cerebral vein, the deep middle cerebral vein and the inferior striate veins. The *anterior cerebral vein* accompanies the anterior cerebral artery and drains the orbital surface of the frontal lobe, anterior portions of the corpus callosum and rostral parts of the cingulate gyrus. The *deep middle cerebral vein*, situated inferiorly in the depths of the lateral sulcus, drains insular and adjacent opercular cortex. The *inferior striate veins* drain ventral portions of the corpus striatum, emerge through the anterior perforated substance and empty into the deep middle cerebral vein (Figs. 4–20, 4–21 and 4–22). In the region of the anterior perforated substance these veins unite with the basal vein which courses caudally around the crus cerebri to join the great cerebral vein. The basal vein receives additional tributaries from the interpeduncular region, the midbrain and the inferior horn of the lateral ventricle. The hypothalamus, and ventral portions of the thalamus, are drained to a considerable extent by the basal veins.

The *occipital vein*, which drains the inferior and medial surface of the occipital lobe and adjacent parietal regions, empties directly into the great cerebral vein. The posterior callosal vein, which extends around the splenium of the corpus callosum, enters the anterior part of the great cerebral vein. This vein drains the posterior part of the corpus callosum and adjacent medial surfaces of the brain.

Angiographic studies (Taveras and Wood, '64) of cerebral veins made by serial roentgenograms reveal that the superficial frontal veins fill slightly before the parietal veins. The deep veins usually are the last to fill and they retain sufficient concentrations of radiopaque material to be visualized for a longer time. From the standpoint of diagnostic radiology, the deep cerebral veins are more important than the superficial veins which exhibit extremely variable configurations. Visualization of the thalamostriate vein and some of its major tributaries can provide information concerning the position and size of the lateral ventricle.

It is evident from the above that the deep veins are concerned primarily with the drainage of the ventricular surface, the choroid plexuses, the deep medullary substance, the caudate nucleus, and the dorsal portions of the lenticular nucleus and thalamus. However, all these structures also can be drained by surface vessels through numerous intracerebral and extracerebral anastomotic veins.

CHAPTER 5

Development And Histogenesis Of The Nervous System

Fertilization to Implantation. The early development and implantation in man parallels that of other mammals. By way of a brief summation, it will be recalled from embryology that the union of the male and female pronuclei (fertilization) results in a newly formed zygote with a restoration of the diploid number of chromosomes (i.e., 46). The zygote then undergoes a series of mitotic divisions (*cleavage*). The cells become smaller with each successive division and are known as blastomeres. Each of the daughter cells contain the full complement of genes, which in the mammalian cell are estimated to be some 20,000 to 40,000 in number. The genes provide for every enzyme and every protein required at all stages of development in each organ. Cell differentiation and maturation in the nervous system depends in large part upon genetic factors, which operate by their control over successive synthesis and release of specific enzymes. Man may be heterozygous for several detrimental genes, so that subsequent malformations and malfunctions of the nervous system often are determined at the time of fertilization.

During the third day following fertilization, while the zygote is passing down the Fallopian tube, cleavage continues to the 12- to 16-cell, or morula, stage. The *morula* consists of a group of centrally located cells (*inner cell mass*) which will give rise to the tissues of the embryo and an outer cell mass which will give rise to the trophoblast, one of the precursors of the placenta. Continued cell divisions of the morula produce an enlarged inner cell mass, and small spaces soon appear between these cells. The minute intercellular spaces coalesce to form a single cavity (blastocoele), and the zygote is now known as a blastocyst. At this stage the trophoblast establishes contact with the epithelial cells of the uterine mucosa. Hence, by the end of the first week, the human zygote has attained approximately 100 cells and, as a blastocyst, has begun its implantation.

Germ Layers to Primitive Streak. In the second week, the cells of the trophoblast penetrate deep into the endometrium of the uterus, and after continued development, they participate in the formation of the definitive placenta. Concurrent changes in the inner cell mass (embryoblast) result in the differentiation of two distinct cell layers: (1) a layer of flattened cells on the surface, facing the lumen of the blastocoele, which now form the *entodermal germ layer;* and (2) a layer of high columnar cells, or *ectodermal germ layer*, which is still in contact with a layer of pale cells now called the cytotrophoblast. These two

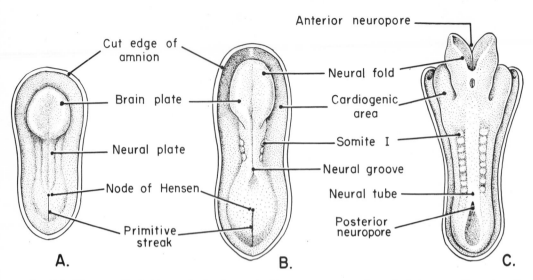

Fig. 5-1. Diagrams illustrating early development of human nervous system. *A*, Late presomite and early neural plate stage (modified from Davis, '23). *B*, Early somite and neural groove stage (modified from Ingalls, '20). *C*, Eight-somite and early neural tube stage (modified from Payne, '24).

layers constitute the *germinal disc* of the blastocyst, which at this stage is interposed between two newly formed cavities (*i.e.*, the amniotic cavity and the secondary yolk sac). At the end of the second week the ectodermal cells in the caudal region of the germinal disc become spherical, proliferate, and migrate toward the midline to form the *primitive streak*. Some of these formative ectodermal cells probably invaginate in the region of the primitive streak to participate later in the formation of an intermediate third layer, or *mesodermal germ layer*. Near the end of the second week, a slight thickening of the entodermal layer in the cephalic region of the embryonic disc forms the *prochordal plate*. The midline region between the primitive streak and the prochordal plate is occupied by the *notochordal process* (derived from the entodermal layer). As more cells are added to the mesodermal layer, it begins to spread laterally. The mesoderm also migrates anteriorly on each side of the midline to meet in front of the prochordal plate (head-fold mesoderm).

In the third week, the cephalic end of the primitive streak shows a marked swelling (Hensen's node) which consists of a small primitive pit surrounded by an elevated area (Fig. 5-1*A*). Soon the noto-chordal process folds into a longitudinal tube, loses its central canal, and becomes detached from the underlying entoderm to form a solid cord (definitive *notochord*). Thus by the middle of the third week the embryonic disc demonstrates a cephalic prochordal plate (which gives rise to the buccopharyngeal membrane) and a primitive streak (the caudal part of which will give rise to the urogenital and anal membranes).

Somite Formation. It is in the expanded cephalic portion of the embryonic disc that the external features of the nervous system first appear late in the third week (Fig. 5-1*B*). The appearance of the neural folds heralds the segmentation of the bilateral strips of paraxial mesoderm into blocks or *somites*. New mesodermal somites will continue to be formed in a craniocaudal sequence, and some 40 somites are normally present by the end of the fourth week (Arey, '38). At the end of the third week, the expanded neural folds and prominent mesodermal somites provide the characteristic early contours of the embryo. This stage also affords a logical starting point for the subsequent development of the nervous system (Fig. 5-1*C*). For a more detailed and pictorial presentation of these early stages of devel-

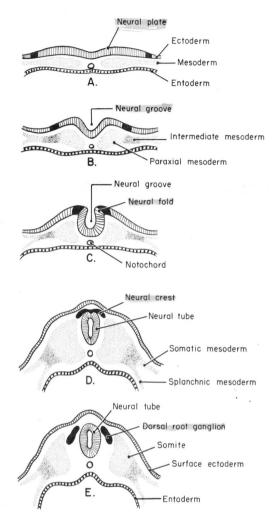

FIG. 5–2. Diagrams of transverse sections of embryos at different ages to show development of the spinal cord. *A*, Neural plate stage. *B*, Early neural groove stage. *C*, Late neural groove stage. *D*, Early neural tube and neural crest stage. *E*, Neural tube and dorsal root ganglion stage.

opment, the student is referred to Patten ('53), Arey ('54), Hamilton, Boyd, and Mossman ('62), and Langman ('63).

Neural Tube. The ectoderm overlying the notochord becomes thickened to form an elongated *neural (medullary) plate*. The primitive neuroblasts, neuroglial elements and neural crest all are derived from the cells of the medullary plate as indicated in Figure 5–4. In the next few days the neural plate invaginates to form

a shallow *neural groove*, which is flanked by two elevated edges called the *neural folds* (Fig. 5–2C). As primitive ectodermal cells continue to proliferate, the neural folds become more prominent, approach each other in the midline, and fuse to form the *neural tube*. Closure of the neural tube begins in the region of the fourth somite (*i.e.*, future cervical region) and continues in both cranial and caudal directions. During neural tube formation, the central canal thus has temporary cranial and caudal connections with the amniotic cavity called *anterior* and *posterior neuropores* (Fig. 5–1C). The anterior neuropore indicates the most cephalic limit of the future brain (*lamina terminalis*) and becomes closed in embryos of 18 to 20 somites. The posterior neuropore disappears later and usually is closed in embryos with 25 to 26 somites. The central nervous system now appears as a closed tube with a narrow caudal portion, the *spinal cord*, and an enlarged cephalic portion, the future *brain*.

Neural Crest. While the midline ectoderm in front of Hensen's node becomes thickened to form the neural plate, the lateral margins of the plate are thinner and continuous with the body ectoderm. The thinned lateral margins of the neural plate (neural crest cells) are approximated as the neural folds meet and fuse. Neural crest cells form a temporary intermediate layer between the neural tube and surface ectoderm (Fig. 5–2D). This temporary layer extends from the cephalic level of the future mesencephalon to the caudal somites. The neural crest cells soon migrate to a posterolateral position on either side of the neural tube (Fig. 5–2E) and become segmented into cell clusters which give rise to the sensory neurons of the dorsal root ganglia of the spinal nerves. Similar cell clusters in the brain region contribute cells to the ganglia of cranial nerves V, VII, VIII, IX, and X (Fig. 5–7B). For example, complete experimental removal of neural crest material from the hindbrain and cervical regions of chick embryos at the 6- to 9-somite stage results in an absence of the intrinsic ganglia within the heart, lungs, esophagus, stomach, and intestines (Yntema and Ham-

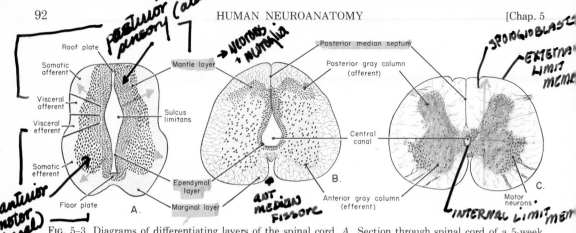

FIG. 5–3. Diagrams of differentiating layers of the spinal cord. *A*, Section through spinal cord of a 5-week human embryo. *B*, Cervical spinal cord of an 8-week human embryo, *C*, Cervical spinal cord of a 10-week human embryo (after Keibel and Mall, '12).

mond, '54). Thus, the neural crest cells form sensory neurons, visceral motor (autonomic) neurons, sheath cells, capsule cells, Schwann cells, and pigment cells, and they may contribute cells to the pia-arachnoid.

Spinal Cord. During closure of the neural tube the walls become thickened, and by the middle of the fourth week the tube has a stratified appearance. The cells and their processes are arranged in three layers: (1) an internal *ependymal layer* composed of columnar cells arranged radially around the central canal, and large ovoid dividing cells (*germinal cells*); (2) a middle *mantle layer* of densely packed primitive neuroblasts derived from the germinal cells of the ependymal layer; and (3) an external *marginal layer* composed of processes from cells in the mantle and ependymal layers (Fig. 5–3).

Continued cell proliferation produces anterior and posterior thickenings in the mantle layer. The anterior thickenings form the larger *basal plates*, or anterior motor horns of the adult cord. The smaller posterior thickenings constitute the *alar plates*, or future posterior sensory horns of the cord (Fig. 5–3). Initially the central canal of the neural tube is somewhat diamond-shaped when observed in transverse section, for it has thin regions above and below known as the *roof* and *floor plates*. A longitudinal groove or *sulcus limitans* extends laterally on each side to further mark the junction between the

anterior motor (basal plate) and posterior sensory (alar plate) areas of the mantle layer. The sulcus limitans extends the length of the primitive spinal cord and continues into the brain stem, where it persists as a prominent sulcus in the floor of the adult fourth ventricle (Figs. 3–5*B* and 5–8). Expansion of the alar plates in a medial direction eventually compresses the posterior portion of the central canal until the two alar plates are in close apposition. The junction line between the two plates (*posterior median septum*) is composed of glia cell processes and intima pia (Figs. 12–1 and 12–2). An invagination, the *anterior median fissure*, in the region of the floor plate, further reduces the size of the central canal (Figs. 3–3 and 5–3). As a result of these changes, the embryonic neural tube is transformed into the gray and white matter configuration of the early spinal cord (Fig. 5–6).

Histogenesis of spinal cord. As the neural tube closes the epithelium thickens and assumes a stratified nuclear appearance due to rapid proliferation of *germinal cells*. These large ovoid cells lie near the central canal and often demonstrate mitotic figures. Rapid cell division produces more and more nuclei which become displaced peripherally so that the primitive cord assumes a three layered appearance (Fig. 5–3*A*). Undifferentiated cells with scanty cytoplasm form the ependymal and mantle layers, and are the stem-cells, or precursors of neurons and neuroglia. The cells

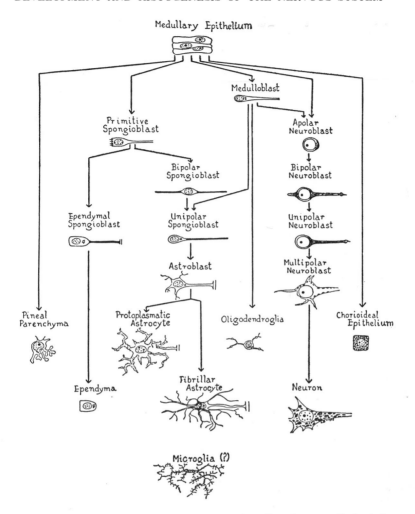

FIG. 5–4. Schema showing histogenesis of neuroglia cells and neurons (Bailey '48)

derived from the primitive medulloblast (neuroblast) and spongioblast are shown in Figure 5–4.

Spongioblasts soon become spindle-shaped bipolar cells that extend through the entire thickness of the tube wall. Their large nuclei are placed close to the lumen and their processes are attached to both the internal and external limiting membranes of the neural tube. Some spongioblasts retain this position and become transformed into ependymal cells (Fig. 5–5). During maturation most ependymal cells lose their attachment to the external limiting membrane and their processes extend only a short distance from the central canal to become anchored in a subependymal glial membrane (Fig. 7–10). Ependymal cells in the adult form the lining of the central canal of the spinal cord and the ventricular surfaces of the brain. The epithelial cells of the choroid plexus (Fig. 7–12) are believed to be modified ependymal cells (i.e., of spongioblast origin). Other spongioblasts in the mantle layer lose their connection with the central canal and assume apolar or unipolar appearances. In later stages of development these detached stem-cells send out new processes and are transformed ultimately into fibrous and protoplasmic astrocytes (Figs. 7–1 and 7–5). Smaller glial cells, the oligodendrocytes, are derived from medulloblasts while the microglia cell comes from

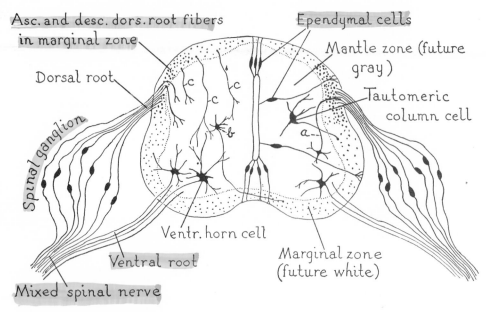

FIG. 5-5. Transverse section through spinal cord and spinal ganglia of a chick embryo. *a*, Efferent fiber; *b*, heteromeric column cell; *c*, collateral. Silver impregnation.

the perivascular mesenchyme which later invades the neural tube. It should be noted that glial cells are present in great numbers before the neuroblasts begin to differentiate. In tissue culture neurons develop normally only when they are embedded in dense glia (Murray '65). Glial cells retain a measure of motility in the adult, whereas neurons are immobile beyond the neuroblast stage. Glial cells also can divide and increase in number, while neurons do not divide after birth and remain in permanent interphase throughout life. The latter is a significant point, for neural pathways, reflexes, and storage of learned information all require a metabolically stable and permanent system of neurons. Structural and functional features of the neuroglial elements are presented in Chapter 7.

Medulloblasts (neuroblasts) of the mantle layer begin to increase in size and soon a fibrillar zone appears in the scanty cytoplasm on the side away from the central canal. This is the apolar stage of the neuroblast (Fig. 5-4). Such large nucleated cells accumulate more cytoplasm and neurofilamentous material. They send out cytoplasmic processes and assume a bipolar appearance which persists for only

a short period. Somewhat later, more cytoplasmic processes develop and the neuroblast becomes transformed into the multipolar shape that is so characteristic of most neurons in the central nervous system (Fig. 6-1). The cell types and fiber arrangement in the mantle and marginal layers at this stage of development are best demonstrated by the Golgi and silver impregnation methods (Fig. 5-5).

Mantle layer. The mantle layer is not found uniformly throughout the neural wall. The floor and roof plates remain reltively thin and furnish only spongioblastic elements. But even in the lateral wall, the neuroblasts are concentrated primarily in the most posterior and the most anterior portions, which correspond to the alar and basal plates, respectively (Fig. 5-5). Between these regions the cells are few and scattered. The mantle layer constitutes the future gray of the spinal cord; the alar portion develops into the posterior horn and the basal plate into the anterior horn.

The neuroblasts of the basal plates become the *efferent peripheral neurons*. Their axons penetrate the marginal layer and external limiting membrane and leave the cord as ventral root fibers which go

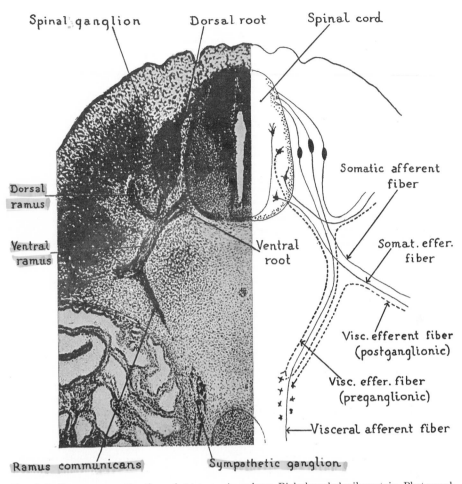

Fig. 5-6. Transverse section through 14-mm. pig embryo. Bielschowsky's silver stain. Photograph.

directly to skeletal muscle or to autonomic ganglia for the innervation of visceral structures (Figs. 5-6 and 12-17). All axons of cells of the alar plate remain within the central nervous system. Some arch anteriorly, cross through the basal plate to the opposite side, and reach the marginal layer, where they ascend or descend for variable distances. Other axons remain on the same side and ascend or descend in the marginal layer. These neurons, whose processes are entirely confined to the central nervous system, constitute the *central*, or *intermediate*, cells. Those whose axons remain on the same side are known as *association cells;* those whose axons cross to the opposite side are *commissural cells.*

As development proceeds, the prolifera-

tion of the germinal cells gradually decreases and ultimately stops altogether. As more and more indifferent cells are transformed into neuroblasts, the nuclear layer progressively diminishes in size and ultimately is reduced to a single layer of columnar ependymal cells. In certain places, as in the anterior commissure of the spinal cord, some of the ependymal cells may retain their embryonal spongioblastic character and extend the whole thickness of the neural wall (Fig. 5-5).

The mantle layer, on the other hand, progressively increases in size and becomes the gray matter of the spinal cord. It is surrounded by a constantly expanding marginal layer which contains the descending and ascending axons of the central cells. At a much later period, most of the axons become myelinated and the marginal layer assumes the whitish, glistening appearance characteristic of the white matter of the adult spinal cord.

Neuron differentiation. In the spinal ganglia, derived from the neural crest, a similar differentiation takes place. Many of the original polygonal or round cells become spindle-shaped and bipolar with the development of two neurofibrillar processes, a central and a peripheral one (Figs. 5–5 and 6–5). The central processes enter the spinal cord as dorsal root fibers and there bifurcate into ascending and descending arms which contribute collaterals to the mantle layer or gray matter (Figs. 5–5 and 12–17).

In human embryos with a crown-to-rump length of 25 mm, many of the neuroblasts have attained the bipolar stage. A few neurons with greater amounts of cytoplasm and distinct neurofilaments appear transitional in shape and often are referred to as pseudounipolar cells (Fig. 6–6). The cytoplasm of the cell body elongates, and the two processes thus become approximated. Ultimately the elongated cell cytoplasm forms the single stem of a T, while the top of the T is formed by the thin central and thicker peripheral processes (Truex, '39; Tennyson, '65). Many neurons are of the unipolar type in spinal ganglia of human 100 mm fetuses. Most of the spinal ganglia cells are true unipolar neurons in the human newborn infant. An occasional bipolar neuron or those in transitional stages may at times be observed in the adult dorsal root ganglia. It is interesting to note that a generous number of ganglionic neuroblasts may be produced initially. Thus, embryonic dorsal root and sympathetic ganglia appear to have an overabundance of neuroblasts when compared to the number of fully differentiated ganglion cells present at birth. For example, Crouse and Cucinotta ('65) made total cell counts of the submandibular ganglia in a graded series of human fetuses and observed a progressive reduction from 12,128 cells at 17 weeks of gestation to 5,988 at full term.

Not all of the cells in the spinal ganglia differentiate into neuroblasts. Some develop into *capsule cells* or *amphicytes* which form a capsule around the bodies of the spinal ganglion cells (Fig. 6–1A). Others wander out along the course of the growing peripheral nerve fibers, envelop them, and ultimately become Schwann cells. These play an active role in the formation of myelin and may be considered as a peripheral type of neuroglia, perhaps most closely related to oligodendrocytes.

Besides the spinal ganglia, there are other peripheral aggregations of nerve cells known as *autonomic* or *sympathetic ganglia* (Figs. 5–6 and 11–2). Arising in part from the neural crest, in part migrating from the anterior part of the cord along the ventral roots, these cells form two ganglionic chains on the anterolateral aspect of the vertebral column (vertebral sympathetic ganglia). Others wander still further to form the ganglia of the mesenteric plexuses (collateral or prevertebral ganglia), while still others actually invade the walls of the viscera, or settle close to them, as the terminal or peripheral autonomic ganglia (Fig. 11–1). Here, too, differentiation occurs in several directions. Some cells enlarge to form the multipolar sympathetic ganglion cells, whose axons terminate in visceral effectors, smooth muscle, heart muscle, and glandular epithelium (Fig. 6–6). Others, as in the case of the spinal ganglia, give rise to amphicytes, which envelop the bodies of one or several ganglion cells. Finally, some differentiate into the chromaffin cells found in the adrenal medulla, carotid bodies, and other portions of the body.

The origin of the autonomic ganglia is still in dispute. While some believe they are formed from the neural crest, others maintain that the largest part are derived from the anterior part of the spinal cord, the cells migrating by way of the ventral roots. It is probable that in mammals, at least, both neural crest and cord contribute to such formation. It has been reasoned that, inasmuch as the sympathetic cells are efferent in character, their origin would most likely be from the visceral efferent part of the spinal cord (Fig. 5–3A).

Segmental Arrangement of Peripheral Nerve Elements. With the differ-

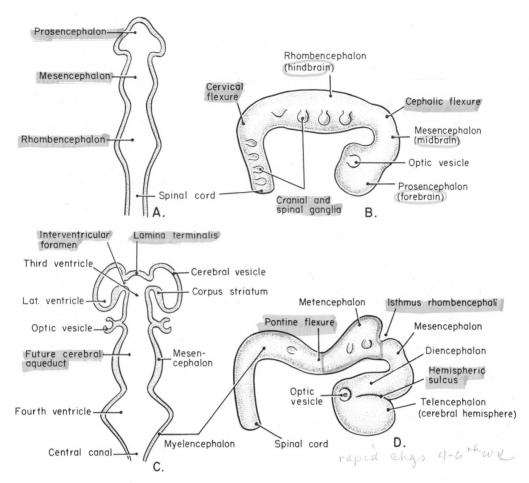

FIG. 5–7. Diagrams of the developing brain vesicles and ventricular system. *A* and *B*, Three brain vesicle stage of a 4-week embryo. *C* and *D*, Five brain vesicle stage of a 6-week human embryo (modified from Hochstetter, '19, and from Langman, '63).

entiation of the various types of nerve cells in early stages of development, a neuronal mechanism that is adequate for complete, if simple, reflex arcs is established. Such arcs consist of afferent, intermediate, and efferent neurons and their peripheral extensions. However, the synaptic junctions of these cells, which make such an arc functional, are as yet unformed.

In embryos of about 10 mm the various components of the peripheral nervous system already are laid down and may be recognized in a transverse section of any typical body segment (Fig. 5–6). The central processes of the spinal ganglion cells form the *dorsal* roots; the ventral root is composed of axons from cells in the anterior gray of the spinal cord (mantle layer). Distal to the ganglion, the ventral root unites with the peripheral processes of the ganglion cells to form a mixed *spinal nerve*, containing afferent and efferent fibers. Each spinal nerve divides into a *dorsal* and a *ventral ramus* and also sends a fiber bundle known as the *ramus communicans* to the vertebral sympathetic chain. The dorsal ramus supplies the muscles and skin of the back; the larger ventral ramus goes to the ventrolateral parts of the body wall. Four functional types of peripheral nerve fibers may be distinguished: *general somatic afferent* (GSA), *general visceral afferent* (GVA), *general somatic ef-*

ferent (GSE), and *general visceral efferent*, (GVE). All of these types of fibers are found in both dorsal and ventral rami. The somatic efferent or "motor" fibers arise from large cells in the anterior gray matter, leave the spinal cord through the ventral roots, and go directly to the skeletal voluntary muscles of the body wall. The somatic afferent or "sensory" fibers are the peripheral processes of spinal ganglion cells, which terminate as receptors in the skin and deeper portions of the body wall. The central processes enter the cord as dorsal root fibers (Fig. 12–17).

The efferent innervation of visceral structures is somewhat different from that of the somatic muscles, for two neurons always are involved in the conduction of impulses from the central nervous system to the effector organs (Figs. 5–6 and 11–2). The *preganglionic visceral efferent* fibers are axons from cells of the spinal cord which pass through the ventral root and ramus communicans to terminate in a vertebral or prevertebral sympathetic ganglion. The axons of sympathetic cells then form the *postganglionic visceral efferent* fibers, which course through the ramus communicans in the reverse direction, join the main branches of the spinal nerve, and are distributed to the smooth muscle and glandular epithelium of the body. In the adult the ramus communicans consists of white and gray portions. The former contains the *myelinated* preganglionic fibers, the latter the *unmyelinated* postganglionic fibers.

Finally, *visceral afferent fibers* convey impulses from the thoracic and abdominal viscera. Like the somatic afferent fibers, they have their cell bodies in the spinal ganglia and enter the cord through the dorsal root (Fig. 12–17).

Brain. Indications of the future brain are present as the neural tube begins to close (Fig. 5–1C). Three primary vesicles or brain regions are evident by the time the neural tube is completely closed. These three early subdivisions are a cephalic *prosencephalon* (forebrain), a middle *mesencephalon* (midbrain), and a caudal *rhombencephalon* (hindbrain). The sulcus limitans is present and indicates the dividing line between motor and sensory areas; it is most prominent in the rhombencephalon. The large cavities within each segment are continuous with the central canal of the spinal cord (Fig. 5–7A). The dilated cavities are the forerunners of the ventricular system, and they will undergo extensive alterations as a result of future cellular proliferation, brain flexures, and growth. The walls of the primary vesicles are thin and epithelial in appearance. Small lateral evaginations (*optic vesicles*) and anterior protrusions (*mammillary eminences*) are present in the forebrain, while the separation of the small midbrain from the larger hindbrain is indicated by the *cephalic flexure* (Fig. 5–7B). Anlagen of the cranial and spinal ganglia from cells of the neural crest are present lateral to the hindbrain and cervical spinal cord. The *cervical flexure* indicates the boundary between hindbrain and spinal cord.

Rapid changes in the brain occur late in the fourth and throughout the fifth week of development. Early in the sixth week, one can identify five brain components due to the appearance of three embryonic landmarks: a transverse rhombencephalic sulcus and a pontine flexure; a deep furrow, the *isthmus rhombencephali;* and on each side, a shallow *hemispheric sulcus* (Fig. 5–7D). The forebrain now demonstrates a cephalic *telencephalon*, or endbrain, and a more caudal part, the *diencephalon* with the attached optic vesicles. The mesencephalon has remained small, while the rhombencephalon has divided into two segments separated by the transverse rhombencephalic sulcus (Fig. 5–10A). The more cephalic *metencephalon* will become the pons and cerebellum, and the caudal *myelencephalon* will form the medulla oblongata (Fig. 5–7D).

The basic pattern of the ventricular system of the brain is evident at this early stage. The roof of the rhombencephalon is extremely thin and the underlying cavity (*fourth ventricle*) appears as a shallow, diamond-shaped depression called the *rhomboid fossa* (Figs. 3–5B and 5–9). With continued growth, the lumen of the midbrain will become narrowed to form the

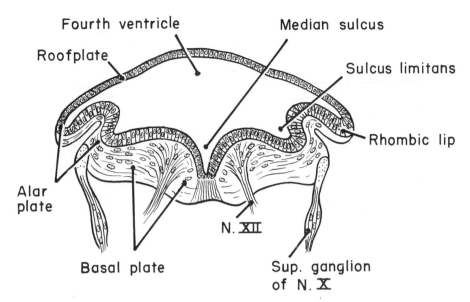

FIG. 5-8. Diagram through medulla of a 5-week human embryo. Note the prominent sulcus limitans separating structures derived from the basal and alar plates.

cerebral aqueduct. Medial growth and expansion of the diencephalon will also reduce the lumen of this segment of the brain to a thin vertical cleft, the *third ventricle*. A large opening (*interventricular foramen*) behind the lamina terminalis provides continuity between the third ventricle and the cavity of the laterally expanding cerebral hemisphere. The primitive *lateral ventricle* within each cerebral hemisphere will become altered extensively by subsequent development (Figs. 5-7 and 5-12).

Each of the five established brain subdivisions undergoes internal organization and presents special features as growth continues. It should be remembered that many of the following embryological events occur simultaneously, as the individual subdivisions are considered briefly.

Myelencephalon. This most caudal brain segment extends between the first spinal nerve of the cervical cord and the early pontine flexure (Fig. 5-7*C* and *D*). As the future medulla oblongata, it differs from the spinal cord in that the walls are pushed laterally at higher levels by the expanding fourth ventricle. As a result the alar plate comes to lie lateral to the basal plate. The sulcus limitans continues

to mark the boundary between these two plates in both gross and microscopic specimens (Figs. 3-5, 5-8 and 14-3). Hence the motor nuclei of cranial nerves IX, X, XI, and XII (derivatives of the basal plate) become located in the floor of the fourth ventricle medial to the sulcus limitans. The sensory nuclei derived from the alar plate lie lateral to the sulcus. The recently acquired pyramid (corticospinal tract) was added medially, while the inferior olive, vestibular nuclei, and inferior cerebellar peduncle are placed more laterally (Figs. 3-5, 14-3 and *A*-5). In the region of the fourth ventricle, the roof plate consists of a single layer of ependymal cells covered by a thin layer of pia mater. These two layers form the tela choroidea, and prolongations project into the ventricle in the region of the transverse rhombencephalic sulcus to form the choroid plexus (Fig. 7-11). Openings in the roof plate appear (4 to 5 months) which establish continuity between the fourth ventricle and the subarachnoid space surrounding the brain stem. The two lateral apertures (foramina of Luschka) connect the lateral recesses of the fourth ventricle with the pontine cistern (Figs. 2-6 and 4-3). A median aperture (foramen of Magen-

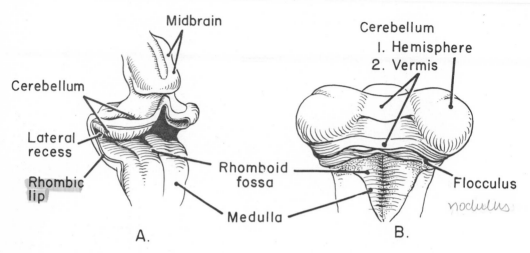

Fig. 5-9. Posterior views of developing cerebellum. *A*, Human embryo of 6 weeks. *B*, Human fetus of 4 months' gestation (after Prentiss and Arey, '20).

die) in the lower roof connects the fourth ventricle with the cerebellomedullary cistern.

Metencephalon. This portion of the hindbrain extends from the pontine flexure to the isthmus rhombencephali (Fig. 5-7D). It consists of an anterior *pons* and a larger *cerebellum*. The pons presents two subdivisions that reflect its phylogenetic development, namely, an older tegmental portion lying in the floor of the fourth ventricle, and a more recent acquisition, the ventral portion (Fig. 5-10B). Cranial nerve nuclei (V, VI, VII, and VIII) and the older fiber systems lie within the tegmentum, while pontine nuclei and newer fiber pathways from the cerebral cortex form the ventral (i.e., basilar) portion.

The posterolateral parts of the two alar plates in the region of the isthmus bend posteriorly and medially to form the *rhombic lips* (Figs. 5-9 and 5-10A). As they enlarge, the lips project caudally over the roof plate of the fourth ventricle and approach each other in the midline to unite; thus they form a transverse *cerebellar plate*. The cerebellar plate soon demonstrates a small midline portion (*vermis*) and two large lateral portions (*cerebellar hemispheres*). A transverse fissure appears on the posterior surface of the cerebellar plate to separate the nodulus from the vermis and the flocculus from the cerebel-

lar hemispheres (Fig. 5-9B). The nodulus and flocculus are the oldest portions of the cerebellum and are intimately connected with the vestibular nuclei. The cranial and caudal portions of the thin metencephalic roof plate remain in the adult brain as the *superior* and *inferior medullary veli* (Fig. 3-12 and A8).

Mesencephalon. The small midbrain extends from the isthmus region to become imperceptibly continuous with the more cephalic diencephalon. It is the least modified of all the brain subdivisions and has two well-marked portions derived from the respective basal and alar plates (Fig. A-25). The more anterior *tegmental portion*, derived from the basal plate, lies below the cerebral aqueduct and contains motor nuclei of the oculomotor and trochlear nerves, as well as phylogenetically older groups of nerve cells and fiber pathways (Figs. 5-10B and A-11). Lying ventral to the tegmental structures are the substantia nigra and the crus cerebri; the latter is composed of more recently acquired nerve fibers that descend to lower levels from the cerebral cortex (i.e., corticospinal, corticobulbar, and corticopontine tracts).

The mantle layer of the alar plate undergoes marked cellular proliferation in the midbrain region. Many of the newly formed cells migrate into the marginal layer, where they become arranged into

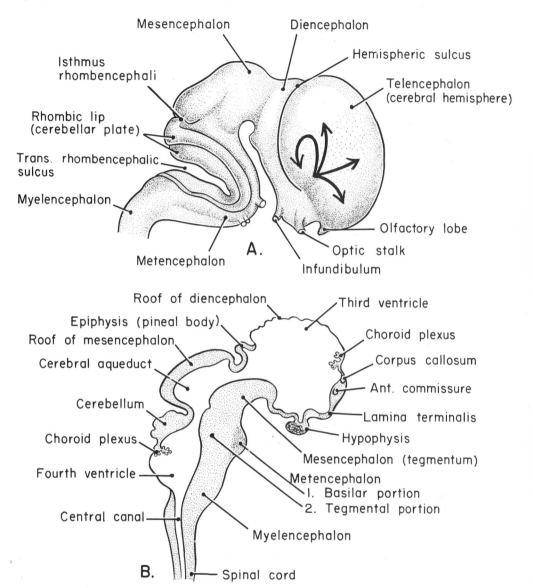

FIG. 5–10. Diagrams of the developing brain vesicles and ventricular system. *A*, Lateral view of cerebral vesicle. *Arrows* indicate directions of growth and expansion of hemisphere. Note the relations of the developing cerebellum. Human embryo of 8 weeks. *B*, Sagittal section through brain of a human fetus of 12 weeks. (Modified from Hochstetter, '19).

stratified neural structures which form a thick roof (tectum) for the cerebral aqueduct (Figs. 3–12, 5–10*B* and *A*–11). The tectum appears first as two longitudinal bands separated by a midline depression. Later a transverse groove divides the bands into the paired *inferior colliculi* (relay nuclei for audition) and paired *supe-*rior colliculi* (relay nuclei for visual impulses). As will be seen in Chapter 16 the superior colliculus retains a rudimentary lamination similar to that of the cerebral cortex.

Diencephalon. This segment is blended with the mesencephalon caudally and with telencephalic structures cranially and lat-

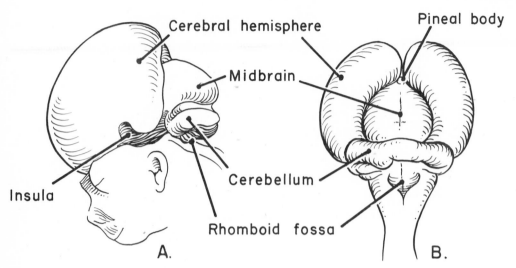

Fig. 5–11. Diagram of cerebral vesicle and brain stem in a human fetus of 12 weeks. A, Lateral view; B, posterior view.

erally. It becomes buried from view in the adult brain by the expanded cerebral hemispheres (Figs. 5–11 and A–26). All the diencephalic structures are derived from the enlarged alar plates, for neither the floor plate nor the basal plate extends beyond the midbrain level. Shallow longitudinal furrows (hypothalamic sulci) soon divide the ventricular surfaces of the rapidly enlarging alar plates into thalamic and hypothalamic regions (Fig. 5–12). In some specimens the two thalami may meet and fuse in the midline and thus form an *interthalamic adhesion* of gray matter which spans the third ventricle. Two nuclear groupings soon appear in the thalamus: a *dorsal group* of association neurons, and a *ventral group* of relay neurons that receive auditory and visual impulses as well as impulses ascending from somesthetic receptors (Fig. 5–12B).

The part of the alar plate that is inferior to the *hypothalamic sulcus* (Fig. 3–13) differentiates into a large number of small hypothalamic nuclei. One of the most prominent nuclear groups is that of the mammillary body. Other hypothalamic derivatives include the infundibulum, posterior lobe of the hypophysis, and optic chiasm. The hypothalamus serves as an important area that regulates a variety of visceral activities through the reticular formation and autonomic nervous system.

The roof plate of the diencephalon is composed of a layer of ependymal cells covered by vascular mesenchyme. These layers project inferiorly to form the choroid plexus of the third ventricle (Figs. 5–12B and 3–13B), while the more caudal part of the roof plate evaginates to form the *pineal body* (epiphysis). It is questionable whether the roof plate, the alar plate, or both, contribute to the formation of the other epithalamic structures (i.e., habenular nuclei, habenular commissure, and posterior commissure).

The *optic nerves* remain associated with the diencephalon and serve as reminders that the eyes develop from this brain vesicle. The hollow *optic vesicle* and optic stalk appear early (Fig. 5–7). In later stages the optic vesicle becomes invaginated to form the two layers of the *optic cup* (similar to pushing one's fist into a hollow rubber ball). The cavity of the vesicle becomes reduced to a mere slit between the two layers. The inner layer develops into the nervous elements of the *retina*, and the cells of this layer soon send nerve fibers back along the optic stalk (optic nerve) to the diencephalon. The thin outer layer of the cup forms the pigmented layer of the adult eye. This mode of development explains why the stratified retina resembles the brain, and the optic nerve fibers are devoid of Schwann

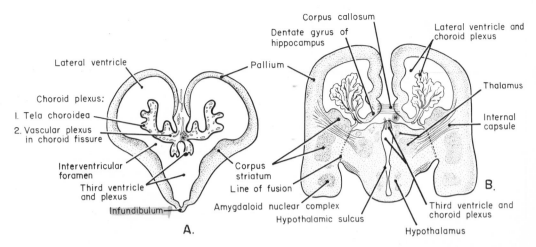

FIG. 5–12. Diagrams of frontal sections through diencephalon, ventricular system, and choroid plexuses of developing brain. A, Invagination of choroid plexuses into lateral and third ventricles. B, Choroid plexuses and secondary fusion of telencephalon with diencephalon. The transverse cerebral fissure is indicated in both A and B by an asterisk (*). (Modified from Hamilton, Boyd, and Mossman, '62).

cell sheaths. For this reason the retina and optic nerves are, literally speaking, "fiber tracts of the brain."

Telencephalon. This most rostral segment of the developing brain is composed of the two evaginating *cerebral vesicles* and their median connection, the *lamina terminalis* (Figs. 5–7 and 5–10). From the cerebral vesicles, three main structures will develop: the *olfactory lobe* (paleopallium), the *corpus striatum*, and the *cerebral cortex* (neopallium). They are derived from the expanded alar plates and enclose the lateral ventricles, which communicate with the third ventricle through the interventricular foramina. The walls of the early vesicle consist of ependymal, mantle, and marginal layers. However, the mantle layer in that part of the evaginating wall which is adjacent to the thalamic area of the diencephalon (Figs. 5–7C and 5–12) soon undergoes a dramatic thickening. The continued proliferation of cells in this region produces a bulge in the lumen of the lateral ventricle and floor of the interventricular foramen. This prominent gray mass in the wall of the cerebral hemisphere marks the embryonic appearance of the basal ganglionic nuclear mass.

The region where the cerebral vesicle is attached to the roof of the diencephalon remains very thin. Here the single layer of ependymal cells and the vascular mesenchyme in the roof of the third ventricle become continuous with similar layers of the lateral ventricle (Fig. 5–12A). A small horizontal cleft thus persists between the cerebral vesicle above and the diencephalon below (i.e., as though one pulled the hemispheres upward and looked forward into the cleft above the pineal body in Figures 5–11 and A–25). This narrow triangular space, lined by a double layer of pia mater and filled with loose mesenchyme (velum interpositum), is the most rostral extension of the *transverse cerebral fissure*. The small *asterisk* (*) in Figure 5–12A and B is located within the transverse cerebral fissure. The lower pial layer of this fissure, as observed in frontal section, forms the roof of the diencephalon and becomes invaginated as the choroid plexus of the third ventricle (Figs. 3–13B and 5–12). The adult cerebral hemisphere also is separated from the cerebellum by the transverse cerebral fissure. The tentorium cerebelli occupies the transverse fissure and helps to separate the inferior surfaces of the hemispheres from the superior surface of the cerebellum (Fig. 4–4).

Thus the choroid plexus of the third ventricle is continuous with the choroid plexus of the lateral ventricle through the interventricular foramen and along the line of vesicle evagination (which persists as the choroidal fissure). Immediately above this line of attachment, the wall of the vesicle becomes thickened to form the *hippocampal ridge* (Fig. 5–12). This thick ridge bulges into the lateral ventricle, where it produces a distinct elevation which is easily identified in the adult brain (Figs. 3–20 and 5–13). Thus the thin walls of the vesicle project laterally (Fig. 5–12), and two modifications have been made along the line of evagination (i.e., choroid plexus and hippocampal formation in the medial roof area, and gray masses of the caudate and lenticular nuclear complex in the floor area adjacent to the thalamus and interventricular foramen).

From this stage of development the cerebral hemispheres grow and expand rapidly—first forward to form the frontal lobe area, then laterally and upward to indicate the future parietal lobe (*arrows* in Fig. 5–10A). Posterior and inferior expansions soon produce the occipital and temporal lobes. The expansions of the cerebral hemispheres bury the diencephalon and posterior surface of the midbrain from view. The anterior, posterior, and inferior expansions during development also explain the curved shape and the relations of several telencephalic structures in the adult brain (e.g., lateral ventricle, choroid plexus, caudate nucleus, and fornix).

The cortex covering the lenticular nucleus remains as a fixed area, the insula. This region becomes buried in the floor of the lateral sulcus by the subsequent overgrowth of adjacent lobes (Fig. 5–13). The large number of nerve fibers entering and leaving the cerebral cortex form a conspicuous fiber pathway (the *internal capsule*) which separates almost completely the deeply placed gray mass (Figs. 3–13 and 5–12B). The medial gray mass becomes the caudate nucleus, and the lateral mass becomes the lenticular nucleus. These two nuclei and the intervening fibers of the internal capsule impart a striated appearance when this region of the adult brain is viewed in transverse section (Fig. 3–26). As noted in Chapter 1, the caudate and lenticular nuclei are collectively referred to as the *corpus striatum*.

Cerebral Cortex. The early evolution of the forebrain is similar in all mammals, and has recently been reviewed (Åström, '67; Bernhard et al., '67; Stensaas, '68; Humphrey, '68; Ravic and Yakovlev, '68). Similar to the spinal cord, the suprastriatal portion of the early telencephalic vesicle appears to be made of three concentric zones during its smooth-surfaced (lissencephalic) stage. A *germinal* or *matrix zone* surrounds the lateral ventricle. Most of the cells will leave this zone and migrate outwards to become nerve and glial cells upon maturation. However, some cells remain in this zone to form the internal limiting membrane, ependyma, and subependymal glial layer. The pale *intermediate zone* will become the white matter of the cerebral hemispheres. It has many radiating fibers and is traversed by neuroblasts and spongioblasts migrating from the matrix zone to the more superficial layer. An outer *cortical zone* or plate represents the prospective neopallium (isocortex). This zone has two distinct layers. The deeper pyramidal layer has many cells and will form layers II to VI of the adult six-layered cortex. The marginal layer is composed mostly of fibers and will become the molecular (plexiform) or most superficial layer (I). In areas of the olfactory cortex (allocortex) the six layers are not present. In these regions the migrant neuroblasts and spongioblasts enter the cortical zone and form a thin nuclear layer close to the surface.

There is some evidence that the neuroblasts invade the cortical zone to form a primitive pyramidal layer before the glial cells arrive (Lorente de Nó, '33). It also has been shown that cells formed at the same time remain in the same part of the pyramidal layer; and that newly formed cells migrate beyond those already present (Angevine and Sidman, '61). Hence, cells in the deeper strata of the pyramidal layer were formed earlier and are older than more superficially located cells. In man the cortical zone becomes highly cellular due to massive neuroblast migrations in the twelfth week. At birth the human neopallium has assumed a stratified appearance as a result of neuron dif-

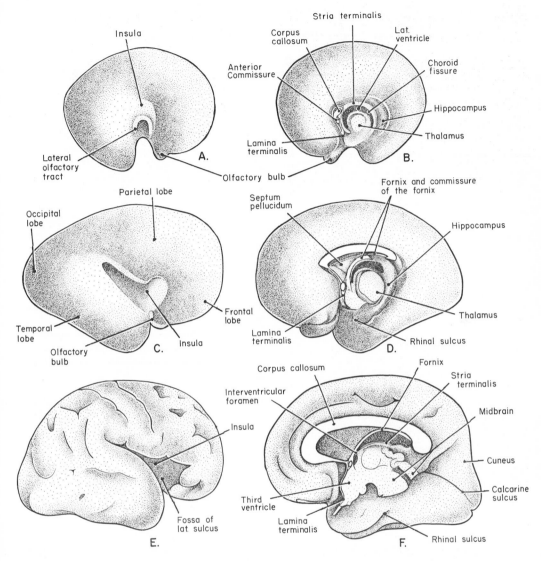

FIG. 5–13. Development of human cerebral hemisphere. A and B, Lateral and medial surfaces of the hemisphere in a fetus of 3 months. C and D, Lateral and medial surfaces of the hemisphere in a fetus at beginning of the fifth month. E and F, Lateral and medial surfaces of the hemisphere at the end of the seventh month. Compare with Figures 4–11 and 4–16. (Modified from Keibel and Mall, '12).

ferentiation and lamina formation by the incoming and outgoing nerve fibers.

Commissures. The medially placed *lamina terminalis* represents the cephalic end of the early neural tube and extends from the roof plate of the diencephalon to the optic chiasm (Figs. 5–10*B* and 5–13). This primitive midline telencephalic structure thus provides the only bridge whereby nerve fibers can pass from one cerebral hemisphere to the other. The first fibers to cross between the two hemispheres (*commissural fibers*) are within the *anterior commissure*. This structure appears in the lower portion of the lamina terminalis by the third month. It connects the olfactory bulb and temporal lobe of the cortex of one side with the same structures of the opposite hemisphere (Figs. 21–3 and 21–6). The small *commissure of the fornix* is the second to appear in the lamina terminalis close to the roof of the diencephalon (Fig. 5–13D). Its fibers connect the cortices of the hippocampal formations with each other.

The largest and most important commissure to cross in the lamina is the *corpus callosum*. The first of these commissural fibers, connecting nonolfactory cortical areas of the two hemispheres, appears as a small bundle rostral to the commissure of the fornix. The size of the corpus callosum parallels the rapid growth and expansion of the neopallium. It first extends anteriorly to connect the frontal lobes and then enlarges posteriorly as the parietal lobes develop. As the constituent fibers increase in number, the corpus callosum arches back over the thin roof of the diencephalon (Figs. 5–13 and A–29). The area between the corpus callosum and the fornix becomes very thin and forms the septum pellucidum. The above commissures and septum pellucidum thus develop within, and represent prolongations of, the embryonic lamina terminalis. The fibers of the *optic chiasm* also cross in the junctional zone between the lamina terminalis and the rostral wall of the diencephalon (Figs. 3–12 and 5–13).

Two small commissures develop caudally at the junction of the roof of the diencephalon and midbrain. The *habenular commissure* appears rostral to the stalk of the pineal body. The *posterior commissure* appears more caudally. They occupy a similar position in the adult brain (Figs. 3–12, 3–13A, A–25).

In the early weeks of gestation the surfaces of the cerebral hemispheres are smooth (lissencephalic). The developing commissures form conspicuous bundles on the cut medial surfaces (Figs. 3–12, 5–13, and A–26). During the sixth and seventh months, the surfaces of the hemispheres grow rapidly and develop convolutions (*gyri*) separated by shallow or deep furrows (*sulci, fissures*). As a result of such surface folds, two-thirds of the cerebral cortex becomes buried in the walls and floor of the sulci and fissures when the brain attains its adult size. Fetal sulci and fissures appear in an orderly sequence; the phylogenetically older sulci appear

first, and more recently acquired sulci appear later (Fig. 5–13E and F). The principal sulci and gyri that form the characteristic pattern of the human cerebral cortex all can be identified in the full-term infant.

In this brief account little detail has been devoted to the mesoderm and its important derivatives. After the neural tube has been formed, it lies deep to the overlying ectoderm and is surrounded on all sides by primitive mesoderm (mesenchyme). This embryonic relationship is shown in Figure 5–6. Here the more darkly stained mesenchyme is seen to the left of the spinal nerve and neural tube. From the surrounding mesoderm the muscles, blood vessels, cartilage, bone, and connective tissue of the body are derived. The mesoderm thus gives rise to several supporting structures of the nervous system (e.g., skull, vertebrae, meninges, intervertebral discs, ligaments, sheaths of peripheral nerves, blood vessels, and microglia). These mesodermal structures are of paramount importance, for they provide not only support, but protection and nourishment, to the nervous system. It is paradoxical that the supporting tissues are, under some circumstances, responsible for serious damage to the nervous system. For example, an artery may rupture with extensive hemorrhage, or the lumen of a vessel may be occluded suddenly and produce anoxia in the area of its neural distribution. Tumors commonly arise from the meninges, from the connective tissue sheaths along peripheral nerves, or from the medulloblast and spongioblast stem cells. An intervertebral disc may rupture posteriorly into the vertebral canal and compress the spinal cord or departing spinal nerve; also fractures of the skull and vertebrae often compress the underlying brain or spinal cord.

We have examined the gross features of the developing and adult central nervous system. The surrounding meninges and all important blood supply also have been presented. Let us now examine the microscopic characteristics of the neuron which forms the structural unit of the nervous system.

CHAPTER 6

The Neuron

In 1891 Waldeyer assembled the known facts about the nerve cell and formulated what is now known as the *neuron doctrine*. Briefly summarized, it states that the individual nerve cell (neuron) is the genetic, anatomic, trophic, and functional unit of the nervous system. All neural reflexes and pathways are composed of individual neuronal units arranged in simple or highly complex circuits.

Each neuron consists of a cell body (perikaryon) from which extend one or more processes. One of the most striking morphological features of the neuron is the presence of the protoplasmic processes, which may become exceedingly elongated. The relation of these long processes to the cell body was poorly understood at first, and nerve tissue long was described as consisting of two elements—nerve cells and nerve fibers. A voluminous literature has accumulated to attest to the continuity of nerve cell and nerve fiber as a single structural unit. Thus the neuron is defined as a nerve cell with all its processes.

Intricate and reliable neurological methods were developed through the years. These technics made it possible to study all of the larger constituents of neurons; however, many minute structural points remained unanswered owing to the limited resolving power of the light microscope. In the last 15 years, the electron microscope and cytochemistry have extended our knowledge and provided answers to many of the fine structural and functional questions about neurons. Such newly acquired information has validated all of the original tenets of the neuron doctrine and will be discussed as the different constituents of the nerve cell are presented.

Neuroanatomical Methods. An appreciation of the microscopic appearance of the different neural components, when stained by appropriate technics, will make the examination of neurons and their adnexa easier and more meaningful. It is essential that fresh nerve tissue be placed in a fluid that results in minimal shrinkage, swelling, and distortion. A good fixative also kills bacteria and renders autolytic enzymes inactive. Perfusion of fixing solutions is possible in animals, whereas several hours usually intervene between death and necropsy in man. Hence, neuronal alterations such as shrinkage, and staining artifacts are often difficult or impossible to avoid in the preparation of human material. Appropriate fixation makes many components of the nerve cell, such as chromatin, receptive to suitable dyes i.e., cresyl violet (Fig. 6–1*E*), or the neurofilaments more permeable to colloidal silver solutions (Fig. 6–1*A*, *B*, *C*). Common neurologic fixatives like formol and alcohols often are used in conjunction with, or followed by, a wide variety of chemicals such as chloral hydrate, ammonia, pyridine, glacial acetic acid and mercuric chloride. Formol fixation followed

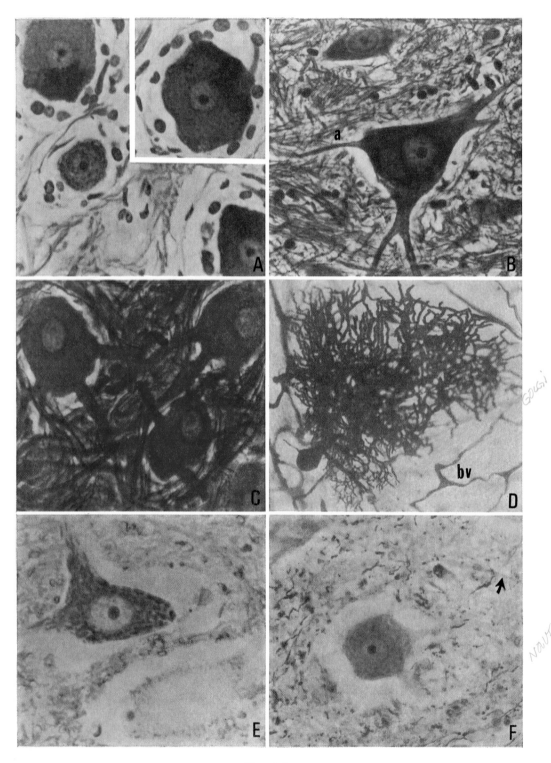

FIG. 6–1

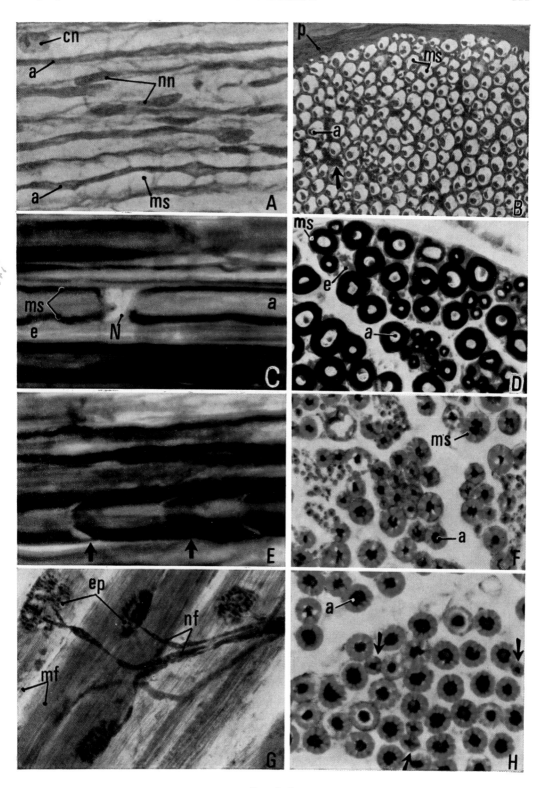

FIG. 6–2

Fig. 6–2 (on previous page)

Fig. 6–2. Size and appearance of nerve fibers stained by different technics. *A*. Longitudinal section of femoral nerve stained with silver protargol. Axons (*a*), Schwann cell (*nn*) and connective tissue (*cn*) nuclei are identified. The myelin sheath (*ms*) is dissolved and remains as a clear space in such silver preparations. ×370. *B*. Cross section of sciatic nerve stained with silver nitrate. Axons (*a*), myelin space (*ms*) and connective tissue of perineurium (*p*) are identified. Small black dots between larger fibers are axons of non-myelinated fibers (arrow). ×130. *C*. Longitudinal section of myelinated nerve fiber and node of Ranvier (*N*) stained with osmic acid and light green. Myelin sheath (*ms*) stains black, axon (*a*) is unstained, and connective tissue of endoneurium (*e*) is green. ×370. *D*. Cross section of lumbar nerve in cauda equina with osmic acid and light green. Endoneurium (*e*) derived from pia mater is green, myelin (*ms*) is black, while axons (*a*) are unstained. ×270. *E*. Longitudinal section of two myelinated nerve fibers with osmic acid and light green. Lower fiber with thicker myelin sheath exhibits Schmidt-Lantermann clefts (*arrows*). ×370. *F*. Cross section of intradural dorsal root sensory fibers with combined Holmes' silver and Luxol blue technics. Axons (*a*) appear dark brown, and myelin sheath (*ms*) is blue. Note variation in size of myelinated and non-myelinated axons. ×270. *G*. Longitudinal section of nerve fibers (*nf*) terminating as motor-end plates (*ep*) on extrafusal skeletal muscle fibers (*mf*). Gold chloride technic. ×145. *H*. Cross section of intradural ventral root motor fibers stained as *F* above. Larger fibers (*A*) terminate as motor-end plates on extrafusal muscle fibers, while smaller gamma efferent axons (*arrows*) end on intrafusal muscle fibers of neuromuscular spindle. ×270.

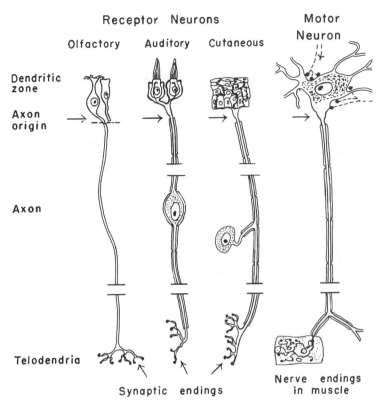

Receptor Neurons

Olfactory   Auditory   Cutaneous

Motor Neuron

Dendritic zone

Axon origin

Axon

Telodendria

Synaptic endings

Nerve endings in muscle

Fig. 6-3. Diagram of three sensory neurons and a motor neuron based on the site of impulse origin rather than location of the cell body. Dendritic zone includes the generation potential in a receptor, as well as excitatory or inhibitory input of synaptic endings (dotted lines on motor neuron) on another nerve cell. The axon and its telodendria are related to conduction and synaptic transmission of a generated nerve impulse. The perikaryon of a neuron is the trophic center primarily concerned with the outgrowth and maintenance of processes, and their metabolic functions other than membrane activity. Note that the cell body may be located either in dendritic zone or the region of the axon. (After Bodian, '62).

neurons and neuroglia are stained black, but these often are shown in great detail against a nearly colorless background (Fig. 6-1D). In addition to neurons and neuroglia the blood vessels also may be stained (Fig. 2-11). The method is largely empirical, the results uncertain, but magnificent neuronal and neuroglial details are revealed in successful preparations (Fig. 7-1).

The illustrations of nerve tissue shown in Figures 6-1 and 6-2 represent but a few of the basic methods used to study the neuron. A wide spectrum of additional technics are now in use, based upon recent advancements in the fields of neurochemistry, autoradiography, fluorescent and electron microscopy. Important contributions have been obtained from each

of the different neurologic methods. Such recent advances are appropriately noted as the neurons and their surrounding tissues are presented in this and subsequent chapters. Additional basic information and procedural steps in the more commonly used neurologic stains can be found in text references edited by Windle, ('57), Baker ('60), Ambrogi ('60), McManus and Mowry ('60), Jones ('61), Gasser, ('61), Humason ('62), Culling ('63) and Adams ('65).

Functional Concept of Neurons. Bodian ('62) has suggested a generalized concept of neuron structure in which *impulse origin*, rather than cell body location, is taken as the focal point. He proposed the term *"dendritic zone"* for the receptor membrane of a neuron (Fig. 6-3). This zone includes the tapering cytoplasmic extensions (dendrites) which receive synaptic endings of other neurons. In some instances membranes of the neuron are differentiated to convert environmental stimuli into local-response-generating activity (i.e., transducer activity of peripheral receptors). The *cell body* (perikaryon) is the focal point of embryonic outgrowth of dendrites and axon, of axon regeneration, and maintains the trophic aspects of neuron activity such as enzyme synthesis in the differentiated neuron. Both location and shape of the cell body becomes less important in this functional concept. It may be multipolar in shape and part of the dendritic zone (e.g., axosomatic synapses on an anterior horn cell), or somewhat removed from the receptor arborizations (bipolar neurons of vestibulocochlear nerve, or unipolar neurons of the cerebrospinal ganglia).

In this light the "*axon*" is a single, often branched and usually elongated, cytoplasmic extension (Fig. 6–3). It may arise from the cell body (axon hillock) or from the base of a dendrite. Impulse origin or the physiological "spike" occurs at or near the origin of the axon, which then conducts the nerve impulse away from the dendritic zone. Axons are ensheathed by neuroglial or Schwann cells—axon diameter and sheath differentiation are both related to speed of conduction. The branched and variously differentiated terminals of axons are "*telodendria*". They may show membrane and cytoplasmic differentiation related to synaptic transmission or neurosecretory activity (Fig. 11–7). Mitochondrial concentrations, synaptic vesicles, or secretory granules are commonly present in their bulblike terminals. The telodendria transmit electrical or chemical signals capable of producing generator potentials in the dendritic zones of other neurons and in muscle. They can also induce stimulatory effects in innervated gland cells, or even in distant cells via a neurohumeral route. It is in keeping with this functional concept that the terms axon, dendrite and cell body are used in this text.

Varieties of Neurons. Neurons show wide variations in size and an infinite variety in the arrangement of their processes. However, nerve cells subserving a similar function or located in a given region of the nervous system often resemble each other structurally (Figs. 6–1, 6–4, 6–5, and 6–6). Thus the *bipolar* neurons are sensory in function and subserve impulses generated by olfactory, visual, vestibular, and auditory receptor endings (Fig. 6–6A). The T-shaped *unipolar neurons* are characteristic of the cerebrospinal ganglia and mesencephalic nucleus of the trigeminal nerve (Figs. 6–1A and 6–6B, C, and D).

Such sensory neurons convey nerve impulses from a variety of specialized and non-specialized receptor endings. *Multipolar neurons* transmit both sensory and motor nerve impulses, and are characteristic of the brain, spinal cord and peripheral autonomic nervous system (Figs. 6–1B–F, 6–4 and 6–6). The primary, secondary and tertiary dendritic branches of some multipolar neurons may be quite elaborate and enormously increase its synaptic surface (Figs. 6–4 and 6–5). A Purkinje cell of the cerebellar cortex serves as an illustrative example. Such dendrites are wide at the base, and taper rapidly. The primary, secondary and tertiary branches have a smooth surface, while the more distal dendritic branches are beset with great numbers of fine spines or *gemmules* (Fig. 6–5). Fox and Barnard ('57) reported the length of the spiny terminals of a single Purkinje cell to be 40,700 microns. The dendritic branchlets with their 61,000 spines have a combined synaptic surface area of 222,000 square microns. In a more recent study of the spiny branchlets in cat, monkey and man Fox et al. ('67) now believe the above estimate of spines to be much too conservative. They now feel the estimate of 61,000 spines on a Purkinje cell should be doubled. In the monkey the dendritic spines are approximately one micron in length, while in man the spines are slightly longer.

Arborizations of neurons in other parts of the CNS are less extensive, yet they too reveal a characteristic pattern of branching. For example, the nerve cells of the inferior olive (Fig. 6–4A) have radiating dendrites with curly branches, whereas

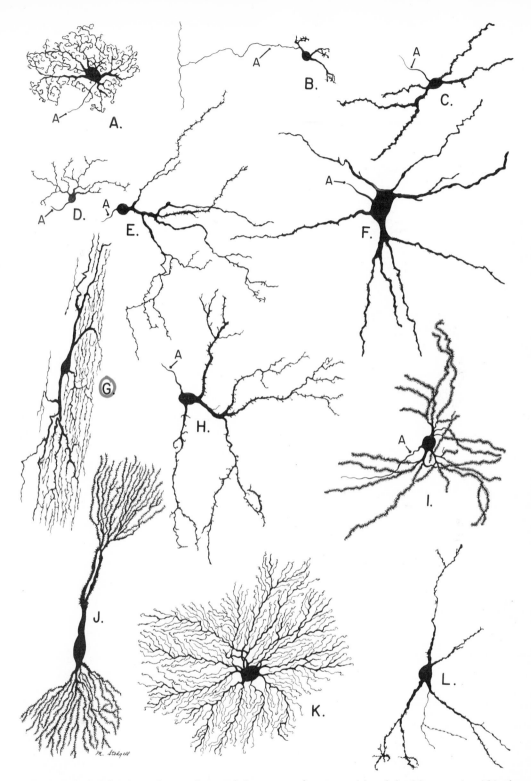

FIG. 6–4. Scaled drawings of some characteristic neurons whose axons (A) and dendrites remain within the central nervous system. *A*, Neuron of inferior olivary nucleus; *B*, granule cell of cerebellar cortex; *C*, small cell of reticular formation; *D*, small gelatinosa cell of spinal trigeminal nucleus; *E*, ovoid cell, nucleus of tractus solitarius; *F*, large cell of reticular formation; *G* spindle-shaped cell, substantia gelatinosa of spinal cord; *H*, large cell of spinal trigeminal nucleus; *I*, neuron, putamen of lenticular nucleus; *J*, double pyramidal cell, Ammon's horn of hippocampal cortex; *K*, cell from thalamic nucleus; *L*, cell from globus pallidus. Golgi preparations, monkey. (Courtesy of Dr. Clement Fox, Wayne State University.)

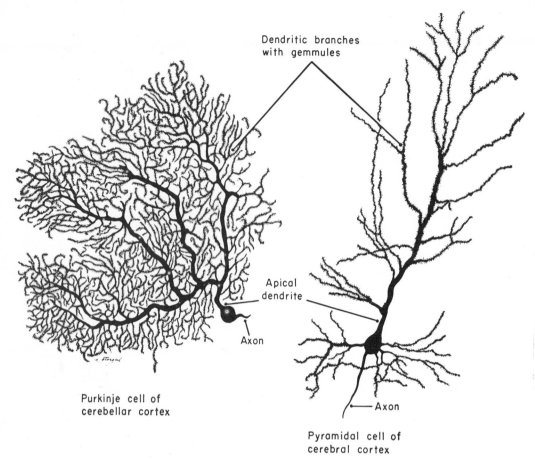

Dendritic branches
with gemmules

Apical
dendrite

Axon

Purkinje cell of
cerebellar cortex

Axon

Pyramidal cell of
cerebral cortex

Fig. 6–5. Scaled drawings of two principal cell types in cerebellar and cerebral cortex. Dendritic branches provide extensive area for synaptic terminals of many other cortical and subcortical neurons. Golgi preparations, monkey. (Courtesy of Dr. Clement Fox, Wayne State University.)

neurons of the thalamus (Fig. 6–4K) have radiating dendrites with longer and less kinked branches. The cells of the *substantia gelatinosa* of the spinal cord are best seen in stained longitudinal sections and demonstrate only a few large dendrites that issue chiefly from one side of the cell body (Fig. 6–4G). Smaller branches of these dendrites then form a compact zone of fine parallel fibers.

It is instructive to compare the profuse dendritic branches of the central sensory and integrating neurons (Fig. 6–4, A, B, D, E, and G through K) with the more robust dendrites of motor neurons (Figs. 6–4, C, F, and L, and 6–6, M, N, and O). This comparison is even more striking if one contrasts the two principal cell types

of the cerebellar and cerebral cortex (Fig. 6–5). The brushlike spread of dendrites of the Purkinje cell is similar to that of other central integrating neurons (Fig. 6–4, A, I, J, and K); yet each has individual characteristics. The large pyramidal cell (Fig. 6–5) also has an extensive dendritic spread and tiny gemmules. However, its basic structure more closely resembles that of a motor neuron (Figs. 6–4, F and L, and 6–6, I and M through O). Successful Golgi preparations permit one to follow the processes of a neuron for considerable distances. The recent studies of Fox and Barnard ('57) and Scheibel and Scheibel ('58a), using this method, provide clearer concepts of neuron structure, dendritic ramification and axonal distribution within the cerebellar cortex, and brain stem reticular formation.

The somatic and visceral neurons of the central and peripheral nervous systems of man can be compared in Figure 6–6. The peripheral processes and axons of such neurons form the peripheral, cranial and spinal nerves. Nerve cells of the sensory and autonomic ganglia are surrounded by a thin nucleated capsule. Although nerve cells do not undergo mitotic division after birth, they probably do increase in size, as their axons and dendrites continue to grow in length. According to length of axon, Golgi (1874) has classified all nerve cells into long axon (Type I) and short axon (Type II) neurons. In the latter, the axon breaks up into an extensive terminal arborization in the immediate vicinity of the cell body.

The length of some nerve axons is quite remarkable. Certain pyramidal cells of the cerebral cortex may send axons to the caudal tip of the spinal cord, i.e., from the top of the head to the lumbar region of the body (Fig. 13–16). Axons of motor neurons in the spinal cord may extend the whole length of the lower extremity to terminate in muscle fibers of the toes. A sensory unipolar neuron situated in the first sacral dorsal root ganglion may send a peripheral fiber to one of the toes, while its central fiber may ascend the whole length of the spinal cord and terminate in the medulla (Fig. 13–6). The total length of such a neuron would be from the toe to the nape of the neck. In a full-grown giraffe, such a fiber would reach the astounding length of over 15 feet.

The size of the neuron body likewise fluctuates within wide limits, from a diameter of 4 micra in the smallest granule cells of the cerebellum (Fig. 6–4B) and cerebral cortex to well over 100 micra in the largest motor cells of the spinal cord. In general, the dimension of the cell body is proportional to the length, thickness, richness of branchings, and terminal arborizations of its dendrites and axon.

The Cell Body (Perikaryon). The neuron body consists of a nucleus surrounded by a mass of cytoplasm whose surface layer forms a delicate plasma membrane. It appears as a fine structure in stained sections when viewed with the light microscope (Fig. 6–1). As observed with the electron microscope, the plasma membrane (*PM* in Fig. 6–8) has a three-layered appearance similar to that of most tissue cells. It delimits sharply the cytoplasm of the neuron (neuroplasm) from adjacent processes of other nerve cells and from neuroglial and connective tissue cells and fibers. The plasma membrane regulates the interchange of materials and ions between the cell and its environment, for it is differentially permeable; i.e., it acts selectively to permit the accumulation within the cell of some solutes and not of others (DeRobertis et al., '65; Robertson, '66). This surface membrane also participates in the reception and transmission of electrical potentials (nerve impulses) from one nerve cell to another (*sy* in Fig. 6–8). It is true that much remains to be learned of the significance and ultrastructure of the neuron plasma membrane and its associated subsurface cisterns (Rosenbluth, '62) and synaptic vesicles. Yet the significance of this essential membrane can not be minimized. Recent studies have provided clearer concepts of neuron structure, which show that the neuron is similar to an enormous gland-like cell that is constantly changing, synthesizing, and producing proteins and lipoproteins with the mediation of ribonucleic acid as an activator and governing molecule (Waelsch, '57; Richter, '57; Hydén, '60). It also has been noted that nerve cells contain more ribonucleic acid than any other cells, with the possible exception of the pancreatic cells in some animals (Brattgård et al., '58). All the ingredients and fluids for such cell synthesis of protein are dependent upon the integrity of the plasma membrane.

The cytoplasm of a neuron in a routinely stained section appears basophilic and has a large, pale nucleus with a prominent nucleolus. After appropriate staining procedures, one also can demonstrate

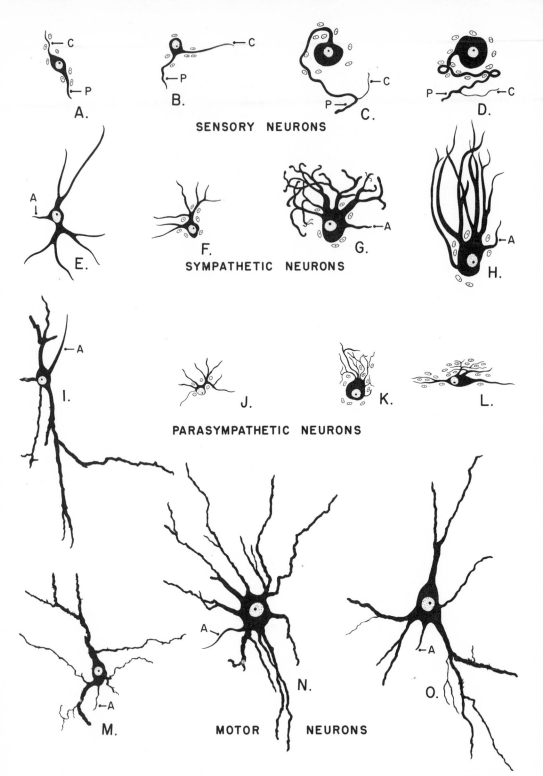

Fig. 6-6. Scaled drawings of representative neurons whose axons (A) are distributed in the peripheral nervous system of man. Capsular nuclei are shown about all ganglion cells. The central (C) and peripheral (P) processes of the sensory neurons are identified. A, Bipolar neuron, nodose ganglion (newborn); B, pseudounipolar neuron, nodose ganglion (newborn); C, unipolar neuron, dorsal root ganglion (newborn) D, unipolar neuron, trigeminal ganglion; E, multipolar neurons of intermediolateral nucleus of spinal cord; F, superior cervical ganglion (newborn); G and H, stellate ganglion; I, dorsal motor nucleus N. X; J, ciliary ganglion (newborn); K, intracardiac ganglion; L, myenteric ganglion; M, nucleus ambiguus; N, motor nucleus N. XII; and O, anterior horn cell.

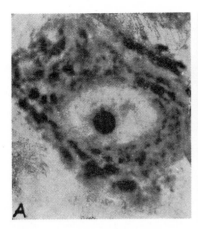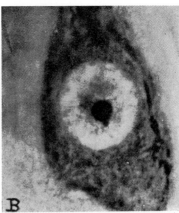

FIG. 6–7. Nucleolar satellite in motor cell of spinal cord (A) and Betz cell of motor cortex (B). Female cat. Cresyl violet. ×1200. (Barr et al., '50.)

within the cytoplasm of nerve cells neurofibrils, chromophil substance (Nissl bodies), Golgi apparatus, mitochondria, at times a central body, and various inclusions such as pigment, fat, and lipids. Neurofibrils are uniquely characteristic of nerve cells, whereas the other cytoplasmic constituents also are observed in other tissue cells. The cytoplasm extends throughout the confines of the cell and all of its processes and, in the axon, is often called axoplasm. As observed by light microscopy, the cytoplasm appears open and somewhat dispersed, whereas it has a compact and crowded appearance in electron micrographs (Fig. 6–8). Many of the neuronal structures seen by light microscopy require specific stains (e.g., neurofibrils, mitochondria, Golgi apparatus, Nissl bodies, and lipids), while most of these same constituents are visualized simultaneously with the higher resolving power in the electron microscope.

Nucleus. This spherical structure, which varies in size from 3 to 18 micra, is usually centrally placed within the cell body. A striking exception is the eccentric position of the nucleus in the cells of the nucleus dorsalis (of Clarke) in the spinal cord (Fig. 12–10). The nucleus often is displaced to one side of the cell in the neurons of the pelvic autonomic ganglia. Bi- and trinucleated neurons may also be observed in these same ganglia.

Small aggregates of desoxyribonucleic acid are scattered in a somewhat homogeneous nucleoplasm and account for the pale appearance of the nucleus (Figs. 6–1 and 6–8). Usually one deeply staining nucleolus occupies a prominent position in the nucleus. The nuclear membrane seen with the light microscope appears sharp and continuous, while electron micrographs reveal it as a double-layered membrane which is periodically interrupted by nuclear pores (*Nuc. M.* in Fig. 6–8). For a more detailed description of nuclear ultrastructure, the student is referred to the studies of Wischnitzer ('60) and of Hay and Revel ('63).

Nucleolus. This basophilic structure contains a large amount of RNA as well as a diffuse coating of DNA. It is known to have positive histochemical reactions for several enzyme systems associated with respiration, energy production and the synthesizing functions of the cell. It is particularly related to the production of nucleic acid and protein in nerve cells. In most electron micrographs the nucleolus shows no limiting membrane and the structure has a dense granular appearance. A "nucleolar satellite" one micron or less in diameter may be found closely apposed to the nucleus in nerve cells from female specimens (Barr et al. '50) as shown in Figure 6–7.

Chromophil Substance. There are two main types of nucleic acid in the cell.

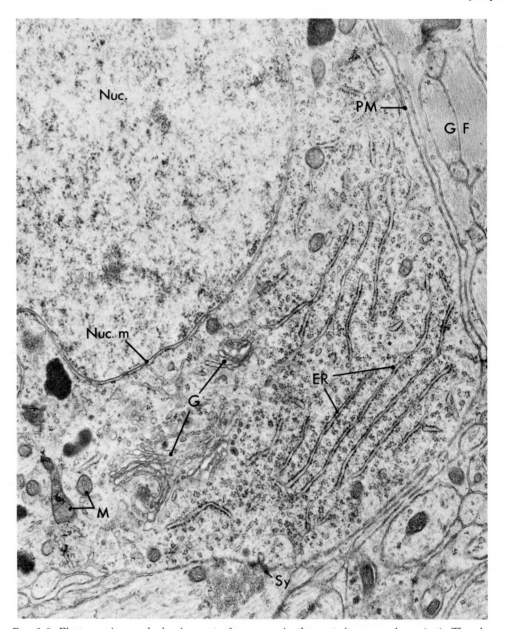

Fig. 6-8. Electron micrograph showing part of a neuron in the posterior gray column (cat). The plasma membrane (*PM*) separates cytoplasmic structures from glial fibers (*GF*) and a synapse (*sy*) which are identified in the adjacent neuropil. Part of the pale nucleus (*Nuc.*) and the nuclear membrane (*Nuc. m*) appear to the upper left. The cytoplasm demonstrates pouches and vesicles of the Golgi complex (*G*), mitochondria (*M*), and an array of individual ribonucleoprotein particles. Some appear as clumps or rosettes, while some ribosomes are attached to the outer surface membranes. The parallel stacks of cisternae of the granular endoplasmic reticulum (*ER*) are characteristic of Nissl bodies. Osmium fixation. ×75,000 (Courtesy of H. J. Ralston, III, Stanford University.)

In one, ribonucleic acid, the sugar of the nucleotide is ribose (pentose); in the other, desoxyribonucleic acid, the sugar is desoxyribose (desoxypentose). Recent cytochemical methods have furnished evidence that nucleoproteins of the √desoxyribose type are found solely in the chromatin, which forms the spireme and chromosomes in mitosis and, during the intermitotic period, is partly represented by chromatin bodies known as karyosomes. The nucleolar satellite apparently also contains desoxyribonucleic acid. On the other hand, the true nucleolus is as a rule a dense, spherical, optically homogenous body that is rich in proteins in which the nucleic acid, when present, is always of the ribose type. Similar ribonucleoproteins are found in the cytoplasm, and there is good evidence for the assumption that the nucleolus plays an important part in cytoplasmic protein formation (Caspersson, '50).

In preparations stained with basic aniline dyes, the *chromophil substance* appears in the form of deeply staining granules or clumps of granules known as *Nissl (tigroid) bodies* (Fig. 6–1E). They are found in the cell bodies and dendrites of all large and many of the smaller cells, but are invariably absent in the axon and in the axon hillock from which that process arises. They are most abundant and sharply defined in the larger cells, whose clear vesicular nucleus contains practically no basichromatin (Figs. 6–1 and 6–7).

The Nissl bodies are larger in motor than in sensory cells, and attempts have been made to distinguish the many neuron types by the size, shape, distribution, and staining capacity of the chromophil granules.

Nissl bodies were long presumed to result from protein precipitation during fixation. However, recent evidence has demonstrated their presence in living cells. In ganglion cells which have been centrifuged with tremendous force, the Nissl bodies become concentrated in the centrifugal pole of the cell without apparently losing their individual discreteness (Beams and King, '35). Bensley and Gersh ('33), using the freeze-dry technic which eliminates many of the artifacts caused by commonly used fixation methods, have obtained Nissl pictures quite similar to those found in the usual histological preparations. Beams and King conclude that "Nissl bodies react like definite masses of greater density imbedded in lighter substance." Deitch and Murray ('56) demonstrated an exact correspondence between the cytoplasmic masses seen by phase-contrast microscopy in tissue culture cells of living chick ganglion cells and in the same cells fixed in 1 per cent buffered osmium tetroxide. They believed the masses to be chromophilic material.

Much of the confusion surrounding the Nissl bodies was resolved by the electron microscopy study of Palay and Palade ('55), in which the Nissl material was identified as masses of granular endoplasmic reticulum. Clusters of punctate ribonucleic acid granules, 10 to 30 millimicra in diameter, were oriented upon and between the cisterns, tubules, and vesicles to form a series of flattened, anastomosing, parallel-arranged sheets or membranes (Fig. 6–8). Dispersed ribonucleic acid granules also can be observed along isolated cisternae within the neuron cytoplasm. With the aid of ultraviolet microscopy and the use of ribonuclease, it has also been shown that ribonucleoprotein is one of the main constituents of the Nissl substance. Treatment of the sections with the enzyme ribonuclease results in the loss of stainability with basic dyes, although the Nissl bodies remain intact.

The available evidence indicates that the Nissl bodies are part of a mechanism for the synthesis of cytoplasmic proteins. This mechanism serves to replace the protein that is constantly consumed during normal physiological activity and to restore the total cell mass when the neuron is suddenly deprived of a large amount of its protoplasm, as in axon amputation (Francoeur and Olszewski '68). Following section of the axon, alterations in the discrete structure of the Nissl bodies can be demonstrated when stained by basic dyes and viewed with light microscopy (Fig. 6–1E). Nissl bodies in the cytoplasm about the nucleus appear dispersed or dissolved, a phenomenon termed *chromatolysis* (see page 142).

Neurofibrils. The neurofibrils are found in *all* nerve cells. As demonstrated by the reduced silver methods, they are delicate, homogeneous threads which are continuous throughout the cell body and its processes (Fig. 6–1B and C). In the cell body they cross and interlace. In the processes they run straight and parallel to each other and are more closely grouped, especially in the axon, which practically constitutes a cable of densely packed neurofibrils. Neurofibrils have been described in the living nerve fibers of several invertebrates and in the living nerve cells of tissue culture (Weiss and Wang, '36; Geiger, '58).

The question whether neurofibrils exist as such in the living cell remained unsolved by the use of the conventional methods of classical histology. Palay and Palade ('55) found nothing in their electron microscopy study comparable in size to the neurofibrillae observed by light microscopy. Similar negative results were obtained in other electron microscopy studies of both the developing and the adult nerve cell bodies and their processes (Palay, '55; Tennyson, '62; Rhodin, '63). However, these and more recent investigators all have observed fibrillar material in the axon, dendrites and perikaryon formed by long tubular elements 200–300 Å in diameter (Peters and Vaughn, '67). Such *neurotubules* have a smooth contour and are of variable length. In the axoplasm of peripheral and central nerves one usually can see neurotubules, as well as strands of canaliculi, vesicles of endoplasmic reticulum and a few ribosomes (Fig. 6–16). In addition to neurotubules there are finer axial components called *neurofilaments* which are about 100 Å in diameter. There is no doubt that the neurotubules and neurofilaments observed in electron microscopy, become aggregated during fixation and form the neurofibrils observed with the light microscope. It is interesting to note that microtubules predominate in dendrites, whereas neurofilaments are few in the initial axon segment but become more common in the distal myelinated segments of axons (Peters, '68). Nerve conduction takes place at the surface membrane of the axon, and neurotubules seem to have no role in the process. Whether the neurotubules are involved in axon growth, the transportation of essential

enzyme systems, or the formation of protein and synaptic vesicles remains unknown. One recent study demonstrated electron-dense, intraluminal granules in the neurotubules of both central and peripheral nerves (Rodriguez-Echandia et al., '68). This observation and the demonstrations of axoplasmic flow (Droz and Leblond, '62; Francoeur and Olszewski, '68) suggests endotubular flow. They are a consistent part of the neuronal cytoskeleton, but their precise function(s) must await further ultrastructural study.

Mitochondria. Granular or filamentous mitochondria are scattered throughout the entire cell body, dendrites, and axon (Fig. 6–9). These organelles occur even in the smallest ramifications and terminals of the neuron and are prominent electron microscopic features wherever intense metabolic activity occurs, such as at synapses and at sensory and motor endings (Palay and Palade, '55; Hartmann, '56; Dempsey, '56). A great amount of knowledge has accumulated on the role of these widely distributed bodies in glycolysis, biosynthesis, cell respiration, and general cell metabolism. Such information has been reviewed by Waelsch ('57). The mitochondria (*M* in Figs. 6–8, 6–19, and 6–21) are recognized easily in most electron micrographs. Their accumulation and breakdown at the nodes of Ranvier have been observed during the early stages of Wallerian degeneration 12 to 24 hours after axonal injury (Webster, '62).

Centrosome. A microcentrum often is demonstrated in neuroblasts. It consists of one or two granules surrounded by a clear cytoplasmic area. In some instances, fine wavy fibrils may radiate from the clear area of cytoplasm. The significance of the centrosome is puzzling, for adult neurons are incapable of cell division. However, Murray and Stout ('47) and Murray ('57) have demonstrated that adult human sympathetic ganglia could survive, migrate, and occasionally divide mitotically in tissue culture. Similar cultures of adult neurons of the human cerebral cortex have been observed to divide

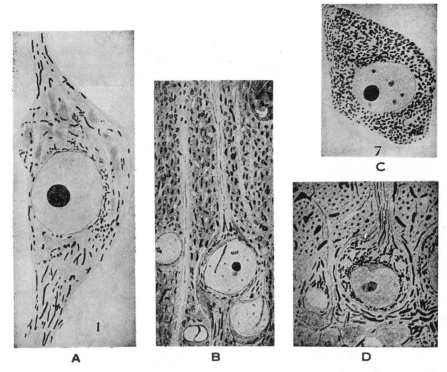

FIG. 6–9. Mitochondria in several types of nerve cells of the white mouse. A, Large anterior horn cells; B, large pyramidal cell from the cortex; C, cell of trigeminal ganglion; D, Purkinje cell of cerebellar cortex.

and survive after six subcultures for periods of 8 to 13 months (Geiger, '58).

Golgi Apparatus. The reticular Golgi complex is highly developed in nerve cells. With special silver-osmium stains, it appears as a complicated perinuclear network which may extend into the base of the larger dendrites (Fig. 6–10). In other cells it may consist of disconnected granules or threads, and in some of the small cells it may be reduced to a single granule (Golgi body). The apparatus reflects altered physiological states and pathological conditions even more sensitively than the chromophil substance. In the cell body of a neuron whose axon has been cut, the substance of the apparatus becomes dispersed toward the periphery and subsequently is fragmented and dissolved (Fig. 6–11). These phenomena have been termed "retispersion" and "retisolution" respectively (Penfield, '20). The reticulated appearance of the Golgi apparatus as observed with the light microscope is quite different from that demonstrated in electron micrographs (G in Fig. 6–8). The apparatus was first equated with the agranular endoplasmic reticulum by Fernández-Morán ('57). He noted its tendency to occur in compact dense lamellae as agranular cisterns and vesicles near the nucleus. The specific role of the Golgi apparatus is by no means known, although it is certain that the apparatus plays an important part in cell metabolism and in the initiation of synthetic activities. Histochemical studies have indicated the presence of a mucopolysaccharide and the enzyme thiamine pyrophosphatase within the Golgi apparatus. Other evidence suggests that the Golgi complex may be the source for new synaptic vesicles, which move distally from the cell body after axonal ligature (van Breemen et al., '58).

Inclusions. In addition to the organelles described above some nerve cells demonstrate dense cytoplasmic bodies and pig-

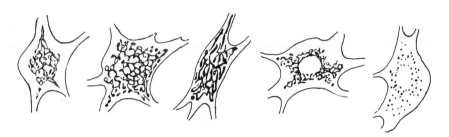

Fig. 6–10. Several forms of the Golgi apparatus in the motor neurons of the spinal cord of a 15-day-old rabbit (after Cajal, '09).

ment granules. Most of the larger adult nerve cells contain a yellowish pigment known as *lipochrome* or *lipofuscin*. It appears in the form of granules which are usually aggregated in a dense mass in some part of the cell body (Fig. 6–1*B*). Occasionally they may be dispersed throughout the cell. They are insoluble in the usual lipoid solvents, are blackened by osmic acid, and stain with Scharlach R. The cells of the newborn do not contain the pigment. It appears about the sixth year in the spinal ganglia, a few years later in the spinal cord, and after the twentieth year in the cerebral cortex. It increases in amount with advancing years, and during senescence it may occupy a large part of the cytoplasm of some neurons (Truex, '40). The lipofuscin in the autonomic ganglia was thought to be related to ceroid (Sulkin, '53, '60). Other histochemical studies indicate there are really three types or granules in the autonomic cells—namely, pigmented, non-pigmented and neurosecretory (Mytilineou et al., '63). The latter consider such material to include a lipoprotein that stores a neurotransmitter (noradrenalin) in an inactive state on the granules.

Granules of a blackish pigment known as *melanin* are found in the substantia nigra, locus ceruleus (nucleus pigmentosus), and certain pigmented cells scattered through the brain stem. It also is found in cerebrospinal and sympathetic ganglion cells (Fig 6–1*A*). Melanin appears at the end of the first year and increases in amount until puberty, after which it apparently remains constant through senescence. Incubation of brain tissue in tritiated-norepinephrine followed by radioautography, reveals a heavy binding of norepinephrine at the surface membranes of pigmented cells of the substania nigra, locus ceruleus, and the dorsal motor nucleus of the vagus nerve (Ishii and Friede, '68). They suggested such binding as due to synaptic endings and may be related to the amount of catecholamines at the surface of the pigmented neurons.

Neurosecretion. One of the characteristics of all nerve cells is that they synthesize their own proteins. Synaptic neurosecretion of acetylcholine and norepinephrine in some neurons has been known for many years. In this sense all neurons may be considered as secretory cells. However, in addition to the above examples, investigators have demonstrated the existence of certain gland-like neurons in both the invertebrate and vertebrate nervous systems (Speidel, '19; Scharrer and Scharrer, '40, '45, '65; Palay, '45). The hypothalamo-hypophyseal system of the vertebrate brain is the classical and best documented of these neuroendocrine mechanisms. These interrelationships have been thoroughly reviewed by Ortmann ('60), Bern and Knowles ('66) and Gabe ('66); see chapter 19. It will suffice to note here that neurosecretory neurons constitute a link in the chain that unites the neural and endocrine systems. They represent the final pathway for conveying neural impulses to the endocrine system.

Neurosecretory neurons are "specialized" in a sense, yet they have retained all of the light and electron microscope

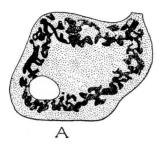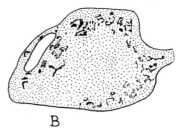

A   B

Fig. 6–11. A, Retispersion in cell of Clarke's column in spinal cord of cat 4 days after cutting its axon. B, Same as A but showing retisolution as well. (Redrawn from Penfield, '20.)

characteristics of ordinary neurons. They demonstrate all the cytoplasmic organelles discussed above including filaments, tubules and the proximo-distal transport of axoplasm. However, the neurofilaments appear to be different in nature along the axon and in its preterminal region. The neurotubes may be 300–500 Å in diameter, and the axons also may demonstrate multilamellate bodies (Bern and Knowles, '66). Some neurosecretory neurons can conduct impulses and have an action potential of long duration (Bern and Yagi, '65). However, these elongated neurons have unusually electron-dense material associated with the Golgi membranes, and a prominent endoplasmic reticulum. It is presumed that "raw" protein material is synthesized by the endoplasmic reticulum which then passes it to the Golgi apparatus where it is packaged (proteinaceous neurosecretory material or NSM). Dense-core granules pass from the perikarya distally along the axon and may be concentrated in the preterminal regions of the fibers. Large masses of secretory material (Herring bodies) are observed along the course of these axons. It is possible that some of the neurosecretory material may even be synthesized in the distal region of the axon. Axon terminals often form bulbous enlargements which serve as storage and release areas for neurosecretory granules.

Inclusions of secretory material can be visualized by several histochemical stains and viewed with the light microscope (e.g. chromhematoxylin-phloxine stain). However, the refined cytological criteria established by electron microscopy provide the most meaningful and identifying features of neurosecretory neurons. The supraoptic and paraventricular hypothalamic nuclei (Figs. 19–16 and A–22) are the best known locations of neurosecretory neurons in the human brain. These modified nerve cells may be said to participate in neurosecretion, whether its axon liberates a hormone into the blood stream, or when it directly regulates the synthesis and release of blood-borne hormones from other parts of the endocrine system. By such participation these neurons link the external and internal environments of the organism with endocrine regulation.

The Nerve Fiber (the Axon and Its Sheaths). The axon is a slender, usually long process which arises from a conical mass of specialized protoplasm known as the implantation cone or axon hillock. It is distinguished from the cell body and dendrites by the complete absence of Nissl bodies, which also are lacking in the axon hillock. Distally each axon breaks up into simple or extensive terminal arborizations, the telodendria. The latter may be synaptic endings on other neurons (e.g., sensory neurons), or effector endings in muscle and glands (Figs. 6–2G, 6–3 and 5 in Fig. 12–17).

In the central nervous system, the axons may be *myelinated* or *unmyelinated*. The former possess a sheath of myelin for at least a portion of their course. The oligodendrocyte forms and maintains the myelin sheath within the brain and spinal cord. In the unmyelinated fibers, the sheath is lacking. In the peripheral nervous system both myelinated and unmy-

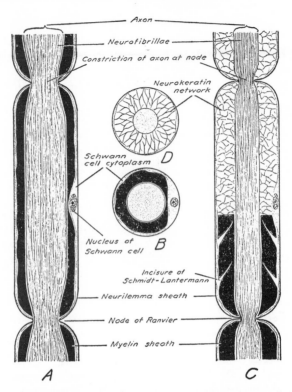

Fig. 6-12. Schematic drawings of peripheral myelinated nerve fibers. In *A* and *B*, the relative diameters of axon and myelin sheaths are based on de Renyi's studies of living nerve fibers. *C* and *D* show them as seen in many fixed preparations. The cross membrane is not shown. (Copenhaver, '64.)

elinated fibers have, in addition, an outer delicate nucleated membrane, the *sheath of Schwann.*

The *peripheral myelinated fiber* is structurally the most differentiated, consisting of axon (axis cylinder), myelin and sheath of Schwann. The myelin sheath is not continuous, but is interrupted at fairly regular intervals; the parts of the fiber free from myelin appear as constrictions known as the *nodes of Ranvier* (Figs. 6-2B and 6-12). In the fresh condition the semifluid axon is broad and homogeneous in appearance, and it occasionally shows faint longitudinal striations. In silver stained preparations, it consists of closely packed, parallel-running neurofibrils imbedded in a scanty amount of homogeneous axoplasm (Fig. 6-2A). In most fixatives the axon usually shrinks down to a thin axial thread, but with special methods of fixation and tissue embedding its normal size may be more nearly approximated.

Between the axon and myelin sheath there is a delicate layer or membrane known as the axolemma (Fig. 6-15). Although difficult to demonstrate histologically, the membrane may be seen clearly in ultraviolet photographs of the living nerve fiber, since the axolemma shows a much greater ultraviolet absorption than the axon and myelin. The axolemma is part of the neuron plasma membrane, and hence it possesses a similar structure and specialized properties. It can be identified easily in high magnification electron micrographs as a delicate membrane surrounding the axon (Figs. 6-15 and 6-16).

Myelin. The myelin sheath is acquired a short distance from the cell body. The proximal portion of the axon is as a rule unmyelinated. The sheath is of varying thickness and is composed of a semifluid, doubly refracting substance known as

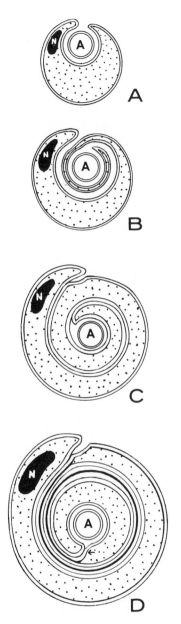

myelin, which in the fresh state has a glistening white appearance. Chemically it is composed of protein and several lipids, such as cholesterol, lecithin, and cerebrosides. According to Schmitt et al., ('41), the myelin sheath consists of thin concentric sheets of protein alternating with layers of lipids. Such a chemical appraisal correlates well with the current electron microscopy knowledge of the lamellae that constitute the definitive myelin sheath (Figs. 6–14 and 6–19). With the limited magnification of light microscopy, it was presumed that peripheral myelinated nerves were enclosed by two separate layers—the myelin and Schwann cell sheaths. The histological appearances of myelinated nerves in cross section, when stained by the osmic acid and silver nitrate methods, are shown in Figures 6–2*B* and *D*. Electron microscopy studies, however, have revealed that myelin was formed primarily by a double-layered infolding of the Schwann cell membrane, which became wrapped spirally around the axon in a few or many concentric layers (Geren, '54; Robertson, '55, '58).

Four stages in the "jelly-roll theory" of myelin formation are depicted in Figure 6–13. In the peripheral nervous system the myelin sheath represents concentric layers of the Schwann cell, while the oligodendrocyte assumes the role of myelin formation within the central nervous system (Bunge, '68). In the latter case one oligodendrocyte may form a myelin layer on more than one axon. It will be noted that the inner surfaces of the plasma membranes come into apposition and fuse to form *major dense lines* which are approximately 30Å thick. Between each major dense line is a less dense *intraperiod line* formed by the union of the outer surfaces of the plasma membranes. This fusion of membranes, accompanied by a reduction in cell cytoplasm, results in the repeating series of light and dark lines observed in electron micrographs (Figs. 6–14 and 6–19). Cytoplasmic remnants of the Schwann cell infolding may at times be identified at the axon-myelin junction (*S* in Fig. 6–19*A*). The primary infolding of the Schwann

Fig. 6–13. Diagram of stages in the development of the myelin sheath about an axon (*A*). Cytoplasm of the Schwann cell is stippled and its nucleus is indicated (*N*). As additional layers of cell cytoplasm become wrapped around the axon (*B* and *C*), the cytoplasm is reduced in amount and the double layered plasma membranes come into apposition (*D*). The outer membrane unit of the Schwann cell will become the future *intraperiod line* of myelin. The dark line (*major dense line*) represents the apposition of the inner (cytoplasmic) surface of the unit membrane as shown in *D*. The internal mesaxon is also indicated (*arrow in D*.)

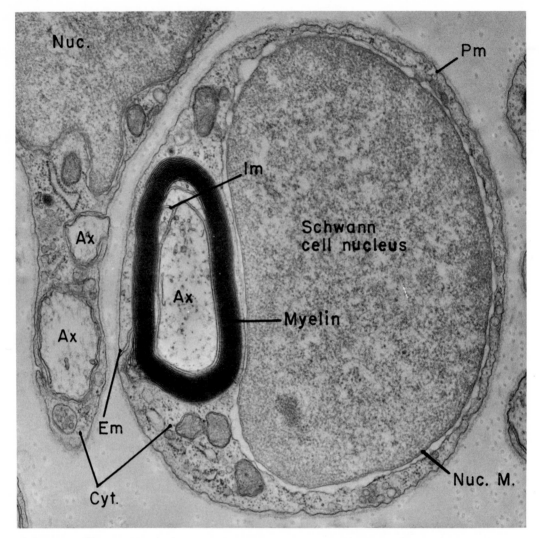

FIG. 6–14. Electron micrograph of a small myelinated nerve fiber from rat dorsal root ganglion matured in tissue culture. The infolding plasma membrane (*PM*) of the Schwann cell forms an external mesaxon (*Em*) continuous with the outermost lamella of the myelin sheath. An internal mesaxon (*Im*) surrounds the axon (*Ax*) and is continuous with the most internal lamella of the myelin sheath. Note the small amount of Schwann cell cytoplasm (*Cyt.*) between the nuclear (*Nuc. M.*) and plasma membranes. At the left are two unmyelinated axons associated with another Schwann cell. Osmium tetroxide fixation, Epon. Lead citrate stain. ×27,000. (Courtesy of Drs. M. B. Bunge and R. P. Bunge, College of Physicians and Surgeons, Columbia University.)

cell membrane often is present as an *internal mesaxon* (*Im* in Fig. 6–14). Continuity between the most superficial lamellae of the myelin sheath and the Schwann cell plasma membrane forms the *external mesaxon* (*Em* in Fig. 6–14).

These intimate relations of Schwann cell and myelin are further amplified by the tissue culture observations of Chu ('54), Peterson and Murray ('55), and Ross et al. ('62). They found that myelination began in isolated segments near the Schwann cell nucleus and extended along the fiber to a node of Ranvier. Remyelination of experimentally injured axons of the cat spinal cord appears to resemble the mechanism of myelination observed along peripheral nerves and in tissue culture (Bunge et al., '61).

Nodes of Ranvier. The myelin sheath is interrupted by constrictions at varying intervals on both central and peripheral axons. These areas can be identified in both the light and electron microscopes as regions where the myelin sheath is deficient (Figs. 6–2C and 6–16). At the nodal gap of peripheral nerves the axolemma is ensheathed by a fine basement membrane and small finger-like processes of the Schwann cell (Rhodin, '63). As shown in Figure 6–15 there are some characteristic differences between the nodes of central and peripheral axons. The internodal distance and nodal gap are both of shorter length on central axons. Such nodes also lack both interdigitating glial processes and a basement membrane. Thus nodes of Ranvier in the central nervous system have a greater extracellular space in the nodal region. The blunt spiral ends of the glial processes appear to fuse with the axolemma adjacent to a central node as shown in Figures 6–15 and 6–16. Peters ('66) believes such paranodal terminations of myelin loops provide close apposition of plasma membranes rather than complete obliteration of the extracellular space about the axon (* in Fig. 6–15). Electron microscopy has provided essential information on the fine structure of the node, and the following studies should be consulted for additional details (Uzman and Nogueira-Graf, '57; Robertson, '59; Peters, '60, '66; Metuzals, '65; and Bunge, '68). The length of the internodal segment varies considerably and is proportional to the diameter of the fiber, the thinner fibers having the shorter internodes. In the peroneal nerve of the rabbit the internodes on fibers 3 to 18 micra in diameter range from 400 to 1500 micra (Vizoso and Young, '48), and these figures probably obtain for other mammals and man. Experimental studies on regenerating fibers, which have much shorter internodes, indicate that there is no particular relation between conduction velocity and internodal length (Young, '49).

At each node of Ranvier the axon is slightly constricted and is traversed by a delicate cross membrane or "Quermembran" which delimits adjacent internodal segments of the axon (Muralt, '46). Muralt has shown that the cross membrane always is demonstrable in the living nerve fiber when viewed in polarized light under proper optical conditions and ascribes to it an important role in the process of nerve excitation. To date Muralt's cross membranes have not been identified in electron micrographs. It will be observed later in the study of physiology that nerve impulses seem to travel by *saltatory transmission*. The flow of electric current, when recorded from a nerve, seems to skip along the nerve fiber from node to node at a rapid rate. An action current generated at one node thus acts as a stimulating current to the next node. It will be recalled that mitochondria tend to accumulate in the nodal areas of axons and provide evidence of heightened metabolic activity at such sites. Collateral branches also take origin from a parent axon at the nodal gap.

Schmidt-Lantermann Clefts. The myelin sheath of each internode is divided at intervals into conical segments by oblique, funnel-shaped clefts, which extend to the axon (Fig. 6–2E). These are best seen in preparations treated with osmic acid but are also constantly visible in the living fiber, when it is viewed in polarized light. Several cone-shaped indentations may occur in a myelin segment between two nodes, while the myelin sheaths of adjacent axons may be devoid of such clefts for long distances. Although long regarded as artifacts, the clefts have recently been observed by electron microscopic studies as shearing defects in the lamellae of the myelin sheath (Robertson, '58; Rhodin, '63; Bunge et al., '67). Such clefts were shown to be areas of local separation of the spirally wrapped myelin lamellae which are nevertheless continuous across the incisure (Fig. 6–17). The light appearing regions between the lamellae consist of Schwann cell cytoplasm. In other preparations, the myelin sheath may exhibit a

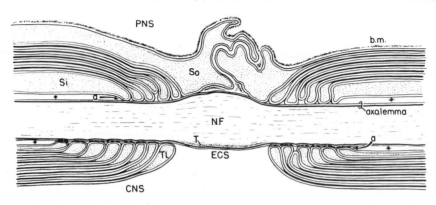

Fig. 6–15. Nodal regions from PNS (*above*) and CNS (*below*). In the PNS the Schwann cell provides both an inner collar (*Si*) and an outer collar (*So*) of cytoplasm in relation to the compact myelin. The outer collar (*So*) is extended into the nodal region as a series of loosely interdigitating processes. Terminating loops of the compact myelin come into close apposition to the axolemma in region near the node apparently providing some barrier (*arrow at a*) for movement of materials into or out of the periaxonal space (marked by *). The Schwann cell is covered externally by a basement membrane. In the CNS the myelin ends similarly in terminal loops (*tl*) near the node and there are periodic thickenings of the axolemma where the glial membrane is applied in the paranodal region. These may serve as diffusion barriers and thus confine the material in the periaxonal space (marked *) so that movement in the direction of the arrow at "a" would be restrained. At many CNS nodes there is considerable extracellular space (*ECS*). Compare with CNS node shown in Figure 6–16. (Courtesy of Dr. R. P. Bunge, '68, and the American Physiological Society.)

delicate trabecular reticulum, the *neuro-keratin network* (Fig. 6–12). The network probably represents a precipitated protein residue of the myelin sheath rather than a true cytoplasmic reticulum. The myelin sheath ends at or near the point where the terminal arborizations, which are always unmyelinated, are given off.

Sheath of Schwann. This sheath of flattened cells forms the myelin of larger fibers. It also provides a thin attenuated cytoplasmic investment on non-myelinated fibers of the cranial and spinal nerves (Figs. 6–18, and 6–19). Schwann cells, like the neurons, are of ectodermal origin (neural crest and neural tube). Each Schwann cell has a flat, oval nucleus surrounded by a thin rim of cytoplasm which contains a Golgi complex and mitochondria (Fig. 6–14). The Schwann cells of both myelinated and non-myelinated nerve fibers are surrounded by a typical basement membrane approximately 250Å in thickness (bm in Fig. 6–15). This is separated from the plasma membrane of the Schwann cell by an interval of 250Å. Ultrastructural studies indicate that the Schwann cell plasma

membrane, with its surrounding basement membrane represents the older term *"neurolemma sheath"* observed in light microscopy (Causey, '60; Thomas, '63). Nathaniel and Pease ('63b) regard only the granular basement membrane surrounding the Schwann cell as equivalent to the neurolemma.

One Schwann cell may have extensive cytoplasmic processes as it presides over, and maintains the integrity of, the segment of myelin between two nodes of Ranvier. If an ultrathin section were cut through a small myelinated nerve fiber to include the nucleus of a Schwann cell, it would reveal ultrastructural relations similar to those shown in Figure 6–14. A longitudinally cut nerve fiber with a thicker myelin sheath is shown in Figure 6–19A. Electron micrographs of adult unmyelinated nerves show one, two, three, or many axons lying within recesses of one Schwann cell (Figs. 6–14 and 6–19B). The plasma membrane of the Schwann cell is closely applied to the axon except for a small periaxonal space of 150–200Å (Bunge, '68). However, at some point around the circumference of each unmye-

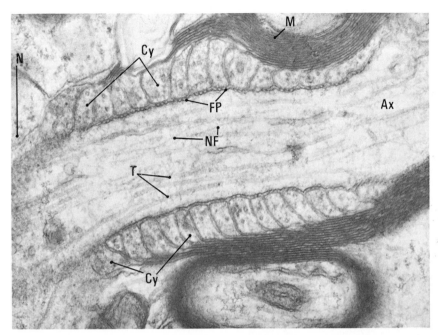

FIG. 6-16. Electron micrograph of node of Ranvier on nerve fiber of spinal cord (cat). The oligoglial cytoplasm (*CY*) forms loops of myelin (*M*) around the axon (*Ax*) at the node (*N*). Fusion points (*FP*) between the myelin and axon membranes are shown also. Neurotubules (*T*) and neurofilaments (*NF*) are identified in the axoplasm. Osmium fixation. ×70,000 (Courtesy of H. J. Ralston, III, Stanford University).

linated axon, the plasma membrane is reflected and extends superficially to form the mesaxon (Fig. 6–19*B*).

Endoneurium. In addition to the above described structures, each peripheral nerve fiber is surrounded by a re-enforcing sheath of delicate connective tissue, the *endoneurium* (*sheath of Henle,* or *of Key and Retzius*). It is composed of delicate collagenous fibers disposed longitudinally for the most part, a homogeneous ground substance, and an occasional flattened fibroblast. A close contact between the endoneurial collagen and the basement membrane of Schwann cells is an inevitable consequence of the ensheathing of nerve fibers in collagen. Actual "collagen pockets" surrounded by Schwann cells have been observed along non-myelinated axons. Thin bundles of collagen usually can be observed within the typical basement membrane surrounding a Schwann cell (Gamble, '64). The endoneurium is continuous with the more abundant connective tissue of the perineurium, which envelops both small and large bundles of fibers within a peripheral nerve trunk (Fig. 6–2*B* and 6–20).

Perineurium. The outermost layers of the perineurium are composed of dense concentric layers of mostly longitudinally arranged strands of collagen. A few fibroblasts and macrophages also are present among the strands. Denney-Brown ('46) noted that the perineural tissue was somewhat peculiar; it consisted of fibroblasts and smooth lamellae that resembled mesothelium. The deeper concentric layers of flattened cells have prominent basement membranes often with closed contacts. The flattened cells also have a slightly granular cytoplasm with scattered mitochondria and rough-walled vesicles. The origin and significance of the perineural cells have attracted the interest of several investigators (Shanthaveerappa and Bourne, '62, '66; Gamble and Eames, '64). The former au-

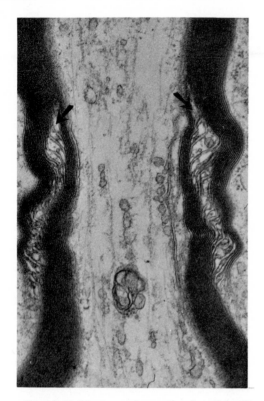

Fig. 6-17. Electron micrograph of a Schmidt-Lantermann cleft (*arrows*). Clear areas consist of Schwann cell cytoplasm. (Courtesy Dr. R. P. Bunge, '67, and Rockefeller University Press.)

thors believe such "perineural epithelium" is derived from the pia-arachnoid and ensheaths all peripheral nerves. They believe it accompanies each fiber to its termination and forms the capsule of its end organ (Figs. 6–20 and 9–11). Their derivation of cells is in keeping with the knowledge that spinal nerves of the human cauda equina demonstrate a pial sleeve or ensheathment and endoneurium (Fig. 6–2G, F). There is evidence which suggests that the squamous cells of the perineural epithelium function as a metabolic and diffusion barrier in the peripheral nerve. It also may play an important role in the degeneration and regeneration of injured peripheral nerves. Waksman ('61) used a variety of large molecular dyes, silver nitrate, toxin, and I[131] labelled proteins to study the blood-nerve barrier in several animals. The peripheral nerve of the rabbit had an effective nerve-barrier which he interpreted as due to the vascular endothelium rather than the mesothelial cells that accompanied the endoneurial connective tissue.

Epineurium. This dense, collagenous layer forms an external connective tissue ensheathment for all peripheral nerve trunks. It is continuous centrally with the dura mater of cranial and spinal nerves. Its fibrous nature further re-inforces the toughness of peripheral nerve trunks. Again the collagen strands are mainly disposed longitudinally, and the component fibers have diameters between 700 and 850 Å. A few elastic fibers and fibroblasts with elongated processes are scattered throughout the epineurium. Axial arteries to peripheral nerves are derived from the large arteries adjacent to nerve trunks. Arteries that provide nourishment to a peripheral nerve, penetrate the epineurium and give off several branches. The smaller arterioles then pursue proximal or distal courses within the perineurium of the nerve trunk. Most of the capillaries supplying the peripheral nerve fibers are located in the endoneurium.

Unmyelinated   Peripheral   Nerve Fibers (Fibers of Remak). These slender axons are enveloped by the thin Schwann cell sheath, its basement membrane, and fine strands of collagen (Figs. 6–18 and 6–19B). The critical point for fiber myelination of an axon in tissue culture is reported to be a diameter of 1 micron (Bunge et al, '67). Axons of thicker diameters are always invested with a myelin sheath. The peripheral axons of most postganglionic sympathetic neurons and many cells of the cerebrospinal ganglia are unmyelinated (Elfvin, '58). Numerous unmyelinated fibers also are found in the gray and white matter of the spinal cord and brain. Here they appear as fine naked axons embedded in glial cell processes with relationships similar to that of the Schwann cells on the peripheral unmyelinated fibers (Luse, '55a and '56a; Bunge et al., '61).

Fiber   Size. Myelinated fibers vary

Fig. 6–18. Three unmyelinated fibers (fibers of Remak) with Schwann cell nuclei (after Cajal, '11).

greatly in size. The fine fibers have a diameter from 1 to 4 micra; those of medium size 5 to 10 micra; and the largest, from 11 to 20 micra. (Fig. 6–2).

Collaterals or branches are given off by most fibers of the central nervous system. They are usually of finer caliber than the parent stem, extend at right angles, and often arise from the proximal unmyelinated part of the axon. In the myelinated portion they are given off at the nodes of Ranvier and become myelinated themselves. In the peripheral nervous system, the fibers of somatic motor neurons, which supply skeletal muscle, branch repeatedly at acute angles before reaching the muscle (Fig. 6–2G). Within the latter the branching may be very extensive, so that a single nerve fiber may furnish motor terminals to many muscle fibers. Many sensory fibers probably branch in a similar manner since their terminal arborizations extend over a considerable area. According to Weddell ('41), a single myelinated fiber may supply sensory endings to more than 300 hair follicle groups. The term "sensory unit" has been suggested for the sensory fiber, including all its terminals.

Myelinated fibers conduct more rapidly than unmyelinated ones. The speed is proportional to the diameter of the fiber and, more especially, to the thickness of the myelin sheath. The myelin sheath may be regarded as insulation, while the extracellular space at the nodes of Ranvier and the periaxonal space provide ready avenues for ionic diffusion. Such a morphologic substrate is required for the rapid reversibility of the excitation processes in order to account for the rapid conduction and relative indefatigability of the myelinated fiber.

Physical and Physiological Grouping of Nerve Fibers. When a wave of excitation, the *nerve impulse*, passes along a nerve fiber, it invariably is accompanied by an electrical change known as the *action potential*, which can be recorded by an appropriate instrument such as the cathode ray oscillograph. The electrical record of an impulse consists of a strong negative deviation of short duration, the *spike potential*, usually followed by two longer but much weaker deviations known as the *negative* and *positive afterpotentials*. Since the traveling electric change and the impulse are inseparable from each other, a study of the electrical phenomena during excitation furnishes the most delicate and accurate information regarding the speed and frequency of the nerve impulse. Thus the speed with which the spike potential travels over the nerve fiber constitutes the conduction velocity of the nerve impulse, and the number of successive potentials traversing the fiber is regarded as representing the frequency of the impulses.

Erlanger and Gasser ('37) have shown that the different fibers in a nerve trunk conduct at greatly varying velocities. The speed of conduction is proportional to the diameter of the fiber and of the myelin sheath. Also each nerve has a characteristic pattern of velocities corresponding to an analogous pattern of fiber diameters in the nerve trunk. As a result of extensive physiological investigations supported by histological studies, nerve fibers have been grouped into four main classes, the A, B, C, and gamma fibers, whose potentials are known as the A, B, C, and gamma waves. Both A and B groups include several subdivisions. Criteria for the classification are fiber diameter, conduction velocity, and nature of the electrical record (Bishop et al., '32; Heinbecker et al., '36; Gasser and Grundfest, '39;

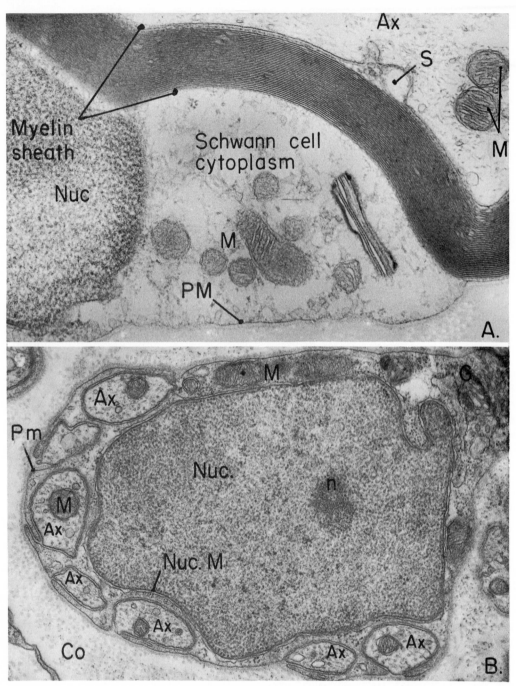

FIG. 6–19. *A*, Electron micrograph showing part of a myelinated nerve fiber in cross section. The Schwann cell cytoplasm and axoplasm (*Ax*) both contain mitochondria (*M*). Note the alternation of dense lamellae with less dense intermediate layers in the myelin sheath. This sheath is composed of thinned out Schwann cell cytoplasm wrapped concentrically around the axon (*Ax*). The innermost layer of the myelin sheath displays a local swelling (*S*). The plasma membrane (*PM*) of the Schwann cell envelops the entire structural complex. Mouse sciatic nerve. ×39,000. *B*, Electron micrograph showing the relationship of several unmyelinated axons (*Ax*) to the plasma membrane (*Pm*) of a Schwann cell. The nuclear membrane (*Nuc. M*), nucleus (*Nuc.*) and nucleolus (*n*) are identified. Mitochondria (*M*) and the Golgi complex (*G*) can be seen within the cytoplasm, while fine collagen fibrils (*Co*) surround the Schwann cell. Mouse sciatic nerve. Phosphate-buffered osmium tetroxide, Epon. Lead tartrate. ×26,000. (Preparations by Dr. J. Rhoden, New York College of Medicine.)

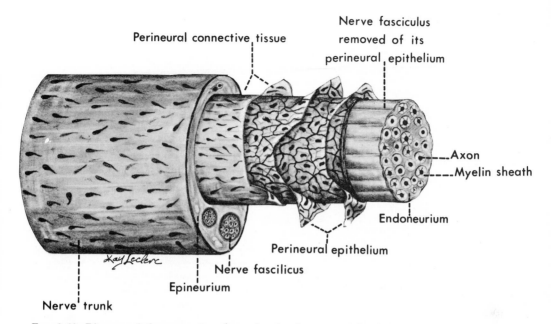

Perineural connective tissue

Nerve fasciculus removed of its perineural epithelium

Axon
Myelin sheath

Endoneurium

Perineural epithelium

Nerve fascilicus

Epineurium

Nerve trunk

Fig. 6-20. Diagram of the connective tissue sheaths about a peripheral nerve. Squamous cells of the perineural epithelium may function as a metabolic and blood-nerve diffusion barrier in the peripheral nerve (Courtesy of Drs. Shanthaveerappa and Bourne, Emory University).

Grundfest, '39, '40; Lloyd, '43; Quensel, '44; Patton, '61).

The A fibers are myelinated, range in diameter from 1 to 20 micra, and conduct at rates of 5 to 120 meters per second, the rate being proportional to the thickness of the fiber. The more finely myelinated B fibers have a diameter up to 3 micra and a conduction rate of about 3 to 15 meters per second, though a higher velocity has been observed in some fibers of this group. The C fibers are unmyelinated and conduct very slowly, about 0.6 to 2 meters per second. It is obvious that there is a certain amount of overlapping, so that a fiber of 2 micra could belong to either A or B, but certain features of the electrical record permit a definite classification. Thus the duration of the spike potential is always much longer in B fibers than in any A fiber, and moreover the B fibers lack a negative afterpotential.

Studies on various types of nerves (muscular, cutaneous, and autonomic) have indicated a general functional grouping of the three fiber types. This grouping must not be regarded too rigidly, since many fibers serving the same function may have widely different calibers. The A fibers include several subdivision. The largest and most rapidly conducting fibers (conduction velocity, 60 to 120 meters per second in man) transmit motor impulses to skeletal muscles while other A fibers carry afferent stretch impulses from these muscles to the central nervous system. The rest of the A fibers, varying considerably in diameter and speed of conduction, carry afferent impulses from cutaneous receptors. The fibers of intermediate size are related to touch and pressure. The finest fibers are believed to transmit impulses of localized pain, and perhaps some of these fibers conduct thermal and tactile impulses.

The B fibers are mainly associated with visceral innervation and are both efferent and afferent. All the preganglionic autonomic fibers belong to this group, and also the postganglionic fibers from the ciliary ganglion, which are partly or wholly myelinated. The more rapidly conducting B fibers transmit afferent impulses from the viscera. The unmyelinated C fibers comprise the efferent postganglionic autonomic fibers and afferent fibers which are

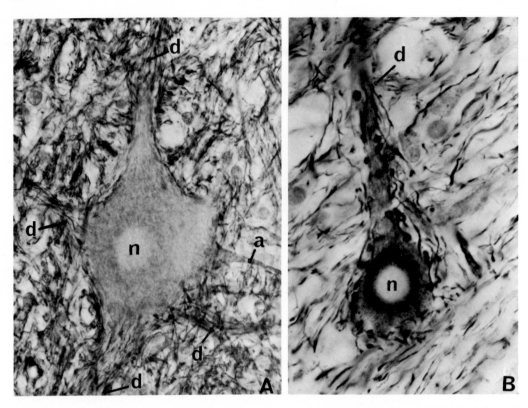

FIG. 6–21. Synaptic endings on human CNS neurons after silver impregnation and observed by light microscopy. Note numerous terminal boutons on the dendrites (*d*, axodendritic synapses) and some of the cell body (axosomatic synapses). The axon (*a*) and nucleus (*n*) are identified in *A* which is a photograph of 650 magnification. The smaller neuron shown in *B* is at a magnification of 920.

believed to conduct impulses of poorly localized pain from the viscera and the periphery.

The Synapse. The simplest segmental reflex requires a chain of at least two neurons (Fig. 13–1). A wave of excitation, the nerve impulse, is set up in a peripheral sensory nerve ending, and it passes along the axon of a ganglion cell into the spinal cord. There it activates a motor neuron, whose impulse travels along the motor fiber and causes a group of muscle fibers to contract (Fig. 12–17). Even such simple reactions have, as a rule, a third or *central* neuron interposed between the afferent and efferent cells (Fig. 13–1). In the more complicated neural circuits the number of such intercalated central neurons may be multiplied tremendously. All neural pathways therefore consist of chains of neurons so related to each other as to make possible the physiological continuity of nerve impulse conduction over the complete circuit. The point of junction of neurons, i.e., where the axonal end arborizations of one neuron come in contact with the cell body or dendrites of another, is known as the *synapse*. Axon terminals upon the dendrite of another neuron are called *axodendritic synapses*, whereas axon terminals upon the cell soma or perikaryon are *axosomatic synapses*. Less frequently axon terminals of one neuron may be located directly on other axonic terminals or on the initial segment of the axon of another neuron (*axoaxonic synapses*).

Synaptic junctions show many structural variations (Fig. 6–21). Most commonly, the axon terminals end in small bulblike expansions or *neuropodia* (*end feet, boutons terminaux*). Each neuropo-

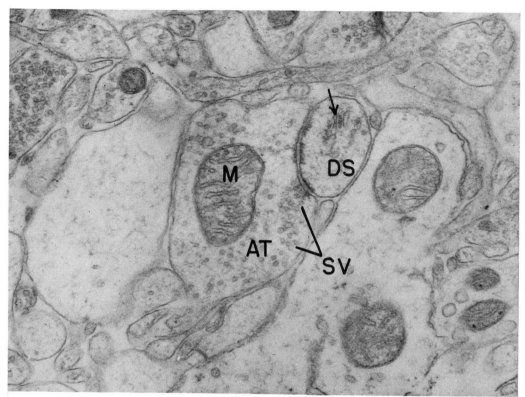

Fig. 6–22. Electron micrograph of an axodendritic synapse in the human cerebral cortex. The saclike enlargement comprising the axon terminal (*AT*) contains a mitochondrion (*M*) and numerous synaptic vesicles (*SV*). The axon terminal is indented by the dendritic spine (*DS*). Profiles of the spine apparatus (*arrow*) are seen *above*, while *to the left* the postsynaptic membrane of the dendritic spine is thickened in three places. Compare with synapse shown in Figure 6–21. Buffered osmium fixation, Epon. ×38,500. (Courtesy of Dr. J. Francis Hartmann, Presbyterian-St. Luke's Hospital, Chicago.)

dium consists of a neurofibrillar loop imbedded in perifibrillar substance; sometimes there are simply small neurofibrillar rings. A large motor cell in the spinal cord may receive several thousand such endings, most of them 1 to 2 micra in diameter. In another type of synapse, the delicate axon terminals do not form end feet but come in lengthwise apposition with the dendrites or cell body, often for considerable distances. The most striking examples are the climbing fibers of the cerebellum. In some cases, unmyelinated axons run at right angles to the dendrites and apparently come in contact with the spiny excrescences or *gemmules* with which the dendrites are beset (Fig. 6–5). It is obvious that one axon may carry impulses to a number of neurons. Conversely a single anterior horn cell may receive impulses from the axons of a great many neurons (i.e., it may receive convergent inputs from several widely separated sources such as different receptors via dorsal root fiber collaterals, or axon terminals from several descending fiber pathways).

Intensive and numerous electron microscopy studies since 1953 have shown that synapses of the vertebrate nervous system possess the following three basic similarities: (1) discontinuity between the cytoplasm of the two apposed membranes of a synapse; (2) direct contact of the presynaptic (plasma membrane of an axon terminal) and subsynaptic membranes, which are separated by only a minute synaptic cleft that is usually 100

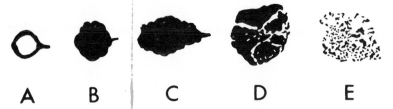

FIG. 6–23. Diagrams showing several stages in the degeneration of end feet in the spinal cord of a cat, following section of a dorsal root. A, Normal end foot. B, C, D, and E, End foot after section of root: B, 2 days; C, 4 days; D and E, 5 days. (After Gibson, '37.)

to 200 Ångströms in width (Fig. 6–22); and (3) the presence, usually, of mitochondria, a tail of neurofilaments, and numerous synaptic vesicles in the axon terminal on the presynaptic side of the synapse (Palay, '56; de Robertis, '59, '60; Gray and Guillery, '61; McLennan, '63). There is strong electron microscopic and chemical evidence that the synaptic vesicles participate in the elaboration of neurotransmitter substances (e.g., epinephrine and acetylcholine) which are released at the synapse and neuromuscular endings (de Robertis and Bennett, '54; de Robertis et al., '62; Thaemert, '63; de Iraldi et al., '63). More detail on the neurotransmitter substances which are released at synaptic junctions is presented in Chapter 11, page 225. One or both of the pre- and sub-synaptic membranes may show small surface areas of increased density, and a "spine apparatus" often can be identified within the dendritic spine (arrow in Fig. 6–22).

Many physiological peculiarities are associated with the synapse. While an activated nerve fiber conducts equally well in either direction (orthodromic and antidromic conduction), impulses are transmitted over the reflex arc, i.e., across the synapse, in one direction only. Thus the impulse travels from the axon of one neuron to the cell body, the dendrites, or more rarely the axon of another, a phenomenon known as dynamic polarization. Hence synapses ensure that nerve fibers normally are used for one-way signal transmission. Some of the other ways in which conduction across the synapse differs from that in a nerve fiber may be briefly mentioned. Over a reflex arc (1) conduction is

slower; (2) the response may persist after cessation of the stimulus (after-discharge); (3) the rhythm of stimulus and the rhythm of response correspond less closely; (4) repetition of a given stimulus may produce a response where a single stimulus will not (summation); (5) greater variability in the threshold value of a stimulus, i.e., the ease with which responses can be elicited; (6) much greater fatigability; (7) greater dependence on oxygen supply and greater susceptibility to anesthetics and drugs; (8) greater refractory period; and (9) re-enforcement or inhibition of one reflex by another.

One of the areas in which electron microscopy has contributed significantly is in defining the ultrastructure of synaptic regions. Biochemical and physiologic data also have converged at the molecular level to elucidate the function of synaptic complexes. Synaptic vesicles contain storage units of transmitter substances such as acetylcholine, norepinephrine and dopamine as well as key metabolic enzymes. Synapses control normal impulse traffic, the amount and pattern of information input, and consequently the behavior of a neuron or groups of neurons. Synapses are the units that provide mutual neuronal interdependence. Although each neuron in its entirety constitutes a "private line" there is no privacy in the central nervous system (Gelfan, '64). For additional details on the synaptic complex the reader is referred to the articles by Eccles ('59), Pappas ('66), DeRobertis ('66), Nathaniel and Nathaniel ('66), Katz ('66), and Guillery ('67).

Degeneration of Nerve Fibers. The cell body is the trophic center of the neu-

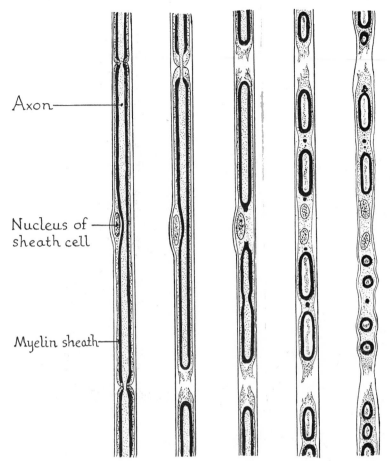

Axon

Nucleus of
sheath cell

Myelin sheath

FIG. 6–24. Diagram showing breakup of myelin and axon during nerve degeneration. Note increase in sheath cell protoplasm and division of the nucleus. (Young, '42.)

ron, and any process detached from it disintegrates. Crushing injuries or interruption of an axon produces detectable changes in the cell body (chromatolysis), as well as in the central and distal stumps of the injured fiber. When an axon is divided, degenerative changes of a traumatic character first affect the cut edges. In the proximal portion of the fiber, which is attached to the cell body, the degenerative changes (retrograde degeneration) extend only a short, though variable distance, depending on the nature of the injury. In a clean cut only one or two internodes may be involved. In more severe injuries, such as gunshot wounds or inflammatory processes, the retrograde degeneration may extend as much as 2 or 3 cm. However, the degeneration is soon succeeded by

reparative processes leading to the formation of new axonal sprouts from the central stump.

In the distal portion, the axon and myelin sheath completely disintegrate, and degeneration occurs throughout the whole length of the fiber, including its terminal arborization. This process is known as *secondary* or *Wallerian degeneration*. The changes as a rule appear simultaneously along the whole length of the nerve fiber distal to the point of injury. Functional failure of the nerve also is abrupt down the length of the distal nerve trunk (Salafsky and Jasinski, '67; Novak and Salafsky, '67). In these studies muscle responses to distal nerve stimulation ceased abruptly 54 to 72 hours after sciatic nerve section, depending on whether

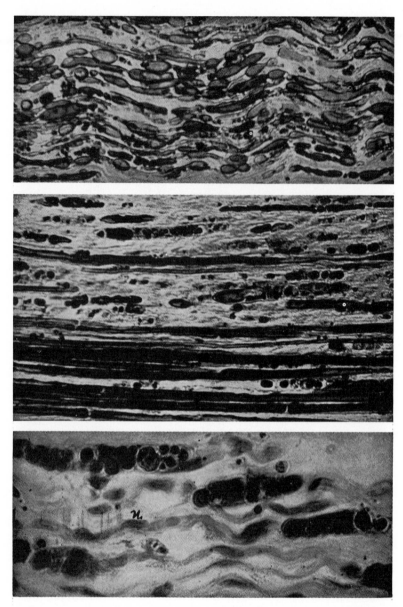

F<small>IG.</small> 6–25. *A*, Distal stump of a nerve cut 3 to 5 days previously. Osmic acid. *B*, Distal stump of a nerve partly cut 12 to 15 days previously. Osmic acid. Normal fibers and two nodes of Ranvier are shown at the *bottom*. *C*, Distal stump of a nerve cut 12 to 15 days previously. Osmic acid and iron hematoxylin. In addition to the clumps or islands of degenerating myelin, several band fibers and their nuclei (*n*) are shown. Photographs.

nerve injury occurred in the thigh or at the level of the knee.

Axonal changes begin almost at once. Electron micrographs of the sciatic nerve following crush injury demonstrate that the initial change is an accumulation of mitochondria in the axoplasm at the nodes of Ranvier. It is followed by a breakdown of the axoplasm and mitochondria (Webster, '62). Twelve hours after injury the axon is swollen and irregular in shape. Within a few days it begins to break up into fragments. However, the breaking up process may con-

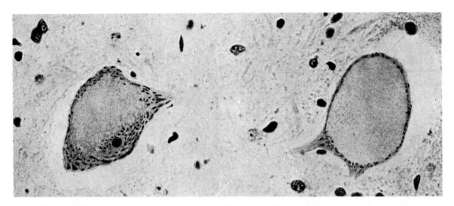

FIG. 6–26. Two motor cells from adult lumbar cord showing "central chromatolysis," nuclear eccentricity, and swelling of cell body. Photograph. The lumbosacral nerve roots had some time previously been crushed in an accident.

tinue for a considerable time in some fibers, and fragments of degenerating axons have been found as late as 3 or 4 weeks after the injury. The synaptic terminals are affected similarly. The neurofibrils lose their staining capacity and assume an irregular shape; by the end of the fifth day many of the fibrils have become broken up to form granules (Fig. 6–23). The myelin sheath likewise degenerates. Two or 3 days after section, constrictions appear which break the myelin into elongated ellipsoid segments, which in turn fragment into smaller ovoid or spherical droplets or granules (Figs. 6–24 and 6–25). The whole process resembles the breakup of a liquid column under surface tension and is ascribed to the fact that the fiber is no longer kept in a turgid condition by neuroplasm pressure emanating from the cell body (Young, '49). This view is supported by the work of Weiss and Hiscoe ('48), who have shown that under normal conditions there is a constant proximo-distal flow of axoplasm from the nucleated portion of the cell. The presumed flow of axoplasm has been substantiated following experimental ligature by the electron microscope studies of van Breemen et al. ('58). The autoradiographic studies of Droz and Leblond ('62) and Francoeur and Olszewski ('68) also indicated that protein synthesized in the nerve cell bodies of the sciatic nerve had migrated distally along the axons.

The myelin changes, at first purely physical, soon are followed by chemical changes as well, the myelin breaking down into simpler intermediate substances, which react to the Marchi stain, and ultimately into neutral fat.

Ultrastructural study again has provided new and essential information. Nineteen hours after peripheral nerve injury there is a loosening of the myelin lamellae (Lee, '63). Myelin disintegration is evident at four days in Schwann cells and well advanced 96 hours after crushing dorsal roots of the cauda equina (Nathaniel and Pease, '63). These authors have elucidated the key roles of the Schwann cell and its basement membrane in both degeneration and regeneration. Schwann cells undergo hypertrophy, demonstrate unusual numbers of ribosomes, multiply in number, become mobile, and form elaborate basement membranes. These cells are almost exclusively responsible for the removal of axon remnants and autodigestion of disintegrated myelin. Their study showed no connective tissue response in the endoneurium, and no leucocytes appeared to participate in the phagocytosis of neuronal debris. The only endoneurial response was a slow accumulation and slight increase in the amount of collagen adjacent to the basement membranes. Newly formed and hypertrophied Schwann cells have extensive tapering and overlapping cytoplasmic processes, which in light microscopy formerly were interpreted as

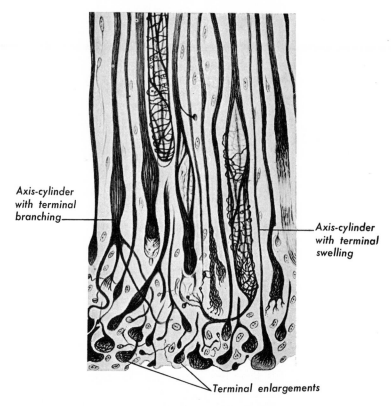

Axis-cylinder
with terminal
branching

Axis-cylinder
with terminal
swelling

Terminal enlargements

FIG. 6–27. Regenerating axons in the central stump of a cat's sciatic nerve 2½ days after section of the nerve (after Cajal, '09).

multinucleated syncytial cords (band fibers).

Nuclear division of the Schwann cells begins around the fourth day and continues actively to about the twenty-fifth, mitosis occurring over the whole length of the fiber. The increase in the number of nuclei is considerable, in some instances as much as 13 times the original population (Abercrombie and Johnson, '47).

Nathaniel and Pease ('63) have demonstrated that during degeneration the Schwann cell plasma and basement membranes become separated from each other to markedly increase the extent and complexity of the extracellular spaces. The reactive Schwann cells also form new elaborately folded and successive basement membranes one inside the other. These Schwann cells and basement membranes thus form numerous extracellular compartments or tubes surrounded by collagen of the endoneurium. Regenerating

axon sprouts from regions above the injury will later enter these extracellular compartments or "tubes" between the basement membrane and Schwann cell. In later stages, especially if no axonal sprouts enter, the tube shrinks considerably and the walls thicken, owing primarily to the increase in the collagen content of the endoneurium. More severe shrinkage of tubes has been reported by Sunderland and Bradley ('50) in the degenerating stumps of the median and ulnar nerves of the opossum. Three months after severance all the fibers were less than 3 or 4 micra in diameter, and after 16 months there were no tubes over 2 micra in caliber.

Retrograde Degeneration. The neuron body whose axon is injured likewise shows marked degenerative changes (Figs. 6–1E and 6–26). The cell body swells and becomes turgescent, the nucleus is displaced toward the periphery, and the

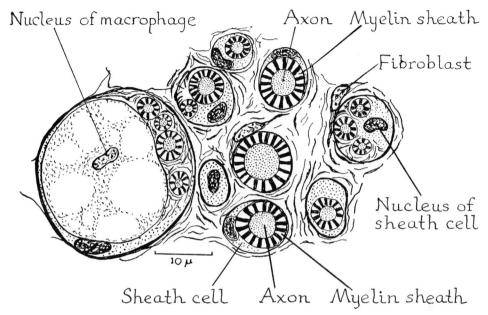

Nucleus of macrophage	Axon	Myelin sheath

Fibroblast

Nucleus of sheath cell

10 μ

Sheath cell	Axon	Myelin sheath

FIG. 6–28. Transverse section of peripheral stump of rabbit nerve which had been severed 150 days previously. The stumps were left unsutured, but a union was established by outgrowth. Most of the tubes contain one or several myelinated fibers surrounded by protoplasm of sheath cell. (After Young, '49.)

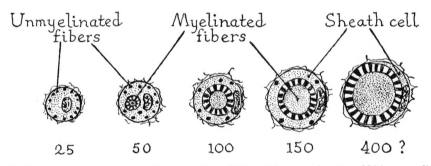

Unmyelinated fibers	Myelinated fibers	Sheath cell

25	50	100	150	400 ?

FIG. 6–29. Diagram showing progress of regeneration within a Schwann tube of a rabbit's nerve distal to a good suture, with approximate number of days for the various stages. At 25 days, there are many fibers at edge of tube; at 50 days, one or two have enlarged and are surrounded by Schwann protoplasm; at 100 days, one myelinated fiber is in center of tube; others are still at periphery. The time of final disappearance of excess fibers and attainment of normal diameter is uncertain. (Young, '49.)

Nissl bodies undergo dissolution. Nissl body breakdown begins in the center of the cell and spreads outward (central chromatolysis). With light microscopy the fixed Nissl material appears to undergo lysis, although the cisternae and ribosomes are only dispersed and less concentrated when the chromatin material is observed with the electron microscope. Ultrastructural changes also have been observed in many of the other neuronal organelles (e.g., mitochondria, endoplasmic reticulum, Golgi apparatus, ribosomes, and lysosomes) following nerve section or X-irradiation of ganglion cells in tissue culture (Masurovsky et al., '67; Holtzman et al., '67; Kirkpatrick, '68). Histochemical changes occur in a number of oxidative and hydrolytic enzymes within chromatolytic and regenerating neurons (Nandy, '68). Such changes reflect a reduction or an increase in glucose metabolism, a breakdown of Golgi bodies, or increased RNA and nucleoprotein synthesis.

The extent and rapidity of these changes depend on the type of neuron involved, on the nature of the lesion, and especially on the location of the injury. A lesion near the cell body produces a greater central effect than one more distantly placed. In other words, the effect depends upon the percentage of the neuron destroyed. If the lesion is very near the cell body, the latter may ultimately die and the proximal portion of the nerve fiber attached to it also degenerates. Chromatolysis in the cell body reaches its maximum 12 to 14 days following injury to the axon. This retrograde alteration of Nissl material (axon reaction) has been employed extensively in neuroanatomical research to locate the cells of origin following injury of axons in central tracts or a peripheral nerve (Figs. 6–1E and 6–26).

Regeneration. If the neuron survives injury, *regeneration* takes place. Recovery in the cell body begins about the third week and is characterized by the appearance of Nissl bodies around the nuclear membrane. The turgescence gradually subsides, the nucleus returns to its central position, and the Nissl bodies are restored to their normal amount and distribution. Full recovery may take from 3 to 6 months, the time depending on the mass of axon to be reconstituted. While this is going on, regenerative processes appear in the axons of the central stump. As early as the tenth hour the axonal terminals begin to swell, owing to pressure emanating from the cell body. Each axon splits into numerous fine strands or fibers (Fig. 6–27) which traverse the scar formed at the site of the injury and reach the Schwann tubes of the degenerating stump. Many of these fibers enter a single tube where they are disposed peripherally (Fig. 6–28). Later some of them move to a more central position and become completely surrounded by the plasma membrane of the sheath cells (Figs. 6–28 and 6–29). Along or within the bands, the regenerating axons grow dis-

tally for long distances to their peripheral destinations. Nathaniel and Pease ('63a) have found by use of the electron microscope that regenerating axonal sprouts reach the extracellular spaces of the membrane envelope as early as four days after a lesion. Although many sprouts initially may occupy the spaces and gutters of the Schwann tube, only one persists and becomes remyelinated. This is usually the largest one, and the smaller axonal sprouts seem to be suppressed. The elimination of excess fibers may take considerable time, and some of them still may be seen in tubes 3 or 4 months after section. Of importance is the fact that the enlargement of one fiber and the elimination of the others occur only if the regenerating axons make sensory or motor contact with appropriate receptor or effector endings in the periphery.

The thin regenerating axons, at first about 0.5 to 3 micra in diameter, gradually enlarge; the increase in diameter advances progressively down the tube, as if propelled by some centrifugal force from the central stump. When the fiber reaches the periphery, growth in length ceases, but the increase in diameter continues until the original thickness is approximated. Myelination may occur as early as the second or third week in some fibers. It likewise advances in a proximo-distal direction, and the process becomes somewhat slower in the more distal regions of the fiber. The myelin is at first laid down as a thin continuous sheath which subsequently becomes broken up into short internodal segments, about 150 to 700 micra in length. In fully regenerated nerve fibers, therefore, the internodes are shorter and more numerous, and there is no longer any definite relation between internodal length and diameter because fibers of varying thickness may possess similar internodal lengths. It should be noted that the time course of the events in degeneration and regeneration overlap each other. As noted above, regeneration of new axon sprouts occurs before axon and myelin disintegration are completed in the distal segment of injured nerves. In

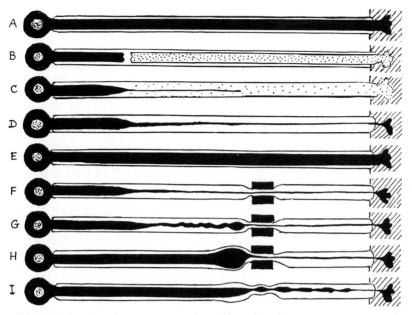

FIG. 6–30. Diagram of stages of nerve regeneration with and without constriction. *A*, Normal fiber; *B* through *E*, ordinary regeneration after simple crushing; *F* through *H*, regeneration after constriction; *I*, after release of constriction. (Weiss and Hiscoe, '48.)

similar fashion regenerating axon sprouts may traverse Schwann tubes which still contain degeneration debris, and regenerated axon sprouts may be in evidence several days before chromatolysis is complete. In fact, Nathaniel and Pease ('63*a*) have observed early remyelination of an axon by a Schwann cell that still had myelin debris.

The growth processes observed during regeneration are truly remarkable. A slender axonal filament ultimately is transformed into a mature fiber whose volume in some instances may be several hundred times the volume of the original filament (Fig. 6–30, *B* through *E*). The manner in which this new axoplasm is formed has been investigated by Weiss and Hiscoe ('48) in a series of ingenious experiments. They fashioned small arterial rings which, when distended, could be slipped over the end of a cut nerve and placed in the desired position. The subsequent contraction of these rings produced localized constrictions with consequent reduction in the diameter of the individual fiber tubes (Fig. 6–30, *F* through *H*). The reduction in the lumen of the tube

does not at first interfere with the advance of the slender regenerating axon, which passes through the constricted zone and makes contact with the periphery. "But when the fiber, as it continues to enlarge, attains the dimensions of the constricted zone, a remarkable difference appears between those parts lying at the distal and at the proximal sides of the narrow neck. The distal segment ceases to grow and remains permanently undersized, while the proximal segment not only continues to enlarge, but near the entrance of the constricted zone, enlarges excessively.... One gets the impression that a column of axoplasm is pressing distad and becomes dammed up where its channel narrows" (Fig. 6–30*H*). The damming increases in intensity with time, and varies with the amount of constriction and the size of the fiber. Morphologically it is expressed in several ways, such as ballooning, beading, telescoping, and coiling of the fibers. On release of the constriction, some of the dammed axoplasm flows into the distal portion, which consequently increases in thickness (Fig. 6–30*I*). The authors conclude that the formation of new axoplasm, i.e., growth in volume, occurs only in the cell body and that this axoplasm is maintained in constant proximo-distal motion that causes the elongation and enlargement of the regenerating fiber.

A knowledge of the mode of nerve regeneration is important as a basis for intelligent surgical treatment. Thus in human trauma it is desirable to approximate the severed ends of the nerve or, if some time has elapsed since the injury, to remove the scar tissue. This forms an obstacle to the passage of the growing axons into the band fibers and thence to their destination. Further details concerning the regenerative processes following injury of peripheral nerves are given on page 213.

Fiber degeneration in the CNS is similar to that observed in the peripheral nerves. However, the degeneration proceeds at a slower pace, and the removal of neural debris by glial cells takes a longer time course. It is known that the large fibers of the corticospinal tract and optic nerve degenerate faster than the fibers of small size (Van Crevel and Verhaart, '63, '63a). Such studies indicate that fibers of equal size tend to possess equal resistance to secondary degeneration. The large fibers degenerate faster, but are resorbed more slowly. Hence the debris of total degeneration in the CNS is in evidence for several months.

Regeneration within the central nervous system of mammals has been restudied in recent years with both anatomical and physiological technics (Sugar and Gerard, '40; Brown and McCouch, '47; Windle and Chambers, '50; Scott and Clemente, '52; Freeman, '52; Campbell et al., '57, '58). Such studies indicate that the central axons of injured nerve cells make abortive attempts to regenerate across an experimental gap in the spinal cord. Factors that influence and often hamper central regeneration are similar to those influencing regeneration in the peripheral nervous system, (e.g., length of gap between severed stumps, hemorrhage, scar formation by ingrowth of connective tissue, and others). Central regeneration is further thwarted by the absence of sheath cells to guide the regenerating axonal sprouts. Sugar and Gerard ('40) found evidence of functional regeneration in adult rats whose thoracic cords had been transected with care to prevent injury to the blood supply. No return of function has been noted in the higher mammals following complete transection of the spinal cord. However, Scott and Clemente ('52) have presented electrophysiological evidence of partial regeneration in severed spinal cords with gaps of less than 1 mm. (cat).

It has been shown that remyelination of experimentally injured axons of the spinal cord can take place in the cat (Bunge et al., '61). Just what effects the described "nerve growth factor" may have upon central nervous system fiber regeneration is a moot question at the present time. Over the years various chemical compounds have been used in an attempt to stimulate the growth of the neurons and their processes. Bueker ('48) first noted that a fragment of mouse sarcoma 180 implanted in the body wall of a 3-day chick embryo became invaded by sensory nerve fibers from the adjacent spinal ganglia. After 4 or 5 days the ganglia appeared to be considerably enlarged. This overall increase resulted from both the number and the size of the sensory neurons, while motor neurons remained unaffected. These initial observations were confirmed by Levi-Montalcini and Hamburger ('51), who also noted that the sympathetic nervous system contributed even more fibers to the tumor graft than did the sensory ganglia. Tissue cultures of chick spinal and sympathetic ganglia, when confronted with explants of a tumor at a distance of a few millimeters, produced an exceedingly dense outgrowth of fibers on the side of the ganglia facing the tumor (Levi-Montalcini et al., '54). An extract prepared from the mouse salivary glands also promoted exuberant nerve growth *in vitro* on chick ganglia, as well as on ganglia from the mouse and rat (Levi-Montalcini and Cohen, '60; Levi-Montalcini and Angeletti, '61). Some of the chemical properties of the nerve growth factor were identified by Cohen

('60). It was nondialyzable, heat labile, destroyed by acid, stable to alkali, had an ultraviolet absorption peak at 279 mμ, and an estimated molecular weight of 44,000. The specific source and precise chemical structure of the protein have not been determined further. An antiserum was produced in rabbits by injection of the nerve growth factor. The antiserum, when injected into young mice, selectively destroyed the sympathetic chain ganglia, especially if the antiserum was administered at birth (Levi-Montalcini and Booker, '60). The source and precise chemical structure of the protein-like nerve growth factor are still obscure. However, that it induces a stimulating effect on the formation of neurites and as much as a sixfold increase in the number and volume of ganglion cells is established and well-documented (Levi-Montalcini and Angeletti, '63). Initial attempts to promote neuron regeneration with the use of nerve growth factor after injury to the cat spinal cord were promising but inconclusive (Scott, '63). For a more complete discussion on regeneration in the central nervous system, the reader is referred to Windle ('55).

CHAPTER 7

Neuroglia, Ependyma And Choroid Plexus

Neuroglia. The glial elements which comprise the interstitial tissue of the CNS long were regarded as a heterogeneous supportive framework for the neurons and a frequent source of tumors. Early studies on nerve tissues prepared by special stains and examined by light microscopy revealed exquisite silhouettes of both the neurons and the neuroglia. Silver and Golgi preparations revealed variations in cell size, and their location and distribution in the brain and spinal cord (Figs. 7–1 and 7–2). Such early work on the neuroglia was reviewed by Del Rio-Hortega ('32), Penfield ('32) and Scheibel and Scheibel ('58a). The use of newer methods has revitalized interest in the neuroglia and changed many of the early morphologic concepts as well. Although we are primarily concerned with the neuroglia of mammals, similar supportive cells are present in all vertebrates and some of the invertebrates (Coggeshall and Fawcett, '64; Bullock and Horridge, '65). The neuroglia in mammals are differentiated into specialized types and outnumber the nerve cells tenfold. Neuroglial elements may comprise almost half the total volume of the human brain—an indication of their important and specialized role.

A great amount of information on neuroglia is contained in a conference volume edited by W. F. Windle ('58). Tissue culture preparations, neurochemistry, neurophysiology, and electron microscopy, used either singly or together, have made outstanding contributions to this previously static field. As a result of such studies, the glial elements must now be considered as a dynamic functional system composed of cells that may be somewhat mobile (Pomerat, '51, '52, '54) and that help regulate fluid and respiratory interchange between the neurons of the central nervous system and their environment. The neurons and glial processes approximate each other so closely in the central nervous system that spaces of only 100 to 200 Å in width separate the contiguous plasma membranes (Dempsey and Luse, '58). In other instances one astrocyte touches the surface of another to form a tight junction (zonula occludens). In such cases the plasmalemmas of the two cells fuse, obliterating the extracellular space for a short distance (Palay, '66). Extracellular spaces of 100 to 150 Å have been observed in the leech (Kuffler and Potter, '64). In this animal the extracellular space accounted for 5% of the nervous system. Although the significance of some information is still obscure, the neuroglial cells of the central nervous system receive collateral terminal nerve endings

Protoplasmic astrocytes of gray matter

Fibrous astrocytes of white matter

FIG. 7–1. Distribution and appearance of astrocytes in gray and white matter of human spinal cord. Smaller nerve cell bodies often are obscured by profuse branches of protoplasmic astrocytes. Blood vessels (*b.v.*) also are stained in such preparations and receive vascular end-feet from adjacent astrocytes. Photograph. Golgi stain. ×175.

(Scheibel and Scheibel, '58), have lower metabolic rates than neurons after stimulation (Hydén and Lange, '62; Hamburger and Hydén, '63), and demonstrate a slow action potential (Tasaki and Chang, '58). Some of the more definitive results will be considered as the individual glial elements are presented.

Neuroglia may be classified structurally as being composed of *macroglia* (i.e., *astrocytes* and *oligodendrocytes*), *ependyma*, and *microglia*. The macroglia and ependymal cells, like the Schwann cells in the peripheral nervous system, are all derived from embryonic ectoderm. The microglia are of mesodermal origin and enter the embryonic brain and spinal cord when these developing structures are penetrated by the blood vessels. No morphological classification is entirely satisfactory, for there are many intermediate forms between oligodendrocytes and as-

trocytes (Glees, '55; Luse, '56; Schultz et al., '57; Palay, '58; Ramon-Moliner, '58; Robertson and Vogel, '62). We have used the term neuroglia in its broadest sense to include: (1) oligodendrocytes, (2) fibrous and protoplasmic astrocytes, (3) microglia (mesoglia), (4) ependyma, and (5) choroid epithelium. To these should be added the Schwann cell capsule, and the satellite cells of the peripheral nervous system, for they probably subserve similar functions for the peripheral nerves and ganglion cells.

Oligodendrocytes. These are the smallest of the macroglial cells and they are found in both the gray and white matter. They are numerous at birth but become less conspicuous in the adult brain and spinal cord. In the light microscope they are characterized by their small, often pear-shaped cell bodies, with rounded eccentric nuclei which are much smaller

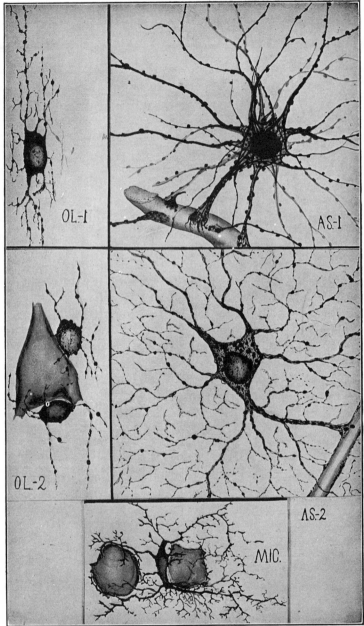

FIG. 7-2. Various types of neuroglia cells. *AS-1*, Fibrous astrocyte with one or two processes forming foot plates against a neighboring blood vessel; *AS-2*, protoplasmic astrocyte with foot plate and containing gliosomes (dark granules) in its body and processes; *MIC*, microglia cell whose delicate spiny processes embrace the bodies of two neurons; *OL-1*, oligodendrocyte in the white matter (interfascicular form); *OL-2*, two oligodendrocytes lying against a nerve cell (perineuronal satellites). (Penfield, '32.)

than the nuclei of astrocytes (Figs. 7-2 and 7-3). Other features include a scanty amount of cytoplasm with no fibrils and only a few delicate processes that extend for a short distance from the cell body. Electron micrographs support the above and show several additional features. The dense chromatin of the nucleus has light patches adjacent to numerous nuclear pores, while the cytoplasm has a crowded appearance, due to large quantities of free ribosomes or ribosome rosettes. Other distinguishing features of their cytoplasm are prominent microtubules, dark and light multivesicular bodies, and granular inclusions. The cytoplasm has mitochondria and a Golgi apparatus, but contains neither fibrils nor glycogen granules (Mugnaini and Walberg, '64; Kruger and Maxwell, '66; Bunge, '68). The plasma membrane of the oligodendrocyte makes closed contacts with adjacent myelin sheaths and the processes of adjacent glial cells.

Three principal types of oligodendroglia can be identified by their location and relationships. *Perineuronal satellite cells* are closely apposed to neuron perikarya, or their dendrites in the gray matter. This type is the most easily identified in adult material (OL in Figs. 7–2 and 7–3). *Interfascicular cells* occur in the white matter and often appear in rows between the myelinated fibers (OL-1 in Fig. 7–2). The interfascicular oligodendrocytes are numerous in the white matter of the fetus and newborn. However, they rapidly diminish in number as myelination progresses. After the myelin sheath is formed, only the nucleus remains, so that in adult material their processes rarely are observed (Fig. 7–3B). The third type, *juxtavascular cells,* are observed less frequently. Cammermeyer ('66) has successfully demonstrated several oligodendrocytes whose delicate processes terminate as end-feet upon adjacent blood vessels. He has suggested that this type may participate in the intrinsic control of blood flow.

Several additional functions have been proposed for oligodendrocytes. It is suggested that they act as: (1) an intermediary in neuronal metabolism, (2) a drainage cell, (3) a massaging device for various tissue elements (4) an energizer to neurons, and lastly, (5) a cell forming the myelin sheath. There is as yet no unanimity of opinion, and little substantiating evidence for most of these presumed func-

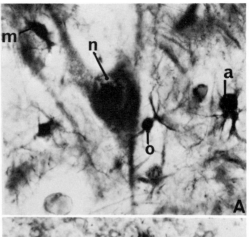

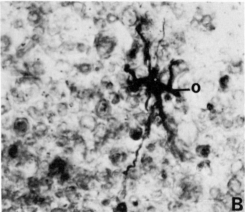

Fig. 7–3. Oligodendrocytes of human spinal cord. *A.* Newborn gray matter to demonstrate relative size of a neuron cell body (*n*), perineuronal (satellite) oligodendrocyte (*o*), astrocyte (*a*) and microglial cell (*m*). Cajal gold sublimate stain. ×565. *B.* Posterior white column of adult cord with oligodendrocyte (*o*). Golgi stain. ×550.

tions. The role of the oligodendrocyte in the myelination and remyelination after injury of central axons, however, does have supporting evidence. The fine structural continuity of the plasma membrane with the myelin sheath, and their active participation in remyelination has been reported in detail by Bunge ('61, '68). These cells are present in great numbers prior to myelin formation, and at this time there is a marked increase in glial enzyme activity (Friede, '61). In view of their cytoplasmic structure and role in myelin formation, these cells may be responsible for the high oxygen consump-

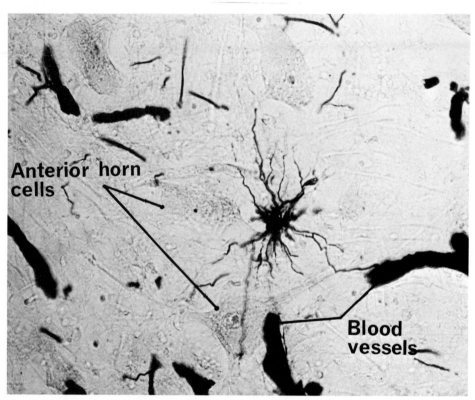

Fig. 7-4. Fibrous astrocyte in gray matter of adult spinal cord. Note perivascular end-foot on blood vessel and processes to adjacent anterior horn cells. Golgi stain. ×310.

tion so essential to the maintenance of myelin integrity (Blunt et al., '67). Astrocytes, as well, may participate in the latter function. It will be recalled that much of our physiological knowledge of membrane potentials and nerve conduction was derived from experiments with the large axon of the squid. Electron microscopic and neurophysiologic studies on the glial relations and functions in the leech and amphibia are equally fundamental and informative (Coggeshall and Fawcett, '64; Kuffler and Potter, '64; Kuffler et al., '66; Orkand et al., '66). Such animals provide simple and available models which can be used to answer many of the currently unresolved questions of neuroglial function. Neurons in tissue culture will continue to afford another productive and valuable method of gleaning much needed information, for as stated by Murray ('65) "developing neurons only differentiate normally when they are densely embedded in glia". In conclusion, it should be noted that in mammals the oli-

godendroglia react to injury by acute swelling, accompanied by marked increases in a variety of osmiophilic organelles, and acid phosphatase activity (Maxwell and Kruger, '66). Their study implied a participation of lysosomal intracellular breakdown of debris rather than phagocytosis by invading microgliocytes. The further changes and role of the oligodendrocyte in many demyelinating diseases of important pathways in man remain to be clarified (see Adams, et al., '65).

Astrocytes. These are the largest, most numerous and most elaborate of all the glial elements. They are abundant in both the gray and white matter of the cord and brain. Their cell bodies have long, wide branched watery processes which invest much of the neuronal perikarya, dendrites and axons, and help isolate their synapses (Figs. 7-4 and 7-5). Each neuron has a specific relationship with the astrocytic processes in its vicinity, ranging from complete encapsulation to none at all

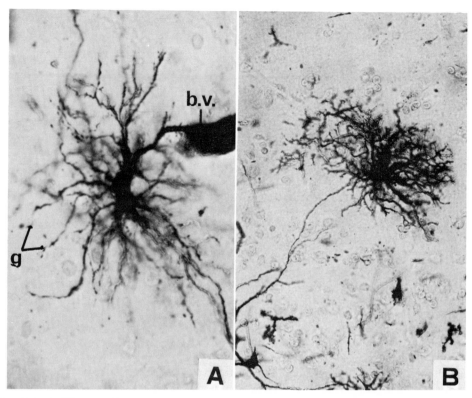

Fig. 7-5. *A*. Fibrous and (*B*) protoplasmic astrocytes in white matter of adult cerebral cortex. Note numerous gliosomes (*g*) in the processes of the fibrous astrocyte and vascular end-foot on blood vessel (*bv*). Photograph. Golgi stain ×550.

(Palay, '66). They form most of the "packing tissue" of the neuropil of the nervous system (Fig. 7-1). They reduce the extracellular space to a series of irregular and interlacing small clefts. Such glial cells also have many small perivascular endfeet that terminate upon blood vessels (Figs. 2-11 and 7-5), and some of their processes form a superficial glial membrane beneath the pia mater of the cord and brain (Fig. 2-3). After Golgi staining these glial cells show a delicate but pervasive framework in which the neural elements appear to be suspended (Fig. 7-1). In sharp contrast to this somewhat rigid image, astrocytes in tissue culture manifest flowing veil-like expansions in all directions, and migrate with a slow, gliding motion (Murray, '65).

Two main types of astrocytes can be distinguished in both light and electron microscopy. The *fibrous astrocyte* (spider cell) is characterized by its thin, less-branched processes which radiate out

from the cell body for considerable distances. These glial elements often are interposed between neurons and adjacent blood vessels and have prominent perivascular feet (Figs. 7-2, 7-4 and 7-5). Fibrous astrocytes are most numerous in the white matter (Fig. 7-1). With appropriate stains the cell body and processes are seen to contain many delicate fibrils. Each intracellular gliofilament is 60 Å in width and of indeterminate length. Such filaments correspond to the thicker fibrils observed in muscle and epithelial cells (i.e., myofibrils and tonofibrils). In the larger processes they are arranged in straight parallel bundles and can be followed for considerable distances. Such gliofibrils also are present in the protoplasmic astrocytes to be described below. Another feature common to both types of astrocytes are small granular swellings along the processes called *gliosomes* (Figs. 7-2, and *g* in 7-5). They occur in the cell body as well, and in electron micrographs they are seen to be clumps of mitochondria which contain a more dense matrix material.

The *protoplasmic astrocytes* (mossy cells) are most numerous and easy to identify in the gray matter (Fig. 7–1). They have numerous freely branching processes, perivascular foot-plates, and often are observed in close proximity to neuronal perikarya and dendrites. If fibrous and protoplasmic astrocytes are examined in Golgi preparations (Fig. 7–5) one can find sharp distinctive cells in each category. In the same sections one also can observe a host of intermediate and transitional cells that defy a precise morphological classification. Electron micrographs have revealed the reason—they represent different forms of the same cell (Maxwell and Kruger, '65). Variations in cell type may in part be a reflection of the cytoarchitectural differences that exist between the gray and white matter of the brain and spinal cord. Electron microscopic features common to both types of astrocytes are the usual cytoplasmic organelles (dense mitochondria, scanty granular and agranular endoplasmic reticulum, gliofilaments, and an abundant watery cytoplasm). The nucleus is finely granular and only moderately dense, and nuclear pores have been identified (Palay, '58; Maxwell and Kruger, '65). Fine structural characteristics which identify the astrocyte alone were described by the latter authors. These include a watery cytoplasm that contains gliofilaments, and dense glycogen granules 150 to 400 Å in diameter.

Astrocytes, the major guardians of the extracellular space of the central nervous system, play an active role in ionic flow and the regulation of normal neuron metabolism. They demonstrate a wide variety of enzymes which suggests they are involved in transport mechanisms between the blood and brain (Adams, '65). For example, stimulation of neurons for short periods leads to an increase in RNA, protein and respiratory enzyme activity, whereas there is a concomitant decrease in these units in the surrounding glial cells. Prolonged stimulation on the other hand decreases the RNA and protein of both neurons and glia. Friede ('62) has suggested a predominantly glycolytic role for the astrocyte which is subject to an adaptive change after a variety of injuries. Early accumulation of cytoplasmic glycogen granules in astrocytes has been demonstrated as a very prompt response to alpha-particle irradiation by both Klatzo et al., ('61) and Maxwell and Kruger ('65). It is not surprising that the astrocytes manifest changes in response to a variety of brain injuries (application of solid carbon dioxide, damage to vascular endothelium, ischemia, irradiation, edema, etc.). They react to injury by undergoing swelling or hypertrophy and are said to be "*reactive astrocytes*" (Fig. 7–6). Such cells exhibit markedly increased staining of their perikarya by the periodic acid-Schiff method for certain oxidative enzymes. In the light microscope the reactive astrocytes appear to persist for many weeks after injury. They can be identified by their increased size, prominent cytoplasmic gliofibrils and enlarged vascular end-feet (Fig. 7–6). Ultrastructural study after alpha-irradiation has confirmed many of the previously suggested astrocytic alterations (Maxwell and Kruger, '65a). These authors observed marked increase in the cytoplasmic glycogen granules within 24 hours. This was accompanied by a great increase in the number of dense mitochondria, and a more moderate increase in the Golgi membrane system. After 7 days the cytoplasm was expanded in volume, and the vascular end-feet were enlarged with even greater amounts of glycogen. Membrane whorls, which appeared to be reduplications of the plasma membrane, also appeared in the vascular end-feet at this stage. They noted that the peak in glycogen content occurred at the time when neuronal degeneration was first clearly evident. Such glycogen accumulations in the astrocyte processes were useful markers which pin-pointed the zone of maximal ionization. Some reactive astrocytes contained multiple nucleoli, but they found no evidence of mitotic divi-

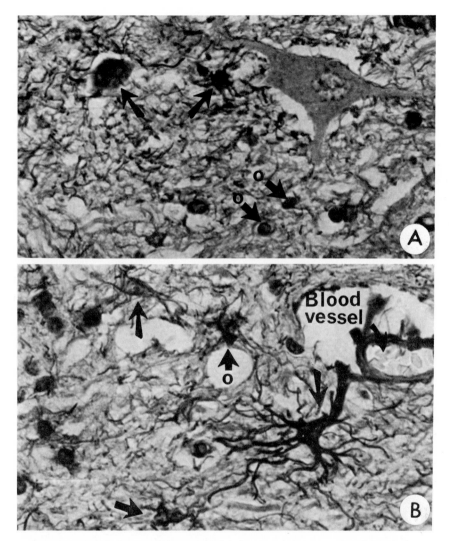

Fig. 7-6. Reactive astrocytes in gray matter of adult human cord four weeks after spinal stereotaxic lesion. *A.* Anterior horn cell with adjacent oligodendrocytes (*o*) and swollen astrocytes (*arrows*). *B.* A prominent and bizarre astrocyte with enlarged vascular end-foot, and several smaller astrocytes with gliofibrils are indicated by arrows. The cell body of an oligodendrocyte (*o*) is identified for comparison of relative sizes. Both photographs are after Holzer stain. ×550.

sion. They also failed to observe any evidence that such swollen astrocytes were engaged in phagocytosis of extracellular debris. The processes of the astrocytes, filled with gliofibrils and diminished quantities of glycogen and mitochondria, were the major elements in the scar of a fully developed laminar lesion. Astrocytes play a similar role in the formation of "glial scars" in man. Whether there is an

actual increase in the number of astrocytes (astrocytosis, hyperplasia) following central nervous system injury remains unresolved.

Microglia. These small elongated components, unlike other types of neuroglia, are presumed to be of mesodermal origin. They enter the nervous system as perivascular mesenchymal cells along with the neural blood vessels. Such undifferenti-

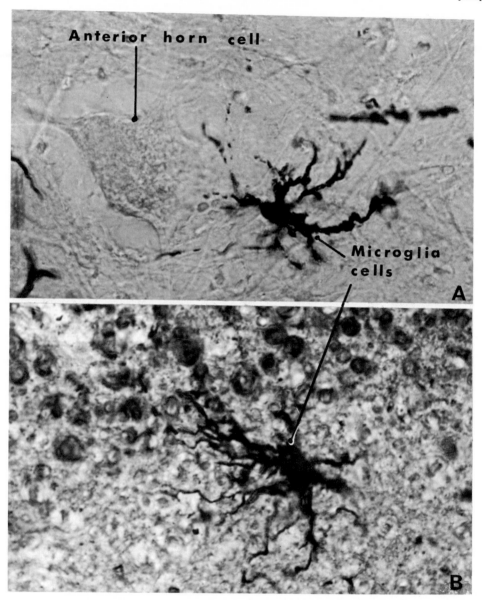

FIG. 7-7. Microglial cells in gray and white matter of adult human cord three weeks after spinal stereo-taxic lesion. *A.* Note thickened and stubby processes extending toward an adjacent anterior horn cell. *B.* Note knobby angular processes of microglial cell extending into the dark zone of degenerating fibers above. Photographs. Golgi stain. ×555.

ated vascular pericytes also may be the source of the macrophages which migrate into the central nervous system following injury and tissue degeneration to phago-cytize the debris (see below). In light mi-croscopy of normal tissue the microglia most often are found in the gray matter as juxtaneuronal cells and less frequently along or near a vascular wall (Fig. 7-7*A*). Approximately ten percent of the cells found in the vicinity of neurons within the gray matter are said to be microglia (Brownson, '56). Small numbers of mi-croglia also are observed in the white matter where their processes wind along or follow an undulating course across

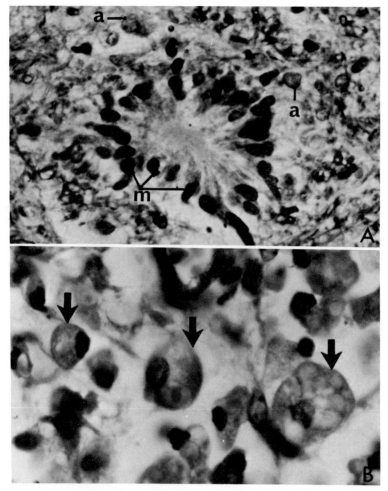

Fig. 7-8. *A*. Carousel formed by numerous microgliocytes (*m*) about a degenerating anterior horn cell four weeks after injury of its axon. Two astrocyte nuclei also are identified (*a*). Adult human cord. Luxol Fast blue-cresyl violet stain. ×555. *B*. Three stages (*arrows*) in the formation of a microglial phagocyte (*gitter cell*). White matter of adult human cord, four weeks after a stereotaxic lesion. Luxol Fast blue-cresyl violet stain. ×655.

myelinated fibers with a remarkable tortuosity (Cammermeyer, '65, '66). A microglia cell has an irregular perikaryon and a few thick processes which often appear to take off from each pole of the cell body. These large antler-like processes divide after variable distances into many smaller branches. Each branch then pursues an irregular and tortuous course either to adjacent neurons, or less often, to a blood vessel wall. The nucleus is ovoid or elongated, which aids in distinguishing the microglia from the oligodendrocyte. The cytoplasm is pervaded by myriads of

minute vacuoles which often gives the cell, or some of its processes, a sieve-like appearance (Fig. 7-7A). Electron micrographs demonstrate an abundance of dense cytoplasm, containing an elongated nucleus, mitochondria, a well developed Golgi complex, one or more dense bodies, and many vacuoles that occupy a large portion of the cytoplasm (Herndon, '64).

Microglia have long been considered the scavengers of the nervous system (i.e., the reticulo-endothelial component of the nervous system). They were presumed to be pleomorphic cells capable of: (1) met-

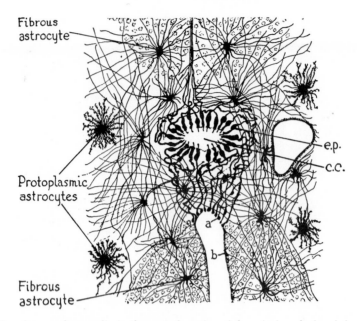

Fibrous astrocyte

Protoplasmic astrocytes

Fibrous astrocyte

e.p.

c.c.

a

b

FIG. 7-9. Ependyma and neuroglia in the central portion of the spinal cord of an infant 8 days old. Golgi impregnation. *a*, Terminal foot plate of ependymal cell; *b*, terminal foot plate of fibrous astrocyte; *c.c.*, central canal; *e.p.*, ependymal cell. (After Cajal, '09.)

amorphosis into a macrophage; (2) undergoing mitotic division and migrating at will through the already formed neuropil; and (3) the ability to autolyze or phagocytize as a microglia cell (Del Rio-Hortega, '32; Penfield, '32). They can rapidly recruit, mobilize and attack invading organisms and thus help remove disintegration products following injury.

The final structural characterization and function of these interesting cells must be written at some future date, for they often are not identified in the limited samples observed by electron microscopy. However, several points merit additional comment. It is difficult to envision even such a small cell as being capable of migrating at will through the tight entanglements of perikarya, axons, dendrites, glial processes and the multitude of capillaries in the neuropil. However, the microglia, or their structural counterparts, rapidly appear in the brain and spinal cord following a variety of insults and injuries (Figs. 7-7*B* and 7-8*A*). Rubinstein et al., ('62) have observed microglial cells in great numbers discretely arranged in the region of experimental injury and edema.

They observed such cellular mobilization as early as 24 hours which persisted for five days following cold injury (−50°C) of the cerebral cortex. They also demonstrated protein inclusions within the microglial cells scattered throughout the edematous white matter of their cortical lesions. Schultz and Pease ('59) observed a similar accumulation of microglial elements in the acute phase 24 hours after stab wounds of the cerebral cortex. The microglia underwent a remarkable transformation within this period; they exhibited a rounded appearance as the cytoplasmic volume increased and became less dense so that the nuclei became more prominent. The nucleoli became very large and there were numerous Golgi membranes. In about one week these changes culminated in the formation of typical macrophages with much pale cytoplasm and no definite processes. An enlarged macrophage in the central nervous system with a foamy cytoplasmic appearance and ingested material is called a "gitter cell". As the cytoplasm of the macrophages became packed with ingested material the nucleus was often pushed to the cell periphery. Such phago-cytosed particles included myelin and lipoid droplets. Gitter cells dominated their lesions for the first week, then decreased in number until 90 days, at which time only an occasional phagocyte was seen.

A similar mobilization is observed in the human nervous system (microglio-cytosis) after neuron injury (Fig. 7–8A). Three stages in the formation of a gitter cell are indicated by arrows in Figure 7–8B. These large vacuolated macrophages may assume gigantic size and a bloated appearance. When suitable fat stains are used (e.g., osmic acid, oil red O, Sudan black, Sudan III or IV) the vacuolated gitter cells display an unusual number of fat droplets of varying size. There is much speculation, but little evidence, to validate the origin of these macrophages. Some investigators consider them to be transformed microglial cells, others believe them to be transformed monocytes. Still others consider the rapidly mobilized cells as being derived from the pia mater or the undifferentiated cells of the perivascular mesenchyme. Maxwell and Kruger ('65a) have presented the strongest evidence to date. They observed a marked fine structure correlation between the vascular pericyte, the microglia, and the gitter cells. They believe the only cerebral element which displays macrophage activity seems to be derived from the vascular pericyte. If such findings are confirmed, the microglia cell may be said to make its original debut and subsequent curtain call from the walls of vessels—namely, the vascular pericyte.

Ependyma. The ependyma lines the central canal of the spinal cord and the ventricles of the brain. In the embryo the processes traverse the entire thickness of the neural tube to become attached to the pia mater and superficial glial membrane (external limiting membrane) by terminal expansions. Most of the processes retract, so that at birth these processes only reach the pia where the neural wall is thin, as in the basal plate region (Fig. 7–9). In fetal life the ependyma consists of several layers of nuclei, and one

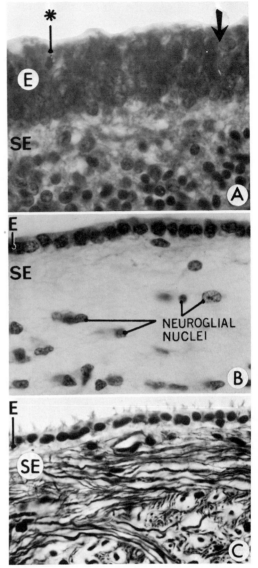

Fig. 7–10. Ependyma of human and rabbit brains. A. Ependymal cells (E) and subependymal glial membrane (SE) in a human fetus of 80 mm C-R length. Mitotic figure (*) and pale germinal cell nuclei (arrow) are indicated. Luxol Fast blue-cresyl violet stain. B. Ependymal cells lining adult human third ventricle. Luxol Fast blue-cresyl violet stain. C. Ciliated ependymal cells lining adult rabbit fourth ventricle. Bodian stain. All photographs ×655.

can see the large pale nuclei of the germinal cells (arrow Fig. 7–10A). Mitotic figures are also easy to identify (*). Cilia are observed in only the embryologic

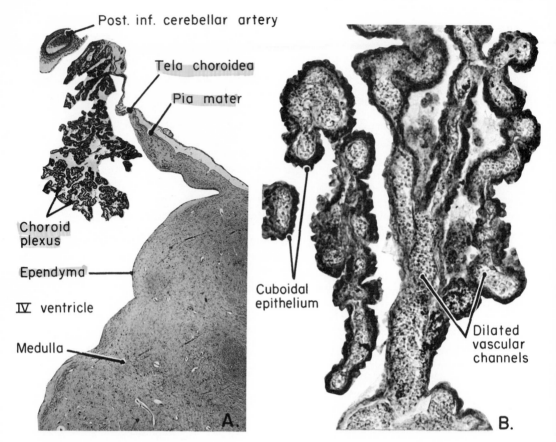

FIG. 7–11. Photographs of human choroid plexus. *A*, Low magnification to show topography and relations of the plexus in the fourth ventricle. *B*, Higher magnification to demonstrate the epithelium and vascularity of two choroid villi.

stages of man, but persist in some adult animals, such as the rabbit and dog (Fig. 7–10*C*). In the human adult the single layer of ependymal cells are cuboidal, while their retracted processes are entwined in the packed astrocytic processes of the *subependymal* (SE in Fig. 7–10) or internal limiting *glial membrane*. There are few places in the nervous system where typical astrocytes and their processes are so concentrated as in this subependymal limiting membrane. During development, the pia-arachnoid pushes a layer of ependymal cells ahead of it, and invaginates into each of the primitive brain ventricles to form the tufted choroid plexuses (Figs. 5–10, 5–12). The points of attachment, composed of pia mater and the cuboid ependymal cells, form the *tela choroidea* of the fourth, third and lateral

ventricles (Fig. 7–11*A*). These points of junction or reflection can be observed in gross brain specimens after the choroid plexus has been removed. The macroscopic torn edge of the ependyma is then referred to as the *tenia choroidea* (Fig. 3–13). At the embryonal transition point between the lamina terminalis and tela choroidea of the third ventricle (rostral wall in midline) in mammals one often finds a peculiar mass called the *subfornical organ*. It is located a slight distance above the anterior commissure and median preoptic area, between the diverging anterior columns of the fornix. This peculiar admixture of tall modified ependymal cells, glia-like cells, nerve cells, fibers and sinusoids appears to be a phylogenetically old structure of unknown function. Akert et al. ('61) have identified this organ in several mammals, and believed it was related to the septal nuclei. Others have ascribed a secretory function, or role in the regulation of water balance to this unique cell cluster. Another lamina of ependymal cells is located below the posterior commissure at the junction of the diencephalon and midbrain (Fig. 16–7). This group of cells forms the *subcommissural organ* and is discussed in Chapter 16 (page 384).

Electron micrographs reveal that the ependymal cell cytoplasm contains small slender mitochondria, vesicles of ergastoplasm, an agranular reticulum, a Golgi complex and compact bundles of fine filaments 90 to 95 Å in diameter, which may be protein (Palay '58; Tennyson and Pappas, '65). Histochemically, the ependymal epithelium exhibits high oxidative activity as reflected by its enzyme content (i.e., acid and alkaline diphosphatase, adenosine triphosphatase). Both structural and chemical reactions reflect the secretory and absorptive functions attributed to the ependymal cells and choroid epithelium (Adams, '65). It will be recalled that the surface layer of ependyma cells and subjacent astrocytes (i.e., subependymal glial membrane) constitute a brain-cerebrospinal fluid barrier (Fig. 2–12).

Choroid epithelium. As noted above the choroid plexuses are formed as a result of the invagination of the ependymal roof plate into the ventricular cavities by the blood vessels of the pia mater (page 103). In human embryos the primordia of all the choroid plexuses develop during the second month of gestation. A mesenchymal invagination into the thin roof area of the fourth ventricle appears first at six weeks. The primordia of the telencephalic choroid plexuses become visible in the seventh week, followed in the eighth week by an invagination into the roof of the third ventricle. It is not surprising that extensive structural alterations in shape and microscopic appearances accompany the different stages of choroid plexus development. Four stages were delimited and described in detail by Shuangshoti and Netsky ('66). For our purposes, it will suffice to note that each

primordium enlarges, becomes lobulated, and each lobule later demonstrates frond-like expansions. In still later stages many villi develop on the surface. The entire lobulated, vascularized mass remains attached by a broad stalk at the point of the original invagination. The covering cells are at first pseudostratified tall epithelial cells 50-60 micra in thickness with a brush border on the luminal surface. At eleven weeks the choroid plexus fills 75 percent of the lateral ventricle, and the covering tall columnar cells have an abundance of cytoplasmic glycogen (Fig. 7–12). At this stage the mesenchyme of the underlying connective stroma becomes extremely loose and accumulates a large amount of mucin. In the interval between 15 and 17 weeks of gestation the entire plexus gradually decreases in size and the primary villi are better developed. The epithelium changes from low columnar to cuboidal and measures 15x15 micra. The loose underlying mesenchyme decreases in amount, while distinct connective tissue fibers (mostly collagen) make their appearance in the stroma. Between 29 weeks and full term the large cuboidal cells are replaced by smaller ones which are 10x10 micra. The cytoplasm loses its glycogen, while meningocytes, foamy cells and fat-laden macrophages are scattered through the stroma. Once removed, the glycogen never reappears as a normal constituent of the adult choroid epithelium. Such disappearance of glycogen after birth, or at the beginning of aerobic oxidation, suggests that the developing nervous tissue uses energy which is released by the anaerobic metabolism of glycogen. Epithelial indentations lining the interlobular clefts may become buried in the stroma during early development and form the choroid cysts observed in the adult human brain (Shuangshoti and Netsky, '66). The gross relations and shapes of these plexuses in the brain are presented on page 34. They appear red due to the blood in the stromal vessels and the fine leaf-like projections endow the choroid plexus with a shaggy surface appearance. Hardened bodies composed of concentric rings of calcium carbonate, calcium and

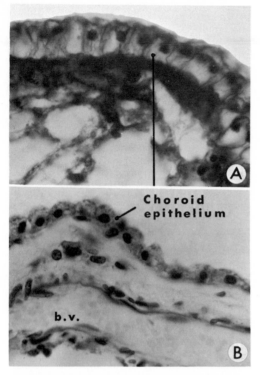

FIG. 7-12. Choroid epithelium of man. *A*. Tall columnar choroid cells in a human fetus of 100 mm C-R length. Holmes' silver with hematoxylin counter-stain. *B*. Cuboidal choroid cells of adult brain. A subjacent blood vessel (*bv*) is identified. Luxol Fast blue-cresyl violet stain. Both photographs are ×655.

magnesium phosphate also occur in the adult choroid plexus (psammoma bodies). They are generally spherical and originate around a group of degenerated cells (Schaltenbrand, '55). Psammomatous bodies are usually of small diameter (0.01–0.15 mm) and appear to increase in number with age.

The histologic appearance of the adult choroid epithelial cells after routine staining is shown in Figures 7–11 and 7–12*B*. They are low cuboidal cells with round and basally located nuclei. The bases of the cells are moderately smooth, while the lateral boundaries interdigitate with adjacent cells and demonstrate terminal bars. Small inpocketings can be seen on all surfaces of the cell (*pinocytosis*) and are regarded as a mechanism whereby

surface solutes can be taken into the cell (cell drinking). An occasional cilia may occur on the apical surface of adult choroid cells. Each cell is bounded by a dense continuous cell membrane. On the ventricular surface, each cell is thrown into elaborate, finger-like extensions 80–90 millimicra in diameter which contain cytoplasmic cores (striated or brush border of light microscopy; *microvilli* in electron micrographs). Microvilli in this instance are a structural device to increase the cell surface and thereby enhance its secretory and possibly absorptive functions (Fig. 7–13). The electron microscopic studies of Tennyson and Pappas ('61, '64, '68) on the developing choroid plexus of the rabbit, suggest such a "dual secretory-absorptive" role. Their ultrastructural observations also confirm and greatly extend the embryological data of light microscopy which was presented above. As shown in one of their electron micrographs (Fig. 7–13) the adult choroidal cell contains numerous mitochondria (*M*), a Golgi complex (*G*), cisternal and tubular elements of the endoplasmic reticulum (*ER*), numerous small vesicles (*V*), dense bodies with a heterogeneous content (*B*) and occasional cilia. These investigators also called attention to the "pores" present in the capillaries of the newborn and adult choroid plexus. However, they found no evidence that thorium dioxide, when injected intravenously, traversed these pores to attain a location within the connective tissue stroma. The authors interpreted such evidence as indicating the existence of a blood-cerebrospinal fluid-barrier for this substance in the newborn rabbit. Histochemical demonstration of phosphatase activity in choroid cells, particularly the intracellular location of adenosine-triphosphatase and acid phosphatase, should be noted. These hydrolytic enzymes play key roles in metabolically active cells; adenosine-triphosphatase participates in the ionic transport at membrane surfaces, and in oxidative phosphorylation within mitochondria. Acid phosphatase is an important constituent of the lysosomes (dense

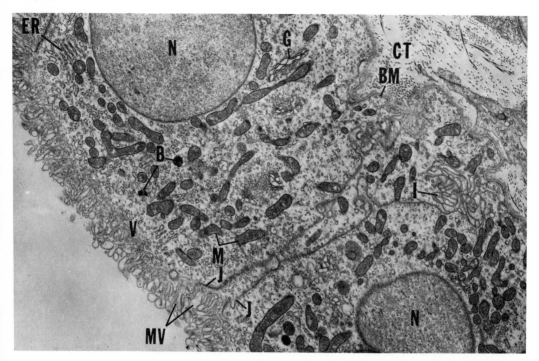

Fig. 7-13. The cuboidal choroid epithelial cells of an adult rabbit have rounded centrally located nuclei (N). The luminal surface is elaborated into multiple polypoid microvilli (MV) while the adjacent cell membranes are closely apposed at the apex (J). The lateral surfaces of the cells are relatively straight except near the base where extensive folds and interdigitations (I) occur. The basal surface is relatively straight or shows slight undulations. The cytoplasm contains a Golgi complex (G), short cisternal or tubular elements of the endoplasmic reticulum (ER), numerous mitochondria (M), vesicles (V), and dense bodies (B) with a heterogeneous content. A basement membrane (BM) separates the epithelium from the connective tissue (CT). ×9000. (Courtesy of Drs. Tennyson and Pappas, '68. In A. Lajtha and D. H. Ford [Eds], Brain Barrier Systems, Progress in Brain Research, 29:63–85. Fig. 1., Elsevier Publishing Co., Amsterdam.)

bodies of electron micrographs) which gives rise to pinocytotic vacuoles and appears to play an important part in transcellular transport and digestion, as well as phagocytosis, necrosis and autolysis (for additional information see Adams, '65).

It should be recalled that the vascular endothelium, choroidal epithelium and their basement membranes act as an effective barrier which prevents large molecular substances from entering the cerebrospinal fluid (e.g., tagged serum proteins, inulin, and fluorescent dyes). However, such substances when injected into the ventricles can slowly pass through the ependyma and subependymal glia to enter the extracellular space of the brain which is guarded by astrocytes (Fig. 2-12). Thus one must consider all the neuroglial elements not only as an impressive structural skeleton, but also as dynamic units that regulate the chemical milieu of nerve cells and thereby participate in neuronal metabolism.

CHAPTER 8

Peripheral Nerves And Their Ganglia

The spinal cord is connected with the various parts of the body by 31 pairs of segmentally arranged spinal nerves: 8 cervical, 12 thoracic, 5 lumbar, 5 sacral, and usually 1 coccygeal. The first cervical nerve emerges between the occipital bone and the atlas, the eighth cervical between the seventh cervical and first thoracic vertebrae. Below the eighth cervical, each spinal nerve emerges from the intervertebral foramen between its own and the next lower vertebra (Fig. 3–2).

Spinal Nerve. Each spinal nerve arises from the cord by two roots, a dorsal afferent root and a ventral efferent one. The two roots traverse the dural sac, penetrate the dura, and reach the intervertebral foramen, where the dorsal root swells into the spinal ganglion which contains the cells of origin of the afferent fibers (Figs. 6–1A and 8–1). Distal to the ganglion, the dorsal and ventral roots unite and emerge from the intervertebral foramen as a *mixed spinal nerve* or *common nerve trunk*, which now contains both afferent and efferent fibers. The dorsal roots are, as a rule, thicker than the ventral ones and vary with the size of their respective ganglia. The only exception is the first cervical nerve, whose dorsal root is greatly reduced and often missing.

Each dorsal root is composed of myeli-

nated and unmyelinated nerve fibers which vary in size from 0.5 to 20 micra. They are the processes of the large, medium-sized, or small dorsal root ganglion cells. The larger myelinated fibers (10 to 20 micra) convey important sensory impulses to the spinal cord from elaborate receptors located in the dermis, subcutaneous connective tissue, muscles, tendons, joint capsules, ligaments, periosteum, and deep fasciae. These large afferent fibers conduct rapidly (5 to 120 meters per second) and, by virtue of their several physiological properties, are classified as the *A fiber* components of peripheral nerves. The smaller myelinated nerve fibers in dorsal roots (0.5 to 10 micra) bring sensory information to the cord from less specialized receptors, and from free nerve endings in the skin, viscera, muscles, and connective tissues of the body. The small, unmyelinated, slow-conducting sensory fibers of the dorsal roots often are classified physiologically as the *C fibers* of peripheral nerves. The diameter spectra of the fibers within a dorsal root are shown in Figure 8–5.

The ventral root of a spinal nerve is composed of myelinated axons that vary in diameter from 3 to 13 micra. The vast majority are the large axons (9 to 13 micra) of large somatic efferent anterior horn

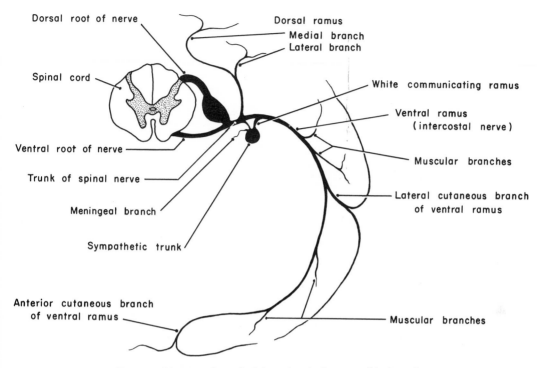

Dorsal root of nerve

Dorsal ramus
Medial branch
Lateral branch

Spinal cord

White communicating ramus

Ventral ramus
(intercostal nerve)

Ventral root of nerve

Muscular branches

Trunk of spinal nerve

Lateral cutaneous branch
of ventral ramus

Meningeal branch

Sympathetic trunk

Anterior cutaneous branch
of ventral ramus

Muscular branches

FIG. 8-1. Diagram of a typical thoracic spinal nerve and its branches

cells of the spinal cord (Figs. 8–5B and 12–17). They conduct rapidly and have functional properties similar to the large sensory A fibers of the dorsal root. Each large A-alpha fiber in the ventral root enters a more peripheral motor nerve and supplies motor impulses to a variable number of *extrafusal muscle fibers* (Fig. 6–2E). Smaller myelinated fibers, 3 to 6 micra in diameter, form a second component of the ventral root (gamma efferent fibers). These are finer axons that arise from smaller multipolar neurons scattered among the larger cells of the anterior gray horn (Figs. 12–13 and 12–17). Each small fiber is a gamma efferent axon. Such small motor axons of ventral roots and motor nerves are designated as "gamma efferents," and they innervate the small *intrafusal fibers* of the neuromuscular spindle (Figs. 9–17 and 12–17). A third fiber component is found only in the ventral roots of spinal nerves T1 to L2 (Fig. 8–6). Such myelinated fibers range from 3 to 10 micra in diameter and are the preganglionic axons

of visceral motor neurons located in the intermediolateral cell column of the spinal cord. These preganglionic visceral efferent fibers leave the ventral root to enter the ganglia of the sympathetic trunk through a white communicating ramus (Figs. 11–1 and 12–17). The preganglionic visceral components of the ventral spinal roots conduct more slowly (3 to 15 meters per second); they are concerned with visceral reflexes and are designated as the *B fibers*. Similar preganglionic visceral efferent fibers (of the parasympathetic part of the autonomic system) are found in the ventral roots of sacral nerves 2, 3, and 4 (Fig. 11–1).

In view of these several fiber components within the dorsal and ventral roots, one obtains a wide variation in the appearance and fiber spectrum as different fascicles of the peripheral nerves are observed microscopically (compare Figs. 6–2 and 8–5).

The Spinal Ganglia. The spinal and autonomic ganglia are part of the periph-

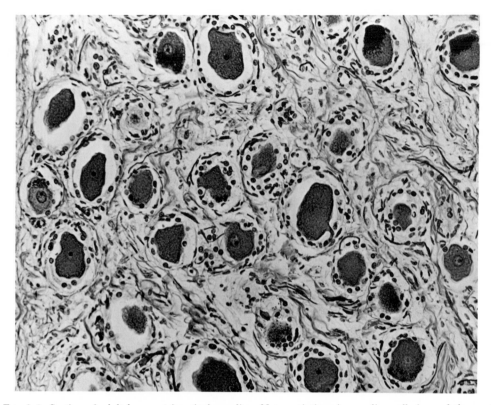

Fɪɢ. 8–2. Section of adult human trigeminal ganglion. Note variations in ganglion cell size and the small dark nuclei of the capsule. Photograph, Bodian stain ×160.

eral nervous system, and they contribute fibers to the peripheral nerves. The majority, if not all, of the afferent fibers, both somatic and visceral, have their cell bodies in the spinal ganglia. These aggregations of unipolar nerve cells form spindle-shaped swellings on the dorsal roots (Figs. 5–6 and 9–1). Each ganglion is surrounded by a connective tissue capsule that is continuous with the epineurium of the spinal nerves. Cells of the spinal ganglia have a peripheral location beneath the capsule. The bundles of nerve fibers entering and leaving the ganglia form a central core. In the trigeminal ganglion the cells and fibers are more loosely arranged and intermeshed (Fig. 8–2). In cerebrospinal ganglia the interneural spaces contain large and small axons, satellite cells, Schwann cells, and blood vessels.

The unipolar neurons are ovoid or spherical in shape, and often have indenta-tions on their surface contour. Their cell diameters range from 20 to over 100 micra. Sensory ganglion cells grown in tissue culture and studied by electron microscopy have all the cytoplasmic organelles possessed by other neurons (Tennyson, '65; Bunge et al., '67; Pineda et al., '67). However, these sensory neurons have less prominent Nissl bodies, and scattered cytoplasmic chromatin; the axon often is coiled to form a "glomerulus" within its surrounding capsule; and each cell has a variable number of adjacent satellite cells. The older literature described two types of ganglion cells on the basis of their staining properties as observed with the light microscope. The larger cells were lighter, while smaller cells often appeared dark (obscure cells; Fig. 8–3). The rapidly preserved tissue of Pineda et al., ('67) failed to demonstrate these two cell types, and such staining variations may reflect differences in cell metabolism at the moment of fixation. Bunge et al. ('67) observed light and dark cells in tissue culture and believed this appearance depended on the amount of cytoplasmic neurofilaments. Angular and indented surface margins of the perikaryon represent interdigitations with the processes of surrounding satellite cells. Such ultrastructural extensions of the perikaryon explain the surface spines and excresences that have been observed in Golgi, silver and methylene blue preparations. These typical, and often bizarre, sensory neurons commonly are observed in ganglia from older individuals (Fig. 8–4). The numerous processes may divide repeatedly or terminate as elaborate end-bulbs within the capsule. Sensory neurons with such supernumerary processes have been mistaken by some investigators as true multipolar (motor) neurons. However, it is relevant to note that no one has yet reported vesicle-containing axon terminals or morphological evidence of synaptic contacts within the dorsal root or trigeminal ganglia. A more detailed study of the sensory ganglia and neuronal variations that accompany senescense have been presented by Warrington and Griffith ('04); Dogiel ('08); Ranson ('12); Truex ('40, '41); Sosa and DeZorilla ('66).

Satellite cells (capsular nuclei) are derived from the embryonic neural crest and, in the adult, form a concentric layer which closely invests the perikaryon and its unmyelinated axonic coils (Wyburn, '58). The round or elongated nuclei of the satellite cells are more dense than the adjacent perikaryon, and are identified easily with the light microscope (Figs. 6–1A, 8–2, 8–4). They have ultrastructural features that distinguish them from Schwann cells. Satellite cells display plasma membrane redundancy in the form of folds on the surface that faces the neuron. Such folds and processes may form several layers and interdigitate with the surface evaginations of the perikaryon. The outer surface of the satellite cell is invested with a basal lamina which is continuous with that investing the myelin at the first internode (Pineda et

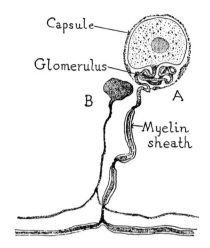

FIG. 8–3. Two cells from vagus ganglion of cat. *A*, Large clear cell; *B*, small "obscure" cell with deeply staining cytoplasm. Ehrlich's methylene blue. (After Cajal, '11.)

al., '67). The capsule of satellite cells separate the perikarya from adjacent ganglionic capillaries, and must be involved in fluid transport mechanisms. They can increase in number after birth, and play an as yet undetermined role in the metabolism of the ganglion cells.

The Mixed Nerve. After union of the dorsal and ventral roots, the common nerve trunk divides into four branches or rami: dorsal ramus, ventral ramus, meningeal ramus, and ramus communicans (Figs. 5–6 and 8–1). The dorsal rami supply the muscles and skin of the back; the larger ventral ones innervate the ventrolateral portion of the body wall and all the extremities. The ramus communicans connects the common spinal trunk with the sympathetic ganglia and consists of white and gray portions (Fig. 11–2). The former contains the myelinated preganglionic fibers from the cord to the sympathetic ganglion, while the gray rami contain the unmyelinated postganglionic fibers which rejoin the ventral rami to be distributed to the body wall. The white rami also contain afferent fibers from the viscera whose cell bodies are situated in the spinal ganglia (Fig. 12–17).

The meningeal branch is a small nerve trunk which usually arises by several

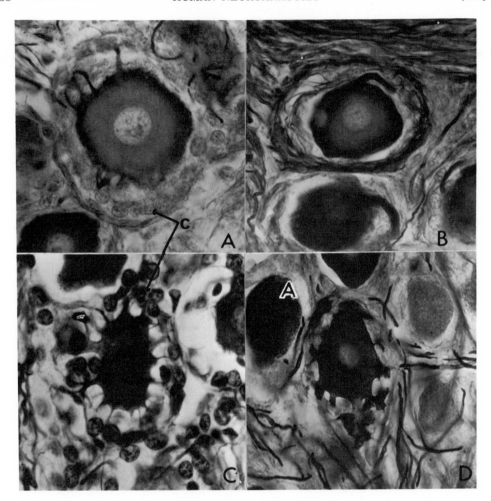

FIG. 8–4. Atypical sensory neurons of adult human trigeminal ganglion. *A*. Fenestrated cell with three looped processes on surface of perikaryon. Satellite and capsular nuclei are identified (*c*). *B*. Pericellular plexus of nerve fibers surrounding unipolar ganglion cell. *C*. Frayed cell (of Cajal) with multiple short processes most of which terminate in the surrounding capsule. Counterstained with hematoxylin to demonstrate capsular nuclei (*c*). *D*. Erethized or irritated cell (of DeCastro). Note thick, palm-leaf expansions or supernumerary processes that issue from perikaryon and axon. Types shown in *A*, *C* and *D* are often observed in sensory ganglia of older individuals (Truex, '40). Cajal silver stain. All photographs ×650.

twigs from both the common trunk and the ramus communicans (Fig. 8–1). It reenters the intervertebral foramen to supply the meninges, blood vessels, and vertebral column.

The dorsal and ventral rami divide into superficial (cutaneous) and deep (muscular) peripheral nerves. These nerve trunks branch repeatedly and become progressively smaller as they extend toward the periphery, ultimately breaking up into

individual nerve fibers which terminate in their respective receptors or effectors. The cutaneous nerves are composed mainly of sensory fibers of various size, but also contain efferent vasomotor, pilomotor, and secretory fibers for the blood vessels, hair, and glands of the skin. In the nerves to muscle there also is a mixture of sensory and motor fibers. Both somatic alpha and gamma efferent fibers go to the skeletal muscle fibers, while numerous large (A) and small afferent fibers pass centrally from receptors in the neuromuscular spindles and tendon organs. Small pain afferents and postganglionic vasomotor (C) fibers to the blood vessels also are found in the nerves that enter each muscle. Thus in each peripheral nerve there are fibers of various categories—myelinated and unmyelinated, large and small, visceral and somatic, sensory and motor.

While each spinal nerve supplies its own body segment, there is considerable intermixture and "anastomosis" of adjacent nerve trunks. The dorsal rami remain relatively distinct, although interconnections between rami of adjacent segments are common in the cervical and sacral regions (Pearson et al., '67). The ventral primary rami, however, form more extensive connections. With the exception of the thoracic nerves, which retain their segmental distribution, the cervical and lumbosacral ventral rami branch and anastomose to form the cervical, brachial, and lumbosacral plexuses (Chapter 10). In these plexuses a regrouping of fibers occurs, so that each of the peripheral nerves which arises from the plexus contains contributions from two, three, or even four ventral rami. The peripheral nerves are therefore "mixed" in a double sense; they consist not only of afferent and efferent fibers, but also of fibers which come from several segments of the spinal cord.

Connective Tissue Sheaths. Morphologically each peripheral nerve consists of parallel-running nerve fibers invested by a thick sheath of rather loose connective tissue, the *epineurium* (Figs. 6–20 and 8–7). From this sheath septa extend into the interior and divide the fibers into bundles or *fascicles* of varying size, each of which is surrounded by a fairly distinct perifascicular sheath or *perineurium* (see page 131). These fascicles do not run like isolated cables but may split at acute angles and connect with adjacent fascicles for an interchange of fibers. As a result, the fascicular arrangement varies in different portions of the same nerve.

From the perineurium delicate strands invade the bundle as intrafascicular connective tissue or *endoneurium*. This tissue separates the fibers into smaller and smaller bundles and ultimately invests each fiber as a delicate tubular membrane. In the epineurial and perineurial connective tissue are blood vessels and spaces lined with endothelium which communicate with lymph channels within the smaller fascicles.

On emerging from the spinal cord, the dorsal and ventral roots receive an investment of connective tissue as they pass through the pia. This tissue is reinforced by additional connective tissue as the roots pass through the arachnoid and dura, the latter becoming continuous with the epineurium of the spinal nerve (root sleeve, Fig. 4–2).

Functional Considerations. The origin, size, course and relations of the spinal nerves to their respective vertebrae should be recalled at this point (Figs. 3–1 and 3–2). Meninges, intervertebral discs, size of the intervertebral foramina, and vertebral mobility often can be correlated anatomically with a variety of spinal nerve root syndromes (Davis, '57). For example, degenerative or ruptured intervertebral discs may lead to compression of spinal nerve roots as they approach the intervertebral foramen, or the foramina may be narrowed due to osteoarthritis. Effects of stress and strain on the erect spine appear first at the weakest points. Here motion occurs and the mechanical impacts of postural strain and trauma usually are recorded (i.e., cervical and lumbar regions). Dorsal roots, except for C_1, are always three times larger than ventral roots. However, the spinal roots vary in size in different regions. The largest are those that participate in the formation of the nerve plexuses that supply the limbs. The sixth cervical is the largest of the cervical nerves and from this point upwards the roots diminish in size. Root size in relation to canal size also has some interesting correlations with attendant liability to mechanical irritation or compression. Cer-

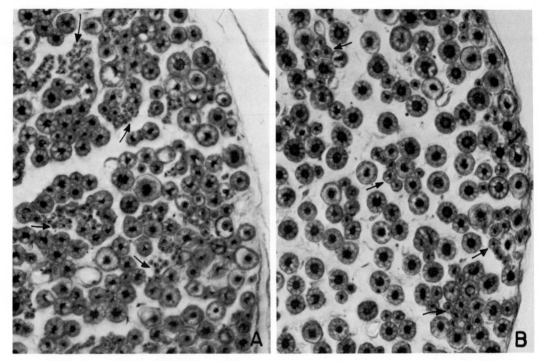

Fig. 8–5. Nerve fibers of dorsal and ventral roots. *A*, Cross section of L4 dorsal root within the dura mater. *Arrows* indicate groups of unmyelinated C fibers. *B*, Cross section of L4 ventral root within the dura mater. *Arrows* indicate axons of smaller gamma efferent neurons to spindle muscle fibers. Larger alpha axons supply groups of skeletal muscle fibers. Holmes' silver-Luxol Fast blue stain. Photograph. ×275.

vical roots occupy only one-fourth of their respective intervertebral foramen. In contrast, from the first lumbar nerve downward the size of the nerve increases in relation to the size of the foramen. The first to third lumbar nerves never completely fill the canal, and the fourth roots rarely do, whereas the fifth lumbar nerve roots frequently fill the intervertebral foramen. Thus one can explain the high incidence of compression in the lumbar region.

Nerve compression by disease or injury can result in a variety of root symptoms and usually is associated with pain. The latter may be a continuous, dull, aching discomfort, or a sharp, radiating pain, usually fleeting, or of short duration. Pain often dominates the clinical picture. If the ventral roots are involved, muscle spasm and vasomotor disturbances may accompany the pain. A knowledge of the radicular (segmental) distribution of the spinal nerves is helpful in evaluating root lesions which may lie in and around the vertebra of a given region.

Injury to the spinal nerves or their peripheral branches causes disturbances of both sensation and movement. Section of a dorsal root in certain instances may produce a loss of all sensation (anesthesia) and loss of all reflexes (areflexia) initiated by appropriate stimuli in the areas supplied by that root. Owing to the overlapping distribution of fibers of adjacent roots, the anesthesia may not be complete unless three contiguous roots are cut (Fig. 10–2). The areflexia is a loss of the superficial and deep kinetic reflexes and it results in a diminution of tone (hypotonia) in the muscles affected.

The various activities of the central nervous system can only be expressed by impulses passing through the efferent peripheral neurons, somatic and visceral, whose axons form the ventral roots. The alpha somatic motor neurons, known as the *lower motor neurons*, constitute the *final common pathway* (Sherrington, '06).

Destruction of the ventral root produces a complete paralysis of reflex and volun-

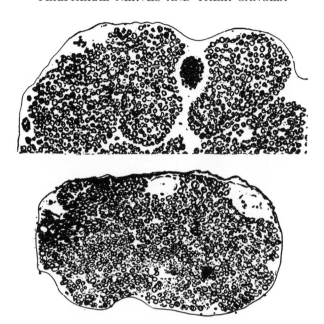

FIG. 8–6. Sections of lumbar (*upper*) and thoracic (*lower*) ventral rootlets. Photograph. Same magnification for both sections. The lumbar root is composed almost entirely of large nerve fibers. In the thoracic root, the coarse fibers are somewhat smaller than in the lumbar root and there are in addition numerous finer myelinated preganglionic autonomic fibers. The greater caliber of the large fibers of the lumbar root is related to the greater length and larger cell bodies of the somatic motor neurons innervating the muscles of the lower extremity, as compared with those innervating the muscles of the trunk. Weigert's myelin stain.

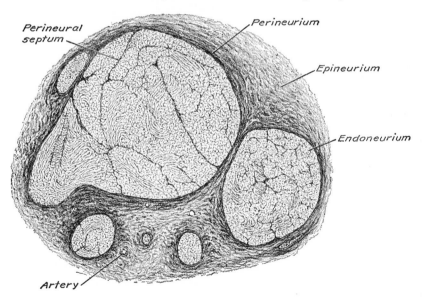

FIG. 8–7. Cross section of sciatic nerve of monkey (Copenhaver, '64)

tary movement, as well as loss of muscle tone (flaccidity) and degenerative atrophy of the skeletal muscle fibers affected. The denervated muscle also shows certain changes in its reaction to electrical stimu-

lation. Healthy muscle responds to stimulation by both the faradic (interrupted) and galvanic (continuous) current. In faradic stimulation, the response lasts as long as the stimulus is applied. In galvanic stimulation the response occurs only on closing or opening the circuit. Normally it is the application of the negative pole or cathode which produces the strongest contraction on closing the current. In the complete reaction of degeneration, which appears 10 to 14 days after nerve injury, the muscle no longer responds to stimulation of its motor nerve. However, the muscle still responds to direct stimulation by sluggish wavelike contractions, but now it is the positive pole or anode which induces the strongest response on closing the current.

If preganglionic visceral fibers also are involved, as in the case of the thoracic and upper lumbar roots, there are sudomotor, vasomotor, and atrophic disturbances expressed by dryness and cyanosis of the skin.

Section of the mixed spinal nerve immediately after union of the dorsal and ventral roots causes combined symptoms of muscular paralysis and sensory loss in the affected area. In the case of peripheral nerves, a knowledge of the exact distribution of each nerve is essential for an understanding of the sensory and motor defects resulting from injury to such a nerve. Familiarity with the structure of the spinal cord aids in understanding the formation and composition of the more complex spinal nerves. A full account of peripheral innervation is given in Chapter 10.

CHAPTER 9

Peripheral Terminations Of Afferent And Efferent Nerve Fibers

For many years major research efforts have been devoted to enlarging our knowledge of the eye, ear and vestibular mechanisms. Interest in the sensory apparatus of olfaction and taste has lagged behind, while renewed interest in the skin has attracted only a few workers from several disciplines. The volume of literature as well as our knowledge of the sensory system, parallels the above research interests.

As adults we each have two square meters of skin and it is so commonplace we take it for granted. Yet it is of primary importance to anyone who desires to understand the sensory input to the spinal cord and brain. Knowledge of the mechanisms of cutaneous sensation can illuminate the diagnosis of neurological disorders and is basic to the interpretation of the symptom of pain. Progress has been made, but too few attempts have been made to correlate the nature of the receptor with the stimulus applied, the message conveyed, and the ultimate sensation produced. The few efforts reported represent an expression of the multiple technical difficulties that are involved in such research. The limited sampling of electron microscopy when coupled with the data obtained by microelectrode recording will one day provide answers to clarify cutaneous sensation. Detailed reviews of

cutaneous innervation have been published by Granit ('56), Gray ('59), Quilliam, ('66), and Sinclair ('67).

The axonic terminals of motor nerves (effectors) are understood best when examined in the light of both their structure and function. This large body of information has been derived largely through the combined efforts of investigators in neuroanatomy, electrophysiology, pharmacology, histochemistry, electron microscopy and clinical evaluations. The fasciculations, spasms, weakness or loss of skeletal muscle activity often are recognized first by the patient. Irritation or injury of visceral motor axons may result in excessive or reduced secretions (salivary, lacrimal and sweat glands), vasoconstriction or dilation of blood vessels, and paralysis of the smooth muscle of the eye. Such obvious clinical symptoms gave impetus to the many studies which have enlarged our understanding of the motor nerves and the characterization of their terminals. Detailed reviews of the current concepts of somatic and visceral motor transmission are presented by Fatt ('59), Von Euler ('59), and Zacks ('64).

RECEPTORS

A wide variety of sensory endorgans have been illustrated morphologically and many of them still bear the names of those who described them. Characterization and distribution of the sensory terminals was attained by the study of tissues following gold and silver impregnations, or the use of methylene blue. The recent identification of adrenergic and cholinergic nerve fibers by the methods of Eränkö ('64, '67) and Falck et al. ('62) have permitted more accurate visualization of these small nerve fibers in their terminal tissue and organ distributions. Receptors may be regarded as miniature transducers which are capable of being aroused by one form of energy much more readily than by others. An appropriate form of energy (adequate stimulus) applied to a receptor results in a "receptor potential", which may in turn initiate an action potential along the parent nerve. Such physiological events have been demonstrated best in the Pacinian corpuscle (Lowenstein and A-Orrego, '58). Receptor endings have numerous mitochondria, microvesicles and neurofilaments, and even acetylcholinesterase in the case of nerve endings related to hairs. Other receptors are associated closely with supportive cells that demonstrate a variety of enzyme activities. Receptors vary from simple axon terminals (Figs. 1 and 2) to highly branched and encapsulated structures. There are many intermediate forms between each of the described classical nerve endings, and one cannot provide a discrete function for each of the receptors presented below. Only the Pacinian corpuscle is known to be activated by compression and deformation (mechanoreceptor). Free nerve endings appear to be the receptors in fetal life, whereas the encapsulated endings appear after birth (Cauna and Mannan, '61). There is evidence also that receptors may continuously break down, and become reorganized throughout life (Cauna, '65). This observation accounts for the variable appearance of corpuscles from older individuals (e.g., Pacinian and Meissner's corpuscles). Lastly, it should be noted that different regions and tissues of the body have marked differences in both the number and type of receptors (e.g., hairy and glabrous skin, muscle, and connective tissue). In short, there is wide variation in the density of receptors per unit of tissue, and a corresponding variance in the types of sensation that one perceives following appropriate stimulation (e.g., the cornea and anal margins are extremely pain-sensitive, whereas the viscera and muscles have a very high pain threshold).

No single classification of receptors has evolved which can adequately correlate the principles of structural organization, distribution and function. The three simple categories suggested by Miller et al., ('58, '60) are the least elaborate and restrictive. They suggested that the entire body is served by a basic triad of sensory nerve endings which are either "free", "expanded-tip" or "encapsulated". Such designations are applicable to the endings in glabrous skin and the subpapillary dermis. These terms also apply to the endings observed in fascia, tendons, ligaments, periosteum and the synovial membrane (Fig. 9–3). However, one encounters difficulty with such categories in hairy skin and muscle spindle receptors where free nerve and expanded-tip endings are also encapsulated.

Sherrington ('06) classified all receptors into three main groups: *exteroceptors*, *proprioceptors*, and *interoceptors* (Fig. 12–17). The exteroceptors, situated on the external surface of the body, receive impressions from the outside which may or may not result in somatic movements. They include touch, light pressure, cutaneous pain and temperature, smell, sight, and hearing. Some of these are *contact receptors*; others, such as smell, sight, hearing, and part of temperature, are activated by distant stimuli and are known as *teloreceptors*.

The conscious proprioceptors receive stimuli from the deeper portions of the body wall, especially from the joints, joint capsules, ligaments, and fascia and give rise to sensations of position and movement. They are primarily concerned with the regulation of movement in response to exteroceptive stimuli. These receptors provide sensory information which is utilized in the cerebral cortex to synthesize a conscious awareness of bodily muscle activity and joint movements (*kinesthetic sense*). Most of the receptors related to the knee and temporomandibular joints are diffuse unencapsulated nerve terminals (Gardner, '44; Keller and Moffett, '68). Other specialized receptors (spindles) in skeletal muscle and tendon are activated by muscle contraction and stretch. Their encoded signals are used for the reflex regulation of muscular activities, either at spinal cord levels (e.g., myotatic, flexor and extensor reflexes) or via the cerebellum for the reflex regulation of muscle tonus and muscle coordination (synergy). The muscle and tendon spindles are somatic receptors, but they contribute no sensory information directly to the cerebral cortex, i.e., they play no direct role in the elaboration of the "kinesthetic sense". The nerve endings in skin, joints, fascia, muscle and tendons all transmit afferent nerve impulses from the soma or body wall. Hence the exteroceptors, conscious proprioceptors, as well as muscle and tendon proprioceptors are grouped together as somatic receptors.

The interoceptors (visceroceptors) are the visceral sense organs that receive and transmit poorly localized sensory impulses related to the visceral activities of digestion, excretion, circulation, and so forth, which are primarily under the control of the autonomic system. They give rise to sensations of taste and visceral pain, to the more obscure forms of visceral sensibility such as hunger, thirst, and sexual feeling; and to the general feelings of well-being or of malaise. Smell, though not interoceptive, has close visceral affiliations and may be considered partly visceral.

Sensibility may also be divided into *superficial* and *deep*. The former obviously coincides with exteroceptive sense, and the latter comprises both interoceptive and proprioceptive sense, including deep pressure. A special form of sensation is the ability to recognize the vibrations of a tuning fork applied to bone, or of a faradic current to the skin. This is usually

FIG. 9-1. Sensory nerve terminations in corneal epithelium (Cajal, '11).

known as *vibratory* sense. The precise nature of its receptors is not known.

An analysis of sensation that is important from a clinical and comparative viewpoint was introduced by Head ('05), who distinguished two types of sensibility, one *protopathic* or affective, the other *epicritic* or discriminative. Head believed that the two had separate receptors, at least for the cutaneous innervation. Protopathic sensation is of a marked affective character, agreeable or disagreeable, but it gives little information of the nature or exact location of the stimulus. In epicritic sensibility, the discriminative element predominates. The stimulus is accurately localized, two points simultaneously applied are properly discriminated, and variations in intensity of stimuli are appreciated. Affective sensations are related primarily to reactions which most directly involve bodily welfare and in which there is reason to believe that the thalamus plays an important part. Consequently they often are termed *vital* or *thalamic*. Discriminative sensibility forms the basis for the complex associative and cognitive reactions of the cerebral cortex; hence it is called *gnostic* or *cortical*. In a general way, pain, temperature, visceral sensibility, and part of touch are predominantly affective, while certain aspects of touch, proprioception, and teleceptive sensibilities are predominantly discriminative.

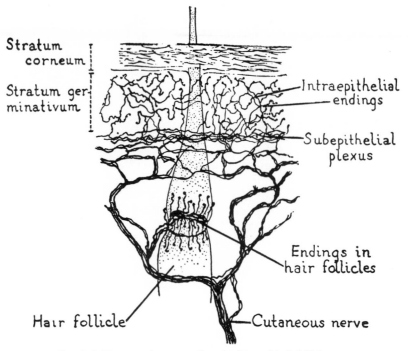

Fig. 9–2. Nerves and nerve endings in skin and hair follicles

From neither category is one or the other element entirely absent.

At the present state of our knowledge we believe two main types of receptors appear to be justified: (1) the *free* and *diffuse endings* which are always unencapsulated, and (2) the *encapsulated* endings or corpuscles, which are enclosed in a capsule of modified supporting cells.

Free Nerve Endings. The free nerve endings are the most widely distributed receptors in the body. They are most numerous in the skin, but also are found in the mucous and serous membranes, muscle, deep fascia, and the connective tissue of many visceral organs. The skin is supplied by many cutaneous nerve trunks composed of myelinated and unmyelinated fibers. Some of the large myelinated fibers are destined for the encapsulated organs described below, but the majority have a relatively small caliber. The fibers of these small nerve trunks separate as they approach the epidermis, lose their myelin sheath, undergo branching, and form extensive unmye-

linated plexuses in the deeper portion of the dermis and immediately beneath the epidermis (Fig. 9–2). From this subepithelial plexus, delicate fibers penetrate the epithelium, divide repeatedly, and form an end arborization of delicate terminal fibrils which wind vertically through the epidermis and end in small knob-like thickenings, upon the surface of the epithelial cells (Figs. 9–1 and 9–2). In the cornea, which has no horny layer, these intraepithelial endings may reach the surface, but in the skin they do not extend beyond the germinative layer. Intraepithelial endings also are found in mucous membranes lined by stratified epithelium, such as the esophagus and bladder. Similar endings may be seen in simple columnar epithelium as well.

Other nerve fibers form unmyelinated arborizations or terminal nets in the connective tissue of the dermis. There is some evidence that the intraepithelial endings are derived from fine myelinated fibers, while the subepidermal arborizations and plexiform nets are in the main

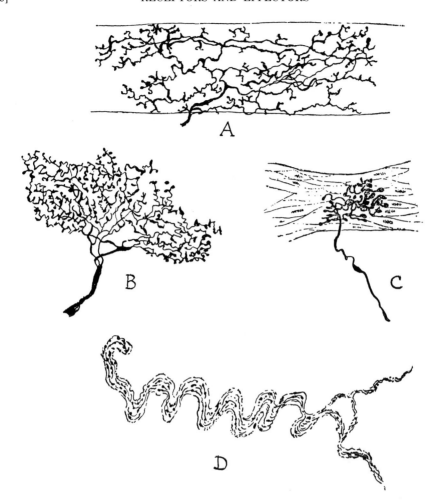

Fig. 9–3. Afferent nerve endings in various visceral structures. *A*, On a large pancreatic blood vessel (after Castro, '22). *B*, In endocardium of dog (after Smirnow, 1895). *C*, In bronchial musculature of child (after Larsell and Dow, '33). *D*, In longitudinal muscle coat of stomach of cat (after Carpenter, '18).

terminals of unmyelinated nerve fibers (Woollard, '35). Such terminal unmyelinated fibers are never naked, but are always invested by Schwann cells (Cauna, '66). Diffuse nerve endings in the form of nerve nets, or arborizations of varying complexity, are distributed widely in visceral organs. They have been described in the serous membranes, heart, bronchial tree, alimentary canal, and blood vessels (Fig. 9–3). Such endings also are found in the choroid plexuses of the brain and in skeletal muscle. For the most part, they are terminals of unmyelinated fibers. Com-plicated arborizations have been found in the smooth muscle of the bronchi by Larsell and Dow, ('33) (Fig. 9–3). These visceral receptors are endings of medium-sized or large myelinated fibers and may initiate proprioceptive bronchial reflexes.

An important type of diffuse cutaneous receptor is represented by the *peritrichial* endings of the hair follicles, which are activated by the movements of hairs. They vary considerably in complexity and are best developed in the vibrissae of certain mammals. In the simpler forms several myelinated fibers approach the hair

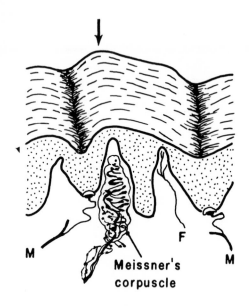

FIG. 9-4. Diagram of the papillary ridge in glabrous skin showing Meissner's corpuscle in a dermal papilla and Merkel's discs (*M*) on the deep
edges of the sweat ridges. A free nerve ending (*F*) is
shown in adjacent papilla. Arrow indicates direction
of most effective epidermal stimulation to elicit
touch and tactile two point discrimination (modified after Cauna, '65).

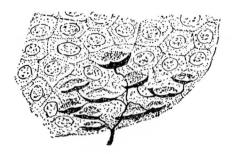

FIG. 9-5. Tactile discs in epithelium of pig's
snout (after Ranvier, 1878).

follicle just below its sebaceous gland, lose
their myelin sheath, and divide into several branches which encircle the outer root
sheath (Fig. 9-2). From these branches
numerous fine fibers run for a short distance upward and downward in the outer
root sheath and terminate in flattened
or bulbous endings. The smallest hair
follicles have at least two stem nerve fibers which form an outer circular plexus
and an inner palisading one formed by
the longitudinally directed fibers. Larger
follicles are supplied by 6 to 10 fibers,
while the largest receive between 20 to
30. In the rabbit each myelinated fiber
sends branches to 4 to 120 hairs, and an
average of 4 different dorsal root fibers
supply each hair (Weddell et al. '55).
Only free epidermal and dermal endings,
and the fibers associated with hair follicles, are found in truly hairy skin.

Besides the intraepithelial endings
described above, which end among or

upon ordinary epithelial cells, the deeper
portion of the germinative layer contains
somewhat more specialized endings known
as the *tactile discs* of Merkel (Figs. 9-4
and 9-5). Each consists of a concave neurofibrillar disc or meniscus closely applied to a single epithelial cell of modified
structure. A single epidermal nerve fiber
may, by repeated branching, give rise to a
number of such discs. These simple endings lie along the deeper sweat ridges between dermal papillae (Fig. 9-4). They are
numerous at birth but gradually diminish
with age. With the electron microscope
the Merkel cell of man and the opossum
can be distinguished from epidermal cells
(Munger, '65, '66). The Merkel cell has a
lobulated nucleus and a massive accumulation of secretory granules (glycoprotein)
in the cytoplasm that is apposed to the
neurite. Cauna ('65) believes them to be
touch receptors which respond to the le-
ver movement that results from deformation of the surface epidermis. In areas of
transition to glabrous skin there is a gradual increase in the number of Merkel's
discs and Meissner's corpuscles. In glabrous skin, such as the volar surface of
the finger, the epidermis and dermal papillae contain a profuse array of free nerve
endings, Merkel's discs and the encapsulated Meissner's corpuscle (Fig. 9-4). The
subpapillary dermis under such skin contains a wide variety of endings including
the end-bulbs of Ruffini, and Krause and
Pacinian corpuscles.

The tendency towards modification of
epithelial cells receiving sensory nerve

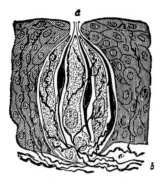

FIG. 9-6. Taste bud from circumvallate papilla of tongue. *a*, Taste pore; *b*, nerve fiber entering taste bud and ending upon neuroepithelial cells. On either side are some free intraepithelial endings (Merkel, 1875).

endings is exemplified in various *neuroepithelial* cells which have special forms and show staining affinities similar to nerve cells. The specific cells of the taste buds (Fig. 9-6), olfactory mucosa, and hair cells in the sensory epithelia of the cochlear and vestibular apparatus are examples of such neuroepithelial cells. Such supportive cells, as well as those forming the lamellae of encapsulated endings have surrounding basement membranes. It remains to be determined whether they are modified epithelial or transformed Schwann cells.

Diffuse Endings. The deep somatic structures of the human body have unencapsulated sensory endings that are more profuse than those observed in visceral structures (Fig. 9-3). Elaborate nerve endings have been demonstrated by Ralston et al. ('60) in the tendons, ligaments, joint capsules, deep fascia, and periosteum of man (Fig. 9-7). Ruffini (1894) originally described an encapsulated fusiform endorgan in the skin and adipose tissue. Although long considered as a corpuscle, its morphology is vague and most investigators have failed to verify its abundant distribution in man. It may well represent a variation of the diffuse, expanded-tip, unencapsulated endings described by Miller et al. ('60). It is conceivable that such extensive nerve endings in the periosteum may be the re-

ceptors for vibratory stimuli, while those found in ligaments, fascia, and joint capsules may record changes in pressure and tension that result from muscular contraction and joint movement. Encoded messages from these diffuse unencapsulated receptors appear to be a most important impulse component carried by the axons of the posterior white column to higher levels. Proprioceptive nerve impulses from these deep receptors play an important role centrally in that they make us aware of the numerous localized body changes that occur during locomotion, standing, sitting or in the performance of a multitude of daily tasks.

Encapsulated Endings. These include the *tactile corpuscles of Meissner*, the *end bulbs*, the *Pacinian corpuscles*, *the Golgi-Mazzoni corpuscles*, the *neuromuscular spindles*, and the *neurotendinous organs* of *Golgi*.

The *tactile corpuscles of Meissner* are elongated ovoid bodies, 90 to 120 micra in length, found in the dermal papillae, close to the epidermis (Fig. 9-8). Each corpuscle is surrounded by a thin, nucleated connective tissue sheath, while the interior consists of many flattened epithelioid cells whose nuclei are placed transversely to the long axis of the corpuscle. From one to four myelinated nerve fibers supply each corpuscle. As each fiber enters, its connective tissue sheath becomes continuous with the fibrous capsule. The myelin sheath disappears and the naked axon winds spirally among the epithelioid cells, giving off numerous branches which likewise spiral, show numerous varicosities, and end in flattened neurofibrillar expansions. Besides the myelinated fibers, the corpuscles also may receive one or more fine unmyelinated fibers. Meissner corpuscles occur mainly in the hairless portion of the skin and are most numerous on the volar surface of the fingers, toes, hands, and feet. In lesser numbers they also are found in the lips, eyelids, tip of the tongue, and volar surface of the forearm. It is now apparent that Meissner's corpuscles are formed in excess of adult requirements, and those that survive pos-

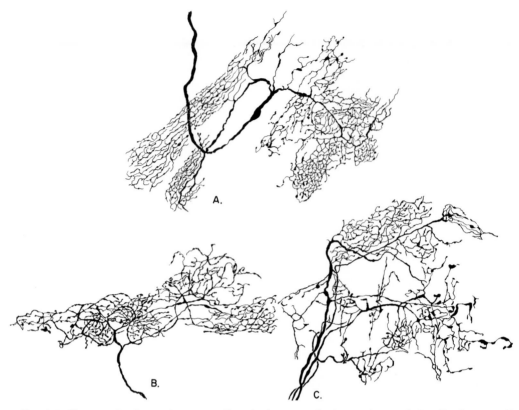

FIG. 9–7. Unencapsulated somatic nerve endings in deep somatic tissues of man. *A*, Patellar ligament; *B*, capsule of knee joint; *C*, periosteum of femur. (after Ralston et al., '60).

sess a capacity for continuous growth and reorganization (Miller et al., '60; Cauna, '65). In young persons nearly every dermal papilla contains a small Meissner corpuscle, 25 micra in length. In older individuals, only a few papillae contain corpuscles which are larger and of more irregular arrangement. These endings always are associated with the papillary ridge which plays an essential role in their stimulation. Their relationship is designed so that the nerve endings are stimulated effectively through one surface elevation of the epidermis, which is in line with the long axis of the corpuscle (arrow in Fig. 9–4). This arrangement makes the Meissner corpuscle particularly suitable for tactile two-point discrimination (Cauna, '65).

The *end bulbs* resemble the tactile corpuscles in structure and are spherical or ovoid bodies which vary greatly in dimension. The simplest and smallest ones are found in the conjunctiva (Oppenheimer et al., '58); the largest in the connective tissue of the external genitalia, where they are known as *genital corpuscles*. In its simplest form (Fig. 9–9*A*), the end bulb consists of a nucleated capsule enclosing a soft gelatinous core in which nuclei may often be seen. One or more myelinated fibers lose their myelin on entering the capsule and give off numerous lateral branches which form a complicated terminal arborization. Some end bulbs may be compound. End bulbs of various forms have a wide distribution, being found in the conjunctiva, mouth, tongue, epiglottis, nasal cavity, peritoneum (and other serous membranes), lower end of rectum, and external genitalia, especially the glans penis and clitoris. They also are found in tendons, ligaments, synovial membranes and in the connective tissue of nerve trunks.

The *Pacinian bodies* (*corpuscles of*

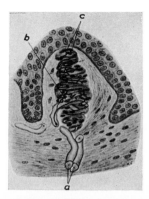

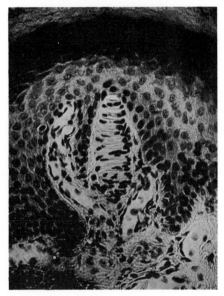

Fig. 9-8. *A*, Meissner's corpuscle from sole of human foot (after Braus, '11); *a*, myelinated fibers; *b*, terminal arborization; *c*, end swellings. *B*, Meissner's corpuscle in dermal papilla of human finger tip. Photograph.

Vater-Pacini) are the largest and most widely distributed of the encapsulated receptors (Figs. 9–10 and 9–11). They are laminated, elliptical structures of whitish color, each supplied by a large myelinated fiber. They differ from the other encapsulated organs mainly in the greater development of their perineural capsule. This capsule is formed by a large number of concentric lamellae; each lamella of the outer bulb consists of a single continuous layer of flattened cells, and is supported by fine collagen fibrils of the interlamellar spaces. The interlamellar spaces

contain a network of fine fibers, blood vessels, and some free cells in a semifluid substance. Blood vessels accompany the nerve fiber to the capsule but ramify only in the outer bulb. At birth the Schwann cell and myelin sheaths are lost as the large nerve fiber enters the inner bulb. However, the capsule continues to grow and enlarge, so that in the human adult both Schwann cell and myelin elements can at times be identified within the inner bulb (Cauna and Mannan, '58, '59). No fine nerves enter the inner bulb with the large fiber. Cauna and Mannan also found that the average length of the corpuscle at birth was from 500 to 700 micra. The size increases gradually throughout life to become 3 to 4 mm. in length. In persons over 70 years of age the corpuscles are less numerous and show regressive changes, becoming smaller and more irregular. Cauna and Mannan conclude that the Pacinian corpuscle is a receptor mechanism for signalling changes in local blood supply rather than changes in pressure. The entire length of the unmyelinated fiber within the corpuscle is sensitive to deformation, and can initiate "all-or-none" responses (Ozeki and Sato, '64, '65). They removed the surrounding capsule and found the mechanoreceptor function was still intact. These authors concluded that the short-lasting receptor potential, obtained from intact corpuscles, must be attributed to the mechanical filtering properties of the lamellae. In addition to pressure the Pacinian corpuscle deep in the limbs may be sensitive as well to vibratory stimuli. The corpuscles are found in subcutaneous tissue, especially of the hand and foot, in the peritoneum, pleura, mesenteries, penis, clitoris, urethra, nipple, mammary glands and pancreas, and in the walls of many viscera. They are especially numerous in the periosteum, ligaments, and joint capsules, and they also occur in muscular septa and occasionally in the muscle itself.

Related to the Pacinian bodies are the lamellated *corpuscles of Golgi-Mazzoni*, found in the subcutaneous tissue of the fingers and on the surface of tendons (Fig. 9–9*B*). They are ovoid bodies with lamel-

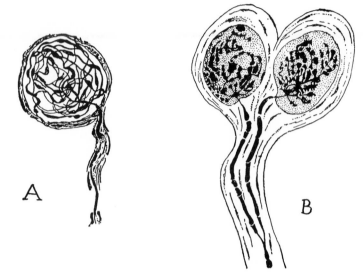

FIG. 9–9. *A*, End bulb of Krause from conjunctiva (Dogiel, 1895). *B*, Compound corpuscle of Golgi-Mazzoni from the subcutaneous tissue of the finger tip (Ruffini, 1894).

lated capsules of varying thickness and a central core of granular protoplasm in which the single myelinated fiber forms a rich arborization with varicosities and terminal expansions.

In the fleshy bellies of skeletal muscles are found complicated nerve endings known as *neuromuscular spindles* (Figs. 9–12, 9–13 and 9–14). Each spindle consists of from 2 to 10 slender striated muscle fibers enclosed within a thin connective tissue capsule and supplied with several nerve fibers which arborize in an exceedingly complicated manner (Fig. 9–12).

The thin muscle fibers within the spindle are known as *intrafusal fibers*. They are tapered at either end and considerably smaller than the adjacent, striated *extrafusal fibers* that produce contractal tension within a muscle (Figs. 9–12 and 9–14). Intrafusal muscle fibers are of two distinct sizes: one is of smaller diameter (10 to 12 micra), is shorter in length (3 to 4 mm.), and has a single chain of central nuclei; the second or larger spindle fibers are about 25 micra in diameter, are 7 to 8 mm. in length, and in the equatorial region are enlarged to accomodate an area of numerous small nuclei ("nuclear-bag" of Barker, '48). The small intrafusal fibers are known as "nuclear-chain fibers", and the larger ones are designated as "nuclear-bag fibers" (Boyd, '62; Barker and Cope, '62). A nuclear-bag fiber with its capsule and associated sensory and motor nerve endings is shown in Figures 9–12 and 9–14. Two or more myelinated afferent fibers enter each spindle. A thick primary afferent fiber forms a spiral, branching, and reticulated ending within the nuclear bag area (primary, annulospiral, or nuclear-bag ending). Silver stained primary and secondary sensory endings on intrafusal muscle fibers are shown in Figure 9–13. The primary receptor has a low threshold to stretching of the muscle or its tendon, and also discharges a volley of impulses when the intrafusal fiber contracts as a result of stimulation by a gamma efferent motor end plate (Fig. 9–14). The neuromuscular spindle is arranged parallel to the extrafusal or contractile fibers of the muscle; hence tension on the spindle is relaxed and afferent volleys from the annulospiral endings cease during active muscle contraction (i.e., the spindle is unloaded, and its receptors are silent). The primary afferent fibers (*Ia* in Fig. 9–12*A*) are 8 to

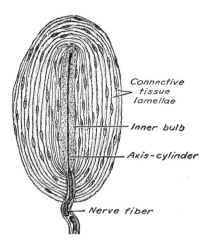

FIG. 9-10. Human Pacinian corpuscle (after Cajal, '11).

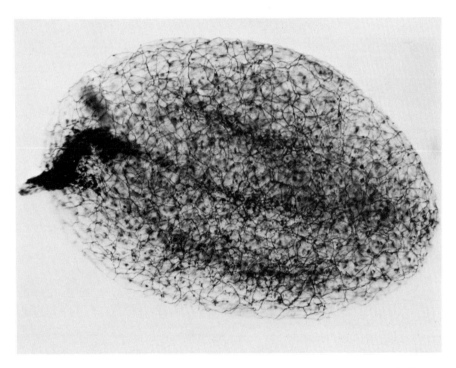

FIG. 9-11. Whole mount of Pacinian corpuscle. Note nuclei of sheets of squamous cells laid one on top of the other, and their continuity with perineural epithelium covering the entering nerve which supplies the corpuscle. Silver nitrate and cresyl violet stain. ×90. (courtesy of Drs. Shanthaveerappa and Bourne, '66, and the Wistar Press).

12 micra in diameter, have fast conduction velocities, and their central processes within the spinal cord participate in the monosynaptic stretch (myotatic) reflex that regulates muscle tone. The myelinated secondary afferent fibers (*II* in Fig. 9-13*B*) with diameters of 6 to 9 micra, also enter the spindle to form small rings, coils, and spraylike varicosities on both sides of the nuclear bag area.

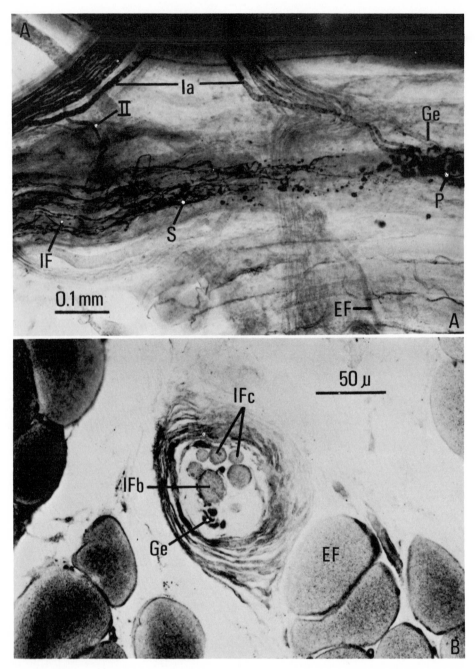

Fig. 9–12. Human intercostal neuromuscular spindle. *A.* Longitudinal squashed preparation showing sensory and motor neural elements related to the intrafusal muscle fibers (*IF*). Compare diameters of sensory fibers (*Ia*) related to primary (*P*, annulospiral) ending, sensory fiber (*II*) of secondary (*S*, flower-spray) ending, and gamma efferent (*Ge*) fiber. An adjacent extrafusal muscle fiber (*EF*) and artery (*A*) are identified. *B.* Cross section of muscle spindle demonstrating its multi-layered capsule and the diameters of the nuclear bag (*IFb*) and nuclear chain (*IFc*) intrafusal muscle fibers. Gamma efferent axons (*Ge*) and extrafusal muscle fibers are identified. Modified DeCastro silver stain. (courtesy of Dr. W. R. Kennedy, University of Minnesota).

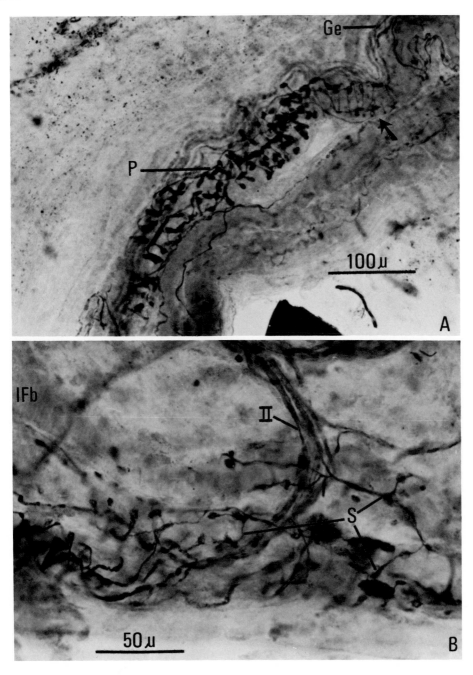

FIG. 9–13. Human intercostal neuromuscular spindles with two types of sensory endings. *A.* Primary (*P*, annulospiral) ending on each intrafusal muscle fiber has a thick axon with many side branches and terminal enlargements. The slender coil (*arrow*) is not seen on all primary endings. Adjacent gamma efferent axons (*Ge*) are identified. *B.* Secondary (*S*, flower-spray) endings found on both bag and chainintrafusal muscle fibers (*IFb*). Architecture is similar to that of primary ending except for the slender, delicate nature of the branches. The axon related to this secondary ending is identified (*II*). Modified DeCastro silver stain. (courtesy of Dr. W. R. Kennedy, University of Minnesota).

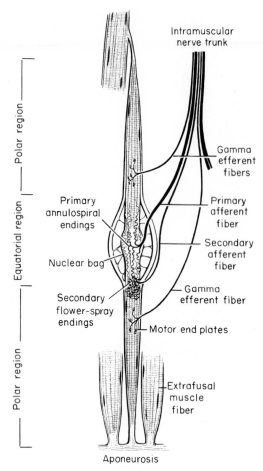

Intramuscular
nerve trunk

Gamma
efferent
fibers

Primary
annulospiral
endings

Primary
afferent
fiber

Secondary
afferent
fiber

Nuclear bag

Secondary
flower-spray
endings

Gamma
efferent fiber

Motor end plates

Extrafusal
muscle
fiber

Aponeurosis

Polar region — Equatorial region — Polar region

Fig. 9–14. Diagram of a nuclear-bag intrafusal muscle fiber within a neuromuscular spindle. The intrinsic sensory and motor nerve endings on the spindle fiber are identified, and the polar and equatorial regions are indicated on the *left*. Normally there are two to ten small and large intrafusal fibers within each neuromuscular spindle. (after Barker, '48.)

These are called secondary, flower-spray, or myotube endings (Fig. 9–13*B*). Both the primary and secondary endings are terminals of sensory fibers, for they degenerate after section of the appropriate dorsal roots. Small fusimotor fibers (gamma efferents) 3 to 7 micra in diameter enter each spindle and terminate. Two kinds of gamma fiber endings upon the intrafusal muscle fibers have been described. Some end as diffuse, multi-terminal "trail fibers", while others terminate in minia-

ture "end plates" (Fig. 9–16). Barker ('67) maintains that both nuclear bag and nuclear chain muscle fibers usually receive each type of gamma motor endings. Boyd ('62) maintains that nuclear bag intrafusal fibers usually receive "plate endings", and nuclear chain muscle fibers usually receive "trail endings". Physiological evidence indicates that the two types of gamma axon terminations subserve different spindle functions, and thereby alter the nerve impulses that are generated subsequently by primary and secondary afferent endings of the neuromuscular spindle. Mixed B fibers have been described that innervate both intrafusal and extrafusal muscle fibers (Bessou et al., '63; Adal and Barker, '65).

As noted above, the contraction of intrafusal muscle fibers by gamma efferent nerves induces discharges in the afferent nerves from the spindle. The fusimotor fibers thus reset the spindle mechanism and thereby regulate the sensitivity of the receptor. Contraction of the spindle fibers contributes nothing per se to the contractile tension of the muscle (Patton, '61). In addition, the neuromuscular spindles receive a variable number of fine unmyelinated fibers which appear to be vasomotor to the small vessels within the spindle. Other fine nerve fibers ramify in the capsule and probably mediate pain impulses.

The recorded dimensions of human muscle spindles fluctuate enormously, the extremes for length being 0.05 and 13 mm. The usual length is 2 to 4 mm. The spindles have been found in practically all muscles and are more numerous in the extremities than in the trunk muscles. They are especially abundant in the small muscles of the hand and foot (lumbricals). Fewer muscle spindles are present in the human extraocular eye muscles. Merrillees et al. ('50) found 71 spindles in a single muscle, while Cooper and Daniel ('49) counted 46 spindles in the inferior rectus muscle. In the goat, Cooper et al. ('51) found 120 muscle spindles in a single muscle. Greene and Jampel ('66) found a maximum of six spindles in a

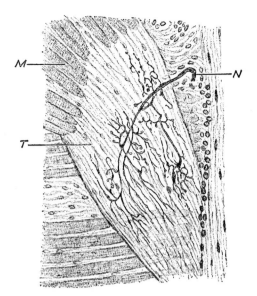

Fig. 9–15. Neurotendinous organ from 6-month human fetus. *M*, Muscle fibers; *N*, nerve fiber; *T*, tendon fibers (after Tello, '22).

single eye muscle of the monkey. In the monkey the spindles were located near the origin of the muscle, or among the small diameter muscle fibers on the outer rim of the muscle. Each spindle contained two to eight intrafusal muscle fibers surrounded by a thin capsule. The intrafusal fibers were 10 micra in diameter, and varied in length from 200 to 450 micra. The diameters of the intrafusal and extrafusal fibers of eye muscles are not as great as in other skeletal muscles, and the surrounding capsules are very thin. For this reason the spindles in the eye muscles are less prominent. Proprioceptive (i.e., stretch) impulses from the extraocular eye muscles of the lamb have been shown to traverse the axons of the ophthalmic nerve, and cells of the trigeminal ganglion enroute to the central nervous system (Manni et al., '66).

Information conveyed centrally from the neuromuscular spindles play a major role in the reflex regulation of muscle tonus and does not reach consciousness. Collaterals from these sensory fibers have monosynaptic junctions with alpha motor neurons while gamma neurons do not (Figs. 12–17, 13–3 and 13–5). More than

one internuncial neuron is interposed between these collaterals and the gamma efferent neurons as shown in Figure 12–17. If the primary fiber (1A) from the annulospiral ending is stimulated there is a central delay of 2 milliseconds before the gamma efferent fiber response is recorded. Hence the annulospiral collaterals use central internuncial neurons to influence gamma efferent neurons, and such connections are polysynaptic (Matthews, '64).

The *neurotendinous organs (of Golgi)* are spindle-shaped structures most commonly found at the junction of muscle and tendon, but occasionally also in the muscular septa and sheaths (Fig. 9–15). They have been demonstrated in practically all muscles. The spindle consists of several tendon fascicles surrounded by a delicate connective tissue capsule. As a rule it is supplied by one, occasionally two or three, myelinated nerve fibers. On penetrating the spindle, the nerve fiber loses its endoneural sheath, which becomes continuous with the capsule, and divides into primary, secondary, and tertiary branches which still retain their myelin sheath. The sensory fibers then split into numerous unmyelinated branches which wind between and around the tendon bundles, giving off side branchlets which again divide repeatedly. All these terminal branches show numerous flat leaflike expansions, the whole ramification appearing as a delicate net enveloping the tendon bundles. In man these spindles have a length of about 1.0 mm, and a thickness of about 100 micra.

Electron microscope studies have demonstrated capillaries both outside and inside the capsule of the tendon organ. Myelinated and unmyelinated endings with many mitochondria are scattered among the collagen filaments within the organ. The collagen filaments and plasma membrane of the nerve endings usually are separated by very thin processes of Schwann cell cytoplasm (Merrillees, '62). The afferent nerve fibers from tendon organ receptors are large fibers of about 12 micra diameter. The tendon organ has a higher threshold to stretch than does the annulospiral ending of the neuromuscular spindle. However, the tendon organ discharges afferent volleys in response to both tendon stretch and muscle contraction. Both muscle and tendon receptors have the physiological properties of large, fast-conducting nerve fibers. In order to distinguish between these two subgroups, the annulospiral afferent nerves are designated as Group 1A, while the tendon organ afferents are referred to as 1B nerve fibers.

Besides the neuromuscular and neurotendinous organs, muscle and tendon have a variety of other sensory structures: free nerve endings, end bulbs, and Pacinian corpuscles. The latter are especially numerous in tendons.

RELATION OF RECEPTORS TO SENSORY MODALITIES

It is generally maintained, though not proven, that each type of receptor is activated by only one kind of physical or chemical change and hence is associated with only one kind of sensory modality. The problem of relating the various receptors to their specific sensory modalities has been an exceedingly difficult one and many important details are still to be elucidated.

It seems probable that painful impulses are received by the diffuse cutaneous end arborizations. Not only would their universal presence and unspecialized terminals indicate this, but also their sole presence in places where stimuli give rise to pain only (e.g., the tympanic membrane of the ear, the cornea of the eye, and the pulp of the teeth). Evidence suggests that the intraepithelial endings derived from fine myelinated fibers are related to sharply localized pain, while poorly localized pain is represented by the subepidermal terminations of unmyelinated fibers (Woolard, '35). It is probable, however, that the intraepithelial fibers also mediate a form of tactile sensibility (Waterston, '33).

Touch is represented by the endings in hair follicles, Meissner's corpuscles, and probably by tactile discs and some other intraepithelial endings. The peritrichial endings, stimulated by movements of the hair give rise to a sensibility quite delicate and discriminative, yet having a marked affective tone. Shaving greatly reduces the sensibility to touch. On the hairless parts of the body tactile stimuli are received primarily by the corpuscles of Meissner, which are probably the chief sense organs of discriminative touch.

The receptors for temperature are not well known, but they are probably end bulbs of various kinds. Possibly some are diffuse endings. It is known that the margin of the cornea is sensitive only to cold and pain, and is provided only with diffuse endings and end bulbs of Krause. Hence the latter and similar subcutaneous end bulbs are believed to be receptors for cold. In the same way, the diffuse unencapsulated nerve endings are believed to be related to warmth.

The different parts of the body surface vary considerably as to their capacity for affective and discriminative sensibility. The skin of the hand and fingers is particularly sensitive, and provides a variety of exteroceptive impulses that are integrated in the cerebral cortex. In other regions such as the back, abdomen, and especially the genitalia, affective sensibility predominates, to the partial exclusion of discriminative aspects of sensation.

The corpuscles of Pacini are found in both deep subcutaneous and visceral structures. Their form and position indicate that they are stimulated by deep pressure and perhaps by vibratory stimuli. It is probable that other lamellated corpuscles, such as those of Golgi-Mazzoni, have a similar function.

The proprioceptive stimuli of position and movement are initiated by the constant or varying tension states of the skeletal muscles, and their tendons, and by the movements of the joints. The changes in tension and pressure are received by the Pacinian and unencapsulated corpuscles found in the joint capsules, ligaments, and periosteum (Fig. 9–7). Such afferent inputs are transmitted to cortical levels where they become utilized to formulate kinesthetic sense (conscious proprioception or kinesthesis). On the other hand, proprioceptive impulses from neuromuscular and tendon spindles are used for regulation of the spinal myotatic reflex, or via cerebellar pathways to regulate muscle tonus and synergy (i.e., such sensory inputs are for subcortical reflex control of skeletal muscle). The subcortical regulation of muscle tone and posture thus provides a background of muscle tone upon which discrete cortical (voluntary) activity, such as locomotion and fine finger movements, are based.

There is much that is still obscure about visceral sensibility. It is known that the viscera are insensitive to many mechanical and chemical stimuli, yet they may be the source of intense pain as well as of the organic sensations of hunger, thirst, and so on. Visceral pain is due mainly to either distension or spasm of the muscle coats. Hence the intramuscular diffuse nerve endings appear to be the receptors for these stimuli (Fig. 9–3). The blood vessels also may give rise to painful sensation, which is likewise due to muscular spasms in their walls and to the resulting stimulation of similar diffuse endings. The totality of stimuli, constantly initiated by these diffuse visceral receptors during normal and abnormal function, probably gives rise to the general affective sensibility of internal well-being or of malaise.

Referred pain. One peculiarity of visceral pain is that painful visceral stimuli are often "felt" in the corresponding somatic segment, or segments of the external body wall, a phenomenon known as "referred pain." Centrally the receptive nuclei for somatic and visceral pain impulses are associated closely within the dorsal gray column of the spinal cord. For this reason, referred pain is most likely due to central mechanisms within the spinal cord, although the precise neurons involved have not been ascertained. A common explanation is that the constant bombardment of pain impulses, from a diseased viscus, lowers the threshold of stimulation of adjacent central (somatic) relay neurons. Normally these relay neurons are concerned with somatic sensations and not concerned with transmission of visceral pain. As a result, normal incoming somatic sensory impulses that terminate in this "sensitized" neuron pool now are relayed to higher centers, where they are misinterpreted as painful stimuli coming from body surfaces.

Sinclair et al. ('48) have suggested that the production of referred pain may be due to the branching of the sensory fibers which conduct painful impulses. One limb of a branched axon goes to the visceral site where the disturbance originates, while others go to the peripheral soma to which the pain is referred.

Referred pains correspond to the dermatomal distribution of a spinal nerve, not to the distribution of a peripheral nerve. The following are some classical examples of a diseased viscus that causes pain to be referred to the overlying soma and dermatome: diaphragm referred to dermatome C4; heart referred to dermatomes C8 to T8; bladder referred to dermatomes T1 to 10; stomach referred to dermatomes T6 to 9; intestine referred to dermatomes T7 to 10; testes, prostate, and uterus referred to dermatomes T10 to 12; kidneys referred to dermatomes T11 to L1; and rectum referred to dermatomes S2 to 4 (Figs. 10–1, 10–7 and 10–8).

EFFECTORS

The endings of the efferent peripheral fibers in the effector organs of the body fall into two groups: somatic efferent and visceral efferent. The somatic efferent terminations represent the motor terminals of myelinated axons whose cell bodies are located in the anterior horn of the spinal cord. These fibers go directly to the skeletal muscles. The visceral endings are terminals of unmyelinated fibers which arise from cells of the various autonomic ganglia. These fibers supply the heart (cardiomotor), visceral muscle (visceromotor), blood vessels (vasomotor), hair

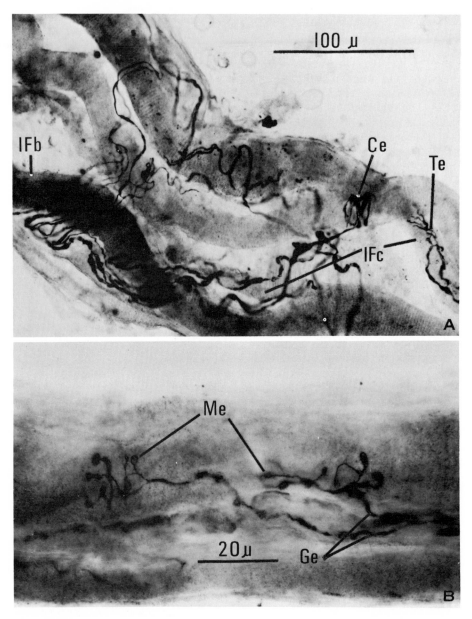

Fig. 9-16. Human intercostal neuromuscular spindle. *A*. Gamma efferent axons near sensory area that demonstrate trail (*Te*) and coiled (*Ce*) endings. In other sections these axons and endings are found on bag (*IFb*) and chain (*IFc*) intrafusal muscle fibers. *B*. Gamma efferent (*Ge*) motor end plates (*Me*) found toward capsular pole of spindle. Pairs of end plates occur frequently. Here two end plates are seen on one bag fiber. Modified DeCastro silver stain. (courtesy of Dr. W. R. Kennedy, University of Minnesota).

(pilomotor), salivary and digestive glands (secretory), and sweat glands (sudomotor).

Somatic Effectors. The somatic efferent fibers terminate upon the skeletal muscle fibers in small, flattened oval expansions, the *motor end plates* or myoneural junction (Figs. 6-2*G* and 9-16). Motor end plates are located in narrow zones in a given muscle. Each end plate always lies in the midportion of the fiber

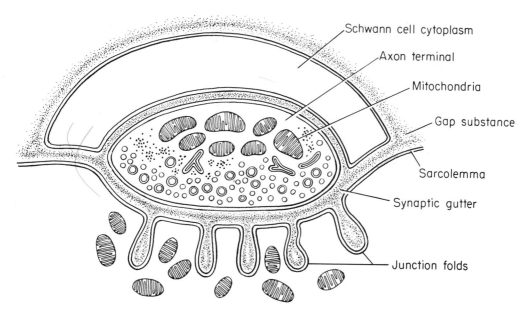

Schwann cell cytoplasm

Axon terminal

Mitochondria

Gap substance

Sarcolemma

Synaptic gutter

Junction folds

Fig. 9–17. Diagram of motor ending on a skeletal muscle fiber as seen in transverse section by electron microscopy. The mitochondria are presumed to play an active role in the synthesis of acetylcholine, whereas the numerous smaller vesicles shown in this diagram may represent a bound state of acetylcholine. Small clusters of dark granules also are found in the axon terminal. Note the separation of axon. Schwann cell, and muscle membranes by gap substance. (modified from Robertson, '56, '60, and from Couteaux, '58).

it supplies. Larger muscle fibers have larger end plates, and in the rabbit and monkey the diameters of end plates differ in "red" and "white" muscle fibers (Coers and Woolf, '59). For example, in red extrafusal fibers the end plates are significantly larger. These muscle fibers are known to be slow reacting and capable of sustained contraction. According to Coers ('55) the mean diameter of adult human limb motor end plates is 32.2 micra. In man most of the end plates have a length of 40 to 60 micra. The myelinated fibers, in their course to the muscle, repeatedly divide, and branch even more extensively as they spread out within the fleshy belly of the muscle. In this manner a single motor nerve fiber provides end plates to a variable number of the large extrafusal muscle fibers (Fig. 6–2G). Each terminal nerve branch loses its myelin sheath as it approaches the sarcolemma of a muscle fiber, while the Schwann cell sheath continues to invest even the smallest terminals. Electron microscopy has confirmed and elucidated many of the structural features of the motor end plate (Reger, '55, '57; Robertson, '56, '60; Couteaux, '58, Zacks, '64). The axoplasm of the small nerve branches contains numerous mitochondria, vesicles, round and oval profiles, small granular elements, and tubular-appearing components of the endoplasmic reticulum. Such nerve terminals do not lie within the sarcoplasm of the muscle fiber, as believed previously, but occupy troughs which are hollowed out by infoldings of the sarcolemma (Fig. 9–17). The floor of the trough is usually corrugated by numerous secondary invaginations of the sarcoplasm (junctional folds). The entire depressed area is called a "synaptic gutter." Within the gutter the axon membrane and sarcolemma remain as discrete structures separated by a gap, or synaptic cleft. The whole ending is covered over by Schwann cell cytoplasm. The membranes of the Schwann cell, axon, and sarcolemma are all separated from each other by a thin layer of moderately electron dense material (gap sub-

FIG. 9–18. Motor nerve terminations in the smooth muscle bands of a bronchus. Rabbit. *tfi*, Terminal fibrils (Larsell and Dow, '33).

stance) which also extends out into the extracellular space around the entire ending.

The synaptic vesicles within the axon terminals of the end plate are presumed to represent the storage form of acetylcholine (Fig. 9–17). With the arrival of a nerve impulse, large numbers of ACH quanta are released through the presynaptic membrane into the synaptic gutter. The liberated acetylcholine is absorbed at selective postsynaptic receptor sites, and alters the permeability of the postsynaptic (sarcolemmal) membrane of the muscle fiber. Depolarization and a muscle action potential result from this series of events. That acetylcholine is the chemical transmitter at motor end plates is supported by several pieces of evidence. Acetylcholine occurs widely in the human nervous system, and is released during nerve stimulation. The enzyme acetylcholinesterase is present in the subneural complex of the motor end plate, and rapidly inactivates released acetylcholine. A large number of microscopic histochemical technics have been used to localize the enzymes of the motor end plate in man and numerous animals. These have been reviewed extensively by McLennan ('63)

and Zacks ('64). If an inadequate amount of acetylcholine is produced (or it is destroyed too rapidly by acetylcholinesterase) muscle contraction is altered and the involved muscles are prone to early fatigue (e.g., myasthenia gravis). If the enzyme acetylcholinesterase is inactivated by anticholinesterase medication (e.g., by neostigmine), the endogenous acetycholine is now preserved at the end plate for longer periods. This rationale when applied to patients with myasthenia gravis often results in a dramatic recovery of muscle strength, and the ability of a muscle to respond to repetitive nerve stimulation.

The axon of one motor neuron supplies a variable number of skeletal muscle fibers. In the larger back muscles (e.g., sacrospinalis, gluteus maximus), a single anterior horn cell may provide motor end plates to over 100 muscle fibers. Each motor neuron to a muscle of the thumb, or an extrinsic eye muscle, may supply only a few skeletal muscle fibers. Namba et al. ('68) have described two kinds of motor endings in the extraocular muscles of man. The superior rectus muscle had both *en plaque* and *en grappe* endings. The levator palpebrae had only *en plaque*

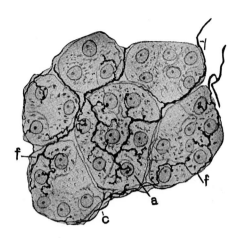

FIG. 9-19. Nerve terminations around and within acini of the pancreas of an adult mouse. c, Periacinous fibers; f, interepithelial and intraepithelial fibers (Castro, '22).

terminals with a mean diameter of 27 micra. As many as 12 *en grappe* endings were found on superior rectus fibers 10 to 20 micra thick. *En grappe* endings had a mean diameter of only 9.6 micra. All the skeletal muscle fibers supplied by one motor neuron and its axon constitute a *motor unit*. A muscle with many motor units for a given number of muscle fibers is capable of more precise movements than a muscle with a few motor units for the same number of muscle fibers. It also follows, that only a few anterior horn cells and motor units are required to maintain reflex muscle tone during periods of rest or sleep. However, many or all motor units may be called into operation when demands are made upon the muscle for maximal contraction.

Visceral Effectors. The unmyelinated autonomic fibers which supply visceral muscle either end in simple arborizations, or first form extensive intramuscular plexuses from which the terminals arise. The terminal fibrils wind between the smooth muscle cells and end in small neurofibrillar thickenings, or delicate loops on the surface of the muscle fibers

(Fig. 9-18). Similar terminals arise from delicate plexuses which surround the tubules or acini of glands, pass between the cells, and terminate upon the plasma membrane of the glandular cells (Fig. 9-19). Terminal endings occupy small troughs in the plasma membranes of both cardiac and smooth muscle fibers, sometimes for long distances. However, no end plates, or specialized endings, have been observed on the terminals of visceral motor fibers by either light or electron microscopy. Groups of tiny axons surrounded by Schwann cell cytoplasm do come into intimate contact with single smooth muscle cells of the small intestine (multiaxonal junctions). In the large intestine (toad) single axons diverge from nerve bundles, and come to lie, free of the Schwann sheath, in shallow grooves in the muscle cell. It is likely that one muscle cell has several widely separated single axon junctions (Roger and Burnstock, '68). Axon terminals have either a predominance of granular or agranular vesicles and numerous mitochondria. A plethora of fine nerve fibers and plexuses have been demonstrated about blood vessels and in a variety of tissues by Falck ('62). He rapidly fixed small bits of tissue by the freeze-dry technic, and exposed the pieces to formaldehyde gas in a closed glass vessel that contained paraformaldehyde. Subsequent paraffin sections, when examined with the fluorescent microscope, revealed an exquisite array of adrenergic nerve fibers and axon terminals. This method has since been used to visualize the course and relations of adrenergic nerve fibers to the smooth muscle within several organs. The meticulous studies of Thaemert ('66, '66a) are equally informative. He has made three dimensional montages from serial section electron micrographs to demonstrate the intricate nerve-muscle fiber relationships in both smooth and cardiac muscle.

CHAPTER 10

Segmental And Peripheral Innervation

SEGMENTAL (RADICULAR) INNERVATION

The "segmental" character of the cord, as evidenced by its spinal nerves, corresponds to the general metamerism of the body, each pair of nerves supplying a body segment (metamere). The ventral roots contain the efferent fibers, which go to the somatic musculature (myotomes) and by way of the autonomic ganglia to the blood vessels (vasoconstrictor), visceral muscle, and glandular epithelium. The dorsal roots contain all the afferent fibers—superficial, deep, and visceral (Fig. 12–17). The cutaneous area supplied by a single dorsal root and its ganglion is called a *dermatome*.

In the adult, the correspondence between neural and body metameres is easily recognized in the trunk region, where each spinal nerve supplies the musculature and cutaneous area of its own segment. Here the dermatomes follow one another consecutively, each forming a band encircling the body from the midposterior to the midanterior line. In the extremities, however, the conditions are more complicated. During development, the metameres migrate distally into the limb buds and arrange themselves parallel to the long axis of the future limb (Fig.

10–1). In each extremity, there is thus formed an axial line along which are placed a number of consecutive segments which have wandered out from the axial portions. The result is that in the trunk and neck portion of the adult the fourth cervical dermatome is in contact with the second thoracic dermatome. For a similar reason, the dermatomes of the first and second lumbar nerves are contiguous anteriorly with the dermatome of the third sacral nerve (Fig. 10–7). The intervening segments have migrated further to form the more distal dermatomes of the extremities (Figs. 10–7 and 10–8). This mode of migration, as well as rotation of the lower extremity, explains the seemingly confused arrangement and sequence of the limb dermatomes (Fig. 10–1*B*).

Sherrington (1893) demonstrated experimentally in the monkey the exact cutaneous areas supplied by the various dorsal roots. Because section of a single root did not produce a marked anesthesia anywhere, he selected a specific root for study and cut two or three adjacent roots above and below. He found that each dermatome overlapped the sensory cutaneous areas of adjacent roots, being coinnervated by the one above and the one below (Fig. 10–2); hence at least three contiguous

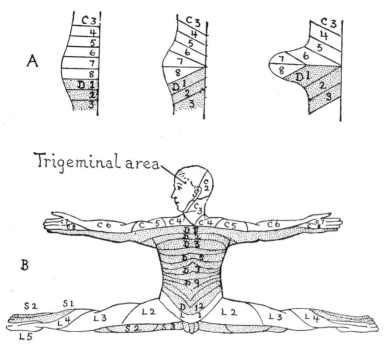

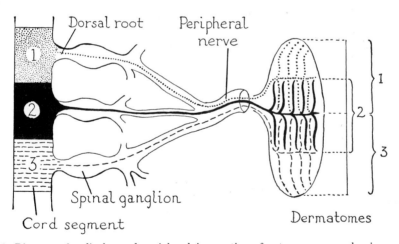

FIG. 10–1. *A*, Schema of migration of metameres during development (after Haymaker, '56). *B*, Segmental arrangement of dermatomes (after Luciani, 1891). *c*, Cervical; *d*, thoracic; *l*, lumbar; *s*, sacral.

FIG. 10–2. Diagram of radicular and peripheral innervation of cutaneous areas showing overlapping of nerve fibers in the dermatomes. (modified from Haymaker, '56.)

roots had to be sectioned to produce a region of complete anesthesia. Pictures similar to those of Sherrington were obtained by irritating single roots or ganglia with strychnine and noting the resulting hypersensitive areas (Dusser de Barenne, '24).

Clinically, Head, ('20) was the first to outline the human dermatomes by studying the areas of cutaneous eruption and hyperalgesia occurring in herpes zoster, a disease which often affects isolated spinal ganglia, and produces vesicular cutaneous eruptions within a single dermatome.

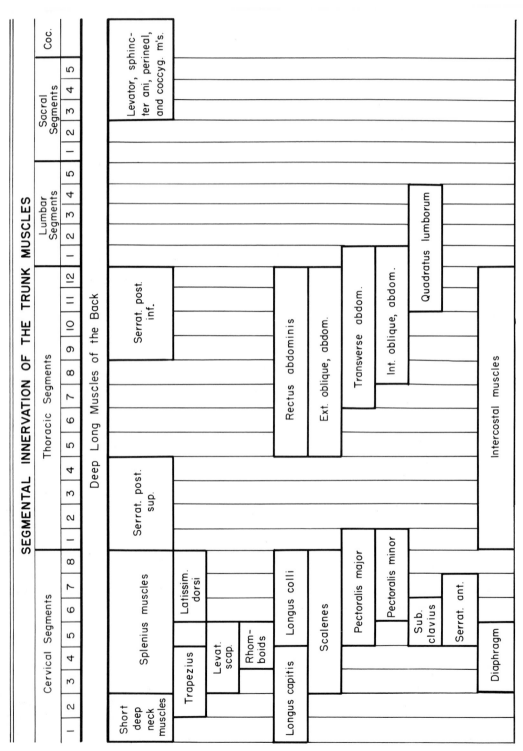

Fɪɢ. 10–3. Segments of spinal cord that contribute somatic motor nerve fibers to individual trunk muscles (after Haymaker, '56).

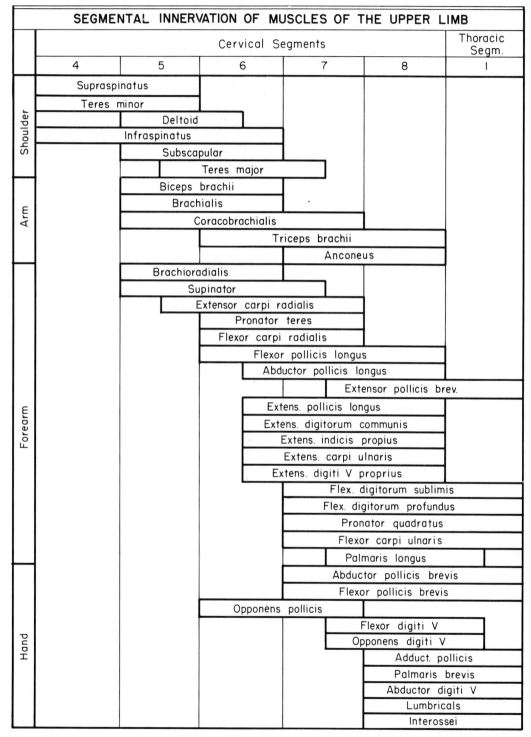

FIG. 10–4. Segments of spinal cord that contribute somatic motor nerve fibers to the individual muscles of shoulder and upper extremity (after Haymaker, '56).

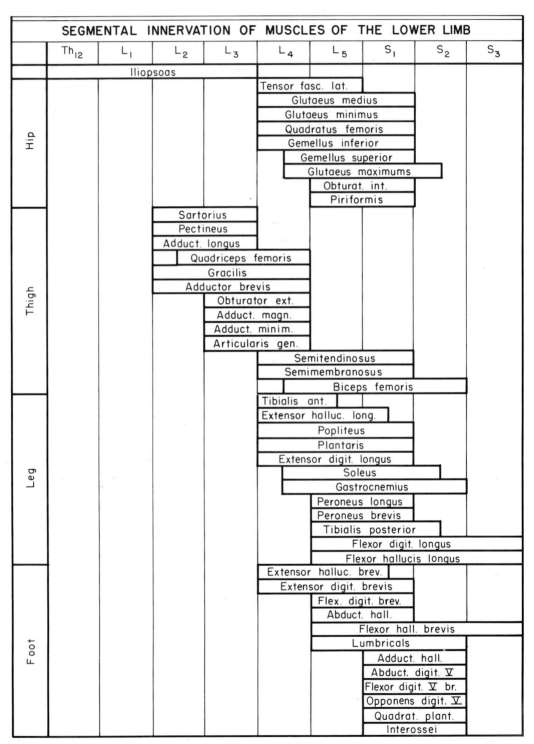

Fig. 10–5. Segments of spinal cord that contribute somatic motor nerve fibers to individual muscles of hip and lower extremity (after Haymaker, '56).

Foerster ('33, '36) has furnished a remarkably complete map of human dermatomes based on numerous resections of dorsal roots for the alleviation of spastic conditions and in cases of root injury due to tumors or other causes. His dermatomal maps correspond closely to those of Head ('20) and show the same overlapping given by Sherrington (1893) for monkeys. Most dermatomes are supplied by fibers of three, occasionally even four, dorsal roots. The only root whose section produces an area of complete anesthesia is that of C2; neither C3 nor the trigeminal nerve invade the back of the head for any extent. It is interesting that the overlapping of adjacent dermatomes is greater for touch than for pain and temperature. The distribution of the human dermatomes is shown in Figs. 10-7 and 10-8.

A somewhat different chart of the human dermatomes was published by Keegan and Garrett ('48), who outlined areas of diminished cutaneous sensibility caused by compression of individual roots. These areas, which they called *primary dermatomes*, did not show any significant overlapping.

The segmental innervation of the skeletal musculature (myotomes) has been worked out in man and animals by: (1) selective stimulation of the ventral roots (Wichmann, '00; Brendler, '68); (2) study of the pathological changes which occur in the anterior horn cells when a ventral root or motor nerve is cut (Fig. 6-1E); or (3) secondary degeneration of peripheral nerve fibers to muscle after central and peripheral lesions. As in the dermatomes, the majority of the muscles, especially those of the extremities, are innervated by two or three, and occasionally even four, ventral roots. Hence injury to a single ventral root may only weaken a muscle or have no apparent effect. Only the very short muscles of the trunk and spinal column and a few others, such as the abductor pollicis, are formed from single myotomes and retain a monosegmental innervation. The peripheral projection of individual spinal cord segments to a specific muscle thus provides a clue to the myotomic origin of skeletal muscle during development. The segmental motor supply to the major trunk and extremity muscles is shown graphically in Figures 10-3, 10-4 and 10-5. Because this information is essential to a full appreciation of muscle physiology, these figures are included for ready reference.

Following is a list of some of the important reflex and visceral activities with the locations in the cord of the anterior horn cells that carry them out.

Movements of the head (by muscles of neck), C1 to C4.

Movements of diaphragm (phrenic center), C3 to C5.

Movements of upper extremity, C5 to T1.

Biceps tendon reflex (flexion of forearm on percussion of biceps tendon), C5 and C6.

Triceps tendon reflex (extension of forearm on percussion of triceps tendon), C6 to C8.

Radial periosteal reflex (flexion of forearm on percussion of distal end of radius), C7 and C8.

Wrist tendon reflexes (flexion of fingers on percussion of wrist tendons), C8 to T1.

Movements of trunk, T1 to T12.

Abdominal superficial reflexes (ipsilateral contraction of subjacent abdominal muscles on stroking skin of upper, middle, and lower abdomen); upper (epigastric), T6 and T7; middle, T8 and T9; lower, T10 to T12.

Movements of lower extremity, L1 to S2.

Cremasteric superficial reflex (elevation of scrotum on stroking skin of inner thigh), T12 to L2.

Genital center for ejaculation, L1 and L2 (smooth muscle); S3 and S4 (skeletal muscles).

Vesical center for retention of urine, T12 to L2.

Patellar tendon reflex or knee jerk (extension of leg on percussion of patellar ligament), L2 to L4.

Gluteal superficial reflex (contraction of glutei on stroking skin over glutei), L4 to S1.

Plantar superficial reflex (flexion of toes on stroking sole of foot), L5 to S2.

Achilles tendon reflex or ankle jerk

(plantar flexion of foot on percussion of Achilles tendon), L5 to S2.

Genital center of erection, S2 to S4.

Vesical center for evacuation of bladder, S3 to S5.

Bulbocavernosus reflex (contraction of bulbocavernosus muscle on pinching penis), S3 to S4.

Anal reflex (contraction of external rectal sphincter on stroking perianal region), S4, S5, and coccygeal.

PERIPHERAL INNERVATION

While each spinal nerve in a general way supplies its own body segment, there is considerable intermixing and anastomosing of adjacent nerve trunks before they reach their peripheral destination. The primary dorsal rami remain relatively distinct, though interconnections are common in the cervical and sacral regions (Pearson et al., '66). The ventral rami, however, form far more elaborate connections. Except for the thoracic nerves, which largely retain their segmental distribution, the cervical and lumbosacral rami innervating the extremities anastomose and branch to form extensive plexuses in which a radical regrouping of fibers occurs. Each of the peripheral nerves arising from these plexuses contains fibers contributed from two, three, four, or even five ventral rami. As a result the cutaneous areas supplied by the peripheral nerves do not correspond with the cutaneous areas supplied by the individual dorsal roots (dermatomes). The peripheral and dermatomal distributions of sensory nerve fibers are contrasted in the anterior and posterior body views shown in Figures 10–7 and 10–8. Similarly, several ventral roots may contribute fibers to a single muscle, and conversely several muscles may receive fibers from a single ventral root. A knowledge of the cutaneous and muscular distribution of the peripheral nerves is of great importance to the neurologist in determining the segmental level of peripheral nerve injuries; hence the more important morphological features are presented briefly. A more complete account will be found in the larger handbooks of anatomy and clinical neurology.

The **dorsal rami** of the spinal nerves innervate the intrinsic dorsal muscles of the back and neck, which constitute the extensor system of the vertebral column, and the overlying skin from vertex to coccyx (Figs 8–1 and 10–8). In the middle of the back the cutaneous area roughly corresponds to that of the underlying muscles, but in the upper and lower portions of the trunk it widens laterally to reach the acromial region above and the region of the great trochanter below. With certain exceptions the dorsal rami have a typical segmental distribution, the field of each overlapping with that of the adjacent segments above and below (Fig. 10–2). Each ramus usually divides into a medial and a lateral branch, both of which may contain sensory and motor fibers, though the lateral branches of the cervical rami are purely motor in character. Deviations are found in the upper two cervical and in the lumbosacral rami. The first or *suboccipital* nerve is purely motor and terminates in the short posterior muscles of the head (rectus capitis and obliquus capitis). The main branch of the second cervical ramus, known as the *greater occipital* nerve, ascends to the region of the superior nuchal line, where it becomes subcutaneous, and supplies the scalp on the back of the head to the vertex, occasionally extending as far as the coronal suture (Fig. 10–8). The nerve is joined by a filament from the third cervical ramus. The lateral branches of the upper three lumbar and upper three sacral rami send cutaneous twigs which supply the upper part of the gluteal area, extending laterally to the region of the great trochanter. These branches are known as the *superior* (lumbar) and *medial* (sacral) *clunial nerves* (Fig. 10–8).

The **ventral rami** of the spinal nerves supply the ventrolateral muscles and the skin of the trunk, as well as the extremities. (Fig. 8–1). With the exception of most thoracic nerves, the ventral rami of adjacent nerves unite and anastomose to form the cervical, brachial, and lumbosacral plexuses.

Cervical Plexus. The cervical plexus is formed from the ventral rami of the four upper cervical nerves. It furnishes cutaneous nerves for the ventrolateral portions of the neck and shoulder and for the lateral portions of the back of the head. The muscular branches supply the deep cervical muscles of the spinal column, the infrahyoid muscles, and the diaphragm. They also aid in the innervation of the trapezius (nerves C1–4) and sternocleidomastoid muscles, which are chiefly supplied by the accessory nerve (N. XI).

The *lesser occipital* nerve (C2 and C3) is distributed to the upper pole of the pinna and to the lateral area on the back of the head, overlapping only slightly the field of the greater occipital nerve (Fig. 10–8). The *great auricular nerve* (C2 and C3) supplies the larger, lower portion of the pinna and the skin over the angle of the mandible. The *transverse colli* (C2 and C3) innervates the ventral and lateral parts of the neck from chin to sternum (supra- and infrahyoid region). The *supraclavicular nerves* (C3 and C4), which have a variable number of branches, are distributed to the shoulder, the most lateral regions of the neck, and the upper part of the breast, where their end branches overlap with those of the second intercostal nerve (Figs. 10–7 and 10–8).

The chief muscular nerve is the *phrenic*, which supplies the diaphragm and is derived mainly from C4, but receives smaller contributions from C3 or C5, or from both (Fig. 10–6). It frequently receives an anastomotic branch from the subclavian nerve of the brachial plexus, which enters the phrenic at a variable height. Hence in high lesions of the phrenic nerve, paralysis of the diaphragm may not be complete. The deep cervical muscles are innervated by direct segmental branches from the ventral rami, as indicated in Figure 10–3.

The hyoid muscles, except those supplied by the cranial nerves, are innervated by twigs from C1 to C3. These twigs unite into a common trunk known as the *ansa cervicalis*. The geniohyoid and thyrohyoid are supplied entirely from C1; the sternohyoid, sternothyroid, and omohyoid, from C2 and C3, as motor twigs from the ansa cervicalis. The cervical plexus also aids in the innervation of the sternocleidomastoid and trapezius muscles. The sternocleidomastoid is supplied mainly by the accessory nerve, with sensory fibers that join it through a branch of C2. The trapezius receives its major motor contributions from the accessory nerve, and additional motor fibers from C2, 3 and 4. Brendler ('68) also demonstrated that C1 may contribute motor fibers to the upper trapezius, while the accessory nerve sends most of the motor fibers to the middle and lower portions of the muscle. These motor and sensory fibers form one or more bundles, and may be intermixed with the supraclavicular nerves.

Paralysis of the short segmental nerves as a result of peripheral nerve injury is relatively rare and usually is associated with involvement of the spinal cord. However, the trapezius and sternocleidomastoid muscles frequently are involved as a result of penetrating stab and bullet wounds of the posterior triangle which injure the accessory nerve. These muscles are superficially located, and palpable so that their respective muscle actions are of diagnostic value. The sternocleidomastoid and trapezius muscles may be involved along with the movements of other axial and limb muscles in association with disease of the basal ganglia. One particularly troublesome disorder is the condition of *torticollis*. Due to muscle spasm the contracted muscle stands out as a large cord, and the head usually is involuntarily rotated toward the normal side. This awkward position may be maintained for long periods of time. Spasmodic torticollis may be associated with early extrapyramidal disease or with neuroses. In the latter cases it is often difficult to distinguish between the functional and purely organic aspects of the disorder. Emotional stress usually aggravates these involuntary muscle movements. Several procedures have been devised to relieve torticollis (e.g., cutting the accessory nerve intra- and extracranially; sectioning ventral roots C1–3; and severing the sternocleidomastoid muscle).

The Brachial Plexus. The nerves supplying the upper extremity and forming the brachial plexus are derived as a rule

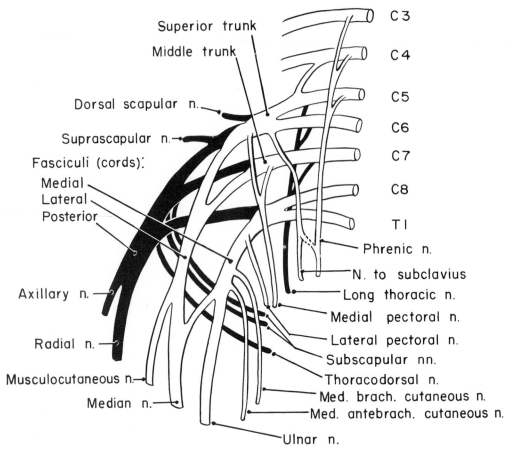

Fɪɢ. 10-6. Diagram of brachial plexus. Cords and peripheral nerves formed by the anterior divisions of ventral primary rami of spinal nerves are *white*. The posterior cord and peripheral nerves formed by the posterior divisions of ventral primary rami of spinal nerves are *black*.

from the ventral rami of the four lower cervical and the first thoracic nerves, with a small contribution from the fourth cervical (Fig. 10-6). There are, however, considerable variations. If the contribution from the fourth cervical is strong and that of the first thoracic negligible, the plexus belongs to the *prefixed* type. It is called *postfixed* when the fourth cervical does not participate at all, but the first thoracic makes a strong contribution and the second thoracic sends a branch. Between these extremes there are many intermediate conditions, depending on the stronger or weaker participation of the fourth cervical, on the one hand, and the second thoracic, on the other. These variations are dependent on embryological factors. The limb buds of both arms and legs may vary

in longitudinal extent and especially in their relative position to the neuraxis. The more cephalic the position of the limbs, the more cephalic will be the nerves contributing to the plexus, and vice versa.

The ventral rami supplying the plexus give rise to three *primary trunks:* C5 and C6 unite to form the *superior trunk;* C8 and T1 form the *inferior trunk;* and C7 is continued as the *medial trunk*. Each trunk splits into a dorsal and a ventral division. The dorsal divisions of all three trunks fuse to form the *posterior cord*, which is situated behind the axillary artery. The ventral divisions of the superior and medial trunk form the *lateral cord*, while the ventral division of the inferior trunk is continued as the *medial cord* (Fig. 10-6).

Many   of   the   nerves   supplying   the

shoulder muscles are given off directly from the ventral rami, or from the primary trunks and their branches before these unite to form the secondary cords. Here also dorsal and ventral nerves are formed. Thus the *dorsal scapular* nerve supplying the rhomboids arises from the dorsal surface of C5, and the *long thoracic* nerve to the serratus anterior arises from the dorsal surface of C5, C6, and C7. From the superior trunk the *suprascapular* nerve (C4, C5, and C6) for the supraspinatus and infraspinatus emerges dorsally, and the small nerve to the subclavius (C5 and C6) arises ventrally. The roots of the *medial and lateral pectoral* nerves (C5 to T1), which innervate the pectoralis major and minor, arise in part from the ventral surface of the superior and medial trunks, and in part from the medial cord (Fig. 10–6).

The three large peripheral nerves of the forearm (radial, median, and ulnar) are formed in the following manner. The posterior cord, which receives contributions from all the plexus nerves, gives off the *thoracodorsal* (C6 to C8) and the *subscapular* nerves (C5 to C8), the former supplying the latissimus dorsi, the latter innervating the teres major and subcapularis. Then the posterior cord splits into its two terminal branches, the larger *radial* nerve and the smaller *axillary* nerve. The lateral and medial cords each split into two branches, thus forming four nerve trunks. The two middle branches, one from the lateral cord and one from the medial cord, unite to form the *median* nerve. The outer branch, derived from the lateral cord, becomes the *musculocutaneous nerve.* The large innermost branch, derived from the medial cord, gives off the purely sensory *medial brachial cutaneous* and *medial antebrachial cutaneous* nerves and is then continued as the *ulnar nerve* (Fig. 10–6).

A brief reference to embryological conditions will aid in explaining the formation of the plexus. During early development the primitive muscle mass of the limb is split into posterior and anterior layers, which are separated by the anlage of the humerus. The primary ventral nerve

rami invading the limb likewise split into posterior and anterior branches to supply corresponding muscles and the overlying skin. Within the primitive musculature, many simple muscles fuse to form larger and more complex ones and become supplied by two or more spinal nerves; as a result, the nerve fibers and plexuses interlace (Fig. 10–6). Such fusion usually occurs within the posterior or the anterior musculature, and the muscles are innervated respectively by posterior or anterior divisions of the nerves. However, at the cephalic (preaxial) and the caudal (postaxial) borders of the limb, some muscles may be derived from both the posterior and the anterior musculature. These are supplied by fibers from both posterior and anterior nerves. A well-known example is the brachialis muscle, which receives branches from the radial and musculocutaneous nerves. Thus the plexus primitively shows a division into posterior and anterior plates. The posterior innervates the posterior or extensor half of the arm and the posterior shoulder muscles; the anterior supplies the volar or flexor half and the anterior muscles of the shoulder. The nerves arising from the posterior plate are the dorsal scapular, long thoracic, suprascapular, subscapular, thoracodorsal, axillary, and radial (black in Fig. 10–6). Those from the anterior plate include the subclavius, pectoral, musculocutaneous, median, and ulnar, as well as the purely sensory medial brachial and medial antebrachial cutaneous nerves.

Following is a summary of the peripheral distribution of the principal upper extremity nerves. The cutaneous areas of each nerve are shown in Figures 10–7 and 10–8. In their peripheral courses, some of the nerves of both the upper and lower extremity are particularly prone to trauma against bone, space occupying lesions, or entrapment by fibrous tissue related to either muscles, adjacent tendons, or ligaments and fascia (see, Kopell and Thompson, '63). Sensory and motor symptoms that accompany such neuropathies depend on whether one is dealing with primarily motor or sensory nerves.

The **axillary nerve** supplies motor

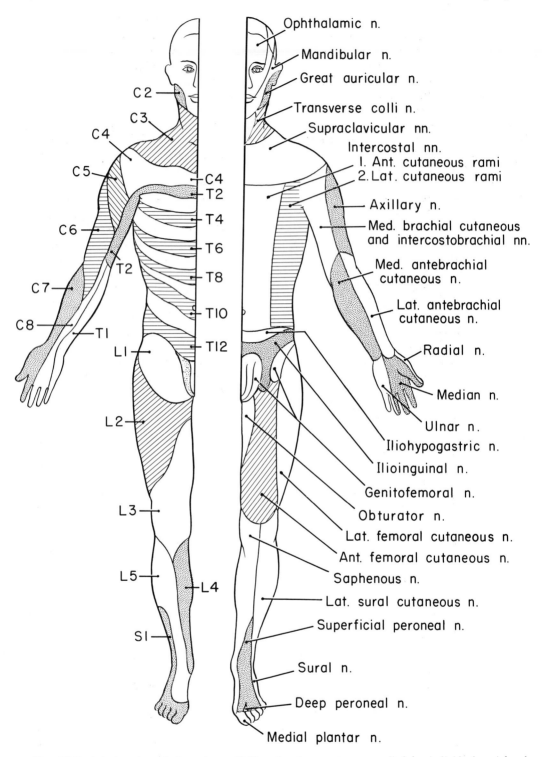

Fig. 10–7. Anterior view of dermatomes (*left*) and cutaneous areas supplied by individual peripheral nerves (*right*).

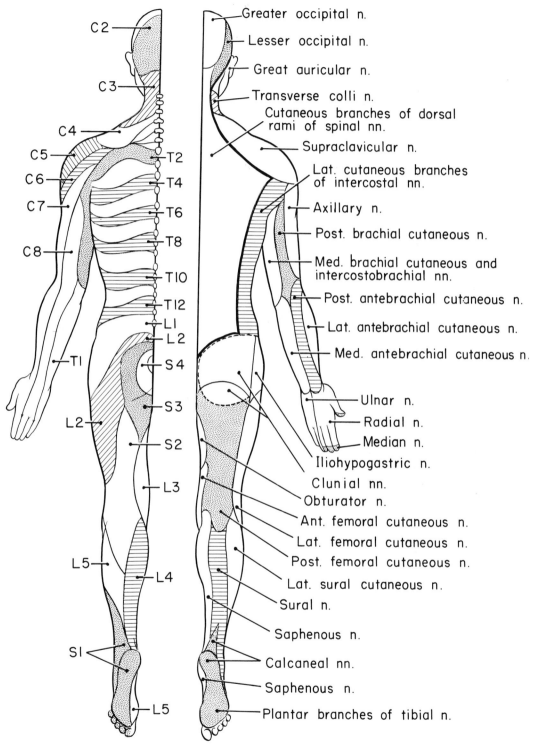

FIG. 10–8. Posterior view of dermatomes (*left*) and cutaneous areas supplied by individual peripheral nerves (*right*).

branches to the deltoid and teres minor muscles and sends the *lateral brachial cutaneous* nerve to the skin of the upper outer surface of the arm, mainly in the deltoid region. After complete section of the axillary nerve, the deltoid muscle is paralyzed and abduction without external rotation is practically impossible. In time deltoid atrophy leads to loss of the round contour normally present at the shoulder. The sensory loss is less extensive, owing to the overlap of neighboring cutaneous nerves.

The **radial nerve** (C5 to T1) supplies motor branches to the triceps muscle and all the extensor muscles of the elbow, hands, and fingers, and to the brachioradialis, supinator, and abductor pollicis longus. In addition, it usually sends a twig to the brachialis. Its cutaneous branches, all distributed to the posterior surface of the extremity, are the *posterior brachial cutaneous nerve* to the arm, the *posterior antebrachial cutaneous* to the forearm, and the *superficial radial nerve* to the radial half of the dorsum of the hand and fingers as far as the distal interphalangeal joints (Fig. 10–8). The segmental innervation of the muscles supplied by the radial nerve is indicated in Figure 10–4.

Injuries of the radial nerve give variable symptoms according to the location of the lesion. Complete section of the nerve above all its branches produces inability to extend the elbow, wrist, fingers, and thumb; wrist drop is the most striking feature. The sensory loss is most marked on the dorsum of the hand and thumb in the territory supplied by the superficial ramus. The anesthesia is negligible on the arm, but usually is present in a narrow strip on the dorsal surface of the forearm from elbow to wrist. The limited sensory loss is due to overlap by the adjacent cutaneous nerves. The most vulnerable points of the radial nerve are its bony relations in the middle third of the humerus and over the lateral epicondyle; the deep branch of the radial nerve in the supinator muscle; and an anomalous intramuscular course of the superficial radial nerve in the forearm.

The **musculocutaneous nerve** (C5 to C7) sends muscular branches to the coracobrachialis, biceps, and brachialis, and continues as the *lateral antebrachial cutaneous* nerve to supply the radial half of the forearm, on both posterior and volar surfaces (Figs. 10–7 and 10–8). In complete section of the nerve, flexion and supination of the forearm are weakened. The lateral portion of the brachialis may be spared since it receives, as a rule, a branch from the radial nerve, and in addition flexion can still be produced by the brachioradialis. The sensory loss is variable in extent. It is poorly defined posteriorly, owing to overlap with the posterior antebrachial cutaneous nerve of the radial. On the volar side, it is more extensive and more nearly approximates the territory supplied by the nerve.

The **median nerve** (C6 to T1, sometimes C5) supplies all the muscles on the volar surface of the forearm except the flexor carpi ulnaris and the ulnar head of the flexor digitorum profundis. In the hand its branches go to the outer lumbricals (I and II) and to the muscles of the thenar eminence, except the adductor pollicis and deep head of the flexor pollicis brevis. The sensory innervation is limited practically to the hand; it comprises the volar surface of the thumb, index, and middle fingers; the radial half of the fourth finger; and corresponding portions of the palm (Fig. 10–7). Posteriorly the nerve supplies the distal phalanx of the index and middle fingers and the radial half of the fourth finger. An inconstant *palmar* branch is distributed to the radial half of the volar surface of the wrist, but this area is usually completely overlapped by the antebrachial branch of the musculocutaneous nerve. The flexor and pronator muscles supplied by the motor branches of the median nerve have a segmental innervation, as indicated in Figure 10–4.

Injury to the nerve along its course in the arm affects all its branches. Complete interruption causes severe impairment of pronation of the forearm and weakened flexion at the wrist. The wasting of the thenar eminence and the abnormal position of the thumb give the hand a characteristic appearance after median nerve injury. Normally the thumb is partially rotated and its metacarpal bone is in a more volar plane than the other metacarpals. In injury of the median nerve the rotation is lost, and the thumb is extended, so that it now lies in the same plane as the rest of the palm (simian hand).

Flexion of the index finger is practically abolished and is only slightly compensated by the flexor action of the interossei at the metacarpophalangeal joint. The middle finger is more variably affected. In the thumb, flexion of the terminal phalanx is completely lost, as are abduction and opposition. Makeshift movements of opposition, without abduction and rotation, can still be effected by the abductor pollicis and the deep head of the flexor brevis (pseudo-opposition). The motor defects are especially brought out in attempts to make a fist. The fourth and fifth fingers flex, but the thumb and index finger, and to a variable degree the middle finger, remain partially extended.

Disturbances of cutaneous sensibility occur in the area supplied by the nerve (Fig. 10-7). Complete anesthesia, is, however, much smaller in extent and is most constant on the volar surface of the index and middle fingers. The median nerve is prone to injury in deep cuts at the wrist and to entrapment as it passes beneath the transverse carpal ligament in company with the flexor tendons (carpal tunnel syndrome). Nerve compression may follow fractures (carpal and distal radial bones) or occur without external stress. Injuries here, as well as lesions of the nerve anywhere along its course may be accompanied by secondary autonomic system overactivity. Following partial or complete median nerve regeneration an intense, persistent "burning pain" may be found over one or more points of the distal course of the nerve (*causalgia*).

The **ulnar nerve** (C8 and T1) supplies the flexor carpi ulnaris and the ulnar head of the flexor digitorum profundis muscles in the forearm. In the hand, it innervates the adductor pollicis, the deep head of the flexor pollicis brevis, the interossei, the two inner lumbricals, and the muscles of the hypothenar eminence. It gives off three cutaneous branches. The *palmar cutaneous* branch supplies the ulnar half of the volar surface of the wrist, an area extensively overlapped by the medial antebrachial cutaneous nerve (Fig. 10-7). The posterior branch goes to the ulnar half of the dorsum of the hand and all of the little finger, and to the proximal phalanx of the ulnar half of the fourth or ring finger. The *superficial volar* branch supplies the volar surface of the fifth, and the ulnar half of the fourth fingers, and the corresponding ulnar portion of the palm (hypothenar region), (Figs. 10-7 and 10-8). The segmental innervation of muscles supplied by the ulnar nerve is indicated in Figure 10-4.

As in the case of the median nerve, injury to the ulnar nerve in the arm region affects its whole distribution. Flexion of the wrist is weakened, as are flexion of the fourth and fifth fingers and adduction of the thumb. There is marked wasting of the hypothenar muscles and of the interossei. The paralysis of these small muscles is particularly disturbing, for it makes execution of the finger movements required for writing, sewing, and other skilled activities exceedingly difficult. The interossei flex the basal phalanges and extend the middle and distal ones. Hence paralysis of the interossei results in: (1) overextension of the basal phalanges by the extensor digitorum communis, and (2) flexion of the middle and distal phalanges by the flexor digitorum sublimis (claw hand).

Sensory disturbances are variable and depend upon the level of nerve injury. Total anesthesia as a rule is limited to the little finger and the hypothenar region. The ulnar nerve is prone to trauma as it crosses the medial epicondyle of the humerus, and to entrapment as it passes from the wrist to enter the hand.

The **medial antebrachial cutaneous nerve** (C8 and T1) supplies the medial half of the forearm, on both posterior and volar surfaces (Figs. 10-7 and 10-8). The extent of the sensory deficits caused by injury varies in individual cases. On the volar side it often reaches to the middle of the arm. On the posterior surface the sensory deficit is somewhat smaller than the area of supply shown in Figure 10–8.

The **medial brachial cutaneous nerve** (T1) usually is associated with the *intercostobrachial* nerve derived from the second and often from the third thoracic (intercostal) nerves. These two nerves supply the axillary region and the inner surface of the arm, the area being considerably larger on the volar surface than on the posterior surface (Figs. 10–7 and 10–8). The area is overlapped extensively by adjacent cutaneous nerves. Injury to one of the nerves produces negligible symptoms or none at all. In injury of both, the anesthesia is limited to the axillary region and medial surface of the upper arm.

Injuries of the Brachial Plexus. The motor and sensory deficits of plexus lesions vary considerably, depending on the extent of the injury, and on whether the primary trunks or secondary cords are involved. In injury of the trunks the symptoms are segmental in character, and two main syndromes may be recognized; one affects the upper and the other the lower primary trunk. The upper trunk (syndrome of Duchenne-Erb) involves the muscles supplied by C5 and C6, namely the deltoid, biceps, brachialis, brachioradialis, supinator, teres major, teres minor, supraspinatus, and infraspinatus. There is difficulty in elevation and external rotation of the arm, accompanied by a severe loss of flexion and supination of the forearm. Owing to the overlap of adjacent roots, the sensory deficit is as a rule limited to the deltoid region and lateral aspect of the arm.

The lower trunk (syndrome of Klumpke or of Duchenne-Aran) is relatively rare and affects primarily the small muscles of the hand innervated by C8 and T1. (Fig. 10–4). The palmaris longus and the long digital flexors usually are involved; hence the chief disabilities are in the finger and wrist movements. The sensory loss is along the medial aspects of the arm, forearm, and hand. If the preganglionic sympathetic fibers of the first thoracic root are included in the injury, there is drooping of the eyelid, diminution in the size of the pupil, and narrowing of the palpebral fissure (Horner's syndrome, see page 232 and Fig. 13–25).

Injuries of the secondary cords produce symptoms similar to those of peripheral nerves, except that several peripheral nerves are affected at the same time. Thus a lesion of the posterior cord involves the radial and axillary nerves and often the thoracodorsal and subscapular nerves (Fig. 10–6). Interruption of the lateral cord affects the musculocutaneous and the lateral portion of the median nerve. Injury to the medial cord involves the ulnar and the medial portion of the median nerve, as well as the medial brachial and antebrachial cutaneous nerves.

The Lumbosacral Plexus. The plexus innervating the lower extremity is as a rule formed by the primary ventral rami of L1 to S2 and the larger portion of S3; frequently there is a small contributing branch from T12 (Figs. 10–9 and 10–10). As in the case of the brachial plexus, there may be anatomical variations. The plexus is *prefixed* when it is supplied by T12 to S2, and *postfixed* when it is formed from roots L2 to S4. There are also many intermediate forms, but the maximum shift in either direction rarely exceeds the extent of a single spinal nerve. These conditions are determined by the individual variations in the position of the limb buds during development. According to Foerster ('29) prefixed plexuses are rare, since in none of his cases did faradic stimulation of the twelfth thoracic nerve produce a contraction of a single muscle in the lower extremity.

The lumbosacral plexus, excluding the pudendal and coccygeal portions, which are not distributed to the leg, is conveniently subdivided into an upper *lumbar* and a lower *sacral* plexus. The **lumbar plexus** is formed by L1, L2, L3, and the larger part of L4, and there is usually a communicating branch from T12 (Fig.

10–9). The more extensive **sacral plexus** is supplied by the smaller portion of L4 (furcal nerve), which joins L5 to form the large lumbosacral trunk, and by S1, S2, and the greater portion of S3 (Fig. 10–10). Except for the uppermost portion supplied mainly by L1, where the conditions are somewhat obscure, both plexuses show an organization into posterior and anterior divisions. The arrangement is simpler than in the brachial plexus. The undivided lumbosacral primary rami do not form interlacing trunks but split directly into posterior and anterior divisions related respectively to the primitive posterior and anterior musculature of the leg. The peripheral nerves to the extremity are formed by the union of a variable number of either posterior or anterior divisions (Figs. 10–9 and 10–10). In the lumbar plexus, the anterior divisions give rise to the iliohypogastric (anterior branch), ilioinguinal, genitofemoral, and obturator nerves; and the posterior divisions give rise to the iliohypogastric (posterior branch), iliopsoas, femoral, and lateral femoral cutaneous nerves. In the sacral plexus, the anterior divisions furnish the tibial nerve and the nerves to the hamstring, quadratus femoris, obturator internus, and gemelli muscles; the posterior divisions form the common peroneal and the superior and inferior gluteal nerves. The posterior femoral cutaneous nerve, which supplies the back of the thigh, receives fibers from both posterior and anterior divisions. As in the case of the arm, muscles derived from both the posterior and the anterior primitive musculature are innervated by both posterior and anterior divisions. Thus the biceps femoris receives branches from the tibial, as well as peroneal portions of the sciatic nerve.

Following is a summary of the peripheral distribution of the principal nerves of the lower extremity. The cutaneous areas supplied by these nerves are shown in Figures 10–7 and 10–8.

The **obturator nerve** (L2 to L4) supplies the adductor muscles of the thigh and the gracilis muscle; it sends an inconstant branch to the pectineus, which more often is innervated by the femoral nerve. Its cutaneous branch is distributed to the inner surface of the thigh (Figs. 10–7 and 10–8), the area being extensively overlapped by adjacent cutaneous nerves. The segmental innervation of the muscles supplied by the obturator nerve is indicated in Figure 10–5.

In injury of the nerve, adduction of the thigh is weakened severely but not completely lost, since the adductor magnus also receives some fibers from the sciatic nerve. The sensory defects usually involve only a small triangular area of the anatomical field. The obturator nerve is vulnerable to entrapment by the obturator membrane as it passes through the obturator canal.

The **femoral nerve** (L2 to L4) sends motor branches to the extensors of the leg, the iliopsoas, the sartorius, and also the pectineus. Occasionally a branch may go to the adductor longus. The cutaneous branches are the *anterior femoral cutaneous* nerves for the thigh and the *saphenous* nerve for the leg and foot (Figs. 10–7 and 10–8). The former supply the anterior and anteromedial surface of the thigh, comprising a relatively large autonomous sensory field. The saphenous nerve sends an infrapatellar branch to the skin in front of the kneecap and then is distributed to the medial side of the leg, the lowermost terminal branches going from the medial margin of the foot to about the proximal phalanx of the great toe.

The segmental innervation of the quadriceps femoris, iliopsoas, sartorius, and pectineus is shown in Figure 10–5.

Injury of the femoral nerve causes inability to extend the leg. If the lesion is high enough to involve the iliopsoas, flexion of the thigh is severely impaired. Sensory disturbances are manifested throughout the field of supply, and there are relatively large areas of total anesthesia. If the thigh nerves alone are involved the anesthesia is most extensive on the anterior surface of the thigh above the knee. In isolated lesions of the saphenous nerve, the anesthetic field extends

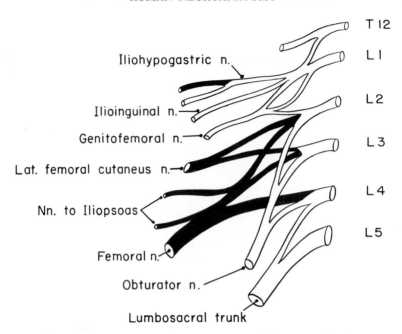

Fig. 10-9. Diagram of lumbar plexus. Peripheral nerves formed by anterior divisions of ventral primary rami are *white;* nerves formed by posterior divisions of ventral primary rami are *black*.

on the inner surface of the leg from just below the knee to the medial margin of the foot. The femoral nerve may become involved secondary to an abcess in the psoas muscle. The terminal sensory branch of the femoral (saphenous nerve) is subject to entrapment as it leaves the subsartorial canal.

The **lateral femoral cutaneous nerve** (L2 and L3) supplies the lateral half of the thigh, from the lateral buttock region to the knee (Figs. 10-7 and 10-8). In spite of considerable overlapping with adjacent cutaneous nerves, injury of this nerve produces a considerable area of anesthesia on the lateral aspect of the thigh.

The cutaneous areas supplied by the *iliohypogastric* (L1), *ilioinguinal* (L1), and *genitofemoral* (L1 and L2) nerves are shown in Figures 10-7 and 10-8. The iliohypogastric and ilioinguinal nerves also send motor fibers to the internal oblique and transverse abdominal muscles. Sensory loss due to injury to one of these nerves is relatively small, or lacking altogether, but such lesions may cause neuralgia.

The **sciatic nerve** (L4 to S3), the largest

nerve in the body, is the chief continuation of all the roots of the sacral plexus. It is composed of the two main leg nerves, the tibial and the common peroneal, enclosed for a variable distance within a common sheath (Fig. 10-10). Emerging from the greater sciatic foramen, or while still within it, the nerve sends branches to the main external rotators of the thigh, namely, the obturator internus, the gemelli, and the quadratus femoris muscles (L4 to S1). Lesions of these nerves are comparatively rare, and external rotation only is weakened, since other external rotators are available. In the region of the thigh, branches are given off to the flexors of the knee (hamstring muscles) and to the adductor magnus, the latter being innervated also by the obturator nerve. These branches, all derived from the tibial portion of the sciatic, often spring from a common trunk, which either runs independently or is loosely incorporated in the medial side of the sciatic nerve. An additional branch from the common peroneal nerve supplies the short head of the biceps femoris muscle. In injuries of the hamstring nerves flexion of the knee is

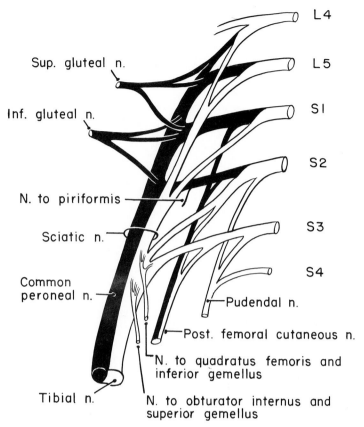

Fig. 10–10. Diagram of lumbosacral plexus. Peripheral nerves formed by anterior divisions of ventral primary rami are *white*; nerves formed by posterior divisions of ventral primary rami are *black*.

impaired severely, but weak flexion still may be produced by the action of the gracilis and sartorius muscles.

The sciatic nerve splits into its two terminal nerves at greatly varying levels of the thigh region. The muscular branches of the common trunk provide motor and sensory fibers to the quadratus femoris, the obturator internus, the gemelli, the semitendinosus, the semimembranosus, and the biceps femoris.

Normal peripheral nerve can be damaged by excessive stretch; as may occur in the roots and cords of the brachial plexus following undue angulation of the head and shoulder or arm traction during delivery. Reaction to stretch in a diseased nerve with a long course such as the sciatic, often produces pain, and paresthesias. One of the best known nerve stretching mechanisms is the straight-leg-raising test (of Lasègue). In a person lying supine with legs extended at the knees, flexion of the thigh at the hip causes stretching of the sciatic nerve. When the nerve is diseased (e.g. neuritis), stretch elicits pain in the distribution of the sciatic nerve (a positive response). The person may attempt to relieve such induced pain in the extended leg by automatically bending the knee to relax the nerve (Kernig sign). Other maneuvers similar to the above can provide evidence of meningitis, intervertebral disc disease, peripheral neuritis, nerve trauma and entrapment in the sciatic notch. This nerve has a prominent axial artery that accompanies it, as well as a large number of postganglionic sympathetic fibers. Injuries of this nerve, like the median nerve described above, are particularly prone to be followed by causalgia.

The **tibial nerve** (L4 to S3) supplies the posterior calf muscles concerned with plantar flexion and inversion of the foot; with plantar flexion of the toes; as well as the intrinsic muscles of the sole, which aid in maintaining the arch of the foot. One cutaneous branch given off in the thigh, the *sural* nerve, is distributed to the posterior and medial surface of the calf, where it is overlapped extensively by the end branchings of the saphenous and lateral sural (peroneal) nerves. The terminal branches of the sural (*lateral calcaneal*) supply the outer margin of the heel and a triangular area on the outer surface of the foot which extends to the lower portion of the Achilles tendon. Other cutaneous branches of the tibial nerve (*medial calcaneal* and *plantar*) supply the back and medial margin of the heel, the plantar surface of the foot and toes, and the dorsal phalanges (Figs. 10–7 and 10–8). The terminal branches of the tibial nerve are the *medial* and *lateral plantar* nerves. The segmental innervation of the calf and plantar muscles supplied by the tibial nerve is indicated in Figure 10–5.

Complete interruption of the tibial nerve above all its branches abolishes plantar flexion of the foot and toes and severely impairs inversion of the foot. Atrophy of the plantar muscles increases the concavity of the plantar arch (pes cavus). Sensory disturbances are neglible in the calf region, in which only a narrow strip may show reduced sensitivity. Total anesthesia is found on the sole of the foot, the plantar surface of the toes, the heel, and often a triangular area on the outer surface of the foot. This nerve is most vulnerable to fractures and dislocations of the medial melleolus, calcaneus and astragalus bones. It also can be compressed as it passes through the osseofibrous canal with three tendons, deep to the flexor retinaculum or deltoid ligament (tarsal tunnel syndrome).

The **common peroneal nerve** (L4 to S2) supplies the lateral and anterior muscles of the leg and the dorsal muscles of the foot, effecting dorsal flexion and eversion of the foot and dorsal flexion of the toes.

The chief cutaneous nerves are the *lateral sural cutaneous* and the *superficial peroneal* nerve (Fig. 10–7). The former, given off in the thigh, is distributed to the outer side of the leg from the knee region to nearly the outer margin of the sole, where it invades the territories of the superficial peroneal and sural nerves. The superficial peroneal nerve supplies the dorsum of the foot and toes to the distal phalanges and a portion of the anterior surface of the leg. A small cutaneous branch of the deep peroneal nerve is distributed to the cleft between the adjacent surfaces of the great and second toe. (Fig. 10–7). The common peroneal nerve divides into its superficial and deep branches as it passes to the lateral side of the neck of the fibula under cover of the peroneus longus muscle. The segmental innervation of the peronei, tibialis anterior, and extensor muscles on the dorsum of the foot is indicated in Figure 10–5.

Complete section of the peroneal nerve causes paralysis of dorsal flexion and eversion of the foot and paralysis of dorsal flexion (extension) of the toes. The most striking feature is inability to elevate the foot and toes (foot drop). If the condition is prolonged, shortening of the Achilles tendon will produce a permanent plantar overflexion and the foot will assume an equinovarus deformity. Sensory defects will be found on the dorsum of the foot, the outer part of the leg, and the skin between the great and second toe. The extent is much smaller than the anatomical field, since the cutaneous areas on both foot and leg are overlapped extensively by the adjacent cutaneous nerves. The common peroneal is subject to injury both by compression and fracture at the neck of the fibula. A terminal branch of the deep peroneal nerve is frequently injured as it crosses the dorsum of the foot. The terminal sensory fibers of the superficial peroneal nerve may become entrapped as they pierce the deep fascia at the distal and lateral part of the leg.

The **superior gluteal nerve** (L4 to S1) supplies the gluteus medius, gluteus minimus, and tensor fasciae latae muscles, which abduct the hip and rotate it internally. These movements are impaired by injury to the nerve.

The **inferior gluteal nerve** (L5 to S2) is distributed to the gluteus maximus, which is the strongest extensor of the hip. Injury causes wasting of the buttock. There is difficulty in rising from a sitting position, walking uphill, or climbing stairs, where powerful contraction of the muscle is required for raising the body.

The **posterior femoral cutaneous nerve** (S1 to S3) gives off several branches (*inferior clunial*) which supply the lower portions of the buttocks, where they overlap with the branches of the lumbar and sacral dorsal rami (superior and medial clunial nerves), (Fig. 10–8). Another small branch (*perineal*) goes to the lower innermost part of the buttock and the dorsal surface of the scrotum (or labia majora) and reaches the inner surface of the thigh. The main nerve supplies the posterior aspect of the thigh, often extending considerably below the knee and widely overlaps the territories of adjacent nerves. Injuries produce a relatively broad strip of anesthesia on the posterior surface of the thigh from the buttocks to the level of the knee.

Regeneration of Injured Peripheral Nerves. Our knowledge of the processes of degeneration and regeneration has been greatly increased in recent years by intensive investigations on mammalian nerves under various experimental conditions. Valuable information was obtained by clinical and surgical studies of the many peripheral nerve injuries resulting from the war. Seddon ('43) distinguishes three types of nerve injury: (1) complete anatomical division; (2) crush or severe compression injuries in which the continuity of the nerve fibers is broken but the sheaths and supporting tissue remain intact; and (3) temporary impairment or block. Nerve section nearly always demands surgical intervention to reestablish continuity. The recovery is more or less successful, but never complete, since many of the regenerating fibers fail to reach their respective end organs. After

nerve crush there also is complete degeneration of the severed nerve fibers. Both nerve section and nerve crush are followed by loss of sensation and movement, wasting of muscles, and reaction of degeneration. However, the damaged nerve fibers and their sheaths are in close anatomical contiguity after nerve crush, and subsequent regeneration usually leads to better recovery. In mild compression or block, there are varying degrees of paralysis, but electrical excitability remains normal. Because the nerve fibers are not severed, there is no peripheral degeneration. Recovery is more rapid; it begins in a few weeks and usually is completed in 2 or 3 months. These three types of nerve injury may appear as separate entities or in various combinations. Since the clinical symptoms after nerve section and crush are the same until regeneration is completed, surgical exploration usually is indicated to determine the nature of the injury (Stookey and Scarff, '43).

In a simple crush, though the continuity of the axons is interrupted, the endoneurium and other supporting tissues remain essentially intact. As a result, regenerating nerve fibers from the central stump can grow distally, traverse the minimal amount of scar tissue between the severed axonal ends, and enter appropriate Schwann cell tubes of the distal stump. After complete anatomical severance, the conditions are quite different at the site of injury. The cut ends are separated by a gap of variable extent which soon becomes filled with connective tissue and sheath cells, so that a scar of union is formed between the stumps. Hemorrhage and the vascular mesenchyme also conribute cells to the scar tissue. These cellular elements in the lesion area can seriously impede the growth of fine sprouts of regenerating axons from the proximal stump of the nerve. An enlarged heterogeneous mass at the cut end of a previously injured nerve is known as a *traumatic neuroma* (amputation or pseudoneuroma). It consists of Schwann cells, connective tissue cells and fibers, macrophages and an abundance of tangled aberrant nerve fibers. Such a skein of "lost" nerve fibers in scar tissue can be a most serious complication following peripheral nerve section or injury. Many of them are still "functional" processes of dorsal root ganglion cells, and these tangled ends still can transmit nerve impulses into the spinal cord. Such neuroma explains why a patient may have localized or "phantom pain" and paresthesias in a previously amputated hand or foot.

The behavior of the Schwann cells after anatomical severance is especially significant. About the fourth day, they become elongated and migrate out of the stumps into the scar, coming mainly from the peripheral stump but, to a lesser extent, also from the central one. These cells arrange themselves end to end, and form strands which traverse the fibrous tissue of the scar and establish continuity between the intact axons and the degenerating tubes of the peripheral stump. In some animals, under suitable conditions, gaps of 2 cm. have been naturally bridged in this manner. In man gaps of several millimeters may be similarly bridged. Under most circumstances, however, the mass of scar tissue is too extensive to be handled by the sheath cells themselves, and surgical intervention is required. Most of the scar tissue is removed and the approximated ends are held in the desired position by epineurial sutures. Meanwhile the central axonal tips swell and produce a number of fine branches which enter the injured area by the third day. At first they appear free in the connective tissue. Soon they apply themselves to the surface of the sheath cell strands and are led to the peripheral stump, where many of the branches enter the old Schwann cell tubes. However, the number of fibers entering the distal tubes is always smaller after section of the nerve than after crush. Moreover, many fibers enter tubes which are structurally unsuitable for full functional maturation. Once the fibers have entered the distal tubes, the further processes of growth and maturation are the same as after crush. These are described in Chapter 6 (page 144).

The rate of nerve regeneration has been studied by a number of investigators. After primary suture of the peroneal nerve in the rabbit, it takes about 7 days for the growing axon tips of the central stump to traverse the scar of the gap and reach the peripheral stump (Gutmann et al., '42; Gutmann and Young, '44). After crush the "scar" delay was about 5 days. Then the fastest axonal tips grew at the rate of 3.5 mm. a day after suture, and 4.4 mm. after a crush. Most of the axons grow distally at 3 mm. a day after the peroneal nerve is crushed, and 2 mm. a day after nerve section and suture. When the fine regenerated axons attain the periphery they increase in diameter and most of them ultimately become remyelinated. If a sufficient number of such fibers reach, and successfully reestablish contact with appropriate sensory and motor end organs, there will be an eventual return of function. The total latent period in the rabbit between nerve regeneration and functional recovery, was 20 days following nerve crush and 36 days after nerve suture.

In the longer nerves of man the process is somewhat slower, though a rate of 4.4 mm. a day for growing axons was found after a crush of one of the digital nerves (Bowden and Gutmann, '44). However, the rate of functional regeneration falls off with the distance traversed, since increase in diameter and myelination occurs more slowly in the distal portions of the fiber. A justifiable assumption for axonal growth in man under ideal conditions is about 3 mm. per day. The average latent period to functional maturity after distal nerve injuries is 20 days after crush and 50 days after suture.

Regeneration can occur when two stumps are sutured after being left apart for a considerable period of time. However, it is generally agreed that functional recoveries after long-delayed sutures usually are unsatisfactory. The difficulties occasioned by long delay are due to a number of factors which interfere with the regenerative processes, and these effects become progressively more serious. Some of the factors may be briefly mentioned.

After a long delay, the distal stump atrophies and the outgrowth of sheath cells is reduced or ceases altogether. Hence good apposition of the cut nerve ends is difficult, and many axons fail to reach the degenerated atrophic Schwann cell tubes of the distal stump. The tubes themselves are greatly shrunken and receive fewer fibers, so that the chances for appropriate peripheral connections are reduced greatly. Myelinization is delayed severely, and increase in diameter is made difficult by the fixation of the thickened endoneurium, which now forms a large portion of the tube. Of special importance is the progressive atrophy of the muscles and end organs. In early stages, where the motor end plates remain intact and connected with the Schwann cell tubes, new fibers can enter directly and restore the original pattern. In late stages with long delay periods, the channels become occluded and the end organs may completely disintegrate. The regenerating fibers often fail to enter the old sensory and motor endings or their previous locations. They then wander along the muscle fibers, ultimately forming new motor end plates of a more primitive character, whose distribution is irregular and different from the original pattern of innervation. The indications are therefore for early suture, perhaps 3 or 4 weeks after injury. At this time sheath cell activity is at its height and the somewhat thickened perineurium permits easier surgical apposition of the injured nerve stumps (Young, '49). After a month the factors mentioned above begin to operate to some extent and become progressively more important. Delays of 6 months or more before suture may seriously interfere with the reparative processes and may possibly prevent them altogether. Failure is not necessarily encountered in all cases. Good recovery is possible after long-delayed suture if enough axons reach appropriate Schwann cell tubes and the muscles are maintained in good condition by appropriate therapy. Sunderland ('50) has reported good restoration of function in human hand and finger muscles which had been denervated for 12 months.

CHAPTER 11

The Autonomic Nervous System

Those portions of the central and peripheral nervous system primarily concerned with the regulation of visceral activities often are termed collectively the *visceral, autonomic,* or *vegetative* nervous system, in contrast to the *somatic* or *cerebrospinal* (Fig. 11–1). Visceral reactions are initiated in the main by internal changes that activate the visceroceptors. Visceral motor responses in the smooth musculature and glands are to a large extent involuntary and unconscious. Such visceral reactions as do reach the conscious level are vague, poorly localized, and predominantly of an affective character. Tactile sensibility is practically absent, and temperature sense is apparently appreciated only in certain places, such as the esophagus, stomach, colon, and rectum. On the other hand, distention, or muscular spasms, of the walls of the hollow viscera or blood vessels may produce severe distress or acute pain.

As defined by Langley ('21) the *autonomic system* was purely visceral motor and consisted of "visceral efferent cells and fibers that pass to tissues other than the skeletal muscle". This rather rigid definition limits the term autonomic to a visceral efferent two neuron system, and excludes all visceral afferent fibers. Yet such sensory fibers accompany most visceral motor fibers and form the afferent

arm of most visceral reflexes. Visceral afferent fibers have their cells of origin in the cerebrospinal ganglia (Fig. 11–2 and 12–17). They, like the higher brain centers, play a constant and dynamic role in the regulation of autonomic activities. In recent years the above limited concept has been liberalized to make the term "autonomic" more synonymous with "visceral", and to include both peripheral and central neural structures (Hess, '48). It behooves all those concerned with visceral function to remember that central neurons and visceral afferent neurons are vital and integrated parts of the autonomic system—regardless of all arbitrary definitions. In similar fashion one should not attempt to sharply delineate the nervous system into somatic and visceral portions. This is a convenient physiological subdivision, but the two are merely different parts of a single integrated neural mechanism. The higher brain centers regulate both somatic and visceral functions, and throughout most neural levels there is intermingling and association of visceral and somatic neurons. Moreover, visceral reflexes may be initiated by impulses passing through somatic afferent fibers and coming from any receptor, and conversely visceral changes may give rise to active somatic movement. Through some mechanism, as yet unexplained, stimulation of peripheral visceral efferent neurons also can alter the activity of somatic sensory receptors.

Interposed in the efferent peripheral pathway between the central nervous system and the visceral structures are aggregations of nerve cells known as the *autonomic ganglia*. The cells of these peripheral ganglia are in synaptic relation with fibers from the spinal cord or brain, and they send out axons which terminate in the visceral effectors: smooth muscle, heart muscle, and glandular epithelium.

Pre- and Postganglionic Neurons. Thus unlike skeletal muscle, which is directly innervated by axons of centrally placed neurons, the transmission of impulses from the central nervous system to the viscera always involves two different neurons (Figs. 11-1 and 11-3). The first neuron, situated in the brain or spinal cord, sends its thinly myelinated axon as a *preganglionic* fiber to an autonomic ganglion, where it synapses with one or more *postganglionic* cells. Such preganglionic fibers of the cranial and spinal nerves are approximately 3 micra in diameter, and they have slow conduction velocities (i.e., 3 to 15 meters per second). Because of their physiological properties, they are designated as the B fibers of peripheral nerves (Patton, '61). The usually unmyelinated axons of autonomic ganglion cells then pass as *postganglionic* fibers to visceral effectors (Fig. 12-17). Postganglionic autonomic axons are of small diameter (0.3 to 1.3 micra), possess slow conduction velocities (0.7 to 2.3 meters per second), and usually are included as the C fibers of peripheral nerves. It is therefore evident that even the simplest visceral reflex arc will involve at least three neurons: afferent, preganglionic visceral efferent and postganglionic visceral efferent (Figs. 11-2 and 12-17).

The autonomic ganglia, which have a wide distribution in the visceral periphery, may be placed in three groups: the *paravertebral*; the *prevertebral* (*collateral*); and the *terminal* or *peripheral*. The paravertebral ganglia are arranged in a segmental fashion along the anterolateral surface of the vertebral column and are connected with each other by longitudinal fibers to form the two *sympathetic trunks* or ganglionated cords (Fig. 11-1). The collateral ganglia are irregular aggregations of cells found in the mesenteric neural plexuses surrounding the abdominal aorta and its larger visceral branches. The terminal ganglia are parasympathetic and are located within, or close to, the structures they innervate. The ganglia show extreme variations as to size and compactness of organization. They are organized into anatomically distinct encapsulated structures, as in the case of the sympathetic trunks and the autonomic ganglia of the head; they form extensive plexuses of nerve cells and fibers, as in the intramural intestinal plexuses; and they are found as small ganglionic masses or scattered cell groups within or near the walls of visceral structures, (e.g., heart, bronchi, pancreas, and urinary bladder).

Three outflows of preganglionic fibers connect the central nervous system with the autonomic ganglia (Fig. 11-1). The *cranial outflow* is represented by preganglionic visceral motor fibers within the oculomotor, facial, glossopharyngeal, and vagus nerves (*blue* in Fig. 11-1). Such visceral fibers terminate in either cranial autonomic ganglia (i.e., ciliary, otic, pterygopalatine, submandibular) or terminal ganglia within the wall of a viscus (e.g., heart, lung, stomach). The *thoracolumbar outflow* is composed of axons from the intermediolateral nucleus of the spinal cord; they pass out by way of the ventral roots of the thoracic and upper two lumbar nerves (*red* in Figs. 11-1 and 11-2). A few may pass through the eighth cervical nerve. These fibers leave the ventral roots as the white rami communicantes, enter the sympathetic trunk, and end in the vertebral ganglia of the trunk or in the collateral mesenteric ganglia. The *sacral outflow* contains preganglionic visceral motor fibers from the sacral autonomic nuclei of the spinal cord. They pass through the ventral roots of the second, third, and fourth sacral nerves and go to the terminal ganglia associated with the pelvic viscera (*blue* in Fig. 11-1).

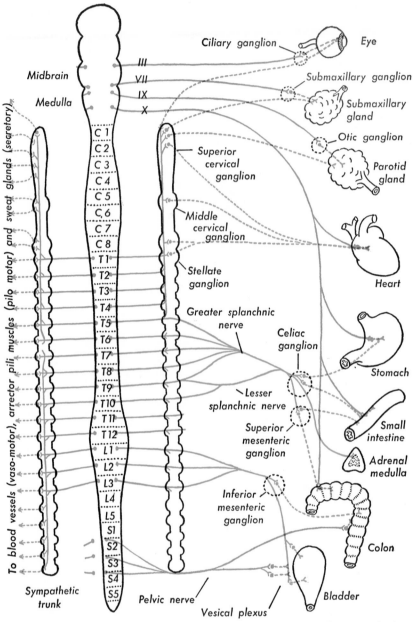

Fig. 11–1. Diagram showing general arrangement of the autonomic system. The sympathetic components are shown in *red*; while the parasympathetic components are in *blue*. *Solid lines* represent preganglionic fibers; *broken lines*, postganglionic fibers. For clearness the sympathetic fibers to the blood vessels, hair, and sweat glands are shown separately on the *left* (Copenhaver, '64).

Most of the viscera receive a double autonomic innervation, the effects of the two being antagonistic but normally integrated. One is through the thoracolumbar division, which supplies all the visceral structures of the body. The other innervation is by the craniosacral division. The cranial portion supplies the visceral structures of the head, and the thoracic and abdominal viscera with the exception of the pelvic organs, which are supplied by the sacral division. The cranial and sacral divisions have other features in common. They react in a similar manner to certain drugs, and their preganglionic fibers run directly to the terminal ganglia. The autonomic thus comprises two main divisions: the *thoracolumbar* or *sympathetic* system (*red* in Figs. 11–1 and 11–2), and the *craniosacral* or *parasympathetic* system (*blue* in Fig. 11–1).

The Sympathetic System. The sympathetic trunks are two ganglionated cords symmetrically placed along the anterolateral aspects of the vertebral column that extend from the base of the skull to the coccyx. The cervical portion contains three ganglia that are formed by the fusion of the original eight segmental ganglia. The *superior cervical ganglion* is the largest of the paravertebral ganglia and is situated near the second and third cervical vertebrae. The small *middle cervical ganglion*, often absent, may lie near the sixth cervical vertebra or close to the *inferior cervical ganglion*. The latter, placed at the lower border of the seventh cervical vertebra, frequently fuses with the first thoracic ganglion to form the cervicothoracic (stellate) ganglion (Fig. 11–1). In the thoracic, lumbar, and sacral regions, the ganglia are segmentally arranged. There are 11 or 12 thoracic, 3 or 4 lumbar, and 4 or 5 sacral ganglia. In the sacral portion, the two trunks gradually approach each other and fuse at the coccyx into the unpaired coccygeal ganglion.

The prevertebral ganglia are irregular ganglionic masses surrounding the visceral branches of the aorta. The largest are the celiac ganglia; the others are the superior mesenteric, aorticorenal, phrenic, and inferior mesenteric ganglia (Fig. 11–1). These will be described in relation to the celiac and subsidiary plexuses.

The sympathetic ganglia receive preganglionic fibers from the spinal cord through the ventral roots of all the thoracic and the upper two lumbar nerves (Sheehan, '41; Pick and Sheehan, '46). These fibers leave the ventral roots, pass through the white rami communicantes, and enter the sympathetic trunk, where they have two general destinations: (1) the paravertebral sympathetic ganglia, or

(2) the prevertebral ganglia. Those that terminate in the paravertebral sympathetic ganglia either end in the first one entered, or pass up or down in the sympathetic trunk giving off collaterals to finally terminate in ganglia above or below the level of their entrance (Fig. 11–1). The preganglionic fibers from the upper five thoracic nerves pass mainly upward, and in the cat, T1 contributes the smallest number of ascending fibers in the cervical sympathetic trunk (Foley and Schnitzlein, '57). Those from the middle thoracic segments (T7 to T10) pass up or down, while those of the lowest thoracic and lumbar pass only downward. The preganglionic fibers that terminate in the prevertebral ganglia do not synapse in the paravertebral ganglia, but merely pass through them and emerge as the splanchnic nerves (Figs. 11–1 and 11–2). Thus while the sympathetic pathway from the spinal cord to the viscera always involves two neurons, there are apparently never more than two, the synapse occurring either in the paravertebral or prevertebral ganglia.

While the white rami communicantes are limited to the thoracic and upper lumbar nerves, each spinal nerve receives a gray ramus communicans from the sympathetic trunk (Fig. 11–2). The gray ramus consists of unmyelinated postganglionic fibers which innervate the blood vessels, hair, and glands of the body wall.

The cervical sympathetic ganglia receive ascending preganglionic fibers from the white rami of the upper thoracic nerves, most of them go to the superior cervical ganglion. From the latter arise numerous gray strands composed of postganglionic fibers (Fig. 11–1). These are distributed as gray rami to the adjacent cranial nerves (IX, X, XI, and XII), to the upper three or four cervical nerves, to the pharynx, and to the external and internal carotid arteries around which the fibers form corresponding plexuses. From the vascular plexuses the postganglionic fibers pass through cranial autonomic ganglia to join branches of the cranial nerves. Such sympathetic postganglionic fibers supply the dilator muscle of the

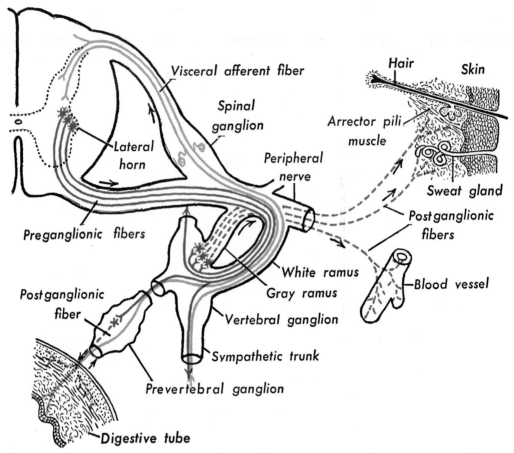

Fig. 11–2. Diagram of neural reflex arcs of the sympathetic system (Copenhaver, '64).

iris; the smooth muscle portion of the levator palpebrae; the orbital muscle of Müller; the blood vessels, sweat glands, and hairs of the head and face; and the lacrimal and salivary glands (Fig. 11–3). Another important branch passes as the superior cervical cardiac nerve to the cardiac plexuses innervating the heart. The middle cervical ganglion, when it lies at the level of the sixth cervical vertebra, supplies gray rami to cervical nerves C5 and C6, and at times also to C4 and C7. When this ganglion is absent or when it is placed close to the inferior cervical ganglion, these spinal nerves receive their gray rami from the sympathetic trunk. The inferior cervical ganglion furnishes gray rami to spinal nerves C7, C8 and T1 (Fig. 11–8). Thus a single ganglion may supply two or more of the lower cervical nerves, and a single nerve

may be supplied by two ganglia. Potts ('24) has found that the lower four cervical nerves may each receive three gray rami derived from the sympathetic trunk and from the middle and inferior cervical ganglia. In addition, the middle and inferior ganglia give off, respectively, the middle and inferior cardiac nerves, which go to the heart by way of the cardiac plexuses (Fig. 11–1).

The thoracic, lumbar, and sacral ganglia furnish gray rami to the remaining spinal nerves. Delicate branches from the upper five or six thoracic ganglia go to the cardiac plexuses as the thoracic cardiac nerves. Other fibers from the inferior cervical ganglion reach the pulmonary plexuses to innervate the bronchial musculature and blood vessels of the lungs (Fig. 11–3). Shorter mediastinal branches from both the thoracic and lumbar gan-

LOCATION OF SOME IMPORTANT AUTONOMIC NEURONS

Structure Supplied	SYMPATHETIC		PARASYMPATHETIC	
	Preganglionic Cell Bodies in CNS Nuclei	Postganglionic Cell Bodies in Peripheral Ganglia	Preganglionic Cell Bodies in CNS Nuclei	Postganglionic Cell Bodies in Peripheral Ganglia
Iris of eye	intermediolateral nuc. in cord segments C8–T2 (3)	sup. cervical ganglion and scattered along carotid plexus	Edinger-Westphal nuc. of midbrain	ciliary ganglion
Lacrimal gland	intermediolateralis nuc. in cord segments T1–2	sup. and middle cervical symp. ganglia	sup. salivatory nuc. in pons	pterygopalatine ganglion
Submandibular and sublingual glands	intermediolateral nuc. in cord segments T1–3(4)	sup. and middle cervical symp. ganglia	sup. salivatory nuc. in pons	submandibular ganglion
Parotid gland	intermediolateral nuc. in cord segments T1–3(4)	sup. and middle cervical symp. ganglia	inf. salivatory nuc. in medulla	otic ganglion
Sweat glands of head and neck	intermediolateral nuc. in cord segments T1–3	3 cervical sympathetic ganglia		
Lungs and bronchi	intermediolateral nuc. in cord segments T1–5	inf. cervical and thoracic (T1–5) symp. ganglia	dorsal motor nuc. N. X	ganglia of pulmonary plexi
Heart	intermediolateral nuc. in cord segments T1–5(6,7)	3 cervical and thoracic (T1–6) symp. ganglia	dorsal motor nuc. N. X	intra-cardiac ganglia of atria
Esophagus	intermediolateral nuc. in cord segments T1–6	thoracic symp. T(1–3) 4-6 ganglia	dorsal motor nuc. N. X	myenteric and submucous plexi
Stomach, small intestine; ascending and transverse colon	intermediolateral nuc. in cord segments T5–11	celiac and sup. mesenteric ganglia	dorsal motor nuc. N. X	myenteric and submucous plexi
Descending colon and rectum	intermediolateral nuc. in cord segments T12–L3	lumbar and inf. mesenteric symp. ganglia	autonomic nuc. of intermediate gray in cord segment S2–4	ganglia of hemorrhoidal myenteric and submucous plexi
Sex organs	intermediolateral nuc. in cord segments T10–L2	lumbar, sacral and inf. mesenteric symp. ganglia	autonomic nuc. of intermediate gray in cord segments S2–4	ganglia along branches of aorta and int. iliac arteries (e.g. ovarian, uterine)
Urinary bladder	intermediolateral nuc. in cord segments T12–L2	lumbar and inf. mesenteric symp. ganglia	autonomic nuc. of intermediate gray in cord segments S2–4	ganglia along vesical branches of int. iliac artery
Sweat glands and blood vessels of lower extremity	intermediolateral nuc. in cord segments L1–2	lumbar and sacral symp. ganglia		

FIG. 11–3. Location of preganglionic and postganglionic autonomic neurons to important visceral structures.

glia form plexuses around the thoracic and abdominal aorta. In addition to these, there are two, sometimes three, important branches known as the *splanchnic nerves* which arise from the thoracic portion of the sympathetic trunk, pierce the diaphragm, and terminate in the prevertebral ganglia of the mesenteric plexuses (Fig. 11–1). The *greater splanchnic nerve* arises by roots from the fifth to the ninth thoracic ganglia and goes to the celiac plexus. The *lesser splanchnic nerve* usually arises by two roots from the tenth and eleventh ganglia, and either unites with the greater splanchnic, or continues as an independent nerve to that portion of the celiac plexus which surrounds the roots of the renal arteries and there terminates in the aorticorenal ganglion. The *smallest splanchnic nerve*, when present, arises from the last thoracic ganglion and goes to the renal plexus. Often this nerve is represented by a branch from the lesser splanchnic nerve. The splanchnic nerves, though appearing as branches of the thoracic ganglia, are composed of preganglionic fibers, which merely pass through the sympathetic trunk on their way to the celiac and mesenteric ganglia (e.g., visceral motor fibers destined for digestive organs and the bladder as shown in Figure 11–1).

The *celiac plexus* is extensive and surrounds the roots of the celiac and superior mesenteric arteries. It extends cranially to the diaphragm, caudally to the renal arteries, and laterally to the suprarenal bodies. It becomes continuous below with the abdominal aortic plexuses. From the main plexus paired and unpaired subsidiary plexuses are given off which accompany the branches of the celiac and superior mesenteric arteries as well as other branches of the abdominal aorta. The paired plexuses include the phrenic, suprarenal, and spermatic (or ovarian); the gastric, hepatic, splenic, and superior mesenteric plexuses are unpaired. Within the celiac plexus are found two relatively large ganglionic masses, the *celiac ganglia*, lying on either side of the celiac artery and connected with each other by delicate fiber strands. Occasionally the two may be so close as to form a single unpaired ganglion encircling the artery. Other ganglionic masses found in the plexus include the paired aorticorenal ganglia and the *superior mesenteric ganglion* lying near the roots of their respective arteries. All these ganglia receive preganglionic fibers from the splanchnic nerves.

Caudally the celiac plexus becomes continuous with the abdominal aortic plexuses lying on either side of the aorta. From these plexuses nerve strands pass to the root of the inferior mesenteric artery and form the inferior mesenteric plexus,

which surrounds that artery and its branches. Within this plexus and lying close to the root of the artery is another prevertebral ganglionic mass the *inferior mesenteric ganglion* (Figs. 11–1 and 11–9). Still further caudally, the abdominal aortic plexuses are continued into the unpaired *hypogastric* or *pelvic plexus*, which also receives strands from the inferior mesenteric plexus. On entering the pelvis the plexus breaks up into a number of subsidiary plexuses adjacent to the rectum, bladder, and accessory genital organs (Fig. 11–9). The preganglionic fibers supplying the pelvic organs come from the white rami of the two upper lumbar nerves and from the lowest thoracic nerve. They pass through the corresponding ganglia of the sympathetic trunk, and terminate in the inferior mesenteric ganglion. The cells of this ganglion then send their postganglionic axons by way of the inferior mesenteric and hypogastric plexuses to the pelvic viscera (Fig. 11–9).

The Parasympathetic System. The preganglionic fibers of the craniosacral division form synaptic relations with postganglionic neurons in cranial autonomic or terminal ganglia. In the *cranial* region four such ganglia are related topographically to the branches of the trigeminal nerve (Fig. 11–1). The *ciliary ganglion* lying against the lateral surface of the optic nerve receives preganglionic fibers from the oculomotor nerve (III) and sends postganglionic fibers to the sphincter of the iris and the smooth muscle of the ciliary body. The *pterygopalatine ganglion*, in the pterygopalatine fossa, and the *submandibular ganglion*, lying over the submandibular gland, receive fibers from the intermediate portion of the facial nerve (VII) (Figs. 11–1 and 15–13). The preganglionic fibers pass by way of the greater petrosal nerve to the pterygopalatine ganglion, and by way of the chorda tympani to the submandibular ganglion. The latter is usually broken up into a submandibular and a sublingual portion. The pterygopalatine ganglion sends postganglionic fibers to the lacrimal glands and to the blood vessels and glands of the mucous membranes of the nose and palate. Postganglionic fibers from the submandibular ganglion go to the submandibular and sublingual glands and also to the mucous membrane of the floor of the mouth. The *otic ganglion* is situated mesially to the mandibular nerve as it leaves the oval foramen. It receives preganglionic fibers from the glossopharyngeal nerve (IX) by way of the lesser petrosal nerve and sends postganglionic fibers to the parotid gland (Fig. 11–1). All of these cranial autonomic ganglia receive nerve filaments from the superior cervical ganglion, passing by way of the internal and external carotid plexuses. These, however, do not synapse with the ganglionic cells but merely pass through the cranial parasympathetic ganglia to furnish sympathetic innervation to the blood vessels, smooth muscle and glands.

The largest source of preganglionic fibers is furnished by the vagus nerve (X), which supplies practically all the thoracic and abdominal viscera except those in the pelvic region (Figs. 11–1 and 11–4). In the thorax, these preganglionic fibers enter the pulmonary, cardiac, and esophageal plexuses to be distributed to the terminal (intrinsic) ganglia of the heart and bronchial musculature. Short postganglionic fibers then go to the heart and bronchial muscle. In the abdomen, the parasympathetic fibers of the vagus nerve go to the stomach, and pass through the celiac and its subsidiary plexuses, to end in the terminal ganglia of the intestine, liver, pancreas, and probably the kidneys. In the alimentary canal these terminal ganglia form the extensive ganglionated plexuses of Auerbach (myenteric) and of Meissner (submucosal). They extend the whole length of the digestive tube from the upper portion of the esophagus to the internal anal sphincter. These plexuses are composed of numerous small aggregations of ganglion cells intimately connected to each other by delicate transverse and longitudinal fiber bundles. From intramural neurons short postganglionic fibers terminate in the smooth muscle and glandular epithelium. The alimentary innervation of the vagus extends as far as the descending colon (Figs. 11–1 and 11–4).

The *sacral* autonomic consists of preganglionic fibers that come from the second, third, and fourth sacral nerves which form the *pelvic nerve* (N. erigens) and go to the terminal ganglia of the pelvic plexuses, as well as to the myenteric and submucosal plexuses of the descending colon and rectum (Fig. 11–1). Postganglionic fibers from these ganglia supply the effectors of the pelvic organs, including the urinary bladder, descending colon, rectum, and accessory reproductive organs. The sacral autonomic fibers innervate those viscera not supplied by the vagus (Figs. 11–4 and 11–9).

The enteric plexuses differ from the other autonomic plexuses in one important respect. They apparently contain some mechanism for local reflex action, since coordinated peristalsis occurs on stimulation of the gut after section of all the nerves which connect these plexuses with the central nervous system. The nature of this reflex mechanism is not fully understood.

It is evident from the above that all the autonomic plexuses consist of complicated intermixtures of sympathetic and parasympathetic fibers which are difficult to distinguish morphologically. It must, however, be emphasized again that the sympathetic preganglionic fibers are interrupted in the paravertebral and prevertebral ganglia, while the parasympathetic preganglionic fibers pass by way of the plexuses to the terminal ganglia.

Visceral Afferent Fibers. There are numerous receptors in the viscera whose afferent fibers, myelinated or unmyelinated, travel centrally by way of the autonomic nerves, both sympathetic and parasympathetic. The largest myelinated fibers come principally from Pacinian corpuscles, the smaller myelinated and the unmyelinated ones from the more numerous diffuse visceral receptors (Fig. 9–3). These sensory fibers from the thoracic, abdominal and pelvic viscera traverse the sympathetic and splanchnic nerves to reach the sympathetic trunk. Here they pass uninterruptedly through the trunk and white communicating rami to their perikarya of origin in the dorsal root ganglia (Figs. 11–2, 11–9 and 12–17). The parasympathetic nerves likewise contain many visceral afferent fibers. The visceral afferent fibers of the vagus, whose cell bodies are in the inferior (nodose) ganglion, are distributed peripherally to the heart, lungs, and other viscera. Similar fibers from the bladder, rectum, and accessory genital organs pass by way of the pelvic nerves and enter the spinal cord through the second, third, and fourth sacral dorsal roots. Their cell bodies are located in the corresponding sacral spinal ganglia. Visceral sensory fibers from the bladder also ascend to enter the spinal cord through the lower thoracic and lumbar spinal nerves (Fig. 11–9). The sacral visceral afferent fibers from the urinary bladder play the dominant role both in reflex control and the mediation of vesical pain impulses. These afferents accompany the sacral parasympathetic outflow and convey the sensory impulses that signal bladder distension. The sensation of a distended bladder is abolished by anesthetic block of the pelvic nerves, resection of these nerves, or the cutting of dorsal roots S2, 3, 4. Visceral afferents from the bladder and adjacent viscera do ascend to the lumbar and lower thoracic dorsal root ganglia, but they appear to play a very minor role in the regulation of the bladder. Resection of the presacral nerve and hypogastric plexus in man is followed subsequently by little or no alteration of vesical function.

The afferent visceral fibers are important for the initiation of various visceral and viscerosomatic reflexes mediated through the spinal cord and brain stem for the regulation and adjustment of vegetative functions. Many of these reactions remain on a subconscious level, but afferent impulses also give rise to visceral sensation, such as visceral pain or distress, nausea, hunger, and other poorly localized visceral sensations. It is the constant stream of afferent visceral impulses that is responsible for the general feeling of internal well being or of malaise.

Visceral pain from most of the abdominal and pelvic organs is carried chiefly by fibers running in the sympathetic nerves. Vagal sensory fibers are concerned with specific visceromotor, vasomotor, and secretory reflexes most of which do not reach consciousness. It should be recalled that pain carried by visceral afferent fibers from diseased or inflamed organs may be "referred" to skin areas supplied by somatic afferent fibers of the same segment (see page 189). The sense of taste is mediated by afferent fibers of the vagus, glossopharyngeal, and facial nerves, while impulses giving rise to hunger probably are carried by the vagus.

Structure of Autonomic Ganglia. The autonomic ganglia are aggregations of multipolar neurons of varying size and shape, each surrounded by a capsule. Trabeculae extending from the capsule form an internal framework which contains numerous, often pigmented perikarya, between which are irregular plexuses of myelinated and unmyelinated fibers (Figs. 6–1C and 11–4). Besides these ganglia, isolated autonomic cells or non-encapsulated aggregations of such cells are found widely distributed throughout the viscera.

The diameter of autonomic cells ranges from 20 to 60 micra, and the number of their branching dendrites is exceedingly variable. There may be as few as three or four on some perikarya, and as many as twenty on others. The cells have a clear ovoid and often eccentric nucleus, delicate neurofibrils, and fine chromophilic bodies. Binucleated or even multinucleated cells are not uncommon. Most of the cells are surrounded by cellular capsules similar to those surrounding spinal ganglion cells (Fig. 6–6).

Some of the cells have short dendrites which ramify within the capsules. These are numerous in the autonomic ganglia of man (Fig. 11–4). Others have long, slender dendrites which pierce the capsule and run for varying distances in the intercellular plexuses. Some cells possess both short and long processes. The intracapsular dendrites may arborize symmetrically on all sides of the cell or they may form interlocking dendritic processes between two or more cells, enclosed within a single capsule (Fig. 11–5). Such cells probably receive common terminal arborizations of preganglionic fibers. The extracapsular dendrites terminate in similar end arborizations at varying distances from the cell body.

Preganglionic fibers end in synaptic relation with the perikarya and dendrites of many postganglionic cells. They branch repeatedly within the ganglion and form pericellular arborizations; some of the terminals end by neurofibrillar rings or loops on the cell body. More common are the axodendritic synapses where the preganglionic fibers end in diffuse arborizations about the intracapsular and extracapsular dendrites. If the superior cervical ganglion (Fig. 11-1) is isolated by section of all incoming preganglionic fibers, the postganglionic perikarya do not degenerate. The isolated postganglionic perikarya may decrease slightly in diameter and show alterations of Nissl substance, endoplasmic reticulum, and mitochondria, but they survive, i.e., the perikarya do not demonstrate a transneuronal degeneration (Hamlyn, '54; Barton and Causey, '58). However, following section of postganglionic axons of the cervical and ciliary ganglia, the perikarya show central chromatolysis and changes in their electrophysiologic properties (Warwick, '54; Barton and Causey, '58; Hunt and Riker, '66).

The capsule cells of the autonomic ganglia are known to contain a variety of enzymes (Truex, '51; Adams, '65). They have been considered as homologous to the oligodendrocytes by Schwyn ('67); to satellite and Schwann cells of dorsal root ganglia by Barton and Causey ('58); or considered as connective tissue fibroblasts and interstitial cells. These supportive cells show a marked hyperplasia following stimulation of the preganglionic fibers for periods of 105 to 180 minutes (Schwyn, '67). Such prolonged stimulation was accompanied by an accelerated nuclear absorption of labelled thymidine-H^3. This author believes the capsule cells participate in neuronal metabolism and DNA turn-over during periods of increased metabolism and synaptic activity.

Chemical Mediation at Synapses. The investigations of Dale ('14), Loewi ('21, '45), Cannon ('29), and many others have demonstrated that autonomic effects are mediated by chemical substances liberated at the postganglionic nerve terminals. Investigation soon revealed that the trans-

mitter at all parasympathetic postganglionic endings was either acetylcholine or a closely related substance. Subsequent studies also showed that acetylcholine was the transmitter agent liberated at the synaptic terminals of all autonomic preganglionic axons, sympathetic as well as parasympathetic. Acetylcholine is now recognized as the mediator of impulses at postganglionic sympathetic nerve endings upon sweat glands, as well as at somatic motor terminations upon skeletal muscle fibers. Acetylcholine probably occurs at the synapses within the brain and spinal cord, too. The brief action of the chemical transmitter in autonomic ganglia, as well as at the somatic neuromuscular junction, corresponds with the demonstration of high concentrations of the enzyme acetylcholineterase at these sites. This enzyme readily hydrolyzes the free unstable acetylcholine to choline and acetic acid. Several chemical substances are now known that inhibit the action of acetylcholinesterase (e.g., atropine, eserine, and neostigmine) and thus prevent the rapid hydrolysis of the free acetylcholine. Much of our knowledge of acetylcholine was acquired through the use of these inhibitor agents. Nerves which liberate this transmitter, or an acetylcholine-like substance, at their terminations are called *cholinergic fibers*. Nerve impulses of cholinergic fibers thus induce rapid, localized responses of short duration in the postjunctional visceral cells.

Stimulation of most sympathetic postganglionic fibers is followed, on the other hand, by the liberation of a different kind of transmitter substance at their terminals (Elliott, '05; Cannon and Rosenblueth, '33, '37; von Euler, '48, '55). The transmitter substance liberated resembled adrenaline, and such axons were designated as *adrenergic fibers*. It is now believed that noradrenaline is the principal agent released by the nerve terminals and that smaller amounts of epinephrine, together with noradrenaline, may be released from chromaffin cells of the adrenal medulla (McLennan, '63). It will be recalled that axon terminals in electron micrographs have large numbers of synaptic vesicles which are presumed to be the precursors

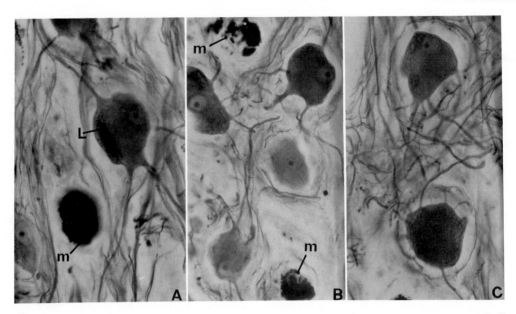

Fig. 11-4. Adult human sympathetic neurons. Note interdigitating dendrites that often form a pericellular plexus. Perikarya show some eccentric nuclei, melanin granules (*m*), and lipofuscin (*L*). The nuclei of the capsule cells are not stained. Cajal silver stain ×490.

or bound packets of transmitter material (Fig. 6–22). Figure 11–7 shows autonomic axon terminals in the cat pineal body which were selectively treated to demonstrate biogenic amines. In this micrograph one can identify small hollow vesicles (*V*3 in Fig. 11–7) as well as dense cored vesicles (*V*1) and laminated bodies (*L*) that reacted positively. Available evidence indicates that the dense or granulated vesicles of the pineal body contain an adrenergic transmitter, whereas the clear, or non-granulated, vesicles are storage sites of acetylcholine and other transmitter substances (see De Robertis et al., '65). Final proof of the specific role of each type of vesicle remains to be established. However, such transmitter substances play an important role in the chemical mediation of the nerve impulse and are another example of neurosecretion (*see* page 124). The enzymatic inactivation of these liberated catecholamines is not as rapid and efficient a process as the liberation and breakdown of acetylcholine. The liberated transmitter substances of most sympathetic postganglionic terminals are more stable and probably diffuse away from the locus of formation and

action. They probably are oxidized and finally disposed of at some distance from, and a considerable time after, their synaptic liberation. As a result of stimulation, adrenergic nerve terminals call forth postjunctional responses that are more slowly induced, more diffuse or widespread, and of a more prolonged duration.

The terms "adrenergic" and "cholinergic" do not correspond completely with "sympathetic" and "parasympathetic," respectively. Thus the postganglionic fibers to the sweat glands (sudomotor fibers) though anatomically part of the sympathetic, are cholinergic. Moreover they react to certain drugs, such as pilocarpine and atropine, in the same way as parasympathetic fibers. It should be recalled that the upper and lower extremities have no parasympathetic nerve fibers. In these regions the sympathetic postganglionic fibers are of two distinct types —most are adrenergic, but those to the sweat glands are cholinergic (Figs. 11–6 and 11–8). There are other instances of mixed autonomic nerves. For example, the splanchnic nerves contain both adrenergic and cholinergic fibers. The latter are destined for the adrenal medulla,

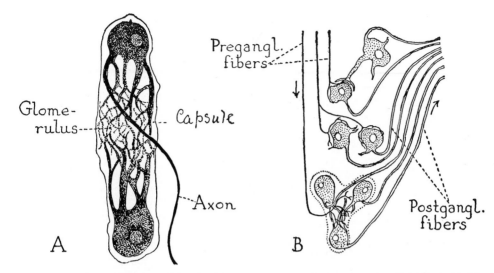

FIG. 11-5. A, Glomerulus formed by dendrites of two sympathetic cells (after Cajal, '11). B, Diagram showing ways by which one preganglionic fiber may come into relation with two or more sympathetic ganglion cells (after Ranson and Billingsley, '18).

IMPORTANT FUNCTIONS OF SOME AUTONOMIC PATHWAYS

FUNCTION	SYMPATHETIC	PARASYMPATHETIC
Iris	dilates the pupil (mydriasis)	constricts the pupil (miosis)
Lacrimal gland	little or no effect on secretion	stimulates secretion
Salivary glands	secretion reduced in amount and viscid	secretion increased in amount and watery
Sweat glands of head, neck, trunk, and extremities	stimulates secretion (cholinergic fibers) nerve fibers	little or no effect on secretion
Bronchi	dilates lumen	constricts lumen
Heart	accelerates rate, augments ventricular contraction	decreases heart rate
GI motility and secretion	inhibits	stimulates
GI sphincters	constricts	relaxes
Sex organs	contraction of ductus deferens, seminal vesicle, prostatic and uterine musculature; vasoconstriction	vasodilation and erection
Urinary bladder	little or no effect on bladder	contracts bladder wall, promotes emptying
Adrenal medulla	stimulates secretion (cholinergic nerve fibers)	little or no effect
Blood vessels of trunk and extremities	constricts	no effect

FIG. 11-6. Sympathetic and parasympathetic actions upon visceral structures.

where acetylcholine is the transmitter substance. Overactivity of both adrenergic and cholinergic fibers is indicative of either autonomic imbalance, irritating lesions, or abnormal regeneration along the course of the fibers. These may be expressed as excessive or abnormal sweating and salivation, alterations in motility

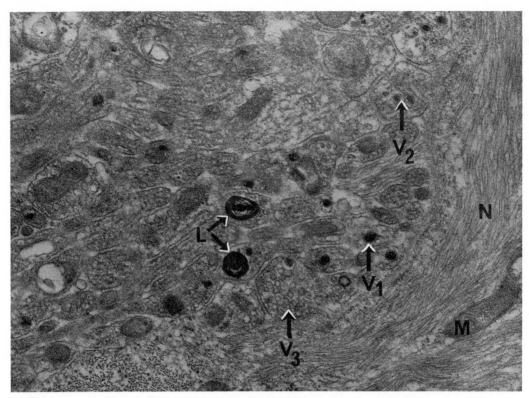

Fig. 11-7. Electron micrograph of autonomic nerve terminals in cat pineal body that was treated to demonstrate biogenic amines. Some dense cored vesicles (*V*1) and laminated bodies (*L*) react positively. Other dense core (*V*2) and hollow vesicles (*V*3) do not react. Mitochondria (*M*) and neurotubules also are identified (courtesy of Dr. J. G. Wood, University of Texas Medical School at San Antonio). ×40,000.

along the gastrointestinal tract, or increased peripheral vasoconstriction as in hypertension. Appropriate drugs are now available that can either enhance or inhibit impulses at the sympathetic and parasympathetic ganglionic synapses, or block the membrane receptor sites upon which the neurotransmitter substances produce their effects (e.g., muscle, heart, glands, blood vessels).

Denervation Sensitization. It was noted above that the postganglionic perikarya and their processes persist following section of the appropriate preganglionic fibers. It is known that section of the preganglionic fibers results in increased sensitivity of the isolated neurons and the tissues they supply to circulating adrenaline. The exact way in which the neuro-effector mechanism is altered remains unknown. However, it was observed that complete section of the postgan-

glionic fibers to an organ or region resulted in far greater sensitization to adrenaline than that which followed complete preganglionic nerve section. Hampel ('35) observed the qualitative responses of the nictitating membrane of the cat to adrenaline on successive days after denervation. He found that the response reached a maximum about eight days after preganglionic denervation. Postganglionic denervation resulted in sensitization responses that were twice as great as those that followed preganglionic section. Similar responses are observed in most other tissues supplied by the adrenergic fibers. Increased sensitivity has been observed as well in structures supplied by the cholinergic fibers (e.g., eye, sweat and salivary glands). The latter become sensitive to acetylcholine, which is equally true of denervated skeletal muscle. This peculiar phenomena often is referred to as

Cannon's ('39) law of denervation: "When in a series of efferent neurons a unit is destroyed, an increased irritability to chemical agents develops in the isolated structure or structures, the effect being maximal in the part directly denervated". Such denervation accounts for the increased sensitization of the superior cervical ganglion cells to acetylcholine which occurs after severance of its preganglionic fibers.

The paralysis after denervation of smooth muscle is very different from that seen in skeletal muscle where there is a persisting flaccid paralysis. Restoration of smooth muscle tone is due in part to the sensitization of the neuro-effector mechanism to circulating epinephrine. The anatomical arrangement of the preganglionic and postganglionic sympathetic vasoconstrictor fibers to the hand and foot serves as an excellent example to illustrate this point (Fig. 11–8). In Reynaud's disease the small arteries and arterioles of the upper extremities, usually the hands, undergo episodic vasoconstriction. As a result, the extremity demonstrates pallor and reactive hyperemia (i.e., an increased amount of blood in a part, or congestion). In chronic cases trophic changes develop with atrophy of the skin and subcutaneous tissues. Long-standing cases may develop skin ulceration or even ischemic gangrene. Removal of the inferior cervical, first and second thoracic sympathetic ganglia, eliminates the vasoconstriction but destroys both the preganglionic, as well as the postganglionic fibers to the forearm and hand (Fig. 11–8A). The smooth muscle of the arteries and arterioles will, in time, regain some vascular tone since the smooth muscle is also highly sensitized by removal of the postganglionic cells and fibers. Better results usually are obtained in the foot following removal of the second and third lumbar sympathetic ganglia (Fig. 11–8B). Here the partial sympathectomy interrupts the preganglionic outflow. However, it leaves intact the postganglionic cells and fibers in the lower lumbar and sacral ganglia which reach the foot through the sciatic nerve and its branches. Thus the vessels of the leg and foot regions are less sensitized to neurohumeral catecholamines.

Central Autonomic Pathways. The important visceral structures innervated by the autonomic system normally maintain a constant internal environment within the organism (homeostasis). Preganglionic neurons within the central nervous system (Figs. 11–1 and 11–3) are maintained in a continuous, but quantitatively variable, state of activity by a multitude of segmental and suprasegmental inputs. Regulation from higher levels is not accomplished by one or even two neuron pathways. There are a series of axonic terminal synapses between several interposed neurons located at successively lower levels (i.e., it is a somewhat diffuse descending multisynaptic pathway). Through this phylogenetically older neuronal system, autonomic fibers from some areas of the cerebral cortex descend to the hypothalamus while others reach the tegmental nuclei of the midbrain (medial forebrain bundle). Axons of tegmental neurons project to reticular neurons, and these in turn project their axons to other reticular nuclei at the same or lower levels. As we shall see later (page 491), there are many afferent pathways that lead into the hypothalamus, as well as efferent hypothalamic tracts that descend into the midbrain, pons, and medulla. Such descending fibers (e.g., mammillotegmental, dorsal longitudinal fasciculus) are part of this diffuse relay system that supplies collaterals and terminals to visceral nuclei of the brain stem. More caudally this descending system also sends terminals to the intermediolateral nuclei in cord segments C8 to L3 (Fig. 11–4). In the midbrain and upper pons, these descending tracts are located dorsally and medially near the central gray matter and floor of the fourth ventricle (Smith and Clarke, '64; Wolf and Sutin, '66; Cheatham and Matzke, '66; Bradley and Conway, '66). In man and most mammals that have been studied, the fibers descending into the upper midbrain stream through the prerubral field and region above the red nucleus. Stereotaxic surgery for dyskinesia in this area of the human brain have re-

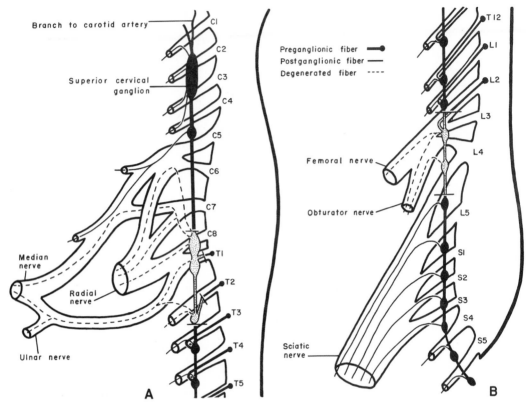

Fig. 11–8. Anatomic course of preganglionic and postganglionic sympathetic vasoconstrictor fibers to the hand and foot. *A*. After cervicothoracic ganglionectomy (inferior cervical, T1 and T2) all of the postganglionic fibers to the hand degenerate. *B*. Resection of sympathetic ganglia L2 and L3 interrupts only descending preganglionic fibers to lower lumbar and sacral sympathetic ganglia. Postganglionic fibers to the sciatic nerve and foot region do not degenerate (modified from White, Okelberry and Whitelaw, '36).

sulted in widespread autonomic deficits (Carmel, '68). These deficits included ptosis (drooping) of the eyelid, miosis (constriction) of the pupil and a loss of sweating (hemianhydrosis) on the same side (ipsilateral) of the body as the lesion site. Such findings in man indicate that these descending fibers are uncrossed axons below the level of the red nucleus. In the caudal pons and medulla, these fibers are located more laterally in the pontine tegmentum and reticular formation of the medulla. Through this descending fiber system, the hypothalamus and other suprasegmental structures help regulate a variety of visceral reflex activities (e.g., blood pressure, body temperature, sweating, secretion, eye, vesicle, rectal, and sexual reflexes). Lesions of these descending central tracts can result in a complete

loss, or altered control of visceral activities at lower segmental levels. For example, lesions in the lateral reticular formation of the medulla interrupt the fibers regulating sympathetic control of the smooth muscle of the eye and may result in a Horner's syndrome.

A most unusual clinical entity described by Riley and his associates ('49, '52, '57, '66) serves as an excellent example of the disseminated and abnormal functional activities of these descending autonomic fibers. The authors originally postulated a central, possibly congenital, diencephalic origin to account for these symptoms in children of Jewish extraction: deficiency of lacrimation; transient and extreme elevation in blood pressure induced by mild anxiety; excessive sweating, and drooling of saliva; and occurrence of sharply demarcated erethymatous blotches on the skin that are bilaterally symmetric (*familial dysautonomia* or *Riley-Day syndrome*). Subsequent study has revealed other essential symptoms that support a diagnosis of this syndrome. These include postural hypotension (on rising from the supine to the upright position); feeding difficulty from birth onward, a relative indifference to pain, erratic control of body temperature, emotional lability, absent corneal reflex and corneal anesthesia, absent deep tendon reflexes, abnormal pupillary response to methacholine, and an abnormal intradermal response to histamine. Hypotonus, poor motor coordination, and developmental retardation may accompany the above findings. The precise pathologic causes remain unknown, but lesions have been noted in the thalamus, reticular formation of pons and medulla, spinal cord, sympathetic ganglia and myenteric plexus (see Riley and Moore, '66). The above constellation of abnormal autonomic, mental, sensory and motor responses imposes serious disabilities upon both the patient and his family.

Bilateral lesions of the lateral white funiculi may result in altered sweating, in regions supplied by the cord segments below the level of such lesions. Control of the bladder and rectum may also be lost. After cord transection the autonomic reflexes are at first depressed (spinal shock), temperature regulation and sweating are absent, and blood pressure falls profoundly. Several weeks later spinal shock wanes, and the more caudal segmental reflexes, along with the somatic reflexes, reappear. However, the recovered visceral reflexes often are altered and sluggish.

Functional Considerations. Gaskell ('16) has pointed out that when a visceral structure is innervated by both the sympathetic and the parasympathetic, the effects of the two are as a rule antagonistic. The sympathetic neurons dilate the pupil, accelerate the heart, inhibit intestinal movements, and contract the vesical and rectal sphincters. The parasympathetic neurons constrict the pupil, slow the heart, further peristaltic movement, and relax the above named sphincters (Fig. 11-6). The apparently haphazard effects on smooth and cardiac muscle produced by each autonomic division in different organs (contraction in one, inhibition in another) are more readily explained when the *overall* activities of the two systems are taken into consideration. The parasympathetic deals primarily with anabolic activities concerned with the restoration and conservation of bodily energy and the resting of vital organs. In the words of Cannon ('29), "a glance at these various functions of the cranial division reveals at once that they serve for bodily conservation; by narrowing the pupil they shield the retina from excessive light; by slowing the heart rate they give the cardiac muscle longer periods for rest and invigoration; and by providing for the flow of saliva and gastric juice, and by supplying the necessary muscular tone for the contraction of the alimentary canal, they prove fundamentally essential to the processes of proper digestion and absorption, by which energy-yielding material is taken into the body and stored. To the cranial division belongs the great service of building up reserves and fortifying the body against times of need and stress." The sacral division supplements the cranial by ridding the body of its intestinal and urinary wastes.

On the other hand, stimulation of the sympathetic component equips the body for the intense muscular action required in offense and defense. It is a mechanism that quickly mobilizes the existing reserves of the body during emergencies or emotional crises. The eyes dilate, respiration is deepened, and the rate and force of the heart is increased. The blood vessels of the viscera and the skin are constricted, the blood pressure is raised, and an ample blood supply is made available to the skeletal muscles, lungs, heart, and brain. The peaceful activities are slowed down or stopped entirely, the blood is drained from the huge intestinal reservoir, peristalsis and alimentary secretion are inhibited, and the urinary and rectal outlets are blocked by contraction of their sphincters.

The two systems are reciprocally inner-vated, and their dual activities are inte-grated into coordinated responses ensuring the maintenance of an adequate internal environment to meet the demands of any given situation. The parasympathetic ac-tivities are initiated primarily by internal changes in the viscera themselves. The sympathetic system is in considerable part activated by exteroceptive impulses that pass over somatic afferent fibers and are initiated by favorable or unfavorable changes in the external environment.

The preganglionic fibers of the sympa-thetic system arise from a continuous cell column in the spinal cord, and a single fiber may form synaptic relations with many cells in different paravertebral or prevertebral ganglia (Fig. 11-5B). Both types of ganglia are placed at considerable distances from the organs innervated, and from them postganglionic fibers are dis-tributed to extensive visceral areas (Figs. 11-1 and 11-9). Such a mechanism per-mits a wide radiation of impulses. The noradrenaline released at most sympathetic terminals further enhances the wide-spread and prolonged effects of sympa-thetic stimulation. Thus, stimulation of a thoracic ventral root, or white ramus, causes erection of hair and vasoconstriction in five, six, or even more segmental skin areas.

In the parasympathetic system the pre-ganglionic neurons are represented by more isolated cell groups whose fibers pass out in separate nerves and go di-rectly to the terminal ganglia within or near the organs. Moreover, each pregan-glionic fiber enters into synaptic relations with fewer postganglionic neurons than is the case in the sympathetic division. Thus in the superior cervical ganglion of the cat, the ratio of preganglionic fibers to postganglionic neurons is about 1:15 or more, while in the ciliary ganglion the ra-tio is only 1:2 (Wolf, '41). Parasympa-thetic action is therefore more discrete and is limited in effect to the portion stimulated. The liberation and rapid hydrolysis of acetylcholine by the para-sympathetic postganglionic fibers is com-patible with such localized autonomic

responses. Thus stimulation of the glosso-pharyngeal nerve increases parotid gland secretion, while stimulation of the oculo-motor nerve constricts the pupil, in each case without the appearance of other para-sympathetic effects.

The functions of the two subdivisions of the autonomic system are most easily understood by contrasting the individual structures innervated and noting the re-ciprocal actions of their dual nerve supply (Fig. 11-6). The autonomic fibers to the eye provide an excellent example of this dual innervation. The sympathetic divi-sion stimulates the smooth muscle fibers of the dilator muscle of the iris, the tarsal muscle, and the orbital muscle (of Mül-ler). The tarsal muscle extends from the levator palpebrae muscle to the tarsal plate of the upper lid and aids in full ele-vation of the upper eyelid. The orbital muscle, at least in lower forms, keeps the ocular bulb forward in the bony orbit. Le-sions in either the central or peripheral sympathetic pathways to the eye lead to the triad of symptoms known as *Horner's syndrome*. As a result of sympathetic in-jury, the parasympathetic innervation is now unopposed, and one may observe con-striction of the ipsilateral pupil (miosis), drooping of the upper eyelid (ptosis), and a sinking in of the eyeball (enophthalmos). Vasodilation and dryness of the skin of the face also may be evident. Sympathetic fibers destined for the eye follow the internal carotid artery, while those to sweat glands on the face course along the branches of the external carotid artery. This dichotomy of postganglionic fibers from the cervical ganglia explains the al-tered patterns of autonomic function that can occur after injuries in the face, deep neck, or within the skull. There may be loss of sweating on the face with preser-vation of sympathetic innervation to the eye or vice versa. Lesions of the cervical sympathetic trunk, inferior cervical gan-glion, or ventral roots of the upper tho-racic nerves interrupt the fibers before they divide to follow separate courses.

Parasympathetic fibers to the eye stim-ulate the sphincter muscle of the iris and thus bring about constriction of the pupil.

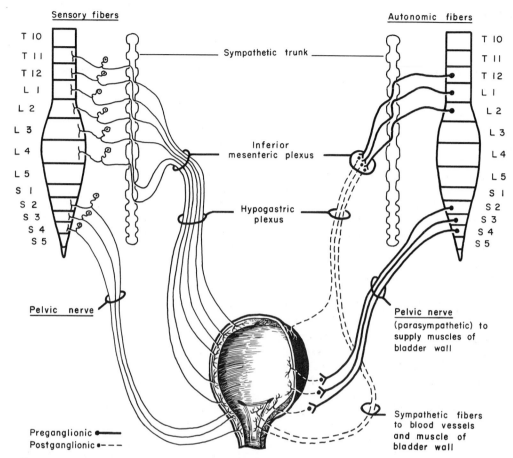

Fig. 11-9. Diagram of the sensory and autonomic innervation of the urinary bladder. The sensory and parasympathetic fibers in the pelvic nerve play the essential role in micturition, along with sacral somatic motor fibers to the pelvic musculature (not included in diagram).

These axons also stimulate the ciliary muscle. Contraction of the circular fibers of the ciliary muscle causes relaxation of the ciliary zonule and thereby decreases the tension of the lens capsule. As a result of such parasympathetic activity, the pupil is constricted and the convexity of the lens is increased for near vision (accommodation).

Innervation of the salivary glands was long believed due solely to secretory fibers in the cranial parasympathetic nerves (Fig. 11-6). Many differences have been found between the several glands of the different species studied, but both parts of the autonomic system send secretory fibers to the salivary glands. Sympathetic fibers provide for vasoconstriction of blood vessels, contraction of the myo-epithelial cells of the ducts and secretory fibers to the demilune gland cells (Babkin, '50). Stimulation of the human sympathetic trunk in the neck, or the injection of adrenaline into the salivary duct, evokes a flow of saliva from the submandibular, but not from the parotid gland. The secretory response to sympathetic stimulation is of short duration when compared to the long acting response that follows parasympathetic stimulation (Emmelin and Stromblad, '54). Parasympathetic fibers in cranial nerves seven and nine provide for vasodilation of the blood vessels and secretory fibers to the alveolar and acinar cells of the parotid, submandibular, sublingual and retrolingual glands. The vagus contains secretory fibers to the glands of the trachea and upper digestive tract. For additional details on the innervation of the salivary glands the reader is referred to the extensive reviews by Babkin, '50; Lundberg, '58; Burgen and Emmelin, '61; and Emmelin, '67.

The motor innervation of the urinary bladder is supplied by fibers in the ventral roots of the sacral nerves (Figs. 11–1 and 11–9). Somatic motor fibers from cord segments and sacral roots 2, 3 and 4 become incorporated in the pudendal nerve. Through a branch, the perineal nerve, the motor fibers maintain tonus of the external vesicle sphincter. Relaxation of the external sphincter muscle precedes the act of urination. Visceral motor fibers of S2, 3, and 4 leave the sacral nerves, and as the *pelvic nerve*, course to the lateral wall of the bladder where the fibers terminate in small vesical ganglia. Short postganglionic parasympathetic fibers to the bladder musculature induce contraction of the detrusor smooth muscle (Fig. 11–9). Relaxation of the external sphincter (somatic nerves) and contraction of the bladder wall (sacral visceral motor) are the two events most essential in micturition. The descending sympathetic fibers in the hypogastric plexus play no essential visceral motor role in the process of urination. They are concerned fundamentally with the innervation of the vesical trigone and lower ureter, vasomotor control, and ejaculation. *Vesical afferents* ascend in the hypogastric nerves and hypogastric plexus to reach the lumbar sympathetic trunk and their perikarya in dorsal roots T10 to L2 (Fig. 11–9). Afferent impulses over these nerves serve as a sensory input to the "vesical center for retention of urine" located in cord segments T12 to L2. It should be recalled that the desire to urinate is dependent upon intravesical pressure rather than fluid-volume content. The vesical capacity and frequency of urination vary with age and are influenced by reflex, psychic and local irritative factors. In children eight to ten years of age the initial desire to void occurs with an intravesical pressure of 9 to 11 cm of water (bladder volume 80–100

ml of urine). In adults with a fluid capacity of 140–180 ml, an intravesical pressure of 15 to 16 cm of water induces the desire to void (Campbell, '57). The most essential sensory fibers from the bladder return to the spinal cord via the pelvic nerve and dorsal roots S2, 3 and 4. These afferents participate in reflexes that are integrated with the "vesical center for bladder evacuation" located in cord segments S3 to S5. The sacral afferent impulses to the cord reach conscious level through the long pathways which are presented in Chapter 13. Bladder function after spinal cord injury is presented on page 296.

A familiarity with the information in Figure 11–6 proves most useful in evaluating the overall functional status of the autonomic nervous system. Vital body processes such as circulation, secretion, digestion, and excretion are essentially autonomic reflex responses. The autonomic system also participates in many somatic-visceral and visceral-somatic reflexes which involve either cranial or spinal nerves (e.g., respiration, pupillary, lacrimal, palatal, pharyngeal, sneeze, cough, swallowing, vomiting, carotid sinus, vasomotor, sudomotor, pilomotor, vesicle, genital, and emotional reflexes). Some of these reflexes will be presented as individual nerves are discussed. Metabolic or mechanical irritations of autonomic nerve fibers in the periphery may cause exaggerations of some of the sympathetic and parasympathetic functions included in Figure 11–6. Partial or complete lesions of autonomic fibers may occur in either the central or the peripheral nervous system (Fig. 13–25). An appreciation of the nuclei, fiber pathways, and resulting reflex deficits from injuries can be most useful as a diagnostic aid in exploring the diffuse distribution of the autonomic system. In the periphery the postganglionic sympathetic fibers that rejoin spinal nerves (Fig. 11–2) have a distribution which compares closely to that of the sensory dermatomes (Richter and Woodruff, '45; DeJong, '58). Hence changes in cutaneous sudomotor and vasomotor reflexes, changes in skin temperature, and increased skin resistance to passage of a minute electric current implicate the involvement of sympathetic nerve fibers. A knowledge of dermatomal and peripheral nerve distributions (Figs. 10–3 to 10–5, 10–7 and 10–8), correlated with the segmental nuclear origins of autonomic neurons (Figs. 11–1 and 11–3), often can provide additional evidence to substantiate both the location and level of a nerve injury.

CHAPTER 12

Internal Structure of the Spinal Cord

The microscopic appearance of the adult spinal cord has become vastly altered from the three-layered tube observed in embryonic development (Fig. 5–3). The incoming and outgoing processes of ganglion cells and intrinsic neurons produce marked changes in the embryonic marginal and mantle layers (Figs. 5–5 and 8–1). The embryonic layers become longitudinal columns of gray and white matter in the adult spinal cord, each having microscopic landmarks and subdivisions (Fig. 3–3). Individual segments of the spinal cord show variations at different levels, for there is great variation in the size and number of fibers in the individual spinal nerves. A knowledge of the microscopic characteristics of the gray and white matter in different regions of the cord is of fundamental importance, if one is to fully understand the material presented in subsequent chapters.

Gray and White Substance. The gray and white matter are composed of neural elements supported by an interstitial framework of neuroglia. The mesodermal structures comprise the blood vessels and their contents. The larger vessels are accompanied by prolongations of pial connective tissue. The gray matter contains the nerve cells, dendrites, and portions of myelinated and unmyelinated fibers. These fibers are axons of nerve cells located in the gray matter and passing to the white matter, or terminal portions of axons in the white entering the gray to terminate. The preponderance of neuron cell bodies, neuroglia, and capillaries imparts a firm consistency to the H-shaped gray substance (Fig. 12–1). This density is enhanced further by the multitude of fine glial processes, fibrils, axon synaptic terminals, and dendrites, which collectively form an intricate meshwork, or *neuropil*, that invests the neurons. In sections prepared with either hematoxylin and eosin or Nissl stains, the gray substance has a highly cellular appearance, whereas the fibrous elements of the neuropil are unstained (Fig. 12–5). In such sections one sees only the neuronal perikarya, glial and endothelial nuclei. The enormous dendritic plexus of the neurons and their associated synaptic endings remain unstained (Fig. 6–21). Lorente de Nó ('53) has estimated that the soma of the perikaryon forms only six per cent of the surface of a neuron. Hence the unstained neuropil of the gray matter in Figure 12–5 is precisely the place where dendritic plexuses are located and 94 per cent of the impulse traffic occurs. The central canal, surrounded by ependymal cells, is located in the cross bar of the H-shaped gray matter (Figs. 12–1 and 12–2). A sharply delineated central canal

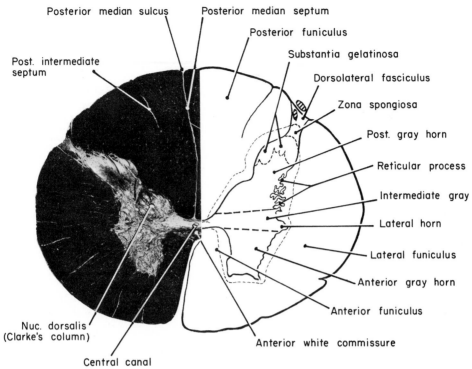

FIG. 12–1. Section through an upper thoracic segment of adult human spinal cord to demonstrate important subdivisions of the gray and white matter. Photograph of Weigert's myelin stain on *left* and schematic drawing on *right*. Area surrounding the gray matter, and limited peripherally by the *dotted line*, is composed of shorter ascending and descending fibers of the fasciculus proprius system.

is seen only in fetal and newborn spinal cords. In the adult the ependymal lining is often discontinuous and the lumen may contain a variety of debris, including round cells, macrophages and neuroglial processes (Fig. 12–2C). Surrounding the central canal are clumps of fibrous astrocytes which are otherwise scarce in the gray matter (Figs. 7–1 and 7–9). The two slender bands of gray matter above and below the central canal form the posterior and anterior gray commissures.

The white matter contains few neuronal cell bodies or dendrites, but is composed of ascending and descending myelinated and unmyelinated nerve fibers. The longitudinally arranged fiber bundles and their supportive neuroglia cells surround the gray matter as the posterior, lateral, and anterior white funiculi. Numerous myelinated axons can be observed entering or leaving the white funiculi as dark fibers in sections stained by the Weigert method

(Figs. 12–1 and 12–15). The structure and distribution of the glial cells are presented in Chapter 7. It need only be recalled here that the processes of the astrocytes form a *superficial glial membrane* which is adherent to the deep surface of the pia mater (Figs. 2–2 and 2–3).

Variations in Spinal Cord at Different Levels. The different levels vary considerably with respect to the shape and size of the spinal cord, the shape and size of the gray matter, and the relative amount of gray and white. These differences are due primarily to variation in the size of the nerve roots. Thus the larger nerves of the extremities produce the cervical and lumbar enlargements and in these segments the two horns of the gray matter are increased in size. Note these enlarged regions of the gray matter in the L4 and C8 segments of Figure 12–3. Similarly the outflow of the preganglionic sympathetic fibers in the thoracic cord is

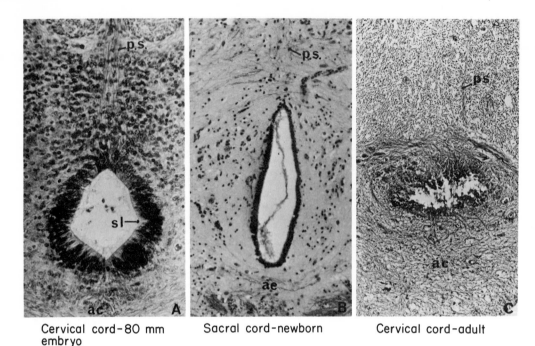

Cervical cord–80 mm embryo   Sacral cord–newborn   Cervical cord–adult

Fig. 12–2. Ependymal cells and central canal of embryonic and adult human spinal cord. The sulcus limitans (*sl* in *A*) becomes lost in the adult. Processes of the ependymal cells entering the posterior median septum (*ps*) can be seen and the fibers of the anterior white commissure are identified (*ac*). *A*. Holmes silver stain ×263. *B*. Luxol fast blue-cresyl violet × 112. *C*. Homes silver-cresyl violet ×108.

represented by the lateral horn (intermediolateral column). Since all levels of the cord are connected with the brain by long ascending and descending fibers, there is naturally an increase in the white matter as we proceed from lower to higher levels. The cervical segments contain the largest number of fibers. This variation in the amount of white matter is the second factor causing differences at various spinal levels. Some of the variants seen at different levels may be observed in the scaled drawings of Figure 12–3.

The length of respective cord segments varies as well as their transverse diameters. Spinal cord segment lengths were measured in the cat and monkey by Thomas and Combs ('62, '65). Their observations parallel those of man. The upper cervical, lower lumbar and sacral segments are the shortest; lower cervical segments are of intermediate length; the thoracic and upper lumbar segments have the greatest lengths.

The *sacral segments* are characterized

histologically by their small overall diameter, by the thick almost quadrangular appearance of the gray matter and its short gray commissure, and by the relatively small amount of white matter in all three of the surrounding white funiculi. The substantia gelatinosa is particularly pronounced in the sacral segments of the spinal cord, and it accounts for the thickened posterior gray column observed at these caudal levels (Figs. 12–4 and 12–5). The posterior spinocerebellar tracts are not present at sacral levels, and as a result the lateral corticospinal tract occupies a superficial position in the posterior portion of the lateral funiculus. Both the gray and white matter are increased in amount at S1 and S2, so that these sacral segments are quite similar in appearance to the L5 segment of the spinal cord.

The *lumbar segments* of the cord, particularly L3, L4, and L5, are enlarged in area and have a transverse diameter of about 12 mm. (Figs. 12–6 and 12–7). There is a considerable increase in the amount

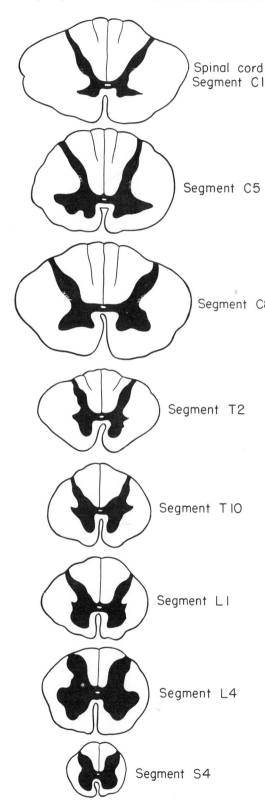

Spinal cord
Segment C1

Segment C5

Segment C8

Segment T2

Segment T10

Segment L1

Segment L4

Segment S4

of white matter, and the gray columns are massive. These changes are the result of the large number of incoming sensory fibers and outgoing motor fibers of the lumbar and sacral plexuses. The anterior gray column is bayed out laterally due to the prominent lateral motor cell columns, and the substantia gelatinosa forms a prominent cap on the posterior gray horn (Fig. 12–7). A rounded nucleus dorsalis (of Clarke) is present in lumbar segments (L1, 2, 3). This prominent group of neurons forms a continuous column of cells from this level upward through segment C8. A transition in appearance is again evident at the L1 level, which is quite similar to the more rostral T12 segment.

The *thoracic segments* display slightly different appearances at higher and lower levels (Figs. 12–3, 12–8 and 12–9). In segments T9 to T12, the anterior gray horn is reduced as compared to that of the lumbar cord. However, it is more prominent than the anterior gray horn observed in segments T2 to T8. It will be recalled that the upper thoracic nerves supply motor fibers only to the axial musculature (i.e., back and intercostals). The lower thoracic nerves supply the same muscles, as well as motor fibers to the abdominal musculature; hence the anterior horn is more pronounced. The small diameter of the slender thoracic segments is due primarily to the marked reduction of gray matter. A posterior intermediate septum (Figs. 12–1 and 12–11) is present in all cord levels above T6 and subdivides the posterior funiculus into two smaller fasciculi (gracilis and cuneatus). In addition to smaller size and thinner gray columns, the thoracic cord segments have other distinguishing features. For example, a prominent gray horn projects into the lateral funiculus at all thoracic levels (Figs. 12–1, 12–3 and 12–8). This gray projection is formed by the intermediolateral nucleus, whose visceral motor axons leave the thoracic cord in ventral spinal roots T1 to L2 (Fig. 12–17).

Fig. 12–3. Diagram of some spinal cord segments at different levels showing variations in shape, size, and topography of the gray and white matter. *Letters and numbers* indicate corresponding segments of the spinal cord.

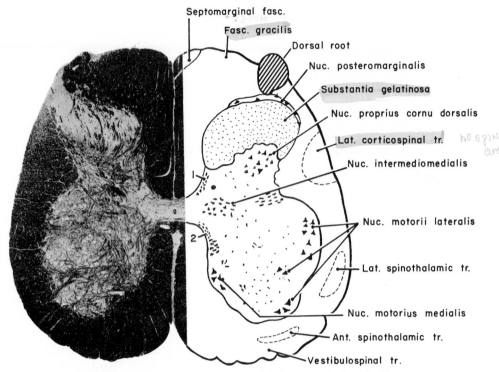

Septomarginal fasc.

Fasc. gracilis

Dorsal root

Nuc. posteromarginalis

Substantia gelatinosa

Nuc. proprius cornu dorsalis

Lat. corticospinal tr.

Nuc. intermediomedialis

Nuc. motorii lateralis

Lat. spinothalamic tr.

Nuc. motorius medialis

Ant. spinothalamic tr.

Vestibulospinal tr.

FIG. 12–4. Section through third sacral segment of adult human spinal cord. The important cell groups and fiber tracts are identified. *1*, Nucleus cornucommissuralis posterior; *2*, nucleus cornucommissuralis anterior. Weigert's myelin stain. Photograph.

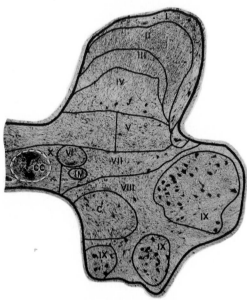

FIG. 12–5. Structural lamination indicated on thick section of human cord segment S4. Structures identified are the commissural nucleus (*C*), central canal (*cc*), and intermediomedial nucleus (*IM*). Compare with Figure 12–4. Thionin stain. Photograph ×15.

On the mesial surface of the posterior gray horn, the nucleus dorsalis (of Clarke) is present at all thoracic levels and may form a rounded eminence (Fig. 12–9). This nucleus is particularly prominent in segments T10 to T12, where one usually can observe many myelinated collaterals entering the nucleus from the posterior funiculus (Figs. 12–1 and 12–8). The large cells of this nucleus have a characteristic appearance. Their large vesicular nuclei are often eccentrically placed, and the coarse chromophilic material is distributed around the periphery of the perikaryon (Fig. 12–10). The clear perinuclear area and eccentric nuclei are normal cell features in this cell group, and should not be interpreted as evidence of chromatolysis. Axons leaving the cells of the nucleus course laterally where they turn upwards as components of the posterior spinocerebellar tract (Figs. 12–16 and 13–15).

The *cervical segments* are easily recognized by their increased size, large amounts of white matter, and the promi-

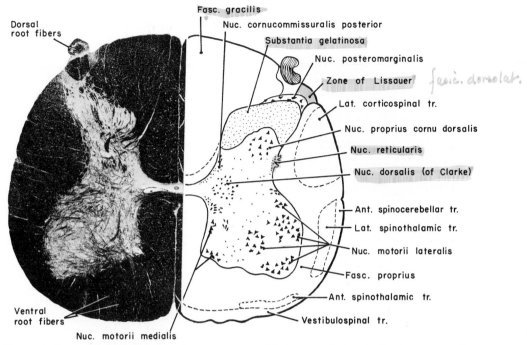

FIG. 12-6. Section through fourth lumbar segment of adult human spinal cord. The important cell groups and fiber tracts are identified. Weigert's myelin stain. Photograph.

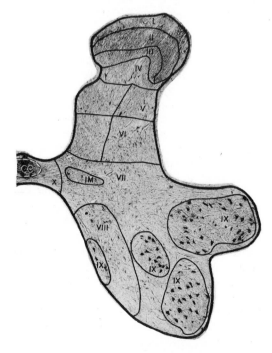

FIG. 12-7. Structural lamination indicated on thick section of human cord segment L5. The central canal (*cc*) and intermediomedial nucleus (*IM*) are identified. Compare with Figure 12-6. Thionin stain. Photograph. ×7.5.

nent appearance of the gray matter, particularly in segments of the cervical enlargement related to the brachial plexus (Figs. 12–3 and 12–11). Segments C7 and C8 are somewhat flattened and have an anteroposterior diameter of 8 to 9 mm, whereas their transverse diameter may be 13 to 14 mm. The anterior gray columns are massive and bayed out to accommodate the lateral motor nuclear groups whose axons innervate the muscles of the upper extremity (Figs. 12–11 and 12–12). The posterior gray column is enlarged, though slender and somewhat tapered. On the lateral border near the base of the posterior gray column, the reticular nucleus forms a series of fine projections into the lateral white funiculus. This serrated area, present at all cervical levels, is called the *reticular process*. A more or less complete septum divides the posterior funiculus into a medial fasiculus gracilis and a lateral fasciculus cuneatus. In the upper cervical segments such as C2 or C1, the gray matter becomes again reduced, but the area of the section is large owing to the great amount of white matter (Fig. 12–14). The transverse diameter of the

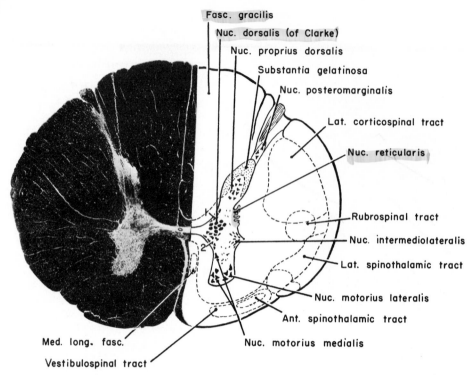

Fasc. gracilis
Nuc. dorsalis (of Clarke)
Nuc. proprius dorsalis
Substantia gelatinosa
Nuc. posteromarginalis
Lat. corticospinal tract
Nuc. reticularis
Rubrospinal tract
Nuc. intermediolateralis
Lat. spinothalamic tract
Nuc. motorius lateralis
Ant. spinothalamic tract
Nuc. motorius medialis
Med. long. fasc.
Vestibulospinal tract

Fig. 12-8. Section through fifth thoracic segment of adult human spinal cord. Important cell groups and fiber tracts are identified. *1*, Nucleus cornucommissuralis posterior; *2*, nucleus cornucommissuralis anterior. Weigert's myelin stain. Photograph.

most rostral cervical segment is about 12 mm.

The Nuclei or Cell Groups. The gray matter contains numerous multipolar cells of varying size and structure which may be grouped into two main classes, the *root cells* and the *column cells*. The root cells, situated in the anterior and lateral gray, are efferent peripheral neurons whose axons pass out of the cord as ventral root fibers to innervate the somatic and visceral effectors. The column cells and their processes, on the other hand, are entirely confined to the central nervous system. They constitute the *central, internuncial, commissural,* and *association* neurons. The majority send their axons to the white matter where, after bifurcating or bending, they form the longitudinal fibers of the white columns. Some are Golgi type II cells, whose short unmyelinated axons do not reach the white matter but terminate in the gray close to their origin. Those cells whose fibers remain on the same side are known as association or *ipsilateral* column cells; those whose axons cross are *contralateral* or *commissural* cells. Some cells may have axons which divide into both crossed and uncrossed terminal branches. The Golgi type II cells may likewise be association or commissural cells, their axons ending in the gray of the same side or crossing over to the gray of the opposite side. Some of the longitudinal fibers arising from the column cells, both crossed and uncrossed, may reach relay nuclei of the brain stem as long ascending tracts (Figs. 13-6 and 13-12). Others ascend or descend variable distances as intersegmental fibers connecting various levels of the cord (Fig. 13-3). Still others may be very short and terminate within a segment. This is especially true of the Golgi cells, which are intrasegmental in character (Fig. 13-1).

The nerve cells are not scattered uniformly through the gray, but are organized in more or less definite columns or

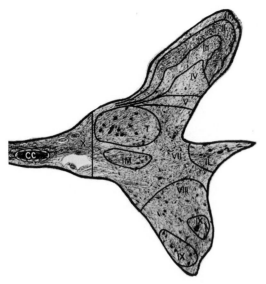

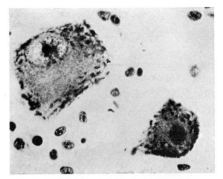

Fig. 12–10. Two cells from nucleus dorsalis (Clarke's column) of human spinal cord. Nissl stain. Photograph.

Fig. 12–9. Structural lamination indicated on thick section of human cord segment T10. The central canal (cc), intermediomedial nucleus (IM) and nucleus dorsalis (T, of Clarke, nucleus thoracicus) are identified. Compare with Figure 12–8. Thionin stain. Photograph. ×14.

nuclei, which may be recognized in transverse sections as separate groups distinguished from each other by their location, size, form, and cellular structure (Figs. 12–6 to 12–12). Some of these cell groups extend the whole length of the cord, though they vary in extent in different levels. Others may be limited to specific cord segments.

Nuclear groups as well as their dendritic patterns are observed best in longitudinal sections of the cord following thionin and Golgi stain procedures. However, this plane of section is difficult for the beginning student to interpret. Transverse sections cut at 80 to 100 micra and stained with thionin provide a more complete picture of neuronal groupings as shown in Figures 12–5, 12–7, 12–9 and 12–12. Such nuclear groups are most prominent in the human newborn; they are less sharply defined in the adult cord—particularly in thin sections which contain only a few cells of a given nucleus. Thicker sections demonstrate more perikarya, but cellular details are lost or compromised.

Lamination. For many years innumer-

able and often conflicting terms were used to locate and describe the nuclear grouping of cells in the spinal cord. Some were based on cell size and appearance (e.g., substantia gelatinosa), others were subdivided on the basis of their location in the gray matter (e.g., motor muclei of the anterior horn). Still others used eponyms, while some believed the only logical terminology should be based on a synaptological principle, (i.e., to class the neurons according to their synaptic connections). In a series of illuminating papers Rexed ('52, '54, '64) described an architectural organization of neurons in the cat spinal cord that has proven most valuable. His several zones have been corroborated and used by other investigators to describe terminal degeneration in this experimental animal. He believed that a similar lamination or zoning of the gray matter existed in all higher mammals. Examination of the spinal cord segments in the newborn and many adult human spinal cords revealed the presence of laminae comparable to those described by Rexed in the cat (Truex and Taylor, '68). This lamination of cell groups in the spinal cord resolved much of the confusion in terminology, and has become a widely used method for localizing axonal degeneration in the mammalian spinal cord.

Thick frozen sections of the human spinal cord from different segmental levels are shown in Figures 12–5, 12–7, 12–9 and 12–12. They are stained to demonstrate neuronal perikarya, and the boundaries of

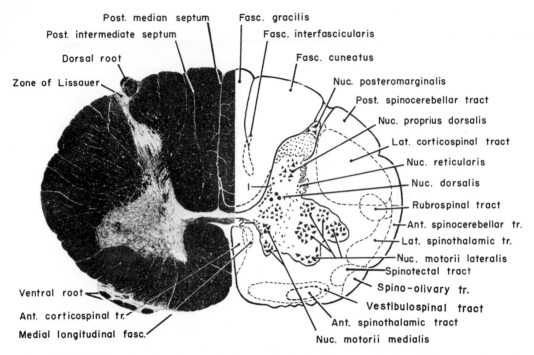

Fasc. gracilis
Post. median septum
Post. intermediate septum
Fasc. interfascicularis
Dorsal root
Fasc. cuneatus
Zone of Lissauer
Nuc. posteromarginalis
Post. spinocerebellar tract
Nuc. proprius dorsalis
Lat. corticospinal tract
Nuc. reticularis
Nuc. dorsalis
Rubrospinal tract
Ant. spinocerebellar tr.
Lat. spinothalamic tr.
Nuc. motorii lateralis
Spinotectal tract
Spino-olivary tr.
Vestibulospinal tract
Ventral root
Ant. corticospinal tr.
Ant. spinothalamic tract
Medial longitudinal fasc.
Nuc. motorii medialis

FIG. 12-11. Section through eighth cervical segment of adult human spinal cord. The important cell groups and fiber tracts are identified. *1*, Nucleus cornucommissuralis posterior; *2*, nucleus cornucommissuralis anterior. Weigert's myelin stain. Photograph.

Rexed's laminae are indicated in each figure. For ease of comparison combined Weigert-Nissl stained nuclear groups are illustrated at each level above those of the laminae. There are differences in laminar configuration between the various segments and regions of the cord. The laminae constitute regions with characteristic properties, but their boundaries are zones of transition, where changes may occur either gradually or abruptly. Only the principal features of individual lamina are included in this brief presentation. Rexed's cytoarchitectonic organization of gray matter is composed of nine cell layers, and region ten surrounds the central canal. Some of the layers correspond to recognized cell columns and nuclei, others are a regional admixture of cells and fibers.

Lamina I is a thin veil of scattered gray substance that caps the surface of the posterior horn and bends around its margins. It has a spongy appearance and is penetrated by many small and large fiber bundles (Figs. 12-4 and 12-5). It contains small, medium and large cells including the nucleus posteromarginalis. The study of Ralston ('68, '68a) indicates there are only a few synaptic endings of dorsal root fibers within this zone.

Lamina II consists of tightly packed small cells and corresponds to the substantia gelatinosa of the earlier literature. It is traversed by many strands of large fibers from the posterior funiculus (Figs. 12-15, 12-16), but has few synaptic endings of dorsal root fibers (Ralston, '68a). The entire lamina has a very low population of glial cells and fibers.

Lamina III forms a band across the posterior horn and consists of less packed and larger neurons. It has a lighter appearance, and the zone has less breadth in man as compared to that of the cat. This zone is rich in myelinated axons, and cells in this layer receive the greatest number of axo-dendritic synapses from entering dorsal root fibers (Ralston, '68a).

Lamina IV is the broadest of the first four layers, and its borders are sometimes diffuse (Figs. 12-5, 12-7 and 12-9). Small

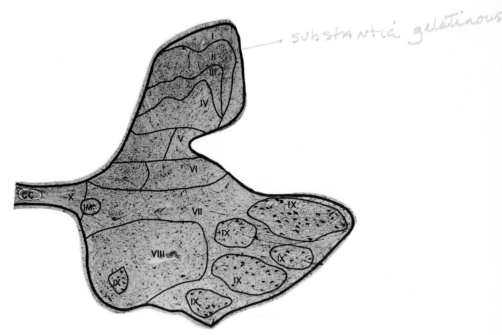

substantia gelatinousa

FIG. 12-12. Structural lamination indicated on thick section of human cord segment C6. The central canal (*cc*) and intermediomedial nucleus (*IM*) are identified. Compare with Figure 12-11. Thionin stain. Photograph. ×9.

to large-sized cells of variable shapes are scattered through this zone and give it a heterogeneous, less compact appearance. Axodendritic and axosomatic synapses of dorsal root fibers are found commonly on the large and medium-sized cells of this layer which includes most of the cells of the nucleus proprius of the posterior horn (Figs. 12-4, 12-6, 12-8, 12-11).

Lamina V is a broad zone extending across the neck of the posterior horn, and has medial and lateral subdivisions except in the thoracic region (Fig. 12-9). Many fiber bundles pass through the lateral zone to give it a reticulated appearance. The lateral part of lamina V (Rexed, '52) is the reticular nucleus, which is particularly prominent at cervical levels (Figs. 12-8 and 12-11). It has more large perikarya with coarse Nissl bodies. The medial zone extends to the posterior funiculus, has fewer and smaller perikarya with small amounts of Nissl substance, and a characteristic pale appearance. Synapses of dorsal root fibers as well as descending suprasegmental fiber pathways have been demonstrated on the neurons of this lamina (e.g. corticospinal fibers).

Lamina VI is a broad layer which is typical only in the cervical and lumbar enlargments (Figs. 12-7 and 12-12). In these levels it is subdivided into small medial and larger lateral zones located at the base of the posterior horn. The medial zone is more compact due to numerous dark-stained medium and small-sized cells. Larger, triangular or star-shaped perikarya are scattered through the less compact lateral zone. Many dorsal root Group I muscle afferents terminate in the medial zone of layer VI, while descending pathways are known to project to cells in the lateral zone (Fig. 12-16). Some axons of cells in the lateral zone leave the gray matter to enter the fasciculus proprius system and lateral white funiculus.

Lamina VII occupies most of the intermediate zone of gray matter (Fig. 12-1), and its boundaries vary at the different cord levels (Figs. 12-7, 12-9, and 12-12). Medium-sized and light stained perikarya predominate in this zone to give a general appearance of homogeneity. Within its boundaries are some long-recognized nuclei such as the nucleus dorsalis (of Clarke, thoracicus) and the intermediolateral and

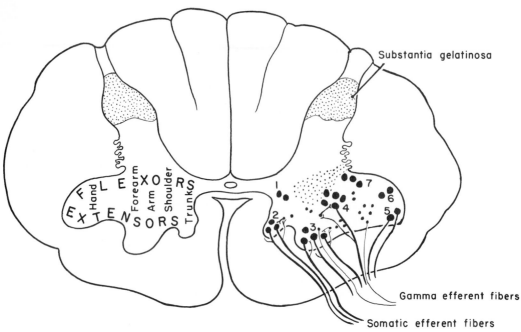

Fig. 12-13. Diagram of motor nuclei in anterior gray horn of lower cervical segment of spinal cord. On the *left* is shown the general location of anterior horn cells that send motor axons to specific muscle groups of the upper extremity. Motor nuclei indicated on the *right* are: *1*, posteromedial; *2*, anteromedial; *3*, anterior; *4*, central; *5*, anterolateral; *6*, posterolateral; *7*, retroposterolateral. Smaller anterior horn cells send axons (gamma efferents) to supply small muscle fibers of neuromuscular spindle. Note the collaterals from somatic efferent axons that return to gray matter and synapse on small medially placed "Renshaw cells." Smaller cells appearing as the *dotted zone* in the intermediate gray indicate the area of the internuncial neuron pool.

intermediomedial nuclei (Figs. 12–8, 12–9). In the lumbar and cervical enlargements lamina VII extends into the anterior horn to include the many internuncial, Renshaw, and gamma efferent neurons known to be present among the larger motor neurons (Fig. 12–13). Within the limits of this most important lamina are large numbers of internuncial cells for dorsal root afferents; descending suprasegmental motor and autonomic pathways, and a variety of segmental reflexes. Axons from perikarya in layer VI will form tracts to the cerebellum and higher centers, while other axons leave the cord in the ventral roots as gamma efferent and preganglionic visceral motor fibers (Figs. 12–16 and 12–17).

Lamina VIII is a heterogeneous mixture of small and medium sized cells, though occasional large perikarya are found scattered in this layer (Figs. 12–5 and 12–9). It is not always sharply delimited from

lamina VII. In the lumbar and cervical enlargements it is confined to the medial part of the anterior horn. Rexed believes the axons from these medially placed neurons are mostly commissural fibers which cross midline in the anterior white commissure (Fig. 12–16). Synaptic terminals of axons in several descending tracts terminate in lamina VIII (e.g., vestibulospinal, reticulospinal, and medial longitudinal fasciculus).

Lamina IX is composed of the largest cells of the spinal cord, namely, the Alpha motor neurons whose axons pass via spinal nerves to supply the skeletal extrafusal muscle fibers (Fig. 12–17). As shown in Figures 12–5, 12–7, and 12–12 the lateral nuclear masses are always sharply delimited. Within each nuclear group one can see also both large and small perikarya that are rich in cytoplasmic Nissl bodies. The medial nuclear masses are often less sharply defined and have a diffuse border with lamina VIII (Figs. 12–7 and 12–9). Many of the motor nuclei have been subdivided and named on the basis of their location in the gray matter as indicated in Figure 12–13. As shown in this figure also, there is a topographic distribution of perikarya whose axons supply the different muscle groups of the extremity.

A. **Somatic Efferent Root Neurons.** These neurons contribute axons to the respective ventral roots of the spinal nerves and are organized into named nuclear groups which may vary from segment to segment (Figs. 12–4, 12–6, 12–8 and 12–11). They have a transverse diameter of 30 to 70 micra, and the cell body may be over 100 micra in length. Such elongated multipolar neurons have 3 to 20 dendrites and axons with diameters of 10 to 13 micra. Each normal cell has a large central vesicular nucleus and coarse Nissl bodies in the cytoplasm (Figs. 6–1E and 6–7A). These somatic efferent neurons are largest in the lumbar and cervical enlargements, for their cell processes (axons) extend to the distal parts of the extremities (Figs. 12–6 and 12–11). Such neurons are smaller in the thoracic segments of the spinal cord (Fig. 12–9). Scattered among the larger anterior horn cells of the anterior gray are smaller cell bodies. Thinner axons from these cells (gamma efferent fibers) supply the slender intrafusal skeletal fibers of the neuromuscular spindle (Figs. 9–14 and 12–13). Other small medially placed neurons in the anterior gray horn have been identified physiologically, but not by anatomical methods to date. These small neurons (Renshaw, '40, '41, '46) presumably receive synaptic terminals from the recurrent axon collaterals of large anterior horn cells. Axons of "Renshaw cells" probably end as synaptic terminals upon the same large cell bodies from which they receive recurrent axon collaterals. Such recurrent collaterals and the involved neurons are shown diagrammatically in Figure 12–13. The Renshaw cells are included (but not identified) in this schema.

As noted above, the large anterior horn cells are organized into medial and lateral groups, and each group has several subdivisions.

1. *Medial nuclear group.* This cell group or column is divisible into a posteromedial and anteromedial group. The latter extends throughout the whole cord and is most prominent in C1, C2, C4, T1, T2, L3, L4, S2, and S3. The nucleus of the hypoglossal nerve in the medulla appears to be a continuation of this column. The posteromedial group is smaller and most distinct in the cervical and lumbar enlargements (Fig. 12–13). It may be missing in the sacral portions of the cord. The medial motor column innervates the short and long muscles attached to the axial skeleton.

2. *Lateral nuclear group.* This motor cell group innervates the rest of the body musculature. In the thoracic segments, it is small and undivided and innervates the intercostal and other anterolateral trunk muscles (Fig. 12–8). In the cervical and lumbar enlargements, it becomes considerably enlarged and a number of subgroups may be distinguished. The group is especially prominent in those segments which participate in the innervation of the most distal portions of the extremities. Here may be distinguished anterolateral, posterolateral, anterior, central, and retroposterolateral groups (Figs. 12–6 and 12–13). The exact innervation of the various extremity muscles by each of these groups has not been completely worked out, but in general the more distal muscles are supplied by the more lateral cell groups. Passing thus from the most mesial part of the anterior horn to its lateral periphery, the successive innervation is spine, trunk, shoulder and hip girdle, upper leg and arm, and lower leg and arm. The retroposterolateral group supplies the muscles of the hand and foot. Experimental denervation studies in animals have produced variable results. Section of specific peripheral motor nerves of the cat showed central neuron chromatolysis in discrete anterior horn nuclei. Cell columns that supplied nerve fibers to the dorsal divisions of the ventral primary ramus were located anterolaterally; cell groups placed posteromedially contributed fibers to the ventral

division of the ventral primary ramus (Romanes, '51). In the monkey, the nerve cells could not be classified functionally on the basis of either their topographic position or morphology (Sprague, '51).

Additional large multipolar neurons are found along the lateral and medial borders of the anterior gray horn in the thoracic, lumbar, and sacral segments of the spinal cord (spinal border cells of Sherrington, 1892). These border cells form the nucleus pericornualis anterior which Cooper and Sherrington ('40) believed to contribute fibers to the anterior spinocerebellar tracts. Similar neurons have been identified in the posterior and intermediate regions of the anterior gray horn of the monkey (propriospinal cells of Sprague, '51).

B. **Visceral Efferent Neurons.** These are the neurons whose axons pass by way of the ventral roots and white rami communicantes to the various sympathetic ganglia. They are ovoid or spindle-shaped cells with thinner shorter dendrites, vesicular nuclei, and finer chromophilic bodies (Figs. 6–6 and 12–9). They are considerably smaller than the somatic motor cells, ranging in size from 12 to 45 micra. In Weigert preparations they appear to be surrounded by a clear homogeneous background resembling the gelatinous substance. They may be divided into two groups.

1. *Intermediolateral nucleus* (Figs. 12–8 and 12–9). This nucleus really consists of several adjacent cell columns. The most lateral apical cell group constitutes the lateral horn. The nucleus begins in the lower portion of C8 and extends caudally through L2 or L3. Axons of neurons in the intermediolateral nucleus leave the cord in the ventral roots of spinal nerves T1 and L3 (Bok, '22; Poliak, '24) to terminate in the ganglionated sympathetic chain, or more peripheral ganglia along the aorta (Figs. 11–1 and 12–17). Each of these preganglionic axons has synaptic endings upon the dendrites and cell bodies of many postganglionic neurons in the above outlying sympathetic ganglia.

2. *Sacral autonomic nuclei.* Scattered small neurons are found along the lateral surface at the base of the anterior gray horn in sacral segments S2, S3, and S4 (Fig. 12–4). Such cells bear a striking resemblance to those found in the intermediolateral nucleus. Axons of these scattered cells leave the cord in the corresponding ventral roots as preganglionic (sacral) parasympathetic fibers. Such axons soon leave the sacral nerves to form short independent "pelvic nerves." These in turn have multiple synapses with many postganglionic cells located in or near the wall of the pelvic viscera (Fig. 11–1). The sacral preganglionic parasympathetic neurons have been localized in the cat and monkey by the use of both morphologic and physiologic methods (Schnitzlein et al., '63). This wedge-shaped column of medium-sized cells lies in the peripheral area of the intermediate gray adjacent to the lateral white funiculus. Most of the axons from cells of this nucleus were 2 to 3 micra in diameter, and the majority of the evoked responses were transmitted at speeds of 6 to 8 meters per second.

C. **Posterior Horn Neurons** (column cells and Golgi type II cells). These cells and their processes are confined entirely to the central nervous system. In the posterior and intermediate gray especially, they receive the collaterals or direct terminations of dorsal root fibers. In turn, they send their axons either directly to anterior horn cells of the same segments or to the white matter, where, by bifurcating, they become ascending and descending longitudinal fibers, forming intersegmental tracts of varying length (Fig. 13–1). The longest fibers reach the brain as parts of suprasegmental pathways (Fig. 13–6). The cells vary in size, form, and internal structure. Some are organized into definite cell groups that are easily distinguishable in transverse sections; others are scattered irregularly in the gray matter.

The *nucleus posteromarginalis (nucleus magnocellularis pericornualis, marginal cells)* forms a thin layer of cells that covers the tip of the posterior horn and is situated in the zona spongiosa or lamina I (Fig. 12–1). They are large, tangentially arranged stellate or spindle-shaped cells reaching a diameter of over 50 micra. Their axons pass into the lateral white funiculus and bifurcate into ascending and descending fibers, probably forming intersegmental pathways. The cells are found throughout the cord; they are most numerous in the lumbosacral segments, less so in the cervical, and least in the thoracic segments. In sections 10 to 20 micra thick, their number varies from 1 or 2 in the thoracic, to 6 or 10 in the lumbar cord (Fig. 12–6).

Beneath the marginal cells is the *substantia gelatinosa* (lamina II) which forms the outer caplike portion of the head of the posterior horn. It extends the whole length of the cord and is largest in the lumbosacral and first cervical segments (Fig. 12–5). Its variations in size are to some extent related to the size of the dorsal roots. The nucleus is composed of rows of small ovoid or polygonal cells with deeply staining nuclei about 6 to 20 micra in diameter (Fig. 6–4*G*). Some unmyelinated or finely myelinated axons end in the substantia gelatinosa. Others pass into the dorsolateral zone of Lissauer, the adjacent lateral white, and the posterior white column. The large number and small size of the cells suggest that they give rise to short, principally intrasegmental fibers. The nucleus constitutes the chief associative center of the posterior horn for incoming impulses.

The head and cervix of the posterior horn is occupied by the *nucleus proprius cornu posterior* (*nucleus centrodorsalis, nucleus magnocellularis centralis*). This nucleus corresponds to lamina III and IV as seen in Figures 12–4 to 12–12. Some are spindle-shaped cells of more than medium size; others are large polygonal cells with numerous dendrites that approach the size of a motor anterior horn cell. This rather poorly defined cell column is found in all segments, the cells being most numerous in the lumbosacral cord. Lateral to this nucleus, the small- and medium-sized cells found in the reticular process (lamina V) have been termed the *nucleus reticularis*, (Figs. 12–6 and 12–11). They send their axons to the same

as well as to the opposite anterolateral white column.

Nucleus dorsalis (*nucleus thoracicus, column of Clarke, nucleus magnocellularis basalis, nucleus spinocerebellaris*) is a striking cell column placed in the medial portion of the base of the posterior horn. The nucleus begins to be well defined in C8 and extends through the thoracic and upper lumbar segments, being most prominent in T10, T12 and L1 (Fig. 12–9). Below L3 it becomes indistinguishable, though occasional cells are found in the lower cord segments as well as in the cervical region. In sections 10 to 20 micra thick, the number of cells ranges from 3 or 4 in the upper thoracic to 10 or 15 in the lower thoracic, and there are about 20 in T12 and L1. Their large, thickly myelinated axons pass uncrossed to the lateral white funiculus, where they ascend to the vermis of the cerebellum as the posterior spinocerebellar tract (Figs. 12–11 and 12–16).

In the intermediate gray a rather diffusely organized cell group constitutes the *nucleus intermediomedialis*, as contrasted with the intermediolateral nucleus. The small- and medium-sized cells, 10 to 24 micra in size, are found in varying numbers throughout the cord (Fig. 12–4) but are most numerous in the upper cervical segments. Their axons pass mostly to the lateral white matter of the same side.

Two less definite cell columns extending the length of the cord are the *nuclei cornucommissurales posterior* and *anterior* (Fig. 12–4). The former, in section, is a thin cell strip occupying the medial margin of the posterior horn and extending along the border of the posterior gray commissure. It lies over the column of Clarke where the latter is present. The anterior is a similar cell group along the medial surface of the anterior horn and anterior gray commissure. These nuclei consist of small- and medium-sized spindle-shaped cells whose axons probably form intersegmental tracts in the posterior and anterior white funiculi, respectively.

Arrangement of Fibers. It has been noted that the white matter is composed

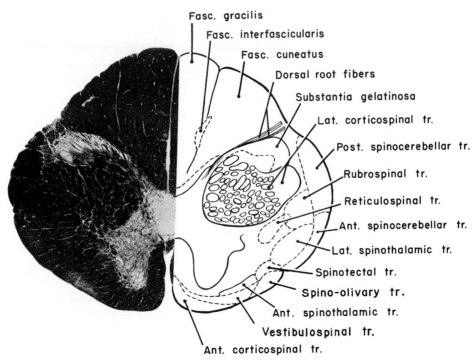

Fasc. gracilis
Fasc. interfascicularis
Fasc. cuneatus
Dorsal root fibers
Substantia gelatinosa
Lat. corticospinal tr.
Post. spinocerebellar tr.
Rubrospinal tr.
Reticulospinal tr.
Ant. spinocerebellar tr.
Lat. spinothalamic tr.
Spinotectal tr.
Spino-olivary tr.
Ant. spinothalamic tr.
Vestibulospinal tr.
Ant. corticospinal tr.

Fig. 12–14. Section through upper portion of first cervical segment of adult human spinal cord. Some of the important fiber tracts are identified. Weigert's myelin stain. Photograph.

principally of longitudinal fibers, while in the gray the fibers have a transverse direction, running from gray to white or vice versa (Figs. 12–14 and 12–15). The reason for the transverse course of these fibers is obvious. The transverse fibers are either fibers of origin or fibers of termination and include: (1) dorsal root fibers entering the cord; (2) axons of column cells passing to the white matter, where they become ascending or descending fibers; and (3) collaterals and terminals of fibers of the white matter, which come from other parts of the spinal cord or from the brain, and enter the gray to terminate there.

The dorsal roots, as already stated, are composed of coarse, thickly myelinated fibers and of finer fibers, many of which are unmyelinated (Figs. 6–2F and 8–5A). The coarse fibers are processes of the larger spinal ganglion cells that bring in impulses from muscle spindles, Golgi tendon organs, Meissner's corpuscles, Pacinian corpuscles, and probably diffuse unencapsulated receptors (position and movement, touch, vibration). These dorsal root fibers are shown in red and black in Figure 12–17. The finer myelinated and unmyelinated fibers, which are processes of the smaller ganglion cells, conduct impulses from diffuse endings, end bulbs, and other encapsulated endings (primarily pain and temperature, but also some touch). Such thin dorsal root fibers are indicated in black in Figure 12–17. The dorsal roots break up into a number of filaments or rootlets which enter the cord in a linear manner. Each of these filaments on entering the cord separates into a smaller lateral bundle composed of fine fibers, which enters the zone of Lissauer, and a larger medial bundle composed of the coarser fibers, which pass into the main portion of the posterior funiculus lying medial to the dorsal horn (Figs. 12–16 and 12–17). Each root fiber bifurcates into a longer ascending and a shorter descending arm as soon as it enters the cord. The fine fibers which pass to the zone of Lissauer divide into very short arms, the longer ascending ones extend only one or

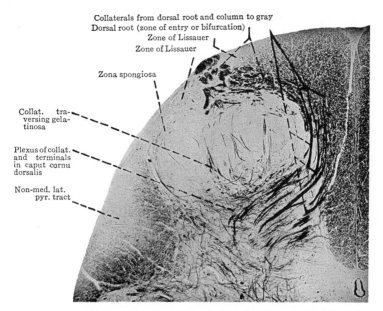

FIG. 12–15. Portion of transverse section of lumbar spinal cord of 5-week-old infant, showing entrance of a dorsal root and its collaterals. Weigert's myelin stain. Photograph.

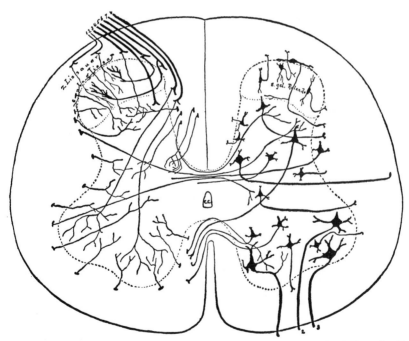

FIG. 12–16. Section through spinal cord, showing arrangement of collaterals (*left*) and cell bodies and their axons (*right*) as seen in Golgi preparations. *1* and *2* represent fine dorsal root fibers passing laterally to the zone of Lissauer. *3* to *8* represent coarse dorsal root fibers passing to the posterior white column. Collaterals from *1* and *2* enter the substantia gelatinosa, those from *3* to *8* enter the substantia gelatinosa, head and neck of the posterior horn, intermediate gray, and anterior horn. Some collaterals from dorsal root fibers of other, probably lower, levels are seen leaving the posterior white column and ending in the dorsal horn, intermediate gray, and column of Clarke. Preganglionic autonomic root cells are not shown. *cc*, Central canal. (after Cajal, '11).

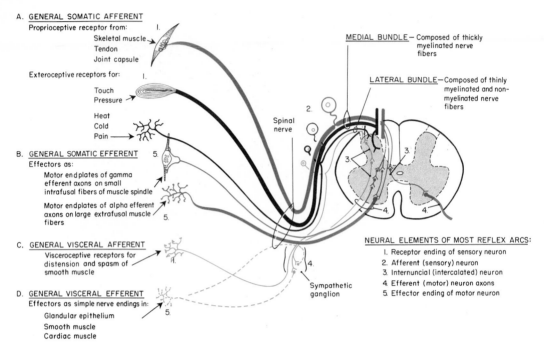

A. GENERAL SOMATIC AFFERENT
Proprioceptive receptor from:
Skeletal muscle
Tendon
Joint capsule

Exteroceptive receptors for:

Touch
Pressure

Heat
Cold
Pain

B. GENERAL SOMATIC EFFERENT
Effectors as:
Motor endplates of gamma
efferent axons on small
intrafusal fibers of muscle spindle
Motor endplates of alpha efferent
axons on large extrafusal muscle
fibers

C. GENERAL VISCERAL AFFERENT
Visceroceptive receptors for
distension and spasm of
smooth muscle

D. GENERAL VISCERAL EFFERENT
Effectors as simple nerve endings in:
Glandular epithelium
Smooth muscle
Cardiac muscle

MEDIAL BUNDLE—Composed of thickly
myelinated nerve
fibers

LATERAL BUNDLE—Composed of thinly
myelinated and non-
myelinated nerve
fibers

Spinal
nerve

Sympathetic
ganglion

NEURAL ELEMENTS OF MOST REFLEX ARCS:
I. Receptor ending of sensory neuron
2. Afferent (sensory) neuron
3. Internuncial (intercalated) neuron
4. Efferent (motor) neuron axons
5. Effector ending of motor neuron

FIG. 12–17. Diagram of functional components of a thoracic spinal nerve, and the arrangement of dorsal root fibers as they enter the spinal cord. Skeletal muscle afferent and efferent fibers are indicated in *red*. Visceral afferent and efferent fibers are shown in *blue*. An afferent fiber from a Pacinian corpuscle (*black*) and a thin pain fiber (*black*) also are shown. Numbers in the diagram correspond to neural elements that form reflex arcs.

two segments (Ranson, '13). The descending and ascending arms ultimately enter, and terminate in, the gray matter. In any transverse section of the cord, bundles of fine fibers composed of collaterals and terminals of the entering roots may be seen passing radially through the substantia gelantinosa, or sweeping around its mesial side to be distributed to the various cell groups of the gray matter. A few fibers terminate in the substantia gelatinosa, while others form terminal plexuses in the caput and cervix of the posterior horn (Figs. 12–15 and 12–16). In the thoracic and upper lumbar segments many myelinated collaterals are seen entering the nucleus dorsalis. Still others can be traced to the intermediate gray, and some go directly to the anterior horn as "sensori-motor" or "direct reflex collaterals" (Figs. 12–17 and 13–3). By means of the last named collaterals, two-neuron reflex arcs are possible, but the number of such collaterals terminating directly on the motor cell is relatively small. Most reflexes have at least one additional central neuron interposed between the afferent and efferent neurons (Figs. 12–17 and 13–1).

The lateral and anterior funiculi are connected with the gray by many transverse fibers. These are all processes of central cells. They are either axons of column cells entering the white matter to become ascending or descending longitudinal fibers, or collaterals and terminals of longitudinal fibers entering the gray to terminate. Many of the fibers cross to the opposite side. The anterior white commissure consists of decussating fibers of column cells which lie near the level of crossing. The much smaller posterior white commissure contains a few crossing axons of column cells and collaterals from the posterior white column.

Finally, in the anterior part of the cord coarser transverse fibers may be seen which are axons of the various somatic motor cell groups. The bundles of somatic motor fibers leave the anterior gray horn, pass through the white matter, and emerge as ventral root fibers (Figs. 12–13 and 12–17). In the thoracic and upper lumbar segments and in some of the sacral ones, the ventral roots also contain a large number of fine myelinated fibers from cells of the lateral horn. These fine fibers constitute the preganglionic fibers of the autonomic system. The visceral sensory and motor fibers are indicated in blue in Figure 12–17.

CHAPTER 13

Fiber Tracts of The Spinal Cord

The ascending and descending fibers of the spinal cord are organized into more or less distinct bundles which occupy particular areas in the white matter. Fiber bundles having the same origin, course, and termination are known as tracts or fasciculi. It is customary to divide the white matter of the spinal cord into three funiculi: posterior, lateral, and anterior. The posterior funiculi lie between the posterior gray horns. The lateral funiculi are located lateral to the butterfly-shaped gray columns, while the small anterior funiculi are situated between the anterior gray horns. Thus a funiculus may contain several fasciculi, but owing to the overlapping and intermingling of fibers, these may not be demarcated sharply. In general, long tracts tend to be located peripherally, while shorter tracts tend to be situated medially.

ARRANGEMENT OF ENTERING AFFERENT FIBERS

All central processes of cells in the dorsal root ganglia enter the spinal cord. Peripheral processes of these cells convey impulses centrally from various types of somatic and visceral receptors. Dorsal root fibers entering the posterolateral aspect of the spinal cord in small fascicles over a considerable distance, have been grouped in two bundles (Ranson, '14). Thick, heavily myelinated fibers of the *medial bundle*

represent the central processes of dorsal root ganglion cells conveying impulses from large encapsulated somatic receptors, such as neuromuscular spindles, neurotendinous organs, Pacinian corpuscles, and Meissner's corpuscles. The smaller, less conspicuous *lateral bundle* is composed of thinly myelinated fibers representing the central processes of smaller ganglion cells related to tactile receptors, thermal receptors, free nerve endings, and other somatic and visceral receptors. Recent evidence based on Golgi studies (Szentágothai, '64) has shown that thinly myelinated fibers from the dorsal root actually pass both medial and lateral to the posterior horn. Upon entering the spinal cord, central processes of each dorsal root ganglion cell divide into ascending and descending branches (Fig. 13–1), which in turn give rise to numerous collateral branches. Most of the collateral branches are given off in the segment of entry, where they participate in intrasegmental reflexes or relay impulses to second order neurons. Primary ascending and descending branches, extending into adjacent spinal cord segments, together with their collaterals, constitute the anatomical basis of intersegmental reflexes and participate in the relay of impulses to secondary sensory pathways (Fig. 13–3). The longer ascending primary branches of the medial bundle enter the ipsilateral posterior funiculus,

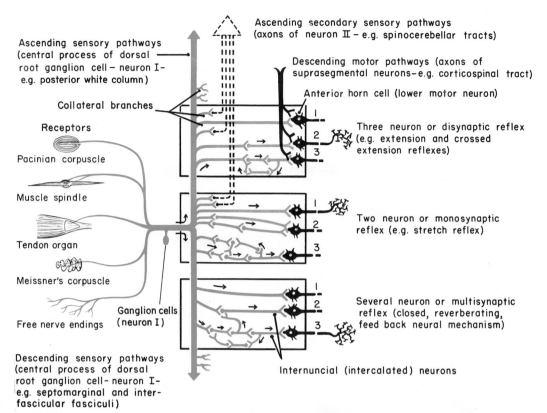

Ascending secondary sensory pathways
(axons of neuron II – e.g. spinocerebellar tracts)

Ascending sensory pathways
(central process of dorsal
root ganglion cell – neuron I–
e.g. posterior white column)

Descending motor pathways (axons of
suprasegmental neurons–e.g. corticospinal tract)

Anterior horn cell (lower motor neuron)

Collateral branches

Receptors

Three neuron or disynaptic reflex
(e.g. extension and crossed
extension reflexes)

Pacinian corpuscle

Muscle spindle

Two neuron or monosynaptic
reflex (e.g. stretch reflex)

Tendon organ

Meissner's corpuscle

Several neuron or multisynaptic
reflex (closed, reverberating,
feed back neural mechanism)

Free nerve endings

Ganglion cells
(neuron I)

Descending sensory pathways
(central process of dorsal
root ganglion cell– neuron I–
e.g. septomarginal and interfascicular fasciculi)

Internuncial (intercalated) neurons

FIG. 13–1. Diagram of major branches and collaterals of dorsal root ganglion cells within three spinal cord segments. On the left are various receptors that generate impulses in response to different kinds of stimuli. Impulses from muscle spindles initiate the myotatic or stretch reflex involving two neurons (monosynaptic reflex). Impulses from the tendon organ initiate disynaptic reflex circuits involving inhibitory mechanisms. Other reflex circuits may involve many neurons (multisynaptic). Also indicated are ascending and descending branches of dorsal root fibers in the posterior white column (see Fig. 13–6) and collateral pathways that project fibers to the cerebellum (see Fig. 13–15).

and many of them ascend without synapse as far as the medulla. Some of the fine, thinly myelinated fibers of the lateral bundle of the dorsal root, conveying impulses of pain, thermal, and light tactile sense, enter the medial part of the *zone of Lissauer (fasciculus dorsolateralis)* (Figs. 12–1, 12–6, and 12–11). The central course and branches of one dorsal root ganglion cell may be far more extensive than shown schematically in red in Figure 13–1.

The zone of Lissauer (fasciculus dorso-lateralis) is composed of: (1) fine myelinated and unmyelinated dorsal root fibers which enter medial parts, and (2) a far larger number of endogenous propriospinal fibers which interconnect different levels of the substantia gelatinosa (Ranson, '14;

Earle, '52; Szentágothai, '64). In Golgi preparations axons of cells in laminae I, II, and III can be followed into lateral parts of the zone of Lissauer. The number of dorsal root fiber collaterals terminating in the substantia gelatinosa is small, although this structure is traversed by fiber bundles passing to laminae III and IV (Szentágothai, '64; Ralston, '65; Stein and Carpenter, '65). It seems likely that afferent impulses excite the substantia gelatinosa polysynaptically via interneurons in deeper portions of the posterior horn. This view is suggested by the rich dendritic arborizations of the large cells of lamina IV which extend in radial fashion throughout the substantia gelatinosa. In addition, marginal cells in lamina I, supplied by small

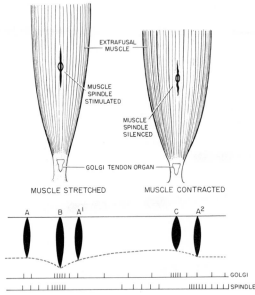

FIG. 13–2. Diagram showing the anatomical and functional relationships of the muscle spindle and the Golgi tendon organ to extrafusal muscle fibers. The muscle spindles are arranged in "parallel" with the extrafusal muscle fibers, so that stretching the muscle causes the spindles to discharge. Contraction of the muscle tends to "unload" or "silence" the muscle spindles. The Golgi tendon organs are arranged in "series" with respect to the extrafusal muscle fibers. Thus, the Golgi tendon organs can be discharged by either a stretch of the tendon or a contraction of the muscle. The threshold of the Golgi tendon organ is relatively higher than that of the muscle spindle. The *lower diagram* summarizes the functional characteristics of the muscle spindle and Golgi tendon in relation to changes in muscle length. At *A*, the muscle is shown at its resting length, and the slow spontaneous discharge of the tendon organ and muscle spindle is indicated. At *B*, the muscle is stretched and both receptors discharge, though the adaptation of the muscle spindle is more rapid. At A^1, the muscle resumes its original length and tension, and there is a temporary reduction in the frequency of spontaneous firing of the muscle spindle. At *C*, where the muscle is contracted and shortened, the muscle spindle is silenced, but the rate of discharge of the tendon organ is increased. At A^2, the muscle is stretched out to its resting length, and the muscle spindles are therefore discharged, while the tendon organs are silenced by the drop in tension (Granit, '55).

dorsal root fibers, also may send axons into the substantia gelatinosa. Studies of the fine structure of the substantia gelatinosa (Ralston, '65) reveal extensive axo-den-

dritic and axo-axonal contacts, but infrequent axo-somatic contacts.

One of the principal sites of termination of large myelinated dorsal root fibers is the dorsal nucleus of Clarke (Fig. 13–4). Clarke's nucleus receives fibers from all ipsilateral spinal roots except cervical roots (Grant and Rexed, '58). Studies of dorsal root afferents to Clarke's nucleus (Liu, '56; Grant and Rexed, '58) indicate: (1) the greatest number of fibers come from dorsal roots of the hindlimb, (2) there is considerable overlap of different dorsal root fibers distributed to the nucleus, and (3) fibers enter the nucleus via both ascending and descending collateral branches of the dorsal root. Synapses of dorsal root afferents upon the cells of Clarke's nucleus appear unique in that preterminal fibers have long parallel contact with the dendrites of Clarke's neurons and unusually large terminal boutons are partially buried in depressions on the cell surface (Szentágothai and Albert, '55). These "giant synapses" between dorsal root fibers and cells of the dorsal nucleus are said to be larger than any other spinal cord synapses. These anatomical observations are in close agreement with physiological studies (Lloyd and McIntyre, '50) showing that selective stimulation of group I afferent fibers establishes synaptic relationships with the cells of Clarke's nucleus.

Collateral branches of dorsal root fibers also are distributed to parts of the anterior horn (Fig. 13–5). According to Sprague ('58) and Sprague and Ha ('64), dorsal root fibers become concentrated especially in the central part of lamina VI; from this region fibers pass in numerous small bundles into lamina IX where they arborize about the soma and dendrites of large motor neurons. Dorsal root fibers also give off collaterals which pass into lamina VIII. Since collaterals of dorsal root fibers passing to laminae VIII and IX traverse broad regions of lamina VII, it is likely that some fibers end upon internuncial neurons in this lamina, as well as on dendrites of motor nuclei which extend beyond the limits of Rexed's lamina IX. Dorsal root fibers from group Ia afferent fibers projecting to lamina IX are involved in the monosynaptic myotatic

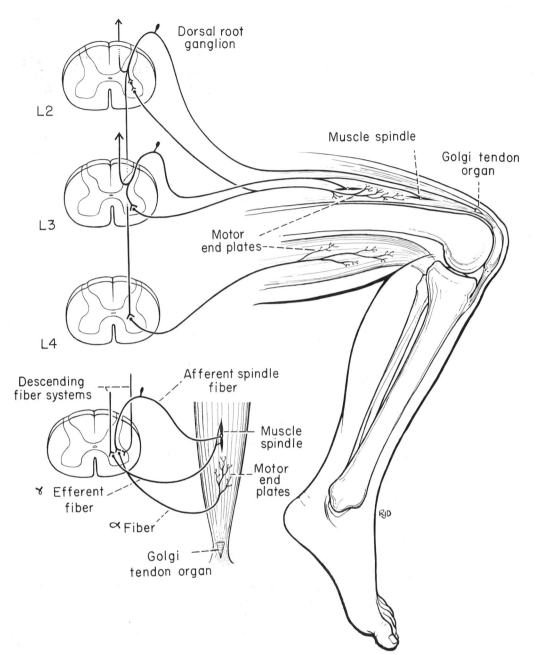

FIG. 13-3. Schematic diagram of patellar tendon reflex. Motor and sensory fibers of the femoral nerve associated with spinal segments L2, L3, and L4 mediate this myotatic reflex. The principal receptors are the muscle spindles, which respond to a brisk stretching of the muscle effected usually by tapping the patellar tendon. Afferent fibers from muscle spindles are shown entering only the L3 spinal segment, while afferent fibers from the Golgi tendon organ are shown entering only the L2 spinal segment. In this monosynaptic reflex, afferent fibers entering spinal segments L2, L3, and L4 and efferent fibers issuing from the anterior horn cells of these levels complete the reflex arc. Motor fibers shown leaving the L4 spinal segment and passing to the hamstring muscles demonstrate the pathway by which inhibitory influences are exerted upon an antagonistic muscle group during the reflex. The *small diagram below* illustrates the gamma loop. Gamma efferent fibers pass to the polar portions of the muscle spindle. Contractions of the intrafusal fibers in the polar parts of the spindle stretch the nuclear bag region and thus cause an afferent impulse to be conducted centrally. The afferent fibers from the spindle synapse upon an alpha motor neuron, whose peripheral processes pass to extrafusal muscle fibers, thus completing the loop. Both alpha and gamma motor neurons can be influenced by descending fiber systems from supraspinal levels. These are indicated separately.

257

reflex (Figs. 13–2 and 13–3). Group Ib and group II afferent fibers generate synaptic potentials in central parts of laminae V, VI and VII (Sprague and Ha, '64).

Spinal Reflexes. The five essential elements required for most spinal reflexes are: (1) peripheral receptors, (2) sensory neurons, (3) internuncial neurons, (4) motor neurons, and (5) terminal effectors. The *myotatic* or *stretch reflex* is a monosynaptic reflex dependent upon two neurons. Stretch-sensitive proprioceptive endings located in muscle (muscle spindle) and tendon (Golgi tendon organ) are the receptors stimulated by a sudden brisk stretch of muscle. The *muscle spindle*, consisting of bundles of specialized slender muscle fibers (intrafusal fibers) surrounded by a connective tissue capsule, is attached to the endomysium of extrafusal muscle fibers. Stretching of the noncontractile nuclear bag region (equatorial region) of the muscle spindle constitutes the mechanical stimulus required to fire the annulospiral or primary afferent fiber of this receptor. Gamma efferent fibers from the smaller anterior horn cells terminating in the polar (contractile) portions of the muscle spindle (intrafusal muscle fibers) bring this receptor under the control of spinal and supraspinal influences. *Golgi tendon organs* are found in tendons close to their muscular attachments. As first pointed out by Fulton and Pi-Suñer ('27–'28), the muscle spindle is arranged in "parallel" with extrafusal fibers, so that stretching of a muscle causes the spindle to discharge, while contraction of the extrafusal fibers tends to "unload" the spindle. The Golgi tendon organ is in "series" with extrafusal muscle fibers and thus can be caused to discharge by either a stretch or a contraction of the muscle (Fig. 13–2). Current physiological belief, based largely upon indirect evidence, indicates that the low threshold muscle spindles are the prime receptors involved in the stretch reflex. However, gamma efferent fibers to the muscle spindle can exert potent influences upon the activity of this receptor. The myotatic reflex can be elicited in almost any muscle by sharply tapping either the muscle, or its tendon, in such a way as

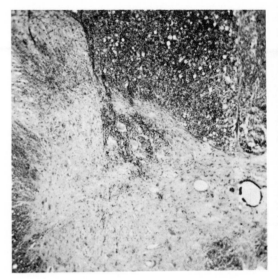

Fig. 13–4. Photomicrograph of degenerated dorsal root fibers in the rhesus monkey projecting directly to the dorsal nucleus of Clarke at L2. Lumbar dorsal roots were sectioned proximal to the dorsal root ganglia. Nauta-Gygax stain. X80.

to produce a brief sudden stretch of the muscle. Thus, striking the tendon of the quadriceps femoris muscle provokes a forceful contraction of the stretched muscle and a quick extension of the leg at the knee (Fig. 13–3). In this example, both the sensory and motor nerve fibers leave and enter the quadriceps muscle as constituents of the femoral nerve. It will be recalled that parts of two, three, or more myotomes are incorporated in each muscle and that two, three, or more spinal nerves and cord segments provide sensory and motor fibers. The femoral nerve is composed of sensory and motor fibers from spinal nerves L2, L3, and L4. Thus, the synapses between these sensory and motor fibers must be within spinal cord segments L2, L3, and L4.

As shown in this schema, the other spinal reflexes have one or more internuncial neurons interposed between sensory and motor neurons (*2* and *3* in Fig. 13–1), and some of these may form complex reverberating circuits. An anterior horn cell (lower motor neuron) thus may be facilitated, or inhibited, by the sum total of all the impulses that play upon it through literally thousands of tiny

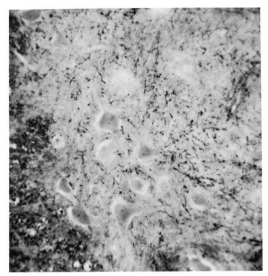

FIG. 13-5. Photomicrograph of terminal degeneration projecting around anterior horn cells at C6 in the rhesus monkey. Cervical dorsal roots were sectioned in this animal. Nauta-Gygax stain. X220.

synaptic end feet. Such synaptic boutons may be terminal endings of incoming sensory fibers, internuncial neurons, or the several descending motor pathways from the brain stem and cortex. This is the basic organization of a spinal cord segment and its attached spinal nerves.

THE LONG ASCENDING TRACTS

I. The Posterior White Columns (*Fasciculus gracilis and fasciculus cuneatus*). Since the posterior funiculus is composed predominantly of dorsal root fibers, both the ascending and descending courses of these fibers are described under this heading.

The more heavily myelinated fibers of the medial bundle of the dorsal root enter the posterior funiculus medial to the posterior horn, where they bifurcate into ascending and descending branches. Ascending fibers from lower levels gradually are shifted medially and posteriorly as they continue upward in the posterior funiculus of the spinal cord. Longer ascending fibers are displaced medially by shorter ascending dorsal root fibers entering the spinal cord at successively higher levels. This arrangement of ascending fibers in the posterior columns produces a laminated arrangement in which the longer sacral fibers are most medial and the shorter cervical fibers are most lateral (Figs. 13-6 and 13-8).

In the cervical and upper thoracic regions of the spinal cord, the posterior funiculus is divided by a posterior intermediate sulcus into a medial *fasciculus gracilis* and a lateral *fasciculus cuneatus* (Figs. 12-11 and 13-6). The former contains the long ascending root fibers from the sacral, lumbar, and lower thoracic ganglia (i.e., from the lower extremity and the lower portion of the trunk). The fasciculus cuneatus consists of similar fibers from the upper thoracic and cervical ganglia representing upper trunk, upper extremity, and neck.

Since many ascending fibers in the posterior columns are relatively short and terminate in the posterior gray column at various intermediate levels, only a portion of the dorsal root fibers terminate in nuclei at medullary levels. Fibers in the posterior columns which reach the medulla constitute the first relay in the largest spinal afferent pathway to the cerebral cortex.

The central processes of dorsal root ganglion cells thus constitute the first neuron (Neuron I, uncrossed) of this ascending pathway. Ascending fibers that reach the medulla within the fasciculus gracilis terminate upon the cells of the nucleus gracilis, while the fibers of the fasciculus cuneatus end about cells of the nucleus cuneatus (Fig. 13-6). The neurons of the nucleus gracilis and cuneatus constitute the second neuron (Neuron II) in this afferent system. The axons of Neuron II sweep ventromedially as *internal arcuate fibers*, cross the midline, and turn upward as a discrete bundle known as the *medial lemniscus*. This crossed tract ascends through the pons and midbrain levels to terminate in the ventral posterolateral nucleus of the thalamus. Relay neurons of this thalamic nucleus (Neuron III) send their axons through the posterior limb of the internal capsule to terminate in the appropriate sensory areas of the cerebral cortex (Fig. 13-6). In this figure one can follow the respective sacral,

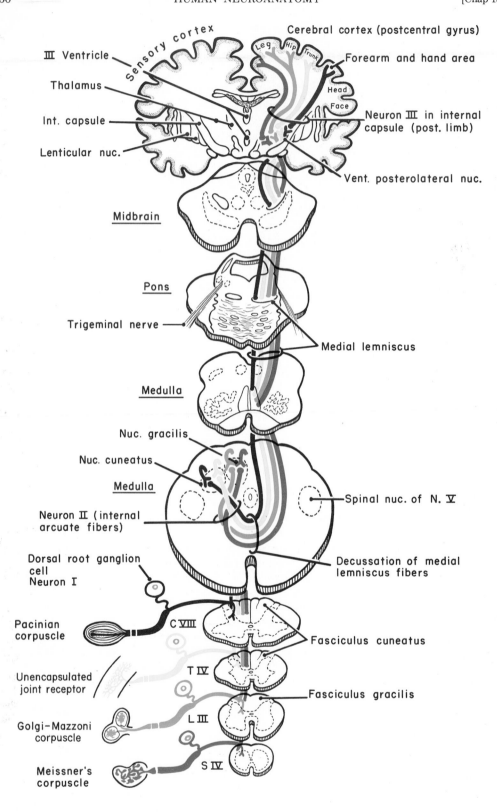

III Ventricle

Thalamus

Int. capsule

Lenticular nuc.

Sensory cortex

Cerebral cortex (postcentral gyrus)

Leg Hip Trunk

Forearm and hand area

Head

Face

Neuron III in internal
capsule (post. limb)

Vent. posterolateral nuc.

Midbrain

Pons

Trigeminal nerve

Medial lemniscus

Medulla

Nuc. gracilis

Nuc. cuneatus

Medulla

Spinal nuc. of N. V

Neuron II (internal
arcuate fibers)

Dorsal root ganglion
cell
Neuron I

Decussation of medial
lemniscus fibers

Pacinian
corpuscle

C VIII

Fasciculus cuneatus

Unencapsulated
joint receptor

T IV

Fasciculus gracilis

Golgi-Mazzoni
corpuscle

L III

Meissner's
corpuscle

S IV

lumbar, thoracic, and cervical fibers as they ascend from their level of entrance in the spinal cord to the sensory (somesthetic) cortex.

The posterior white columns are among the newer acquisitions of the nervous system, and they receive principally impulses from the arms and legs. In animals without extremities, they are poorly developed and consist mainly of shorter fibers. When we consider the great importance of the upper extremity, especially the hand, as an organ for discriminative sensibility and acquisition of skill, and of the lower extremity for the maintenance of erect posture, it is not surprising that this phylogenetically younger fiber system constitutes the principal path for the conduction of discriminative (epicritic) sensibility related to cortical function.

Long ascending fibers in the posterior columns convey impulses concerned with touch-pressure and kinesthesis (i.e., sense of position and movement). These fibers constitute part of a highly specific sensory pathway in which single elements are responsive to one, or the other of these forms of physiological stimuli, but not to both (Rose and Mountcastle, '59). Fibers of this system are highly specific with respect to place, and endowed with an exquisite capacity for temporal and spatial discrimination. Thus, these fibers conduct impulses from tactile receptors necessary for the proper discrimination of two points simultaneously applied (spatial discrimination) and for exact tactile localization. Rapid successive stimuli, produced by applying a tuning fork to a bony prominence or skin, result in a sense of vibration. "Vibrating sense" is not a specific sensory modality, but a temporal modulation of tactile sense (Calne and Pallis, '66). The end organs involved in perception of vibratory sense probably are Pacinian corpuscles found in subcutaneous connective tissue and in periosteum. Impulses conveying this form of temporally modulated tactile sense are considered to ascend in both the posterior and lateral columns of the spinal cord (Calne and Pallis, '66). The ascending impulses in the posterior columns conducted from receptors on joint surfaces and in joint capsules, which are excited by movement, are of great importance because they convey information concerning the position of different parts of the body (kinesthesis).

Lesions of the posterior columns naturally abolish or diminish these forms of sensibility, and the symptoms appear on the same side as the lesion. Mere contact and pressure are apparently normal; but tactile localization is poor, and two-point discrimination and vibratory sense are lost or diminished. There is loss of appreciation of differences in weight and inability to identify objects placed in the hand by feeling them. These symptoms are most acute on the fingers and more acute on the extremities than on the trunk. Position and movement sense is severely affected, especially in the distal parts of the extremities. Small passive movements are not recognized as movements at all, but as touch or pressure. Even in long excursions the direction and extent of the movement may not be perceived. Loss of position sense greatly impairs the performance of voluntary motor function. This sensory loss causes movements to be clumsy, uncertain, and poorly coordinated (posterior column ataxia).

Since a fiber severed from its cell of origin degenerates, injury to these central ascending fibers of the posterior white column will produce microscopic evidences of fiber degeneration. These large myelinated fibers frequently are involved totally, or in part, by toxins, or by demyelinating or metabolic diseases. Sections prepared by the Weigert method yield a "negative picture of myelin de-

---

Fig. 13-6. Diagram of the formation and course of the posterior white columns and the medial lemniscus. Fibers in the posterior white columns in the spinal cord are uncrossed, while all fibers of the medial lemniscus are crossed. Impulses mediated by this pathway concern discriminative tactile sense (touch and pressure) and kinesthetic sense (i.e., sense of position and movement). *Letters* and *numbers* indicate segmental levels of the spinal cord.

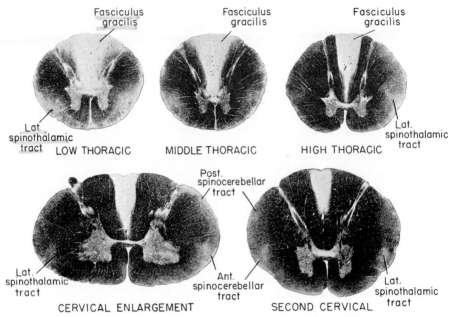

FIG. 13-7. Transverse sections of human spinal cord crushed some time previously in the lumbosacral region. In the posterior columns the progressive diminution of the degenerated area is due to passage into the gray matter of short and medium length ascending arms of lumbosacral dorsal root fibers. The progressive increase in normal fibers adjacent to the posterior horns is due to the addition of ascending arms of dorsal root fibers entering above the level of the injury. Weigert's myelin stain.

generation" after injury, for only the normal intact fibers are stained (Figs. 13-7 and 13-10). A knowledge of tract formation (Fig. 13-6) enables one to distinguish which region of the spinal cord may have been injured sometime prior to death. The series shown in Figure 13-7 was made following injury in the lumbosacral region, and the antemortem neurological signs and symptoms involved the lower extremities and pelvis. Note the decrease of ascending degeneration in the fasciculus gracilis as it ascends to the second cervical segment. Also observe the progressive increase of normal fibers that have entered the cord above the level of the injury. Contrast the appearance of the second cervical segments shown in Figures 13-7 and 13-10. The antemortem posterior column symptoms were far more extensive in the patient with a cervical cord crush (Fig. 13-10). Here all ascending posterior column fibers were interrupted bilaterally, including part of the sensory fibers from the brachial plexus. Note

that only a few normal cervical fibers have entered the fasciculus cuneatus above the level of injury.

Sections of the cord prepared by the Marchi method demonstrate a "positive picture of fiber degeneration" (Figs. 13-8 and 13-9). In such preparations the degenerated myelin sheaths stain as fine brown or black granules. The ascending degeneration, after destroying only the dorsal roots of L1, T12, and T11, is shown in Figure 13-8. In such an injury outside the spinal cord, normal sacral and lumbar fibers remain and are visible in the most medial part of the fasciculus gracilis. The fasciculus cuneatus is completely normal. A section of the cervical cord after lumbar injury (Fig. 13-9) shows that degeneration is limited to the most medial fibers within the fasciculus gracilis.

The Marchi method yields important information concerning the course of large well myelinated tracts, but it does not provide information concerning the terminations of degenerated fibers. Great

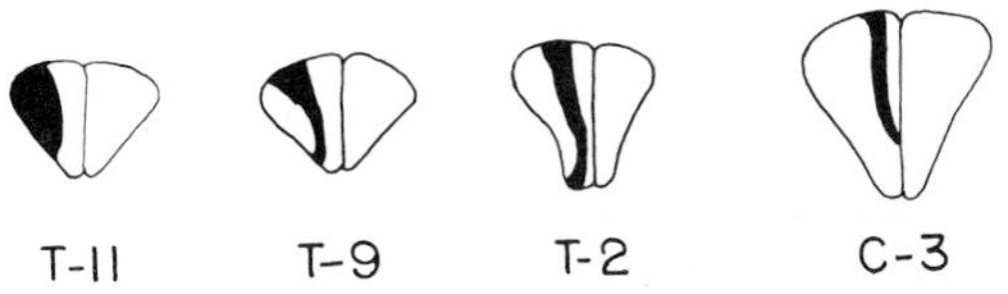

FIG. 13–8. Ascending degeneration after section of dorsal roots L1, T12, and T11. Marchi method (after Foerster, '36).

care must be used in interpreting Marchi preparations, for this method often produces deceiving artifacts (Smith, '51, '56).

Evidence of degeneration in the posterior columns also can be detected in Nissl-stained sections after a considerable period of time. Relatively dense gliosis is present in the areas of degenerated fibers (Fig. 13–11).

The descending branches of the dorsal root fibers vary in length, and become displaced medially and somewhat posteriorly as they pass to lower segments of the cord. They are relatively shorter fibers, but some may descend a distance of ten or more segments. In the cervical and most of the thoracic cord they form a small plug-shaped bundle, the *fasciculus interfascicularis* or *comma tract of Schultze,* lying in the middle of the posterior funiculus (Figs. 13–6 and 13–23). In the lumbar region they descend near the middle of the posterior septum in the *septomarginal fasciculus (oval area of Flechsig),* which in the sacral cord occupies a small triangle near the postero-median periphery (*triangle of Phillippe-Gombault;* Fig. 12–4). Besides the descending root fibers, the above named fascicles also contain descending fibers from cells of the posterior horn.

II. The Anterior Spinothalamic Tract. For many years it has been assumed that the spinothalamic tracts arose primarily from the large cells of the proper sensory nucleus (i.e., nucleus centrodorsalis, laminae III and IV of Rexed, '52) of the dorsal horn; axons of these cells were considered to cross obliquely in the anterior white commissure and ascend contralaterally as part of the spinothalamic system. Studies (Pearson, '52; Szentágothai, '64) of Golgi stained preparations have failed to reveal any fibers arising from cells of lamina IV that could be followed into the anterior white commissure. Thus it seems unlikely that spinothalamic fibers arise from the proper sensory nucleus. Available evidence suggests that fibers crossing in the anterior white commissure and entering the spinothalamic system arise mainly from laminae VI, VII and perhaps from lamina VIII (Szentágothai, '64). The manner in which cells of the proper sensory nucleus make contact with the cells of origin of the spinothalamic system is unknown.

In spite of these gaps in our knowledge, it seems well established that spinothalamic fibers cross in the anterior white commissure, and that the decussation takes place through several spinal segments. Fibers ascending contralaterally in the anterior and anterolateral funiculi form the anterior spinothalamic tract (Fig. 13–12). Fibers of the anterior spinothalamic tract are somatotopically arranged so that those originating from the most caudal segments of the spinal cord are situated laterally with respect to those from more rostral spinal segments. A small number of uncrossed fibers may ascend in the anterior spinothalamic tract; these are not indicated in Figure 13–12.

Fibers of the anterior spinothalamic tract usually are described as ascending without interruption to thalamic levels. As this tract ascends in the brain stem a conspicuous reduction in the number of fibers is evident. In the medulla the tract is located dorsolaterally to the inferior olivary nucleus, where it appears to join the lateral spinothalamic tract. At medullary levels some fibers of this tract, or collaterals, project into the dorsolateral part of the brain stem reticular formation, while others appear to terminate about cells of the lateral reticular nucleus of the medulla, a cerebellar relay nucleus. Fibers projected to these locations explain the attenuation of the tract in the lower brain stem. At levels through the upper pons and midbrain, the tract becomes closely associated with the medial lemniscus. Fibers of this ascending

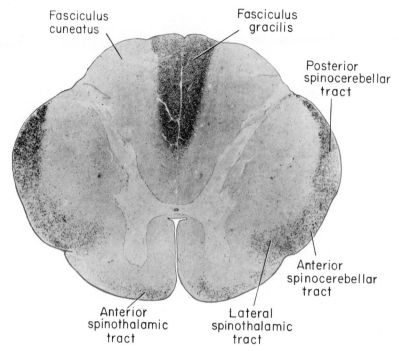

Fig. 13-9. Section through second cervical segment of a human spinal cord which had been crushed several weeks previously in the upper lumbar region. The ascending degenerating fibers are seen as *black granules*. Marchi stain. Photograph.

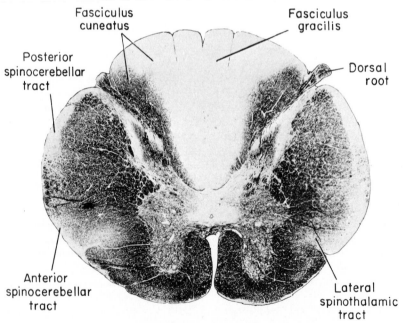

Fig. 13-10. Section through second cervical segment of a human spinal cord which had been crushed some time previously in the lower cervical region. Owing to the high level of the injury, practically all the fibers of the spinocerebellar and spinothalamic tracts have undergone degeneration. Also degenerated are all ascending root fibers in the posterior white column except those of dorsal root fibers which have entered above the upper level of the lesion (about C6). Weigert's myelin stain. Photograph.

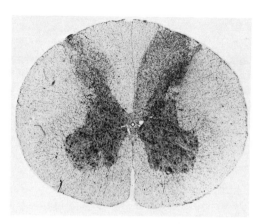

Fig. 13–11. Photomicrograph of the fifth cervical spinal segment in a rhesus monkey following multiple cervical dorsal rhizotomies on the right and section of the C5 dorsal root on the left. Intense gliosis sharply outlines the fasciculus cuneatus on the right, while more restricted gliosis on the left occupies the area of degenerated C5 dorsal root fibers. Nissl stain. ×10.

sensory system terminate upon cells of the ventral posterolateral nucleus of the thalamus. From this thalamic nucleus impulses are relayed to the cerebral cortex.

The anterior spinothalamic tract transmits impulses of light touch to higher levels of the neuraxis. Light touch is the sensation provoked by stroking an area of skin devoid of hair (glabrous skin) with a feather or wisp of cotton. This sensation supplements deep touch (pressure) and discriminative tactile sense conveyed in the posterior white columns. Because tactile sensation is transmitted centrally by both the posterior white columns and the anterior spinothalamic tracts, clinically this sensory modality is of limited value in localizing injuries of the spinal cord. Injury to the anterior spinothalamic tract in the spinal cord produces little, if any, disturbance in tactile sensibility, though sensory thresholds may be raised. The pleasant or unpleasant character of certain sensations, however, is considered to be related to conduction in the anterolateral funiculi. Bilateral destruction of these columns may cause complete loss of such affective qualities as itching, tickling, and libidinous feeling (Foerster and Gagel, '32).

III. The Lateral Spinothalamic Tract. Closely related to the anterior spinothalamic tract is the lateral spinothalamic tract. It is treated separately in view of its tremendous clinical importance. Its component fibers are more concentrated than those in the anterior spinothalamic tract, and it contains more numerous long fibers that go directly to the thalamus. The receptors of pain and thermal sense represent peripheral endings of the small- and medium-sized dorsal root ganglion cells, whose thin central processes enter the zone of Lissauer (Fig. 13–13). Statements made in regard to the cells of origin of the anterior spinothalamic tract apply also to the lateral spinothalamic tract. Thus it seems likely that cells of laminae VI, VII and perhaps VIII give rise to axons that cross in the anterior white commissure and ascend in the opposite lateral funiculus, as the lateral spinothalamic tract. Fibers of this tract cross obliquely to the opposite side within the segment of entry, although some may ascend one segment before crossing. Fibers of this tract are medial to those of the anterior spinocerebellar tract (Fig. 13–23).

The fibers show an anteromedial segmental arrangement in the lateral spinothalamic tract. The most lateral and posterior fibers represent the lowest portion of the body, whereas the more medial and anterior fibers are related to the upper extremity and neck (Fig. 13–13). As shown on the left of level C8, there is also a lamination of the sensory modalities within this tract; fibers concerned with thermal sense are posterior while pain fibers are located more anteriorly. Injuries of this compact pathway ordinarily affect both pain and thermal sense. At higher brain stem levels this tract sends numerous collaterals into the reticular formation and tegmentum.

Detailed studies of anterolateral cordotomy in the monkey (Bowsher, '57, '61; Mehler, et al., '60) indicate that the thalamic projections of the spinothalamic system are more complex than classic studies suggest. Unilateral anterolateral cordotomy produces: (1) predominantly

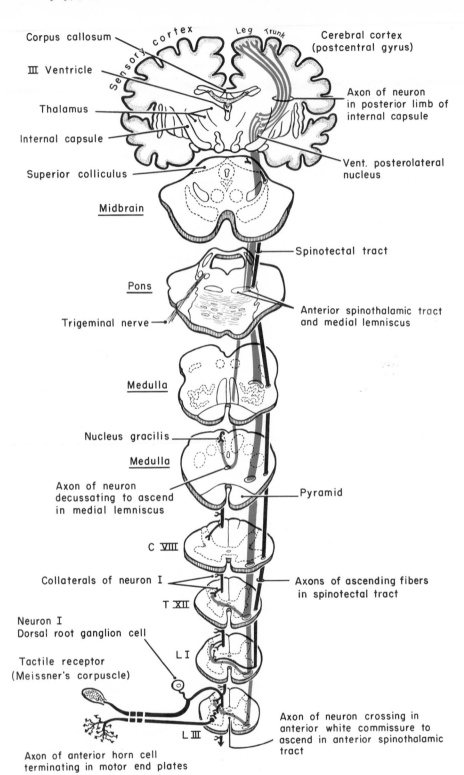

FIG. 13–12. Diagram of the anterior spinothalamic and tectospinal tracts. Although the precise cells of origin of these tracts are not known, spinothalamic fibers are considered to arise mainly from laminae VI, VII and VIII of Rexed. The anterior spinothalamic tract conveys impulses of light touch. *Letters* and *numbers* indicate segmental spinal levels.

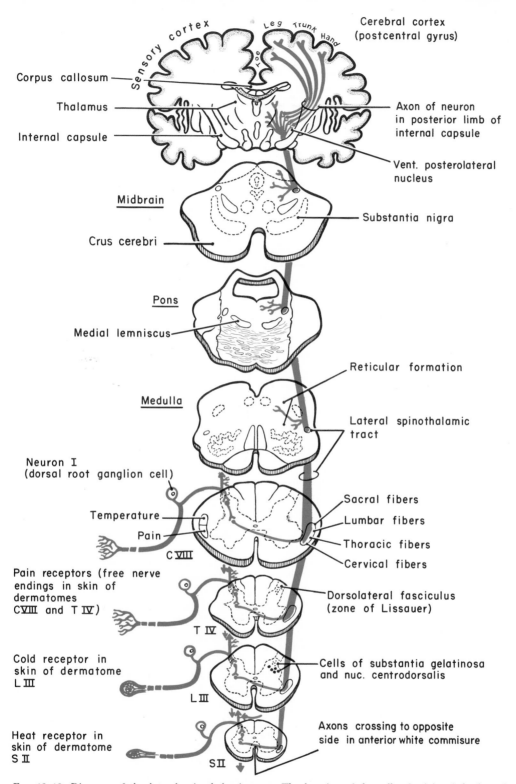

VPL
Po
Intra
Lamiuta
Nuc.

FIG. 13-13. Diagram of the lateral spinothalamic tract. The location of the cells of origin of the lateral spinothalamic tract appears to be in laminae VI, VII and VIII of Rexed, but fibers of this tract usually cross to the opposite side within one segment. Fibers of the lateral spinothalamic tract have a more complex termination in the thalamus than indicated here. The lateral spinothalamic tract conveys impulses of pain and thermal sense and has a somatotopic lamination. *Letters* and *numbers* indicate segmental spinal levels.

ipsilateral degeneration in the ventral posterolateral nucleus, and (2) bilateral degeneration in certain intralaminar nuclei and in a posterior thalamic region near the magnocellular part of the medial geniculate bodies. These anatomical observations, confirmed by physiological studies (Poggio and Mountcastle, '60; Whitlock and Perl, '61; Perl and Whitlock, '61) indicate that in the ventral posterolateral nucleus: (1) the body surface is represented in an orderly topographic manner, (2) cells of this nucleus are related to small specific receptive fields contralaterally, and (3) most cells are not activated by noxious stimuli. In the posterior thalamic region there is no topographic representation; cells in this region are activated from large receptive fields, both ipsilaterally and contralaterally, and respond readily to noxious stimuli.

Unilateral section of this tract produces a complete loss of pain and thermal sense (analgesia and thermoanesthesia) on the opposite side of the body. This contralateral sensory loss extends to a level one segment below that of the lesion, owing to the oblique crossing of fibers (Fig. 13–25). The anesthesia involves the superficial and deep portions of the body wall, but not the viscera, which appear to be represented bilaterally. The anogenital region is not markedly affected in unilateral lesions. After a variable period there is often some return of pain sensibility, due perhaps to the presence of uncrossed spinothalamic fibers. Such pain impulses also may ascend by shorter relays along spinospinal and spinoreticular pathways. A return of thermal sense also may be encountered.

In certain instances bilateral surgical section of the lateral spinothalamic tracts (cordotomy) is performed on selected patients to relieve pain and produce a complete and more enduring sensory loss. The spinothalamic and trigeminothalamic pathways both may be destroyed by one laterally placed lesion in the medulla or midbrain, where these two tracts occupy a superficial position (Figs. 13–13 and 15–17). Interruption of both tracts at the midbrain levels results in a loss of pain and thermal sense over the face, neck, trunk, and extremities on the opposite side of the body.

Nathan and Smith ('51) have presented evidence that in man the fibers subserving the sensation of bladder fullness and desire to micturate, and the pain fibers from the bladder, urethra, and lower ureter are all located in the lateral spinothalamic tract. They believe that fibers mediating touch, pressure, or tension in the urethra ascend in the posterior white column.

It is evident from the above that the sensory impulses brought in by the dorsal roots are organized in the spinal cord into two main systems, discriminative (epicritic) and affective (vital, protopathic); the former are related to the long fibers of the posterior white columns and the latter to the shorter root fibers and the anterolateral white column. Discriminative sensibility carried by the longest fibers remains uncrossed in the spinal cord. Pain and thermal impulses conveyed by the shortest fibers in the zone of Lissauer cross almost at once via the lateral spinothalamic tract.

This distribution of afferent impulses accounts for the curious sensory dissociation occurring in hemisection of the spinal cord (Brown-Séquard), where there is loss of pain and thermal sense on the opposite half of the body below the level of the lesion, while the sense of position and movement, two-point discrimination, and vibration are lost on the same side as the lesion (Fig. 13–28).

Experimental studies in the cat, which is said to lack an uninterrupted spinothalamic tract (Busch, '61), suggest that a *spinocervical tract* may serve as its homologue (Morin, '55; Morin and Catalano, '55; Taub, '64; Taub and Bishop, '65). Cells of origin of the spinocervical tract (Taub, '64), considered to lie in the nucleus proprius of the posterior horn (portions of laminae III and IV), give rise to uncrossed fibers which ascend in the superficial part of the posterolateral funiculus. These ascending fibers project to the ipsilateral lateral cervical nucleus, a

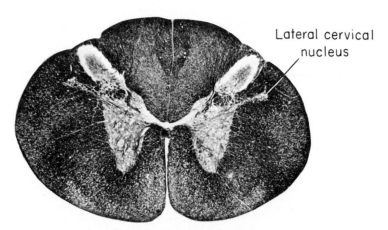

Lateral cervical
nucleus

Fig. 13-14. Transverse section of the first cervical spinal segment in the cat showing the lateral cervical nucleus. Cells of this nucleus receive fibers of the spinocervical tract, considered as the feline equivalent of the spinothalamic tract, and project impulses to the reticular formation and thalamus. Weil stain. ×16.

longitudinal cell column anterolateral to the posterior horn in the lateral funiculus of the C1 and C2 segments of the cat's spinal cord (Rexed and Brodal, '51). The lateral cervical nucleus (Fig. 13-14) projects fibers to the contralateral inferior olivary complex, reticular formation, and thalamus. Single units of the spinocervical tract show spontaneous activity and respond to hair movement and thermal cutaneous stimuli with a uniformly low threshold. The spinocervical tract, containing 2000 to 3000 fibers, 10 to 14μ in diameter, is the most rapidly conducting pathway in the feline spinal cord. Its integrity is essential for the earliest portion of the cortically evoked potential in somatic sensory areas I and II. Anatomical studies suggest that the spinocervical tract may convey impulses related to painful stimuli. It has been postulated that this rapidly conducting pathway may play a role in central alerting, in preparation for pain perception and for the subsequent activation of central descending inhibitory mechanisms. Physiological data indicate that the spinocervical tract is independent of the posterior spinocerebellar tract (Taub and Bishop, '65).

IV. The Spinotectal Tract. The cells of origin of the small spinotectal tract, like those of the spinothalamic system, are not known. Fibers of this crossed tract, located in the anterolateral part of the

spinal cord (Figs. 13-12 and 13-23), ascend in the spinal cord and brain stem in close association with the spinothalamic system (Poirier and Bertrand, '55). At midbrain levels fibers of the spinotectal tract project medially into the deep layers of the superior colliculus and to lateral regions of the central gray substance. While the functional significance of the spinotectal tract is largely conjecture, certain evidence suggests that it may be part of a multisynaptic pathway transmitting nociceptive impulses (Mehler et al., '60). This view is supported by observations (Magoun et al., '37; Spiegel et al., '54) of behavioral reactions which suggest painful sensations as a consequence of stimulation of the superior colliculus and periaqueductal gray.

V. The Posterior Spinocerebellar Tract. This prominent uncrossed ascending tract, situated along the posterolateral periphery of the spinal cord (Figs. 13-9, 13-15 and 13-23), arises from the large cells of Clarke's column (dorsal nucleus) which extend from the third lumbar (L3) to the eight cervical (C8) segment. Afferent fibers reach the nuclei via the dorsal roots (Fig. 13-4). The large cells of Clarke's nucleus give rise to large fibers which pass laterally in the ipsilateral white matter and ascend the entire length of the spinal cord. In the medulla fibers of this tract become incorporated in the in-

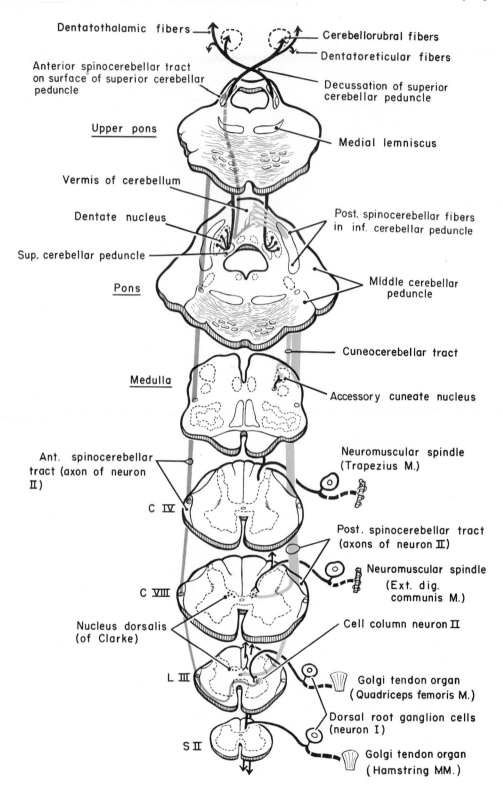

Dentatothalamic fibers

Cerebellorubral fibers

Dentatoreticular fibers

Anterior spinocerebellar tract
on surface of superior cerebellar
peduncle

Decussation of superior
cerebellar peduncle

Upper pons

Medial lemniscus

Vermis of cerebellum

Dentate nucleus

Post. spinocerebellar fibers
in inf. cerebellar peduncle

Sup. cerebellar peduncle

Pons

Middle cerebellar
peduncle

Cuneocerebellar tract

Medulla

Accessory cuneate nucleus

Ant. spinocerebellar
tract (axon of neuron
II)

Neuromuscular spindle
(Trapezius M.)

C IV

Post. spinocerebellar tract
(axons of neuron II)

Neuromuscular spindle
(Ext. dig.
communis M.)

C VIII

Nucleus dorsalis
(of Clarke)

Cell column neuron II

L III

Golgi tendon organ
(Quadriceps femoris M.)

Dorsal root ganglion cells
(neuron I)

S II

Golgi tendon organ
(Hamstring MM.)

ferior cerebellar peduncle, enter the cerebellum, and terminate in both cephalic and caudal portions of the vermis. The tract first appears in the upper lumbar cord (L3) and increases in size until the upper limit of Clarke's nucleus is reached (C8). Since the column of Clarke is not present in lower lumbar and sacral spinal segments, impulses entering via these caudal dorsal roots, and destined for the cerebellum, are first conveyed rostrally in the fasciculus gracilis by ascending branches of dorsal root fibers; at higher levels where Clarke's column is present, these fibers leave the fasciculus gracilis and enter the dorsal nucleus (Figs. 12–15 and 13–15).

Experimental evidence (Liu, '56; Grant and Rexed, '58) indicates that Clarke's nucleus receives both ascending and descending collaterals of dorsal root fibers, and a single dorsal root may supply afferent fibers to Clarke's nucleus in as many as six or seven spinal segments. Thus, there is extensive overlapping of afferent fibers of certain dorsal roots in their termination in Clarke's nucleus. Clarke's nucleus receives afferent fibers via dorsal roots from all parts of the body except the head and neck (C1 to C4 dorsal roots), but functionally this nucleus appears related primarily to the hindlimb and caudal part of the body.

Fibers of the posterior spinocerebellar tract have conduction velocities ranging from 30 to 110 m/sec. (Lloyd and McIntyre, '50; Oscarsson, '65). Fibers of this tract terminate almost exclusively ipsilaterally in the cerebellar vermal cortex (Grant, '62). Cerebellar areas of fiber termination in the anterior lobe correspond to Larsell's lobules I-IV (Fig. 17–1), while those in posterior areas end mainly in parts of the pyramis and paramedian lobule. According to physiological studies

(Snider and Stowell, '44, Carrea and Grundfest, '54; Combs, '56) these cerebellar cortical areas represent mainly the hindlimb.

This uncrossed pathway from periphery to cerebellum is composed of two neurons, the spinal ganglion cells, and the cells of Clarke's column (dorsal nucleus) (Fig. 13–15). Extensive degeneration studies in man have emphasized that the anterior and posterior spinocerebellar tracts are difficult to delimit as they form the margins of the lateral funiculus in the spinal cord. Many fibers of the anterior spinocerebellar tract move posteriorly as they ascend and become incorporated within the posterior spinocerebellar tract (Smith, '57).

Impulses relayed to the cerebellum via the posterior spinocerebellar tract arise from stimulation of stretch receptors in muscle, the muscle spindles, and the Golgi tendon organs. Neurons of Clarke's column receive monosynaptic excitation by group Ia and Ib afferent fibers via the dorsal root ganglion and often there is additional excitation from group II muscle spindle afferents (Oscarsson, '65). There is no evidence that the posterior spinocerebellar tract is activated by stimulation of low threshold joint receptors. The synaptic linkage between group I afferents and the dorsal nucleus allows transmission of impulses at high frequencies, and it has been shown that little spatial summation is required for eliciting a discharge in the posterior spinocerebellar tract. The majority of neurons in Clarke's column are activated by either Ia or Ib afferents, but some apparently receive excitation from both types of afferents. The occasional convergence of Ia and Ib excitation is said to be of little functional significance. There is also evidence indicating that certain exteroceptive impulses may be transmitted by the posterior spinocerebellar

Fɪɢ. 13–15. Diagram of the anterior (red) and posterior (blue) spinocerebellar tracts and the cuneocerebellar tract (blue). Impulses conveyed by the posterior spinocerebellar tract arise from muscle spindles and Golgi tendon organs. Crossed fibers of the anterior spinocerebellar tract are considered to arise from cells in parts of laminae V, VI and VII of Rexed, and are activated by impulses from Golgi tendon organs. The cuneocerebellar tract, arising from cells of the accessory cuneate nucleus in the medulla, is considered the upper limb equivalent of the posterior spinocerebellar tract. The rostral spinocerebellar tract, considered the upper limb equivalent of the anterior spinocerebellar tract in the cat, is not shown. Letters and numbers indicate segmental spinal levels.

tract (Oscarsson, '65). These exteroceptive impulses are related to touch and pressure receptors in the skin, and slowly adapting pressure receptors in foot pads.

Thus, the posterior spinocerebellar relays impulses from stretch receptors, touch receptors and pressure receptors directly from spinal levels to particular parts of the cerebellum. The tract is somatotopically organized in its course and termination, and transmission is relatively little influenced by supraspinal mechanisms. Present information suggests that impulses conveyed by this tract are utilized in the fine coordination of posture and movement of individual limb muscles.

VI The Anterior Spinocerebellar Tract. Situated along the lateral periphery of the spinal cord anterior to the posterior spinocerebellar tract, and posterior to the site of emergence of ventral root fibers (Fig. 13–15), is the anterior spinocerebellar tract. Medial to this tract is the lateral spinothalamic tract. The tract makes its first appearance in the lower lumbar spinal cord. In upper cervical spinal segments some fibers of the tract appear to become incorporated within the posterior spinocerebellar tract (Smith, '57). In the human brain stem the anterior spinocerebellar tract appears quite small.

Fibers of the anterior spinocerebellar tract were considered by Cooper and Sherrington ('40) to arise in lumbar spinal segments from cells in the periphery of the anterior horn, known as "spinal border cells" or the *nucleus pericornualis anterior*. Recent investigations (Hubbard and Oscarsson, '62) in the cat indicate that cells of origin of this tract occupy the lateral part of the base and neck of the posterior horn and the lateral part of the intermediate zone (i.e., parts of laminae V, VI and VII of Rexed). These cells form a column that extends caudally as far as sacral segments (Grant '62), or coccygeal segments (Ha and Liu, '68). The investigations of Ha and Liu ('68) indicate that the cells of origin of the anterior spinocerebellar tract are widely distributed in the dorsolateral part of the anterior gray. While some of these cells are "spinal border cells," they do not form the principal part of the cell column. Morphologically

these neurons are almost impossible to distinguish from motor neurons in Nissl preparations of normal spinal cord. In the cat, cells of this scattered cell column extend rostrally to the L1 segment; there is no "forelimb" component. Fibers of the anterior spinocerebellar tract are less numerous than those of the posterior spinocerebellar tract, are composed of uniformly large fibers (11–20μ), have conduction velocities of 70 to 120 m/sec., and virtually all are crossed.

This pathway to the cerebellum is composed of two neurons: Neuron I in the dorsal root ganglia, and Neuron II in the cell column at the base of the anterior and posterior horns in lumbar spinal segments. Fibers of Neuron II cross in the spinal cord, and ascend through the spinal cord, medulla and pons. At upper pontine levels the tract enters the cerebellum by coursing along the dorsal surface of the superior cerebellar peduncle (Figs. 13–15 and 17–18). Although physiological studies (Carrea and Grundfest, '54; Combs, '56) indicate that fibers of this ascending system cross initially at spinal levels and recross again within the cerebellum, anatomical studies in man indicate that only a small number of these fibers cross in the cerebellum (Smith, '61). Experimental studies (Lundberg and Oscarsson, '62; Grant, '62; Oscarsson, '65) show that the majority of fibers of this tract in the cat terminate contralaterally, with about 10 percent ipsilateral and about 15 percent, after branching, ending both ipsilaterally and contralaterally. Within the cerebellar cortex, fibers of this tract have a rostrocaudal distribution similar to that of the posterior spinocerebellar tract, except that the main area of termination is in the anterior lobe (lobules I to IV; Grant, '62; Oscarsson and Uddenberg, '64).

Cells which give rise to the anterior spinocerebellar tract receive monosynaptic excitation and inhibition from ipsilateral and contralateral flexor reflex afferents (Oscarsson, '65). Fibers of this tract are activated by afferent impulses from Golgi tendon organs with receptive fields which often include one synergic muscle group at each joint of the ipsilateral limb. It is presumed that the fibers of this system convey information concerning movement or posture of the whole limb rather than information about changes of tension in individual muscles. The significance of polysynaptic excitation and inhibition received via flexor reflex afferents remains obscure. Transmission of impulses in the anterior spinocerebellar tract is said to be controlled by supraspinal systems that might allow selection of information from either tendon organ afferents or flexor reflex afferents.

The effects of injury to these tracts in the spinal cord are difficult to judge, since other tracts are involved simultaneously. Injury to the cerebellum itself results in reduced muscular tone and in an incoordination of muscular action producing disturbances of posture and movement (cerebellar ataxia or asynergia). There is no loss of proprioceptive sense as a consequence of these lesions since impulses projected to the cerebellum do not enter the conscious sphere.

VII. Cuneocerebellar Tract. Since the column of Clarke is not present above C8, large fibers of cervical spinal nerves entering above this level ascend ipsilaterally in the fasciculus cuneatus. Fibers conveying impulses from group Ia muscle afferents and some cutaneous afferents pass to the *accessory cuneate nucleus*, a group of large cells in the dorsolateral part of the medulla with cytological features similar to those of the dorsal nucleus of Clarke (Figs. 13–15 and 14–12). The accessory cuneate nucleus receives afferents via the dorsal roots from T7 to C1 (Shriver et al., '68). Cells of the accessory cuneate nucleus give rise to the cuneocerebellar tract, the upper limb equivalent of the posterior spinocerebellar tract. Fibers of this tract, posterior external arcuate fibers, enter the cerebellum as a component of the inferior cerebellar peduncle and terminate in the ipsilateral cerebellar cortex (lobule V). These cerebellar afferent fibers are distributed to the forelimb area of the intermediate zone in the anterior lobe and to forelimb areas of the pyramis and paramedian lobule (Fig. 17–1).

In the cat another spinocerebellar pathway, the *rostral spinocerebellar tract*, has been identified (Oscarsson, '64, '65; Oscarsson and Uddenberg, '64) as the ipsilateral forelimb equivalent of the anterior spinocerebellar tract. The position of the cells of origin of this tract is unknown, but they are located rostral to the column of Clarke in the cervical spinal cord, and give rise to an uncrossed tract having an anterior position in the spinal cord which reaches the cerebellum via both the inferior and superior cerebellar peduncles. This tract resembles the anterior spinocerebellar tract, except that it is uncrossed; fibers of the tract are distributed mainly to ipsilateral parts of the anterior lobe (lobules I to V) of the cerebellum (Fig. 17–1).

Thus, in addition to the posterior and anterior spinocerebellar tracts, related primarily to the hindlimbs and caudal parts of the body, there are two equivalent tracts, the cuneocerebellar and the rostral spinocerebellar, that relay sensory information from the forelimbs and rostral parts of the body (Oscarsson, '65). The posterior spinocerebellar and cuneocerebellar tracts are similar and convey information from muscle spindles, tendon organs (not demonstrated in cuneocerebellar tract), and touch and pressure receptors in the skin. The anterior spinocerebellar and rostral spinocerebellar tracts are similar in that they convey impulses from tendon organ afferents and flexor reflex afferents, both from wide receptive fields.

VIII. Spinoreticular Fibers. Recent investigations indicate that impulses from the spinal cord project to widespread regions of the brain stem reticular formation. Spinoreticular fibers originate from all spinal levels, presumably from cells located in the posterior horn (Brodal, '49; Morin et al., '51; Mehler et al., '56; Rossi and Brodal, '57). These fibers ascend in the anterolateral funiculus, and those terminating in the medullary reticular formation are preponderantly uncrossed (Fig. 13–20). In the medulla these fibers terminate chiefly upon cells of the nucelus reticularis gigantocellularis and parts of the lateral reticular nucleus. The lateral reticular nucleus of the medulla is known to project to specific portions of the cerebellum, indicating that some fibers in this pathway may be concerned with the transmission of exteroceptive impulses to the cerebellum. Most of the large cells of the nucleus reticularis gigantocellularis project to spinal levels. Spinoreticular fibers passing to pontine levels are distributed bilaterally and are less numerous than those terminating in the medulla. Most of these fibers end in the nucleus reticularis pontis caudalis (Brodal, '57). A small number of spinoreticular fibers have been found in the mesencephalic reticular formation (O'Leary et al., '58). Functionally, the spinoreticular fibers represent an important component of a phylogenetically old, polysynaptic system which plays a significant role in the maintenance of the state of consciousness and awareness. This complex, referred to as the ascending reticular system (Moruzzi and Magoun, '49), is considered in more detail in Chapter 16.

IX. Other Ascending Fiber Systems in the Spinal Cord. In addition to the ascending fiber systems mentioned in preceding sections, several other ascending pathways have been described. While the existence of these anatomical pathways seems certain, relatively little is known of their functional significance.

A spinocortical tract has been described in man and experimental animals (Brodal and Walberg, '52; Nathan and Smith, '55a). Fibers of this tract arise from all levels of the spinal cord, but the contribution from the cervical region is greatest. Lesions involving the lateral and anterior corticospinal tracts produce ascending degeneration which can be followed cephalically. Some of these ascending fibers appear to cross in the spinal cord, but the majority cross in the pyramidal decussation. The course of these fibers in the brain stem follows the corticospinal tract, but in a reverse direction. Degenerated spinocortical fibers have been traced through the brain stem, the internal capsule and into the lower layers of the cerebral cortex. Although the function of these fibers is unknown, it has been postulated that they may subserve certain reflexes which have centers in the cerebral cortex.

Other ascending fiber systems described

include the spino-olivary, spinovestibular, and spinopontine. Spino-olivary fibers originate from all levels of the spinal cord, ascend largely in the anterior funiculus, and terminate mostly in specific parts of the dorsal and medial accessory olivary nuclei. Somewhat more than half of these fibers cross in the medulla. Since fibers from the inferior olivary nuclei project to the cerebellum, the spino-olivary fibers would seem to constitute a component of a spinocerebellar pathway which presents certain similarities to that of the posterior spinocerebellar tract (Brodal et al., '50).

A moderate number of spinal fibers projecting largely upon the dorsal part of the lateral vestibular nucleus constitute a spinovestibular fiber system. These fibers ascend ipsilaterally in the spinal cord from levels as far caudally as lumbar segments (Pompeiano and Brodal, '57b). Fibers of this tract are partially intermingled with those of the posterior spinocerebellar tract.

Spinopontine fibers ascend with the spinocortical fibers previously described. These fibers, which appear to be collaterals of the spinocortical tract, terminate upon pontine nuclei. It has been suggested that they may be concerned with transmission of certain exteroceptive impulses to the cerebellum.

THE LONG DESCENDING TRACTS

I. The Corticospinal or Pyramidal Tracts. These tracts consist of all fibers which: (1) originate from cells within the cerebral cortex, (2) pass through the medullary pyramid, and (3) enter the spinal cord. They constitute the largest and most important descending fiber system in the human neuraxis. Each tract is composed of over a million fibers of which some 700,000 are myelinated (Lassek and Rasmussen, '39; Lassek, '42, '54). Approximately 90% of these myelinated fibers have a diameter of 1 to 4 micra; most of the remaining myelinated fibers range in caliber from 5 to 10 micra, but include among them some 30,000 to 40,000 very large fibers having a thickness of 10 to 22 micra. The large fibers arise mainly from the giant pyramidal cells of Betz in the precentral gyrus (area 4 of Brodmann, Fig. 22–4), but some undoubtedly arise from adjacent cortical areas. These corticofugal fibers converge in the corona radiata and pass downward through the internal capsule, crus cerebri, pons, and medulla (Fig. 13–16). As this large tract descends in the brain stem, it passes close to the emerging root fibers of cranial nerves III, VI and XII. Corticobulbar fibers conveying impulses to motor nuclei of the brain stem are closely associated with corticospinal fibers in the internal capsule and brain stem. The corticospinal tract comes to the surface in the medulla as the pyramid. At the junction of medulla and cord, the fibers undergo an incomplete decussation giving rise to three tracts: (1) a large lateral or crossed corticospinal tract, (2) an anterior uncrossed corticospinal tract, and (3) a small uncrossed lateral corticospinal tract (not illustrated in Fig. 13–16).

The majority of the fibers, 75 to 90 per cent, cross in the pyramidal decussation and descend in the posterior part of the lateral funiculus as the lateral or crossed pyramidal tract, lying between the posterior spinocerebellar tract and the lateral fasciculus proprius (Figs. 13–17, 13–18, and 13–19). In lower lumbar and sacral spinal segments, caudal to where the posterior spinocerebellar tract is found, fibers of the corticospinal tract reach the lateral surface of the spinal cord (Fig. 13–19). In the uppermost cervical segments some fibers occupy, for a short distance, an aberrant position external to the posterior spinocerebellar fibers. The tract extends to the lower-most part of the cord and progressively diminishes in size as more and more fibers leave to terminate in the gray matter.

A smaller portion of the pyramidal fibers descend uncrossed as the anterior or direct pyramidal tract (bundle of Türck), occupying an oval area adjacent to the anterior median fissure (Figs. 13–16, 13–17 and 13–18). It normally extends only to the upper thoracic cord, though fibers have been traced to the lower thoracic and even the lumbar region, and inner-

vates primarily the muscles of the upper extremities and neck. This tract is found only in man and the higher apes, and its size shows considerable variations, owing to the fact that the proportion of decussating fibers is not constant. In extreme cases they may be absent altogether, practically all of the fibers crossing in the pyramidal decussation. In other isolated cases, the pyramidal fibers of one or both sides may not cross at all and may give rise to huge anterior pyramidal tracts (Verhaart and Kramer, '52).

Besides the two tracts discussed, there are other uncrossed corticospinal fibers which form the *anterolateral pyramidal tract* of Barnes ("Fibres pyramidales homolaterales superficielles" of Déjérine). This tract is composed of fine fibers which descend more anteriorly in the lateral funiculus.

Fibers of the crossed lateral corticospinal tract enter the gray matter laterally in the region of the intermediate zone. Silver impregnation studies (Nyberg-Hansen and Brodal, '63) in the cat show that entering fibers divide into dorsomedial and ventromedial components. Fibers of the dorsomedial component are distributed to laminae IV, V, and part of VI, while the ventromedial component supplies fibers to lamina VI and the dorsal part of lamina VII. In the cat no degenerated fibers are found in lamina IX, where large motor anterior horn cells are located. In the monkey Liu and Chambers ('64) describe corticospinal fibers passing into lamina VII and into the base of both the posterior and anterior horns. A few fibers of the lateral corticospinal tract have been described as crossing in the posterior and anterior gray commissures to end in the intermediate gray and the dorsomedial and central parts of the contralateral anterior horn. The majority of axons in the anterior corticospinal tract have been found to cross in the anterior white commissure and to terminate in the intermediate gray and the centromedial part of the anterior horn. Fibers of the uncrossed lateral corticospinal tract remain uncrossed and terminate in the base of the posterior horn, the intermediate gray and central parts of the an-

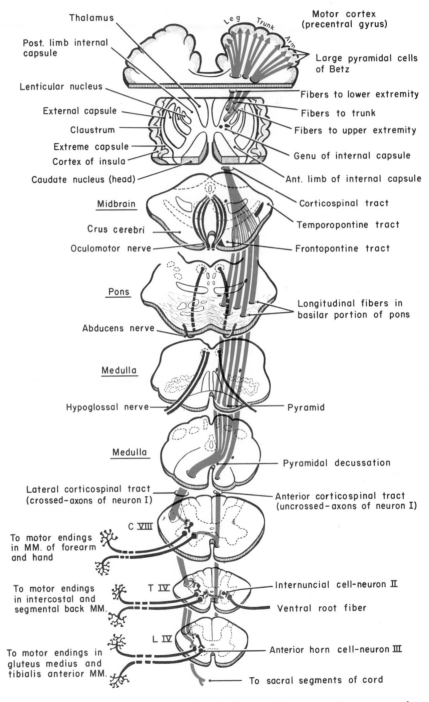

Fig. 13-16. Diagram of lateral and anterior corticospinal tracts—the upper motor neuron pathways to the anterior horn cells (voluntary motor activity and skilled acts). The locations of the corticobulbar tracts appear in each level of the brain stem as *black areas* (*right side*). *Letters* and *numbers* indicate corresponding segments of spinal cord.

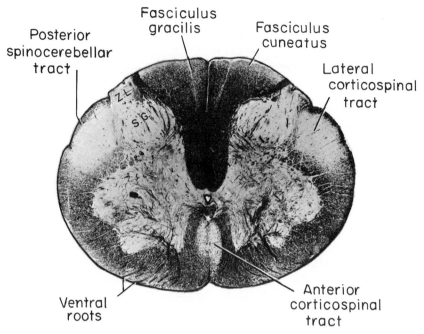

FIG. 13-17. Section through cervical enlargement of spinal cord of 7- to 8-month human fetus. The pyramidal tracts are unmyelinated at this stage and hence are unstained. *S.G.*, Substantia gelatinosa; *Z.L.*, zone of Lissauer. Weigert's myelin stain. Photograph.

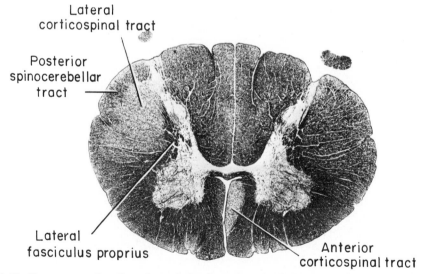

FIG. 13-18. Transverse section through cervical enlargement of spinal cord of a hemiplegic man. The lateral corticospinal tract of one side and the anterior corticospinal tract of the other side are degenerated. Weigert's myelin stain. Photograph.

terior horn. According to Liu and Chambers ('64) corticospinal fibers arising in the precentral gyrus terminate in the intermediate gray and the base of the posterior and anterior horns, while fibers arising from the postcentral gyrus terminate primarily in the dorsal horn, especially the nucleus proprius. In the monkey several authors (Hoff and Hoff, '34; Kuypers, '60; Liu and Chambers, '64) report that some corticospinal fibers end in direct synaptic contact with anterior horn cells, although

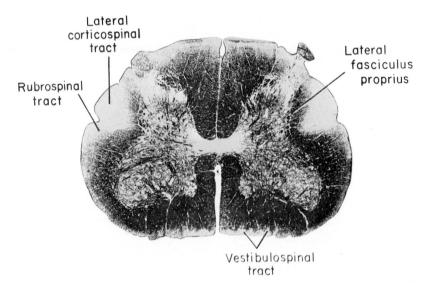

Fig. 13-19. Section through fourth lumbar segment of a human spinal cord which had been crushed some time previously in the lower cervical region. The degenerated long descending tracts are unstained. Note that the lateral corticospinal tract reaches the lateral periphery of the cord. Weigert's myelin stain. Photograph.

the majority of fibers are said to terminate on internuncial neurons in the intermediate zone. This species difference between cat and monkey is supported by electrophysiological evidence (Lloyd, '41; Bernhard et al., '53; Bernhard and Bohm, '54; Hern and Phillips, '59; Hern et al., '60; Preston and Whitlock, '61; Landgren et al., '62) indicating monosynaptic activation of motor neurons by corticospinal fibers in the monkey, but not in the cat. Some physiological (Bernhard, '54; Preston and Whitlock, '60, '61) and anatomical (Kuypers, '60; Liu and Chambers, '64) studies suggest a somatotopical organization in the monkey in which fibers from the precentral gyrus pass to epi-axial motor neurons, but not to axial motor neurons. The contralateral projection is to neurons innervating distal (chiefly) and proximal limb muscles. The ipsilateral cortical projection is to motor neurons innervating proximal limb muscles. Although some fibers from the postcentral gyrus pass directly to spinal motor neurons, they are far fewer in number.

It has been estimated that about 55 per cent of all pyramidal fibers end in the cervical cord, 20 per cent in the thoracic, and 25 per cent in the lumbosacral segments (Weil and Lassek, '29). This would suggest that pyramidal control over the upper extremity is much greater than over the lower. Myelination of the corticospinal fibers begins near birth and is not completed until the end of the second year.

The pyramidal tract conveys impulses to the spinal cord which result in volitional movements, especially isolated individual movements of the fingers and hand which form the basis for the acquisition of manual skills. Destruction of the tract produces a loss of voluntary movement that is most marked in the distal parts of the extremities. The proximal joints and grosser movement are less severely and permanently affected. At the onset of a vascular accident involving corticospinal fibers, there is a loss of tone in the affected muscles. But after a period of days or sometimes weeks, the muscles gradually become more resistant to passive movement (spasticity), and the deep tendon (myotatic) reflexes, especially in the leg, are increased in force and amplitude (hyperreflexia). On the other hand, the superficial reflexes, such as the abdominals, cremasteric, and normal plantar, are lost or diminished.

In individuals of advanced age there is

a tendency for the abdominal reflexes to be absent. These reflexes are absent more often in females than in males (Madonick, '57). Absence of the superficial abdominal reflexes is not in itself indicative of neurological disease. The abnormal plantar response, elicited by stroking the sole of the foot with a blunt instrument, is characterized by extension of the great toe and fanning of the other toes (*sign of Babinski*). The normal plantar response is a brisk flexion of all toes. The Babinski sign usually is indicative of injury to the corticospinal system, but it is not an infallible sign. The extensor toe response commonly can be elicited in the newborn infant, the sleeping or intoxicated adult, or following a generalized seizure. It also may be absent in some patients with lesions of the corticospinal tract (Nathan and Smith, '55).

After a prolonged interval, most individuals with lesions involving the corticospinal tract show considerable restitution of gross muscle movements about the shoulder and hip. Residual defects are most marked in the distal parts of the extremities. In time motor disturbances and alterations of reflex activity associated with the lesion often diminish, and may almost disappear.

The cause of the spasticity usually occurring in human hemiplegia is still a subject of considerable controversy. Lesions of the pyramidal tract in cats and monkeys produce a hypotonic paralysis, or paresis of discrete movements, though in the chimpanzee the hypotonia is more obscure (Tower, '49). Similarly, Fulton and Kennard ('34) have reported that ablation of the motor area (area 4) in monkeys and chimpanzees produces paralysis of a flaccid character. When the motor area (area 4) and the pre-motor area (area 6) are both ablated there is a slight increase in resistance to passive movements, but usually not of the degree that characterizes true spasticity (see Chapter 22, page 572).

It must be remembered that the corticospinal tract is a complex fiber system arising from extensive cortical areas, and only part of it originates from the giant pyramidal cells of Betz in the precentral gyrus. These cells are relatively few in number, about 25,000 according to Campbell ('05), some 34,000 in the more careful count of Lassek ('40). They probably furnish the larger fibers, 10 to 22 micra in diameter, whose number has been estimated at about 40,000 (Lassek and Rasmussen, '39). The more numerous finer fibers come in considerable part from other cortical regions. Thus there are at least two components in the pyramidal tract, a large-fibered component from the motor area, and a fine-fibered one mainly from other areas. Lesions of the entire pyramidal tract involve both components; ablation of the motor area alone destroys only the large-fibered one (Häggquist, '37). It is probable that fibers of the Betz cells are concerned with the finer isolated movements of the distal parts of the extremities, which are primarily affected in pyramidal lesions. The more numerous finer fibers may be related to grosser movement and tonic control, and injury to them may be the cause of the increase in muscle tone and the hyperactive deep tendon reflexes. These fibers are not, however, "extrapyramidal." They form an integral part of the pyramidal tract—its largest portion—descending uninterruptedly from the cerebral cortex through the medullary pyramids to the spinal cord. They come from cortical areas which also give rise to extrapyramidal fibers (i.e., fibers which are relayed in subcortical nuclei before reaching the spinal cord).

The pyramidal cells and their axons constitute the "upper motor neurons" in contrast to the "lower motor neurons" (anterior horn cells), which directly innervate the skeletal muscle. The symptoms of a pyramidal lesion—loss of volitional movement, spasticity, increased deep tendon reflexes, loss of superficial reflexes, and the sign of Babinski—therefore often are designated as "upper motor neuron" paralysis (spastic or supranuclear paralysis). In "lower motor neuron" paralysis, there is loss of all movement, reflex and voluntary, as well as loss of tone and rapid atrophy of the affected muscles.

Paralysis of both arm and leg on one

side is termed a *hemiplegia*, that of a single limb a *monoplegia*. *Diplegia* denotes the paralysis of two corresponding parts on opposite sides, such as both arms, though when both legs are involved the term *paraplegia* is used. Paralysis of all four extremities is known as *tetraplegia*, or *quadraplegia*.

II. The Reticulospinal Tracts. These tracts constitute a system of relatively fine fibers originating mainly from the pontine and medullary reticular formation which descend in the anterior and anterolateral portions of the spinal cord (Fig. 13–20). Fibers in these tracts originate from the medial two-thirds of the reticular formation of the medulla and pons (Brodal, '57). The greatest number of fibers appear to arise from the areas dorsal and rostral to the inferior olivary nucleus (i.e., nucleus reticularis gigantocellularis) and from levels of the pons (i.e., nucleus reticularis pontis caudalis and nucleus reticularis pontis oralis). The contribution from the pontine reticular formation is almost entirely homolateral, while that from the medulla is mainly, but not exclusively homolateral. Fibers from the pontine reticular formation form the major descending component of the medial longitudinal fasciculus in the brain stem; in the spinal cord these fibers descend chiefly in the medial part of the anterior funiculus. A few fibers from the pontine reticular formation cross to the opposite side in the anterior white commissure (Nyberg-Hansen, '65). Medullary reticulospinal fibers, bilateral, but mainly uncrossed, are located primarily in the anterior part of the lateral funiculus. Reticulospinal fibers from these two regions of the brain stem are not sharply segregated in the spinal cord.

Although initial experimental studies (Bodian, '46; van Beusekom, '55; Brodal, '57) suggested that reticulospinal tracts did not descend caudal to thoracic spinal segments, more recent data (Staal, '61; Nyberg-Hansen, '65; Petras, '67) indicate that these fibers descend the entire length of the spinal cord. Pontine reticulospinal fibers, more numerous than those from the medulla, terminate in lamina VIII and adjacent parts of lamina VII. Medullary reticulospinal fibers terminate chiefly in lamina VII, though a few fibers terminate in lamina IX. Reticulospinal fibers from both the pons and medulla terminate on cells of all sizes and on both somata and dendrites. The above evidence suggests that impulses arising from the reticular formation which influence gamma motor neuron activity probably are mediated at segmental levels largely by internuncial neurons in laminae VII and VIII (Eldred et al., '53; Eldred and Fujimori, '58). The regions of termination of pontine reticulospinal fibers are similar to those of fibers of the vestibulospinal tract; both of these fiber systems convey impulses considered to be facilitatory to extensor motor neurons. Medullary reticulospinal fibers terminate in parts of the gray laminae that also receive fibers from rubrospinal and corticospinal tracts.

Information concerning the reticulospinal tracts in man is very meager (Nathan and Smith, '55), and conclusive data are not available. Autonomic fibers from higher levels of the neuraxis probably descend in close association with both the reticulospinal and corticospinal tracts to end about visceral motor cells of the intermediate gray matter.

Experimental studies have demonstrated that stimulation of the brain stem reticular formation can: (1) facilitate or inhibit voluntary movement, cortically induced movement, and reflex activity; (2) influence muscle tone; (3) affect inspiratory and expiratory phases of respiration; (4) exert pressor or depressor effects on the circulatory system; and (5) exert depressant effects on the central transmission of sensory impulses. Areas of the medullary reticular formation from which medullary reticulospinal fibers arise appear to correspond closely with the regions from which inspiratory, inhibitory, and depressor effects have been obtained (Pitts et al., '39; Pitts, '40; Amoroso et al., '54; Torvik and Brodal, '57). Areas of the brain stem reticular formation related to facilitatory influences, expiratory effects, and pressor vasomotor phenomena are mainly rostral to the medulla and appear to extend beyond those regions which give rise

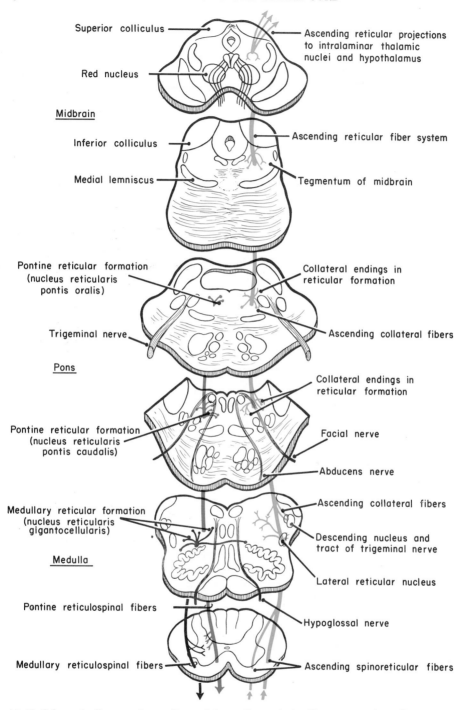

Fig. 13–20. Schematic diagram of ascending and descending reticular fiber systems. Ascending spinoreticular and collateral reticular projections are shown on the *right* (*blue*). This system gives off collateral fibers at various brain stem levels and is augmented by rostrally projecting reticular fibers. Pontine reticulospinal fibers (medial reticulospinal tract, *red*) are uncrossed and originate largely from the nucleus reticularis pontis caudalis. Medullary reticulospinal fibers (lateral reticulospinal tract, *black*) are predominantly uncrossed and arise from the nucleus reticularis gigantocellularis. Fibers from these sources are not sharply segregated in the spinal cord. (Based upon Olszewski and Baxter, '54; Brodal, '57; and Nauta and Kuypers; '58.)

to direct reticulospinal fibers (Brodal, '57). Thus, some facilitatory influences from the upper brain stem reticular formation probably are not transmitted directly to spinal levels by reticulospinal pathways.

Recent studies have shown that the reticular formation can influence muscle tone by acting upon gamma motor neurons which innervate the contractile portions of the muscle spindle (Eldred et al., '53; Granit, '55). Inhibitory effects on the muscle spindle are obtained most easily from the medullary reticular formation, while facilitatory effects are elicited from more rostral regions. It is probably by this means that the reticulospinal systems can modify tendon reflex activity. The reticular formation and its great functional significance will be considered in more detail in Chapter 16.

III. The Vestibulospinal Tract. This tract originates from the lateral vestibular nucleus which receives fibers from the vestibular division of the eighth cranial nerve and from specific parts of the cerebellum. Practically all cells of the lateral vestibular nucleus contribute to the formation of this tract, which, partially intermingled with ascending spinothalamic fibers, descends uncrossed in the anterior periphery of the spinal cord. In cervical segments the majority of the fibers are situated in the anterior part of the lateral funiculus, but in caudal spinal segments more fibers are found in the anterior funiculus (Figs. 13–19, 13–21, and 13–23). The studies of Pompeiano and Brodal ('57a) indicate that the vestibulospinal tract, which arises from both large and small cells within the lateral vestibular nucleus, is somatotopically organized. Cells in different portions of the nucleus project fibers to specific parts of the spinal cord. The ventrorostral region of the nucleus projects fibers to cervical spinal segments, while cells in the dorsocaudal part of the nucleus pass to lumbosacral spinal segments. Fibers passing to thoracic spinal segments are derived from intermediate regions of the nucleus. While there is some overlap between regions sending fibers to particular spinal segments, the evidence for this somatotopical arrangement is definite. Fibers of the vestibulospinal tract descend the entire length of the spinal cord. Cervical and lumbar spinal segments receive the greatest number of vestibulospinal fibers; thoracic segments receive fewer fibers. Vestibulospinal fibers enter the gray matter and are distributed to all parts of lamina VIII and the medial and central parts of lamina VII (Nyberg-Hansen and Mascitti, '64). These fibers form axo-dendritic and axo-somatic synaptic contacts with all types of cells within these laminae, although axo-dendritic synapses are most numerous. No vestibulospinal fibers appear to terminate directly on motor neurons, except in the thoracic cord, where a few fibers may end upon cells of the anteromedial group. Although fibers in this tract in man probably are less numerous than in other mammals, it is still a tract of considerable size and functional significance.

There is no evidence that fibers from the inferior, medial or superior vestibular nuclei contribute fibers to the vestibulospinal tract. No fibers from the lateral vestibular nucleus reach the spinal cord via the medial longitudinal fasciculus (Carpenter et al., '60; Nyberg-Hansen, '64).

The vestibulospinal tracts relay impulses to the spinal cord from the vestibular end organ and from specific portions of the cerebellum. Cerebellar efferent fibers from portions of the cerebellar vermis (Walberg and Jansen, '61) and from the fastigial nuclei (Walberg et al., '62) terminate in a specific manner upon portions of the lateral vestibular nucleus. From the above description, it is apparent that vestibular influences upon the spinal cord are mediated largely by the vestibulospinal tract. There is considerable evidence that the vestibular nuclei, especially the lateral nucleus, exert a facilitatory influence upon the reflex activity of the spinal cord and spinal mechanisms which control muscle tone. This perhaps is best exemplified in experimental decerebrate animals by the reduction of rigidity which follows lesions in the lateral vestib-

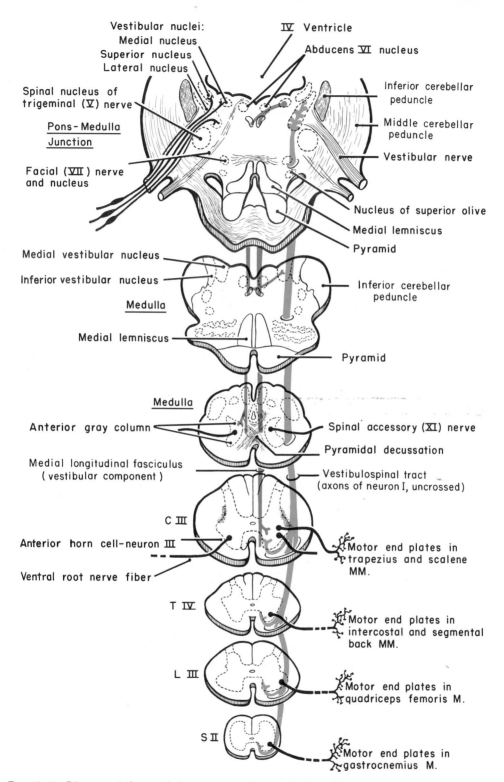

Fig. 13–21. Diagram of the vestibulospinal tract (*blue*) and descending vestibular fibers in the medial longitudinal fasciculus (*red*). Fibers of the vestibulospinal tract have a somatotopic origin in the lateral vestibular nucleus, descend the length of the spinal cord and terminate predominantly in lamina VIII of Rexed. Descending vestibular fibers in the medial longitudinal fasciculus arise from the medial vestibular nucleus. In the lower brain stem these fibers are bilateral, but in the cervical spinal cord they are ipsilateral. *Letters* and *numbers* indicate segmental spinal levels.

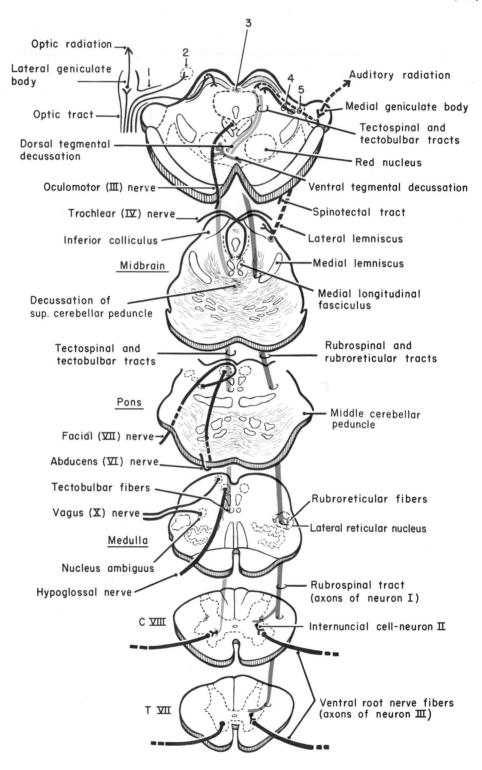

Optic radiation

Lateral geniculate body

Optic tract

Dorsal tegmental decussation

Oculomotor (III) nerve

Trochlear (IV) nerve

Inferior colliculus

Midbrain

Decussation of sup. cerebellar peduncle

Tectospinal and tectobulbar tracts

Pons

Facial (VII) nerve

Abducens (VI) nerve

Tectobulbar fibers

Vagus (X) nerve

Medulla

Nucleus ambiguus

Hypoglossal nerve

C VIII

T VII

Auditory radiation

Medial geniculate body

Tectospinal and tectobulbar tracts

Red nucleus

Ventral tegmental decussation

Spinotectal tract

Lateral lemniscus

Medial lemniscus

Medial longitudinal fasciculus

Rubrospinal and rubroreticular tracts

Middle cerebellar peduncle

Rubroreticular fibers

Lateral reticular nucleus

Rubrospinal tract (axons of neuron I)

Internuncial cell-neuron II

Ventral root nerve fibers (axons of neuron III)

ular nucleus or interruption of the vestibulospinal tract in the spinal cord. Another experimental study (Pompeiano, '60) has shown that electrical stimulation of points in the lateral vestibular nucleus produces increases in extensor muscle tone which may be localized to forelimb or hindlimb, depending upon the position of the electrode within the nucleus. These physiological findings offer confirmation of the anatomically described somatotopical origin of fibers in the lateral vestibular nucleus. Sasaki et al. ('62) have demonstrated that following stimulation of the lateral vestibular nucleus in the cat excitatory postsynaptic potentials can be recorded intracellularly from extensor motor neurons, while the effects on flexor motor neurons are insignificant. Anatomical data suggest that these facilitatory effects must be mediated via interneurons in laminae VII and VIII. The abundant fibers from the cerebellum which project in a specific manner to the vestibular nuclei suggest that significant cerebellar influences upon muscle tone and posture also are mediated to spinal levels via the vestibulospinal tract.

Clinically, examples of impulses conveyed by the vestibulospinal tract are seen in the tendency to fall after being rapidly rotated and in the "past-pointing" reaction. In the latter, after being rotated in a certain direction, vertical voluntary movements tend to deviate in the direction of prior rotation, and the person misses objects he endeavors to touch with his eyes closed.

IV. The Rubrospinal Tract. The rubrospinal tract is a relatively small bundle of fibers arising from cells of the red nucleus, a well-defined structure in the central part of the mesencephalic tegmentum (Figs. 13–22, 16–1 and 16–4). The red nucleus is a large oval cell mass which in transverse sections has a circular appearance (Fig. 16–1). This nucleus usually is divided into a rostral parvocellular part and a caudal magnocellular part; the extent of these two divisions show variations in size in different animals. In man the magnocellular part of the nucleus is relatively small. Although many authors consider the rubrospinal tract to arise exclusively from the large cells in the caudal pole of the nucleus, evidence (Pompeiano and Brodal, '57) for the cat indicates that cells of all sizes in the caudal three-fourths of the nucleus give rise to axons that project to spinal levels. In the monkey (Kuypers and Lawrence, '67) the rubrospinal tract arises largely from the magnocellular region which occupies the caudal third of the red nucleus. Rubrospinal fibers are given off from the medial border of the red nucleus, cross the median raphe immediately in the ventral tegmental decussation, and descend to spinal levels, where fibers lie anterior to, and partially intermingled with, fibers of the lateral corticospinal tract (Figs. 13–22 and 13–23). Fibers of the rubrospinal tract arise somatotopically from the red nucleus (Pompeiano and Brodal, '57). Fibers projecting to cervical spinal segments arise from dorsal and dorsomedial parts of the nucleus, while fibers passing to lumbosacral regions of the spinal cord arise from ventral and ventrolateral parts of the red nucleus. Thoracic spinal segments receive fibers that originate from intermediate regions of the nucleus. While the rubrospinal tract extends the length of the spinal

FIG. 13–22. Diagram of the rubrospinal (*red*) and tectospinal (*blue*) tracts. Rubrospinal fibers arise somatotopically from the red nucleus, cross in the ventral tegmental decussation and descend to spinal levels where fibers terminate in parts of laminae V, VI and VII of Rexed. Crossed rubrobulbar fibers project to parts of the facial nucleus (not shown) and to the lateral reticular nucleus of the medulla (rubroreticular fibers). Uncrossed rubrobulbar fibers (not shown) descend in the central tegmental tract and terminate in the dorsal lamella of the ipsilateral principal olivary nucleus. Tectospinal fibers arise from deep layers of the superior colliculus, cross in the dorsal tegmental decussation and descend initially ventral to the medial longitudinal fasciculus. At medullary levels these fibers become incorporated in the medial longitudinal fasciculus. Fibers of the tectospinal tract descend only to lower cervical spinal segments. Numbered midbrain structures include: *1*, the brachium of the superior colliculus; *2*, the pretectal area; *3*, commissure of the superior colliculus; *4*, spinotectal tract; and *5*, collicular fibers from the lateral lemniscus.

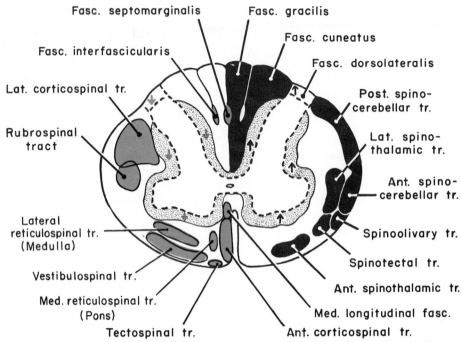

Fig. 13–23. Diagram of ascending (*black*) and descending (*red*) pathways of the spinal cord. The fasciculus proprius system (*stippled*) and dorsolateral fasciculus contain both ascending and descending nerve fibers.

cord in most mammals, it has not been demonstrated below thoracic spinal segments in man (Stern, '38). Conclusions that the rubrospinal tract in man is rudimentary are based partially on the fact that cells of the human red nucleus are small. It seems likely that many of the rubrospinal fibers in man are thin and poorly myelinated, thus making their identification difficult. In the cat cervical spinal segments receive the greatest number of rubrospinal fibers and thoracic segments receive a smaller number of fibers than do lumbar segments (Hinman and Carpenter, '59; Nyberg-Hansen and Brodal, '64). Fibers of this tract enter the spinal gray laterally and radiate in fan-shaped fashion into the lateral half of lamina V, lamina VI, and dorsal and central parts of lamina VII. These fibers terminate on somata and dendrites of large and small cells within these laminae (Nyberg-Hansen and Brodal, '64).

In their descent through the brain stem, some collateral fibers of the rubrospinal tract are given off which project to the cerebellum (Courville and Brodal,

'66), the facial nucleus (Courville, '66a) and the lateral reticular nucleus of the medulla (Walberg, '58; Hinman and Carpenter, '59; Courville, '66a). The red nucleus also gives rise to uncrossed rubral efferent fibers that project to parts of the principal inferior olivary nucleus; these fibers are referred to as uncrossed rubrobulbar fibers (Walberg, '56).

The red nucleus receives fibers from the cerebellum and cerebral cortex. Studies (Rinvik and Walberg, '63) of corticorubral fibers in the cat indicate that these fibers arise from the "motor" cortex, pass ipsilaterally, and terminate in all parts of the red nucleus on dendrites and cell somata. Corticorubral fibers are somatotopically organized with respect to both origin and termination. Thus, together corticorubral and rubrospinal fibers constitute a somatotopically organized nonpyramidal pathway between the motor cortex and various spinal levels. All parts of the red nucleus receive crossed cerebellar efferent fibers via the superior cerebellar peduncle. Fibers from the dentate nucleus project mainly to the rostral third of the red nucleus, while fibers from part of the interposed nucleus (equivalent to the emboliform and globose nucleus in man) pass to the caudal two-thirds of the nucleus (Courville, '66b; Massion, '67). Rubral afferent fibers from part of the interposed nucleus (anterior part) are somatotopically organized.

Stimulation of the red nucleus (Pompeiano, '56, '57) in the cat produces flexion in either the forelimb or hindlimb on the opposite side, depending upon which part of the nucleus is stimulated. Flexion limited to a single limb is explained by the somatotopic organization of fibers in the rubrospinal tract. Microelectrode studies (Sasaki et al., '60) have demonstrated that stimulation of cells in the red nucleus produces excitatory postsynaptic potentials in contralateral flexor alpha motor neurons, and inhibitory postsynaptic potentials in extensor alpha motor neurons. The most important function of the rubrospinal tract is the control of muscle tone in flexor muscle groups (Massion, '67). Since rubrospinal fibers do not end directly upon anterior horn cells, impulses conveyed by these fibers could be mediated in one of two ways: (1) by spinal interneurons which in turn facilitate flexor alpha motor neurons, or (2) by effects upon gamma motor neurons which indirectly influence alpha motor neurons through the gamma loop (Fig. 13–3).

V. The Tectospinal and Tectobulbar Tracts. These two tracts arise from neurons in the deeper layers of the superior colliculus, which is primarily an optic relay center. Fibers contributing to the formation of these tracts sweep anteromedially about the periaqueductal gray and cross the midline anterior to the medial longitudinal fasciculus in the *dorsal tegmental decussation*. In the upper brain stem these tracts descend near the median raphe anterior to the medial longitudinal fasciculus; at medullary levels tectospinal fibers become incorporated within the medial longitudinal fasciculus (Fig. 13–22). In the older literature tectospinal fibers are referred to as the predorsal bundle. In the spinal cord

tectospinal fibers descend in the most anterior part of the anterior funiculus near the anterior median fissure. The majority of fibers terminate in the upper four cervical spinal segments, but a few reach lower cervical segments (Altman and Carpenter, '61; Nyberg-Hansen, '66; Petras, '67). Tectospinal fibers enter the ventromedial part of the anterior horn and radiate into laminae VIII, VII and parts of lamina VI (Nyberg-Hansen, '66). None of these fibers terminate directly upon large motor neurons. The functional significance of the tectospinal tract is not known, but it is presumed to mediate reflex postural movements in response to visual and perhaps auditory stimuli.

Tectobulbar fibers are distributed to posterior areas of the mesencephalic reticular formation bilaterally and to the medial regions of the contralateral pontine and medullary reticular formation. A prominent bundle of uncrossed *tectopontine* fibers passes to the posterolateral pontine nuclei (Altman and Carpenter, '61).

VI. The Medial Longitudinal Fasciculus (MLF). The posterior part of the anterior funiculus contains a composite bundle of descending fibers that originates from different nuclei at various brain stem levels and is collectively referred to as the *medial longitudinal fasciculus* (abbreviated MLF). Such descending fibers represent only a portion of the brain stem tract that is designated by the same name, but is composed of both ascending and descending fibers. In the brain stem and spinal cord, fibers of this tract are always near the median raphe and immediately ventral to the cerebral aqueduct, fourth ventricle, or central canal. Descending fibers of the medial longitudinal fasciculus in the spinal cord originate from the medial vestibular nucleus, the reticular formation, the superior colliculus (tectospinal fibers), and the interstitial nucleus of Cajal (interstitiospinal fibers). Fibers of this bundle form a well-defined tract only in the upper cervical segments of the spinal cord (Figs. 13–21 and 13–23). Below that level most fibers are difficult to follow, although fibers have been traced to sacral levels. Most of these fibers are believed to terminate among internuncial neurons in the most medial part of the anterior horn.

Vestibular fibers descending in the medial longitudinal fasciculus arise only from the medial vestibular nucleus, are predominantly ipsilateral in the spinal cord, and terminate in the dorsal part of lamina VIII and adjacent parts of lamina VII (Nyberg-Hansen, '64; McMasters et al., '66). The largest component of descending fibers in the medial longitudinal fasciculus at spinal levels is the pontine reticulospinal tract; these fibers descend the length of the spinal cord. Fibers of the interstitiospinal tract are largely uncrossed, descend in the most posterior part of the anterior funiculus near the anteromedian fissure and terminate in dorsal parts of lamina VIII and neighboring parts of lamina VII (Staal, '61; Nyberg-Hansen, '66). While most of the fibers of this tract are given off in upper portions of the spinal cord, some fibers project as far caudally as sacral levels.

VII. The Olivospinal Tract. This tract is considered to be a complex tract composed of fine fibers which stain lightly in Weigert preparations. This bundle, located on the anterior surface of the spinal cord at the zone of transition between the lateral and anterior funiculi, is partially traversed by ventral root fibers. While this tract has been described as containing descending fibers from the inferior olivary nucleus, the evidence is not conclusive. Some fibers from higher levels traversing this area have been considered as part of the anterolateral corticospinal tract (Barnes, '01; Déjérine, '01). Experimental studies indicate that this tract contains primarily spino-olivary fibers ascending to the medial and dorsal accessory olivary nuclei (Brodal et al., '50).

VIII. Descending Autonomic Pathways. The descending tracts described in the preceding pages are parts of pathways by which impulses ultimately reach the voluntary striated muscles through the somatic anterior horn cells. The spinal cord also contains descending fibers which come in relation with the intermediolateral column and other preganglionic cell groups for the innervation of visceral structures (smooth muscle, heart muscle, and glandular epithelium). The highest coordinating center of this pathway is the hypothalamus, which in turn is under the influence of visceral neurons within portions of the cerebral cortex and thalamus. Other important autonomic centers lie in the tegmentum of the midbrain, pons and medulla. These descending paths are diffuse and probably are interrupted by relay neurons. In the spinal cord these fibers descend mainly in the anterior and anterolateral portions of the white matter, in close relation to the lateral fasciculus proprius system, and the reticulospinal tracts.

IX. The Fasciculi Proprii. Equally as important as the long ascending and descending tracts are the shorter fiber systems which form part of the intrinsic reflex mechanism of the cord. In its simplest form a spinal reflex arc may consist of only two neurons, an afferent peripheral neuron (spinal ganglion cell) and an efferent peripheral neuron (anterior horn cell) with a single synapse in the gray (Fig. 13–1). These monosynaptic reflexes are as a rule uncrossed and usually involve only one segment or closely adjacent ones (i.e., they are primarily segmental reflexes). This same reflex arc, which is dependent upon impulses from the muscle spindles, plays a vital role in the unconscious neural control of muscular contraction during movement and the maintenance of posture. It has been suggested (Merton, '53) that this reflex arc behaves as a servo-mechanism, or automatic control, which is activated by an "error signal" occurring in a closed loop and possessing power amplification. The closed loop consists of the muscle spindle, group Ia afferent fibers, the synapse with alpha motor neurons, and alpha fibers innervating extrafusal muscle (Fig. 13–3). The power amplification is provided by the contraction of extrafusal muscle. Thus, contraction of the muscle opposes applied tension and tends to maintain the muscle at a constant length. The "error signal" may be considered to be the difference in the frequency of firing of the primary endings when the muscle is unloaded, and when it is loaded (Matthews, '64).

However, only part of the collaterals of dorsal root fibers terminate directly upon anterior horn cells (Hoff, '32; Foerster et al., '33; Sprague and Ha, '64). Hence in most reflex arcs there is at least one central or internuncial neuron interposed between the afferent and efferent neurons. These central cells then send their axons to the motor cells of the same segment, or to higher and lower segments, for the completion of various intersegmental arcs. Many of the fibers are axons of internuncial cells which ascend or descend in the white columns of the same side. Others come from commissural cells and pass to the white matter of the opposite side. All these ascending and descending fibers, crossed and uncrossed, which begin and end in the spinal cord and connect its various levels, constitute the *spinospinal* or *fundamental* columns (*fasciculi proprii*) of the spinal cord (Figs. 12–1 and 13–23). To this spinal reflex mechanism also belong the descending root fibers of the interfascicular and septomarginal bundles, which previously were described, and the collaterals and many terminals of ascending dorsal root fibers. Impulses entering the cord at any segment may travel along these fibers to higher or lower levels before connecting directly or through internuncial neurons with the anterior horn cells (Fig. 13–1).

The spinospinal fibers are found in all funiculi; posterior, anterior, and lateral. They occupy the area adjacent to the gray matter, and between the gray matter and the more peripherally placed long tracts with which they intermingle. They are most numerous in the anterolateral white columns. In the posterior funiculus they form a narrow zone along the posterior commissure and adjacent portions of the posterior horn. In general, the shortest fibers lie nearest the gray and connect adjacent segments. The longer fibers lie more peripherally and continue up or down through several segments.

It must be kept in mind that under normal circumstances there are no *isolated* reflexes, and that every neural reaction involving any given arc always influences, and is influenced by, other parts of the nervous system. The primitive nervous system is organized for the production of generalized muscle movements and total response. Studies of fetal behavior suggest that local reflexes appear later (Herrick and Coghill, '15; Coghill, '29; Hooker, '44).

The Ascending and Descending Tracts. A series of schematic diagrams have represented the ascending and descending tracts of the spinal cord described in this chapter. It should be emphasized that at different levels of the spinal cord these tracts occupy slightly different positions and that they show variations in size depending upon the particular level. Considerable intermingling and overlapping of fiber pathways are found at all spinal levels. Major ascending and descending spinal pathways are diagramed schematically in Figure 13–23.

The anterior horn cells and their axons, which innervate striated muscle, constitute an anatomical and physiological unit referred to as the *final common pathway* or the *lower motor neuron.* Cells of the anterior horn can be influenced directly by impulses transmitted by descending fiber systems and by impulses conveyed by dorsal root afferents. Although all of the descending fibers which can influence the activity of the lower motor neuron constitute upper motor neuron systems, the overwhelming clinical importance of the *corticospinal tract* has caused it to be equated with the *upper motor neuron.* The nonpyramidal descending fibers (i.e., rubrospinal, vestibulospinal, reticulospinal, tectospinal, and the medial longitudinal fasciculus) constitute the oldest part of the descending motor system and exert regulatory control over mechanisms which influence muscle tone, reflex activity, posture, and synergistic automatic movement patterns of a somewhat stereotyped nature. These influences upon motor function have been blended with the highly versatile, refined, and skilled motor control considered to be mediated by the corticospinal system.

LESIONS AND DEGENERATION IN
THE SPINAL CORD

The origin, course, and terminations of most of the ascending sensory paths, as well as of the descending corticospinal tract, are the most documented pathways in the nervous system of man and higher mammals (Nathan and Smith, '55; van Beusekom, '55). However, much anatomical and physiological information remains to be ascertained, particularly for some of the small and diffuse pathways that descend from higher levels into the spinal cord. Additional facts are constantly being amassed by studies of material chiefly from three sources: (1) experimental lesions in animals followed by neuroanatomical staining technics; (2) neurophysiological stimulation and recording of neuron potentials, with subsequent histological examination; and lastly, (3) antemortem and postmortem neuropathological studies of human nerve tissue after injury, or surgical procedures.

In determining the fiber tracts, the method of secondary or Wallerian degeneration has been especially valuable (Fig. 13–24). When a nerve fiber is cut, not only does the part severed from the cell body undergo complete degeneration, but the cell body itself exhibits certain pathological changes, such as central chromatolysis, swelling, and nuclear eccentricity. Thus if the spinal cord is cut or injured, all the ascending fibers will degenerate above the level of injury ("ascending" degeneration). Their cell bodies, located below the injury, may show the pathological changes (Figs. 6–1E and 6–26). Below the level of injury the descending fibers will degenerate ("descending" degeneration), since their cell bodies are above the cut. In the same way the central continuations of the dorsal root fibers may be determined by following their secondary degeneration in the cord after section of the dorsal roots proximal to the spinal ganglia. (Fig. 13–24). Although chromatolysis of spinal ganglion cells might be expected following surgical section of the dorsal root in this location, only very minimal cell changes are seen (Hare and Hinsey, '40). However, section

of the mixed spinal nerve produces retrograde cell changes in the spinal ganglia and in the anterior horns. The location of the cell bodies whose axons form the ventral roots may be similarly determined by cutting the ventral root and ascertaining which cell bodies in the cord show retrograde changes (axon reaction). The Marchi, Nauta, and Glees (Nauta and Gygax, '51, '54; Glees and Nauta, '55) methods are used extensively to give precise information, particularly when small numbers of degenerating nerve fibers are being traced within the brain and spinal cord (Figs. 13–4 and 13–5).

It should now be obvious that cutting a dorsal root of a spinal nerve (i.e., dorsal rhizotomy) will abolish all of its incoming sensory impulses as well as interrupt the afferent arms of some segmental reflexes (Fig. 13–24). Due to the overlap of dermatomes in the periphery, destruction of one dorsal root does not result in diminished cutaneous innervation (hypesthesia); three consecutive dorsal roots must be destroyed before there is complete *anesthesia* in a dermatome (Fig. 10–2). Muscle tone also is dependent upon the integrity of segmental reflexes, although two or more segments usually supply a single muscle. For example, total resection of dorsal root C5 will result in severe loss of muscle tone in the supraspinatus and rhomboid muscles (derived from cervical myotomes 4 and 5—mostly 5). Such a lesion also diminishes, but does not abolish, reflex tone in the deltoid, subscapularis, biceps brachii, brachialis, and brachioradialis muscles (derived from cervical myotomes 5 and 6). However, if dorsal roots C5 and C6 are both destroyed, all proprioceptive sensory nerve fibers from these muscles are lost and there are no reflexes (*areflexia*). As a result the normal tone of these muscles is abolished completely (*atonia*). These muscles can still contract, however, for their ventral root fibers remain intact.

The difference in the physiological deficits occurring with dorsal rhizotomies involving all roots to a limb and those sparing certain roots is impressive. Mott

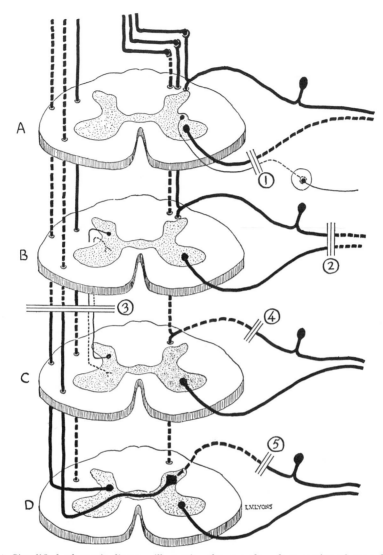

Fig. 13–24. Simplified schematic diagram illustrating the secondary degeneration of nerve fibers separated from their perikarya by lesions of the spinal roots or spinal cord. *A*, *B*, *C*, and *D*, various levels of the spinal cord. *1*, *2*, *3*, *4*, and *5*, various lesions severing nerve fibers. The portions undergoing secondary degeneration are indicated by *broken lines* (after a figure from Ranson, '36).

and Sherrington (1895) showed that complete deafferentation of an extremity resulted in virtual paralysis of the limb. Monkeys with such rhizotomies could not use the deafferented limb for walking, climbing, or grasping. The motor deficits resulting from incomplete deafferentation of an extremity are quite different. If only one dorsal root distributing cutaneous afferents to any part of the hand or foot remained intact, little motor deficit resulted. These authors differentially sec-

tioned certain dorsal roots and found that if cutaneous afferents alone were left intact, little impairment of function resulted. However, when muscle afferents were intact and cutaneous afferents were sectioned, the hand was virtually useless. From these studies, it was concluded that, "afferent impulses, both from the skin and from muscle, especially the former, as related to the palm or sole, are necessary for the carrying out of the highest level movements." Subsequent investigations (Lassek, '53) indicate that preservation of the C7 dorsal root appears to be of the greatest significance for use of the upper extremity. According to Twitchell ('54) monkeys with incomplete deafferentation of the arm direct movement of the limb by contact alone. These observations serve to emphasize the important role that different sensory inputs play in the integration of motor function.

Injury to the emerging ventral root of a spinal nerve produces deficits in segmental motor responses due to interruption of somatic efferent axons (Figs. 12–17, 13–24, and 13–25). If a thoracic or upper lumbar spinal nerve is injured, visceral efferent neurons (and reflexes) also would be involved (Figs. 11–1 and 11–2). Thus the destruction of the C8 spinal ventral root would partly paralyze the small muscles of the hand (via median and ulnar nerves), whereas a lesion of both ventral roots C8 and T1 would produce a complete flaccid paralysis and atrophy of these muscles (pages 169 and 206). The inclusion of ventral root T1 in the injury also interrupts most of the preganglionic visceral efferent fibers en route to the superior cervical sympathetic ganglion (Figs. 12–17 and 13–25). Loss of these visceral motor fibers to the smooth muscle of the eye and levator palpebrae muscle results in a triad of clinical symptoms known as Horner's syndrome (page 232). This syndrome usually is accompanied by altered sweating on the face. It should be noted that destruction of either the anterior horn cells (e.g., poliomyelitis), or their peripheral axons, results in a lower motor neuron lesion (Fig. 13–25), which deprives the appropriate muscles of the tonic influence of motor nerves.

If the mixed nerve is injured distal to the junction of the dorsal and ventral root (Fig. 13–24), the combined sensory and motor losses enumerated above will be present. It should be noted that if such combined nerve lesions are extensive, they may be followed by trophic changes in the skin (smoothness, dryness) and in capillary circulation (cyanosis). The trophic alterations presumably are due to the loss of peripheral vasomotor and afferent nerve fibers.

The ventral root fibers may be injured centrally along with secondary ascending sensory pathways. The ependymal cells and glial elements about the central canal (Fig. 12–2) at times undergo degenerative changes and liquefaction which result in a small, central cavity (syringomyelia). Frequently the initial destruction is confined to the crossing fibers of the spinothalamic tracts. Later the cavity may enlarge in a lateral, posterior, cranial, or caudal direction, and it may destroy adjacent fiber tracts or gray matter. A typical example of such a case is illustrated schematically in Fig. 13–25. Here the lesion interrupts the crossing fibers of the lateral spinothalamic tract in cord segments C8 and T1. Injured axons distal to the point of the lesion are separated from their cells of origin and undergo degeneration (*broken lines* in Fig. 13–25). Destruction of these crossing fibers from both sides of the cord results in a detectable bilateral loss of pain and thermal sense in the distribution of spinal nerves and dermatomes of C8–T1. All pain and temperature fibers of T1 are destroyed, but some of the C8 fibers are spared inasmuch as a few fibers ascend and cross in the C7 cord segment. This type of lesion results in a "dissociated sensory" loss since tactile, pressure, and position sense remain intact. The remainder of the lateral spinothalamic tract contains normal fibers that have crossed the spinal cord in segments either above or below the area of the lesion. In this case, the lateral extension of the cavity also has destroyed the anterior gray horn and nerve fibers passing through it (Fig. 13–25). A patient with such a lesion would have symptoms and signs of a unilateral lower motor neuron lesion and a Horner's syndrome in addition to the sensory disturbances. These neurological findings aid in localizing the lesion in cord segments C8 and T1.

A different type of spinal cord disease (amyotrophic lateral sclerosis) may involve both the upper and lower motor neurons. This is a progressive degenera-

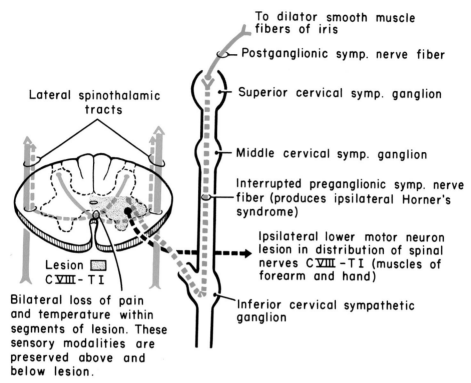

To dilator smooth muscle fibers of iris

Postganglionic symp. nerve fiber

Superior cervical symp. ganglion

Lateral spinothalamic tracts

Middle cervical symp. ganglion

Interrupted preganglionic symp. nerve fiber (produces ipsilateral Horner's syndrome)

Ipsilateral lower motor neuron lesion in distribution of spinal nerves C VIII - T I (muscles of forearm and hand)

Lesion C VIII - T I

Inferior cervical sympathetic ganglion

Bilateral loss of pain and temperature within segments of lesion. These sensory modalities are preserved above and below lesion.

FIG. 13-25. Diagram of syringomyelia with lateral extension into anterior gray horn of spinal cord. *Arrows* show direction of impulse conduction; *broken lines* indicate degenerated nerve fibers.

tive disease of unknown etiology, occurring with greatest frequency in the fifth and sixth decades of life, characterized by degeneration of the corticospinal tracts and the anterior horn cells. When degeneration of anterior horn cells begins in the cervical region (Fig. 13-26), the disease manifests itself by progressive muscular atrophy in the upper extremities, usually in the small intrinsic hand muscles, and spastic weakness of the muscles of the trunk and lower extremities. Muscular weakness usually is symmetrical and in the terminal phases of the disease becomes generalized. Fasciculations (i.e., involuntary twitching of muscle fascicles) in affected muscles can be observed and felt by the patient and the examiner. Myotatic irritability of affected muscles persists until atrophy is complete. Late in the course of this progressive disease the above findings may be accompanied by functional disturbances of the bladder and rectum due to injury of descending autonomic fibers en route to lumbar and

sacral segments of the cord. Such fibers lie close to both the reticulospinal and the corticospinal tracts and can be looked upon as "suprasegmental" to the visceral nuclei of the spinal cord.

The large myelinated fibers of the posterior and lateral funiculi of the spinal cord are frequently involved simultaneously in certain neurological diseases (e.g., subacute combined degeneration, multiple sclerosis, and Friedreich's disease). The posterior white columns and the lateral corticospinal tracts are affected most often, although the adjacent spinocerebellar tracts and other pathways also may be involved (Fig. 13-27). Lesions in other regions of the nervous system can precede or accompany the demyelinating process shown here in the cervical cord. Essential findings depend upon the level of the cord lesion and the amount of the destruction within the different tracts. This cervical lesion (Fig. 13-27) results in more extensive signs than a similar lesion in the lumbar region of the spinal cord,

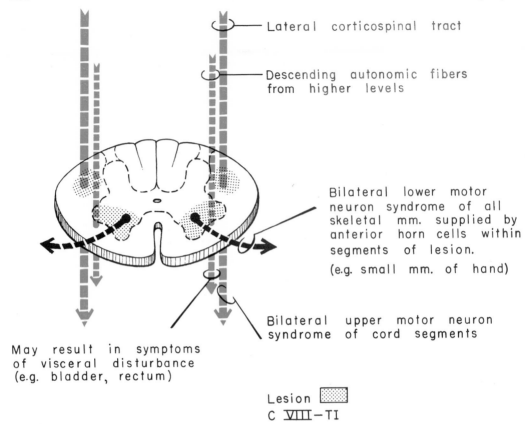

Lateral corticospinal tract

Descending autonomic fibers from higher levels

Bilateral lower motor neuron syndrome of all skeletal mm. supplied by anterior horn cells within segments of lesion.

(e.g. small mm. of hand)

Bilateral upper motor neuron syndrome of cord segments

May result in symptoms of visceral disturbance (e.g. bladder, rectum)

Lesion

C VIII–TI

FIG. 13–26. Diagram of a spinal cord lesion in amyotrophic lateral sclerosis. *Arrows* show direction of impulse conduction; *broken lines* indicate degenerated nerve fibers.

for in the cervical region more ascending sensory and descending motor fibers are destroyed. Destruction of the posterior white columns produces marked sensory deficits in the hands, trunk, and lower extremities (page 261). Injury of the corticospinal tracts at this level results in release phenomena characteristic of an upper motor neuron lesion (page 278) in the same body areas. Concomitant involvement of descending autonomic fibers may produce additional visceral disturbances. The tottering, stiff gait is characteristic of the patient who has paresis, as well as sensory deficits.

Hemisection of the spinal cord is probably the most instructive spinal lesion for teaching purposes, in spite of the fact that precise lesions of this kind are encountered only rarely in clinical neurology. The signs and symptoms associated with hemisection of the spinal cord constitute the *Brown-Séquard syndrome*

(Fig. 13–28). Neurological findings in the illustrated hemisection would include: (1) loss of sensory impulses in the posterior white columns below the lesion on the same side; (2) upper motor neuron lesion below the level of injury on the same side; (3) lower motor neuron symptoms and vasomotor paralysis in areas supplied by the injured segments on the side of the lesion; (4) bilateral loss of pain and thermal sense within the area of the lesion; and (5) loss of pain and thermal sense below T12 on the opposite side of the body (i.e., lower extremity, genitals, and perineum). With a lesion at cord segment T12, sensory and pyramidal symptoms would be manifested through spinal nerves of the lumbar and sacral plexuses. The lower motor neuron damage at cord segment T12 would produce no significant loss in motor function or reflex activity.

Complete and incomplete transections of the human spinal cord may result from

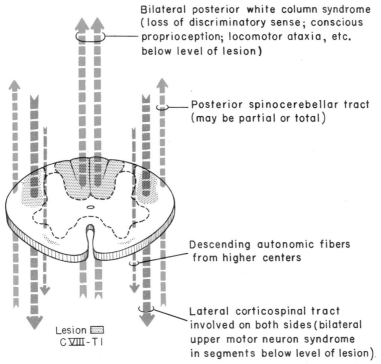

Bilateral posterior white column syndrome
(loss of discriminatory sense; conscious
proprioception; locomotor ataxia, etc.
below level of lesion)

Posterior spinocerebellar tract
(may be partial or total)

Descending autonomic fibers
from higher centers

Lesion
C VIII - T I

Lateral corticospinal tract
involved on both sides (bilateral
upper motor neuron syndrome
in segments below level of lesion)

FIG. 13–27. Diagram of spinal cord degeneration characteristically seen in subacute combined sclerosis (i.e., combined system disease). Arrows indicate the direction of impulse conduction. *Broken lines* indicate fiber systems which degenerate in this disease. The extent of degeneration in the posterior spinocerebellar tract is variable.

missile wounds or fracture-dislocation of vertebrae. Similar damage may follow ischemic necrosis due to occlusion or interruption of radicular arteries that supply the vulnerable upper thoracic segments (Fig. 4–1) of the spinal cord (Bolton, '39; Mettler, '48; Zülch, '54). Neoplasms also may compress the cord as they enlarge and secondarily compromise the blood supply. In such spinal cord lesions, the symptoms are severe and the complications are numerous, regardless of the level of injury.

Complete transection of the spinal cord is followed by loss of all sensibility below the injury since all ascending pathways are destroyed. Total anesthesia extends up to and includes the level of transection. There is a loss of all voluntary movement (absolute paralysis) below the level of the lesion due to interruption of all descending pathways. In view of the acute cord injury, there may even be suppression of sensory and motor func-

tions and loss of reflexes in several cord segments above the level of spinal transection. Such suppression usually lasts no longer than 2 weeks (Haymaker, '56).

Below the transection all somatic and visceral reflex activity, including muscle tone, is abolished for a variable period of time. This severe depression or collapse of intrinsic cord function is known as "spinal shock." Reflex activity within the isolated caudal segments may begin to reappear within a few days, or may not become evident until 6 weeks after injury. Once reasserted, caudal to the transection, the deep reflexes increase in intensity until they obviously are exaggerated. Superficial reflexes rarely are observed though the Babinski response can be elicited bilaterally. The caudal spinal segments, released from the control of suprasegmental structures, initiate and maintain a marked increase in reflex muscle tone (hypertonus). Such uncontrolled muscle tone leads to alternating

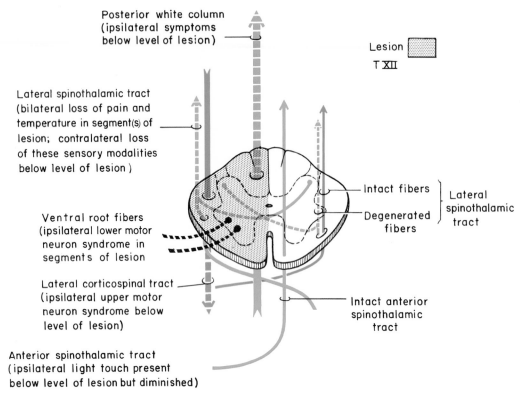

Posterior white column
(ipsilateral symptoms
below level of lesion)

Lesion

T XII

Lateral spinothalamic tract
(bilateral loss of pain and
temperature in segment(s) of
lesion; contralateral loss
of these sensory modalities
below level of lesion)

Intact fibers

Lateral
spinothalamic
tract

Degenerated
fibers

Ventral root fibers
(ipsilateral lower motor
neuron syndrome in
segments of lesion

Lateral corticospinal tract
(ipsilateral upper motor
neuron syndrome below
level of lesion)

Intact anterior
spinothalamic
tract

Anterior spinothalamic tract
(ipsilateral light touch present
below level of lesion but diminished)

Fig. 13–28. Diagram of spinal cord hemisection. This lesion results in a Brown-Séquard syndrome. *Arrows* show direction of impulse conduction; *broken lines* indicate degenerated nerve fibers.

spasms of the flexor and extensor muscles. Eventually there is a predominant contraction of either the extensor or flexor muscles of the paralyzed limbs. The position assumed by the paralyzed limbs during the early stages of paraplegia is believed by some to be an important factor in determining whether flexor or extensor spasms will eventually predominate. In paraplegics who have survived 2 years or longer, Guttmann ('46, '52) noted that extensor spasms predominate over flexor spasms in the majority of cases (65 per cent) and that persistent flaccid paralysis is less common (18 per cent). Kuhn's extensive study ('50) of the functional capacity of the isolated human spinal cord indicated that extensor muscle spasms may become predominant as early as 6 months after injury and may continue for years. Under certain conditions, some patients with extreme ex-

tensor muscle spasm can stand momentarily without mechanical support.

Bladder and bowel functions are disturbed in all transections of the cord, for they are no longer under voluntary control. Interruption of descending autonomic fibers, particularly those en route to parasympathetic nuclei in the sacral cord (S3, 4, and 5), leads to loss of rectal motility. There are reflex spasms of the external anal sphincters and fecal retention. Defecation occurs involuntarily after long intervals. If cord segments S3, 4, and 5 are destroyed, there is a permanent paralysis of the external sphincter and fecal incontinence. When these sacral segments are involved, there is in addition paralytic incontinence, and usually bladder distention, impotence, and perianal or saddle anesthesia. However, normal sensory and motor function is retained in the lower extremities (conus medullaris syndrome).

Bladder disturbances usually occur in three phases after cord transection. At the outset there is always *retention*, due to paralysis of the muscular bladder wall (detrusor muscle), and spasm of the vesicle sphincter. Two or 3 weeks later (range, 2 days to 18 months) the second phase or *overflow incontinence* is observed. This phase consists of an intermittent dribbling of urine and is due to gradual hypertrophy of the detrusor smooth muscle. The muscle now can overcome the resistance of the external sphincter for short periods of time. In most cases continued hypertrophy of the bladder wall eventually permits the bladder to expel small amounts of urine automatically, providing bladder infections have not intervened. This is the third phase, known as *automatic micturition*. Such automaticity of the bladder is poor if the lumbar segments are involved, and absent (paralytic incontinence) when the sacral segments are destroyed.

In partial or incomplete transection of the spinal cord, some of the ascending or descending fibers escape injury. The sensory deficits may not correspond to the level of motor loss, and some voluntary function may return within a week or two. Vasomotor and visceral disturbances are usually less pronounced, and irritative sensory phenomena are more common (e.g., pains, paresthesias, hyperesthesias). Marked priapism is more likely to accompany an incomplete transection of the cord. Haymaker ('56) has stated that the only reliable criterion of total transection, in the early stages after spinal injury, is "a complete flaccid paraplegia with areflexia and complete sensory loss which lasts longer than 2 to 5 days".

CHAPTER 14

The Medulla

The medulla, the most caudal segment (myelencephalon) of the brain stem, represents a conical, expanded continuation of the upper cervical spinal cord. Externally the transition from spinal cord to lower medulla is gradual without sharp demarcation. The caudal limit of the medulla is rostral to the highest rootlets of the first cervical spinal nerve at about the level of the foramen magnum. Above the level of transition, the medulla increases in size and its external features become distinctive (see page 34). Changes in the external appearance of the medulla are due chiefly to structural rearrangements and development of structures peculiar to the medulla. The development of the fourth ventricle causes structures previously located posteriorly to be shifted posterolaterally, while the appearance of the pyramids on the anterior surface partially obliterates the anterior median sulcus. The oval eminences posterolateral to the pyramids, produced by the inferior olivary nuclei, give the medulla above the zone of transition a characteristic configuration. The gross features of the brain stem are shown in anterior and posterior views in Figures 14–1 and 14–2.

While the spinal cord throughout most of its length presents a relatively uniform internal organization, graded sections through the medulla disclose numerous important changes from level to level. Among the principal changes taking place in the medulla are the following: (1) the development of the fourth ventricle, representing the rostral continuation of the central canal of the spinal cord, (2) the replacement of the butterfly-shaped central gray of the spinal cord by larger aggregations of cellular groups and interlacing fibers constituting the reticular formation, (3) the termination of ascending first order fibers contained in the fasciculi gracilis and cuneatus upon their respective nuclei, and the formation of a composite second order lemniscal pathway, (4) the gradual replacement of spinal fibers in the zone of Lissauer by descending spinal trigeminal fibers, (5) the decussation of the pyramids, (6) the development of cranial nerve nuclei, their interconnecting fiber systems, and their afferent and efferent root fibers, and lastly, (7) the appearance of complex groups of relay nuclei, part of which belong to the reticular formation, that project fibers to the cerebellum. In the floor of the fourth ventricle the sulcus limitans can be seen lateral to the median sulcus. This groove continues to demarcate afferent and efferent cell columns (Fig. 14–3) as it did in the developing spinal cord (Fig. 5–3A). The reticular formation, phylogenetically one of the oldest portions of the neuraxis, represents the core of the brain stem. Structurally, it is composed of complex collections of cells of different sizes, types, and shapes forming both diffuse cellular aggregations and circumscribed nuclei. Fibers entering, leaving, and traversing the reticular core seemingly pass haphazardly in all directions. However, studies of Golgi-stained preparations of this region (Scheibel and Scheibel, '58) indicate that fibers and cellular groups are organized in specific patterns. The reticular formation of the medulla is continuous with that of the pons and higher levels of the brain stem.

A schematic arrangement of the functional components of the cranial nerves of the medulla, and the cell columns to which they are related, is shown in Figure 14-3. This schema resembles that present in the spinal cord, though development of the fourth ventricle has shifted somatic and visceral afferent regions laterally. While the functional components of a typical spinal nerve are four in number [i.e., general somatic afferent (GSA), general visceral afferent (GVA), general visceral efferent (GVE) and general somatic efferent (GSE); Fig. 12-17], three additional functional components are present in cranial nerves [i.e., special somatic afferent (SSA), special visceral afferent (SVA) and special visceral efferent (SVE)]. It is not considered necessary to divide somatic efferent fibers into special and general components. The above schema for the functional components of the cranial nerves will facilitate study and should lead to a more comprehensive understanding.

Within the medulla special somatic afferent (SSA) cranial nerves are represented by the auditory and vestibular components of the eighth nerve entering posterolaterally (Figs. 14-1, 14-3 and 14-5). General somatic afferent (GSA) fibers from components of cranial nerves V, VII, IX, and X descend in the spinal trigeminal tract (Fig. 14-5). Fibers conveying taste (special visceral afferent (SVA)), consisting of components of cranial nerves VII, IX, and X, form a well-defined tract, the fasciculus solitarius (Figs. 14-3, 14-4, 14-5 and 14-16). Cells of the nucleus ambiguus, located in the ventrolateral part of the reticular formation dorsal to the nucleus of the inferior olive (Figs. 14-3, 14-4, 14-5, 14-12 and 14-18), supply special visceral efferent (SVE) fibers which innervate the muscles of the pharynx and larynx via cranial nerves IX, X, and XI.

Since these neurons supply muscles derived from the mesoderm of the third and fourth branchial arches (branchiomeric muscles), they are referred to as branchiomeric cranial nerves. Other motor nuclei, having similar locations in the pons, provide special visceral efferent (SVE) fibers to muscle derivatives of the first and second branchial arches via cranial nerves V and VII (Figs. 14-4 and 14-5). The general visceral efferent (GVE) components (parasympathetic) constituting parts of cranial nerves III, VII, IX, and X are indicated in *yellow* in Figures 14-4 and 14-5. The hypoglossal nuclei located in the floor of the fourth ventricle (Figs. 14-2, 14-3, 14-4 and 14-16) give rise to somatic efferent (GSE) fibers which supply the muscles of the tongue. Other cranial nerve nuclei in higher brain stem segments supplying somatic efferent (GSE) fibers are the abducens, trochlear, and oculomotor nerves. These nuclei are arranged in linear order in the brain stem, near the midline and close to the ventricular surface (Fig. 14-5). Schematic diagrams showing the nuclei and intramedullary course of most of the cranial nerves are given in Figures 14-4 and 14-5. These diagrams should be used for reference here and at higher brain stem levels. Figure 14-6 indicates the level and plane of section of most of the brain stem photomicrographs described in this and succeeding chapters.

JUNCTION OF SPINAL CORD AND MEDULLA

At the junction of the spinal cord and medulla (Figs. 14-7 and A-1) sections resemble those of the upper cervical spinal cord with certain modifications. The substantia gelatinosa has increased in size, and coarse myelinated fibers can be found in the zone of Lissauer. At this level the zone of Lissauer contains fine ascending root fibers from the uppermost cervical nerves and coarser descending fibers of the trigeminal nerve (N. V) which enter at pontine levels and descend in the dorsolateral part of the brain stem. Some of these descending spinal trigeminal fibers can be found as low as the second cervical segment, where they terminate directly,

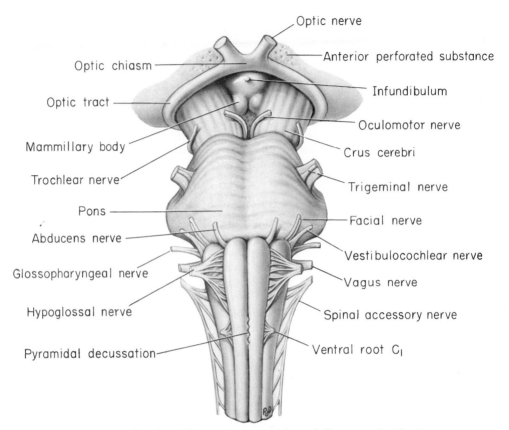

FIG. 14-1. Drawing of the anterior aspect of the medulla, pons and midbrain

or by collaterals, in parts of the substantia gelatinosa.

A conspicuous increase in the amount of gray surrounding the central canal is evident. The lateral corticospinal tract has become clearly separated from the medial longitudinal fasciculus by its passage into the posterior part of the lateral funiculus. It is broken up into a number of obliquely or transversely cut bundles, between which are strands of gray matter. A few fibers of the spinal portion of the spinal accessory nerve can be seen arching posterolaterally to emerge from the lateral aspect of the spinal cord between the dorsal and ventral roots (Figs. 14–7 and A–1). Axons of somatic motor neurons in the anterior horn emerge as ventral root fibers of the first cervical nerve. Rostrally these cells extend into the lower medulla (Fig. 14–10) where they are known as the supraspinal nucleus (Jacobsohn, '08). Fiber

tracts in the white matter have the same arrangement as in cervical spinal segments.

CORTICOSPINAL DECUSSATION

The most conspicuous features of sections through this level (Figs. 14–8, 14–9, and A–2) are the decussation of the pyramidal tracts, the first appearance of the nuclei of the posterior columns, and the development of the medullary reticular formation. The central gray has increased in size and lies mostly dorsal to the central canal.

Bundles of pyramidal fibers cross the midline ventral to the central gray and project dorsolaterally across the base of the anterior horn. These fibers cross in interdigitating bundles having a downward, as well as transverse, direction; in transverse sections these bundles are cut obliquely, so that in some sections more pyramidal fibers may be present on one

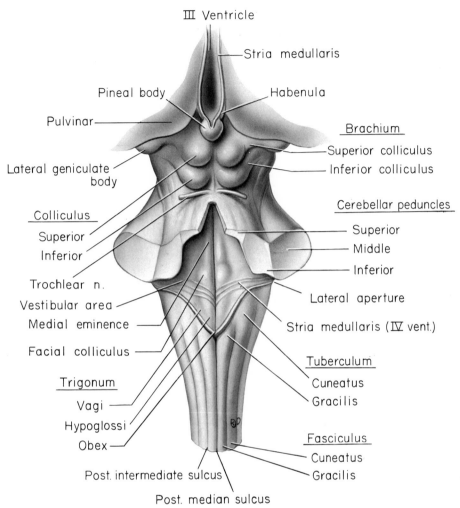

III Ventricle

Stria medullaris

Pineal body   Habenula

Pulvinar

Brachium

Superior colliculus

Inferior colliculus

Lateral geniculate
body

Cerebellar peduncles

Colliculus

Superior   Superior

Inferior   Middle

Inferior

Trochlear n.

Vestibular area   Lateral aperture

Medial eminence   Stria medullaris (IV vent.)

Facial colliculus

Tuberculum

Trigonum   Cuneatus

Vagi   Gracilis

Hypoglossi

Obex   Fasciculus

Cuneatus

Post. intermediate sulcus   Gracilis

Post. median sulcus

FIG. 14–2. Drawing of the posterior aspect of the brain stem with the cerebellum removed

side. The pyramidal, or corticospinal tract, is a massive bundle of fibers arising mainly from cells in the primary motor and somesthetic cortex, which undergoes an incomplete decussation in the lower medulla and enters the spinal cord. The largest number of fibers (nearly 90%) cross and descend in the posterior part of the lateral funiculus, as the lateral corticospinal tract (Fig. 13–16). Fibers of the anterior corticospinal tract retain their original position and project uncrossed into the anterior funiculus of the spinal cord. Some uncrossed fibers pass into the lateral funiculus on the same side. In a series of ascending sections the pyramidal decussation naturally is seen in reverse.

The pyramidal decussation forms the anatomical basis for the voluntary motor control of one half of the body by the opposite cerebral hemisphere. Injury of the pyramidal tract anywhere above the decussation may cause paralysis of the contralateral extremities.

The greatly enlarged substantia gelatinosa is capped externally by the zone of Lissauer. The zone no longer contains ascending spinal root fibers but is composed of descending afferent fibers of the trigeminal nerve (N. V), which terminate directly or by collaterals in the gelatinous substance. This fiber bundle now constitutes the *spinal trigeminal tract*, and the substantia gelatinosa similarly becomes the

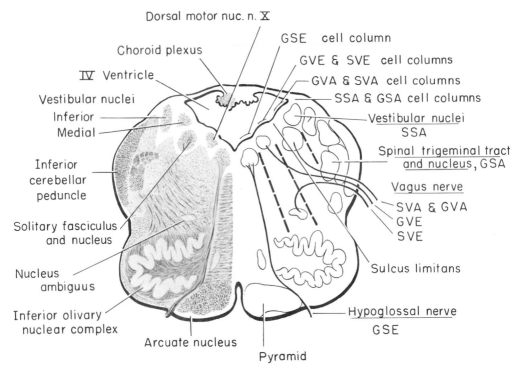

Fig. 14–3. Schematic transverse section of the medulla showing its basic features. Cell columns related to functional components of the cranial nerves are indicated on the right. Functional components of cranial nerves are both general and special. The vestibular nuclei shown at this level (and auditory nuclei at higher levels) form the special somatic afferent (SSA) cell columns. The spinal trigeminal nucleus forms the general somatic afferent (GSA) cell column and receives fibers from cranial nerves with this functional component (i.e., N.V, N.VII, N.IX, N.X). Functional components of the vagus nerve (except GSA) are shown in relation to particular nuclei. The hypoglossal nucleus (and the nuclei of N.VI, N.IV and N.III at higher brain stem levels) gives rise to general somatic efferent (GSE) fibers. Heavy dashes separate the nuclei of the various cell columns on the *right* side.

spinal trigeminal nucleus (Figs. 14–5, 14–8 and 14–16).

The anterior horn is still recognizable; at this level it contains groups of motor neurons which contribute fibers to the first cervical, and the spinal accessory nerves. On the medial border of the anterior horn is the medial longitudinal fasciculus which has been pushed laterally by the fibers of the pyramidal decussation (Figs. 14–8 and 14–9). On the ventral and lateral borders of the anterior horn are fibers of the vestibulospinal tract. The gray between the spinal trigeminal nucleus and the anterior horn has lost its definite continuity and is composed of scattered cells and intermingled fiber bundles. Fibers present in this area are corticospinal and short intersegmental fibers, comparable

to those of the fasciculi proprii. This area of intermingled gray and white is the most caudal part of the brain stem reticular formation; it is said to be continuous with small islands of gray in the reticular process at spinal levels.

In the posterior white columns nuclear masses have appeared in the fasciculi gracilis and cuneatus. These are the nuclei of the posterior funiculi, known respectively as the *nucleus gracilis* and *nucleus cuneatus*. The long ascending branches of the cells in the dorsal root ganglia, coursing in the posterior funiculus, terminate upon these nuclei (Figs. 13–1, 13–6 and 14–2). At these levels the fasciculus cuneatus is massive and the small caudal part of the nucleus cuneatus protrudes into the ventral part of the fasciculus (Figs. 14–8 and

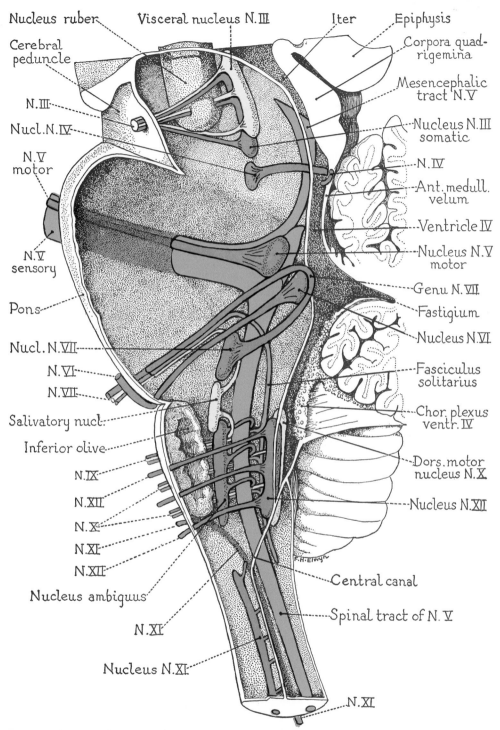

Nucleus ruber

Visceral nucleus N. III

Iter

Epiphysis

Cerebral peduncle

Corpora quadrigemina

N. III

Mesencephalic tract N. V

Nucl. N. IV

Nucleus N. III somatic

N. V motor

N. IV

Ant. medull. velum

Ventricle IV

N. V sensory

Nucleus N. V motor

Pons

Genu N. VII

Fastigium

Nucl. N. VII

Nucleus N. VI

N. VI

Fasciculus solitarius

N. VII

Salivatory nucl.

Chor. plexus ventr. IV

Inferior olive

N. IX

Dors. motor nucleus N. X

N. XII

Nucleus N. XII

N. X

N. XI

N. XII

Nucleus ambiguus

N. XI

Central canal

Nucleus N. XI

Spinal tract of N. V

N. XI

F. H. Elwyn

FIG. 14–4. Nuclei and intramedullary course of some of the cranial nerves, somewhat schematic, viewed from the median sagittal surface. The right brain stem is represented as a hollow from which all other brain structures have been removed. General somatic (GSE) and special visceral (SVE) efferent components of cranial nerves innervating striated muscles are shown in *red*. General visceral efferent (GVE) components of cranial nerves III, VII, IX and X, representing preganglionic parasympathetic fibers, are shown in *yellow*. General somatic (GSA) and general visceral (GVA) afferent components of cranial nerves are shown in *blue* (after Braus-Elze, '32).

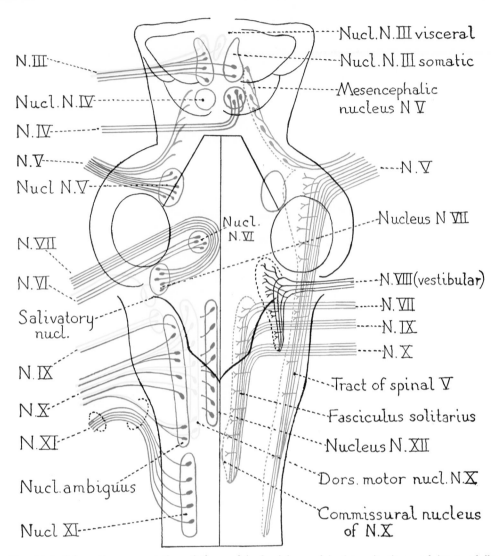

N.Ⅲ

Nucl.N.Ⅳ

N.Ⅳ

N.Ⅴ

Nucl N.Ⅴ

N.Ⅶ

N.Ⅵ

Salivatory nucl.

N.Ⅸ

N.Ⅹ

N.Ⅺ

Nucl.ambiguus

Nucl Ⅺ

Nucl.N.Ⅲ visceral

Nucl.N.Ⅲ somatic

Mesencephalic nucleus NⅤ

Nucl. N.Ⅵ

Nucleus NⅦ

N.Ⅴ

N.Ⅷ(vestibular)

N.Ⅶ

N.Ⅸ

N.Ⅹ

Tract of spinal Ⅴ

Fasciculus solitarius

Nucleus N.Ⅻ

Dors. motor nucl.N.Ⅹ

Commissural nucleus of N.Ⅹ

FIG. 14–5. Schematic representation of the nuclei of origin, nuclei of termination, and intramedullary course of the infratentorial cranial nerves projected on the posterior surface of the brain stem. Color coding is the same as in Fig. 14–4: *red*, general somatic (GSE) and special visceral (GVE) efferent components; *yellow*, general visceral efferent (GVE, parasympathetic) components; *blue*, general somatic (GSA) and general visceral (GVA) afferent components; *black*, special somatic afferent (SSA, vestibular).

14–9). The nucleus gracilis is larger, occupies a more central position and is capped dorsally and laterally by fibers of the fasciculus gracilis. As progressively higher levels are reached, increasing numbers of fibers terminate in these nuclei. The nuclei increase in size while the fasciculi show a corresponding decrease (Fig. 14–10). At levels through the caudal part of the inferior olivary complex, the entire fasciculus gracilis and most of the fascic-

ulus cuneatus have been replaced by their respective nuclei (Figs. 14–11 and 14–12).

In animals three cytologically distinct regions of the nucleus gracilis have been recognized (Cajal, '09; Taber, '61; Kuypers and Tuerk, '64): (1) a reticular region rostral to the obex characterized by a loose organization of cells, (2) a "cell nest" region caudal to the obex characterized by cell clusters, and (3) a caudal region characterized by few cells occurring singly or

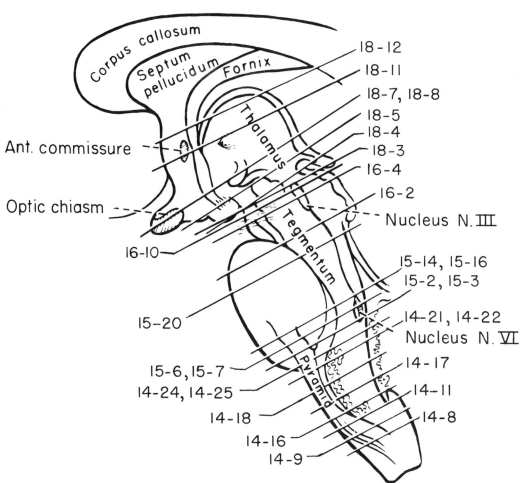

FIG. 14–6. Outline of paramedian sagittal section of brain stem, showing level and plane of the transverse sections of the figures indicated. For identification of structures, see Figure 18–1.

in small clusters. Ascending dorsal root fibers project somatotopically to the nucleus gracilis (Ferraro and Barrera, '35; Walker and Weaver, '42; Hand, '66). According to Hand ('66) lumbosacral dorsal root fibers exhibit a somatotopic lamination chiefly in the "cell nest" region, while terminations in the reticular region are diffuse with impressive intersegmental overlap. Certain physiological studies in the cat suggest that neurons in the nucleus gracilis exhibit rostrocaudal differences with respect to: (1) the size of the peripheral receptive fields which supply afferent input (Gordon and Paine, '60; McComas, '63), and (2) segregation of sensory modality (Kuhn, '49; Perl et al., '62; Gordon and Jukes, '64; Winter, '65). Rostral

portions of the nucleus (i.e., reticular region) are said to be related to deep pressure and joint movement, while the "cell nest" and caudal regions of the nucleus are related to hair and skin receptors. Other physiological data (Kruger et al., '61), based upon single neuron analysis of posterior column nuclei, provide no evidence of rostrocaudal differentiation in terms of either somatotopy or modality segregation. The latter finding supports other experimental studies (Mountcastle and Powell, '59; Poggio and Mountcastle, '60) which indicate that: (1) the somatotopic organization of the posterior columns and the medial lemniscus is maintained at the level of the posterior column nuclei, and (2) neural elements devoted to

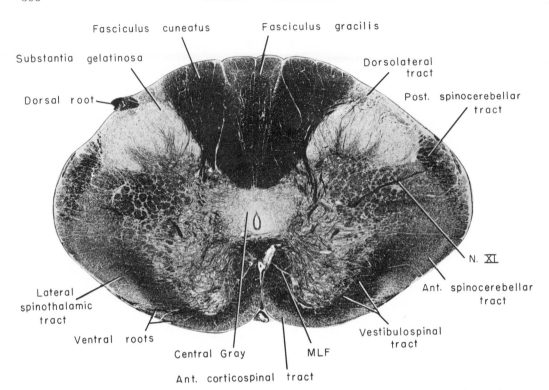

Fasciculus cuneatus

Fasciculus gracilis

Substantia gelatinosa

Dorsolateral tract

Dorsal root

Post. spinocerebellar tract

Lateral spinothalamic tract

N. XI

Ant. spinocerebellar tract

Ventral roots

Vestibulospinal tract

Central Gray

MLF

Ant. corticospinal tract

Fig. 14–7. Transverse section through uppermost portion of spinal cord of 1-month infant. Weigert's myelin stain. Photograph.

kinesthesis and tactile sense are intermingled in a single and mutual somatotopic pattern. Studies (Carpenter et al., '68) in the monkey indicate that lower thoracic, lumbar, and sacrococcygeal dorsal roots project in overlapping somatotopic fashion throughout the rostrocaudal extent of the nucleus gracilis. Zones of the nucleus gracilis receiving terminal dorsal root fibers are organized, so that: (1) roots of the lumbar enlargement project to irregular-shaped areas in the central core region of the nucleus, (2) lower thoracic and upper lumbar roots project in serial fashion to narrow, oblique laminae lateral to the core region, and (3) sacral and coccygeal dorsal roots project in serial fashion to crescent-shaped laminae in dorsomedial parts of the nucleus. The areas of the terminal projection zones in the nucleus gracilis are related to the size of the dorsal root and the number of ascending fibers they contribute to the fasciculus gracilis.

The nucleus cuneatus also exhibits regional differences in its cytoarchitecture (Meesen and Olszewski, '49; Olszewski and Baxter, '54). According to Kuypers and Tuerk ('64) dorsal areas of the cuneate nucleus contain clusters of round cells with many bushy dendrites while basal areas contain triangular, multipolar and fusiform cells with long sparse dendrites. These authors considered the round cell clusters to receive afferents principally from distal parts of the body and to be related to small cutaneous receptive fields. Triangular and multipolar cells were considered to receive afferents primarily from proximal parts of the limb and trunk, and were regarded as being related to larger cutaneous receptive fields. These studies suggested that dorsal root fibers have a dual termination with some fibers ending in cell clusters and others among basal triangular cells.

A systematic study (Shriver et al., '68) of dorsal root projections to the cuneate nucleus in the monkey has shown that: (1) fibers from C1 through T1 terminate in both exclusive and overlapping zones,

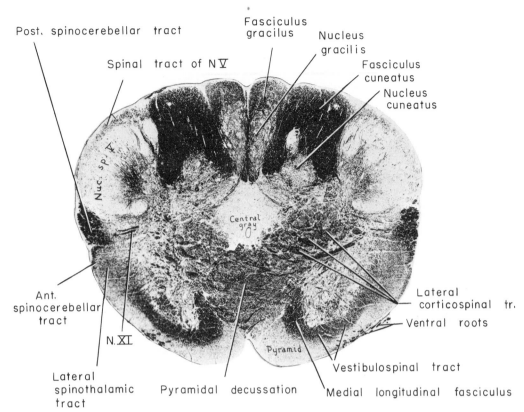

Post. spinocerebellar tract

Spinal tract of N V

Fasciculus gracilis

Nucleus gracilis

Fasciculus cuneatus

Nucleus cuneatus

Nucl. sp. V

Central gray

Ant. spinocerebellar tract

N. XI

Lateral spinothalamic tract

Pyramidal decussation

Pyramid

Lateral corticospinal tr.

Ventral roots

Vestibulospinal tract

Medial longitudinal fasciculus

FIG. 14–8. Transverse section of medulla of 1-month infant through the decussation of the pyramidal tracts. Weigert's myelin stain. Photograph.

(2) fibers from C5 through C8 terminate in a central core region about which other dorsal root fibers terminate in oblique serial laminae, (3) rostral dorsal root fibers (C1 through C4) terminate in ventrolateral regions, and caudal dorsal root fibers (T1 through T7) terminate in dorsomedial regions (Figs. 14–13 and 14–14). Comparisons of the patterns of dorsal root terminations in the nuclei gracilis and cuneatus in the monkey (Carpenter et al., '68) suggest that in the nucleus gracilis: (1) overlapping terminations are more extensive and irregular than in the cuneate nucleus, and (2) there is less autonomous terminal representation of individual dorsal root fibers in the nucleus gracilis.

Tracts in the lateral and anterior white substance of the caudal medulla occupy the same relative positions as in upper cervical spinal segments. Short intersegmental fibers have become incorporated within the reticular formation.

DECUSSATION OF THE MEDIAL LEMNISCUS

In transverse sections of the medulla above the pyramidal decussation (Figs. 14–11, 14–12 and A–3), the nucleus gracilis reaches its greatest extent, and practically all fibers of the fasciculus gracilis have terminated in portions of the nucleus. Although the nucleus cuneatus is much larger than in Figures 14–9 or 14–10, a considerable number of fibers of the fasciculus cuneatus remain dorsal to the nuclei. From the nuclei gracilis and cuneatus, myelinated fibers arise which sweep ventromedially around the central gray. These fibers, known as *internal arcuate fibers*, cross the median raphe and contralaterally form a well-defined ascending bundle, the *medial lemniscus*. This large ascending fiber bundle can be readily followed through the brain stem to its termination in the ventral posterolateral nucleus of the thalamus (Fig. 13–6). The medial

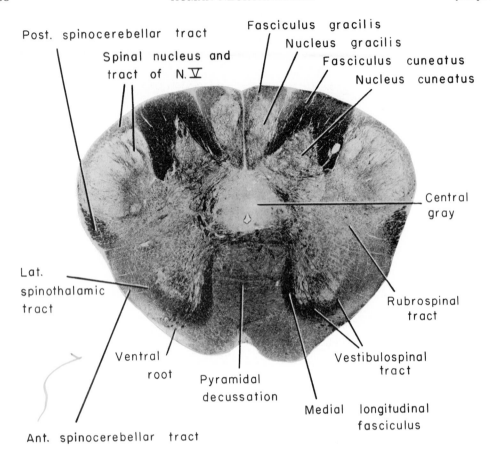

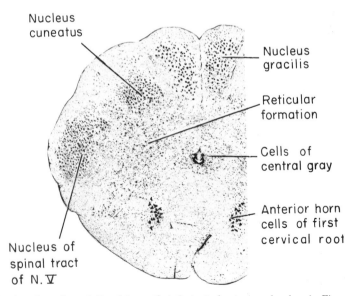

Fig. 14–10. Section through medulla of 1-month infant at about same level as in Figure 14–8. Cresyl violet. Photograph, with cell groups blocked in schematically.

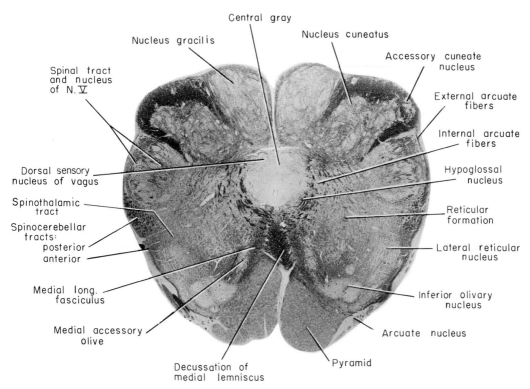

FIG. 14-11. Transverse section of medulla of 1-month infant through the decussation of the medial lemniscus. Weigert's myelin stain. Photograph.

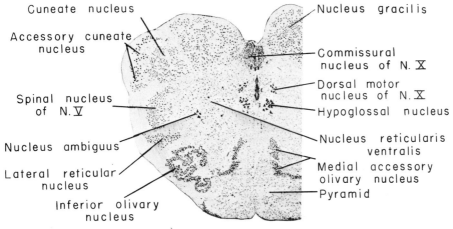

FIG. 14-12. Section through medulla of 1-month infant about same level as in Figure 14-11. Cresyl violet. Photograph, with cell groups blocked in schematically.

lemniscus constitutes the second neuron of the posterior column pathway conveying kinesthetic sense and discriminative touch to higher levels of the neuraxis. The decussation of the medial lemniscus provides part of the anatomical basis for sensory representation of half of the body in the contralateral cerebral cortex. Consequently, injury to the medial lemniscus causes characteristic kinesthetic and tactile deficits on the opposite side of the body.

CUNEATE NUCLEUS

Fig. 14–13. Photomicrograph of terminal degeneration in the cuneate and accessory cuneate nuclei in the monkey following section of the fifth (A) and sixth (B) cervical dorsal roots. Compare localization of degeneration with that plotted in Figs. 14–14 and 14–15. Nauta-Gygax stain. X16.

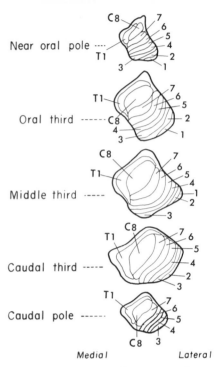

Fig. 14–14. Diagram of the somatotopic terminations of cervical and T1 dorsal root fibers in the cuneate nucleus in the monkey. The nucleus is shown in drawings of transverse sections from the right side. Thoracic dorsal root fibers T2 through T7 terminate in overlapping fashion along the dorsomedial margin of the nucleus (Shriver et al., '68).

Lateral to the cuneate nucleus is a group of large cells similar to those of the dorsal nucleus of Clarke (see p. 249), known as the *accessory cuneate* nucleus (Figs. 13–15, 14–11, 14–12, A–3 and A–4). This nucleus is considered to be the medullary equivalent of the dorsal nucleus (Sherrington, 1893a; Pass, '33; Brodal, '41). These nuclei share the following anatomical and functional features: (1) cells are morphologically similar with eccentric nuclei, (2) afferent fibers are derived from dorsal roots, (3) both nuclei give rise to uncrossed cerebellar afferent fibers, (4) both nuclei relay impulses from muscle spindles, type II muscle afferents, and cutaneous afferents (Oscarsson, '65). Although impulses from Golgi tendon organs are relayed via the dorsal nucleus, similar relays have not been established for the accessory cuneate nucleus. Ascending fi-

bers conveyed by the fasciculus cuneatus and terminating in the accessory cuneate nucleus are derived from the same dorsal root ganglia as those projecting to the cuneate nucleus, namely those of cervical and upper thoracic spinal segments. Dorsal root fibers, projecting to the accessory cuneate nucleus, terminate somatotopically (Liu, '56; Shriver et al., '68), in overlapping laminae. In the monkey (Shriver et al., '68) the pattern of termination of fibers from C1 through T1 dorsal roots in the accessory cuneate nucleus is similar to that of the cuneate nucleus in that fibers from: (1) C5 through C8 terminate in the central core region about which other dorsal root fibers terminate in oblique serial laminae, (2) rostral roots terminate in ventrolateral regions, while those from

ACCESSORY CUNEATE NUCLEUS

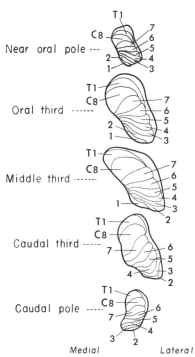

FIG. 14-15. Diagram of the somatotopic termination of cervical and T1 dorsal root fibers in the accessory cuneate nucleus in the monkey. The nucleus is shown in drawings of transverse sections from the right side. Fibers from these roots partially overlap the terminal zone of the next highest root. Thoracic dorsal root fibers T2 through T7 terminate in overlapping fashion along the dorsolateral margin of the nucleus (Shriver et al., '68).

more caudal roots end in dorsomedial regions, and (3) all of these roots, except C1 and C2, terminate throughout the rostrocaudal extent of the nucleus (Figs. 14–13 and 14–15). Fibers from the above mentioned dorsal roots terminating in the accessory cuneate nucleus end in both exclusive and overlapping zones; fibers from one dorsal root partially overlap the territory of the next highest root. Upper thoracic dorsal root fibers (other than T1) exhibit greater overlap and terminate in smaller zones in the lateral part of the nucleus.

Although fibers from parts of the fasciculus cuneatus terminate upon cells of the accessory cuneate nucleus, these cells do not contribute fibers to the medial lemnis-

cus. Cells of the accessory cuneate nucleus give rise to uncrossed cuneocerebellar fibers that at higher levels enter the cerebellum via the inferior cerebellar peduncle (Fig. 13–15). Fibers of the cuneocerebellar tract, conveying impulses from receptors in muscles of the upper extremity and neck, represent the upper limb equivalent of the posterior spinocerebellar tract.

The *spinal trigeminal tract*, consisting of afferent trigeminal root fibers which enter the brain stem at upper pontine levels and descend, occupies the region which at spinal levels constitutes the *zone of Lissauer* (Figs. 14–8, 14–9, 14–10, 14–11, 14–16 and 14–17). These fibers, originating from cells of the trigeminal ganglion, have a definite topographic organization within the tract. Central descending processes of cells are organized, so that: (1) fibers of the mandibular division are most dorsal, (2) fibers of the ophthalmic division are most ventral, and (3) fibers of the maxillary division occupy an intermediate position. Clinicopathological studies (Taylor et al., '22; Smyth, '39; Falconer, '49) suggest that fibers of the separate divisions extend caudally for different distances, with those of the mandibular division terminating at medullary levels and those of the ophthalmic division terminating in upper cervical spinal segments. Experimental studies (Torvik, '56; Kruger and Michel, '62; Kerr, '63; Rhoton et al., '66) indicate that there is little difference in the caudal extent of fibers in the different trigeminal divisions, and that some fibers from all divisions extend into upper cervical spinal segments. As this tract descends it becomes progressively smaller as fibers leave the tract and terminate in the adjacent spinal trigeminal nucleus. In the rostral medulla a surprisingly large number of trigeminal fibers in the dorsal part of the spinal trigeminal tract project medially to terminate in a restricted ventrolateral part of the nucleus solitarius (Torvik, '56; Kerr, '61, '63; Rhoton et al., '66).

A number of general somatic afferent fibers from the vagus, glossopharyngeal

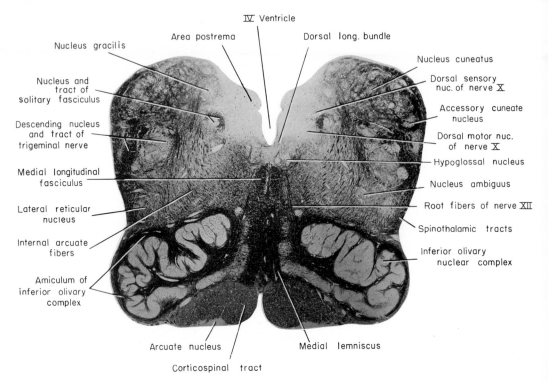

IV Ventricle
Area postrema
Nucleus gracilis
Dorsal long. bundle
Nucleus cuneatus
Nucleus and tract of solitary fasciculus
Dorsal sensory nuc. of nerve X
Accessory cuneate nucleus
Descending nucleus and tract of trigeminal nerve
Dorsal motor nuc. of nerve X
Hypoglossal nucleus
Medial longitudinal fasciculus
Nucleus ambiguus
Lateral reticular nucleus
Root fibers of nerve XII
Spinothalamic tracts
Internal arcuate fibers
Inferior olivary nuclear complex
Amiculum of inferior olivary complex
Arcuate nucleus
Medial lemniscus
Corticospinal tract

FIG. 14–16. Transverse section of medulla of 1-month infant through lower part of inferior olivary nucleus. Weigert's myelin stain. Photograph.

and facial nerves enter and descend in the spinal trigeminal tract. Vagal and glossopharyngeal fibers descend in the dorsomedial part of the tract for a considerable distance and terminate in the magnocellular division of the caudal part of the spinal trigeminal nucleus (Torvik, '56; Kimmel et al., '61; Kerr, '62; Rhoton et al., '66). Only a modest number of facial nerve fibers enter the spinal trigeminal tract.

The *spinal trigeminal nucleus*, which lies along the medial border of the tract, extends from the level of entry of the trigeminal root in the pons to the second cervical spinal segment (Fig. 15–17). Fibers from the spinal trigeminal tract terminate upon cells of the nucleus at various levels throughout its extent. Cytoarchitecturally the spinal trigeminal nucleus has been subdivided into three parts (Olszewski, '50): (1) an oral part extending caudally to the level of the rostral pole of the hypoglossal nucleus, (2) an interpolar part extending caudally to the

level of the obex, and (3) a caudal part which begins at the level of the obex, closely resembles the posterior horn of the spinal cord, and extends caudally as far as the second cervical spinal segment. The inner medial part of the caudal subdivision, containing irregularly arranged medium-sized cells of triangular or multipolar shape, constitutes the magnocellular (division) subnucleus. Fibers in different parts of the spinal trigeminal tract terminate within sharply circumscribed sectors of the spinal trigeminal nucleus. A number of descending trigeminal fibers pass beyond the spinal trigeminal nucleus to terminate in dorsal parts of the reticular formation and portions of the solitary nucleus.

Descending fibers in the spinal trigeminal tract convey impulses concerned with pain, thermal, and tactile sense from the face, forehead, and mucous membranes of the nose and mouth. While other portions of the trigeminal complex are concerned with tactile sense, the spinal trigeminal

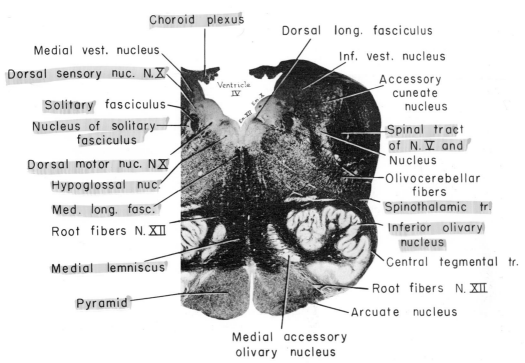

Choroid plexus

Dorsal long. fasciculus

Medial vest. nucleus

Inf. vest. nucleus

Dorsal sensory nuc. N.X

Accessory cuneate nucleus

Ventricle IV

Solitary fasciculus

Spinal tract of N. V and Nucleus

Nucleus of solitary fasciculus

Dorsal motor nuc. NX

Olivocerebellar fibers

Hypoglossal nuc.

Spinothalamic tr.

Med. long. fasc.

Inferior olivary nucleus

Root fibers N. XII

Central tegmental tr.

Medial lemniscus

Root fibers N. XII

Pyramid

Arcuate nucleus

Medial accessory olivary nucleus

FIG. 14–17. Transverse section of adult medulla through inferior olive somewhat higher than in Figure 14–16. Weigert's myelin stain. Photograph. *Em.X*, eminentia vagi; *Em. XII*, eminentia hypoglossi.

tract and nucleus appear to be the only part of this complex concerned with the perception of pain and thermal sense. The most decisive evidence for this modality segregation is that medullary trigeminal tractotomy markedly reduces pain and thermal sense without impairing tactile sense (Sjöqvist, '38). Physiological studies (Kruger and Michel, '62a) indicate that it is extremely difficult to isolate or identify neurons in the spinal trigeminal nucleus uniquely concerned with transmission of impulses related to pain, while virtually all neurons in this nucleus can be excited by delicate tactile stimuli. These authors have suggested that the representation of pain in the spinal trigeminal nucleus may involve tactile neurons excited by small fibers which are known to convey impulses related to painful sensations in certain circumstances.

From the spinal nucleus fibers arise which form the secondary trigeminal tracts. These fibers arise, a few at each level, and cross through the reticular formation to the opposite side. Most of these fibers ascend to thalamic levels in association with the contralateral medial lemniscus; others appear to terminate upon cells of the reticular formation. These are trigeminothalamic fibers which constitute the second neuron in the sensory pathway from face to cortex (Fig. 15–17).

Other uncrossed fibers ascend and descend on the same side, forming reflex connections with the motor nuclei of the hypoglossal, vagus, facial, and other cranial nerves (Figs. 15–17 and 15–19). Since the spinal trigeminal tract and nucleus are located not far from the spinothalamic tract, injury to the dorsolateral region of the medulla produces the curious clinical picture of an alternating hemianalgesia and hemithermo-anesthesia of the face and body. There is loss or diminution of pain and thermal sense on the same side of the face, and on the opposite side of the body and neck.

Nuclei belonging to the hypoglossal (N. XII) and vagus (N. X) nerves are located in the central gray surrounding the central canal. Within the ventral part of the central gray, small clusters of large neurons constitute part of the hypoglossal nuclei (Figs. 14–11 and 14–12). Dorsolateral to the hypoglossal nuclei, smaller cell groups form the caudal poles of the dorsal motor nuclei of the vagi. Dorsal to the central canal is the commissural nucleus of the vagus.

Immediately rostral to the obex on each side of the fourth ventricle is the *area postrema* (Fig. 14–16), a slightly rounded eminence containing astroblast-like cells, arterioles, sinusoids, and probably some apolar or unipolar neurons (Cammermeyer, '47; Brizzee and Neal, '54). The area postrema in the dog has been demonstrated to function as an emetic chemoreceptor trigger zone that responds to apomorphine and intravenous digitalis glycosides (Borison and Wang, '49, '53). The area postrema receives fibers from the nucleus solitarius (Morest, '60), as well as some fibers ascending in the posterior and lateral columns of the spinal cord (Morest, '67). It is suggested that some impulses transmitted by ascending spinal pathways from viscera may play a role in the physiology of vomiting. Axons from neurons in the area postrema have been traced into caudal parts of the medial nucleus solitarius (Morest, '67).

The reticular formation at the level of the decussation of the medial lemniscus occupies the region ventral to the posterior column nuclei and the spinal trigeminal complex and dorsolateral to the pyramid (Fig. 14–11). It contains numerous cells of various sizes arranged in more or less definite groups and is traversed by both longitudinal and transverse fiber bundles. At this level it is traversed by numerous internal arcuate fibers and smaller bundles of secondary trigeminal fibers. Peripheral to the reticular formation the long tracts retain their relative lateral and anterior positions. Fibers of the medial longitudinal fasciculus are dorsal to the pyramids and lateral to the decussation of the medial lemniscus.

One of the distinct reticular nuclei, the *lateral reticular nucleus of the medulla*, is located ventrolaterally (Fig.

14–11). This nucleus begins caudal to the inferior olivary complex and extends rostrally to midolivary levels (Figs. 14–12 and 14–16). In man this nucleus consists of a large ventral cell group dorsolateral to the inferior olive and a small subtrigeminal cell group beneath the spinal trigeminal nucleus (Walberg, '52). Neurons composing these nuclear groups project fibers to specific portions of the cerebellum via the ipsilateral inferior cerebellar peduncle. The lateral reticular nucleus of the medulla receives afferent fibers from the spinal cord via spinoreticular pathways and collaterals from the spinothalamic tracts. Crossed descending rubrobulbar fibers also terminate upon cells of this nucleus (Walberg, '58; Hinman and Carpenter, '59). Physiological data suggest that exteroceptive impulses may be conveyed to the cerebellum via the lateral reticular nucleus (Morin and Gardner, '53; Combs, '56).

On the anterior aspect of the pyramid is the *arcuate nucleus*, whose position varies somewhat in different levels (Figs. 14–16 and 14–18). In rostral portions of the medulla the nucleus enlarges considerably (nucleus precursorius pontis) and appears to become continuous with the nuclei of the pons. Afferent fibers to this nucleus probably are derived from the cerebral cortex, and efferent fibers from it project as ventral external arcuate fibers to the cerebellum. Fibers from this small nucleus are thought to be crossed.

Dorsolateral to the pyramids new nuclear masses have appeared (Figs. 14–11, 14–12 and A–26) which become more extensive in the succeeding levels. They represent the caudal part of the inferior olivary complex.

LOWER AND MIDOLIVARY LEVELS OF THE MEDULLA

Transverse sections through the lower and midolivary levels of the medulla present the most characteristic features of the medulla (Figs. 14–16, 14–17, 14–18, A–4, and A–5). The central canal has opened into the fourth ventricle, which widens progressively at higher levels. The tela choroidea and choroid plexus

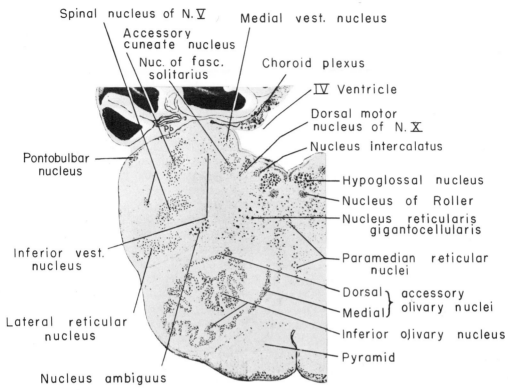

Spinal nucleus of N. Ⅴ   Medial vest. nucleus

Accessory
cuneate nucleus

Nuc. of fasc.
solitarius

Choroid plexus

Ⅳ Ventricle

Dorsal motor
nucleus of N. Ⅹ

Nucleus intercalatus

Pontobulbar
nucleus

Hypoglossal nucleus

Nucleus of Roller

Nucleus reticularis
gigantocellularis

Inferior vest.
nucleus

Paramedian reticular
nuclei

Dorsal⎫ accessory
Medial⎭ olivary nuclei

Lateral reticular
nucleus

Inferior olivary nucleus

Pyramid

Nucleus ambiguus

FIG. 14–18. Section through midolivary region of adult medulla. Cresyl violet. Photograph, with schematic representation of main cell groups.

form a thin roof over the ventricle, while the floor of the fourth ventricle contains several rounded eminences formed by specific nuclear groups. The medial eminence, or *trigonum hypoglossi*, is produced by the nucleus of N. XII; the intermediate eminence, known as the *trigonum vagi*, overlies certain vagal nuclei; the lateral eminence in the fourth ventricle is the *area vestibularis*, which is occupied by the caudal poles of the medial and inferior vestibular nuclei (Figs. 14–2, 14–17 and 14–18).

Although the nucleus gracilis has disappeared at this level and the nucleus cuneatus is greatly reduced in size, internal arcuate fibers can be seen sweeping ventromedially through the reticular formation to enter the contralateral medial lemniscus. At this level the medial lemnisci occupy triangular areas on each side of the median raphe, bounded ventrally by the pyramids and laterally by the inferior olivary nuclei. Dorsal to the medial

lemnisci on each side of the median raphe are the medial longitudinal fasciculi (Figs. 14–16 and 14–17). The spinal trigeminal nucleus and tract, somewhat inconspicuous in Weigert-stained sections, retain the same general position; the accessory cuneate nucleus is dorsal, and the fibers forming the inferior cerebellar peduncle are lateral.

Inferior Olivary Nuclear Complex. The most striking new structure is the convoluted gray band of cells known as the inferior olivary nuclear complex. The complex consists of: (1) the *principal inferior olivary nucleus*, appearing as a folded bag with the opening or hilus directed medially; (2) a *medial accessory olivary nucleus* along the lateral border of the medial lemniscus; and (3) a *dorsal accessory olivary nucleus*, dorsal to the main nucleus. These nuclei are composed of relatively small, round or pear-shaped cells with numerous short branching dendrites. Axons of these cells are distributed to all parts of the opposite side of the cerebellum, and constitute an olivo-cerebellar fiber system. Fibers emerging from the inferior olivary nucleus fill the interior of the bag-shaped nucleus, pass through the hilus, traverse the medial lemnisci, and course both through and around the opposite inferior olivary nuclei. Contralaterally these fibers traverse the reticular formation and parts of the spinal trigeminal complex to enter the inferior cerebellar peduncle. The accessory olivary nuclei and the most medial part of the main olivary nucleus are phylogenetically the oldest and project their fibers largely to the cerebellar vermis. The larger convoluted lateral portion of the main nucleus projects its fibers to the opposite cerebellar hemisphere (neocerebellum). As more and more olivocerebellar fibers are given off, the inferior cerebellar peduncle increases in size. While this peduncle is a composite bundle containing fibers from a large number of specific nuclei, olivo-cerebellar fibers constitute the largest component of this bundle (Figs. 14–17, 14–21, and 17–20).

The main olivary nucleus is surrounded by a dense band of myelinated fibers, the *amiculum olivae*, composed largely of axons terminating in the nucleus. Descending fibers terminating upon cells of the inferior olivary complex arise from the cerebral cortex, the red nucleus, and the periaqueductal gray of the mesencephalon (Mettler, '44; Wallberg, '56). Cortico-olivary fibers appear to arise from frontal, parietal, temporal, and occipital cortex, descend in most of their course with corticospinal fibers, and terminate bilaterally, primarily upon the ventral lamella of the principal olive. Rubro-olivary fibers and fibers arising from the periaqueductal gray of the mesencephalon enter a composite bundle known as the central tegmental tract and descend (Figs. 14–17, 14–24 and 15–3). These uncrossed fibers terminate in different portions of the principal olive. Rubro-olivary fibers end in the dorsal lamella, while fibers from the periaqueductal gray terminate in parts of the ventral lamella (Walberg, '56). Spino-olivary fibers, ascending in the anterior funiculus of the spinal cord, terminate largely on parts of the dorsal and medial accessory olivary nuclei; more than half of these fibers cross in the medulla. The inferior olivary nuclear complex is the largest of the medullary cerebellar relay nuclei.

The tracts ventrolateral to the reticular formation have been pushed dorsally by the olivary nuclei. The anterior spino-cerebellar, rubrospinal, and spinothalamic tracts occupy the lateral periphery between the inferior cerebellar peduncle and the olive. Fibers of the vestibulospinal tract are scattered along the posterior surface of the inferior olive. Posteriorly on each side of the medial raphe lie the medial longitudinal fasciculi, containing descending fiber bundles of mixed origin. Descending fibers in this tract are derived primarily from certain vestibular nuclei and portions of the brain stem reticular formation, but some fibers originate from nuclei in the midbrain. The interstitial nucleus of Cajal (interstitiospinal tract) contributes a small number of fibers to the dorsomedial part of the medial longitudinal fasciculus. Tectospinal fibers from the superior colliculus form a loosely organized group of fibers in the ventral part of the bundle.

Medullary Reticular Formation. The term "reticular formation" is a somewhat vague designation given a variety of special connotations; it originated in anatomy to describe portions of the brain stem core characterized structurally by a wealth of cells of various sizes and types, arranged in diverse aggregations, and enmeshed in a complicated fiber network. In a sense, the reticular formation constitutes a matrix within which "specific" nuclei and tracts are embedded. Cajal ('11) considered reticular neurons to be composed largely of third order sensory neurons and, to a lesser extent, of second order motor neurons. Phylogenetically the reticular formation is very old. In primitive forms it may represent the largest part of the central nervous system. In higher vertebrates the reticular core of the brain stem constitutes a mass of considerable proportions, owing in part to the process of encephalization. Although some authors have regarded the reticular formation as a diffusely organized brain stem component, anatomical studies (Brodal, '57) indicate that it is not diffusely organized, and that it can be subdivided into specific regions, possessing distinctive cytoarchitecture, fiber connections, and intrinsic organization. In spite of this, these regions cannot be considered as entirely independent entities, since complex fiber connections provide innumerable possibilities for interaction between the various subdivisions.

Golgi-stained sections of the reticular formation have yielded important information concerning its intrinsic organization. Such studies (Scheibel and Scheibel, '58) indicate that almost all reticular axons project for some distance in both rostral and caudal directions. A large number of these emit branching collaterals along their course which terminate in a variety of different types of endings. The majority of primary bifurcating axons are oriented in the longitudinal axis of the brain stem, but project collateral branches in all directions. Many of these collateral fibers arborize extensively about cranial nerve nuclei, and in some instances they may end upon both motor and sensory nuclei.

Physiological data indicate that the reticular formation is predominantly a polysynaptic pathway involving chains of neurons which fire successively. The inability to demonstrate short-axoned, Golgi type II cells in the reticular formation in Golgi-stained material (Scheibel and Scheibel, '58) suggests that the polysynaptic transmission of impulses probably is due to lateral dispersion along collateral fibers. Impulses conducted rapidly in the reticular core (Adey et al., '57) appear to be transmitted by long projecting axons of reticular neurons. Thus the organizational pattern of the reticular formation suggests that a single reticular neuron may convey impulses both rostrally and caudally, may exert its influences both locally and at a distance, and may participate in both rapid and slow conduction of impulses.

The reticular formation proper begins in the medulla a little above the decussation of the pyramids (Figs. 14-10 and 14-11). One of the particularly discrete nuclei of the reticular formation, the *lateral reticular nucleus* of the medulla, has been described. In sections through the lower medulla, the area dorsal to the caudal half of the inferior olivary nucleus and medial to the lateral reticular nucleus is the location of the *nucleus reticularis ventralis* (Fig. 14-12). At higher levels the reticular area located medial and dorsal to the rostral half of the inferior olivary nucleus is occupied by the *nucleus reticularis gigantocellularis* (Olszewski and Baxter, '54; Figs. 14-18 and A-5). The latter nucleus is the rostral continuation of the nucleus reticularis ventralis. The nucleus reticularis gigantocellularis is a relatively large nuclear complex composed of characteristic large cells, as well as medium and small cells (Fig. 14-18). Giant cells in this nucleus are not as conspicuous in man as in lower forms. Descending fibers from this reticular nucleus form the medullary reticulospinal tract described earlier (Fig. 13-20).

At the midolivary levels of the medulla small groups of cells are situated near the midline, dorsal to the inferior olivary complex. These cells, which have been subdivided into a dorsal, a ventral, and an accessory group, constitute the *paramedian reticular nuclei* (Fig. 14-18). Experimental studies (Brodal, '53) have shown that these reticular neurons project most of their fibers to the cerebellum.

The *nucleus reticularis parvicellularis* is a small-celled reticular nucleus situated dorsolaterally, medial to the spinal trigeminal nucleus and ventral to the vestibular area. This portion of the reticular formation has been referred to as the "sensory" part (Brodal, '57), since numerous studies have shown that collateral fibers from secondary sensory systems terminate in this region.

Afferent Fibers to the Medullary Reticular Formation. While the exact cells of origin of spinoreticular fibers have not been established, it is accepted generally that these fibers ascend almost exclusively in the anterolateral funiculus (Mehler et al., '56; Rossi and Brodal, '57). These fibers terminate largely in the caudal and lateral portions of the medullary reticular formation, including the caudal half of the nucleus reticularis gigantocellularis. Although some fibers of this system project to more rostral regions of the brain stem reticular formation, fibers passing to the nucleus reticularis parvicellularis appear scanty.

A large number of spinothalamic fibers have been shown to terminate in a somatotopic fashion upon cells of the lateral reticular nucleus of the medulla (Brodal, '49). Since almost all cells of this nucleus give rise to fibers which pass to specific parts of the cerebellum, this nucleus is considered primarily as a reticular relay nucleus in a spinocerebellar pathway. Physiological data support the thesis that exteroceptive impulses may be relayed to the cerebellum via this route (Combs, '56).

Other important sources of afferents to the reticular formation are collateral fibers from second order sensory neurons, such as spinothalamic fibers, secondary auditory pathways, secondary fibers from the nucleus of the solitary fasciculus, secondary trigeminal pathways, and secondary vestibular pathways. Collaterals from these diverse sources appear to terminate largely in the lateral region of the reticular formation, which has been referred to as the "sensory" part. It is notable that few, if any, collaterals from the medial lemniscus enter the brain stem reticular formation. Except for a modest number of primary trigeminal fibers (Torvik, '56; Carpenter and Hanna, '61), primary sensory fibers do not appear to terminate in the reticular formation.

Cerebellar fibers projected to the medullary reticular formation appear to terminate primarily in the region of the paramedian reticular nuclei. Fibers originating in the fastigial nuclei reach this region via the uncinate fasciculus (Thomas et al., '56; Carpenter et al., '58), while fibers from the dentate nucleus pass via the descending division of the superior cerebellar peduncle (Carpenter and Nova, '60).

Corticoreticular fibers originate from widespread areas of the cerebral cortex, but the majority of these fibers arise from the sensorimotor areas (Rossi and Brodal, '56). These fibers for the most part terminate in areas of the reticular formation which give rise to reticulospinal fibers, the *nucleus reticularis pontis oralis*, the *nucleus reticularis pontis caudalis*, and the *nucleus reticularis gigantocellularis* (Figs. 13–20 and 14–18). Corticoreticular fibers are both crossed and uncrossed.

According to Golgi studies of afferents to the brain stem reticular formation, most of the long ascending and descending fiber systems, making connections in various regions, emit collateral or terminal fibers in planes perpendicular to the long axis of the brain stem. As a consequence of this arrangement, it seems likely that impulses from a wide variety of sources converge upon the reticular nuclei. The area of maximal overlap of afferent fields occurs in the medullary reticular formation, which gives rise to the largest number of long ascending and descending axons.

Efferent Fibers from the Medullary Reticular Formation. Ascending reticular fibers from the medulla arise from cells dorsal to the rostral half of the inferior olive and are localized in the medial two-thirds of the reticular formation. While most of these fibers originate from the nucleus reticularis gigantocellularis, some may arise from the nuclei reticularis ventralis and lateralis. These fibers ascend mainly in the area of the central tegmental fasciculus and are for the most part uncrossed. Degeneration studies (Nauta and Kuypers, '58) indicate that they terminate in the intralaminar, and reticular nuclei of the thalamus. This same area of the reticular formation also projects descending fibers to spinal levels (Torvik and Brodal, '57; Fig. 13–20).

Efferent fibers from the paramedian reticular nuclei and the lateral reticular nuclei project to specific portions of the cerebellum. Fibers arising in the paramedian reticular nuclei, preponderantly uncrossed, terminate largely in the vermis of the anterior lobe (Brodal, '53). Cerebellar areas receiving fibers from the lateral reticular nucleus include hemispheral regions and the flocculonodular lobule.

The medullary reticular formation, exclusive of the cerebellar projecting nuclei, may be divided into medial and lateral regions. The medial two-thirds of the reticular formation gives rise to most of the long ascending and descending fiber systems, while cells in the lateral third project axons medially and dendrites laterally. Morphological data suggest that the lateral regions of the reticular formation may serve "receptive" and/or "associative" functions, while the medial regions, capable of transmitting impulses to both spinal and higher brain stem levels, may be primarily the "effector" area (Brodal, '57).

Inferior Cerebellar Peduncle. This peduncle is a composite group of tracts and fibers which assemble along the posterolateral border of the medulla and first form a distinct bundle at about mid-olivary levels (Fig. A–4). Throughout the upper medulla the addition of fibers increases the size of the structure until it forms a large, well-defined mass of myelinated fibers (Figs. 14–21, 14–22, 14–25, and A–5). Tracts and fibers forming this peduncle originate in the medulla and spinal cord. The posterior spinocerebellar tract moves dorsally and enters the inferior cerebellar peduncle directly. Crossed olivocerebellar fibers, originating from all parts of the inferior olivary complex, constitute quantitatively the largest group of fibers that enter the inferior cerebellar peduncle (Fig. 14–17, 14–21, 14–25, and 17–20). A number of medullary nuclei contribute a relatively smaller number of fibers to the inferior cerebellar peduncle. These nuclei include: (1) the lateral reticular nucleus of the medulla, (2) the accessory cuneate nucleus, (3) the paramedian reticular nuclei, (4) the arcuate nucleus, and (5) the perihypoglossal nuclei (i.e., the nucleus intercalatus, the nucleus of Roller, and the nucleus prepositus) (Figs. 14–18 and 14–21). Fibers from the lateral reticular nucleus and the accessory cuneate nucleus are uncrossed, while those from the other nuclei are both crossed and uncrossed. At higher levels, the infe-

rior cerebellar peduncle becomes covered laterally by fibers of the middle cerebellar peduncle (Figs. 14–25 and 15–2).

On the posterolateral aspect of the inferior cerebellar peduncle a small group of closely packed, medium-sized cells can be seen (Fig. 14–18). These cells constitute the caudal portion of the *pontobulbar nucleus*. At more rostral levels this cell column assumes a progressively more ventral position, until at the junction of pons and medulla it forms a fairly large cell mass ventral to the inferior cerebellar peduncle (Figs. 14–22 and 14–24). The cells of this nucleus resemble those in the ventral portion of the pons and have been regarded as a caudal extension of the pontine nuclei.

The cranial nerves of this portion of the brain stem are the *hypoglossal* (N. XII), the *vagus* (N. X), and the *glossopharyngeal* (N. IX).

THE HYPOGLOSSAL NERVE

The hypoglossal nerve is a motor nerve (GSE) innervating the somatic skeletal musculature of the tongue. It also appears to contain some afferent fibers, since the muscle spindles of the tongue degenerate following section of the nerve. These afferent fibers may be derived in part from inconstant ganglion cells found on the hypoglossal roots (Tarkhan and Abd-El-Malek, '50), but their principal source is still obscure. During fetal life the nerve apparently contains dorsal root fibers related to a small ganglion, but these disappear at a later period.

The nucleus of N. XII forms a column of typical multipolar motor cells about 18 mm. long that occupies the central gray of the medial eminence. It begins below the caudal tip of the inferior olive and extends rostrally to the region of the striae medullares. Within the nucleus coarse myelinated fibers can be seen, which are the root fibers of the motor cells, and a network of finer fibers representing terminals of axons ending in the nucleus. The root fibers gather on the ventral surface of the nucleus, forming a series of rootlets which pass ventrally, lateral to the medial lemniscus, and emerge on the surface in the anterolateral (preolivary) sulcus between the pyramid and the inferior olivary complex (Figs. 14-1, 14-13, 14-17 and A-4).

The hypoglossal nuclei receive numerous fibers and collaterals from reticular neurons, which form delicate plexuses within and around the nuclei. Some of these fibers constitute the terminal part of a "corticobulbar" fiber system effecting voluntary movements of the tongue. Fibers from the reticular formation are crossed and uncrossed. Other fibers to these nuclei probably are secondary glossopharyngeal, vagal, and trigeminal fibers which mediate reflex tongue movements in response to stimuli from lingual oral, and pharyngeal mucous membranes (i.e., taste, touch, thermal sense, and pain). Fibers from visceral centers also may terminate in the hypoglossal nuclei.

Immediately dorsolateral to the hypoglossal nucleus is a small bundle of fibers in the periventricular gray known as the *dorsal longitudinal fasciculus* (Schütz, 1891) (Figs. 14-16 and 14-17). This is a composite bundle of fibers consisting of ascending and descending components which remain poorly defined. While the prevailing direction of conduction in this bundle appears to be in an ascending direction (Burgi and Bucher, '60), descending fibers arising from medial and periventricular hypothalamic cell groups have been identified (Krieg, '32; Ingram, '40; Nauta, '58). It has been suggested, but not established, that some descending fibers may terminate in the dorsal motor nucleus of the vagus.

In the central gray of the ventricular floor are several nuclear masses whose functions and connections are not understood completely. The *nucleus intercalatus*, situated between the hypoglossal nucleus and dorsal motor nucleus of the vagus, is composed predominantly of small cells and a scattering of larger cells (Fig. 14-18). Rostral to the hypoglossal nucleus is the *nucleus prepositus* (Figs. 14-21 and 14-22), which extends from the oral pole of the hypoglossal nucleus almost to the abducens nucleus. It is composed of relatively large cells and a few smaller cells resembling those of

the nucleus intercalatus, with which it is continuous at more caudal levels. The *nucleus of Roller*, composed of relatively large cells, lies ventral to the rostral pole of the hypoglossal nucleus and adjacent to its root fibers (Fig. 14-18). Collectively, the nucleus intercalatus, nucleus prepositus and nucleus of Roller constitute the so-called perihypoglossal nuclei.

Injury to the hypoglossal nerve produces a lower motor neuron paralysis of the ipsilateral half of the tongue with loss of movement, loss of tone, and atrophy of the muscles affected. Since the genioglossus muscle effects protrusion of the tongue to the opposite side, the tongue, when protruded, will deviate to the side of the injury.

The juxtaposition of the emerging root fibers of N. XII and the pyramidal tract is the anatomical basis of the *inferior* or *hypoglossal alternating hemiplegia* resulting from ventral lesions of this area (Fig. 13-16). This syndrome consists of: (1) a lower motor neuron paralysis of the ipsilateral half of the tongue, and (2) a contralateral hemiplegia.

SPINAL ACCESSORY NERVE

The accessory nerve usually is divided into cranial and spinal portions which form, respectively, the internal and external branches of the nerve (Fig. 14-19). The cranial root of the nerve arises from neurons in the caudal pole of the nucleus ambiguus (SVE). Axons of these cells emerge from the lateral surface of the medulla caudal to the lowest filaments of the vagus nerve. The cranial fibers of the accessory nerve join the vagus nerve and, as motor fibers of the inferior (recurrent) laryngeal nerve, innervate the intrinsic muscles of the larynx. The spinal portion of the accessory nerve originates from a cell column in the anterior horn extending from the fifth (or sixth) cervical segment to about the middle of the pyramidal decussation. Caudally cells of this column occupy a lateral process of the anterior horn, but at higher levels they tend to assume a more central position. Root fibers from these cells arch posterolaterally to emerge from the lateral aspect of the

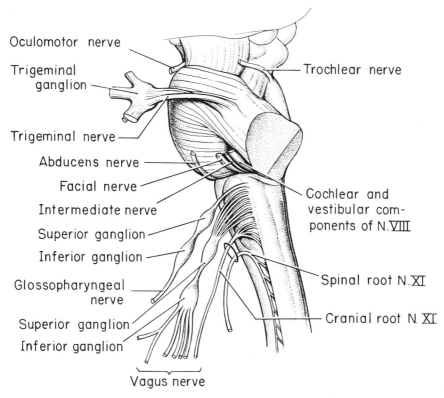

Oculomotor nerve

Trigeminal ganglion

Trochlear nerve

Trigeminal nerve

Abducens nerve

Facial nerve

Intermediate nerve

Superior ganglion

Inferior ganglion

Cochlear and vestibular components of N. VIII

Glossopharyngeal nerve

Superior ganglion

Inferior ganglion

Spinal root N. XI

Cranial root N. XI

Vagus nerve

FIG. 14-19. Semidiagrammatic sketch of brain stem and cranial nerves showing the peripheral ganglia

spinal cord between the dorsal and ventral roots (Fig. 14-7). Rootlets of the spinal part of the accessory nerve unite to form a common trunk (external branch) which ascends in the spinal canal posterior to the denticulate ligaments, enters the skull through the foramen magnum, and ultimately exits from the skull via the jugular foramen, together with the vagus and glossopharyngeal nerves (Fig. 14-19). The spinal nucleus of N. XI, like all motor nuclei, receives direct and indirect fiber projections from a variety of sources which mediate reflex activity related to cephalogyric movements. The spinal portion of the accessory nerve supplies the sternocleidomastoid and upper parts of the trapezius muscles. Although contractions of the sternocleidomastoid muscle turn the head to the opposite side, unilateral lesions of N. XI usually do not produce any abnormality in the position of the head. Weakness in rotating the head to the opposite side can be brought out on testing; when the neck is flexed, the chin tends to turn slightly to the paralyzed side. Paralysis of the upper part of the trapezius muscle is evidenced by: (1) downward and outward rotation of the upper part of the scapula, and (2) a moderate sagging of the shoulder on the affected side (see p. 201). Weakness of the upper part of the trapezius muscle also can be tested by having the patient shrug his shoulders against resistance.

THE VAGUS NERVE

The vagus nerve (N. X) is both efferent and afferent. It contains: (1) *general somatic afferent (GSA) fibers* distributed through the auricular branch of the vagus to the skin in back of the ear and the posterior wall of the external auditory meatus (these fibers have their cell bodies in the *superior ganglion* of the vagus nerve or jugular ganglion of the root (Fig. 14-19)); (2) *general visceral afferent (GVA) fibers* from the pharynx, larynx, trachea, esophagus, and thoracic and abdominal viscera, as well as *some special visceral afferent* (*SVA*) *fibers* from scattered taste buds in the region of the epiglottis (the cell bodies of these visceral fibers are in the larger *inferior ganglion* or nodosal ganglion of the trunk (Fig. 14–19)); (3) *general visceral efferent* (*GVE; preganglionic*) *fibers* to terminal parasympathetic ganglia innervating the thoracic and abdominal viscera; and (4) *special visceral efferent* (*SVE; branchiomotor*) *fibers* to the voluntary striated muscles of the larynx and pharynx.

The *dorsal motor nucleus* (preganglionic neurons) occupies the medial portion of the trigonum vagi (Figs. 14–3, 14–16 and 14–18). It is a column of cells extending both cranially and caudally a little beyond the hypoglossal nucleus. The nucleus is composed of relatively small, spindle-shaped cells among which are larger cells with coarser chromophilic bodies and scattered pigment. The functional significance of the several cell types is not clear. The cells which give rise to secretory fibers have not been determined definitely for the vagus, but probably lie more ventrally in the dorsal part of the reticular formation. In more rostral portions of the medulla, a group of such cells known as the *inferior salivatory nucleus* contributes secretory fibers to the glossopharyngeal nerve. The axons of the cells from the dorsal motor nucleus pass ventrolaterally, traverse the spinal trigeminal nucleus and tract, and emerge on the lateral surface of the medulla between the olive and the inferior cerebellar peduncle (Figs. A–4 and A–5).

The dorsal motor nucleus contains relatively few myelinated fibers, indicating that most of the terminals entering it are unmyelinated. These are principally secondary fibers from the sensory nuclei of the glossopharyngeal and vagus nerves, and from visceral centers.

The *nucleus ambiguus* is a column of cells in the reticular formation about halfway between the spinal trigeminal nucleus and the inferior olive (Figs. 14–3, 14–4, 14–5, 14–18, and A–4). It extends from about the caudal border of the lemniscal decussation to the level of the striae medullares; the uppermost portion contributes fibers to the glossopharyngeal nerve. The nucleus is composed of typical multipolar lower motor neurons whose axons innervate the muscles of the larynx and pharynx. These axons have an arched intramedullary course (Fig. 14–3, 14–4, 14–23 and A–5). They pass obliquely dorsally and medially, join the other fibers of the vagus, and then bending abruptly outward, pass with them to the lateral surface of the medulla. The nucleus receives various terminals, among which are both crossed and uncrossed corticobulbar fibers for the voluntary control of swallowing and phonation (Fig. 14–23). The nucleus receives impulses from the pharyngeal and laryngeal muscles for tonic control, and from secondary vagal, glossopharyngeal, and trigeminal fibers. Fibers in these three nerves convey impulses from the oral, pharyngeal, and respiratory mucosa that mediate various reflexes, such as coughing, vomiting, and pharyngeal and laryngeal reflexes.

Afferent vagal fibers enter the medulla in association with emerging efferent fibers. Cutaneous fibers contained in the auricular branch of the vagus nerve enter the dorsal part of the spinal trigeminal tract along with similar general somatic afferent fibers of other branchiomeric cranial nerves. These fibers terminate in caudal portions of the spinal trigeminal nucleus. More numerous visceral afferent fibers pass dorsomedially to the nucleus solitarius where some fibers terminate; other fibers bifurcate into small ascending and large descending components which enter the solitary fasciculus (Fig. 14–4). Descending vagal fibers in the fasciculus solitarius gradually diminish, as collaterals and terminals are given off to the cells of the nucleus solitarius, but some fibers descend caudal to the obex where the solitary nuclei of the two sides join to form the commissural nucleus of the vagus (Figs. 14–5 and 14–12). A considerable number of descending vagal fibers decussate and enter the contralateral half of the commissural nucleus (Rhoton et al., '66).

The *fasciculus solitarius* is formed by

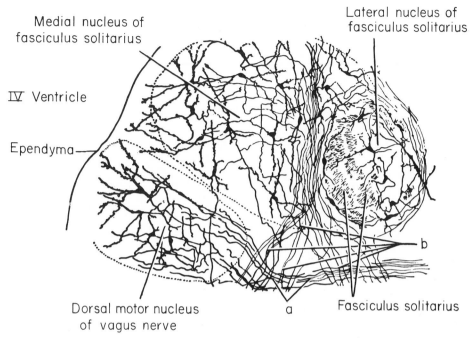

Medial nucleus of
fasciculus solitarius

Lateral nucleus of
fasciculus solitarius

Ⅳ Ventricle

Ependyma

b

Dorsal motor nucleus
of vagus nerve

a

Fasciculus solitarius

Fig. 14–20. The vagal nuclei in the floor of the fourth ventricle based upon a drawing of a Golgi preparation of newborn cat (Cajal, '09). Efferent (preganglionic) fibers from the dorsal motor nucleus of the vagus nerve are indicated by *a*, while *b* indicates fibers from the medial and lateral (sensory) nuclei of the fasciculus solitarius forming secondary vagoglossopharyngeal pathways. The medial nucleus of the fasciculus solitarius extends caudally to the fourth ventricle and merges with the corresponding cell group on the opposite side, forming the commissural nucleus of the vagus nerve (Fig. 14–12). The lateral nucleus of the fasciculus solitarius extends rostrally, increases in size, and parallels the fasciculus solitarius throughout most of its length.

visceral afferent fibers contributed by the vagus, glossopharyngeal and facial nerves. Glossopharyngeal fibers convey impulses of taste from the posterior third of the tongue; afferent facial nerve fibers convey similar impulses from the anterior two-thirds of the tongue. Although facial nerve fibers enter at more rostral levels, some of these fibers descend in upper parts of the fasciculus solitarius and terminate in portions of the solitary nucleus above the obex. The upper portion of the fasciculus solitarius, rostral to the entry of the vagus nerve, contains fibers related primarily to taste, while caudal portions of the fasciculus contain mainly general visceral afferent fibers from structures innervated by the vagus nerve. Thus the fasciculus solitarius constitutes a composite bundle of descending visceral afferent fibers comparable to the spinal trigeminal tract

which contains general somatic afferent fibers.

The *nucleus solitarius*, in which fibers of the fasciculus solitarius terminate, can be divided into two parts: (1) a medial portion, dorsolateral to the dorsal motor nucleus of the vagus, referred to as the "dorsal sensory nucleus of the vagus," and (2) a lateral portion situated along the lateral border of the fasciculus solitarius referred to as the "ventral nucleus of the fasciculus solitarius (Figs. 14–16, 14–17 and 14–20). The medial portion, consisting of a column of small densely packed cells within a fine intrinsic fiber plexus, extends rostrally to levels slightly above the oral pole of the dorsal motor nucleus of the vagus; this portion of the nucleus extends caudal to the fourth ventricle where it merges with the same cell group of the opposite side to form the commissural nucleus of the vagus (Torvik, '56). The lateral portion of the nucleus consists of slightly larger multipolar cells scattered in a rich fiber plexus; some cells lie ventrolateral to, or within, the fasciculus solitarius, while at rostral levels portions of the nucleus completely surround the fasciculus. Rostrally the lateral portion of the nucleus increases in size and extends almost to the inferior border of the pons. This portion of the nucleus parallels the fasciculus solitarius throughout most of its length, but in caudal regions cells diminish in number and are difficult to delimit from neurons of the reticular formation. The rostral enlarged (lateral) portion of the nucleus solitarius, which receives special visceral afferent (taste) fibers mainly from the facial and glossopharyngeal nerves, is referred to as the *gustatory nucleus* (Nageotte, '06; Rhoton et al., '66).

The secondary fibers forming part of the afferent taste pathways to the thalamus and cortex are not well established. These fibers appear to cross and ascend largely in association with the medial lemniscus (Allen, '27). According to Morest ('67) the caudal part of the medial nucleus solitarius, which receives mainly nongustatory visceral afferents, does not project fibers to the thalamus. The most significant projections from this part of the nucleus solitarius are to portions of the dorsal and lateral reticular formation of the medulla which have been implicated in the central regulation of respiratory, cardiovascular and emetic functions. Other secondary fibers from the sensory nuclei of N. X and N. IX go to various motor nuclei of the cranial and spinal nerves. As already stated, such fibers go to the hypoglossal and salivatory nuclei for lingual and secretory reflexes, either directly or through intercalated neurons. Other impulses from the pharyngeal, respiratory, and alimentary mucous membranes passing to the nucleus ambiguus probably are involved in pharyngeal and laryngeal reflexes. Additional impulses go to the dorsal motor nucleus of N. X, the phrenic nucleus in the cervical cord, and the nuclei of the intercostal muscles in the thoracic cord involved in coughing,

vomiting, and respiration. The connections with the spinal cord centers innervating the respiratory muscles probably are in large part mediated by intercalated reticular neurons in the vicinity of the nucleus solitarius (reticulospinal fibers).

It has been established for the cat and the monkey that the maintenance of rhythmic respiratory movements is mediated by diffusely arranged cell groups in the reticular formation dorsal to the olivary region and roughly longitudinally coextensive with the sensory and motor nuclei of the vagus nerve (Pitts, '46). The cells of this *"respiratory center"* not only are activated by vagal and other neural impulses, but also are affected directly by changes in their chemical environment (CO_2 accumulation, etc.). Ventral cell groups lying immediately above the inferior olive are concerned with inspiratory movements, while more dorsal ones are concerned with expiration. The activities of the respiratory center are subject to regulation from higher neural levels in the brain stem and the cerebral cortex.

Bilateral destruction of the vagus nerves is rapidly fatal in man unless immediate precautions are instituted to prevent asphyxia, for there is complete laryngeal paralysis. Paralysis and atonia of the esophagus and stomach induce pain and an incoercible vomiting with the hazards of aspiration. There also is a loss of vagal respiratory reflexes, dyspnea, and cardiac acceleration.

A unilateral lesion of the vagus nerve is followed by ipsilateral paralysis of the soft palate, pharynx, and larynx, which results in hoarseness, dyspnea, and dysphagia. During phonation the soft palate is elevated on the normal side and the uvula deviates to the normal side. The palatal reflex is lost on the lesion side. Anesthesia of the pharynx and larynx results in an ipsilateral loss of the cough reflex. Destruction of visceral motor fibers of the vagus results in an ipsilateral loss of the carotid sinus reflex.

THE GLOSSOPHARYNGEAL NERVE

The glossopharyngeal nerve (N. IX), though emerging at a somewhat higher

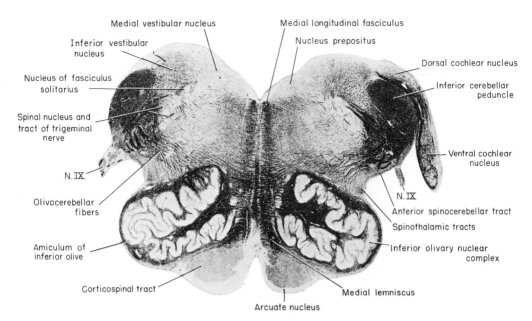

Medial vestibular nucleus

Inferior vestibular nucleus

Nucleus of fasciculus solitarius

Spinal nucleus and tract of trigeminal nerve

N. IX

Olivocerebellar fibers

Amiculum of inferior olive

Corticospinal tract

Medial longitudinal fasciculus

Nucleus prepositus

Dorsal cochlear nucleus

Inferior cerebellar peduncle

Ventral cochlear nucleus

N. IX

Anterior spinocerebellar tract

Spinothalamic tracts

Inferior olivary nuclear complex

Medial lemniscus

Arcuate nucleus

FIG. 14-21. Transverse section of medulla of 1-month infant through the cochlear nuclei and ninth nerve. Weigert's myelin stain. Photograph.

level (Figs. 14-19, 14-21, and 14-22), is intimately related to the vagus nerve. These two nerves have common intramedullary nuclei of origin and termination and similar functional components. Like the vagus nerve, the glossopharyngeal nerve has both afferent and efferent fibers. Functional components of the glossopharyngeal nerve include: (1) a few *general somatic afferent* (GSA) *fibers*, (2) *general visceral afferent* (GVA) *fibers*, (3) *special visceral afferent* (SVA) *fibers* (taste), (4) *general visceral efferent* (GVE) *fibers*, and (5) *special visceral efferent* (SVE) *fibers*. General somatic afferent fibers, innervating a small cutaneous area back of the ear, are distributed through the auricular branch of the vagus nerve. Cell bodies giving rise to these peripheral fibers are in the superior ganglion located within the jugular foramen (Fig. 14-19). Central processes of these cells terminate in the spinal trigeminal nucleus.

The cell bodies of the visceral afferent fibers are in the larger inferior ganglion. Some of these fibers are general visceral afferent fibers conveying tactile, pain, and thermal sense from the mucous membranes of the posterior portion of the tongue,

tonsil, and Eustachian tube. More numerous are the special visceral afferent fibers from the taste buds on the posterior third of the tongue. After entering the medulla, these fibers contribute to the upper portion of the fasciculus solitarius and terminate in the rostral part of its nucleus, the gustatory nucleus. Of interest is a special sensory branch, the *carotid* or *sinus nerve*, which innervates the carotid sinus, a dilatation of each common carotid at its bifurcation into the internal and external carotid arteries. Elevation of carotid arterial pressure initiates afferent impulses in the carotid sinus receptors, which are conveyed along the sinus nerve to the medulla. Centrally these afferent fibers of the glossopharyngeal nerve send collaterals to the dorsal motor nucleus of the vagus nerve. Preganglionic axons from this vagal nucleus pass distally in the vagus nerve to terminate about ganglion cells in the atria of the heart. Short postganglionic fibers continue to the adjacent sinoatrial and atrioventricular nodes, as well as to the atrial heart muscle. This glossopharyngeal-vagus reflex pathway is constantly regulating arterial pressure; stimulation of the sinus nerve produces slowing

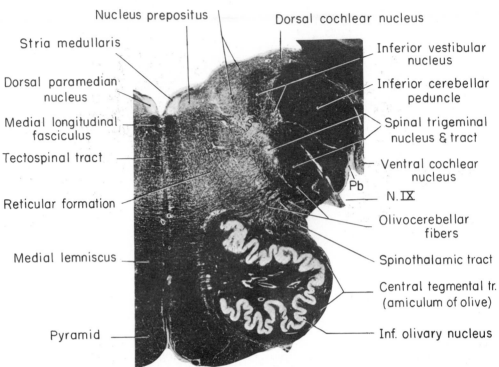

Fig. 14–22. Transverse section through the upper medulla at the level of the cochlear nuclei and the root fibers of the glossopharyngeal nerve. *S* indicates the lateral nucleus of the fasciculus solitarius. Weigert's myelin stain. Photograph.

of the heart and a fall in blood pressure. In elderly people, particularly patients with arteriosclerosis, the carotid sinus reflex may be hypersensitive. In such cases slight pressure on the carotid bifurcation may induce bradycardia, convulsions, and even loss of consciousness (carotid sinus syndrome).

General visceral efferent fibers arise from the inferior salivatory nucleus (Figs. 14–4 and 14–5) and pass via the lesser petrosal nerve to the otic ganglion where preganglionic fibers terminate. Postganglionic fibers originating from cells of the otic ganglion convey secretory impulses to the parotid gland. Cells of the inferior salivatory nucleus are virtually impossible to distinguish from reticular neurons, but they are considered as separate rostral cell groups equivalent to the dorsal motor nucleus of the vagus.

Special visceral efferent fibers, arising from the rostral part of the nucleus ambiguus, innervate the stylopharyngeus

muscle, and perhaps portions of the superior pharyngeal constrictor muscle (Figs. 14–4 and 14–5). This motor component of the glossopharyngeal nerve is quite small.

Pure lesions of the glossopharyngeal nerve alone are infrequent. The major symptoms of ninth nerve involvement include loss of the pharyngeal (gag) and carotid sinus reflexes and loss of taste in the posterior third of the tongue. Glossopharyngeal neuralgia, like trigeminal neuralgia, is characterized by excruciating, paroxysmal pain within the distribution of its sensory fibers. In glossopharyngeal neuralgia the trigger zone usually is in the pharynx, and the pain radiates to the Eustachian tube, the middle ear, or the region behind the ear. It is most often initiated by coughing or swallowing.

CORTICOBULBAR FIBERS

Corticofugal fibers projecting into the lower brain stem are referred to as *corticobulbar fibers*. These fibers arise mainly from the precentral and postcentral gyri, and are distributed to: (1) sensory relay nuclei, (2) parts of the reticular formation, and (3) certain motor cranial nerve nuclei in man and primates. Sensory relay nuclei receiving corticobulbar fibers include the nuclei gracilis and cuneatus, the sensory trigeminal nuclei, and the nucleus of the solitary fasciculus (Brodal et al., '56; Torvik, '56; Walberg, '57; Kuypers, '58, '58a, '58b, '60, Kuypers et al., '61; Kuypers and Tuerk, '64; Zimmerman et al., '64). Corticobulbar fibers to the posterior column nuclei leave the pyramid, and enter these nuclei by, either passing among the fibers of the medial lemniscus, or by traversing the reticular formation. After unilateral cortical lesions degenerated terminal fibers are distributed bilaterally to the posterior column nuclei, but are most numerous contralaterally. There are suggestions of somatotopic projections between portions of the precentral and postcentral gyri and the nuclei gracilis and cuneatus, but considerable overlap also is evident (Kuypers, '58b). According to Zimmerman et al. ('64), the projection from the primary somesthetic cortex in the rat is such that fibers from the forelimb cortical area pass to the nucleus cuneatus and those from the hindlimb area terminate in the nucleus gracilis. Studies of corticobulbar fibers projecting to the nuclei gracilis and cuneatus in the cat (Kuypers and Tuerk, '64) indicate that these fibers are distributed preferentially to portions of the nuclei containing loosely organized cells, and that few fibers from the cortex terminate in "cell nest" regions which receive ascending fibers from spinal dorsal roots. Fibers to all trigeminal sensory nuclei and the nucleus solitarius are derived from widespread cortical regions with the largest number arising from the frontoparietal region (Brodal et al., '56). Corticobulbar projections to trigeminal sensory nuclei appear to be non-topological (Zimmerman et al., '64), though Kuypers ('58b) suggests that in primates these fibers arise mainly from the postcentral gyrus. Corticofugal fibers to the nucleus solitarius terminate chiefly in its rostral part, near levels where facial and trigeminal afferents end.

Corticobulbar projections to the pos-terior column nuclei, and other sensory relay nuclei underlie a physiological mechanism by which descending cortical impulses can influence the transmission of ascending sensory impulses at the second neuron level. Both excitatory and inhibitory influences upon these sensory relay nuclei can be produced following stimulation of the cerebral cortex (Hagbarth and Kerr, '54; Hernandez-Peon and Hagbarth, '55; Levitt et al., '60; Jabbur and Towe, '61; Gordon and Jukes, '64a). Experimental studies (Gordon and Jukes, '64, '64a) of descending cortical influences upon the nucleus gracilis suggest that excitatory and inhibitory influences are exerted differentially upon portions of the nucleus which are distinguishable on the basis of the size of the receptive field and sensory modality represented. Corticofugal inhibitory influences were found mainly in middle portions of the nucleus where individual cells responded to movement of hair, light touch to foot pads, pressure at the base of a claw, or subcutaneous pressure. These cells exhibited small receptive fields and were inhibited by stimuli applied outside the physiological receptive field (i.e., surround inhibition). Corticofugal excitatory effects were found mainly in the rostral, and the deep part of the middle region of the nucleus where individual cells responded mainly to touch and pressure. These cells with rather large receptive fields did not show the phenomenon of surround inhibition.

Corticoreticular fibers projecting to the lower brain stem arise from broad areas of the cerebral cortex, but the largest number originates from the motor, premotor, and somesthetic areas (Rossi and Brodal, '56a). These fibers descend with those of the corticospinal tract, but leave this bundle to enter the brain stem reticular formation. The largest number of these fibers terminate in two well circumscribed areas, one in the medulla, another in the pons. Terminations in the medulla are in the area of the nucleus reticularis gigantocellularis, while the pontine area of termination is mainly within the nucleus reticularis pontis oralis. Corticoreticular fibers are distributed bilaterally, but with a slight contralateral predominance (Zim-

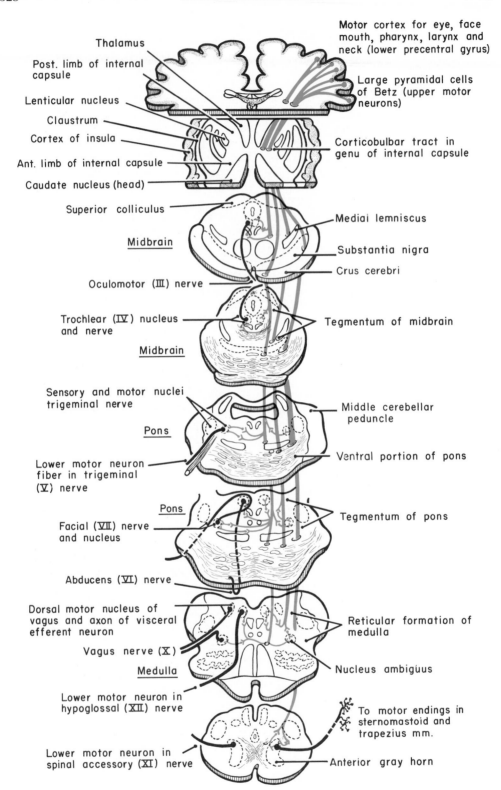

Thalamus

Post. limb of internal capsule

Lenticular nucleus

Claustrum

Cortex of insula

Ant. limb of internal capsule

Caudate nucleus (head)

Motor cortex for eye, face mouth, pharynx, larynx and neck (lower precentral gyrus)

Large pyramidal cells of Betz (upper motor neurons)

Corticobulbar tract in genu of internal capsule

Superior colliculus

Midbrain

Oculomotor (III) nerve

Medial lemniscus

Substantia nigra

Crus cerebri

Trochlear (IV) nucleus and nerve

Midbrain

Tegmentum of midbrain

Sensory and motor nuclei trigeminal nerve

Pons

Lower motor neuron fiber in trigeminal (V) nerve

Middle cerebellar peduncle

Ventral portion of pons

Pons

Facial (VII) nerve and nucleus

Tegmentum of pons

Abducens (VI) nerve

Dorsal motor nucleus of vagus and axon of visceral efferent neuron

Vagus nerve (X)

Medulla

Reticular formation of medulla

Nucleus ambiguus

Lower motor neuron in hypoglossal (XII) nerve

Lower motor neuron in spinal accessory (XI) nerve

To motor endings in sternomastoid and trapezius mm.

Anterior gray horn

merman et al., '64). Some corticoreticular fibers also project to reticular cerebellar relay nuclei, such as the reticulotegmental nucleus in the pons, the lateral reticular nucleus, and the paramedian reticular nuclei of the medulla. Regions of the reticular formation receiving corticofugal fibers give rise to: (1) long ascending and descending projections (Brodal and Rossi, '55; Torvik and Brodal, '57), (2) projections to the cerebellum (Brodal, '53; Combs, '56), and (3) abundant collateral fibers that project to cranial nerve nuclei (Scheibel and Scheibel, '58).

The motor cranial nerve nuclei innervating striated muscle receive impulses from the cerebral cortex via corticobulbar pathways. These fibers arise mainly from portions of the precentral gyrus, descend through the internal capsule and brain stem in association with the corticospinal tract, and constitute the upper motor neurons for the motor cranial nerve nuclei. Most fibers regarded as "corticobulbar" are distributed to neurons in the reticular formation which in turn relay impulses to the motor cranial nerve nuclei. In experimental studies (Walberg, '57a; Kuypers, '58; Zimmerman et al., '64) in the cat and rat, it has not been possible to trace terminal degeneration directly into any motor cranial nerve nucleus. These findings present a parallel to that accepted for the spinal cord, in that relatively few corticospinal fibers terminate directly upon anterior horn cells (Phalen and Davenport, '37; Szentágothai-Schimert, '41; Lloyd, '41). This indirect system is supplemented in man and primates by corticobulbar fibers that project directly to certain motor nuclei, namely, the trigeminal, the facial, the hypoglossal and the supraspinal (Kuypers, '58a). Fiber projections to the motor trigeminal and hypoglossal nuclei are bilateral and nearly equal (Fig. 14–23). Direct cortical projec-

tions to the facial nucleus are bilateral, but fibers passing to ventral cell groups, which innervate lower facial muscles, are most abundant contralaterally. These observations are thus in accord with clinical observations regarding one central type of facial palsy to be discussed fully in the next chapter. Many of the direct corticobulbar fibers correspond to what early authors referred to as aberrant pyramidal bundles. An example of these obliquely running fascicles, frequently seen in the medulla and lower pons, is shown coursing into the pontine tegmentum in Fig. 15–15. The more numerous corticoreticular fibers represent part of the phylogenetically older indirect corticobulbar pathway in which neurons of the reticular core serve as internuncials. Direct corticobulbar fibers found in man and primates represent a more recently developed parallel system.

Thus, the supranuclear innervation of the motor cranial nerve nuclei is largely bilateral and more complex than that present at spinal levels. Bilateral projections are most evident to those nuclei innervating muscle groups which as a rule cannot be contracted voluntarily on one side (Fig. 14–23). These include the laryngeal, pharyngeal, palatal, and upper facial muscles. This same principle applies to the muscles of mastication and the extraocular muscles. Because unilateral stimulation of the motor cortex produces isolated contraction of contralateral lower facial muscles, certain cell groups of the facial nucleus are considered to receive predominantly crossed corticobulbar fibers. The fact that unilateral stimulation of the motor cortex causes turning of the head to the opposite side has been interpreted as indicating that corticofugal fibers to nuclei innervating the sternocleidomastoid muscle probably are uncrossed, since contraction of this muscle turns the head to the opposite side. It seems likely that

---

Fig. 14–23. Diagram of "corticobulbar" pathways in the brain stem. Fibers of this principal upper motor neuron pathway to the motor cranial nerve nuclei arise in the cerebral cortex; pass caudally in the internal capsule, the crus cerebri, and the ventral portion of the pons; and are distributed largely to neurons in the reticular formation bilaterally. Reticular neurons conveying the impulses to the motor cranial nerve nuclei correspond to the intercalated or internuncial neurons found at spinal levels. In man and primates this indirect system is paralleled by more recently developed direct corticobulbar fibers distributed to the motor trigeminal, facial, and hypoglossal nuclei (Kuypers, '58a).

some uncrossed corticospinal fibers (Figs. 13-16 and 13-18) may project impulses to spinal accessory cell groups innervating this muscle and the upper part of the trapezius muscle, although direct fibers to these cells appear meager (Kuypers, '58a). Eye movements elicited by electrical stimulation of the cerebral cortex are always conjugate, indicating that the supranuclear innervation of the nuclei of the extraocular muscles is bilateral.

Because cortical control of motor cranial nerve nuclei is largely bilateral, unilateral lesions interrupting corticobulbar fiber systems (upper motor neuron) produce comparatively mild forms of paresis. Slight weakness of tongue (genioglossus muscle) and jaw movements (pterygoid muscles) contralateral to the lesions usually can be detected. Weakness in these muscles is expressed by modest deviation of the tongue and jaw to the side opposite the lesion. However, marked weakness of lower facial muscles contralateral to the lesion is evident when the patient attempts to show the teeth, purse the lips, or puff out the cheeks.

Bilateral lesions involving corticobulbar fiber systems produce a syndrome known as *pseudobulbar palsy*. This syndrome is characterized by paralysis or weakness of muscles which control swallowing, chewing, breathing, and speaking, and may occur with little or no paralysis in the extremities, if lesions are localized. Loss of emotional control characterized by unrestrained and inappropriate outbursts of laughing and crying frequently form a part of the syndrome; these symptoms appear as the physiological expression of rather extensive bilateral lesions in the upper brain stem or at higher levels. Although there is marked paresis of the muscles of mastication and in the muscles of the face, tongue, pharynx and larynx, these muscles do not atrophy, since the lower motor neurons remain intact. After prolonged periods of time, contractures may appear in the muscles of the lips, tongue and palate (Haymaker, '56).

Cranial nerves V, VII, and IX through XII may be involved, together or in varying combinations, as a result of bilateral interruption of the corticobulbar tracts centrally (Fig. 14-23). Bilateral lesions involving "corticobulbar pathways" above pontine levels usually are the result of extensive demyelinating disease, vascular disease, thrombosis, or neoplasms.

UPPER MEDULLA AND JUNCTION OF MEDULLA AND PONS

The fourth ventricle reaches its maximum width at the level of the lateral recesses (Figs. 14-1, 14-24 and A-6). These lateral extensions of the fourth ventricle pass external to the inferior cerebellar peduncle and the cochlear nuclei, which form its medial wall and floor (Fig. A-5). The lateral wall of each recess is formed by the *peduncle of the flocculus*, a part of the floccular lobe of the cerebellum lying close to the lateral surface of the medulla (Fig. 14-24). Cranial nerves present at this level are the glossopharyngeal (N. IX) and the cochlear root of N. VIII.

The hypoglossal and dorsal motor nucleus of the vagus are not present at these levels, though the rostral portion of the nucleus ambiguus is present and contributes visceral efferent fibers to the glossopharyngeal nerve. Afferent fibers of N. IX enter the posterolateral aspect of the medulla ventral to the inferior cerebellar peduncle, traverse parts of the spinal trigeminal tract and nucleus, enter the fasciculus solitarius, and in part terminate upon upper portions of the nucleus of that tract, the gustatory nucleus. Other fibers descend to lower levels. Above the level of entrance of N. IX the fasciculus solitarius cannot be distinguished readily, for it consists only of a small descending bundle of root fibers of N. VII.

Root fibers of the *cochlear* nerve, conveying impulses from the organ of Corti in the cochlea, enter the posterolateral margin of the upper medulla. Primary auditory fibers terminate upon two nuclear masses associated closely with the auditory nerve, the *ventral and dorsal cochlear nuclei*. The dorsal cochlear nucleus forms a prominence, the *tuberculum acusticum*, along the lateral border of the rhomboid fossa (Figs. 14-22, 14-25 and A-6). Cells of the dorsal cochlear nucleus are small,

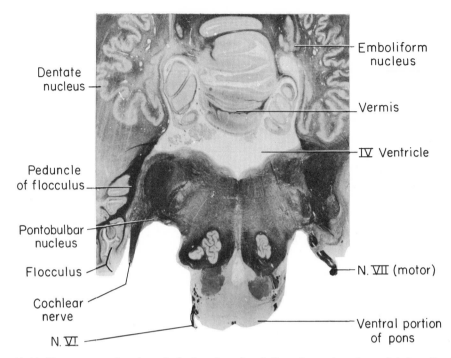

FIG. 14–24. Transverse section through the junction of medulla and pons in a 1-month infant. Portions of the cerebellum containing large parts of the intracerebellar nuclei are attached. Structures in and around the tegmentum are identified in Fig. 14–25. Weigert's myelin stain. Photograph.

ovoid, and fusiform, while those of the ventral nucleus are large, round cells with a dark-staining cytoplasm. Secondary auditory fibers arise from the dorsal and ventral cochlear nuclei and ascend to higher levels. These fibers become apparent at levels rostral to the cochlear nuclei.

In the floor of the fourth ventricle medial to the inferior cerebellar peduncle are two of the vestibular nuclei, the medial and the inferior (Figs. 14–21 and 14–22). The triangular-shaped area occupied by these nuclei is dorsal to the medullary reticular formation and the spinal trigeminal tract and nucleus. The *medial vestibular nucleus*, which stains poorly in Weigert preparations, is lateral to the nucleus prepositus and the sulcus limitans. The *inferior vestibular nucleus*, located further laterally, adjacent to the inferior cerebellar peduncle, is characterized by small bundles of dark-staining fibers (Figs. 14–21 and 14–22). Secondary fibers originating from these vestibular nuclei enter the reticular formation, pass toward the

median raphe, and become incorporated in the medial longitudinal fasciculus. These fibers largely cross to the opposite side where they divide into ascending and descending branches in the medial longitudinal fasciculus; the largest number of these branches ascend to higher levels. The inferior vestibular nucleus has abundant reciprocal connections with the vestibular portions of the cerebellum, but projects few, if any, fibers to spinal levels (Carpenter et al., '60). The medial vestibular nucleus may participate in such visceral reflexes as nausea and vomiting occurring in response to excessive labyrinthine stimulation. The vestibular nerve, which supplies afferent fibers to these nuclei, enters the brain stem at higher levels.

The main inferior olivary nuclei are still large and send bundles of olivocerebellar fibers to the opposite inferior cerebellar peduncles, which have grown to massive proportions. The arcuate nuclei practically envelop the pyramids and may represent the most caudal portion of the pontine nuclei (*nucleus precursorius pontis*). In favorable preparations the *striae medullares* (of the medulla) are seen passing transversely over the ventricular floor and dipping into the raphe (Fig. 14–22). These fibers probably arise from the arcuate nucleus, cross the midline, and ascend dorsally in the raphe; they then pass laterally over the ventricular floor to terminate in the flocculus of the cerebellum (arcuatocerebellar tract).

In the upper medulla the medial lemniscus reaches its full extent. It forms a vertical band of heavily myelinated fibers on either side of the raphe dorsal to the pyramids (Fig. 14–22). The formation and course of this tract are shown in Figure 13–6. The lateral and anterior spinothalamic tracts occupy a retro-olivary position (Fig. 14–22). Corticobulbar fibers leave the pyramids and pass dorsally into the reticular formation (Fig. 14–23); intercalated neurons lying in the reticular formation in turn project upon motor cranial nerve nuclei (Walberg, '57a).

Owing to the proximity of the pyramid and medial lemniscus in the inter-olivary region of the medulla, injury of this area may affect both tracts and produce a severe contralateral anesthesia (touch, kinesthesis, vibration) and hemiplegia (upper motor neuron paralysis).

The medial longitudinal fasciculus (abbreviated MLF), tectospinal, and tectobulbar tracts occupy an area dorsal to the medial lemniscus on each side of the median raphe. The tracts are partially separated by lighter-stained areas representing the raphe nuclei. At somewhat higher levels this position is occupied by the inferior central nucleus (Figs. 14–25 and 15–3). Other descending tracts, such as the rubrospinal and vestibulospinal, are difficult to distinguish in Weigert-stained material. The rubrospinal tract is located in the retro-olivary area ventral to the spinal trigeminal tract and nucleus. Vestibulospinal fibers originating from the lateral vestibular nucleus do not form a compact bundle at this level, but are present in the area dorsal to the inferior olivary complex; at more caudal levels these fibers also enter the retro-olivary area.

In the superficial gray of the medial eminence is a strip of closely packed small cells known as the *nuclei of the medial eminence* (Fig. 15–4). The functions of these nuclei are unknown, but it seems likely that they may be related to visceral reflex pathways since they may receive fibers from the dorsal longitudinal bundle of Schütz, the medial vestibular nucleus, or both. They may send fibers to the reticular formation, the hypoglossal nucleus, dorsal motor nucleus of the vagus, and secretory nuclei. Ventral and caudal to this small-celled column are groups of larger cells, the most conspicuous of which is the *nucleus prepositus*, found in the place previously occupied by the hypoglossal nucleus (Figs. 14–22 and 14–25).

The junction of medulla and pons (Figs. 14–24, 14–25, and A–6) is characterized by: (1) gradual passage of the inferior cerebellar peduncle into the white matter of the cerebellum, (2) reduction in size and ultimate disappearance of the inferior olivary nucleus, (3) gradual incorporation of the corticospinal tracts within the ventral portion of the pons, (4) enlargement of the reticular formation, (5) gradual shifting of the position of the medial lemniscus, and (6) the appearance of other cranial nerves at this higher level. Sections through this junctional area usually include the cerebellum, which forms the roof of the fourth ventricle. In these sections the cerebellar *vermis* and intracerebellar nuclei (i.e., the *nucleus dentatus* and *nucleus emboliformis*) can be seen (Figs. 14–24 and A–6).

As the inferior cerebellar peduncle enters the medullary core of the cerebellum, it is covered externally by the fibers of the middle cerebellar peduncle, which arise from the ventral part of the pons. The development of the ventral portion of the pons envelops the medullary pyramids. The blind end of the anterior median fissure overhung by the pons is known as the *foramen cecum posterior* (Fig. 14–25). The attenuated rostral pole of the inferior olivary nucleus is flanked laterally by the fibers of the central tegmental tract and medially and ventrally by the medial lemniscus. The medial lemniscus gradually becomes flattened

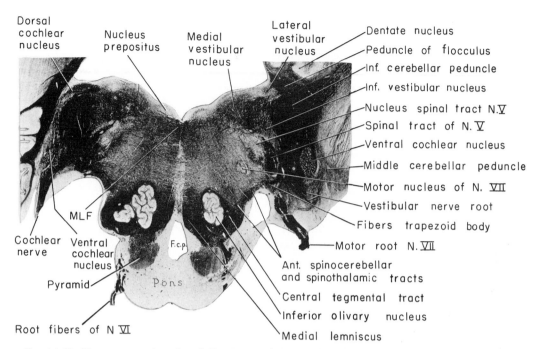

FIG. 14–25. Transverse section of medulla of 1-month infant, through caudal border of pons. *F.c.p.*, Foramen cecum posterior; *MLF*, medial longitudinal fasciculus. Weigert's myelin stain. Photograph.

dorsoventrally and lies along the ventral border of the pontine tegmentum (Fig. 13–6). The light-staining area separating the medial lemnisci and the medial longitudinal fasciculi is occupied by the inferior central nucleus (nucleus of the raphe).

Cranial nerves present at the junction of the medulla and pons are the cochlear, vestibular, facial, and abducens. The cochlear, vestibular, and facial nerves are grouped together at the cerebellopontine angle, formed by the junction of the medulla, pons, and cerebellum. The cochlear nerve is the most caudal and lateral, while the facial nerve is the most rostral and medial. The cochlear nerve has disappeared on the right side in Figures 14–24 and 14–25, though the rostral pole of the ventral cochlear nucleus is present. On the left side the relationships between the cochlear nerve and the dorsal and ventral cochlear nuclei are evident (Fig. 14–25). Vestibular nerve fibers entering the medulla pass between the inferior cerebellar peduncle and the spinal trigeminal tract. The vestibular area, to which these fibers

are directed, is larger and now includes a small caudal part of the *lateral vestibular nucleus* dorsal to the inferior vestibular nucleus. In the lateral reticular formation, the caudal tip of the motor nucleus of the facial nerve occupies a position similar to that of the nucleus ambiguus at lower levels. Root fibers of the facial nerve emerge from the brain stem medial to the vestibular nerve. Fibers of the abducens nerve emerge anteriorly, lateral to the pyramid at the junction of medulla and pons. The nuclei of the facial and abducens nerves, located dorsally in the pontine tegmentum, will be discussed in the next chapter.

Experimentally, electrical stimulation of the lateral part of the medullary reticular formation and adjacent periventricular gray in lower animals (Wang, '55) produces elevation of arterial blood pressure and cardiac acceleration, probably as a consequence of activating sympathetic effectors. Descending pathways mediating these responses lie in the anterior and lateral funiculus of the spinal cord and are largely homolateral. Stimulations in the region of the obex, and in a wide area medial and ventral to the sympathetic area, produce a slowing of the heart rate. Part of this response appears to be vagal, but other evidence also suggests an inhibition of sympathetic neurons. Similar studies indicate that inspiratory and expiratory responses can be obtained from stimulations of circumscribed areas of the medulla (Ngai and Wang, '57).

Multiple medullary structures may be simultaneously involved by vascular lesions, neoplasms, or other disease processes. Symptoms and signs resulting from such lesions bear a close correlation to the specific neural structures involved, and their nature depends in part upon whether the lesions are irritative or destructive. Although vascular lesions are subject to considerable variation in location and extent, the distribution of the principal blood vessels within the medulla shows some constant features (Figs. 4–12 and 4–13). Lesions involving structures in the dorsolateral part of the medulla (lateral

medullary syndrome) are probably the most common at this level and give rise to a constellation of symptoms and signs that are readily recognizable (Currier et al., '61). While the classic feature of this syndrome is loss of pain and thermal sense in the ipsilateral half of the face and the contralateral half of the trunk and extremities, a variety of other severe symptoms occur. These include vertigo, nausea, vomiting, dysphonia, dysphagia, face and body pain, weakness of the face, disturbance of equilibrium, and hiccup. In the past this syndrome has been attributed largely to occlusion or disease of a single vessel, the posterior inferior cerebellar artery, but new data (Baker, '61) indicate that involvement of the vertebral artery and its smaller penetrating branches plays an equally important role in the production of the syndrome. Particular attention should be given to the neuronal structures which lie within the area of distribution of both the posterior inferior cerebellar and vertebral arteries (Figs. 4–12 and 4–13).

CHAPTER 15

The Pons

Rostral portions of the hindbrain are covered ventrally by massive collections of cells, the pontine nuclei, and large bundles of myelinated fibers coursing transversely which enlarge this portion of the brain stem and give it a characteristic configuration. The pons consists of two parts, a pars dorsalis and pars ventralis (Fig. 15–1). The *dorsal portion*, constituting the pontine tegmentum, is continuous with the reticular formation of the medulla and contains specific cranial nerve nuclei, ascending and descending tracts, and large portions of the reticular formation. The *ventral portion*, referred to as the basilar portion or the pons proper, contains the corticospinal tracts, corticopontine fibers and the pontine nuclei which give rise to crossed, transversely oriented fibers on the ventral surface of this brain stem segment.

CAUDAL PONS AND PONTINE TEGMENTUM

The Ventral Portion of the Pons consists of transverse and longitudinal fibers between which are numerous groups of small- and medium-sized polygonal cells, the *pontine nuclei*. Longitudinal fibers in the ventral portion of the pons are: (1) corticospinal, (2) corticobulbar, and (3) corticopontine (Figs. A–7, A–8 and A–9). The largest groups of longitudinal fibers, the corticospinal tracts, traverse the pons, enter the medullary pyramids, decussate incompletely, and pass into the spinal cord (Figs. 13–16, and A–28) 2. Corticobul-

bar fibers separate from the corticospinal tracts and enter the reticular formation of the pontine tegmentum. Impulses pass to the motor cranial nerve nuclei via intercalated neurons. While bundles of corticospinal fibers present a compact arrangement at the rostral and caudal pontine levels, in the middle regions of the pons the bundles are broken up into a number of small fascicles by transversely oriented pontine fibers. Other longitudinal fibers descending from the pallium and terminating upon pontine nuclei are corticopontine fibers. These fibers arise from the cortex of the frontal (frontopontine), temporal (temporopontine), parietal (parietopontine), and occipital (occipitopontine) lobes, descend without crossing, and end upon homolateral pontine nuclei. The corticopontine fibers are numerous in the upper portion of the pons, where they form bundles difficult to distinguish from the pyramidal tracts (Figs. 15–16 and 15–20). Their number gradually diminishes as fibers terminate in the pontine nuclei. In the most caudal portions of the pons only a few of them are left. The corticopontine fibers and the transverse fibers to be described below do not become myelinated until some time after birth and are not distinguishable in brain sections of a 4-week infant stained by the Weigert technic. They are shown in the adult pons in Figures 15–3, 15–16, and 15–20.

The transversely oriented fibers are

335

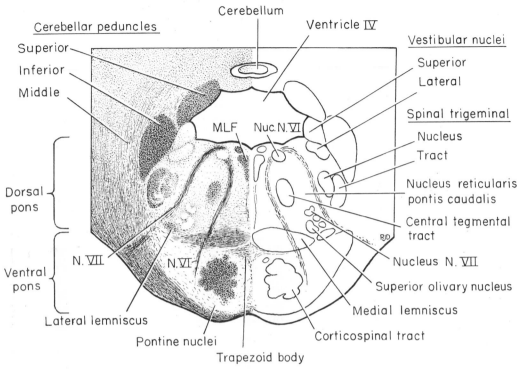

FIG. 15-1. Semidiagramatic drawing of a transverse section of the pons at the level of the abducens nucleus. The dorsal portion of the pons, constituting the tegmentum, contains the reticular formation, cranial nerve nuclei and ascending and descending tracts. The ventral portion of the pons contains the pontine nuclei, massive bundles of corticofugal fibers, and the transverse fibers of the pons which form the middle cerebellar peduncle.

axons of pontine nuclei (Fig. 15-4) which cross to the opposite side and form the massive *middle cerebellar peduncle*. These fibers pass dorsal and ventral to the corticospinal tract; the more dorsal fibers form the *deep layer*, while the more ventral ones constitute the *superficial layer* of the pons (Fig. A-26). Fibers of the middle cerebellar peduncle sweep dorsolaterally and somewhat caudally to enter the medullary core of the cerebellum superficial to the inferior cerebellar peduncle. The ventral portion of the pons thus may be considered as a relay station in an extensive, phylogenetically new, two neuronal pathway from the cerebral cortex to the cerebellar cortex. The first neuron in the cerebral cortex projects an uncrossed corticopontine fiber to the pontine nuclei. The second pontine neuron sends a crossed pontocerebellar fiber to the cortex of the opposite cerebellar hemisphere via the

middle cerebellar peduncle. A small number of fibers from the superior colliculus project ventrally and caudally to terminate upon dorsolateral pontine nuclei (Altman and Carpenter, '61).

Certain nuclei in the pontine tegmentum, like the reticulotegmental nucleus, project fibers into the ventral part of the pons which enter the cerebellum via the middle cerebellar peduncle (Figs. 15-21, A-8 and A-9). These fibers are regarded as tegmentocerebellar. Other vertically oriented fibers (Fig. 15-15) passing from the ventral portion of the pons into the tegmentum have been considered as aberrant pyramidal fibers projecting to motor cranial nerve nuclei. These fibers appear to be corticobulbar or corticoreticular fibers.

The pontine nuclei are numerous, closely packed cellular aggregations of varying extent placed between the trans-

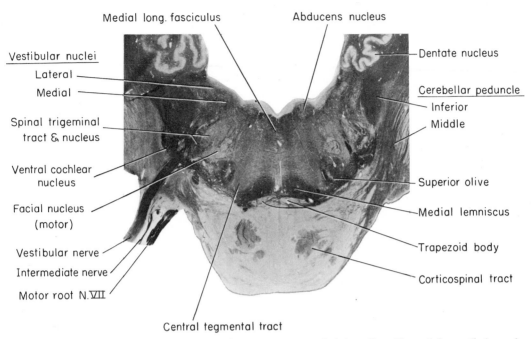

Medial long. fasciculus　　　　　Abducens nucleus

Vestibular nuclei　　　　　　　　　　　　　　　　　Dentate nucleus

　　Lateral

　　Medial　　　　　　　　　　　　　　　　　　　Cerebellar peduncle

　　　　　　　　　　　　　　　　　　　　　　　　　Inferior

Spinal trigeminal　　　　　　　　　　　　　　　　Middle
　tract & nucleus

Ventral cochlear
　nucleus　　　　　　　　　　　　　　　　　　　　Superior olive

Facial nucleus　　　　　　　　　　　　　　　　Medial lemniscus
　(motor)

Vestibular nerve　　　　　　　　　　　　　　　Trapezoid body

Intermediate nerve

Motor root N. VII　　　　　　　　　　　　　　Corticospinal tract

Central tegmental tract

Fig. 15–2. Slightly asymmetrical section of the pons of a 1-month infant. Root fibers of the vestibular and facial nerves are present on the left. Weigert's myelin stain. Photograph.

verse and longitudinal fibers (Fig. 15–4). In caudal regions the cells form a ring around the compact pyramidal tract, which more rostrally is broken up into smaller bundles by islands of pontine cells. In a general way the cells may be grouped into lateral, medial, dorsal, and ventral nuclear masses (Fig. 15–7). In the lateral groups the polygonal cells are relatively large- or medium-sized; in the paramedian region they are smaller. Their dendrites ramify around adjacent cell bodies, and their axons, almost entirely crossed, form the middle cerebellar peduncle. Among these cells are found curiously shaped Golgi type II cells whose dendrites are beset with numerous hairlike processes, and whose short, branching axons terminate in the vicinity of the cell body.

The Dorsal Portion of the Pons, known as the pontine tegmentum, is the direct continuation of the medulla. The position and configuration of the medial lemniscus are strikingly different compared with those at medullary levels. This tract now forms a flattened, almost elliptical mass on

each side of the median raphe near the dorsal border of the ventral portion of the pons. These bundles are separated from the ventral portion of the pons by the transversely oriented auditory fibers composing the trapezoid body (Figs. 15–2, 15–3 and A–8). The medial longitudinal fasciculi and tectospinal tracts retain their dorsal position on each side of the median raphe. An enlarged nucleus of the raphe, the inferior central nucleus, occupies the midline region between these structures. The spinal trigeminal nucleus and tract, as well as the spinothalamic and anterior spinocerebellar tracts, are in essentially the same positions as in medullary sections, but appear more internally located since they are covered externally by the middle cerebellar peduncle. The vestibular nuclei continue to occupy a triangular-shaped area in the floor of the fourth ventricle. The pontine reticular formation, ventral to the vestibular nuclei, medial to the spinal trigeminal nucleus, and dorsal to the medial lemniscus, is more extensive than the medullary reticular formation. The medial two-thirds of the

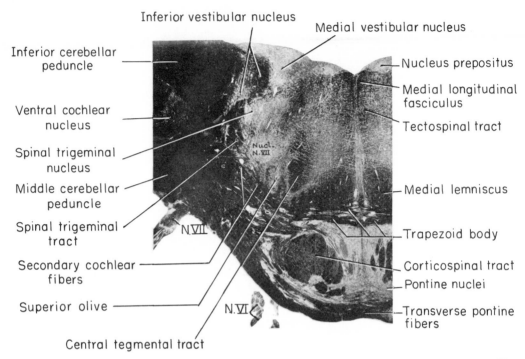

Inferior vestibular nucleus

Medial vestibular nucleus

Inferior cerebellar peduncle

Nucleus prepositus

Medial longitudinal fasciculus

Ventral cochlear nucleus

Tectospinal tract

Spinal trigeminal nucleus

Nucl. N.VII

Middle cerebellar peduncle

Medial lemniscus

Spinal trigeminal tract

N.VII

Trapezoid body

Secondary cochlear fibers

Corticospinal tract

Pontine nuclei

Superior olive

N.VI

Transverse pontine fibers

Central tegmental tract

Fig. 15-3. Transverse section of the adult pons at the level of emergence of the facial nerve root. Weigert's myelin stain. Photograph.

pontine reticular formation is represented by the *nuclei reticularis pontis caudalis* and *oralis* (Olszewski and Baxter, '54). The nucleus reticularis pontis caudalis, in the caudal pons, replaces the nucleus reticularis gigantocellularis of the medulla and extends rostrally to the level of the motor trigeminal nucleus. This nucleus contains a number of large cells in addition to various types of smaller cells. Descending fibers from this nucleus constitute the uncrossed pontine reticulospinal tract (Fig. 13-20). Lateral to the nucleus reticularis pontis caudalis is the nucleus parvicellularis, which has the same structure as described at medullary levels. The nucleus reticularis pontis oralis is present in more rostral sections of the pons; the transitional zone between this nucleus and the caudal pontine reticular nucleus is indistinct. This nuclear mass extends into the caudal mesencephalic reticular formation, but giant cells are found only in the caudal parts. In the subependymal area the nucleus of the *medial eminence* and the *dorsal parame-*

dian nucleus are found (Figs. 14-2 and 15-4). The reticular formation dorsal to the lateral part of the medial lemniscus contains the central tegmental tract—a large, relatively discrete bundle (Figs. 15-1 and 15-3). Descending fibers of this composite tract originate from the midbrain tegmentum, the periaqueductal gray, and the red nucleus. These fibers form the amiculum olivae and terminate in specific portions of the inferior olivary complex (Fig. A-29). Since all efferent fibers from the inferior olivary complex decussate and project to the cerebellum, these descending fibers form part of a complex pathway by which impulses from the midbrain are conveyed to the contralateral half of the cerebellum. A much larger ascending component of the central tegmental tract arises from medial portions of the brain stem reticular formation.

In addition to the structures described, the pontine tegmentum contains a number of cranial nerve nuclei and nuclei related to specific sensory systems. These include the cochlear and vestibular com-

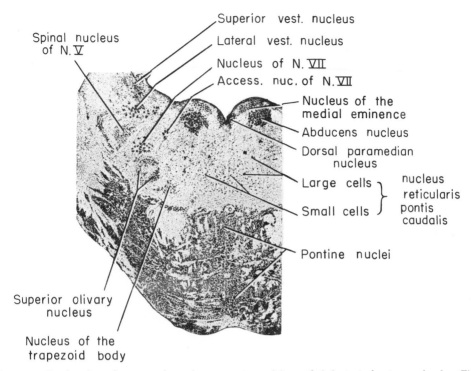

Spinal nucleus
of N. V

Superior vest. nucleus

Lateral vest. nucleus

Nucleus of N. VII

Access. nuc. of N. VII

Nucleus of the
medial eminence

Abducens nucleus

Dorsal paramedian
nucleus

Large cells ⎤
              ⎬ nucleus
Small cells ⎦ reticularis
                pontis
                caudalis

Pontine nuclei

Superior olivary
nucleus

Nucleus of the
trapezoid body

FIG. 15-4. Section through pons and pontine tegmentum of 3-month infant at about same level as Figure 15-2. Cresyl violet. Photograph, with schematic representation of cell groups.

ponents of N.VIII, the motor and sensory components of the facial nerve, the abducens nerve, and large portions of the trigeminal nuclear complex. Root fibers of the vestibulocochlear and facial nerves enter the caudal pons at the cerebellopontine angle formed by the junction of the medulla, pons and cerebellum (Fig. 14–19). Fibers of the cochlear nerve root pass dorsally, lateral to the inferior cerebellar peduncle, to terminate upon cells of the dorsal and ventral cochlear nuclei (Fig. 14–25). Vestibular root fibers, slightly medial and rostral to those of the cochlear nerve, enter caudal portions of the pons by passing between the inferior cerebellar peduncle and the spinal trigeminal tract (Figs. 15–2 and 15–5). Primary vestibular fibers are distributed differentially within the vestibular nuclear complex in the floor of the fourth ventricle; a small number of vestibular fibers project to specific parts of the cerebellum via the juxtarestiform body, a structure medial to the inferior cerebellar peduncle (Fig. 15–6). Ventral to the ves-

tibular nerve are the intermediate and facial nerves (Figs. 15–2 and 15–5). The intermediate nerve contains mainly special visceral afferent (taste; SVA) and general visceral efferent (parasympathetic; GVE) fibers. The larger motor root of the facial nerve is the most rostral and medial cranial nerve in the cerebellopontine angle.

The *motor nucleus of N. VII* appears as a pear-shaped gray mass in the lateral part of the reticular formation immediately dorsal to the superior olive (Figs. 15–2, 15–3, and 15–4). Within it may be seen the usual plexus of fine terminals and the coarser fibers which give origin to the facial root. The root fibers form a complicated intramedullary loop whose continuity cannot be seen in any one section (Figs. 14–4, 14–5, 15–6, and 15–7). Emerging as fine bundles of fibers from the dorsal surface of the nucleus, they proceed dorsomedially to the floor of the ventricle. There they form a compact longitudinal bundle which ascends for a distance of about 2 mm. medial to the abducens nucleus and

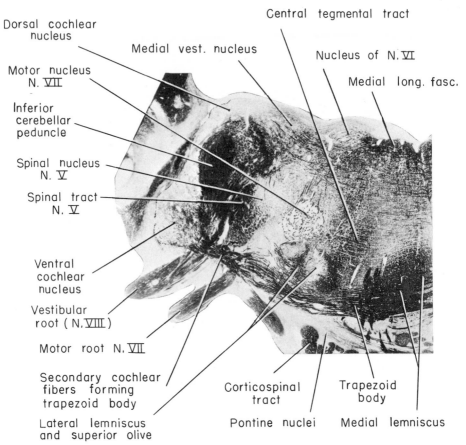

Dorsal cochlear nucleus

Central tegmental tract

Medial vest. nucleus

Nucleus of N. VI

Motor nucleus N. VII

Medial long. fasc.

Inferior cerebellar peduncle

Spinal nucleus N. V

Spinal tract N. V

Ventral cochlear nucleus

Vestibular root (N. VIII)

Motor root N. VII

Secondary cochlear fibers forming trapezoid body

Corticospinal tract

Trapezoid body

Lateral lemniscus and superior olive

Pontine nuclei

Medial lemniscus

FIG. 15–5. Section of left half of pons and pontine tegmentum of 3-year-old child whose brain showed a complete absence of the left cerebellar hemisphere and middle cerebellar peduncle. The origin of the trapezoid fibers from the ventral cochlear nucleus is clearly shown. Note also fibers of the dorsal acoustic stria passing into the tegmentum from the dorsal cochlear nucleus (Strong, '15). Weigert's myelin stain. Photograph.

dorsal to the medial longitudinal fasciculus (Fig. 15–7). At the cranial border of the abducens nucleus the bundle makes a sharp lateral turn over the dorsal surface of the abducens nucleus, forming the *internal genu* of the facial nerve. Fibers of the motor root of the facial nerve pass ventrolaterally, medial to the spinal trigeminal complex, and emerge from the brain stem near the caudal border of the pons (Fig. 14–1).

The *abducens nucleus (N. VI)* is a rounded gray cellular mass in the lateral part of the medial eminence of the fourth ventricle. Together with the genu of the facial nerve, it forms the rounded prominence in the ventricular floor known as the *colliculus facialis* (Figs. 14–2 and 15–4).

Its root fibers exit from the medial surface of the abducens nucleus and descend to emerge at the caudal border of the pons (Fig. 14–1).

3. THE VESTIBULOCOCHLEAR NERVE

The vestibulocochlear nerve (N. VIII) consists of two parts: (1) the *pars cochlearis*, which conveys auditory impulses from the cochlea, and (2) the *pars vestibularis*, which conveys impulses from the utricle, saccule, and semicircular canals, and is concerned with equilibrium, postural mechanisms, and muscle tone. These two divisions of the vestibulocochlear nerve run together from the internal auditory meatus to the cerebellopontine angle, where they enter the brain stem. Each of

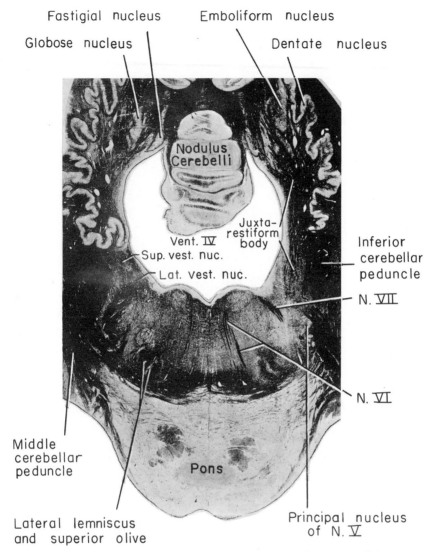

Fastigial nucleus　　Emboliform nucleus

Globose nucleus　　　　　Dentate nucleus

Nodulus Cerebelli

Juxta-restiform body

Vent. IV

Sup. vest. nuc.

Lat. vest. nuc.

Inferior cerebellar peduncle

N. VII

N. VI

Middle cerebellar peduncle

Pons

Lateral lemniscus and superior olive

Principal nucleus of N. V

Fig. 15-6. Section through pons, pontine tegmentum, and part of cerebellum, just below entrance of trigeminal nerve. One-month infant. Weigert's myelin stain. Photograph.

these nerves enters the brain stem separately and has its own central connections.

a.　The Cochlear Nerve and Nuclei. The larger cochlear division of N. VIII enters the brain stem lateral and somewhat caudal to the vestibular division (Fig. 3-7). Its fibers originate in the *spiral ganglion*, an aggregation of bipolar cells situated in the modiolus of the cochlea. The longer central processes of these cells form the cochlear nerve, while the short peripheral ones end in relation to the hair cells of the organ of Corti (Figs. 15-8 and 15-9). Fibers

of the cochlear nerve terminate upon two nuclear masses, the *dorsal* and *ventral cochlear nuclei*, located on the external surface of the inferior cerebellar peduncle just caudal to where fibers of this peduncle enter the cerebellum (Figs. 14-21 and 14-25). Although the dorsal and ventral cochlear nuclei represent a more or less continuous cell mass dorsolateral and lateral to the inferior cerebellar peduncle, they have distinctive cells and cytoarchitectural organization. The dorsal cochlear nucleus forms an eminence on the

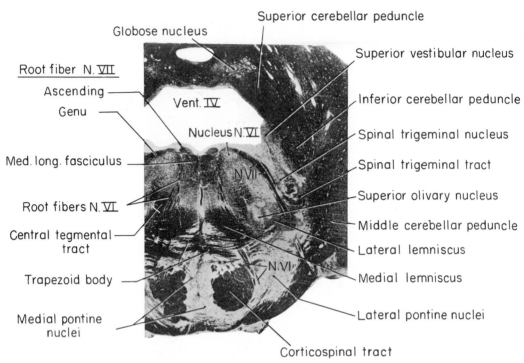

Globose nucleus
Superior cerebellar peduncle
Superior vestibular nucleus
Root fiber N. VII
Ascending
Genu
Vent. IV
Nucleus N. VI
Inferior cerebellar peduncle
Spinal trigeminal nucleus
Med. long. fasciculus
N.VII
Spinal trigeminal tract
Root fibers N. VI
Superior olivary nucleus
Central tegmental tract
Middle cerebellar peduncle
Lateral lemniscus
Trapezoid body
N.VI
Medial lemniscus
Medial pontine nuclei
Lateral pontine nuclei
Corticospinal tract

Fig. 15–7. Transverse section of the adult pons through the abducens nucleus showing the root fibers of the abducens and facial nerves. Weigert's myelin stain. Photograph.

most lateral portion of the ventricular floor known as the *acoustic tubercle*. In most mammals this nucleus appears distinctly laminated in Nissl preparations (Powell and Erulkar, '62). Beneath the ependyma is a molecular layer of small round cells. Deep to this is a layer of spindle cells, two or three cells thick, regularly arranged with their long axes perpendicular to the surface. The innermost polymorphic layer is the thickest and consists of sparsely distributed medium and relatively large pyramidal cells. In man the above described lamination often is indistinct. Cells of the ventral cochlear nucleus are oval, or round, medium-sized cells with relatively large amounts of cytoplasm, fine evenly distributed Nissl substance, and very short processes. There is no lamination as in the dorsal cochlear nucleus, but variations of cellular arrangement are present in different parts of the nucleus. Cells in medial portions of the nucleus are smaller, rounder, and more compactly arranged than in the lateral portion. In the cat the ventral cochlear

nucleus has been divided into anterior and posterior parts on the basis of cellular arrangements (Rose et al., '59).

Primary auditory fibers, representing the central processes of the spiral ganglion, enter the cochlear nuclei, bifurcate in an orderly sequence, and are distributed to both dorsal and ventral cochlear nuclei (Lorente de Nó, '33a). Experimental studies (Powell and Cowan, '62) indicate that after partial and complete lesions of the cochlea, degenerated fibers can be found in both parts of the cochlear nuclear complex. Fibers to the dorsal cochlear nucleus terminate about cells in the deep polymorphic layer and on the deep dendrites of the spindle cells. In the ventral cochlear nucleus, cochlear fibers end in fine pericellular plexuses and boutons surrounding cell somata (Rasmussen, '57).

One of the characteristic features of the auditory system is the pattern of *tonotopic localization* evident at various levels. In the cochlea it has been shown that high tones are received in the basal coils, while the apical portion is sensitive to low

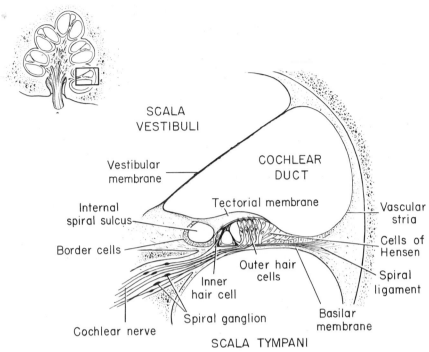

SCALA
VESTIBULI

COCHLEAR
DUCT

Vestibular
membrane

Tectorial membrane

Vascular
stria

Internal
spiral sulcus

Cells of
Hensen

Border cells

Outer hair
cells

Spiral
ligament

Inner
hair cell

Basilar
membrane

Cochlear nerve

Spiral ganglion

SCALA TYMPANI

FIG. 15–8. Drawing of a radial section through the cochlea showing the cochlear duct, the basilar membrane, the organ of Corti, and the tectorial membrane. The *small diagram in the upper left* is an axial section of the cochlea. The *area enclosed in the rectangle* is reproduced in detail in the large drawing.

frequencies (Crowe, '35; Tasaki, '54). Anatomical studies suggest that apical cochlear fibers terminate in ventral parts of the dorsal cochlear nucleus and in the ventral nucleus, while fibers from basal portions of the cochlea end in the dorsal part of the dorsal cochlear nucleus (Lewy and Kobrak, '36). Physiological evidence (Rose et al., '59; Rose, '60), based upon microelectrode studies of frequency sensitive neurons in the cochlear nuclear complex, indicates that each major division possesses its own frequency sequence, and that each division seems to have a full tonal spectrum. In all three divisions of the cochlear complex in the cat (i.e., dorsal nucleus and anterior and posterior parts of the ventral nucleus) neurons responding to higher frequencies are dorsal while those responding to lower frequencies are ventral. Thus, there appears to be multiple tonotopic representation in the cochlear nuclear complex which suggests that primary cochlear fibers bifurcate and terminate in an orderly dorso-

ventral sequence throughout the complex.

Secondary auditory pathways in the brain stem are exceedingly complex and many details regarding their exact composition and course are uncertain. Further, most of the available information concerning these pathways is based upon studies in animals. Secondary auditory fibers arising from the dorsal and ventral cochlear nuclei are grouped into three acoustic striae (Barnes et al., '43; Ades, '59). The *ventral acoustic stria* arises from the ventral cochlear nucleus, courses medially along the ventral border of the pontine tegmentum to form the trapezoid body (Figs. 15–5 and 15–9). Many of these fibers pass through or ventral to the medial lemniscus, cross the raphe, and reach the dorsolateral border of the opposite *superior olive*, where they turn upward to form a longitudinal ascending bundle known as the *lateral lemniscus*. Other trapezoid fibers terminate in the homolateral and contralateral nuclei of the su-

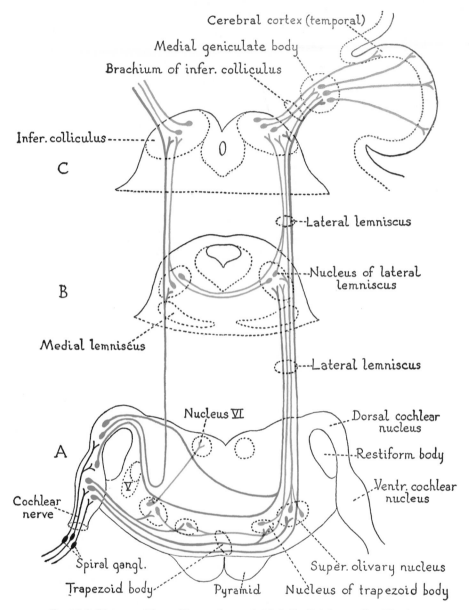

Fig. 15–9. Diagram of the auditory pathway. *A*, Medulla; *B*, isthmus; *C*, midbrain

perior olive and the trapezoid body, two nuclear masses interposed in the secondary cochlear pathway. From these nuclei fibers arise which join the lateral lemniscus of the same and the opposite sides.

The *dorsal* and *intermediate acoustic striae* arise respectively from the dorsal cochlear nucleus and from the dorsal part of the ventral cochlear nucleus. Both of these striae pass medially dorsal to the inferior cerebellar peduncle (Fig. 15–9). The dorsal stria crosses the median raphe ventral to the medial longitudinal fasciculus and fibers pass ventrally to join the lateral lemniscus of the opposite side. Fibers of the intermediate stria course medially through the reticular formation in an intermediate position, cross the midline and enter the contralateral lateral lemniscus. The dorsal stria is larger than the intermediate stria and the ventral stria is larger than the other two combined. In their passage through the tegmentum there is a diminution in the number of fibers in the various striae due to terminations in the reticular formation, the superior olivary nuclei, and the trapezoid nuclei. The superior olivary and trapezoid nuclei give rise to a number of tertiary auditory fibers which ascend mainly in the lateral lemniscus of the same side (Stotler, '53). Thus the lateral lemniscus consists primarily of crossed secondary fibers contributed by the three auditory striae and tertiary fibers from the superior olive and trapezoid nuclei. No direct fibers from the cochlear nuclei ascend in the ipsilateral lateral lemniscus (Barnes et al., '43). The number of ascending fibers in the lateral lemniscus is small compared with the total number of fibers arising from the dorsal and ventral cochlear nuclei.

The *trapezoid body* forms a conspicuous bundle of transverse fibers in the ventral part of the pontine tegmentum (Figs. 15–3, 15–5, and 15–7). These fibers arise principally from the ventral cochlear nucleus and, in a gentle arc, sweep medially toward the raphe. Most of these fibers cross to the opposite side, passing through or ventral to the medial lemniscus, and reach the ventrolateral portion of the tegmentum. Here they turn sharply in a longitudinal direction to form a new ascending fiber bundle, the lateral lemniscus (Fig. 15–9). The turn is made just dorsolateral to a nuclear mass known as the *superior olive* (Figs. 15–7 and A–27). This is a cellular column, about 4 mm. long, extending from the level of the facial nucleus to the motor nucleus of the trigeminal nerve; it is in close contact ventrally with the lateral portion of the trapezoid body. It contains several distinct cell groups: an S-shaped principal nucleus composed of medium-sized polygonal cells, and a wedge-shaped medial accessory nucleus of closely packed somewhat larger fusiform cells (Figs. 15–3 and 15–4). The superior olive receives collaterals of secondary cochlear fibers and contributes fibers to the trapezoid body and lateral

lemniscus. From its dorsal surface a bundle of fibers, the *peduncle of the superior olive*, passes dorsomedially toward the abducens nucleus (Figs. 15–2 and A–7).

Other smaller cellular aggregations related to the trapezoid body are difficult to see in Weigert preparations (Fig. 15–5). They include the *trapezoid nucleus*, which is scattered among the trapezoid fibers medial to the superior olive, and the *internal* and *external preolivary nuclei*, which lie ventral to the superior olive. All these nuclei appear to be intercalated cell groups in the secondary auditory pathways (Fig. A–7).

The *lateral lemniscus*, the principal ascending auditory pathway in the brain stem, courses rostrally in the lateral part of the tegmentum. Initially this bundle lies lateral to the superior olivary complex (Figs. 15–7 and 15–9), but at isthmus levels its position is more dorsal (Fig. 15–20).

Interposed in the course of the lateral lemniscus in the upper portion of the pons are other more diffuse cellular aggregations which constitute the *nucleus of the lateral lemniscus* (Fig. 15–9). To these the lemniscus contributes some terminals, or at least collaterals, and probably receives additional fibers from them. The lateral lemniscus then reaches the midbrain, where most of the fibers terminate either directly, or by collaterals, in the inferior colliculus. Some fibers may reach the colliculus of the opposite side through the commissure of the inferior colliculi. The small number of remaining fibers in the lateral lemniscus probably project directly to the medial geniculate body (Woollard and Harpman, '40). Thus fibers from the inferior colliculus, and a few from the lateral lemniscus, constitute the *brachium of the inferior colliculus* (Fig. 15–9).

It is evident from the above that the auditory pathway receives contributions from a number of intercalated nuclear masses and has a more complex composition than sensory systems considered heretofore; it also has a considerable ipsilateral component consisting of ascending fibers arising mainly from the superior olivary complex. It is difficult to state the

audit efferent system

number of neurons involved in the auditory pathway from periphery to cortex, but the principal ones are: (1) cells of the spiral ganglion whose central processes form the cochlear nerve, (2) secondary fibers from the dorsal and ventral cochlear nuclei which form the three auditory striae and contribute a number of crossed fibers to the lateral lemniscus, (3) the nuclei of the superior olivary complex and the trapezoid body that contribute to the lateral lemnisci, (4) the nucleus of the lateral lemniscus which receives and contributes fibers to the bundle of the same name, (5) the inferior colliculus which receives fibers from the lateral lemniscus and projects via its brachium to the medial geniculate body, and (6) the medial geniculate body, which gives rise to geniculocortical fibers (auditory radiations) that project to the transverse temporal gyri of Heschl. Whether the fibers contributed by all of these nuclei convey impulses which ultimately reach the cerebral cortex remains undetermined. There is evidence (Winkler, '21) that some crossed fibers in the dorsal and intermediate acoustic striae may pass directly to the medial geniculate body. Thus a relatively small number of auditory impulses may be conveyed to the cortex via tertiary neurons. Most of the auditory impulses reaching the auditory cortex are conveyed by higher order neurons. Physiological data (Rose and Woolsey, '58; Ades, '59) concerning the tonotopic representation of auditory impulses at the cortical level are discussed in Chapter 22 (p. 565).

Because of the large number of intercalated nuclei in the course of the auditory pathway (i.e., superior olive, trapezoid nucleus, nucleus of the lateral lemniscus, inferior colliculus), the reflex cochlear connections are exceedingly complex and not fully understood. It seems likely that all of the relay nuclei along the auditory pathway are involved to some degree in reflex circuits by which various motor phenomena occur in response to cochlear stimulation. Considerable experimental evidence suggests that a descending conduction system, from the auditory cortex to the cochlea (Rasmussen, '60), is associated with the classical ascending auditory system. One of the most interesting cochlear reflex connections is the *peduncle of the superior olive* or the *efferent cochlear bundle* described by Rasmussen ('46). Fibers of the crossed component, originating from the medial accessory superior olive and the area dorsal to it, pass dorsally, cross beneath the genu of the facial nerve, and exit from the brain stem in association with the vestibular nerve. A smaller homolateral component appears to arise from the principal superior olive. Peripherally these crossed and uncrossed fibers ultimately re-enter the cochlear nerve via the vestibulocochlear anastomosis. In the cochlear nerve these fine fibers proceed to the organ of Corti, where they appear to make synaptic contact with the hair cells (Rasmussen, '63; Smith and Rasmussen, '63). Electrophysiological studies (Galambos, '56) have shown that stimulation of the fibers of the efferent cochlear bundle causes a suppression of auditory nerve activity.

In addition to the efferent cochlear bundle, which represents essentially a feedback system to the primary sensory receptor, other evidence (Rasmussen, '60) indicates that the cochlear nuclei receive descending efferent fibers from various relay nuclei in the auditory pathway. Structures giving rise to these fibers include the inferior colliculus, the nuclei of the lateral lemniscus, and the principal superior olive. These descending pathways may inhibit impulses concerned with certain frequencies of the auditory spectrum and in this way result in a relative enhancement of those impulses not subject to inhibition. This phenomenon is referred to as auditory sharpening.

Additional secondary and higher order auditory fibers enter the brain stem reticular formation and may be involved in reflex closing of the eyes and turning of the head in response to a loud noise. The nucleus of the lateral lemniscus gives rise to fibers which decussate and enter the inferior colliculus of the opposite side. The inferior colliculi are interconnected via commissural fibers and probably some fibers project to the superior colliculi. Recent physiological studies (Rose et al.,

'66) suggest that some neurons of the inferior colliculus are sensitive to interaural time relationships of binaurally applied stimuli, while others are sensitive to small interaural intensity differences. These data indicate that certain neurons in the inferior colliculus may be concerned with the localization of a sound source.

Destruction of the cochlear nerve, or of both cochlear nuclei, causes complete *deafness* on the same side. Since the secondary cochlear pathways are both crossed and uncrossed, lesions of one lateral lemniscus or of the auditory cortex cause a bilateral diminution of hearing (partial deafness) that is most marked in the contralateral ear. Removal of one temporal lobe causes an impairment of sound localization on the opposite side, especially as regards judgment of the distance from which the sound is coming (Penfield and Evans, '32).

Conduction deafness due to disease of the middle ear should be distinguished from nerve deafness. In conduction deafness the ossicular chain fails to transmit vibrations from the tympanum to the oval window and to the scala vestibuli and scala media (i.e., cochlear duct; Fig. 15–8). When the ossicular chain is broken, vibrations of the tympanum pass via the air of the middle ear to the round window; this is inefficient because it lacks the impedence matching of the ossicular chain and most of the sound energy is lost. Hearing loss due to interruption of the ossicular chain ranges between 30 decibels, for low tones, to 65 decibels in the middle range. Fixation of the ossicular chain resulting from middle ear infections, or otosclerosis, is more common than interruptions of the ossicular chain. In otosclerosis even air conduction via the round window is impaired because this membrane is thickened. Early in the course of the disease patients with otosclerosis have, either a loss of appreciation of low tones, or a mild loss in the entire auditory range. Later there is a marked perceptive deficit for high tones. Tinnitus, without vertigo, is common and many patients hear better in the presence of loud noises (*paraacusis*).

The Vestibular Nerve and Nuclei. The vestibular portion of the inner ear consists of three *semicircular canals*, the *utricle* and the *saccule* (Fig. 15–10). Receptors in these structures are concerned with equilibrium, and orientation in three-dimensional space. The semicircular canals, concerned with kinetic equilibrium, are arranged at right angles to each other and represent approximately the three planes of space. One end of each canal has a dilatation, the ampulla, containing a ridge or crista oriented transversely. The columnar epithelium of the *crista ampullaris* is composed of neuroepithelial hair cells which constitute the vestibular receptor. The utricle and saccule each have a similar patch of sensory epithelium, the *macula utriculi* and *macula sacculi*, but here the hair cells are in contact with a gelatinous covering containing small calcareous concretions or particles, the *otoliths*. The utricle and saccule together constitute the so-called "otolith organ."

The cristae of the semicircular canals are stimulated by rotatory movement (i.e., angular acceleration) which causes movement of endolymphatic fluid and deflection of hairs of the sensory epithelium. Endolymphatic flow is greatest in the pair of canals most nearly perpendicular to the axis of rotation. The utricular macula, concerned primarily with static equilibrium, responds to changes in gravitational forces, and to linear acceleration. Macular impulses convey information regarding the position of the head in space, the hair cells being stimulated by the otolithic particles, whose position varies under the influence of gravity. The functional role of the saccular macula in static equilibrium has not been resolved. Destruction of the sacculae does not produce any detectable disturbance in the rabbit (Versteegh, '27) or in the frog (Tait and MacNally, '25). The experiments of Ashcroft and Hallpike ('34) demonstrated that the nerve from the saccular macula in the frog did not respond to tilting or rotation, but did respond accurately to vibratory stimuli up to 500 cycles per second. These data have been interpreted as indicating that the saccule in man may be concerned with the reception of vibratory stimuli.

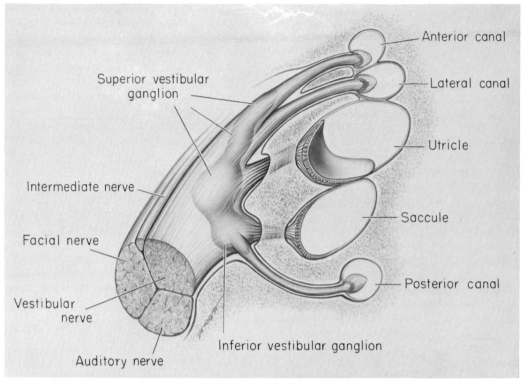

Fig. 15–10. Semischematic drawing of the vestibular ganglia and peripheral branches innervating anatomically distinctive portions of the labyrinth. Cells in the superior vestibular ganglion are arranged in a spiral fashion. Cells in the superior and distal portion of this ganglion innervate the cristae of the anterior and lateral semicircular canals. The broader proximal part of the superior vestibular ganglion contains cells which innervate the macula of the utricle. Cells of the inferior vestibular ganglion innervate the macula of the saccule and the crista of the posterior semicircular canal. The superior and inferior vestibular ganglia are joined by an isthmus of cells. The relationships between the facial, intermediate, vestibular and auditory nerves are shown on the left (Stein and Carpenter, '67).

Anatomical studies (Lorente de Nó, '33a; Stein and Carpenter, '67) clearly show that the nerve fibers from the saccular macula do not join the cochlear nerve and that they are distributed to the vestibular nuclei in a manner similar to that of nerve fibers from the utricular macula and the semicircular canals. Although the function of the saccule is not fully understood, it should be considered as a part of the vestibular end organ.

The maculae and cristae are innervated by cells of the vestibular ganglion (ganglion of Scarpa), an aggregation of bipolar cells located in the internal auditory meatus. The vestibular ganglion can be divided into superior and inferior vestibular ganglia which are connected by a narrow isthmus (Fig. 15–10). The shorter peripheral processes of these cells go to the maculae and cristae while the longer central ones form the vestibular nerve, which enters the cerebellopontine angle medial to the cochlear nerve. Vestibular root fibers pass dorsally between the inferior cerebellar peduncle and the spinal trigeminal tract, and bifurcate into short ascending and long descending branches which are distributed to the vestibular nuclei (Fig. 14–5). Some primary vestibular fibers (i.e., root fibers) continue without interruption to particular parts of the cerebellum; these fibers reach the ipsilateral half of the cerebellum via the juxtarestiform body (Fig. 15–6) and project mainly to the cortex of the nodulus, uvula and flocculus (Brodal and Høivik, '64). The largest number of primary vestibular fibers terminate differentially in the four vestibular nuclei in the floor of the fourth ventricle. The vestibular nuclei are the inferior, lateral, medial, and superior. Because of the long rostrocaudal extent of the vestibular nuclei, usually only two nuclei can be seen in any one transverse section (Figs. A–4, A–5 and A–6).

The **inferior vestibular nucleus** begins caudally in the medulla medial to the accessory cuneate nucleus and extends rostrally medial to the inferior cerebellar peduncle to the point near the entrance of the vestibular nerve root. Cytoarchitecturally the nucleus is composed of small- and medium-sized cells except in its most rostral part, where scattered large cells resemble those characteristic of the lateral vestibular nucleus. In the ventrolateral and caudal parts of the nucleus, a number of rather large cells form several densely packed groups. These cells (*group f* of Brodal and Pompeiano, '57) are of particular interest because they do not receive primary vestibular fibers and many of them project fibers to the cerebellum. In fiber-stained sections, the inferior vestibular nucleus is characterized by bundles of longitudinally oriented fibers, large parts of which are descending primary vestibular fibers. In fiber-stained sections the descending fiber bundles facilitate the delineation of the inferior and medial vestibular nuclei, which have a similar cytoarchitecture near their mutual border (Figs. 14–22 and 15–3).

The **lateral vestibular nucleus** (Deiters' nucleus), located laterally in the ventricular floor at the level of entrance of the vestibular nerve, extends rostrally to the level of the abducens nucleus. This nucleus is readily identified by its multipolar giant cells with coarse Nissl granules. Although most of the cells of this nucleus are regarded as giant cells, considerable variations in cell size are found. The nucleus also contains a number of smaller cells of varying types. Cells of all sizes are intermingled throughout the nucleus except in a small dorsolateral protrusion that consists only of medium-sized cells. There are some regional differences in the relative number and size of giant cells, which are most abundant in the caudal part of the nucleus.

The **medial vestibular nucleus** occupies the floor of the fourth ventricle medial to the inferior and lateral vestibular nuclei. Its rostral and caudal boundaries are indistinct. Rostrally it fuses dorsolaterally with the superior vestibular nucleus, and it becomes small at the level of the abducens nucleus.

Cells of the medial vestibular nucleus are small and medium-sized, closely packed, and fairly evenly distributed. Dorsolaterally some of the larger cells resemble those of the lateral vestibular nucleus, though none are true giant cells. The medial and inferior vestibular nuclei can be distinguished readily at all levels in myelin-stained preparations because bundles of longitudinally coursing fibers are not present in the medial vestibular nucleus (Fig. 15–3).

The **superior vestibular nucleus** lies dorsal and mostly rostral to the lateral vestibular nucleus in the angle formed by the floor and the lateral wall of the fourth ventricle. The superior cerebellar peduncle forms the dorsolateral border of the nucleus throughout most of its rostrocaudal extent. The mesencephalic and principal sensory nuclei of the trigeminal nerve are adjacent to the nucleus medially and ventrally, respectively, in its rostral two-thirds. The rostral pole of the nucleus is difficult to delimit. Cells of this nucleus are loosely scattered, medium and small-sized, and round or spindle-shaped. Larger stellate cells in the central part of the nucleus form clusters. Primary vestibular fibers terminate largely in the central part of the nucleus. Besides the main vestibular nuclei described above, there are several smaller accessory nuclei (Brodal and Pompeiano, '57), one of which consists of strands of cells between the root fibers of the vestibular nerve (interstitial nucleus of the vestibular nerve; Fig. 15–12).

Primary vestibular fibers project to all four vestibular nuclei and the interstitial

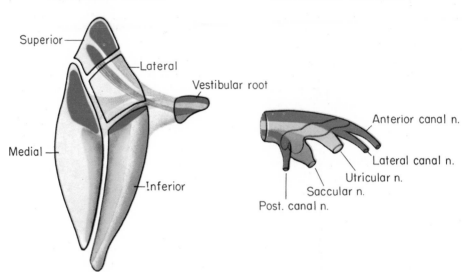

FIG. 15-11. Diagramatic representation of the relationships between portions of the vestibular ganglia and central fibers projecting to parts of the vestibular nuclear complex. The vestibular ganglia are shown in a modified transverse plane, while the vestibular nerve root and the vestibular nuclear complex are drawn in a stylized fashion, as they would appear in horizontal sections of the brain stem. Only the principal central projections of distinctive parts of the vestibular ganglia are shown. Portions of the vestibular ganglia innervating the cristae of the semicircular canals (*red*) project primarily to the superior vestibular nucleus and rostral parts of the medial vestibular nucleus. Portions of the superior vestibular ganglion (*yellow*) innervating the macula of the utricle project central fibers primarily to parts of inferior and medial vestibular nuclei. Fibers from portions of the inferior vestibular ganglion innervating the macula of the saccule (*blue*), project mainly to dorsolateral parts of the inferior vestibular nucleus. Some cells in the vestibular ganglia project fibers to parts of all vestibular nuclei, so that each specific part of the labyrinth has a unique as well as common projection, within the vestibular nuclear complex (Stein and Carpenter, '67).

nucleus of the vestibular nerve, but their distribution is differential (Fig. 15-11). Upon entering the brain stem, primary vestibular fibers bifurcate into ascending and descending branches. Ascending branches supply the superior vestibular nucleus, rostral parts of the medial vestibular nucleus, and give off collaterals to the ventral part of the lateral vestibular nucleus. Descending branches form the so-called descending root of the vestibular nerve, which provides fibers to the inferior vestibular nucleus and collaterals to the caudal parts of the medial vestibular nucleus. Quantitatively the largest number of primary vestibular fibers pass to the inferior vestibular nucleus. Terminal degeneration is not distributed equally to all of the regions of the vestibular nuclei following section of the vestibular nerve. Certain areas in each of the

vestibular nuclei do not receive primary vestibular fibers (Walberg et al., '58). In the superior vestibular nucleus, primary vestibular fibers terminate mainly in the central regions of the nucleus. In the lateral vestibular nucleus, primary vestibular fibers are found only in the ventral part of the nucleus and these fibers do not appear to establish synaptic contact with the giant cells, though many of these fibers end upon small cells and their processes. The dorsal half of the lateral vestibular nucleus is the largest regional area in this nuclear complex that is devoid of primary vestibular fibers (Lorente de Nó, '33a; Walberg et al., '58). The medial vestibular nucleus receives primary vestibular fibers throughout large regions of its rostral part, but caudally terminations are mainly in lateral regions near the inferior vestibular nucleus (Fig. 15-11). Primary vestibular fibers are found throughout the rostrocaudal extent of the inferior vestibular nucleus, except in its ventrolateral part (Figs. 15-11 and 15-12). Of the so-called accessory vestibular nuclei, only the interstitial nucleus of the vestibular nerve receives primary vestibular fibers.

One technically difficult problem has concerned the central projection of cells in the vestibular ganglia innervating particular parts of the labyrinth. This problem has been approached successfully in the monkey (Stein and Carpenter, '67) by producing small lesions in discrete parts of the ganglia (Fig. 15-10) and tracing degeneration: (1) distally, to the sensory epithelium, and (2) centrally, in the brain stem. Data from this study indicate that cells of the superior vestibular ganglion, innervating the cristae of the anterior and lateral canals, give rise to central fibers which: (1) occupy rostral and lateral parts of the vestibular root, and (2) project mainly to the superior vestibular nucleus and oral portions of the medial vestibular nucleus (Fig. 15-11). Cells of the superior vestibular ganglion, innervating the macula of the utricle, mainly descend in the dorsomedial part of the inferior vestibular nucleus. Collaterals of these fibers pass to dorsolateral parts of the medial vestibular nucleus caudally. Cells of the inferior vestibular ganglion, innervating the crista of the posterior canal, pass in caudal parts of the vestibular root and terminate mainly in portions of the superior and medial vestibular nuclei. Central fibers from cells of the inferior vestibular ganglion, innervating the saccular macula, mainly descend in dorsolateral parts of the inferior vestibular nucleus. Cell groups within the vestibular ganglia, innervating selectively individual receptor components of the labyrinth, have major unique central projections within the ipsilateral vestibular nuclei and less extensive projections to all parts of the complex. The interstitial nucleus of the vestibular nerve appears distinctive in that parts of this nucleus receive fibers from all cell groups of the vestibular ganglia (Fig. 15-12).

Primary vestibulocerebellar fibers pro-

ject beyond the vestibular nuclei to the ipsilateral cerebellar cortex. These fibers terminate as mossy fibers in the cortex of the nodulus, uvula and flocculus (Brodal and Høivik, '64). A small number of fibers reach parts of the paraflocculus and the lingula. There is no conclusive evidence that these fibers terminate in the fastigial nucleus.

The vestibular system and its fiber projections constitute one of the most widely dispersed special sensory systems in the neuraxis. Fiber projections of this sensory system pass to all spinal and brain stem levels, and to specific parts of the cerebellum. The vestibular nuclei, which receive primary vestibular fibers, and fibers from particular parts of the cerebellum, serve as a distributing center for secondary pathways.

Secondary Vestibular Fibers. The vestibular nuclei give rise to secondary vestibular fibers which project to specific portions of the cerebellum, certain motor cranial nerve nuclei, and to all spinal levels. In addition to the primary vestibulocerebellar fibers described above, there are a large number of secondary vestibulocerebellar fibers which originate from specific portions of the inferior and medial vestibular nuclei (Fig. 15-12). These fibers arise from lateral and caudal parts of these nuclei, traverse the juxtarestiform body, and project to the nodulus, uvula, flocculus and the fastigial nuclei. Within the cerebellum these fibers are distributed bilaterally, but with ipsilateral preponderance, except for those fibers passing to the flocculus. The latter fibers are distributed ipsilaterally (Brodal and Torvik, '57). The fastigial nuclei and certain portions of the cerebellar cortex give rise to fibers that project back to the vestibular nuclei to be distributed in a selective manner (Thomas et al., '56; Carpenter, '59; Walberg et al., '62). These efferent cerebellar fibers plus both primary and secondary vestibulocerebellar fibers mainly course medial to the inferior cerebellar peduncle in the *juxtarestiform body*. The vestibular nuclei serve as one of the important relay stations for the transmission of impulses to and from the cerebellum.

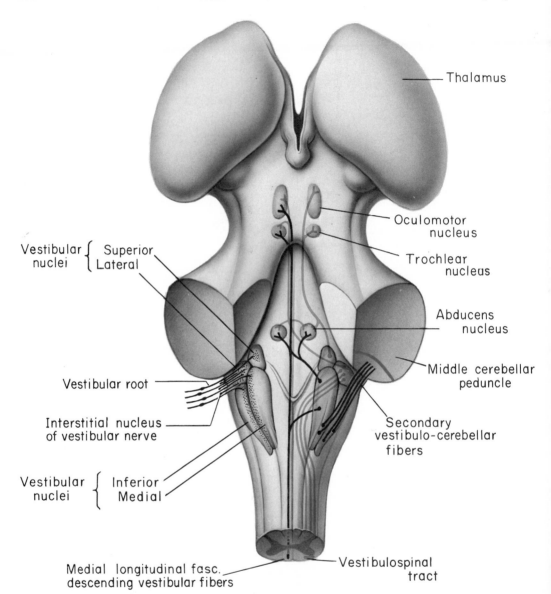

Fig. 15-12. Schematic diagram of some of the principal fiber projections of the vestibular system. On the *left* the relationships and spatial disposition of the four main vestibular nuclei are indicated. Among the afferent root fibers are the cells of the interstitial nucleus of the vestibular nerve. *Dotted areas* in the vestibular nuclei represent the regions of the nuclear complex which receive the largest number of primary vestibular fibers. These areas are: (1) the ventral half of the lateral vestibular nucleus, (2) the lateral part of the medial vestibular nucleus, (3) the dorsomedial part of the inferior vestibular nucleus, and (4) the central part of the superior vestibular nucleus. On the *right* the course of secondary vestibular fibers from individual nuclei is shown. Fibers from the superior vestibular nucleus (*red*) ascend ipsilaterally in the medial longitudinal fasciculus. Fibers from the medial vestibular nucleus (*black*) enter the medial longitudinal fasciculus to partially ascend and partially descend. Although these fibers are shown as totally crossed, uncrossed fibers also are present. Descending fiber projections from the lateral vestibular nucleus (*blue*) form the vestibulospinal tract; ascending fibers from this nucleus (*blue*) appear to be largely crossed and ascend in the medial longitudinal fasciculus. Again some of the uncrossed ascending fibers are not shown. Secondary vestibulocerebellar fibers (*black*) arise from caudal parts of the inferior and medial vestibular nuclei. A small number of fibers from the rostral part of the inferior vestibular nucleus ascend in the medial longitudinal fasciculus, but these are not shown.

The cells of the lateral vestibular nucleus give rise to the uncrossed vestibulospinal tract, which descends throughout the entire length of the spinal cord in the anterior and lateral funiculi (Figs. 13–21 and 15–12). These fibers arise from cells of all sizes within the nucleus and are somatotopically organized (Pompeiano and Brodal, '57a). Cells in the dorsocaudal parts of the nucleus supply fibers to lumbosacral spinal segments, while fibers arising from cells in the rostroventral parts of the nucleus project to cervical spinal levels. In the brain stem, these fibers do not have a direct course. Upon leaving the lateral vestibular nucleus the fibers pass ventromedially and caudally, successively occupying positions dorsomedial to the motor nucleus of N. VII and the nucleus ambiguus; from a retro-olivary locus fibers pass into the spinal cord. The vestibulospinal tract, derived exclusively from the lateral vestibular nucleus, has a more important relationship with the spinal cord than any other descending vestibular fiber system. The lateral vestibular nucleus also receives a large number of afferent fibers from the fastigial nucleus and the cortex of the cerebellar vermis (Fig. 17–17) which are somatotopically organized. Although crossed and uncrossed fastigiovestibular fibers are distributed differentially and asymmetrically within the lateral vestibular nucleus, they both supply regions which project to all spinal levels (Fig. 17–17). Most of these fibers establish synaptic contact only with the smaller cells of the lateral vestibular nucleus. Cerebellovestibular fibers from the vermis, largely the anterior lobe, are distributed ipsilaterally and terminate mainly in the dorsal halves of the lateral and inferior vestibular nuclei. These fibers terminate upon cells of all sizes, but in the lateral vestibular nucleus the majority make synaptic contact with large cells (Walberg and Jansen, '61). Thus, the lateral vestibular nucleus receives impulses from the vestibular nerve and the cerebellum and conveys impulses to spinal levels that mediate responses in axial and appendicular musculature (Brodal et al., '62). Impulses relayed to spinal levels via the lateral vestibular nucleus have important facilitating influences upon muscle tone and reflex activity.

Medial Longitudinal Fasciculus (MLF). Fibers from all of the vestibular nuclei pass medially in the region of the abducens nucleus and enter the medial longitudinal fasciculus. Vestibular fibers in the medial longitudinal fasciculus are both crossed and uncrossed and many bifurcate into ascending and descending branches (Fig. 15–12).

Descending vestibular fibers in the medial longitudinal fasciculus projecting to spinal levels arise primarily, if not exclusively, in the medial vestibular nucleus. These fibers, both crossed and uncrossed, descend in the medial longitudinal fasciculus until they reach the pyramidal decussation, where they shift ventrolaterally to enter the sulcomarginal region of the anterior funiculus. In their course they may project fibers into the lower brain stem reticular formation. It has been suggested that some of these fibers reach visceral motor nuclei, and other autonomic cell groups participating in the reflex phenomena that occur with excessive labyrinthine stimulation (e.g., nausea, vomiting, vasomotor reactions, facial pallor, palpitation, and perspiration). In the spinal cord these fibers are predominantly ipsilateral and do not project caudal to cervical spinal segments. The superior, lateral and inferior vestibular nuclei do not contribute descending fibers to the medial longitudinal fasciculus that reach spinal levels (Pompeiano and Brodal, '57; Carpenter, '60; Nyberg-Hansen, '64).

The medial longitudinal fasciculus also contains nonvestibular descending fibers. These include fibers from: (1) the interstitial nucleus of Cajal (interstitiospinal tract), (2) the superior colliculus (tectobulbar and tectospinal tracts, sometimes referred to as the predorsal bundle), (3) the pontine reticular formation (reticulospinal tract), and (4) more rostral brain stem nuclei projecting to particular portions of the inferior olivary complex. The small number of fibers in the interstitiospinal and tectospinal tracts project largely to cervical spinal segments. The largest group of descending fibers in the medial longitudinal fasciculus are the reticulo-spinal fibers, and most of these probably arise from the pontine reticular formation. Reticulospinal fibers descend to lumbo-sacral segments of the spinal cord (Fig. 13–20).

Ascending fibers in the medial longitudi-nal fasciculus are almost exclusively ves-tibular and arise from portions of all ves-tibular nuclei and the interstitial nucleus of the vestibular nerve (Brodal and Pom-peiano, '57a). These ascending vestibular fibers project primarily to portions of the nuclei of the extraocular muscles (i.e., the abducens, trochlear and oculomotor) and bring the innervation of these muscles under the influence of vestibular, and pos-sibly cerebellar regulation. A small num-ber of ascending fibers in the medial lon-gitudinal fasciculus bypass the oculomotor nucleus to terminate in the interstitial nucleus of Cajal (lateral to the medial longitudinal fasciculus near the oculo-motor nucleus, Figs. 16–11 and 16–13). Al-though it seems likely that vestibular impulses are projected rostrally to dien-cephalic levels, relatively few secondary vestibular fibers reach the diencephalon. Tertiary vestibular fibers probably exist, but information concerning them is meager.

Ascending fibers in the medial longitudi-nal fasciculus, arising from individual vestibular nuclei, have both differential and overlapping projections to the nuclei of the extraocular muscles (McMasters et al., '66). Fibers from the superior ves-tibular nucleus ascend exclusively (Fig. 15–12), enter the ipsilateral medial longi-tudinal fasciculus rostral to the abducens nucleus, and project primarily to the trochlear nucleus and the dorsal nucleus of the oculomotor complex (i.e., inferior rectus muscle, Fig. 16–9). Ascending fibers from the medial and lateral vestibular nuclei enter the medial longitudinal fas-ciculus at the level of the abducens nu-cleus, are both crossed and uncrossed, and project bilaterally, asymmetrically, and differentially to the nuclei of the extraocu-lar muscles. Projections of the medial ves-tibular nucleus are particularly prominent to: (1) the contralateral trochlear nucleus,

(2) the contralateral intermediate cell column (i.e., inferior oblique muscle), and (3) the ipsilateral ventral nucleus (i.e., medial rectus muscle) of the oculomotor complex (Fig. 16–9). Ascending fibers from the lateral vestibular nucleus appear to arise only from ventral parts of the nucleus and have prominent projections to: (1) the contralateral abducens and trochlear nu-clei, and (2) asymmetrical portions of the oculomotor nuclear complex. Ascending fibers from the inferior vestibular nucleus in the medial longitudinal fasciculus are relatively sparse. No ascending secondary vestibular fibers in the MLF appear to project to the caudal central nucleus (i.e., the levator palpebrae muscle; Fig. 16–9), or to the visceral nuclei of the oculomotor complex.

Besides the above listed fibers, it is pre-sumed that there are other fibers in the medial longitudinal fasciculus concerned with the mediation of conjugate horizon-tal eye movements which interconnect the nuclei of the extraocular muscles (Crosby, '50, '53). Whether these fibers arise from the vestibular nuclei or from other sources (e.g., parabducens nucleus) is unknown.

The medial longitudinal fasciculus, to-gether with the tectospinal and tectobul-bar tracts, represents a complex system of fibers which becomes myelinated very early in development. This bundle extends from the rostral part of the midbrain to the caudal medulla, where fibers pass into the sulcomarginal part of the anterior funiculus of the spinal cord. The caudal extent of this composite bundle in the spinal cord has not been established, but the majority of vestibular fibers in this bundle appear to end in cervical segments. Below the level of the abducens nuclei almost all fibers of the bundle are de-scending; above these nuclei ascending fibers predominate. In spite of the com-plex constitution of the medial longitudi-nal fasciculus and the fact that fibers enter and leave it at various locations, this bun-dle appears to form a functional entity.

Functional Considerations. Physiolog-ical studies (Szentágothai, '50; Fluur, '59; Cohen et al., '64) indicate that secondary vestibular fibers contained in the medial longitudinal fasciculus are essential for most conjugate eye movements. The investigations cited have shown that selective stimulation of individual semicircular canals, or of the nerves from the canals, produces conjugate deviations of the eyes in specific directions. Primary responses obtained by this type of stimulation are abolished following section of the medial longitudinal fasciculi rostral to the abducens nuclei. The fact that nystagmus produced by labyrinthine stimulation is not abolished by section of the medial longitudinal fasciculi (Lorente de Nó, '28, '31; Spiegel, '29; Bender and Weinstein, '44) suggests that vestibular impulses involved in this phenomenon may pass via the reticular formation.

Clinically, lesions involving the medial longitudinal fasciculus rostral to the abducens nuclei produce a disturbance of conjugate horizontal eye movements known as *anterior internuclear ophthalmoplegia* (Spiller, '24; Spiegel and Sommer, '44; Cogan et al., '50; Christoff et al., '60). The salient features of this syndrome are: (1) a paresis or paralysis of ocular adduction on attempted lateral gaze, but with preservation of ocular convergence, and (2) horizontal nystagmus, either more pronounced or exclusively present in the abducting eye. In most of the clinical cases examined pathologically, brain stem lesions have been so extensive as to preclude reliable anatomical correlations. Available data indicate that paresis of ipsilateral ocular adduction occurs with unilateral lesions of the medial longitudinal fasciculus. These findings have been confirmed experimentally in the monkey (Bender and Weinstein, '44, '50; Shanzer et al., '59). Recent studies (Carpenter and McMasters, '63; Carpenter and Strominger, '65) indicate that the syndrome in the monkey can be produced by lesions involving only the most medial fibers in the medial longitudinal fasciculus near, or rostral to, the abducens nucleus. Ascending degeneration resulting from unilateral lesions in the MLF rostral to the abducens nucleus is confined to the ipsilateral medial longitudinal fasciculus and is distributed differentially to the ventral nucleus of the oculomotor complex, a cell group that innervates the ipsilateral medial rectus muscle. Large bilateral lesions of the medial longitudinal fasciculi between the abducens nuclei in the monkey produce bilateral paresis of all horizontal eye movements (both abducting and adducting eye movements), without impairment of vertical eye movements or ocular convergence.

The mechanisms governing equilibrium (i.e., the maintenance of appropriate positions of the body in space) are largely of a reflex character and are activated by afferent impulses from several sources. Among the more important of these are the general proprioceptive impulses from the muscles, joints and tendons of the neck, trunk, and lower limbs, and the special proprioceptive impulses from the vestibular end organ. Impulses from the retina which project to the visual cortex also make an important contribution to spatial orientation. In this equilibratory complex, the labyrinth constitutes a highly specialized proprioceptive mechanism that is stimulated by the *position* or *changes in position* of the head. When the head is moved, either by contraction of the neck muscles or by shifting the body as a whole, the cristae are stimulated and, through the central vestibular connections, effect the reflex compensatory adjustments of the eyes and limbs needed for the particular movement (kinetostatic reflexes). The new attitude, as long as the position of the head remains unchanged, is sustained by impulses originating in the macula of the utricle. The sustaining (static) reflexes are initiated by the gravitational pull of the otolithic membrane on the macular hair cells.

The vestibulospinal tracts and descending fibers from the pontine reticular formation exert a strong excitatory influence upon muscle tone, particularly extensor tone. Normally muscle tone is maintained by a balance of inhibitory and facilitatory influences from higher centers, a large part of which are considered to be mediated by the brain stem reticular formation. If the influences of these higher centers are removed in an experimental animal, such as the cat, by transection of the brain stem at the intercollicular level (i.e., between the superior and inferior colliculi), a condition known as *decerebrate rigidity* develops. This condition is characterized by tremendously increased tone in the antigravity muscles. Increased muscle tone seen in this condition appears to be an expression of facilitation of gamma motor neurons, which thereby increase the rate of firing of muscle spindles; this in turn influences the firing of alpha motor neurons to maintain the tonic state. In this type of experimental preparation, the facilitatory pathways of the reticular formation and the vestibulospinal tract remain active, while inhibitory elements of the reticular formation no longer function. Inhibitory regions of the reticular formation are considered to be dependent upon descending impulses from higher levels, while the facilitating regions of the reticular formation receive impulses from ascending afferent systems. Thus, this type of midbrain transection removes the input to the reticular inhibitory system, but has little effect upon the reticular facilitating system or the descending vestibular system. This form of rigidity can be abolished by a variety of different lesions, including destruction of the vestibular nuclei and section of the anterior part of the spinal cord.

Labyrinthine stimulation, irritation, or disease cause vertigo, and objective signs such as unsteadiness, staggering, postural deviation, deviations of the eyes, and nystagmus. In some instances nausea, vomiting, vasomotor changes and prostration occur. The term *vertigo* refers to a subjective sense of rotation, either of the individual or his environment; this term should not be regarded as a synonym for dizziness or giddiness. *Nystagmus*, one of the most prominent objective signs, is a rhythmic involuntary oscillation of the eyes characterized by alternate slow and rapid ocular excursions. Clinically, nystagmus is named for the direction of the rapid phase, but the slow phase is the primary physiological movement. The nausea and vomiting which occur with motion sickness are the result of stimulation of the utricle. Since the labyrinths are antagonistic to each other, the elimination of one causes the other to be overactive until accommodation takes place.

Tests for vestibular function, based upon stimulation of the semicircular canals or vestibular nerve endings, include: (1) the rotating-chair test (Bárány chair), (2) the caloric test (i.e., thermal stimulation which changes the temperature of the endolymph), and (3) the galvanic test which stimulates nerve endings directly. In the first of these testing procedures, the slow phase of the nystagmus, deviation of the eyes, postural deviation, and past-pointing are all in the direction of the previous rotation, and can be correlated with the direction of endolymphatic flow. The sensation of vertigo is in the opposite direction (DeJong, '58). It is not possible to test the otoliths directly.

THE FACIAL NERVE

The facial nerve, and its intermediate component, contain both efferent and afferent fibers (Fig. 15–13). Functional components of this nerve include: (1) special visceral efferent (SVE, branchiomotor) fibers, (2) general visceral efferent (GVE) fibers, (3) special visceral afferent (SVA) fibers of taste, and probably (4) a few general somatic afferent (GSA) fibers. Special visceral efferent fibers innervate the superficial skeletal muscles of the face and scalp (mimetic musculature), the platysma, the stylohyoid, the posterior belly of the digastric muscle, and the stapedius muscle. General visceral efferent fibers supply the submandibular and pterygopalatine ganglia, which innervate the submandibular, sublingual, and lacrimal glands, as well as glands in the mucous membranes of the nose and roof of the mouth. Special visceral afferent fibers conveying taste from the anterior two-thirds of the tongue have their cell bodies in the *geniculate ganglion*. General somatic afferent fibers also arise from cells in the geniculate ganglion; together with similar fibers from N. IX and N. X, they innervate the external auditory meatus and the skin back of the ear.

The fibers supplying the facial muscles

form the large motor root (SVE). The afferent fibers and general visceral efferent
fibers constitute the intermediate nerve
(Wrisberg), which emerges between the
facial motor root and the vestibular nerve
(Fig. 15–2). General somatic afferent (GSA)
fibers from the intermediate nerve enter
the dorsal part of the spinal trigeminal
tract and descend.

There are some observations which suggest that the facial nerve may carry impulses of deep pain and deep pressure
from the face (Hunt, '15). In some cases
in which the trigeminal nerve was cut for
the relief of facial neuralgia, deep pain
sense due to pressure apparently persisted, but on the other hand, such pain is
sometimes diminished in lesions of the
facial nerve. The question is not settled,
but investigations suggest that both deep
and superficial pain probably are mediated exclusively by the trigeminal nerve
(Smyth, '39).

The *motor (branchiomotor) nucleus* of
N. VII is a column of typical multipolar
motor cells. It is about 4 mm. long and
occupies a lateral position similar to that
of the nucleus ambiguus (Figs. 14–3, 14–18
14–23 and 15–2). Efferent fibers emerge
from the dorsal surface of the nucleus,
project dorsomedially into the floor of the
fourth ventricle and ascend longitudinally
as a compact bundle medial to the abducens nucleus and dorsal to the medial longitudinal fasciculus (Fig. 15–7). Near the
rostral pole of the abducens nucleus, facial
root fibers make a sharp lateral bend over
the surface of the abducens nucleus, pass
ventrolaterally medial to the spinal trigeminal complex, and emerge from the
brain stem near the caudal border of the
pons (Figs. 15–2, 15–6, 15–7 and A–7).
Root fibers looping around the abducens
nucleus form the *internal genu* of the
facial nerve.

The facial nucleus is composed of several distinct cell groups (Papez, '27; Vraa-
Jensen, '42; Courville, '66b) which appear
to innervate specific facial muscles. Most
authors recognize at least 4 cell groups,
designated as dorsomedial, ventromedial,
intermediate, and lateral. The dorsomedial
cell group appears to give rise to the pos-

terior auricular nerve which innervates
auricular muscles and the occipital muscle. The ramus colli which innervates the
platysma muscle arises from the ventromedial cell group. The temporal and zygo-
matic branches of the facial nerve, related
to the intermediate cell group, supply the
frontalis, orbicularis oculi, the corrugator
supercilli and the zygomaticus. The lateral cell group gives rise to the buccal
branches which innervate the buccinator
muscle and the buccolabial muscles. It is
uncertain as to which cell groups innervate the stylohyoid, the posterior belly
of the digastric muscle, and the stapedius
muscle (Courville, '66b). Comparisons of
the cell groups of the facial nucleus in
animals and man (Vraa-Jensen, '42) reveal
a close correspondence except that in man
the lateral cell group (buccolabial muscles) is especially prominent, while the
medial cell group is very small.

A few muscle spindles have been described in facial muscles (Bowden and
Mahran, '56; Voss, '56). The presence of
muscle spindles suggests the existence of
gamma efferent fibers, and leads to the
assumption that gamma neurons are mixed
with alpha neurons in the facial nucleus.

The facial motor nucleus receives afferent fibers from a number of sources.
Among these are: (1) secondary trigeminal fibers from the spinal trigeminal nucleus (Cajal, '09; Carpenter and Hanna,
'61) involved in corneal and other trigem-
inofacial reflexes, (2) direct corticobulbar
fibers (Fig. 14–23) which project bilaterally but with important regional differences (Kuypers, '58a), (3) indirect corticobulbar fibers which convey impulses to
the facial nucleus via relays in the reticular formation (Walberg, '57a; Kuypers, '58,
'58a), and (4) crossed rubrobulbar fibers
(Courville, '66a) which project only to cell
groups (i.e., dorsomedial and intermediate) innervating the upper facial muscles.
In addition it seems likely that descending
fibers from the mesencephalic reticular
formation project ipsilaterally to portions
of the facial nucleus (Courville, '66a). Secondary or tertiary auditory fibers, considered to reach the facial nucleus, are
thought to mediate certain acousticofacial

reflexes. These reflexes include closing of the eyes in response to a sudden loud noise, and contraction of the stapedius muscle to dampen the movements of the ear ossicles. Clinical evidence (Monrad-Krohn, '24, '39) suggests that impulses from the thalamus or globus pallidus may reach portions of the facial nucleus indirectly, since lesions in these structures may produce a *mimetic* or *emotional* type facial palsy. The pathways involved are unknown, but it has been suggested that such impulses may be mediated by brain stem reticular neurons.

The *visceral motor nucleus*, known as the *superior salivatory nucleus*, is difficult to distinguish and apparently is represented by a scattered group of cells in the dorsolateral part of the reticular formation. The cells extend caudally to the rostral tip of the nucleus ambiguus, the more caudal cells constituting the inferior salivatory nucleus of the glossopharyngeal nerve. In Figure 14–4 these two nuclei are indicated schematically as a single cell column. The superior salivatory nucleus, and probably other accessory cells, send out preganglionic fibers which leave the brain stem by way of the intermediate nerve. Peripherally, part of these preganglionic parasympathetic fibers pass via the chorda tympani to the submandibular ganglion; postganglionic fibers supply the submandibular and sublingual salivary glands (Fig. 15–13). Other preganglionic fibers enter the major petrosal nerve and reach the pterygopalatine ganglion, from which postganglionic secretory and vasomotor fibers go to the lacrimal gland and to the mucous membranes of the nose and roof of the mouth. Fibers projecting to the superior salivatory nucleus involved in lacrimal and salivary reflexes are poorly defined, mainly because of the difficulties in identifying this nucleus.

Visceral afferent fibers of the facial nerve originate from cells of the *geniculate ganglion* located at the external genu of the facial nerve (Fig. 15–13). These fibers, which convey principally taste impulses from the anterior two-thirds of the tongue, form part of the nervus intermedius, which enters the brain stem between the fibers of the motor root of N. VII and the vestibular root of N. VIII (Fig. 15–2). Centrally these fibers enter the fasciculus solitarius and terminate in the upper portion of the nucleus of that bundle.

Lesions of the facial nerve (Bell's palsy) producing paralysis of facial movements, and sometimes disturbances of taste and secretory function, may involve fibers of the nerve within the brain stem or in their peripheral course. The particular deficits which result depend upon the location of the lesion and its extent. A complete lesion of the motor part of the facial nerve as it emerges from the stylomastoid foramen (*A*, Fig. 15–13) produces paralysis of all ipsilateral facial movements. The patient is unable to wrinkle the forehead, close the eye, show the teeth, purse the lips, or whistle. On the side of the lesion the palpebral fissure is widened, the nasolabial fold is flattened, and the corner of the mouth droops. Although corneal sensation is present, the corneal reflex is lost on the side of the lesion because motor fibers participating in this reflex are destroyed. A lesion of this nerve distal to the geniculate ganglion (*B*, Fig. 15–13) produces all of the deficits found with a lesion at *A*, plus impairment of secretions from the sublingual and submandibular salivary glands, hyperacusis, and sometimes impairment of taste over the anterior two-thirds of the tongue. Impairment of salivary secretion results from interruption of preganglionic parasympathetic fibers from the superior salivatory nucleus. *Hyperacusis* is caused by paralysis of the stapedius muscle, which normally functions to dampen the oscillations of the ear ossicles. Taste may not always be impaired by such lesions since some fibers may take an aberrant course with the major petrosal nerve. Lesions of the facial nerve proximal to the geniculate ganglion (*C*, Fig. 15–13) produce all of the deficits encountered with lesions at *A* and *B* and, in addition, invariably result in complete loss of taste over the anterior two-thirds of the tongue. Lacrimation also is impaired on the side of the lesion as a consequence of destruction of parasym-

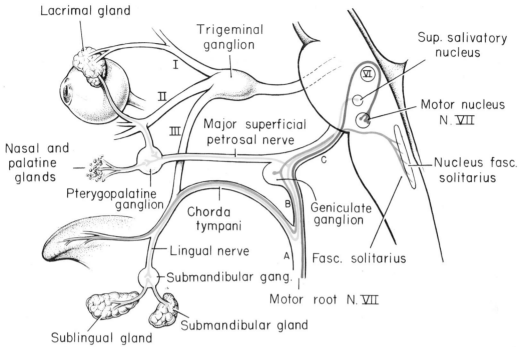

FIG. 15-13. Diagram showing the functional components, organization, and peripheral distribution of the facial nerve. Special visceral efferent fibers (motor) are shown in *red*. General visceral efferent fibers (parasympathetic) are in *yellow*, and special visceral afferent fibers are in *blue*. A, B, and C denote lesions of the facial nerve at the stylomastoid foramen, distal to the geniculate ganglion, and proximal to the geniculate ganglion. Disturbances resulting from lesions at these locations are described in the text (pages 358–359).

pathetic fibers to the pterygopalatine (sphenopalatine) ganglion. With complete lesions in this location no regeneration of sensory fibers takes place. Aberrant regeneration of preganglionic parasympathetic fibers may cause lacrimation in response to a salivary stimulus (syndrome of "crocodile tears").

Central lesions involving corticobulbar and corticoreticular fibers projecting upon reticular neurons, which in turn discharge upon cells of the facial nucleus, produce a marked weakness of muscles in the lower half of the face contralaterally, especially in the perioral region. Muscles of the upper facial region concerned with wrinkling the forehead, frowning, and closing the eyes are not affected. The accepted explanation of this upper motor neuron paralysis is that corticobulbar fibers projecting to the upper part of the facial nucleus (supplying muscles of the upper face and forehead) are distributed bilateral, while corticobulbar projections

to the lower part of the facial nucleus (supplying muscles of the lower face) are predominantly crossed. Although a completely satisfactory explanation is still lacking as to why a capsular hemiplegia in man is accompanied by paresis only in the lower facial muscles, the anatomical observations of Kuypers ('58a) support the accepted thesis. This author found direct bilateral corticobulbar projections to the facial nucleus, but noted that ventral cell groups (regarded as innervating lower facial muscles) of the contralateral facial nucleus received more fibers than the same cell groups of the ipsilateral facial nucleus.

Even in the presence of a central type facial paralysis, as described above, mimetic or emotional innervation of th facial muscles may be preserved. In sponse to a genuine emotional sti the muscles of the lower face tract symmetrically while smili ing. Actually, contractions cles on the paretic side may begin earlier and last longer than on the normal side (Monrad-Krohn, '39). Mimetic or emotional innervation of facial muscles is largely involuntary. Available evidence suggests that impulses from higher levels of the neuraxis, other than those arising in the cerebral cortex, must reach the facial nuclei and bring about emotional facial expression. The neural mechanism for emotional facial innervation appears distinct and separate from that controlling voluntary facial movement. Thus two different types of central facial paresis are recognized, one concerned with voluntary facial movement, and another involving emotional facial expression. Each of these types of central facial paresis can occur alone since the central pathways are different, but with certain lesions both voluntary and mimetic facial paralyses can occur together. The neuroanatomical pathways mediating emotional facial innervation are unknown; clinically it has been suggested that the globus pallidus and portions of the thalamus may be involved in this reflex facial innervation.

THE ABDUCENS NERVE

The abducens is the motor nerve (GSE) innervating the lateral rectus muscle of the eye. The nucleus forms a column, about 3 mm. in length of typical somatic motor cells in the lateral part of the medial eminence (Figs. 15-4 and 15-7). Fibers of the facial nerve form a complicated loop about the nucleus. Root fibers of the abducens nerve emerge from the medial aspect of the nucleus and pass ventrally through the pontine tegmentum and lateral to the corticospinal tract (Figs. 15-1, 15-6 and 15-7). They emerge from the brain stem at the caudal border of the pons (Figs. 14-1, 14-4, and A-7). The nucleus receives, and is traversed by, crossed and uncrossed vestibular fibers from the inferior, medial, and lateral vestibular nuclei entering the medial longitudinal fasciculi (Fig. 15-12). Impulses conveyed by these fibers may be concerned with the vestibular control of lateral eye movements. Corticobulbar fibers convey impulses to abducens nuclei bilaterally via

intercalated neurons in the reticular formation (Fig. 14-23).

Lesions of the abducens nerve in the brain stem, or in its long intracranial course cause ipsilateral paralysis of the lateral rectus muscle. Owing to the unopposed action of the medial rectus muscle, the eye is strongly adducted. The contralateral eye is unaffected and can move in all directions. The patient has diplopia (double vision) on attempting to gaze to the side of the lesion; two images are seen side by side. This is called horizontal diplopia. Diplopia results because light reflected by an object in the visual field does not fall upon corresponding points of the two retinae.

Discrete unilateral lesions of the abducens nucleus produce a weakness, or paralysis, of lateral gaze toward the side of the lesion. The syndrome of "lateral gaze paralysis" differs from a simple paralysis of the lateral rectus muscle in that both eyes are forcefully and conjugately directed to the side opposite the lesion, and movement of the eyes laterally toward the side of the lesion is severely limited, or impossible. The head may be tilted slightly to the opposite side. Ocular convergence usually is preserved. The abducens nucleus thus appears unique among the motor cranial nerve nuclei, since it is the only cranial nerve in which disturbances associated with lesions of root fibers and motor nucleus are not identical. This curious finding requires an explanation.

All ocular movements, whether horizontal, vertical, or rotatory, require reciprocal activity in the extraocular muscles producing these movements. Conjugate lateral gaze requires simultaneous and appropriate contractions of the lateral rectus on one side and the medial rectus of the opposite side. The central neural mechanism underlying conjugate lateral movements of the eyes is not fully understood, but it is generally agreed that fibers in the medial longitudinal fasciculus interconnecting the abducens nucleus and portions of the oculomotor nuclear complex are essential for these movements. It has been postulated that cells in the reticular formation adjacent to, or in, the abducens nucleus may give rise to these fibers. This cell group, referred to as the *parabducens nucleus*, often is called the pontine "center for lateral gaze." Although the theoretical existence of the parabducens nucleus has been acknowledged (Crosby, '53; Peele, '61), there is no definitive description or experimental evidence substantiating it as an entity. It also has been suggested that ascending vestibular fibers which are known to traverse and terminate in the abducens nuclei, and to project rostrally in the medial longitudinal fasciculus, might be implicated in the syndrome of "lateral gaze paralysis." Since oculomotor fibers supplying the medial rectus muscle are uncrossed (Fig. 16–9; Warwick, '53), it would be expected that ascending fibers from the pontine "center for lateral gaze" must cross in the vicinity of the abducens nucleus. In any case, axons destined for the contralateral medial longitudinal fasciculus are interrupted, and coordinating impulses do not reach appropriate cell groups in the oculomotor nucleus. It should be recalled that unilateral lesions of the medial longitudinal fasciculus rostral to the abducens nucleus produce a fragment of the syndrome of *lateral gaze paralysis*, namely paralysis of adduction in the ipsilateral eye. Thus, lateral gaze paralysis due to lesions in the region of the abducens nucleus would appear to be a combination of two factors: (1) paralysis of the ipsilateral lateral rectus due to destruction of cells in the abducens nucleus, and (2) paralysis of adduction in the contralateral medial rectus muscle due to interruption of fibers destined for the medial longitudinal fasciculus and specific parts of the contralateral oculomotor nucleus.

Discrete lesions in the abducens nucleus in the monkey (Carpenter et al., '63) produce ascending degeneration which is most profuse in the contralateral medial longitudinal fasciculus; these ascending fibers are distributed differentially to the ventral nucleus of the oculomotor complex, a cell group innervating the medial rectus muscle on that side. Lesions of the

medial longitudinal fasciculus rostral to the abducens nucleus (Carpenter and Strominger, '65) produce paresis of ipsilateral ocular adduction (i.e., anterior internuclear ophthalmoplegia) and similarly distributed degeneration in the ipsilateral oculomotor nucleus. Available evidence suggests that the paresis of ocular adduction, which forms a part of the "lateral gaze paralysis" syndrome, and anterior internuclear ophthalmoplegia probably have a common basis, namely, interruption of fibers of the medial longitudinal fasciculus at different locations and on different sides of the median raphe. However, lesions limited to individual vestibular nuclei do not produce paresis of ocular adduction (McMasters et al., '66). Thus it seems likely that the ascending fibers of the medial longitudinal fasciculus whose interruption produces these ocular disturbances probably do not arise from the vestibular nuclei.

Because of the proximity of emerging root fibers of the abducens nerve to the corticospinal tract, lesions in the caudal pons involving both of these structures produce the so-called *middle alternating hemiplegia*. This syndrome is characterized by paralysis of the ipsilateral lateral rectus muscle and a contralateral hemiplegia. This condition resembles the *inferior alternating hemiplegia* seen with comparable medullary lesions which involve the hypoglossal nerve and the medullary pyramid.

ROSTRAL PONS AND PONTINE TEGMENTUM

Transverse sections through the upper pons at the level of root fibers of the trigeminal nerve (Figs. 15–14, 15–15, 15–16, and A–8) reveal important changes when compared with sections at lower pontine levels (Figs. 15–2, 15–3, and 15–7). The fourth ventricle is narrower, though its roof is still formed by the cerebellum. Within the cerebellum portions of all the deep cerebellar nuclei can be seen (Fig. 15–14), and fibers of the inferior and middle cerebellar peduncles enter the cerebellum close to each other (Fig. 15–14). At slightly higher levels fibers of the

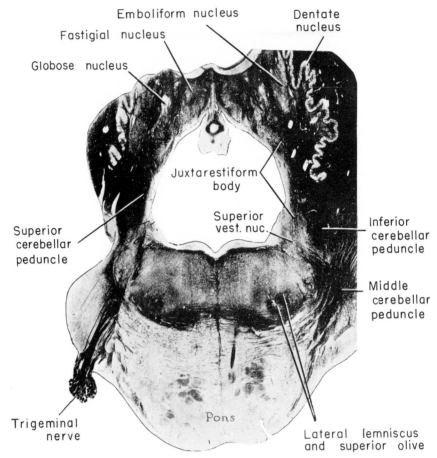

Fig. 15–14. Section of pons, pontine tegmentum, and part of cerebellum through the root of the trigeminal nerve. One-month infant. Weigert's myelin stain. Photograph.

superior cerebellar peduncle form the dorsolateral wall of the fourth ventricle (Fig. 15–16).

The ventral portion of the pons is larger than at lower levels but still contains transverse and longitudinal fibers, as well as large masses of pontine nuclei. Corticospinal and corticopontine tracts here consist of numerous fiber bundles less compactly arranged than in the caudal pons. Fibers within the raphe of the pons are probably reticulocerebellar fibers arising from cells in the pontine tegmentum. The more laterally placed fibers projecting dorsally, previously regarded exclusively as aberrant pyramidal fiber bundles, probably also contain corticobulbar fibers passing to reticular neurons (Fig. 15–15).

In the dorsal part of the pons the medial lemniscus is traversed by the transverse fibers of the trapezoid body. Lateral to the medial lemniscus and closely associated with fibers of the trapezoid body is the rostral pole of the superior olivary nucleus (Fig. 15–14). Ventrolaterally the lateral lemniscus is becoming a well-defined bundle (Figs. 15–15 and 15–16). The spinothalamic and anterior spinocerebellar tracts are located lateral to the medial lemniscus. The position of the medial longitudinal fasciculus is unchanged from lower levels. Longitudinally cut fibers of the facial genu appear lateral to the medial longitudinal fasciculus (Fig. 15–15). Fibers of the central tegmental tract form a fairly discrete bundle in the reticular formation dorsal to the lateral part of the medial lemniscus (Fig. 15–15).

The Pontine Reticular Formation, still

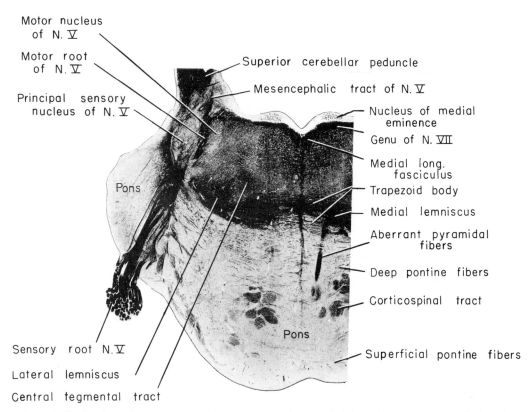

Motor nucleus of N. V

Motor root of N. V

Principal sensory nucleus of N. V

Pons

Sensory root N. V

Lateral lemniscus

Central tegmental tract

Superior cerebellar peduncle

Mesencephalic tract of N. V

Nucleus of medial eminence

Genu of N. VII

Medial long. fasciculus

Trapezoid body

Medial lemniscus

Aberrant pyramidal fibers

Deep pontine fibers

Corticospinal tract

Pons

Superficial pontine fibers

FIG. 15–15. Section of pons and pontine tegmentum of 1-month infant through entrance of trigeminal nerve. Weigert's myelin stain. Photograph.

occupying the central core of the tegmentum, is somewhat reduced in size. Dorsal to the facial genu the nucleus of the medial eminence remains. The central reticular area contains the *nucleus reticularis pontis oralis*, the rostral continuation of the more caudal pontine reticular nucleus (Fig. 15–18). This cell group extends rostrally into the caudal mesencephalon, where its oral boundaries become indistinct. The more caudal part of this nuclear mass contains scattered giant cells, like those which characterize the medial two-thirds of the medullary reticular formation. Some of the larger cells at this level give rise to the uncrossed reticulospinal fibers; others give rise to ascending fibers which pass rostrally in the central tegmental tract. In many instances a single cell with a dichotomizing axon projects fibers both rostrally and caudally. Ascending fibers from parts of the nuclei reticularis pontis oralis and caudalis appear to pass to the intralaminar nuclei of

the thalamus. These ascending fibers and those originating from more caudal brain stem regions participate in activation of the cerebral cortex.

In the ventral part of the tegmentum immediately dorsal to the medial lemnisci is a moderately large group of multipolar cells known as the *nucleus reticularis tegmenti pontis*, or the reticulotegmental nucleus (Fig. 15–18). These cells are considered as a medial tegmental extension of the pontine nuclei, which they resemble. Experimental studies (Brodal and Jansen, '46) have shown that these nuclei project virtually all of their fibers to the cerebellum. Projections to the cerebellar vermis are both crossed and uncrossed, while those to the hemisphere are entirely crossed. In the raphe region dorsal to the reticulotegmental nucleus is the *superior central nucleus*, a closely packed aggregation of relatively small cells. This nucleus is more prominent at isthmus levels (Figs. 15–18 and 15–20).

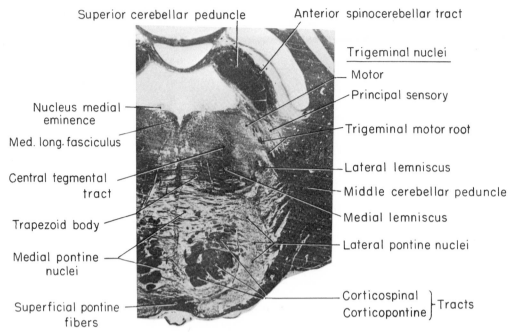

Fig. 15–16. Transverse section of adult pons through motor trigeminal nucleus. Weigert's myelin stain. Photograph.

Afferent root fibers of the trigeminal nerve traverse the lateral portion of the pons, reach the dorsolateral pontine tegmentum, and terminate in specific nuclei of the trigeminal nerve. Lateral to the entering root fibers is a large gray cellular mass, the *nucleus sensorius principalis* of the trigeminal nerve (Fig. 15–18). Small groups of root fibers can be seen entering this nucleus (Figs. 15–14 and 15–15). Medial to the trigeminal root fibers and the principal sensory nucleus is a smaller oval collection of large cells whose efferent fibers exit medial to the afferent fibers. This is the *motor nucleus* of the trigeminal nerve. A small bundle of afferent fibers coursing dorsally between the motor and sensory nuclei toward the ventricular surface constitutes the *mesencephalic tract of the trigeminal nerve*. Although these are afferent fibers, they arise from large unipolar cells situated in the central gray matter along the lateral border of the ventricle (Figs. 15–15 and 15–18). Cells of the mesencephalic nucleus of the trigeminal nerve are best seen at somewhat higher levels (Figs. 15–21 and 15–22).

THE TRIGEMINAL NERVE

The trigeminal, the largest cranial nerve, contains both sensory and motor fibers. *General somatic afferent (GSA) fibers* convey both exteroceptive and proprioceptive impulses. Exteroceptive impulses of touch, pain and thermal sense are transmitted from: (1) the skin of the face and forehead, (2) the ectodermal mucous membranes of the nose, the nasal sinuses and the oral cavity, (3) the teeth, and (4) extensive portions of the cranial dura. Proprioceptive impulses (deep pressure and kinesthesis) are conveyed from the teeth, peridontium, the hard palate and temporomandibular joint receptors. In addition afferent fibers convey impulses arising from stretch receptors in the muscles of mastication. *Special visceral efferent fibers* (SVE; branchiomotor) innervate the muscles of mastication, the tensor tympani and the tensor veli palatini. Afferent fibers constitute the sensory root (portio major) while efferent fibers form the smaller motor root (portio minor).

The afferent fibers, with the exception of those associated with proprioception and stretch receptors, have their cell bodies in the large, flattened, crescent-shaped *trigeminal ganglion* (See p. 369 concerning the extraocular muscles). This semilunar-shaped ganglion, placed on the cerebral surface of the petrous bone in the middle cranial fossa, is composed of typical unipolar ganglion cells (Truex, '40; Figs. 15–17 and 15–19). The peripheral processes of these cells form the three main divisions of the trigeminal nerve: ophthalmic, maxillary, and mandibular. The first two are wholly sensory, but incorporated in the mandibular branch is the entire motor root supplying the muscles of mastication. The ophthalmic branch innervates the forehead, upper eyelid, cornea, conjunctiva, dorsum of the nose, and mucous membranes of the nasal vestibule and the frontal sinus. The maxillary division supplies the upper lip, lateral and posterior portions of the nose, upper cheek, anterior portion of the temple, and mucous membranes of the nose, upper jaw, upper teeth, and roof of the mouth to the palatopharyngeal arch. Sensory fibers of the mandibular branch are distributed to the lower lip, chin, posterior portions of the cheek and the temple, external ear, and mucous membranes of the lower jaw, lower teeth, cheeks, anterior two-thirds of the tongue, and floor of the mouth. All three branches contribute sensory fibers to the dura. The dura of the posterior fossa also is innervated by fibers from the tenth cranial and the upper three spinal nerves (Penfield and McNaughton, '40; Kimmel, '61).

The central processes of cells in the trigeminal ganglion form the sensory root which passes through the lateral part of the pons and enters the tegmentum, where many fibers divide into short ascending and long descending arms. Other fibers descend or ascend without bifurcation (Windle, '26). The short ascending fibers and their collaterals terminate in the principal sensory nucleus lying dorsolateral to the entering fibers. The long descending branches form the spinal trigeminal tract, whose longest fibers reach the uppermost cervical segments of the spinal cord; terminals and collat-

erals to the spinal trigeminal nucleus are given off en route (Fig. 15–19).

The *spinal trigeminal nucleus* is a long column of cells that extends caudally from slightly below the root entry zone into the uppermost cervical spinal segments (Fig. 15–19). Rostrally the nucleus merges with the principal sensory nucleus, while caudally it merges imperceptibly into the substantia gelatinosa. The spinal trigeminal tract lies along the lateral border of the nucleus throughout its extent; in the upper cervical spinal cord fibers of this tract are intermingled with fibers of the dorsolateral fasciculus (zone of Lissauer). Throughout the lower pons fibers of the tract are covered laterally by the inferior and middle cerebellar peduncles; in the upper medulla the tract lies medial to the inferior cerebellar peduncle, but in the caudal medulla, and upper cervical region the tract is more superficial and nearly touches the dorsolateral surface (Fig. 15–17).

Within the spinal trigeminal tract there is a definite topographical grouping of fibers from the three main peripheral divisions that is widely accepted (Woodburne, '36; Kerr, '63). Fibers from the ophthalmic division are most ventral, fibers from the maxillary division are intermediate and mandibular fibers are most dorsal. This laminar orientation is said to be due to a medial rotation of the trigeminal root that brings fibers of the ophthalmic division ventral, while fibers of the mandibular division reach a dorsal position. While certain evidence (Smyth, '39; McKinley and Magoun, '42) has suggested that fibers of the various divisions of the trigeminal nerve descend in the spinal trigeminal tract for different distances, more extensive studies (Torvik, '56; Darian-Smith and Mayday, '60; Kruger and Michel, '62; Kerr, '63) indicate that the laminar arrangement of fibers from the different trigeminal divisions persists throughout the length of the tract with little or no intermingling of fibers.

Fibers from the spinal trigeminal tract terminate upon cells of the spinal trigeminal nucleus at all levels. According

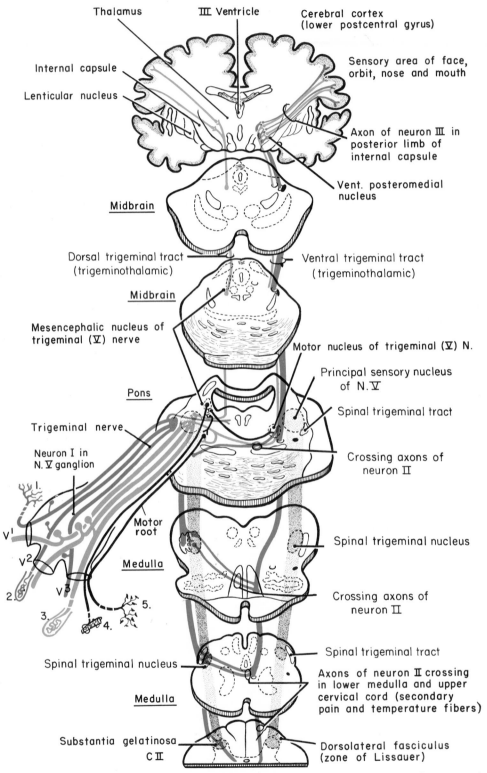

Thalamus

III Ventricle

Cerebral cortex
(lower postcentral gyrus)

Internal capsule

Lenticular nucleus

Sensory area of face,
orbit, nose and mouth

Axon of neuron III in
posterior limb of
internal capsule

Vent. posteromedial
nucleus

Midbrain

Dorsal trigeminal tract
(trigeminothalamic)

Ventral trigeminal tract
(trigeminothalamic)

Midbrain

Mesencephalic nucleus of
trigeminal (V) nerve

Motor nucleus of trigeminal (V) N.

Principal sensory nucleus
of N. V

Pons

Spinal trigeminal tract

Trigeminal nerve

Neuron I in
N. V ganglion

Crossing axons of
neuron II

V¹

Motor
root

V²

Spinal trigeminal nucleus

Medulla

2.

V³

Crossing axons of
neuron II

3.

5.

4.

Spinal trigeminal tract

Spinal trigeminal nucleus

Axons of neuron II crossing
in lower medulla and upper
cervical cord (secondary
pain and temperature fibers)

Medulla

Substantia gelatinosa
C II

Dorsolateral fasciculus
(zone of Lissauer)

FIG. 15–17. Diagram of the secondary trigeminal tracts. The ventral trigeminal tract (*red*) conveys primarily pain and thermal sense. These fibers originate from the spinal trigeminal nucleus, cross in the lower

to Kerr ('63) fibers of the tract project into that part of the spinal trigeminal nucleus immediately adjacent to it, so that a clear-cut segregation of fibers within the nucleus exists for each division with virtually no overlap. A considerable number of fibers from the mandibular division of the spinal trigeminal tract project dorsomedially into the nucleus solitarius (Torvik, '56; Kerr, '61, '63; Rhoton et al., '66), a finding suggesting that some of the descending fibers in this tract may participate in visceral functions. In addition the spinal trigeminal tract contains some general somatic afferent fibers from the facial, glossopharyngeal and vagus nerves (see, p. 312), most of which occupy dorsomedial locations.

Cytoarchitecturally the spinal trigeminal nucleus has been subdivided into three parts (Olszewski, '50): (1) a *pars oralis* extending caudally to the rostral third of the inferior olivary nucleus, (2) a *pars interpolaris* extending from the pars oralis to the decussation of the pyramids, and (3) a *pars caudalis* extending as far down as the second cervical spinal segment. Elaborate physiological studies (Wall and Taub, '62) in the cat reveal that a somatotopic map of the face exists at all levels within the spinal trigeminal nucleus. Throughout the nucleus the face is represented in upside down fashion with the jaw dorsal and the forehead ventral. The pars oralis receives impulses from the head, mouth, nose and eyes, has small receptive fields, and the dominant representation is of internal structures. The pars interpolaris has small receptive fields and is related mainly to cutaneous facial regions. The pars caudalis has large receptive fields and responds to light pressure over proximal parts of the face (i.e., forehead, cheeks and region of the jaw angle). In addition to fibers of the tri-

geminal nerve and general somatic afferent fibers from other branchiomeric cranial nerves, the spinal trigeminal nucleus receives corticobulbar fibers (Brodal et al., '56; Kuypers, '58; Kuypers and Tuerk, '64; Zimmerman et al., '64). These fibers arise mainly from the frontoparietal cortex and are predominantly crossed. Physiological studies (Darian-Smith and Yokota, '66) indicate that corticobulbar fibers projecting to the pars oralis and pars caudalis mediate both inhibitory and excitatory effects. Current observations suggest that inhibitory effects are presynaptic in nature.

There is considerable clinical evidence that lesions of the spinal trigeminal tract result chiefly in loss, or diminution, of pain and thermal sense in the area innervated by the trigeminal nerve, but apparently do not affect tactile sensibility. It is probable that the nonbifurcating descending fibers mediate exclusively pain and thermal sense, while the bifurcating ones convey tactile sensibility. Hence in lesions of the spinal trigeminal tract many tactile fibers may be destroyed, but the ascending branches of these fibers still reach the principal sensory nucleus and touch remains intact. Clinically there is no doubt that pain and thermal sense are handled entirely by the spinal trigeminal tract and nucleus, while touch and two-point discrimination are in large part related to the principal sensory nucleus (Fig. 15–17). However, physiological studies (Wall and Taub, '62; Kruger and Michel, '62a) indicate that is is extremely difficult to isolate and identify neurons in the spinal trigeminal nucleus uniquely concerned with impulses related to pain. Neurons at nearly all levels of the nucleus respond to tactile stimuli (Kruger and Michel, '62).

The composition, location and relation-

brain stem at various locations, and ascend in association with the contralateral medial lemniscus. Secondary trigeminothalamic fibers from the principal sensory nucleus, conveying touch and pressure (*blue*), ascend by two separate pathways. Fibers from the ventral part of the principal sensory nucleus of N. V cross and ascend in association with the contralateral medial lemniscus. Fibers from the dorsomedial part of the same nucleus ascend uncrossed as the dorsal trigeminal tract. Both the ventral and dorsal trigeminal tracts project to the ventral posteromedial nucleus of the thalamus. The brain stem location of the ascending lateral spinothalamic tract is indicated in *black* on the *right side*. The ophthalmic (V^1), maxillary (V^2), and mandibular (V^3) divisions of the trigeminal nerve are identified. *1*, Free nerve ending; *2*, thermal receptor; *3*, Meissner's corpuscle; *4*, neuromuscular spindle; *5*, motor end plate in muscle of mastication.

ships of the spinal trigeminal tract and nucleus are of considerable diagnostic and surgical importance. It should be noted that the overlap between the cutaneous areas supplied by the three peripheral divisions of the trigeminal nerve is slight and in sharp contrast to the extensive overlap characteristic of spinal dermatomes. Neurosurgical studies (Sjöqvist, '38) have demonstrated that trigeminal tractotomy can relieve various forms of facial pain including trigeminal neuralgia (tic douloureux). The importance of this procedure is that it selectively eliminates, or greatly reduces, pain and thermal sense without impairing tactile sense. Meticulous examination of such patients (Walker, '39a; Weinberger and Grant, '42) frequently reveals that tactile sense is mildly impaired and that there is not a complete loss of any sensory modality. One notable advantage of this procedure is that corneal sensation is not abolished, and the corneal reflex is not lost (though it may not be as brisk). The fact that section of this tract caudal to the level of the obex has produced complete facial analgesia is cited as supporting the thesis that the caudal part of the nucleus is concerned chiefly with pain.

Trigeminal root fibers conveying impulses for tactile and pressure sense ascend and enter the principal sensory nucleus; some of these fibers are ascending branches of bifurcating fibers, while others are direct fibers. The *principal sensory nucleus* lies lateral to the entering trigeminal root fibers, has an ovoid configuration in transverse sections, and consists of small to medium-sized neurons with relatively large nuclei (Fig. 15–18). Caudally this nucleus merges with the pars oralis of the spinal trigeminal nucleus and the level of transition is indistinct (Fig. 15–19). Root fibers terminating in this nucleus are distributed in a manner similar to that described for the spinal trigeminal nucleus. Fibers of the ophthalmic division terminate ventrally, fibers of the maxillary division are intermediate, and fibers of the mandibular division are most dorsal (Kerr, '63). According to Wall and Taub ('62), cells of

the principal sensory nucleus have large receptive fields, show high spontaneous activity, and respond to a wide range of pressure stimuli with little adaptation.

Another source of afferent trigeminal fibers is a slender column of cells found in the lateral margin of the central gray of the upper fourth ventricle and aqueductal region which constitutes the *mesencephalic nucleus of the trigeminal nerve* (Figs. 15–18, 15–19 and 15–22). This nucleus, extending from the level of the trigeminal motor nucleus to the rostral midbrain, is composed primarily of large unipolar neurons. Careful study (Pearson, '49, '49a) of neurons in this nucleus has revealed many bipolar and multipolar cells as well, but most cells resemble those of the dorsal root ganglion. However, unlike dorsal root ganglion cells, they lie within the central nervous system, are not encapsulated, and often have more than one process. The principal processes of these cells form a slender sickle-shaped bundle, the *mesencephalic tract of the trigeminal nerve* (Figs. 15–15, 15–17, 15–19, 15–22 and A–8), which descends to the level of the trigeminal motor nucleus, provides collaterals to motor cells, and appears to emerge as part of the motor root. Cells of this nucleus commonly are regarded as afferent peripheral neurons which have been "retained" within the central nervous system, but proof that these cells arise from the neural crest in mammals is still lacking (Pearson, '49, '49a).

Afferent fibers of the mesencephalic nucleus of the trigeminal nerve convey proprioceptive impulses (pressure and kinesthesis) from the teeth, peridontium, hard palate, muscles of mastication and joint capsules (Allen, '19, '25; Pfaffmann, '39; Corbin, '40; Corbin and Harrison, '40). It appears likely that these fibers may be concerned with the mechanism which controls the force of the bite. The mesencephalic nucleus also receives afferent impulses from stretch receptors in the muscles of mastication. Action potentials can be recorded in the mesencephalic nucleus in response to stretching the masticatory muscles (Corbin and Harrison, '40; Cooper et al., '53). Scattered

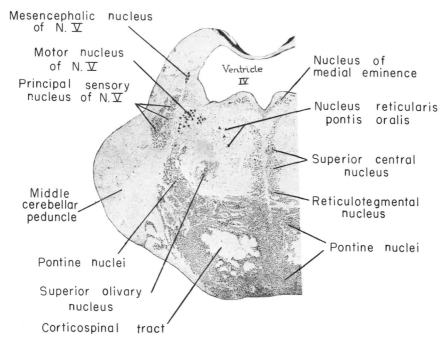

Mesencephalic nucleus
of N. Ⅴ

Motor nucleus
of N. Ⅴ

Principal sensory
nucleus of N. Ⅴ

Ventricle
Ⅳ

Nucleus of
medial eminence

Nucleus reticularis
pontis oralis

Superior central
nucleus

Reticulotegmental
nucleus

Middle
cerebellar
peduncle

Pontine nuclei

Pontine nuclei

Superior olivary
nucleus

Corticospinal tract

Fig. 15–18. Section through pons and pontine tegmentum of 1-month infant at about same level as Figure 15–15. Cresyl violet. Photograph, with cell groups schematically blocked in.

ganglion cells found along the motor root appear related to the mesencephalic nucleus and are considered to convey impulses from stretch receptors in the mylohyoid and diagastric muscles. Although most afferent fibers of the mesencephalic nucleus course peripherally with fibers of the motor root, experimental evidence (Corbin, '40) indicates that some fibers from this nucleus pass peripherally in all three divisions of the trigeminal nerve. At least one author (Peele, '61) considers some cells of the mesencephalic nucleus to be homologous to cells of the dorsal nucleus of Clarke, but some impulses relayed by this nucleus reach consciousness and must be relayed to thalamic levels.

Pearson ('49) has established that the connections of the mesencephalic nucleus are more extensive than was supposed formerly. Some fibers leave the mesencephalic tract and enter the white matter of the cerebellum, possibly connecting with the deep cerebellar nuclei. Other fibers have been traced to the roof of the cerebral aqueduct, especially to the region of the superior colliculi; still others have

been considered to go to the nuclei of N. III and N. IV, either synapsing there or continuing as root fibers in these nerves. Cells resembling those of the mesencephalic nucleus also are found scattered at the base of the cerebellum and to a smaller extent in the roof of the cerebral aqueduct.

Some authorities believe that deep sensibility of the lingual, facial, and extraocular muscles is mediated by fibers of the fifth nerve. Experimental studies (Cooper et al., '53, '53a) in the goat, an animal with numerous muscle spindles in the extraocular muscles, suggested that stretching of the extraocular muscles produces short, and delayed, latency responses in the mesencephalic nucleus. More recent studies in the lamb indicate that a localized part of the trigeminal ganglion contains cells whose afferent fibers convey impulses from muscle spindles in the extraocular muscles (Manni et al., '66). Cells, in a part of the ganglion which forms the ophthalmic branch, respond with a sustained increase in discharge rate when the extraocular muscles are stretched; the discharge ceases as soon

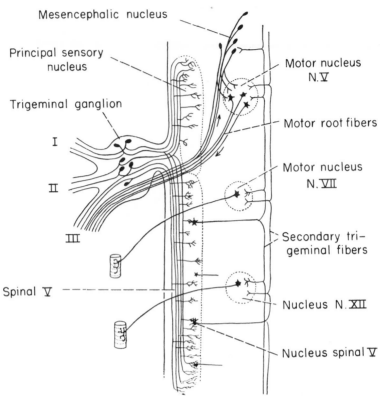

Fig. 15–19. Diagram of the trigeminal nuclei and some of the trigeminal reflex arcs. *I*, Ophthalmic division; *II*, maxillary division; *III*, mandibular division (modified from Cajal, '09).

as the stretched muscles are released. These short latency responses are abolished by section of the ophthalmic branch of the trigeminal nerve. Deep sensibility from the face also is considered to be mediated by the trigeminal nerve, but the possibility remains that this may be supplemented by facial nerve afferents. In spite of considerable research, many important questions remain concerning the afferent innervation of muscles and deep structures of the head.

The *motor nucleus of the trigeminal nerve* is an ovoid column of typical multipolar motor cells that lies medial to the principal sensory nucleus (Fig. 15–18). Its coarse efferent fibers emerge internal to the entering sensory root and pass underneath the trigeminal ganglion to become incorporated in the mandibular branch (Figs. 15–17 and 15–19). Among the terminals ending in the nucleus are collaterals from the mesencephalic root and other afferent trigeminal fibers. These

fibers furnish a two-neuron arc for reflex control of the jaw muscles. Additional secondary trigeminal fibers, both crossed and uncrossed, provide reflex control of the jaw muscles to superficial stimuli, especially from the lingual and oral mucous membrane. As in the case of other motor cranial nerve nuclei, many corticobulbar fibers do not terminate directly upon cells of the motor trigeminal nucleus but pass to reticular neurons, which in turn project to motor cells (Figs. 14–23).

Secondary Trigeminal Pathways. Secondary trigeminal pathways originate from cells in the principal sensory and spinal trigeminal nuclei. Collaterals from incoming sensory fibers, as well as axons from cells in these nuclei, provide numerous largely uncrossed fiber projections to motor nuclei of the brain stem (Fig. 15–19).

Axons from cells within the spinal trigeminal nucleus pass ventromedially in the reticular formation, cross the median raphe, and enter the contralateral medial lemniscus (Smyth, '39; Walker, '39, '42; Nauta and Kuypers, '58; Carpenter and Hanna, '61). Some efferent fibers from the spinal trigeminal nucleus pass into the parvicellular part of the reticular formation, and others arborize about cells of the nucleus reticularis gigantocellularis; a moderate number of fibers project to the cerebellum via the inferior cerebellar peduncle. The principal secondary trigeminal fibers from this nucleus ascend in the brain stem in close association with the contralateral medial lemniscus and terminate in a selective way about cells of the ventral posteromedial (VPM) nucleus of the thalamus. Axons of cells in the spinal trigeminal nucleus that cross and ascend with the contralateral medial lemniscus form the *ventral trigeminal tract* (*ventral trigeminothalamic tract*). It should be recalled that the spinal trigeminal tract and nucleus also relay pain and thermal sensations from the somatic afferent fibers of the facial, glossopharyngeal, and vagus nerves.

The relationship of the spinal trigeminal tract and nucleus to the spinothalamic tracts in the brain stem should be noted in Figure 15–17. The location of the latter tract is represented in *solid black* on the right side at each level. Vascular lesions in the lower medulla involving structures in the dorsolateral area frequently interrupt these pathways and produce a syndrome characterized by: (1) loss of pain and thermal sense over the face ipsilaterally, and (2) loss of pain and thermal sense, and impairment of tactile sensation over the contralateral half of the body. The involvement of other structures in this region produces additional neurological deficits that confirm the location of the lesion (see page 334).

Trigeminal root fibers conveying impulses for tactile sense and pressure ascend without bifurcating and terminate upon cells of the principal sensory nucleus (Fig. 15–19). Some tactile impulses are mediated by bifurcating fibers, one branch of which descends in the spinal trigeminal tract. Secondary trigeminal fibers originating from the principal sensory nucleus are both crossed and uncrossed. Cells in the dorsomedial part of the nucleus give rise to a small bundle of uncrossed fibers which ascends to ipsilateral thalamic nuclei (Torvik, '57; Carpenter, '57a). These uncrossed fibers constituting the *dorsal trigeminal tract* (von Economo, '11; Winkler, '21; Papez and Rundles, '37; Walker, '39; Verhaart, '54) ascend in the dorsal pontine tegmentum; at mesencephalic levels they occupy a position near the periaqueductal gray (Fig. 15–17). At the level of the fasciculus retroflexus the fibers make a ventrolateral bend and enter the medial part of the ventral posteromedial (VPM) nucleus of the thalamus. Because afferent fibers terminating in the dorsal part of the principal sensory nucleus are associated primarily with the mandibular division (Kerr, '63), it has been suggested that fibers of the dorsal trigeminal tract may subserve a unique function.

Neurons in the ventral part of the principal sensory nucleus of N. V give rise to a larger crossed bundle of trigeminothalamic fibers which ascends in association with the contralateral medial lemniscus (Wallenberg, '05; Winkler, '21; Papez and Rundles, '37; Walker, '39; Russell, '54; Torvik, '57). These crossed secondary trigeminal fibers also terminate in the ventral posteromedial (VPM) nucleus of the thalamus.

As previously mentioned the mesencephalic nucleus of the trigeminal nerve is anomalous in that the primary sensory neurons are found in this brain stem nucleus rather than in the trigeminal ganglion. While there is convincing evidence that fibers from this nucleus convey impulses from pressure, joint and stretch receptors, the pathway by which these impulses are transmitted centrally remains obscure. It has been suggested that collateral fibers passing to the principal sensory nucleus might relay conscious impulses from pressure and joint receptors (Brodal, '59); it is possible that impulses conveying these sensory modalities may ascend in the dorsal trigeminal tract (Crosby et al., '62). Impulses from stretch receptors probably are conveyed to the cerebellum via direct trigeminocerebellar fibers (Woodburne, '36; Pearson, '49).

The numerous secondary *reflex* fibers arising from the terminal nuclei of N. V ascend and descend in the dorsolateral part of the reticular formation, giving off terminals or collaterals to various motor nuclei (Fig. 15–19). They are largely uncrossed. These fibers provide connections for many reflexes initiated by stimulation of the skin of the face, the oral and nasal mucous membranes, and muscles, tendons, and bones of the jaw and face. Among the more important of these reflexes, and the motor nuclei to which the secondary fibers go, are: (1) the *corneal reflex*, to the motor nucleus of N. VII, (2) the *lacrimal* or *tearing* reflex, to the superior salivatory nucleus of N. VII, (3) *sneezing*, to the nucleus of N. XII, the nucleus ambiguus, and associated respiratory nuclei of the cord, i.e., phrenic, intercostal, and others, (4) *vomiting*, to the dorsal motor nucleus of N. X, the nucleus ambiguus, and other nuclei, including the motor nucleus of N. V, (5) *salivary reflexes*, to the salivatory nuclei of Nn. VII and IX, and (6) *oculocardiac* reflex (slowing of the heart elicited by pressure on the eyeball), to the dorsal motor nucleus of N. X. Secondary fibers also go to the hypoglossal nucleus for reflex tongue movements following stimulation of the tongue and oral mucous membrane. To effect the corneal reflex, impulses from the cornea pass to the facial nuclei of both sides through crossed and uncrossed secondary trigeminal fibers; stimulation of one cornea thus produces blinking and closure of both eyes (consensual reflex). In injury of the trigeminal nerve (ophthalmic branch), there is an absence of reflex eye closure on both sides when the involved cornea is stimulated; but in lesions of the facial nerve, only the direct (ipsilateral) reflex is lost since the arc for the consensual (contralateral) reflex is still intact.

ISTHMUS OF THE HINDBRAIN

The narrow portion of the hindbrain situated rostral to the cerebellum and merging with the midbrain is known as the *isthmus rhombencephali*. The most cephalic levels of this region, near the junction with the midbrain, demonstrate characteristic features (Figs. 15–20, 15–21 and A–9). As in more caudal sections three regions are distinguishable, namely, a roof, the tegmentum, and a ventral pontine portion. The roof consists of a thin white membrane, the *superior medullary velum*, which covers the most superior portion of the fourth ventricle. The fourth ventricle is greatly reduced in size and begins to resemble the *cerebral aqueduct* of the midbrain. The ventricle is bounded ventrally and laterally by the central gray matter. The root fibers of the *trochlear nerve* (N. IV) decussate in the superior medullary velum. They originate from nuclei which lie more rostrally in the ventral part of the central gray. The fibers arch dorsally and somewhat caudally around the fourth ventricle, decussate in the roof, and emerge caudal to the inferior colliculus (Fig. 14–2). Only the decussation is seen at this level. This nerve innervates the superior oblique muscle of the eye.

The ventral portion of the pons is considerably larger than the tegmental portion (Figs. A–26 and A–27). The pontine nuclei are extensive, and the pyramidal and corticopontine tracts are broken up into numerous bundles.

In the tegmentum the mesencephalic tract of the trigeminal nerve forms a slender, sickle-shaped bundle in the lateral part of the central gray (Fig. 15–20). Mingled with it may be seen the oval cells of the mesencephalic nucleus, and ventral to this is the relatively large *locus ceruleus* (*nucleus pigmentosus pontis*) that is characteristic of the uppermost pontine levels. This structure consists of a considerable aggregation of closely packed pigmented cells appearing near the superior end of the principal sensory nucleus of N. V and extends some distance into the midbrain. It is composed of medium-sized polygonal cells containing melanin pigment. In spite of its large size, the significance of this pigmented nucleus is not known. It is believed by some that the nucleus is intimately re-

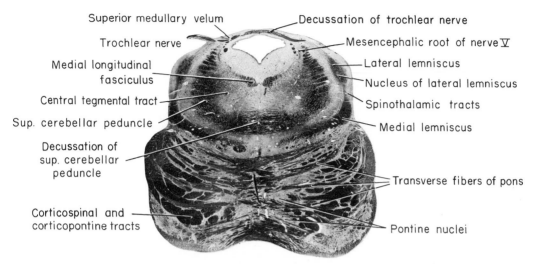

Superior medullary velum — Decussation of trochlear nerve

Trochlear nerve — Mesencephalic root of nerve Ⅴ

Medial longitudinal fasciculus — Lateral lemniscus

— Nucleus of lateral lemniscus

Central tegmental tract — Spinothalamic tracts

Sup. cerebellar peduncle — Medial lemniscus

Decussation of sup. cerebellar peduncle

— Transverse fibers of pons

Corticospinal and corticopontine tracts

— Pontine nuclei

Fig. 15–20. Section of the isthmus of an adult brain at the level of the decussation and exit of the trochlear nerve. Weigert's myelin stain. Photograph.

lated to the trigeminal nuclei, either receiving afferent fibers from, or contributing fibers to, the motor root. Most of its axons combine to form a tract, the *bundle of Probst*, which descends in the dorsolateral part of the reticular formation and may make connections with the nucleus intercalatus or the dorsal motor nucleus of the vagus. Certain studies (Johnson and Russell, '52; Baxter and Olszewski, '55) suggest that the nucleus may be associated functionally with the pontine pneumotaxic center.

The lateral lemniscus lies near the surface in the lateral part of the tegmentum, forming the major part of the external structure known as the *trigonum lemnisci*. Groups of cells among its fibers constitute the *nucleus of the lateral lemniscus*, one of several intercalated nuclei in the auditory pathway (Figs. 15–9, 15–20 and 15–21). The medial lemniscus is a flattened band extending transversely in the lateroventral part of the tegmentum, and the spinothalamic tract is in its usual position between the two lemnisci. Included in the medial lemniscus and spinothalamic tracts are the secondary trigeminal, vagal and glossopharyngeal fibers. The dorsal trigeminal tract ascends in the dorsal part of the reticular formation, lateral to the medial longitudinal fasciculus (Fig.

15–17). All these secondary cranial nerve tracts carry tactile, proprioceptive, pain, and temperature sensations from the head and mouth, and possibly visceral sensibility. Thus at this level the principal afferent suprasegmental paths form a peripheral shell of fibers enclosing the tegmentum, and representing general body and head sensibility as well as audition.

The Superior Cerebellar Peduncle has entered the tegmentum, where it forms a large crescent-shaped bundle in the lateral part of the reticular formation. The superior cerebellar peduncle, which arises from the dentate, emboliform, and globose nuclei, forms the most important efferent fiber system of the cerebellum. Emerging from the cerebellum, it first forms the dorsolateral wall of the fourth ventricle, then dips into the pontine tegmentum, and in the caudal midbrain, undergoes a complete decussation (Figs. 15–20, 16–2 and 17–14). Many of its fibers end in the red nucleus; others continue directly to the ventral lateral nucleus of the thalamus (Figs. 17–14 and 19–4). A relatively small number of fibers of the superior cerebellar peduncle descend lateral to the superior central nucleus to terminate in the reticulotegmental nucleus in the upper pons, and the paramedian reticular nuclei in the medulla

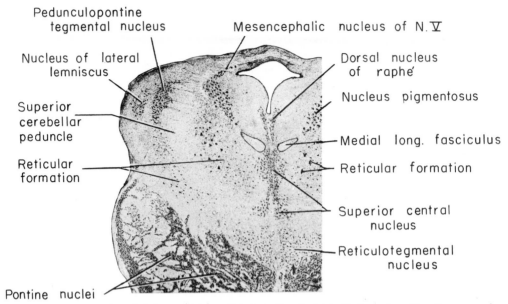

Fig. 15–21. Section through isthmus of 3-month infant. Cresyl violet. Photograph, with cell groups schematically blocked in.

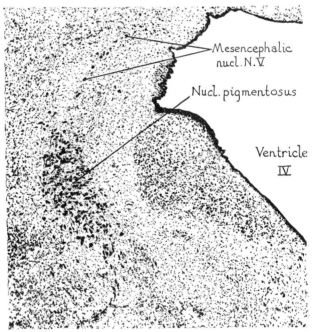

Fig. 15–22. Portion of pontine tegmentum in oral region of pons (isthmus). Twelve-week infant. Nissl stain. Photograph.

(Carpenter and Nova, '60). These cerebelloreticular fibers form part of a cerebelloreticular feedback pathway, since these reticular nuclei project fibers to parts of the cerebellum (Fig. 17–14).

The central tegmental tract is large and occupies a truly central position. The anterior spinocerebellar tract now lies on the surface, external to the superior cerebellar peduncle, and its fibers appear to be cut longitudinally (Fig. 17–18). This tract has an aberrant course to the cerebellum. It ascends in the lateral part of the reticular formation to the uppermost limit of the pons, and at this point turns caudally, forming a loop on the external surface of the superior cerebellar peduncle (Figs. 3–7, 13–15 and 15–16). Then, accompanying the latter, but in a reverse direction, it descends in the superior medullary velum to terminate in the vermis of the anterior lobe of the cerebellum. Only the turn or bend of the fibers is seen at this level.

The medial longitudinal fasciculus and tectospinal tract are in their usual positions. The rubrospinal tract has shifted to a more medial position, lying dorsal to the medial lemniscus. It is more easily distinguished as a definite tract in the caudal portions of the midbrain near its origin from the red nucleus (Fig. 13–22).

The cell groups of the reticular formation are most extensive near the raphe (Fig. 15–21). Most ventral in this region is the *reticulotegmental nucleus*, already described; it is considered to be a tegmental extension of the pontine nuclei (Jacobson, '09). Dorsal to these nuclei, but near the median raphe, is the *superior central nucleus*, a large aggregation of closely packed small and medium-sized cells. On each side of the midline, dorsal to the medial longitudinal fasciculus, is the *dorsal nucleus of the raphe*, a narrow band of cells which merges above with the larger and more complex *dorsal tegmental nucleus* of the midbrain (Fig. 16–3).

The main body of the reticular formation is divided into medial and lateral portions by the superior cerebellar peduncle. In the lateral part a dense collection of medium-sized cells constitutes the *pedunculopontine tegmental nucleus*, which is closely applied to the external surface of the superior cerebellar peduncle. Compact and diffuse portions of this nucleus extend rostrally into the caudal midbrain (Olszewski and Baxter, '54; Fig. 16–3). This nucleus receives cortical projections from the precentral gyrus (Kuypers and Lawrence, '67) and descending fibers from the globus pallidus (Nauta and Mehler, '66; Carpenter and Strominger, '67). Elsewhere the reticular formation appears diffusely organized, though scattered within it, especially in its medial portion, are large multipolar cells (Fig. 15–21).

At this point the student will find it instructive to review the blood supply of the medulla and pons (Chapter 4, p. 74). Being familiar with the internal organization of the hindbrain and the connections of the cranial nerves, should give the reader a better appreciation of the neurological syndromes which follow sudden occlusion of arteries of the vertebro-basilar system. Other lower brain stem lesions associated with syringobulbia, demyelinating diseases, and tumors frequently begin in localized regions and produce specific neurological signs and symptoms. Neurological disturbances associated with these conditions usually develop slowly and generally are progressive.

CHAPTER 16

The Mesencephalon

The mesencephalon, or midbrain, the smallest and least differentiated division of the brain stem, consists of three parts: (1) the *tectum* or quadrigeminal plate, dorsal to the cerebral aqueduct, (2) the massive *crura cerebri* on the ventrolateral surfaces, and (3) the *tegmentum*, centrally, representing the rostral continuation of the pontine tegmentum. The cerebral aqueduct, surrounded by the central gray substance (i.e., periaqueductal gray) separates the tectum from the tegmentum (Fig. 16–1) The term *cerebral peduncle*, according to the accepted nomenclature, denotes one half of the midbrain, excluding the tectum. The cerebral peduncle consists of two parts: (1) a dorsal part, the tegmentum, and (2) a ventral part, the crus cerebri. These two parts of the cerebral peduncle are separated from each other by a large pigmented nuclear mass, the *substantia nigra* (Fig. A–27). The midbrain contains the nuclei of the trochlear and oculomotor nerves and important neural structures concerned with ocular reflexes and eye movements. Relay nuclei constituting important parts of the auditory and visual systems are prominent, along with pathways interrelating higher and lower portions of the neuraxis. The principal nuclear masses and fiber pathways can be observed and studied at two typical levels, namely, the levels of the inferior and superior colliculi. The latter level is shown diagramatically in Figure 16–1.

INFERIOR COLLICULAR LEVEL

Sections of the midbrain at the level of the inferior colliculus (Figs. 16–2 and 16–3) show several conspicuous changes when compared with transverse sections at isthmus levels (Figs. 15–20, A–9 and A–10). Comparison of these brain stem levels reveals the following: (1) the narrow rostral part of the fourth ventricle has become the cerebral aqueduct, (2) the superior medullary velum, containing the decussating fibers of the trochlear nerves, is replaced by the inferior colliculi, (3) fibers of the superior cerebellar peduncles have migrated ventromedially to decussate (Figs. 16–2 and A–10), and (4) the ventral portion of the pons is reduced in size and has become organized into two massive groups of fibers, the crura cerebri (Fig. A–10). In some sections the pigmented nuclei of the substantia nigra are present dorsal to the crura cerebri (Fig. 16–3).

The mesencephalic tract and nucleus of N. V., locus ceruleus (nucleus pigmentosus), medial lemniscus, spinothalamic tract, and spinotectal tract are in the same positions as in previous sections (Figs. 16–2 and 16–3). Fibers of the lateral lemniscus, located near the surface in the lateral part of the tegmentum at isthmus levels (Figs. 15–20 and A–9) have moved dorsally at rostral levels to enter the inferior colliculus; part of these fibers envelop the inferior colliculus and form its capsule. While most fibers of the lateral lemniscus terminate in the inferior colliculus, a

376

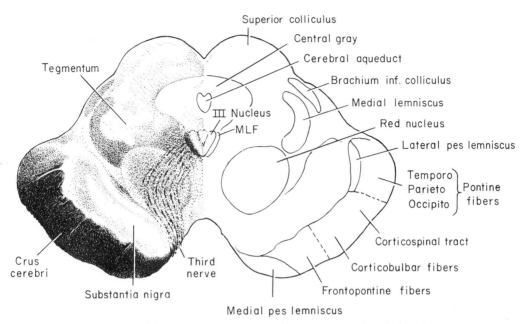

Fig. 16–1. Schematic transverse section through upper portion of midbrain.

small number bypass it and project to the medial geniculate body. Fibers arising from the inferior colliculus and direct fibers of the lateral lemniscus pass to the medial geniculate body via the *brachium* of the *inferior colliculus*. The brachium of the inferior colliculus thus constitutes the fiber bundle by which auditory impulses are conveyed from the midbrain to their specific relay nucleus in the thalamus. At isthmus levels fibers of the superior cerebellar peduncle form a large compact bundle medial to the lateral lemniscus (Fig. 15–20). Beginning at the isthmus and continuing through the caudal midbrain, fibers of this peduncle gradually shift ventromedially and undergo a complete decussation in the ventral tegmentum. As fibers of the superior cerebellar peduncle migrate ventromedially towards their decussation, fibers of this bundle are intermingled with those of the dorsal trigeminal and central tegmental tracts (Fig. A–28). For this reason it is difficult to distinguish these tracts in normal Weigert preparations at the level of the inferior colliculus, even though these tracts maintain essentially the same positions as at more caudal levels. Fibers of the rubrospinal tract lie ventral to the decussation of the

superior cerebellar peduncles and relatively close to the midline (Fig. 16–2). In their caudal descent fibers of this tract move laterally along the dorsal margin of the medial lemniscus.

The Trochlear Nerve

The nucleus of the trochlear nerve is a small compact cell group in the ventral part of the central gray that appears to indent the dorsal surface of the medial longitudinal fasciculus (Fig. 16–3). The nucleus consists of a column of typical somatic motor cells that in essence constitute a small caudal appendage to the oculomotor nuclear complex. Root fibers emerging from the nucleus curve dorsolaterally and caudally in the outer margin of the central gray and reach the superior medullary velum, where they decussate completely and exit from the brain stem (Figs. 15–20 and A–9). Peripherally the slender nerve root curves around the lateral surface of the brain stem, passes between the superior cerebellar and posterior cerebral arteries, and enters the cavernous sinus. This cranial nerve innervates the superior oblique muscle that serves to: (1) intort the eye when abducted,

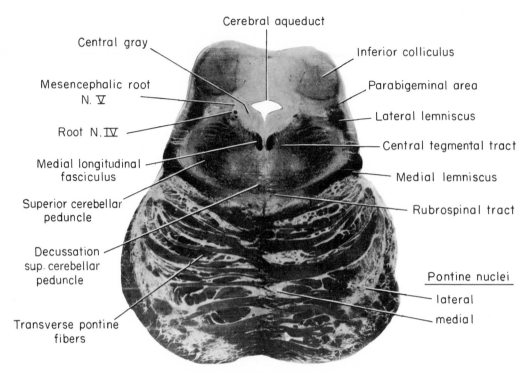

FIG. 16–2. Transverse section of the adult midbrain through the inferior colliculus. Large fascicles of corticospinal and corticopontine fibers (unlabeled), cut in cross section, are located among the bundles of transverse pontine fibers. Photograph. Weigert's myelin stain.

and (2) depress the eye when adducted. Lesions involving the trochlear nerve alone are unusual and detection of resulting disturbances of extraocular movement is difficult. Diplopia resulting from such a nerve lesion is vertical and maximal on attempted downward gaze to the opposite side. Patients with trochlear nerve lesions complain especially of difficulty in walking downstairs. Tilting of the head to the opposite side, seen in some patients with trochlear nerve lesions, is a posture which compensates for the weakness of ocular intortion on the lesion side (Cogan, '56).

The Inferior Colliculi. Each inferior colliculus consists of an ovoid cellular mass, the *nucleus of the inferior colliculus*, and a thin cellular layer, or cortex, on the surface external and medial to the nucleus (Fig. 16–3). The nucleus is composed of small and medium-sized cells, the latter sending their axons into the brachium of the inferior colliculus. It receives afferent fibers from the lateral lemniscus, from the colliculus of the opposite side, and

from the medial geniculate body via the inferior brachium (Fig. 15–9). Many fibers of the lateral lemniscus, coming mainly from the superior olive and the nucleus of the lateral lemniscus, terminate directly in the colliculus, some crossing to the colliculus of the opposite side. Other lemniscal fibers, probably from the dorsal cochlear nucleus, send collaterals to the colliculus; the fibers themselves project to the medial geniculate body.

Efferent fibers arising from the inferior colliculus project largely to the small-celled portion of the medial geniculate body via the brachium of the inferior colliculus. Other collicular fibers pass to the opposite inferior colliculus, to the superior colliculus, or they form descending pathways which project to the nuclei of the lateral lemniscus and other relay nuclei in the auditory system (Rasmussen, '60). The exact location of all of the descending fibers has not been ascertained. Evidence indicates that relatively few, if any, tectospinal fibers originate in the in-

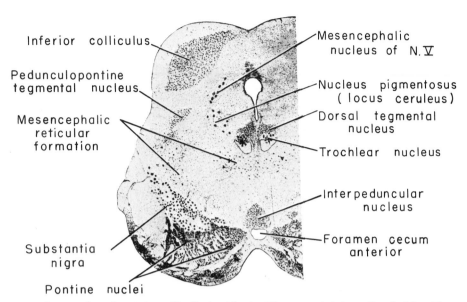

Inferior colliculus

Pedunculopontine tegmental nucleus

Mesencephalic reticular formation

Substantia nigra

Pontine nuclei

Mesencephalic nucleus of N. V

Nucleus pigmentosus (locus ceruleus)

Dorsal tegmental nucleus

Trochlear nucleus

Interpeduncular nucleus

Foramen cecum anterior

FIG. 16-3. Section through inferior colliculi of midbrain. Three-month infant. Cresyl violet. Photograph, with schematic representation of main cell groups.

ferior colliculus (Woollard and Harpman, '40).

The inferior colliculi are thus both relay stations in the auditory pathway and reflex acoustic centers. They are phylogenetically newer parts of the brain stem related primarily to the cochlear apparatus and to the projection of auditory impulses to higher levels of the neuraxis.

Physiological studies (Rose et al., '63) in the cat indicate that a definite tonotopic localization is present in the inferior colliculus. Neurons in the central nucleus of the inferior colliculus are arranged in an orderly manner with respect to frequencies. Advancement of an electrode from its point of penetration (dorsal, caudal and lateral) in a ventral, oral and medial direction consistently gives a sequence of frequencies from low to high in the central nucleus. In the lateral part of the inferior colliculus near its capsule frequencies follow a sequence from high to low, the reverse of that seen in the central nucleus. Other data (Rose et al., '66) have demonstrated that there are neurons in the inferior colliculus whose response is a sensitive function of interaural time relationships. Since it is well known that time and sound intensity cues are utilized for localization of sound sources, these data

suggest that the inferior colliculus may play a significant role in this function.

Ventrolateral to the inferior colliculus is a fairly well-defined zone known as the *parabigeminal area*, lying between the lateral lemniscus and the periphery (Fig. 16-2). It is composed mainly of obliquely, or transversely running fibers, among which are scattered cells or groups of cells constituting the *parabigeminal nucleus*. Its connections are obscure, but apparently some fibers from the nucleus go to the lateral nuclei of the pons. The more numerous fibers gathered at the lateral periphery of the area are regarded by some as corticopontine fibers from the occipital cortex.

Tegmental and Interpeduncular Nuclei. The narrow aqueduct, somewhat triangular in section, is surrounded by a broad layer of central gray substance that contains numerous diffusely grouped cells. In the rapheal region several nuclei are present at this level (Fig. 16-3). The dorsal nucleus of the raphe has expanded into the *dorsal tegmental nucleus*, composed of many small and some larger cells. It lies in the central gray dorsal to the trochlear nucleus. Immediately ventral to the medial longitudinal fasciculus, the cells near the raphe constitute the *ventral* *tegmental nucleus*, which appears to be a continuation of the superior central nucleus of the pons.

In the rapheal region of the ventral tegmentum is the *interpeduncular nucleus*, a collection of medium-sized, multipolar, slightly pigmented cells (Fig. 16–3). This nucleus, situated immediately dorsal to the interpeduncular fossa, is prominent in most mammals, but comparatively small in man. Fibers from the habenular nucleus project to the interpeduncular nucleus via the fasciculus retroflexus (Fig. 18–5 and 18–6); some fibers in this bundle bypass the interpeduncular nucleus and are distributed to the superior central nucleus, the dorsal tegmental nucleus and caudal regions of the central gray (Nauta, '58). The dorsal tegmental nucleus also receives fibers from the interpeduncular nucleus and from the mammillary bodies (via the mammillotegmental tract). The dorsal tegmental nucleus appears intimately related to the *dorsal longitudinal fasciculus* (of Schütz), a small but complex pathway in the ventromedial part of the central gray. Although the prevailing direction of conduction appears to be ascending in this bundle, it contains some descending elements, but few of these reach medullary levels. The pathways described above constitute part of the complex system by which impulses related to the limbic system are projected to midbrain levels. These impulses are thought to be concerned primarily with visceral functions.

Corticofugal fibers (corticospinal, corticopontine, and corticobulbar) on the ventral surface of the brain stem undergo a rearrangement and are beginning to form the *crus cerebri* (Fig. 16–3). At slightly higher levels these fibers are separated from the tegmentum by a mass of gray matter, the *substantia nigra* (Figs. 16–4, A–10 and A–11).

SUPERIOR COLLICULAR LEVEL

Sections through the rostral half of the midbrain show the following principal features: (1) the tectum is formed by the superior colliculi, (2) the tegmentum contains the oculomotor nuclei, the red nuclei and the midbrain reticular formation, and (3) the crura cerebri, containing concentrated bundles of pallial efferent fibers, form the most ventral part, and are separated from the tegmentum by the substantia nigra (Figs. 16–1, 16–4, and A–11).

The cerebral aqueduct is surrounded by a broad band of central gray which has a gelatinous appearance in Weigert-stained preparations. Near the ventral border of the central gray in a V-shaped trough is the oculomotor nuclear complex. This nuclear complex appears on both sides of the median raphe between the diverging fascicles of the medial longitudinal fasciculi. The oculomotor complex is composed of several nuclear groups, not all of which can be seen in any one section. In sections through the caudal part of the oculomotor nucleus, two large lateral cell columns can be seen along the medial borders of the medial longitudinal fasciculi, as well as a midline wedge-shaped group of cells known as the *caudal central nucleus* (Figs. 16–4 and A–11). At more rostral levels the lateral cell column becomes more extensive, while the caudal midline nuclear group disappears. In the rostral part of the nuclear complex two small cell groups appear dorsomedial to the lateral cell columns; these groups constitute the visceral nuclei of the complex, the *nuclei of Edinger-Westphal*. Root fibers of the oculomotor nerve issue from the ventrolateral border of the nucleus, course through and around the red nucleus, and converge medially to exit from the brain stem in the interpeduncular fossa (Figs. 16–4 and A–11). The oculomotor nucleus and nerve are discussed on pages 384–388.

At this level (Fig. 16–4) fibers of the superior cerebellar peduncle have decussated completely. In some caudal sections crossed fibers of this peduncle form a large oval bundle in the area immediately caudal to the red nucleus (Figs. A–10 and A–26). At more rostral levels these fibers partially traverse and terminate in the red nucleus, and many form a capsule about this nucleus. Fibers passing through the red nucleus project upon thalamic nuclei.

The lateral lemniscus, which has ter-

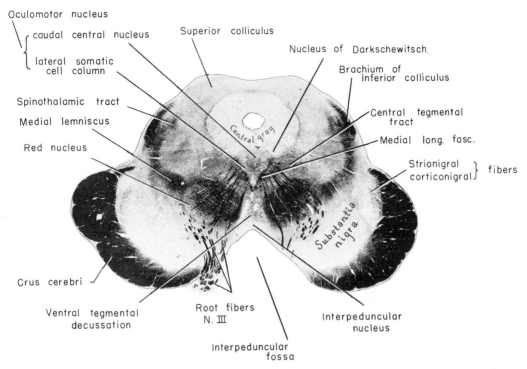

Oculomotor nucleus

caudal central nucleus

lateral somatic cell column

Superior colliculus

Nucleus of Darkschewitsch.

Brachium of inferior colliculus

Spinothalamic tract

Medial lemniscus

Red nucleus

Central gray

Central tegmental tract

Medial long. fasc.

Strionigral ⎱ fibers
corticonigral⎰

Substantia nigra

Crus cerebri

Ventral tegmental decussation

Root fibers N. III

Interpeduncular nucleus

Interpeduncular fossa

FIG. 16–4. Transverse section of adult midbrain through exit of Nerve III. Weigert's myelin stain. Photograph.

minated in the inferior colliculus, now is replaced by the brachium of the inferior colliculus, which lies on the lateral surface of the tegmentum. The brachium of the inferior colliculus is composed mainly of fibers from the inferior colliculus, which terminate in the medial geniculate body (Fig. 15–9). Axons from cells of this nucleus constitute the last relay of the cochlear path to the temporal cortex.

The medial lemniscus has been displaced laterally by the superior cerebellar peduncle and the red nucleus; it appears now as a curved bundle lying above the substantia nigra and extending dorsally near the lateral border of the tegmentum (Figs. 16–1 and 16–4). The lateral spinothalamic tract is distinguishable as a small bundle close to the dorsal tip of the medial lemniscus, with which it practically fuses. At this level ascending sensory tracts from spinal cord and medulla are in close continuity (Figs. 13–12, 13–13 and 15–17). Spinotectal fibers, which run close to the spinothalamic tracts, detach

themselves in this region and enter the superior colliculus (Figs. 3–7 and 13–12).

The medial longitudinal fasciculus at the level of the superior colliculus consists predominantly of ascending secondary vestibular fibers which project to nuclear subdivisions of the oculomotor complex. In transverse sections of the midbrain the fasciculi diverge slightly as its fibers pass along the lateral borders of the oculomotor nuclear complex. There is a diminution in the size of these fasciculi at successively rostral levels through the upper midbrain; these fasciculi disappear completely in the junctional region between the midbrain and diencephalon.

Superior Colliculi and Pretectal Area. The superior colliculi are two flattened eminences which form the rostral half of the tectum. In submammalian vertebrates the optic tectum, a structure homologous with the mammalian superior colliculus, has a complex laminated structure resembling that of the cerebral cortex and it is a primary way station in the optic tract.

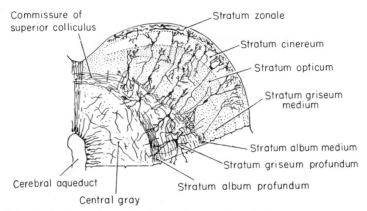

FIG. 16–5. Cellular lamination and organization of the superior colliculus based upon reconstruction from Golgi preparations taken from an 8-month human fetus.

Beginning with reptiles, the importance of the superior colliculus diminishes progressively as an increasing number of optic fibers establish more extensive connections with the thalamus and cortex. In man these structures have become greatly reduced in size and serve primarily as reflex centers concerned with eye movements. In addition the superior colliculi may receive fibers conveying general somatic sensibility, especially painful sensations.

Each colliculus still shows in a rudimentary form the complex laminated structure found in lower forms and consists of several alternating layers of gray and white matter (Figs. 13–22, 16–5 and 16–6). These layers, proceeding from the external surface inward, are: (1) an outer, mainly fibrous layer, the *stratum zonale*, (2) the *stratum cinereum*, or superficial gray layer, (3) the *stratum opticum*, or superficial white layer, and (4) the remaining layers, called collectively the *stratum lemnisci*, which may be subdivided into middle gray and white layers and deep gray and white layers (Figs. 16–5 and 16–6). The stratum zonale is composed of fine nerve fibers arising mainly from the occipital cortex and entering through the brachium of the superior colliculus. Among the fibers are small, mostly horizontal cells with tangentially or centrally directed axons. The stratum cinereum consists of radially arranged cells whose dendrites pass peripherally and whose axons project inward. The

larger cells lie deepest. The corticotectal fibers, mentioned above, and most of the optic fibers terminate in this layer. The stratum opticum is composed of optic fibers from the retina and the lateral geniculate body. These fibers enter through the brachium of the superior colliculus and terminate mainly in the stratum cinereum; some fibers, however, go to deeper layers of the colliculus. Among these fibers are scattered cells whose axons pass into the next layer. The stratum lemnisci receive spinotectal fibers (Mehler et al., '60) and some fibers from the lateral lemniscus and the inferior colliculus. The stratum lemnisci contain many medium-sized and large stellate cells.

Thus, the superior colliculus receives afferent fibers from the pallium, the lateral geniculate body, and the retina which terminate in the superficial layers. Spinotectal and other afferent fibers end in the deeper layers. Efferent fibers from the superior colliculus arise from large and medium-sized cells in deeper layers. *Tectoreticular fibers* are projected bilaterally into the dorsal parts of the mesencephalic reticular formation, though ipsilateral fibers are more abundant. Axons from some of the large cells sweep ventromedially around the central gray, decussate completely in the dorsal tegmental decussation, and are distributed to nuclei in the pontine and medullary reticular formation near the midline. Although some of

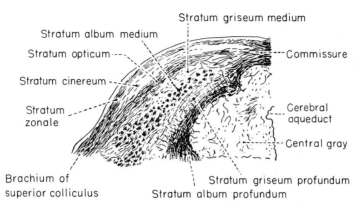

Stratum griseum medium

Stratum album medium

Stratum opticum

Commissure

Stratum cinereum

Stratum
zonale

Cerebral
aqueduct

Central gray

Brachium of
superior colliculus

Stratum griseum profundum

Stratum album profundum

Fig. 16-6. Drawing of the myelinated fiber structure of the adult superior colliculus based upon Weigert-stained sections.

these fibers project into the immediate vicinity of the nucleus of Darkschewitsch and the interstitial nucleus of Cajal, few, if any, enter the oculomotor nuclear complex (Papez and Freeman, '30; Rasmussen, '36; Marburg and Warner, '47; Szentágothai, '50). Crossed descending fibers from the superior colliculus (referred to in the older literature as the predorsal bundle) become incorporated in the medial longitudinal fasciculus at medullary levels and continue caudally as the *tectospinal tract* (Fig. 13–22). A prominent, compact bundle of uncrossed *tectopontine fibers* (Altman and Carpenter, '61) passes caudally beneath the inferior colliculus to terminate in the dorsolateral pontine nuclei. Experimental studies (Jefferson, '58) have demonstrated that stimulation of the superior colliculus in the cat provokes a typical EEG arousal response (see p. 398), suggesting that visual activation of the cerebral cortex may be mediated by tectoreticular fiber systems. Available data suggest that the tectopontine fibers may relay optic impulses to the cerebellum as described physiologically by Snider ('50). Experimental evidence (Altman and Carpenter, '61) also has demonstrated that tectofugal fibers project to parts of the lateral geniculate body (ventral part), the medial geniculate body, the pretectum, and the most caudal portions of the pulvinar.

Electrical stimulation of the superior colliculus results in contralateral conjugate deviation of the eyes followed by turning of the head (Faulkner and Hyde, '58). Studies of the influence of barbiturate anesthesia upon these responses suggest that this coordinating mechanism involves the functional integrity of the interneurons of the brain stem reticular formation. Vertical eye movements, particularly upward ones, are said to be evoked by stimulation of the superior colliculus, indicating that this colliculus may serve as a "center for vertical gaze" (Riley, '30; Crosby and Henderson, '48).

Recent studies (Sprague and Meikle, '65) in the cat indicate that unilateral lesions of the superior colliculus produce: (1) relative neglect of stimuli in the contralateral visual field, (2) ipsiversive forced circling, and (3) heightened responses to stimuli in the ipsilateral visual field. These disturbances were not associated with changes in pupillary size or accommodation. Analysis of these disturbances suggested that contralateral visual neglect was associated with involvement of the brachium of the superior colliculus and interruption of tectothalamic projections, while motor disturbances resulted from interruption of tectospinal fibers.

Immediately rostral to the superior colliculus, in the region of the junction of midbrain and thalamus, is the *pretectal area*, which usually is considered a part of the mesencephalon (Figs. 18–4 and A–12). This area, composed of several indistinct groups of small and large cells, re-

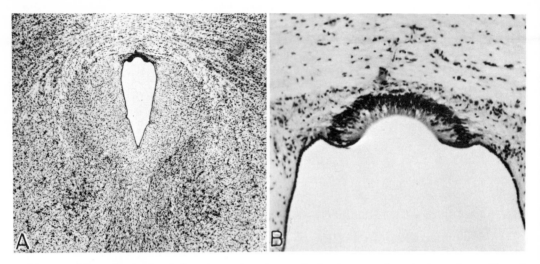

FIG. 16–7. Photomicrographs of the subcommissural organ in the rhesus monkey. *A*, shows the position of the structure in the roof of the aqueduct beneath the posterior commissure. *B*, contrasts the tall columnar cells of the subcommissural organ with the cells of the ependyma. Nissl stain, ×16, ×100.

ceives fibers from the optic tract, the lateral geniculate body, and the posterior parietal cortex (Clark, '32), and sends fibers to the mesencephalic tegmentum. Ranson and Magoun ('33) have demonstrated that the pretectal area, and not the superior colliculus, is the midbrain center for the pupillary light reflex.

The region of transition from midbrain to diencephalon is marked dorsally by the *posterior commissure*. The posterior commissure lies immediately rostral to the superior colliculus at the place where the cerebral aqueduct becomes the third ventricle (Figs. 18–1 and 18–4). Although the posterior commissure is a fairly good sized bundle and appears to contain several different fiber components, its composition is understood poorly. The posterior commissure is considered to contain: (1) fibers from the pretectal nuclei, (2) fibers from the nucleus of the posterior commissure (Fig. 16–11), (3) commissural fibers interconnecting the superior colliculi (Fig. 18–3), and (4) possibly fibers from the interstitial nucleus, the nucleus of Darkschewitsch and the habenular nuclei (Figs. 16–11 and 18–5). Fibers from the pretectal nuclei cross in the posterior commissure and pass to the contralateral Edinger-Westphal nucleus; these fibers convey impulses involved in the pupillary light reflex.

The ependyma of the cerebral aqueduct immediately beneath the posterior commissure is modified to form a special plate of cells, the *subcommissural organ* (Wislocki and Leduc, '53). The subcommissural organ (Fig. 16–7) consists of tall columnar ciliated cells which appear to have a secretory function. Evidence reviewed by Gilbert and Glaser ('61) suggests that the subcommissural organ may secrete aldosterone and serve as a volume receptor. The subcommissural organ is regarded as the only neurosecretory structure in the midbrain, and one of the few areas of the brain not included in the blood-brain barrier. This structure would seem capable of responding quickly to changes in effective circulating blood volume. Lesions of the subcommissural organ in rats result in an immediate and drastic reduction of water consumption, and marked dehydration; because dehydration is more intense than could be accounted for on the basis of adipsia alone, an increase in the renal excretion of salt and water is postulated (Gilbert, '60).

THE OCULOMOTOR NERVE

The oculomotor nerve is an efferent nerve supplying: (1) general somatic efferent (GSE) fibers to all of the extraocular muscles except the lateral rectus and the

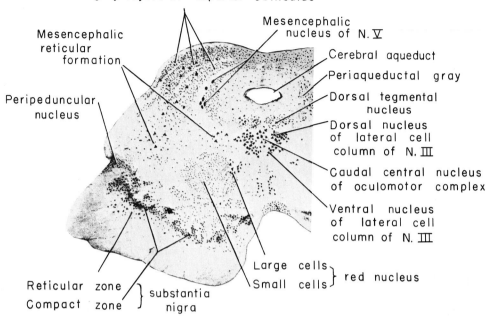

External, middle and deep
gray layers of superior colliculus

Mesencephalic
nucleus of N. V

Mesencephalic
reticular
formation

Cerebral aqueduct

Periaqueductal gray

Dorsal tegmental
nucleus

Peripeduncular
nucleus

Dorsal nucleus
of lateral cell
column of N. III

Caudal central nucleus
of oculomotor complex

Ventral nucleus
of lateral cell
column of N. III

Large cells ⎫
Small cells ⎬ red nucleus
              ⎭

Reticular zone ⎫
Compact zone ⎬ substantia nigra
              ⎭

Fig. 16–8. Section through superior colliculi of midbrain. Three-month infant. Cresyl violet. Photograph in which the main cell groups have been schematically blocked in.

superior oblique, and (2) preganglionic parasympathetic efferent (GVE) fibers to the ciliary ganglion. Extraocular muscles innervated by the oculomotor nerve include the levator palpebrae; the superior, medial, and inferior recti; and the inferior oblique. Visceral efferent fibers of the oculomotor nerve pass to the ciliary ganglion, whose postganglionic fibers are distributed to the smooth muscle of the ciliary body and the sphincter of the iris via the short ciliary nerves. Somatic efferent fibers of the nerve conduct impulses which produce elevation of the eyelid, vertical eye movements, converging eye movements and also participate in conjugate horizontal eye movements. The visceral component of the third nerve is concerned functionally with: (1) constriction of the pupil by contraction of the sphincter muscles of the iris, and (2) contraction of the ciliary muscle, which relaxes the suspensory ligament of the lens and causes the lens to become more convex. Constriction of the pupil, a normal response to light flashed into the eye, is referred to as the *pupillary light reflex*.

Pupillary constriction also occurs in association with convergence of the eyes and the alterations of lens diameter necessary for near vision. *Accommodation* for near vision requires pupillary constriction, convergence, and an increase in the diameter of the lens (produced by contraction of the ciliary muscle).

The *oculomotor nuclear complex* is located ventral to the central gray in a V-shaped trough formed by the diverging fibers of the medial longitudinal fasciculi (Figs. 16–1, 16–4 and 16–8). It extends from the rostral pole of the trochlear nucleus to the cephalic level of the superior colliculus. The oculomotor nuclear complex can be divided into somatic and visceral cell groups. Paired, large-celled *lateral nuclear groups*, and an unpaired paramedian cell group, the *caudal central nucleus*, constitute the somatic motor nuclei. Each lateral somatic nuclear group is composed of obliquely oriented columns of cells closely applied to the medial surfaces of the medial longitudinal fasciculi. These cell columns extend virtually the entire length of the nuclear

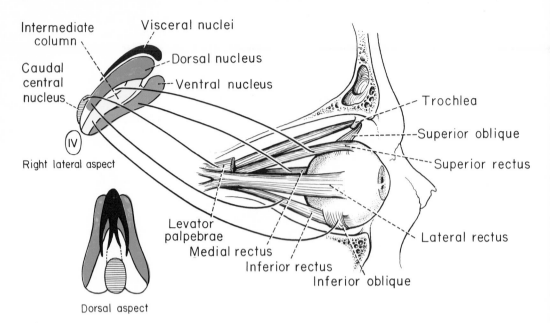

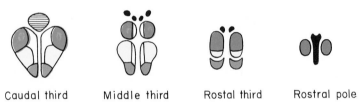

FIG. 16–9. Schematic representation of the localization of the extraocular muscles within the oculomotor nuclear complex, based upon studies in the rhesus monkey (Warwick, '53). Cell columns composing the complex are shown in lateral and dorsal views and in transverse sections through various levels. The visceral motor (parasympathetic) cell columns are shown in *black*. The ventral nucleus (*blue*) innervates the medial rectus muscle. The dorsal nucleus (*red*) innervates the inferior rectus muscle. The intermediate cell column (*yellow*) innervates the inferior oblique muscle. The cell column (*white*) medial to the dorsal and intermediate cell columns innervates the superior rectus muscle. The caudal central nucleus (*lined*) supplies fibers to the levator palpebrae superioris. Fibers innervating the medial rectus, inferior rectus, and inferior oblique muscles are uncrossed; fibers supplying the levator palpebrae muscle are both crossed and uncrossed, while those to the superior rectus muscle are crossed. The *drawing in the upper right* shows the positions of all of the extraocular muscles in relation to the globe and the bony orbit.

complex. In different locations small groups of cells infiltrate the fiber bundles of the MLF to variable depths. Most observers agree that the lateral nuclear groups can be divided in certain regions into dorsal and ventral cell columns. Caudally these cell columns merge so that the oculomotor complex in transverse sections has a triangular configuration (Figs. 16–4, 16–8 and 16–9). In the middle third of the complex, the dorsal and ventral cell columns are more distinct and the

complex has nearly a rectangular appearance in transverse sections (Fig. 16–9). Rostrally the dorsal cell column is larger than the ventral cell column, and extends beyond it to the rostral pole of the complex.

The caudal central nucleus is a collection of medium-sized cells located in the median raphe dorsal to the lateral somatic cell columns. This nucleus is present only in the caudal third of the oculomotor complex (Figs. 16–4, 16–8, and 16–9).

The visceral nuclei of the oculomotor complex include the *nucleus of Edinger-Westphal* and the *anterior median nucleus*, which are composed of small ovoid or spindle-shaped cells (Figs. 16–9 and 16–11). These cells resemble those of the dorsal motor nucleus of the vagus nerve. The *Edinger-Westphal nucleus* consists of collections of small cells located dorsal and dorsomedial to the lateral somatic cell columns in the rostral two-thirds of the oculomotor complex. Rostroventral to the Edinger-Westphal nucleus there is a vertically disposed group of small cells between the rostral parts of the lateral somatic cell columns. This cell group is the *anterior median nucleus*, regarded by some as the rostral continuation of the Edinger-Westphal nucleus (Warwick, '54). The visceral nuclei of the oculomotor complex give rise to uncrossed preganglionic parasympathetic (GVE) fibers which pass to the ciliary ganglion.

Some small cells, occupying the median raphe in the caudal two-thirds of the oculomotor nuclear complex (between dorsal and ventral lateral cell columns), have been referred to as the *nucleus of Perlia*. This nucleus has been considered to be associated with ocular convergence. Neither Clark ('26), nor Warwick ('55) could identify this nucleus as an entity in the monkey, and there is considerable doubt concerning its postulated function as a center for ocular convergence.

Attempts to determine cell groups within the oculomotor nucleus that innervate specific extraocular muscles have yielded contradictory results. Most of these studies have been made in animals and have been based upon retrograde cell changes resulting from extirpation of individual extraocular muscles. Practically all authors agree that localized representation of individual muscles exists within the oculomotor nucleus. However, different schemes show common features, but few are identical. Until recently the schemes of oculomotor nuclear organization proposed by Bernheimer (1897), Edinger ('00), and Brouwer ('18) have been the most widely accepted. The most extensive and complete investigation of the representation of the extraocular muscles in the oculomotor complex is that of Warwick ('53). His scheme of representation within the oculomotor nucleus is entirely different from that proposed by Bernheimer in that he considers the complex to be composed of longitudinally arranged cell columns rather than chains of separate nuclei (Fig. 16–9). According to Warwick, the levator palpebrae is innervated by cells of the caudal central nucleus, which gives rise to crossed and uncrossed fibers. Cells providing innervation of the superior rectus muscle are located in the most medial part of the caudal two-thirds of the complex and give rise to fibers which are crossed. Cells of the oculomotor complex which innervate the inferior rectus, the medial rectus, and the inferior oblique muscles project uncrossed fibers into the oculomotor nerve. The inferior rectus muscle is innervated by a long column of cells in the dorsolateral part of the complex. A column of ventrally located neurons innervates the medial rectus muscle, while cells of an intermediate cell column provide innervation for the inferior oblique muscle.

Although the specific innervation of the intrinsic eye muscles is not understood fully, it is generally accepted that preganglionic parasympathetic (GVE) fibers projecting to the ciliary ganglion originate from the Edinger-Westphal nucleus. According to Warwick ('54), the anterior median nucleus is a cephalic prolongation of the Edinger-Westphal cell column and an integral part of this parasympathetic component. Both of these nuclei give rise to uncrossed preganglionic fibers passing to the ciliary ganglion. Postganglionic fibers from the ciliary ganglion reach the intrinsic ocular musculature via the short ciliary nerves. The largest part of these fibers pass to the ciliary body; only a small fraction (3 per cent) are said to innervate the sphincter of the iris.

Neuromuscular spindles have been described in the extraocular muscles (Cooper and Daniel, '49; Cooper et al., '55) which are thought to act as low threshold stretch receptors. It has been postulated that impulses from these muscle spindles are conveyed by fibers arising from: (1) ganglion-like cells along the root of the oculomotor nerve (Tozer and Sherrington, '10; Pearson, '44), or (2) cells of the mesencephalic nucleus of the trigeminal nerve (Abd-El-Malek, '38; Cooper et al., '55). Recent experimental studies provide impressive evidence that cells in a part of the trigeminal ganglion (which form the ophthalmic branch) convey afferent impulses from muscle spindles in the extraocular muscles (Manni et al., '66).

The root fibers arising from the oculomotor nucleus pass ventrally in a number of bundles, some coursing medial to, and some traversing, the red nucleus. Ventrally the fibers converge and emerge in the interpeduncular fossa on the anterior aspect of the midbrain. This spreading of the root fibers through and around the red nucleus is an expression of the intraradicular expansion of the red nucleus during embryological development.

The oculomotor nucleus receives terminals and collaterals from the medial longitudinal fasciculus (Fig. 15–12), most of which originate from vestibular nuclei (McMasters et al., '66), as well as fibers from the interstitial and commissural nuclei. In addition it probably receives fibers from the reticular formation which convey impulses from a variety of sources, including the cerebral cortex. Fibers from the superior colliculus appear to reach the oculomotor nuclei via the interstitial nucleus of Cajal and the nucleus of Darkschewitsch (Figs. 16–11 and 16–12). This system of fibers places eye movements under the control of collicular optic reflex centers and thereby under the eye movement centers in the cerebral cortex which project fibers to the superior colliculus. A relatively small number of cerebello-oculomotor fibers, arising from the dentate nucleus, cross in the decussation of the superior cerebellar peduncle and enter portions of the lateral cell columns of the oculomotor complex (Carpenter and Strominger, '64). Most of these fibers project to the medial cell group that innervates the superior rectus muscle. Impulses to the visceral component

of the oculomotor nucleus concerned with the pupillary light reflex do not come from the superior colliculi, but from the pretectum. Corticobulbar fibers probably do not project directly to the oculomotor nucleus but to intercalated neurons in the reticular formation. The vestibular fibers reflexly correlate the position of the eyes with those of the head, while the internuclear fibers in the medial longitudinal fasciculus associate the abducens and oculomotor nuclei in the performance of conjugate lateral eye movements.

The fact that the conjugate eye movements—lateral, vertical, and converging—cannot be dissociated voluntarily, or reflexly, suggests that the pyramidal, and all other fibers, act on internuncial cells. These in turn integrate the various motor neurons used in the eye movements. This certainly would seem to be the case with the conjugate lateral movements, which are controlled by two widely separated nuclei—N. VI for the lateral rectus, and N. III for the medial rectus.

Lesions of the third nerve produce an ipsilateral lower motor neuron paralysis of the muscles supplied by the nerve. There is an external strabismus (squint) due to the unopposed action of the lateral rectus muscle, inability to move the eye vertically or inward, drooping of the eyelid (ptosis), dilatation of the pupil (mydriasis), loss of the pupillary light reflex and convergence, and loss of accommodation of the lens. The nearness of the emerging root fibers of N. III to the corticospinal tract in the crus cerebri may lead to the inclusion of both structures in a single lesion, which causes an alternating hemiplegia similar to those already described for the sixth and twelfth nerves (Fig. 13–16). In this case, there is an ipsilateral lower motor neuron paralysis of muscles innervated by N. III, combined with a contralateral hemiplegia. Since at this level the corticobulbar and corticospinal fibers are close to each other, there also may be contralateral paresis (weakness) of the muscles innervated by the cranial nerves, especially those of the lower face and tongue. This constitutes the *superior* or *oculomotor alternating hemiplegia* clinically known as *Weber's syndrome*.

PUPILLARY REFLEXES

When a beam of light is thrown on the retina of one eye, both pupils contract. The response of the eye stimulated is called the *direct reaction*, that of the opposite eye the *consensual reaction*. The pathway for the *pupillary light reflex* consists of the following neurons: (1) fibers from retinal ganglion cells, which pass through the optic nerve and tract, enter the brachium of the superior colliculus, and project to the pretectal area, (2) axons of pretectal cells, which partially cross through the posterior commissure, sweep ventrally along the central gray matter, and terminate in the Edinger-Westphal nucleus of the same and opposite side, (3) preganglionic fibers from the Edinger-Westphal nucleus, which course in N. III to the ciliary ganglion, and (4) postganglionic fibers from the ciliary ganglion which pass to the smooth muscle fibers of the sphincter of the iris.

When the gaze is suddenly shifted from a distant to a near object, the *accommodation-convergence reaction* occurs. Contraction of the medial recti muscles causes convergence of the eyes; contraction of the ciliary muscle effects a thickening of the lens (*accommodation*, see p. 385); and as an aid to the sharper definition of the image, the pupils constrict. In this instance pupillary constriction is an associated part of a more elaborate reflex response that involves both smooth and skeletal muscle fibers. The retinal impulses must first reach the visual cortex. Descending cortical impulses then pass directly, or by way of the frontal eye centers of the cerebral cortex, to the "convergence center" of the oculomotor nuclei. Since the pupilloconstrictor pathways for light and accommodation are distinct, they may be involved separately by isolated lesions. This occurs in certain diseases, such as central nervous system syphilis (tabes dorsalis), in which there is loss of pupillary constriction (miosis) to light, but not to accommodation. In this condition the pupil is small (less than 2.5 mm.), fails to constrict in bright light, and dilates imperfectly to atropine; yet the pupil has a brisk response during convergence and accommodation. A small immobile pupil with these properties is known as an *Argyll-Robertson pupil*. Many contemporary authors place the responsible lesion in the afferent visual pathway after the retinal fibers leave the optic tract to enter the pretectal area (Figs. 13–22 and 18–4). However, a unilateral Argyll-Robertson pupil is not infrequent, and a single pathological or experimental lesion in the brain stem can not explain satisfactorily this peculiar ophthalmological finding. Some believe the lesion involves efferent pathways for pupillary constriction (Naquin, '54). Others attribute the fixed Argyll-Robertson pupil to abnormalities of the blood vessels, nerves, and smooth muscle within the iris (Langworthy and Ortega, '43; Apter, '54a). The pathways serving accommodation remain intact.

In intense illumination, contraction of the pupil may be accompanied by closure of the eyelids, lowering of the brows, and general contractions of the face, designed to shut out the maximal amount of light. In so far as they are not volitional, these probably are reflex movements mediated through the superior colliculi and the tectobulbar tracts.

The central pathway for pupillary dilatation is not known completely. Dilatation occurs reflexly on shading the eye or scratching the side of the neck with a pin, and it is a constant feature in severe pain and extreme emotional states. Experimental evidence points to a path from the frontal cortex to the posterior region of the hypothalamus, which is one of the highest autonomic centers of the brain stem. Descending fibers from the hypothalamus passing in the reticular formation (and periventricular region) terminate upon reticular neurons in the lower brain stem, which in turn give rise to fibers that project to spinal levels. Impulses conveyed by these fibers, and probably relayed by spinal internuncial neurons, reach cells of the intermediolateral cell column in upper thoracic spinal (C8-T1) segments. The latter send preganglionic fibers by way of the upper two or three rami communicantes and the sympathetic trunk to the superior cervical ganglion, from which postganglionic fibers go to the dilator muscle of the iris (Fig. 13–25). Interruption of these descending fibers, which probably course in the dorsolateral tegmentum, at any level of the brain stem caudal to the hypothalamus will produce a *Horner's syndrome*. In a Horner's syndrome due to a brain stem lesion, the pupil shows relatively little dilatation to adrenalin, but if the lesion producing this syndrome involves postganglionic sympathetic fibers, adrenalin causes mydriasis and lid retraction on the affected side but not on the normal side. This hypersensitivity of the pupil to adrenalin seen with lesions involving the postganglionic fibers is an example of denervation sensitivity (Cogan, '56). See page 228 for a discussion of denervation sensitivity.

NUCLEI OF THE MESENCEPHALIC TEGMENTUM

The midbrain tegmentum, the region ventral to the cerebral aqueduct and dorsal to the substantia nigra, contains the trochlear and oculomotor nuclei, the mesencephalic reticular formation, the red nuclei, and many scattered collections of cells. The functional significance of many smaller cell groups remains obscure. The most conspicuous structure in the midbrain tegmentum at the level of the superior colliculus is the red nucleus.

The Red Nucleus. The red nucleus, recognized as a part of the mesencephalic reticular formation, has been distinguished as an entity because of special anatomical characteristics. In fresh specimens it has a pinkish-yellow color said to be due to its relatively high vascularity. The "capsule" of the nucleus, formed by fibers of the superior cerebellar peduncle, its central position within the mesencephalic reticular formation, and its color serve to sharply define the structure (Figs. 16–4, 16–8, 16–10, A–11, A–26, and A–27). The nucleus is a large ovoid column of cells

extending from the caudal margin of the superior colliculus into the caudal diencephalon (Figs. 20–10 and A–12). In transverse sections the nucleus has a characteristic circular appearance.

Since the classic comparative studies of Hatschek ('07), it has been customary to recognize magnocellular (paleoruber) and parvocellular (neoruber) portions of the red nucleus. The magnocellular part tends to occupy more caudal parts of the structure; it is more extensive in lower mammals and has been considered by some as the only cellular group which gives rise to the rubrospinal tract. The small-celled, or parvocellular, portion forms the bulk of the nucleus (Fig. 16–8); its development has been considered to parallel the growth of the deep cerebellar nuclei, particularly the dentate nucleus. Between the cells of the nucleus are numerous small bundles of myelinated fibers which give a punctate appearance to the nucleus in transverse sections. These are primarily fibers from the superior cerebellar peduncle which traverse the nucleus, as well as terminate in parts of it. The red nucleus is traversed in several directions by different bundles of fibers. Fibers of the superior cerebellar peduncle traverse it in a caudorostral direction. Oculomotor root fibers pass through it en route to the interpeduncular fossa, and fibers of the fasciculus retroflexus traverse its rostral pole medially (Fig. 18–4).

Afferent fibers projecting to the red nucleus are derived from two principal sources, the deep cerebellar nuclei and the cerebral cortex. Fibers from both of these sources appear to terminate somatotopically within the red nucleus. Fibers of the superior cerebellar peduncle, arising from the dentate, emboliform and globose nuclei, undergo a complete decussation in the caudal midbrain and both enter and surround the contralateral red nucleus. According to Jansen and Jansen ('55) approximately half of the fibers arising from the dentate nucleus pass rostrally beyond the red nucleus, while little more than 10% of those arising from the interposed nuclei (i.e., emboliform and globose) project beyond the red nucleus. All parts of the red nucleus receive fibers from the dentate and interposed nuclei in the cat. On the basis of discrete lesions in the interposed nucleus (anterior part) in the cat, it is evident that fibers from this nucleus project to the caudal two-thirds of the red nucleus in a somatotopic fashion (Fig. 17–15; Courville, '66b). There is a complex mediolateral and caudorostral correspondence between portions of the interposed and the red nuclei. Since lesions destroying both the dentate and interposed nuclei produce degeneration in all parts of the contralateral red nucleus, it may be inferred that fibers from the dentate nucleus project particularly to rostral parts of the red nucleus (Fig. 17–14). The caudal portions of the red nucleus, which are linked somatotopically with the contralateral interposed nucleus (and paravermal cerebellar cortex), project somatotopically to spinal levels. Thus, indirect pathways are present by which impulses from the cerebellar cortex and interposed nucleus can be conveyed somatotopically to spinal levels via the red nucleus. This indirect pathway involves two midbrain decussations (i.e., the superior cerebellar peduncle and the rubrospinal tract).

Corticorubral fibers, mainly from the precentral gyrus (Rinvik and Walberg, '63; Kuypers and Lawrence, '67), project somatotopically upon cells in all parts of the red nucleus. These fibers are uncrossed. Fibers from the "motor" cortical forelimb area terminate in the dorsal part of the red nucleus, while fibers from the cortical hindlimb area end in the ventral part of the red nucleus. These regions of the red nucleus project fibers, respectively, to cervical and lumbosacral regions of the spinal cord (Pompeiano and Brodal, '57). Thus, corticorubral and rubrospinal fiber systems together constitute a somatotopically organized nonpyramidal pathway from the motor cortex to spinal levels.

The established efferent projections of the red nucleus are to the spinal cord, the brain stem and the cerebellum. Experimental data for the cat (Pompeiano and Brodal, '57) indicate that rubrospinal fibers arise chiefly, but not exclusively, from cells of all sizes in the caudal three-fourths of the red nucleus. In general, cells in dorsomedial parts of the nucleus project fibers to cervical spinal segments, while cells in ventral and ventrolateral locations project to lumbosacral spinal segments; fibers passing to thoracic regions of the spinal cord arise from intermediate parts of the red nucleus. Cervical spinal segments receive the largest number of rubrospinal fibers, probably as many as project to all other spinal regions. According to Kuypers and Lawrence ('67), the rubrospinal tract in the monkey arises almost exclusively from the caudal magnocellular part of the nucleus.

Rubrospinal fibers issue from the medial margin of the red nucleus, cross the median raphe in the *ventral tegmental decussation* (*of Forel*), and descend in the brain stem close to the branchiomeric motor cranial nerve nuclei (Fig. 13–22). In the upper pons some crossed descending rubral efferent fibers separate from the rubrospinal tract, traverse portions of the trigeminal nuclei, and enter the cerebellum in association with the superior cerebellar peduncle. These *rubrocerebellar fibers*, originally described as projecting to the dentate nucleus (Brodal and Gogstad, '54; Hinman and Carpenter, '59), have been traced to the nucleus interpositus (anterior part) (Courville and Brodal, '66). This direct (and crossed) rubrocerebellar feedback appears to be somatotopically organized. Other crossed descending rubral efferent fibers leave the rubrospinal tract in the lower brain stem and enter parts of the facial nucleus and the lateral reticular nucleus of the medulla. Rubral efferent fibers project only to the dorsomedial and intermediate cell groups of the facial nucleus (Courville, '66a), cell groups which innervate upper facial muscles. In the medulla crossed rubral efferent fibers project to parts of the lateral reticular nucleus (Walberg, '58; Courville, '66a), a cerebellar relay nucleus previously described (Fig. 13–22). Except for these fibers, which may be considered as *rubrobulbar*, no crossed descending rubral efferent fibers end upon

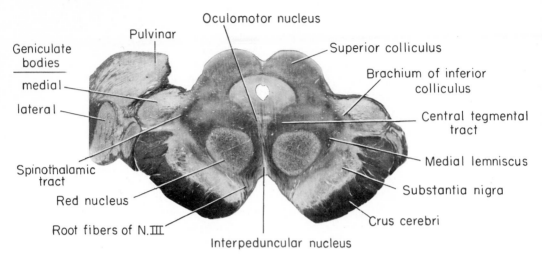

FIG. 16-10. Transverse section of the adult midbrain through the superior colliculus. Caudal portions of the thalamus are seen dorsolaterally. Weigert's myelin stain. Photograph.

portions of the brain stem reticular formation. Rubrospinal fibers in the retro-olivary area of the medulla pass caudally to enter the lateral funiculus of the spinal cord; the most dorsally situated fibers in the tract are intermingled with those of the lateral corticospinal tract.

Uncrossed descending rubral efferent fibers enter the central tegmental tract and project to the dorsal lamella of the principal inferior olivary nucleus (Walberg, '56). These fibers, referred to as *rubro-olivary fibers*, constitute the largest contingent of the so-called rubrobulbar fibers. It is possible that some of these fibers may terminate in, or give off collaterals to, the brain stem reticular formation. From the above discussion it is apparent that descending rubral efferent fibers, other than those in the rubrospinal tract, are organized to project impulses to the cerebellum via: (1) direct rubrocerebellar fibers, or (2) rubrobulbar fibers which pass to cerebellar relay nuclei (i.e., the lateral reticular nucleus of the medulla and parts of the principal inferior olivary nucleus).

Information concerning ascending rubral efferent fibers is less specific because these fibers are intermingled with those of the superior cerebellar peduncle. Available evidence (Carpenter, '56; Pompeiano and Brodal, '57; Kuypers and Lawrence, '67) indicates that the majority of ascending

fibers from the red nucleus arise from rostral portions of the nucleus. Because lesions in the red nucleus (Hinman and Carpenter, '59) produce degeneration in essentially the same thalamic nuclei as lesions of the superior cerebellar peduncle, it is presumed that their projection is similar. The only convincing anatomical evidence that the red nucleus projects ascending fibers is based upon studies of retrograde cell changes in the nucleus produced by lesions at more rostral levels (Preisig, '04; von Monakow, '09; Pompeiano and Brodal, '57; Kuypers and Lawrence, '67). Electrophysiological evidence (Conde, '66) has confirmed connections between the rostral part of the red nucleus and the thalamus. The conclusion that no rubral efferent fibers project to diencephalic levels (Poirier and Bouvier, '66) does not appear to be consistent with available evidence.

It is evident from the above that the red nucleus is a way station interposed in a variety of complex pathways. It would appear to relay cerebellar impulses to the diencephalon and the spinal cord, as well as to participate in various neural mechanisms by which some cerebellar impulses can be fed back to the cerebellum. Impulses from the cerebral cortex also can be conveyed to the spinal cord and cerebellum via the red nucleus.

There is considerable evidence that in

lower mammals (cats and dogs) the mid-brain contains a center for the integration of complex postural reflexes which enable an animal to change from an abnormal to a normal position (righting reactions). This center may be located in the magnocellular portion of the red nucleus and in the adjacent reticular formation. Destruction of the superior colliculi or of the substantia nigra does not interfere with these reactions, but they are abolished when the ventral tegmental decussation is severed. It is doubtful if the same conditions obtain in man, where the magnocellular part of the nucleus is greatly reduced. In man the righting reactions, and postural orientation are mediated to a large extent by retinal impulses which are integrated in cortical centers.

Conflicting statements in the literature suggest that stimulation of the red nucleus in animals produces flexion of ipsilateral forelimb and extension of the contralateral forelimb. This reaction, generally known as "the tegmental response" frequently can be obtained from regions of the mesencephalic reticular formation dorsal and lateral to the red nucleus. The studies of Pompeiano ('56, '57) indicate that stimulation of the red nucleus *per se* elicits flexion in the contralateral extremities, which appears to be mediated by the rubrospinal tract (Pompeiano and Brodal, '57). It has been demonstrated that stimulation of the red nucleus in the decerebrate cat gives rise to: (1) excitatory postsynaptic potentials in the contralateral flexor alpha motor neurons, and (2) inhibitory postsynaptic potentials in contralateral extensor alpha motor neurons. The functional relationship of rubrospinal fibers to gamma motor neurons is not clear.

Because the red nucleus receives a large proportion of its afferents from the cerebellum by way of the superior cerebellar peduncle, it is possible to relate certain phenomena associated with cerebellar stimulation to the red nucleus. These observations concern mainly the nucleus interpositus, which projects the majority of its fibers to the caudal two-thirds of the contralateral red nucleus. Reciprocal somatotopic relationships exist between the nucleus interpositus and the contralateral red nucleus (Courville and Brodal, '66; Courville, '66b). Stimulation of specific parts of the nucleus interpositus (anterior part) in decerebrate preparations produces flexion in either the ipsilateral forelimb or hindlimb (Pompeiano, '59, 60a; Maffei and Pompeiano, '62). These flexor responses are mediated by the red nucleus and occur ipsilaterally because of the double crossing of the fiber systems involved (i.e., superior cerebellar peduncle and rubrospinal tract). The above responses are in turn structurally and functionally related to specific regions of cerebellar cortex which project upon the nucleus interpositus.

Clinically, unilateral lesions of the mesencephalic tegmentum involving the red nucleus are described as producing a syndrome characterized by contralateral motor disturbances that are variously designated as tremor, ataxia and choreiform activity, and an ipsilateral oculomotor palsy. The motor disturbances associated with this syndrome, known as the syndrome of Benedikt since the time of Charcot, have been attributed to destruction of the red nucleus. Experimentally produced lesions in the red nucleus in a variety of different animals (von Economo and Karplus, '09; Rademaker, '26; Mussen, '27; Ingram and Ranson, '32; Carpenter, '56) have not produced physiological disturbances equivalent to those reported in man. Isolated lesions of the red nucleus in the monkey (Carpenter, '56) produce transient tremor and ataxia, enduring hypokinesis, and ipsilateral oculomotor disturbances. It is of interest that unilateral lesions in the red nucleus in monkeys with virtually complete degeneration of the contralateral superior cerebellar peduncle produce no additional neurological disturbances (Carpenter, '57). These findings suggest that motor disturbances resulting from lesions of the mesencephalic tegmentum, including the red nucleus, probably are a consequence of interruption of cerebellar efferent fibers, rather than destruction of cells in the red nucleus. It also has been found that, in the monkey, neither lesions of the red nucleus nor section of the rubrospinal tract in the spinal cord abolishes cerebellar disturbances produced by prior lesions of the deep cerebellar nuclei. These experiments suggest that impulses mediating experimentally induced cerebellar disturbances are not transmitted to spinal levels via the rubrospinal tract.

Mesencephalic Reticular Formation. The midbrain reticular formation is somewhat less extensive than the pontine reticular formation caudal to it. While the red nucleus is recognized as a distinctive part of the reticular formation, classically it is customary to reserve this term for structures lateral and dorsal to the red nucleus. According to detailed studies (Olszewski, '54; Olszewski and Baxter, '54), the principal reticular nuclei of the mesencephalon are: (1) the *nucleus tegmenti pedunculopontinus* (pedunculopontine nucleus), (2) the *nucleus cuneiformis*, and (3) the *nucleus subcuneiformis*. The pedunculopontine nucleus lies in the lateral part of the midbrain tegmentum ventral to the inferior colliculus (Fig. 16–3). The nucleus consists of two parts, a compact part located dorsolaterally and a small-celled diffuse part located ventrally. Fibers of the superior cerebellar peduncle traverse portions of the nucleus as they shift ventromedially to decussate. Although the connections of this nucleus are poorly understood, it would appear to be important in the integration of motor activities since it receives descending pallidotegmental fibers (Fig. 20–8; Nauta and Mehler, '66; Carpenter and Strominger, '67) as well as corticofugal fibers from the precentral gyrus (Kuypers and Lawrence, '67). The nuclei cuneiformis and subcuneiformis lie between the tectum, dorsally, and the pedunculopontine nucleus. At more rostral levels only the cuneiform and subcuneiform nuclei are found. Medial to the latter nuclei are the fibers of the central tegmental tract. Also seen at this level is the interpeduncular nucleus, which occupies a small triangular space dorsal to the interpeduncular fossa (Figs. 16–3, 16–4, and 16–10). Cells of this nucleus are very small, spindle-shaped, lightly staining, and compactly arranged. The interpeduncular nucleus receives fibers of the fasciculus retroflexus from the habenular nuclei (Figs. 16–8, 18–5 and 18–6).

The central gray substance (periaqueductal gray) surrounding the cerebral aqueduct is composed of small oval or spindle-shaped cells. Other tegmental nuclei usually considered in conjunction with the reticular formation are: (1) *the interstitial nucleus of Cajal*, (2) *the nucleus of Darkschewitsch*, (3) *the nuclei of the posterior commissure*, and (4) *the dorsal tegmental nucleus*. The *interstitial nucleus of Cajal* consists of medium-sized multipolar cells located among, and ventrolateral to, the fibers of the medial longitudinal fasciculus in the rostral mesencephalic tegmentum; it is lateral to the rostral part of the oculomotor nucleus and extends beyond the superior pole of this nucleus (Figs. 16–11 and 16–12). The interstitial nucleus receives fibers from the vestibular nuclei that ascend in the medial longitudinal fasciculus (Fig. 16–13), as well as fibers from the superior colliculus. Efferent fibers from the interstitial nucleus descending in the dorsomedial part of the medial longitudinal fasciculus (Busch, '61) project to the medial vestibular nucleus (Pompeiano and Walberg, '57) and the spinal cord. Uncrossed fibers from this nucleus which reach spinal levels constitute the interstitiospinal tract. Such fibers, which are not numerous, are present in the sulcomarginal area. The *nucleus of Darkschewitsch*, which some authors have erroneously called the nucleus of the posterior commissure, is a rather indistinct cell group just inside the ventrolateral border of the central gray matter (Figs. 16–11 and 16–12). It lies dorsal to the interstitial nucleus of Cajal and the medial longitudinal fasciculus. The small cells of the nucleus, generally resembling those of the periaqueductal gray, begin at the caudal pole of the oculomotor nucleus and extend rostrally beyond it. Although the anatomical connections of the nucleus of Darkschewitsch are not known fully, several studies indicate that fibers from the medial longitudinal fasciculus (Carpenter and Hanna,

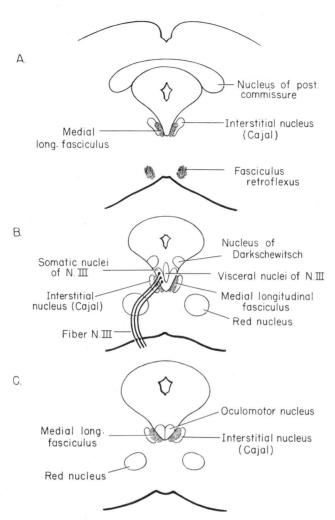

A.

Nucleus of post.
commissure

Interstitial nucleus
(Cajal)

Medial
long. fasciculus

Fasciculus
retroflexus

B.

Nucleus of
Darkschewitsch

Somatic nuclei
of N. III

Visceral nuclei of N. III

Interstitial
nucleus (Cajal)

Medial longitudinal
fasciculus

Red nucleus

Fiber N. III

C.

Oculomotor nucleus

Medial long.
fasciculus

Interstitial nucleus
(Cajal)

Red nucleus

Fig. 16–11. Schematic diagrams of the nuclei in the periaqueductal region in the cat showing the locations of the nucleus of the posterior commissure, the nucleus of Darkschewitsch, and the interstitial nucleus of Cajal (after Pompeiano and Walberg, '57). Diagrams are arranged in caudal (*lower*) to rostral (*upper*) sequence. *A*, The nucleus of the posterior commissure lies dorsal to the central gray and is associated with fibers of the posterior commissure. *B*, The nucleus of Darkschewitsch lies within the central gray dorsal to the medial longitudinal fasciculus. *C*, Cells of the interstitial nucleus of Cajal are situated lateral to the medial longitudinal fasciculus and among its fibers. This nucleus extends rostrally beyond the oculomotor nuclear complex.

'62) and the superior colliculus (Papez and Freeman, '30; Rasmussen, '36; Marburg and Warner, '47; Altman and Carpenter, '61) pass to the region of the nucleus. Szentágothai ('50) has suggested that impulses from the superior colliculus may reach the oculomotor complex via the nuclei of Darkschewitsch and Cajal (Figs. 16–11 and 16–12). The studies of Pompeiano and Walberg ('57) indicate that

fibers from the nucleus of Darkschewitsch do not descend in the medial longitudinal fasciculus and do not project to the vestibular nuclei. The *nucleus of the posterior commissure*, like the interstitial nucleus of Cajal, lies outside the periaqueductal gray (Fig. 16–11). It is situated dorsal to the central gray from levels of the mid-oculomotor region to the frontal border of the posterior commissure. This nucleus

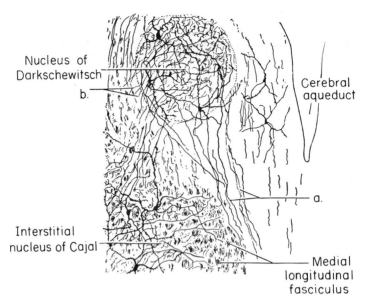

FIG. 16–12. Relationships of the nucleus of Darkschewitsch and the interstitial nucleus of Cajal to the central gray (surrounding the cerebral aqueduct) and the medial longitudinal fasciculus. Collateral fibers terminating in the nucleus of Darkschewitsch are indicated by *b*, while fibers indicated by *a* are leaving this nucleus. Drawing based upon Golgi preparations from a newborn kitten (after Cajal, '11).

is associated with the fibers of the posterior commissure. The *dorsal tegmental nucleus* lies within the central gray, dorsal to the trochlear nucleus and the oculomotor complex (Fig. 16–3). Fibers from this nucleus and from a collection of more caudally located cells known as the *ventral tegmental nucleus* ascend to the mammillary bodies, the lateral hypothalamic areas, the preoptic area, and the septal area (Guillery, '56; Nauta and Kuypers, '58). These fibers travel in the dorsal longitudinal fasciculus (of Schütz), the mammillary peduncle, and some continue rostrally in the medial forebrain bundle (Fig. 18–6).

FUNCTIONAL CONSIDERATIONS OF THE RETICULAR FORMATION

In previous chapters the anatomical organization of the medullary and pontine reticular formation was described. It will be recalled that the medullary reticular formation consists essentially of three zones: (1) a median region containing the nuclei of the raphe and the paramedian reticular nuclei, (2) a medial region constituting roughly the medial two-thirds

of the reticular formation and regarded as an "effector" area, and (3) a smaller lateral region referred to as the "sensory" or "receptive" part because of the large number of collateral fibers projected to it from secondary sensory pathways. The pontine reticular formation appears to have essentially the same divisions, except that the "sensory" portion is smaller and clearly evident only in the caudal pons. Electrophysiological investigations in animals have yielded important information concerning the functions of the reticular formation. Magoun and Rhines ('46, '47) found that electrical stimulation of the ventromedial zone of the medullary reticular formation inhibited or reduced most forms of motor activity. Stimulation in this region produced inhibition of the patellar tendon reflex, the flexion reflex of the foreleg, and the blink reflex. In addition, it caused inhibiton of extensor muscle tone in decerebrate animals and inhibited responses to stimulation of the motor cortex in intact animals. All inhibitory effects were bilateral, but ipsilateral inhibition sometimes could be obtained at a lower threshold. No inhibitory effects could be elicited from the most lateral part of the medullary reticular formation. Regions of the medullary reticular formation from which inhibitory responses are obtained correspond closely to the area occupied by the nucleus reticularis gigantocellularis (except for its most rostral part) and part of the nucleus reticularis ventralis. Since these nuclei give rise to medullary reticulospinal fibers, it would appear that these inhibitory influences are mediated directly by this fiber system (Torvik and Brodal, '57). This thesis is further supported by the fact that medullary inhibition can still be obtained by electrical stimulation following chronic midbrain and pontine hemisection (Niemer and Magoun, '47). Nevertheless, there is evidence that higher centers projecting to medullary reticular units may produce inhibition of motor activity and of extensor muscle tone. Such higher centers are thought to include the anterior lobe of the cerebellum, the corpus striatum, and certain cortical regions (Magoun and Rhines, '47).

A far greater region of the reticular formation facilitates or augments reflexes at lower levels, and cortically induced movements in response to electrical stimulation. This facilitatory area extends rostrally uninterruptedly from the upper medulla through the pontine and mesencephalic tegmentum into the hypothalamic, subthalamic, and intralaminar thalamic regions of the diencephalon. Bilateral facilitatory effects can be evoked at any level within this long stretch of the reticular formation. The facilitatory region of the reticular formation includes many areas from which no direct reticulospinal projections arise. Facilitatory effects produced by stimulation of the rostral and dorsal parts of the nucleus reticularis gigantocellularis, or of the nuclei reticularis pontis caudalis and oralis, presumably could reach spinal levels by direct reticulospinal fibers originating in these nuclei. Descending polysynaptic pathways would appear to mediate facilitatory effects obtained from regions of the midbrain and diencephalon, which have no direct reticulospinal projections.

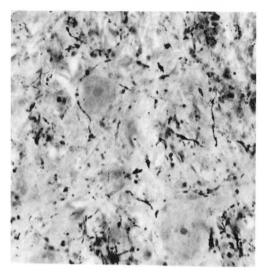

Fig. 16–13. Photomicrograph of terminal fiber degeneration passing around cells of the interstitial nucleus of Cajal. Ascending degeneration passing to this nucleus resulted from a lesion in the medial longitudinal fasciculus. Monkey. Nauta-Gygax stain. ×560.

The descending influences of the brain stem reticular formation are not limited to inhibition and facilitation of reflex activity or somatic motor function. As commented upon earlier, respiratory responses can be obtained by electrical stimulation of the reticular formation. Maximal inspiratory responses can be obtained from stimulating points within the nucleus reticularis gigantocellularis (Torvik and Brodal, '57), while expiratory effects are evoked chiefly from the parvocellular reticular nucleus in the medulla. Vasomotor depressor effects generally are obtained from areas within the nucleus reticularis gigantocellularis and the most rostral part of the nucleus reticularis ventralis. Pressor effects usually are evoked by stimulations outside of the reticular regions which project fibers to spinal levels.

While it is well known that alpha motor neurons can be influenced by stimulation of the reticular formation, the investigations of Granit ('55) indicate that these effects are not necessarily due to reticulospinal volleys impinging directly upon these neurons, since activity of gamma motor neurons can influence alpha motor neurons through the gamma loop (Fig.

13–3). Granit and Kaada ('52) demonstrated that repetitive electrical stimulation of the facilitating regions of the brain stem tegmentum increased the efferent discharge of gamma motor neurons, and increased the rate of discharge from the muscle spindle. On the other hand, inhibition of the gamma discharge was produced by stimulating the medullary inhibitory region. These data suggest that a large part of the excitation of alpha motor neurons results from firing of the gamma efferents, which are actively controlled by the reticular formation. The inhibition of extensor muscle tone in a decerebrate animal by stimulation of the medullary reticular formation (Terzuolo and Terzian, '53) is a dramatic example of this potent influence.

The discovery that the activity of the muscle spindle could be modified by descending reticular influences suggested that the reticular formation might affect the initiation and transmission of other sensory impulses. Hagbarth and Kerr ('54) demonstrated that synaptic transmission of sensory impulses in the spinal cord could be depressed by stimulation of the reticular formation. Likewise, potentials evoked in the posterior column nuclei following stimulation of the posterior columns could be depressed or abolished by stimulation of the reticular formation (page 327). Although findings suggest that the inhibitory influence of the reticular formation acts upon the second order sensory neurons, it is possible that some of these effects may be a consequence of stimulation of corticofugal fibers projecting to sensory relay nuclei. Many of the latter fibers traverse portions of the reticular formation.

Moruzzi and Magoun ('49) have demonstrated that the facilitatory region of the brain stem reticular formation also acts in an ascending direction to influence the spontaneous electrical activity of the cerebral cortex. The pioneer investigations of Berger ('29, '30) showed that in man and lower mammals wakefulness, sleep, alertness, and relaxation were characterized by strikingly different electroencephalographic patterns. Wakefulness and alertness are characterized by fast low voltage activity, while sleep is associated with the appearance of slow high voltage waves (see p. 584). The observations of Moruzzi and Magoun that stimulation of the brain stem reticular formation desynchronizes and activates the electroencephalogram (EEG) in a manner paralleling arousal from sleep, or alerting to attention, have been confirmed by a number of investigators. The ascending reticular activating system has been shown to respond to peripheral, splanchnic, trigeminal, and vagal nerve stimulation, as well as to auditory, vestibular, visual, and olfactory stimuli (Bremer, '36; Gerebtzoff, '40; McKinley and Magoun, '42; Moruzzi and Magoun, '49; Starzl et al., '51a; French et al., '52; Dell, '52; French et al., '53; Bernhaut et al., '53).

Further physiological studies (Moruzzi and Magoun, '49; Starzl and Whitlock, '52; French et al., '53) have shown that interruption of the long ascending sensory pathways in the brain stem does not prevent impulses from reaching the reticular activating system and provoking the characteristic EEG arousal response. Lesions in the rostromedial midbrain tegmentum abolish the EEG arousal elicited by sensory stimulation (French and Magoun, '52; Magoun, '52), even though the long ascending sensory pathways are intact. These data suggest that two functionally distinct, but interrelated, pathways must project to diencephalic levels. The long ascending sensory pathways, located laterally with respect to the reticular core, constitute the *lemniscal system*, which is concerned largely with the transmission of specific sensory impulses to particular thalamic relay nuclei. The lemniscal systems (i.e., the medial lemniscus, lateral lemniscus, spinothalamic tracts, and secondary trigeminal projections) are regarded as oligosynaptic specific sensory pathways. Although electrical stimulation of the lemniscal systems produces arousal (Starzl et al., '51; French et al., '52; Magoun, '63), this is not considered to be a direct effect. The second pathway, the *ascending reticular activating system*, occupies more medial areas of the brain stem reticular formation and receives collateral fibers from surrounding specific sensory systems. Physiologically this system is regarded as a multineuronal, polysynaptic system within which collaterals from sensory systems lose their specific identity. The continuous subliminal facilitating effect of these nonspecific afferents upon the reticular activating system appears to be responsible for wakefulness, alerting, and arousal.

Anatomical and physiological data appear to be in agreement concerning the distribution of collaterals from secondary sensory fibers within the reticular formation. These collaterals are given off by secondary fibers in the auditory and vestibular systems, as well as from the nuclei of the solitary tract, the trigeminal nuclei, the vagal nuclei, and the spinothalamic tracts. Visual impulses would appear to reach the reticular formation via tectoreticular fibers (Altman and Carpenter, '61). Anatomically it is significant that direct spinoreticular fibers are more numerous than collaterals from the spinothalamic tracts and that they have a wider distribution within the reticular formation. The medial lemniscus, unlike other long ascending systems, does not contribute collateral fibers to the reticular activating system. Experimental studies (Rossi and Zirondoli, '55; Roger et al., '56) indicate that the secondary trigeminal collaterals given off at pontine levels are a particularly potent source of tonic influence to the reticular activating system and exceed in importance that contributed by other cranial nerves.

Lastly, it has been shown that the cerebral cortex plays a role in altering the state of consciousness and alertness by influencing reticular neurons that mediate the arousal responses (Jasper et al., '52; Bremer and Terzuolo, '54; French et al., '55). Such a role has been suggested by the well-known arousal effect of psychical stimuli. Areas of the cerebral cortex from which the arousal responses can be obtained by nonconvulsive electrical stimulation include loci on the orbitofrontal surface, the frontal convexity, the sensorimotor cortex, the posterior parietooccipital cortex, the superior temporal gyrus, and the cingulate gyrus. It appears likely that corticoreticular fibers, which originate from all parts of the cerebral cortex, convey excitatory impulses to the reticular neurons, whose ascending discharge produces the arousal response. Anatomical evidence (Rossi and Brodal, '56) indicates that corticoreticular fibers are projected most abundantly to two regions of the brain stem reticular formation: (1) a pontine region corresponding to the nucleus reticularis pontis oralis, and (2) a medullary region corresponding to the nucleus reticularis gigantocellularis.

As noted earlier, the more lateral regions of the brain stem reticular formation are regarded as the "sensory" part, while the larger, more medial region, which projects numerous long ascending and descending fibers, is considered as the "effector" portion. In spite of the fact that physiological studies support the view that ascending transmission in the reticular formation involves chains of neurons which fire successively, it has not been possible to demonstrate short-axoned, Golgi type II cells in the reticular formation (Scheibel and Scheibel, '58). Since anatomical studies (Brodal and Rossi, '55) indicate that approximately one-third of the cells in the "effector" reticular regions give rise to long ascending fibers in the reticular core, it appears likely that these fibers actually form the structural basis of the ascending reticular activating system. Rapidly conducted impulses in the reticular core would appear to be transmitted by long ascending axons, while slowly conducted impulses probably are conveyed by fine caliber axons, or by circuitous pathways provided by laterally dispersed collaterals. The main ascending pathway of the brain stem reticular formation appears to be the *central tegmental fasciculus*, a large composite bundle that also contains descending fiber systems (Brodal, '57; Nauta and Kuypers, '58). This bundle occupies a large part of the bulbar tegmentum, but at mesencephalic levels it is displaced dorsally so that its fibers occupy a position adjacent to the central gray and dorsal to the red nucleus. At diencephalic levels the central tegmental tract projects into the subthalamic region and to the intralaminar nuclei of the thalamus. Although the areas of origin of ascending fibers within this system have not been delineated precisely, most evidence indicates that ascending fibers originate throughout the longitudinal extent of the medulla and pons (Brodal and Rossi, '55); reticular pathways ascending beyond the midbrain appear to arise largely from levels rostral to the inferior olivary nuclei. According to Nauta and Kuypers ('58), the central tegmental tract also contains an abundance of short ascending fibers which appear to form a multineuronal system for intrareticular conduction.

Ascending reticular projections to the hypothalamus arise from medial regions of the caudal midbrain and are distinct from those contained in the central tegmental tract (Nauta and Kuypers, '58). These projections are represented largely by two fiber bundles: (1) the dorsal longitudinal fasciculus (Schütz) situated near the central gray, and (2) fibers of the mammillary peduncle, which originate in the medial tegmental region (Fig. 18–6) and terminate in the mammillary body and lateral hypothalamic region (Nauta, '58).

Anatomical and physiological data are in agreement concerning the diencephalic projections (hypothalamus, subthalamic region, and intralaminar nuclei of the thalamus) of the ascending reticular activating system, but the manner in which these structures influence the activity of the cerebral cortex is not definitely established (French et al., '52; Rossi and Zanchetti, '57; Bowsher, '66). While the EEG arousal response undoubtedly is mediated in part by the projection systems of the intralaminar nuclei (Moruzzi and Magoun, '49), subsequent data (Starzl et al., '51) indicate that thalamic relay nuclei may be involved and that alternate extrathalamic pathways also may be implicated. This subject will be treated in more detail in Chapter 19.

It is significant that bilateral interruption of lemniscal systems in the brain stem still leaves the animal with an electrocorticogram characteristic of the wakeful state. After lesions in the upper reticular core which spare the lemniscal system, the electroencephalogram changes to that of the sleeping state. After lesions in the rostral midbrain interrupting somatic and auditory pathways (without destroying the ascending reticular system), tactile and auditory stimuli produce an EEG arousal, though no tactile or auditory impulses reach the thalamus by the specific sensory pathways. The central reticular core might be regarded as a common system of neurons with multiple relays which are discharged equivalently by all sensory systems projecting collaterals to it. Such a common system would not be involved in the conscious perception of any one sensory modality, but would be involved with afferent functions common to all types of sensory experience, namely, alerting and attracting attention. The nonspecific sensory impulses ascending in the reticular activating system would appear to function by sharpening the attentive state of the cortex and creating optimal conditions for the conscious perception of sensory impulses mediated by the classical pathways.

There is evidence that a differential susceptibility of these two systems to the action of depressant drugs contributes to a considerable degree in the production of the anesthetic state (French et al., '53; Brazier, '54; Arduini and Arduini, '54; Killam and Killam '58). The undiminished persistence of impulses in the lemniscal systems, and the blocking of impulses in the ascending reticular core, in anesthetic states (e.g., ether and certain barbiturates) suggest that many effects may be due to alterations of synaptic transmission in the multineuronal activating system.

Long term experimental studies (Sprague et al., '63) of cats with extensive rostral midbrain lesions interrupting the specific lemniscal pathways bilaterally produce consistent alterations of behavior. Such animals exhibit: (1) a marked reduction of somatic and autonomic signs of affective behavior, (2) marked inattention to, and poor localization of, many visual, auditory, tactile and nociceptive stimuli, (3) stereotyped, hyperexploratory behavior, largely independent of stimuli in the external environment, and (4) changes in eating, grooming, excretory and sexual habits. In spite of these changes, these animals show essentially normal behavioral and EEG arousal.

Substantia Nigra. The substantia nigra is the most voluminous nuclear mass of the human mesencephalon, extending throughout its length and into the caudal diencephalon (Figs. 16–10 and 20–10). It is rudimentary in lower vertebrates, makes its definite appearance in mammals, and reaches its greatest development in man. In sections two zones are distinguishable: a dorsal compact or black zone, and a ventral reticular zone, which has a reddish-brown color in the fresh condition similar to that of the globus pallidus (Fig. 16–8). The compact zone appears as an irregular band of closely packed, large polygonal or pyramidal cells containing granules of melanin pigment. Pigmented cells are found in the substantia nigra of a wide variety of mammals (Marsden, '61); the intensity of the pigmentation in primates is greater than in any other order and reaches maximum intensity in man. In man pigmented cells in the substantia nigra do not appear until the fourth or fifth year. The compact zone extends to the most caudal part of the midbrain, where it is covered ventrally by the pontine nuclei (Fig. 16–3). The reticular zone, also known as the stratum intermedium, lies close to the crus cerebri and is composed of scattered cells of irregular shape that are rich in iron but contain no melanin pigment. Islands of such cells may be seen penetrating between the fibers of the crus cerebri. Within the stratum intermedium, especially in its lateral portion, are many bundles of descending myelinated fibers coming chiefly from the corpus striatum (Fig. 16–4). This zone extends upward into the diencephalon, where it lies ventral to the subthalamic nucleus (Figs. 18–5 and 20–10).

Dorsal to the substantia nigra and ventrolateral to the red nucleus, is a region containing scattered cells of various sizes and shapes, among which are large cells with melanin pigment. It is not certain whether some of these belong to the substantia nigra or to the tegmentum, but many

authorities regard this region as a diffusely organized extension of the compact zone. Lateral to the substantia nigra a layer of small cells, the *peripeduncular nucleus*, caps the dorsal surface of the crus cerebri (Fig. 16–8).

In spite of the large size and prominence of the substantia nigra, the fiber connections of this important nucleus are not fully known. Afferent fibers to the substantia nigra arise from the cerebral cortex and the neostriatum (i.e., caudate nucleus and putamen).

Corticonigral fibers (Déjerine, '01; von Economo, '02; von Monakow, '14; Verhaart and Kennard, '40; Mettler, '47) have been considered one of the largest groups of afferent fibers passing to the substantia nigra. Levin ('44) estimated that approximately one-third of the corticofugal fibers from the precentral region entered the stratum intermedium of the substantia nigra. Recent experimental studies (Rinvik, '66) in the cat indicate that the number of corticofugal fibers projecting to the substantia nigra is much smaller than earlier studies suggested. Fibers from the gyrus proreus (homologue of the frontal lobe rostral to area 4) and "secondary sensory area" project to the medial and lateral regions of the nigral complex. The primary "sensorimotor" cortex projects fibers mainly to the middle third of the nigra, while fibers from the supplementary motor area appear to end in the medial two-thirds of the nigra. Corticonigral fibers from the primary "sensorimotor" cortex appear to end mainly in the neuropil of the nigra, but fibers from other areas terminate in close relationship to cell bodies and their processes.

Strionigral fibers have been described by many authors (Morgan, '27; Rundles and Papez, '37; Papez, '42; Verhaart, '50), but their extensive nature and spatial organization were not appreciated until the investigations of Voneida ('60) and Szabo ('62). Fibers from the head of the caudate nucleus pass to rostromedial parts of the substantia nigra (Voneida, '60), while fibers from the putamen project to lateral and caudal parts of the nucleus (Szabo, '62). Fibers from the neostriatum to the nigra are said to terminate mainly in the reticular zone, but some fibers appear to establish connections with cells in the compact zone (Nauta and Mehler, '66; Szabo; 67). Most authors (Ranson and Ranson, '42; Verhaart, '50) report that no fibers from the globus pallidus project to the substantia nigra, but the question must be regarded as unresolved, because experimentally it is virtually impossible to produce a lesion in the globus pallidus without producing some injury to the putamen. If pallido-nigral fibers exist, they probably are rela-tively sparse and may have a restricted area of termination (Nauta and Mehler, '66). Subthalamonigral fibers have been described (Woodburne et al., '46; Whittier and Mettler, '49) in normal and Marchi-stained preparations, but this connection remains in doubt (Carpenter and Stro-minger, '67).

Efferent fiber projections from the sub-stantia nigra described in the older litera-ture include: (1) *nigrostriatal fibers*, (2) *nigropallidal fibers*, and (3) *nigrotegmental fibers*. Although *nigrostriatal* fibers appear to be favored as one of the principal efferent bundles from this nucleus, evi-dence for their existence is based almost entirely upon retrograde cell changes occurring in the nigra following striatal lesions (Holmes, '01; Dresel and Rothman, '25; Ferraro, '25; Morrison, '29; Mettler, '43). Attempts to trace degenerated fibers from lesions in the substantia nigra into the striatum usually have not been suc-cessful (Ranson and Ranson, '42; Mettler, '42; Rosegay, '44; Cole et al., '64; Car-penter and McMasters, '64; Afifi and Kaelber, '65; Carpenter and Strominger, '67).

Although it has not been possible by accepted anatomical methods to trace fibers from the substantia nigra to the striatum (Cole et al., '64; Afifi and Kaelber, '65; Carpenter and Strominger, '67), data based upon a histochemical fluorescence method (Falck, '62; Falck et al., '62) sug-gest the existence of a nigrostriatal dopa-mine neuronal system. Using the above fluorescence technic it was found that the striatum has a very high dopamine content

(Andén et al., '64; Fuxe and Andén, '66) and that the large cells of the substantia nigra store a primary catecholamine, prob-ably dopamine. Following lesions in the substantia nigra, dopamine nerve terminals in the striatum disappear after about 8 days. Large striatal lesions are said to cause retrograde chromatolysis of nigral neurons and a marked decrease in amine levels. These observations appear highly significant in view of the fact that brains of patients with parkinsonism (paralysis agitans) show a virtual absence of dopa-mine in the striatum and substantia nigra (Hornykiewicz, '66).

Nigropallidal fibers have been estab-lished by experimental studies (Ranson and Ranson, '42; Kimmel, '42; Mettler, '43; Fox and Schmitz, '44; Woodburne et al., '46; Carpenter and McMasters, '64) using different methods. Evidence from the most recent studies (Cole et al., '64; Car-penter and Strominger, '67) suggests that these fibers are not numerous and that most of them terminate in the medial segment of the globus pallidus (Fig. 16–14).

Fibers regarded as *nigrotegmental* (Papez, '42) appear to be pallidotegmen-tal fibers, and so-called *nigrotectal fibers* (Foix and Nicolesco, '25) are regarded now as primarily corticotectal fibers that traverse portions of the nigra *en route* to the superior colliculus.

The most profuse and impressive projec-tions of the substantia nigra are to specific portions of the thalamus (Cole et al., '64; Afifi and Kaelber, '65; Carpenter and Strominger, '67). These *nigrothalamic fibers* pass rostrally through Forel's field H and enter the ventromedial aspect of the thalamus; fibers are distributed to the medial part of the ventral lateral nucleus (VLm) and to the magnocellular part of the ventral anterior nucleus (VAmc; Figs. 16–14 and 19–4). The full significance of this thalamic projection is not known, but it is of interest that there is little or no terminal overlap of nigrothalamic and pallidothalamic projections (Fig. 20–8).

The substantia nigra is regarded as an important extrapyramidal, or nonpyram-idal, nucleus, largely because it is one of

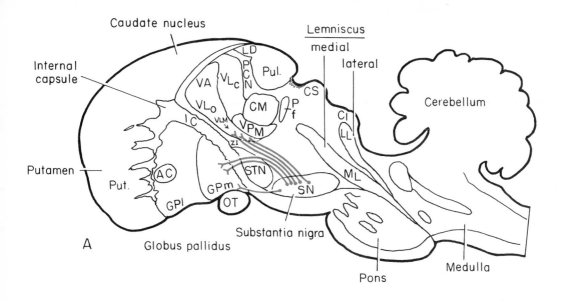

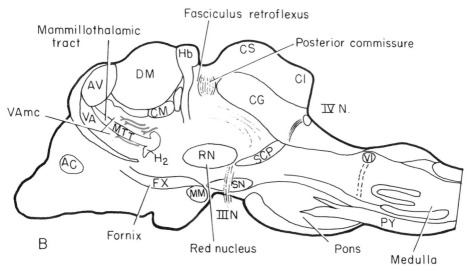

Fig. 16–14. Schematic drawings of the efferent projections (*red*) of the substantia nigra in sagittal sections. Ascending fibers from the substantia nigra (SN) course dorsal to the subthalamic nucleus (STN) to terminate in the medial part of the ventral lateral (VLm) and the magnocellular part of the ventral anterior (VAmc) thalamic nuclei. Efferent fibers from the substantia nigra also project to the globus pallidus (GPm). Drawing *A*, lateral to drawing *B*, shows a sagittal section passing through large parts of the basal ganglia (i.e., caudate nucleus, putamen and globus pallidus), thalamus and lower brain stem. Drawing *B*, relatively close to the midline, shows more medial regions of the thalamus and brain stem. The magnocellular part of the ventral anterior nucleus (VAmc) of the thalamus partially surrounds the mammillothalamic tract. Drawings are based upon studies in the rhesus monkey (Carpenter and Strominger, '67). Abbreviations indicate the following: AC, anterior commissure; AV, anterior ventral thalamic nucleus; CG, central gray; CI, inferior colliculus; CM, centromedian thalamic nucleus; CS, superior colliculus; DM, dorsomedial thalamic nucleus; GPL and GPm, lateral and medial segments of the globus pallidus; H2, lenticular fasciculus; Hb, habenular nucleus; LD, lateral dorsal thalamic nucleus; MM, mammillary body; OT, optic tract; PCN, paracentral thalamic nucleus; Pf, parafascicular nucleus; Pul, pulvinar; Py, medullary pyramid; SCP, superior cerebellar peduncle; VA, ventral anterior thalamic nucleus; VLc and VLo, ventral lateral thalamic nucleus (caudal and oral parts); VPM, ventral posteromedial thalamic nucleus; ZI, zona incerta.

the structures of this system that is affected with a high degree of consistency in paralysis agitans (Tretiakoff, '19; Foix, '21; Hassler, '39; Heath, '47). Several authors (Biemond and Sinnege, '55; Martin, '59; Jung and Hassler, '60) have suggested that the rigidity and akinesia of the parkinsonian syndrome may be related to pathological changes in the substantia nigra. It is of interest that discrete lesions of the substantia nigra in the monkey destroying up to 40 per cent of the nucleus do not produce alterations of muscle tone, impairment of associative movements, tremor, or any detectable form of dyskinesia (Carpenter and McMasters, '64). Larger, more extensive lesions involving portions of the substantia nigra, other midbrain structures and portions of the temporal lobe are reported to produce hypokinesis, general poverty of movement and a tendency to assume immobile postures (Stern, '66).

Crus Cerebri. The most ventral part of the midbrain contains a massive band of descending corticofugal fibers, the *crus cerebri*. According to Déjerine ('01), the medial three-fifths of the crus cerebri contain somatotopically arranged corticospinal and corticobulbar fibers. Other authors (Flechsig, '05; von Monakow, '05; Quensel, '10) indicate that smaller portions of the central part of the crus cerebri contain these fibers. Fibers in the most lateral part of the central region are concerned with the lower extremity; the larger middle region contains fibers concerned with the upper extremity; and the most medial fibers of the central region are associated with the musculature of the face, pharynx, and larynx. The extreme medial and lateral portions of the crus cerebri contain *corticopontine fibers*. Frontopontine fibers are medial, while corticopontine fibers from the temporal, parietal, and occipital cortices are located laterally (Fig. 16–1).

Besides the above named tracts, there often are two fiber bundles which descend partly within the crus cerebri and partly in the region of the medial lemniscus, known as *pes-lemnisci* (Fig.

16–1). The *medial* or *superficial pes-lemniscus* detaches itself from the lateral portion of the crus cerebri, winds ventrally around the crus, and forms a semilunar fiber bundle medial to the frontal corticopontine tract (Fig. 16–1). At lower levels the fibers leave the crus cerebri, pass dorsally through the substantia nigra, and descend in or near the ventromedial portion of the medial lemniscus. The *lateral* or *deep pes-lemniscus* detaches itself from the dorsal surface of the crus, runs for some distance in the lateral portion of the substantia nigra, then turns dorsally and descends in the region of the medial lemniscus (Fig. 16–1). Certain authors (Déjerine, '01; Verhaart, '35) regarded these bundles as aberrant corticospinal fibers which during phylogenesis became separated from the main tract by the increasing development of the dorsal pontine nuclei. According to Kuypers ('58a) fibers of the pes lemnisci can be traced caudally through the pons to the level of the pyramidal decussation. A number of these fibers are distributed to the tegmentum of the pons and medulla. These fibers, which are undoubtedly corticobulbar, appear to project mainly into the reticular formation; few, if any, of these fibers pass directly to motor cranial nerve nuclei. For a more complete discussion of corticobulbar fibers see p. 329, and Figure 14–23.

At this juncture it is recommended that the blood supply of the midbrain be reviewed (Chapter 4, p. 78). A more complete understanding of the structural organization of the midbrain should emphasize the importance of the vessels that supply this part of the brain stem. The principal vessels supplying parts of the midbrain include the posterior cerebral, the superior cerebellar, the posterior communicating and the anterior choroidal arteries (Figs. 4–13 and 4–14). The numerous veins draining large portions of the diencephalon and basal regions enter the great cerebral vein in regions dorsal to the midbrain (Fig. 4–18). These veins and their tributaries are of major importance.

CHAPTER 17

The Cerebellum

Although the cerebellum is derived embryologically from ectodermal thickenings about the cephalic borders of the fourth ventricle, known as the rhombic lip, this portion of the neuraxis functions in a suprasegmental manner (Figs. 5–9 and 5–11). The cerebellum is concerned primarily with mechanisms that influence coordination of somatic motor activity, equilibrium, and muscle tone. Afferent fibers projecting to the cerebellum, entering largely via the middle and inferior cerebellar peduncles, originate from cell groups in the spinal cord and from specific brain stem nuclei which relay impulses from the cerebral cortex, the reticular formation, and certain cranial nerves. While the functional influences of the cerebellum are exerted at both segmental and suprasegmental levels, the cerebellum does not give rise to any known tract that projects directly to spinal levels. Thus, cerebellar influences upon segmental parts of the nervous system are indirect and are mediated by groups of neurons that relay impulses downward and to other parts of the nervous system.

The gross anatomy of the cerebellum already has been described in Chapter 3 (page 38). From this discussion, it will be recalled that the cerebellum consists of: (1) a superficial gray mantle, the *cerebellar cortex*; (2) an internal white mass, the *medullary substance*; and (3) four pairs of *intrinsic nuclei* (Figs. 17–2, 17–3 and 17–11). Grossly the cerebellum may be divided into a median portion, the *vermis*, and two expanded lateral lobes or *hemispheres*. The cerebellar cortex is composed of numerous narrow *laminae* or cerebellar *folia*, which in turn possess secondary and tertiary infoldings. Five deeper fissures divide the cerebellar vermis and hemispheres into lobes and lobules which can be identified in gross specimens as well as in midsagittal section (Figs. 3–8 and 3–10). These fissures are (1) the *primary*, (2) the *posterior superior*, (3) the *horizontal*, (4) the *prepyramidal*, and (5) the *posterolateral* (prenodular). They form the basis for all subdivisions of the cerebellum (Fig. 17–1).

On developmental and functional bases, the cerebellum can be divided into three distinct parts. The *archicerebellum*, represented by the *nodulus*, the *two flocculi*, and their peduncular connections (i.e., *flocculonodular lobe*), is the oldest part of the cerebellum and is the subdivision most closely related to the vestibular nerve and nuclei (*blue* in Fig. 17–1). The flocculonodular lobe is separated from the corpus cerebelli by the posterolateral fissure, which is the first fissure to develop in the cerebellum. The *paleocerebellum*, consisting of all parts of the cerebellum rostral to the primary fissure, frequently is referred to as the *anterior lobe* of the cerebellum (*red* in Fig. 17–1). In lower forms, the paleocerebellum forms most of the cerebellum, while in man it constitutes a small subdivision which receives

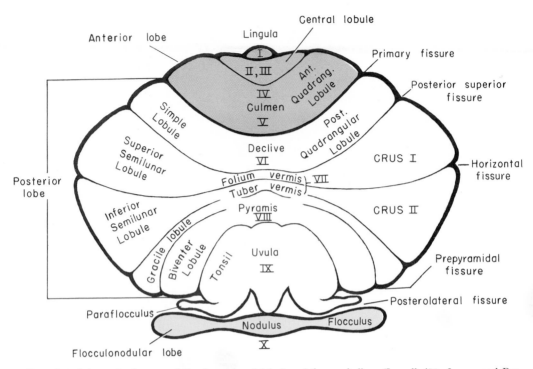

FIG. 17-1. Schematic diagram of the fissures and lobules of the cerebellum (Larsell, '51; Jansen and Brodal, '58; Angevine et al., '61). Portions of the cerebellum caudal to the posterolateral fissure (*blue*) represent the flocculonodular lobule (archicerebellum), while portions of the cerebellum rostral to the primary fissure (*red*) constitute the anterior lobe (paleocerebellum). The neocerebellum lies between the primary and posterolateral fissures. *Roman* numerals refer to portions of the cerebellar vermis only.

impulses primarily from stretch receptors. The paleocerebellum receives the spinocerebellar and cuneocerebellar tracts and is the part of the cerebellum considered to be most concerned with the regulation of muscle tone. Influences upon muscle tone mediated via the fastigial nuclei and cerebellovestibular projections reach spinal levels via the vestibulospinal and reticulospinal tracts. Impulses from the emboliform nucleus modify muscle tone by projecting upon cells of the red nucleus which in turn project to spinal levels (Massion, '67). These fibers are shown in Figure 17-15.

Phylogenetically the newest and the largest portion of the human cerebellum is the *neocerebellum*. It includes all parts of the cerebellum between the primary and posterolateral fissures in both the vermis and lateral lobes and comprises the posterior lobe (Fig. 17-1). The lateral part of the cerebellum between the primary

fissure and the posterior superior fissure is known as the *simple lobule*. The portions of the lateral lobe between the posterior superior fissure and the gracile lobule constitute the *ansiform lobule*. The horizontal fissure divides the ansiform lobule into *crus I* (superior semilunar lobule) and *crus II* (inferior semilunar lobule). Between the prepyramidal and posterolateral fissures are the biventer lobule and the cerebellar tonsil in the hemisphere, and the pyramis and uvula in the vermis. The neocerebellum is the portion of the cerebellum considered to be related primarily to coordination of skilled movements initiated at cortical levels.

The cerebellum is attached to the medulla, the pons, and the midbrain by three cerebellar peduncles (Fig. 3-7). These compact fiber bundles interconnect the archicerebellum, paleocerebellum, and neocerebellum with the spinal cord, brain stem, and higher levels of the neuraxis.

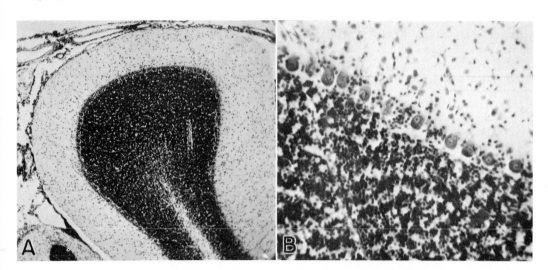

Fig. 17-2. Sections through a folium of monkey cerebellar cortex. In *A* the relative thickness of the three cerebellar layers can be seen. Light spaces in the dark staining granular layer are the "cerebellar islands" containing the glomeruli. A single row of Purkinje cells above the granular layer is shown in *B*. Photograph, Nissl stain, ×50, ×20.

The extensive nature of these connections suggests that the cerebellum serves as a great integrative center for the coordination of muscular activity. Before examining the afferent and efferent fibers of the cerebellum, it will be profitable to consider the structure of the cerebellar cortex.

STRUCTURE OF THE CEREBELLAR CORTEX

The most striking features of the cerebellar cortex are: (1) its relative simplicity and uniformity, (2) its well defined three layered structure, and (3) the five different neuron types which form it. This uniformly structured cortex, present in all parts of the cerebellum, extends across the midline without evident demarcation. The cortex is composed of three layers: (1) an outer *molecular layer*, (2) an inner *granular layer*, and (3) between these a ganglionic or *Purkinje cell layer* (Fig. 17-2, 17-4, 17-5 and 17-6).

The molecular layer consists principally of dendritic arborizations, densely packed thin axons coursing parallel to the long axis of the folia and two types of neurons (Fig. 17-5 and 17-6). The cell density of this layer is low. The two types of cell bodies in the molecular layer are the basket cell and the outer (superficial) stellate cell. The dendritic ramifications of both of these neurons are confined to the molecular layer, as are the axons of the outer stellate cells. The axons of the basket cells lie mainly in the molecular and Purkinje cell layers, but penetrate short distances into the granular layer. The cell processes of both cells are oriented transversely to the long axis of the folia. The *outer stellate cells*, located in the outer two-thirds of the molecular layer, have small cell bodies, short thin dendrites, and fine unmyelinated axons (Fig. 17-5 and 17-6). The short thin dendrites ramify near the cell body, and fine unmyelinated axons extend transversely to the folia to establish synaptic contacts with Purkinje cell dendrites. The *basket cells* (or deep stellate cells) are situated in the vicinity of the Purkinje cell bodies (Figs. 17-4, 17-5 and 17-6). These cells give rise to numerous branching dendrites that ascend in the molecular layer, and elaborate unmyelinated axons arising from one side of the cell body and coursing transversely to the folia. The axons of the basket cells, passing in the same plane as the dendritic arborizations of the Purkinje cells, give off one or more descending collaterals which form intricate terminal arborizations

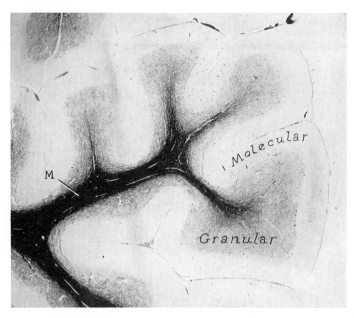

F IG. 17–3. Section through portion of adult cerebellum showing several secondary folia. *M*, Medullary core. Weigert's myelin stain. Photograph.

about the somata of about 10 Purkinje cells. A single descending axon collateral may furnish terminal arborizations for more than one Purkinje cell, and Purkinje cells may receive axonal collaterals from several different basket cells. Basket cell axons divide and form a dense plexus about the Purkinje cell axon hillock (Bell and Dow, '67). Thus a single basket cell may come in synaptic relationship with many Purkinje cells situated in the transverse plane of the folium, its axon even extending to a neighboring folium (Fig. 17–5). It is evident from the above that besides the relatively few cells, the molecular layer is composed primarily of unmyelinated dendritic and axonal processes. These processes include the dendrites of the Purkinje cells, the transversely running axons of the granule cells, the axons of the outer stellate cells, the sagittally oriented axons of the basket cells, and the dendrites of basket and Golgi type II cells. Section of all these processes gives to the molecular layer its finely punctate appearance. Only in its deepest portion is there a narrow horizontal plexus of myelinated fibers composed of axonal collaterals of Purkinje cells (Fig. 17–5).

The Purkinje cell layer consists of a single sheet of large flask-shaped cells that are relatively uniformly arranged along the upper margin of the granular layer (Figs. 17–2, 17–5, 17–6 and 17–7). Purkinje cells have a clear vesicular nucleus with a deeply staining nucleolus and irregular Nissl granules usually arranged concentrically (Fig. 17–4). Each cell gives rise to an elaborate dendritic tree which arborizes in a flattened fanlike fashion in a plane at right angles to the long axis of the folium (Figs. 17–5, 17–7 and 17–8). The dendritic tree arises from the neck of the cell as two or three large primary dendrites which branch repeatedly. In the depth of a furrow the dendritic branches form a broad angle approximating 180 degrees, while near the crest of a folium dendritic branches form more acute angles (Eccles et al., '67). The full extent of the dendritic arborization can be appreciated only in sagittal sections of the cerebellum. Primary and secondary dendritic branches have a smooth surface, but tertiary branches are characterized by short rather thick spines, densely and regularly distributed over all surfaces. These thick dendritic spines are referred to as "spiny

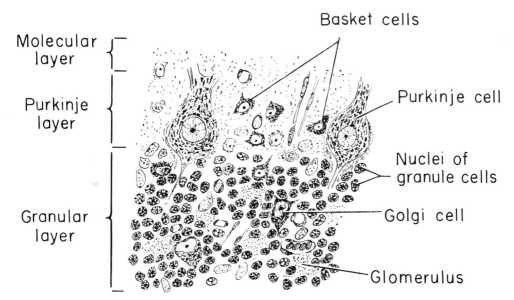

FIG. 17–4. Drawing of portions of the three layers of the human cerebellar cortex. Nissl stain (after Cajal, 11).

branchlets" (Fox and Barnard, '57) or "gemmules" (Fig. 17–8). The axon arises from the part of the Purkinje cell opposite to the dendrites, acquires a myelin sheath, and passes through the granular layer to enter the underlying white matter (Figs. 17–5 and 17–6); most, but not all, of these axons pass to the deep cerebellar nuclei. Purkinje cell axons give rise to recurrent Purkinje collaterals (Fig. 17–5) which establish axo-somatic contacts with Golgi type II cells in the granular layer (Hámori and Szentágothai, '66). Some Purkinje cell collaterals may make synaptic contact with basket cells but present evidence is not conclusive. Occasionally somewhat smaller, aberrantly placed Purkinje cells may be found in the granular or molecular layers. Since the axons of the Purkinje cells are the only ones to enter the white matter, it is evident that all impulses entering the cerebellum must converge on these cells to reach the efferent cerebellar paths.

The granular layer in ordinary stains presents the appearance of closely packed chromatic nuclei, not unlike those of lymphocytes; irregular light spaces here and there constitute the so-called "cerebellar islands" or "glomeruli" (Figs. 17–2, 17–4,

17–5 and 17–6). The *granule cells* are so prodigious in number (3 to 7 million granule cells per cubic millimeter of granular layer, Braitenberg and Atwood, '58) that the residual space seems insufficient to accommodate their processes, fibers of passage, and other intrinsic cells. Granule cell nuclei are round, or oval, in shape and range in diameter from 5μ to 8μ; chromatin granules are aggregated against their nuclear membrane as well as clustered centrally. The nakedness of granule cell nuclei is said to be due to: (1) the complete absence of discrete Nissl granules, and (2) the thinness of the rimming cytoplasm (Fox et al., '67). In silver preparations these cells give rise to four or five short dendrites, which arborize in claw-like endings within the "glomeruli" (Fig. 6–4B). The unmyelinated axons of granule cells ascend vertically into the molecular layer, where each bifurcates into two branches which run parallel to the long axis of the folium. These parallel fibers practically fill the whole depth of the molecular layer and run transversely to the dendritic expansions of the Purkinje cells. They traverse layer after layer of these expansions, like telegraph wires strung along the branches of a tree, and extend

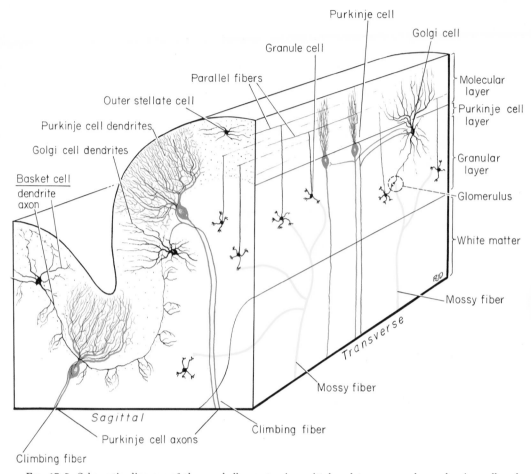

Fig. 17–5. Schematic diagram of the cerebellar cortex in sagittal and transverse planes showing cell and fiber arrangements. Purkinje cells and cell processes (i.e., axons and dendrites) are shown in *blue*. Mossy fibers are in *yellow*; climbing fibers are shown in *red*. Golgi cells, basket cells, and outer stellate cells are in *black*. While the dendritic arborizations of Purkinje cells are oriented in a sagittal plane, dendrites of the Golgi cells show no similar arrangement. Layers of the cerebellar cortex are indicated.

laterally in a folium (Fig. 17–5). Electron microscopic observations (Gray, '61; Fox et al., '64; Hámori and Szentágothai, '66) have shown that each dendritic spine of the Purkinje cell dendritic tree receives a synaptic connection from a parallel fiber in the so-called "crossing-over" synapse. In 1957 Fox and Barnard estimated that each Purkinje cell in the cerebellar cortex of the monkey had a total of 60,000 dendritic spines and that from 200,000 to 300,000 parallel fibers projected through the territory of its dendritic tree. More recent studies in cat, monkey and man (Fox et al., '67) indicate that the early estimate of 60,000 spines on a single Purkinje cell

should be doubled. Each parallel fiber, extending about 1.5 mm. from its bifurcation, has been estimated to traverse the dendritic trees of up to 500 Purkinje cells. The parallel fibers of the granule cells also make "crossing-over" synaptic contacts with the dendrites of outer stellate, basket, and Golgi type II cells in the molecular layer (Fig. 17–6).

The *Golgi type* II cell usually is found in the upper part of the granular layer, but it is seen also in other parts of this layer. These cells have vesicular nuclei and definite chromophilic bodies (Fig. 17–4). The dendritic branches of the Golgi cell extend throughout all layers of the

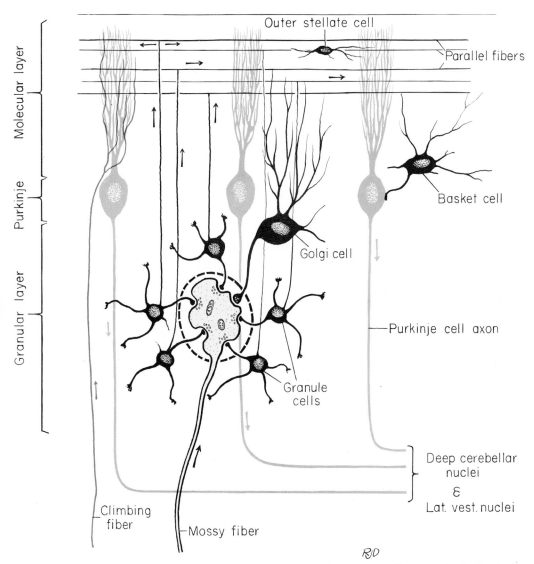

FIG. 17–6. Schematic diagram of the cellular and fiber elements of the cerebellar cortex in the longitudinal axis of a folium. Excitatory inputs to the cerebellar cortex are conveyed by the mossy fibers (*yellow*) and the climbing fibers (*red*). The broken line represents a glia lamella ensheathing a glomerulus, containing: (a) a mossy fiber rosette, (b) several granule cell dendrites, and (c) one Golgi cell axon. Axons of granule cells ascend to the molecular layer, bifurcate, and form an extensive system of parallel fibers which synapse on the spiny processes of the Purkinje cells. Purkinje cells and their processes are shown in *blue*. Climbing fibers traverse the granular layer and ascend the dendrites of the Purkinje cells where they synapse on smooth branchlets. Arrows indicate the directions of impulse conduction. Outer stellate and basket cells are shown in the molecular layer, but the axons of the basket cells which ramify about Purkinje cell somata are not shown (based upon Gray, '61; Eccles et al., '67).

cerebellar cortex, but are most extensive in the molecular layer. Unlike the dendrites of the Purkinje cell, arborizations are not restricted to a single plane (Figs. 17–5 and 17–6). In the molecular layer Golgi cell dendrites are contacted by parallel fibers; the cell body is in contact with collaterals of climbing fibers and recurrent collaterals of Purkinje cells (Scheibel and Scheibel, '54; Hámori and

Szentágothai, '66). It has been estimated that there is one Golgi cell for every 10 Purkinje cells (Bell and Dow, '67). The axonal arborization of the Golgi cell is extremely dense; it extends throughout the width of the granular layer but is restricted laterally to a region immediately beneath the cell body. The axons of Golgi type II cells have complex relationships with the terminals of mossy fibers and the dendrites of granule cells.

The "cerebellar islands" within the granular layer each contain a complex synaptic structure known as a *glomerulus* (Figs. 17-4, 17-5, 17-6 and 17-9). A cerebellar glomerulus is a nodular structure formed by: (1) one mossy fiber rosette, (2) the dendritic terminals of numerous granule cells, (3) the terminals of Golgi cell axons, and (4) proximal parts of Golgi cell dendrites. The center of the glomerulus contains a single mossy fiber rosette with which the dendrites of about 20 different granule cells interdigitate (Fig. 17-9). The axons of the Golgi cells form a plexus on the outer surface of the granule cell dendrites. The whole structure is encased by a single glial lamella (Eccles et al., '67; Bell and Dow, '67). Physiological evidence (Eccles et al., '66c) indicates that in the glomerulus, the mossy fiber-granule cell synapse is excitatory while the Golgi axon-granule cell junction is inhibitory. Thus a glomerulus is basically a cluster in which two types of presynaptic fibers enter into a complex relationship with one postsynaptic element. The granule cell and its dendrites constitute the postsynaptic element. The Golgi cell functions as a negative feedback to the mossy fiber-granule cell relay; the main excitatory input to the Golgi cell is derived from the parallel fibers (Fig. 17-6).

Nerve Fibers. Afferent fibers to the cerebellar cortex are supplied by tracts entering the cerebellum mainly via the inferior and middle cerebellar peduncles. These include the spinocerebellar, the cuneocerebellar, the olivocerebellar, the vestibulocerebellar and the pontocerebellar tracts as well as numerous smaller bundles of cerebellar afferent fibers. In addition there are cerebellar association fibers (Eager, '63a, '65) that pass from one folium to adjacent folia, and longer association fibers that connect different cortical regions on the same side. Structurally two types of afferent terminals are found in the cerebellar cortex, mossy fibers and climbing fibers.

1) The *mossy fibers*, so-called because of the appearance of their terminations in the embryo, are the coarsest fibers in the white matter. While still in the white matter, they bifurcate repeatedly into numerous branches, and enter the granular layer, where the branches of a single fiber often go to adjacent folia. They pass into the granular layer, lose their myelin sheath, and give off many fine collaterals. Fine lobulated enlargements, with the appearance of rosettes, occur along the course of the branches and at their terminals (Figs. 17-5, 17-6, and 17-9). A single mossy fiber rosette forms the center of each cerebellar glomerulus (Fig. 17-9). In the glomerulus they come into synaptic relationship with granule cell dendrites and Golgi cell axon terminals.

2) The *climbing fibers* pass from the white matter through the granular layer and past the Purkinje cell bodies to reach the main dendrites of the latter. There they lose their myelin sheath and split into a number of small fibers which climb ivy-like along the dendritic arborization of the Purkinje cell, whose branchings they closely imitate (Figs. 17-5 and 17-6). Climbing fibers contact only the smooth branches of the dendrites; they do not contact the spiny branchlets on which parallel fibers synapse (Fox et al., '67). Although Cajal considered each climbing fiber to be related to a single Purkinje cell, Scheibel and Scheibel ('54) have demonstrated that many fine collaterals leave the parent fiber and end on portions of the soma or primary dendrites of adjacent Purkinje cells. Light and electron microscopic studies (Scheibel and Scheibel, '54; Hámori and Szentágothai, '66) indicate that climbing fiber collaterals also make contact with stellate, basket, and Golgi cells. The climbing fiber system is remarkably specific. Each climbing fiber possesses an extensive all-or-

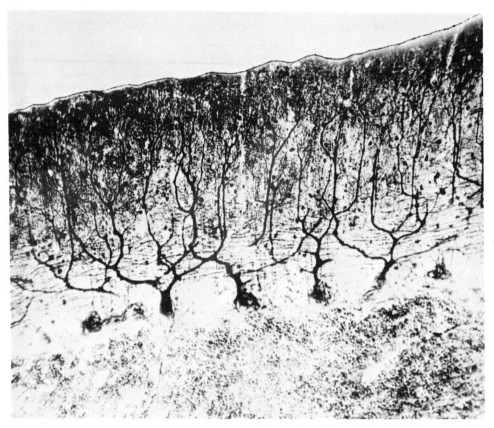

FIG. 17-7. Sagittal section through cerebellar cortex showing Purkinje cell bodies and their main dendritic processes. Fine parallel fibers in deeper portions of the molecular layer are basket cell axons. Cajal's silver stain. Photograph.

none excitatory connection with the Purkinje cell dendrites. Whenever the climbing fiber discharges, the Purkinje cell also discharges (Eccles et al., '64, '66).

The respective sources of the mossy and climbing fibers have been difficult to determine. Experimental evidence indicates that the mossy fibers degenerate following interruption of spinocerebellar and pontocerebellar tracts, and lesions involving primary and secondary vestibulocerebellar fibers (Miscolczy, '31, '34; Snider, '36; Mettler and Lubin, '42; Brodal, '54; Brodal and Høivik, '64). The mossy fibers constitute the principal afferent system to the cerebellar cortex and are the mode of termination of most cerebellar afferent systems. The climbing fibers have been the center of great interest since their discovery by Cajal in 1888 because of their remarkable one-to-

one relationship with dendritic branches of the Purkinje cell. These fibers have been thought to be recurrent axonal collaterals of Purkinje cells (Lorente de Nó, '24), or recurrent axons of the deep cerebellar nuclei (Carrea et al., '47). It now is believed that most climbing fibers arise from the inferior olivary complex (Szentágothai and Rajkovits, '59). Golgi studies (Scheibel and Scheibel, '54) have demonstrated that individual climbing fibers establish contact with almost every type of neuron in the cerebellar cortex. Ultrastructural observations of climbing fibers (Hámori and Szentágothai, '66) show that these fibers establish synaptic contacts with: (1) cell bodies and proximal parts of the dendrites of Golgi cells, (2) cell bodies of basket cells, (3) cell bodies of outer stellate cells, and (4) dendrites of Purkinje cells.

FIG. 17–8. Photograph of a single Purkinje cell and virtually all of its rich dendritic arborizations. ×300. (Courtesy of C. A. Fox, School of Medicine, Wayne State University).

C. **Structural Mechanisms.** The intricate geometric relationships of the structural elements in the cerebellar cortex have furnished many hypotheses concerning intracortical impulse transmission and the possible functions of individual neurons. Recent studies of the microphysiology of cerebellar neurons have yielded spectacular findings. These observations indicate that the climbing fiber has an extremely powerful excitatory synaptic action on the primary and secondary dendrites of the Purkinje cell (Eccles et al., '64, '66). On the basis that different endings of the same neuron probably mediate similar effects, it seems likely that climbing fibers also excite basket cells and Golgi type II neurons. Stimulation of the superficial parallel fibers, representing axons of granule cells, produces excitation of Purkinje cells via crossing-over synapses with Pur-

kinje cell dendrites (Eccles et al., '66a). However, stimulation of deeper parallel fibers produces less marked excitatory effects on Purkinje cells because of the concomitant inhibitory influences of basket and outer stellate cells. Available evidence (Eccles et al., '66b) indicates that the outer stellate cells, basket cells, and Golgi type II cells are inhibitory interneurons in the cerebellar cortex. Inhibitory influences of the outer stellate cells affect dendrites of Purkinje cells in the molecular layer (Fig. 17–5). Basket cell inhibition appears to be effected by axosomatic synapses on Purkinje cell somata. Golgi type II cells appear to inhibit the afferent input to the cerebellar cortex at the mossy fiber-granule cell relay in the glomeruli (Eccles et al., '66a). Inhibitory influences of the outer stellate and basket cells would be mediated in a plane trans-

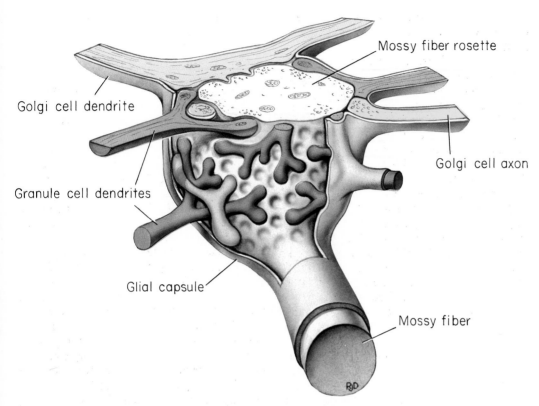

Mossy fiber rosette

Golgi cell dendrite

Golgi cell axon

Granule cell dendrites

Glial capsule

Mossy fiber

FIG. 17-9. Schematic reconstruction of a cerebellar glomerulus based upon electron microscopic studies. A cerebellar glomerulus is formed by one mossy fiber rosette, the dendritic terminals of numerous granule cells (*red*), and terminals of Golgi cell axons (*yellow*). Proximal parts of Golgi cell dendrites (*blue*) also enter the glomerulus and establish broad synaptic contacts with the mossy fiber rosette. The entire nodular structure is ensheathed in a glial capsule. In this reconstruction the glomerulus is shown in horizontal section, and in a schematic three-dimensional view (based upon Eccles et al., '67).

verse to the folia; outer stellate cell inhibition would be relatively localized, but basket cell inhibition would involve 10–12 Purkinje cells (Fig. 17–5). Because Golgi cell axons reach glomeruli throughout the depth of the granular layer, they could inhibit input via mossy fibers to parallel fibers for a distance of about 3 mm. longitudinally, and over a distance of 5 or 6 Purkinje cells transverse to the folium (Figs. 17–5, 17–6 and 17–9). Although Purkinje cell axons represent the principal discharge pathway from the cerebellar cortex, recurrent axonal collaterals exert important influences upon Golgi cells and basket cells (Fig. 17–5). Present evidence suggests that these axonal collaterals have a disinhibitory influence upon these cells (Hámori and

Szentágothai, '66). The cerebellar cortex thus has an exceedingly elaborate structural and functional organization in which multiple interactions influence input, conduction, synaptic articulations, and the output which ultimately must pass via Purkinje cell axons to the deep cerebellar nuclei. It has been estimated that the human cerebellar cortex contains 15 million Purkinje cells (Braitenberg and Atwood, '58). The combined surface area of the dendritic branchlets and spines of one Purkinje cell in the monkey is said to be about 220,000 square microns (Fox and Barnard, '57). A synaptic area of such magnitude on each of 15 million cells provides an index of the elaborate activity of the cerebellar cortex. The fact that all parts of the cerebellar cortex have a similar structure has been interpreted to mean that specific functions are not precisely localized.

2.   Purkinje cell axons represent the efferent pathway from the cerebellar cortex. These axons project mainly to the deep cerebellar nuclei, though some fibers from certain cortical areas by-pass the deep cerebellar nuclei and project to portions of the vestibular nuclear complex. Direct cerebellovestibular fibers arise from the flocculonodular lobe (Dow, '36, '38) and from portions of the vermis both anteriorly and posteriorly (Walberg and Jansen, '61; Eager, '63). Recent investigations (Ito and Yoshida, '64, '66; Ito et al., '64; Ito et al., '66; Eccles et al., '67) indicate that the entire output of the cerebellar cortex is inhibitory. Thus the axons of the Purkinje cells inhibit the cells with which they synapse, namely those of the deep cerebellar nuclei and portions of the vestibular nuclei.

The majority of cerebellar cortical association fibers are short interconnections extending no more than two or three folia. Long association pathways have been traced only from the paravermal cortex, the lateral culmen and the lateral cortex of crus II (Eager, '63a). Anatomically the cortex of the vermis appears independent of that of the lateral hemispheres in that association fibers in vermal cortex pass only to adjacent vermal folia, and the cortex of the lateral hemispheres does not project to the vermis (Clarke and Horsley, '05; Jansen, '33; Eager, '63a). Paravermal and lateral cortical areas of the anterior lobe give rise to long association fibers passing to the posterior folia of crus II on the same side. Long association fibers, crossing the midline, arise from lateral crus II, and terminate in folia of the contralateral crus II, the paramedian lobule and parts of the paraflocculus (Eager, '63). Long and short association fibers in the cerebellar cortex are regarded as myelinated axonal collaterals of Purkinje cells (Fox et al., '67).

Neuroglia. While most of the neuroglial elements in the cerebellar cortex are similar to those present in other parts of the central nervous system, the Purkinje cell layer contains modified astrocytes known as the Golgi epithelial cells (Cajal, '11) or Bergmann cells. Bergmann cells are a special form of astrocyte, indigenous to the molecular layer (Penfield, '32), with a "candelabra" shape, that give rise to several ascending processes. The upward prolongations of these processes coursing perpendicularly in the molecular layer terminate at the surface of the cortex (i.e., limiting glial membrane) in conical expansions, the bases of which are directed toward the folial surface. Bergmann fibers are located between the dendritic arborizations of consecutive Purkinje cells. Processes of Bergmann fibers insulate the smooth branchlets of Purkinje cell dendrites from passing parallel fibers (Fox et al., '67). This insulation is absent only where climbing fibers come into synaptic relationship with the smooth branchlets. The feathered cells of Fañanas are another variety of astroglia found in the deeper portions of the molecular layer, clustered close to Purkinje cell dendrites (Fig. 17–10). These special glial cells seem functionally similar to the Bergmann cells, but their processes do not reach the limiting glial membrane (Sotelo, '67). Oligodendroglia are very sparse in the molecular layer, but are found in other layers. In the granular layer astrocytes are principally of the protoplasmic type, while in the white matter they are of the fibrous type.

2.   THE DEEP CEREBELLAR NUCLEI

Imbedded in the white matter of each half of the cerebellum are four nuclear masses (Figs. 15–6, 15–14 and 17–11). The most medial of these, and phylogenetically the oldest, is the **nucleus fastigii,** located near the midline in the roof of the fourth ventricle. It consists of a lateral older portion containing large multipolar cells and a medial newer portion of smaller cells.

The nucleus dentatus, the largest of the deep cerebellar nuclei, lies in the white matter of the cerebellar hemisphere close to the vermis. It is a convoluted band of gray having the shape of a folded bag with the opening or hilus directed me-

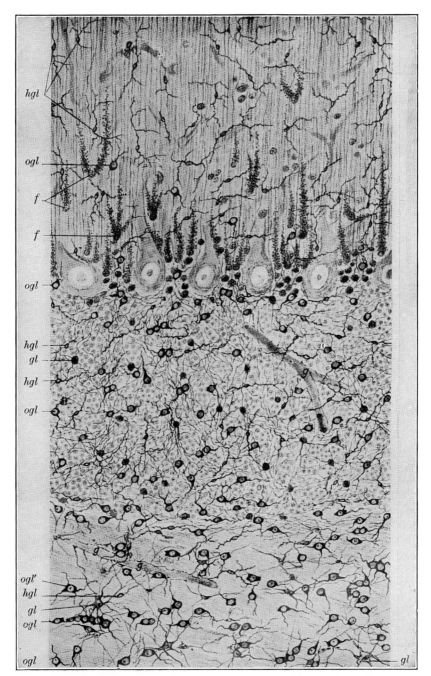

FIG. 17-10. Arrangement of neuroglia cells in human cerebellar cortex. *f*, Cells of Fañanas; *gl*, astroglia; *hgl*, microglia; *ogl*, *ogl'*, oligodendrocytes. (Jakob, '28, after Schröder.)

dially and dorsally. In transverse section it has an appearance similar to that of the inferior olivary nucleus. It is found as a definite nucleus only in mammals, and it becomes greatly enlarged in man and the anthropoid apes. A dorsomedial older portion may be distinguished from a newer and larger ventrolateral portion. The nucleus is composed mainly of large multipolar cells with branching dendrites.

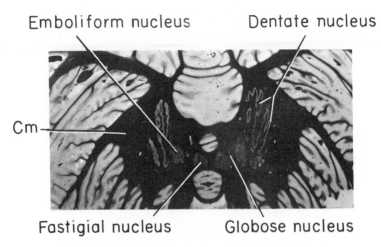

Fig. 17–11. Horizontal section through adult cerebellum showing portions of the deep cerebellar nuclei and the corpus medullare (Cm). Weigert's myelin stain. Photograph.

These cells have a high iron content. Their axons acquire a myelin sheath while still in the nucleus and pass out as fibers of the superior cerebellar peduncle. Between these cells are small stellate ones whose axons apparently arborize within the nucleus. Afferent fibers from the Purkinje cells enter laterally and form a dense fiber plexus, the amiculum, around the nucleus.

The nucleus emboliformis is a wedge-shaped gray mass close to the hilus of the dentate nucleus and often difficult to delimit from the latter. It is composed of clumps of cells resembling those of the dentate nucleus (Fig. 17–11).

The nucleus globosus consists of one or more rounded gray masses lying between the fastigial and emboliform nuclei. It likewise contains large and small multipolar cells. In lower mammals the globose and emboliform nuclei form essentially a single structure referred to as the *nucleus interpositus*. Flood and Jansen ('61) have distinguished two parts of the nucleus interpositus in the cat: (1) an anterior nucleus interpositus close to the dentate nucleus that appears homologous to the emboliform nucleus, and (2) a posterior nucleus interpositus located more medially that appears homologous to the globose nucleus.

Quantitatively the largest number of afferent fibers to the deep cerebellar nu-

clei arise from Purkinje cells in the cerebellar cortex. All parts of the cerebellar cortex project upon the intrinsic nuclei. The pattern of corticonuclear projection indicates that anterior and posterior vermal areas project fibers to the fastigial nuclei (Jansen and Brodal, '40, '42; Eager, '63). The paravermal cortex projects fibers mainly to the ipsilateral intermediate nuclei (i.e., the globose and emboliform), although fibers from some portions of this cortical region pass to parts of the dentate nucleus. Cortex of the lateral hemispheres gives rise to fibers projecting throughout the length of the dentate nucleus, and to caudal parts of the intermediate nuclei. Portions of the paraflocculus project fibers to the intermediate nuclei and to caudal parts of both fastigial nuclei. The intrinsic cerebellar nuclei in addition receive direct afferent fibers from specific portions of the inferior olivary nuclear complex. Olivocerebellar fibers, comprising one of the largest cerebellar afferent systems, pass to all parts of the cerebellar cortex and to the deep cerebellar nuclei. Other afferent fibers to the intrinsic cerebellar nuclei include: (1) secondary vestibular fibers to the fastigial nuclei, and (2) a small number of rubrocerebellar fibers to the interposed nuclei (Courville and Brodal, '66). If the Purkinje cells are inhibitory, as present evidence indicates, the deep cerebellar nuclei must be provided with some excitatory input. It is assumed that the deep cerebellar nuclei receive excitatory influences via collaterals of cerebellar afferents. It seems likely that the principal, but not the exclusive, source of this excitation may come from the inferior olivary complex (Eccles, '66; Fox et al., '67). Thus, the deep cerebellar nuclei probably receive both excitatory and inhibitory impulses. The current assumption is that in these neurons tonic facilitation predominates over inhibition, and thus maintains a tonic discharge of impulses directed toward brain stem neurons (Eccles et al., '67).

3   CORPUS MEDULLARE AND FIBER CONNECTIONS

The corpus medullare is a compact mass of white matter, continuous from hemisphere to hemisphere, that is covered everywhere by the cerebellar cortex. It consists of afferent projection fibers to the cerebellar cortex, efferent projection fibers from the cerebellar cortex, and to a lesser extent, association fibers connecting the various portions of the cerebellum. Many fibers—afferent, efferent, and associative—cross to the other side, the commissural fibers being concentrated in two cerebellar commissures: a posterior commissure in the region of the fastigial nuclei, and an anterior commissure in front of the dentate nuclei.

The corpus medullare is continuous with the three peduncles which connect the cerebellum with the brain stem: the *inferior cerebellar peduncle*, which connects with the medulla; the *middle cerebellar peduncle*, which connects with the pons; and the *superior cerebellar peduncle*, which connects with the midbrain (Figs. 3-7 and 3-8B). Medially and ventrally, near the roof of the ventricle, the corpus medullare splits into two white lamina—inferior and superior—which separate at an acute angle to form a tentlike recess (fastigium) in the roof of the fourth ventricle. The inferior lamina is a thin white plate which passes backward over the nodulus as the inferior medullary velum. It becomes continuous with the tela choroidea and the choroid

plexus of the fourth ventricle and, with them, forms the roof of the lower half of that ventricle (Fig. 3-10). Laterally the inferior medullary velum extends to the flocculi and actually forms the narrow bridge connecting these structures with the nodulus (Fig. 3-8).

The largest part of the medullary substance is continued into the superior lamina, which forms the superior medullary velum (Fig. 3-8). The latter is a thin white plate joining the two superior cerebellar peduncles; together these structures form the roof and lateral walls of the upper part of the fourth ventricle.

Afferent Fibers. The fiber connections of the cerebellum have been investigated by electrophysiological (oscillographic) methods which have confirmed anatomical findings and, in addition, have indicated some connections for which the exact anatomical pathways are still poorly known. The heightened activity of a group of neurons, resulting from electrical stimulation, can be recorded electrically as potential changes or "spikes." This activity is transmitted by axons to the nuclear groups in which they terminate. As a result, these nuclear groups are activated, and similar potential changes appear in their electrical record. If the pathway involves a number of neurons, the activity will be transmitted through successive nuclei to the terminal cell groups. Thus if the stimulation of a certain region in the cerebral cortex evokes potentials in a definite area of the cerebellar cortex, it is concluded that anatomical connections exist between the two areas. Similarly, stimulation of afferent peripheral fibers, or their endings, will evoke potentials in those parts of the brain which form the terminal stations of the afferent pathway. These methods do not disclose the exact anatomical location of the fiber systems and nuclei, or the number of neurons involved in a pathway. However, a suggestion of the number of synapses involved may be determined by the latency of the response (i.e., the time elapsed between the stimulus and the appearance of the electrical waves).

Afferent cerebellar fibers are nearly

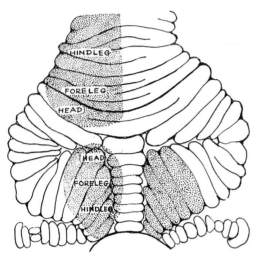

FIG. 17–12. Tactile areas of the cerebellum of the monkey as mapped out by discrete movement of hairs on the left side of the animal (Snider, '50).

3. *cerebellar connections*

three times more numerous than efferent ones (Snider, '50). They convey impulses from the periphery and from various levels of the neuraxis via relay nuclei in the brain stem. Most of the fibers enter the cerebellum through the inferior and middle cerebellar peduncles, though a small number enter in association with the superior cerebellar peduncle. The inferior peduncle consists of a larger, entirely afferent portion—the restiform body—and a smaller, medial, juxtarestiform portion that contains both afferent and efferent fibers, and is concerned primarily with vestibulocerebellar and cerebellovestibular connections (Fig. 15–14). With the exception of some rubrocerebellar, vestibulocerebellar and olivocerebellar fibers, which go to the deep cerebellar nuclei, all afferent fibers terminate in the cerebellar cortex.

The afferent fibers which connect the cerebellum with the periphery, directly or indirectly, convey mainly special proprioceptive impulses from the vestibular end organ and impulses from stretch receptors in muscles and tendons (Lloyd and McIntyre, '50; Oscarsson, '65). However, electrophysiological experiments on several species, including the monkey, have shown that exteroceptive impulses, such as tactile, auditory, and visual im-

pulses, likewise reach the cerebellum, though the fiber tracts conveying them are not fully known (Snider, '50). The projection of exteroceptive impulses to the cerebellar cortex is somatotopically organized in a definite way. Tactile stimulation evokes potential changes in the anterior lobe and simple lobule of the same side and in the paramedian lobules of both sides. The paramedian lobule corresponds to the gracile lobule (Fig. 17–1) but according to the accepted nomenclature, is regarded as a part of the inferior semilunar lobule (Angevine et al., '61). The leg is represented in the central lobule, the arm in the culmen, and the head in the simple lobule. The orientation is reversed in the paramedian lobules, the leg area lying most caudally and the head area most rostrally (Fig. 17–12). Similarly, auditory and visual stimulation evokes potentials in limited areas of the cerebellar cortex, i.e., in the simple lobule, folium, and tuber and immediately adjacent portions of the hemispheres (Fig. 17–13). The meaning of this localized projection is not altogether clear.

a) *Vestibulocerebellar fibers*, entering largely through the juxtarestiform body, include: (1) primary vestibular fibers from the vestibular nerve root that pass to the ipsilateral nodulus, flocculus, uvula, and ventral paraflocculus (Brodal and Høivik, '64), and (2) secondary vestibular fibers that originate from the inferior vestibular nucleus and, to a lesser extent, from parts of the medial vestibular nucleus. Primary and secondary vestibulocerebellar fibers appear to have similar distributions, but the number of secondary fibers is much greater. In addition secondary vestibular fibers pass bilaterally to the nodulus, uvula and the fastigial nuclei (Brodal and Torvik, '57; Carpenter et al., '59).

b) The *posterior spinocerebellar tract* enters the cerebellum as part of the inferior cerebellar peduncle and projects upon the rostromedial part of the anterior lobe (lobules I to IV, Fig. 17–1) and the lateral part of the pyramis and the paramedian lobule (Grant, '62a; Oscarsson, '65). Most of these fibers have been found to termi-

3. afferents to cerebellum (con't)

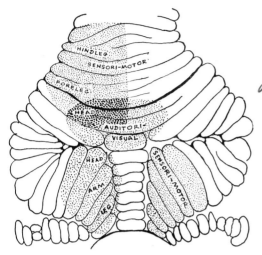

FIG. 17–13. Corticocerebellar projections in the monkey (*Macaca mulatta*). Note the head, arm, and leg areas receiving projections from the sensorimotor cortex. Note also the overlap of the head area with the area receiving projections from the audiovisual cortex (Snider, '50).

nate ipsilaterally. The posterior spinocerebellar tract conveys impulses from stretch receptors via group Ia and Ib muscle afferents, exteroceptive impulses from touch and pressure receptors in the skin, and slow adapting pressure receptors (Oscarsson, '65). There is no evidence that fibers of this tract convey impulses from low threshold joint receptors.

c) The *anterior spinocerebellar tract* has an aberrant course in that it ascends in the brain stem to rostral pontine levels and enters the cerebellum in association with the superior cerebellar peduncle (Figs. 13–15, 15–16 and 17–18). Fibers initially located dorsolateral to the superior cerebellar peduncle arch medially over this largely efferent bundle to enter the cerebellum. These fibers pass to essentially the same cortical areas as those of the posterior spinocerebellar tract. However, the main area of termination is in the anterior lobe; only a few fibers reach the pyramis and paramedian lobule (Grant, '62a). The majority of the fibers of this tract terminate in the cerebellum contralaterally with respect to the tract in the spinal cord (and ipsilateral to the cells of origin); about 15% of the fibers

terminate both ipsilaterally and contralaterally (Smith, '61; Grant, '62a; Oscarsson, '65). The anterior spinocerebellar tract mainly conveys impulses from group Ib afferent fibers.

d) *Cuneocerebellar fibers* from the accessory cuneate nucleus in the lower medulla enter the inferior cerebellar peduncle and pass to the posterior part of the anterior lobe, (lobule V, Fig. 17–1), the anterior folia of the simple lobule, the paramedian lobule, and the depths of the prepyramidal fissure in the posterior vermis (Grant, '62). Fibers of this afferent system are ipsilateral. The accessory cuneate nucleus may be regarded as the medullary equivalent of the dorsal nucleus of Clarke in the spinal cord. The cuneocerebellar tract, the forelimb equivalent of the posterior spinocerebellar tract, conveys impulses from group Ia muscle afferents and exteroceptive impulses from cutaneous afferents (Fig. 13–15). Receptive fields for cutaneous afferent impulses are smaller than those associated with the posterior spinocerebellar tract (Oscarsson, '65).

e) The *rostral spinocerebellar tract*, identified in the cat (Oscarsson, '64a, '65), is the forelimb functional equivalent of the anterior spinocerebellar tract, but is uncrossed. The fibers of this tract arise from cells rostral to the dorsal nucleus of Clarke, ascend in the anterior part of the spinal cord, and enter the cerebellum via both the inferior and superior cerebellar peduncles. Fibers of this tract are distributed almost exclusively to the anterior lobe of the cerebellum in lobules I to V (Fig. 17–1). Fiber terminations are predominantly ipsilateral, but some collateral branches pass to corresponding regions on the opposite side (Oscarsson, '65, '67). This tract is activated monosynaptically by group Ib muscle afferents and polysynaptically by flexor reflex afferents.

f) *Reticulocerebellar fibers.* Two distinct reticular nuclei in the medulla give rise to reticulocerebellar fibers, which enter the cerebellum via the inferior cerebellar peduncle. The lateral reticular nucleus of the medulla projects uncrossed fibers to the anterior lobe and the paramedian lobule. In general the projection to the vermis is more abundant than to other parts of the cerebellum. Spinal afferent fibers contained in the anterolateral funiculus are known to terminate in a specific manner upon the small-celled part of this nucleus and certain adjacent parts. Anatomical (Brodal, '49) and physiological (Combs, '56) evidence indicates that the lateral reticular nucleus is a relay in a spinocerebellar pathway transmitting somatotopically organized impulses to specific parts of the cerebellum. Reticulocerebellar fibers from this nucleus appear to mediate tactile impulses, and perhaps other types of impulses, to the cerebellum. The lateral reticular nucleus also receives fibers from the red nucleus and the fastigial nucleus, and thus, in part, functions in a cerebelloreticular feedback system.

The paramedian reticular nuclei of the medulla give rise to fibers which pass largely to the vermis of the anterior lobe, the pyramis, and the uvula, though some of them appear to terminate in the fastigial nuclei (Brodal, '53). These fibers are mostly uncrossed. The significance of this fiber system is not known, though it appears to be part of a cerebelloreticular feedback. Another group of medullary nuclei not belonging to the reticular formation appears to have a cerebellar projection which in principle is similar to that of the paramedian reticular nuclei. These are the perihypoglossal nuclei described in Chapter 14 (page 320).

Impulses transmitted to the cerebellum from higher levels of the neuraxis are mediated by pontocerebellar fibers, and, in part, by olivocerebellar fibers (Fig. 17–19). Some reticulocerebellar fibers also subserve a similar function.

Olivocerebellar fibers form the largest component of the inferior cerebellar peduncle. They arise from the contralateral inferior olivary nucleus and are distributed to all parts of the cerebellar cortex in an orderly pattern. In man, fibers from the medial portion of the olive and the accessory olives go to all portions of the vermis. A much larger component from

the lateral portion of the principal olivary nucleus is distributed to the cerebellar hemisphere. The dorsal part of the olive projects to the superior surface of the cerebellum, while the ventral part projects to its inferior surface (Holmes and Stewart, '08). The olivocerebellar projection in young cats and rabbits has been worked out in detail by Brodal ('40). The intracerebellar nuclei, as well as all parts of the cortex, receive olivary fibers, and the distribution is localized exquisitely, each portion of the olive projecting to a specific cerebellar area.

The inferior olivary nucleus is a highly developed complex in man; its specific functions are unknown, though its importance is obvious since it is the source of the climbing fibers that have potent excitatory synapses on Purkinje cell dendrites (Szentágothai and Rajkovits, '59; Hámori and Szentágothai, '66; Eccles et al., '64, '66). The principal part of this nucleus receives descending fibers from the central tegmental tract, a composite bundle originating from multiple nuclei. Descending fibers in this tract passing to the principal part of the inferior olivary nucleus arise from the red nucleus, the central gray substance, and the midbrain tegmentum. Fibers from the sensorimotor cortex pass to the ventral lamella of the principal olive via the crus cerebri and the pyramid (Walberg, '56). Spino-olivary fibers project to specific parts of the medial and dorsal accessory olivary nuclei. Electrophysiological studies (Eccles, '66) have shown that portions of the inferior olivary complex receiving fibers from the spinal cord are excited by impulses from groups Ia and II muscle afferents from the contralateral hindlimb. Thus the spino-olivary-olivocerebellar pathway in many respects resembles the posterior spinocerebellar tract (Brodal et al., '50), though conduction via this pathway is much slower. From this discussion it is obvious that the inferior olivary nucleus constitutes a massive cerebellar relay complex interrelating the spinal cord and suprasegmental structures with all parts of the cerebellum (Figs. 17–19 and 17–20). The massive *pontocerebellar tract* or middle cerebellar peduncle conveys impulses from the cerebral cortex to the cerebellum. The pontine nuclei receive cortical fibers from the frontal and temporal lobes and, to a lesser extent, from the parietal and occipital lobes. In the cat there is evidence that corticopontine fibers arising from the sensorimotor cortex project in a somatotopical manner onto two longitudinally oriented cell columns within the pontine nuclei (Brodal, '68). The fibers from the temporal cortex terminate in the caudal pons, those from the frontal cortex in the cranial portion of the pons. In man the pontocerebellar fibers are almost entirely crossed (Fig. 17–20*B*) and are distributed primarily to the ansoparamedian lobe and probably to the folium and tuber. According to Brodal and Jansen ('46), both uncrossed and crossed pontine fibers go to all parts of the vermis except the nodulus. Thus, while the neocerebellum receives the bulk of the pontocerebellar fibers, a considerable number of fibers go to the paleocerebellum as well.

Anatomically, the pontocerebellar projection does not show a definite pattern of localization. Electrical stimulation of the cerebral cortex in cats and monkeys evokes potentials in extensive cerebellar areas. These potentials are more definite and widespread from the motor and sensory cortex, but they may be elicited also from parietal, temporal, and occipital regions (Dow, '42). Several investigators have obtained remarkably localized cerebellar projections, from certain cortical areas. The results have been summarized by Snider ('50). The motor area (area 4) and the somatic sensory areas (areas 3, 1, and 2) project to the anterior lobe and the simple lobule. Within the cerebellum the cortical leg area projects to the central lobule, the arm area to the culmen, and the face area to the simple lobule (Fig. 17–13). These are the same cerebellar regions which receive tactile impulses from the leg, arm, and face, respectively. Similarly the auditory and visual areas of the cortex project to the simple lobule, folium, and tuber. Again these are the cerebellar regions receiving auditory and

visual impulses from the periphery. The probable meaning of these projections will be discussed in the section on cerebellar function.

The reticulotegmental nucleus of the pons (Fig. 15–18), located in the ventromedial pontine tegmentum, has been regarded as a dorsally displaced part of the pontine nuclei (Jacobsohn, '09; Brodal and Jansen, '46). Fibers from this reticular nucleus pass into the cerebellum via the middle cerebellar peduncle and are distributed to all parts of the vermis, except the nodulus, and to the ansoparamedian lobule. The reticulotegmental nucleus receives some spinal afferents as well as corticofugal fibers descending in the crus cerebri. Fibers of the descending division of the superior cerebellar peduncle terminating in this nucleus (Fig. 17–14) appear to be part of a cerebelloreticular feedback system (Carpenter and Nova, '60).

i) Both primary and secondary *trigeminocerebellar* fibers from different subdivisions of the trigeminal nuclear complex have been described. Although primary trigeminocerebellar fibers have been observed in lower vertebrates (Larsell, '23, '47; Woodburne, '36; Herrick, '48), their areas of termination in the cerebellum have not been established, and such fibers in mammals do not appear numerous. Secondary trigeminocerebellar fibers from the mesencephalic nucelus of N. V (Pearson, '49, '49*a*), studied in human fetal material, enter the cerebellum in association with the superior cerebellar peduncle and appear to be distributed to the dentate and the emboliform nuclei. These fibers are believed to conduct impulses from stretch receptors in the muscles of mastication and possibly also from the facial and extraocular muscles. Secondary trigeminocerebellar fibers from the principal sensory and spinal trigeminal nuclei (Woodburne, '36; Larsell, '47*a*; Carpenter and Hanna, '61) enter the cerebellum via the inferior cerebellar peduncle. Fibers from these nuclei terminate in the upper culmen and declive (Whitlock, '52; Carpenter and Hanna, '61). Electrophysiological studies (Snider

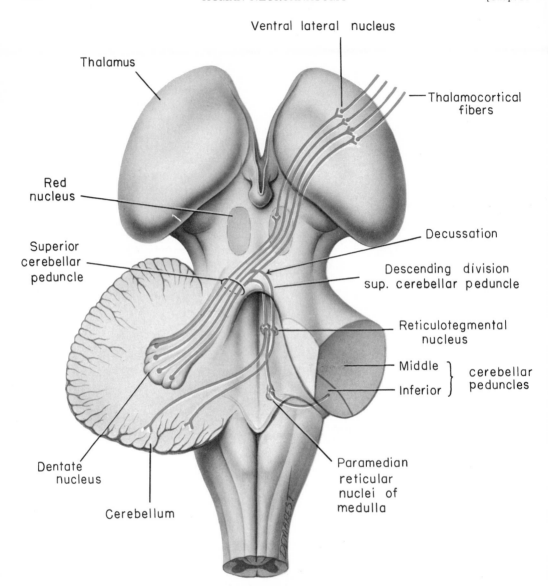

FIG. 17–14. Diagram of the efferent fibers of the dentate nucleus. These fibers, contained in the superior cerebellar peduncle, all decussate in the caudal mesencephalon. Ascending fibers project to the rostral part of the red nucleus and to the ventrolateral (VLo) nucleus of the thalamus. Fibers of the descending division of the superior cerebellar peduncle project to the reticulotegmental nucleus and the paramedian reticular nuclei of the medulla. Descending fibers of the superior cerebellar peduncle constitute part of a cerebello-reticular system that conveys impulses back to the cerebellum.

and Stowell, '44) confirm these same terminal areas.

Tectocerebellar fibers, described as originating largely from the inferior and superior colliculi and entering the cerebellum in association with the superior cerebellar peduncle, do not appear to be accepted by all authors. Certainly the terminal distribution of these thin and probably unmyelinated fibers within the cerebellum is not established. Tectocerebellar fibers and their termination have attracted attention because Snider and Stowell ('44) have shown that optic and auditory impulses give rise to action potentials in specific portions of the cere-

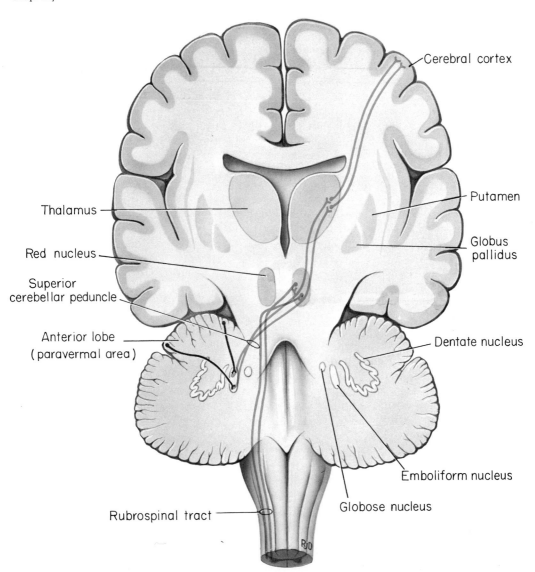

FIG. 17-15. Schematic diagram of connections between the emboliform nucleus (anterior interposed nucleus) and the red nucleus. Axons of Purkinje cells (*black*) in the paravermal cortex of the anterior lobe of the cerebellum project somatotopically upon the emboliform nucleus. The most rostral cortical regions, concerned with the lower extremity (Figs. 17-12 and 17-13), project to the rostral part of the emboliform nucleus, while caudal regions, concerned with the upper extremity, project to caudal parts of this nucleus. Fibers from the emboliform nucleus (*blue*) project via the superior cerebellar peduncle to caudal portions of the contralateral red nucleus, and to the ventral lateral nucleus of the thalamus. Projections from the emboliform nucleus to the red nucleus terminate somatotopically. Rubrospinal fibers (*red*) arising from dorsomedial regions of the red nucleus project to cervical spinal segments, while fibers from ventrolateral parts of this nucleus project to lumbosacral spinal segments. Thus the somatotopic linkage is maintained from cerebellar cortex to spinal levels (Courville, '66; Massion, '67).

bellar cortex (Fig. 17-13). While it is possible that these impulses may be mediated by direct tectocerebellar fibers, anatomical evidence suggests that impulses from the superior colliculus pass via tectopontine fibers to pontine nuclei (Altman and Carpenter, '61), which in turn project to areas of the cerebellar cortex. The cerebellar projection area of the pontine nuclei receiving tectopontine fibers corresponds to loci from which optic and auditory responses have been evoked (Snider and Stowell, '44; Brodal and Jansen, '46).

Efferent Fibers. The principal efferent tracts of the cerebellum arise from the deep cerebellar nuclei. Two distinct and separate efferent systems are recognized on the basis of the nuclei of origin, the course of fibers, and the terminal projection areas. Fibers from the dentate, emboliform, and globose nuclei form the largest cerebellar efferent fiber system, the *superior cerebellar peduncle* (Figs. 15–14, 15–20, 16–2, and 17–14). This system of fibers emerges from the hilus of the dentate nucleus to form a compact bundle along the dorsolateral wall of the upper part of the fourth ventricle. Studies in the monkey suggest that fibers from the nucleus interpositus and dorsal part of the dentate nucleus occupy the dorsal two-thirds of the peduncle, while fibers in the ventral part of the peduncle arise from the ventrolateral part of the dentate nucleus (Carpenter and Stevens, '57). At levels of the isthmus (Fig. 15–20), fibers of the superior cerebellar peduncle sweep ventromedially into the pontine tegmentum, and at the level of the inferior colliculus, all fibers decussate. The largest part of these fibers ascends to enter and surround the contralateral red nucleus.

Experimental anatomical studies (Jansen and Jansen, '55) indicate that approximately half of the fibers of the superior cerebellar peduncle arising in the dentate nucleus pass beyond the red nucleus. Of the fibers arising from the interposed nuclei only a little more than 10% appear to pass beyond the red nucleus. Thus, both the dentate and interposed nuclei give rise to rubral afferent fibers. While fibers arising from the dentate nucleus are more numerous, a relatively larger proportion of fibers from the interposed nuclei appear to end upon, or give off collaterals to, the contralateral red nucleus. Fibers from the dentate nucleus terminate mainly in the rostral third of the red nucleus while fibers from the interposed nuclei

project to the caudal two-thirds of this nucleus (Angaut and Bowsher, '65; Courville, '66). According to Courville ('66) fibers from the anterior part of the interposed nucleus in the cat (which probably corresponds to the emboliform nucleus in man, Flood and Jansen, '61) project somatotopically upon cells of the red nucleus. Two patterns of fiber organization have been recognized between these nuclei: (1) fibers distributed in a mediolateral sequence in the red nucleus have a caudorostral pattern of origin in the nucleus interpositus, and (2) fibers terminating in a rostrocaudal arrangement in the red nucleus have a corresponding lateromedial origin in the nucleus interpositus. However, only fibers from the interposed nucleus terminating in a mediolateral arrangement in the red nucleus are regarded as having a somatotopic distribution (Pompeiano and Brodal, '57; Courville, '66; Massion, '67). Thus rostral parts of the interposed nucleus project to hindlimb regions of the red nucleus (ventral and ventrolateral areas), while caudal parts of the nucleus project to forelimb regions of the red nucleus (dorsal and dorsomedial areas; Fig. 17–15). Because of the topographical projections of cerebellar cortex upon the deep cerebellar nuclei (Jansen and Brodal, '58; Eager, '63) which are organized as three longitudinal zones, connections exist between: (1) the paravermal cortex and the red nucleus through the interposed nucleus and (2) hemispheric cerebellar cortex and the red nucleus through the dentate nucleus (Massion, '67).

The majority of the fibers in the superior cerebellar peduncle (arising from the dentate nucleus) ascend to the ventral lateral (VLo) nucleus of the thalamus (Jansen and Brodal, '58; Figs. 17–14 and 19–4*B*). Physiological studies (Appelberg, '60; Eccles et al., '67) indicate that a number of axons from the interposed nucleus also project to the ventral lateral nucleus of the thalamus after giving off collaterals to the red nucleus. In addition to this main thalamic projection some fibers of the superior cerebellar peduncle pass to the more rostral intralaminar thalamic nuclei (Ranson and Ingram, '32; Mehler et al., '58; Carpenter and Strominger, '64). It is of interest that small localized lesions in the dentate nucleus produce degeneration distributed over the same areas of VLo and the intralaminar nuclei as virtually total ablation of the dentate nucleus, though the amount of degeneration is less (Carpenter, '67). The ventral lateral (VLo) nucleus of the thalamus projects in topical fashion to Brodmann's area 4 (Figs. 17–19, 19–4, 19–5 and 22–4); medial parts of the nucleus send fibers to the face area, lateral parts send fibers to the leg area, and fibers from intermediate regions pass to cortical areas corresponding to arm and trunk (Walker, '38a, '49).

A relatively small number of cerebellar efferent fibers from the dentate nucleus decussate in the caudal mesencephalon, pass dorsally and are distributed differentially within the lateral somatic cell columns of the contralateral oculomotor nuclear complex (Carpenter and Strominger, '64). Most of these fibers terminate about cells which innervate the superior rectus muscle on the opposite side (Fig. 16–9). These cerebello-oculomotor fibers appear to constitute a unique example of cerebellar efferent fibers projecting directly to a lower motor neuron. Another small group of fibers in the superior cerebellar peduncle decussate with the main bundle and descend in the ventromedial tegmentum of the brain stem near the median raphe. These fibers, constituting the descending division of the superior cerebellar peduncle, project largely to the reticulotegmental and the paramedian reticular nuclei (Carpenter and Nova, '60). Because these nuclei are known to project to the cerebellum, it seems likely that this component of the superior cerebellar peduncle may serve as part of a cerebelloreticular feedback system (Fig. 17–14).

Cerebellar efferent fibers originating from the fastigial nuclei emerge from the cerebellum via the *uncinate fasciculus* (*Russell*) and the *juxtarestiform body* (Figs. 17–16, 17–17 and 17–18). Fastigial efferent fibers in the uncinate fasciculus, both crossed and uncrossed, arch around the superior cerebellar peduncle. Fibers of this bundle originating from the rostral part of the fastigial nucleus are uncrossed, while the more numerous fibers from the caudal part of the nucleus are mostly crossed (Carpenter, '59; Walberg et al., '62). Fibers forming the descending component of the uncinate fasciculus sweep ventromedially to be distributed differentially in parts of all of the vestibular nuclei and in dorsomedial parts of the reticular formation of the pons and medulla (Figs. 17–16 and 17–17). Within the vestibular nuclei crossed fibers of the uncinate fasciculus are distributed to the peripheral parts of the superior vestibular nucleus, the ventralmost part of the medial vestibular nucleus, and the ventrolateral portions of the lateral and inferior vestibular nuclei. Some descending fibers of this system have been traced to the lateral reticular nucleus of the medulla (Walberg and Pompeiano, '60) and to the perihypoglossal nuclei (Walberg, '61).

Uncrossed fastigial efferent fibers contained in the uncinate fasciculus, and to a larger extent in the juxtarestiform body, arise from the rostral part of the fastigial nucleus and project largely to the vestibular nuclei, where they have a distribution distinctly different from that of the crossed fibers. In the inferior, medial, and lateral vestibular nuclei these fibers terminate in more dorsal areas which do not receive crossed fastigial efferent fibers. The above account, based on the investigations of Walberg et al. ('62), indicates relatively little overlap in the areas of terminal distribution of crossed and uncrossed fastigial efferent fibers in the vestibular nuclei. Only in the superior vestibular nucleus are these areas similar. The differential distribution of these fibers upon the lateral vestibular nucleus seems especially significant, since vestibulospinal fibers originating from this nucleus show a somatotopical arrangement (Pompeiano and Brodal, '57). These findings thus appear to offer an anatomical explanation concerning somatotopical localization

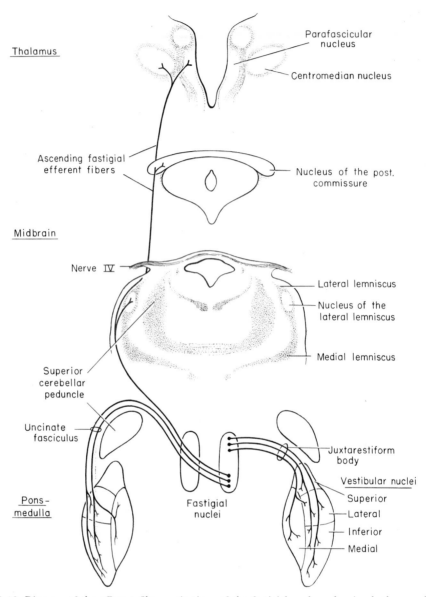

Fɪɢ. 17–16. Diagram of the efferent fiber projections of the fastigial nucleus showing both ascending and descending fibers. The differential distribution of fastigiovestibular fibers is based upon the investigations of Walberg et al. ('62). Descending fastigial fibers to the reticular formation are not shown.

within the vermis of the cerebellum (Fig. 17–17).

A smaller portion of the fibers of the uncinate fasciculus ascend in the dorsolateral part of the brain stem and project fibers to the nucleus of the lateral lemniscus, the nucleus of the posterior commissure, and a number of thalamic nuclei (Fig. 17–16; Thomas et al., '56; Carpenter et al., '58).

Cerebellovestibular fibers. Although the flocculonodular lobe is classically regarded as the "vestibulocerebellum," primary vestibulocerebellar fibers have a more extensive distribution in that they also project to ventral parts of the uvula and to the ventral paraflocculus (Brodal and Høivik, '64). All of these parts of the "vestibulocerebellum," considered in its broadest sense, project fibers to the ves-

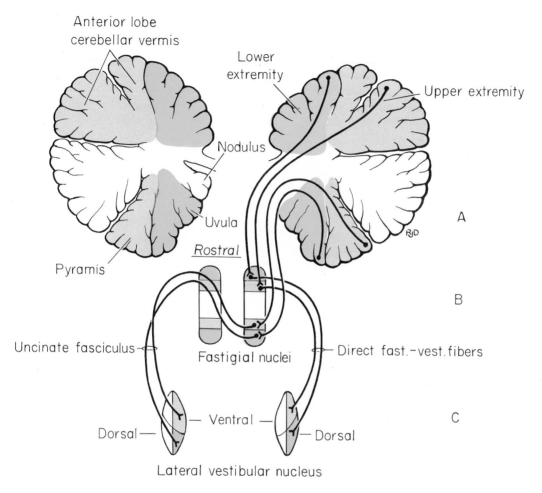

FIG. 17-17. Diagram of the somatotopic arrangements of the projections of the anterior and posterior cerebellar vermis upon the fastigial nuclei and the projections of the fastigial nuclei upon the lateral vestibular nuclei. The cerebellar vermis in *A* is shown in midsagittal section with areas concerned with the lower extremity in *red* and those concerned with the upper extremity in *blue* (See Figs. 17–12 and 17–13). The fastigial nuclei in *B* are shown in horizontal section, while the lateral vestibular nuclei in *C* are shown in sagittal planes. The direct fastigiovestibular fibers which arise mainly from the rostral part of the fastigial nucleus are shown on the right: these fibers project mainly to dorsal parts of the lateral vestibular nucleus. Fibers of the uncinate fasciculus, arising mainly from caudal parts of the fastigial nucleus, are crossed and project to ventral parts of the lateral vestibular nucleus. These somatotopic relationships were determined in the cat by anatomical and physiological studies (Walberg et al., '62). *Blue* areas of the cerebellar vermis, fastigial nuclei and lateral vestibular nuclei are concerned with the upper extremity; *red* areas refer to the lower extremity.

tibular nuclear complex, except the paraflocculus (Angaut and Brodal, '67). The flocculus and nodulus project fibers to portions of all four main vestibular nuclei; the uvula gives rise to fibers passing to portions of the superior, lateral and inferior vestibular nuclei. These fibers have an ipsilateral distribution.

Cerebellar Connections. Although cerebellar influences upon other parts of the nervous system are mediated by a number of relay nuclei at all levels of the

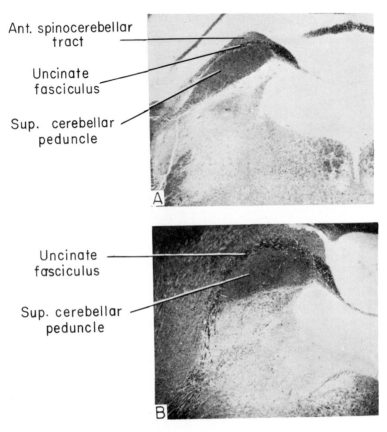

Ant. spinocerebellar tract

Uncinate fasciculus

Sup. cerebellar peduncle

Uncinate fasciculus

Sup. cerebellar peduncle

FIG. 17–18. Degeneration of fibers in the uncinate fasciculus of the monkey following a lesion of the contralateral fastigial nucleus. In *B*, all of the crossed fibers can be seen arching around the superior cerebellar peduncle near the site of emergence. Ascending fibers of the uncinate fasciculus are shown in *A* between the superior cerebellar peduncle and the anterior spinocerebellar tract. Marchi stain. Photograph.

brain stem, many of the structures receiving cerebellar impulses are known to project fibers back to the cerebellum. These complex pathways are referred to as feedback systems, and appear similar to those found in electronic systems which provide controlling and regulating effects. Cerebellar efferent fibers in the superior cerebellar peduncle project impulses upon the contralateral motor cortex through the mediation of thalamic nuclei. The motor cortex in turn gives rise to frontopontine fibers, which convey impulses back to the contralateral cerebellar hemisphere via the pontine nuclei and the middle cerebellar peduncle (Fig. 17–19). Other areas of the cerebral cortex also influence the activity of the cerebellum via corticopontine and pontocerebellar pathways. The central tegmental tract

conveys impulses from the red nucleus and the midbrain tegmentum which reach the contralateral cerebellar hemisphere by way of parts of the inferior olivary nuclear complex. Some fibers of the superior cerebellar peduncle that descend in the brain stem terminate upon reticular nuclei, which project fibers back to the cerebellum (Fig. 17–14). Efferent fibers from the red nucleus project directly to the interposed nucleus (Courville and Brodal, '66), as well as to relay nuclei (i.e., contralateral lateral reticular nucleus of the medulla and ipsilateral inferior olivary nucleus) of the brain stem that give rise to cerebellar afferent fibers. In addition, fastigial efferent fibers contained in the uncinate fasciculus and the juxtarestiform body project profusely and differentially upon the vestibular nuclei (Figs. 17–16

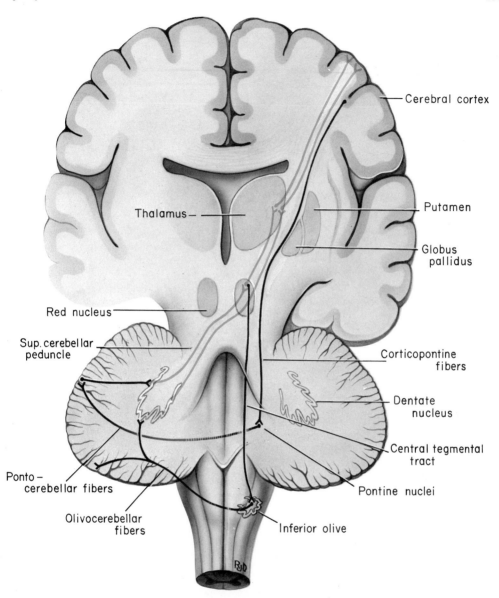

Fig. 17-19. Diagram of some of the principal afferent and efferent cerebellar connections. Cerebellar efferent fibers from the dentate nucleus are shown in *blue*. Corticopontine and pontocerebellar fibers (*black*) represent the most massive cerebellar afferent system. The principal inferior olivary nucleus receives uncrossed descending fibers from the red nucleus and periaqueductal gray via the central tegmental tract. Cortico-olivary fibers (not shown) pass via the medullary pyramids. Olivocerebellar fibers (*black*) cross, enter the inferior cerebellar peduncle, and are distributed to: (a) the cerebellar cortex as climbing fibers, and (b) the deep cerebellar nuclei.

and 17-17). Parts of the inferior and medial vestibular nuclei give rise to secondary vestibular fibers that project back to the cerebellum (Fig. 15-12). Similar relationships appear to exist between parts of the cerebellum and the lower brain stem reticular formation. Even though the functional significance of each of these multiple feedback systems is not fully understood, the systems are considered to play an important role in the integrative functions of the cerebellum.

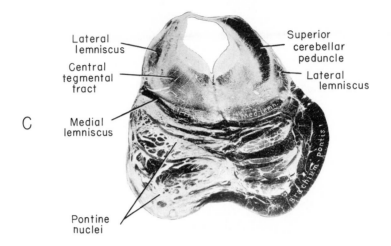

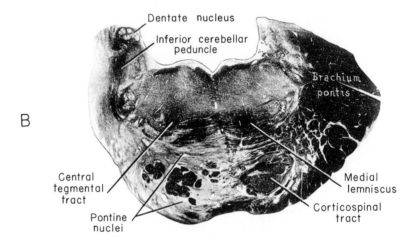

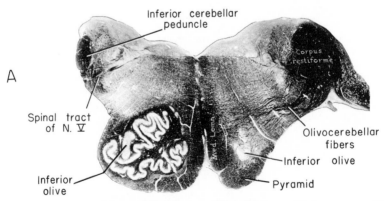

Fig. 17–20. Transverse sections of the medulla (A), pons (B), and isthmus (C) from a case of left cerebellar agenesis (Strong, '15). These sections clearly demonstrate the crossed nature of olivocerebellar and ponto-cerebellar fibers. Weigert's myelin stain. Photograph.

Some of the neocerebellar connections in man are especially brought out in Figure 17–20, which shows sections through the medulla, pons, and isthmus from an individual in whom the left cerebellar hemisphere, except the flocculus, failed to develop (hemicerebellar agenesis). There was also a correlated agenesia of all the afferent and efferent pathways to and from the left cerebellar hemisphere. The spinocerebellar and the vestibular connections were normal, since the vermis and flocculi were intact. On the other hand, the left dentate nucleus was represented by a minute structure; the right inferior olive was greatly reduced; and the right red nucleus (not shown) and pontine nuclei were practically absent. As a result, the left inferior cerebellar peduncle was greatly reduced by the absence of olivocerebellar fibers. The left superior cerebellar peduncle was represented by a few scattered fibers, and the left middle cerebellar peduncle was virtually absent. Similarly lacking were the right central tegmental and corticopontine tracts. As a result the right crus cerebri was composed only of pyramidal fibers. A survey of these preparations emphasizes the fact that in man fibers of the middle cerebellar peduncle and the olivocerebellar fibers are practically all crossed.

FUNCTIONAL CONSIDERATIONS

The cerebellum is concerned with the coordination of somatic motor activity, the regulation of muscle tone, and mechanisms that influence and maintain equilibrium. Afferent cerebellar pathways convey impulses from a variety of different receptors, including the organs of special sense, but special attention has been directed to cerebellar afferent systems that convey impulses from stretch receptors in muscles and tendons, and from the labyrinth. Although Sherrington referred to the cerebellum as "the head ganglion of the proprioceptive system," the cerebellum is not concerned with the conscious appreciation of muscle, joint and tendon sense, or any specific sensory modality. The cerebellum receives a massive input from the stretch receptors (i.e., the muscle spindle and Golgi tendon organ) via the spinocerebellar and cuneocerebellar tracts, while few impulses from these receptors are projected to the cerebral cortex (Matthews, '64).

It is widely accepted that stretch receptors probably play no role in the conscious perception of "position sense." The principal function of the stretch receptors appears to be in the unconscious neural control of muscular tone both during movement and steady contraction. The stretch receptors provide the cerebellum with information concerning the state of the muscles. The cerebellum, which receives the major part of the afferent input from the stretch receptors, appears to be part of a neural mechanism providing regulating and controlling influences that: (1) effect gradual alterations of muscle tension for proper maintenance of equilibrium and posture, and (2) assures the smooth and orderly sequence of muscular contraction characteristic of voluntary skilled movements. The superb physiological studies of Oscarsson ('65) suggest that the posterior spinocerebellar and cuneocerebellar tracts convey information which may be used in the fine coordination of posture and movement of individual limb muscles, while information conveyed by the anterior spinocerebellar and rostral spinocerebellar tracts may be utilized in postural adjustments involving the entire body, or an entire limb.

Each movement requires the coordinated action (synergy) of a group of muscles. The agonist is the muscle which provides the actual movement of the part, while the antagonist is the opposing muscle which must relax to permit movement. Associated with these are other synergic or, fixating muscles, which fix neighboring or even distant joints to the extent needed for the desired movement. The maintenance or change of posture similarly involves the cooperation of synergically acting muscle groups.

Such synergic units obviously must have a complex reciprocal innervation, as they receive both inhibitory and excitatory impulses which effect the alterations in muscular tension needed for any specific movement. While other neural centers probably are involved in this reciprocal innervation, the cerebellum may be regarded as the highest center for its finest automatic regulation. Its function is to furnish optimum tension states for all the muscles during both rest and activity. It plays an integral, though masked, role in all simple and complex skeletal muscle actions. The entire cerebellum works efficiently behind the scenes in the maintenance of posture and in walking, standing, sitting, and running, as well as in the performance of discrete and often complex movements of the limbs or digits.

There are certain principles concerning disturbances resulting from cerebellar lesions. These general principles are: (1) cerebellar disturbances, resulting from lesions in the cerebellum, occur ipsilateral to the lesion, (2) cerebellar disturbances usually occur as a constellation of intimately related phenomena, (3) cerebellar disturbances due to nonprogressive pathological changes show a gradual but definite attenuation with time, and (4) cerebellar disturbances resulting from cerebellar lesions probably are the physiological expression of intact neural structures deprived of the controlling and regulating influences of the cerebellum. To a degree the severity of the disturbances reflects the magnitude of the lesion, but it is known from experimental studies that extensive lesions confined to the neocerebellar cortex may cause only transient or minimal disturbances (Keller et al., '37; Carrea and Mettler, '47). Lesions involving the deep cerebellar nuclei, particularly the dentate nuclei, or the superior cerebellar peduncle, produce the most severe and enduring cerebellar disturbances.

Lesions of the cerebellar hemispheres (neocerebellum) primarily affect the isolated finer movements of the extremities (i.e., pyramidally induced movements). The muscles are flabby (*hypotonia*) and tire easily. The marked hypotonia associated with cerebellar disease may be related to interruption of afferent input from stretch receptors, or to destruction of efferent pathways that have facilitating influences on these receptors. There are severe disorders of movement (*asynergia*) expressed in faulty range, direction, and force of muscular contractions. Most striking is the inability to gauge distances properly (*dysmetria*); the movements overshoot, fall short of the mark, or they err in direction and pass it by (*past-pointing*). Cerebellar asynergia may be brought out in many tests. When the elbow of a normal man is made to flex against resistance and the arm is suddenly released, overflexion is arrested by the contraction of the triceps. In cerebellar disease the contraction of the triceps is delayed; as a result flexion is uncontrolled, and the patient may hit himself in the face or chest (*rebound phenomenon*). There is inability to execute rapid alternating movements, such as pronation and supination of the hand (*adiadochokinesis*), and movements which require simultaneous action at several joints may be broken up into a series of successive movements, each involving a single joint (*decomposition of movement*). Thus when asked to touch his nose with a finger raised above his head, the patient will first lower his arm and then flex the elbow to reach his nose.

The irregularities of muscular contraction probably are responsible for the coarse tremor during voluntary movement that is often demonstrable in cerebellar disease (Holmes, '39). The tremor classically associated with cerebellar lesions occurs only during voluntary or associated movements, has a coarse irregular quality, and occurs ipsilateral to the lesion. This type of tremor, referred to as "*intention tremor*," is not present at rest, becomes evident on purposeful movement, and is seen predominantly in the extremities. It appears to involve primarily the proximal appendicular musculature, but the tremor is transmitted mechanically to distal parts of the limbs. It is most evident in the upper extremities, mainly because weight-bearing in the lower extremities partially masks the disturbance. Cerebellar tremor frequently is contrasted with the tremor of paralysis agitans which is referred to as "static" or "resting tremor," meaning that the tremor is present when no voluntary or associated movements are in progress. Although each of these types of tremor has unmistakable features and occurs as part of distinctly different syndromes, Holmes ('22) noted that "resting tremor" may occur in association with cerebellar lesions. Certain developments in our understanding of tremor associated with cerebellar lesions indicate that the basic neural mechanisms involved in cerebellar tremor may be similar in some respects to those that underlie other forms of tremor (Carpenter, '61).

Ataxia, another asynergic disturbance seen in association with neocerebellar lesions, results in a bizzare distortion of basic movement patterns. This phenomenon, involving especially the axial muscles and muscles of the shoulder and pelvic girdles, produces marked disturbances in walking. It is characterized by muscle contractions which are highly irregular in force, amplitude and direction and which occur asynchronously in different parts of the body. Both cerebellar tremor and ataxia are most conspicuous and enduring when either the dentate nucleus or the superior cerebellar peduncle is destroyed. Patients with neocerebellar lesions also have unsteadiness in standing, particularly when the feet are close together; this occurs whether the eyes are open or closed. In standing the patient usually assumes a stance in which the legs are spread apart because this affords greater stability. The gait is broadbased and the patient reels, lurches, and frequently stumbles. With unilateral lesions there is a tendency to veer to the side of the lesion.

Nystagmus is commonly seen in association with cerebellar disease and is most pronounced when the patient moves his eyes laterally toward the side of the lesion. Cerebellar nystagmus is regarded as a fixation nystagmus in that it is most pronounced when eyes are fixed accurately on some small object. According to Holmes ('22) nystagmus results directly from lesions of the cerebellum and probably is the physiological expression of impairment of cerebellar mechanisms that control the synergy and tone of the extraocular muscles. However, it must be remembered that many pathological processes which affect the cerebellum also involve the brain stem and especially the vestibular nuclei located in the floor of the fourth ventricle.

Lesions of the cerebellum, particularly extensive lesions, produce disturbances of phonation and articulation. *Speech disturbances* are characterized by a slow, monotonous voice, and an unnatural separation of syllables uttered in a slurred and explosive manner.

Lesions involving portions of the posterior cerebellar vermis (i.e., nodulus and uvula) and probably portions of the flocculus produce what has been called the *archicerebellar syndrome*. Such lesions affect the axial musculature and the bilateral movements used for locomotion and maintenance of equilibrium. The patient sways and is generally unsteady when standing; when walking he staggers and has a tendency to fall backwards or to either side. The gait resembles that of a drunken individual in that it is broadbased, jerky, and highly incoordinate. If the muscles involved in speech are affected, articulation is jerky and words are slurred; the words are often shot out with unnecessary force. Nystagmus and abnormal attitudes, if present, are usually ascribed to injury of the vestibular structures. Muscle tone is little affected, there is usually no tremor, and there is no incoordination of arm or leg movements when the patient is resting in bed. This particular syndrome most commonly occurs in children as a consequence of a midline cerebellar tumor (medulloblastoma) that probably arises from cell-rests in the inferior medullary velum at the base of the nodulus.

Experimental studies (Tyler and Bard, '49) indicate that ablations of the nodulus in dogs, demonstrated to be susceptible to motion sickness, render these animals immune to the emetic effects of motion. These findings suggest that the emetic responses of motion sickness involve neural mechanisms independent of the forebrain.

Lesions of the anterior lobe of the cerebellum (paleocerebellum) in the dog and cat produce severe disturbances of posture and increased extensor muscle tone. These animals exhibit an extreme opisthotonus, tight closure of the jaw, hyperactive deep tendon reflexes, increased positive supporting mechanisms, and periodic tonic seizures. Those that survive these lesions regain the ability to walk without swaying of the head or trunk, and can perform voluntary movements without evident tremor (Fulton, '49a). Conclusive information concerning ablations of the anterior lobe of the cerebellum in primates does not appear to be available. A clinical syndrome in man corresponding to that described in experimental animals has not been defined. The closest related phenomenon would appear to be the so-called "tonic seizure," which usually is related to compression of the brain stem. Other experimental studies (Bremer, '22) have shown that ablations of the anterior lobe of the cerebellum produce an exaggeration of decerebrate rigidity in the cat.

In what is now a classical experiment, Sherrington (1898) demonstrated that electrical stimulation of the anterior lobe of the cerebellum could inhibit the extensor muscle tone in a decerebrate animal. This experiment, confirming the early work of Loewenthal and Horsley (1897), indicated an important inhibitory action of the paleocerebellum upon muscle tone. Studies summarized by Moruzzi (Dow and Moruzzi, '58) indicate that facilitating effects also can be obtained by stimulation of the anterior lobe of the cerebellum, and that the rate of stimulation is critical in determining whether inhibition or facilitation occurs. With square wave stimulation, it was found that low repetitive rates (2 to 10 cycles per second) caused a slow increase in ipsilateral extensor muscle tone, while rapid stimulation (30 to 300 cycles per second) produced a relaxation of the muscles in the ipsilateral limbs. These apparently opposite effects originally were interpreted as indicating that inhibitory and facilitatory neurons were intermingled in the cortex of the anterior lobe of the cerebellum. Further studies of these interesting phenomena (summarized by Brodal et al., '62) indicate that these inhibitory and facilitatory influences must involve different parts of the fastigial nuclei and their fiber projections, as well as cerebellovestibular fiber projections

(Fig. 17–17). Following lesions in the region of the rostrolateral part of the fastigial nucleus, stimulation of the ipsilateral vermis of the anterior lobe with high frequency square waves (300 cycles per second) produced a clear-cut increase in extensor rigidity on the side stimulated. This finding suggested that most of the inhibitory pathways had been interrupted by the fastigial lesion, while the facilitatory pathways remained intact. Following lesions in the region of the rostromedial part of the fastigial nucleus, stimulation of the vermis of the anterior lobe with low frequency square waves (2 to 10 cycles per second) caused inhibitory effects upon ipsilateral decerebrate rigidity, indicating that facilitatory fiber systems were interrupted by the fastigial lesion. After a unilateral total lesion of the fastigial nucleus, stimulation of the surface of the ipsilateral vermis of the anterior lobe yielded no responses (Sprague and Chambers, '53, '54), and the same effect was seen when the lesion was limited to the rostral part of the ipsilateral fastigial nucleus (Moruzzi and Pompeiano, '56). Although a complete anatomical basis for these physiological observations cannot be provided, it seems likely that: (1) inhibitory influences obtained from stimulating the vermis of the anterior lobe of the cerebellum are mediated via the fastigial nucleus and act in part upon the ipsilateral reticular formation, and (2) facilitatory influences obtained from stimulation of the vermis of the anterior lobe are mediated by parts of the fastigial nucleus that act upon the vestibular nuclei, particularly the lateral vestibular nucleus (Brodal et al., '62). Cerebellovestibular fibers which pass through regions near the rostrolateral part of the fastigial nucleus (Walberg and Jansen, '61), have been demonstrated to exert an inhibitory influence upon cells of the lateral vestibular nucleus (Ito and Yoshida, '66; Ito et al., '66; Eccles et al., '67). This is an example of direct cerebellar cortical inhibition upon cells of the lateral vestibular nucleus. As yet there is no anatomical evidence indicating a direct fiber projection from the cerebellar cortex to the reticular formation.

Studies in the cat of the physiological

effects of discrete lesions in the fastigial nucleus upon the extensor rigidity associated with decerebration have demonstrated that fastigial efferent fibers exert potent influences upon muscle tone. Sprague and Chambers ('53) observed that isolated unilateral destruction of the fastigial nucleus caused an inhibition of ipsilateral extensor muscle tone in the decerebrate cat. This finding was confirmed by Moruzzi and Pompeiano ('56) who further demonstrated that: (1) unilateral destruction of the rostral pole of the fastigial nucleus caused an ipsilateral inhibition of extensor muscle tone, (2) unilateral destruction of the caudal pole of the fastigial nucleus caused an inhibition of contralateral extensor muscle tone, and (3) bilateral total, or symmetrical, destruction of the fastigial nuclei caused extensor rigidity to be reestablished symmetrically (if lesions were produced serially) or to be essentially unchanged (if simultaneously produced). These findings initially were explained on the basis of interruption of predominantly uncrossed or crossed components of fastigial efferent fibers presumed to have a facilitatory influence upon portions of the reticular formation which can alter muscle tone. Because the fastigial efferent fiber projection system to the vestibular nuclei is more abundant than that to the reticular formation and has a definite somatotopic pattern of termination in the lateral vestibular nucleus (Walberg et al., '62), it seems likely that asymmetrical interruptions of fastigiovestibular fiber systems primarily account for the observed modifications of muscle tone (Fig. 17–17). Bilateral symmetrical, or total, lesions of the fastigial nuclei interrupt fastigiovestibular fiber systems equally on both sides, and under these circumstances muscle tone is not modified. These observations indicate that fastigiovestibular fiber systems are not essential for the maintenance of extensor muscle tone in decerebrate rigidity, but that asymmetrical withdrawal of the facilitating influences mediated by this system causes detectable differences in muscle tone.

Other cerebellar mechanisms which can influence muscle tone involve the paravermal cortex, the nucleus interpositus and the contralateral red nucleus (Massion, '67); all of these structures are connected by somatotopically organized fibers. Stimulation of the rostral part of the interposed nucleus (anterior part) produces flexion in the ipsilateral hindlimb of the cat, while stimulation of the caudal part of this nucleus produces flexion in the ipsilateral forelimb (Pompeiano, '59; Maffei and Pompeiano, '62). These responses occur ipsilaterally because fibers of both the superior cerebellar peduncle and the rubrospinal tract are crossed (Fig. 17–15). Intracellular recordings in the red nucleus demonstrate that stimulation of the nucleus interpositus produces excitatory postsynaptic potentials with a monosynaptic latency (Tsukahara et al., '64; Massion, '67). The pathway between the interposed nucleus and the red nucleus is regarded as purely excitatory and impulses conveyed by this system have an important facilitatory influence upon flexor muscle tone; these impulses are conveyed to spinal levels by the rubrospinal tract. Although the Purkinje cell output from the cerebellar cortex is inhibitory, variations in the activity of these cells are responsible for the inhibition or activation of cells in the interposed nucleus which directly effect cells of the contralateral red nucleus.

With the development of the pallium and corticospinal system, the importance of the cerebellum is increased greatly. It receives a massive cortical projection via the pontine nuclei which is related mainly to the neocerebellum. There is correspondingly an increased development of the dentate nuclei, superior cerebellar peduncle and the red nuclei, representing components of the principal pathway connecting the cerebellar outflow with the thalamus and cerebral cortex. Functionally the neocerebellum is concerned primarily with the regulation of coordinated voluntary motor activity. The most marked disturbances of neocerebellar function are seen only during voluntary movement; they disappear, or diminish, at rest, or following lesions which destroy significant parts of the corticospinal system.

The maintenance of equilibrium depends upon sensory inputs which can modify muscle tone and influence posture through reflex mechanisms or voluntary muscular activity. Sensory impulses concerned with the conscious regulation of posture and equilibrium involve primarily the visual system and kinesthetic receptors (located in joints and joint capsules) which transmit impulses to the somesthetic areas of the cerebral cortex. The vestibular and spinocerebellar systems convey impulses which play important roles in the automatic or reflex regulation of muscle tone. While some impulses from the vestibular end organ undoubtedly reach higher levels of the neuraxis, a large part of these impulses, and most of the impulses from stretch receptors, project to the cerebellum.

Experimental studies in the monkey demonstrate that cerebellar dyskinesia, produced by lesions in the deep cerebellar nuclei, can be abolished by surgical section of the dorsal half of the lateral funiculus of the spinal cord at high cervical levels (Carpenter and Correll, '61). Selective section of the anterior half of the lateral funiculus and the anterior funiculus of the spinal cord in these animals has no appreciable effect on the dyskinesia. Bilateral selective destruction of the posterior funiculi tends to exaggerate ataxia and asynergic disturbances, including tremor. These data suggest that impulses essential to the neural mechanism of experimental cerebellar dyskinesia in the monkey are transmitted to segmental levels via the lateral corticospinal tract. Since no fibers of the corticospinal tract are infrapallial in origin, and most are crossed, this implies that the neocerebellum must exert its regulating and controlling influences upon the contralateral motor cortex through the mediation of certain thalamic relay nuclei. This hypothesis is in accord with the well-established finding that neocerebellar disturbances occur ipsilateral to cerebellar lesions.

Clinical experiences indicate that lesions in the contralateral thalamic nuclei can significantly modify and ameliorate cerebellar dyskinesia in man (Cooper and Poloukhine, '59; Cooper, '60; Martin, '60). Experimental studies (Carpenter and Hanna, '62a) in the monkey have demonstrated that lesions destroying significant parts of the ventral lateral nucleus of the thalamus can reduce the tremor associated with cerebellar lesions without destroying fibers of the corticospinal tract and without producing paresis. Thus, this thalamic nucleus must be concerned with the mediation of certain cerebellar disturbances (Fig. 17–19). Physiological evidence also suggests that the cerebellothalamic cortical relay system may play an important role in the unconscious regulation of muscle tone. It seems likely that some impulses from stretch receptors may be conveyed to higher integrative levels of the neuraxis by these fibers. Further, it seems likely that surgical interruption of the relay fibers of this system at thalamic levels may be responsible for the reduction in muscle tone seen in patients with paralysis agitans.

Historically there have been two opposing concepts of cerebellar function. Bolk ('06), after a detailed comparative study of the mammalian cerebellum, concluded that there was a discrete somatotopic localization in the cerebellum, each cerebellar lobule controlling specific muscle groups. A similar though more restricted view was held by van Rijnberk ('26), who found that the head and neck muscles had their center in the simple lobule, while the arm muscles had theirs in the superior, and the leg muscles in the inferior portion of the ansoparamedian lobule. On the other hand, Luciani (1891) and Sherrington ('06) maintained that the cerebellum functioned as a whole in muscular coordination and that its various parts did not control individual muscles. Sherrington pointed out that the cerebellum is a "mechanism that deals with the innervation, not of this or that piece of musculature, but with the innervation of the musculature of the body as a whole" (Fulton, '49). This "unitarian" concept of cerebellar function, still dominant in clinical neurology, found strong support in the work of Golgi and Cajal. They demonstrated histologically that, unlike the cerebral cortex, the cerebellar cortex was remarkably uniform in structure throughout its whole extent. Clinically there is little evidence of functional localization as far as the extremities are concerned, neocerebellar lesions producing ipsilateral symptoms in both arm and leg (Holmes, '39).

Experimental investigations on animals, including the monkey and chimpanzee, indicate that the cerebellum possesses a remarkable degree of functional localization, especially in the anterior lobe, simple lobule, and tuber. These investigations also suggest that cerebellar influence is not related solely to the control of muscular coordination, but is exerted in practically all neural functions, both sensory and motor. The results of these investigations have been critically reviewed by Snider ('50).

The afferent impulses reaching the cerebellum through the corticopontocerebellar pathway are, in part, projected from specific cortical to specific cerebellar areas. The motor and somatic sensory areas of the cortex are related to the anterior lobe and simple lobule in such a manner that the cortical leg area projects impulses to the central lobule, the cortical arm area to the culmen, and the cortical face area to the simple lobule (Fig. 17-13). These same areas receive tactile impulses from the leg, arm, and face, respectively. The auditory and visual areas of the cortex project to the simple lobule, folium, and tuber, and these again are the cerebellar regions which receive auditory and optic impulses from the periphery.

Impulses from the red nucleus and reticular formation reach the cerebellum mainly by way of the central tegmental tract and by olivocerebellar fibers and, to a lesser extent, by the reticulocerebellar fibers. The fact that olivocerebellar fibers are distributed in a very specific manner to all parts of the cerebellum (Brodal, '40) suggests that these projections to the cerebellum are of great functional significance.

On the efferent side, the cerebellum projects impulses to neural centers, which in turn project back to the cerebellum. Here too a remarkable degree of somatotopic and functional localization is evident, especially in the indirect cerebellar projections to the cerebral cortex. It has been known for some time that stimulation of the anterior lobe will inhibit, or facilitate, the reflex movement of decerebrate animals. Snider and Eldred ('52) were able to map out localized areas for the control of leg, arm, and facial movements, which they found were identical with the tactile receiving areas.

Studies by Sprague and Chambers ('54) indicate that stimulation of either paleocerebellar structures or the medial reticular formation of the cat can induce reciprocal postural responses. Stimulation of vermal areas and the cortex of the anterior lobe resulted in ipsilateral facilitation of foreleg flexor muscles and inhibition of the extensor muscles. In the opposite limb, stimulation produced facilitation of the extensor muscles and inhibition of the flexor muscles. These changes in the limb muscles were accompanied by turning of the head and body to the side of stimulation. More variable postural effects were observed following stimulation of the lateral areas of the cerebellar cortex and lateral reticular formation. These postural adjustments include facilitation of both ipsilateral extension and contralateral flexion. The above experimental results provide evidence that the cerebellum influences posture in a reciprocal manner.

The cerebellar projections which pass by way of the thalamus to the motor area of the cerebral cortex have been known for a long time. The experimental studies of Henneman et al. ('48) and of Hampson ('49) on cats and monkeys have demonstrated that the cerebellum also projects to the various sensory areas of the cortex. Electrical stimulation of the anterior lobe, simple lobule, and paramedian lobules evokes responses in both the motor and the somatic sensory areas. In a similar way the central lobule projects to the cortical leg area, the culmen to the cortical arm area, and the simple lobule to the cortical face area. Similarly, stimulation of the cerebellar "audiovisual" area (simple lobule and tuber) evokes responses in the cortical auditory area and in parts of the cortical visual area.

Recent advances concerning the structural and functional components of the cerebellar cortex (summarized by Eccles et al., '67) suggest that in some way the cerebellum functions as a type of computer particularly concerned with smooth and effective control of movement. Present evidence suggests that the cerebellum integrates and organizes information flowing into it via numerous neural pathways, and that cerebellar output participates in the control of motor function by the transmission of impulses to: (1) brain stem nuclei (i.e., lateral vestibular and red nuclei) that project to spinal levels, and (2) thalamic nuclei which can modify the activity of cortical regions concerned with motor function. Every part of the cerebellar cortex receives directly, or indirectly, two extremely different inputs, that of the mossy fibers, and that of the climbing fibers. Although these inputs differ in their structural and functional characteristics, they appear to convey very similar sensory information to particular areas of the cerebellar cortex. The only output of the cerebellar cortex, conveyed by Purkinje cell axons, is inhibitory. This inhibition is exerted upon the deep cerebellar nuclei and the lateral vestibular nucleus. The output of the deep cerebellar nuclei is excitatory, a fact which implies that excitatory, as well as inhibitory, impulses must reach these nuclei. Excitatory impulses are thought to be conveyed to these nuclei via collaterals of both climbing and mossy fibers, as well as from other extracerebellar sources. The established fact that the cerebellar cortex transforms all input into inhibition, precludes the possibility of dynamic storage of information by impulses circulating in complex neuronal pathways, as in the cerebral cortex. The absence of reverberatory chains of neurons in the cerebellar cortex appears to enhance its performance as a special kind of computer, in that it can provide a quick and clear response to the input of any particular set of information. Available data suggest that the cerebellum processes its input information rapidly, conveys its output indirectly to other parts of the nervous system, and has virtually no short-term dynamic memory.

CHAPTER 18

Topography of the Diencephalon and Basal Ganglia

The rostral end of the brain stem is the diencephalon, a nuclear complex composed of several major subdivisions. Although the diencephalon is relatively small, constituting less than 2 percent of the neuraxis (Jenkins and Truex, '63), it has long been regarded as the key to the understanding of the organization of the central nervous system. Adjacent to the diencephalon, but separated from it by fibers of the internal capsule, are the basal ganglia. The basal ganglia represent subcortical derivatives of the telencephalon, but parts of the basal ganglia appear in many transverse sections through the diencephalon. The gross topography of these large nuclear masses and the internal capsule can be reviewed in Figures 3–5, 3–6, 3–11, 3–13, and 3–26 through 3–27. Although portions of the epithalamus, hypothalamus, and metathalamus (medial and lateral geniculate bodies) can be recognized in gross specimens, most components of the subthalamus (Fig. 3–13*B*) and the nuclear subdivisions of the thalamus can be studied only in microscopic preparations.

Because the diencephalon is one of the most complex divisions of the neuraxis, it is essential to become familiar with its topography and the relationships of its components before discussing the detailed anatomy and its functional implica-

tions. The region can be approached best through a graded series of photomicrographs of transverse sections. The level and plane of each section are indicated in Figs. 18–1 and 18–2.

MIDBRAIN-DIENCEPHALIC JUNCTION

Rostral transverse sections of the midbrain reveal the addition of several discrete nuclear masses of the caudal thalamus closely surrounding the posterior and lateral surfaces of the mesencephalon. These structures include the *medial* and *lateral geniculate bodies* and the *pulvinar*. External to all of these is the *retrolenticular* portion of the internal capsule (Figs. 18–3, 18–4, and A-12). The pineal body lies dorsally between the superior colliculi, while portions of the mammillary bodies can be seen in the interpeduncular fossa (Fig. 18–3). Fibers from thalamic nuclei pass laterally into the internal capsule, through which they are distributed to various parts of the cerebral cortex. The internal capsule also contains corticofugal fibers projecting to thalamic nuclei. Thus *thalamocortical* and *corticothalamic* fibers constitute a large part of the internal capsule referred to as the *thalamic radiations*.

Fibers of the optic tract enter the ventral surface of the lateral geniculate

441

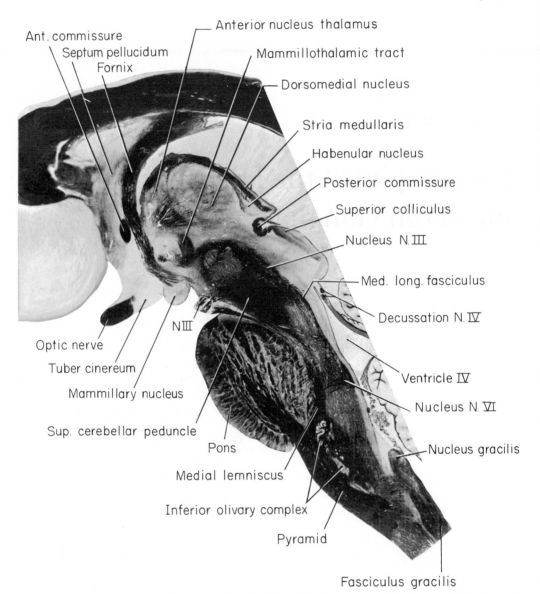

Fig. 18-1. Sagittal section of brain stem through pillar of fornix and root of third nerve. Weigert's myelin stain. Photograph.

body, where most of them terminate (Fig. 18-3). Some optic fibers, however, continue beyond the lateral geniculate body to form the *brachium of the superior colliculus*, which terminates in the optic strata of the superior colliculi and in the pretectal area. These fibers mediate reflex adjustment of eye, neck, and body muscles to optic stimulation (Fig. 13-22). The lateral geniculate body gives rise to a large number of fibers which pass lat-

erally into posterior parts of the internal capsule. These fibers form the geniculocalcarine tract (i.e., optic radiations), which project to the visual cortex (Figs. 19-11, 19-12 and 19-13).

Internal to the lateral geniculate body is the medial geniculate body, which receives the fibers of the brachium of the inferior colliculus. From its lateral surface fibers gather to form the geniculotemporal tract (auditory radiations),

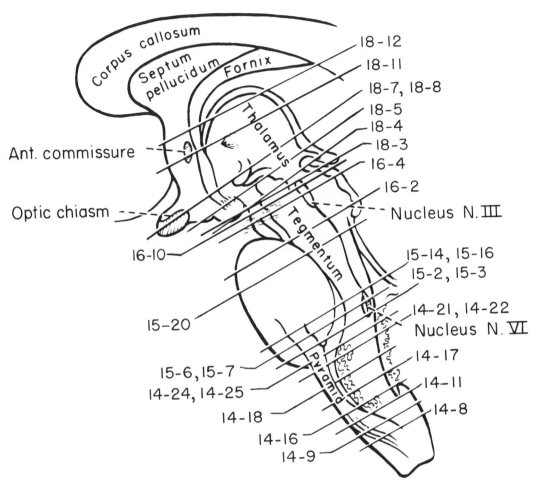

FIG. 18-2. Outline of paramedian sagittal section of brain stem, showing level and plane of the transverse sections of the figures indicated. For identification of structures see Figure 18–1.

which enters the internal capsule and projects to the temporal cortex, thus completing the auditory pathway (Figs. 15–9 and 19–9).

The pulvinar is a large nuclear mass dorsal to the medial geniculate body. Its dorsal surface is covered by a thin plate of fibers, the *stratum zonale*. Fibers passing laterally from this nucleus contribute to the retrolenticular portion of the internal capsule (Fig. 19–8) and are distributed to the posterior parietal and occipitotemporal cortex. The innermost portion of the internal capsule, wedged between the pulvinar and lateral geniculate body, forms a triangular area known as the *zone of Wernicke*. This zone, composed of a mixture of transverse and longi-

tudinal fibers (Fig. 18–3), mainly contains the optic radiations. After leaving the lateral geniculate body, these fibers course forward for variable distances and then loop backward to project to the occipital cortex (Figs. 19–11, 19–12 and 19–13). Intermingled with these are fibers from the pulvinar and the medial geniculate body.

In the midbrain root fibers of the third nerve have disappeared, but rostral portions of the oculomotor nucleus remain. Still present are cells of the Edinger-Westphal and anterior median nuclei. Rostral portions of the red nucleus are defined clearly by a fibrous capsule, formed principally by fibers of the superior cerebellar peduncle. Lateral to the

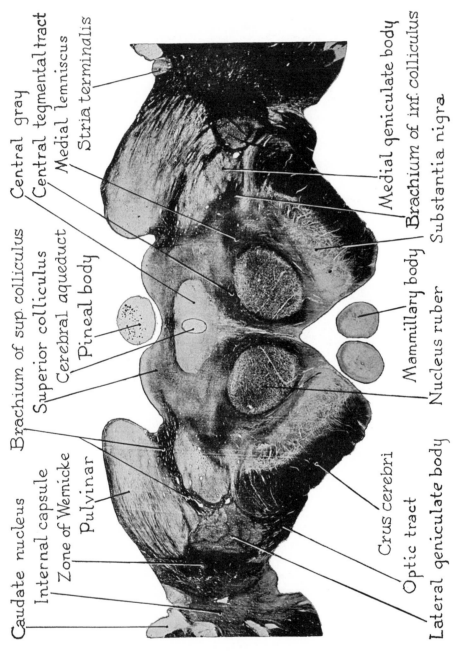

Fig. 18–3. Transverse section through junction of midbrain and thalamus. Weigert's myelin stain. Photograph.

Caudate nucleus
Internal capsule
Zone of Wernicke
Pulvinar

Brachium of sup. colliculus
Superior colliculus
Cerebral aqueduct
Pineal body

Central gray
Central tegmental tract
Medial lemniscus
Stria terminalis

Medial geniculate body
Brachium of inf. colliculus
Substantia nigra

Mammillary body
Nucleus ruber

Crus cerebri
Optic tract
Lateral geniculate body

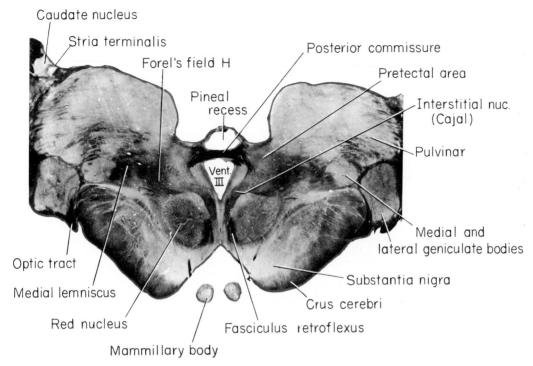

FIG. 18-4. Transverse section of the brain stem at the junction of mesencephalon and diencephalon. The posterior thalamic zone, which receives impulses from many sources concerned with painful and noxious stimuli, lies medial to the medial geniculate body at approximately this level. This cell group lies caudal to the ventral posterior thalamic nucleus (Fig. 18-5). Weigert's myelin stain. Photograph.

red nucleus are the medial lemniscus and the spinothalamic tracts. The reticular formation appears greatly reduced, as does the central tegmental tract. The medial longitudinal fasciculus is difficult to distinguish from the medial capsule of the red nucleus. The crus cerebri occupies the same position as in more caudal levels. Dorsal to it is the diminished substantia nigra.

Sections through more rostral levels (Figs. 18-4 and A-12) reveal a great expansion of the diencephalic nuclei, as well as significant, though less marked, changes in the midbrain. The pulvinar is much larger, while the medial geniculate body is smaller. The lateral geniculate body appears larger, and some fibers of the optic tract can be seen entering this structure. Lateral to the pulvinar is the tail of the caudate nucleus, separated from the pulvinar by fibers of the *stria terminalis* (stria semicircularis; Fig. 3-13). The stria terminalis occupies a shal-

low groove near the ventricular surface referred to as the terminal sulcus. The cerebral aqueduct expands into the deeper third ventricle; the posterior commissure marks the boundary between midbrain and diencephalon. Above the commissure is the stalk of the pineal body, enclosing the pineal recess of the third ventricle. The superior colliculi are replaced by the pretectal areas, believed to be centers for the pupillary light reflex (Fig. 18-4). This area, which receives fibers from the optic tract and the lateral geniculate body, projects fibers bilaterally to the Edinger-Westphal nuclei. The connections of the pretectal area and posterior commissure have been discussed in Chapter 16 (page 383).

The oculomotor nuclei and their root fibers have largely disappeared, though some portions of the most rostral visceral nuclei of the oculomotor complex may be present in the light-staining midline area below the ventricle. Lateral to this most

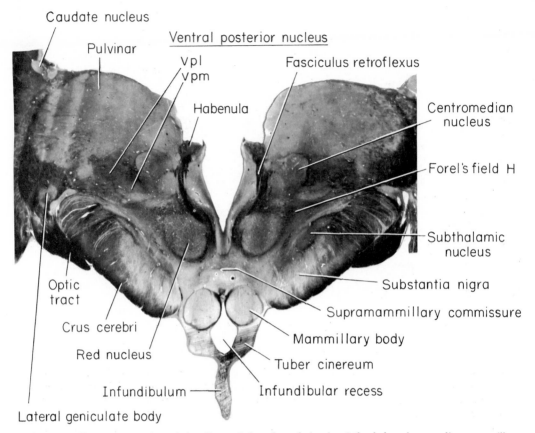

Caudate nucleus

Pulvinar

Ventral posterior nucleus

Vpl
Vpm

Habenula

Fasciculus retroflexus

Centromedian
nucleus

Forel's field H

Subthalamic
nucleus

Optic
tract

Substantia nigra

Supramammillary commissure

Crus cerebri

Mammillary body

Red nucleus

Tuber cinereum

Infundibulum

Infundibular recess

Lateral geniculate body

FIG. 18–5. Transverse section of the diencephalon through levels of the habenular ganglia, mammillary bodies, and infundibulum. VPL and VPM indicate the ventral posterolateral and ventral posteromedial nuclei of the thalamus. Weigert's myelin stain. Photograph.

rostral part of the oculomotor complex is a collection of relatively large cells, the *interstitial nucleus of Cajal* (Figs. 16–11, 16–12 and 18–4). This nuclear group receives a large number of ascending fibers from the medial longitudinal fasciculus (Fig. 16–13) and gives rise to a small number of descending fibers, which pass to the medial vestibular nucleus and the spinal cord (interstitiospinal tract). The area lateral to the posterior commissure and ventral to the pretectum contains the *nuclei of the posterior commissure*. *The nucleus of Darkschewitsch* (Fig. 16–11) lies within the periaqueductal gray, dorsal to the interstitial nucleus of Cajal.

The medial portion of the red nucleus is traversed by a vertical fiber bundle, the *fasciculus retroflexus* or *habenulopeduncular tract*. These fibers arise from the

habenular nucleus, situated at a somewhat more rostral level, and pass backward and downward to end in the interpeduncular nucleus and other midbrain nuclei. The tract is a link in a reflex pathway connecting the visceral areas of the forebrain with nuclei of the brain stem (Figs. 18–5 and 18–6).

The medial lemniscus, spinothalamic, and secondary trigeminal tracts spread out diffusely, prior to terminating in the ventral thalamic nuclei; these nuclei in turn project to the cerebral cortex. The capsular fibers of the red nucleus likewise change from a longitudinal to a transverse direction and form a radiating bundle that extends from the dorsolateral surface of the red nucleus toward the ventral portion of the thalamus. This is the beginning of the *tegmental field H of Forel* or *prerubral field*, composed at this

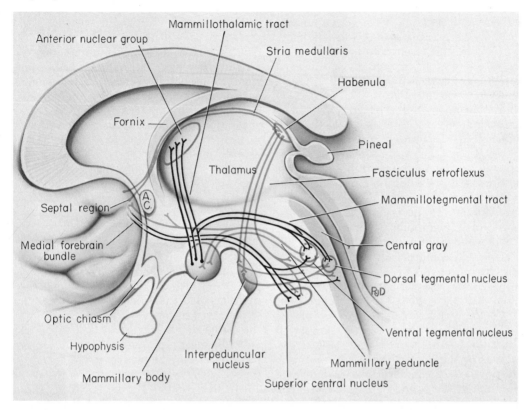

FIG. 18–6. Semischematic diagram of limbic pathways interrelating the telencephalon and diencephalon with medial midbrain structures. The medial forebrain bundle and efferent fibers of the mammillary body are shown in *black*. The *medial forebrain bundle* originates from the septal and lateral preoptic region, traverses the lateral hypothalamic area and projects into the midbrain tegmentum. The mammillary princeps divides into two bundles, the mammillothalamic tract and the mammillotegmental tract. Ascending fibers of the *mammillary peduncle*, arising from the dorsal and ventral tegmental nuclei, are shown in *red*; most of these fibers pass to the mammillary body, but some continue rostral to the lateral hypothalamus, the preoptic regions and the medial septal nucleus. Fibers arising from the septal nuclei project caudally in the medial part of the *stria terminalis* (*blue*) to terminate in the medial habenular nucleus. Impulses conveyed by this bundle are distributed to midbrain tegmental nuclei via the fasciculus retroflexus (based on Nauta, '58).

level mainly of rubrothalamic and dentatothalamic fibers. Cells scattered among the fibers of Forel's field H and along its dorsal border constitute the *nucleus of the tegmental field of Forel* (nucleus of the prerubral field; Fig. 19–2).

CAUDAL DIENCEPHALON

Transverse sections through the habenular nuclei and the mammillary bodies (Fig. 18–5) reveal the structural organization of the caudal diencephalon. The *habenular nuclei* are two small gray masses forming triangular eminences on the dorsomedial surfaces of the thalami.

These nuclei receive fibers mainly from the septal nuclei and the preoptic area via the striae medullares (Figs. 3–5*B*, 3–13, 18–1 and 18–6). Some fibers crossing to the opposite side in the *habenular commissure* are not illustrated in Figure 18–5, but can be seen in Figures 3–5 and 3–13*A*. Axons from the habenular nuclei form a well-defined bundle, the *fasciculus retroflexus*, which passes ventrally and caudally to terminate in the interpeduncular nuclei. The fasciculus retroflexus passes through the rostromedial part of the red nucleus.

The third ventricle appears greatly en-

larged, and parts of it are seen in two
locations (Figs. 18–5 and A-13). The main
part of the third ventricle is present dorsally, where it is covered by a thin roof
extending between the habenular nuclei
and the striae medullares. The margins of
this attachment (not shown in Fig. 18–5)
on each side constitute the *tenia thalami*.
A small part of the third ventricle, referred to as the *infundibular recess*, is
present ventral to the mammillary bodies
and dorsal to the infundibulum. The mammillary bodies, tuber cinereum, and infundibulum are parts of the hypothalamus. Each mammillary body consists of
a larger *medial nucleus* and a smaller lateral portion composed of the *intermediate*
and *lateral nuclei* (Fig. 19–15). The mammillary body receives some fibers from the
basal olfactory areas of the brain, and
corticomammillary fibers by way of the
fornix from the hippocampal formation
(Figs. 18–1 and 18–6). It also receives collaterals or terminals from other ascending
tracts; these fibers form the *peduncle* of
the mammillary body (Fig. 18–6). The
mammillary body gives rise to the *fasciculus mammillaris princeps* which splits to
form two distinct tracts (Fig. 18–6). The
larger *mammillothalamic tract* (*bundle
of Vicq d'Azyr*) passes diagonally upward
and forward to terminate in the anterior
nuclear group of the thalamus. The
smaller *mammillotegmental tract* curves
caudally and passes to certain tegmental
nuclei of the midbrain.

The small rostral pole of the substantia nigra lies dorsal to the medial part of
the crus cerebri. Dorsolateral to the nigra
is a lens-shaped gray mass, the *subthalamic nucleus*, (corpus Luysi; Fig. 18–5).
Dorsal to the mammillary bodies a few
fibers of the *supramammillary commissure* (posterior hypothalamic decussation)
can be seen crossing the midline.

The red nucleus is smaller and flanked
dorsolaterally by tegmental field H of
Forel. Between the dorsal capsule of the
subthalamic nucleus and the tegmental
field is a narrow band of gray matter
known as the *zona incerta*. Like the nucleus of the field of Forel, it may be regarded as a continuation of the midbrain
reticular formation (Figs. 18–7 and 18–8).

A progressive increase in the size of the
thalamus is evident (Figs. 18–5 and A-13).
The pulvinar has reached its greatest extent and part of the lateral thalamic nuclear group, with which the pulvinar is
continuous rostrally, also may be present.
Ventral to the pulvinar are the ventral
thalamic nuclei and the *centromedian
nucleus;* the latter nucleus is delimited
sharply by a thin fibrous capsule. The
medial geniculate body has disappeared
and the lateral geniculate is greatly reduced.

DIENCEPHALON AND BASAL GANGLIA
(LEVEL OF OPTIC CHIASM)

Transverse sections through the central
part of the diencephalon (Figs. 18–1, 18–7,
and 18–8) demonstrate three major subdivisions of the diencephalon: (1) the
thalamus, (2) the hypothalamus, and (3)
the subthalamic region. Portions of the
epithalamus, represented by the striae
medullares, the habenular nuclei, and the
pineal body, can be seen in Figures 18–3,
18–4, 18–5 and 18–8. In addition, these
sections show the lenticulothalamic portion of the internal capsule and, lateral
to this, parts of the basal ganglia.

The narrow third ventricle, extending
from the region immediately ventral to
the striae medullares to the optic chiasm,
completely separates the thalami. A shallow groove on the ventricular surface, the
hypothalamic sulcus (Figs. 3–11, 3–12,
and 3–13B), separates the dorsal thalamus
from the hypothalamus. The dorsal surface of the thalamus is covered by the
stratum zonale. At the junction of the
dorsal and medial thalamic surfaces, fibers
of the striae medullares are cut transversely and appear as small bundles of
myelinated fibers. These fibers pass caudally to terminate in the habenular nuclei (Fig. 18–1). The dorsal thalamus is
divided into medial and lateral nuclear
groups by a delicate band of myelinated
fibers, the *internal medullary lamina* of
the thalamus. In the lateral nuclear group,
ventral and lateral (dorsal) nuclear masses
can be distinguished (Figs. 18–8, 19–2 and
19–3). The ventral nuclear mass, extending nearly the entire length of the thalamus, is divisible into three separate

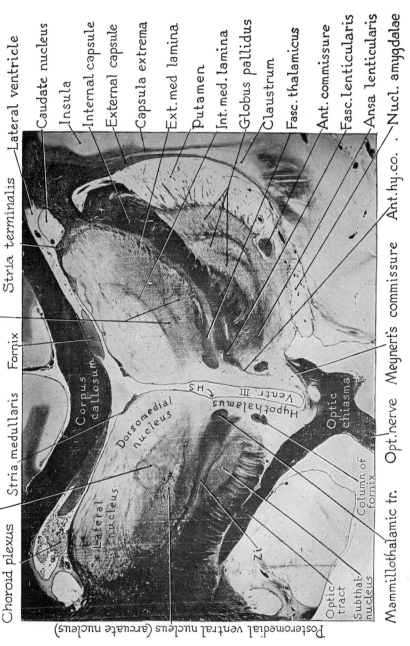

Fig. 18-7. Transverse section through diencephalon and basal ganglia at level of optic chiasm. The right side is cut at a higher level than the left. *Ant.hy.co.*, Anterior hypothalamic commissure; *Hs*, hypothalamic sulcus; *Zi*, zona incerta. The gray stripe separating the external medullary lamina of the thalamus from the internal capsule constitutes the reticular nucleus, which ventrally becomes continuous with the zona incerta. Weigert's myelin stain. Photograph.

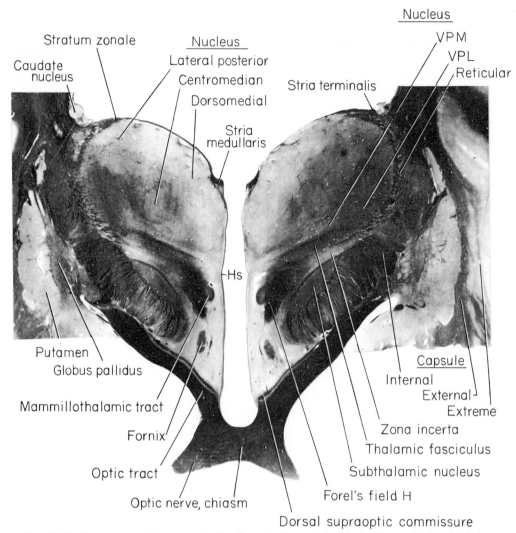

Fig. 18–8. Transverse section through the diencephalon and basal ganglia at the level of the optic chiasm. HS indicates the hypothalamic sulcus in the wall of the third ventricle. VPM and VPL refer to the ventral posteromedial and ventral posterolateral nuclei of the thalamus. Weigert's myelin stain. Photograph.

nuclei: (1) a caudal, *ventral posterior nucleus*, (2) an intermediate, *ventral lateral nucleus*, and (3) a rostral, *ventral anterior nucleus*. The ventral posterior nucleus is subdivided into a *ventral posterolateral nucleus*, located laterally, and a *ventral posteromedial nucleus*, located medially (Figs. 19–3 and 19–4). The ventral posteromedial nucleus sometimes is referred to as the *arcuate* or *semilunar nucleus*. The two parts of the ventral posterior nucleus constitute the thalamic nuclei upon which fibers of the medial lemniscus, the spinothalamic tracts, and the secondary trigeminal tracts terminate (Fig. 19–4).

The lateral nuclear mass of the thalamus, located dorsal to the ventral nuclear mass discussed above, also is divided into three separate nuclei: (1) a greatly expanded caudal part, the *pulvinar*, (2) an intermediate part, the *lateral posterior nucleus*, and (3) a more rostral part, the *lateral dorsal nucleus* (Fig. 19–4). While it is easy to identify the pulvinar (Figs. 18–3, 18–4, 18–5, and A–13), the distinction between the lateral posterior and the lateral dorsal nuclei is more difficult.

The medial nuclear group of the thalamus, located medial to the internal medullary lamina, contains the *dorsomedial nu-*

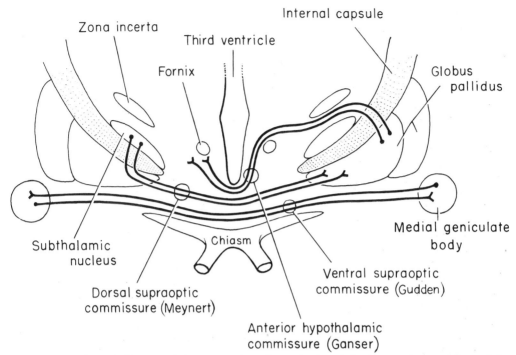

FIG. 18-9. Schematic diagram of the supraoptic and anterior hypothalamic commissures. Fibers of the *anterior hypothalamic commissure* (Ganser), presumed to arise from the medial segment of the globus pallidus, arch ventromedially over the fornix to enter the hypothalamus. The *dorsal supraoptic commissure* (Meynert) consists of fibers which arise from the subthalamic nucleus, perforate the internal capsule and cross to the opposite side along the dorsal borders of the optic tract and optic chiasm; these fibers pass into the contralateral globus pallidus. The *ventral supraoptic commissure* (Gudden) interconnects portions of the medial geniculate bodies.

cleus, a nuclear mass intimately related to the cortex of the frontal lobe. Wedged between the dorsomedial nucleus and the ventral nuclei caudally is the centromedian nucleus, the largest of the intralaminar nuclei (Figs. 18-5, 18-7, 18-8, and A-13). The internal medullary lamina partially splits to surround this nucleus.

Along the lateral border of the thalamus, near the internal capsule, is a narrow band of myelinated fibers, the *external medullary lamina* of the thalamus. Cells located between, and external to, these fibers form a thin outer envelope, the *reticular nucleus* of the thalamus. Ventrally the reticular nucleus appears to become continuous with the zona incerta (Figs. 18-7, 19-2 and 19-3).

The hypothalamus is present on both walls of the third ventricle below the hypothalamic sulcus (Figs. 3-13B, 18-7 and 18-8). This important subdivision of the diencephalon extends from the region

of the lamina terminalis (Figs. 3-11 and 19-14) to the caudal border of the mammillary bodies. The columns of the *fornix,* in passing to the mammillary body, roughly divide the hypothalamic nuclei into medial and lateral nuclear groups. The fornix, which arises from the hippocampal formation in the temporal lobe, represents one of the largest afferent systems to the hypothalamus. It will be considered with the rhinencephalon and limbic system in Chapter 21. Dorsal to the columns of the fornix are the well-delimited fiber bundles of the *mammillothalamic tract.* Fibers of this tract originate in the mammillary body, course diagonally upward and rostrally, and terminate in the anterior nuclear group of the thalamus (Figs. 3-20, 18-6, 18-8, and 20-4).

The fibers of the optic nerve partially decussate in the optic chiasm, beyond which the continuations of the optic fibers are known as the optic tract. Dorsal to the optic chiasm several bundles of fine fibers cross the midline; these fibers constitute the hypothalamic decussations. The largest of these is the *dorsal supraoptic commissure* or *decussation* (Meynert) which consists of fibers that arise from the subthalamic nucleus and pass to the contralateral globus pallidus (Carpenter and Strominger, '67). Immediately ventral to the above commissure is the *ventral supraoptic commissure* (Gudden) which is applied closely to the dorsal surface of the optic chiasm and tract. Fibers of this commissure apparently are related to auditory pathways since they can be traced laterally into the medial geniculate body and its capsule. A third commissure, located somewhat more rostrally, is the *anterior hypothalamic commissure* or *decussation* (Ganser; Figs. 18–7 and 18–9) whose entire composition is not known. Fibers of this commissure project ventromedially from Forel's field H, arch over the fibers of the fornix and enter the hypothalamus. It is presumed that these fibers arise from the medial segment of the globus pallidus.

The subthalamic region, located ventral to the dorsal thalamus and lateral to the hypothalamus, contains: (1) the *subthalamic nucleus* (corpus Luysi), (2) the *zona incerta*, (3) the *lenticular fasciculus*, (4) the *thalamic fasciculus*, and (5) *tegmental field H of Forel* (prerubral field). The subthalamic nucleus is a small, lens-shaped structure obliquely oriented, medial to the peduncular portion of the internal capsule. Fibers of the lenticular fasciculus are found mainly along the rostral border of the subthalamic nucleus, but a few fibers also are present along the dorsomedial border of this nucleus (Figs. 18–7 and 18–8). The zona incerta, dorsal to the lenticular fasciculus, is a narrow strip of gray matter that serves as an important landmark in this intricate region. Because of this landmark, fibers of the thalamic fasciculus situated dorsal to the zona incerta can be distinguished readily from those of the lenticular fasciculus that course between the zona incerta and the subthalamic nucleus. Tegmental field H of Forel, medial to both the subtha-

lamic nucleus and the zona incerta, occupies a location similar to that of the red nucleus at midbrain levels. Fibers in this area are largely dentatothalamic, rubrothalamic, and pallidofugal. Fibers from the dentate and red nuclei pass primarily to the ventral lateral nucleus of the thalamus. Pallidofugal fibers arising in the globus pallidus reach this field by either passing through the internal capsule (lenticular fasciculus) or coursing ventromedially around it. Pallidal efferent fibers traversing the internal capsule, mainly at levels rostral to the subthalamic nucleus, form the lenticular fasciculus (also known as Forel's field H_2). Pallidal efferent fibers that sweep ventromedially around the internal capsule form the *ansa lenticularis* (Fig. 20–5). The lenticular fasciculus and the ansa lenticularis merge in tegmental field H of Forel. From tegmental field H pallidofugal fibers project rostrally and laterally in the thalamic fasciculus (also known as Forel's field H_1).

Lateral to the internal capsule are two large nuclear masses derived from the telencephalon and collectively referred to as the *lenticular nucleus*. The largest and most lateral, the *putamen*, appears lightly stained and is traversed by small fascicles of myelinated fibers directed ventromedially (Fig. 18–7). The smaller and more medial component of the lenticular nucleus is the *globus pallidus*. Near the dorsal border of the putamen incomplete bridges of striatal gray extend across the internal capsule toward the *caudate nucleus*. In more rostral sections the putamen and caudate nucleus become continuous with each other (Figs. 18–11 and 18–12). The caudate nucleus and putamen have essentially the same cytological structure, though bundles of myelinated fibers are more prominent in the putamen. Collectively the caudate nucleus and the putamen form the newest phylogenetic portion of the basal ganglia, the *neostriatum* (striatum).

Medial to the putamen throughout most, but not all, of its extent is the *globus pallidus*. This structure, rich in myelinated fibers, is divided into two principal segments by a *medial medullary lamina*.

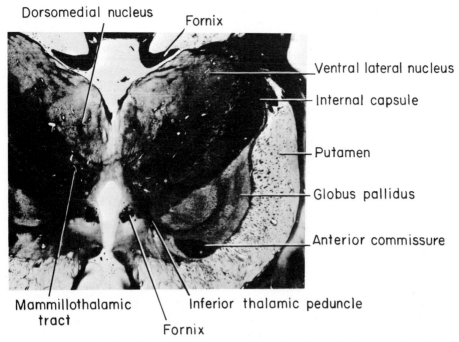

FIG. 18-10. Transverse section through the diencephalon and basal ganglia demonstrating fibers of the inferior thalamic peduncle. The inferior thalamic peduncle consists of fibers from the amygdaloid complex, temporal neocortex, and possibly the substantia innominata which project to the dorsomedial nucleus of the thalamus, as well as fibers from the thalamus which project to the hypothalamus and amygdaloid complex. The inferior thalamic peduncle, plus fibers interconnecting the amygdala and hypothalamus, constitute the *ansa peduncularis*. Weigert's myelin stain. Photograph.

A thin band of fibers constituting the *lateral medullary lamina* is found on the external surface of the globus pallidus at its junction with the putamen. The globus pallidus, phylogenetically older than the striatum, is referred to as the *paleostriatum*, and its equivalent is well developed in lower vertebrates.

Structures Lateral to the Corpus Striatum. External to the putamen is a band of mainly longitudinally coursing fibers, the *external capsule*, flanked laterally by a plate of gray matter, the *claustrum*, whose function and connections are not understood. The claustrum is regarded by some as a detached portion of the putamen, and by others as belonging to the cortex of the insula. The latter is separated from the claustrum by a layer of subcortical white matter known as the extreme capsule (Fig. 20-2). Investigations of these structures (Berke, '60) indicate that the most important components of

the external capsule may be corticotegmental fibers arising from frontal, temporal, anterior parietal, and insular cortex that course ventrally and caudally to reach the midbrain tegmentum by a sublenticular route. In their course these fibers are said to give fibers to the putamen. The extreme capsule appears to be primarily a cortical association bundle interconnecting frontal, insular, and temporal cortex. The small compact fiber bundle indenting the ventral surface of the lenticular nucleus (Fig. 18-7) is the anterior commissure; fibers of this commissure can be seen crossing the midline rostral to the fornices in Figure 18-11.

THALAMUS AND CORPUS STRIATUM
(LEVEL OF ANTERIOR COMMISSURE)

Transverse sections through the thalamus and corpus striatum at the level of the anterior commissure (Fig. 18-2) present certain structural features reminiscent of both coronal and horizontal sections through this region. The section, seen in Figure 18–11, passes rostral to the hypothalamus and clearly demonstrates the division of the thalamus into medial and lateral nuclear groups. Medial to the internal medullary lamina are the large *dorsomedial nucleus* and the central (periventricular) gray substance, containing a number of poorly delimited cell groups known collectively as the *midline thalamic nuclei* or the *periventricular thalamic nuclei* (Fig. 19–2). The portion of the thalamus lateral to the internal medullary lamina contains the ventral lateral nucleus (Figs. 18–10 and 18–11). The ventral lateral nucleus receives fibers from the dentate nucleus and from the globus pallidus. The medial lemniscus and other sensory tracts already have terminated at a caudal level in the ventral posterior nucleus.

Dorsally another gray mass appears above the medial and lateral nuclear groups of the thalamus. This is the *anterior thalamic nuclear group* which is partially surrounded by a distinct capsule (Fig. 18–11). These nuclei receive the mammillothalamic tract (Fig. 18–6) and direct fibers from the fornix. The striae medullares are still present along the dorsomedial margins of the thalami. Central portions of the anterior commissure are present and the relationships of this structure to rostral parts of the globus pallidus and putamen are evident. The columns of the fornices are near the midline caudal to the anterior commissure. The anterior commissure mainly interconnects portions of the temporal lobe cortex.

Situated ventral to the globus pallidus and the ansa lenticularis is a gray cellular mass known as the *substantia innominata* (Reichert) or the *basal nuclei of Meynert* (Figs. A–18 and A–22). This cellular area lies dorsal to the optic tract and extends rostrally under the anterior commissure. Cells of the substantia innominata are large, multipolar neurons which in man contain a yellow lipochrome pigment which increases with advancing age. Scattered cells of the substantia innominata also extend into the medial and lateral medullary laminae of the globus pallidus.

A massive fiber bundle projecting dorsomedially from the amygdalopyriform complex traverses the gray matter of the substantia innominata (Nauta and Mehler, '66). This fiber system is the *ansa peduncularis*, a complex grouping of fibers which divides into two principal components: (1) one which continues medially into the preoptico-hypothalamic region, and (2) another which curves dorsally around the medial margin of the internal capsule to enter the ventromedial aspect of the thalamus. The latter component is called the *inferior thalamic peduncle* (Fig. 18–10). The composition of the ansa peduncularis is extremely complex; it includes the following components: (1) amygdalothalamic fibers to the dorsomedial thalamic nucleus, (2) fibers from the orbitofrontal cortex to the thalamus and hypothalamus, (3) fibers from the amygdalopyriform complex to the substantia innominata and lateral preoptico-hypothalamic region, (4) fibers from the temporal cortex to the dorsomedial thalamic nucleus, (5) fibers from the thalamus projecting to the hypothalamus and amygdala, and (6) hypothalamo-amygdaloid fibers. Although the substantia innominata has been considered by some authors to contribute fibers to the ansa lenticularis, experimental evidence indicates that the ansa lenticularis and the ansa peduncularis are entirely separate neural pathways. The ansa lenticularis forms one of the principal pallidofugal pathways. The ansa peduncularis represents a composite system of reciprocal connections between the amygdalo-pyriform complex, the substantia innominata, the preoptico-hypothalamic region and parts of the dorsomedial nucleus of the thalamus.

Fibers of the mammillothalamic tract stand out as a discrete bundle at the boundary between medial and lateral thalamic nuclei (Figs. 18–1, 18–10 and 18–11). These fibers project to the anterior nuclear group of the thalamus.

The lenticular nucleus is large, especially the putamen; the latter structure now is medially continuous with the head of the caudate nucleus. The boundary

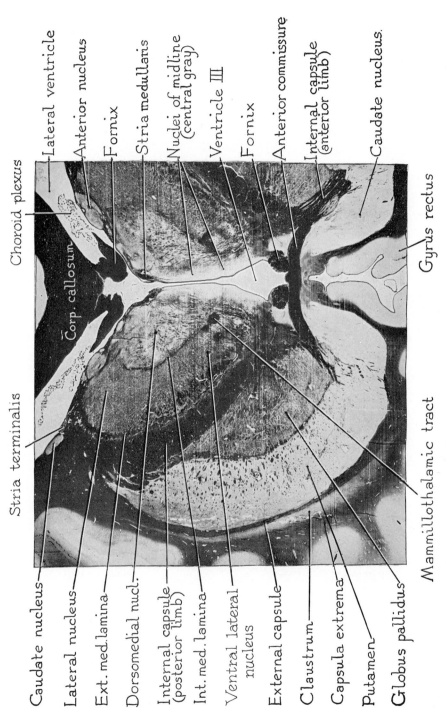

Fig. 18–11. Transverse section through the diencephalon and basal ganglia at the level of the anterior commissure. Weigert's myelin stain. Photograph.

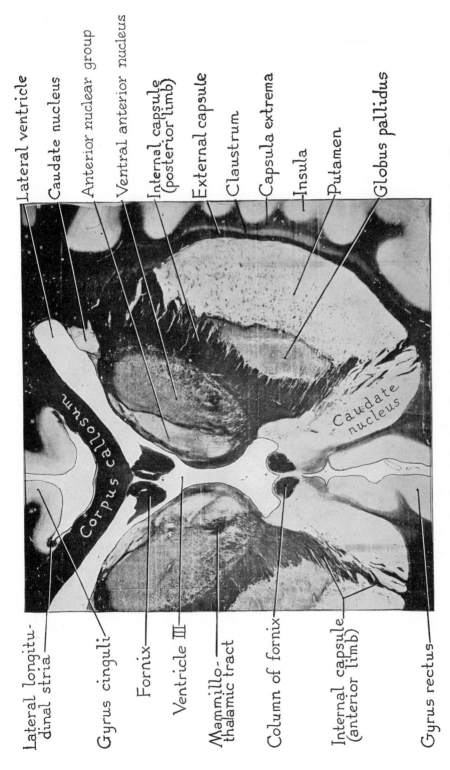

Lateral ventricle
Caudate nucleus
Anterior nuclear group
Ventral anterior nucleus
Internal capsule (posterior limb)
External capsule
Claustrum
Capsula extrema
Insula
Putamen
Globus pallidus

Lateral longitu- dinal stria
Gyrus cinguli
Fornix
Ventricle III
Mammillo- thalamic tract
Column of fornix
Internal capsule (anterior limb)
Gyrus rectus

Corpus callosum

Caudate nucleus

FIG. 18–12. Transverse section through basal ganglia and rostral portion of thalamus. Weigert's myelin stain. Photograph.

zone between them is marked by a bundle of longitudinally cut fibers which represent the beginning of the anterior limb of the internal capsule. The tail of the caudate nucleus is still present and occupies its previous position, immediately lateral to the stria terminalis.

In more rostral transverse sections (Fig. 18–12) the dorsomedial nucleus of the thalamus is no longer seen. The thalamus, greatly reduced in size, consists of the *anterior nuclear* group and the most rostral portion of the lateral nuclear group, the *ventral anterior nucleus* (Fig. 19–4). These nuclei are separated by the internal medullary lamina. Some fibers of the mammillothalamic tract can be seen entering the anterior nuclear groups of the thalamus.

The putamen appears much larger at this level, but the globus pallidus is smaller. The portion of the globus pallidus remaining is the lateral segment. Ventrally the putamen is practically fused with the head of the caudate nucleus. The junctional zone between the two is perforated by fibers of the internal capsule (anterior limb). The internal capsule forms a shallow V whose apex is directed medially (Fig. 19–8). The larger posterior portion between thalamus and lenticular nucleus constitutes the posterior limb; the ventral portion between the caudate and lenticular nuclei constitutes the anterior limb, or lenticulocaudate portion. The external capsule, claustrum, and extreme capsule are in the same position as at other levels.

ROSTRAL CORPUS STRIATUM

In sections rostral to the thalamus (Figs. 18–2, 18–11 and 18–12) the anterior limb of the internal capsule is bounded medially by the head of the caudate nucleus and laterally by the putamen. In the extreme rostral region (Fig. A–24), the caudate nucleus (i.e., head) is much larger than the putamen. The globus pallidus has disappeared. Putamen and caudate nucleus are connected by numerous gray bridges which extend across the internal capsule.

The third ventricle has disappeared and the lateral ventricles are now represented by their most rostral portions, the anterior horns (Figs. A–23 and A–24). The lateral wall of the anterior horn of each ventricle is formed by the caudate nucleus, the roof and floor, respectively, by the body and rostrum of the corpus callosum. The thin medial wall separating the two ventricles is the *septum pellucidum*, composed of two thin plates of neural tissue, the *laminae of the septum pellucidum* (Fig. 3–11). Between the two laminae there is a space of variable extent, the *cavum of the septum pellucidum*. Each lamina consists of fibers covered superficially by a layer of gray matter.

This introduction to the diencephalon and basal ganglia is provided to facilitate the more detailed anatomical discussion of these regions which follows. Frequent reference should be made to text figures and the atlas section.

CHAPTER 19

The Diencephalon

The diencephalon extends from the region of the posterior commissure rostrally to the region of the interventricular foramen. Laterally it is bounded by the posterior limb of the internal capsule, the tail of the caudate nucleus and the stria terminalis (Fig. 19-1). The third ventricle separates the diencephalon into two symmetrical parts, except in the region of the *interthalamic adhesion* (massa intermedia), where the medial surfaces of the thalami may be in continuity (Fig. 3-13). The diencephalon is divisible into four major parts: the epithalamus, the thalamus, the hypothalamus, and the subthalamus or ventral thalamus. The medial and lateral geniculate bodies, constituting distinctive subdivisions of the thalamus, are referred to as the *metathalamus*.

THE EPITHALAMUS

The epithalamus comprises the pineal body, the habenular trigones, the striae medullares, and the epithelial roof of the third ventricle (Fig. 3-13). The habenular ganglion in man consists of a smaller medial and a larger lateral nucleus (Figs. 18-5 and 18-6). The medial nucleus consists of small, closely packed, deeply staining round cells; in the lateral nucleus, the cells are larger, paler, and more loosely arranged. The ganglion receives the terminals of the stria medullaris (Figs. 18-1 and 19-1) and gives origin to the habenulopeduncular tract or fasciculus

retroflexus, which terminates in the interpeduncular nucleus (Fig. 18-5). The *stria medullaris* is a complex bundle composed of fibers arising from: (1) the septal nuclei, (2) lateral preoptic region (Nauta, '58), (3) the anterior thalamic nuclei, and (4) possibly, the globus pallidus (Nauta and Mehler, '66). The septal nuclei which receive fibers from both the hippocampal formation and the amygdaloid nuclear complex project profusely to the medial habenular nucleus. Fibers from the lateral preoptic nucleus and the globus pallidus pass to the lateral habenular nucleus (Fig. 18-6). Some of the strial fibers cross to the opposite side in the habenular commissure. Thus the stria medullaris, habenula, and fasciculus retroflexus form segments of visceral efferent pathways which convey impulses to parts of the brain stem.

The *pineal body* or *epiphysis* is a small, cone-shaped body attached to the roof of the third ventricle in the region of the posterior commissure (Fig. 19-1). It appears to be a rudimentary gland whose function in the adult is not fully known. It consists of a network of richly vascular connective tissue trabeculae in the meshes of which are found glia cells and, cells of a peculiar type, the *pineal* or *epiphysial cells*. These are cells of variable size with a pale nucleus, granular argentophilic cytoplasm, and relatively few branching processes. They may represent modified nerve cells, since they are

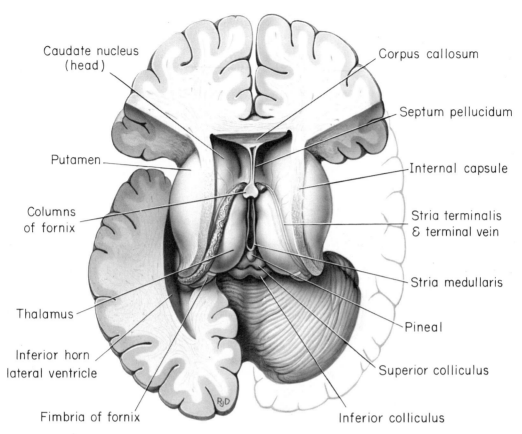

Caudate nucleus
(head)

Corpus callosum

Septum pellucidum

Putamen

Internal capsule

Columns
of fornix

Stria terminalis
& terminal vein

Stria medullaris

Thalamus

Pineal

Inferior horn
lateral ventricle

Superior colliculus

Fimbria of fornix

Inferior colliculus

FIG. 19-1. Drawing of a brain dissection showing gross relationships of the thalamus, internal capsule, basal ganglia and the ventricular system.

not stained by glia stains. True nerve cells do not appear to be present, though occasional cells with typical Nissl bodies have been observed by some investigators. The gland is said to receive fibers from the stria medullaris, habenular ganglion, and posterior commissure; the fibers terminate in a plexus between the epiphysial cells.

Although the functions of the pineal body are not completely known, present information (Thiéblot, '65) indicates that it is an endocrine gland. Experimental and clinical evidence suggests that the pineal body directly or indirectly inhibits gonadal function. If this effect is indirect, it is probably mediated by way of the anterior hypophysis. The resultant effect seems to be inhibition of pituitary gonadotrophin. Pinealectomy in experimental animals or pineal tumors in young males cause precocious development of

the gonads. After the age of 16 calcareous bodies frequently are present in the pineal body. These calcareous bodies, consisting of calcium and magnesium phosphates and carbonates, form large conglomerations which often are visible in skull roentgenographs. Identification and measurements of the position of the pineal body in skull films can provide useful information, especially in the diagnosis of space occupying intracranial lesions.

THE THALAMUS

The Thalamic Nuclei and their Connections. The thalamus is divided by a nearly vertical plate of fibers, the internal medullary lamina, into a medial and a lateral portion each containing several nuclear masses (Figs. 18–7 and 18–8).

The nuclei are particularly difficult to visualize in three dimensions. In addition, the nomenclature is complex, and in some instances the fiber connections and the significance of the smaller thalamic nuclei remain unknown. In a general way, depending upon their fiber connections, most of the major thalamic nuclei can be classified either as specific relay nuclei (R), or as association nuclei (A). The specific relay nuclei project to, and receive fibers from, well defined cortical areas considered to be related to specific functions. The association nuclei of the thalamus do not receive direct fibers from ascending systems, but project to association areas of the cortex. Other thalamic nuclei have predominantly, or exclusively, subcortical (SC) connections. Physiological studies suggest that certain thalamic nuclei may have diffuse cortical connections, but these have not been established. The following classification of thalamic nuclei is based upon functional and morphological data drawn from many sources, but especially from the works of Clark ('32), Walker ('38, '66), Olszewski ('52), and Russell ('55). The major nuclear groups of the thalamus and the most important nuclei are in bold faced type. The abbreviations most frequently used to designate these nuclear subdivisions are in parentheses. Letters in italics indicate specific relay nuclei (R), association nuclei (A), and nuclei with subcortical (SC) projections.

A. **Anterior Nuclear Group**
   1. **Anteroventral nucleus** (AV) R
   2. Anterodorsal nucleus (AD) R
   3. Anteromedial nucleus (AM)

B. **Medial Nuclear Group**
   Dorsomedial nucleus (DM)
   a. parvocellular part A
   b. magnocellular part SC

C. **Midline Nuclear Group**
   1. Paratenial nucleus
   2. Paraventricular nucleus
   3. Reuniens nucleus
   4. Rhomboidal nucleus

D. **Intralaminar Nuclear Group**
   1. **Centromedian nucleus** (CM) SC
   2. **Parafascicular nucleus** (PF) SC
   3. Paracentral nucleus SC
   4. Central lateral nucleus SC
   5. Central medial nucleus SC

E. **Lateral Nuclear Group**
   1. **Lateral dorsal nucleus** (LD) A
   2. **Lateral posterior nucleus** (LP) A
   3. **Pulvinar** (P) A
      a. medial part
      b. lateral part
      c. inferior part

F. **Ventral Nuclear Group**
   1. **Ventral anterior nucleus** (VA)
      a. parvocellular part (VApc) R
      b. magnocellular part (VAmc) SC
   2. **Ventral lateral nucleus** (VL)
      a. **oral part** (VLo) R
      b. caudal part (VLc) R
      c. medial part (VLm) R
   3. **Ventral posterior nucleus** (VP) R
      a. **ventral posterolateral** (VPL) R
         aa. oral part (VPLo) R
         bb. caudal part (VPLc) R
      b. **ventral posteromedial** (VPM) R
         aa. parvocellular part (VPMpc) R
      c. ventral posterior inferior (VPI) R

G. **Metathalamus**
   1. **Medial geniculate body** (MG) R
      a. parvocellular part (MGpc) R
      b. magnocellular part (MGmc)
   2. **Lateral geniculate body** (LG) R
      a. dorsal part R
      b. ventral part

H. **Unclassified Thalamic Nuclei**
   1. Submedial nucleus
   2. Suprageniculate nucleus
   3. Limitans nucleus

I. **Thalamic Reticular Nucleus** (RN) SC

The gross appearance of the dorsal surface of the diencephalon exposed by dissection is shown in Fig. 19–1. This illustration demonstrates the relationships of the thalamus and epithalamus to surrounding structures. Figures 19–2 and 19–3 show portions of many major thalamic nuclei at two important levels. The major subdivisions of the thalamus together with the established afferent and efferent thalamic projections are diagramed in Figure 19–4. The cortical projection areas of the thalamic nuclei are diagramatically represented in Figure 19–5. Examples of ascending thalamic afferent systems have been provided in diagrams for spinal pathways (Figs. 13–6, 13–12 and 13–13) and for certain pathways originating in the brain stem (Figs. 15–9 and 15–17) and cerebellum (Figs. 17–14, 17–15 and 17–19). Review of these schematic diagrams will contribute to your understanding of thalamic organization. The illustrations in Chapter 18 and in the atlas section provide additional material worthy of reference.

The internal medullary lamina divides the thalamus into anterior, medial and lateral nuclear groups (Fig. 19–4A). The anterior nuclear group, lying rostrally, is partially flanked medially and laterally by this lamina. The medial nuclear group, represented mainly by the dorsomedial nucleus (DM), lies everywhere medial to this medullary lamina. The lateral nuclear mass, situated between the internal and external medullary laminae, is divided into two tiers or étages. The dorsal tier, constituting the lateral nuclear group, occupies a more caudal position than the ventral tier. Nuclei of the lateral nuclear group are the lateral dorsal (LD), lateral posterior (LP), and the pulvinar (P). The ventral tier nuclei, the most significant functional group of the lateral nuclear mass, are divided into three nuclei, the ventral anterior (VA), the ventral lateral (VL), and the ventral posterior (VP). The metathalamus, consisting of the medial (MG) and lateral (LG) geniculate bodies, lies caudal to the ventral tier nuclei and has close relationships with the upper midbrain and the pulvinar. The intralaminar nuclei lie mainly within the internal medullary lamina. The thalamic reticular nucleus (RN) forms an outer envelope or shell about the lateral aspect of the thalamus.

The **anterior nuclear group** lies beneath the dorsal surface of the most rostral part of the thalamus, where it forms a distinct swelling, the anterior tubercle. It consists of a large principal nucleus, the anteroventral (AV), and accessory nuclei, the anterodorsal (AD) and anteromedial (AM). The round or polygonal cells composing these nuclei are of medium or small size; they have little

chromophilic substance and a moderate amount of yellow pigment. The anterior nuclei receive the mammillothalamic tract and send fibers to the mammillary body (Clark and Boggon, '33) by the same bundle (thalamomammillary; Fig. 19–4B. According to Fry et al. ('63), fibers from the medial mammillary nucleus project to the ipsilateral anteroventral and anteromedial nuclei, while the lateral mammillary nucleus projects bilaterally to the anterodorsal nucleus, but not to other subdivisions of the nuclear group. The anterior nuclei of the thalamus are said to receive as many direct fibers from the fornix as from the mammillothalamic tract (Powell et al., '57). The cortical projections of the anterior nuclei are to the cingulate gyrus (areas 23, 24, and 32) via the anterior limb of the internal capsule (Fig. 19–5). These cortical areas appear to send reciprocal projections back to the anterior nuclei (Meyer et al., '47; Freeman and Watts, '48). Fibers passing from the anterior nuclei to the habenular ganglion via the stria medullaris also have been described by some investigators.

The **dorsomedial nucleus** (DM) occupies most of the area between the internal medullary lamina and the periventricular gray (Figs. 19–2, 19–3 and 19–4A). Two cytologically distinct regions of the nucleus are recognized: (1) a magnocellular portion, located rostrally and dorsomedially, consisting of fairly large, polygonal, deeply staining cells; and (2) a larger dorsolateral and caudal parvocellular portion made up of small, pale-staining cells which tend to occur in clusters (Sheps, '45; Olszewski, '52; Dekaban, '53). The nucleus has extensive connections with the centromedian and other intralaminar nuclei and with the lateral nuclear groups. The medial magnocellular division of the dorsomedial nucleus receives fibers from the amygdaloid complex and projects fibers via the inferior thalamic peduncle (Fig. 18–10) to the lateral preoptic and hypothalamic regions, the substantia innominata, the rostral pole of the amygdaloid complex, the nucleus of the diagonal band and the olfactory tubercle. The

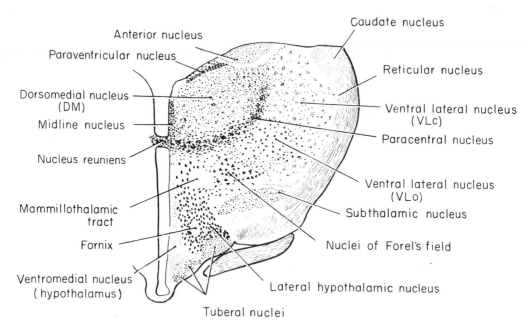

Fig. 19-2. Drawing of a transverse Nissl section through the diencephalon at the level of the tuber cinereum showing nuclei of the thalamus and hypothalamus (modified from Malone, '10).

caudal orbitofrontal cortex also has connections with the medial division of the dorsomedial nucleus (Nauta, '62). The much larger parvocellular portion is connected by a massive projection with practically the entire frontal cortex rostral to areas 6 and 32 (Figs. 19-4 and 19-5). After extensive prefrontal cortical lesions, or lesions interrupting fibers to this region, nearly all small cells of the dorsomedial nucleus degenerate (Walker, '36; Sheps, '45; Meyer et al., '47; Freeman and Watts, '48; McLardy, '50). Fibers projected by the parvocellular part of this nucleus are organized in such a way that cells in the rostral and caudal parts of the nucleus project to corresponding parts of the prefrontal cortex (Mettler, '47). The dorsomedial nucleus is regarded as an important relay station between the hypothalamus and the prefrontal cortex, and is concerned with integration of certain somatic and visceral impulses (Walker, '59). Some impulses relayed to the prefrontal cortex may enter consciousness and may thus influence or produce various feeling tones. Psychosurgical studies suggest that the dorsomedial nucleus may mediate impulses of an affective nature,

and though these vary greatly among individuals, they may constitute part of the emotional experience that contributes to the formation of personality.

The **midline nuclei** are more or less distinct cell clusters which lie in the periventricular gray matter of the dorsal half of the ventricular wall and in the interthalamic adhesion (Figs. 19-2 and 19-3). They are small and difficult to delimit in man, but in the lower vertebrates they, together with some of the intralaminar nuclei, form the largest part of the thalamus (paleothalamus). They consist of small, fusiform, rather darkly staining cells resembling preganglionic autonomic neurons (Malone, '10) and are believed to be concerned with visceral activities. Their scanty connections are mainly with the hypothalamic region by fine myelinated and unmyelinated fibers which run in the periventricular gray substance. They also are related to the magnocellular portion of the dorsomedial nucleus and to the intralaminar nuclei. The more distinct of the midline cell groups include the *paratenial nucleus*, near the stria medullaris, and the *paraventricular nucleus*, in the dorsal ventricular wall. In an attempt

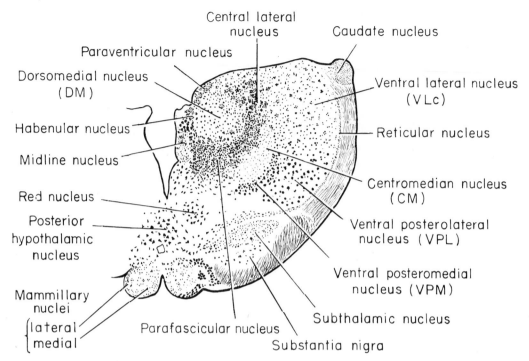

Central lateral
nucleus

Caudate nucleus

Paraventricular nucleus

Dorsomedial nucleus
(DM)

Ventral lateral nucleus
(VLc)

Habenular nucleus

Reticular nucleus

Midline nucleus

Centromedian nucleus
(CM)

Red nucleus

Ventral posterolateral
nucleus (VPL)

Posterior
hypothalamic
nucleus

Ventral posteromedial
nucleus (VPM)

Mammillary
nuclei
{ lateral
{ medial

Parafascicular nucleus

Subthalamic nucleus

Substantia nigra

FIG. 19–3. Drawing of a transverse Nissl section through the diencephalon at the level of the habenular nuclei and the mammillary bodies showing the nuclei of the thalamus and hypothalamus (modified from Malone, '10).

to homologize these ill-defined nuclei with the more developed nuclei of lower mammals, some authorities recognize several cell groups in this periventricular gray: the *nucleus reuniens*, the *rhomboidal nucleus*, and the *median central nucleus*. The reuniens, rhomboidal, and median central nuclei all bear definite close relationships with the interthalamic adhesion (massa intermedia), when present. The latter structure is reported to be absent in about 30 per cent of human brains (Morel, '47).

The **intralaminar nuclei** (Figs. 19–2 and 19–3) are cell groups of variable extent infiltrating the internal medullary lamina, which separates the medial from the lateral thalamic mass. Their cells, though varying in size in the different nuclei, are usually fusiform and darkly staining, and they resemble those of the midline nuclei. Their fiber connections are intricate and incompletely understood (Fig. 19–4*B*).

While most of the intralaminar nuclei

are small and their boundaries indistinct, the *centromedian nucleus* (CM) is a large and sharply defined cell group (Figs. 18–5, 18–7 and 18–8). This prominent nucleus is located in the middle third of the thalamus between the dorsomedial nucleus above and the ventral posterior nucleus below (Figs. 18–7 and 19–3). It is almost completely surrounded by fibers of the internal medullary lamina, except along its medial border, where it merges by interdigitations with the parafascicular nucleus (Fig. 19–3). It is composed of small, loosely arranged, ovoid or round cells containing a considerable amount of yellow pigment. Cells in the lateral portion of the nucleus are small, while those in more medial regions bordering the dorsomedial nucleus are larger and more densely arranged. There has been considerable controversy concerning precise delimitation of the centromedian nucleus, particularly with respect to the border separating it from the parafascicular nucleus. According to Mehler ('66) only the

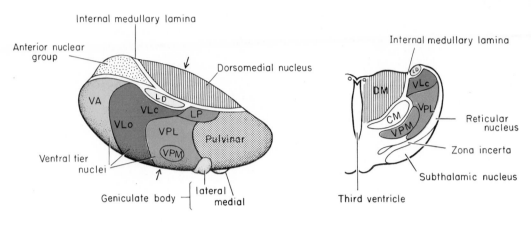

A.

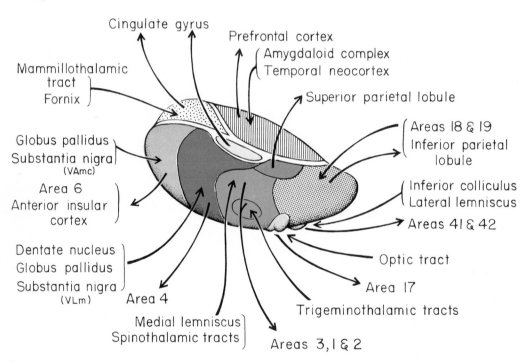

B.

Fig. 19-4. Schematic diagram of the major thalamic nuclei. An oblique dorsolateral view of the thalamus and its major subdivisions is shown on the left in *A*. A transverse section of the thalamus at level of arrows is shown on the right in *A* and indicates: (a) the relationships between VPM and VPL, and (b) the location of CM with respect to the internal medullary lamina of the thalamus. In *B*, the principal afferent and efferent projections of particular thalamic subdivisions are indicated. While most cortical areas project fibers back to the thalamic nuclei from which fibers are received, not all of these are shown.

ventrolateral small-celled region should be identified as the centromedian nucleus.

The *parafascicular nucleus* (PF) lies medial to the centromedian nucleus and ventral to the caudal part of the dorso-

medial nucleus (Figs. 18–5 and 19–3). Caudally the boundary between the parafascicular nucleus and the centromedian nucleus is indistinct and somewhat arbitrary. The most distinguishing

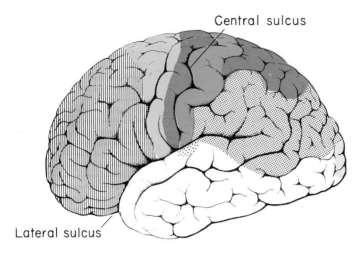

Central sulcus

Lateral sulcus

Lateral surface

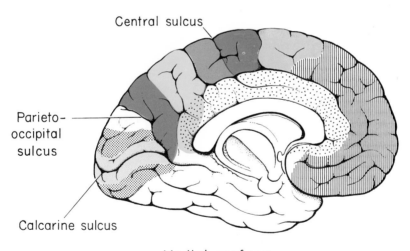

Central sulcus

Parieto-
occipital
sulcus

Calcarine sulcus

Medial surface

Fig. 19–5. Diagram of the left cerebral hemisphere showing the cortical projection areas of the thalamic nuclei. The color code is the same as that used in Fig. 19–4. Information concerning the cortical projection areas of some thalamic nuclei is incomplete, and has been approximated.

feature of the parafascicular nucleus is that its cells surround the dorsomedial part of the fasciculus retroflexus; portions of the nucleus medial and lateral to this tract show no cytological differences (Walker, '38).

The paracentral, central lateral, and central medial nuclei are all associated with the internal medullary lamina of the thalamus. The paracentral nucleus lies along the lateral border of the dorsomedial nucleus rostrally (Fig. 19–2); caudally, it is fused with the central lateral nucleus in its dorsal part and with the central medial nucleus in its medial part (Toncray and Krieg, '46).

Although it is widely recognized that the brain stem reticular formation probably is one of the principal sources of afferent impulses to the intralaminar nuclei

of the thalamus, considerable controversy has developed concerning the manner in which these impulses are transmitted rostrally. This controversy centers
around discrepancies between the results
of anatomical and physiological investigations. According to physiological findings
(Moruzzi and Magoun, '49; Starzl et al.,
'51), transmission of ascending impulses in
the reticular formation takes place via a
series of reticular neurons with short
axons. This type of impulse transmission
involves a large number of neurons, is
polysynaptic, and is said to account for
the long latency of responses. As mentioned previously (Chapter 16), Golgi
studies of the intrinsic organization of the
reticular core (Scheibel and Scheibel,
'58) do not reveal neurons with short
axons (Golgi type II cells) within the
reticular formation, although such neurons
might be expected on the basis of physiological evidence. Anatomical studies
(Brodal and Rossi, '55; Papez, '56; 56a;
Brodal, '57; Nauta and Kuypers, '58;
Scheibel and Scheibel, '58) indicate that
"effector" regions of the reticular formation give rise to long ascending fibers
which enter the area of the central tegmental tract. Areas of the reticular formation from which the largest number of
ascending fibers in this system originate
correspond to parts of the nucleus reticularis gigantocellularis and nucleus reticularis ventralis (medulla) and to the nucleus reticularis pontis caudalis (pons)
(Figs. 13–20, 14–12, 14–18, and 15–4). The
most complete study of the diencephalic
projection of this system is that of Nauta
and Kuypers ('58) based upon silver staining methods. These authors traced fibers
to the central tegmental fasciculus into:
(1) the centromedian-parafascicular nuclear complex, as well as the paracentral
and central lateral nuclei, and (2) the
subthalamic region. These ascending
reticular projections are said to be chiefly
ipsilateral. The above findings have been
confirmed in nearly every detail by Golgi
studies (Scheibel and Scheibel, '58). Because action potentials in the brain stem
reticular formation have been recorded
with stimulation of almost every type of

receptor, it has been presumed that
activation of the ascending reticular system is due to "collateral" excitation derived from specific sensory pathways
(Chapter 16).

As mentioned earlier (Chapter 13) with
respect to the spinothalamic tract, anterolateral cordotomy (Mehler et al., '60;
Bowsher, '61) produces ascending degeneration which passes not only to the ventral posterolateral nucleus and the
magnocellular part of the medial geniculate body, but also to the intralaminar
thalamic nuclei. Unilateral anterolateral
cordotomy produces bilateral degeneration
in these nuclei which is greatest ipsilaterally, except in the intralaminar nuclei
where nearly equal bilateral degeneration is seen. Within the intralaminar
nuclei these fibers are distributed to parts
of the parafascicular nuclei and throughout the central lateral nuclei (Fig. 19–3).
It appears that these spinal afferents to
parts of the intralaminar nuclei follow
pathways in the brain stem that are independent of the classic spinothalamic
trajectory (Mehler et al., '60) and probably are related to a phylogenetically older
system.

The centromedian nucleus (CM) receives a large number of pallidal efferent
fibers that separate from the thalamic
fasciculus at nearly right angles (Nauta
and Mehler, '66; Carpenter and Strominger, '67). A considerable part of these fibers may be collaterals of pallidofugal
fibers passing to the ventral anterior and
ventral lateral thalamic nuclei (Fig. 20–8).
The centromedian nucleus also receives
corticofugal fibers from the motor cortex
(area 4) that are distributed throughout
the nucleus (Petras, '64; Mehler, '66); this
projection appears significantly larger than
that from the pallidum. There is additional evidence (Astruc, '64) indicating
that Brodmann's area 6 and 8 provide
afferent fibers to central lateral and parafascicular nuclei.

Other afferent fibers to the intralaminar
nuclei appear to originate from the dentate nucleus (Hassler, '50; Cohen et al.,
'58) and from the fastigial nucleus
(Thomas et al., '56; Carpenter et al., '58).

Although fibers of the superior cerebellar peduncle have been described as passing to the centromedian nuclei, most of these fibers merely pass through this nucleus to the more rostral intralaminar nuclei (Mehler et al., '58; Carpenter, '67). These fibers appear to terminate in the central lateral nucleus.

While all of the efferent projections of the intralaminar nuclei are not known, it appears established that one of the principal projections of the centromedian nucleus is to the putamen (Mettler, '47; Freeman and Watts, '47; McLardy, '48; Droogleever-Fortuyn and Stefens, '51; Nauta and Whitlock, '54; Powell and Cowan, '56). According to Powell and Cowan ('56), the parafascicular nucleus also projects to the putamen, while the smaller and most rostral intralaminar nuclei project fibers to the caudate nucleus. These thalamostriatal fibers follow a wide curved path through the ventral anterior and rostral reticular nuclei of the thalamus, but do not appear to establish terminal connections within the ventral anterior nucleus (Mehler, '66). Some of these fibers, however, may terminate in portions of the reticular nucleus. The majority of these afferent projections to the striatum course dorsal to the globus pallidus. According to Nauta and Whitlock ('54), some fibers from the intralaminar nuclei terminate in the ventral lateral nucleus of the thalamus.

The intralaminar nuclei of the thalamus have long been regarded as having no cortical projections. This conclusion is based upon the absence of retrograde cell changes in these nuclei following virtually complete decortication (Walker, '38, '38a; Sheps, '45; Combs, '49; Powell, '52) and the absence of degeneration traceable from lesions in the centromedian nucleus to any part of the cortex (Clark and Boggon, '33, '33a; Nauta and Whitlock, '54). These observations have been difficult to reconcile with abundant physiological studies indicating that the intralaminar nuclei are of extreme importance in the control and alteration of electrocortical activity over broad regions of the cerebral cortex. Recently Bowsher ('66) has de-

scribed projections from the centromedian nucleus that passed beyond the thalamus into the subcortical white matter. It has been suggested that if direct fibers from the intralaminar nuclei to the neocortex exist, they may be collaterals of fibers projecting to the striatum. The striking development of the centromedian nucleus in primates, including man, in relation to that of the principal nuclei, which also demonstrate progressive differentiation, suggests that the centromedian nucleus may constitute a complex intrathalamic regulating mechanism (Clark, '32; Purpura and Cohen, '62; Cohen et al., '62).

The **lateral nucleus** begins as a narrow strip some distance from the anterior limit of the thalamus, enlarges posteriorly, and merges caudally with the pulvinar. It consists of two small gray masses, the lateral dorsal and lateral posterior nuclei (Fig. 19-4A).

The **lateral dorsal nucleus** (LD), which lies on the dorsal surface of the thalamus, extends along the upper margin of the internal medullary lamina (Fig. 19-4). Topographically this nucleus has been considered as a posterior extension of the anterior nuclear group (Locke et al., '61; Walker, '66). While many authors accept that this nucleus projects to the posterior parietal cortex, recent data indicate that its fibers pass mainly to the cingulate gyrus, though some pass to the supralimbic cortex of the parietal lobe. Afferent fibers to this nucleus are poorly understood.

The **lateral posterior nucleus** (LP) lies caudal to the lateral dorsal nucleus and dorsal to the ventral posterior nucleus (Fig. 19-4). The small cells of this nucleus have a homogeneous appearance and project to the parietal cortex. The input to this nucleus presumably is derived from internuncial neurons of adjacent primary relay nuclei, especially the ventral posterior nucleus (Walker, '66). Posteriorly the nucleus is difficult to delimit from the pulvinar.

These nuclei receive few ascending sensory fibers, but they possess reciprocal connections with a rather extensive area of the cortex. The lateral dorsal nucleus sends and receives fibers from the precuneal cortex, while the lateral posterior nucleus is intimately connected with the superior parietal lobule (areas 5 and 7).

The **pulvinar** (P) is a large mass forming the posterior portion of the thalamus. Caudally it overhangs the geniculate bodies and dorsolateral surface of the midbrain (Figs. 18-3, 18-4, and 18-5). The pulvinar usually is divided into a narrow lateral nucleus, a large medial nucleus, and a more primitive inferior nucleus. The lateral nucleus of the pulvinar is traversed by fibers passing to and from the external medullary lamina. The medial nucleus occupies the dorsomedial two-thirds of the pulvinar, while the inferior nucleus is the portion adjacent to the lateral geniculate body. The pulvinar does not receive long ascending sensory fibers; its input appears to be derived from internuclear relationships with other thalamic nuclei, especially the medial and lateral geniculate bodies and perhaps the ventral posterior nucleus. The cortical projections of the different parts of the pulvinar are specific (Simpson, '52; Walker, '66). The medial nucleus projects to the posterior parietal region, while the lateral nucleus sends fibers mainly to posterior parts of the temporal lobe. The inferior nucleus of the pulvinar sends fibers to the area surrounding the striate cortex (Fig. 19-5).

The **ventral nuclear mass** of the thalamus usually is divided into three separate nuclei: the *ventral anterior*, the *ventral lateral*, and the *ventral posterior*. The ventral anterior nucleus is the most rostral and smallest of this group. The ventral posterior nucleus, the largest and most posterior of the group, is further subdivided into the *ventral posterolateral* and *ventral posteromedial* nuclei. Although the *medial* and *lateral geniculate bodies* together constitute the *metathalamus*, these well-defined nuclear masses may be considered as a caudal continuation of the ventral nuclear mass. The ventral nuclear group and the metathalamus constitute the largest division of the thalamus concerned with relaying impulses from other portions of the neuraxis to specific parts

of the cerebral cortex. The most caudal parts of this complex are concerned with relaying impulses of specific sensory systems to cortical regions, while more rostral nuclei (ventral anterior and ventral lateral nuclei) relay impulses from the basal ganglia and cerebellum.

The **ventral anterior nucleus** (VA) lies in the extreme rostral part of the ventral nuclear mass where it is bounded anteriorly and ventrolaterally by the reticular nucleus. Rostrally this nucleus occupies the entire thalamic region lateral to the anterior nuclear group (Fig. 18-12), but caudally it becomes restricted to a more medial region. The mammillothalamic tract passes through the ventral anterior nucleus but does not form its medial border. The nucleus is composed of large and medium-sized multipolar cells arranged in clusters. The clustering of cells is particularly evident in rostrolateral parts of the nucleus due to thick myelinated fiber bundles coursing longitudinally within the nucleus.

A distinctive part of the nucleus adjacent to the mammillothalamic tract and along the ventral border of the nucleus is composed of large, dark, densely arranged cells. This subdivision, called the magnocellular part (VAmc; Olszewski, '52), extends further caudal than the principal part of the ventral anterior nucleus (VApc). Thus there are two distinctive cytological subdivisions of the ventral anterior nucleus. Each of these subdivisions appears to receive fibers from different sources. Afferent fibers to the ventral anterior nucleus (VA) arise from the medial segment of the globus pallidus and reach the nucleus via the lenticular fasciculus and ansa lenticularis (Ranson and Ranson, '42; Papez, '42; Nauta and Mehler, '66; Scheibel and Scheibel, '66a). These fibers enter the thalamic fasciculus, turn dorsolaterally and are distributed in a rostrolateral direction within the ventral anterior nucleus. Pallidofugal fibers also pass to medial and oral parts of the ventral lateral nucleus.

The magnocellular part of the ventral anterior nucleus (VAmc) receives a significant fiber projection from the substantia nigra (Cole et al., '64; Afifi and Kaelber, '65; Carpenter and Strominger, '67). These fibers pass medially and rostrally through Forel's field H and enter the thalamus from its medioventral aspect (Figs. 16–14 and 19–4B).

Other afferent fibers to the ventral anterior nucleus appear to be: (1) collaterals of corticofugal fibers, (2) ascending fibers from the brain stem reticular formation, and (3) collateral fibers arising from intralaminar and midline thalamic nuclei (Scheibel and Scheibel, '66a). The latter afferent projections appear to account for the characteristics of the nonspecific thalamic system exhibited by this nucleus.

Virtually all the information concerning efferent projections from the ventral anterior nucleus is based upon studies of cell loss and retrograde cell changes following different cortical lesions. Although some experimental studies (Bard and Rioch, '37; Papez, '38) indicate that all cells of the ventral anterior nucleus degenerate following hemidecortication, observations in man (Powell, '52) reveal that over 50 per cent of them remain following hemispherectomy. Data from Golgi studies confirm this finding (Scheibel and Scheibel, '66a). Critical study of cell changes in the thalamus resulting from large hemispheric lesions in man (Angevine et al., '62) suggests that this nucleus projects in part to the anterior insular cortex. Descriptions by most authors suggest that VAmc, or part of it, probably does not project to the cerebral cortex (Yakovlev et al., '66; Carpenter, '67).

Subcortical projections of VA have been alluded to by many authors. Physiological evidence (Starzl and Magoun, '51) suggests a subcortical projection to the caudate nucleus as well as to the opposite ventral anterior nucleus. According to the Scheibels ('66a), the most profuse cell type in the ventral anterior nucleus is a multipolar brush cell. The most frequent trajectory of axons from these cells appears to be a rostral one passing through the thalamic reticular nucleus and into the caudate nucleus. In addition some of these cells project axons caudally, or across the midline.

Physiological data (Starzl and Magoun, '51; Jasper et al., '52; Jasper, '54) indicate that the ventral anterior nucleus may be functionally related to the intralaminar nuclei of the thalamus in that recruiting responses in widespread cortical areas can be evoked by repeated low frequency stimulation of the nucleus. It is of particular interest that the ventral anterior nucleus seems to exhibit characteristics of both the specific and the nonspecific thalamic nuclei.

The **ventral lateral nucleus** (VL), caudal to the ventral anterior nucleus, is composed of small and large neurons that show considerable differences in various parts of the nucleus (Fig. 19–4). This nucleus has been subdivided into three main parts (Olszewski, '52): (1) pars oralis (VLo), (2) pars caudalis (VLc), and (3) pars medialis (VLm). The largest subdivision (VLo) consists of numerous deep staining cells arranged in clusters. The pars caudalis (VLc) is less cellular but formed of scattered large cells. The pars medialis (VLm) begins ventral to VA and extends caudally to the subthalamic region. Cerebellar efferent fibers contained in the superior cerebellar peduncle decussate in the mesencephalon and project profusely to the contralateral ventral lateral nucleus, pars oralis (Olszewski, '52). These fibers arise mainly from the dentate nucleus. The pars oralis also receives pallidofugal fibers via the thalamic fasciculus (Nauta and Mehler, '66).

The ventral lateral nucleus of the thalamus receives a considerable number of fibers from the precentral cortex (Clark, '32; Levin, '36, '49; Verhaart and Kennard, '40; Mettler, '47). These corticofugal fibers pass to both the pars oralis and the pars caudalis of VL. Thus corticofugal fibers pass to regions of the nucleus that receive fibers from the cerebellum as well as to regions which do not. Connections of the ventral lateral nucleus with the precentral cortex are reciprocal and topically arranged. Medial parts of the nucleus send fibers to the face area, lateral parts send fibers to the leg area, and fibers from intermediate portions of the nucleus pass to cortical regions representing the arm and trunk (Walker, '38, '49). Most of these fibers pass to area 4, but some may reach area 6. This topical arrangement of thalamocortical fibers passing to the precentral cortex is considered as the anatomical expression of the functional independence of different body parts in the primary motor area. The fact that impulses from the cerebellum are projected to the motor cortex via the ventral lateral nucleus suggests that cerebellar influences upon motor function may be effected primarily at a cortical level. Different regions of the medial part of the ventral lateral nucleus (VLm) receive afferent fibers from the substantia nigra and a smaller number from the globus pallidus.

The **ventral posterior nucleus** (VP), whose cells are among the largest in the thalamus, is composed of two main portions, *the posteromedial* and the *posterolateral* (Figs. 19-3 and 19-4). The ventral posterior nucleus is regarded universally as the largest primary somatic relay nucleus of the thalamus.

The **ventral posterolateral nucleus** (VPL) has been subdivided into a pars oralis (VPLo), characterized by very large, relatively uniform cells sparsely distributed, and a pars caudalis (VPLc) containing large and small cells, and characterized by a wide range of cell size and a high cellular density. Both divisions of the nucleus contain medium-sized fiber bundles radiating in an oblique dorsal direction.

Two principal long ascending systems project to VPL, the medial lemniscus (Clark, '36; Walker, '38a; Rasmussen and Peyton, '48; Matzke, '51; Bowsher, '58, '61) and the spinothalamic tracts (Clark, '36; Walker, '38a; Berry et al., '50; Bowsher, '57, '61; Mehler et al., '60). Fibers of the medial lemniscus course through the brain stem without supplying collateral or terminal fibers to the reticular formation, and terminate exclusively in the ventral posterolateral nucleus (Fig. 19-4B). These fibers terminate profusely in all parts of the nucleus in a pattern presenting a sharp contrast with the parcellated distribution of the spinothalamic fibers. Fibers arising from the nucleus gracilis terminate lateral to those of the nucleus cuneatus (Clark, '36; Walker, '38a). Fibers of the medial lemniscus establish predominantly axodendritic contacts throughout the rostrocaudal extent of VPL.

Spinothalamic fibers in the monkey enter the caudal part of the nucleus and spread out laterally on the inner surface of the external medullary lamina; from this location bundles of fibers invade more medial regions of the nucleus (Mehler et al., '60). Other impressive contrasts between these ascending sensory pathways might be mentioned. The spinothalamic tracts contribute a large number of fibers and collaterals to the bulbar reticular formation, project fibers to both a ventral relay nucleus (ventral posterolateral) and the nonspecific nuclei (intralaminar nuclei) of the thalamus. According to Bowsher ('57), spinothalamic fibers, interrupted by anterolateral cordotomy in man, project bilaterally to the ventral posterolateral nuclei.

Physiological studies (Mountcastle and Henneman, '49, '52; Rose and Mountcastle, '52, '59; Poggio and Mountcastle, '60) indicate the precise and orderly fashion in which the contralateral body surface is represented in the ventral posterolateral nucleus (external portion of the ventrobasal complex). There is a complete, though distorted, image of the body form; volume representation of a given part of the body is related to its effectiveness as a tactile organ (i.e., to its innervation density). Cervical segments are represented most medially and sacral segments most laterally. The thoracic and lumbar regions are represented only dorsally, while the regions concerned with the distal parts of the limbs extend ventrally. Each neuron of this complex is related to a restricted, specific and unchanging receptive field on the contralateral side of the body. Each neuron of the ventrobasal complex can be activated by either tactile stimulation of the skin, or mechanical alteration of deep structures (especially joint rotation), but by only one of these. These neurons are regarded as place specific, modality specific, and concerned, almost exclusively, with the perception of tactile sense and position sense (kinesthesis). Few cells of the ventrobasal complex appear to be activated by noxious stimuli (Poggio and Mountcastle, '60). Although the terminology used by these authors differs from that used here, it is generally accepted that these superbly defined principles apply to man. The inner portion of the ventrobasal complex, known as the ventral posteromedial nucleus, contains the representation of the contralateral head, face and intraoral structures.

The **ventral posteromedial nucleus** (VPM), known also as the arcuate or semilunar nucleus, is located medial to the posterolateral nucleus; the adjacent centromedian nucleus forms its medial boundary (Figs. 18–7, 18–8, and 19–4). The ventral posteromedial nucleus (VPM) contains one distinct subdivision in its medial apical region composed of small, light-staining, densely packed cells. This subdivision is known as the pars parvocellularis (VPMpc). The precise boundaries of VPM are best defined on the basis of its fiber connections. The ventral posteromedial nucleus receives afferent systems concerned with the head, face and intraoral structures. Ascending secondary trigeminal fibers include: (1) crossed fibers from the spinal and principal sensory trigeminal nuclei, which ascend in association with the medial lemniscus (Carpenter and Hanna, '61), and (2) uncrossed fibers of the dorsal trigeminal tract (Carpenter, '57a; Torvik, '57) originating from the dorsal part of the principal sensory nucleus of N. V. Impulses from stretch receptors in the facial musculature also are believed to reach the ventral posteromedial nucleus, but the pathways involved are not known. Experimental evidence (Mountcastle and Henneman, '52; Berry et al., '56) indicates that tactile impulses from the face and intraoral structures are transmitted bilaterally to parts of the ventral posteromedial nucleus. Even though the central pathways conveying impulses mediating gustatory sense are not known, it seems likely that secondary fiber systems originating from the nucleus solitarius reach the medial part of the ventral posteromedial nucleus (VPMpc), since

electrical stimulation of the chorda tympani and glossopharyngeal nerves evokes localized responses (Blomquist et al., '62) in this nucleus. According to Rose and Mountcastle ('52) and Mountcastle and Henneman ('52), VPMpc was not found to respond to tactile stimuli of body surfaces. Benjamin and Akert ('59) have shown that ablations of the cortical taste area in the rat produce retrograde degeneration of thalamic neurons confined to VPMpc. Gustatory representation in thalamic neurons in the rat, cat and monkey (Blomquist et al., '62) is said to be bilateral, but apparently is predominantly ipsilateral in the cat and monkey. Emmers ('64) has found that the most medial portion of the thalamic taste projection does not relay any tactile afferent impulses and suggests that gustatory sense has an independent representation in the thalamus.

Lesions in the ventral posteromedial nucleus in experimental animals impair taste (Blum et al., '43; Patton et al., '44; Andersson and Jewell, '57). Some evidence supports this thesis in that degenerated fibers from lesions in the nucleus solitarius can be traced to the ventral posteromedial nucleus (Allen, '23). These fibers are described as ascending in association with the contralateral medial lemniscus. Clinical evidence (Adler, '33) suggests that gustatory sense in the thalamus may be represented only contralaterally.

The ventral posterior nucleus has a precise topical projection to the cortex (Clark and Boggon, '35; Walker, '38a; Clark and Powell, '53; Kruger and Porter, '58). Fibers project to the postcentral gyrus so that dorsal portions of the gyrus receive fibers from the lateral part of VPL; lower portions of the gyrus near the lateral sulcus are supplied by fibers from VPM. Intermediate parts of VP project to intermediate parts of the postcentral gyrus. This thalamocortical projection correlates precisely with the termination of ascending somatosensory systems in the ventral posterior nuclear complex. Cortical areas 3, 1 and 2 receive the specific projections of VPL and VPM, with the majority of the cells projecting to area 3.

Caudal to the ventral posterior nucleus

there is a transitional diencephalic zone with a complex and varied cellular morphology. This posterior zone lies ventral to the lateral posterior nucleus and medial to the principal part of the medial geniculate body (Fig. 18–4). Part of this region contains the large cells of the magnocellular part of the medial geniculate body. This region is of interest because it receives spinothalamic fibers (Mehler et al., '60; Bowsher, '61) and appears to be concerned with the perception of painful and noxious stimuli (Poggio and Mountcastle, '60). Spinothalamic fibers project bilaterally about cells in this region. Physiological evidence (Poggio and Mountcastle, '60) indicates that cells in this region are activated by somatic sensory stimuli, but that mechano-receptive cells are not place specific and there is no orderly projection of the body image within this region. Cells of this region are not modality specific in that many cells may respond to tactile, vibratory or auditory stimuli. None of the cells in this thalamic region has been observed to be activated by gentle rotation of joints. The majority of cells in this region respond to noxious stimuli. Neurons responding to nociceptive stimuli are related to large, and usually bilateral, receptive fields. Thalamic neurons of this region, which includes the magnocellular part of the medial geniculate body, are considered to project in a sustaining fashion upon the second somatic area of the cortex (Rose and Woolsey, '58). It seems likely that cells of this posterior thalamic region have a diverse sensory input and that it may be the locus of complex sensory interactions.

The **medial geniculate** (MG) **body** consists of a ventral nucleus composed of large, closely packed polygonal cells (magnocellular part), and a large dorsal nucleus of more loosely arranged smaller cells (parvocellular part; Figs. 16–10, 18–3, 18–4, and 19–4). The dorsal part of the nucleus, which is concerned only with audition, receives ascending auditory fibers originating from the trapezoid nuclei, the superior olivary nuclei, the nuclei of the lateral lemniscus, and the inferior colliculus. Most of these fibers arise from the inferior colliculus, but some reach the nucleus directly, via the lateral lemniscus. The principal cortical projection of the medial geniculate body is to the superior temporal convolution (transverse gyrus of Heschl) via the geniculotemporal or auditory radiations (Figs. 19–4 and 19–5). This cortical projection area (area 41) has a tonotopic localization in which high tones are appreciated in medial regions and low tones in anterior and lateral regions. Some fibers from the medial geniculate nucleus also pass to the ventral and lateral thalamic nuclei, as well as to the pulvinar. In addition the dorsal part of the medial geniculate body projects fibers or collaterals to the inferior colliculus, the nucleus of the lateral lemniscus, the trapezoid body, and the superior olivary nucleus (Ades, '41). One of the characteristic features of the auditory pathways (Rasmussen, '60) is that ascending fibers connecting the nuclei at various levels are to a degree paralleled by similar, though less extensive, descending pathways, which may serve as a regulatory feedback mechanism. The magnocellular part of the medial geniculate body is reported to be unresponsive to supramaximal click stimuli (Rose and Galambos, '52), but as previously mentioned, part of this subdivision is related to the posterior thalamic region which receives a polysensory input. Ventral regions of the medial geniculate body give rise to fibers of the ventral supraoptic decussation (Gudden) which cross to the opposite side and terminate in the medial geniculate body and its capsule (Fig. 18–9).

The **lateral geniculate** (LG) **body** which is intimately associated with the optic tract, consists in most mammals of a dorsal and a ventral nucleus. The former is connected with the ventral thalamic nucleus, pulvinar, and striate area of the cortex. The ventral nucleus apparently represents a subthalamic structure related to the zona incerta. In man the ventral nucleus is represented by scattered cells lying medial to the main nucleus among the entering fibers of the optic tract. The principal nucleus is a laminated mass with the shape of a horseshoe, whose hilus

Dorsolateral

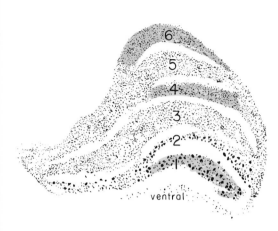

Ventromedial

Fig. 19–6. Drawing of the cellular lamination of the lateral geniculate body. Laminae *1* and *2* constitute the magnocellular layers; the *ventral* nucleus is shown *below*. Crossed fibers of the optic tract terminate in laminae *1, 4,* and *6*; uncrossed fibers terminate in laminae *2, 3,* and *5.*

is directed ventromedially (Fig. 19–6). It is composed of six concentrically arranged cell layers that are separated by intervening fiber bands. The four outer layers consist of small- and medium-sized cells; in the two narrower, inner layers the cells are large and more loosely arranged (magnocellular nucleus of Malone, '10). According to the scheme of numbering shown in Figure 19–6; crossed fibers of the optic tract terminate on laminae 1, 4, and 6, while uncrossed fibers end in laminae 2, 3, and 5. Phylogenetically, the nucleus first differentiates into three cell layers. It becomes six-layered in forms where the optic tracts show a partial decussation, the uncrossed and crossed portions each terminating upon three different laminae (Minkowski, '13; Clark, '32).

The lateral geniculate nucleus is the main end station of the optic tract. It projects to the calcarine cortex (area 17) by the geniculocalcarine tract or visual radiations, and it receives corticogeniculate fibers from the same area. Its internuclear connections are with the pulvinar and the ventral and lateral thalamic nuclei. It also sends fibers to the superior colliculi and

pretectal area by way of the brachium of the superior colliculus.

The **thalamic reticular nucleus** (RN) is a thin neuronal shell which surrounds the lateral, antero-superior, and antero-inferior aspects of the dorsal thalamus. This thalamic nuclear envelope develops embryologically from the mantle layer of the subthalamus and migrates dorsally between the external medullary lamina of the thalamus and the internal capsule (Kuhlenbeck, '48; Dekaban, '54). Thus, this nucleus actually is a derivative of the ventral thalamus, although it surrounds the lateral aspect of the dorsal thalamus. Cells of this nucleus are said to resemble those of adjacent thalamic nuclei (Walker, '38). According to Scheibel and Scheibel ('66) Golgi studies of the reticular nucleus show that its neurons are similar to those of the brain stem reticular formation in that they are multipolar, vary in size from medium to large, and lie immersed in a complex neuropil. Dendrites of cells are long, relatively unramified and without specific orientation. The main axons of the majority of cells turn caudally and penetrate deeply into the thalamus, although some axons appear to run exclusively within the reticular nucleus. About one-fifth of the axons from cells in the reticular nucleus, directed caudally, are said to enter the mesencephalic tegmentum and end among clusters of reticular neurons. Golgi preparations (Scheibel and Scheibel, '66) provide no evidence that fibers of this nucleus have cortical terminations. Although cells in the reticular nucleus are said to undergo degeneration following cortical ablations (Rose and Woolsey, '43; Rose, '52), degeneration occurs late and is less severe than in cortically dependent thalamic nuclei. It has been suggested that cell changes and cell loss in the reticular nuclei under these conditions may be transneuronal. The reticular nucleus of the thalamus receives cortical afferent fibers which are organized topographically (Carman et al., '64). Thus the reticular nucleus of the thalamus does not appear to be part of a nonspecific thalamic pathway to the cortex. Since its major projections are to specific and nonspecific

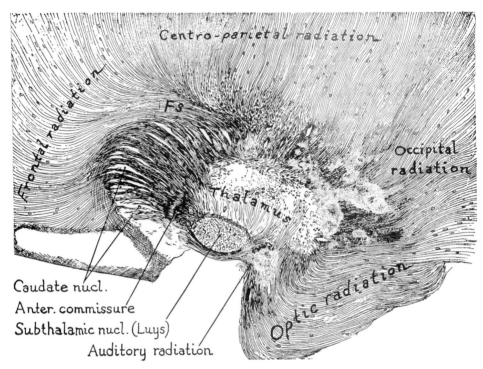

Fig. 19-7. The thalamic radiations. Composite picture drawn from photographs of serial sections and dissections, *Fs*, Fasciculus subcallosus of frontal radiation (after J. Rosett, '33).

thalamic nuclei, it may serve to integrate intrathalamic activities.

THE THALAMIC RADIATIONS AND INTERNAL CAPSULE

Fibers which reciprocally connect the thalamus and the cortex constitute the thalamic radiations. These thalamocortical and corticothalamic fibers form a continuous fan that emerges along the whole lateral extent of the caudate nucleus. Fiber bundles, radiating forward, backward, upward and downward, form large portions of various parts of the internal capsule (Figs. 19-7, 19-8 and 19-10). Though the radiations connect with practically all parts of the cortex, the richness of connections varies considerably for specific cortical areas. Most abundant are the projections to the frontal granular cortex, the precentral and postcentral gyri, the calcarine area, and the gyrus of Heschl. The posterior parietal region and adjacent portions of the temporal lobe also have rich thalamic connections, but relatively scanty radiations go to other cortical areas,

especially the temporal lobe (Walker, '38) (Fig. 19-5).

The thalamic radiations usually are grouped into four subradiations designated as the thalamic *peduncles* or *stalks* (Figs. 19-7 and 19-12). The *anterior* or *frontal peduncle* connects the frontal lobe with the medial and anterior thalamic nuclei. The *superior* or *centroparietal peduncle* connects the Rolandic area and adjacent portions of the frontal and parietal lobes with the ventral thalamic nuclei. The fibers, carrying general sensory impulses from the body and head, form part of this radiation and terminate in the postcentral gyrus (Figs. 19-4, 19-5, and 19-9). The *posterior* or *occipital peduncle* connects the occipital and posterior parietal convolutions with the caudal portions of the thalamus. It includes the optic radiations (geniculocalcarine) from the lateral geniculate body to the calcarine cortex (striate area). The *inferior* or *temporal peduncle* is relatively small and includes the scanty connections of the thalamus with the temporal lobe and the insula. Included in this

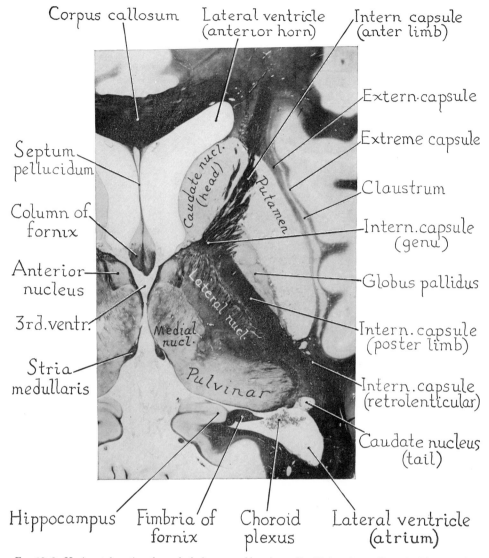

Corpus callosum   Lateral ventricle   Intern capsule
                   (anterior horn)   (anter limb)

Extern·capsule

Extreme capsule

Septum
pellucidum

Caudate nucl.
(head)

Putamen

Claustrum

Column of
fornix

Intern.capsule
(genu)

Anterior
nucleus

Lateral nucl.

Globus pallidus

3rd.ventr.

Medial
nucl.

Intern.capsule
(poster limb)

Stria
medullaris

Pulvinar

Intern.capsule
(retrolenticular)

Caudate nucleus
(tail)

Hippocampus   Fimbria of   Choroid   Lateral ventricle
               fornix   plexus   (atrium)

FIG. 19–8. Horizontal section through thalamus and basal ganglia. Weigert's myelin stain. Photograph.

are the auditory radiations (geniculotemporal) from the medial geniculate body to the transverse temporal gyrus of Heschl (Fig. 19–9).

The cerebral hemisphere is connected with the brain stem and spinal cord by an extensive system of projection fibers—some afferent, others efferent. These fibers arise from the whole extent of the cortex, enter the white substance of the hemisphere, and appear as a radiating mass of fibers, the *corona radiata*, which converges toward the brain stem (Figs. 3–18 and 3–19). On reaching the latter they form a broad, compact fiber band, the *internal capsule*, flanked medially by the thalamus and caudate nucleus and laterally by the lenticular nucleus (Fig. 19–9). Thus the internal capsule is composed of all the fibers, afferent and efferent, which go to, or come from, the cerebral cortex. A large part of the capsule is obviously composed of the thalamic radiations described above. The rest is composed mainly of efferent cortical fiber systems, which descend to lower portions of the brain stem and to

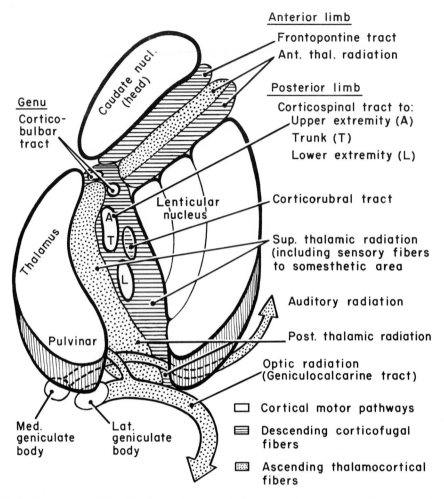

FIG. 19-9. Components of the right internal capsule. This diagram has the same orientation as Fig. 19-8 with which it should be compared. The blood supply of the internal capsule is shown in Fig. 4-11. The blood supply of the basal ganglia and thalamus is diagramed in Fig. 4-10.

the spinal cord. These include the corticospinal, corticobulbar, corticoreticular, and corticopontine tracts and smaller bundles to the hypothalamus, substantia nigra, red nucleus, and certain other gray masses of the brain stem. Below the level of the thalamus these descending systems constitute the crus cerebri of the midbrain (Fig. 13–16).

The internal capsule, as seen in a horizontal section, is composed of a shorter *anterior* and a longer *posterior limb*, which meet at an obtuse angle, forming a junctional zone known as the *genu* (Figs. 19–8 and 19–9). The anterior limb lies between the lenticular and caudate nuclei. The

posterior limb of the internal capsule, or the *lenticulothalamic* portion, lies between the lenticular nucleus and the thalamus. A *retrolenticular* part of the internal capsule extends caudally for a short distance behind the lenticular nucleus. In this caudal region a number of fibers passing beneath the lenticular nucleus to reach the temporal lobe collectively form the *sublenticular* portion of the internal capsule.

The *anterior limb* of the internal capsule contains the anterior thalamic radiation or peduncle, the prefrontal corticopontine tract, and fibers from the orbital cortex to the hypothalamus. The *genu* contains corticobulbar and corticoreticular fibers.

The *posterior limb* of the internal capsule contains: (1) corticospinal fibers, (2) frontopontine fibers, (3) the superior thalamic radiation, and (4) relatively smaller numbers of corticotectal, corticorubral and corticoreticular fibers. Corticospinal fibers are organized in a specific manner so that those closest to the genu are concerned with cervical portions of the body while succeeding, more caudal regions are related to the upper extremity, trunk and lower extremity, respectively. Fibers of the superior thalamic radiation, located caudal to the corticospinal fibers, project impulses concerned with general somatic sense to the postcentral gyrus.

The *retrolenticular portion* of the posterior limb contains the posterior thalamic radiations, including among others the geniculocalcarine (optic) radiations, parietal and occipital corticopontine fibers, and fibers from the occipital cortex to the superior colliculi and pretectal region. The *sublenticular portion*, difficult to separate from the retrolenticular, contains the *inferior thalamic peduncle*, (Fig. 18-10), the geniculotemporal (auditory) radiations, and corticopontine fibers from the temporal and the parietooccipital area.

Thalamocortical and corticofugal fibers within the internal capsule occupy a comparatively small, compact area (Fig. 19-9). Lesions in this area produce more widespread disability than lesions in any other region of the nervous system. Thrombosis or hemorrhage of the anterior choroidal, striate, or capsular branches of the middle cerebral arteries (Fig. 4-11) are responsible for most injuries to the internal capsule. Vascular lesions in the posterior limb of the internal capsule result in contralateral hemianesthesia (or hemihypesthesia) of the head, trunk, and limbs due to injury of thalamocortical fibers en route to the sensory cortex. There is also a contralateral hemiplegia (hemiparesis) due to injury of the corticospinal tracts. If the genu of the internal capsule is included in the injury, corticobulbar fibers also are destroyed (see page 326). Lesions in the posterior third of the posterior limb may include the optic and auditory radiations. In such instances there may be a contralateral triad consisting of hemianesthesia, hemianopsia, and hemihypacusis. More extensive vascular lesions may include the thalamus or corpus striatum, so that affective changes and extrapyramidal symptoms may be added to those characteristic of injury to the internal capsule.

THE VISUAL PATHWAY

The *retina* arises as an evaginated portion of the brain, the optic pouch, which secondarily is invaginated to form the two-layered optic cup. The outer layer gives rise to pigmented epithelium. The inner layer forms the neural portion of the retina, from which are differentiated the bipolar rod and cone cells, the bipolar and horizontal neurons confined within the retina itself, and the multipolar ganglionic neurons whose axons form the optic nerve (Fig. 19-10). The inner layer thus constitutes a fiber tract connecting two parts of the brain. Its fibers possess no Schwann sheaths, and its connective tissue investments represent continuations of the meningeal sheaths of the brain: i.e., pia, arachnoid, and dura.

The rod and cone cells are visual receptors which react specifically to physical light. The cones, numbering some 7,000,000 in the human eye, have a higher threshold of excitability and are stimulated by light of relatively high intensity. They are responsible for sharp vision and for color discrimination in adequate illumination. The rods, whose number has been estimated at more than 100,000,000, react to low intensities of illumination and subserve twilight and night vision. Close to the posterior pole of the eye, the retina shows a small, circular, yellowish area, the *macula lutea*, in direct line with the visual axis. The macula represents the retinal area for central vision, and the eyes are fixed in such a manner that the retinal image of any object is always focused on the macula. The rest of the retina is concerned with paracentral and peripheral vision. In the

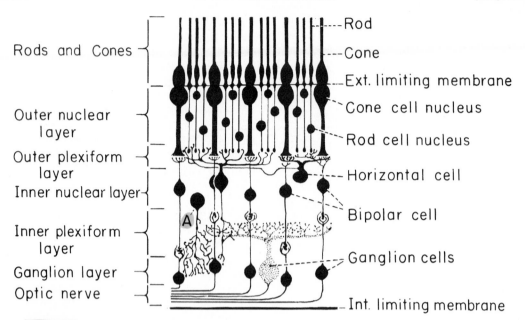

Rods and Cones

Outer nuclear layer

Outer plexiform layer

Inner nuclear layer

Inner plexiform layer

Ganglion layer

Optic nerve

Rod

Cone

Ext. limiting membrane

Cone cell nucleus

Rod cell nucleus

Horizontal cell

Bipolar cell

Ganglion cells

Int. limiting membrane

FIG. 19-10. Neural elements of the human retina as schematically drawn from Golgi preparations. *A* represents an amacrine cell (modified from Walls, '63).

macular region the inner layers of the retina are pushed apart, forming a small central pit, the *fovea centralis*, which constitutes the point of sharpest vision and most acute color discrimination. Here the retina is composed entirely of closely packed slender cones.

The nerve impulses from the rods and cones are transmitted to the bipolar neurons, which in turn establish synaptic relations with the dendrites or bodies of the multipolar ganglionic cells. The axons of the latter, at first unmyelinated, are arranged in fine radiating bundles which run parallel to the retinal surface and converge at the optic disc to form the optic nerve. On emerging from the eyeball the fibers at once acquire a myelin sheath, and there is a consequent increase in the size of the optic nerve.

The optic nerves enter the cranial cavity through the optic foramen and unite to form the optic chiasm, beyond which they are continued as the optic tracts. Within the chiasm a partial decussation occurs, the fibers from the nasal halves of the retina crossing to the opposite side, and those from the temporal halves of the retina remaining uncrossed

(Fig. 19-11). It must be remembered that in binocular vision each visual field, right and left, is projected upon portions of both retinae. Thus the images of objects in the right field of vision (red in Fig. 19-11) are projected on the right nasal and the left temporal half of the retina. In the chiasm the fibers from these two retinal portions are combined to form the left optic tract, which represents the complete right field of vision. By this arrangement the whole right field of vision is projected upon the left hemisphere, and the left visual field upon the right hemisphere.

Each optic tract sweeps outward and backward, encircling the hypothalamus and the rostral portions of the crus cerebri. Most of its fibers terminate in the lateral geniculate body, though a smaller portion continues as the brachium of the superior colliculus to the superior colliculi and pretectal area (Fig. 19-11). Although numerous authors suggest the existence of retinohypothalamic fibers (Marburg, '42), a recent survey of a group of different vertebrates (Kiernan, '67), using a variety of technics, has failed to demonstrate these fibers. Of all these terminal

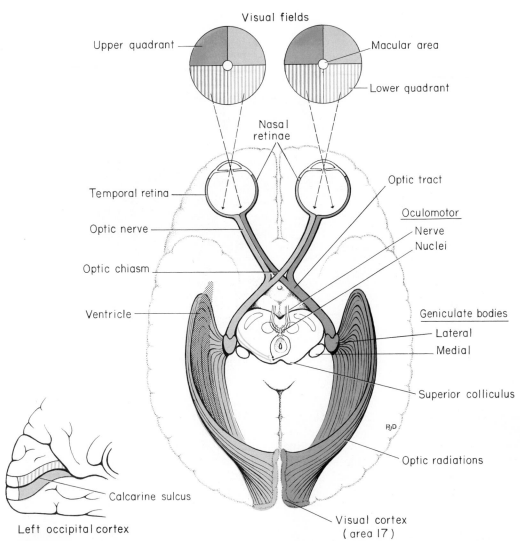

Fig. 19–11. Diagram of the visual pathways viewed from the ventral surface of the brain. Light from the upper half of the visual field falls on the inferior half of the retina. Light from the temporal half of the visual field falls on the nasal half of the retina, while light from the nasal half of the visual field falls on the temporal half of the retina. The visual pathways from the retina to the striate cortex are shown. The plane of the visual fields has been rotated 90 degrees toward the reader. The insert shows the projection of the quadrants of the visual field upon the left calcarine (striate) cortex. The macular area of the retina is represented nearest the occipital pole. Fibers mediating the pupillary light reflex leave the optic tract and project to the pretectal region; other fibers relay impulses indirectly to the visceral nuclei of the oculomotor complex.

nuclei only the lateral geniculate body appears to receive fibers concerned with visual perception. The lateral geniculate body gives rise to the geniculocalcarine tract, which forms the last relay of the visual path. The other nuclei subserve various optic reflexes. The pretectal area (Fig. 18–4) is concerned with the light reflex (page 389), the superior colliculi with reflex movement of the eyes and head in response to optic stimuli.

The *geniculocalcarine* tract arises from the lateral geniculate body, passes through the retrolenticular portion of the

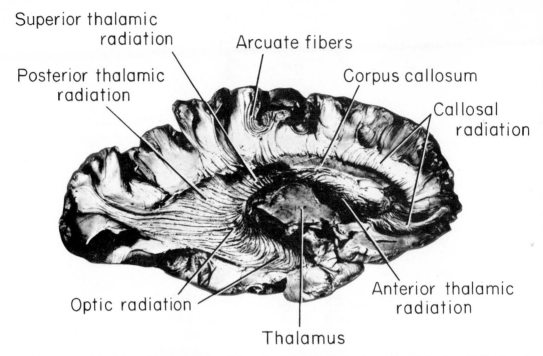

Superior thalamic radiation

Arcuate fibers

Posterior thalamic radiation

Corpus callosum

Callosal radiation

Optic radiation

Anterior thalamic radiation

Thalamus

FIG. 19–12. Dissection of brain from medial surface, showing internal capsule (thalamic radiations) and portions of callosal radiation. Photograph.

internal capsule, and forms the optic radiations, which end in the striate cortex (area 17), located on the medial surface of the occipital lobe. These fibers terminate on both sides of the calcarine sulcus (Fig. 19–5). All fibers of this radiation do not reach the cortex by the shortest route (Figs. 19–11 and 19–12). The most dorsal fibers pass almost directly backward to the striate area. Those placed more ventrally first turn forward and downward into the temporal lobe, and spread out over the rostral part of the inferior horn of the lateral ventricle; these fibers then loop backward, and run close to the outer wall of the lateral ventricle (external sagittal stratum) to reach the occipital cortex. The most ventral fibers make the longest loop; some of these extend into the uncal region of the temporal lobe before turning backwards (Fig. 19–11).

The retinal areas have a precise point-to-point relationship with the lateral geniculate body, each portion of the retina projecting on a specific and topographically limited portion of the geniculate. The fibers from the upper retinal quadrants (representing the lower visual field) terminate in the medial half, those from the lower quadrants in the lateral half of the geniculate body. The macular fibers occupy the central portion, flanked medially and laterally by fibers from the paracentral and peripheral retinal areas. A similar point-to-point relation exists between the geniculate body and the striate cortex. The medial half of the lateral geniculate body, representing the upper quandrants (lower visual fields), projects to the superior lip of the calcarine sulcus, and the fibers form the superior portion of the optic radiations (Fig. 19–11). The lateral half of the lateral geniculate body, representing the lower retinal quadrants (upper visual field) projects to the inferior lip of the calcarine sulcus. These fibers occupy the inferior portion of the optic radiations. The macular fibers, which constitute the intermediate part of the optic radiations, terminate in the caudal third of the calcarine cortex. Those from the paracentral and peripheral retinal areas end in respectively more rostral portions.

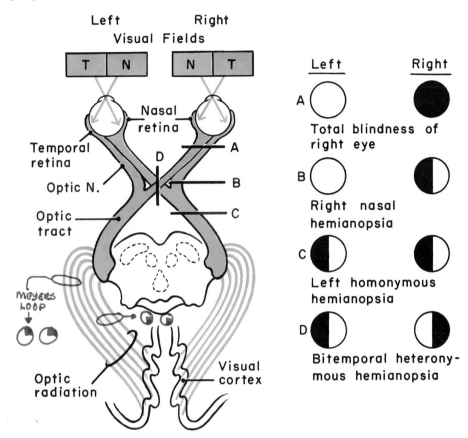

FIG. 19-13. Diagram of common lesions within the visual pathway. On the *left*, *A* through *D* indicate lesions. Corresponding visual field defects are shown on the *right* (modified from Haymaker, '56).

Experimental studies (Kuffler, '53) with stationary spots of light indicate that the receptive fields of ganglion cells in the retina are organized in concentric zones with either an "on" or "off" type of discharge in the center and the reverse in the periphery. The receptive fields of neurons in the lateral geniculate body appear similar with stationary spots of light (Hubel and Wiesel, '61). However, studies (Hubel and Wiesel, '62, '63) of single units in the striate cortex reveal that receptive fields at this level are not concentric and are particularly sensitive to "slits" of light or moving visual patterns oriented in certain directions.

Clinical Considerations. Injury to any part of the optic pathway produces visual defects whose nature depends on the location and extent of the injury. During examination each eye is covered in turn as the retinal quadrants of the opposite eye are tested. Visual defects are said to be *homonymous* when restricted to a single visual field, right or left, and *heteronymous* when parts of both fields are involved. It is evident that homonymous defects are caused by lesions on one side anywhere behind the chiasm, i.e., optic tract, lateral geniculate body, optic radiations, and visual cortex. Complete destruction of any of these structures results in a loss of the whole opposite field of vision (*homonymous hemianopsia*, Fig. 19-13C); partial injury produces *quadrantic homonymous* defects. Lesions of the temporal lobe, by compressing or destroying the looping fibers in the lower portion of the optic radiations, are likely to produce such quandrantic defects in the upper visual field. Injury to the parietal lobe may involve the more superiorly placed fibers of the radiations and cause similar defects in the lower field of vision.

Lesions of the chiasm may cause several kinds of heteronymous defects. Most commonly the crossing fibers from the nasal portions of the retina are involved, with consequent loss of the two temporal fields of vision (*bitemporal hemianopsia*; Fig. 19–13D). Rarely, both lateral angles of the chiasm may be compressed; in such cases the non-decussating fibers from the temporal retinae are affected, and the result is loss of the nasal visual fields (*binasal hemianopsia*). Injury of one optic nerve naturally produces blindness in the corresponding eye with loss of the pupillary light reflex (Fig. 19–13A). The pupil will, however, contract consensually to light entering the other eye, since the pretectal reflex center is related to both Edinger-Westphal nuclei. The pupillary reflex will not be affected by lesions of the visual pathway above the brachium of the superior colliculus (Fig. 19–11).

FUNCTIONAL CONSIDERATIONS OF THE THALAMUS

All sensory impulses, with the sole exception of the olfactory ones, terminate in the gray masses of the thalamus, from which they are projected to specific cortical areas by the thalamocortical radiations.

Though olfactory impulses project directly to the rhinencephalic cortex, higher order projections of this system ultimately reach portions of the thalamus, such as the anterior nuclear group and the habenular nucleus. Appreciation of olfactory stimuli does not depend upon thalamic relays; hence higher order olfactory projections to the thalamus are not concerned directly with this special sense. While portions of the dorsal thalamus serve as primary relay nuclei in various sensory pathways in which impulses are projected to specific regions of the cerebral cortex, the structure and organization of the thalamus indicate that its function is more complex and elaborate than that of a simple relay station. It seems certain that the thalamus is the chief sensory integrating mechanism of the neuraxis, but its functions are not limited to this. There is abundant evidence that specific parts of the thalamus play a dominant role in the maintenance and regulation of the state of consciousness, alertness, and attention, through widespread functional influences upon the activity of the cerebral cortex. The thalamus is concerned not only with general and specific types of awareness, but with certain emotional connotations that accompany, or are associated with, most sensory experiences. Other data suggest that some thalamic nuclei serve as integrative centers for motor functions, since they receive the principal efferent projections from the cerebellum and the basal ganglia.

The *specific sensory relay nuclei* of the thalamus are in the ventral tier of the lateral nuclear group. These include the medial and lateral geniculate bodies and the two divisions of the ventral posterior nucleus. The medial geniculate body receives fibers from the inferior colliculus and, to a lesser extent, from the lateral lemniscus. The dorsal parvocellular part of the nucleus, concerned mainly with audition, projects fibers via the geniculotemporal radiations to the transverse temporal gyrus of Heschl. The lateral geniculate body, receiving both crossed and uncrossed fibers of the optic tract, gives rise to the geniculocalcarine fibers, which project in a specific way to the cortex surrounding the calcarine sulcus (see page 480). As mentioned earlier, the two divisions of the ventral posterior nucleus project to the cortex of the postcentral gyrus. In the postcentral gyrus all parts of the body are represented in a definite sequence (Penfield and Rasmussen, '50); this cortical region is referred to as the *primary somesthetic area* (somatic sensory area I). The sensory representation of the body in somatic sensory area I is duplicated in reverse sequence at the base of the postcentral gyrus along the border of the lateral fissure (Penfield and Boldrey, '37; Woolsey, '58). This second topographical body representation, known as *somatic sensory area II* (somatic area II), receives fibers from the posterior part of the ventral posterior nucleus and the transitional posterior thalamic zone caudal to it (Fig. 18-4), that is sometimes identified as the magnocellular part of the medial geniculate body (Knighton, '50; Rose and Woolsey, '58; Poggio and Mountcastle, '60; Mehler, '66a). Some intercalated thalamic neurons also may project impulses to this area (Rose and Mountcastle, '59). While ablation experiments indicate that somatic area II is not essential for somatic discrimination, the observations of Poggio and Mountcastle ('60) indicate that somatic area II is concerned in a special way with pain sensibility. This finding does not mean that pain sensations project exclusively to this area, for it is well known that electrical stimulation of the postcentral gyrus in man often can evoke painful sensations, and ablations of the postcentral gyrus may eliminate certain types of pain.

The relatively simple impulses from peripheral receptors do not pass through the thalamus without modification. Many of the impulses become synthesized and integrated at a thalamic level before being projected to specific cortical areas. According to Head and Holmes ('11) and Foerster ('27), crude sensory modalities such as touch, thermal sense, and pain may be injured separately below thalamic levels, but at thalamic levels, and above, they become intimately fused and can no longer be segregated. Thus, the sensory cortex probably has little, if any, direct association with peripheral sensory receptors and is dependent upon the modified and integrated sensory impulses it receives from the thalamus. In animals which have no pallium, or only a poorly developed one, the thalamus probably constitutes the highest sensory correlation center in which somatic and visceral impulses are integrated.

The thalamus represents the neurological substratum of a crude sort of awareness, such as the recognition of touch (mere contact), temperature, pain, and of the affective quality of sensation, i.e., its pleasantness or unpleasantness. In certain lesions of the thalamus, or of the thalamocortical connections, after a brief initial stage of complete contralateral anesthesia, pain, crude touch, and some temperature sense return. However, tactile localization, two-point discrimination, and the sense of position and movement are lost or severely impaired. The sensations recovered are poorly localized and are accompanied by a great increase in "feeling tone," most commonly of an unpleasant character. Though the threshold of excitability is raised on the affected side, tactile and thermal stimuli previously not unpleasant now evoke disagreeable sensations (dysesthesias), not easily characterized by the patient. He cannot endure innocuous cutaneous stimulation, yet he cannot tell the nature of the exciting stimulus. Occasionally the reverse occurs: a previously indifferent stimulus evokes a most pleasant feeling. These feeling states may even be induced by other sensations, for instance auditory ones (Head, '20). Thus one patient could not go to church because listening to the hymns produced the most disagreeable sensations on his affected side. The dysesthesias may become intensified into spontaneous intractable pains which appear spasmodically, often without any apparent peripheral irritation. The pains are difficult to localize and may not respond even to powerful narcotic drugs.

It has already been stated that there are two aspects to sensation: the discriminative and the affective. In the former, stimuli are compared with respect to intensity, locality, and relative position in space and time—i.e., they are localized, and integrated into perceptions of form, size, and texture; movements are judged as to extent, direction, and sequence. It is this aspect of sensation which is related primarily to the specific sensory relay nuclei and the restricted cortical areas to which they project. With respect to the general somatic sensory relay nuclei (i.e., VPL and VPM) it is important to recall that these nuclei represent a complete, though distorted, image of the body, and the relationship between the periphery and portions of this complex is very precise. This specificity is similar to that which exists in the primary sensory cortex. These neurons also are modality specific, being concerned mainly with tactile and position sense, and responding to either superficial mechanical stimulation of the skin, mechanical distortion of deep tissues, or joint rotation, but not to more than one of these. It seems unlikely that afferent impulses from stretch receptors are conveyed to these nuclei, or that these receptors play a significant role in the perception of joint position. The visual thalamic relay nuclei likewise are organized in a specific manner in which point for point relationships exist between the receptor organ and the thalamic nuclei. The auditory thalamic relay nuclei probably are organized in a specific manner, but precise details concerning the tonotopic arrangement in the medial geniculate body are lacking (Whitfield, '67).

On the other hand there is the "affective" side of sensation: pain, agreeableness, and disagreeableness. Pain is a subjective sensation with considerable affective quality that often is difficult to describe and almost impossible to measure. The localization of different types of pain is often inexact and clinical judgment of its intensity must take into account the personality of the patient. Temperature and many tactile sensations likewise have a marked affective tone. This is especially true for all visceral sensations, in which the discriminative element is practically absent. This affective quality, which forms the basis of general bodily well-being or *malaise* and of the more intense emotional states, is believed to be "appreciated" by the thalamus rather than the cortex, though it may be profoundly modified and controlled by the latter. The appreciation of pain, crude touch, and some temperature sense is retained even after complete destruction of the sensory cortical areas of both sides.

In addition to the specific sensory relay nuclei described above, there are other *cortical relay nuclei* in the thalamus. These include: (1) the anterior nuclei, (2) the ventral lateral nucleus, and (3) the ventral anterior nucleus (in part). The anterior nuclei of the thalamus receive what is probably the largest efferent fi-

ber bundle from the hypothalamus—the mammillothalamic tract (Figs. 3–20, 18–1, 18–6, and 18–11). These nuclei in turn project to the cingulate gyrus, a cortical area demonstrated to produce a variety of visceral responses upon stimulation (Kremer, '47; Ward, '48). In this connection it seems pertinent to recall that fibers from the cingulate gyrus also pass to the anterior nuclei of the thalamus, and that thalamomammillary fibers (Clark and Boggon, '33) are contained within the mammillothalamic fasciculus.

The ventral lateral nucleus of the thalamus, which receives cerebellar, rubral and pallidal efferent fibers, relays impulses from these sources to the precentral gyrus. These complex pathways from the cerebellum and basal ganglia to the precentral cortex via VL constitute major neural systems involved in motor function, yet the precise nature of the impulses conveyed by them is not known. Since most of the group I muscle afferent impulses are relayed to the cerebellum (Lloyd and McIntyre, '50; Oscarsson, '65) and volleys confined to group I muscle afferents evoke little, or no response in the somatic sensory cortex (Mountcastle and Powell, '59), it seems reasonable to suspect that this cerebellothalamic cortical relay system may play an important role in the unconscious regulation of muscle tone. In this manner impulses from stretch receptors may be conveyed indirectly to higher integrative levels of the neuraxis. Further, it seems likely that interruption of relay fibers in this system at thalamic levels may be responsible for the reduction in muscle tone that occurs in patients with paralysis agitans after stereotaxic surgery.

Cerebellar dyskinesia resulting from lesions of the dentate nucleus appears to be the physiological expression of removal of controlling cerebellar influences which normally act upon thalamic nuclei. In this sense neocerebellar disturbances might be regarded as a "release phenomenon" in which the ventral lateral nucleus of the thalamus is released, and functions in an abnormal fashion. This hypothesis may explain why lesions in VL ameliorate cerebellar dyskinesia in man and monkeys (Carpenter and Hanna, '62).

Although the ventral anterior nucleus is known to receive a large number of fibers from the globus pallidus and some fibers from the substantia nigra, available evidence indicates that only part of the cells of this nucleus project upon the cerebral cortex. The projection areas of the principal part of the ventral anterior nucleus (VApc) appear to be the anterior insular cortex (Angevine et al., '62) and frontal cortical area 6 (Freeman and Watts, '47). As mentioned before this nucleus also has subcortical projections and is related functionally with the intralaminar nuclei. The ventral anterior nucleus exhibits characteristics of both the specific and the nonspecific thalamic nuclei.

The cortical relay nuclei of the thalamus present certain common features: all receive substantial numbers of afferent fibers from specific parts of the neuraxis; all project to well defined cortical areas; and all undergo degenerative cell changes following ablations of their cortical projection areas. These nuclei constitute the *specific thalamic nuclei*. Low frequency electrical stimulation of individual specific sensory thalamic nuclei and certain specific relay nuclei (i.e., the ventral lateral nucleus) elicits a primary response followed by an augmenting sequence of surface potentials from the primary cortical projection area. Characteristically, *augmenting responses*: (1) have a short latency, (2) are diphasic and increase in magnitude during the initial four or five stimuli of a repetitive train, and (3) are localized to the primary cortical projection area of the specific thalamic nucleus stimulated (Dempsey and Morison, '42).

The *association nuclei of the thalamus* receive no direct fibers from the ascending systems, but have abundant connections with other diencephalic nuclei. They project largely to association areas of the cerebral cortex in the frontal and parietal lobes and, to a lesser extent, in the occipital and temporal lobes. The principal association nuclei include the dorsomedial nucleus (DM), the lateral dorsal nucleus

(LD), the lateral posterior nucleus (LP), and the pulvinar (P) (Fig. 19-5). The dorsomedial nucleus, the most prominent gray mass of the medial thalamus, is highly developed in primates, especially man (Fig. 19-4). It is connected with the lateral thalamic nuclei, the hypothalamus, and the amygdaloid nuclear complex; moreover, it has a strong reciprocal connection with the frontal granular cortex (Fig. 19-5). It has been suggested that in this nucleus somatic impulses forming the basis for discriminative cortical sensibility are blended with the feeling tone engendered by visceral activities. These somatovisceral impulses are projected to the prefrontal cortex, which constitutes a large, phylogenetically new cortical area highly developed only in man. While the significance of the prefrontal cortex is not fully understood, it has been regarded as the place where the discriminative cortical activities attain their highest elaboration.

Large injuries to the frontal lobes of both hemispheres are likely to cause defects in complex association, as well as certain changes in behavior, expressed by loss of acquired inhibitions and more direct and excessive emotional responses. Similar alterations in emotional behavior are produced when the pathways between the dorsomedial nucleus and the frontal cortex are severed (e.g., in frontal lobotomy).

The lateral dorsal and lateral posterior nuclei receive afferent fibers principally from the ventral nuclei and apparently are concerned with complex somesthetic association mechanisms related to various parts of the body. These nuclei project largely to parietal association areas (Fig. 19-5). The pulvinar, considered as an outgrowth of the lateral posterior nucleus, appears relatively late in phylogenetic development. Development of this huge nuclear mass seems to be correlated with increasing complexity in the integration of somatic and special senses, especially vision and audition. The cortical projections of this thalamic nuclear mass are to portions of the posterior parietal and occipitotemporal cortex.

The *intralaminar and midline nuclei*

of the mammalian dorsal thalamus for a long time have constituted an unexplored and poorly understood region. Phylogenetically these nuclei are older than the specific relay nuclei, composing such a large and conspicuous part of the human thalamus. In man and primates many of these nuclei are small and indistinct. Most of them are regarded anatomically as having no cortical projections, though they appear to have connections with other thalamic nuclei (Nauta and Whitlock, '54), the hypothalamus (Bodian, '40), the globus pallidus (Nauta and Mehler, '66) and the striatum (Powell and Cowan, '56). As previously described, most of the afferent fibers to the intralaminar nuclei ascend from the brain stem in the central tegmental fasciculus, a composite bundle containing predominantly long axons originating from neurons in the reticular formation. Stimulation of the ascending reticular activating system and various kinds of sensory stimuli (see Chapter 16) result in a generalized desynchronization and activation of the electroencephalogram, and behavioral arousal. These phenomena are comparable to those associated with arousal from natural sleep. It is presumed that the electroencephalographic (EEG) arousal response, which produces dramatic effects upon cortical activity, is mediated, at least in part, by the intralaminar nuclei. Physiological studies suggest that impulses producing these changes in cortical activity reach the cortex via a diffuse thalamic projection system (Moruzzi and Magoun, '49; Jasper, '49; Starzl and Magoun, '51; Jasper et al., '52), the exact nature of which has not been established. Anatomical evidence (Nauta and Kuypers, 58; Scheibel and Scheibel, '58) indicates that ascending reticular fibers also pass to the hypothalamus and the subthalamic region, suggesting that the so-called diffuse thalamic projection system should not be regarded as the only relay by which impulses from the reticular formation can influence electrocortical activity. It is possible that some impulses to the cerebral cortex may follow alternate extrathalamic pathways involving

basal diencephalic nuclei that project fibers into the internal capsule (Starzl et al., '51).

The classical studies of Dempsey and Morison ('42, '43) and of Morison and Dempsey ('42) showed that stimulation of the so-called nonspecific thalamic nuclei, and the basal diencephalic region, produced widespread and pronounced effects upon electrocortical activity. The *nonspecific*, or *diffuse*, thalamic nuclei include the intralaminar and midline nuclei, and, in part, the ventral anterior nucleus of the ventral tier. Repetitive stimulation of these thalamic nuclei alters spontaneous electrocortical activity over large areas and, under certain conditions, resets the frequency of brain waves by eliciting responses that are time-locked to the thalamic stimulus. The most characteristic effect of stimulating the nonspecific thalamic nuclei is the *recruiting response*. When the frequency of stimulation is in the range of 6 to 12 cycles per second, predominantly surface negative cortical responses rapidly increase to a maximum (by the fourth to sixth stimulus of the train) and then decrease over a broad area; continued stimulation causes the evoked responses to wax and wane. Stimulation of one of the nonspecific thalamic nuclei causes all others to be activated in a mass excitation (Starzl and Magoun '51). Bilateral cortical responses do not appear to be dependent upon transmission by fibers of the corpus callosum or anterior commissure, nor does spread from one cortical area to another depend upon intracortical propagation (Morison and Dempsey, '42; Jasper, '49). Available evidence suggests that cortical spread involves intrathalamic activities, including conduction across midline gray masses of the thalamus. Although stimulating the nonspecific thalamic nuclei produces changes in electrocortical activity over broad areas, these effects are not indiscriminate or equal in all cortical areas. Responsive cortical zones appear to be relatively specific in the frontal, cingulate, orbital, parietal, and occipital association areas. The so-called diffuse thalamic projection system appears capable of exerting a massive influence mainly upon areas of the associational cortex, but with a great preponderance of its effects upon the frontal association cortex (Starzl and Whitlock, '52). No recruiting responses or other evoked potentials are recorded in rhinencephalic structures (i.e., olfactory tubercle, pyriform lobe, amygdaloid complex, or hippocampal formation) upon stimulation of the intralaminar nuclei. Some evidence (Green and Arduini, '54) indicates that stimuli producing desynchronization in neocortical areas evoke a series of slow undulating waves in the hippocampal formation that might be interpreted as a specialized form of arousal reaction.

Stimulation of the nonspecific thalamic nuclei demonstrates that these nuclei also exert a potent influence upon subcortical structures, particularly the thalamic association nuclei, such as the dorsomedial nucleus, the lateral dorsal nucleus, the lateral posterior nucleus, and the pulvinar (Starzl and Whitlock, '52). Effects may be observed also in the anterior nuclei. Stimulation of midline thalamic nuclei is capable of eliciting recruiting activities in mesencephalic reticular regions, which apparently do not depend on cortical connections (Schlag and Faidlerbe, '61). Recruiting responses are observed in the head of the caudate nucleus upon thalamic stimulation of this system (Starzl and Magoun, '51; Starzl and Whitlock, '52; Verzeano et al., '53), but they are found only rarely in the putamen and not at all in the globus pallidus. It is of interest that stimulation of the head of the caudate nucleus produces recruiting responses in the nonspecific thalamic nuclei and in the cerebral cortex (Shimamoto and Verzeano, '54). Attempts to analyze the functional relationships between subcortical structures and the nonspecific thalamic nuclei have shown that recruiting responses are not dependent upon: (1) the thalamic association nuclei, (2) the specific relay nuclei of the thalamus, or (3) the striatum, if these structures are destroyed individually (Hanberry and Jasper, '53; Hanberry et al., '54; Koella and Gellhorn, '54; Kerr and O'Leary, '57).

The above statement should not be interpreted as meaning that recruiting responses remain after all of these structures have been destroyed together. Additional evidence indicates that bilateral destruction of the globus pallidus does not impair recruiting responses produced by thalamic stimulation (Spiegel et al., '57; Szekely, '57).

The early observation of Moruzzi and Magoun ('49) that cortical recruiting responses induced by low frequency stimulation of the nonspecific thalamic nuclei could be reduced, or blocked, by stimulation of the bulbar reticular formation appears to provide experimental evidence that the nonspecific nuclei of the thalamus are within the sphere of influence of the ascending reticular formation. This finding together with anatomical evidence (Nauta and Kuypers, '58; Scheibel and Scheibel, '58) strongly supports the thesis that EEG arousal reactions elicited by ascending reticular volleys are mediated, at least in part, via the nonspecific thalamic nuclei. However, these responses also may be mediated by extrathalamic pathways which pass lateral to the hypothalamus and subthalamus to enter the internal capsule (Starzl et al., '51). Physiological evidence for this route is provided by the persistence of generalized cortical activation upon high frequency stimulation of the reticular formation after destruction of the thalamus.

Some idea of the complex physiological relationship between the brain stem reticular formation and nonspecific thalamic nuclei is provided by the antagonistic effects of reticular activation on the recruiting responses and other varieties of electrocortical synchronization elicited by stimulation of the nonspecific thalamus, as noted above. However, it must be pointed out that electrocortical synchronization also may be obtained by stimulation of caudal as well as rostral regions of the brain stem reticular formation and that, conversely, electrocortical desynchronization may be obtained with high frequency stimulation of nonspecific thalamic nuclei. The overt electroencephalographic effects appear to depend in part on both the frequency and the intensity of stimulation at different sites within the mesencephalic and diencephalic reticular system (Moruzzi, '63).

Physiological evidence (Cohen et al., '62; Frigyesi and Purpura, '64; Purpura et al., '66) indicates that transmission of cerebellofugal impulses projecting to the motor cortex via the ventral lateral nucleus of the thalamus may be markedly altered by synaptic activities at multiple sites. Of the pathways studied, those arising in the nonspecific thalamic nuclei appear especially potent. Low frequency stimulation (8 per second) of the nonspecific thalamic nuclei produces short-latency facilitation and prolonged inhibition of specific evoked responses in VLo, the motor cortex, and the corticospinal tract. Present findings suggest that the modulation of cerebellar influences on the motor cortex may be the consequence of facilitatory and inhibitory effects of the nonspecific thalamic nuclei upon synaptic activities in the ventral lateral nucleus.

The thalamus is played upon by two great streams of afferent fibers: the peripheral and the cortical. The former brings sensory impulses from all parts of the body concerning changes in the external and internal environment of the individual. The cortical connections link the thalamus with the associative memory mechanism of the pallium and bring it under cortical control. The thalamus has subcortical efferent connections with the hypothalamus and striatum (i.e., caudate nucleus and putamen) through which the thalamus can influence visceral and somatic effectors. The functional nature of these subcortical efferent thalamic pathways is unknown, but they are considered to serve primarily affective reactions. These pathways, like the thalamus itself, are under the control of the cerebral cortex. Corticothalamic projections usually are considered to exert inhibitory influences upon thalamic activity. It has been suggested that corticothalamic fibers may constitute part of a complex neural mechanism for the selective regulation of the integrative actions of the thalamus, permitting certain sub-divisions to function while inhibiting the activity of others.

THE HYPOTHALAMUS

The hypothalamus comprises the ventral walls of the third ventricle below the hypothalamic sulci and the structures of the ventricular floor, including the optic chiasm, the tuber cinereum with the infundibulum, and the mammillary bodies. Anteriorly it passes without sharp demarcation into the basal olfactory area (diagonal gyrus of the anterior perforated substance), and caudally it is similarly continuous with the central gray matter and tegmentum of the midbrain. It may be conveniently described as extending from the region of the optic chiasm to the caudal tip of the mammillary bodies (Fig. 19-14). The region immediately in front of the chiasm, extending to the lamina terminalis and anterior commissure, is known as the *preoptic area* and, though belonging to the forebrain, it is closely related to hypothalamic structures. Dorsal to the hypothalamus is the thalamus; lateral and caudal to the hypothalamus is the subthalamic region (Fig. 3-13B).

The Hypothalamic Nuclei. Pervading the whole area is a diffuse matrix of cells constituting the central gray substance, in which are found a number of more or less distinct nuclear masses. A sagittal plane passing through the anterior pillar of the fornix roughly separates the medial and lateral hypothalamic areas. The lateral area, which abuts upon the subthalamic region and internal capsule, is narrow in its rostral and caudal portions, but in the region of the tuber cinereum it expands considerably (Fig. 19-15). It contains scattered groups of large, darkly staining cells—the *lateral hypothalamic nucleus*—and two or three sharply delimited, circular cell groups known as the *nuclei tuberis* (tuberales), which often produce small visible eminences on the basal surface of the hypothalamus. They consist of small, pale, multipolar cells surrounded by a delicate fiber capsule about which are found the large cells of the lateral hypothalamic nucleus (Fig. 19-15).

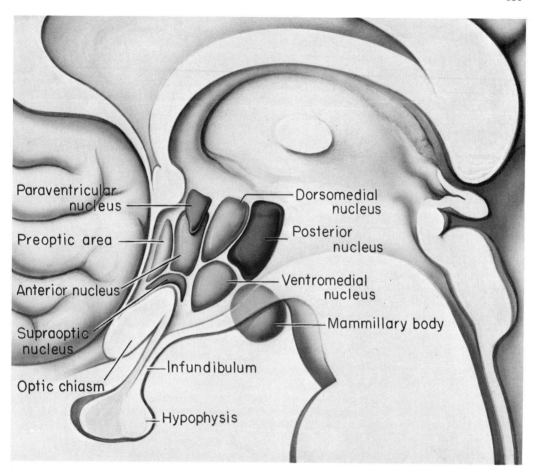

Fig. 19-14. Schematic diagram of the medial hypothalamic nuclei. Nuclei in the anterior or supraoptic region of the hypothalamus are in *blue*. The paraventricular and supraoptic nuclei are *dark blue*; the anterior nucleus of the hypothalamus is *light blue*. Nuclei of the middle, or tuberal, region of the hypothalamus are *yellow*. Nuclei of the caudal, or mammillary, region of the hypothalamus are shades of *red*. The preoptic area lies rostral to the anterior hypothalamic region.

In a cephalocaudal direction three hypothalamic regions may be recognized: (1) an anterior or *supraoptic region*, lying above the chiasm and continuous in front with the preoptic area, (2) a middle or *tuberal region*, and (3) a caudal or *mammillary region*, which is continuous caudally with the central gray of the cerebral aqueduct.

The poorly differentiated preoptic area forms the central gray of the most rostral part of the third ventricle. Clark et al. ('38) distinguished a medial preoptic nucleus of rather densely grouped small cells, and a lateral nucleus in which the medium-sized cells are more diffusely arranged (Figs. 19-14 and 19-15).

The supraoptic region contains two of the most striking and sharply defined hypothalamic nuclei, the *paraventricular nucleus* and the *supraoptic nucleus*, which have certain common features as to cell structure and fiber connections (Figs. 19-14 and 19-15). They are both composed of large, often bipolar, dark staining cells. The Nissl substance is distributed peripherally, and in the cytoplasm inclusions of colloidal material are found, which are regarded by some as evidence of secretory activity. Both nuclei send fibers to the posterior lobe of

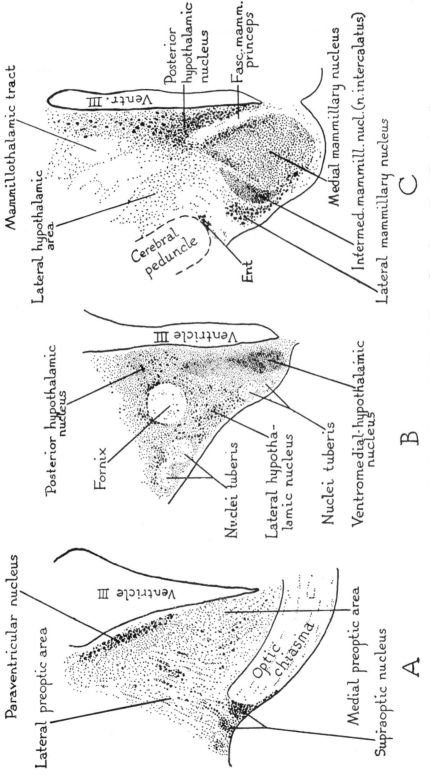

Fig. 19-15. Transverse sections through supraoptic (*A*), infundibular (*B*), and mammillary (*C*) portions of human hypothalamus (after Clark et al., '38). *Ent*, entopeduncular nucleus.

the hypophysis. The paraventricular nucleus is a fairly broad, flat, vertical plate of densely packed cells occupying a considerable portion of the wall of the third ventricle. Rostrally it extends almost to the optic chiasm, while dorsally it approaches the hypothalamic sulcus. The ventrally placed supraoptic nucleus straddles the lateral portion of the optic chiasm (Fig. 19-14). Scattered cells or small cell groups appear to form an incomplete bridge between the two nuclei. The less differentiated central gray of this region, known as the *anterior hypothalamic nucleus*, merges imperceptibly with the preoptic area.

In the tuberal region where the hypothalamus reaches its widest extent, the fornix separates the medial and the lateral hypothalamic areas. The medial portion forms the central gray substance of the ventricular wall, in which there may be distinguished a *ventromedial* and a *dorsomedial nucleus* that are poorly delimited from each other (Fig. 19-14). These nuclei are composed of uniformly small ovoid cells. In the caudal part of this region many large oval or rounded cells are scattered in a matrix of smaller ones; collectively they constitute the *posterior hypothalamic nucleus*. The large cells, especially numerous in man, extend caudally over the mammillary body to become continuous with the periventricular gray and tegmentum of the midbrain. These cells resemble those of the lateral hypothalamic area, and often are included with them in a single and more extensive nuclear mass, the *mammilloinfundibular nucleus* (Malone, '10). Large cells in this location are believed to furnish most of the efferent hypothalamic fibers to the lower portions of the brain stem.

The mammillary portion consists of the mammillary bodies, and the dorsally located cells of the posterior hypothalamic nucleus. In man the mammillary body consists almost entirely of the large, spherical *medial mammillary nucleus*, composed of relatively small cells invested by a capsule of myelinated fibers. Lateral to this is the small *intermediate (intercalated) mammillary nucleus*

composed of smaller cells. Even further lateral is a well-defined group of large cells, the *lateral mammillary nucleus*, which probably represents a condensation of cells from the posterior hypothalamic nucleus (Figs. 19-15C and 19-16C).

The most characteristic features of the human hypothalamus are the sharply circumscribed tuberal nuclei, the large size of the medial mammillary nuclei, and the extensive distribution of the large cells in the posterior and lateral hypothalamic areas.

Connections of the Hypothalamus. The hypothalamus, in spite of its small size, has extensive and complex fiber connections. Some fibers are organized into definite and conspicuous bundles, while others are diffuse and difficult to trace.

The **afferent connections of the hypothalamus** which have been established are: (1) The *medial forebrain bundle*, a complex group of fibers arising from the basal olfactory regions, the periamygdaloid region, and the septal nuclei, that pass to, and through, the lateral parts of the hypothalamus. Some fibers of this bundle continue caudally into the midbrain tegmentum (Fig. 18-6). Nuclei whose fibers form this bundle receive impulses from the olfactory bulb. This tract is well developed in lower vertebrates, but in man it is small and inconspicuous. (2) *Hippocampo-hypothalamic fibers* originating from the hippocampal formation, that form the fornix (Figs. 21-4, 21-6 and 21-7). Fibers of the fornix project mainly to the mammillary body, terminating largely in the medial mammillary nucleus. However, precommissural fibers of the fornix are distributed to the septal nuclei, the lateral preoptic region, the nucleus of the diagonal band, and the dorsal hypothalamic area (Nauta, '56). (3) *Cortico-hypothalamic fibers*, arising from various portions of the frontal lobe, that pass directly to the hypothalamus. A considerable projection from the posterior orbital cortex is distributed to several hypothalamic nuclei (Ward and McCulloch, '47; Meyer, '49; Sachs et al., '49; Clark and Meyer, '50; Wall et al., '51; Showers, '58; Nauta, '62). Fibers to

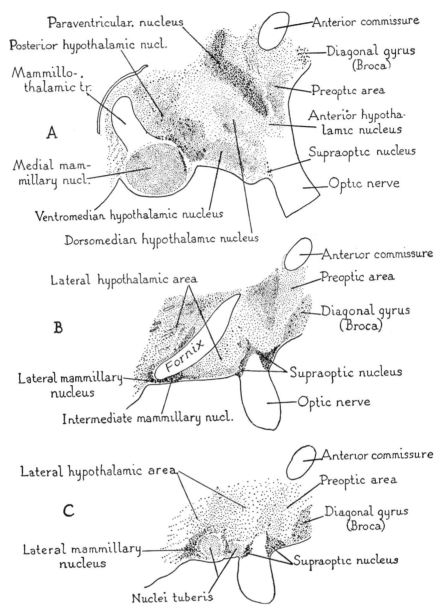

Fig. 19–16. Sagittal sections of human hypothalamus. *A*, Near median (ventricular) surface; *B*, through anterior column of fornix; *C*, near lateral border of hypothalamus (after Clark et al., '38).

the lateral preoptic and hypothalamic regions appear to follow the medial forebrain bundle (Nauta, '62). (4) *Amygdalo-hypothalamic fibers* that follow two pathways to the hypothalamus: (a) the stria terminalis, and (b) a course ventral to the lentiform nucleus. The stria terminalis arises mainly from the caudal half of the amygdaloid complex, and its fibers are distributed to the medial preoptic nucleus, the anterior hypothalamic nucleus, and the diffuse part of the supra-optic nucleus. Ventral amygdalofugal fibers spread medially and rostrally under the lentiform nucleus to reach the lateral preoptic, hypothalamic, and septal regions (Nauta, '61). (5) *Thalamo-hypothalamic fibers* that arise chiefly from the

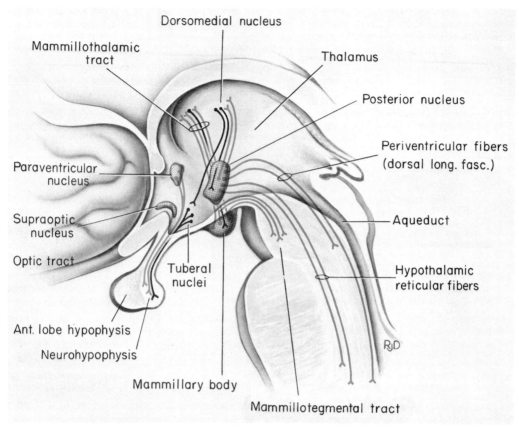

Fig. 19–17. Diagram showing some of the efferent hypothalamic pathways. Color code is the same as in Fig. 19–14. The terminations of the mammillotegmental tract are shown in detail in Fig. 18–6.

magnocellular portion of the dorsomedial nucleus, and from the midline thalamic nuclei. These nuclei project via the inferior thalamic peduncle to the lateral preoptic and hypothalamic regions, as well as to rostral portions of the amygdaloid complex (Nauta, '62). (6) Fibers of the *mammillary peduncle*, arising from the dorsal and ventral tegmental nuclei of the midbrain (Guillery, '56), that project mainly to the lateral mammillary nucleus (Fig. 18–6). In its course the mammillary peduncle passes rostrally through the rootlets of the third nerve and lies lateral to the interpeduncular nucleus. A few of these fibers ascend in the medial forebrain bundle beyond the hypothalamus. The afferent connections of the dorsal and ventral tegmental nuclei are incompletely known, but some mammillo-

tegmental fibers reach these nuclei, thus forming a feedback circuit.

In the older literature there are descriptions of pallidohypothalamic fibers passing to the ventromedial nucleus. Recent studies with silver staining technics (Nauta and Mehler, '66) have failed to demonstrate this pathway. Available evidence suggests that the so-called pallidohypothalamic tract is composed mainly of aberrant fibers of the ansa lenticularis which rejoin the principal pallidofugal system and ascend to the thalamus.

Efferent hypothalamic fibers emerge from the mammillary bodies, the periventricular gray and the tuberal region (Fig. 19–17). From the medial mammillary nucleus, and to a lesser extent the lateral and intermediate mammillary nuclei, arises a well-defined bundle, the *fascicu-*

lus mammillaris princeps. This bundle passes dorsally for a short distance and divides into two components: the *mammillothalamic tract* and the *mammillotegmental tract* (Figs. 18–6 and 19–17). The mammillothalamic tract contains fibers from the medial mammillary nucleus that project to the ipsilateral anteroventral and anteromedial nuclei, and fibers from the lateral mammillary nucleus that pass bilaterally to the anterodorsal nuclei (Fry et al., '63). A few fibers of this tract apparently course in the reverse direction (i.e., from the anterior nuclear group of the thalamus to the mammillary body). Since the anterior nuclear group of the thalamus is connected reciprocally with the cingulate gyrus (Figs. 19–4 and 19–5), hypothalamic impulses can influence this cortical region, and the hypothalamus is brought indirectly under the control of the cingulate region. The mammillotegmental tract curves caudally into the midbrain tegmentum. Fibers of this tract terminate in the dorsal and ventral tegmental nuclei (Fig. 18–6).

The *periventricular fibers* arise primarily from the large cells of the posterior hypothalamic nucleus and to some extent also from the nuclei of the tuberal and supraoptic regions. These finely myelinated and unmyelinated fibers pass dorsally in the periventricular gray. Some of these fibers terminate in the dorsomedial thalamic nucleus and in some of the midline nuclei, where they intermingle with fibers which pass from these thalamic nuclei to the hypothalamus (Figs. 19–4*B* and 19–17). This two-way connection brings the hypothalamus into relationship with the frontal granular cortex, since the latter is reciprocally connected with the dorsomedial thalamic nucleus.

The majority of the periventricular fibers turn caudally and descend to lower portions of the brain stem. Their exact course is not fully understood. A few run dorsal to the cerebral aqueduct and terminate in the midbrain tectum. A larger number descend ventral to the cerebral aqueduct in the subependymal portion of the central gray and form a part of the dorsal bundle of Schütz (Fig. 19–17). Descending fibers in the dorsal longitudinal fasciculus are distributed to the ventral half of the central gray and to the dorsal tegmental nucleus. According to Nauta ('58), none of the descending bundles of this system extend beyond the level of the abducens nucleus. As mentioned previously (p. 380), the prevailing direction of conduction in this fiber system is ascending. Other hypothalamic efferent fibers descend in the reticular formation of the brain stem, probably to medullary levels. Few, if any, of these fibers project to spinal levels.

The connections of the hypothalamus with the posterior lobe of the hypophysis are well established for man (Pines, '25; Stengel, '26; Greving, '35). They are unmyelinated fibers which arise principally from the supraoptic and paraventricular nuclei and form a well-defined bundle, the *supraopticohypophysial tract* (Fig. 19–17). A smaller bundle, the *tuberohypophysial tract*, is contributed by the medial cells of the tuber cinereum.

It is evident from the above that the efferent descending hypothalamic fibers represent essentially connections with lower autonomic centers innervating visceral structures. The hypothalamus is under thalamic and pallial control, and in turn influences the activity of these centers. Pallial control is in part mediated by direct corticohypothalamic fibers. Greater pallial control is mediated by way of the dorsomedial and anterior thalamic nuclei, which connect the frontal and cingulate cortex with the hypothalamus. Since the dorsomedial and the anterior thalamic nuclei are connected reciprocally with both cortex and hypothalamus, these pathways are also important channels through which hypothalamic influences can be transmitted to the cortex.

In addition to the connections mentioned above, there is physiological evidence that certain regions of the hypothalamus are intimately related to, and integrated with, the reticular system of the brain stem. Stimulation of the lateral and posterior hypothalamus facilitates reflex and cortically induced movements. It evokes the same activating effects upon the electrical activities of the cortex as are obtained from stimulation of the mesencephalic and subthalamic regions.

Functional Considerations. A large accumulation of experimental evidence and clinical observations have demonstrated beyond doubt that the hypothalamus and immediately adjoining regions are related to all kinds of visceral activities. The most diverse disturbances of autonomic functions, such as water balance, internal secretion, sugar and fat metabolism, and temperature regulation, all can be produced by stimulation or destruction of hypothalamic areas. Even the mechanism for normal sleep may be altered profoundly by such lesions. It is established that the hypothalamus is the chief subcortical center for the regulation of both sympathetic and parasympathetic activities. These dual activities are integrated into coordinated responses which maintain adequate internal conditions in the body. It is highly improbable that each of the autonomic activities has its own discrete center in view of the small size of the hypothalamus and the complex nature of these activities. However, a specific function has been established for the supraoptic and periventricular nuclei. There is a fairly definite topographical organization as regards the two main divisions of the autonomic system. Control of parasympathetic activities is related to the anterior and medial hypothalamic regions (supraoptic and preoptic areas) and the ventricular portion of the tuber cinereum. Stimulation of this region results in increased vagal and sacral autonomic responses, characterized by reduced heart rate, peripheral vasodilation, and increased tonus and motility of the alimentary and vesical walls.

Of the several nuclei found in this region, the supraoptic and paraventricular nuclei definitely are concerned with the maintenance of body water balance (Figs. 19-15A and 19-16B). Destruction of these nuclei, or their hypophysial connections, invariably is followed by the condition known as *diabetes insipidus*, in which there is increased secretion of urine (polyuria) without an increase in the sugar content of the urine. The antidiuretic hormone is secreted directly by the cells of the supraoptic and paraventricular nuclei. The secretion is conducted to the posterior lobe along the unmyelinated axons of the supraopticohypophysical tract (Bargmann et al., '50). Experimental evidence indicates that the antidiuretic hormone is stored in the posterior lobe of the pituitary. The production of antidiuretic hormone varies in accordance with changes in the osmotic pressure of the blood. An increase in the osmotic pressure of the blood which supplies the supraoptic nuclei increases the activity of these neurons and the release of antidiuretic hormone. In states of experimental dehydration there is a depletion of the hormone in the posterior lobe and increased secretory activity in the supraoptic and paraventricular nuclei. After re-establishment of water balance, there is a re-accumulation of the hormone in the posterior lobe (Hild, '56).

The lateral and posterior hypothalamic regions are concerned with the control of sympathetic responses. Stimulation of this area, especially the posterior portion, from which most of the descending efferent fibers arise, activates the thoracolumbar outflow and results in the heightened metabolic and somatic activities characteristic of states of emotional stress, combat, or flight. These responses are expressed by dilation of the pupil, piloerection, acceleration of the heart rate, elevation of blood pressure, increase in the rate and amplitude of respiration, somatic struggling movements, and inhibition of the gut and bladder. All these signs of emotional excitement also are readily elicited when the hypothalamus is released from cortical control. Thus removal of the cortex, or interruption of the cortical connections with the hypothalamus, induces many of the above visceral symptoms collectively designated as "sham rage" (Fulton and Ingraham, '29; Bard, '39). On the other hand, destruction of the posterior hypothalamus produces emotional lethargy, abnormal sleepiness, and a fall in temperature due to the reduction of general visceral (and somatic) activities.

The coordination of sympathetic and

parasympathetic responses is strikingly shown in the regulation of body temperature. This complex function involving widely spread physical and chemical processes apparently is mediated by two hypothalamic mechanisms, one concerned with the dissipation of heat and the other with its production and conservation. There is considerable experimental evidence that the anterior hypothalamus, especially the preoptic area, is sensitive to increases in temperature, and sets in motion the mechanism for dissipating the excess heat. In man this consists mainly in profuse sweating and vasodilation of the cutaneous blood vessels. These actions permit the rapid elimination of heat by convection and radiation from the surface of the engorged blood vessels and by the evaporation of sweat. In animals with fur this is supplemented to a considerable degree by rapid respiratory movements of shallow amplitude (panting); the heat loss is effected mainly by the warming of rapidly successive streams of inspired air. Lesions involving the anterior part of the hypothalamus abolish the neural control of mechanisms concerned with the dissipation of heat and result in hyperthermia. This hyperthermia (hyperpyrexia) may result from tumors in or near the anterior hypothalamic and preoptic areas.

The posterior hypothalamus, on the other hand, is sensitive to conditions of decreasing body temperature and institutes measures for the conservation and increased production of heat. The cutaneous blood vessels are constricted and sweat secretion ceases, so that heat loss through radiation and evaporation is reduced. Simultaneously there is augmentation of visceral activities, and the somatic muscles become involved in the involuntary movements of shivering. All these activities tremendously increase the processes of oxidation, with a consequent production and conservation of heat. Bilateral lesions in posterior regions of the hypothalamus usually produce a condition in which body temperature varies with the environment (poikilothermia) since such lesions effectively destroy descending pathways concerned with both the conservation and dissipation of heat.

These two intrinsically antagonistic mechanisms do not function independently but are continually interrelated and balanced against each other to meet the changing needs of the body, the coordinated responses always being directed to the maintenance of a constant optimum temperature.

There is considerable evidence that the hypothalamus is largely responsible for maintaining and regulating the activity of the anterior pituitary gland. The paucity of nerve fibers in the anterior lobe of the pituitary makes it seem unlikely that hypothalamic influences are mediated by direct neural pathways. Experimental data (Harris, '55, '56) indicate that hypothalamic influences upon the anterior pituitary probably are transmitted by humoral mediators via the hypophysial portal system. The hypothalamus appears intimately concerned with the mechanisms that cause secretion of gonadotrophic, adrenocorticotrophic (ACTH), and thyrotrophic (TSH) hormones. Electrical stimulation of the hypothalamus in the rabbit reportedly causes the discharge of gonadotrophic hormone (Markee et al., '46; Harris, '48) and of ACTH (DeGroot and Harris, '50). Similar direct stimulation of the pituitary gland does not elicit these responses, presumably because the humoral part of this pathway is not electrically excitable. Other evidence supporting the thesis that the hypothalamus controls the anterior hypophysis is derived from studies in which the anterior pituitary has been transplanted in experimental animals to body sites some distance from the sella turcica. Under these conditions the anterior pituitary gland shows only slight autonomous activity with respect to the secretion of ACTH and TSH; the secretion of follicle-stimulating hormone (FSH) ceases. Thus the anterior pituitary stands in marked contrast to other endocrine organs, such as the ovary, testis, thyroid, and adrenal cortex, which may be transplanted to distant sites and function in a relatively normal manner (Harris, '56).

It has been known for a long time that certain lesions near the base of the brain are associated with obesity. Experimental investigations (Hetherington and Ranson, '40; Stevenson, '49; Anand and Brobeck, '51, '51a; Ingram, '52) indicate that localized bilateral lesions in the hypothalamus involving primarily, or exclusively, the ventromedial nucleus in the tuberal region produce hyperphagia. Such animals eat voraciously, consuming two or three times the usual amount of food. Obesity appears to be the direct result of increased food intake. Lesions destroying portions of the lateral hypothalamic nucleus bilaterally impair or abolish the desire to feed in hyperphagic and normal animals (Ingram, '56). These data suggest that the ventromedial nucleus of the hypothalamus is concerned with *satiety*, while the lateral hypothalamic nucleus may be regarded as a *feeding center*. Most animals with hyperphagia due to hypothalamic lesions exhibit savage behavior and rage reactions.

The hypothalamus is regarded as one of the principal centers concerned with emotional expression. Since it is acknowledged that the physiological expression of emotion is dependent, in part, upon both sympathetic and parasympathetic components of the autonomic nervous system, it is evident that the hypothalamus, intimately relating both of these, probably is involved directly or indirectly in most emotional reactions. As mentioned above, lesions in the ventromedial nucleus of the hypothalamus produce savage behavior and extreme rage reactions (Wheatley, '44). Stimulation of the hypothalamus in unanesthetized cats with implanted electrodes (Masserman, '43; Hess, '54) provokes responses resembling rage and fear which can be increased by graded stimuli of different intensities and which cease immediately on withdrawal of the stimulus. These reactions, referred to by some as "pseudoaffective," are "stimulus-bound" in that they are present only during the period of stimulation. There are indications that different types of responses are elicited from different parts of the hypothalamus; flight responses are most readily evoked from lateral regions of the anterior hypothalamus, while aggressive responses characterized by hissing, snarling, baring of teeth, and biting are more commonly seen with stimulation of the region of the ventromedial nucleus (Nakao, '58). Because the emotional reactions provoked by electrical stimulation of the hypothalamus are directed, it seems likely that the cerebral cortex and thalamus play important roles in these responses. In these reactions the hypothalamus cannot be regarded as a simple efferent mechanism influencing only lower levels of the neuraxis.

THE SUBTHALAMUS

The subthalamus, also known as the ventral thalamus, is bounded dorsally by the thalamus, ventrally and laterally by the peduncular part of the internal capsule, and medially and rostrally by the hypothalamus (Figs. 3–13B, 18–7 and 18–8). Caudally the subthalamic region becomes continuous with the tegmentum and basilar portion of the midbrain, and it contains the rostral portions of the red nucleus and substantia nigra. The more prominent fiber bundles of the subthalamus, many of them fibers of passage, are the tegmental field of Forel (prerubral field, field H), the ansa lenticularis, the fasciculus lenticularis (field H_2), and the thalamic fasciculus (field H_1) (Figs. 18–7, 18–8 and 20–5). The intrinsic gray masses include the subthalamic nucleus, the zona incerta, and the nucleus of the tegmental field of Forel. Although the subthalamus, or ventral thalamus, is a component of the diencephalon, the principal nuclei and fiber tracts in this region are related closely to the basal ganglia. For this reason the subthalamic nucleus and the fiber tracts associated with it will be considered with the basal ganglia in the next chapter.

CHAPTER 20

The Basal Ganglia

In close relationship to parts of the diencephalon, but separated from it by the internal capsule, are the large nuclear masses that consititue the basal ganglia (Figs. 20–1 and 20–2). The basal ganglia represent subcortical nuclei derived from the telencephalon. Structures composing the basal ganglia are the *caudate nucleus*, the *putamen*, the *globus pallidus*, and the *amygdaloid nuclear complex*. Because the terms designating components of the basal ganglia are used in various ways, it is appropriate to clarify them at the outset. The amygdaloid nuclear complex, phylogenetically the oldest part of the basal ganglia, is known as the *archistriatum*. This structure, located internal to the uncus in the temporal lobe, has olfactory connections and is related to the hypothalamus and brain stem structures concerned with visceral functions. The *globus pallidus*, consisting of medial and lateral segments oriented along the lateral surface of the internal capsule, is designated the *paleostriatum*, but commonly is referred to simply as the pallidum. The term, *neostriatum*, refers to the caudate nucleus and putamen, which together form the largest and newest component of the basal ganglia. The neostriatum commonly is called the striatum. Collectively the neostriatum (striatum) and the paleostriatum (pallidum) form the *corpus striatum*. The globus pallidus plus the putamen are referred to as the lentiform nucleus, mainly for descriptive purposes; the use of this term for other purposes is regrettable for it groups together, in an incomplete way, two structures that are anatomically and physiologically distinct.

The amygdaloid nuclear complex is a gray mass situated in the dorsomedial portion of the temporal lobe, in front and partly above the tip of the inferior horn of the lateral ventricle (Fig. 21–9). It is covered by a layer of rudimentary cortex and is caudally continuous with the uncus of the parahippocampal gyrus (Figs. 20–1, 20–2, 21–4 and 21–7).

The amygdaloid complex usually is divided into two main nuclear masses, a corticomedial nuclear group and a basolateral nuclear group (Crosby and Humphrey, '41; Gloor, '60; Crosby et al., '62). A rather poorly defined central nucleus sometimes is regarded as a separate subdivision, but frequently is included as part of the corticomedial nuclear group. In man the *corticomedial nuclear group* constitutes a dorsal or dorsomedial part of the complex due to a medial rotation of the temporal lobe. Nuclear subdivisions of the corticomedial group include: (1) the anterior amygdaloid area, (2) the nucleus of the lateral olfactory tract, (3) the medial amygdaloid nucleus, (4) the cortical amygdaloid nucleus, and (5) the central amygdaloid nucleus. The nucleus of the lateral olfactory tract is the least well developed of the amygdaloid nuclei in man. The anterior amygdaloid area, representing the most rostral part of the amygdaloid complex, is rather poorly differentiated (Fox, '40). The corticomedial amygdaloid nuclear group lies closest to the putamen and tail of the caudate nucleus.

The largest and best differentiated part of the amygdaloid complex in man is the *basolateral nuclear group*. Subdivisions of this nuclear group are: (1) the lateral amygdaloid nucleus, (2) the basal amygdaloid nucleus, and (3) an accessory basal amygdaloid nucleus. The amygdaloid complex is related medially to the area olfactoria and laterally to the claustrum, while dorsally it is hidden partially by the lentiform nucleus. Caudally the amygdaloid complex is in contact with the tail of the caudate nucleus, which sweeps anteriorly in the roof of the inferior horn of the lateral ventricle (Figs. 3–23 and 20–4). The amygdaloid complex is found in all mammals and has been homologized with the olfactory striatum (archistriatum) of submammalian forms.

Among the afferent connections of the amygdaloid complex, only olfactory fibers are well defined anatomically. Fibers originating in the olfactory bulb project via the lateral olfactory tract to terminate in the corticomedial nuclear group (Adey and Meyer, '52; Allison, '54; Gloor, '60). No fibers from the lateral olfactory tract appear to enter the basolateral nuclear group. The basolateral amygdaloid nuclei receive an indirect olfactory input via relays in the prepyriform cortex. Thus nearly all parts of the amygdaloid nuclear complex receive either direct, or indirect olfactory pathways. The central nuclear group appears to be the only exception (Powell et al., '65).

Anatomical evidence concerning nonolfactory sensory afferents to the amygdaloid complex is meager, though electrophysiological studies suggest such connections. Evoked potentials can be elicited in the amygdaloid complex in response to stimulation of nearly all sensory receptors (Gerard et al., '36; Machne and Segundo, '56). These responses are recorded mainly in the basolateral nuclear group. Impulses originating from distant parts of the body surface, as well as impulses concerned with different sensory modalities, were found to converge upon the same cells (Gloor, '60). Additional subcortical structures projecting afferent fibers to the amygdaloid complex include the brain stem reticular formation (Machne and Segundo, '56), the pyriform cortex (Fox, '40), and perhaps parts of the inferior temperal gyrus (Whitlock and Nauta, '56).

The most prominent efferent pathway from the amygdaloid complex is the *stria terminalis* (stria semicircularis) (Figs. 3–5B, 3–13A, 18–7, 18–8, 18–11, 19–1 and 21–4). Fibers of this bundle originate mostly from the caudal half of the amygdaloid complex, arch along the entire medial border of the caudate nucleus and terminate in the medial preoptic, anterior hypothalamic nucleus, and the region of the nucleus supraopticus diffusus (Nauta, '61). Some of these fibers appear to enter the ventromedial nucleus of the hypothalamus (Hall, '63; Heimer and Nauta, '67; Dreifuss et al., '68). A few fibers of the stria terminalis, arising from the rostral half of the amygdala, terminate in the bed nucleus of the stria terminalis.

The *ventral amygdalofugal projection* passes medial and forward, ventral to the lentiform nucleus. These fibers pass to the substantia innominata, the lateral preoptic and hypothalamic regions, the septal region, the nucleus of the diagonal band (Broca) and the olfactory tubercle. A prominent component of this system bypasses the preoptic region and enters the inferior thalamic peduncle (Fig. 18–10). Fibers of this component terminate in the magnocellular division of the dorsomedial nucleus of the thalamus. The ventral amygdalofugal pathway also contains an amygdalocortical component that terminates in the paraterminal gyrus and the rostral cingulate gyrus (Fig. 21–4). Accord-

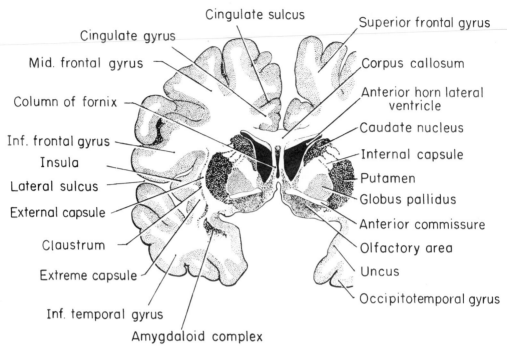

FIG. 20-1. Frontal section of the brain passing through the columns of the fornix and the anterior commissure. At this level the lateral segment of the globus pallidus lies mainly dorsal to the fibers of the anterior commissure.

ing to Nauta ('61), amygdaloid efferent fibers emerging from lateral ventral parts of the complex distribute fibers to rostral parts of the superior, middle and inferior temporal gyri, the ventral insular cortex, the claustrum, the rostral putamen and the caudal orbitofrontal cortex.

Electrical stimulation of the olfactory bulb evokes potentials over the entire extent of the amygdaloid complex (Berry et al., '52), but this complex is only part of a larger cortical and subcortical field activated by such stimuli. Additonal structures activated by olfactory bulb stimulation include parts of the striatum, thalamus, hippocampal formation, and brain stem. In these areas there is extensive overlap of olfactory-evoked potentials and responses evoked from other sensory systems. Even though the amygdaloid complex receives an olfactory input, the importance of this complex for olfactory sense is uncertain. Most evidence suggests that the amygdaloid complex cannot be closely related to olfactory sense since it is well developed in anosmatic aquatic mammals,

and bilateral destruction of it does not impair olfactory discrimination (Swann, '34; Allen, '41).

Striking changes in emotional and sexual behavior have been observed in animals and man after extensive bilateral lesions of the temporal lobes, uncus, hippocampus, and amygdaloid nuclei (Klüver and Bucy, '39; Bard and Mountcastle, '48; Terzian and Ore, '55; Green et al., '57; Green, '58; Gloor, '60). These studies suggest that the amygdaloid complex and adjacent rhinencephalic structures are related to brain stem mechanisms that regulate visceral activity and emotional behavior. Destruction of these visceral centers in man presumably results in a loss of fear and rage reactions, increased sexual activity, homosexual tendencies, excessive eating, and severe deficiencies in memory (*Klüver-Bucy syndrome*). The deficits in memory probably are not due to destruction of the amygdaloid complex, but to concomitant destruction of adjacent structures in the temporal lobe (see page 540).

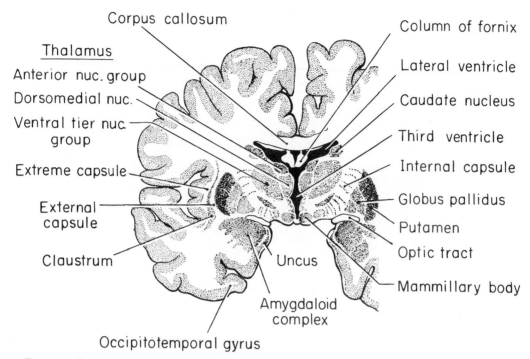

Corpus callosum

Column of fornix

Thalamus

Lateral ventricle

Anterior nuc. group

Dorsomedial nuc.

Caudate nucleus

Ventral tier nuc.
group

Third ventricle

Extreme capsule

Internal capsule

External
capsule

Globus pallidus

Putamen

Claustrum

Optic tract

Uncus

Mammillary body

Amygdaloid
complex

Occipitotemporal gyrus

FIG. 20–2. Frontal section of the brain passing through the level of the mammillary bodies. In this section the main nuclear groups of the thalamus are evident, as well as both segments of the globus pallidus and the subthalamic nucleus. The amygdaloid nuclear complex lies medial to the uncus and below the lenticular nucleus.

The **claustrum** is a thin plate of gray matter lying in the medullary substance of the hemisphere between the lenticular nucleus and the cortex of the insula, and separated from these structures by two white lamina: the external capsule medially, and the extreme capsule laterally (Figs. 3–26, 18–11, 20–1 and 20–2). Some consider it a part of the striatum, but there is considerable evidence that it originated from the deep layers of the insular cortex, from which it secondarily splits off. Its functions and connections are obscure.

2.   The Corpus Striatum. Arising as a single gray mass during early development, the corpus striatum becomes secondarily divided by the fibers of the internal capsule into two cellular masses, the *lenticular nucleus* and the *caudate nucleus*. This separation is incomplete, for rostrally the head of the caudate nucleus is ventrally continuous with the putamen, and dorsally portions of the caudate nucleus and putamen are connected by a number of slender gray bridges across the internal capsule (Figs. 20–3 and 20–4).

α. The caudate nucleus is an elongated, arched, gray mass related throughout its extent to the ventricular surface of the lateral ventricle (Figs. 19–1, 20–4 and 20–9). Its enlarged anterior portion or *head* lies rostral to the thalamus and bulges into the anterior horn of the lateral ventricle. Its long, attenuated caudal portion or *tail* extends along the dorsolateral border of the thalamus, from which it is separated by the terminal sulcus. In the latter are lodged the stria terminalis and terminal vein (Figs. 4–18 and 19–1). On reaching the caudal limit of the thalamus, the tail arches ventrally and runs forward in the roof of the inferior horn of the lateral ventricle to reach the amygdaloid nucleus (Figs. 20–4 and 21–7).

b. The lenticular nucleus has the size and form of a Brazil nut. In frontal sections this nucleus appears as a wedge whose broad, somewhat convex base is directed laterally and its blade medially. It has no

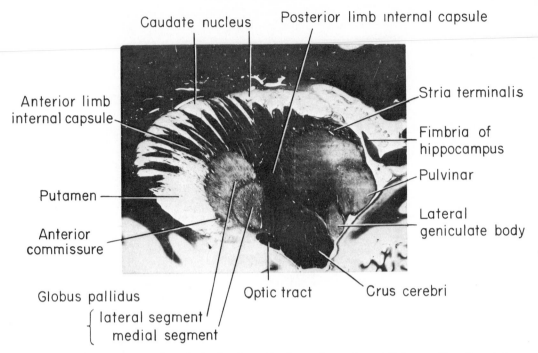

Fig. 20-3. Sagittal section through the basal ganglia, internal capsule and thalamus. Note the relationships of the caudate nucleus to the fibers of the anterior limb of the internal capsule. Weigert's myelin stain. Photograph.

ventricular surface but lies deeply buried in the white matter of the hemisphere, closely applied to the lateral surface of the internal capsule, which separates it from the caudate nucleus and the thalamus (Figs. 20-1 and 20-2). A vertical plate of white matter, the lateral medullary lamina, divides the nucleus into an outer larger portion, the *putamen,* and an inner portion the *globus pallidus.*

The putamen, the largest and most lateral part of the basal ganglia, lies between the external capsule and the lateral medullary lamina of the globus pallidus. In transverse sections it appears lightly stained and is traversed by numerous fascicles of myelinated fibers directed ventromedially toward the globus pallidus. The caudate nucleus and putamen, which are continuous rostrally, have essentially the same cytological structure. Cells of the neostriatum are of two types: small round, or spindle-shaped cells and large multipolar cells. The smaller cells outnumber the large ones by about 20 to 1. Axons of the smaller cells either terminate

within the striatum or pass medially to the globus pallidus. Myelinated fibers from the large multipolar neurons project to both segments of the globus pallidus (Nauta and Mehler, '66; Szábo, '67), and to the pars reticularis of the substantia nigra (Szábo, '62).

The globus pallidus forms the smaller and most medial segment of the lentiform nucleus. This structure, which lies medial to the putamen throughout most of its extent, is divided into two principal segments by a medullary lamina. A thin lateral medullary lamina is found on the external surface of the pallidum at its junction with the putamen. The globus pallidus, phylogenetically older than the striatum, is well developed in lower vertebrates. Many bundles of myelinated fibers traverse the globus pallidus, hence in fresh preparations it appears paler than the putamen or caudate nucleus. Cells of the globus pallidus are mainly large multipolar neurons of the motor type. The axons of these cells form the principal efferent fiber system of the corpus striatum.

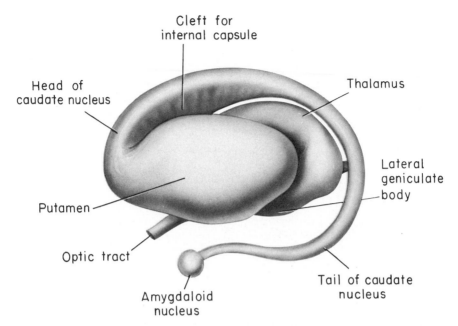

Cleft for
internal capsule

Head of
caudate nucleus

Thalamus

Putamen

Lateral
geniculate
body

Optic tract

Amygdaloid
nucleus

Tail of caudate
nucleus

FIG. 20-4. Semischematic drawing of the isolated striatum, thalamus, and amygdaloid nucleus showing:
(1) the continuity of the putamen and head of the caudate nucleus rostrally, and (2) the relationships between the tail of the caudate nucleus and the amygdaloid nucleus. The cleft occupied by fibers of the internal capsule is indicated. The anterior limb of the internal capsule is situated between the caudate nucleus
and the putamen, (Fig. 3–23, and 20–3) while the posterior limb of the internal capsule lies between the
lentiform nucleus and the thalamus.

3. **Striatal afferent fibers** arise primarily
from the cerebral cortex and the intralaminar thalamic nuclei, and certain evidence suggests some afferents may arise
from the substantia nigra.

Corticostriate fibers. Although certain
authors in the older literature regarded
the striatum as independent of the cerebral cortex, recent studies leave little
doubt as to the existence of corticostriate
fibers. The question as to whether or not
the striatum receives fibers from the cerebral cortex remained unanswered for many
years because of a lack of a suitable histological technic for demonstrating degenerated axons. The observation that, at
least, the intrastriatal portion of the corticostriate fibers is unmyelinated probably accounts for many discrepancies and
the failure of the Marchi method to demonstrate these fibers. Silver staining
methods indicate that nearly all regions
of the cortex contribute fibers to the striatum (Webster, '61, '65; Carman et al.,
'63). The most comprehensive study of

corticostriate connections (Carman et al.,
'63) done in the rabbit indicates that corticostriate fibers are organized in both
dorsoventral and mediolateral dimensions.
The anterior half of the hemisphere, including the sensorimotor cortex, is related
to a larger part of the striatum than is the
posterior half of the hemisphere. The
greater part of the cortex is connected to
both the caudate nucleus and the putamen, but cortex along the dorsomedial
margin of the hemisphere projects exclusively to the dorsal part of the caudate
nucleus. It further has been found (Carman et al., '65) that in the rat, cat and
rabbit the sensorimotor cortex projects
bilaterally to the caudate nucleus and
putamen. Fibers projecting contralaterally, cross the midline in the corpus callosum, and enter the caudate nucleus via
the subcallosal fasciculus, and the putamen via the external capsule. Most of
these fibers pass to caudal parts of the
head of the caudate nucleus and corresponding parts of the putamen. Cortico-

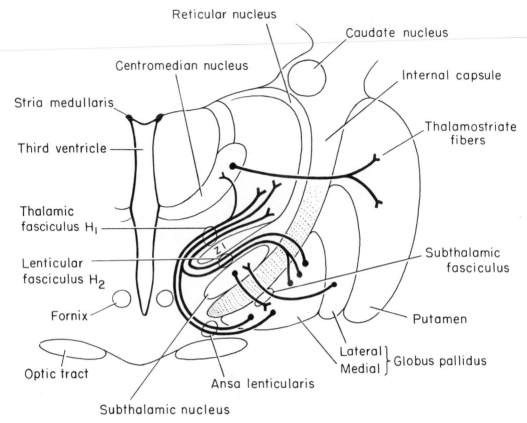

Reticular nucleus

Caudate nucleus

Centromedian nucleus

Internal capsule

Stria medullaris

Thalamostriate fibers

Third ventricle

Thalamic fasciculus H₁

Subthalamic fasciculus

Lenticular fasciculus H₂

Fornix

Putamen

Lateral } Globus pallidus
Medial }

Optic tract

Ansa lenticularis

Subthalamic nucleus

Fɪɢ. 20–5. Schematic diagram of the pallidofugal fiber systems in a transverse plane. Fibers of the ansa lenticularis issue from the ventral surface of the medial pallidal segment, curve medially and rostrally around the internal capsule and enter the prerubral field. Fibers of the lenticular fasciculus (H_2) issue from the dorsal surface of the medial pallidal segment, traverse the posterior limb of the internal capsule, and pass rostral and dorsal to the subthalamic nucleus to enter the prerubral field. The ansa lenticularis and the lenticular fasciculus merge in the prerubral field (Field H of Forel, not labeled here), and project dorsolaterally as a component of the thalamic fasciculus. Fibers of the thalamic fasciculus (H_1) pass dorsal to the zona incerta (ZI). The subthalamic fasciculus consists of pallidosubthalamic fibers arising from the lateral pallidal segment, and subthalamopallidal fibers that terminate in the medial pallidal segment. Fibers of both components of this bundle traverse the internal capsule. Indicated above are thalamostriate fibers passing from the centromedian nucleus to the putamen. Comparisons of this diagram should be made with Figs. 20–6, 20–7 and 20–8.

striate fibers from regions other than the sensorimotor cortex have only an ipsilateral projection.

Thalamostriate fibers constitute one of the largest and most important groups of afferent fibers passing to the caudate nucleus and putamen (Fig. 20–5). The largest number of these fibers originate from the centromedian nucleus, traverse the internal capsule, and enter the putamen (Mettler, '47; Nauta and Whitlock, '54; Powell and Cowan, '56). The most conclusive

study of this subject (Powell and Cowan, '56) shows that the centromedian nucleus projects exclusively to the putamen and that cells in particular parts of the nucleus pass to selective parts of the putamen. None of these fibers appear to project to the globus pallidus or the claustrum. The parafascicular nucleus also projects fibers to the putamen and shows a similar organization within its projection. Afferent fibers to the caudate nucleus originate from the smaller intralaminar thalamic nuclei (medial central, paracentral, and lateral central) found in more rostral and dorsal locations.

Nigrostriate fibers have been described in the literature as one of the principal afferent fiber systems to the striatum (Monakow, 1895; Holmes, '01; Dresel and Rothman, '25; Ferraro, '25, '28; Morrison, '29; Mettler, '43), but data concerning these fibers are not complete. The concept of nigrostriate fibers is based almost entirely upon retrograde cell changes produced in the substantia nigra following large striatal lesions. Attempts to trace fiber degeneration from lesions in the substantia nigra to the striatum in Marchi preparations (Ranson and Ranson, '42; Mettler, '42; Rosegay, '44) and silver impregnated material (Carpenter and McMasters, '64; Cole et al., '64; Afifi and Kaelber, '65; Carpenter and Strominger, '67) either have failed to demonstrate these fibers, or indicated that they are extremely sparse. However, use of the fluorescence technic for the demonstration of cellular monoamines (Falck, '62; Carlsson et al., '62) suggests that cells in the pars compacta of the substantia nigra may send axons to the striatum. After lesions in the substantia nigra or internal capsule the histochemical fluorescence and dopamine content of the striatum are markedly reduced (Andén et al., '64; Poirier and Sourkes, '65).

Striatal efferents project to the globus pallidus and the substantia nigra. Available evidence suggests that none of these fibers enter either the lenticular fasciculus or the ansa lenticularis.

Striopallidal fibers are topographically organized in both dorsoventral and rostrocaudal sequences and radiate into various parts of the pallidum like spokes of a wheel (Fig. 18–7). Experimental studies in the monkey (Nauta and Mehler, '66; Szábo, '67) indicate that putaminopallidal fibers terminate in both pallidal segments, but other data (Cowan and Powell, '66), based upon the distribution of gliosis in the pallidum following striatal lesions, suggest that different parts of the striatum may project selectively to portions of the medial and lateral pallidal segments. According to Szábo ('67) the precommissural part of the putamen appears to project exclusively to the globus pallidus while other regions of the striatum project to both globus pallidus and substantia nigra. Striopallidal fibers from the caudate nucleus pass ventrally through the internal capsule, while fibers from the putamen project medially to the globus pallidus.

Strionigral fibers. Although many reports of strionigral fibers were based primarily upon descriptions of normal material (Edinger, 1899; Holmes, '01; Morgan, '27; Rundles and Papez, '37; Papez, '38, '42), experimental studies (Voneida, '60; Szábo, '62, '67) with the Nauta technic have confirmed these observations. Lesions in the caudate nucleus and putamen produce degeneration which passes mainly to the reticular zone of the substantia nigra. Fibers from the head of the caudate nucleus project to medial and rostral parts of the nigra. Putaminonigral fibers also are topographically organized and project primarily to parts of the reticular zone. Fibers from the dorsal parts of the putamen terminate in dorsal and medial parts of the substantia nigra. Ventral parts of the putamen project to ventrolateral regions of the substantia nigra. While most of the strionigral fibers terminate in the reticular part of the nucleus, small numbers of fibers appear to end upon cells of the compact part (Nauta and Mehler, '66; Szábo, '67).

Pallidal afferent fibers are derived from a number of nuclei, most of which are considered to play an important role in motor integration. The largest number of pallidal afferent fibers arise from cells in the caudate nucleus and putamen and project topographically upon both segments of the globus pallidus. These fibers are discussed under the section entitled striopallidal fibers. Subthalamopallidal fibers interdigitate with fibers of the internal capsule as they pass ventrolaterally to enter the medial segment of the globus pallidus. Within the medial pallidal segment these fibers sweep

Mammillothalamic tract　　　　Lenticular fasciculus

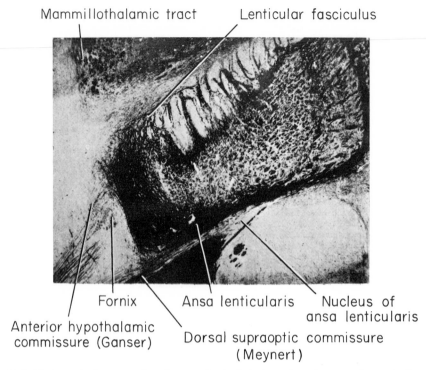

Fornix　　　　Ansa lenticularis　　　Nucleus of
　　　　　　　　　　　　　　　　　　　　　　ansa lenticularis

Anterior hypothalamic
commissure (Ganser)　　　　Dorsal supraoptic commissure
　　　　　　　　　　　　　　　　　　(Meynert)

FIG. 20–6. Photograph demonstrating the ansa lenticularis in a decorticate monkey. All fibers of the internal capsule have degenerated so that pallidofugal fibers are especially prominent. Weigert's myelin stain. (Courtesy of Dr. F. A. Mettler and The C.V. Mosby Company, St. Louis.)

ventrally toward the inferior border of the pallidum (Fig. 20–5). Some of these fibers enter both the medial and lateral medullary lamina. Quantitatively the largest number of these fibers end in the medial segment of the globus pallidus (Carpenter and Strominger, '67). Nigropallidal fibers arise largely from clusters of large cells in the compact zone, ascend, and traverse the peduncular portion of the internal capsule to terminate in the medial pallidal segment (Ranson and Ranson, '42; Kimmel, '42; Mettler, '43; Fox and Schmitz, '44; Woodburne et al., '46; Carpenter and McMasters, '64; Carpenter and Strominger, '67).

Whether or not corticofugal fibers terminate in the globus pallidus appears to be unresolved. Although some authors (Riese, '25; Glees, '45; Knook, '65) claim that the cortex projects to the pallidum, other authors (Webster, '61; Petras, '65), using silver staining methods, have been unable to demonstrate corticopallidal fibers. It also remains questionable whether any fibers from the thalamus project to the globus pallidus, even though such fibers have been described (Papez, '42; Showers, '58).

Pallidofugal fiber systems are of major importance because they represent the principal efferent system of the corpus striatum. Impulses from nuclei projecting upon the globus pallidus are ultimately transmitted from the pallidum by an intricate pallidofugal fiber system. Pallidal efferent fibers can be divided into four bundles: (1) the *lenticular fasciculus*, (2) the *ansa lenticularis*, (3) the *pallidotegmental fibers*, and (4) the *pallidosubthalamic fibers*. The first three of the above arise exclusively from the medial pallidal segment (Ranson and Ranson, '42; Nauta and Mehler, '66; Carpenter and Strominger, '67). Pallidosubthalamic fibers arise predominantly, but not exclusively, from the lateral pallidal segment (Carpenter et al., '68). Pallidofugal fibers are arranged in a rostrocaudal sequence with the ansa lenticularis most

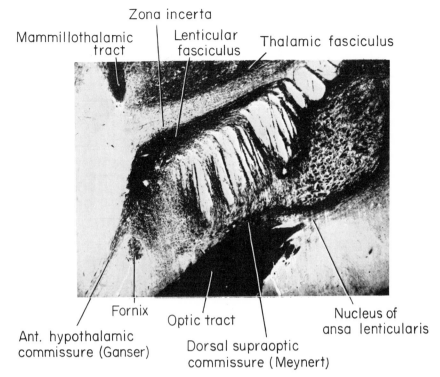

Zona incerta

Mammillothalamic   Lenticular   Thalamic fasciculus
        tract   fasciculus

Fornix   Optic tract   Nucleus of
                                                ansa lenticularis

Ant. hypothalamic   Dorsal supraoptic
commissure (Ganser)   commissure (Meynert)

FIG. 20-7. Photograph demonstrating the lenticular fasciculus in a decorticate monkey. Fibers of this bundle can be seen passing through the degenerated internal capsule. At this level, immediately rostral to the subthalamic nucleus, the lenticular fasciculus lies on the inner aspect of the internal capsule ventral to the zona incerta. Weigert's myelin stain. (Courtesy of Dr. F. A. Mettler and The C. V. Mosby Company, St. Louis.)

rostral, the lenticular fasciculus in an intermediate position, and pallidosubthalamic fibers most caudal.

The ansa lenticularis arises from ventral portions of the medial segment of the globus pallidus and forms a well defined bundle on the ventral surface of the pallidum (Figs. 20-5 and 20-6). These fibers sweep ventromedially and rostrally around the posterior limb of the internal capsule, and then course posteriorly to enter Forel's field H.

The lenticular fasciculus is formed in dorsal parts of the medial pallidal segment, issues from the dorsomedial margin of the pallidum slightly caudal to the ansa lenticularis, and traverses the ventral parts of the internal capsule in a number of small fascicles (Figs. 20-5 and 20-7). These fibers cross through the internal capsule immediately rostral to the subthalamic nucleus and form a relatively

large and discrete bundle ventral to the zona incerta. Although most of the lenticular fasciculus lies rostral to the subthalamic nucleus, some fibers of this bundle can be seen coursing along the dorsal border of this nucleus at more caudal levels. Fibers of the lenticular fasciculus are referred to as Forel's field H_2. While fibers of the lenticular fasciculus pursue a distinctive course through the internal capsule, they pass medially and caudally to join fibers of the ansa lenticularis in Forel's field H (prerubral field). The major part of the fibers of the lenticular fasciculus (H_2) and the ansa lenticularis which merge in Forel's field H ultimately enter the thalamic fasciculus (Forel's field H_1) located dorsal to the zona incerta.

Thalamic fasciculus. Pallidofugal fibers from Forel's field H pass rostrally and laterally along the dorsal surface of the zona incerta where they form part of

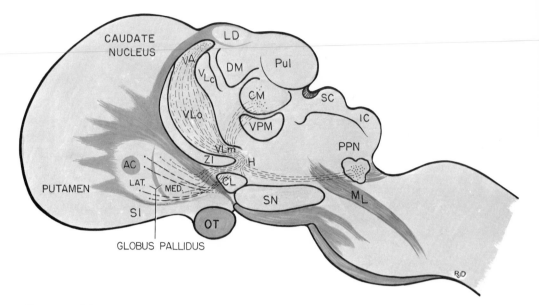

FIG. 20-8. Schematic diagram of the efferent projections and terminations of pallidofugal fibers arising from the medial (*red*) and lateral (*black*) pallidal segments shown in a sagittal plane. Fibers of the ansa lenticularis and lenticular fasciculus (Fig. 20-5) merge in field H of Forel. The bulk of these fibers pass in the thalamic fasciculus to the ventral lateral (VLo and VLm) and ventral anterior (VA) thalamic nuclei. Some fibers separate from this bundle and pass to the centromedian (CM) nucleus. Descending pallidofugal fibers from the medial pallidal segment form the pallidotegmental bundle; these fibers terminate upon cells of the pedunculopontine nucleus (PPN). Pallidosubthalamic fibers arising mainly from the lateral pallidal segment are shown in *black*. Other abbreviations used are: AC, anterior commissure; CL, subthalamic nucleus; DM, dorsomedial nucleus; H, Forel's field H; IC, inferior colliculus; LD, lateral dorsal nucleus; ML, medial lemniscus; OT, optic tract; Pul, pulvinar; SC, superior colliculus; SI, substantia innominata; SN, substantia nigra; VLc, ventral lateral nucleus, pars caudalis; VPM, ventral posteromedial nucleus; ZI, zona incerta.

the thalamic fasciculus (Figs. 20-5 and 20-7). Some of the fibers of the lenticular fasciculus merely make a "C" shaped loop around the medial part of the zona incerta and enter the thalamic fasciculus. The thalamic fasciculus is a complex bundle containing pallidothalamic fibers, as well as rubrothalamic and dentatothalamic fibers which ascend through the prerubral region. Fibers of this composite bundle pass dorsolaterally over the zona incerta to enter parts of the rostral ventral tier thalamic nuclei. In the region dorsal to the zona incerta, where fibers of this bundle are distinct and separate from those of the lenticular fasciculus (Figs. 20-5 and 20-7), the thalamic fasciculus is designated as bundle H$_1$ of Forel. Pallidofugal fibers in the thalamic fasciculus project rostrally and dorsally into the ventral anterior (VA) and ventral lateral (VLo and VLm) thalamic nuclei (Fig.

20-8. Some of the pallidofugal fibers separate from the thalamic fasciculus and course dorsally, caudally and medially to enter the centromedian (CM) nucleus of the thalamus. In their course, these latter fibers pass through portions of the ventral posteromedial (VPM) nucleus of the thalamus. Fibers projecting to the centromedian nucleus, in part, may be collaterals of fibers passing to the rostral ventral tier thalamic nuclei (Nauta and Mehler, '66). Dentatothalamic fibers coursing with the thalamic fasciculus pass largely to the ventral lateral (VLo) nucleus of the thalamus, but some of these cerebellar efferent fibers project to the more rostral intralaminar nuclei.

Thus, each of these thalamic afferent systems has: (1) overlapping projections to parts of the ventral lateral (VLo) nucleus, and (2) distinctive projections to the intralaminar thalamic nuclei. It has

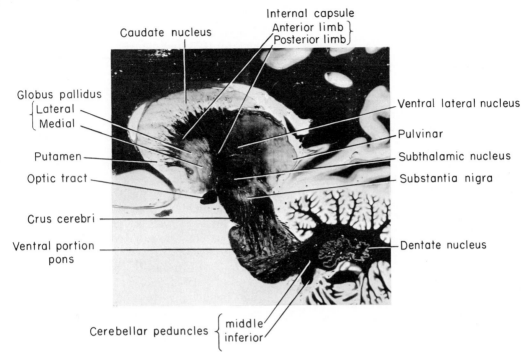

Caudate nucleus

Internal capsule
Anterior limb ⎱
Posterior limb ⎰

Globus pallidus
{ Lateral
{ Medial

Putamen

Optic tract

Crus cerebri

Ventral portion
pons

Ventral lateral nucleus

Pulvinar

Subthalamic nucleus

Substantia nigra

Dentate nucleus

Cerebellar peduncles { middle
{ inferior

FIG. 20-9. Sagittal section through the basal ganglia, thalamus, upper brain stem and cerebellum. Relationships between the basal ganglia, the subthalamic nucleus, and the substantia nigra are evident. Weigert's myelin stain. Photograph.

been suggested that some degree of integration of cerebellar and pallidal impulses probably occurs in the ventral lateral (VLo) nucleus of the thalamus. It is highly significant that the ventral lateral nucleus of the thalamus projects upon the motor cortex (area 4).

A small number of pallidal efferent fibers, emerging from the point of union of the lenticular fasciculus and the ansa lenticularis, pass ventromedially over the columns of the fornix and project towards the hypothalamus. These fibers, regarded as *pallidohypothalamic*, have been described as projecting to the ventromedial nucleus in the tuberal region of the hypothalamus (Ranson and Ranson, '42). These fibers are partially intermingled with those of the anterior hypothalamic decussation (Fig. 18-9; Ganser's commissure) but have not been traced across the midline (Fig. 20-7). According to Nauta and Mehler ('66), fibers, previously **regarded** as pallidohypothalamic fibers, take off in the direction of the

hypothalamus but loop back to join the principal bundle of pallidofugal fibers in their projection to certain thalamic nuclei. A small number of pallidofugal fibers caudal to the level of formation of the thalamic fasciculus are distributed to cells in Forel's field H (nucleus campi Foreli, or prerubral field (Fig. 20-8); Papez, '42; Woodburne et al., '46; Johnson and Clementi, '59). There are no pallidofugal fibers that pass to the red nucleus or the zona incerta.

Pallidotegmental fibers constitute a small group of descending pallidofugal fibers (Fig. 20-8), derived from the medial segment of the globus pallidus, that project to caudal mesencephalic levels (Nauta and Mehler, '66). These fibers become identifiable as a separate bundle dorsomedial to the subthalamic nucleus. This loosely organized bundle descends along the ventrolateral border of the red nucleus for some distance and then sweeps dorsolaterally into the midbrain tegmentum where its fibers are partially intermingled with those of the medial lemniscus. At levels through the inferior colliculus (Fig. 16–3) pallidotegmental fibers terminate upon large cells of the pedunculopontine nucleus (Fig. 20–8). No pallidofugal fibers appear to descend to more caudal regions of the brain stem.

Evidence supporting the existence of *pallidonigral fibers* is conflicting. Grunstein ('11), Wilson ('14), Foix and Nicolesco ('25), and Johnson and Clemente ('59) regard such fibers as established, but Ranson and Ranson ('42), Verhaart ('50), and Smith (Martin, '59) were unable to confirm these observations. Available evidence suggests that most of the fibers considered to be pallidonigral may actually be nigropallidal or strionigral.

The subthalamic fasciculus consists of pallidofugal fibers that pass through the internal capsule to enter the subthalamic nucleus, and of fibers from the subthalamic nucleus that project back to the globus pallidus. *Pallidosubthalamic fibers* arising from the lateral segment of the globus pallidus project exclusively upon cells of the subthalamic nucleus (Ranson and Ranson, '42; Nauta and Mehler, '66; Carpenter and Strominger, '67). These fibers are topographically organized, predominantly in mediolateral and dorsoventral sequences (Carpenter et al., '68), so that: (1) rostral and central regions project fibers to the rostral two-thirds of the subthalamic nucleus, (2) rostral regions project fibers primarily to the medial half of the nucleus, (3) central regions project fibers primarily to the lateral half of the nucleus, and (4) caudal regions of the lateral pallidal segment project fibers to caudal and dorsal parts of the nucleus. A small number of pallidal efferent fibers originating in the medial segment appear to terminate in the caudomedial part of the subthalamic nucleus. Pallidosubthalamic fibers traverse ventromedial and caudal parts of the internal capsule, caudal to both the ansa lenticularis and the lenticular fasciculus (Figs. 20–5 and 20–8). *Subthalamopallidal fibers* traverse the same part of the internal capsule in the opposite direction, and are distributed primarily to parts of the medial pallidal segment (Carpenter and Strominger, '67).

THE SUBTHALAMIC REGION

The subthalamus, briefly mentioned in chapter 19, lies ventral to the thalamus, medial to the internal capsule and lateral and caudal to the hypothalamus. Nuclei found within the subthalamic region include the subthalamic nucleus, the zona incerta and the nuclei of the tegmental fields of Forel (nucleus campi Foreli, Forel's field H). Prominent fiber bundles passing through this region include the ansa lenticularis, the lenticular fasciculus (Forel's field H_2), the thalamic fasciculus (Forel's field H_1), and the subthalamic fasciculus, as well as multiple fiber systems passing through the prerubral area (Forel's field H).

The subthalamic nucleus (corpus Luysi), located on the inner surface of the peduncular portion of the internal capsule, has the shape of a thick biconvex lens (Figs. 18–7, 18–8, 19–2, 20–8, 20–9 and 20–10). Caudally the medial part of the nucleus overlies the most rostral portions of the substantia nigra. Cells of the subthalamic nucleus are spindle-shaped, pyramidal, or round with branching processes. Cells vary in size, shape and concentration in different parts of the nucleus, and all contribute to a rich neuropil. In medial parts of the nucleus cells tend to be round, smaller, and more concentrated than in lateral regions. The nucleus has a café-au-lait color in fresh sections, and a rich blood supply derived from branches of the posterior communicating, posterior cerebral, and anterior choroidal arteries (Foix and Hillemand, '25).

Although there is no structure with which the subthalamic nucleus can be homologized in reptiles and birds (Huber and Crosby, '29), the nucleus has a consistent distribution in mammals. This nucleus is rudimentary in carnivores, but well developed in primates. While the nucleus is small in the monkey, its relative size is essentially the same as in man (Whittier and Mettler, '49a; von Bonin and Shariff, '51). Its principal afferent fibers come from the lateral segment of the globus pallidus via the subthalamic fasciculus. These fibers have a

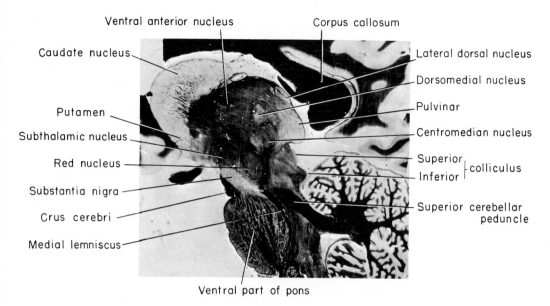

Ventral anterior nucleus   Corpus callosum

Caudate nucleus

Lateral dorsal nucleus

Dorsomedial nucleus

Pulvinar

Putamen

Centromedian nucleus

Subthalamic nucleus

Red nucleus

Superior ⎱
Inferior ⎰ colliculus

Substantia nigra

Crus cerebri

Superior cerebellar peduncle

Medial lemniscus

Ventral part of pons

FIG. 20–10. Sagittal section through medial regions of the basal ganglia, thalamus and upper brain stem showing the relationships of caudate nucleus and putamen as well as those of the subthalamic nucleus, the red nucleus and the substantia nigra. Weigert's myelin stain. Photograph.

specific topographical distribution within the nucleus. It has been suggested that the medial part of the nucleus may receive some fibers from the substantia innominata (Nauta and Mehler, '66), but most of the fibers from this source only enter the capsule of the nucleus. Data obtained from studies of human frontal lobotomy (Meyer et al., '47; Meyer, '49) suggest that corticofugal fibers project to the subthalamic nucleus. According to Petras ('65), ablations of area 4 produce abundant degeneration in Forel's fields H_1 and H_2 and the zona incerta but only modest degeneration in the subthalamic nucleus. Ablations of cortical areas 3, 1 and 2 produce only sparse degeneration in Forel's fields and the zona incerta and no degeneration in the subthalamic nucleus. Experimental studies (Verhaart and Kennard, '40; Mettler, '47b; Levin, '49) utilizing the Marchi method have failed to demonstrate corticofugal fibers passing into the subthalamic nucleus.

Efferent fibers from the subthalamic nucleus traverse the internal capsule and project mainly to caudal parts of the medial segment of the globus pallidus (Fig. 20–5). A few of these fibers enter the medial and lateral medullary laminae

of the pallidum. A small number of efferent fibers traverse the apex of the globus pallidus, enter the dorsal supra-optic decussation, and pass into the contralateral globus pallidus (Fig. 18–9; Carpenter and Strominger, '67). Some authors believe that the subthalamic nucleus sends fibers to the substantia nigra (Glees and Wall, '46; Whittier and Mettler, '49a), but this connection remains in doubt. No fibers from the substantia nigra project to the subthalamic nucleus (Cole et al., '64; Carpenter and McMasters, '64). So-called subthalamotegmental fibers (Papez, '42; Woodburne et al., '46) appear to actually be pallidotegmental fibers. No fibers from the subthalamic nucleus project to the thalamus.

In man relatively discrete lesions in the subthalamic nucleus, usually hemorrhagic, give rise to violent, forceful, and persistent choroid movements, referred to as *hemiballism*. These unusually violent involuntary movements occur contralateral to the lesion and involve primarily the proximal musculature of the upper and lower extremities, though they may involve the facial and cervical musculature as well (Jakob, '23; Martin, '27; von

Santha, '28; Martin and Alcock, '34; Whittier, '47).

The *zona incerta* is a strip of gray matter situated between the thalamic and lenticular fasciculi (Figs. 18–8, 20–5 and 20–7). It is composed of diffuse cell groups which laterally are continuous with the thalamic reticular nucleus. This zone receives corticofugal fibers from the precentral cortex; its efferent projections are unknown.

The lenticular fasciculus, ansa lenticularis, and the thalamic fasciculus constitute the largest and best defined fiber bundles of passage in the subthalamic region. Scattered along and between the fibers of the ansa lenticularis are strands of cells which collectively constitute the so-called *nucleus of the ansa lenticularis* (Riley, '43).

The *prerubral field* or Forel's field H (Fig. 20–8) contains pallidofugal fibers and scattered cells which constitute the nucleus of the prerubral field (nucleus campi Foreli). The nuclei of the prerubral field, together with similar cells scattered along pallidofugal pathways, have been referred to collectively as the *subthalamic reticular nucleus*.

THE EXTRAPYRAMIDAL MOTOR SYSTEM

Since the term basal ganglia refers to the subcortical telencephalic nuclei, neurologists have found it convenient to use the term "extrapyramidal" motor system to group together the basal ganglia and certain related brain stem nuclei, considered to subserve somatic motor functions. Even though there are many objections to the use of this term, which was coined but not defined by Wilson ('12), it has been used widely for half a century and serves to emphasize important functional relationships between the basal ganglia and specific brain stem nuclei. Because the term "extrapyramidal" literally includes the entire central nervous system, except the corticospinal system, a more practical and precise designation is needed. Nuclei of the brain stem forming a part of this so-called system, in addition to the basal ganglia, include: (1) the subthalamic nu-

cleus, (2) the substantia nigra, (3) the red nucleus, and (4) the brain stem reticular formation. Since phylogenetically the development of the nuclei of this system antedates the development of the neopallium, the extrapyramidal motor system constitutes an older system than the corticospinal system. It is of interest that the older motor system is defined with respect to the pyramidal system, even though the latter is present only in mammals. In reptiles and birds the neopallium is rudimentary, and descending fibers from the cortex are few in number. The corpus striatum, on the other hand, is an old part of the forebrain that is found in all vertebrates. The paleostriatum, comparable to the globus pallidus, is already well developed in fish. It receives mainly olfactory impulses and gives rise to the "basal forebrain bundle," which discharges into the thalamus, hypothalamus, and midbrain (i.e., a lateral forebrain bundle). This bundle is probably homologous in mammals with the ansa lenticularis and lenticular fasciculus. In reptiles and birds a neostriatum—the caudate and putamen of higher vertebrates—develops and receives impulses mainly from the thalamus. In birds the whole striatal complex becomes highly differentiated and enlarged to form the most massive portion of the cerebrum. It seems certain that in animals without a cortex, or with a poorly developed one, the corpus striatum is a most important center. Upon the integrity of the striatum depends the normal, largely instinctive activities of these forms, such as locomotion, defense, feeding, and courting. Motor activities in these submammalian forms are highly stereotyped and resemble well patterned reflex movements. In birds these activities are practically unaffected after ablation of the primitive cortex, but they are severely impaired by lesions of the corpus striatum (Rogers, '22). Thus in submammalian forms the diencephalon and corpus striatum together constitute the highest sensorimotor integrating mechanism of the forebrain. The thalamus of such animals represents the receptive center; the corpus striatum and hypothalamus are related to motor control. The corpus striatum probably discharges through intercalated nuclei to the somatic efferent neurons; the hypothalamus is connected similarly with the visceral effectors. These reactions are determined on the afferent side by sensory stimuli of an affective rather than discriminative nature, and they are expressed in movements which are gross, postural, and stereotyped.

With the evolution of the neopallium in mammals the functions of the corpus striatum seem to become subordinated to those of the cerebral cortex and are brought into balance with the activities of the motor area. However, the old motor system continues to be utilized for many of the more or less automatic movements concerned with postural adjustments, defensive reactions, and feeding. Many mammals are able to perform their normal activities after destruction of both pyramidal tracts. Even chimpanzees recover sufficiently to feed themselves and to execute movements of walking and climbing. Whether the human striatum has similar functions is still a disputed question. Destruction of the pyramidal tract in man causes a far more complete and lasting paralysis, but the grosser movements are affected less severely and recover to a considerable extent. According to Wilson ('28), the corpus striatum maintains a postural background for voluntary activities, reinforcing and steadying movements, and postures of cortical origin, but is incapable of initiating such movements. Others maintain that even in man the grosser, more automatic, volitional movements, as well as postural adjustments, are mediated through the extrapyramidal system; these movements are affected most severely in diseases of the corpus striatum.

Thus the cerebral cortex projects to lower motor centers through two main channels: (1) long fibers in the corticospinal tract concerned primarily with fine, isolated, versatile movements which form the basis for acquisition of motor skills, and (2) short fibers passing to extrapyramidal nuclei, which are concerned with mechanisms for postural adjustments and gross movement patterns that are largely reflex in character. Through hypothalamic connections the cortex also is related to the regulation of autonomic functions. These areas do not discharge directly to the lower motor neurons but utilize the existing, though modified, mechanisms of the old motor system. The two systems do not function independently, but are in constant balance with each other; the smooth execution of nonpostural pyramidal movements implies a concomitant regulation and modification of the postural mechanisms.

Clinically two basic types of disturbances are associated with diseases of the so-called extrapyramidal system. These disturbances are: (1) various types of abnormal involuntary movements, referred to as *dyskinesia*, and (2) disturbances of muscle tone. Types of dyskinesia occurring in association with these diseases include *tremor, athetosis, chorea,* and *ballism.* *Tremor* is a rhythmical, alternating, abnormal involuntary activity having a relatively regular frequency and amplitude. A major clinical criterion used to describe and classify different tremors is whether the tremor occurs "at rest" or during voluntary movement. The type of tremor commonly seen in paralysis agitans (Parkinsonism), involving primarily the digits and the lips, occurs during the absence of voluntary movement. During the course of voluntary movements the tremor ceases. Tremor classically associated with cerebellar lesions becomes evident during voluntary and associated movements and ceases when the patient is "at rest." Although this criterion is of great importance in clinical neurology, it is acknowledged that tremor "at rest" and tremor during voluntary movement sometimes occur together in various degrees in association with diseases involving primarily, either the basal ganglia, or the cerebellum. *Athetosis* (Hammond, 1871) is the term used to designate slow, writhing, vermicular involuntary movements involving particularly the extremities, but in many instances also the muscles of the face and neck. The movements blend with each other to give the appearance of a continuous mobile spasm. Athetoid movements involving primarily the axial musculature produce severe torsion of the neck, shoulder girdle, and pelvic girdle. This disturbance, referred to as *torsion spasm* or *torsion dystonia*, is considered by some (Jakob, '25; Alexander, '42) as a form of athetosis; differences between torsion dystonia and athetosis are considered to be due largely to inherent mechanical differences between axial and appendicular musculature. *Chorea* is a brisk, graceful, series of successive involuntary movements of considerable complexity which resemble fragments of purposeful voluntary movements. These movements involve primarily the distal portions of the extremities, the muscles of facial expression, the tongue, and the deglutitional musculature. *Ballism*, a violent, forceful, flinging movement, involves primarily the proximal appendicular musculature, and muscles about the shoulder and pelvic girdles. It represents the most violent form of dyskinesia known. Although athetosis, chorea, and ballism each present distinguishing features, basic resemblances among these forms of dyskinesia probably are greater than their differences (Charcot, 1879; Wilson, '25; Mettler, '55; Carpenter, '58). Characteristics common to these dyskinesias include: (1) variable amplitude and frequency, (2) occurrence of movements in immediate and delayed sequence, (3) variations in the duration of single movements, and (4) a highly integrated, complex activity pattern. While each of these types of involuntary motor activity is specialized to a degree, there are indications that athetosis, chorea, and ballism may form a spectrum of choreoid activity in which athetosis and ballism represent extreme forms possessing distinguishing characteristics.

Although it is customary to associate increased muscle tonus with most extrapyramidal syndromes, this is not always found. The initial symptom of paralysis agitans is frequently a rigidity of the muscles, which gradually increases over a period of years. The augmentation of muscle tone is not selective, as in hemiplegia, but is present to a nearly equal degree in antagonistic muscle groups (i.e., in both flexor and extensor muscles). The rigidity in the early stages can be demonstrated by passively flexing or extending the muscles of the extremities, or by attempting to rotate the hand in a circular fashion at the wrist. These movements are interrupted by a series of jerks, referred to as cog-wheel phenomenon. In later stages of the disease rigidity may be so severe as to completely incapacitate the patient. Athetosis usually is associated with variable degrees of paresis and spasticity. It is suggested that the slow, writhing character of this dyskinesia may be due in part to the spasticity. Although muscle tone is increased greatly during athetoid movements and persists after the completion of the movement, muscle tone may thereafter gradually diminish (Herz, '31). Chorea and ballism usually are associated with variable degrees of hypotonus (Martin, '27).

The various types of dyskinesia and excesses of muscle tone associated with diseases of the basal ganglia are regarded as positive disturbances since they involve an excess of neural activity and the expenditure of energy (Martin, '59). Such disturbances cannot arise directly from destruction of specific neural structures, but must represent the functional capacity of surviving intact structures. According to this thesis, which is supported by experimental and clinical data, positive disturbances (i.e., tremor, athetosis, chorea, and ballism) are believed to be the result of release phenomena. A lesion in one structure removes the controlling and regulating influences which that structure previously exerted upon an associated neural mechanism, and thus leads to overactivity of the second neural structure. This theory forms the basis of most neurosurgical attempts to alleviate and abolish dyskinesia and excesses of muscle tone without producing paresis. However, not all of the disturbances associated with diseases of the basal ganglia can be regarded as positive phenomena, particularly in paralysis agitans. Patients with paralysis agitans also exhibit a mask-like face, infrequent blinking of the eyes, a slow dysarthric speech, a stooped posture, a slow shuffling gait, loss of associated movements (e.g., swing of the arms while walking), and general poverty of movement. Some patients may have excessive secretion of saliva, unusual oiliness of the skin, difficulty in holding the head erect, and disturbances of equilibrium. According to certain authors (Martin and Hurwitz, '62; Martin et al., '62; Martin, '67), the negative symptoms of Parkinsonism largely concern disorders of postural fixation, equilibrium, locomotion, phonation, and articulation. Negative symptoms are considered to be deficits due to loss of function of destroyed neural structures.

Clinicopathological studies of most forms of dyskinesia categorized as extrapyramidal indicate widespread neuropathological changes. In these disorders the basal ganglia suffer severe pathological alterations, but specific brain stem nuclei and parts of the cerebral cortex may be affected also. In paralysis agitans, pathological changes most consistently affect the substantia nigra, but significant alterations are found also in the globus pallidus, the cerebral cortex, and the brain stem reticular formation (Benda and Cobb, '42; Heath, '47; Denny-Brown, '62). Athetosis most frequently is associated with pathological processes involving the striatum and cerebral cortex, though lesions are sometimes found in the globus pallidus and thalamus (Carpenter, '50). Hemiathetosis may develop after a hemiparesis, or in association with it, as a consequence of a necrotizing cerebrovascular lesion destroying portions of the internal capsule and striatum. Athetoid activity occurs contralateral to the lesion. With respect to chorea, there is relatively little information available, except that concerning chronic progressive chorea, or Huntington's chorea. This hereditary disease is characterized by an insidious onset in adult life. Pathological changes are widespread but have a special predilection for the cerebral cortex and striatum. Ballism appears to be the only form of dyskinesia resulting from a discrete lesion. The lesion usually is confined to the subthalamic nucleus or its immediate connections (Whittier, '47).

Attempts to produce dyskinesia in experimental animals by creating lesions in the basal ganglia have been notoriously unsuccessful (Wilson, '14; Liddell and Phillips, '40; Mettler, '42). Experimental attempts to provoke dyskinesia in animals by striatal or pallidal lesions have been criticized on the basis of Meltzer's ('06–'07) principle of physiological safety. This principle states that in biological organisms more tissue is found in individual organs and structures than is required for the maintenance of their essential functions. If this principle is applied to the neuraxis, it would seem to mean that a lesion cannot be expected to produce the symptoms and signs characteristic of a specific tissue deficit unless the amount of destruction includes some of the irreducible minimum necessary for normal function. Failure to produce athetoid or choreoid activity in animals by striatal lesions has been said to be due to the rather limited volumes of tissue destroyed. This explanation does not appear valid in all cases. Wilson ('14) succeeded in destroying selectively virtually the entire putamen in the monkey without producing dyskinesia. This suggests that the striatum (caudate nucleus and putamen) must have a high limit of physiological safety, or that it may function to some degree bilaterally. The experiments of Mettler ('42) indicate that large bilateral striatal lesions produce forced progression and cursive hyperkinesia. This form of hyperactivity implies that the striatum normally may inhibit other neural mechanisms subserving motor function. Unilateral lesions of the globus pallidus in monkeys produce minimal disturbances of motor function. Bilateral lesions of the globus pallidus, inflicted simultaneously, produce profound hypokinesis, loss of associated movements, and disturbances of posture. Bizarre and enforced postures are maintained for long periods of time, with only feeble, or ineffective attempts to establish a normal attitude. These animals bear certain striking resemblances to patients with paralysis agitans, but there is no tremor or rigidity. Since the effects of bilateral pallidal lesions are so severe compared with those resulting from unilateral lesions, it is suspected that the globus pallidus may function bilaterally (Martin, '59). Available evidence indicates that the globus pallidus makes a significant positive contribution to motor function.

Anatomically the globus pallidus appears to be a focal structure upon which many pathways concerned with nonpyramidal motor function converge. This suggests that the globus pallidus may serve as one of the important subcortical sites involved in the integration of nonpyramidal motor function. The fact that quantitatively the largest number of pallidofugal fibers pass to the thalamus indicates that specific subdivisions of the thalamus probably serve as the principal subcortical structure concerned with integration of motor functions. Certainly, portions of the thalamus receive the principal efferent fiber systems from the cerebellum and basal ganglia and constitute the primary relay nuclei by which impulses are projected to the cerebral cortex. The validity of this thesis is dramatically demonstrated by the gratifying amelioration of various forms of dyskinesia, in selected patients, following stereotaxic lesions produced in either the globus pallidus or the ventral lateral (VLo) nucleus of the thalamus (Wycis and Spiegel, '52; Spiegel and Wycis, '54, '58; Cooper, '56, '60; Narabayashi et al., '56). Destruction of portions of the globus pallidus appears most effective in relieving contralateral rigidity in paralysis agitans, while thalamic lesions are often most successful in alleviating contralateral tremor. Similar clinical evidence indicates that lesions in these locations can ameliorate symptoms in dystonia (Cooper, '57, '59; Cooper and Bravo, '58), chorea (Spiegel and Wycis, '50), and ballism (Talairach et al., '50; Roeder and Orthner, '56; Cooper, '57; Martin and McCaul, '59; Andy and Brown, '60). Small lesions interrupting pallidofugal fiber systems also yield beneficial results (Spiegel and Wycis, '54). It is of considerable interest that thalamic lesions, which destroy parts of the ventral lateral nucleus, are effective in ameliorating intention tremor associated with cerebellar disease and multiple sclerosis (Cooper and Poloukhine, '59; Cooper, '60a, '60b; Martin, '60).

The only form of dyskinesia, other than cerebellar tremor, produced in experimental animals which resembles that occurring in man, is that resulting from discrete lesions in the subthalamic nucleus. In the monkey violent choreoid and ballistic activity occurs contralateral to localized lesions in the subthalamic nucleus which: (1) destroy approximately 20 per cent of the nucleus, and (2) preserve the integrity of surrounding pallidofugal fiber systems (Whittier and Mettler, '49a; Carpenter et al., '50). Studies of this experimental dyskinesia (Carpenter et al., '50; Carpenter and Mettler, '51; Carpenter and Brittin, '58; Carpenter et al., '60; Carpenter, '61; Strominger and Carpenter, '65; Carpenter et al., '65; Stein and Carpenter, '65) indicate that subthalamic dyskinesia in the monkey resulting from lesions in the subthalamic nucleus can be abolished contralaterally without producing paresis by lesions destroying: (1) portions of the medial segment of the globus pallidus, (2) the lenticular fasciculus, or (3) the ventral lateral nucleus of the thalamus. This form of dyskinesia can be abolished, but with concomitant paresis, by ablations of the contralateral motor cortex (area 4), or by surgical section of the ipsilateral corticospinal tract at high cervical spinal levels. No significant modification of this form of dyskinesia in the monkey results contralaterally from: (1) ablation of area 6, (2) destruction of the centromedian nucleus, (3) destruction of portions of the substantia nigra, or (4) large lesions in the red nucleus. Selective partial cordotomies in animals with this form of dyskinesia indicate that surgical interruption of the rubrospinal, vestibulospinal and reticulospinal tracts have little or no effect upon ipsilateral dyskinesia. Finally, multiple dorsal root sections (i.e., dorsal rhizotomy), virtually abolishing afferent input from an entire extremity, not only does not abolish the dyskinesia in the deafferented limb, but cause an increase in amplitude of the dyskinesia. This increase in amplitude appears to be due to loss of conscious proprioceptive sense, and increased loss of muscle tone.

These experimental results have been interpreted to mean that the subthalamic nucleus normally exerts inhibitory and regulating influences upon the globus pallidus. A lesion in the subthalamic nucleus releases the globus pallidus from this controlling influence; removal of this controlling influence is expressed physiologically by bursts of irregular, forceful, large amplitude ballistic movements on the opposite side of the body. Available evidence suggests that impulses from the globus pallidus reach the ipsilateral motor cortex through the ventral lateral (VLo) nucleus of the thalamus. Dyskinesia occurs contralaterally because impulses responsible for this dyskinesia are conveyed to segmental levels of the spinal cord via the corticospinal tract (Carpenter et al., '60), and most fibers of this system decussate at medullary levels. These experimental results, relative to the effects of pallidal and thalamic lesions, have been confirmed upon human ballism (Talairach et al., '50; Roeder and Orthner, '56; Martin and McCaul, '59).

Attempts to abolish various forms of dyskinesia, and excesses of muscle tone by surgery are based on the thesis that these disturbances are the physiological expression of release phenomena. This implies that disease or pathological alterations of certain neural structures has removed inhibitory influences normally acting upon other intact neural structures, and that this overactivity, or excessive function, is responsible for the dyskinesia. Thus, attention has been focused upon the globus pallidus and the ventral lateral nucleus of the thalamus since these structures appear to be of greatest importance in the subcortical integration of nonpyramidal motor function.

Finally there is abundant evidence that the cerebral cortex must play an important role in neural mechanisms of dyskinesia. It is well known that almost all forms of abnormal involuntary movement cease during sleep and are abolished by general anesthesia. Most forms of dyskinesia are exaggerated in situations where the patient becomes self-conscious, overly anxious, or excited. The fact that ablations of motor cortex and interruption of the corticospinal tract at various locations abolish dyskinesia suggests that impulses from centers considered to be responsible for dyskinesia must be transmitted to segmental levels via the corticospinal tract (Bucy, '57, '58, '59; Carpenter et al., '60). These findings imply that the so-called extrapyramidal system is not a complete and independent motor unit.

There is certain information which suggests that the medial and lateral segments of the globus pallidus each may have unique functions. Anatomically the efferent projections of the pallidal segments are distinctive; the medial pallidal segment gives rise to the largest and most widely distributed pallidofugal fibers. Lesions in the medial pallidal segment are effective in modifying experimental dyskinesia while those in the lateral pallidal segment are not. Other evidence from pathological studies (Carpenter and Strominger, '65) suggests that extensive destruction of the lateral pallidal segment may provoke choreoid dyskinesia. It has been postulated that the dyskinesia occurring with such lesions is due to the interruption of efferent fibers from that pallidal segment which projects exclusively to the subthalamic nucleus (Papez et al., '42).

CHAPTER 21

Rhinencephalon, Olfactory Pathways, and Limbic System

RHINENCEPHALON

The term *rhinencephalon* refers to the olfactory brain. Although some authors use this term broadly to include those regions of the brain concerned with both the reception and integration of olfactory impulses, it is apparent that not all regions of the brain from which potentials can be recorded in response to olfactory stimulation are concerned exclusively with olfactory sense. Higher order pathways of the olfactory system are complex and subject to modifying influences from many sources. Thus some of these pathways, involving multiple synapses, are subject to other influences and have lost their original olfactory specificity. For this reason use of the term "rhinencephalon" should be restricted to those structures of the central nervous system that receive fibers from the olfactory bulb (Brodal, '63). In this strict sense the rhinencephalon includes the olfactory bulb, tract, tubercle and striae, the anterior olfactory nucleus, parts of the amygdaloid complex, and parts of the prepyriform cortex. The term rhinencephalon, in this restricted sense, is equivalent to the *paleopallium* or primitive olfactory lobe (Valverde, '65). The *archipallium*, the oldest cortical derivative, is represented by the hippocampal formation, the dentate gyrus, the fasciolar gyrus and the indusium griseum (supracallosal gyrus).

Although the rhinencephalon is large and conspicuous in the lower vertebrates (Fig. 1-4), including many macrosmatic mammals, in man it is overshadowed and comparatively reduced by the tremendous development of the neopallium. The hippocampal formation, conversely, reaches its greatest development in microsmatic man and is well formed in certain anosmatic aquatic mammals (e.g., porpoise, whale).

BASAL OLFACTORY STRUCTURES

The *olfactory lobe* makes its appearance in the second month as a narrow longitudinal bulge on the basal surface of the developing cerebral hemisphere, ventral and medial to the basal ganglia (Fig. 5-10A). It is distinctly demarcated from the lateral surface of the pallium by the *rhinal sulcus* and soon differentiates into anterior and posterior portions. The anterior portion, at first containing an extension of the lateral ventricle, elongates into a tubular stalk which becomes solid by the end of the third month, and forms the rudiment of the olfactory tract and bulb. The posterior portion differentiates into the olfactory area (anterior perforated substance) and certain other olfactory structures closely related to the anteromedial portion of the temporal lobe, collectively known as the *pyriform lobe*.

During the second month, a longitudinal thickening, the *hippocampal ridge*, appears

518

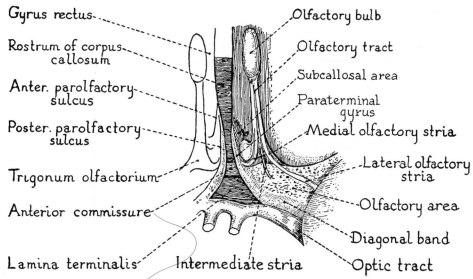

Gyrus rectus

Rostrum of corpus callosum

Anter. parolfactory sulcus

Poster. parolfactory sulcus

Trigonum olfactorium

Anterior commissure

Lamina terminalis

Intermediate stria

Olfactory bulb

Olfactory tract

Subcallosal area

Paraterminal gyrus

Medial olfactory stria

Lateral olfactory stria

Olfactory area

Diagonal band

Optic tract

FIG. 21-1. Olfactory lobe as seen on the inferior surface of the human brain. The optic nerves and chiasm have been folded backward.

on the medial wall of the hemisphere a short distance from the dorsal margin (Fig. 5–12). This ridge soon folds into the hemisphere, producing the *hippocampal fissure* on the medial surface, and a corresponding elevation in the ventricular wall. When the pallium curves inferiorly and forward to form the temporal lobe, the hippocampal fissure and associated structures increase in length and finally extend from the region of the interventricular foramen to the tip of the inferior horn. The hippocampal ridge develops into the *hippocampal formation* (Figs. 21–6, 21–7 and 21–8). It is the most ancient portion of the pallium and is present in amphibians. Hence it is known as the *archipallium*, as distinguished from the more recently acquired *neopallium*, which is highly developed only in mammals.

The structures of the olfactory lobe are limited to the inferior surface of the cerebral hemisphere. The *olfactory bulb* is a flattened ovoid body resting on the cribriform plate of the ethmoid bone, its dorsal surface pressed into the anterior portion of the olfactory sulcus (Figs. 3–15 and 21–1). Delicate fascicles of fine unmyelinated fibers, the *fila olfactoria*, pass from the nasal fossa through the apertures of the cribriform plate and enter the ventral surface of the bulb. These fila, the central

processes of the bipolar receptor cells in the olfactory mucous membrane, collectively constitute the *olfactory nerve* (N. I). Thus the olfactory bulb serves as the terminal "nucleus" of the olfactory nerve.

The *olfactory tract* is a narrow white band lying in the olfactory sulcus. It extends from the olfactory bulb to the anterior perforated substance, where it enlarges to form the *olfactory trigone* by dividing into two roots, the *lateral* and *medial olfactory striae* (Fig. 21–1). In cross section each olfactory tract is triangular in shape, with its apex directed into the olfactory sulcus (Fig. 3–15). A less definite intermediate stria often dips directly into the anterior perforated substance. The olfactory tract consists principally of secondary olfactory fibers from cells of the bulb; these fibers are covered dorsally by a layer of primitive cortex that is greatly reduced in man. The cells of this gray layer receive collaterals from the secondary olfactory fibers and in turn contribute fibers to the olfactory tract (Fig. 21–2). Scattered cells caudal to the olfactory bulb are designated collectively as the *anterior olfactory nucleus* (Fig. 21–3). The olfactory tract thus contains both secondary and tertiary myelinated fibers which pass into the olfactory striae. The olfactory striae likewise are covered by a thin coating of

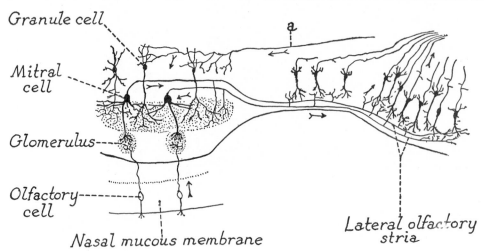

FIG. 21-2. Diagram showing structure of olfactory bulb and olfactory tract. *a*, Fiber to bulb from opposite olfactory tract (after Cajal, '11).

gray substance that is greatly reduced in man and hence are known as the *lateral* and *medial olfactory gyri*. They tend to blend almost imperceptibly with the basal frontal cortex, the anterior perforated substance, and the prepyriform cortex. Certain centrifugally directed fibers are found in each olfactory tract. These fibers arise from cells in the anterior olfactory nucleus, cross in the anterior part of the anterior commissure and project to the opposite anterior olfactory nucleus and olfactory bulb (Clark and Warwick, '46; Valverde, '65; Figs. 21-2, 21-3 and 21-6).

At the point of division of the olfactory tract into lateral and medial olfactory striae, there is a rhomboid-shaped region, bounded by the olfactory trigone and the optic tract, known as the *anterior perforated substance* (Figs. 21-1 and 21-7). This region is studded with numerous perforations made by entering blood vessels. The posterior border of this region, near the optic tract, has a smooth appearance and forms an oblique band, *the diagonal band of Broca* (Fig. 21-1). In macrosmatic animals, especially those with well-developed snouts or muzzles, the rostral portion of the area is marked by a prominent elevation, *the olfactory tubercle* (Fig.

21-4). Only rudiments of this structure are present in man. The region of the olfactory tubercle receives fibers from the olfactory bulb, the anterior olfactory nucleus, and the amygdaloid nuclear complex. It projects fibers into the stria medullaris and the medial forebrain bundle.

The medial olfactory stria extends to the medial hemispheric surface and becomes continuous with a small cortical field known as the *subcallosal area* (parolfactory area), located beneath the rostrum of the corpus callosum (Figs. 21-1 and 21-4). This area is limited in front by the anterior parolfactory sulcus, while behind it is separated by the posterior parolfactory sulcus from another strip of cortex, the *paraterminal gyrus* (subcallosal gyrus), which is closely applied to the rostral lamina of the corpus callosum.

The subcallosal area and the paraterminal gyrus together constitute the *septal area* (paraterminal body). The term septal area refers to the cortical part of this region. The subcortical part of the septal region consists of the *medial* and *lateral septal nuclei*, which are found rostral to the anterior commissure (Fig. 21-4). The medial septal nucleus becomes continuous with the nucleus and tract of the diagonal

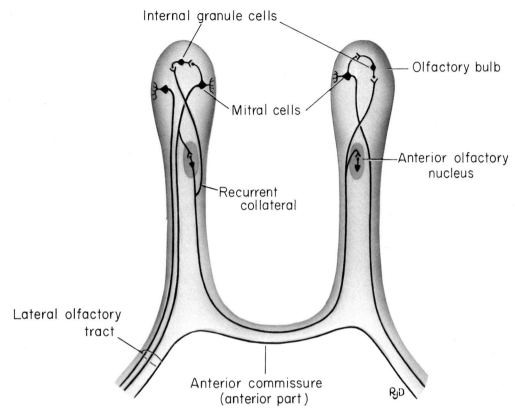

Internal granule cells

Olfactory bulb

Mitral cells

Anterior olfactory
nucleus

Recurrent
collateral

Lateral olfactory
tract

Anterior commissure
(anterior part)

RjD

Fig. 21-3. Schematic diagram of interconnections of the olfactory bulbs and anterior olfactory nuclei. Collaterals of mitral cell axons synapse upon apical dendrites of pyramidal-shaped cells of the anterior olfactory nucleus. These cells give rise to fibers that cross in the anterior part of the anterior commissure (Fig. 21-6) and synapse upon cells in the contralateral anterior olfactory nucleus and internal granule cells in the olfactory bulb. Recurrent collaterals of axons of the anterior olfactory nuclei project back to the ipsilateral olfactory bulb to terminate upon internal granule cells, which can in turn activate mitral cells. The principal axons of mitral cells enter the lateral olfactory tract (based on Valverde, '65).

band (Fig. 21-1) and thus establishes connections with the amygdaloid nuclear complex (Fig. 21-4). The lateral septal nucleus appears continuous over the anterior commissure with scattered neurons of the septum pellucidum. The septal nuclei receive a large number of afferent fibers from the hippocampal formation via the fornix (Nauta, '56, '58) and some fibers from the amygdaloid complex. The medial septal nucleus also receives fibers from the medial midbrain reticular formation; these fibers ascend in the mammillary peduncle (Fig. 21-5) and continue rostrally in the medial forebrain bundle (Guillery, '56, '57; Nauta and Kuypers, '58). It is uncertain whether the septal nuclei receive olfactory impulses. Evidence suggests that

fibers from the olfactory tubercle passing to the septal region are largely nonolfactory. Efferent fibers from the septal nuclei enter the medial part of the stria medullaris and pass to the habenular nucleus (Figs. 21-4 and 21-5). In addition axons from these nuclei enter the medial forebrain bundle to be distributed caudally to the entire lateral extent of the hypothalamic region; some fibers of this group extend into the midbrain tegmentum (Nauta, '56, '58). The medial septal nucleus projects fibers back to the hippocampal formation via the fornix (Daitz and Powell, '54). The studies of Nauta ('56, '58) indicate that the septal region constitutes a nodal area in the limbic projection system through which primary hippocampal and amygdaloid

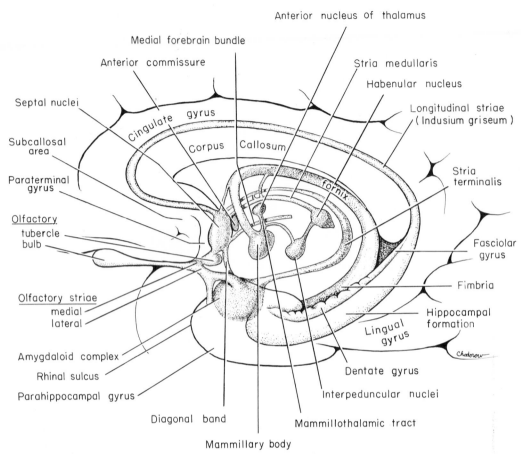

FIG. 21–4. Semischematic drawing of rhinencephalic structural relationships as seen in medial view of the right hemisphere. Both deep and superficial structures are indicated. Modified from a drawing by Krieg ('53).

projections appear to overlap. Two distinct and separate pathways originating from this region conduct impulses to the midbrain tegmentum. These tracts are: (1) the stria medullaris which synapses upon the habenular nuclei (which in turn give rise to the fasciculus retroflexus), and (2) the medial forebrain bundle (Fig. 21–5).

The lateral olfactory stria passes laterally across the anterior perforated substance towards the lateral sulcus and reaches the inferior apex of the insula (Fig. 21–4). There it loops sharply backward, the loop forming the limen of the insula, and passes medially in the floor of the fissure to terminate in the uncus and anterior portion of the parahippocampal gyrus. Some fibers also end in the amygdaloid nucleus, which lies buried beneath

the uncus, above and in front of the tip of the inferior horn of the lateral ventricle (Figs. 21–7 and 21–9). The lateral olfactory stria, the uncus, and the anterior part of the parahippocampal gyrus constitute the so-called *pyriform lobe*, which is more highly developed in macrosmatic mammals. The rostral part of the parahippocampal gyrus is rolled inward and upward as a consequence of the tremendous development of the neopallium. The rostromedial protrusion of this gyrus is the *uncus* (Figs. 3–20 and 21–7). The shallow rhinal sulcus, a rostral continuation of the collateral fissure, separates the anterior part of the parahippocampal gyrus from the more lateral neocortex (Figs. 3–15 and 21–8). In man the caudal limits of this area are indistinct, and it is uncertain how much of

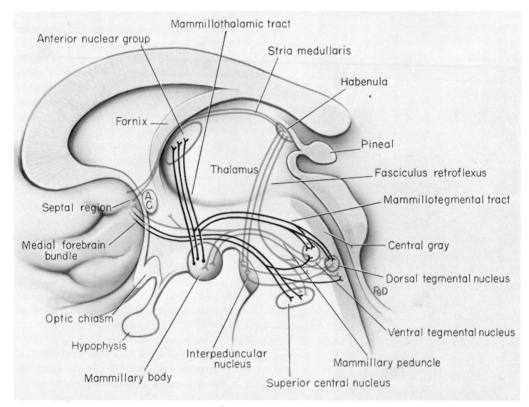

Mammillothalamic tract

Anterior nuclear group

Stria medullaris

Habenula

Fornix

Pineal

Thalamus

Fasciculus retroflexus

Mammillotegmental tract

Septal region

Medial forebrain
bundle

Central gray

Dorsal tegmental nucleus

Optic chiasm

Ventral tegmental nucleus

Hypophysis

Interpeduncular
nucleus

Mammillary peduncle

Mammillary body

Superior central nucleus

Fig. 21-5. Semischematic diagram of limbic pathways interrelating the telencephalon and diencephalon with medial midbrain structures. The medial forebrain bundle and efferent fibers of the mammillary body are shown in *black*. The *medial forebrain bundle* originates from the septal and lateral preoptic region, traverses the lateral hypothalamic area and projects into the midbrain tegmentum. The mammillary princeps divides into two bundles, the mammillothalamic tract and the mammillotegmental tract. Ascending fibers of the *mammillary peduncle*, arising from the dorsal and ventral tegmental nuclei, are shown in *red;* most of these fibers pass to the mammillary body, but some continue rostrally to the lateral hypothalamus, the preoptic regions and the medial septal nucleus. Fibers arising from the septal nuclei project caudally in the medial part of the *stria medullaris* (*blue*) to terminate in the medial habenular nucleus. Impulses conveyed by this bundle are distributed to midbrain tegmental nuclei via the fasciculus retroflexus (based on Nauta, '58).

the parahippocampal area should be included.

The *pyriform lobe*, so named because of its pear shape in certain species, is divided into several regions. These include the *prepyriform*, the *periamygdaloid*, and the *entorhinal areas*. The prepyriform area, often referred to as the lateral olfactory gyrus, extends along the lateral olfactory stria to the rostral amygdaloid region (Fig. 21-4). Since its afferent fibers are derived from the lateral olfactory stria, it is regarded as an olfactory relay center. The periamygdaloid area is a small region dor-

sal and rostral to the amygdaloid nuclear complex; it is intimately related to the prepyriform area. The entorhinal area, the most posterior part of the pyriform lobe, corresponds to area 28 of Brodmann and constitutes a major portion of the anterior parahippocampal gyrus in man (Fig. 22-4). This area, relatively large in primates and in man, is composed of a six-layered cortex of a transitional type. The entorhinal cortex does not receive direct fibers from the olfactory bulb or tract (Cajal, '11; Humphrey, '36; Fox, '40; Clark and Meyer, '47; Powell et al., '65).

OLFACTORY PATHWAYS

Olfactory Receptors. The olfactory membrane is a yellowish brown patch of specialized epithelium in the upper part of the nasal cavity. Olfactory receptors are located in this membrane. Small sensory cells scattered among supporting cells in the olfactory epithelium have two processes, a coarse peripheral one passing to the surface and a fine central one projecting through the basement membrane (Fig. 1-3B). From the coarse peripheral processes a variable number of short olfactory hairs arise. The delicate central processes, which constitute the unmyelinated *olfactoria fila*, converge to form small fascicles and pass from the nasal cavity via foramina in the cribriform plate of the ethmoid bone. These exceedingly small fibers, said to have the slowest conduction rate of any nerves, enter the ventral surface of the olfactory bulb. The olfactory fila, representing the central processes of bipolar cells in the olfactory epithelium, collectively constitute the *olfactory nerve* (N. I).

Olfactory Bulb. This flattened ovoid body resting on the cribriform plate of the ethmoid bone is the terminal "nucleus" of the olfactory nerve. Most of the fibers of the olfactory nerve enter the anterior tip of the olfactory bulb. Structurally the olfactory bulb has a laminar organization, but in man it is difficult to demonstrate the laminar pattern found in lower mammals. Within the gray matter of the olfactory bulb are several types of nerve cells, the most striking of which are the large, triangular *mitral cells*, so named because of their resemblance to a bishop's mitre (Figs. 21-2 and 21-3). Primary olfactory fibers synapse with the brushlike terminals of vertically descending dendrites of the mitral cells to form the *olfactory glomeruli*. Smaller cells of the olfactory bulb, known as *tufted cells*, similarly have a number of dendrites, one of which participates in the formation of the glomerulus. Granular cells of various sizes found throughout the olfactory bulb appear to serve associative functions. The fact that the arrangement of afferent fibers in the olfactory bulb does not appear to be localized in any patterned way (Clark and War-

wick, '46) suggests that olfactory sense lacks the localizing features characteristic of other sensory systems. Axons of the mitral and tufted cells enter the olfactory tract as *secondary olfactory fibers*. Caudal to the olfactory bulb are scattered groups of neurons, intermediate in size between mitral and granular cells, that form the *anterior olfactory nucleus* (Fig. 21-3). Some cells of this loosely organized nucleus are found along the olfactory tracts near the base of the hemisphere. Dendrites of these cells pass among the fibers of the olfactory tract, from which they receive impulses. Axons of the cells of the anterior olfactory nucleus pass centrally, cross in the anterior part of the anterior commissure (Fig. 21-6), and enter the contralateral anterior olfactory nucleus and olfactory bulb (Powell et al., '65; Valverde, '65; Fig. 21-3). These neurons are thought to serve as part of a reinforcing mechanism for olfactory impulses.

Olfactory Tract. This tract passes towards the anterior perforated substance and divides into well-defined *lateral* and *medial olfactory striae*. A thin covering of gray substance over the olfactory striae composes the *lateral* and *medial olfactory gyri*. The lateral olfactory stria and gyrus pass along the lateral margin of the anterior perforated substance to reach the prepyriform region (Fig. 21-4). Fibers of the lateral olfactory stria arising in the olfactory bulb give collaterals to the anterior olfactory nucleus and the olfactory tubercle. These fibers terminate in the prepyriform cortex and in parts of the amygdaloid nuclear complex (Fig. 21-4). The terminations of these fibers are said to be axodendritic in relation to pyramidal cells of the plexiform layer of the prepyriform cortex, and axosomatic in the cortical and medial amygdaloid nuclei (Allison, '53). Terminations also are present in the nucleus of the lateral olfactory tract, and in parts of the anterior amygdaloid nucleus (White, '65), both of which constitute subdivisions of the corticomedial nuclear group (see p. 498). The prepyriform cortex and the periamygdaloid area, which receive fibers from the lateral olfactory stria, constitute the *primary olfactory cortex*. Olfaction appears to be unique among the sensory systems in that impulses in this system reach the cortex without being relayed in the thalamus.

The prepyriform cortex projects fibers to the entorhinal cortex (area 28), the basal and lateral amygdaloid nuclei, the lateral preoptic area, the nucleus of the diagonal band, the medial forebrain bundle, and to parts of the dorsomedial nucleus of the thalamus (Powell et al., '65). The entorhinal cortex is regarded as a *secondary olfactory cortical area* (Fig. 21–11 and 22–4), though no fibers of the lateral olfactory tract project directly to this area. Efferent fibers from the entorhinal cortex are projected to the hippocampal formation, and to the anterior insular and frontal cortex via the uncinate fasciculus. No fibers from the prepyriform cortex pass to the hippocampal formation.

Different parts of the amygdaloid nuclear complex receive olfactory inputs. Direct projections from the olfactory bulb pass to the cortical and medial amygdaloid nuclei, while indirect, but substantial, olfactory impulses pass to the basal and lateral amygdaloid nuclei, via relays in the prepyriform cortex. It is of interest that direct and indirect olfactory pathways to the amygdaloid complex terminate in different components and that these two pathways probably influence the entire amygdaloid complex, except the central nucleus.

Fibers originating from the cells of the anterior olfactory nucleus project: (1) peripherally to internal granule cells of the ipsilateral olfactory bulb, and (2) via the lateral olfactory tract and the anterior part of the anterior commissure to the contralateral anterior olfactory nucleus and olfactory bulb (Lohman, '63; Valverde, '65; Powell et al., '65). Impulses from the anterior olfactory nucleus on one side thus reach internal granule cells of the olfactory bulb on both sides, and the contralateral anterior olfactory nucleus. Internal granule cells in the olfactory bulb relay impulses to mitral cells (Fig. 21–3).

The medial olfactory stria and gyrus, which are less distinct in man, become continuous with the subcallosal area and the paraterminal gyrus. Some of the fibers in this stria may reach the olfactory tubercle and the anterior perforated substance. It appears doubtful if any fibers arising from the olfactory bulb project directly to the bed nucleus of the stria terminalis or the septal nuclei.

Reflex Connections. Although the septal area receives fibers from the olfactory tubercle, these fibers probably do not convey olfactory impulses. The olfactory tubercle, the nucleus of the diagonal band, the septal area (subcallosal area and paraterminal gyrus) and the substantia innominata receive ventral amygdalofugal fibers (Nauta, '61). Other ventral amygdalofugal fibers, which probably arise mainly from the basolateral amygdaloid nuclear group (Valverde, '65; Cowan et al., '65), project to the lateral preoptic and lateral hypothalamic regions. The amygdaloid complex also gives rise to the fibers of the stria terminalis. The *stria terminalis,* arising from both the corticomedial and the basolateral amygdaloid nuclear groups, arches along the entire medial border of the caudate nucleus (Fig. 19–1) and projects its fibers mainly to the bed nucleus of the stria terminalis. However, part of these fibers are distributed to the medial preoptic nucleus and anterior hypothalamic areas (Nauta, '61; Cowan et al., '65). Amygdaloid projections to the septal area, the lateral preoptic region and the lateral hypothalamic region may serve to lead impulses originating in the amygdaloid complex into both the medial forebrain bundle and the stria medullaris. By virtue of synaptic relationships with cells which project fibers into the medial forebrain bundle and the stria medullaris, connections are established by which impulses can be transmitted to extensive areas of the midbrain tegmentum (Fig. 21–5). The ventral amygdalofugal pathway thus appears comparable to the fornix system in that it furnishes the first link in a multisynaptic pathway by which impulses can be transmitted to specific parts of the brain stem reticular formation.

Direct hippocampal projections contained in the precommissural fornix pass to the septal nuclei and the preoptic region. Part of these direct fibers, continuing beyond these nuclei and the mammillary body, are distributed to rostral parts of the midbrain central gray. The latter fibers represent a direct hippocampo-mesencephalic projection (Nauta, '58). Fibers arising from the septal nuclei enter the medial part of the stria medullaris and project to the medial habenular nucleus. Part of the caudally continuing fibers of the precommissural fornix are joined by numerous fibers from the septal nuclei to form a large part of one of the most massive roots of the medial forebrain bundle (Zuckerkandl's "olfactory bundle of Ammon's horn"). The hippocampal component of this bundle probably does not extend beyond the lateral preoptic region, but septal fibers are distributed to the entire extent of the lateral hypothalamic region, and some project via the medial forebrain bundle into the ventral midbrain tegmentum (Nauta, '58). Fibers of the postcommissural fornix traverse the hypothalamus and project mainly to the medial mammillary nucleus. Thus there are three main pathways by which impulses from the amygdaloid complex and hippocampal formation can be relayed into the midbrain tegmentum. These pathways are the medial forebrain bundle, the mammillotegmental tract, and the stria medullaris. Fibers of the stria medullaris synapse in the habenular nuclei which in turn give rise to the fasciculus retroflexus (habenulopeduncular tract) which passes to the interpeduncular nucleus (Figs. 16–3, 18–5 and 21–5).

The medial forebrain bundle, the mammillotegmental tract and the fasciculus retroflexus are regarded as having dual distributions in the midbrain. Each of these pathways has: (1) a lateral component terminating in central and lateral tegmental regions, and (2) a medial component distributed to medial and paramedian regions of the midbrain. Fibers contained in the medial forebrain bundle, projecting to lateral tegmental regions, represent one of the main pathways by which impulses from the lateral hypothalamus influence visceral motor nuclei in more caudal parts of the brain stem. Medially projecting fibers of the medial forebrain bundle are distributed to the ventral tegmental area, the superior central nucleus and caudal parts of the central gray substance. Fibers of the mammillotegmental tract pass to both the dorsal and ventral (deep) tegmental nuclei. Most of the fibers of the fasciculus retroflexus terminate in the interpeduncular nucleus which in turn projects fibers to reticular nuclei in the midbrain tegmentum, particularly the superior central and dorsal tegmental nuclei. Some fibers of the fasciculus retroflexus by-pass the interpeduncular nucleus and continue dorsocaudally directly to the superior central nucleus and the central gray (Nauta, '58).

Fibers from the dorsal tegmental nucleus, as well as fibers from medial and periventricular hypothalamic cell groups, and ventral parts of the central gray, join the dorsal longitudinal fasciculus (Schütz) and descend. Although fibers of this bundle are considered by certain authors (Ingram, '40) to descend to lower brain stem nuclei, the number of descending fibers dwindles rapidly caudal to the midbrain. Conduction in this bundle appears to be predominantly in an ascending direction. The majority of ascending fibers in the dorsal longitudinal fasciculus are distributed to periventricular and medial hypothalamic cell groups and to the dorsal hypothalamic area.

The mammillary peduncle (Fig. 21–5), arising from both the dorsal and ventral tegmental nuclei, constitutes another ascending bundle related to the limbic system. Although most of the fibers of this bundle project to the mammillary body, part of the fibers continue rostrally in the medial forebrain bundle and enter the lateral hypothalamic and preoptic regions, and the medial septal nucleus.

Descending fibers of these systems appear to interrelate certain autonomic and somatic nuclei of the brain stem with olfactory and hypothalamic centers. By this rather diffuse system, which involves a number of complex relays and intercalated nuclei, somatic and visceral effectors are brought under reflex olfactory and hypothalamic control. It seems likely that many of the complex somatic and visceral phenomena observed in response to experimental stimulation of the amygdaloid complex (Gloor, '60) may be mediated by amygdalofugal impulses that are relayed to the brain stem reticular formation (see discussion pp. 540). Indirect pathways relating the hippocampal formation to the brain stem reticular formation appear to subserve, in part, similar functions, but impulses conveyed by this system seem to play a particularly important role in modulating basic patterns of cortical activity. It should be emphasized that part of these fibers, and those from the lateral hypothalamus, project to tegmental regions occupied by diffuse and multineuronal components of the reticulothalamic system that have widespread activating influences upon the cerebral cortex.

Clinical Considerations. The ability of the human nose, in concert with the brain, to discriminate thousands of different odor qualities is well known, but the physiological and psychological bases for such discriminations are unknown. Olfactory discrimination does not appear to be based upon morphologically distinct types of receptors, but there is some evidence (Mozell, '64) that certain odors may be distinguished by their relative effectiveness in stimulating particular regions of the olfactory epithelium. Current theories suggest that spatial and temporal factors probably play important roles in the neural coding of olfactory responses (Moulton and Beidler, '67).

From a clinical viewpoint the importance of the olfactory system is slight in man, since this special sense plays a less essential role than in lower vertebrates. In certain instances valuable clinical information can be obtained by testing olfactory sense by appropriate methods. Olfaction is tested in each nostril separately by having the patient inhale or sniff nonirritating volatile oils or liquids with characteristic odors. Substances which stimulate gustatory end organs, or peripheral endings of the trigeminal nerve in the nasal mucosa, are not appropriate for testing olfaction. Comparisons between the two sides are of great importance. While the olfactory nerves are rarely the seat of disease, they frequently are involved by disease or injury of adjacent structures. Fractures of the cribriform plate of the ethmoid bone or hemorrhage at the base of the frontal lobes may cause tearing of the olfactory filaments. The olfactory nerves may be involved as a consequence of meningitis or abscess of the frontal lobe. Unilateral anosmia may be of important diagnostic significance in localizing intracranial neoplasms, especially meningiomas of the sphenoidal ridge or olfactory groove. Hypophysial tumors affect the olfactory bulb and tract only when they extend above the sella turcica. Olfactory "hallucinations" frequently are a consequence of lesions involving or irritating the parahippocampal gyrus, the uncus, or adjoining areas around the amygdaloid nuclear complex. The olfactory sensations which these patients experience usually are described as disagreeable in character and may precede a generalized convulsion. Such seizures are referred to as "uncinate fits."

[handwritten margin note: UNCINATE ATTACKS]

THE ANTERIOR COMMISSURE

The anterior commissure crosses the median plane as a compact fiber bundle immediately in front of the anterior columns of the fornix (Figs. 18-1, 18-11, 21-6, 21-7 and A-25). Proceeding laterally it splits into two portions. The small anterior, or olfactory portion, greatly reduced in man, loops rostrally and connects the gray substance of the olfactory tract on one side with the olfactory bulb of the opposite side. Fibers in this part of the anterior commissure arise from the anterior olfactory nucleus, cross to the opposite side, and project to the contralateral anterior olfactory nucleus and to granule cells in the olfactory bulb (Fig. 21-3). It has been suggested (Powell and Cowan, '63) that these centrifugal fibers may subserve reflex control of activity in the olfactory bulb, and in principle may be comparable to the gamma efferent system at spinal levels.

The larger posterior portion forms the bulk of the anterior commissure. From its central region fibers of the anterior

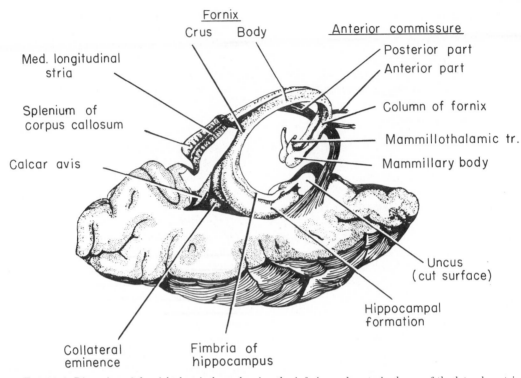

FIG. 21–6. Dissection of the right hemisphere showing the inferior and posterior horns of the lateral ventricle, the hippocampal formation, the configuration of the fornix, and the anterior and posterior parts of the anterior commissure (after Rauber-Kopsch, '43).

commissure pass laterally and backward through the most inferior parts of the lateral segment of the globus pallidus and putamen, a relationship most obvious in sagittal sections of the brain (Figs. A–31 and A–32). Further laterally the fibers of the anterior commissure enter the external capsule and come into apposition with the inferior part of the claustrum. On entering the external capsule the fibers of the commissure twist so that posterior fibers pass ventrally. Fibers of the posterior portion of the anterior commissure mainly interconnect the middle temporal gyri, although some pass into the inferior temporal gyrus (Fox et al., '48). Similar findings have been reported in physiological studies in the monkey (McCulloch and Garol, '41) and in the chimpanzee (Bailey et al., '41). The findings of Whitlock and Nauta ('56), who used silver impregnation methods, appear similar to those of Fox and his associates.

THE HIPPOCAMPAL FORMATION

The hippocampal formation is laid down in the embryo on the medial wall of the hemisphere along the hippocampal fissure, immediately above and parallel to the choroidal fissure, which marks the invagination of the choroid plexus into the ventricle. With the formation of the temporal lobe, both these fissures are carried downward and forward, each forming an arch extending from the region of the interventricular foramen to the tip of the inferior horn of the lateral ventricle. The various parts of the hippocampal arch do not develop to the same extent. The upper or anterior portion of the hippocampal fissure is invaded by the crossing fibers of the corpus callosum and ultimately becomes the callosal fissure, which separates this massive commissure from the overlying pallium. The corresponding part of the hippocampal formation, which lies above the corpus callosum, undergoes lit-

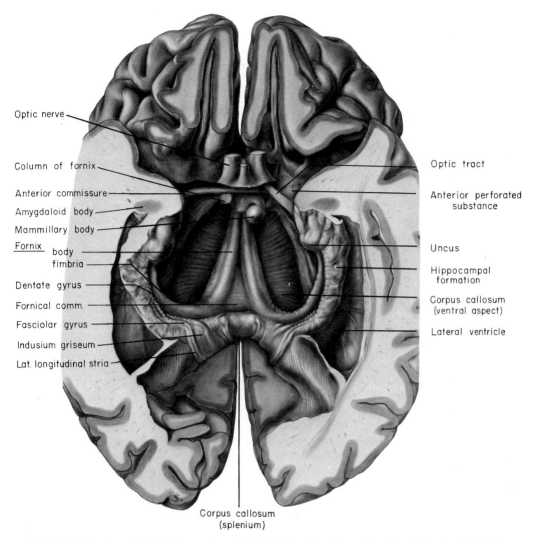

Optic nerve

Column of fornix

Anterior commissure

Amygdaloid body

Mammillary body

Fornix   body
          fimbria

Dentate gyrus

Fornical comm.

Fasciolar gyrus

Indusium griseum

Lat. longitudinal stria

Optic tract

Anterior perforated
substance

Uncus

Hippocampal
formation

Corpus callosum
(ventral aspect)

Lateral ventricle

Corpus callosum
(splenium)

FIG. 21-7. Dissection of the inferior surface of the brain showing the configuration of the fornix, the hippocampal formation, the dentate gyrus, and related structures. (Mettler, *Neuroanatomy*, 2nd Ed., 1948. Courtesy of Dr. F. A. Mettler and The C. V. Mosby Company, St. Louis.)

tle differentiation; in the adult, it forms a thin vestigial convolution, the *indusium griseum* (Fig. 21-7). The lower temporal portion of the arch, which is not affected by the corpus callosum, differentiates into the main structures of the hippocampal formation. The hippocampal fissure deepens; and the invaginated portion, which bulges deeply into the inferior horn, becomes the *hippocampus*, while the lips of the fissure give rise to the *dentate* and the *parahippocampal gyri*. The relationships

of these structures are best illustrated in a frontal section through this area, or in special dissections (Figs. 21-7 and 21-8). Proceeding from the collateral sulcus, the *parahippocampal gyrus* extends to the hippocampal fissure, where it dips into the ventricle to form the *hippocampal formation*. The latter curves dorsally and medially and, on reaching the medial surface, curves inward again to form a semilunar convolution, the *dentate gyrus* or *fascia dentata* (Fig. 21-9). The whole ventricu-

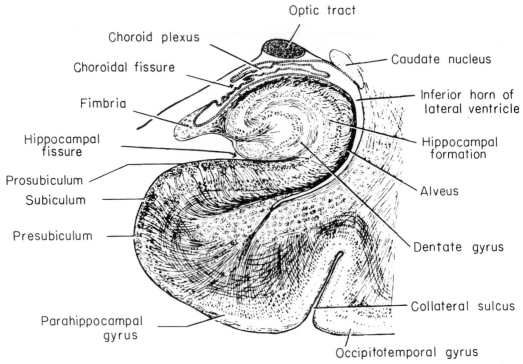

Fig. 21-8. Transverse section through human hippocampus and parahippocampal gyrus

lar surface of the hippocampal formation is covered by a white layer, the *alveus*, which is composed of axons from cells of the hippocampus (Fig. 21–11). These fibers converge on the medial surface of the hippocampus to form a flattened band, the *fimbria*, lying medial to the hippocampus and the dentate gyrus. Fibers from the alveus entering the fimbria constitute the beginning of the fornix system (Figs. 21–4, 21–6 and 21–7). The free thin border of the fimbria is directly continuous with the epithelium of the choroidal fissure, which lies immediately above it. The choroid plexus, invaginated into the ventricle along this fissure, partly covers the hippocampus (Fig. 21–8). The superior portion of the parahippocampal gyrus adjoining the hippocampal fissure is known as the *subiculum*, and the area of transition between it and the parahippocampal gyrus, as the *presubiculum* (Fig. 21–8). The presubiculum, subiculum, prosubiculum, hippocampal formation, and dentate gyrus all belong to the archipallium, which has an allocortical structure. The larger inferior portion of the parahippocampal gyrus,

which is bounded by the collateral sulcus, is neopallial and has the general structure of the isocortex.

When the hippocampal fissure is opened up, the *dentate gyrus* is seen as a narrow, notched band of cortex between the hippocampal fissure below and the fimbria above (Fig. 21–7). In sagittal sections (Fig. 21–9) the relationships between the hippocampal formation, the dentate gyrus, the amygdaloid nucleus, and the inferior horn of the lateral ventricle can be readily appreciated. Traced backward, the gyrus accompanies the fimbria almost to the splenium of the corpus callosum. There it separates from the fimbria, loses its notched appearance, and as the delicate *fasciolar gyrus*, passes on to the superior surface of the corpus callosum. It spreads out into a thin gray sheet representing a vestigial convolution, the *indusium griseum* or *supracallosal gyrus* (Figs. 21–4 and 21–7). Imbedded in the indusium griseum are two slender bands of myelinated fibers which appear as narrow longitudinal ridges on the superior surface of the corpus callosum. These are the *medial*

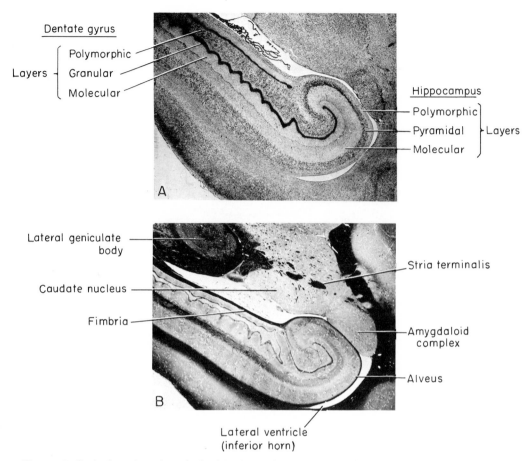

Dentate gyrus

Layers { Polymorphic / Granular / Molecular

Hippocampus
— Polymorphic ⎫
— Pyramidal   ⎬ Layers
— Molecular   ⎭

A

Lateral geniculate body

Caudate nucleus

Fimbria

Stria terminalis

Amygdaloid complex

Alveus

B

Lateral ventricle
(inferior horn)

FIG. 21-9. Sagittal sections through the hippocampal formation and dentate gyrus in the rhesus monkey showing the relationships of these structures to the inferior horn of the lateral ventricle, the neostriatum and the amygdaloid nuclear complex. In *A*, the cellular layers of the hippocampal formation and dentate gyrus are identified. In *B*, the alveus, fimbria, tail of the caudate nucleus, stria terminalis, amygdaloid complex and part of the lateral geniculate body are identified. *A*, Nissl stain, X8; *B*, Weil stain, X9.

and *lateral longitudinal striae (Lancisii)*, which constitute the white matter of these vestigial convolutions. The indusium griseum and the longitudinal striae extend the whole length of the corpus callosum, pass over the genu, and become continuous with the parateminal gyrus, which is in turn prolonged into the diagonal band of Broca (Fig. 21-1). Traced forward, the dentate gyrus extends into the notch between the uncus and hippocampal gyrus. Here it makes a sharp dorsal bend and passes as a smooth band across the inferior surface of the uncus. This terminal portion is known as the *band of Giacomini*, and the part of the uncus lying posterior to it often is designated as the *intralimbic gyrus*.

The cortical zones from the parahippocampal gyrus through the presubiculum, the subiculum, and the prosubiculum to the hippocampal formation and the dentate gyrus show a gradual transition from a six- to a three-layered cellular organization (Fig. 21-8). Although the entorhinal region (area 28) is six-layered cortex, it represents a transitional form not typical of neocortex. In more medial cortical areas certain layers of the entorhinal cortex drop out and undergo rearrangement, so that the cortex of the *hippocampal formation* has only three fundamental layers. These are the *polymorphic layer*, the *pyramidal layer* and the *molecular layer* (Fig. 21-9). Several secondary laminae are formed by the arrangement of axons and

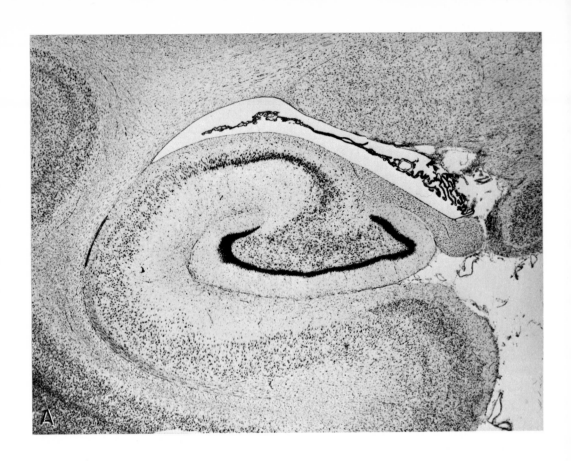

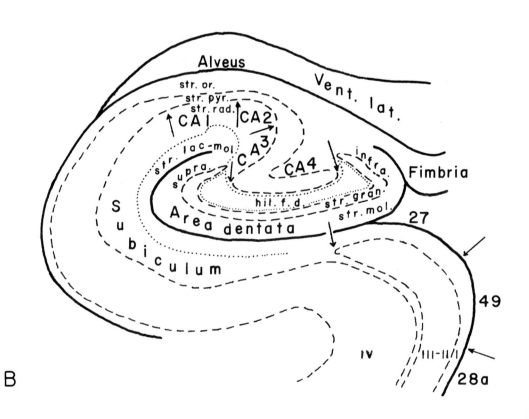

dendrites of cells within the fundamental layers. Immediately beneath the ependyma of the ventricle is the alveus. Recognized laminae passing inward from the alveus are: (1) the stratum oriens, (2) the stratum pyramidale, (3) the stratum radiatum, (4) the stratum lacunosum and (5) the stratum moleculare (Fig. 21–10). The last three laminae are considered to correspond to the molecular layer of the neocortex (Lorente de Nó, '33, '34). The most characteristic layer of the hippocampal formation is the pyramidal layer consisting of large and small pyramidal and Golgi type II cells (Fig. 21–11). Large and small pyramidal cells exhibit many morphological differences, especially in dendritic development. Some of the cells are described as double pyramids because of the rich dendritic plexuses arising from both poles (Fig. 6–4J). Basal and apical dendrites of the pyramidal cells enter adjacent layers, while axons of these cells pass through the stratum oriens to enter the alveus (Fig. 21–11). The stratum oriens, containing fibers and polymorphic cells, has been divided into outer and inner zones. Cells of the outer zone distribute axons to the molecular layer. Cells of the inner zone send some axons into the alveus, while others ramify within this layer or pass into the pyramidal layer. The stratum radiatum is made up largely of interlacing and branching processes which appear to radiate from the bordering pyramidal layer. The stratum lacunosum and stratum moleculare, sometimes considered as a single lamina, contain a rich plexus of fibers from other layers.

Although the architectonics of the hippocampal formation is uniform throughout its extent, there are variations in cell morphology, differences in the relative development of various cortical regions, and differences in the pathways followed by various fiber systems. On the basis of these differences Lorente de Nó ('34) subdivided the hippocampal formation into sectors designated as CA1, CA2, CA3 and CA4. The position of these various sectors is shown in Figure 21–10.

The *dentate gyrus*, like the hippocampus, consists of three layers: a *molecular layer*, a *granular layer* and a *polymorphic layer* (Figs. 21–9 and 21–10). Layers of the dentate gyrus are arranged in a "U" or "V" shaped configuration in which the open portion is directed toward the fimbria in transverse sections (Figs. 21–8 and 21–11). Thus layers are present on both sides of sector CA3 of the hippocampus which extends into the hilus of the dentate gyrus. The molecular layer of the dentate gyrus is continuous with that of the hippocampus in the depths of the hippocampal fissure. The granular layer, made up of closely arranged spherical or oval neurons, gives rise to axons which pass through the polymorphic layer to terminate upon dendrites of pyramidal cells in the hippocampus. Dendrites of granule cells enter mainly the molecular layer. Cells of the polymorphic layer are of several types, including modified pyramidal cells and so-called basket cells. The dentate gyrus does not give rise to fibers passing beyond the hippocampal formation (Raisman et al., '66).

The *area dentata* (Blackstad, '56) is bounded by imaginary lines extending from the tip of the pyramidal cell layer of the hippocampus to the extremities of the granular layer of the dentate gyrus (Fig. 21–10). Within this line is the hilus of the fascia dentata containing polymorphic neurons; this region has been designated as sector CA4 by Lorente de Nó. The term, *fascia dentata*, applies only to the molecular and granular layers of the area dentata.

Fig. 21–10. Hippocampal region in the rhesus monkey in horizontal section showing the respective layers of the hippocampal formation and dentate gyrus. *A*, Nissl stain. Photograph, X20. In *B*, the layers are drawn and the sectors of the hippocampal formation according to Lorente de Nó ('33, '34) are indicated. Abbreviations used are: 28a, entorhinal area; hilf. d., hilus fasciae dentatae; 49, parasubiculum; 27, presubiculum; str. gran., stratum granulosum; str. lac-mol., stratum lacunosum-moleculare; str. mol., stratum moleculare; st. or., stratum oriens; str. pyr., stratum pyramidale; str. rad., stratum radiatum; supra and infra, suprapyramidal and infrapyramidal limbs of the stratum granulosum. Roman numerals refer to layers of cortical areas 27, 49 and 28a. The assistance of Dr. J. B. Angevine of the University of Arizona, College of Medicine, is acknowledged for delimiting the cell layers and sector boundaries.

Recent studies of the hippocampal region utilizing autoradiographic technics (Angevine, '65) have provided new information concerning the development and migration of neurons in this cortical region. This technic is based upon the injection of tritiated thymidine into pregnant animals, which becomes incorporated into the DNA of premitotic cells. Thymidine-H^3 remains in the nuclei of daughter cells as a permanent label, providing a radioactive marking of neuroblasts. This makes it possible to study the proliferation and migration of neuroblasts destined for various parts of the brain. Studies of neurogenesis show that active displacement and migration of neurons is the rule. Neurons in all components of the hippocampal formation but one arise in a general, but not rigid, "inside-out" sequence. The outstanding exception in this cortical region is the granular layer of the dentate gyrus. Granule cells originating prenatally, or perinatally, migrate to the granular layer in an "outside-in" pattern, and postnatally granule cells arise by proliferation of deeply situated neuroblasts in the granular layer itself.

This "inside-out" sequence of neuron origin applies to the majority of cells in most cortical areas. Thus neurons arising late in gestation, and destined for superficial locations in a given cortical area, must traverse an extensive population of neurons which originated at earlier times. This same sequence of cell differentiation has been demonstrated in the hippocampal formation in human embryos (Humphrey, '66).

Even though the hippocampal formation has in the past been considered as an important olfactory center, there is no decisive evidence to support this concept (Brodal, '47). The anatomical connections of this structure indicate that it does not receive fibers from the olfactory bulb or the anterior olfactory nucleus (Rose and Woolsey, '43a; Fox et al., '44; Clark and Meyer, '47) and suggest that it is largely an effector structure.

Afferent fibers to the hippocampal formation arise mainly from the entorhinal area (Cajal, '11; Lorente de Nó, '33, '34), a portion of the pyriform lobe which does not receive direct olfactory fibers. Fibers from the entorhinal area (area 28) are distributed to the dentate gyrus and hippocampus in their entire posterior portion (Lorente de Nó, '34). Fibers arising from the medial part of the entorhinal area follow the so-called "alvear path" to enter the hippocampus from its ventricular surface (Fig. 21–11). These fibers are distributed to the deep layer of the subiculum and to sector CA1 of the hippocampus. Fibers from the lateral parts of the entorhinal cortex pursue the so-called "perforant path" and traverse the subiculum (Fig. 21–11). These fibers are distributed to all sectors of the hippocampus except the region transitional to the dentate gyrus (CA4). Afferent fibers following these pathways establish synaptic contacts with dendrites of pyramidal cells in the hippocampus, but do not come into direct contact with the granule cells in the dentate gyrus (Raisman et al., '65).

Other afferent fibers to the hippocampal formation have been described. The medial septal nucleus projects fibers via the fimbria (Daitz and Powell, '54) to sectors CA3 and CA4 of the hippocampus and to the dentate gyrus. The cingulum (Fig. 3–21), a massive fiber bundle derived from cells of the cingulate cortex, projects to the presubiculum and the entorhinal area (Raisman et al., '65), but not to the hippocampal formation. Since the entorhinal area projects to the hippocampus proper, these findings imply that impulses from the cingulate cortex are relayed to the hippocampus via the entorhinal area. Although it has been postulated that the indusium griseum contributes fibers to the hippocampus, these fibers are not numerous. In addition, some fibers crossing in the hippocampal commissure may interconnect the two hippocampi. None of these afferent pathways to the hippocampal formations appear to transmit olfactory impulses.

Fornix. This band of white fibers constitutes the main efferent fiber system of the hippocampal formation, including both projection and commissural fibers (Figs. 21–6 and 21–7). It is composed of ax-

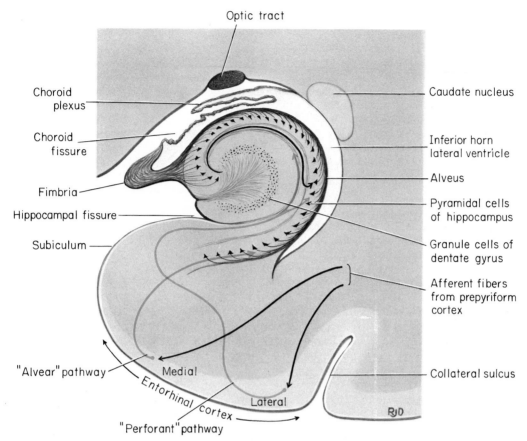

FIG. 21-11. Semischematic diagram of the hippocampal formation, dentate gyrus and entorhinal area. In the dentate gyrus only the granular layer is indicated. In the hippocampal formation only pyramidal cells and their axons projecting into the alveus are shown. Afferent fibers from prepyriform cortex projecting to the entorhinal cortex are shown in *black*. Projections of the entorhinal cortex to the hippocampal formation follow two pathways: (1) the lateral region gives rise to fibers which follow the so-called "perforant" pathway (*red*), and (2) the medial region gives rise to fibers which follow the so-called "alvear" pathway (*blue*). Axons of pyramidal cells in the hippocampal formation entering the alveus pass to the fimbria of the hippocampus. The dentate gyrus gives rise to fibers that project only to the hippocampal formation. (Based on Lorente de N6, '34, and a schematic diagram by Peele, '61.)

ons from the large pyramidal cells of the hippocampus, which spread over the ventricular surface as the *alveus* and then converge to form the *fimbria*. Proceeding backward, the fimbriae of the two sides increase in thickness. On reaching the posterior end of the hippocampus, they arch under the splenium of the corpus callosum as the *crura* of the fornix, at the same time converging toward each other. In this region a number of fibers pass to the opposite side, forming a thin sheet of crossing fibers, the *fornical commissure* (hippocampal commissure, or psalterium),

a structure rather poorly developed in man (Figs. 3–21 and 21–7). The two crura then join to form the *body of the fornix*, which runs forward under the corpus callosum to the rostral margin of the thalamus. Here the bundles separate again, and as the *anterior columns of the fornix*, arch ventrally in front of the interventricular foramina and caudal to the anterior commissure. The fimbriae, thin bands of fibers situated laterally, accompany the fornices throughout most of their extent (Figs. 21–6 and 21–7), but rostrally they become incorporated within the main bundles as the latter form the anterior columns of the fornix. Approximately half of the fibers descend caudal to the anterior commissure as the *postcommissural fornix* (Daitz and Powell, '54; Powell et al., '57). Remaining fibers of the fornix pass rostral to the anterior commissure as the *precommissural fornix*.

Fibers of the postcommissural fornix traverse the hypothalamus en route to the mammillary body, but in their course give off fibers to the thalamus. Fornix fibers passing directly to the mammillary body terminate mainly in the medial nucleus. Fibers leaving the postcommissural fornix in the rostral hypothalamus are distributed mainly to the anterior, and the rostral intralaminar thalamic nuclei (Guillery, '56; Nauta, '56; Valenstein and Nauta, '59). According to Powell et al. ('57), the anterior nuclei of the thalamus receive as many direct fibers from the fornix as from the mammillothalamic tract. Some postcommissural fornix fibers descend caudally beyond the mammillary bodies to enter the midbrain tegmentum (Guillery, '56; Nauta, '56, '58). Precommissural fornix fibers, constituting a less compact bundle than the postcommissural fibers, are distributed to the septal areas, the lateral preoptic area, the anterior part of the hypothalamus, and the nucleus of the diagonal band (Nauta, '56).

Recent studies (Raisman et al., '66) provide new data concerning the differential origin and distribution of hippocampal efferent fibers contained in the fornix and fimbria. *Postcommissural fornix fibers* arise from hippocampal sectors CA1 (anterior part) and CA2. Those from the anterior part of CA1 project via the fornix to terminate in the anterior thalamic nuclei and the medial and lateral mammillary nuclei. Sector CA2 distributes fibers via the fimbria to essentially the same nuclei. *Precommissural fornix* fibers arise from the posterior part of CA1 and from sectors CA3 and CA4. Fibers from sectors CA3 and CA4 are distributed via the fimbria, while those from sector CA1 (posterior part) pass via both the fornix and fimbria. These precommissural fibers terminate ipsilaterally in the medial septal nuclei,

and bilaterally in the lateral septal nuclei and the diagonal band nuclei. The dentate gyrus does not appear to have any extrahippocampal projection.

The above anatomical connections indicate the complex pathways by which impulses from the hippocampal formation can be projected to different parts of the neuraxis. Thus, both direct and indirect pathways connect the hippocampal formation with certain thalamic nuclei (i.e., the anterior and the intralaminar), the hypothalamus, and the midbrain reticular formation (Fig. 21-5). The anterior nucleus of the thalamus in turn projects to the cingulate gyrus, from which impulses can reach the hippocampus via the cingulum and the entorhinal cortex. One of many circuitous pathways involving the hippocampus is thus completed.

Functional Considerations. Although the hippocampal formation is a very large structure and considerable information is available concerning its anatomical connections, relatively little is known about its function. There appears to be abundant anatomical and physiological evidence that the hippocampus has no olfactory function (Brodal, '47). Comparative anatomists have long known that development of the hippocampus in mammals does not proceed parallel to the development of olfaction. The hippocampus and dentate gyrus are well developed in cetaceans that are said to be completely anosmatic, and lack olfactory bulbs and nerves (Addison, '15; Ries and Langworthy, '37). Animal experiments have shown that olfactory discrimination is not affected by ablations of the hippocampus (Swann, '34, '35), and that olfactory-conditioned reflexes persist after removal of the hippocampus (Allen, '40, '41).

Localized lesions in the hippocampus and local stimulation of this structure in conscious cats tend to produce similar phenomena (Green, '60). Behavioral changes observed in these animals resemble those occurring in psychomotor epilepsy, and it seems likely that the abnormal fears, hyperesthesia, and pupillary dilatation seen, may represent fragments of a complete seizure. The behavioral changes noted initially after lesions tend to disappear within several weeks, but recur at a later time. The hippocampus is recognized as having an exceedingly low threshold for seizure activity, and the afterdischarge is prolonged (Green and Shimamoto, '53; MacLean, '57, 57a; Green, '60). Seizure discharges spread from the hippocampus to other parts of the limbic lobe (see page 538) and ultimately to the neocortex.

There is considerable evidence indicating that the hippocampus may be concerned with recent memory (Green, '64). Relatively large bilateral lesions of the hippocampus (Bechterew, '00; Glees and Griffith, '52; Victor et al., '61) appear to be associated with profound impairment of memory for recent events and with relatively mild behavioral changes, such as persistent inactivity, indifference, and loss of initiative. Memory for remote events usually is unaffected. Although general intellectual functions may remain at a fairly high level, these patients demonstrate an inability to learn new facts and skills. These findings are in accord with those found after bilateral resection of the medial parts of the temporal lobe. According to Scoville and Milner ('57), lesions of the most anterior portion of the temporal lobe do not impair memory; impairment of memory occurs only when the lesions extend far enough posteriorly to involve the hippocampal formation, the dentate gyrus, and parts of the parahippocampal gyrus. It is generally felt that loss of memory occurs only if lesions of the hippocampal formation and parahippocampal gyrus are bilateral (Penfield and Milner, '58), but some patients may show mild verbal disorders or disturbances of memory following resections of parts of the temporal lobe of the dominant hemisphere. In these cases unsuspected lesions of the opposite hippocampus have been thought to be present. There is some evidence suggesting that in certain cases of senile dementia, characterized mainly by loss of memory, the most prominent lesions are found in the hippocampus. Experimental studies (Stepien et al., '60; Orbach et al., '60) in the monkey indicate that bilateral removals of the amygdaloid complex and portions of the hippocampus impair memory and learning that depend upon visual and auditory discriminations. Experiments in the rat (Kaada et al., '61) showed that bilateral lesions of the hippocampus, the fornix, and mammillary bodies result in severe disturbances of recent memory, as demonstrated by interference with maze learning and retention.

Even though the fornix contains most of the efferent fibers from the hippocampal formation, evidence that interruption of these fibers produces memory loss is meager. No discernible deficits of memory have been reported after section of both fornices in the monkey (Garcia-Bengochea et al., '51) or in man (Dott, '38; Akelaitis et al., '42; Akelaitis, '43). One human case reported by Sweet et al. ('59) showed severe and lasting memory loss, apathy, and lack of spontaneity following section of both columns of the fornix to facilitate removal of a third ventricular tumor. The mammillary bodies, like the fornix, would seem to be implicated in memory function, but it must be remembered that the entire projection of the fornix does not reach the mammillary bodies. According to Thompson and Hawkins ('61), bilateral lesions in the mammillary nuclei do not affect memory in the rat; but lesions in the lateral hypothalamic area or the caudal portion of the fasciculus retroflexus significantly impair memory. Korsakoff's psychosis, appearing as a sequel to Wernicke's encephalopathy and probably caused by a thiamine deficiency associated with alcoholism, is characterized by severe impairment of memory without clouding of consciousness. Lesions in this syndrome almost always involve the mammillary bodies and adjacent areas (Symonds, '66). However, it has been suggested that the amnesia of Korsakoff's syndrome is present only if there is additional involvement of the thalamus (Victor, '64).

Although it is not possible to further define the functions of the hippocampus, there are suggestions that it also may be concerned with: (1) emotional reactions or control of emotions, (2) certain visceral activities, and (3) regulation of reticular-activating influences upon the cerebral cortex (Green, '64). Particularly prominent among concepts relating the hippocampal formation to emotion is the theory proposed by Papez ('37), which attempts to provide an anatomical basis for emotion. Realizing that the term "emotion" denotes both subjective feelings and the expression of these feelings by appropriate autonomic and somatic responses, Papez concluded, as have others, that the cortex is essential for subjective emotional experience and that emotional expression must be dependent upon the integrative actions of the hypothalamus. He expressed the belief that the hippocampal formation and its principal projection system, the fornix, provide one of the main pathways by which impulses from the cortex reach the hypothalamus. Impulses reaching the hypothalamus could be projected caudally through the brain stem to effector structures, as well as rostrally to thalamic, and ultimately, cortical levels. The "central emotive process of cortical origin" was considered to be built up in the hippocampal formation, and transmitted to the mammillary bodies, the anterior nuclei of the thalamus, and the cingulate gyrus. He regarded the cingulate cortex as the receptive region for impulses concerned with emotion and suggested that radiation of impulses from the cingulate gyrus to other cortical regions added emotional coloring to the psychic process. This circuitous interrelation between cortex and diencephalon was thought to explain how emotional responses could result from either psychic or hypothalamic activity. Although this hypothesis has been criticized from several different viewpoints, it has served as a potent stimulus for further research and has drawn attention to the so-called limbic system.

LIMBIC SYSTEM

On the medial surface of the cerebral hemisphere, a large arcuate convolution formed primarily by the cingulate and parahippocampal gyri surrounds the rostral brain stem and interhemispheric commissures. These gyri, which encircle the

upper brain stem, constitute what Broca (1878) referred to as the *grand lobe limbique*. Specifically, *the limbic lobe* includes the subcallosal, cingulate, and parahippocampal gyri, as well as the underlying hippocampal formation and dentate gyrus (Fig. 21–12). From a phylogenetic and cytoarchitectural point of view, the limbic lobe consists of *archicortex* (hippocampal formation and dentate gyrus), *paleocortex* (pyriform cortex of the anterior parahippocampal gyrus), and *juxtallocortex* or *mesocortex* (cingulate gyrus). The latter represents a type of cortex that is transitional between allocortex and neocortex. Some authors (Kaada, '60) in addition have included the cortex of the posterior orbital surface of the frontal lobe, the anterior insular region, and the temporal polar region, because of cytoarchitectural and functional similarities. One of the striking features of the limbic lobe is the constancy of its gross and microscopic structure throughout phylogeny, compared with that of the expanding neopallium which surrounds it (MacLean, '54). Although the cortical areas designated as the limbic lobe have some common structural characteristics, the extent to which they form a functional unit is not understood.

An even more extensive and inclusive designation is the *limbic system*. This term is used to include all of the limbic lobe (Fig. 21–12) as well as associated subcortical nuclei (Fig. 21–4), such as the amygdaloid complex, septal nuclei, hypothalamus, epithalamus, anterior thalamic nuclei, and parts of the basal ganglia (MacLean, '52, '54). Nauta ('58) regards the medial tegmental region of the midbrain as part of the limbic system, since anatomical connections, both ascending and descending, relate this region to the hippocampal formation and the amygdaloid complex. The septal nuclei, the lateral preoptic region, and the hypothalamus (Fig. 19–14) appear to constitute a nodal area in the integration of the limbic system. The principal pathways interrelating the thalamic nuclei and the brain stem reticular formation with the hippocampus and amygdaloid complex appear

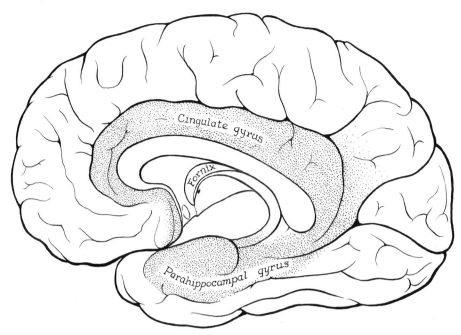

FIG. 21–12. Drawing of the medial surface of the hemisphere. *Shading* indicates the limbic lobe which encircles the upper brain stem. Although the cortical areas designated as the limbic lobe have some common structural characteristics, the extent to which they form a functional unit is not clear.

to come together in this region (Figs. 21–4 and 21–5).

The role of the cerebral cortex in the subjective aspects of emotion has been emphasized repeatedly, yet the neocortex appears to have relatively few hypothalamic connections and comparatively little autonomic representation. The intimate relationship of the limbic lobe with the hypothalamus, and the inclusion of these neural structures within the limbic system, have caused many authors to refer to the limbic system as the "visceral brain." Papez's proposed mechanism of emotion, which implicated structures of the limbic system, received experimental support from the studies of Klüver and Bucy ('39) on monkeys deprived of parts of both temporal lobes. Lesions in these animals destroyed the entire amygdaloid complex, large portions of the parahippocampal gyrus, the hippocampal formation, and the temporal neocortex. Following these extensive temporal lobe lesions, previously wild and intractable monkeys became docile and showed no evidence of fear or anger. These animals further displayed an apparent "psychic blindness;" a compulsion to examine objects visually, tactually, and orally; bizarre sexual behavior; and certain changes in dietary habits. They appeared unable to discriminate between food and potentially dangerous objects. Almost all objects were examined, smelled, and mouthed; if the object was not edible, it would be discarded. Animals appeared hypersexed and sought partnerships indiscriminately with male and female animals. Tendencies to explore objects orally and the docile behavior persisted for years in these animals (Klüver, '52). The above constellation of disturbances has become known as the *Klüver-Bucy syndrome*. It has been described in man following large bilateral removals of portions of the temporal lobes (Terzian and Ore, '55; Terzian, '58).

Further attempts to explore the relationships between specific symptoms and structures within the temporal lobe have yielded conflicting results. According to Bard and Mountcastle ('48), bilateral anterior temporal lobe ablations in the cat, similar to those described above, produce savage behavior and easily provoked rage reactions. These differences in behavior might be attributed to species differences, except for the fact that other investigators (Schreiner and Kling, '53; Brady et al., '54) have reported docile behavior in the cat following lesions of the amygdaloid complex and pyriform cortex. Perhaps the best explanation for these discrepancies is that the structures removed were not completely analogous in the different studies (Kaada, '60).

Bilateral lesions fairly well confined to the amygdaloid complex in monkeys and cats consistently produce disturbances of emotional behavior (Thomson and Walker, '51; Anand and Brobeck, '52; Poirier, '52; Pribram and Bagshaw, '53; Green et al., '57; Gloor, '60). The animals become placid and display no reactions of fear, rage, or aggression. Previously dominant and abusive animals became tame and did not retaliate to the threats or molestations of other animals. Hypersexuality has been noted as a prominent feature in some experimental studies (Schreiner and Kling, '54; Green et al., '57), but not in all. There are some indications that hypersexual behavior may occur only when the lesions concomitantly involve the pyriform cortex, since amygdaloid lesions sparing this region do not alter sexual behavior. In most instances hypersexual behavior following bilateral lesions develops after a latent period of several weeks. Castration will prevent hypersexuality, or cause it to disappear, following bilateral amygdalectomy (Schreiner and Kling, '54), but this should not necessarily be interpreted as indicating that an increased production of sex hormone is the basic cause of hypersexuality in these animals (Gloor, '60). Observations in man concerning the effects of bilateral lesions in the amygdaloid complex indicate that these lesions cause a decrease in aggressive and assaultive behavior (Green et al., '51; Pool, '54; Scoville, '54). Reports concerning stereotaxic lesions in the amygdaloid complex in man (Narabayashi et al., '63) suggest that such lesions produce a marked reduction in emotional excitability and tend to normalize social behavior and adaptation of in-dividuals with severe behavior disturbances. Unilateral lesions in some cases proved sufficient to bring about definite improvement. Bilateral lesions did not produce signs and symptoms suggestive of the Klüver-Bucy syndrome, and no disturbances of memory were observed.

Electrical stimulation of the amygdaloid complex in animals consistently produces a variety of visceral, somatic, behavioral, and endocrine changes (Kaada, '51; MacLean and Delgado, '53; Shealy and Peele, '57; Gloor, '60). Visceral and autonomic responses include alterations of respiratory rate, rhythm, and amplitude, as well as inhibition of respiration. Cardiovascular responses involve both increases and decreases in arterial blood pressure and occasionally alterations of heart rate. Gastrointestinal motility and secretion may be inhibited or activated, and both defecation and micturition may be induced. Piloerection, salivation, pupillary changes, and alterations of body temperature can occur. These responses are both sympathetic and parasympathetic in nature. Somatic responses obtained by stimulation of the amygdaloid complex include turning of the head and eyes to the opposite side, and complex rhythmic movements related to chewing, licking and swallowing. The most pronounced behavioral changes elicited in unanesthetized animals are reactions of attention, fear, and rage. Endocrine responses include the release of gonadotropic hormone and ACTH from the pituitary. In man stimulation of the amygdaloid complex frequently produces confusional states, disturbances of awareness, and amnesia for events taking place during the stimulation (Feindel and Penfield, '54). It is of special interest that the widely varied somatomotor and autonomic effects resulting from electrical stimulation of the amygdaloid complex constitute a relatively insignificant part of the syndrome produced by bilateral lesions in this complex.

Various visceral, somatic, and behavioral responses also are obtained by electrical stimulation of the anterior cingulate cortex and the orbital-insular-temporal cortex. Elevation, as well as depression, of arterial blood pressure results from electrical stimulation of these regions in experimental animals (Kaada et al., '49; Anand and Dua, '56; Kaada, '60). Points from which pressor and depressor effects can be obtained frequently are only a few millimeters apart; most authors report that declines in blood pressure are more frequent and of greater magnitude. Effects upon arterial pressure do not appear to be secondary to associated respiratory changes. Other autonomic responses obtained in experimental animals include inhibition of peristalsis in the pyloric antrum, pupillary dilatation, salivation, and bladder contraction. Perhaps the most striking effect of stimulating these regions is profound inhibition of respiratory movements (Smith, '45), which involves mainly the inspiratory phase of the respiratory cycle, occurs almost instantaneously, and cannot be held in abeyance for longer than 35 seconds. Acceleration of respiratory movements, produced most readily in the dog, can be elicited by stimulating portions of the cingulate gyrus posterior to the zone yielding maximum inhibitory effects (Kaada, '60).

Somatic effects obtained by stimulating the anterior cingulate and the orbital-insular-temporal cortex include: (1) inhibition of spontaneous movements, (2) inhibition and facilitation of cortically induced and reflex movements, and (3) chewing, licking, and swallowing movements. Inhibition of spontaneous movements is associated with muscular relaxation and inhibition of respiration. Cortically induced movements appear to be more readily facilitated than spinal reflexes. According to some authors (Showers and Crosby, '58; Showers, '59), a pattern of somatotopic movements obtained by stimulating the anterior cingulate region in the monkey can be elicited in reverse order in the posterior cingulate region; a double somatic representation is thus indicated in this area. These movements are obtained only under light anesthesia and can be induced after ablations of the motor areas.

The behavioral changes observed in un-anesthetized animals with stimulation of the cingulate gyrus, which are referred to as an "arrest reaction," consist of an immediate cessation of other activities, an expression of attention or surprise, and movements of the head and eyes to the opposite side (Kaada, '51, '60). Animals remain alert during stimulations and respond to external stimuli. Stimulation of posterior cingulate areas may induce sexual reactions, enhanced grooming, and seemingly pleasurable reactions (MacLean, '54, '58). Neither unilateral nor bilateral ablations of the cingulate cortex, or of the cortex of the orbital-insular-temporal polar region, appear to disturb basic somatomotor or autonomic functions to any marked degree. These ablations do not alter: (1) voluntary or reflex motor performance, (2) muscle tone, or (3) respiratory, cardiovascular, or gastrointestinal functions (Kaada, '60). Some observers have noted alterations of body temperature, piloerection, and increased sudomotor activity following lesions of the anterior and posterior cingulate cortex in the monkey (Showers and Crosby, '58).

Experiments have shown that electrical stimulation of certain parts of the limbic system via implanted electrodes in unanesthetized rats, cats, and monkeys produce apparently pleasurable effects (Olds and Milner, '54; Brady, '60). In these studies the experimental arrangement is such that the animals can deliver an electrical stimulus to localized areas of their own brains by pressing a pedal or bar. Self-stimulations of the septal region, the anterior preoptic area, and the posterior hypothalamus by bar pressing may be at rates as high as 5000 per hour in the rat (Olds, '60). The compulsive behavior seen in these situations, where the only reward is an electric shock to a localized region of the brain, suggests that the stimulus may provide a primary reinforcement for drives related to food or sex. Repeated self-stimulation may occur in the monkey from electrodes implanted in a variety of subcortical sites, such as the head of the caudate nucleus, the amygdaloid complex, the medial forebrain bundle, and the midbrain reticular formation (Brady, '60). Self-stimulation of certain regions of the thalamus and hypothalamus may produce unpleasant or avoidance reactions, but these regions appear relatively small in number compared to those from which some gratification appears to result.

It is apparent that the functions of the so-called limbic system are complex and multiple, that wide differences exist between the separate parts, and that the functions of the separate parts may be expressed through distinctive neural structures. Visceral functions appear to predominate in the amygdaloid complex, the anterior cingulate gyrus, and the cortex of the orbital-insular-temporal region. Amygdaloid efferent fibers contained in the stria terminalis and the ventral amygdalofugal pathways (see p. 499) projecting to the septal region, the preoptic region and portions of the hypothalamus probably mediate most of the responses produced by stimulation of the amygdaloid complex. However, it must be recalled that amygdalofugal fibers also project to the dorsomedial nucleus of the thalamus via the inferior thalamic peduncle and to specific cortical regions (Nauta, '61). Although the limbic system has been referred to as the "visceral brain," there are some parts of the system in which no visceral function has been demonstrated. Finally, numerous somatic functions appear to be intermingled inseparably with visceral functions.

CHAPTER 22

The Cerebral Cortex

STRUCTURE OF THE CORTEX

The early stages in the histogenesis of the pallium resemble those of other parts of the neural tube. During the first two months the wall of the pallium remains relatively thin and is composed of an ependymal, a mantle, and a marginal layer. At the end of the second month cells begin to wander from the mantle layer into the marginal zone, where they form a superficial gray layer, the *cerebral cortex*. As the cerebral cortex gradually thickens by the addition and differentiation of the migrating cells, it assumes a laminated appearance. The cells become organized into horizontal layers, and between the sixth and eighth months, six such layers may be distinguished (Brodmann, '09). This six-layered cellular arrangement is characteristic of the entire neopallial cortex, which is referred to as *neocortex, isocortex* (Vogt and Vogt, '19), or *homogenetic cortex* (Brodmann, '09). The *paleopallium* (olfactory cortex) and the *archipallium* (hippocampal formation and dentate gyrus) do not show six layers in either the developing or adult stage. Together the paleopallium and archipallium constitute the *allocortex* or *heterogenetic cortex*.

The cerebral cortex has an area of approximately 2,200 sq. cm. (2.5 sq. feet), but only about a third of this is found on the free surface; the remaining two-thirds are hidden in the depths of the sulci. The thickness of the cortex varies from about 4.5 mm in the precentral gyrus to about 1.5 mm in the depths of the calcarine sulcus. The cortex is always thickest over the crest of a convolution and thinnest in the depth of a sulcus. It has been estimated that besides nerve fibers, neuroglia, and blood vessels, the cerebral cortex contains nearly 14 billion neurons (Economo, '29).

The cerebral cortex contains: (1) terminals of afferent fibers from other parts of the nervous system (e.g., thalamocortical fibers), (2) association and commissural neurons whose axons interrelate cortical regions of the same or opposite hemisphere, and (3) projection neurons whose axons conduct impulses to other parts of the neuraxis (e.g., corticospinal, corticoreticular, or corticopontine fibers). Most projection fibers arise from the deeper layers of the cortex, while the association fibers come mainly, though not exclusively, from the more superficial ones. A striking feature of pallial structure is that the number of projection fibers is relatively small, compared with the enormous number of cortical neurons. The great majority of the cortical cells are concerned with associative functions.

Cortical Cells and Fibers. The principal types of cells found in the cortex are pyramidal, stellate, and fusiform neurons (Figs. 6–5, 22–1, and 22–2). The *pyramidal cells*, which are most characteristic of the cortex, have the form of a pyramid or isosceles triangle whose up-

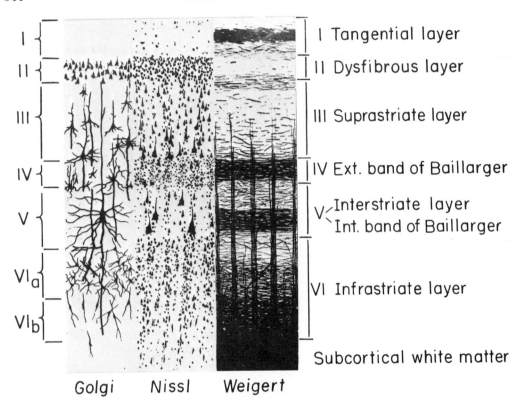

FIG. 22-1. The cell layers and fiber arrangement of the human cerebral cortex. Semischematic (after Brodmann, '09).

per pointed end is continued toward the surface of the brain as the *apical dendrite*. Besides the apical dendrite, a number of more or less horizontally running *basal dendrites* spring from the cell body and arborize in the vicinity of the cell. The axon emerges from the base of the cell and descends toward the medullary substance, either terminating in the deeper layers of the cortex, or entering the white matter as a projection, or association fibers. The pyramidal cells have a large vesicular nuclei and prominent Nissl granules. They usually are classified as small, medium, and large neurons. The height of the cell body varies from 10 or 12 micra for the smaller neurons to 45 or 50 micra for the larger ones. The giant pyramidal cells of Betz may be more than 100 micra in height. These cells are found in the motor area of the precentral gyrus.

The *stellate* or *granule cells* are, as a rule, small and have a polygonal or triangular shape. They have dark-staining nuclei and scanty cytoplasm, and vary in size from 4 to 8 micra. These cells have a number of dentrites passing in all directions and a short axon which ramifies close to the cell body (Golgi type II). Other larger stellate cells have longer axons which may enter the medullary substance. Some resemble pyramidal cells in that they have an apical dendrite which extends to the surface. These cells are known as *stellate pyramidal cells*, or *star pyramids* (Lorente de Nó, '49). Stellate cells are found throughout all layers of the cortex but are especially numerous in layer IV.

The *fusiform* or *spindle cells* are found mainly in the deepest layer, with their long axis usually vertical to the surface. The two poles of the cell are continued into dendrites; the lower dendrite arborizes within the layer, while the upper one ascends toward the surface, often reaching the superficial layer. The axon arises from the middle or lower part of

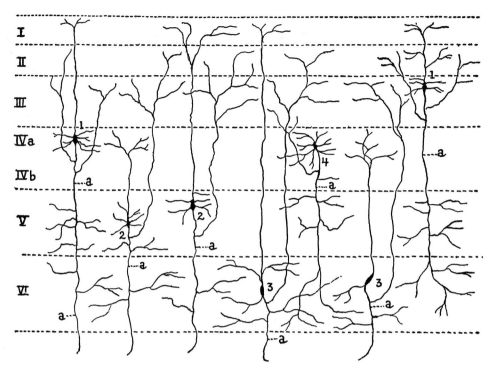

FIG. 22-2. The dendritic and axonal branchings of several types of cortical neurons with descending axons. Semischematic. *1*, Pyramidal cells of superficial layers; *2*, pyramidal cells from ganglionic layer; *3*, spindle cells; *4*, stellate cells; *a*, axon. Based on data by Cajal ('11) and Lorente de Nó ('49).

the cell body, and enters the white matter as a projection or association fiber.

Other cell types found in the cortex are the *horizontal cells of Cajal*, and the *cells with ascending axons*, known as the *cells of Martinotti* (M in Fig. 22-3). The former are small fusiform or pear-shaped cells found in the most superficial layer; their long axons run horizontally for considerable distances and arborize within that layer. Martinotti cells, present in practically all layers, are small triangular or polygonal cells whose axons are directed toward the surface and extend variable distances. Some arborize in the same layer; others send collaterals to a number of layers. It is evident from the above that projection and subcortical association fibers are continuations of descending axons from the pyramidal, fusiform, and larger stellate cells. Golgi (type II) granule cells, horizontal cells, and Martinotti cells are concerned entirely with intracortical connections.

Fibers in the cerebral cortex are dis-

posed both radially and tangentially. The former are arranged in delicate radiating bundles running vertically from the medullary substance toward the cortical surface (Fig. 22-1). They include the axons of pyramidal, fusiform, and stellate cells, which leave the cortex as projection or association fibers, and the entering afferent projection and association fibers, which terminate within the cortex. Ascending axons of the Martinotti cells likewise have a vertical course. The tangential fibers, running horizontal to the surface, are composed principally of the terminal branches of the afferent projection and association fibers, the axons of the horizontal and granule cells, and the terminal branches of collaterals from the pyramidal and fusiform cells. The horizontal fibers represent, in large part, the terminal portions of the radial fibers, which bend horizontally to come into synaptic relation with cortical cells. The tangential fibers are not distributed evenly throughout the thickness of the cortex but are concentrated at varying depths into horizontal bands, or plexuses, separated by layers with relatively few fibers (Fig. 22–1). The two most prominent bands are known as the *bands of Baillarger*, which are visible to the naked eye as delicate white stripes in sections of the fresh cortex.

The Cortical Layers. A striking feature of cortical structure is its lamination. In sections stained by the Nissl method, cell bodies are not uniformly distributed, but are arranged in superimposed horizontal layers. Each layer is distinguished by the types, density, and arrangements of its cells. In preparations stained for myelin, a similar lamination is visible; in this case it is determined primarily by the disposition of the horizontal fibers, which differ in amount and density for each cellular layer (Fig. 22–1). In the neopallial cortex or isocortex, which forms over 90% of the hemispheric surface, six fundamental layers are recognized (Brodmann, '09), and some of these are subdivided into two or more sublayers. Proceeding from the surface of the cortex toward the medullary substance these layers include: (I) the molecular layer, (II) the external granular layer, (III) the external pyramidal layer, (IV) the internal granular layer, (V) the internal pyramidal, or ganglionic layer, and (VI) the multiform layer.

I. The *molecular* or *plexiform layer* contains relatively few cells of two kinds: cells with horizontal axons and Golgi type II cells. Within it are found the terminal dendritic ramifications of the pyramidal and fusiform cells from the deeper layers, and the axonal endings of Martinotti cells. All these dendritic and axonal branches form a fairly dense tangential fiber plexus—hence the name plexiform layer.

II. The *external granular layer* consists of numerous closely packed small cells of triangular or pyramidal shape whose apical dendrites terminate in the molecular layer. Their axons descend to the deeper cortical layers, where many terminate, though some enter the white matter as association fibers. The layer

is rather poor in myelinated fibers; it contains the basal dendrites of its own cells and the terminals of axon collaterals from more deeply lying cells. The dendritic processes of pyramidal and fusiform cells pass through it to reach the molecular layer.

III. The *external pyramidal layer* is composed mainly of typical well-formed pyramidal neurons. Two sublayers are recognized: a superficial layer of medium-sized pyramids and a deeper layer of larger ones. Their apical dendrites go to the first layer, while most of their axons enter the white matter, chiefly as association or commissural fibers. Some axons may end within the cortex. Intermingled with the pyramidal neurons are many granule cells and Martinotti cells. In the most superficial part of the layer there are a greater number of horizontal myelinated fibers constituting the band of Kaes-Bechterew.

Lorente de Nó ('49) places the larger, deeper pyramids in layer IV, where they are designated as the sublayer of stellate pyramidal cells. According to him these cells, in addition to their numerous short dendrites, which give them a stellate appearance, possess apical dendrites which give off branches to layer IV and then ascend unbranched to the molecular layer.

IV. The *internal granular layer* is composed chiefly of closely packed stellate cells. Many of these are very small and have short axons ramifying within the layer. Other larger cells have descending axons which terminate in deeper layers, or may enter the white substance. The whole layer is permeated by a dense horizontal plexus of myelinated fibers, forming the external band of Baillarger (Fig. 22–1), considered to be mainly the terminal ramifications of thalamocortical fibers.

V. The *internal pyramidal* or *ganglionic layer* consists principally of medium-sized and large pyramidal neurons intermingled with granule and Martinotti cells. The apical dendrites of the larger pyramids ascend to the molecular layer; those of the smaller ones ascend only to layer IV, or may even arborize within the ganglionic layer (Figs. 22–2 and 22–3). The axons enter the white matter chiefly as projection fibers and, to a lesser extent, as association fibers. A considerable number of callosal fibers are furnished by the smaller pyramidal cells. The rich horizontal fiber plexus in the deeper portion of this layer constitutes the internal band of Baillarger.

VI. The *multiform layer* or *layer of fusiform cells* contains predominantly spindle-shaped cells whose long axes are perpendicular to the cortical surface. It also contains granule, Martinotti, and stellate cells. Like the pyramidal neurons of layer V, the spindle cells also vary in size; the larger ones send a dendrite into the molecular layer. The dendrites of the smaller ones ascend only to layer IV, or arborize within the fusiform layer itself. Thus the dendrites of many pyramidal and spindle cells from layers V and VI come in direct relation with the endings of sensory thalamocortical fibers, which ramify chiefly in the internal granular layer. Axons of the spindle cells enter the white substance, both as projection and association fibers. It is maintained that many of the short arcuate association fibers connecting adjacent convolutions are furnished by the deep stellate cells of layer VI (Lorente de Nó, '49). The multiform layer may be subdivided into an upper sublayer of more densely packed larger cells, and a lower one in which the smaller cells are loosely arranged. The whole layer is pervaded by fiber bundles which enter or leave the medullary substance (Fig. 22–3).

Besides the horizontal cellular lamination, the cortex also exhibits a vertical radial arrangement of the cells, which gives the appearance of slender vertical cell columns passing through the whole thickness of the cortex (Fig. 22–9). This vertical lamination, quite distinct in the parietal, occipital, and temporal lobes, is practically absent in the frontal lobe. The arrangement into vertical cell columns is produced by the radial fibers of the cortex, just as the horizontal lamination is largely determined by the distribution of the tangential fibers.

Many authorities believe that a distinction should be made between the *supragranular* and *infragranular layers* of the cortex. The former, which include layers II and III, are the latest to arise, the most highly differentiated, and the most extensive in man (Kaes, '07). The fibers which they receive or send out are chiefly associative in character; hence they are believed to be concerned mainly with cortical associative mnemonic functions. The infragranular layers, composed of layers V and VI, are well developed in other mammals, and are directly connected with subcortical structures by descending projection systems. It has been shown by Nissl that when the cortex of newborn rabbits is isolated from the rest of the nervous system, the infragranular layers fail to increase during subsequent development, while the growth of the supragranular cortex remains unaffected. The older layers appear to be concerned with the more fundamental cortical activities, which are primarily of a motor character. The internal granular layer, which intervenes between the supragranular and infragranular cortex, receives chiefly the afferent projection fibers. The supragranular layers are lacking in the archipallium and paleopallium.

The Interrelation of Cortical Neurons. The structure of the cerebral cortex as seen in Nissl or myelin sheath-stained sections is very incomplete, for these sections show only the type and arrangement of cell bodies, or the course and distribution of myelinated fibers. These methods give no information regarding terminal dendritic and axonal arborizations, which constitute the synaptic junctions through which nerve impulses are transmitted. An understanding of the neuronal relationships, and hence of the intracortical conduction circuits, can be obtained only by impregnation methods which give a total picture of the cell body and all its processes. By the use of such methods the distribution of the dendritic and axonal terminals has been worked out by a number of investigators, notably Cajal. Lorente de Nó has given a detailed account for the elementary pattern of cortical organization that is applicable for the parietal, temporal, and occipital isocortex. According to this investigator, the arrangement of the axonal and dendritic branchings forms the most constant feature of cortical structure. The following paragraphs are based largely on Lorente de Nó's ('49) account.

The afferent fibers to the cortex include projection fibers from the thalamus, association fibers from other cortical areas of the same side, and commissural fibers from the opposite side. The thalamocortical fibers, especially the specific afferent ones from the ventral tier thalamic nuclei and the geniculate bodies, pass unbranched to layer IV (Figs. 13–6, 13–12, 13–13, and 15–17). Here the axons form a dense terminal plexus; some of the fibers extend to layer III where they arborize (Fig. 22–3B). Fibers of the so-called nonspecific thalamocortical system, which is related to the ascending reticular activating system, presumably reach the cerebral cortex, though histological data concerning the origin, course, and termination of these afferent fibers are meager (Hanberry and Jasper, '53; Nauta and Whitlock, '54; Bowsher, '66). It is thought that these impulses may be mediated in the cerebral cortex by the nonspecific afferent fibers with diffuse connections described by Lorente de Nó ('49). According to Jasper ('60), the synaptic termination of fibers of this nonspecific system in the cortex is chiefly axodendritic and widely distributed in all layers, but the principal physiological effects appear to be within the superficial layers. Evidence favors the concept that recruiting waves recorded from the cerebral cortex may be a reflection of dendritic electrical activity, which implies that they are graded responses not dependent on the all-or-none firing of cortical cells (Clare and Bishop, '56; Purpura and Grundfest, '56). The association and callosal fibers, on the other hand, give off some collaterals to layers V and VI, and ramify mainly in layers II and III, and to a lesser extent in layer IV. The further course of the entering impulses naturally depends on the axonal branching of the cells which have synaptic relations with the afferent fibers.

The cortical neurons, with respect to the direction and extent of their fiber processes, may be grouped into cells with descending, ascending, horizontal, and short axons. The last three types serve wholly for intracortical connections (Fig. 22–3). The cells with descending axons (pyramidal, fusiform, and larger stellate cells) furnish all the efferent projection and association fibers, but in addition their axonal collaterals form an extensive system of intracortical connections. The descending axons which do not reach the medullary substance have only intracortical branches.

The pyramidal cells of layers II, III, and IV have a similar pattern of dendritic and axonal branchings (Fig. 22–2). They have a number of basilar dendrites which arborize in the same layer, and an apical dendrite which ends in the molecular layer. Their descending axons in part terminate in the deeper layers of the cortex, and, in part, are continued as association or callosal fibers. During their descent they give off a few recurrent collaterals to their own layers, chiefly II and III, and numerous horizontal collaterals to V and VI, where they contribute to the horizontal plexuses. Thus, these axonal ramifications chiefly connect layers II and III with V and VI.

The pyramidal and fusiform cells of layers V and VI have a very characteristic pattern of dendritic and axonal branchings. All the pyramidal cells of layer V give off basilar dendrites to their own layer and an apical dendrite which, in most cases, extends to the molecular layer. There are, however, medium-sized pyramidal neurons, whose apical dendrites terminate in layer IV, and short pyramidal cells, whose dendrites all ramify in layer V (Fig. 22–2). The spindle cells of layer VI have similar branches; ascending dendritic shafts terminate respectively in layers I and IV, while other dendrites arborize in layer VI. The dendritic terminals of the medium pyramidal and spindle cells thus come into direct contact with the endings of specific afferent fibers in layer IV. The axons of pyramidal and spindle neurons, and those of many deep stellate cells, are continued as projection, association, or callosal fibers, and they have collateral branchings of a definite character. All these axons send horizontal collaterals to layers V and VI, where they contribute to the horizontal plexuses, especially those of layer V (internal band of Baillarger). Many have, in addition, one or more recurrent collaterals which ascend unbranched through layer IV and arborize in layers II and III; some even extend to the molecular layer (Fig. 22–2). The horizontal plexuses of layers III and II are formed in part by these recurrent collaterals. Thus impulses reaching efferent cells of the deeper layers may spread horizontally within these layers, or they may return by the recurrent collaterals to the superficial layers, especially II and III.

Added to this extensive system of intracortical connections furnished by the cells with descending axons are the more intricate arborizations of the cells with short, ascending, or horizontal axons. These small cells, which are less numerous in lower mammals, have become tremendously increased in man. They are small stellate cells with numerous short dendrites whose axons break up into dense terminal arborizations close to the cell body. Synaptically, their short axons are related to the bodies of many pyramidal cells with descending axons. The cell and all its processes are confined to one layer, though the axon may extend horizontally for a short distance before ramifying. The short axon cells (Golgi type II) are most concentrated in layer IV, but are found in large numbers in all the layers. The cells with horizontal axons are found chiefly in the molecular layer; their long axons often run for considerable distances and make contact with the dendritic terminals of many pyramidal and fusiform cells (Fig. 22–3). The cells of Martinotti also are present in every layer except the most superficial one. Their dendrites usually are confined to a single layer, and their ascending axons vary in length and distribution. Some Martinotti cells from layers V and VI arborize chiefly in layers III and II. Others extend to the surface and may send collaterals to all the layers through which they pass. Thus while the horizontal and short axon cells have intralaminar connections, the Martinotti cells interconnect the various lamina. Through these cortical circuits nerve impulses reaching the cells of the deeper layers can be returned again and again to the more superficial ones.

From the arrangement of the cell processes described above, it is evident that any vertical strip of cortex may be regarded as an elementary functional unit in which all the necessary elements (afferent, internuncial, and efferent) for the formation of complete cortical circuits are present. The simplest vertical unit, theoretically, would involve a single synapse, such as the synaptic junction of an afferent fiber with the apical dendrite of a pyramidal cell (Fig. 22–3). Superimposed upon this fundamental cortical arc are vertical chains of varying complexity that involve progressively larger numbers of synapses. The character of the axonal branchings indicates that in such complex circuits, entering impulses are repeatedly switched from superficial to deeper layers, and vice versa. The impulses may return again and again to the same cells before ultimately leaving the cortex through efferent fibers. These vertical chains are interconnected by short neuronal links, represented primarily by the short axon granule cells whose processes arborize within a single layer. Through these short links, cortical excitation may spread horizontally and involve a progressively larger number of vertical units (Fig. 22–3). Thus a specific afferent fiber may not only fire vertical columns of cells in its immediate vicinity, but may reach more distant units through Golgi type II cell relays. These vertical units are fundamentally similar in all mammals. However, the columns of cells with short relays increase in complexity in the higher forms, especially man, whose cortex contains enormous numbers of short axon cells. According to Cajal, the intricacy and delicacy of functioning of the human brain is expressed anatomically by the large number of its small cells.

CORTICAL AREAS

The cerebral cortex does not have a uniform structure throughout. It has been

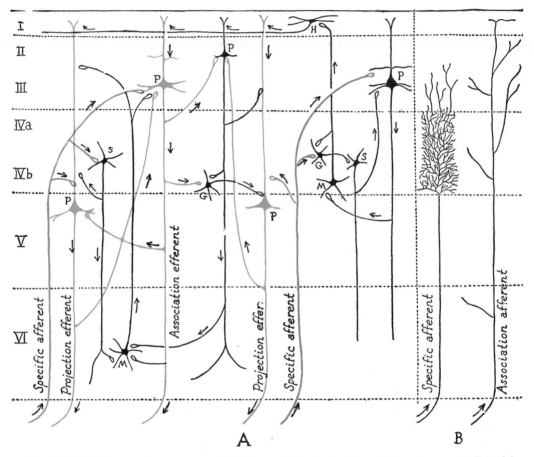

FIG. 22–3. *A*, Diagram showing some of the intracortical circuits. Synaptic junctions are indicated by *loops*. *Red*, Afferent thalamocortical fibers; *blue*, efferent cortical neurons; *black*, intracortical neurons; *G*, granule cell; *H*, horizontal cell; *M*, Martinotti cell; *P*, pyramidal cell; *S*, stellate cell; *B*, mode of termination of afferent cortical fibers. Based on data by Lorente de Nó ('49).

mapped and divided into a number of distinctive areas that differ from each other in total thickness, in the thickness and density of individual layers, and in the arrangement and number of cells and fibers. In certain areas the structural variations are so extreme that the basic six-layered pattern is practically obscured. Such areas are termed *Heterotypical*, as opposed to *homotypical*, which describes cortex in which the six layers are easily distinguished (Brodmann, '09). Histological surveys based on differences in the arrangement and types of the cells, and in the pattern of the myelinated fibers have furnished several fundamentally similar cortical maps, in which the number of distinctive areas has been estimated vari-

ously. Campbell ('05) described some 20 cortical fields; Brodmann ('09) increased the number to 47, and Economo ('29) to 109; the Vogts ('19) parcelled the human cerebral cortex into more than 200 areas. Even the last number is apparently insufficient, since other investigators have found a number of distinctive cytoarchitectural fields in regions previously considered homogeneous (Beck, '29; Rose, '35). Brodmann's chart, which is the most widely used for reference, is shown in Figure 22–4. This cytoarchitectural map of the human cortex can be compared with the lateral view of the brain shown in Figure 22–5.

According to Economo ('29), all cortical structure is reducible to five fundamental

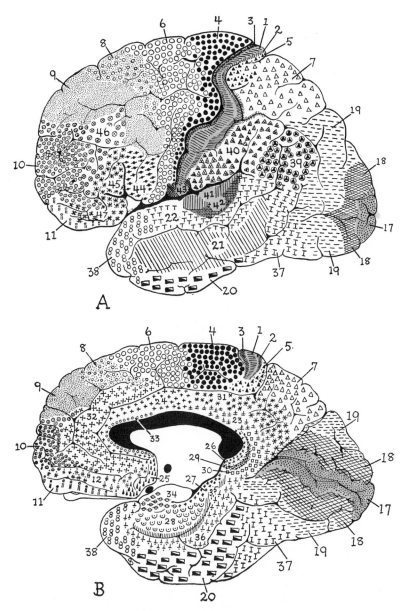

FIG. 22-4. Cytoarchitectural map of human cortex. *A,* Convex surface; *B,* medial surface (after Brodmann, '09).

types, based primarily on the relative development of granule and pyramidal cells. Types 2, 3, and 4, known respectively as the frontal, parietal, and polar types, are homotypical and constitute by far the largest part of the cortex. Types 1 (agranular) and 5 (granulous) are heterotypical and limited to smaller specialized regions (Figs. 22–6 and 22–7).

Agranular type cortex (type 1) is distinguished by its thickness and the virtual absence of granule cells (Figs. 22–6 and 22–8, *A and B*). Pyramidal cells of layers III and V are well developed and large. Even the smaller cells in layers II and IV are predominantly pyramidal-shaped, making it difficult to distinguish individual layers. The agranular type cortex is

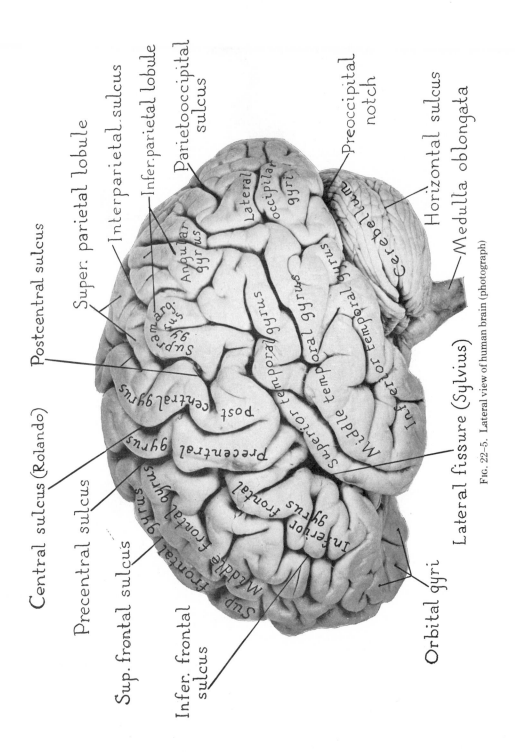

FIG. 22–5. Lateral view of human brain (photograph)

Central sulcus (Rolando)

Precentral sulcus

Sup. frontal sulcus

Infer. frontal sulcus

Orbital gyri

Lateral fissure (Sylvius)

Medulla oblongata

Horizontal sulcus

Preoccipital notch

Parietooccipital sulcus

Infer. parietal lobule

Interparietal sulcus

Super. parietal lobule

Postcentral sulcus

Angular gyrus

Lateral occipital gyri

Cerebellum

Inferior temporal gyrus

Middle temporal gyrus

Superior temporal gyrus

Supramarginal gyrus

Post central gyrus

Precentral gyrus

Inferior frontal gyrus

Middle frontal gyrus

Sup. frontal gyrus

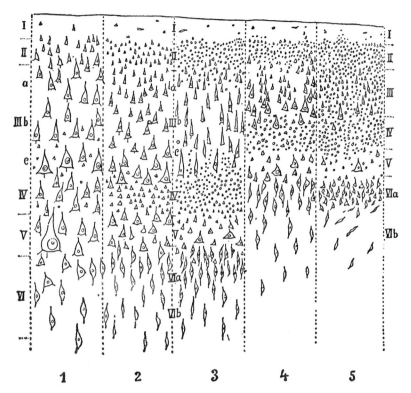

FIG. 22-6. The five fundamental types of cortical structure. *1*, Agranular; *2*, frontal; *3*, parietal; *4*, polar; *5*, granulous (koniocortex) (Economo, '29).

represented classically by the cortex of the precentral gyrus.

Frontal type cortex (type 2) is relatively thick and shows six distinct layers. Pyramidal cells of layers III and V are large and well developed, as are the spindle cells of layer VI (Fig. 22-6). Although the granular layers are distinct, they are narrow and composed primarily of loosely arranged small triangular cells.

Parietal type cortex (type 3) is characterized by even more distinctive cortical layers due to the greater thickness and cell density of the granular layers (Figs. 22-6 and 22-9, *A* and *B*). In this type of cortex, the pyramidal layers are thinner and their cells are smaller and more irregularly arranged.

Polar type cortex (type 4), found near the frontal and occipital poles, is characterized by its thinness, its well developed granular layers, and its comparative wealth of cells. Near the frontal pole pyramidal cells may be seen in layers III and V, but in occipital areas pyramidal cells are smaller and less numerous.

Granulous type cortex or *koniocortex* (type 5) is extremely thin cortex composed mainly of densely packed granule cells (Figs. 22-6 and 22-9C). These are found not only in layers II and IV, but the other layers, especially layer III, show large numbers of such small cells and a consequent reduction of the pyramidal cells. The most striking example of this type is the calcarine cortex, in which there is even a duplication of the internal granular layer (Fig. 22-9C).

The general distribution of these five types of cortex is shown in Figure 22-7. The agranular type cortex covers the caudal part of the frontal lobe in front of the central sulcus, the anterior half of the gyrus cinguli, and the anterior portion of the insula. A narrow strip is found also in the retrosplenial region of the gyrus cinguli and is continued along the parahippocampal gyrus and uncus. Since the chief effer-

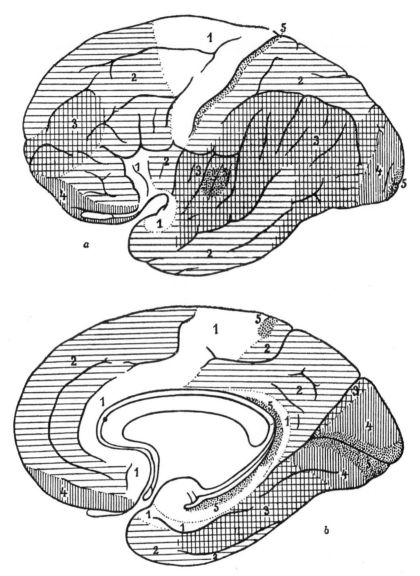

Fig. 22-7. Distribution of the five fundamental types of cortex over the convex (a) and the medial (b) surfaces of the hemisphere. 1, Agranular; 2, frontal; 3, parietal; 4, polar; 5, granulous (korniocortex) (Economo, '29).

ent fiber systems arise from these regions, especially from the precentral gyrus, the agranular cortex may be considered as efferent or motor type cortex (Figs. 13–16 and 14–23). Similarly the koniocortex may be regarded as primarily sensory in character, since it is found only in the areas receiving the specific sensory thalamo-cortical projections. These areas include the anterior wall of the postcentral gyrus, the walls and lips of the calcarine sul-

cus, and the transverse temporal gyrus (Heschl). Again there is a narrow strip of koniocortex in the retrosplenial region and along the dorsal wall of the hippocampal fissure.

By far the largest part of the hemispheric surface is covered by homotypical cortex. Frontal type cortex is spread over the larger anterior part of the frontal lobe, the superior parietal lobule, the precuneus, and most of the middle and inferior temporal gyri. Parietal type cortex includes chiefly the inferior parietal lobule, the superior temporal gyrus, the occipito-temporal gyrus, and the anterior convex parts of the occipital lobe. Polar type cortex, as already stated, covers the areas near the frontal and occipital poles. The thalamic connections of these areas are mainly with the association nuclei such as the dorsomedial, lateral dorsal, lateral posterior, and the pulvinar.

Practically every part of the cerebral cortex is connected with subcortical centers by afferent and efferent projection fibers. Strictly speaking there are no circumscribed cortical areas which are purely associative or projective in character. In a general way, however, there are regions from which the more important descending tracts arise. Directly or through intercalated centers, these tracts reach the lower motor neurons for the initiation and control of both somatic and visceral activities (Penfield and Jasper, '54). These primarily efferent or motor areas, from which muscular movements can be elicited by electrical stimulation, are concentrated chiefly in the precentral part of the frontal lobe, but they also are found to a lesser extent in the cortex of other lobes. Similarly those specific cortical regions which receive direct thalamocortical sensory fibers from the ventral tier thalamic nuclei and from the geniculate bodies represent the primary receptive or sensory areas. The remaining cortical areas which constitute the largest part of the cerebral cortex are referred to as "association areas." Afferent fibers to the association areas are derived from association nuclei of the thalamus and from primary sensory areas of the cortex.

SENSORY AREAS OF THE CEREBRAL CORTEX

Primary Sensory Areas. The localized regions to which impulses concerned with specific sensory modalities are projected are the primary sensory areas of the cerebral cortex. Although certain aspects of sensation probably enter consciousness at thalamic levels, the primary sensory areas are concerned especially with the integration of sensory experience and with the discriminative qualities of sensation. With the exception of olfaction, impulses involved in all forms of sensation reach localized areas of the cerebral cortex via thalamocortical projection systems. The organization of the thalamus is such that all of the specific sensory relay nuclei are located caudally in the ventral tier (see p. 482 and Figs. 19-4 and 19-5). The cortical projections of the specific sensory relay nuclei are to localized areas of the parietal, occipital, and temporal lobes. Although there is probably a primary cortical receptive area for each sensory modality, each modality is not represented separately, and the primary sensory areas for some forms of sensation are poorly defined. Established primary sensory areas in the cerebral cortex are: (1) *the somesthetic area*, consisting of the postcentral gyrus and its medial extension in the paracentral lobule (areas 3, 1, and 2), (2) *the visual* or *striate area*, located along the lips of the calcarine sulcus (area 17), and (3) *the auditory area*, located on the two transverse gyri (Heschl; areas 41 and 42; see Fig. 21-4). The *gustatory area* appears to be localized to the most ventral part (opercular) of the postcentral gyrus (area 43). The primary *olfactory area* consists of the allocortex of the prepyriform and periamygdaloid regions and is not assigned numbers under the Brodmann parcellation. A vestibular projection to the human cerebral cortex has not been established, but it seems likely that vestibular impulses from the thalamus may project to portions of the temporal lobe (Penfield and Rasmussen, '50). Woolsey ('58) suggests that in lower forms the primary motor and sensory areas of the cortex are relatively large compared with the association cortex, while in higher forms this situation appears reversed.

Neurophysiological studies (Mountcastle, '57; Powell and Mountcastle, '59a) of the somatic sensory cortex indicate that a vertical column of cells extending across all cellular layers constitutes the elementary functional cortical unit. This thesis is supported by the following observations: (1) neurons of a particular vertical column

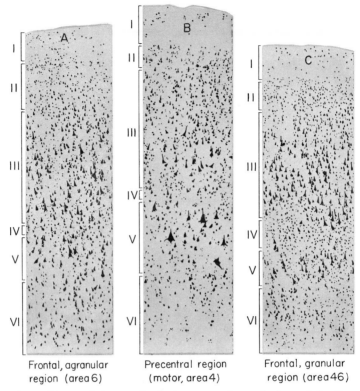

Frontal, agranular
region (area 6)

Precentral region
(motor, area 4)

Frontal, granular
region (area 46)

Fɪɢ. 22-8. Cytoarchitectural pictures of several representative cortical areas (after Campbell, '05)

all are related to the same, or nearly the same, peripheral receptive field, (2) neurons of the same vertical column are activated, as a rule, by the same peripheral stimulus, and (3) all cells of such a vertical column discharge at more or less the same latency following a brief peripheral stimulus. These observations indicate that the topographical pattern present on the cortical surface extends throughout its depth. Physiological studies (Hubel and Wiesel, '62, '63) of the striate (visual) cortex also demonstrate that discrete columns of cells extending from the surface to the white matter are responsive to restricted retinal stimulation in the form of long narrow rectangles of light ("slits"), dark bars against a light background, or straight-line borders that have a particular orientation. Microelectrode recordings indicate that the columns of cells are radially arranged and perpendicular to the cortical layers, but show variations in size and cross-sectional shape. Maps of the striate cortex indicate that receptive field orientation varies in a continuous manner as the surface of the cortex is traversed. Although this concept of a vertical columnar organization is supported both anatomically and physiologically, it does not imply that these vertical cell columns are isolated functional units (see page 349).

Secondary Sensory Areas. The primary sensory areas of the cerebral cortex undoubtedly receive the principal projections of the specific sensory relay nuclei of the thalamus, and are the focal regions in the cerebral cortex where specific sensory modalities are most extensively and critically represented. Evidence suggests that near each primary receptive area there are cortical zones which also receive sensory inputs directly, or indirectly, from the thalamus. These cortical zones, adjacent to primary sensory areas, but outside of the principal projection area of the specific sensory relay nuclei of the thalamus, are referred to as the *secondary sensory areas*. These areas have been defined and mapped in experimental animals by re-

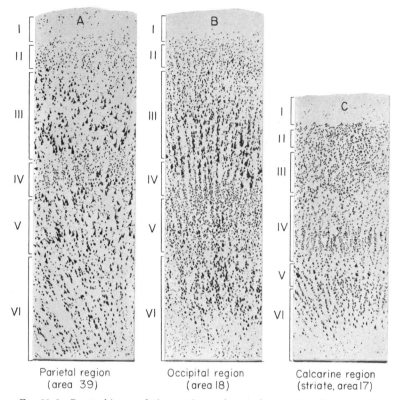

I

II

III

IV

V

VI

Parietal region
(area 39)

I

II

III

IV

V

VI

Occipital region
(area 18)

I

II

III

IV

V

VI

Calcarine region
(striate, area 17)

FIG. 22–9. Cytoarchitectural picture of several cortical areas (after Campbell. '05)

cording evoked potentials in response to peripheral stimulation (Adrian, '40, '41; Woolsey and Walzl, '42; Woolsey and Fairman, '46; Thompson et al., '50). Studies of these secondary sensory areas indicate that sequential representation of parts of the body, or of the tonotopic pattern in the case of the auditory areas, is not the same as in the primary areas (Woolsey, '58; Rose and Woolsey, '58). The secondary sensory areas are smaller than the primary sensory areas, and the order of representation is the reverse of that found in the primary areas. Removals of the primary somesthetic area do not abolish potentials evoked in the secondary somatic sensory area (Woolsey and Wang, '45; Buser and Borenstein, '56). Evidence suggests that ablations of secondary sensory areas produce relatively minor sensory disturbances compared with those resulting from ablations of primary sensory areas. In the monkey ablations of the secondary somatic area do not appear to interfere with the performance tests based upon somesthetic

discrimination (Orbach and Chow, '59). Secondary sensory areas, which have been defined primarily in experimental animals, include: (1) a secondary somatic sensory area (somatic area II), located ventral to the primary sensory and motor areas along the superior lip of the lateral sulcus, (2) a secondary auditory area (auditory area II), located ventral to the primary auditory area (auditory area I) in the cat (Rose and Woolsey, '58; Ades, '59), and (3) a secondary visual area (visual area II), described in the rabbit, cat, and monkey (Talbot and Marshall, '41; Woolsey, '47; Thompson et al., '50; Hubel and Wiesel, '65) as anterolateral to visual area I, and identical to the area defined anatomically as area 18. A secondary somatic sensory area has been demonstrated in man (Penfield and Rasmussen, '50), stimulation of which produces various sensations in the upper and lower extremities. Representation of the extremities is chiefly contralateral, though ipsilateral representation also is present. In man no cortical representation for the face, tongue, mouth, or throat has been found in somatic area II. Because of the intimate functional relationships between the primary and secondary sensory areas, these will be discussed together for the various forms of sensation.

The primary somesthetic area, subserving general somatic sensibility, superficial as well as deep, is located in the postcentral gyrus and in the posterior part of the paracentral lobule. Histologically the gyrus is composed of three narrow strips of cortex (areas 3, 1, 2) which differ in their architectural structure (Fig. 22–4). In the postcentral region there is a definite antero-posterior gradient of morphological change, but the gradient is not uniformly gradual. The anterior part, area 3, is clearly distinguishable from the posterior part; areas 1 and 2 show more gradual morphological changes. Area 3, for the most part, lies along the posterior wall of the central sulcus; its transition with area 4 anteriorly is not sharp and it lies in the posterior part of the depth of the central sulcus. The cortex of area 3 is characterized by its thinness and by the fact that layers II, III and IV tend to fuse or blend with each other (Powell and Mountcastle, '59). Cell layers II, III and IV are composed of densely packed granulous cells (Economo, '29). Areas 1 and 2, forming respectively the crown and posterior wall of the postcentral gyrus, have a six-layered structure characteristic of homogenetic cortex. The most marked differences between area 3 and area 1 are found in layer III; cells in layer III all become pyramidal in shape and there is a reduction in cell density. The transition from area 1 to area 2 is not sharply defined, but is characterized by an increase in the thickness of the cortex and an increase in the number of large pyramidal cells in layers III and V. The transition from area 2 to areas 5 and 7 is gradual; in the latter areas layers II and IV are sharply demarcated and a pronounced columnar arrangement of cells is seen.

The postcentral gyrus receives the thalamic projections from the ventral posterior nuclei, which relay impulses from the medial lemniscus, the spinothalamic

tracts, and the secondary trigeminal tracts. Experimental studies (Clark and Powell, '53) in the monkey indicate that areas 3, 1, and 2 receive the specific cortical projection from the ventral posterolateral and ventral posteromedial nuclei. The majority of the cells of the ventral posterior nuclei project to area 3. Area 1, however, receives the exclusive projections of only about 30 per cent of the cells in these nuclei, but it also receives collaterals of fibers passing to area 3. Most of the fibers projecting to area 2 appear to be collaterals of fibers passing primarily to areas 3 and 1. The various regions of the body are represented in specific portions of the postcentral gyrus, the pattern corresponding to that of the motor area (Fig. 22–10). Thus the face area lies in the most ventral part, while above it are the sensory areas for the hand, arm, trunk, leg, and foot in the order named; the lower extremity extends into the paracentral lobule. The cortical areas representing the hand, face, and mouth regions are disproportionally large. The digits of the hand, particularly the thumb and index finger, are well represented. The cortical area related to sensations from the face occupies almost the entire lower half of the postcentral gyrus; the upper part of the face is represented above, while the lips and mouth are represented below. The tongue and pharyngeal region are localized in more ventral areas. According to Penfield, sensations from intra-abdominal structures are represented near the opercular surface of the postcentral gyrus. Most of our information concerning the pattern of representation in the somesthetic cortex has been obtained from stimulating this region in patients operated upon under local anesthesia (Penfield and Boldrey, '37; Penfield and Rasmussen, '50; Penfield and Jasper, '54). In attempts to present a readily apparent visual pattern of the sequence of sensory representation in the cerebral cortex, Penfield has drawn a "sensory homunculus" relating different parts of the body to appropriate areas of the cortex. The "sensory homunculus" corresponds to the "motor homunculus" (Fig. 22–10).

Using the evoked potential technic,

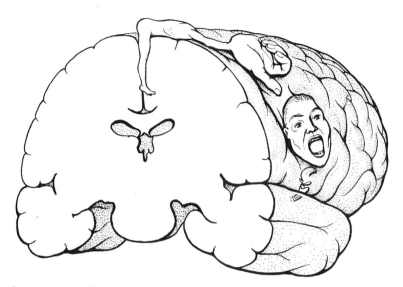

FIG. 22-10. Somatotopic localization of parts of the body in the motor cortex. Parts of the body are drawn in proportion to the extent of their cortical representation. The resulting disproportionate figure is called the motor "homunculus." A similar pattern of localization with respect to somesthetic sense is found in the postcentral gyrus (after Penfield and Rasmussen, '50).

Adrian ('41) found that touch, pressure, and movements were the only stimuli which evoked well-marked responses in the contralateral postcentral gyrus in the cat. No responses were observed to pain or thermal stimuli. Pressure applied to a foot produced a sustained discharge which increased in frequency as the pressure was increased and gradually declined with a constant stimulus. Tactile stimuli produced brief discharges that were not sustained. The fact that one cortical locus frequently could be activated by touching hairs within a relatively large skin area indicates a considerable degree of convergence at a cortical level. This convergence of pathways in the sensory cortex was observed also by Marshall et al., ('41). These authors found that one cortical point could be activated maximally, and also submaximally, from a considerable area of skin. It would appear that a restricted stimulus can activate a number of afferent units projecting to the cortex and that slight differences in latency may be due to spread of excitation among thalamic neurons. Cortical responses were evoked contralaterally from all stimuli, except in the face area, where some ipsilateral responses were recorded.

Physiological studies (Powell and Mountcastle, '59a; Mountcastle and Powell, '59) in the monkey indicate that the majority of neurons in the postcentral gyrus are activated by mechanical stimulation, and are selectively excited by stimulation of receptors within either skin or deep tissues, but not by stimulation of both. Over 90 percent of the neurons in area 2 are related to receptors in deep tissues of the body, while the majority of neurons in area 3 are activated only by cutaneous stimuli; different neurons in area 1 are related to either cutaneous or deep receptors. This differential representation of sensory modalities appears closely correlated with the gradient of morphological change that characterizes these three cytoarchitectural areas. Further evidence (Mountcastle and Powell, '59a) indicates that afferent impulses from receptors in joint capsules and pericapsular tissues, stimulated by joint movement, are conveyed by the posterior columns, the medial lemniscus, and thalamic relay neurons to particular cell columns in the postcentral gyrus. Impulses conveyed by this system subserve position sense and kinesthesis. Stretch receptors in muscle and tendons do not provide information useful in the perception of joint position; further most of the afferent impulses from stretch receptors are projected to the cerebellum (Oscarsson, '65). Studies of cell columns of the postcentral gyrus responsive to cutaneous stimuli (Mountcastle and Powell, '59a) indicate that receptive fields on the body surface are constant. The size and position of the receptive fields are not changed by variations in the depth of anesthesia. Further, there is no evidence that the position of the stimulus within the receptive field is coded in terms of the temporal characteristics of the response. The majority of cortical neurons driven by cutaneous stimuli adapt quickly to steady stimuli. The above observations pertain only to the somatic afferent system composed of primary dorsal root afferents in the posterior columns, lemniscal fibers arising from the posterior column nuclei, and thalamocortical fibers arising from the ventral posterolateral nucleus. This is a system of great synaptic security, poised for action at high frequency levels, and possessing the neural attributes required for discriminatory functions.

Although fibers of the spinothalamic tract project to the ventral posterolateral nucleus of the thalamus, fibers of this system also project bilaterally upon posterior portions of the thalamus near the magnocellular part of the medial geniculate body (Mehler et al., '60; Bowsher, '61; Whitlock and Perl, '61). Cells of this posterior thalamic region differ from those of the ventral posterior nuclear complex in that they are not place or modality specific. These cells have large receptive fields, frequently bilateral, and the majority of cells respond to noxious stimuli (Poggio and Mountcastle, '60). Experimental evidence (Knighton, '50; Mehler, '66a) indicates that cells in this posterior thalamic region project to the secondary somatic sensory area (somatic area II). However, cortical cells with properties similar to those of the posterior thalamic region probably are not confined to somatic area II. Mountcastle and Powell ('59a) observed a small percentage of cells in the postcentral gyrus of the monkey which responded only to noxious stimuli and were related to wide receptive fields.

Stimulation of the postcentral gyrus in man produces sensations described by the patient as numbness, tingling, or a feeling of electricity. Occasionally the patient may report a sensation of movement in a particular part of the body, though no actual movement is observed. A sensation of pain is rarely produced by these stimulations. Sensations described are referred to contralateral parts of the body, except in response to stimulations of the face area. Evidence suggests that the face and tongue may be represented bilaterally. It is of interest that essentially the same sensations can be elicited by stimulating the precentral gyrus. According to Penfield and Rasmussen ('50), 25 per cent of the locations giving sensory responses are in the precentral gyrus, but the ratio of sensory responses obtained from the postcentral gyrus to those from the precentral gyrus varies in different parts of the sensory sequence. Sensation referable to the eyes is obtained, almost exclusively, by stimulating the precentral gyrus, while sensation in the lips is associated almost invariably with stimulations of the postcentral gyrus. Sensory responses are reported only rarely with stimulations at points greater than 1 cm. from the central sulcus. That stimulation of the precentral gyrus still produces sensory responses after removal of the postcentral gyrus indicates that these responses are not dependent upon the postcentral gyrus or collateral fibers to it. Even though sensation can be produced by stimulating the precentral gyrus, ablation of it produces no clinically detectable sensory deficits.

There are other observations which suggest that the somesthetic cortical area is not limited to the postcentral gyrus, but may include portions of the superior and inferior parietal lobules. The clinical observations of Foerster ('36) indicate that destructive processes in the superior parietal lobule are followed by sensory disturbances similar to those associated with lesions of the postcentral gyrus. Other authors (Penfield and Rasmussen, '50) report no detectable somatic sensory deficits following cortical removals of large parts of the superior and inferior lobules in the nondominant hemisphere, though their patient tended to ignore the contralateral hand and had difficulty performing complex maneuvers with it.

Available evidence indicates that position sense and kinesthesis are represented only contralaterally. Whether the discriminative aspects of tactile sensibility are represented bilaterally in the human cortex is not known definitely. Clinically the sensory deficits caused by lesions in the postcentral gyrus are detectable only on the opposite side.

The sensory cortex is not concerned primarily with the recognition of crude sensory modalities, such as pain, thermal sense, and mere contact. These apparently enter consciousness at the level of the thalamus, and their appreciation is retained even after complete destruction of the sensory area. "The sensory activity of the cortex... endows sensation with three discriminative faculties. These are: (1) recognition of spatial relations, (2) a graduated response to stimuli of different intensity, (3) appreciation of similarity and difference in external objects brought into contact with the surface of the body" (Head, '20). Hence in lesions of the primary somesthetic area there is loss of appreciation of passive movement, of two point discrimination, and of ability to differentiate various intensities of stimuli. In severe lesions the patient, though aware of the stimulus and its sensory modality, is unable to locate accurately the point touched, to gauge the direction and extent of passive movement, and to distinguish between different weights, textures, or degrees of temperature; as a result, he is unable to identify objects by merely feeling them (astereognosis). The more complicated the test, the more evident the sensory defect becomes. With all this there is a variability of response so that a definite threshold for a given sensation cannot be established.

Somatic sensory area II (somatic area II), as described in experimental animals, lies along the superior bank of the lateral sulcus and extends posteriorly into the parietal lobe (Woolsey, '58). Representation of the various parts of the body is in reverse sequence to that found in the primary somesthetic area, and the regions of the two face areas are adjacent (Fig. 22–11). Parts of the body are represented bilaterally in the secondary somatic sensory area, although contralateral representation predominates. In man the face, tongue, mouth, and throat regions have not been verified as yet in somatic area II, presumably because of proximity to the primary face area (Penfield and Rasmussen, '50). Stimulation of somatic area II in the unanesthetized patient produces sensations in the extremities similar to those obtained by stimulating the primary somesthetic cortex. The secondary somatic sensory area in animals appears to coincide with the so-called secondary motor area (Welker et al., '57). The studies of Penfield indicate that the concept of a precise secondary motor area in man is not yet justified.

Somatic area II appears to have functional characteristics of both the lemniscal and spinothalamic systems. Representation of the body form in somatic area II is nearly as detailed as that in the postcentral gyrus (Woolsey, '58), and single unit analysis (Carreras and Levitt, '59) has revealed many cells in this area to be both mode and place specific. Other functional characteristics of this area resemble those of the posterior thalamic nuclei in that they are neither place specific, nor modality specific, and they respond to more than one form of somatic stimulation. Certain cells in this cortical area respond only to noxious peripheral stimuli. Although our understanding of the functional significance of somatic area II is incomplete, present evidence suggests it is related primarily to the spinothalamic system (or ascending sensory pathways which conduct impulses in the anterolateral portion of the spinal cord), and may be concerned in some special way with pain sensibility (Poggio and Mountcastle, '60). This statement should not be interpreted as implying that impulses concerned with pain do not reach the postcentral gyrus. In a broad sense it suggests that while the lemniscal system (ventral posterolateral thalamic nucleus and the postcentral gyrus) and the spinothalamic system (posterior thalamic region and somatic area II) each have predominant characteristics, each also possesses to a certain extent the properties of the other system.

The primary visual area (area 17) is located in the walls of the calcarine sulcus and adjacent portion of the cuneus and lingual gyrus. It occasionally extends around the occipital pole on to the lateral surface of the hemisphere (Figs. 19–5 and 22–4). The exceedingly thin cortex of this area (1.5 to 2.5 mm.) is the most striking example of the heterotypical granulous cortex (type 5). Layers II and III are narrow and contain numerous small pyramidal cells that are hardly larger than typical granule cells (Fig. 22–9C). Layer IV, which is very thick, is subdivided by a light band into three sublayers. The upper and lower sublayers are packed with small granule cells. In the middle, lighter layer, fewer small cells are scattered between the large stellate cells (giant stellate cells of Meynert). This light layer is occupied by the greatly thickened outer band of Baillarger, here known as the band of Gennari. This band, visible to the naked eye in sections of the fresh cortex, has given this region the name—*area striata* (Fig. 22–12). Layer V is relatively narrow and poor in small cells, but scattered among these cells are isolated large pyramidal cells which may reach a height of 60 micra (Fig. 22–9C).

The visual cortex receives the geniculocalcarine tract, whose course and exact projection have been discussed in an earlier chapter (Fig. 19–11; see page 478). Geniculocalcarine fibers pass in the *external sagittal stratum* which is separated from the wall of the inferior and posterior horns of the lateral ventricle by the *internal sagittal stratum*, and by fibers of the corpus callosum designated as the *tapetum* (Fig. 3–24). Fibers of the internal sagittal stratum are corticofugal fibers passing from the occipital lobe to the superior colliculus and the lateral geniculate body (Altman, '62). The macular fibers terminate in the caudal third of the calcarine area, and those from the paracentral and peripheral retinal areas end in respectively more rostral portions. The representation of the macular area in the occipital cortex appears relatively large compared with the macular area of the lateral geniculate body. Because some unilateral lesions of the visual cortex result in a sparing of macular vision, certain authors have suggested that the macula is represented bilaterally. Anatomical evidence supports the thesis that parts of each macular area are represented only in the visual cortex of one hemisphere, since unilateral lesions of the visual cortex result in retrograde cell changes, or cell loss, only in the ipsilateral lateral geniculate body. Clinically, sparing of macular vision associated with vascular lesions involving the occipital cortex usually is attributed to collateral circulation provided by branches of the middle cerebral artery. Following occlusion of the posterior cerebral artery, these collateral vessels frequently are sufficient to preserve some macular vision. Similar collateral circulation apparently is not present in the cortical area representing paracentral and peripheral parts of the retina. Complete unilateral destruction of the visual cortex in man produces a contralateral homonymous hemianopsia in which there is blindness in the ipsilateral nasal field and the contralateral temporal field. Thus a lesion in the right visual cortex produces a left homonymous hemianopsia (Figs. 19–11 and 19–13). Lesions involving portions of the visual cortex, such as the inferior calcarine cortex, produce an *homonymous quadranopsia*, in which blindness results in the superior half of the visual field contralaterally. Homonymous hemianopsia can result from lesions involving all fibers of either the optic tract or the optic radiations (Fig. 19–13C), but lesions in these locations tend to be incomplete and the visual field defects in the two eyes are rarely identical. Frequently patients are unaware of homonymous hemianopsia and complain of bumping into people and objects on the side of the visual field defect. Bilateral destruction of the striate areas causes total blindness in man, but other mammals, such as dogs and monkeys, retain the ability to distinguish light intensities after ablations of the visual cortex (Klüver, '42; Glees, '61; Snyder et al., '66).

An image falling upon the retina initiates a tremendously complex process that results in vision. The transformation of a retinal image into a perceptual image occurs partly in the retina but mostly in the brain. The complexity of this process makes the achievement of a camera seem very modest. Recent elegant experimental studies by Hubel and Wiesel in the cat have provided the first real insight into the functional organization of the visual cortex. The receptive field of a cell in the visual system is defined as the region of the retina (or visual field) over which one can influence the firing of that cell. In the cat's retina two types of ganglion cells can be distinguished (Kuffler, '53): (1) those with concentric "on" center receptive fields (i.e., excitatory), and (2) those with concentric "off" center receptive fields (i.e., inhibitory). The lateral geniculate body also has cells of these two types (Hubel and Wiesel, '61). The striate cortex, anatomically far more complex than the retina or lateral geniculate body, does not have cells with concentric receptive fields. Cells of the striate cortex show marked specificity in their responses to restricted retinal stimulation (Hubel and Wiesel, '59, '62, '63). The most effective stimulus shapes are long narrow rectangles of light ("slits"), dark bars against a light background ("dark bars") and straight-line borders separating areas of different brightness ("edges"). A given cell responds vigorously when an appropriate stimulus is shone on its receptive field, or moves across it, provided the stimulus is presented in a specific orientation. This orientation is referred to as the "receptive-field axis orientation" and it is critical and constant for any particular cell, but it may differ for different cells.

The visual cortex is subdivided into discrete columns extending from the surface to the white matter; all cells within each column have the same receptive field axis orientation. The many varieties of cells in the striate cortex have been grouped into two main functional types, but it is apparent that other subtypes or varieties also exist. The main functional cell types are referred to as "simple" and "complex." "Simple" type cells respond to slits of light having the proper receptive-field axis of orientation. A slit of light oriented vertically in the visual field may activate a given "simple" cell, whereas the same cell will not respond, though other cells will respond, if the orientation of the slit of light is moved out of the vertical position. "Complex" type cells, like "simple" cells, respond best to "slits," "bars" or "edges", provided the orientation is suitable, but unlike "simple" cells, they respond with sustained firing to moving lines. The retinal region over which a "simple" type cell can be influenced, is, like the fields of retinal and geniculate cells, divided into "on" and "off" areas. In "simple" cells these "on" areas are not circular but are narrow rectangles, adjoined on each side by larger "off" regions. The magnitude of the "on" response depends upon how much of the region is covered by the stimulating light. A narrow slit of light that just fills the elongated "on" region produces a powerful "on" response; stimulation with a slit of light having a different orientation produces a weaker response, because it includes part of the antagonistic "off" regions. A slit of light at right angles to the optimum orientation for a particular cell, usually produces no response. Thus a large spot of light covering the whole retina evokes no response in "simple" cortical cells, because "on" and "off" effects apparently balance. A particular cortical cell's optimum receptive-field axis orientation appears to be a property built into the cells by its anatomical connections. The receptive-field orientation differs from one cell column to the next, and may be vertical, horizontal or oblique. There is no evidence that any one orientation is more common than any other.

Available evidence (Hubel and Wiesel, '62) suggests that "simple" cells receive their impulses directly from the lateral geniculate body. Presumably a typical "simple" cell receives an input from a large number of lateral geniculate neurons whose "on" centers are arranged in a straight line. Thus, for each area of the retina stimulated, each line, and each orientation of the stimulus, there is a particular set of "simple" striate cortical cells that respond. Changing any of the stimulus arrangements will cause an entirely new and different population of "simple" striate cells to respond.

Although "complex" cells in the striate cortex have some characteristics similar to those of simple cells, their receptive fields cannot be mapped into antagonistic "on" and "off" regions. "Complex" cells respond to slits of light with a particular orientation, but when the slit is moved, without changing its orientation, the "complex" cells continue to fire. It is believed (Hubel and Wiesel, '62) that a "complex" cell receives its input from a large number of "simple" cells—all of which have the same receptive field axis of orientation. These findings imply that a vast network of intracortical connections relate "simple" and "complex" cells in the striate cortex in a very specific fashion, and that similar arrangements must exist for all receptive-field orientations. Since columns of cells constitute the fundamental functional units of the cortex, each small region of the visual field must be represented in the striate cortex many times, in column after column of cells with different receptive field orientations.

The secondary visual area (visual area II) has been mapped in the rabbit, cat, and monkey by recording the potentials evoked by flashing photic stimulation of the retina (Talbot and Marshall, '41; Woolsey, '47; Thompson et al., '50). Visual area II is a smaller mirror image representation of the primary visual area, located anterolaterally, which appears to be anatomically identical to area 18 in the cat (Fig. 22-11). Lateral to visual areas I and II is a third systematic projection of the contralateral visual field (visual area III) which in the cat appears to be identical with area 19 (Hubel and Wiesel, '65). Cells in visual area I (area 17) project to both visual area II (area 18), and visual area III (area 19) bilaterally, indicating that visual impulses to the latter areas are transmitted from visual area I, the only area receiving direct

fibers from the lateral geniculate body. Cells in visual areas II and III, like those in visual area I, respond best to slits, dark bars and edges which have a specific orientation. The majority of cells in visual area II are "complex" and approximately half of the cells in visual area III are "complex"; other cells in these areas, referred to as "hypercomplex", demonstrate more elaborate response properties. Both visual areas II and III are organized in columns, extending from the surface to the white matter, containing both "complex" and "hypercomplex" cells, all of which have the same receptive-field orientation. These cells, however, differ in the precise position and arrangement of receptive fields. "Hypercomplex" cells behave as though their input comes from: (1) two sets of complex cells—one excitatory and one inhibitory, or (2) other "hypercomplex" cells of a lower order. In visual area III there are columns in which some cells have one receptive-field orientation, others with an orientation at 90 degree to the first, and still others which respond to both of these orientations. The majority of cells in visual areas II and III are driven from both eyes. Thus, there appears to be as much binocular representation in visual areas II and III as in visual area I.

Area 18 is six-layered granular cortex which lacks the band of Gennari and rostrally merges with area 19 without distinct demarcation (Figs. 22-4 and 22-9B). This area interrelates areas 17 and 19 of the same and opposite hemispheres by association and commissural fibers. Projection fibers from area 18 enter the superior longitudinal and inferior occipitofrontal fasciculi (Fig. 3-17). According to Crosby and Henderson ('48), corticotectal and corticomesencephalic fibers orginating from area 18 play an important role in the neural mechanism of vertical and oblique eye movements resulting from electrical stimulation of this region. Similar corticotectal fibers from area 19 project to the ipsilateral superior colliculus. Stimulation of area 19 in the monkey may produce conjugate deviation of the eyes upward, downward, or horizontally, de-

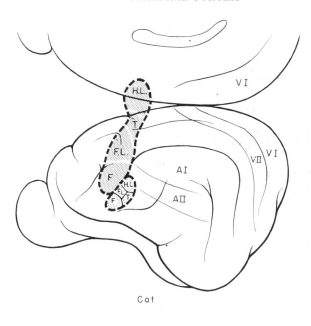

Cat

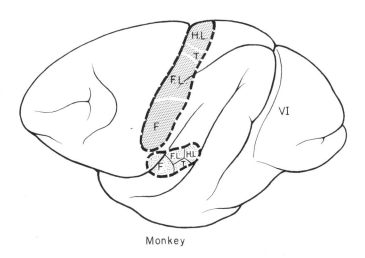

Monkey

░░ Primary sensory area   ░░ Secondary sensory area

FIG. 22–11. Diagrams of the primary and secondary cortical sensory areas in the cat and monkey. Somatotopic representation of different parts of the body are indicated in the primary and secondary somatic sensory areas: *F*, face area; *T*, trunk; *FL*, forelimb; *HL* hindlimb. Primary and secondary auditory (*AI* and *AII*) and visual (*VI* and *VII*) areas in the cat brain are shown. The medial aspect of the cat brain is represented *above* (after Woolsey, '58).

pending on the site stimulated (Crosby and Henderson, '48). Areas 18 and 19 are regarded as essential for eye movements induced by visual stimuli (i.e., following eye movements) and for visual fixation.

The primary auditory area (areas 41 and 42) is located on the two transverse gyri (Heschl) which lie on the dorsal surface of the superior temporal convolution, buried in the floor of the lateral sulcus (Figs. 19–5 and 22–4). The middle part of the anterior transverse gyrus and a portion of the posterior gyrus constitute the principal auditory receptive areas

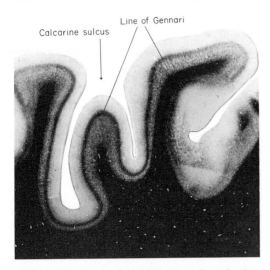

Calcarine sulcus   Line of Gennari

FIG. 22-12. Frontal section through calcarine cortex (area striata) showing extent of line of Gennari. Weigert's myelin stain. Photograph.

(area 41). Remaining parts of the posterior transverse gyrus and adjacent portions of the superior temporal gyrus compose area 42, which is largely an auditory association area. In order to visualize these gyri in an intact brain, it is necessary to separate widely the banks of the lateral sulcus (Fig. 3–14). These two cortical areas are cytoarchitecturally distinct. Although area 41 is typical koniocortex, resembling that of areas 3 and 17, it is relatively thick (3 mm) and distinguished by the thickness of the granular layers. Granular cells are arranged in perpendicular columns. Area 42 is six-layered cortex of the parietal type (type 3, Fig. 22–6). A distinguishing feature is the presence of a number of large pyramidal cells in layer III.

The auditory area receives geniculotemporal fibers (auditory radiations) from the medial geniculate body. The auditory radiations reach their cortical projection site by passing through the sublenticular portion of the internal capsule (Fig. 19–9). The greater part of the auditory radiations projects to area 41, though fibers also project to area 42. One of the characteristic features of the auditory system is its tonotopic localization. The tonotopic localization present in the cochlea appears to be preserved to a degree through all of the

relay nuclei of the auditory system (Rose and Woolsey '58; Ades, '59), even though the ascending auditory pathways are exceedingly complex, and fibers arising from various nuclei are both crossed and uncrossed. This does not mean that the frequency specificity of portions of the end organ is retained without change throughout the auditory pathway, even though various segments of the audible spectrum retain their relative positions with respect to each other. The number of neurons exhibiting frequency specificity varies at different levels of the auditory system. While a large proportion of the fibers of the auditory nerve show a sharply restricted frequency specificity at threshold intensity, the number of neurons retaining this characteristic progressively diminishes at higher levels of the auditory pathway. This means that at higher levels of this system there is a progressively increasing proportion of neural elements not directly concerned with the parameter of stimulus frequency, even though they respond to complex sounds (i.e., noise click) covering broad bands of the audible spectrum (Ades, '59).

In the cerebral cortex two areas showing tonotopic localization have been defined in the cat by determining the loci of potentials evoked in response to stimulation of nerve fibers in the cochlea, or different sound frequencies (Woolsey and Walzl, '42; Ades, '43, '59). The pattern of tonotopic localization in these two areas has been studied in detail. In the more dorsal area, referred to as auditory area I, the basal coils of the cochlea (high frequencies) are represented rostrally, and the apical region of the cochlea (low frequencies) caudally. In the more ventral area (auditory area II) the tonotopic localization is reversed (Fig. 22–13). A third cortical zone designated as EP (i.e., posterior ectosylvian area) lies posterior to auditory area I and II and appears to be related functionally to auditory area I. Anatomical studies of ablations of these auditory areas have provided information concerning the origin of afferent fibers from the medial geniculate body (Rose and Woolsey, '49, '58). Auditory area I receives an essential projection from the anterior portion of the principal division of the medial geniculate body, while auditory areas II and EP receive only sustaining projections from the pars principalis of the medial geniculate body. This conclusion is based on the fact that removals of auditory area I cause severe degeneration in the anterior part of the principal division of the medial geniculate body, while ablations of auditory area II and EP do not cause marked cellular changes. However, simultaneous ablations of auditory areas I, II, and EP result in more profound cellular degeneration in the medial geniculate body than ablations of auditory area I alone. Auditory areas I and II have also been identified in the monkey (Ades and Felder, '42; Pribram et al., '54), although studies of the primate brain are less numerous. In the chimpanzee tones of low frequency are represented anterolaterally, while tones of high frequency are represented posteromedially (Bailey et al., '43). It seems likely that a similar tonotopic localization exists in man.

Electrical stimulation of the cortical areas in the temporal lobe near the primary auditory area (i.e., areas 42 and 22) in man produces sounds described as the noise of a cricket, a bell, or a whistle. These sounds are elementary tones which may be high or low pitched, continuous or interrupted, but always devoid of complicated or changing qualities (Penfield and Rasmussen, '50). Most of these auditory responses are referred to the contralateral ear.

One of the distinctive features of the auditory system, in contrast to other sensory systems, is the large number of actual and potential sites at which impulses from one side can be transmitted to contralateral relay nuclei. The largest and most important fiber crossing is in the trapezoid body at the level of the cochlear nuclei, but others also are present (Fig. 15-9), including fibers from auditory cortical areas that cross in the corpus callosum (Mettler, '32). Physiological studies (Woolsey and Walzl, '42; Ades and Brookhart, '50; Rosenzweig, '54) in-

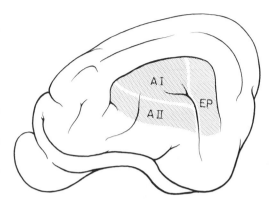

Fig. 22–13. Diagram of the auditory areas in the cat. In the primary auditory area (*AI*) the basal coils of the cochlea are represented rostrally, and the apical part of the cochlea caudally. A reverse tonotopic pattern is found in the secondary auditory (*AII*). Area *EP* (posterior ectosylvian area) represents a third auditory area (after Ades, '59).

dicate that each cochlea is represented bilaterally in the auditory cortex, although some slight differences exist between the two sides. Rosenzweig ('54) has demonstrated that although the cortical effects of stimulating each ear separately are nearly the same, significant differences occur when the position of the stimulus is varied with respect to the ears during bilateral stimulation. When the sound is presented at one side, the cortical response is greatest in the contralateral hemisphere. If the sound is presented in a median plane, the cortical activity in the two hemispheres is equal. These studies suggest a correlation between auditory localization and differential responses in the auditory cortex.

Because audition is represented bilaterally at a cortical level, unilateral lesions of the auditory cortex cause only a partial deafness. The deficits, however, are bilateral, and the greatest loss is contralateral. According to Penfield and Evans ('34), removal of one temporal lobe impairs sound localization on the opposite side, especially judgment of the distance of sounds. Clinically, unilateral lesions of the auditory cortex are difficult to recognize. Experimental studies indicate that bilateral ablations of auditory areas I, II, and EP in the cat do not abolish auditory localization of sound in space, though discriminations of this kind are impaired (Neff et al., '56; Neff and Diamond, '58). Bilateral ablations of the auditory cortical areas mentioned above reportedly have little or no effect on the ability of cats to discriminate changes in frequency (Meyer and Woolsey, '52; Butler et al., '57; Neff and Diamond, '58). Meyer and Woolsey ('52) reported that following bilateral ablations of auditory areas I, II, and EP, and somatic area II, cats could not relearn to discriminate changes in frequency, but could discriminate changes in sound intensity. Studies by Goldberg and Neff ('61) suggest that cats can relearn an auditory frequency discrimination after more extensive cortical ablations that include all the areas mentioned above and portions of insular-temporal cortex as well. Although ability to localize sound in space depends to a degree upon the auditory cortex, it is not affected by section of the corpus callosum and is affected very little by section of the commissure of the inferior colliculus, but it is severely affected by section of the trapezoid body (Neff and Diamond, '58; Jerger, '60).

Brodmann's area 22, bordering the primary auditory area (Fig. 22–4) and representing typical six-layered isocortex, receives fibers from areas 41 and 42 and has connections with areas of the parietal, occipital, and insular cortex (Bailey et al., '43; Sugar et al., '48, '50). Lesions of area 22 in the dominant hemisphere, or bilateral lesions, produce word deafness or sensory aphasia (see page 586). Although patients with these lesions can hear, they cannot interpret the meaning of sounds, especially speech. This form of sensory aphasia usually is associated with lesions in the posterior part of area 22.

The gustatory area has not been established conclusively, though numerous cortical locations for taste sensibility have been suggested. Clinical and experimental evidence indicates that taste sensibility probably is represented in the parietal operculum (area 43) and in the adjacent parainsular cortex (Börnstein, '40, 40a; Patton and Ruch, '46; Penfield and Rasmussen, '50; Bagshaw and Pribram, '53). Ablations of the precentral and

postcentral opercula in the monkey and chimpanzee reportedly cause a loss of taste. Similar lesions involving the anterior insular cortex, the postcentral operculum, and the anterior supratemporal cortex in the monkey impair taste sensibility (Bagshaw and Pribram, '53). Stimulations of the parietal operculum (Penfield and Boldrey, '37) and adjacent insular cortex (Penfield and Rasmussen, '50) in conscious patients produce gustatory sensations. A particularly interesting report of an epileptic patient who experienced a gustatory aura characterized by a sour or bitter taste, frequently is cited as providing information concerning localization of taste in the cerebral cortex (Shenkin and Lewey, '44). Although this patient could recognize bitter and salty substances bilaterally, he was unable to perceive sweet substances on one side of his tongue. A vascular anomaly was found in the parietal opercular region contralateral to the taste deficit.

Electrophysiological studies (Landgren, '61; Emmers et al., '62; Blomquist et al., '62; Emmers, '64) in the rat, cat, and squirrel monkey indicate that afferent taste impulses conveyed by the chorda tympani and glossopharyngeal nerves are projected to the most medial and caudal part of the ventral posteromedial nucleus of the thalamus. In the rat this projection was bilateral and symmetrical; in the cat and squirrel monkey this projection was predominantly ipsilateral. Direct lesions, destroying this thalamic region, produce gustatory deficits in the monkey (Blum et al., '43; Patton et al., '44) and goat (Andersson and Jewell, '57). Available evidence suggests that thalamic cell groups subserving taste probably are separated spatially from those related to other sensory modalities (Emmers, '66). Anatomical studies (Benjamin and Akert, '59) in the rat indicate that unilateral ablations of the cortical area in which potentials could be evoked by stimulating the chorda tympani and glossopharyngeal nerves (i.e., the parietal operculum) did not impair normal taste discrimination. Bilateral ablations of this area produced a partial loss of taste. Ablations of this cortical taste area produced retrograde degeneration of thalamic neurons confined to the most medial sub-division of the ventral posteromedial (VPM) nucleus. It remains questionable whether this subdivision of the ventral posteromedial thalamic nucleus corre-sponds precisely with the parvocellular part (VPMpc) described by Olszewski ('52). The gustatory representation in the cerebral cortex is adjacent to the somes-thetic area for the tongue (Cohen et al., '57), suggesting that taste may not have an exclusive primary receiving area. Although some cortical neurons in the taste area respond only to tactile, thermal, or taste stimuli, others respond to more than one form of stimulation (Landgren, '57; '61). Different observations in the squirrel monkey (Benjamin, '63) suggest cortical areas concerned with taste may be sep-arated from somesthetic areas; however, ablations of these areas have failed to pro-duce detectable impairment of gustatory sense in this animal.

Vestibular representation in the cere-bral cortex is poorly defined in comparison with other sensory modalities. In man, electrical stimulation of portions of the superior temporal gyrus, particularly re-gions rostral to the auditory area, provoke sensations of turning movements of the whole body, referred to as *vertigo* (Penfield and Rasmussen, '50). These sensations are comparatively mild in contrast with the violent vertigo produced by direct stimula-tion of the labyrinth. Nausea is compara-tively infrequent during these vertiginous sensations, and when present may be the result of spread of the stimulus to portions of the underlying insular cortex. Less dis-tinct illusions of body movement have been reported following stimulation of parietal cortex (Penfield, '57). Sensations of dizzi-ness may be elicited from stimulating a variety of cortical sites, though these sensations most commonly are associated with subcortical stimulation.

Experimental studies of the vestibular system indicate that vestibular impulses are projected to cortical areas in the cat, dog, and monkey. Either electrical stimu-lation of the vestibular nerve, or rotation of the animal, evokes potentials at cortical levels (Kempinsky, '51; Mickle and Ades, '52; Andersson and Gernandt, '54). In the cat responses are evoked in the anterior ectosylvian gyrus and the posterior bank of the anterior suprasylvian gyrus, regions which correspond to portions of the tem-poral lobe in primates. Cortical responses following stimulation of the vestibular nerve are principally contralateral. More recent physiological studies (Fredrickson et al., '66) indicate that vestibular im-pulses in the monkey project contralat-erally to a region of the postcentral gyrus, between the primary and secondary somes-thetic areas. These studies were based upon stimulation of the vestibular nerve before and after section of the roots of cranial nerves V, IX, X and XI. This find-ing suggests that at the cortical level in primates, the vestibular projection may be related more closely to somatosensory proprioceptive afferents than to the au-ditory system.

EFFERENT CORTICAL AREAS

Corticofugal fibers originating from vari-ous parts of the cerebral cortex are con-cerned with the initiation of voluntary movement, the integration of motor func-tions, the modification of reflex activity, the modulation of sensory input, and the regu-lation of the state of consciousness and attention. These fibers, originating largely from the deeper layers of the cerebral cortex, are projected widely to the spinal cord, the brain stem, and subcortical telencephalic nuclei. The principal cortico-fugal fibers can be grouped under the following designations: (1) corticospinal, (2) corticoreticular, (3) corticopontine, (4) corticothalamic, and (5) corticonuclear (a composite grouping of different fibers passing to the basal ganglia, the hypo-thalamus, the substantia nigra, the red nucleus, and various sensory relay nuclei). Cortical efferent fibers projecting to other cortical areas of the same hemisphere are designated as associational, while those projecting to cortical areas of the opposite hemisphere are commissural.

The Primary Motor Area. Area 4 of Brodmann, commonly designated as the motor area, is located on the anterior wall of the central sulcus and adjacent portions of the precentral gyrus (Fig. 22–4). Broad at the superior border of the hemisphere, where it spreads over a considerable part of the precentral gyrus, it constantly narrows inferiorly and, at the level of the inferior frontal gyrus, is practically limited to the anterior wall of the central sulcus. On the medial surface of the hemisphere it comprises the anterior portion of the paracentral lobule. The unusually thick cortex of the motor area (3.5 to 4.5 mm.) is agranular in structure, and its ganglionic layer contains the giant pyramidal cells of Betz, whose cell bodies may reach a height of 60 to 120 micra (Figs. 6–5 and 22–8B). These cells are largest in the paracentral lobule, and smallest in the inferior opercular region. The density of Betz cells also varies in different parts of area 4 (Lassek, '40). Approximate percentages of Betz cells in different topographical subdivisions of area 4 are: 75 per cent in the leg area, 18 per cent in the arm area, and 7 per cent in the face area. According to Lassek ('40, '47), 34,000 giant pyramidal cells with cross sectional areas between 900 and 4,100 square micra have been counted in area 4 in the human brain. Cytoarchitecturally area 4 represents a modification of the typical six-layered isocortex in which the pyramidal cells in layers III and V are increased in number and the internal granular layer is obscured. For this reason the cortex is called agranular.

The rostral border of area 4 has been distinguished physiologically as a distinct subdivision, referred to as area 4S (Hines, '36, '37). Ablation of this narrow strip of cortex along the rostral border of area 4 in the monkey is said to produce a transient spastic paralysis. Stimulation of area 4S has been reported to inhibit extensor muscle tone. Subsequent studies indicated that area 4S was one of a number of cortical areas from which suppressor effects could be obtained in response to stimulation (Dusser de Barenne and McCulloch, '39). Although various investigators have suggested that this subdivision can be distinguished from other parts of area 4, anatomically it is not regarded as a separate entity. Physiological aspects of this region

are discussed in more detail on pages 580–581.

The corticospinal tract, which is considered to transmit impulses for highly skilled volitional movements to lower motor neurons, arises in large part from area 4. The larger corticospinal fibers are probably the axons of giant pyramidal cells, for these cells undergo chromatolysis following section of the pyramid (Holmes and May, '09; Levin and Bradford, '38). Since the number of fibers in the human corticospinal tract at the level of the pyramid is approximately one million, axons of the giant cells of Betz could account for only a little over 3 per cent of these fibers, assuming that each cell gives rise to a single corticospinal fiber (Lassek, '40). Studies of the fiber spectrum of the human corticospinal tract, indicating about 30,000 fibers with diameters between 9 and 22 micra (Lassek and Rasmussen, '39, '40; Lassek, '54), strongly support the view that these fibers are the parent axons of the giant pyramidal cells. Approximately 90 per cent of the fibers of the corticospinal tract range from 1 to 4 micra in diameter. Of the total number of fibers in the tract, about 40 per cent are poorly myelinated. The more numerous small fibers of the corticospinal tract are considered to arise from smaller cells in this and other cortical regions. Interruption of the corticospinal tract also gives rise to chromatolytic cell changes in small pyramidal cells in the III and V layers, not only in area 4, but also in areas 3, 1, 2, and 5 (Levin and Bradford, '38). Data concerning the cortical areas which contribute fibers to the corticospinal tract and the extent of their individual contributions are variable and incomplete. Ablations of area 4 in the monkey cause degeneration of 27 to 40 per cent of the corticospinal tract, including virtually all of the large myelinated fibers (Lassek, '42, '54). Other authors have reported smaller percentages of degenerated fibers after similar ablations (Häggqvist, '37), but none report complete degeneration of the corticospinal tract (Mettler, '44a; Welch and Kennard, '44). Ablations of parietal cortex (areas 3, 1, 2, 5, and 7) also provoke degeneration of myelinated fibers in the corticospinal tract (Minkowski, '23–'24; Peele, '42). Combined ablations of the precentral and postcentral gyri cause degeneration of 50 to 60 per cent of the fibers in the corticospinal tract (Lassek, '42; Russell and DeMyer, '61). Although corticospinal fibers arising from area 6 have been described (Hoff, '35; Kennard, '35), some authors (Mettler, '35; Levin, '36; Verhaart and Kennard, '40) have questioned this finding. A careful quantitative study of the origin of corticospinal fibers in the monkey based on silver staining methods (Russell and DeMyer, '61) seems to have resolved this question. These authors found that virtually all fibers of the corticospinal tract arise from area 4, area 6, and parts of the parietal lobe. Approximate percentages of corticospinal fibers arising from these areas were as follows: (1) area 4, 31%, (2) area 6, 29%, and (3) parietal lobe, 40%. Complete decortication, or hemispherectomy, causes all fibers of the corticospinal tract to degenerate in man (Lassek and Evans, '45) and in the monkey (Mettler, '44a; Russell and DeMyer, '61).

Electrical stimulation of the motor area evokes discrete isolated movements on the opposite side of the body. Usually the contractions involve the functional muscle groups concerned with a specific movements, but individual muscles, even a single interosseus, may be contracted separately. While the pattern of excitable foci is the same for all mammals, the number of such foci, and hence the number of discrete movements, is increased greatly in man. Thus flexion or extension at a single finger joint, twitchings at the corners of the mouth, elevation of the palate, protrusion of the tongue, and even vocalization, expressed in involuntary cries or exclamations, all may be evoked by careful stimulation of the proper areas. Charts of motor representation, which are in substantial agreement, have been furnished by a number of investigators (Foerster, '36a, 36b; Penfield and Boldrey, '37; Scarff; '40; Penfield and Rasmussen, '50; Penfield and Jasper, '54). These data concerning the human brain were collected during neurosurgical procedures in which patients were operated upon under local anesthesia. The location of centers for specific movements may vary from individual to individual, but the sequence of motor representation appears constant; e.g., the point which on stimulation produces a movement of the pharynx always lies nearer to the lateral sulcus than that producing a movement of the lips, and so on. Ipsilateral movements have not been observed in man, but bilateral responses occur in the muscles of the eyes, face, tongue, jaw, larynx, and pharynx. According to Penfield and Boldrey ('37), the center for the pharynx (swallowing) lies in the most inferior opercular portion of the precentral gyrus; it is followed, from below upward, by centers for the tongue, jaw, lips, larynx, eyelid, and brow, in the order named. Next come the extensive areas for finger movements, the thumb being lowest and the little finger highest; these are followed by areas for the hand, wrist, elbow, and shoulder. Finally in the most superior part are the centers for the hip, knee, ankle, and toes. The last named are situated at the medial border and extend into the paracentral lobule, which also contains the centers for the anal and vesicle sphincters (Fig. 22–10).

For a long time there was considerable controversy regarding the location of representation of the lower extremity, due mainly to difficulties in stimulating the medial surface. According to Foerster ('36a), the paracentral lobule contains foci related to the foot, the toes, the bladder and the rectum. Penfield and Boldrey ('37) reported leg movements in 23 cases produced by stimulation of superior portions of the precentral gyrus, but Scarff ('40) was unable to elicit any leg movements by stimulating the lateral surface of the hemisphere. According to Scarff ('40) the leg, as a rule, is represented only on the medial surface of the hemisphere (i.e., in the paracentral lobule). This upward shift of the motor area, which appears unique to man, is considered to be due to the great expansion of cortical areas on the lateral surface of the hemisphere representing the tongue, mouth, lips, face and upper extremity (Fig. 22–14).

The movements elicited by electrical

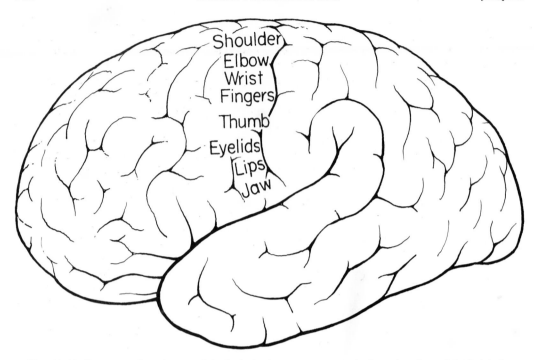

Fig. 22–14. Representation of parts of the body in the motor area on the lateral surface of the hemisphere. According to Scarff ('40), the leg usually is represented only in the anterior part of the paracentral lobule.

stimulation of the motor cortex probably are not equivalent to voluntary movements, although they are interpreted as "volitional" by the patient. These movements are never skilled movements, comparable to those of complex acquired movements, but consist largely of either simple flexions or extensions at one or more joints. The threshold in different topographical parts of area 4 varies. The region representing the thumb appears to have the lowest threshold, while the face area has the highest threshold. Excessive stimulation of area 4 produces either a focal seizure, or one resembling a Jacksonian convulsion.

Ablations of the motor cortex in mammals produce increasingly greater neurological deficits at progressively higher levels of the phylogenetic scale (Walker and Fulton, '38). In the cat removals of the motor cortex, or even hemidecortication, do not impair the animal's ability to walk upon recovery from anesthesia. Ablations of area 4 in the monkey produce a contralateral flaccid paralysis, marked hypotonia, and areflexia. Within a relatively short time myotatic reflexes reap-

pear, along with withdrawal responses to nociceptive stimuli (Fulton and Keller, '32). Recovery of movement begins in proximal musculature and progresses distally, but the digits tend to remain permanently paralyzed. Studies by Travis ('55) in the monkey confirm these findings, except that recovery of motor function in the distal parts of the extremity was as rapid as that in proximal parts. Although considerable improvement of motor function occurred, skilled movements were performed slowly and with some deliberation. Atrophy present in the paretic limbs during the period of greatest disuse, disappeared after maximal functional recovery. No significant spasticity developed in these animals. The results of other authors (Denny-Brown and Botterell, '48; Denny-Brown, '60) differ from the above in that some degree of spasticity accompanied the paretic manifestations after all lesions of the precentral gyrus in the monkey. Relatively mild spasticity developed first in proximal muscle groups and was described as most enduring following total ablations.

Because the precentral gyrus gives rise to a large number of nonpyramidal fibers, and is the source of only a part of the corticospinal tract, it is instructive to compare the motor deficits described above with those which follow surgical section of the pyramids. Selective pyramidotomy in the monkey and chimpanzee, accomplished by an anterior approach, produces a contralateral paresis which is somewhat more severe in the chimpanzee than in the monkey (Tower, '40, '49). In neither animal is the paresis so severe that the affected limbs are useless. The relatively stereotyped movements of progression are impaired, and there is a severe poverty of movement. The usage which survives is stripped of all the finer qualities which contribute to the skill, precision, and versatility of motor performance. Although remaining stereotyped movements are useful, execution of purposeful movements appears to require deliberation and critical attention. Pyramidotomy is associated with hypotonia, and loss of superficial abdominal and cremasteric reflexes. The myotatic reflexes are increased in threshold and somewhat pendular. Tonic neck reflexes are absent, and clonus does not occur. A forced grasp reflex is prominent and may be so severe as to interfere with climbing. In the chimpanzee, a persistent and enduring Babinski sign can be elicited. Observations on monkeys with bilateral pyramidal lesions by Lawrence and Kuypers ('68) also indicate that considerable recovery of independent limb movements occurs, but recovery of individual finger movements never returns. All movements are slower and the muscles fatigue more rapidly than in normal animals. These findings indicate that corticospinal pathways conduct impulses concerned with speed and agility of movement, and fractionation of movements, as exemplified by individual finger movements. Motor function remaining after bilateral pyramidotomy must be mediated by brain stem pathways projecting to spinal levels.

Lesions of the motor cortex in man produce neurological deficits similar to those described in the primate, though anatomical details are not so precise. Since conclusions based upon pathological lesions of various types are difficult to interpret, reliable data are limited to instances in which all, or parts, of the precentral gyrus have been removed surgically (Foerster, '36a; Bucy, '49, '59; Penfield and Rasmussen, '50). Ablations limited to the "arm" or "leg" area of the precentral gyrus result in a paralysis of a single limb (i.e., monoplegia). The ultimate loss of movement is always greatest in the distal muscle groups, but motor recovery in the affected limb usually is more complete than that associated with nearly total lesions of the motor area (Bucy, '49). Immediately after complete or partial lesions of the precentral gyrus, there is a flaccid paralysis of the contralateral limbs or limb, marked hypotonia, and loss of superfical and myotatic reflexes. Within a relatively short time the Babinski sign can be elicited. The myotatic reflexes generally return early in an exaggerated form. There are differences of opinion concerning whether removals of area 4 in man result in a permanent spastic paralysis (Foerster, '36a; Bucy, '49, '59; Penfield and Rasmussen, '50). According to Bucy ('49), the spasticity is not severe and is less intense than that commonly associated with hemiplegias resulting from large capsular lesions. Although there is considerable restitution of function in proximal muscle groups, relatively little recovery of skilled motor function occurs in the smaller distal muscles of the extremities. The neural mechanisms underlying this partial recovery of function are not known.

The Premotor Area. This area (area 6) lies immediately in front of the motor area. It likewise runs dorsoventrally along the whole lateral aspect of the frontal lobe and is continued on the medial surface to the sulcus cinguli (Fig. 22-4). Near the superior border it is quite broad and includes the caudal portion of the superior frontal gyrus. Proceeding inferiorly the premotor area narrows, and at the operculum is limited to the precentral gyrus. Its histological structure resembles that of the motor area; it is composed principally of large well-formed pyramidal cells, but there are no giant cells of Betz (Fig.

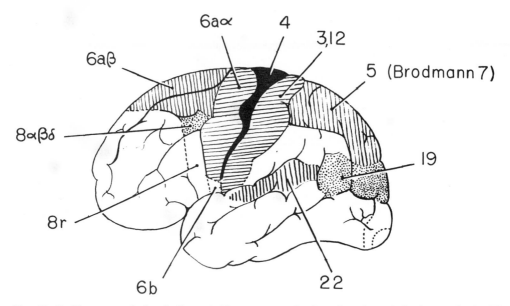

Fig. 22-15. The areas of electrically excitable cortex on the lateral surface of the human brain. The motor area is shown in *black*, and the extrapyramidal areas are *hatched* except for the eye fields, which are *stippled* (after Foerster, '36*b*).

22-8*A*). The presence of pyramidal cells in layers III and V and the narrowness of layer IV make it difficult to distinguish an internal granular layer. For this reason area 6, like area 4, is referred to as agranular frontal cortex. Area 6 has been subdivided into various portions, as shown in Figure 22-15 (Foerster, '36*b*). According to this parcellation, area 6*aα* lies immediately rostral to area 4 along the convexity of the hemisphere, while area 6*aβ* occupies the region of the superior frontal gyrus on both the lateral and medial surfaces of the hemisphere. A small area designated as 6*b* lies in front of the face area.

Electrical stimulation of area 6*aα* in man produces responses similar to those obtained from area 4, though stronger currents are required (Foerster, '31, '36*a*). The isolated movements produced by stimulating this area apparently depend upon transmission of impulses to area 4, because they cannot be elicited after destruction of area 4. It is probable that area 6*aα* discharges via the corticospinal tract. Stimulation of area 6*aβ* elicits more general movement patterns characterized by rotation of the head, eyes, and trunk to the opposite side, and synergic patterns

of flexion, or extension in the contralateral extremities. These general movement patterns appear independent of area 4, since they can be obtained after its removal. It is suggested that these responses are mediated by nonpyramidal fiber systems. Stimulation of area 6*b* is reported to produce rhythmic coordinated movements of a complex type involving facial, masticatory, laryngeal, and pharyngeal musculature. Portions of area 6*aβ* on the medial aspect of the hemisphere are considered as part of the supplementary motor area (page 575).

Unilateral ablations of area 6, including portions on the medial aspect of the hemisphere, produce transient grasp reflexes in the monkey (Richter and Hines, '32). Bilateral removals of these portions of area 6 are said by some authors (Richter and Hines, '34) to produce permanent involuntary grasping in the monkey, but most investigators indicate that grasp reflexes are temporary, though they persist longer than after unilateral ablations (Kennard and Fulton, '33; Welch and Kennard, '44). Unilateral destruction of area 6*aβ* in man produces little or no motor deficit (Foerster, '36*a*). Evidence in man and monkey emphasizes that only lesions involving the supplementary motor areas produce grasping phenomena (Erickson and Woolsey, '51; Travis, '55a). Ablations of area 6, not involving the precentral or supplementary motor areas, do not produce paresis, grasp reflexes, or hypertonia.

Experimental studies in the monkey have suggested that combined ablations of areas 4 and 6 produce a contralateral spastic paralysis (Kennard and Fulton, '33; Fulton and Kennard, '34; Kennard, '49). Similar findings were reported in man following ablations of area 6, which undoubtedly included parts of area 4, as well as so-called area 4S (Kennard et al., '34). Attempts to clarify these results by Hines ('37) indicated that removal of area 4S in the monkey produced a temporary paresis but a permanent increase in tone in the contralateral antigravity muscles. Ablations of the posterior part of area 4 resulted in a contralateral flaccid paresis. These studies suggested that ablation of area 4S probably was responsible for the release phenomena expressed as spasticity. Subsequent investigations (Travis, '55a) explain the spasticity resulting from combined lesions of area 4 and 6 on the basis of simultaneous destruction of precentral and supplementary motor areas, which are known to produce a contralateral spastic paralysis. This same investigator has shown that bilateral removals of area 4S in the monkey do not produce spasticity until the lesions in the strip area (4S) encroach upon the supplementary motor area. These results not only appear to resolve a long-standing controversy, but eliminate apparent discrepancies concerning the effects of ablations of motor cortex and pyramidotomy.

Supplementary Motor Area. Observations by early investigators indicated that motor responses in different parts of the body could be elicited by electrical stimulation of the medial surface of the frontal lobe rostral to the primary motor area. This motor area, identified in the human brain, has been designated as the supplementary motor are (Penfield and Rasmussen, '50). The supplementary motor area

in man and monkey occupies the medial surface of the superior frontal gyrus rostral to area 4. Detailed descriptions of somatotopic representation within the supplementary motor area of the monkey have been provided by Woolsey et al., ('52). The sequential representation of body parts in this area is shown in Figure 22–16. The threshold for stimulation of the supplementary motor area in man and monkeys is slightly higher than for the precentral region, but the motor effects clearly are not due to spread of excitation across the cortex. Stimulation of the supplementary motor area in man produces raising of the opposite arm, turning of the head and eyes, and bilateral synergic contractions of the muscles of the trunk and legs. Movements provoked by stimulation of the supplementary motor area have been divided into three types: (1) assumption of postures, (2) maneuvers consisting of a series of complex patterned movements, and (3) infrequent rapid incoordinate movements. The whole pattern of movement seems to be bilateral and synergistic, but most movements are described as tonic contractions of the postural type. Other responses obtained included pupillary dilatation, cardiac acceleration, vocalization, and occasional sensory phenomena. Although the visceral responses resemble those commonly obtained from the cingulate gyrus, these are not regarded as due to spread of the stimulus. Unilateral ablations of the supplementary motor area in man produce no permanent deficit in the maintenance of posture or the capacity for movement (Penfield and Rasmussen, '50; Penfield and Welch, '51).

Systematic studies in the monkey of removals of the supplementary motor area alone, and in combination with the precentral motor area, have contributed information concerning its function (Travis, '55, '55a). Unilateral ablations of the supplementary motor area in the monkey produce weak transient grasp reflexes in the contralateral limbs, and moderate bilateral hypertonia of the shoulder muscles, but no detectable paresis. Bilateral simultaneous ablations of this area result in

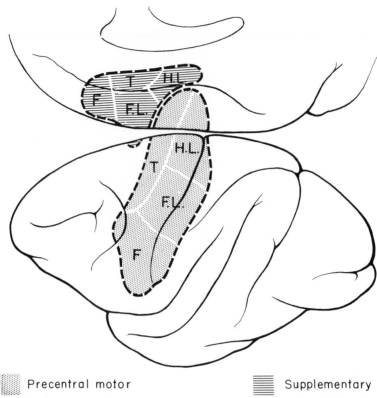

Precentral motor   Supplementary

FIG. 22-16. Diagram of the precentral and supplementary motor areas in the monkey. The somatotopical representation of different parts of the body are shown: *F*, face area; *T*, trunk; *FL*, forelimb; *HL*, hindlimb. The precentral motor area on the lateral convexity extends over onto the medial aspect of the hemisphere; the *outlined area* shown posterior to the central sulcus represents cortex hidden in the depths of the central sulcus. The supplementary motor area, largely on the medial aspect of the hemisphere, is shown *above* (after Travis, '55*a*).

disturbances of posture and tonus, but produce no paresis. Gradually increasing hypertonia develops during an interval of 2 to 4 weeks to the point of muscle contracture. The hypertonia is mainly in flexor muscles. Myotatic reflexes are hyperactive, and clonus can be demostrated. The developed spasticity demonstrates a topographical localization according to the portions of the supplementary motor area removed. Ablations of the supplementary motor area and the precentral motor area on the same side result in an immediate contralateral hypotonic paresis with impaired myotatic reflexes. Within a period of 2 weeks, the hypotonus changes to hypertonus and the myotatic reflexes become exaggerated. These studies indicate that spasticity can be dissociated from paresis and paralysis, and that these phenomena need not always occur together. As men-

tioned previously, these physiological findings concerning the supplementary motor area appear to explain the controversy regarding ablations of areas 4 and 6, and the relationships of so-called area 4S to muscle tonus. All evidence indicates that the supplementary motor area is a bilaterally functioning entity concerned primarily with mechanisms of posture and movement. Other observations (Coxe and Landau, '65) following bilateral simultaneous ablations of the supplementary motor area in the monkey indicate that such lesions produce a milder increase in muscle tone, inconsistent reflex changes, and no evidence of joint contracture. The explanation for these discrepancies is not obvious, but differences in the location and extent of the cortical lesions seems likely.

The neural pathways underlying responses from the supplementary motor area are poorly understood. Ablations of the supplementary motor area apparently do not produce degeneration passing to the spinal cord. Physiological study of efferent pathways from this motor area indicate that electrical stimulation of the supplementary motor area in the monkey evokes potentials in the region of the corticospinal tracts on both sides of the spinal cord (Bertrand, '56). The apparent bilateral features of this system are striking and appear to explain why unilateral lesions of the supplementary motor area cause only minor deficits. Penfield and Jasper ('54) report that motor responses from the supplementary motor area can be elicited after removal of the precentral gyrus.

According to Bates ('53), stimulation of this motor area in man, following hemispherectomy, induces ipsilateral movements similar to those which can be produced voluntarily.

Frontal Eye Fields. In front of the premotor area is a cortical region particularly concerned with voluntary eye movements. The frontal eye field in man occupies principally the caudal part of the middle frontal gyrus (corresponding to parts of area 8, shown in Figure 22-15) and extends into contiguous portions of the inferior frontal gyrus. The entire frontal eye field does not lie within a single cytoarchitectonic area. Cytoarchitecturally, area 8 is typical six-layered isocortex of the frontal type in which the granular layers are distinct (Fig. 22-6). Electrical stimulation of the frontal eye field in man causes strong conjugate deviation of the eyes, usually to the opposite side (Foerster, '31; Penfield and Rasmussen, '50). This cortical field is believed to be a center for voluntary scanning movements of the eyes.

Some studies in man and primates indicate a double representation of specific eye movements in each frontal eye field (Lemmen et al., '59; Crosby, '53; Crosby et al., '62). These authors divide the frontal eye field into upper (frontal eye field I) and lower (frontal eye field II) parts; frontal eye field II has a mirror image arrangement, compared to frontal eye field I. Patterns of eye movements elicited by stimulation of these fields in orderly sequence include: (1) deviation downwards and to the opposite side, (2) divergence, (3) conjugate deviation to the opposite side, and (4) deviation upward and to the opposite side. Voluntary eye movements in response to a visual stimulus require that impulses be relayed from area 17. These impulses are thought to be relayed via the inferior occipitofrontal fasciculus. Unilateral lesions of the frontal lobe involving the frontal eye field usually cause the eyes to be conjugately deviated toward the side of the lesion; this deviation is transient except in the unconscious patient. The manner in which impulses from the frontal eye fields are conveyed to brain stem nuclei is not known, though it seems likely that corticoreticular or corticotectal fibers are involved.

Nonpyramidal corticofugal fibers consist largely of corticoreticular, corticopontine, corticothalamic, and corticonuclear fibers (page 569). *Corticoreticular* fibers appear to originate from all parts of the cerebral cortex, but the largest number arise from the motor and premotor areas (Rossi and Brodal, '56). Inferior cortical areas (basal) and parts of the cortex on the medial surface of the hemisphere also contribute to the corticoreticular projection, but very few fibers arise from the auditory and visual areas. Only a few of these fibers arise from the temporal and occipital cortex. Corticoreticular fibers probably descend in association with fibers of the corticospinal tract, but they leave this bundle to enter specific areas of the brain stem reticular formation. The number of corticoreticular fibers is not large. The major part of these fibers terminate in two fairly well circumscribed areas, one in the medulla, another in the pons. The terminal area in the medulla corresponds to the nucleus reticularis gigantocellularis, while the pontine area coincides with the nucleus reticularis pontis oralis (Fig. 13-20). Unilateral cerebral lesions produce an approximately equal distribution of degenerated corticoreticular fibers on both sides of the reticular formation. The reticular areas receiving corticoreticular fibers correspond to areas which give rise to both reticulospinal fibers (Torvik and Brodal,

'57) and ascending reticular fibers projecting rostrally to mesencephalic levels (Brodal and Rossi, '55). Some corticoreticular fibers also reach reticular cerebellar relay nuclei, such as the reticulotegmental nucleus, the lateral reticular nucleus, and the paramedian reticular nuclei of the medulla.

Impulses mediated by certain corticoreticular fibers probably pass via intercalated reticular neurons to motor cranial nerve nuclei and in this sense can be regarded as corticobulbar fibers (see p. 326). The studies of Kuypers ('58a, '58b, and '58c) indicate that in the primate and man a direct corticobulbar projection to certain motor cranial nerve nuclei (trigeminal, facial, and hypoglossal) also exists. Thus corticobulbar fibers are represented by a phylogenetically older indirect pathway involving reticular neurons, and a more recent direct corticobulbar pathway, which seems to be characteristic only in primates (Fig. 14–23).

Corticoreticular fibers also may play a role in motor phenomena observed in response to stimulation of the cortex after section of the pyramids in the cat. According to Tower ('36), stimulation of the motor cortex under these conditions produces an inhibition of any movement previously present in the contralateral limbs. These inhibitory responses may be mediated by activation of inhibitory regions of the medullary reticular formation. More intense stimulation under these conditions produces mass movements. Finally it seems likely that corticoreticular fibers convey impulses to the reticular formation which play a role in initiating and maintaining the state of alertness and attention by influencing the ascending reticular activating system.

Another important system of efferent cortical fibers is represented by the extensive corticopontine tracts, which arise from the frontal, temporal, parietal, and occipital regions of the cortex. These tracts have been investigated in man and the monkey (Meyer et al., '47; Beck, '50; Nyby and Jansen, '51). The massive *frontopontine tract* (bundle of Arnold) arises mainly from the lateral and superior convexity of the whole prefrontal cortex (areas 10, 9, 8, 45, and 46), with the exception of the orbital region and the extreme frontal pole. A smaller contingent comes from the precentral region (areas 4 and 6). The prefrontal fibers pass through the anterior limb of the internal capsule, and the precentral ones through the posterior limb. On reaching the midbrain, the frontopontine tract forms the medial fifth of the crus cerebri, and is distributed to the medial pontine nuclei (Fig. 17–19). Other corticopontine tracts arise from the superior, middle, and inferior temporal gyri (*temporopontine*), and from the superior and inferior parietal lobules (*parietopontine*). A smaller *occipitopontine* bundle comes chiefly from area 18 of the occipital lobe (Nyby and Jansen, '51). The temporal, parietal, and occipital fibers, collectively known as the *bundle of Türck*, descend through the retrolenticular and sublenticular portions of the internal capsule. These fibers occupy the lateral fifth of the crus cerebri and are distributed mainly to the lateral and dorsolateral cell groups of the pons. Through these tracts the cerebral cortex is brought into intimate association with the synergic regulating mechanism of the cerebellum. The transient ataxia and hypotonia sometimes observed in frontal and temporal lesions may be due to injury of these corticocerebellar connections.

Corticothalamic fibers constitute a large group of cortical efferent fibers, but information is incomplete concerning the origins and terminations of these fibers. In general, cortical areas receiving projections from specific thalamic nuclei contribute efferent fibers which pass back to the same nuclei. Areas of granular frontal cortex project primarily to the dorsomedial nucleus of the thalamus, though some fibers pass to the submedial nucleus (Clark, '48; Meyer, '49). Particularly prominent among these fibers are those arising from frontal areas 9 and 10. According to Mettler ('47), corticofugal fibers to the dorsomedial nucleus come from areas 11, 9, 8, and 6 in the monkey. Most of these fibers reach the thalamus via the anterior limb of the internal capsule. Fibers from the cingulate gyrus pass to the anterior nucleus of the thalamus (Pribram and Fulton, '54; Showers, '59). Most of these fibers come from the supracallosal part of the cingulate gyrus at the transition of areas 24 and 23 and pass through the anterior thalamic radiations.

Corticothalamic fibers from the precentral area project to the ventral lateral nucleus of the thalamus (Clark, '32; Levin, '36, '49; Verhaart and Kennard, '40; Mettler, '47b; Hines, '49). Olszewski ('52) makes an important point that cortical efferent fibers from the precentral gyrus pass to both the pars oralis and the pars caudalis of the ventral lateral nucleus. Thus corticofugal fibers pass to regions of this nucleus that receive fibers from the cerebellum and globus pallidus (VLo), as well as to regions (VLc) which do not. Observations by Petras ('64) add details concerning a rather substantial cortical projection from areas 4 and 6 to the intralaminar nuclei. Area 4 projects mainly to the centromedian nucleus, while area 6 projects to the parafascicular and paracentral nuclei.

Efferent fibers from the parietal cortex in the monkey pass by way of the sensory radiations to the thalamic nuclei, from which they receive fibers. Corticothalamic fibers from the primary somesthetic cortex project to the ventral posterolateral and posteromedial nuclei, and have been described as ending in a somatotopic fashion within these nuclei (Peele, '42; Krieg, '54). A similar arrangement has been reported in the cat, though fibers from somatic area II project to the caudal extension of the ventral posteromedial nucleus (Stratford, '54). Fibers from parts of the auditory cortex project back to the medial geniculate body through sublenticular parts of the internal capsule (Papez, '36; Riley, '43; Krieg, '47; Walther and Rasmussen, '60). These fibers appear to pass to the magnocellular part of the medial geniculate body. The striate cortex, area 17, sends axons to the lateral geniculate body and to the lateral posterior nucleus of the thalamus (Nauta and Bucher, '54; Altman, '62).

While reciprocal relationships exist between the principal thalamic nuclei and their cortical projection sites, a different relationship pertains to the reticular and intralaminar thalamic nuclei. The thalamic reticular nucleus, which forms an envelope about the lateral surface of the thalamus, receives afferents from almost all areas of the cerebral cortex (Carman et al., '64). These corticothalamic fibers are organized so that rostral cortical regions project to rostral parts of the reticular nucleus and posterior cortical regions project to posterior portions of the nucleus. There is no evidence that the reticular nucleus of the thalamus projects to the cerebral cortex (Scheibel and Scheibel, '66). The intralaminar thalamic nuclei, like the reticular thalamic nucleus, do not project to the cerebral cortex, but they receive corticofugal fibers. According to Powell and Cowan ('67), most of the prefrontal cortex projects fibers to the rostral intralaminar thalamic nuclei. The premotor and motor cortex project fibers to centromedian and parafascicular nuclei; parietal and occipital cortex do not project fibers to the intralaminar thalamic nuclei.

Other nonpyramidal corticofugal fibers, collectively grouped together as corticonuclear fibers, pass to the neostriatum, the hypothalamus, and certain brain stem nuclei. Cortical projections to the neostriatum and extrapyramidal nuclei are discussed in Chapter 20 (page 503). Corticohypothalamic fibers in the monkey arise largely from the lateral and orbital surfaces of the frontal lobe, and are chiefly homolateral. Areas 8 and 10 project fibers to the supraoptic nucleus, while fibers to the paraventricular nucleus come from areas 10 and 47 and from the posterior and medial parts of the orbital surface. The posterior hypothalamic nucleus receives fibers from areas 45 and 47, and from the posterior orbital cortex (Ward and McCulloch, '47). Area 6 sends fibers to the mammillary bodies and the lateral and posterior hypothalamic nuclei. Particularly abundant connections to several hypothalamic nuclei, the preoptic nuclei, and the medial forebrain bundle arise from the posterior orbital cortex (Meyer, '49; Sachs et al., '49; Clark and Meyer, '50; Showers, '59). In addition, the hypothalamus receives indirect projections via the magnocellular part of the dorsomedial nucleus.

Corticofugal fibers, arising largely from the precentral and postcentral gyri, that leave the corticospinal tract in the lower brain stem and terminate upon certain secondary sensory relay nuclei, convey direct cortical impulses that modify the central propagation of afferent impulses (Hagbarth and Kerr, '54; Hernández-Péon and Hagbarth, '55). These fibers pass to the nuclei gracilis and cuneatus, the sensory trigeminal nuclei, and the nucleus of the solitary fasciculus (Brodal et al., '56; Torvik, '56; Walberg, '57; Kuypers, '58; '58a, '58b, '60; Kuypers et al., '61). These corticobulbar fibers are discussed in Chapter 14 (page 326).

Corticofugal fibers. The preceding descriptions and discussion indicate the extensive nature of fiber systems emerging from the cerebral cortex and descending to other parts of the neuraxis. The multiplicity of fibers originating from certain cortical areas suggests diverse but related functions. Obviously electrical stimulation of most cortical areas results in simultaneous activation of multiple fiber systems. Most of the cortical efferent fibers can be grouped into three principal efferent systems. The first and largest is the *corticospinal system*, which is concerned primarily with the fine, nonpostural, discrete movements of skilled activity. The second system, composed of *nonpyramidal corticofugal fibers* projecting to parts of the neostriatum, the thalamus, the hypothalamus, extrapyramidal brain stem nuclei, the reticular formation of the brain stem, and certain sensory relay nuclei, is concerned with the integration of somatic and visceral activities at all levels of the neuraxis. The third system of fibers, the *corticopontocerebellar system*, relates widely separated cortical areas with the cerebellum. It is through the integrative action of all these systems that the cerebral cortex makes its impressive contribution to the overall function of the nervous system.

Phenomenon of Cortical Suppression. Certain specific areas of the cerebral cortex, whose electrical stimulation is said to suppress the spontaneous electrical activity of area 4 and to inhibit responses from the motor cortex, have been described as suppressor areas. The first suppressor area in the monkey was defined as a narrow strip of cortex (so-called area 4S) lying between areas 4 and 6 (Hines, '36, '37). Area 4S is not generally recognized as a separate entity in cytoarchitectonic studies of the cortex. Subsequent studies based upon strychnine neuronography and electrical stimulation revealed several other areas (8S, 2S, 19S, and 24) from which suppressor effects could be elicited in the monkey and chimpanzee (Dusser de Barenne et al., '42; McCulloch, '49). Although the predominant effect of stimulating these areas is suppression of motor responses, some data indicate that the suppressor areas also influence afferent impulses to the cortex, and lead to a reduction in the amplitude of the EEG (Barker and Gellhorn, '47).

The phenomenon of cortical suppression appears to be somewhat inconstant and variable, depends to a degree on the depth of anesthesia, begins several minutes after the application of the stimulus, and persists for a relatively long time (i.e., up to 30 minutes). It has been postulated that suppressor activity of these cortical areas involves corticocaudate fibers. Direct corticocaudate projections from all suppressor areas have been demonstrated physiologically in the monkey and chimpanzee (Dusser de Barenne et al., '42). The concept of specific localized suppressor areas in the cortex has been challenged with the implication that the suppression observed in stimulating these areas probably is identical with that of the spreading depression of Leão (Sloan and Jasper, '50; Druckman, '52). The latter phenomenon is not restricted to specific cortical areas, but is related to experimental interferences. Leão ('44) described a depression of cortical rhythms in the rabbit which spreads slowly outward from the site of a weak mechanical, electrical, or chemical stimulus to the cortex. Neither evoked potentials nor motor responses to cortical stimulation could be observed when the depression reached the sensorimotor cortex. Species differences in susceptibility of the cortex to spreading depression have been noted in that depression is more easily produced in the rabbit than the cat and is seen only occasionally in the monkey. Substantial evidence indicates that cortical depression results from exposure of the brain to less than optimal physiological conditions, such as dehydration, cooling, or prolonged experimentation (Marshall, '50; Marshall and Essig, '51; Marshall et al., '51; Marshall, '59). The existence of specific suppressor areas in the cerebral cortex of either animals or man appears doubtful.

GENERAL CONSIDERATION OF CORTICAL FUNCTIONS

Cerebral Dominance. Although the two cerebral hemispheres appear as mirror images, or duplicates of each other, there are many functions which are not represented equally at a cortical level. This appears true even though impulses from receptors on each side of the body seem to project nearly equally, though largely contralaterally, to symmetrical cortical areas, and certain information received in the cortex of one hemisphere can be transferred to the other via interhemispheric commissures (Meyers, '56). In certain higher functions, believed to be cortical in nature, one hemisphere appears to be the "leading" one and, in this sense, is referred to as the *dominant hemisphere*. With respect to most of the higher functions, cerebral dominance appears to be one of degree (Zangwill, '60). According to Henschen ('26), cerebral dominance probably is most complete in relation to the complex and highly evolved aspects of language. Handedness also is related to cerebral dominance, though its relationship is less clear-cut than has been assumed in the past. It seems likely that handedness is a graded characteristic. Left-handedness, in particular, is less definite than right-handedness, and less regularly associated with dominance in either hemisphere. There also appears to

be a group of disturbances related to language that are said to be commonly associated with imperfectly developed cerebral dominance. These include the improper development of reading, writing, and drawing abilities, poor spatial judgment, and imperfect directional control (Zangwill, '60). In true right-handed individuals, it is nearly always the left hemisphere which is dominant and governs language and related processes; but the converse of this is not necessarily true. The degree of cerebral dominance appears to vary widely, not only among individuals, but with respect to different functions. Although a degree of "cerebral ambilaterality" would appear to be a distinct advantage with respect to recovery of speech following a unilateral cerebral injury, it appears to carry the risk or possibility of difficulty in learning to read, spell, and draw. The relationship between handedness and speech is perhaps a more natural one than is commonly realized, since some gesturing often accompanies speech and in certain situations may substitute for it. Although most clinicians relate handedness and speech to the dominant hemisphere, Penfield and Roberts ('59) report that there is no difference in the incidence of aphasia after operation on the left hemisphere between left- and right-handed patients, provided patients with cerebral injury occurring early in life are excluded. With this same exclusion there is said to be no significant difference in the frequency of aphasia after operations on the right hemisphere between right- and left-handed patients. Nevertheless, these authors regard the left hemisphere as dominant for speech regardless of handedness. Cerebral dominance is considered to have a genetic basis, but its hereditary determination probably is not absolute. Pathological and psychological factors also influence handedness, and many determining factors remain unknown.

Many cortical functions are concerned only with contralateral regions of the body, and unilateral lesions affecting these functions produce a disturbance contralaterally, regardless of cerebral dominance. This appears particularly true of the primary motor and sensory areas. It also is the case with lesions of the parietal cortex which result in *astereognosis*, or inability to recognize the form, size, texture, and identity of an object by touch alone. In certain parietal lobe lesions there is evidence that particular deficits occur more commonly in the nondominant hemisphere. One such syndrome is characterized by a disorder of the body image in which the patient: (1) fails to recognize part of his own body, (2) fails to appreciate the existence of hemiparesis, and (3) neglects to wash, shave, or cover the part of his body which he denies (Critchley, '53).

Interhemispheric Transfer. Though the corpus callosum is the largest of the interhemispheric commissures, relatively little has been known of its functions until recently. The first convincing evidence regarding its function was the demonstration of its importance in interhemispheric transfer of visual discrimination learning in cats with longitudinal section of the optic chiasm (Meyers, '56). Following section of the optic chiasm and corpus callosum, cats trained with one eye masked were unable to remember simple visual discriminations learned with the first eye. The untrained eye could be trained to make a reverse type of discrimination that did not interfere with the patterned discrimination learned on the opposite side. This apparent functional independence of the surgically separated cerebral hemispheres with respect to learning, memory, and other gnostic activity has been the stimulus for considerable investigation (Mountcastle, '62). The results originally suggested that section of the corpus callosum prevented the spread of learning and memory from one hemisphere to the other. It was as if each hemisphere existed independently and had a complete amnesia for the experience of the other (Sperry, '62). Extension of these transfer studies in the monkey from visual to somesthetic and motor learning (Sperry, '61, '62) have indicated that the independence of the surgically separated hemispheres may be less clear-cut than

originally supposed, and that in some instances strong transfer of learning can occur from one hemisphere to the other.

Observations of the functional effects of surgical separation of the hemispheres in man (Gazzaniga et al., '65; Gazzaniga and Sperry, '67) by complete transection of the corpus callosum, anterior and hippocampal commissures, and separation of the thalamic adhesion (massa intermedia) have been reported. These patients show a striking functional independence of the gnostic activities of the two hemispheres. Perceptual, cognitive, mnemonic, learned and volitional activities persist in each hemisphere, but each can proceed outside the realm of awareness of the other hemisphere. Subjective experiences of each hemisphere are known to the other only indirectly through lower level and peripheral effects. Disconnection of the hemispheres produces little disturbance of ordinary, daily behavior, temperament, or intellect. Functional deficits tend to be compensated for by development of bilateral motor control from each hemisphere, as well as by the bilaterality in some of the sensory pathways. Information perceived exclusively, or generated exclusively, in the minor (right) hemisphere could be communicated neither in speech, nor in writing; it was expressed entirely by nonverbal responses. There was no detectable impairment of speech or writing with reference to information processed in the major (left) hemisphere. These authors found linguistic expression to be organized almost exclusively in the dominant hemisphere. In contrast to the above, comprehension of language both spoken and written, was found to be represented in both hemispheres, with the minor hemisphere a little less proficient.

Nonspecific Thalamocortical Relationships. Even though anatomical details concerning the manner in which impulses from the nonspecific thalamic nuclei reach the cortex are poorly understood, there is abundant physiological evidence that these nuclei play an important role in the regulation of the electrical activity of the cerebral cortex. The fact that repetitive stimulation of the nonspecific thalamic nuclei gives rise to widespread, diffuse cortical responses of a recruiting nature (Dempsey and Morison, '42, '43; Morison and Dempsey, '42) has served to distinguish this system from the short latency, local cortical responses which characterize the specific thalamic nuclei. The ascending reticular activating system, related physiologically to alerting, attention, and general excitement, appears to exert its activating influences upon broad areas of the cerebral cortex, in part through the mediation of the nonspecific thalamic nuclei. This conclusion is based on the fact that cortical recruiting responses can be blocked by stimulation of portions of the ascending reticular activating system (Moruzzi and Magoun, '49; Machne et al., '55). EEG arousal responses also may reach the cortex by extrathalamic pathways (Starzl et al., '51).

Lorente de Nó ('49) described two types of cortical afferent fibers. Specific afferent fibers, forming the main projection system from the sensory relay nuclei of the thalamus, were described as terminating principally in layer IV of the cortex. What he referred to as "unspecific" fibers originated from: (1) undetermined regions of the thalamus independent of the specific thalamic nuclei, and (2) cortical cells giving rise to transcortical and commissural fibers. The nonspecific fibers ("unspecific") tended to terminate in all layers of the cortex. Most of these nonspecific fibers are regarded as terminating axodendritically in the cortex. Although the view is widely held that the nonspecific cortical afferents described by Lorente de Nó have their origin in the intralaminar thalamic nuclei, this thesis is not based upon direct evidence (Powell and Cowan, '67). Electrophysiological evidence suggests that a large proportion of the nonspecific thalamocortical fibers probably terminate in the more superficial layers of the cerebral cortex (Jasper, '60), although activation of cortical neurons at all depths has been observed during recruiting responses. According to current concepts, the recruiting waves recorded in the cortex following repetitive stimulation of the nonspecific thalamic nuclei probably represent dendritic responses or activity (Clare and Bishop, '56; Purpura and Grundfest, '56). These responses do not depend upon all-or-none firing of cortical cells; they are graded; and they have no refractory period. The absence of a refractory period implies that these waves may be summated over wide ranges, with amplitude and duration being functions of the stimulus. Recruiting responses are attributed to axodendritic depolarizing and hyperpolarizing postsynaptic potentials, mainly in the superficial layers of the cortex (Purpura, '59). Microelectrode studies indicate that recruiting responses can be obtained in the absence of unit discharges in the depths of the cortex.

Repetitive stimulation of the nonspecific thalamic nuclei produces changes in electrocortical activity over broad areas. These nonspecific thalamic nuclei are capable of exerting a massive excitation, mainly upon areas of associational cortex with a great preponderance of effects upon frontal associational cortex (Starzl and Whitlock, '52). These cortical responses are not dependent upon transmission by fibers of the corpus callosum or upon intracortical propagation. It seems generally accepted that the nonspecific thalamocortical projection system regulates the local and general excitability of the cortex and therefore the state of consciousness and awareness. As Magoun ('54) has stated, "It is not easy for the physiologist to put his finger upon consciousness, though it is present abundantly and for long periods." The most pronounced alterations of consciousness accompany the transition from sleep to wakefulness. Recordings of the electrical activity of the cerebral cortex provide objective evidence of this marked change of the conscious state. Although the whole brain must participate in what is called consciousness, the reticular formation and the nonspecific thalamocortical system appear to be the principal integrators, since it is through these systems that the cortical electrical activity is regulated (Gastaut, '54; Jasper, '58).

Sleep. Although at least four stages of sleep are recognized (Lindsley, '60; Kleitman, '63), the electrical activity of the brain of the sleeping mammal demonstrates two opposite, recurring, and closely interconnected forms (Jouvet, '67). One form, referred to as *slow sleep*, is characterized by synchronized cortical activity consisting of spindles (11–16 cycles/sec.), and/or high voltage slow waves. There is no specific behavioral criteria for slow sleep because the relationship between synchronized, or slow cortical activity, and sleep behavior is not absolute. During slow sleep, tone remains in the neck muscles, spinal reflex activity is present, and changes in autonomic activity are minimal. The EEG in the other form, known as *paradoxical sleep*, shows low voltage fast activity, which resembles that of the alert waking state. Paradoxical sleep occurs intermittently after variable periods of slow sleep and has precise behavioral criteria: (1) abolition of antigravity muscle tone (especially in cervical muscles), (2) depression of spinal reflex activity, (3) characteristic autonomic changes (i.e., reduction in blood pressure, bradycardia, and irregular respiration), and (4) bursts of rapid eye movements (REM). The fact that paradoxical sleep is "deeper" than slow sleep, but associated with an EEG pattern similar to that of the waking state gave rise to the term paradoxical sleep. So-called REM sleep (paradoxical sleep) occurs periodically during a night of sleep, with longer periods during the latter part of the night. If the subject is awakened during or immediately after a period of rapid eye movements, in 80 percent of the instances, the subject will report that he has been dreaming, and can relate the content of the dream (Lindsley, '60).

At one time physiological sleep was interpreted as the expression of a functional deafferentation of the ascending reticular arousal system which eliminated its waking influences. Current theory postulates the existence of synchronizing and sleep-inducing structures in the lower brain stem. It seems possible that these structures may include a group of serotonergic neurons located in the raphe nuclei (Jouvet, '67). The experiments of Rossi ('63) and Rossi et al., ('63) suggest that the triggering mechanism underlying the low voltage fast activity of paradoxical sleep are located in the pontine reticular formation. Ascending impulses conveyed by fibers arising from the medial and inferior vestibular nuclei have been shown to be of critical importance for the REM occurring during paradoxical sleep (Pompeiano and Morrison, '65).

Cortical Functioning. One of the most striking features of the human brain is its elaborate neural mechanism for the more complex correlation and discrimination of sensory impulses, and the greater utilization of former reactions. The principal function of this mechanism may be termed *associative memory* and the reactions it uses, *mnemonic* (memory) *reactions*. In man, the acquired changes which occur in the cortex after birth permit the neurons to alter subsequent stimuli reaching the cortex. This ability to retain, modify, and reuse neuronal chains provides the basis of conscious and unconscious memory, of personal experience, and of individually acquired neural mechanisms. Other animals utilize individual experience and thus "learn." However, it is very doubtful if any animal other than man summates experience by transmitting it to other individuals and new generations. The symbolization necessary for this summation undoubtedly requires the great complexity of the pallial mechanism for associative memory. It has been estimated that the cerebral cortex contains nearly 14 billion nerve cells, and by far the greater number of these may be utilized for the above activities.

In a general way, the central sulcus divides the brain into a posterior receptive portion and an anterior portion related more closely to efferent or motor functions. In the posterior part are all the primary receptive areas, which receive specific sensory impulses from the lower centers of the brain and hence indirectly from the peripheral sensory receptors. Impulses entering these primary areas produce sensations of a sharply defined character, such as distinct vision and hearing, sharply localized touch, and ac-

curate sensations of position and movement. However, these sensations have not
attained the perceptual level necessary
for the recognition of an object. This requires the integration of primary stimuli
into progressively more complicated sensory patterns. The regions in immediate
contact with the receptive centers, known
as *parasensory areas*, serve for the combination and elaboration of the primary impulses into more complex unisensory perceptions that are capable of recall under
appropriate conditions. In the more distant association areas the various sensory
fields overlap, e.g., the inferior parietal
lobule and adjacent portions of the occipital and temporal lobes. In these areas
the combinations are still more complicated and are expressed as multisensory
perceptions of a progressively higher order. Thus tactile and kinesthetic impulses are built up into perceptions of
form, size, and texture (stereognosis). Visual impulses are similarly compounded
into perceptions of visual object recognition. Hence any object comes to be represented ultimately by a constellation of
memories compounded from several sensory channels as a result of previous experience. When sensory impulses initiated by feeling or seeing an object are
capable of exciting these memory constellations, the object is "recognized," i.e.,
remembered as having been seen or felt
before. This arousal of the associative
mnemonic complexes by afferent cortical
impulses may be termed "gnosis," and it
forms the basis of understanding and
knowledge. Disorders of this mechanism
caused by lesions in the association areas
usually are known as gnostic disturbances
or *agnosias*. The tactile, visual, or auditory stimuli evoked by an object no
longer arouse the appropriate memories;
hence the object and its uses appear un-
familiar and strange. When such gnostic
disturbances involve the far more complicated associative mechanisms underlying the comprehension of language,
they form part of a complex known as the
aphasias. Closely related to both agnosia
and aphasia is another group of disorders
characterized by difficulty, or inability,
in performing learned complex or skilled
movements even though no paralysis, sensory loss, or ataxia is present. These disorders, which affect the motor side of
higher sensory-motor integration, are referred to as the *apraxias*. One must real-
ize that there are only two ways in which
a patient can show that he recognizes an
object: (1) by naming the object or de-
scribing its use, and (2) by demonstrating
its use. These simple methods demonstrate that the disorder of function in agnosia in part underlies both aphasia and
apraxia. If the patient can demonstrate
the use of an object, but is unable to
name or describe it, he has an aphasia. If
he can name or describe an object, but
does not know how to use it, he has an
apraxia.

Agnosia. The term agnosia means a failure to recognize. Various types of agnosias
have been defined according to the particular sensory channel which is affected.
Of the many types of agnosia classified on
this basis with respect to both objects and
space, three may properly be considered
here, namely, *tactile agnosia*, *visual agnosia*, and *auditory agnosia*.

Tactile agnosia is a failure to recognize
objects by means of tactile and proprioceptive sensibilities when both are normal in the part of the body being tested.
Astereognosis is the inability to recognize
objects owing to sensory impairment at a
cortical level. According to Brain ('61),
tactile agnosis is associated especially
with lesions of the supramarginal gyrus in
the left cerebral hemisphere, which may
be the dominant hemisphere for tactile
recognition.

Visual agnosia is a failure to recognize
objects that cannot be attributed to a defect of visual acuity or to intellectual impairment. Although a patient with visual
agnosia is unable to recognize an object
by sight, he may recognize it by other
sensibilities, and he can still recognize
people. The disability usually is limited
to small objects and varies somewhat from
day to day. In some instances the visual
agnosia may extend to surroundings, and
it then results in spatial disorientation.
Lesions associated with visual agnosia

alexia => angular gyrus

involve the lateral visual association areas in the dominant hemisphere. The term *alexia* denotes a special form of visual agnosia in which the patient is unable to read because he fails to recognize written or printed words. Lesions in this syndrome interrupt pathways conveying impulses from the visual cortex of both sides to the angular gyrus of the left hemisphere.

Auditory agnosia is the term used to describe the condition in which a patient with unimpaired hearing fails to recognize or distinguish what he hears. This type of agnosia may involve speech, musical sounds, or familiar noises, such as the telephone bell or running water. One form of auditory agnosia, known as word deafness, constitutes a type of receptive aphasia. Lesions associated with auditory agnosia involve parts of the superior temporal convolution posteriorly (area 22) in the dominant hemisphere, though these disturbances are more severe when the injury is bilateral.

Aphasia. This disorder is characterized by receptive and expressive disturbances in the faculty of using symbols and signs to communicate. It results from organic neural lesions involving cerebral memory mechanisms for language without impairment of cortical or subcortical structures essential for the relay of impulses, or the innervation of speech organs (i.e., the muscles of the larynx, tongue, and lips). The aphasias usually are divided into two basic types: receptive (sensory) and expressive (motor). In receptive aphasia the disturbance involves an impairment in the appreciation of the meanings of both spoken and written words. Expressive aphasia is characterized by impairment or lack of ability to express thoughts in a meaningful way in speech or writing. Less severe forms of expressive aphasia may involve primarily the incorrect choice of words, or grammatical confusion. The division of the aphasias into these two types suggests a more clear-cut distinction than our understanding permits, since certain common disturbances of memory and language must be involved in both types. While relatively pure receptive or expressive forms of aphasia do

occur, mixed varieties are the most common. Certain patients with severe expressive forms of aphasia may be capable of making meaningful gestures which suggest some degree of thought comprehension.

It is extremely difficult to locate precisely the site, or sites, of lesions which result in different forms of aphasia. Most evidence suggests that the disorder is associated with lesions involving the posterior temporoparietal region, and the so-called Broca's area (portions of the pars opercularis and triangularis of the inferior frontal gyrus) in the dominant hemisphere (Penfield and Roberts, '59; Brain, '61). Penfield and Roberts ('59) report that any large lesion in the posterior temporoparietal region that involves the cortex and underlying projection areas of the thalamus causes a severe aphasia. Although Broca's speech area has long been considered the cortical site of lesions in expressive aphasia, several observers have questioned its significance (Marie, '06; Mettler, '49; Jefferson, '50). According to these authors, this area can be sacrificed in the adult without eventual loss of normal speech. Penfield and Roberts ('59) also suggest that it is less important than the posterior temporoparietal region.

Apraxia. The inability to perform certain learned complex movements, in the absence of paralysis, sensory loss, or disturbance of coordination, is known as apraxia. Since complex voluntary movements require the utilization of cerebral processes in formulating the nature of the act to be performed, movements of this nature are considered separate from those which are more or less automatic. Formulation of these movement complexes is largely unconscious and appears to depend upon memory constellations of similar acts previously performed. Complex learned movement patterns are organized in space and time, and follow intricate sequences requiring close attention. Multiple sensory systems contribute to the skill of these movement patterns. Apraxia has been regarded as a disorganization of the underlying complex movement patterns. Many varieties of apraxia have been pro-

Voncida ?

posed as distinct entities, though some tend to have common features.

Kinetic apraxia is characterized by an inability to execute fine acquired motor movements; there is no paresis, and automatic and associated movements can be carried out. This disturbance may be confined to one limb. It has been interpreted as an expressive defect and most frequently is associated with lesions of the precentral cortex. The defect usually occurs contralateral to the lesion (De Jong, '58).

Ideomotor apraxia is caused by an interruption of pathways between the center for formulation of a motor act and the motor areas necessary for its execution. Although the patient may know what he wants to do, he is unable to do it. He can perform many complex acts automatically, but he may fail to perform the same acts on command. Spontaneous gestures may be normal. Ideomotor apraxia is often bilateral and affects the extremities equally. It is said to be associated with lesions of the parietal lobe, particularly the supramarginal gyrus, in the dominant hemisphere.

Ideational apraxia is the term used to describe loss of ability to formulate the ideational plan for the execution of the components of a complex act. While simple isolated movements may be performed normally, the component movements of a complex act are not synthesized into a purposeful plan and individual movements may be performed in a faulty sequence. Since kinesthetic memory and appreciation of the act to be performed are defective, ideational apraxia may be a variety of agnosia. This form of apraxia has been considered to result from lesions in the dominant parietal lobe, or in the corpus callosum, but frequently it is associated with rather diffuse pathological processes.

Constructional apraxia is a disorder characterized by loss of visual guidance, impairment of the visual image, and disturbances of revisualization. A patient suffering from this form of apraxia is unable to reproduce simple geometric figures by drawing or by the arrangement of blocks. Although this form of apraxia is

included with expressive disorders of motor function, it is rarely a pure motor disorder. As a rule the patient is unaware of his inability to perceive spatial relationships. This variety of apraxia appears to be related to interruption of pathways between the occipital and parietal cortex (Critchley, '53).   *ANGULAR GYRUS*

Certain curious combinations of agnosia and apraxia occur as a consequence of lesions involving primarily the inferior parietal lobe, usually in the dominant hemisphere (Gerstmann, '40; Critchley, '53). This syndrome is characterized by: (1) finger agnosia, (2) right-left disorientation, (3) agraphia or dysgraphia, and (4) acalculia or dyscalculia. Patients suffering from this syndrome have difficulty in differentiating their fingers, in naming the individual fingers, and in pointing to particular fingers. Right-left disorientation, unlike finger agnosia, may affect all parts of the body, as well as inanimate objects and other individuals. The disturbance in writing does not extend to copying, which can be accomplished without difficulty. Inability to solve arithmetical problems is most evident with written figures, but it involves mental calculations as well.

Prefrontal Cortex. The frontal lobe rostral to areas 6 and 8 represents a relatively late phylogenetic acquisition which is well-developed only in primates, especially in man. These areas of cortex, including that on the orbital surface, are referred to as the prefrontal cortex. Areas of cortex on the lateral convexity of the brain (particularly areas 9 and 10) receive a large number of fibers from the dorsomedial nucleus of the thalamus, which bring impulses from autonomic centers of the hypothalamus. These areas are connected by the cingulum and the uncinate fasciculus with anterior portions of the temporal lobe and, directly or indirectly, with parietal and adjacent occipitotemporal association areas. It is the opinion of some that complex memory patterns formed in areas caudal to the central sulcus may be transmitted to the prefrontal areas and synthesized into mnemonic constellations, which perhaps form the basis of abstract thinking and of certain higher intellectual activities. In the prefrontal region, these highly discriminative cortical activities are blended with the activities of the hypothalamus and medial nuclear groups of the thalamus, which represent more primitive affective components of consciousness, and probably play an important role in emotional responses. Russell ('48) believes that the prefrontal areas are not primarily concerned with memory or general intelligence, but rather with the establishment and conditioning of emotional reactions. They are of great importance during childhood and the growing years, when behavioral patterns are being formed. Emotional reactions become less prominent after maturity, when behavior patterns have become established.

A procedure known as prefrontal *lobotomy* or *leucotomy* was used widely some years ago in attempts to modify the behavior of severely psychotic patients. The basic operation involved sectioning of the fiber connections to and from the prefrontal area, and it usually was performed bilaterally. Lobotomy, introduced by Moniz ('36), became popular in the United States and elsewhere in the 1940's (Freeman and Watts, '49). This neurosurgical procedure permitted many institutionalized patients to return home and even to resume their former activities. Moreover, a considerable number of lobotomies were performed for the relief of chronic intractable pain of organic origin when other measures, such as massive doses of narcotics and even cordotomy, had proved of no avail (Falconer, '48; Freeman and Watts, '49; Scarff, '49). After the operation, the patient no longer complained spontaneously of pain and no longer appeared to be in distress, though when asked, he acknowledged that pain was still present. Relief was apparently due to removal of the anxiety and fear that usually are associated with pain. Since prefrontal lobotomy, and numerous technical variations of it (Mettler, '49; Green et al., '52), was performed on a large number of patients, it afforded an opportunity to study the associated intellectual and behavioral effects of these lesions.

The results of numerous lobotomies have been critically discussed in a number of publications (Freeman and Watts, '49; Partridge, '50; Denny-Brown, '51). These studies are difficult to evaluate because of lack of agreement concerning the extent of the changes in behavior and intellect. Most striking are the alterations in emotional behavior, which were characterized by Freeman and Watts as a lessening of "consciousness of the self", and a narrowing of the patient's mental horizon to the immediate present and to his own person. The patient is easily amused, careless in personal habits, unconcerned in social relations, and little affected by criticism. His emotional reactions are abrupt, transient, and superficial, and they often are accompanied by outspoken tactlessness. Pain and hardship are not associated with anxiety, nor is there much concern about financial or domestic difficulties. There is inability to gauge or appreciate the gravity of a situation and to maintain a responsible attitude towards it. These are the most enduring changes which can be attributed to the operation, and they probably are responsible for the successful abolition of morbid anxiety and obsessional states (Freeman and Watts, '49).

Intellectual damage is especially difficult to evaluate. General memory returns rapidly, and standard psychometric tests are accurately performed. Nearly all agree that the capacity for abstract thought is reduced and that the patient develops a more concrete attitude. Easy distractibility is common, judgment is poor, and initiative is reduced. Mental concentration and the capacity for sustained intellectual effort are impaired, especially with respect to solving complex problems. The most reliable data concerning the effects of lobotomy upon intelligence are those obtained from nonpsychotic patients in whom this procedure was done for relief of pain. On the basis of thorough studies of patients before and after operation, Rylander ('48) concluded that intellectual and emotional deterioration may be severe. The results of the operation necessarily depend upon the intelligence of the patient and the extent of the operative procedure. This conclusion appears to be supported by others (Koskoff et al., '48). Other forms of prefrontal lobe surgery, such as topectomy and orbitofrontal lobotomy, are not reported to produce such severe impairment of intellectual function (Landis et al., '50; Green et al., '52). The fact that the extent of intellectual deterioration following prefrontal lobotomy cannot be measured in specific terms reflects the exceedingly complex nature of what is called intellect and suggests that the criteria used to evaluate it may not be adequate.

In spite of the difficulties in evaluating the behavior changes and the intellectual alterations of prefrontal lobotomy, many patients were considered to have benefited from the operation. Perhaps the greatest problem, and one of the reasons why this form of psychosurgery is done only rarely now, was the difficulty in determining preoperatively which patients might be expected to be improved by it. Another important factor in the decline of psychosurgery was the introduction of the so-called tranquilizing drugs which have facilitated the treatment of severe behavioral disorders.

The structure and function of the basic features of the human nervous system have been presented, and the reader has had an opportunity to form certain concepts regarding detailed and overall aspects of this system. Although the functions of the nervous system are spectacular, it must be admitted that its gross appearance is not impressive. The human nervous system has evolved slowly, and although many of the details of its anatomical structure appear firmly established, concepts concerning the functional significance and interrelation of its various subdivisions change as a result of continuing research. Many so-called "electronic brains" have been constructed which can perform certain functions faster and more efficiently than the human brain. The more complex the performed function, the more elaborate the programming of the computer must be. "Electronic brains" are impressive in appearance and function; yet they do not approach in versatility or scope the fantastic potentialities of the human brain. The human brain is unique in that it can provide its own programming; in fact, it is programmed throughout life by our daily experiences. It seems likely that "electronic brains" will in the future perform many more of the functions now performed by human brains, but this change must be regarded as a redistribution of labor, not a replacement. The "electronic brain" is after all only one of the many expressions of the ingenuity of the human brain.

BIBLIOGRAPHY

ABD-EL-MALEK, S. 1938. On the presence of sensory fibers in the ocular nerves. J. Anat., **72:** 524–530.

ABERCROMBIE, M., AND JOHNSON, M. L. 1947. The effect of reinnervation on collagen formation in degenerating sciatic nerves of rabbits. J. Neurol. Neurosurg. & Psychiat., **10:** 89–92.

ADAL, M. N., AND BARKER, D. 1965. Intramuscular branching of fusimotor fibres. J. Physiol., **177:** 288–299.

ADAMS, C. W. M. 1965. Disorders of neurons and neuroglia. In C. W. M. ADAMS (Editor), *Neurohistochemistry*. Elsevier Publishing Company, Amsterdam. Ch. 10, pp. 403–436. (See also Ch. 1–8, pp. 1–332)

ADAMS, C. W. M., IBRAHIM, M. Z. M., AND LEIBOWITZ, S. 1965. Demyelination. In C. W. M. ADAMS (Editor), *Neurohistochemistry*. Elsevier Publishing Company, Amsterdam. Ch. 11, pp. 437–487.

ADDISON, W. H. F. 1915. On the rhinencephalon of *Delphinus delphis*. J. Comp. Neurol., **25:** 497–522.

ADES, H. W. 1941. Connections of the medial geniculate body in the cat. Arch. Neurol. & Psychiat., **45:** 138–144.

ADES, H. W. 1943. A secondary acoustic area in the cerebral cortex of the cat. J. Neurophysiol., **6:** 59–64.

ADES, H. W. 1959. Central auditory mechanisms. In J. FIELD (Editor), *Handbook of Physiology*, Section I, Vol. I. American Physiological Society, Washington, D. C. Ch. 24, pp. 585–613.

ADES, H. W., AND BROOKHART, J. M. 1950. The central auditory pathway. J. Neurophysiol., **13:** 189–205.

ADES, H. W., AND FELDER, R. 1942. The acoustic area of the monkey (*Macaca mulatta*). J. Neurophysiol., **5:** 49–54.

ADEY, W. R., AND MEYER, M. 1952. Hippocampal and hypothalamic connexions of the temporal lobe in the monkey. Brain, **75:** 358–384.

ADEY, W. R., SEGUNDO, J. P., AND LIVINGSTON, R. B. 1957. Corticofugal influences on intrinsic brain stem conduction in cat and monkey. J. Neurophysiol., **20:** 1–16.

ADLER, A. 1933. Zur Topik des Verlaufes der Geschmackssinnsfasern und anderer afferenter Bahnen im Thalamus. Ztschr. ges. Neurol. u. Psychiat., **149:** 208–220.

ADRIAN, E. D. 1940. Double representation of the feet in the sensory cortex of the cat. J. Physiol., **98:** 16P–18P (abstract).

ADRIAN, E. D. 1941. Afferent discharges to the cerebral cortex from peripheral sense organs. J. Physiol., **100:** 159–191.

ADRIAN, E. D. 1943. Afferent areas of the cerebellum connected with the limbs. Brain, **66:** 289–315.

AFIFI, A., AND KAELBER, W. W. 1965. Efferent connections of the substantia nigra in the cat. Exper. Neurol., **11:** 474–482.

AITKEN, H. F. 1909. A report on the circulation of the lobar ganglia made to Dr. James B. Ayer (with a postscript by J. B. Ayer, M.D.). Boston Med. & Surg. J., **160:** Suppl. 18.

AKELAITIS, A. J. 1943. Study of language function (tactile and visual lexia and graphia) unilaterally following section of the corpus callosum. J. Neuropath. & Exper. Neurol., **2:** 226–262.

AKELAITIS, A. J., RISTEEN, W. A., HERREN, R. Y., AND VAN WAGENEN, W. P. 1942. Studies on corpus callosum; contribution to study of dyspraxia and apraxia following partial and complete section of corpus callosum. Arch. Neurol. & Psychiat., **47:** 971–1008.

AKERT, K., POTTER, H. D., AND ANDERSON, J. W. 1961. The subfornical organ in mammals. I. Comparative and topographic anatomy. J. Comp. Neurol., **116:** 1–14.

ALEXANDER, L. 1942. The vascular supply of the striopallidum. A. Res. Nerv. & Ment. Dis., Proc., **21:** 77–132.

ALLEN, W. F. 1919. Application of the Marchi method to the study of the radix mesencephalica trigemini in the guinea pig. J. Comp. Neurol., **30:** 169–216.

ALLEN, W. F. 1923. Origin and destination of the

tractus solitarius in the guinea pig. J. Comp. Neurol., **35:** 273–311.

ALLEN, W. F. 1925. Identification of the cells and fibers concerned in the innervation of the teeth. J. Comp. Neurol., **39:** 325–343.

ALLEN, W. F. 1927. Experimental-anatomical studies on the visceral bulbospinal pathway in the cat and guinea pig. J. Comp. Neurol., **42:** 393–456.

ALLEN, W. F. 1940. Effects of ablating the frontal lobes, hippocampi, and occipito-parieto-temporal (excepting pyriform areas) lobes on positive and negative olfactory conditioned reflexes. Am. J. Physiol., **128:** 754–771.

ALLEN, W. F. 1941. Effect of ablating the pyriform-amygdaloid areas and hippocampi on positive and negative olfactory conditioned reflexes and on conditioned olfactory differentiation. Am. J. Physiol., **132:** 81–92.

ALLISON, A. C. 1953. The morphology of the olfactory system in the vertebrates. Biol. Rev. Cambridge Phil. Soc., **28:** 195–244.

ALLISON, A. C. 1954. The secondary olfactory areas in the human brain. J. Anat., **88:** 481–488.

ALTMAN, J. 1962. Some fiber projections to the superior colliculus in the cat. J. Comp. Neurol., **119:** 77–95.

ALTMAN, J., AND CARPENTER, M. B. 1961. Fiber projections of the superior colliculus in the cat. J. Comp. Neurol., **116:** 157–178.

AMBROGI, L. P. 1960. *Manual of Histologic and Special Staining Technics*. Ed. 2. McGraw-Hill Book Company, Inc., New York. pp. 157–174.

AMOROSO, E. C., BELL, F. R., AND ROSENBERG, H. 1954. The relationship of the vasomotor and respiratory regions in the medulla oblongata of the sheep. J. Physiol., **126:** 86–95.

ANAND, B. K., AND BROBECK, J. R. 1951. Hypothalamic control of food intake in rats and cats. Yale J. Biol. & Med., **24:** 123–140.

ANAND, B. K., AND BROBECK, J. R. 1951a. Localization of a "feeding center" in the hypothalamus of the rat. Proc. Soc. Exper. Biol. & Med., **77:** 323–324.

ANAND, B. K., AND BROBECK, J. R. 1952. Food intake and spontaneous activity of rats with lesions in the amygdaloid nuclei. J. Neurophysiol., **15:** 421–430.

ANAND, B. K., AND DUA, S. 1956. Circulatory and respiratory changes induced by electrical stimulation of limbic system (visceral brain). J. Neurophysiol., **19:** 393–400.

ANDÉN, N. E., CARLSSON, A., DAHLSTRÖM, A., FUXE, K., HILLARP, N. A., AND LARSSON, K. 1964. Demonstration and mapping out of nigro-neostriatal dopamine neurons. Life Sc., **3:** 523–530.

ANDERSSON, B., AND JEWELL, P. A. 1957. Studies on the thalamic relay for taste in the goat. J. Physiol., **139:** 191–197.

ANDERSSON, S., AND GERNANDT, B. E. 1954. Cortical projection of vestibular nerve in cat. Acta oto-laryng., **116**(suppl.): 10–18.

ANDY, O. J., AND BROWN, J. S. 1960. Diencephalic coagulation in the treatment of hemiballismus. S. Forum, Proc. Clin. Cong. Am. Coll. Surgeons, **10:** 795–799.

ANGAUT, P., AND BOWSHER, D. 1965. Cerebellorubral connexions in the cat. Nature, **208:** 1002–1003.

ANGAUT, P., AND BRODAL, A. 1967. The projection of the "vestibulocerebellum" onto the vestibular nuclei in the cat. Arch. ital. Biol., **105:** 441–479.

ANGEVINE, J. B. 1965. Time of neuron origin in the hippocampal region. An autoradiographic study in the mouse. Exper. Neurol., Suppl., **2:** 1–70.

ANGEVINE, J. B., MANCALL, E. L., AND YAKOVLEV, P. I. 1961. *The Human Cerebellum. An Atlas of Gross Topography in Serial Sections*. Little, Brown & Company, Boston.

ANGEVINE, J. B., LOCKE, S., AND YAKOVLEV, P. I. 1962. Limbic nuclei of thalamus and connections of limbic cortex: IV. Thalamocortical projection of the ventral anterior nucleus in man. Arch. Neurol., **7:** 518–528.

ANGEVINE, J. B., AND SIDMAN, R. L. 1961. Autoradiographic study of cell migration during histogenesis of cerebral cortex in the mouse. Nature, **192:** 766–768.

APPELBERG, B. 1960. Localization of focal potentials evoked in the red nucleus and ventrolateral nucleus of the thalamus by electrical stimulation of the cerebellar nuclei. Acta physiol. scandinav., **51:** 356–370.

APTER, J. T. 1954. The significance of the unilateral Argyll-Robertson Pupil. Part I. A report of 13 cases. Am. J. Ophth., **38:** 34–43.

APTER, J. T. 1954a. The significance of the unilateral Argyll-Robertson Pupil. Part II. A critical review of the theories of its pathogenesis. Am. J. Ophth., **38:** 209–222.

ARDUINI, A., AND ARDUINI, M. G. 1954. Effect of drugs and metabolic alterations on brain stem arousal mechanisms. J. Pharmacol. & Exper. Therap., **110:** 76–85.

AREY, L. B. 1938. The history of the first somite in human embryos. Carnegie Inst. Washington, Contrib. Embryol., **27:** 233–269.

AREY, L. B. 1954. *Developmental Anatomy*, Ed. 6. W. B. Saunders Company, Philadelphia.

ASHCROFT, D. W., AND HALLPIKE, C. S. 1934. On the function of the saccule. J. Laryng. & Otol., **49:** 450–460.

ÅSTRÖM, K. E. 1967. On the early development of the cortex in fetal sheep. In C. G. BERNHARD

AND J. P. SCHADÉ (Editors), *Developmental Neurology, Progress in Brain Research*. Vol. 26. Elsevier Publishing Company, New York, pp. 1–59.

ASTRUC, J. 1964. Corticofugal fiber degeneration following lesions of area 8 (frontal eye field) in Macaca mulatta. Anat. Rec., **148:** 256.

BABKIN, B. P. 1950. Significance of the double innervation of the salivary glands. In B. P. BABKIN (Editor), *Secretory Mechanism of the Digestive Glands*, Ed. 2. P. B. Hoeber Company, New York. Ch. 27, pp. 733–766.

BAGSHAW, M. H., AND PRIBRAM, K. H. 1953. Cortical organization in gustation (*Macaca mulatta*). J. Neurophysiol., **16:** 499–508.

BAILEY, P. 1948. *Intracranial Tumors*, Ed. 2. Charles C Thomas, Publisher, Springfield, Ill., p. 212.

BAILEY, P., VON BONIN, G., GAROL, H. W., AND MC-CULLOCH, W. S. 1943. Functional organization of temporal lobe of monkey (*Macaca mulatta*) and chimpanzee (*Pan satyrus*). J. Neurophysiol., **6:** 121–128.

BAILEY, P., GAROL, H. W., AND McCULLOCH, W. S. 1941. Cortical origin and distribution of corpus callosum and anterior commissure in the chimpanzee (*Pan satyrus*). J. Neurophysiol., **4:** 564–571.

BAKAY, L. 1952. Studies on blood-brain barrier with radioactive phosphorus. Arch. Neurol. & Psychiat., **68:** 629–640.

BAKAY, L. 1956. *The Blood-Brain Barrier*. Charles C Thomas, Publisher, Springfield, Ill., pp. 1–30.

BAKER, A. B. 1961. Cerebrovascular disease. IX. The medullary blood supply and the lateral medullary syndrome. Neurology, **11:** 852–861.

BAKER, J. R. 1960. *Cytological Technique. Methuen's Monographs on Biological Subjects.* John Wiley and Sons, New York.

BARD, P. 1939. Central nervous mechanisms for emotional behavior patterns in animals. A. Res. Nerv. & Ment. Dis., Proc., **19:** 190–218.

BARD, P., AND MOUNTCASTLE, V. B. 1948. Some forebrain mechanisms involved in expression of rage with special reference to suppression of angry behavior. A. Res. Nerv. & Ment. Dis., Proc., **27:** 362–404.

BARD, P., AND RIOCH, D. M. 1937. A study of 4 cats deprived of neocortex and additional portions of the forebrain. Bull. Johns Hopkins Hosp., **60:** 73–147.

BARGMANN, W., HILD, W., ORTHMANN, R., AND SCHIEBLER, T. H. 1950. Morphologische und experimentelle Untersuchungen über das hypothalamischhypophysäre System. Acta neuroveg., **1:** 233–275.

BARKER, D. 1948. The innervation of the mus-cle-spindle. Quart. J. Microscop. Sci., **89:** 143–186.

BARKER, D. 1967. The innervation of mammalian skeletal muscle. In A. V. S. DE REUCK AND J. KNIGHT (Editors), *Myotatic, Kinesthetic and Vestibular Mechanisms*. Little, Brown and Company, Boston, pp. 3–15.

BARKER, D., AND COPE, M. 1962. The innervation of individual intrafusal muscle fibers. In D. BARKER (Editor), *Symposium on Muscle Receptors*. Hong Kong University Press, Hong Kong, pp. 263–269.

BARKER, S. H., AND GELLHORN, E. 1947. Influence of suppressor areas on afferent impulses. J. Neurophysiol., **10:** 133–138.

BARNARD, J. W., AND WOOLSEY, C. N. 1956. A study of localization in the corticospinal tracts of monkey and rat. J. Comp. Neurol., **105:** 25–50.

BARNES, S. 1901. Degenerations in hemiplegia: with special reference to a ventrolateral pyramidal tract, the accessory fillet and Pick's bundle. Brain, **24:** 463–501.

BARNES, W. T., MAGOUN, H. W., AND RANSON, S. W. 1943. The ascending auditory pathway in the brain stem of the monkey. J. Comp. Neurol., **79:** 129–152.

BARR, M. L. 1939. Some observations on the morphology of the synapse in the cat's spinal cord. J. Anat., **74:** 1–11.

BARR, M. L., BERTRAM, L. F. AND LINDSAY, H. A. 1950. The morphology of the nerve cell nucleus according to sex. Anat. Rec., **107:** 283–297.

BARTON, A. A., AND CAUSEY, G. 1958. Electron microscopic study of the superior cervical ganglion. J. Anat., **92:** 399–407.

BATES, J. A. V. 1953. Stimulation of the medial surface of the human cerebral hemisphere after hemispherectomy. Brain, **76:** 405–447.

BAXTER, D. W., AND OLSZEWSKI, J. 1955. Respiratory responses evoked by electrical stimulation of pons and mesencephalon. J. Neurophysiol., **18:** 276–287.

BEAMS, H. W., AND KING, R. L. 1935. The effect of ultracentrifuging the spinal ganglia cells of the rat, with special reference to Nissl bodies. J. Comp. Neurol., **61:** 175–184.

VON BECHTEREW, W. V. 1900. Demonstration eines Gehirns mit Zerstörung der vorderen und inneren Theile der Hirnrinde beider Schläfenlappen. Neurol. Centralbl., **19:** 990–991.

BECK, E. 1929. Die myeloarchitektonische Felderung des in der Sylvischen Furche gelegenen Teiles des menschlichen Schläfenlappens. J. Psychol. u. Neurol., **36:** 1–21.

BECK, E. 1950. The origin, course and termination of the prefronto-pontine tract in the human brain. Brain, **73:** 368–391.

BELL, C. C., AND DOW, R. S. 1967. Cerebellar

circuitry. Neurosc. Res. Progr. Bull., **5:** (no. 2) 121–222.

BENDA, C. E., AND COBB, S. 1942. On the pathogenesis of paralysis agitans (Parkinson's disease). Medicine, **21:** 95–142.

BENDER, M. B., AND WEINSTEIN, E. A. 1944. Effects of stimulation and lesion of the median longitudinal fasciculus in the monkey. Arch. Neurol. & Psychiat., **52:** 106–113.

BENDER, M. B., AND WEINSTEIN, E. A. 1950. The syndrome of the median longitudinal fasciculus. A. Res. Nerv. & Ment. Dis., Proc. **28:** 414–420.

BENJAMIN, R. M. 1963. Some thalamic and cortical mechanisms of taste. In Y. ZOTTERMAN (Editor), *Olfaction and Taste.* The Macmillian Company, New York, pp. 309–329.

BENJAMIN, R. M., AND AKERT, K. 1959. Cortical and thalamic areas involved in taste discrimination in the albino rat. J. Comp. Neurol., **111:** 231–260.

BENSLEY, R. R., AND GERSH, I. 1933. Studies on cell structure by the freezing-drying method. III. The distribution of cells of the basophil substances, in particular the Nissl substance of the nerve cell. Anat. Rec., **57:** 369–385.

BERGER, H. 1929. Ueber das Elektrenkephalogramm des Menschen. Arch. Psychiat., **87:** 527–570.

BERGER, H. 1930. Ueber das Elektrenkephalogramm des Menschen. J. Psychol. u. Neurol., **40:** 160–179.

BERKE, J. J. 1960. The claustrum, the external capsule, and the extreme capsule of the Macaca mulatta. J. Comp. Neurol., **115:** 297–331.

BERN, H. A., AND KNOWLES, F. G. W. 1966. Neurosecretion. In L. M. MARTINI AND W. F. GANONG (Editors), *Neuroendocrinology.* Academic Press, New York, Ch. 5, pp. 139–186.

BERN, H. A., AND YAGI, K. 1965. Electrophysiology of neurosecretory systems. In *Proceedings of the 2nd International Congress of Endocrinology.* Excerpta Medica International Congress, Section 83 (Part I), pp. 577–583.

BERNHARD, C. G. 1954. The corticospinal system. D. NACHMANSOHN AND H. H. MERRITT (Editors), *Nerve Impulse,* Transactions of the Fifth Conference, J. Macy, Jr. Foundation, New York, pp. 95–134.

BERNHARD, C. G., AND BOHM, E. 1954. Cortical representation and functional significance of the cortico-motoneuronal system. Arch. Neurol. & Psychiat., **72:** 473–502.

BERNHARD, C. G., BOHM, E., AND PETERSEN, I. 1953. Investigations on the organization of the corticospinal system in monkeys. Acta physiol. scandinav., **29:** 79–103.

BERNHARD, C. G., KOLMODIN, G. M. AND MEYERSON, B. A. 1967. On the prenatal development of function and structure in the somesthetic cortex of the sheep. In C. G. BERNHARD AND J. P.

SCHADÉ (Editors), *Developmental Neurology, Progress in Brain Research.* Vol. 26. Elsevier Publishing Company, New York, pp. 78–91.

BERNHAUT, M., GELLHORN, E. AND RASMUSSEN, A. T. 1953. Experimental contributions to problem of consciousness. J. Neurophysiol., **16:** 21–35.

BERNHEIMER, S. 1897. Experimentelle Studien zur Kenntnis der Innervation der inneren und äusseren vom Oculomotorius versorgten Muskeln des Auges. Von Graefes Arch. Ophthal., **44:** 481–525.

BERRY, C. M., ANDERSON, F. D., AND BROOKS, D. C. 1956. Ascending pathways of the trigeminal nerve in cat. J. Neurophysiol., **19:** 144–153.

BERRY, C. M., HAGAMEN, W. D., AND HINSEY, J. C. 1952. Distribution of potentials following stimulation of olfactory bulb in cat. J. Neurophysiol., **15:** 139–145.

BERRY, C. M., KARL, R. S., AND HINSEY, J. C. 1950. Course of spinothalamic and medial lemniscal pathways in the cat and rhesus monkey. J. Neurophysiol., **13:** 149–156.

BERTRAND, G. 1956. Spinal efferent pathways from the supplementary motor area. Brain, **79:** 461–473.

BESSOU, P., EMONET-DÉNAND, F., AND LAPORTE, Y. 1963. Occurrence of intrafusal muscle fibre innervation by branches of slow A motor fibres in the cat. Nature, **198:** 594–595.

VAN BEUSEKOM, G. T. 1955. *Fibre Analysis of the Anterior and Lateral Funiculi of the Cord in the Cat.* Eduard Ijdo N. V., Leiden, pp. 1–136.

BIEMOND, A., AND SINNEGE, J. L. 1955. Tabes of Friedrich with degeneration of the substantia nigra, a special type of hereditary parkinsonism. Confinia neurol., **15:** 129–142.

BLACKSTAD, T. W. 1956. Commissural connections of the hippocampal region in the rat, with special reference to their mode of termination. J. Comp. Neurol., **105:** 417–538.

BLOMQUIST, A. J., BENJAMIN, R. M., AND EMMERS, R. 1962. Thalamic localization of afferents from the tongue in squirrel monkey (*Saimiri sciureus*). J. Comp. Neurol., **118:** 77–87.

BLUM, M., WALKER, A. E., AND RUCH, T. C. 1943. Localization of taste in the thalamus of *Macaca mulatta.* Yale J. Biol. & Med., **16:** 175–192.

BLUNT, J. J., WENDELL-SMITH, C. P., PAISLEY, P. B., AND BALDWIN, F. 1967. Oxidative enzyme activity in macroglia and axons of cat optic nerve. J. Anat., **101:** 13–26.

BODIAN, D. 1936. A new method for staining nerve fibers and nerve endings in mounted paraffin sections. Anat. Rec., **65:** 89–97.

BODIAN, D. 1937. The structure of the vertebrate synapse. A study of the axon endings on Mauthner's cell and neighboring centers in the goldfish. J. Comp. Neurol., **68:** 117–160.

BODIAN, D. 1940. Studies on the diencephalon of

the Virginia opossum. II. The fiber connections in normal and experimental material. J. Comp. Neurol., **72**: 207–297.

BODIAN, D. 1946. Experimental evidence on the cerebral origin of muscle spasticity in acute poliomyelitis. Proc. Soc. Exper. Biol. & Med., **61**: 170–175.

BODIAN, D. 1962. The generalized vertebrate neuron. Science, **137**: 323–326.

BÖRNSTEIN, W. S. 1940. Cortical representation of taste in man and monkey. I. Functional and anatomical relations of taste, olfaction and somatic sensibility. Yale J. Biol. & Med., **12**: 719–736.

BÖRNSTEIN, W. S. 1940a. Cortical representation of taste in man and monkey. II. Localization of cortical taste area in man and method of measuring impairment of taste in man. Yale J. Biol. & Med., **13**: 133–156.

BORISON, H. L., AND WANG, S. C. 1953. Physiology and pharmacology of vomiting. Pharmacol. Rev., **5**: 193–230.

BOLK, L. 1906. *Das Cerebellum der Säugethiere.* E. F. Bohn, Harlem.

BOLTON, B. 1939. The blood supply of the human spinal cord. J. Neurol. & Psychiat., **2**: 137–148.

VON BONIN, G., AND SHARIFF, G. A. 1951. Extrapyramidal nuclei among mammals. J. Comp. Neurol., **94**: 427–438.

BORISON, H. L., AND WANG, S. C. 1949. Functional localization of central coordinating mechanisms for emesis in cat. J. Neurophysiol., **12**: 305–313.

BOWDEN, R. E. M., AND GUTMANN, E. 1944. Denervation and re-innervation of the human voluntary muscle. Brain, **67**: 273–313.

BOWDEN, R. E. M., AND MAHRAN, Z. Y. 1956. The functional significance of the pattern of innervation of the muscle quadratus labii superioris of the rabbit, cat and rat. J. Anat., **90**: 217–227.

BOWSHER, D. 1957. Termination of the central pain pathway: the conscious appreciation of pain. Brain, **80**: 606–622.

BOWSHER, D. 1958. Projections of the gracile and cuneate nuclei in Macaca mulatta: An experimental degeneration study. J. Comp. Neurol., **110**: 135–155.

BOWSHER, D. 1961. The termination of secondary somatosensory neurons within the thalamus of Macaca mulatta: An experimental degeneration study. J. Comp. Neurol., **177**: 213–227.

BOWSHER, D. 1966. Some afferent and efferent connections of the parafascicular-center median complex. In D. P. PURPURA AND M. D. YAHR (Editors), *The Thalamus.* Columbia University Press, New York, pp. 99–108.

BOYD, I. A. 1962. The nuclear-bag fibre and nuclear-chain fibre systems in the muscle spindles of the cat. In D. BARKER (Editor), *Symposium on*

Muscle Receptors. Hong Kong University Press, Hong Kong, pp. 185–190.

BOYD, I. A. 1962a. The structure and innervation of the nuclear-bag fibre system and the nuclear-chain fibre system in mammalian muscle spindles. Phil. Tr. Roy. Soc. London, ser. B, **245**: 81–136.

BRADLEY, W. E., AND CONWAY, C. J. 1966. Bladder representation in the pontine-mesencephalic reticular formation. Exper. Neurol., **16**: 237–249.

BRADY, J. V. 1960. Temporal and emotional effects related to intracranial electrical self-stimulation. In S. R. RAMEY AND D. S. O'DOHERTY (Editors), *Electrical Studies on the Unanesthetized Brain.* Paul B. Hoeber, Inc., New York. Ch. 3, pp. 52–77.

BRADY, J. V., SCHREINER, L., GELLER, I., AND KLING, A. 1954. Subcortical mechanisms in emotional behavior: The effect of rhinencephalic injury upon the acquisition and retention of a conditioned avoidance response in cats. J. Comp. Physiol. & Psychol., **47**: 179–186.

BRAIN, R. 1961. *Speech Disorders. Aphasia, Apraxia and Agnosia.* Butterworth, London, 184 pp.

BRAITENBERG, V., AND ATWOOD, R. P. 1958. Morphological observations on the cerebellar cortex. J. Comp. Neurol., **109**: 1–27.

BRATTGÅRD, S. O., EDSTRÖM, J. E., AND HYDÉN, H. 1958. The productive capacity of the neuron in retrograde reaction. Exper. Cell Res., Suppl. **5**: 185–200.

BRAZIER, M. A. B. 1954. The action of anaesthetics on the nervous system, with special reference to the brain stem reticular system. In J. F. DELAFRESNAYE (Editor), *Brain Mechanisms and Consciousness* (Symposium). Blackwell Scientific Publications, Oxford, pp. 163–193.

VAN BREEMEN, V. L., ANDERSON, E., AND REGER, J. F. 1958. An attempt to determine the origin of synaptic vesicles. Exper. Cell Res., Suppl. **5**: 153–167.

BREMER, F. 1922. Contributions á l'étude de la physiologie du cervelet. La fonction inhibtrice du palaeo-cérébellum. Arch. internat. physiol., **19**: 189–226.

BREMER, F. 1936. Nouvelles recherches sur le mécanisme du sommeil. Comp. rend. Soc. biol., **122**: 460–464.

BREMER, F., AND TERZUOLO, C. 1954. Contribution a l'etude des mécanismes physiologiques du maintien de l'activité vigile du cerveau. Interaction de la formation réticulée et de l'écorce cérébrale dans le processus du réveil. Arch. internat. physiol., **62**: 157–178.

BRENDLER, S. J. 1968. The human cervical myotomes: Functional anatomy studied at operation. J. Neurosurg., **28**: 105–111.

BRIZZEE, K. R., AND NEAL, L. M. 1954. A re-evaluation of the cellular morphology of the area postrema in view of recent evidence for a chemoreceptor function. J. Comp. Neurol., **100**: 41–62.

BROCA, P. 1878. Anatomie comparée circonvolutions cérébrales. Le grand lobe limbique et la scissure limbique dans la série des mammifères. Rev. anthropol., Ser. 2, **1**: 384–498.

BRODAL, A. 1940. Experimentelle Untersuchungen über die olivocerebellare Lokalisation. Ztschr. ges. Neurol. u. Psychiat., **169**: 1–153.

BRODAL, A. 1941. Die Verbindungen des Nucleus cuneatus externus mit dem Kleinhirn beim Kaninchen und bei der Katze. Experimentelle Untersuchungen. Ztschr. ges. Neurol. u. Psychiat., **171**: 167–199.

BRODAL, A. 1947. The hippocampus and the sense of smell. Brain, **70**: 179–222.

BRODAL, A. 1948. The origin of the fibers of the anterior commissure in the rat. Experimental studies. J. Comp. Neurol., **88**: 157–205.

BRODAL, A. 1949. Spinal afferents to the lateral reticular nucleus of the medulla oblongata in the cat. An experimental study. J. Comp. Neurol., **91**: 259–295.

BRODAL, A. 1953. Reticulo-cerebellar connections in the cat. An experimental study. J. Comp. Neurol., **98**: 113–153.

BRODAL, A. 1954. Afferent cerebellar connections. In J. JANSEN AND A. BRODAL (Editors), *Aspects of Cerebellar Anatomy*. J. G. Tanum, Oslo, Ch. 2, pp. 82–188.

BRODAL, A. 1957. *The Reticular Formation of the Brain Stem. Anatomical Aspects and Functional Correlations*. Charles C Thomas, Publisher, Springfield, Ill., 87 pp.

BRODAL, A. 1959. *The Cranial Nerves. Anatomy and Anatomico-clinical Correlations*. Charles C Thomas, Publisher, Springfield, Ill.

BRODAL, A. 1963. General discussion of the terminology of the rhinencephalon. In W. BARGMANN AND J. P. SCHADÉ. (Editors), *The Rhinencephalon and Related Structures. Progress in Brain Research*, Vol. 3. Elsevier Publishing Company, Amsterdam, pp. 237–244.

BRODAL, A., AND GOGSTAD, A. C. 1954. Rubrocerebellar connections. An experimental study in the cat. Anat. Rec., **118**: 455–486.

BRODAL, A., AND HØIVIK, B. 1964. Site and mode of termination of primary vestibulo-cerebellar fibres in the cat. Arch. ital. Biol., **102**: 1–21.

BRODAL, A., AND JANSEN, J. 1946. The ponto-cerebellar projection in the rabbit and cat. J. Comp. Neurol., **84**: 31–118.

BRODAL, A., AND POMPEIANO, O. 1957. The vestibular nuclei in the cat. J. Anat., **91**: 438–454.

BRODAL, A., AND POMPEIANO, O. 1957a. The origin of ascending fibers of the medial longitudinal fasciculus from the vestibular nuclei: An experimental study in the cat. Acta Morphol. Neerlando-scandinav., **1**: 306–328.

BRODAL, A., POMPEIANO, O., AND WALBERG, F. 1962. *The Vestibular Nuclei and Their Connections, Anatomy and Functional Correlations*. Charles C Thomas, Publisher, Springfield, Ill.

BRODAL, A., AND ROSSI, G. F. 1955. Ascending fibers in brain stem reticular formation of cat. Arch. Neurol. & Psychiat., **74**: 68–87.

BRODAL, A., SZABO, T., AND TORVIK, A. 1956. Corticofugal fibers to sensory trigeminal nuclei and nucleus of solitary tract. J. Comp. Neurol., **106**: 527–555.

BRODAL, A., AND TORVIK, A. 1957. Über den Ursprung der sekundären vestibulo-cerebellaren Fasern bei der Katze. Eine experimentell-anatomische Studie. Arch. Psychiat., **195**: 550–567.

BRODAL, A., AND WALBERG, F. 1952. Ascending fibers in the pyramidal tract of cat. Arch. Neurol. & Psychiat., **68**: 755–775.

BRODAL, A., WALBERG, F., AND BLACKSTAD, T. 1950. Termination of spinal afferents to inferior olive in cat. J. Neurophysiol., **13**: 431–454.

BRODAL, P. 1968. The corticopontine projection in the cat. I. Demonstration of a somatotopically organized projection from the primary sensorimotor cortex. Exper. Brain Res., **5**: 210–234.

BRODMANN, K. 1909. *Vergleichende Lokalisationlehre der Grosshirnrinde in ihren Prinzipien dargestellt auf Grund des Zellenbaues*. J. A. Barth, Leipzig, 324 pp.

BROUWER, B. 1918. Klinisch-anatomische Untersuchungen über den Oculomotoriuskern. Ztschr. ges. Neurol. u. Psychiat., **40**: 152–193.

BROWN, J. O., AND McCOUCH, G. P. 1947. Abortive regeneration of the transected spinal cord. J. Comp. Neurol., **87**: 131–138.

BROWNSON, R. H. 1956. Perineuronal satellite cells in the motor cortex of aging brains. J. Neuropath. Exper. Neurol., **15**: 190–195.

BUCHSBAUM, R. 1948. *Animals Without Backbones*. University of Chicago Press, Chicago.

BUCY, P. C. 1949. Effects of extirpation in man. In P. C. BUCY (Editor), *The Precentral Motor Cortex*, Ed. 2. University of Illinois Press, Urbana. Ch. 14, pp. 353–394.

BUCY, P. C. 1957. Principes physiologiques et résultats des interventions neurochirurgicales dans les affections dites extrapyramidales. I. Relationship of the "pyramidal tract" and abnormal involuntary movements. In *Premier Congrès International des Sciences Neurolo-*

giques. *Première Journée Commune, Bruxelles, Juillet, 1957.* Pergamon Press, London, pp. 101–107.

BUCY, P. C. 1958. The cortico-spinal tract and tremor. In W. S. FIELDS (Editor), *Pathogenesis and Treatment of Parkinsonism.* Charles C Thomas, Publisher, Springfield, Ill., Ch. 11, pp. 271–293.

BUCY, P. C. 1959. The surgical treatment of abnormal involuntary movements. Neurologia, **1:** 1–15.

BUCY, P. C. 1959a. The basal ganglia and skeletal muscular activity. In G. SCHALTENBRAND AND P. BAILEY (Editors), *Introduction to Stereotaxis, with an Atlas of the Human Brain,* Vol. I. Georg Thieme, Stuttgart, pp. 331–353.

BUEKER, E. D. 1948. Implantation of tumors in the hind limb field of the embryonic chick, and the developmental response of the lumbosacral nervous system. Anat. Rec., **102:** 369–389.

BULL, J. W. D. 1961. Use and limitations of angiography in the diagnosis of vascular lesions of the brain. Neurology, **11:** 80–85.

BULLOCK, T. H., AND HORRIDGE, G. A. 1965. *Structure and Function in the Nervous Systems of Invertebrates,* Vols. 1 and 2. W. H. Freeman and Company, San Francisco.

BUNGE, M. B., BUNGE, R. P., PETERSON, E. R., AND MURRAY, M. R. 1967. A light and electron microscope study of long term organized cultures of rat dorsal root ganglia. J. Cell Biol., **32:** 439–466.

BUNGE, M. B., BUNGE, R. P., AND RIS, H. 1961. Ultrastructural study of remyelination in an experimental lesion in adult cat spinal cord. J. Biophys. & Biochem. Cytol., **10:** 67–94.

BUNGE, R. P. 1968. Glial cells and the central myelin sheath. Physiol. Rev., **48:** 197–251.

BURGEN, A. S. V., AND EMMELIN, N. G. 1961. Innervation of the glandular elements. In A. S. V. BURGEN AND N. G. EMMELIN (Editors), *Physiology of the Salivary Glands.* Williams and Wilkins Company, Baltimore, Ch. 3, pp. 38–71.

BURGI, S., AND BUCHER, V. M. 1960. *Markhaltige Faserverbindungen im Hirnstamm der Katze.* J. Springer Verlag, Berlin.

BUSCH, H. F. M. 1961. *An Anatomical Analysis of the White Matter in the Brain Stem of the Cat.* Thesis, University of Leiden. Te Assen Bij Van Gorcum and Company, N. V., Leiden, 116 pp.

BUSER, P., AND BORENSTEIN, P. 1956. Données sur la répartition des réponses sensorielles corticales (somethésiques, visuelles, auditives) chez le chat cur arisé non anesthésie. J. Physiol., Paris, **48:** 419–421.

BUTLER, R. A., DIAMOND, I. T., AND NEFF, W. D. 1957. Role of auditory cortex in discrimination of changes in frequency. J. Neurophysiol., **20:** 108–120.

CAJAL, S. RAMÓN Y. 1909, 1911. *Histologie du système nerveux de l'homme et des vertébrés.* Norbert Maloine, Paris, 2 vols.

CAJAL, S. RAMÓN Y. 1928. *Degeneration and Regeneration of the Nervous System,* Vol. I. Translation by R. M. May. Oxford University Press, London, pp. 27–40.

CALNE, D. B., AND PALLIS, C. A. 1966. Vibratory sense: A critical review. Brain, **89:** 723–746.

CAMMERMEYER, J. 1947. Is the human area postrema a neuro-vegetative nucleus? Acta Anat., **2:** 294–320.

CAMMERMEYER, J. 1965. Histiocytes, iuxtavascular mitotic cells and microglia cells during retrograde changes in the facial nucleus of rabbits of varying age. Ergebn. Anat. Entwicklungsgesch., **38:** 195–229.

CAMMERMEYER, J. 1966. Morphologic distinctions between oligodendrocytes and microglial cells in the rabbit cerebral cortex. Am. J. Anat., **118:** 227–448.

CAMPBELL, A. W. 1905. *Histological Studies on the Localization of Cerebral Function.* Cambridge University Press, New York, 360 pp.

CAMPBELL, J. B., BASSETT, C. A. L., HUSBY, J., AND NOBACK, C. R. 1957. Regeneration of adult mammalian spinal cord. Science, **126:** 929.

CAMPBELL, J. B., BASSETT, C. A. L., HUSBY, J., AND NOBACK, C. R. 1958. Axonal regeneration in the transected adult feline spinal cord. S. Forum, Proc. Clin. Cong. Am. Coll. Surgeons, **8:** 528–532.

CAMPBELL, M. F. 1957. Neuromuscular uropathy. In M. F. CAMPBELL (Editor), *Principles of Urology.* W. B. Saunders Company, Philadelphia, Ch. 9, pp. 337–378.

CANNON, W. B. 1929. *Bodily Changes in Pain, Hunger, Fear and Rage. An Account of Recent Researches into the Function of Emotional Excitement.* D. Appleton and Company, New York.

CANNON, W. B. 1939. A law of denervation. Am. J. M. Sc., **98:** 737–750.

CANNON, W. B., AND ROSENBLUETH, A. 1933. Studies on activity in endocrine organs; sympathin E and sympathin I. Am. J. Physiol., **104:** 557–574.

CANNON, W. B., AND ROSENBLUETH, A. 1937. *Autonomic Neuro-Effector Systems.* The Macmillan Company, New York.

CARLSSON, A., FALCK, B., AND HILLARP, N. A. 1962. Cellular localization of brain monoamines. Acta physiol. scandinav., **56:** Suppl. 196, 1–28.

CARMAN, J. B., COWAN, W. M., AND POWELL, T. P. S. 1963. The organization of corticostriate connexions in the rabbit. Brain, **86:** 525–562.

CARMAN, J. B., COWAN, W. M., AND POWELL, T. P. S. 1964. Cortical connexions of the thalamic reticular nucleus. J. Anat., **98:** 587–598.

CARMAN, J. B., COWAN, W. M., AND WEBSTER, K. E.

1965. A bilateral cortico-striate projection. J. Neurol. Neurosurg. & Psychiat., **28:** 71–77.

CARMEL, P. W. 1968. Sympathetic deficits following thalamotomy. Arch. Neurol., **18:** 378–387.

CARPENTER, F. W. 1918. Nerve endings of sensory type in the muscular coat of the stomach and small intestine. J. Comp. Neurol., **29:** 553–560.

CARPENTER, M. B. 1950. Athetosis and the basal ganglia. Arch. Neurol. & Psychiat., **63:** 875–901.

CARPENTER, M. B. 1956. A study of the red nucleus in the rhesus monkey. Anatomic degenerations and physiologic effects resulting from localized lesions of the red nucleus. J. Comp. Neurol., **105:** 195–250.

CARPENTER, M. B. 1957. Functional relationships between the red nucleus and the brachium conjunctivum. Physiologic study of lesions of the red nucleus in monkeys with degenerated superior cerebellar brachia. Neurology, **7:** 427–437.

CARPENTER, M. B. 1957a. The dorsal trigeminal tract in the rhesus monkey. J. Anat., **91:** 82–90.

CARPENTER, M. B. 1958. The neuroanatomical basis of dyskinesia. In W. S. FIELDS (Editor), *Pathogenesis and Treatment of Parkinsonism.* Charles C Thomas, Publisher, Springfield, Ill., Ch. 2, pp. 50–85.

CARPENTER, M. B. 1959. Lesions of the fastigial nuclei in the rhesus monkey. Am. J. Anat., **104:** 1–34.

CARPENTER, M. B. 1960. Fiber projections from the descending and lateral vestibular nuclei in the cat. Am. J. Anat., **107:** 1–22.

CARPENTER, M. B. 1961. Brain stem and infratentorial neuraxis in experimental dyskinesia. A. M. A. Arch. Neurol., **5:** 504–524.

CARPENTER, M. B. 1967. Ventral tier thalamic nuclei. In D. WILLIAMS (Editor), *Modern Trends in Neurology.* Butterworths, London. pp. 1–20.

CARPENTER, M. B., ALLING, F. A., AND BARD, D. S. 1960. Lesions of the descending vestibular nucleus in the cat. J. Comp. Neurol., **114:** 39–50.

CARPENTER, M. B., BARD, D. S., AND ALLING, F. A. 1959. Anatomical connections between the fastigial nuclei, the labyrinth and the vestibular nuclei in the cat. J. Comp. Neurol., **111:** 1–26.

CARPENTER, M. B., AND BRITTIN, G. M. 1958. Subthalamic hyperkinesia in the rhesus monkey. Effects of secondary lesions in the red nucleus and brachium conjunctivum. J. Neurophysiol., **21:** 400–413.

CARPENTER, M. B., BRITTIN, G. M., AND PINES, J. 1958. Isolated lesions of the fastigial nuclei in the cat. J. Comp. Neurol., **109:** 65–90.

CARPENTER, M. B., AND CORRELL, J. W. 1961. Spinal pathways mediating cerebellar dyskinesia in the rhesus monkey. J. Neurophysiol., **24:** 534–551.

CARPENTER, M. B., CORRELL, J. W., AND HINMAN, A. 1960. Spinal tracts mediating subthalamic hyperkinesia. Physiological effects of partial selective cordotomies upon dyskinesia in the rhesus monkey. J. Neurophysiol., **23:** 288–304.

CARPENTER, M. B., FRASER, R. A. R., AND SHRIVER, J. E. 1968. The organization of pallidosubthalamic fibers in the monkey. Brain Res., **11:** 522–559.

CARPENTER, M. B., AND HANNA, G. R. 1961. Fiber projections from the spinal trigeminal nucleus in the cat. J. Comp. Neurol., **117:** 117–132.

CARPENTER, M. B., HANNA, G. R. 1962. Lesions of the medial longitudinal fasciculus in the cat. Am. J. Anat., **110:** 307–332.

CARPENTER, M. B., AND HANNA, G. R. 1962a. Effects of thalamic lesions upon cerebellar dyskinesia in the rhesus monkey. J. Comp. Neurol., **119:** 127–148.

CARPENTER, M. B., AND McMASTERS, R. E. 1963. Disturbances of conjugate horizontal eye movements in the monkey. II. Physiological effects and anatomical degeneration resulting from lesions in the medial longitudinal fasciculus. Arch. Neurol., **8:** 347–368.

CARPENTER, M. B., AND McMASTERS, R. E. 1964. Lesions of the substantia nigra in the rhesus monkey. Efferent fiber degeneration and behavioral observations. Am. J. Anat., **114:** 293–320.

CARPENTER, M. B., McMASTERS, R. E., AND HANNA, G. R. 1963. Disturbances of conjugate horizontal eye movements in the monkey. I. Physiological effects and anatomical degeneration resulting from lesions of the abducens nucleus and nerve. Arch. Neurol., **8:** 231–247.

CARPENTER, M. B., AND METTLER, F. A. 1951. Analysis of subthalamic hyperkinesia in the monkey with special reference to ablations of agranular cortex. J. Comp. Neurol., **95:** 125–158.

CARPENTER, M. B., NOBACK, C. R., AND MOSS, M. L. 1954. The anterior choroidal artery. Its origins, course, distribution and variations. A.M.A. Arch. Neurol. & Psychiat., **71:** 714–722.

CARPENTER, M. B., AND NOVA, H. R. 1960. Descending division of the brachium conjunctivum in the cat: A cerebello-reticular system. J. Comp. Neurol., **114:** 295–305.

CARPENTER, M. B., STEIN, B. M., AND SHRIVER, J. E. 1968. Central projections of spinal dorsal roots in the monkey. II. Lower thoracic, lumbosacral and coccygeal dorsal roots. Am. J. Anat., **123:** 75–118.

CARPENTER, M. B., AND STEVENS, G. H. 1957. Structural and functional relationships between the deep cerebellar nuclei and the brachium conjunctivum in the rhesus monkey. J. Comp. Neurol., **107:** 109–164.

CARPENTER, M. B., AND STROMINGER, N. L. 1964. Cerebello-oculomotor fibers in the rhesus monkey. J. Comp. Neurol., **123:** 211–230.

CARPENTER, M. B., AND STROMINGER, N. L. 1965. The medial longitudinal fasciculus and disturbances of conjugate horizontal eye movements in the monkey. J. Comp. Neurol., **125**: 41–66.

CARPENTER, M. B., AND STROMINGER, N. L. 1967. Efferent fibers of the subthalamic nucleus in the monkey. A comparison of the efferent projections of the subthalamic nucleus, substantia nigra and globus pallidus. Am. J. Anat., **121**: 41–72.

CARPENTER, M. B., STROMINGER, N. L., AND WEISS, A. H. 1965. Effects of lesions in the intralaminar thalamic nuclei upon subthalamic dyskinesia. A study in the rhesus monkey. Arch. Neurol., **13**: 113–125.

CARPENTER, M. B., WHITTIER, J. R., AND METTLER, F. A. 1950. Analysis of choreoid hyperkinesia in the rhesus monkey. Surgical and pharmacological analysis of hyperkinesia resulting from lesions in the subthalamic nucleus of Luys. J. Comp. Neurol., **92**: 293–332.

CARREA, R. M. E., AND GRUNDFEST, H. 1954. Electrophysiological studies of cerebellar inflow. I. Origin, conduction and termination of ventral spino-cerebellar tract in monkey and cat. J. Neurophysiol., **17**: 208–238.

CARREA, R. M. E., AND METTLER, F. A. 1947. Physiologic consequences following extensive removals of the cerebellar cortex and deep cerebellar nuclei and effect of secondary cerebral ablations in the primate. J. Comp. Neurol., **87**: 169–288.

CARREA, R. M. E., REISSIG, M., AND METTLER, F. A. 1947. The climbing fibers of the simian and feline cerebellum. J. Comp. Neurol., **87**: 321–365.

CARRERAS, M., AND LEVITT, M. 1959. Microelectrode analysis of the second somatosensory cortical area in the cat. Fed. Proc., **18**: 24.

CASPERSON, T. 1950. *Cell Growth and Cell Function, a Cytological Study.* W. W. Norton and Company, New York, 185 pp.

CAUNA, N. 1965. The effects of aging on the receptor organs of the human dermis. In W. MONTAGNA (Editor), *Advances in Biology of Skin*, Vol. 6. *Aging.* Pergamon Press, New York, pp. 63–69.

CAUNA, N. 1966. Fine structure of the receptor organ and its probable functional significance. In A. V. S. DEREUCK AND J. KNIGHT (Editors), *Touch, Heat and Pain.* Ciba Foundation Symposium. Little, Brown and Company, Boston, pp. 117–127.

CAUNA, N., AND MANNAN, G. 1958. The structure of human digital Pacinian corpuscles (Corpuscula lamellosa) and its functional significance. J. Anat., Part 1, **92**: 1–20.

CAUNA, N., AND MANNAN, G. 1959. Development and postnatal changes of digital Pacinian corpuscles (Corpuscula lamellosa) in the human hand. J. Anat., **93**: 271–286.

CAUNA, N., AND MANNAN, G. 1961. Organization and development of the preterminal nerve pattern in the palmar digital tissues of man. J. Comp. Neurol., **117**: 309–328.

CAUSEY, G. 1960. *The Cell of Schwann.* E. and S. Livingston Ltd., Edinburgh.

CHARCOT, J. M. 1879. *Lectures on the Diseases of the Nervous System.* Translated by G. Sigerson. Henry C. Lea, Philadelphia, p. 390.

CHEATHAM, M. L., AND MATZKE, H. A. 1966. Descending hypothalamic medullary pathways in the cat. J. Comp. Neurol., **127**: 369–380.

CHRISTOFF, N., ANDERSON, P. J., NATHANSON, M., AND BENDER, M. B. 1960. Problems in anatomic analysis of lesions of the median longitudinal fasciculus. A.M.A. Arch. Neurol., **2**: 293–304.

CHU, L. W. 1954. Cytological study of anterior horn cells isolated from human spinal cord. J. Comp. Neurol., **100**: 381–413.

CLARE, M. H., AND BISHOP, G. H. 1956. Potential wave mechanisms in cat cortex. Electroencephalog. and Clin. Neurophysiol., **8**: 583–602.

CLARK, W. E. L. 1926. The mammalian oculomotor nucleus. J. Anat., **60**: 426–448.

CLARK, W. E. L. 1932. The structure and connections of the thalamus. Brain, **55**: 406–470.

CLARK, W. E. L. 1936. The termination of ascending tracts in the thalamus of the macaque monkey. J. Anat., **71**: 1–40.

CLARK, W. E. L. 1948. The connections of the frontal lobes of the brain. Lancet, **1**: 353–356.

CLARK, W. E. L., BEATTIE, J., RIDDOCH, G., AND DOTT, N. M. 1938. *The Hypothalamus.* Oliver and Boyd, Edinburgh.

CLARK, W. E. L., AND BOGGON, R. H. 1933. On the connections of the anterior nucleus of the thalamus. J. Anat., **67**: 215–226.

CLARK, W. E. L., AND BOGGON, R. H. 1933a. On the connections of the medial cell group of the thalamus. Brain, **56**: 83–98.

CLARK, W. E. L., AND BOGGON, R. H. 1935. The thalamic connections of the parietal and frontal lobes of the brain in the monkey. Phil. T. Roy. Soc., London, ser. B, **224**: 313–359.

CLARK, W. E. L., AND MEYER, M. 1947. The terminal connexions of the olfactory tract in the rabbit's brain. Brain, **70**: 304–328.

CLARK, W. E. L., AND MEYER, M. 1950. Anatomical relationships between the cerebral cortex and the hypothalamus. Brit. M. Bull., **6**: 341–345.

CLARK, W. E. L., AND POWELL, T. P. S. 1953. On the thalamocortical connexions of the general sensory cortex of Macaca. Proc. Roy. Soc., London, ser. B, **141**: 467–487.

CLARK, W. E. L., AND WARWICK, R. T. 1946. The pattern of olfactory innervation. J. Neurol. Neurosurg. & Psychiat., **9**: 101–111.

CLARKE, R. H., AND HORSLEY, V. 1905. On the intrinsic fibers of the cerebellum, its nuclei and its efferent tracts. Brain, **28**: 13–29.

COERS, C. 1955. Les variations structurelles normales et pathologiques de la jonction neuromusculaire. Acta neurol. (belg.), **55**: 741–866.

COERS, C., AND WOOLF, A. L. 1959. *The Innerva-*

tion of Muscle: A Biopsy Study. Blackwell Scientific Publications, Oxford.

COGAN, D. G. 1956. *Neurology of the Ocular Muscles*, Ed. 2. Charles C Thomas, Publisher, Springfield, Ill.

COGAN, D. G., KUBIK, C. S., AND SMITH, W. L. 1950. Unilateral internuclear ophthalmoplegia. Report of eight clinical cases with one postmortem study. Arch. Ophth., **44:** 783–796.

COGGESHALL, R. E., AND FAWCETT, D. W. 1964. The fine structure of the central nervous system of the leech, *Hirudo medicinalis*. J. Neurophysiol., **27:** 229–289.

COGHILL, G. E. 1914. Correlated anatomical and physiological studies of the growth of the nervous system of amphibia. I. The afferent system of the trunk of Amblystoma. J. Comp. Neurol., **24:** 161–223.

COGHILL, G. E. 1929. *Anatomy and the Problem of Behavior*. Oxford University Press, London.

COHEN, B., HOUSEPIAN, E. M., AND PURPURA, D. P. 1962. Intrathalamic regulation of activity in a cerebellocortical projection pathway. Exper. Neurol., **6:** 492–506.

COHEN, B., SUZUKI, J. I., AND BENDER, M. B. 1964. Eye movements from semicircular nerve stimulation in the cat. Ann. Otol. Rhin. & Laryng., **73:** 153–169.

COHEN, D., CHAMBERS, W. W., AND SPRAGUE, J. M. 1958. Experimental study of the efferent projections from the cerebellar nuclei to the brain stem of the cat. J. Comp. Neurol., **109:** 233–259.

COHEN, M. J., LANDGREN, S., STROM, L., AND ZOTTERMANN, Y. 1957. Cortical reception of touch and taste in the cat. Acta physiol. scandinav., **40:** Suppl. 135, 50 pp.

COHEN, S. 1960. Purification of a nerve-growth factor promoting protein from the mouse salivary gland and its neuro-cytotoxic antiserum. Proc. Nat. Acad. Sc., **46:** 302–311.

COLE, M., NAUTA, W. J. H., AND MEHLER, W. R. 1964. The ascending efferent projections of the substantia nigra. Tr. Am. Neurol. A., **89:** 74–78.

COMBS, C. M. 1949. Fiber and cell degeneration in the albino rat brain after hemidecortication. J. Comp. Neurol., **90:** 373–402.

COMBS, C. M. 1956. Bulbar regions related to localized cerebellar afferent impulses. J. Neurophysiol., **19:** 285–300.

CONDE, H. 1966. Analyse électrophysiologique de la voie dentato-rubro-thalamique chez le chat. J. Physiol. Paris, **58:** 218–219.

COOPER, I. S. 1956. *Neurosurgical Alleviation of Parkinsonism*. Charles C Thomas, Publisher, Springfield, Ill.

COOPER, I. S. 1957. Relief of juvenile involuntary movement disorders by chemopallidectomy. J. A. M. A., **164:** 1297–1301.

COOPER, I. S. 1959. Dystonia musculorum defor-

mans alleviated by chemopallidectomy and chemopallidothalamectomy. A.M.A. Arch. Neurol. & Psychiat., **81:** 5–19.

COOPER, I. S. 1960. Results of 1,000 consecutive basal ganglia operations for parkinsonism. Ann. Int. Med., **52:** 483–499.

COOPER, I. S. 1960*a*. Neurosurgical relief of intention tremor due to cerebellar disease and multiple sclerosis. Arch. Phys. Med. & Rehab., **41:** 1–4.

COOPER, I. S. 1960*b*. Neurosurgical alleviation of intention tremor of multiple sclerosis and cerebellar disease. New England J. Med., **263:** 441–444.

COOPER, I. S., AND BRAVO, G. J. 1958. Anterior choroidal artery occlusion, chemopallidectomy and chemothalamectomy in parkinsonism: A consecutive series of 700 operations. In W. S. FIELDS (Editor), *Pathogenesis and Treatment of Parkinsonism*. Charles C Thomas, Publisher, Springfield, Ill. Ch. 15, 325–352.

COOPER, I. S., AND POLOUKHINE, N. 1959. Neurosurgical relief of intention (cerebellar) tremor. J. Am. Geriatrics Soc., **7:** 443–445.

COOPER, S., AND DANIEL, P. M. 1949. Muscle spindles in human extrinsic eye muscles. Brain, **72:** 1–24.

COOPER, S., DANIEL, P. M., AND WHITTERIDGE, D. 1953. Nerve impulses in the brainstem of the goat. Short latency responses obtained by stretching the extrinsic eye muscles and the jaw muscles. J. Physiol., **120:** 471–490.

COOPER, S., DANIEL, P. M., AND WHITTERIDGE, D. 1953*a*. Nerve impulses in the brainstem of the goat. Responses with long latencies obtained by stretching the extrinsic eye muscles. J. Physiol., **120:** 491–513.

COOPER, S., DANIEL, P. M., AND WHITTERIDGE, D. 1955. Muscle spindles and other sensory endings in the extrinsic eye muscles; the physiology and anatomy of these receptors and their connections with the brain stem. Brain, **78:** 564–583.

COOPER, S., AND SHERRINGTON, C. S. 1940. Gower's tract and spinal border cells. Brain, **63:** 123–134.

COPENHAVER, W. M. 1964. *Bailey's Textbook of Histology*, Ed. 15. Williams and Wilkins Company, Baltimore, 633 pp.

CORBIN, K. B. 1940. Observations on the peripheral distribution of fibers arising in the mesencephalic nucleus of the fifth cranial nerve. J. Comp. Neurol., **73:** 153–177.

CORBIN, K. B., AND HARRISON, F. 1940. Function of the mesencephalic root of the fifth cranial nerve. J. Neurophysiol., **3:** 423–435.

CORNING, H. K. 1922. *Lehrbuch der Topographischen Anatomie für Studierende und Ärzte*. J. F. Bergmann, Munich and Wiesbaden, pp. 609–614.

COURVILLE, J. 1966. Somatotopical organization of the projection from the nucleus interpositus anterior of the cerebellum to the red nucleus. An experimental study in the cat with silver impregnation methods. Exper. Brain Res., **2**: 191–215.

COURVILLE, J. 1966a. Rubrobulbar fibres to the facial nucleus and the lateral reticular nucleus (nucleus of the lateral funiculus). An experimental study in the cat with silver impregnation methods. Brain Res., **1**: 317–337.

COURVILLE, J. 1966b. The nucleus of the facial nerve; the relation between cellular groups and peripheral branches of the nerve. Brain Res., **1**: 338–354.

COURVILLE, J., AND BRODAL, A. 1966. Rubrocerebellar connections in the cat: An experimental study with silver impregnation methods. J. Comp. Neurol., **126**: 471–485.

COUTEAUX, R. 1958. Morphological and cytochemical observations on the postsynaptic membrane at motor end plates and ganglionic synapses. Exper. Cell Res., Suppl. **5**: 294–322.

COWAN, W. M., AND POWELL, T. P. S. 1966. Striopallidal projection in the monkey. J. Neurol. Neurosurg. & Psychiat., **29**: 426–439.

COXE, W. S., AND LANDAU, W. M. 1965. Observations upon the effect of supplementary motor cortex ablation in the monkey. Brain, **88**: 763–772.

CRAGG, B. G. 1961. Olfactory and other afferent connexions of the hippocampus in the rabbit, rat and cat. Exper. Neurol., **3**: 588–600.

VAN CREVEL, H., AND VERHAART, W. J. C. 1963. The rate of secondary degeneration in the central nervous system. I. The pyramidal tract of the cat. J. Anat., **97**: 429–449.

VAN CREVEL, H., AND VERHAART, W. J. C. 1963a. The rate of secondary degeneration in the central nervous system. II. The optic nerve of the cat. J. Anat., **97**: 451–464.

CRITCHLEY, M. 1953. *The Parietal Lobes*. Edward Arnold, London, 479 pp.

CROSBY, E. C. 1950. The application of neuroanatomical data to the diagnosis of selected neurosurgical and neurological cases. J. Neurosurg., **7**: 566–583.

CROSBY, E. C. 1951. The mammalian midbrain and isthmus regions. Part II. The fiber connections. C. The hypothalamo-tegmental pathways. J. Comp. Neurol., **94**: 1–32.

CROSBY, E. C. 1953. Relations of brain centers to normal and abnormal eye movements in the horizontal plane. J. Comp. Neurol., **99**: 437–480.

CROSBY, E. C., AND HENDERSON, J. W. 1948. The mammalian midbrain and isthmus regions. II. Fiber connections of the superior colliculus. B. Pathways concerned in automatic eye movements. J. Comp. Neurol., **88**: 53–91.

CROSBY, E. C., AND HUMPHREY, T. 1941. Studies of the vertebrate telencephalon. II. The nuclear pattern of the anterior olfactory nucleus, tuberculum olfactorum and the amygdaloid complex in adult man. J. Comp. Neurol., **74**: 309–352.

CROSBY, E. C., HUMPHREY, T., AND LAUER, E. W. 1962. *Correlative Anatomy of the Nervous System*. Macmillan Company, New York, 731 pp.

CROUSE, G. S., AND CUCINOTTA, A. J. 1965. Progressive neuronal differentiation in the submandibular ganglia of a series of human fetuses. J. Comp. Neurol., **125**: 259–272.

CROWE, S. J. 1935. Symposium on tone localization in the cochlea. Ann. Otol. Rhin. & Laryng., **44**: 737–837.

CULLING, C. F. A. 1963. *Handbook of Histopathological Techniques*, Ed. 2. Butterworths, London, pp. 348–375.

CURRIER, R. D., GILES, C. L., AND DEJONG, R. N. 1961. Some comments on Wallenberg's lateral medullary syndrome. Neurology, **11**: 778–791.

DAITZ, H. M., AND POWELL, T. P. S. 1954. Studies of the connections of the fornix system. J. Neurol. Neurosurg. & Psychiat., **17**: 75–82.

DALE, H. H. 1914. The action of certain esters and ethers of choline, and their relation to muscarine. J. Pharmacol., **6**: 147–190.

DANDY, W. E. 1947. *Intercranial Arterial Aneurysms*. Comstock Publishing Company, Ithaca, N. Y., 147 pp.

DARIAN-SMITH, I., AND MAYDAY, G. 1960. Somatotopic organization within the brain stem trigeminal complex of the cat. Exper. Neurol., **2**: 290–309.

DARIAN-SMITH, I., AND YOKOTA, T. 1966. Corticofugal effects on different neuron types within the cat's brain stem activated by tactile stimulation of the face. J. Neurophysiol., **29**: 185–206.

DAVIDOFF, L. M., AND DYKE, C. G. 1951. *The Normal Encephalogram*, Ed. 3. Lea and Febiger, Philadelphia, pp. 167–170.

DAVIS, C. L. 1923. Description of a human embryo having 20 paired somites. Contrib. Embryol., **15**: 1–51.

DAVIS, D. 1957. *Radicular Syndromes With Emphasis on Chest Pain Simulating Coronary Disease*. Year Book Publishers, Inc., Chicago, pp. 17–160.

DAVSON, H. 1960. Intracranial and intraocular fluids. In J. FIELD (Editor), *Handbook of Physiology*, Section 1, Vol. III, *Neurophysiology*, American Physiological Society, Washington, D. C., Ch. 71, pp. 1761–1788.

DEITCH, A. D., AND MURRAY, M. R. 1956. Nissl substance of living and fixed spinal ganglion cells; phase contrast study. J. Biophys. & Biochem. Cytol., **2**: 433–444.

DEJERINE, J. 1901. *Anatomie des centres nerveux*, Vol. 2. J. Rueff, Paris, 720 pp.

DEJONG, R. N. 1958. *Neurologic Examination*. Paul B. Hoeber, Inc., New York, pp. 664–683 and 834–867.

DEKABAN, A. 1953. Human thalamus. An anatomical, developmental and pathological study. I. Division of the human adult thalamus into nuclei by use of the cyto-myelo-architectonic method. J. Comp. Neurol., **99:** 639–683.

DEKABAN, A. 1954. Human thalamus. An anatomical developmental and pathological study. II. Development of the human thalamic nuclei. J. Comp. Neurol., **100:** 63–97.

DELL, P. 1952. Corrélations entre le système vegetatif et le système de la vie de relation: mésencéphale, diencephale et cortex cerebral. J. Physiol., Paris, **44:** 471–557.

DEMPSEY, E. W. 1956. Variations in the structure of mitochondria. J. Biophys. & Biochem. Cytol., **2:** Suppl. 4, 305–312.

DEMPSEY, E. W., AND LUSE, S. 1958. Fine structure of the neuropil in relation to neuroglia cells. In W. F. WINDLE (Editor), *Biology of Neuroglia*. Charles C Thomas, Publisher, Springfield, Ill., pp. 99–108.

DEMPSEY, E. W., AND MORISON, R. S. 1942. The production of rhythmically recurrent cortical potentials after localized thalamic stimulation. Am. J. Physiol., **135:** 293–300.

DEMPSEY, E. W., AND MORISON, R. S. 1943. The electrical activity of a thalamocortical relay system. Am. J. Physiol., **138:** 283–298.

DENNY-BROWN, D. 1946. Importance of neural fibroblasts in the regeneration of nerve. Arch. Neurol. & Psychiat., **55:** 171–215.

DENNY-BROWN, D. 1951. The frontal lobes and their functions. In A. FEILING (Editor), *Modern Trends in Neurology*. Paul B. Hoeber, Inc., New York, pp. 13–89.

DENNY-BROWN, D. 1960. Motor mechanisms—introduction: the general principles of motor integration. In J. FIELD (Editor), *Handbook of Physiology*, Section I, Vol. II. American Physiological Society, Washington, D. C. Ch. 32, pp. 781–796.

DENNY-BROWN, D. 1962. *The Basal Ganglia and Their Relation to Disorders of Movement*. Oxford University Press, London.

DENNY-BROWN, D., AND BOTTERELL, E. H. 1948. The motor functions of the agranular frontal cortex. A. Res. Nerv. & Ment. Dis., Proc., **27:** 235–345.

DOGIEL, A. S. 1908. *Der Bau der Spinalganglien des Menschen und der Säugetiere*. Gustav Fischer, Jena.

DOTT, N. M. 1938. Surgical aspects of the hypothalamus. In W. E. L. CLARK *ET AL.* (Editors),

The Hypothalamus. Oliver and Boyd, Edinburgh, pp. 131–185.

DOW, R. S. 1936. The fiber connections of the posterior parts of the cerebellum in the rat and cat. J. Comp. Neurol., **63:** 527–548.

DOW, R. S. 1938. Efferent connections of the flocculonodular lobe in *Macaca mulatta*. J. Comp. Neurol., **68:** 297–305.

DOW, R. S. 1942. Cerebellar action potentials in response to stimulation of the cerebral cortex in monkeys and cats. J. Neurophysiol., **5:** 121–136.

DOW, R. S. AND MORUZZI, G. 1958. *The Physiology of the Cerebellum*. University of Minnesota Press, Minneapolis.

DREIFUSS, J. J., MURPHY, J. T., AND GLOOR, P. 1968. Contrasting effects of two identified amygdaloid efferent pathways on single hypothalamic neurons. J. Neurophysiol., **31:** 237–248.

DRESEL, K., AND ROTHMAN, H. 1925. Völliger Ausfall der Substantia nigra nach Exstirpation von Grosshirn und Striatum. Ztschr. ges. Neurol. u. Psychiat., **94:** 781–789.

DROOGLEEVER-FORTUYN, J., AND STEFENS, R. 1951. On the anatomical relations of the intralaminar and midline cells of the thalamus. Electroencephalog. & Clin. Neurophysiol., **3:** 393–400.

DROZ, B., AND LEBLOND, C. P. 1962. Migration of protein along axons of the sciatic nerve. Science, **137:** 1047–1048.

DRUCKMAN, R. 1952. A critique of "suppression" with additional observations in the cat. Brain, **75:** 226–243.

DUSSER DE BARENNE, J. G. 1924. Experimental researches on sensory localization in the cerebral cortex of the monkey. Proc. Roy. Soc., London, ser. B, **96:** 272–291.

DUSSER DE BARENNE, J. G., GAROL, H. W., AND McCULLOCH, W. S. 1942. Physiological neuronography of the corticostriatal connections. A. Res. Nerv. & Ment. Dis., Proc., **21:** 246–266.

DUSSER DE BARENNE, J. G., AND McCULLOCH, W. S. 1939. Suppression of motor response upon stimulation of area 4S of the cerebral cortex. Am. J. Physiol., **126:** 482.

EAGER, R. P. 1963. Efferent cortico-nuclear pathways in the cerebellum of the cat. J. Comp. Neurol., **120:** 81–103.

EAGER, R. P. 1963a. Cortical association pathways in the cerebellum of the cat. J. Comp. Neurol., **121:** 381–393.

EAGER, R. P. 1965. The mode of termination and temporal course of degeneration of cortical association pathways in the cerebellum of the cat. J. Comp. Neurol., **124:** 243–257.

EAGER, R. P., AND BARRNETT, R. J. 1966. Morphological and chemical studies of Nauta-stained degenerating cerebellar and hypothalamic fibers. J. Comp. Neurol., **126:** 487–510.

EARLE, K. M. 1952. The tract of Lissauer and its possible relation to the pain pathway. J. Comp. Neurol., **96:** 93–111.

ECCLES, J. C. 1959. Neuron physiology—introduction. In J. FIELD (Editor), *Handbook of Physiology,* Section I, Vol. I. American Physiological Society, Washington, D. C., Ch. 2, pp. 59–74.

ECCLES, J. C. 1966. Functional organization of the cerebellum in relation to its role in motor control. In R. GRANT (Editor), *Muscular Afferents and Motor Control.* Almquist & Wiksell, Stockholm, pp. 19–36.

ECCLES, J. C., ITO, M., AND SZENTÁGOTHAI, J. 1967. *The Cerebellum as a Neuronal Machine.* J. Springer Verlag, New York.

ECCLES, J. C., LLINÁS, R., AND SASAKI, K. 1964. Excitation of cerebellar Purkinje cells by the climbing fibers. Nature, **203:** 245–246.

ECCLES, J. C., LLINÁS, R., AND SASAKI, K. 1966. The excitatory synaptic action of climbing fibres on the Purkinje cells of the cerebellum. J. Physiol., **182:** 268–296.

ECCLES, J. C., LLINÁS, R., AND SASAKI, K. 1966*a*. Parallel fibre stimulation and responses induced thereby in the Purkinje cells of the cerebellum. Exper. Brain Res., **1:** 17–39.

ECCLES, J. C., LLINÁS, R., AND SASAKI, K. 1966*b*. The inhibitory interneurones within the cerebellar cortex. Exper. Brain. Res., **1:** 1–16.

ECCLES, J. C., LLINAS, R., AND SASAKI, K. 1966*c*. The mossy fibre-granule cell relay of the cerebellum and its inhibitory control by Golgi cells. Exper. Brain Res., **1:** 82–101.

VON ECONOMO, C. F. 1902. Die zentralen Bahnen des Kau- und Schluckaktes. Arch. ges Physiol., **91:** 629–643.

VON ECONOMO, C. F. 1911. Über dissoziierte Empfindungslähmung bei Ponstumoren und über die zentralen Bahnen des sensiblen Trigeminus. Jahrb. Psychiat. u. Neurol., **32:** 107–138.

VON ECONOMO, C. F. 1929. *The Cytoarchitectonics of the Human Cerebral Cortex.* Oxford Medical Publications, London, 186 pp.

VON ECONOMO, C. F., AND KARPLUS, J. P. 1909. Zur Physiologie und Anatomie des Mittelhirns. Arch. Psychiat., **46:** 275–356.

EDINGER, L. 1899. *The Anatomy of the Central Nervous System in Man and in Vertebrates in General.* F. A. Davis Company, Philadelphia. Ch. 19, pp. 295–300.

EDINGER, L. 1900. *Vorlesungen über den Bau der nervösen Centralorgane des Menschen,* Ed. 6. F. C. W. Vogel, Leipzig.

ELDRED, E., AND FUJIMORI, B. 1958. Relations of the reticular formation to muscle spindle activation. In H. H. JASPERS *ET AL.* (Editors), *Reticu-*

lar Formation of the Brain. Little, Brown and Company, Boston, pp. 275–283.

ELDRED, E., GRANIT, R., AND MERTON, P. A. 1953. Supraspinal control of the muscle spindles and its significance. J. Physiol., **122:** 498–523.

ELFVIN, L. G. 1958. The ultrastructure of unmyelinated fibers in the splenic nerve of the cat. J. Ultrastructure Res., **1:** 428–454.

ELLIOTT, K. A. C., AND JASPER, H. H. 1949. Measurement of experimentally induced brain swelling and shrinkage. Am. J. Physiol., **157:** 122–129.

ELLIOTT, T. R. 1905. The action of adrenalin. J. Physiol., **32:** 401–467.

ELMAN, R. 1923. Spinal arachnoid granulations with especial reference to the cerebrospinal fluid. Bull. Johns Hopkins Hosp., **34:** 99–104.

ELZE, C. 1932. Centrales Nervensystem. In H. BRAUS, *Anatomie des Menschen. Ein Lehrbuch für Studierende und Ärzte,* Vol. III. J. Springer, Berlin, p. 234.

EMMELIN, N. 1967. Nervous control of salivary glands. In C. F. CODE (Editor), *Handbook of Physiology,* Section 6. Vol. II. Secretion. American Physiological Society, Washington, D.C., Ch. 37, pp. 595–632.

EMMELIN, N., AND STROMBLAD, B. C. R. 1954. A method of stimulating and inhibiting salivary secretion in man. Acta physiol. scandinav., **31:** Suppl. 114, 12–13.

EMMERS, R. 1964. Localization of thalamic projection of afferents from the tongue of the cat. Anat. Rec., **148:** 67–74.

EMMERS, R. 1966. Separate relays of tactile, thermal and gustatory modalities in the cat thalamus. Proc. Soc. Exper. Biol. & Med., **121:** 527–531.

EMMERS, R., BENJAMIN, R. M., AND BLOMQUIST, A. J. 1962. Thalamic localization of afferents from the tongue in albino rat. J. Comp. Neurol., **118:** 43–48.

ERÄNKÖ, O. 1964. Histochemical demonstration of catecholamines by fluorescence induced by formaldehyde vapour. J. Histochem. & Cytochem., **12:** 487–489.

ERÄNKÖ, O. 1967. Histochemistry of nervous tissues: catecholamines and cholinesterases. Ann. Rev. Pharmacol., **7:** 203–222.

ERICKSON, T. C., AND WOOLSEY, C. N. 1951. Observations on the supplementary motor area of man. Tr. Am. Neurol. A., **76:** 50–56.

ERLANGER, J., AND GASSER, H. S. 1937. *Electrical Signs of Nervous Activity.* University of Pennsylvania Press, Philadelphia, 221 pp.

VON EULER, U. S. 1948. Identification of the sympathomimetic ergone in adrenergic nerves of cattle (sympathin N) with laevo-noradrenaline. Acta physiol. scandinav., **16:** 63–74.

von Euler, U. S. 1955. *Noradrenaline.* Charles C Thomas, Publisher, Springfield, Ill.

von Euler, U. S. 1959. Autonomic neuroeffector transmission. In J. Field (Editor), *Handbook of Physiology*, Section I, Vol. I. American Physiological Society, Washington, D.C., Ch. 7, pp. 215–237.

Falck, B. 1962. Observations on the possibilities of the cellular localization of monoamines by a fluorescence method. Acta physiol. scandinav., 56: Suppl. 197, 1–25.

Falck, B., Hillarp, N. A., Thieme, G., and Torp, A. 1962. Fluorescence of catecholamines and related compounds condensed with formaldehyde. J. Histochem. & Cytochem., 10: 348–354.

Falconer, M. A. 1948. Relief of intractable pain of organic origin by frontal lobotomy. A. Res. Nerv. & Ment. Dis., Proc., 27: 706–722.

Falconer, M. A. 1949. Intramedullary trigeminal tractotomy and its place in treatment of facial pain. J. Neurol. Neurosurg. & Psychiat., 12: 297–311.

Farquhar, M. G., and Hartmann, J. F. 1957. Neuroglial structure and relationships as revealed by electron microscopy. J. Neuropath. & Exper. Neurol., 16: 18–39.

Fatt, P. 1959. Skeletal neuromuscular transmission. In J. Field (Editor), *Handbook of Physiology*, Section I, Vol. I. American Physiological Society, Washington, D. C., Ch. 6, pp. 199–213.

Faulkner, R. F., and Hyde, J. E. 1958. Coordinated eye and body movements evoked by brainstem stimulation in decerebrated cats. J. Neurophysiol., 21: 171–182.

Feindel, W., and Penfield, W. 1954. Localization of discharge in temporal lobe automatism. Arch. Neurol. & Psychiat., 72: 605–630.

Fernández-Morán, H. 1957. Electron microscopy of nervous tissue. In D. Richter (Editor), *Metabolism of the Nervous System*. Second International Neurochemical Symposium, Aarhus, Denmark, 1956. Pergamon Press, New York, pp. 1–34.

Ferraro, A. 1925. Contributa sperimentale allo studio della substantia nigra normale e dei suoi rapporti con la corteccia cerebrale e con il corpo striato. Arch. Gen. Neurol. Psichiat., 6: 26–117.

Ferraro, A. 1928. The connections of the pars suboculomotoria of the substantia nigra. Arch. Neurol. & Psychiat., 19: 177–180.

Ferraro, A., and Barrera, S. E. 1935. Posterior column fibers and their terminations in the *Macacus rhesus*. J. Comp. Neurol., 62: 507–530.

Fink, R. P., and Heimer, L. 1967. Two methods for selective silver impregnation of degenerating axons and their synaptic endings in the central nervous system. Brain Res. 4: 369–374.

Flechsig, P. 1905. Einige Bemerkungen über die Untersuchungsmethoden der Grosshirnrinde, insbesondere des Menschen. Arch. Anat. u. Entwicklungsgeschichte, 337–444.

Flood, S., and Jansen, J. 1961. On the cerebellar nuclei in the cat. Acta anat., 46: 52–72.

Fluur, E. 1959. Influences of semicircular ducts on extraocular muscles. Acta Oto-laryng., Suppl. 149: 1–46.

Foerster, O. 1927. *Die Leitungsbahnen des Schmerzgefühls und die chirurgische Behandlung der Schmerzzustände.* Urban und Schwarzenberg, Berlin.

Foerster, O. 1931. The cerebral cortex in man. Lancet, 2: 309–312.

Foerster, O. 1933. The dermatomes in man. Brain, 56: 1–39.

Foerster, O. 1936. Sensible cortical Felder. In O. Bumke and O. Foerster (Editors), *Handbuch der Neurologie*, Vol. 6. J. Springer, Berlin, pp. 358–448.

Foerster, O. 1936a. Motor cortex in man in the light of Hughlings Jackson's doctrines. Brain, 59: 135–159.

Foerster, O. 1936b. Symptomatologie der Erkrankungen des Grosshirns. Motorische Felder und Bahnen. In O. Bumke and O. Foerster (Editors), *Handbuch der Neurologie*, Vol. 6. J. Springer, Berlin, pp. 1–357.

Foerster, O. 1936c. Symptomatologie der Erkrankungen des Rückenmarks und seiner Wurzeln. In O. Bumke and O. Foerster (Editors), *Handbuch der Neurologie*, Vol. 5. J. Springer, Berlin, pp. 1–400.

Foerster, O., and Gagel, O. 1932. Die Vorderseitenstrangdurchschneidung beim Menschen. Eine klinischpathophysiologisch-anatomische Studie. Ztschr. ges. Neurol. u. Psychiat., 138: 1–92.

Foerster, O., Gagel, O., and Sheehan, D. 1933. Veränderungen an den Endösen im Rückenmark des Affen nach Hinterwurzeldurchschneidung. Ztschr. Anat., 101: 553–565.

Foix, C. 1921. Les lésions anatomiques de la maladie de Parkinson. Rev. neurol., 37: 593–600.

Foix, C., and Hillemand, J. 1925. Les artères de l'axe encéphalique jusqu'au diencéphale inclusivement. Rev. neurol., 44: 705–739.

Foix, C., and Nicolesco, J. 1925. *Les Noyaux gris centraux et la région mesencephalo-sous-optique.* Masson et Cie, Paris, 578 pp.

Foley, J. M., Kinney, T. D., and Alexander, L. 1942. The vascular supply of the hypothalamus in man. J. Neuropath. & Exper. Neurol., 1: 265–296.

Foley, J. O., and Schnitzlein, H. N. 1957. The contributions of individual thoracic spinal nerves to the upper cervical sympathetic trunk. J. Comp. Neurol., 108: 109–120.

Fox, C. A. 1940. Certain basal telencephalic centers in the cat. J. Comp. Neurol., **72:** 1–62.

Fox, C. A., and Barnard, J. W. 1957. A quantitative study of the Purkinje cell, dendritic branchlets and their relationship to afferent fibers. J. Anat., **91:** 299–313.

Fox, C. A., Fisher, R. R., and DeSalva, S. J. 1948. The distribution of the anterior commissure in the monkey (*Macaca mulatta*). Experimental studies. J. Comp. Neurol., **89:** 245–277.

Fox, C. A., Hillman, D. E., Siegesmund, K. A., and Dutta, C. R. 1967. The primate cerebellar cortex: A Golgi and electron microscope study. In C. A. Fox and R. S. Snider (Editors), *Progress in Brain Research, The Cerebellum,* Vol. 25. Elsevier Publishing Company, Amsterdam. pp. 174–225.

Fox, C. A., Hillman, D. E., Siegesmund, K. A., and Sether, L. A. 1966. The primate globus pallidus and its feline and avian homologues: A Golgi and electron microscopic study. In R. Hassler and H. Stephan (Editors), *Evolution of the Forebrain. Phylogenesis and Ontogenesis of the Forebrain.* Georg Thieme Verlag, Stuttgart, pp. 237–248.

Fox, C. A., McKinley, W. A., and Magoun, H. W. 1944. An oscillographic study of olfactory system of cats. J. Neurophysiol., **7:** 1–16.

Fox, C. A., and Schmitz, J. T. 1944. The substantia nigra and the entopeduncular nucleus in the cat. J. Comp. Neurol., **80:** 323–334.

Fox, C. A., Siegesmund, K. A., and Dutta, C. R. 1964. The Purkinje cell dendritic branchlets and their relation with the parallel fibers: light and electron microscopic observations. In M. M. Cohen and R. S. Snider (Editors), *Morphological and Biochemical Correlates of Neural Activity.* Harper and Row, New York, Ch. 7, pp. 112–141.

Francoeur, J., and Olszewski, J. 1968. Axonal reaction and axoplasmic flow as studied by radioautography. Neurology, **18:** 178–184.

Frantzen, E., and Olivarius, B. I. F. 1957. On thrombosis of the basilar artery. Acta psychiat. & neurol. scandinav., **32:** 431–439.

Fredrickson, J. M., Figge, U., Scheid, P., and Kornhuber, H. H. 1966. Vestibular nerve projection to the cerebral cortex of the rhesus monkey. Exper. Brain Res. **2:** 318–327.

Freeman, L. W. 1952. Return of function after complete transection of the spinal cord of the rat, cat and dog. Am. Surgeon, **136:** 193–205.

Freeman, W., and Watts, J. W. 1947. Retrograde degeneration of the thalamus following prefrontal lobotomy. J. Comp. Neurol., **86:** 65–93.

Freeman, W., and Watts, J. W. 1948. The thalamic projection to the frontal lobe. A. Res. Nerv. & Ment. Dis., Proc., **27:** 200–209.

Freeman, W., and Watts, J. W. 1949. *Psychosurgery, Intelligence, Emotion and Social Behavior Following Prefrontal Lobotomy for Mental Disorders,* Ed. 2. Charles C Thomas, Publisher, Springfield, Ill., 337 pp.

French, J. D., von Amerongen, F. K., and Magoun, H. W. 1952. An activating system in the brain stem of monkey. A.M.A. Arch. Neurol. & Psychiat., **68:** 577–590.

French, J. D., Hernández-Peon, R., and Livingston, R. B. 1955. Projections from cortex to cephalic brain stem (reticular formation) in monkey. J. Neurophysiol., **18:** 74–95.

French, J. D., and Magoun, H. W. 1952. Effects of chronic lesions in central cephalic brain stem of monkeys. A.M.A. Arch. Neurol. & Psychiat., **68:** 591–604.

French, J. D., Verzeano, M., and Magoun, H. W. 1953. An extralemniscal sensory system in the brain. A.M.A. Arch. Neurol. & Psychiat., **69:** 505–518.

French, J. D., Verzeano, M., and Magoun, H. W. 1953a. The neural basis of the anesthetic state. A.M.A. Arch. Neurol. & Psychiat., **69:** 519–529.

Friede, R. 1961. A histochemical study of DPN-diaphorase in human white matter; with some notes on myelination. J. Neurochem., **8:** 17–30.

Friede, R. L. 1962. The cytochemistry of normal and reactive astrocytes. J. Neuropath. & Exper. Neurol., **21:** 471–478.

Friedmann, U., and Elkeles, A. 1932. Weitere Untersuchungen über die Permeabilität der Bluthirnschranke. Z. ges. Exper. Med., **80:** 212–234.

Frigyesi, T. L., and Purpura, D. P. 1964. Functional properties of synaptic pathways influencing transmission in the specific cerebello-thalamocortical projection system. Exper. Neurol., **10:** 305–324.

Fry, W. J., Krumins, R., Fry, F. J., Thomas, G., Borbely, S., and Ades, H. 1963. Origins and distribution of some efferent pathways from the mammillary nuclei of the cat. J. Comp. Neurol., **120:** 195–258.

Fulton, J. F. 1949. *Physiology of the Nervous System,* Ed. 3. Oxford Medical Publications, New York.

Fulton, J. F. 1949a. *Functional Localization in the Frontal Lobes and Cerebellum.* Clarendon Press, Oxford.

Fulton, J. F., and Ingraham, F. D. 1929. Emotional disturbances following experimental lesions of the base of the brain (pre-chiasmal). J. Physiol., **67:** 27–28.

Fulton, J. F., and Keller, A. D. 1932. *The Sign of Babinski. A Study of the Evolution of Cor tical Dominance in Primates.* Charles C Thomas, Springfield, Ill., 165 pp.

FULTON, J. F., AND KENNARD, M. A. 1934. A study of flaccid and spastic paralysis produced by lesions of the cerebral cortex in primates. A. Res. Nerv. & Ment. Dis., Proc., **13:** 158–210.

FULTON, J. F., AND PI-SUÑER, J. 1927–28. A note concerning the probable function of various afferent end-organs in skeletal muscle. Am. J. Physiol., **83:** 554–562.

FUXE, K., AND ANDÉN, N. E. 1966. Studies on central monoamine neurons with special reference to the nigro-neostriatal dopamine neuron system. In E. COSTA ET AL. (Editors), *Biochemistry and Pharmacology of the Basal Ganglia.* Raven Press, Hewlett, N. Y., pp. 123–129.

GABE, M. 1966. *Neurosecretion.* Translated by R. Crawford. Pergamon Press, Ltd., Oxford, pp. 427–736.

GALAMBOS, R. 1956. Suppression of auditory nerve activity by stimulation of efferent fibers to cochlea. J. Neurophysiol., **19:** 424–437.

GALLOWAY, J. R., AND GREITZ, T. 1960. The medial and lateral choroid arteries: An anatomic and roentgenographic study. Acta radiol., **53:** 353–356.

GAMBLE, H. J. 1964. Comparative electron-microscopic observations on the connective tissues of a peripheral nerve and a spinal nerve root in the rat. J. Anat., **98:** 17–25.

GAMBLE, H. J., AND EAMES, R. A. 1964. An electron microscope study of the connective tissues of human peripheral nerve. J. Anat., **98:** 655–663.

GARCIA-BENGOCHEA, F., CORRIGAN, R., MORGANE, P., RUSSELL, D., AND HEATH, R. 1951. Studies on the function of the temporal lobes: I. The section of the fornix. Tr. Am. Neurol. A., **76:** 238–239.

GARDNER, E. 1944. The distribution and termination of nerve fibers in the knee joint of the cat. J. Comp. Neurol., **80:** 11–32.

GARVEN, H. S. D. 1925. The nerve endings in the Panniculus carnosus of the hedgehog, with special reference to the sympathetic innervation of striated muscle. Brain, **48:** 380–441.

GASKELL, W. H. 1961. *The Involuntary Nervous System.* Longmans, Green and Company, London.

GASSER, G. 1961. *Basic Neuro-Pathological Technique.* Blackwell Scientific Publications, Oxford, pp. 39–74.

GASSER, H. S., AND GRUNDFEST, H. 1939. Axon diameters in relation to the spike dimensions and the conduction velocity in mammalian A fibers. Am. J. Physiol., **127:** 393–414.

GASTAUT, H. 1954. The brain stem and cerebral electrogenesis in relation to consciousness. In

J. F. DELAFRESNAYE (Editor), *Brain Mechanisms and Consciousness.* Blackwell Scientific Publications, Oxford, pp. 249–279.

GAZZANIGA, M. S., BOGEN, J. E., AND SPERRY, R. W. 1965. Observations on visual perception after disconnexion of the cerebral hemispheres in man. Brain, **88:** 221–236.

GAZZANIGA, M. S., AND SPERRY, R. W. 1967. Language after section of the cerebral commissures. Brain, **90:** 131–148.

GEIGER, R. S. 1958. Subcultures of adult mammalian brain cortex *in vitro.* Exper. Cell Res., **14:** 541–566.

GELFAN, S. 1964. Neuronal interdependence. In J. C. ECCLES AND J. P. SCHADÉ (Editors), *Progress in Brain Research, Organization of the Spinal Cord,* Vol. 11. Elsevier Publishing Company, Amsterdam, pp. 238–260.

GERARD, R. W., MARSHALL, W. H., AND SAUL, L. J. 1936. Electrical activity of the cat's brain. Arch. Neurol. & Psychiat., **36:** 675–738.

GEREBTZOFF, M. A. 1940. Recherches sur la projection corticale du labyrinth. I. Des effets de la stimulation labyrinthique sur l'activité électrique de l'écorce cérébrale. Arch. internat. physiol., **50:** 365–378.

GEREN, B. B. 1954. The formation from the Schwann cell surface of the myelin in peripheral nerves of chick embryos. Exper. Cell Res., **7:** 558–562.

GERSTMANN, J. 1940. Syndrome of finger agnosia; disorientation for right and left, agraphia and acalculia. Arch. Neurol. & Psychiat., **44:** 398–408.

GIBSON, C. W. 1937. Degeneration of the boutons terminaux in the spinal cord: an experimental study. Arch. Neurol. & Psychiat., **38:** 1145–1157.

GILBERT, G. J. 1960. The subcommissural organ. Neurology, **10:** 138–142.

GILBERT, G. J., AND GLASER, G. H. 1961. On the nervous system integration of water and salt metabolism. Arch. Neurol., **5:** 179–196.

GILLILAN, L. 1958. The arterial blood supply of the human spinal cord. J. Comp. Neurol., **110:** 75–103.

GLEES, P. 1945. The interrelation of the striopallidum and the thalamus in the macaque monkey. Brain, **68:** 331–346.

GLEES, P. 1946. Terminal degeneration within the central nervous system as studied by a new silver method. J. Neuropath., **5:** 54–59.

GLEES, P. 1955. *Neuroglia; Morphology and Function.* Blackwell Scientific Publications, Oxford, 111 pp.

GLEES, P. 1961. *Experimental Neurology.* Oxford University Press, London. 532 pp.

GLEES, P., AND GRIFFITH, H. B. 1952. Bilateral destruction of the hippocampus (cornu ammonis) in a case of dementia. Monatsschr. Psychiat. u. Neurol., **123:** 193–204.

GLEES, P., AND NAUTA, W. J. H. 1955. A critical review of studies on axonal and terminal degeneration. Monatsschr. Psychiat. u. Neurol., **129:** 74–91.

GLEES, P., AND WALL, P. D. 1946. Fibre connections of the subthalamic region and the centromedian nucleus of the thalamus. Brain, **69:** 195–211.

GLOOR, P. 1960. Amygdala. In J. FIELD (Editor), *Handbook of Physiology*, Section 1, Vol. II. American Physiological Society, Washington, D. C. Ch. 57, pp. 1395–1420.

GOLDBERG, J. M., AND NEFF, W. D. 1961. Frequency discrimination after bilateral ablation of cortical auditory areas. J. Neurophysiol., **24:** 119–128.

GOLDBY, F., AND HARRISON, R. J. 1961. Editors, *Recent Advances in Anatomy*, Ser. 2. Little, Brown and Company, Boston. Ch. 7, pp. 247–273.

GOLGI, C. 1894. *Untersuchungen über den feineren Bau des centralen und peripherischen Nervensystems.* Gustav Fischer, Jena.

GORDON, G., AND JUKES, M. G. M. 1964. Dual organization of exteroceptive components of the cat's gracile nucleus. J. Physiol., **173:** 263–290.

GORDON, G., AND JUKES, M. G. M. 1964a. Descending influences on the exteroceptive organization of the cat's gracile nucleus. J. Physiol., **173:** 291–319.

GORDON, G., AND PAINE, P. H. 1960. Functional organization in nucleus gracilis of the cat. J. Physiol., **153:** 331–349.

GRANIT, R. 1955. *Receptors and Sensory Perception.* Yale University Press, New Haven.

GRANIT, R., AND KAADA, B. R. 1952. Influence of stimulation of central nervous structures on muscle spindles in cat. Acta physiol. scandinav., **27:** 130–160.

GRANT, G. 1962. Projection of the external cuneate nucleus onto the cerebellum in the cat: An experimental study using silver methods. Exper. Neurol., **5:** 179–195.

GRANT, G. 1962a. Spinal course and somatotopically localized termination of the spinocerebellar tracts. An experimental study in the cat. Acta physiol. scandinav., **56:** Suppl. 193, 1–45.

GRANT, G., AND REXED, B. 1958. Dorsal spinal root afferents to Clarke's column. Brain, **81:** 567–576.

GRAY, E. G. 1961. The granule cells, mossy synapses and Purkinje spine synapses of the cerebellum: Light and electron microscopic observations. J. Anat., **95:** 345–356.

GRAY, E. G., AND GUILLERY, R. W. 1961. The basis for silver staining of synapses of the mammalian spinal cord: A light and electron microscope study. J. Physiol., **157:** 581–588.

GRAY, J. A. B. 1959. Initiation of impulses at receptors. In J. FIELD (Editor), *Handbook of Physiology*, Section I, Vol. I. American Physiological Society, Washington, D. C., Ch. 4, pp. 123–145.

GRAZER, F. M., AND CLEMENTE, C. D. 1957. Developing blood-brain barrier to trypan blue. Proc. Soc. Exper. Biol. & Med., **94:** 758–760.

GREEN, J. D. 1958. The rhinencephalon: aspects of its relation to behavior and the reticular activating system. In H. H. JASPERS ET AL. (Editors), *Reticular Formation of the Brain.* Henry Ford Hospital International Symposium. Little, Brown and Company, Boston, pp. 607–619.

GREEN, J. D. 1960. The hippocampus. In J. FIELD (Editor), *Handbook of Physiology*, Section I, Vol. II. American Physiological Society, Ch. 56, pp. 1373–1389.

GREEN, J. D. 1964. The hippocampus. Physiol. Rev., **44:** 561–608.

GREEN, J. D., AND ARDUINI, A. A. 1954. Hippocampal electrical activity in arousal. J. Neurophysiol., **17:** 533–557.

GREEN, J. D., CLEMENTE, C. A., AND DE GROOT, J. 1957. Rhinencephalic lesions and behavior in cats. J. Comp. Neurol., **108:** 505–545.

GREEN, J. D., AND SHIMAMOTO, T. 1953. Hippocampal seizures and their propagation. Arch. Neurol. & Psychiat., **70:** 687–702.

GREEN, J. R., DUISBERG, R. E. H., AND McGRATH, W. B. 1951. Focal epilepsy of psychomotor type. A preliminary report of observations on effects of surgical therapy. J. Neurosurg., **8:** 157–172.

GREEN, J. R., DUISBERG, R. E. H., AND McGRATH, W. B. 1952. Orbitofrontal lobotomy with reference to effects on 55 psychotic patients. J. Neurosurg., **9:** 579–587.

GREENE, J., AND JAMPEL, R. 1966. Muscle spindles in the extraocular muscles of the Macaque. J. Comp. Neurol., **126:** 547–550.

GREVING, R. 1935. Makroskopische Anatomie und Histologie des vegetativen Nervensystems. In O. BUMKE AND O. FOERSTER (Editors), *Handbuch der Neurologie*, Vol. I. J. Springer, Berlin, pp. 811–886.

DE GROOT, J., AND HARRIS, G. W. 1950. Hypothalamic control of the anterior pituitary gland and blood lymphocytes. J. Physiol., **111:** 335–346.

GRUNDFEST, H. 1939. The properties of mammalian B fibers. Am. J. Physiol., **127:** 252–262.

GRUNDFEST, H. 1940. Bioelectric potentials. Ann. Rev. Physiol., **2:** 213–242.

GRUNSTEIN, A. M. 1911. Zur Frage von den Leitungsbahnen des Corpus striatum. Neurol. Centralbl., **30:** 659–665.

GUILLERY, R. W. 1956. Degeneration in the posterior commissural fornix and the mammillary peduncle of the rat. J. Anat., **90:** 350–370.

GUILLERY, R. W. 1957. Degeneration in the hypothalamic connexions of the albino rat. J. Anat., **91:** 91–115.

GUILLERY, R. W. 1967. A light and electron microscopic study of neurofibrils and neurofilaments at neuro-neuronal junctions in the lateral geniculate nucleus of the cat. Am. J. Anat., **120:** 583–604.

GUTMANN, E., GUTTMANN, L., MEDAWAR, P. B., AND YOUNG, J. Z. 1942. Rate of regeneration of nerve. J. Exper. Biol., **19:** 14–44.

GUTMANN, E., AND YOUNG, J. Z. 1944. The re-innervation of muscle after various periods of atrophy. J. Anat., **78:** 15–43.

GUTTMANN, L. 1946. Rehabilitation after injuries to spinal cord and cauda equina. Brit. J. Phys. Med., **9:** 162–171.

GUTTMANN, L. 1952. Studies on reflex activity of the isolated cord in the spinal man. J. Nerv. & Ment. Dis., **116:** 957–972.

HA, H., AND LIU, C. N. 1968. Cell origin of the ventral spinocerebellar tract. J. Comp. Neurol., **133:** 185–205.

HÄGGQVIST, G. 1937. Faseranalytische Studien über die Pyramidenbahn. Acta psychiat. et neurol., **12:** 457–466.

HAGBARTH, K. E., AND KERR, D. I. B. 1954. Central influences on spinal afferent conduction. J. Neurophysiol., **17:** 295–307.

HAMBURGER, A., AND HYDÉN, H. 1963. Inverse enzymatic changes in neurons and glia during increased function and hypoxia. J. Cell Biol., **16:** 521–525.

HALL, E. A. 1963. Efferent connections of the basal and lateral nuclei of the amygdala in the cat. Am. J. Anat., **113:** 139–151.

HAMILTON, W. J., BOYD, J. D., AND MOSSMAN, H. W. 1962. *Human Embryology. Prenatal Development of Form and Function.* Williams and Wilkins Company, Baltimore. Ch. 12, pp. 315–388.

HAMLYN, L. H. 1954. The effect of preganglionic section on the neurons of the superior cervical ganglion in rabbits. J. Anat., **88:** 184–191.

HAMMOND, W. A. 1871. *A Treatise on Diseases of the Nervous System.* D. Appleton and Company, New York, pp. 655–662.

HÁMORI, J., AND SZENTÁGOTHAL, J. 1966. Identification under the electron microscope of climbing fibers and their synaptic contacts. Exper. Brain Res., **1:** 65–81.

HAMPEL, C. W. 1935. The effect of denervation on the sensitivity to adrenine of the smooth muscle in the nictitating membrane of the cat. Am. J. Physiol., **61:** 611–621.

HAMPSON, J. L. 1949. Relationships between cat cerebral and cerebellar cortices. J. Neurophysiol., **12:** 37–50.

HANBERY, J. A., AJMONE-MARSAN, C., AND DILWORTH, M. 1954. Pathways of non-specific thalamo-cortical projection system. Electroencephalog. and Clin. Neurophysiol., **6:** 103–118.

HANBERY, J., AND JASPER, H. 1953. Independence of diffuse thalamo-cortical projection system shown by specific nuclear destruction. J. Neurophysiol., **16:** 252–271.

HAND, P. J. 1966. Lumbosacral dorsal root terminations in the nucleus gracilis of the cat. Some observations on terminal degeneration in other medullary sensory nuclei. J. Comp. Neurol., **126:** 137–156.

HARE, W. K., AND HINSEY, J. C. 1940. Reaction of dorsal root ganglion cells to section of peripheral and central processes. J. Comp. Neurol., **73:** 489–502.

HARRIS, G. W. 1948. Electrical stimulation of the hypothalamus and the mechanism of neural control of the adenohypophysis. J. Physiol., **107:** 418–429.

HARRIS, G. W. 1955. *Neural Control of the Pituitary Gland.* Edward Arnold and Company, London.

HARRIS, G. W. 1956. Hypothalamic control of the anterior lobe of the hypophysis. In W. S. FIELDS. ET AL. (Editors), *Hypothalamic-Hypophysial Interrelationships.* (Symposium). Charles C Thomas Publisher, Springfield. Ill., pp. 31–42.

HARTMANN, J. F. 1956. Electron microscopy of mitochondria in the central nervous system. J. Biophys. & Biochem. Cytol., **2:** Suppl., 373–378.

HASSLER, O. 1966. Deep cerebral venous system in man. A microangiographic study on its areas of drainage and its anastomoses with the superficial cerebral veins. Neurology, **16:** 505–511.

HASSLER, O. 1967. Venous anatomy of human hindbrain. Arch. Neurol., **16:** 404–409.

HASSLER, O. 1967a. Arterial pattern of human brain stem. Normal appearance and deformation in expanding supratentorial conditions. Neurology, **17:** 368–375.

HASSLER, R. 1939. Zur pathologischen Anatomie des senilen und des parkinsonistischen Tremor. J. Psychol. u. Neurol., **49:** 193–230.

HASSLER, R. 1950. Über Kleinhirnprojektionen zum Mittelhirn und Thalamus beim Menschen. Deutsche Ztschr. Nervenh., **163:** 629–671.

HATSCHEK, R. 1907. Zur vergleichenden Anatomie des Nucleus ruber tegmenti. Arb. Neurol. Inst. Wiener Univ., **15:** 89–135.

HAUGSTED, H. 1956. Occlusion of the basilar artery. Diagnosis by vertebral angiography during life. Neurology, **6:** 823–828.

HAY, E. D., AND REVEL, J. P. 1963. The fine structure of the DNP component of the nucleus. An electron microscope study ultilizing autoradiography to localize DNA synthesis. J. Cell Biol., **16:** 29–51.

HAYMAKER, W. 1956. *Bing's Local Diagnosis in*

Neurological Diseases. C. V. Mosby Company, St. Louis, pp. 57–62 and 105–112.

HAYMAKER, W., AND WOODHALL, B. 1945. *Peripheral Nerve Injuries; Principles of Diagnosis.* W. B. Saunder Company, Philadelphia, 227 pp.

HEAD, H. 1905. The afferent nervous system from a new aspect. Brain, **28**: 99–116.

HEAD, H. 1920. *Studies in Neurology.* Oxford University Press, London, 2 vols.

HEAD, H., AND HOLMES, G. 1911. Sensory disturbances from cerebral lesions. Brain, **34**: 102–254.

HEATH, J. W. 1947. Clinicopathologic aspects of Parkinsonian states. A.M.A. Arch. Neurol. & Psychiat., **58**: 484–497.

HEIMER, L., AND NAUTA, W. J. H. 1967. The hypothalamic distribution of the stria terminalis in the rat. Anat. Rec., **157**: 259.

HEINBECKER, P., BISHOP, G. H., AND O'LEARY, J. L. 1936. Functional and histologic studies of somatic and autonomic nerves of man. Arch. Neurol. & Psychiat., **35**: 1233–1255.

HENNEMAN, E., COOKE, P., AND SNIDER, R. S. 1948. Cerebellar projections to the cerebral cortex in cat and monkey. Am. J. Physiol., **155**: 443.

HENSCHEN, S. E. 1926. On the function of the right hemisphere of the brain in relation to the left in speech, music and calculation. Brain, **49**: 110–123.

HERN, J. E. C., LANDGREN, S., AND PHILLIPS, C. G. 1960. Corticofugal discharges evoked by surface-anodal and surface-cathodal stimulation of the baboon's brain. J. Physiol., **154**: 70P–71P.

HERN, J. E. C., AND PHILLIPS, C. G. 1959. Cortical thresholds for minimal synaptic action on cat motoneurons. J. Physiol., **149**: 24P–25P.

HERNÁNDEZ-PEON, R., AND HAGBARTH, K. E. 1955. Interaction between afferent and cortically induced reticular responses. J. Neurophysiol., **18**: 44–55.

HERNDON, R. M. 1964. The fine structure of the cerebellum. II. The stellate neurons, granule cells and glia. J. Cell Biol., **23**: 277–293.

HERREN, R. Y., AND ALEXANDER, L. 1939. Sulcal and intrinsic blood vessels of human spinal cord. Arch. Neurol. & Psychiat., **41**: 678–687.

HERRICK, C. J. 1948. *The Brain of the Tiger Salamander.* University of Chicago Press, Chicago, Ill., pp. 141–142 and 175.

HERRICK, C. J., AND COGHILL, G. E. 1915. The development of reflex mechanisms in Amblystoma. J. Comp. Neurol., **25**: 65–85.

HERZ, E. 1931. Die amyostatischen Unruheerscheinungen. J. Psychol. u. Neurol., **43**: 3–182.

HESS, W. R. 1948. *Die Funktionelle Organisation des Vegetativen Nervensystems.* Benno Schwabe and Company, Basel.

HESS, W. R. 1954. *Diencephalon, Autonomic and*

Extrapyramidal Functions. Grune and Stratton, Inc., New York, 79 pp.

HETHERINGTON, A. W., AND RANSON, S. W. 1940. Hypothalamic lesions and adiposity in the rat. Anat. Rec., **78**: 149–172.

HILD, W. 1956. Neurosecretion in the central nervous system. In W. S. FIELDS *ET AL.* (Editors), *Hypothalamic-Hypophysial Interrelationships.* Charles C Thomas, Publisher, Springfield, Ill., pp. 17–25.

HINES, M. 1936. The anterior border of the monkey's (*Macaca mulatta*) motor cortex and the production of spasticity. Am. J. Physiol., **116**: 76.

HINES, M. 1937. The "motor" cortex. Bull. Johns Hopkins Hosp., **60**: 313–336.

HINES, M. 1949. Significance of the precentral motor cortex. In P. C. BUCY (Editor), *The Precentral Motor Cortex.* University of Illinois Press, Urbana, Ill., Ch. 18, 461–494.

HINMAN, A., AND CARPENTER, M. B. 1959. Efferent fiber projections of the red nucleus in the cat. J. Comp. Neurol., **113**: 61–82.

HOCHSTETTER, F. 1919. *Beiträge zur Entwicklungsgeschichte des menschlichen Gehirns,* Vol. I. F. Deuticke, Vienna and Leipzig.

HOFF, E. C. 1932. Central nerve terminals in the mammalian spinal cord and their examination by experimental degeneration. Proc. Roy. Soc. London, ser. B, **111**: 175–188.

HOFF, E. C. 1932a. The distribution of the spinal terminals (boutons) of the pyramidal tract, determined by experimental degeneration. Proc. Roy. Soc. London, ser. B, **111**: 226–237.

HOFF, E. C. 1935. Corticospinal fibers arising in the premotor area of the monkey. Distribution of bouton terminations. Arch. Neurol. & Psychiat., **33**: 687–697.

HOFF, E. C., AND HOFF, H. E. 1934. Spinal termination of the projection fibers from the motor cortex of primates. Brain, **57**: 454–474.

HOLMES, G. 1901. The nervous system of the dog without a forebrain. J. Physiol., **27**: 1–25.

HOLMES, G. 1922. The Croonian Lectures on the clinical symptoms of cerebellar disease and their interpretation. Lancet, **1**: 1177–1182.

HOLMES, G. 1939. The cerebellum of man. Brain, **62**: 1–30.

HOLMES, G., AND MAY, W. P. 1909. On the exact origin of the pyramidal tract in man and other mammals. Brain, **32**: 1–43.

HOLMES, G., AND STEWART, T. G. 1908. On the connections of the inferior olive with the cerebellum in man. Brain, **31**: 125–137.

HOLMES, W. 1943. Silver staining of nerve axons in paraffin sections. Anat. Rec., **86**: 157–187.

HOLTZMAN, E., NOVIKOFF, A. B., AND VILLARERDE, H. 1967. Lysosomes and GERL in normal and chromatolytic neurons of the rat ganglion nodosum. J. Cell Biol., **33:** 419–435.

HOOKER, D. 1944. *The Origin of Overt Behavior.* University of Michigan, Ann Arbor, Mich.

HORNYKIEWICZ, O. 1966. Metabolism of brain dopamine in human parkinsonism: neurochemical and clinical aspects. In E. COSTA *ET AL.* (Editors), *Biochemistry and Pharmacology of the Basal Ganglia.* Raven Press, Hewlett, N. Y., pp. 171–185.

HUBBARD, J. I., AND OSCARSSON, O. 1962. Localization of the cell bodies of the ventral spinocerebellar tract in lumbar segments of the cat. J. Comp. Neurol., **118:** 199–204.

HUBEL, D. H., AND WIESEL, T. N. 1959. Receptive fields of single neurons in the cat's striate cortex. J. Physiol., **148:** 574–591.

HUBEL, D. H., AND WIESEL, T. N. 1961. Integrative action in the cat's lateral geniculate body. J. Physiol., **155:** 385–398.

HUBEL, D. H., AND WIESEL, T. N. 1962. Receptive fields, binocular interaction and functional architecture in the cat's visual cortex. J. Physiol., **160:** 106–154.

HUBEL, D. H., AND WIESEL, T. N. 1963. Shape and arrangement of columns in cat's striate cortex. J. Physiol., **165:** 559–568.

HUBEL, D. H., AND WIESEL, T. N. 1965. Receptive fields and functional architecture in two nonstriate visual areas (18 and 19) of the cat. J. Neurophysiol., **28:** 229–289.

HUBER, G. C., AND CROSBY, E. C. 1929. Somatic and visceral connections of the diencephalon. A. Res. Nerv. & Ment. Dis., Proc., **9:** 199–248.

HUMASON, G. L. 1961. *Animal Tissue Techniques.* W. H. Freeman and Company, San Francisco, pp. 189–217.

HUMPHREY, T. 1936. The telencephalon of the bat. The non-cortical nuclear masses and certain pertinent fiber connections. J. Comp. Neurol., **65:** 603–711.

HUMPHREY, T. 1966. Correlations between the development of the hippocampal formation and the differentiation of the olfactory bulbs. Alabama J. M. Sc., **3:** 235–269.

HUMPHREY, T. 1968. The development of the human amygdala during early embryonic life. J. Comp. Neurol., **132:** 135–166.

HUNT, C. C., AND RIKER, W. K. 1966. Properties of frog sympathetic neurons in normal ganglia and after axon section. J. Neurophysiol., **29:** 1096–1114.

HUNT, J. R. 1915. The sensory field of the facial nerve: A further contribution to the symptomatology of the geniculate ganglion. Brain, **38:** 418–446.

HYDÉN, H. 1960. The neuron. In J. BRACHET AND A. E. MIRSKY (Editors), *The Cell: Biochemistry, Physiology, Morphology,* Vol. IV.

Academic Press, Inc., New York. Ch. 5, pp. 215–323.

HYDÉN, H., AND HARTELIUS, H. 1948. Stimulation of the nucleoprotein production in the nerve cells by malononitrile and its effects on psychic function in mental disorder. Acta psychiat. et neurol., Suppl. **48:** 5–117.

HYDÉN, H., AND LANGE, P. W. 1962. A kinetic study of the neuron-glia relationship. J. Cell Biol., **13:** 233–237.

INGALLS, N. W. 1920. A human embryo at the beginning of segmentation with special reference to the vascular system. Contrib. Embryol., **11:** 61–90.

INGRAM, W. R. 1940. Nuclear organization and chief connections of the primate hypothalamus. A. Res. Nerv. & Ment. Dis. Proc., **20:** 195–244.

INGRAM, W. R. 1952. Brain stem mechanisms in behavior. Electroencephalog. & Clin. Neurophysiol., **4:** 397–406.

INGRAM, W. R. 1956. The hypothalamus. Clin. Symposia, **8:** 117–156.

INGRAM, W. R., AND RANSON, S. W. 1932. Effects of lesions in the red nuclei in cats. Arch. Neurol. & Psychiat., **28:** 483–512.

DE IRALDI, A. P., H. F. DUGGAN, AND DEROBERTIS, E. 1963. Adrenergic synaptic vesicles in the anterior hypothalamus of the rat. Anat. Rec., **145:** 521–531.

ISHII, T., AND FRIEDE, R. L. 1968. Tissue binding of tritiated-norepinephrine in pigmented nuclei of human brain. Am. J. Anat., **122:** 139–144.

ITO, M., OBATA, K., AND OCHI, R. 1966. The origin of cerebellar-induced inhibition of Deiters neurones. II. Temporal correlation between the trans-synaptic activation of Purkinje cells and the inhibition of Deiters neurones. Exper. Brain Res., **2:** 350–364.

ITO, M., AND YOSHIDA, M. 1964. The cerebellar-evoked monosynaptic inhibition of Deiters neurones. Experientia, **20:** 515.

ITO, M., AND YOSHIDA, M. 1966. The origin of cerebellar-induced inhibition of Deiters neurones. I. Monosynaptic initiation of the inhibitory postsynaptic potentials. Exper. Brain Res., **2:** 330–349.

ITO, M., YOSHIDA, M., AND OBATA, K. 1964. Monosynaptic inhibition of the intracerebellar nuclei induced from the cerebellar cortex. Experientia, **20:** 575–576.

JABBUR, S. J., AND TOWE, A. L. 1961. Cortical excitation of neurones in dorsal column nuclei of cat, including an analysis of pathways. J. Neurophysiol., **24:** 499–509.

JACOBSOHN, L. 1908. Über die Kerne des menschlichen Rückenmarks. Aus dem Anhang zu den Abhandlungen der königl. preuss. Akademie der Wissenschaften, 72 pp.

JACOBSOHN, L. 1909. Über die Kerne des menschlichen Hirnstamms. Aus dem Anhang zu den Abhandlungen der königl. preuss. Akademie der Wissenschaften, 1: 1–70.

JAKOB, A. 1923. *Die Extrapyramidalen Erkrankungen.* Springer, Berlin.

JAKOB, A. 1925. The anatomy, clinical syndromes and physiology of the extrapyramidal system. Arch. Neurol. & Psychiat., 13: 596–620.

JAKOB, A. 1928. Das Kleinhirn. In W. VON MÖLLENDORFF (Editor), *Handbuch der mikroskopischen Anatomie des Menschen,* Vol. IV. Julius Springer, Berlin, pp. 674–916.

JANE, J. A., MASTERTON, R. B., AND DIAMOND, I. T. 1965. The function of the tectum for attention to auditory stimuli in the cat. J. Comp. Neurol., 125: 165–191.

JANSEN, J., AND BRODAL, A. 1940. Experimental studies on the intrinsic fibers of the cerebellum. II. The corticonuclear projection. J. Comp. Neurol., 73: 267–321.

JANSEN, J. 1933. Experimental studies on the intrinsic fibers of the cerebellum. I. The arcuate fibers. J. Comp. Neurol., 57: 369–400.

JANSEN, J. AND BRODAL, A. 1942. Experimental studies on the intrinsic fibers of the cerebellum. The cortico-nuclear projection in the rabbit and in the monkey (*Macacus rhesus*). Norske Vid.-Akad. Avh. Mat.-Naturv., No. 3, 1–50.

JANSEN, J., AND BRODAL, A. 1958. Das Kleinhirn. In W. VON MÖLLENDORFF (Editor), *Handbuch der mikroskopischen Anatomie des Menschen,* Vol. III. Julius Springer, Berlin, pp. 1–323.

JANSEN, J., AND JANSEN, J., JR. 1955. On the efferent fibers of the cerebellar nuclei in the cat. J. Comp. Neurol., 102: 607–632.

JASPER, H. H. 1949. Diffuse projection systems: The integrative action of the thalamic reticular system. Electroencephalog. & Clin. Neurophysiol., 1: 405–420.

JASPER, H. H. 1954. Functional properties of the thalamic reticular system. In J. F. DELAFRESNAYE (Editor), *Brain Mechanisms and Consciousness* (Symposium). Blackwell Scientific Publications, Oxford, pp. 374–395.

JASPER, H. H. 1958. Recent advances in our understanding of ascending activities of the reticular system. In H. H. JASPER ET AL. (Editors), *Reticular Formation of the Brain.* Henry Ford Hospital International Symposium. Little, Brown and Company, Boston. Ch. 15, pp. 319–331.

JASPER, H. H. 1960. Unspecific thalamocortical relations. In J. FIELD (Editor), *Handbook of Physiology,* Section I, Vol. II. American

Physiological Society, Washington, D. C. Ch. 53, pp. 1307–1321.

JASPER, H. H., AJMONE-MARSAN, C., AND STOLL, J. 1952. Corticofugal projections to the brain stem. A. M. A. Arch. Neurol. & Psychiat., 67: 155–171.

JEFFERSON, G. 1950. Localization of function in the cerebral cortex. Brit. M. Bull., 6: 333–340.

JEFFERSON, G. 1958. Discussion: Ch. 2, SCHEIBEL, M. E., AND SCHEIBEL, A. B., Substrates for integrative patterns in the reticular core. In H. H. JASPER ET AL. (Editors), *Reticular Formation of the Brain.* Henry Ford Hospital International Symposium. Little, Brown and Company, Boston, pp. 65–68.

JENKINS, T. W., AND TRUEX, R. C. 1963. Dissection of the human brain as a method for its fractionation by weight. Anat Rec., 147: 359–366.

JERGER, J. F. 1960. Observations on auditory behavior in lesions of the central auditory pathways. A. M. A. Arch. Otolaryng., 71: 797–806.

JOHNSON, T. N., AND CLEMENTE, C. D. 1959. An experimental study of the fiber connections between the putamen, globus pallidus, ventral thalamus and midbrain tegmentum in cat. J. Comp. Neurol., 113: 83–101.

JOHNSON, F. H., AND RUSSELL, G. V. 1952. The locus caeruleus as a pneumotaxic center. Anat. Rec., 112: 348.

JONES, R. M. 1961. *McClung's Handbook of Microscopical Technique,* Ed. 3. Hafner Publishing Company, New York, pp. 346–431.

JOUVET, M. 1967. Neurophysiology of the states of sleep. Physiol. Rev., 47: 117–177.

JUNG, R., AND HASSLER, R. 1960. The extrapyramidal motor system. In J. FIELD (Editor), *Handbook of Physiology,* Section I, Vol. II. American Physiological Society, Washington, D. C., Ch. 35, pp. 863–927.

KAADA, B. R. 1951. Somatomotor, autonomic and electrocorticographic responses to electrical stimulation of "rhinencephalic" and other structures in primates, cat and dog. Acta physiol. scandinav., 24: Suppl., 83, 285 pp.

KAADA, B. R. 1960. Cingulate, posterior orbital, anterior insular and temporal pole cortex. In J. FIELD (Editor), *Handbook of Physiology,* Section I, Vol. II. American Physiological Society, Washington, D. C. Ch. 55, pp. 1345–1372.

KAADA, B. R., PRIBRAM, K. H., AND EPSTEIN, J. A. 1949. Respiratory and vascular responses in monkeys from temporal pole, insula, orbital surface and cingulate gyrus. J. Neurophysiol., 12: 347–356.

KAADA, B. R., RASMUSSEN, E. W., AND KVEINI, O. 1961. Effects of hippocampal lesions on maze learning and retention in rats. Exper. Neurol., **3**: 333–355.

KAES, T. 1907. *Die Grosshirnrinde des Menschen in ihren Massen und in ihrem Fasergehalt*, Vol. I. Gustav Fischer, Jena, 64 pp., 92 plates.

KAPLAN, H. A. 1956. Arteries of the brain. Acta radiol., **46**: 364–370.

KAPLAN, H. A. 1958. Vascular supply of the base of the brain. W. S. FIELDS (Editor), *Pathogenesis and Treatment of Parkinsonism*. Charles C Thomas, Publisher, Springfield, Ill. Ch. 6, pp. 138–155.

KAPLAN, H. A. 1961. Collateral circulation of the brain. Neurology, **11**: 9–15.

KAPLAN, H. A., AND FORD, D. H. 1966. *The Brain Vascular System*. Elsevier Publishing Company, Amsterdam, 230 pp.

KAPPERS, C. U. A., HUBER, G. C., AND CROSBY, E. C. 1936. *The Comparative Anatomy of the Nervous System of Vertebrates, Including Man*, Vol. 2. Macmillan Company, New York, pp. 1358–1400.

KATZ, B. 1966. *Nerve, Muscle and Synapse*. McGraw-Hill Book Company, New York.

KEEGAN, J. J., AND GARRETT, F. D. 1948. The segmental distribution of the cutaneous nerves of the limbs of man. Anat. Rec., **102**: 409–437.

KEIBEL, F., AND MALL, F. P. 1912. *Manual of Human Embryology*, Vol. II. J. P. Lippincott, Company, Philadelphia. Ch. 14, pp. 1–144.

KELLER, A. D., ROY, R. S., AND CHASE, W. P. 1937. Extirpation of the neocerebellar cortex without eliciting so-called cerebellar signs. Am. J. Physiol., **118**: 720–733.

KELLER, J. H., AND MOFFETT, B. C., JR. 1968. Nerve endings in the temporomandibular joint of the Rhesus Macaque. Anat. Rec., **160**: 587–594.

KEMPINSKY, W. H. 1951. Cortical projection of vestibular and facial nerves in cat. J. Neurophysiol., **14**: 203–210.

KENNARD, M. A. 1935. Corticospinal fibers arising in the premotor area of the monkey as demonstrated by the Marchi method. Arch. Neurol. & Psychiat., **33**: 698–711.

KENNARD, M. A. 1949. Somatic functions. In P. C. BUCY (Editor), *The Precentral Motor Cortex*, Ed. 2. University of Illinois Press, Urbana, Ill. Ch. 9, pp. 243–276.

KENNARD, M. A., AND FULTON, J. F. 1933. The localizing significance of spasticity, reflex grasping and the signs of Babinski and Rossolimo. Brain, **56**: 213–225.

KENNARD, M. A., VIETS, H. R., AND FULTON, J. F. 1934. The syndrome of the premotor cortex in man: Impairment of skilled movement, forced grasping, spasticity and vasomotor disturbances. Brain, **57**: 69–84.

KERR, F. W. L. 1961. Structural relation of the trigeminal spinal tract to upper cervical roots and the solitary nucleus in the cat. Exper. Neurol., **4**: 134–148.

KERR, F. W. L. 1962. Facial, vagal and glossopharyngeal nerves in the cat. Afferent connections. Arch. Neurol., **2**: 264–281.

KERR, F. W. L. 1963. The divisional organization of afferent fibers of the trigeminal nerve. Brain, **86**: 721–732.

KERR, F. W. L., AND O'LEARY, J. L. 1957. The thalamic source of cortical recruiting in the rodent. Electroencephalog. & Clin. Neurophysiol., **9**: 461–476.

KETY, S. S., AND SCHMIDT, C. F. 1948. The nitrous oxide method for the quantitative determination of cerebral blood flow in man: Theory, procedure and normal values. J. Clin. Invest. **27**: 484–492.

KEY, A., AND RETZIUS, G. 1875. *Studien in der Anatomie des Nervensystems und des Bindegewebes*. Samson and Wallin, Stockholm.

KIERNAN, J. A. 1967. On the probable absence of retino-hypothalamic connections in five mammals and an amphibian. J. Comp. Neurol., **131**: 405–408.

KILLAM, K. F., AND KILLAM, E. K. 1958. Drug action on pathways involving the reticular formation. In H. H. JASPER ET AL. (Editors), *Reticular Formation of the Brain*. Henry Ford Hospital International Symposium. Little, Brown and Company, Boston. Ch. 4, pp. 111–122.

KIMMEL, D. L. 1942. Nigro-striatal fibers in cat. Anat. Rec., **82**: 425.

KIMMEL, D. L. 1959. The cervical sympathetic rami and the vertebral plexus in the human fetus. J. Comp. Neurol., **112**: 141–162.

KIMMEL, D. L. 1961. Innervation of spinal dura mater and dura mater of the posterior cranial fossa. Neurology, **9**: 800–809.

KIMMEL, D. L., KIMMEL, C. B., AND ZARKIN, A. 1961. The central distribution of afferent nerve fibers of the facial and vagus nerves in the guinea pig. Anat. Rec., **139**: 245.

KIRKPATRICK, J. B. 1968. Chromatolysis in the hypoglossal nucleus of the rat: An electron microscopic analysis. J. Comp. Neurol., **132**: 189–212.

KLATZO, I., MIGUEL, J. TOBIAS, C., AND HAYMAKER, W. 1961. Effects of alpha-particle irradiation on the rat brain, including vascular permeability and glycogen studies. J. Neuropath. & Exper. Neurol., **20**: 459–483.

KLEITMAN, N. 1963. *Sleep and Wakefulness*. University of Chicago Press, Chicago.

KLÜVER, H. 1942. Visual Mechanisms. *Bio-*

logical Symposia, Vol. 7. J. Cattell Press, Lancaster, Pa.

KLÜVER, H. 1952. Brain mechanisms and behavior with special reference to the rhinencephalon. Lancet, **72:** 567–574.

KLÜVER, H., AND BARRERA, E. 1953. A method for the combined staining of cells and fibers in the nervous system. J. Neuropath. & Exper. Neurol., **12:** 400–403.

KLÜVER, H., AND BUCY, P. 1939. Preliminary analysis of functions of the temporal lobes in monkeys. Arch. Neurol. & Psychiat., **42:** 979–1000.

KNIGHTON, R. S. 1950. Thalamic relay nucleus for the second somatic sensory receiving area in the cerebral cortex of the cat. J. Comp. Neurol., **92:** 183–192.

KNOOK, H. L. 1965. *The Fibre-Connections of the Forebrain*. Van Gorcum and Co., Te Assen, 477 pp.

KOELLA, W. P., AND GELLHORN, E. 1954. The influence of diencephalic lesions upon the action of nociceptive impulses and hypercapnia on the electrical activity of the cat's brain. J. Comp. Neurol., **100:** 211–235.

KOPELL, H. P., AND THOMPSON, W. A. L. 1963. *Peripheral Entrapment Neuropathies*. Williams and Wilkins Company, Baltimore.

KOSKOFF, Y. D., DENNIS, W., LAZOVIK, D., AND WHEELER, E. T. 1948. The psychological effects of frontal lobotomy performed for alleviation of pain. A. Res. Nerv. & Ment. Dis. Proc., **27:** 723–753.

KREMER, W. F. 1947. Autonomic and somatic reactions induced by stimulation of the cingulate gyrus in dogs. J. Neurophysiol., **10:** 371–379.

KRIEG, W. J. S. 1932. The hypothalamus of the albino rat. J. Comp. Neurol., **55:** 19–89.

KRIEG, W. J. S. 1947. Connections of the cerebral cortex. I. The albino rat. C. Extrinsic connections. J. Comp. Neurol., **86:** 267–394.

KRIEG, W. J. S. 1953. *Functional Neuroanatomy*. Blakiston Company, New York, 658 pp.

KRIEG, W. J. S. 1954. Connections of the cerebral cortex. II. The macaque. E. The postcentral gyrus. J. Comp. Neurol., **101:** 101–165.

KRUGER, L., AND MAXWELL, D. S. 1966. Electron microscopy of oligodendrocytes in normal rat cerebrum. Am. J. Anat., **118:** 411–436.

KRUGER, L., AND MICHEL, F. 1962. A morphological and somatotopic analysis of single unit activity in the trigeminal sensory complex of the cat. Exper. Neurol., **5:** 139–156.

KRUGER, L., AND MICHEL, F. 1962a. Reinterpretation of the representation of pain based on physiological excitation of single neurons in the trigeminal sensory complex. Exper. Neurol., **5:** 157–178.

KRUGER, L., AND PORTER, P. 1958. A behavioral study of the functions of the Rolandic cortex

in the monkey. J. Comp. Neurol., **109:** 439–469.

KRUGER, L., SIMINOFF, R., AND WITKOVSKY, P. 1961. Single neuron analysis of dorsal column nuclei and spinal nucleus of trigeminal in cat. J. Neurophysiol., **24:** 333–349.

KUFFLER, S. W. 1953. Discharge patterns and functional organization of mammalian retina. J. Neurophysiol., **16:** 37–68.

KUFFLER, S. W., NICHOLS, J. G., AND ORKLAND, R. K. 1966. Physiological properties of glial cells in the central nervous system of Amphibia. J. Neurophysiol., **29:** 768–787.

KUFFLER, S. W., AND POTTER, D. D. 1964. Glia in the leech central nervous system: physiological properties and neuron-glia relationships. J. Neurophysiol., **27:** 290–320.

KUHLENBECK, H. 1948. The derivatives of the thalamus ventralis in the human brain and their relation to the so-called subthalamus. Mil. Surgeon, **102:** 433–447.

KUHN, R. A. 1949. Topographical pattern of cutaneous sensibility in the dorsal column nuclei of the cat. Tr. Am. Neurol. A., **74:** 227–230.

KUHN, R. A. 1950. Functional capacity of the isolated human spinal cord. Brain, **75:** 1–51.

KUYPERS, H. G. J. M. 1958. An anatomical analysis of cortico-bulbar connexions to the pons and lower brain stem in the cat. J. Anat., **92:** 198–218.

KUYPERS, H. G. J. M. 1958a. Corticobulbar connexions to the pons and lower brain-stem in man. An anatomical study. Brain, **81:** 364–388.

KUYPERS, H. G. J. M. 1958b. Some projections from the peri-central cortex to the pons and lower brain stem in monkey and chimpanzee. J. Comp. Neurol., **110:** 221–256.

KUYPERS, H. G. J. M. 1958c. Pericentral cortical projections to motor and sensory nuclei. Science, **128:** 662–663.

KUYPERS, H. G. J. M. 1960. Central cortical projections to motor and somato-sensory cell groups. Brain, **83:** 161–184.

KUYPERS, H. G. J. M., HOFFMAN, A. L., AND BEASLEY, R. M. 1961. Distribution of cortical "feedback" fibers in the nuclei cuneatus and gracilis. Proc. Soc. Exper. Biol. & Med., **108:** 634–637.

KUYPERS, H. G. J. M., AND LAWRENCE, D. G. 1967. Cortical projections to the red nucleus and the brain stem in the rhesus monkey. Brain Res., **4:** 151–188.

KUYPERS, H. G. J. M., AND TUERK, J. D. 1964. The distribution of cortical fibres within the nuclei cuneatus and gracilis in the cat. J. Anat., **98:** 143–162.

LANDGREN, S. 1957. Convergence of tactile, thermal and gustatory impulses on single cortical cells. Acta physiol. scandinav., **40**: 210–221.

LANDGREN, S. 1961. The response to thalamic and cortical neurons to electrical and physiological stimulation of the cat's tongue. In W. A. ROSENBLITH (Editor), *Sensory Communication.* Massachusetts Institute Technology Press, Cambridge, pp. 437–453.

LANDGREN, S., PHILLIPS, C. G., AND PORTER, R. 1962. Minimal synaptic actions of pyramidal impulses on some alpha motoneurones of the baboon's hand and forearm. J. Physiol., **161**: 91–111.

LANDIS, C., ZUBIN, J., AND METTLER, F. A. 1950. The functions of the human frontal lobe. J. Psychol., **30**: 123–138.

LANGLEY, J. N. 1921. *The Autonomic Nervous System,* Vol. 1. W. Heffer and Sons, Cambridge.

LANGMAN, J. 1963. *Medical Embryology.* Williams and Wilkins Company, Baltimore.

LANGWORTHY, O. R., AND ORTEGA, L. 1943. The iris. Medicine, **22**: 287–361.

LARSELL, O. 1923. The cerebellum of the frog. J. Comp. Neurol., **36**: 89–122.

LARSELL, O. 1947. The cerebellum of myxinoids and petromyzonts, including developmental stages in the lampreys. J. Comp. Neurol., **86**: 395–446.

LARSELL, O. 1947a. The development of the cerebellum in man in relation to its comparative anatomy. J. Comp. Neurol., **87**: 85–129.

LARSELL, O. 1951. *Anatomy of the Nervous System,* Ed. 2. Appleton-Century-Crofts, Inc., New York, 520 pp.

LARSELL, O., AND DOW, R. S. 1933. Innervation of the human lung. Am. J. Anat., **52**: 414–438.

LASSEK, A. M. 1940. The human pyramidal tract. II. A numerical investigation of the Betz cells of the motor area. Arch. Neurol. & Psychiat., **44**: 718–724.

LASSEK, A. M. 1942. The human pyramidal tract. IV. A study of the mature, myelinated fibers of the pyramid. J. Comp. Neurol., **76**: 217–225.

LASSEK, A. M. 1942a. The pyramidal tract. The effect of pre- and postcentral cortical lesions on the fiber components of the pyramids in monkey. J. Nerv. & Ment. Dis., **95**: 721–729.

LASSEK, A. M. 1947. The pyramidal tract: Basic considerations of corticospinal neurons. A. Res. Nerv. & Ment. Dis., Proc., **27**: 106–128.

LASSEK, A. M. 1953. Potency of isolated brachial dorsal roots in controlling muscular physiology. Neurology, **3**: 53–57.

LASSEK, A. M. 1954. *The Pyramidal Tract.* Charles C Thomas, Publisher, Springfield, Ill., 166 pp.

LASSEK, A. M., AND EVANS, J. P. 1945. The human pyramidal tract. XII. The effect of hemispherec-tomies on the fiber components of the pyramids. J. Comp. Neurol., **83**: 113–119.

LASSEK, A. M., AND RASMUSSEN, G. L. 1939. The human pyramidal tract. A fiber and numerical analysis. Arch. Neurol. & Psychiat., **42**: 872–876.

LASSEK, A. M., AND RASMUSSEN, G. L. 1940. A comparative fiber and numerical analysis of the pyramidal tract. J. Comp. Neurol., **72**: 417–428.

LAWRENCE, D. G., AND KUYPERS, H. G. J. M. 1968. The functional organization of the motor system in the monkey. I. The effects of bilateral pyramidal lesions. Brain, **91**: 1–14.

LEÃO, A. A. P. 1944. Spreading depression of activity in the cerebral cortex. J. Neurophysiol., **7**: 359–390.

LEE, J. C. Y. 1963. Electron microscopy of Wallerian degeneration. J. Comp. Neurol., **120**: 65–79.

LEMMEN, L. J., DAVIS, J. S., AND RADNOR, L. L. 1959. Observations on stimulation of the human frontal eye field. J. Comp. Neurol., **112**: 163–168.

LEVI-MONTALCINI, R., AND ANGELETTI, P. V. 1961. Growth control of the sympathetic system by a specific protein factor. Quart. Rev. Biol., **36**: 99–108.

LEVI-MONTALCINI, R., AND ANGELETTI, P. V. 1963. Essential role of the nerve growth factor in the survival and maintenance of dissociated sensory and sympathetic embryonic nerve cells *in vitro.* Develop. Biol., **7**: 653–659.

LEVI-MONTALCINI, R., BOOKER, B. 1960. Excessive growth of the sympathetic ganglia evoked by a protein isolated from mouse. Proc. Nat. Acad. Sc., **46**: 373–391.

LEVI-MONTALCINI, R., AND COHEN, S. 1960. Effects of the extract of the mouse submaxillary salivary glands on the sympathetic system of mammals. Ann. New York Acad. Sc., **85**: 324–341.

LEVI-MONTALCINI, R., AND HAMBURGER, V. 1951. Selective growth stimulating effects of mouse sarcoma on the sensory and sympathetic nervous system of the chick embryo. J. Zool., **116**: 321–362.

LEVI-MONTALCINI, R., MEYER, H., AND HAMBURGER, V. 1954. *In vitro* experiments on the effects of mouse sarcomas 180 and 37 on the spinal and sympathetic ganglia of the chick embryo. Cancer Res., **14**: 49–57.

LEVIN, P. M. 1936. The efferent fibers of the frontal lobe of the monkey (*Macaca mulatta*). J. Comp. Neurol., **63**: 369–419.

LEVIN, P. M. 1949. Efferent fibers. In P. C. BUCY (Editor), *The Precentral Motor Cortex,* Ed. 2. University of Illinois Press, Urbana, Ill. Ch. 5, pp. 133–148.

LEVIN, P. M., AND BRADFORD, F. K. 1938. The

exact origin of the corticospinal tract in the monkey. J. Comp. Neurol., **68:** 411–422.

LEWY, F. H., AND KOBRAK, H. 1936. Neural projection of cochlear spirals on primary acoustic centers. Arch. Neurol. & Psychiat., **35:** 839–852.

LEVITT, M., CARRERAS, M., CHAMBERS, W. W., AND LIU, C. N. 1960. Pyramidal influence on unit activity in . posterior column nuclei of cat. Physiologist, **3:** 103.

LIDDELL, E. G. T., AND PHILLIPS, C. G. 1940. Experimental lesions in the basal ganglia of the cat. Brain, **63:** 264–274.

LINDSLEY, D. B. 1960. Attention, consciousness, sleep and wakefulness. In J. FIELD (Editor), *Handbook of Physiology*, Section I, Vol. III. American Physiological Society, Washington, D. C., pp. 1553–1593.

LIU, C. N. 1956. Afferent nerves to Clarke's and the lateral cuneate nuclei in the cat. Arch. Neurol. & Psychiat., **75:** 67–77.

LIU, C. N., AND CHAMBERS, W. W. 1964. An experimental study of the corticospinal system in the monkey (Macaca mulatta). The spinal pathways and preterminal distribution of degenerating fibers following discrete lesions of the pre- and postcentral gyri and bulbar pyramid. J. Comp. Neurol., **123:** 257–284.

LLOYD, D. P. C. 1941. The spinal mechanisms of the pyramidal system in cats. J. Neurophysiol., **4:** 525–546.

LLOYD, D. P. C. 1943. Conduction and synaptic transmission of reflex response to stretch in spinal cats. J. Neurophysiol., **6:** 317–326.

LLOYD, D. P. C., AND McINTYRE, A. K. 1950. Dorsal column conduction of group I muscle afferent impulses and their relay through Clarke's column. J. Neurophysiol., **13:** 39–54.

LOCKE, S., ANGEVINE. J. B., AND YAKOVLEV, P. I. 1961. Limbic nuclei of thalamus and connections of limbic cortex. II. Thalamo-cortical projections of the lateral dorsal nucleus in man. Arch. Neurol., **4:** 355–364.

LOEWENSTEIN, W. R., AND ALTAMIRANO-ORREGO, R. 1958. The refractory state of the generator and propagated potentials in a Pacinian corpuscle. J. Gen. Physiol., **41:** 805–824.

LOEWENTHAL, M., AND HORSLEY, V. 1897. On the relations between the cerebellum and other centres (namely cerebral and spinal) with special reference to the action of antagonistic muscles. Proc. Roy. Soc. London, ser. B, **61:** 20–25.

LOEWI, O. 1921. Über humorale Übertragbarkeit der Herznervenwirkung. Arch. ges. Physiol., **189:** 239–242.

LOEWI, O. 1945. Chemical transmission of nerve impulses. Sc. in Progr., **4:** 98–119.

LOHMAN, A. H. M. 1963. The anterior olfactory lobe of the guinea pig. Acta anat. **53:** Suppl. 49, 1–109.

LORENTE DE NÓ, R. 1924. Études sur le cerveau postérieur. Trav. Lab. recherches biol. Univ. Madrid, **22:** 51–65.

LORENTE DE NÓ, R. 1928. *Die Labyrinthreflexe auf die Augenmuskeln nach einseitiger Labyrinthexstirpation nebst einer kurzen Angabe über den Nervenmechanismus der vestibulären Augenbewegungen.* Urban and Schwarzenberg, Vienna.

LORENTE DE NÓ, R. 1931. Ausgewählte Kapitel aus der vergleichenden Physiologie des Labyrinthes: Die Augenmuskelreflexe beim Kaninchen und ihre Grundlagen. Ergebn. Physiol., **32:** 73–242.

LORENTE DE NÓ, R. 1933. Studies on the structure of the cerebral cortex. I. The area entorhinalis. J. Psychol. u. Neurol., **45:** 381–438.

LORENTE DE NÓ, R. 1933a. Anatomy of the eighth nerve. The central projection of the nerve endings of the internal ear. Laryngoscope, **43:** 1–38.

LORENTE DE NÓ, R. 1933b. Vestibulo-ocular reflex arc. Arch. Neurol. & Psychiat., **30:** 245–291.

LORENTE DE NÓ, R. 1934. Studies on the structure of the cerebral cortex. II. Continuation of the study of the ammonic system. J. Psychol. u. Neurol., **46:** 113–177.

LORENTE DE NÓ, R. 1949. The structure of the cerebral cortex. In J. F. FULTON (Editor), *Physiology of the Nervous System*, Ed. 3. Oxford University Press, New York, pp. 288–330.

LORENTE DE NÓ, R. 1953. Symposium discussion. In J. L. MALCOLM AND J. A. B. GRAY (Editors), *The Spinal Cord*. Ciba Foundation Symposium. Little, Brown and Company, Boston, pp. 40–41.

LUCIANI, L. 1891. *Il cervelletto: nuovi studi di fisiologia normale e patologica.* Le Monnier, Florence.

LUNDBERG, A. 1958. Electrophysiology of the salivary glands. Physiol. Rev., **38:** 21–40.

LUNDBERG, A., AND OSCARSSON, O. 1962. Functional organization of the ventral spino-cerebellar tract in the cat. IV. Identification of units by antidromic activation from the cerebellar cortex. Acta physiol. scandinav., **54:** 252–269.

LUSE, S. A. 1956. Electron microscopic observations of central nervous system. J. Biophys. & Biochem. Cytol., **2:** 531–542.

LUSE, S. A. 1956a. Formation of myelin in the central nervous system of mice and rats, as studied with the electron microscope. J. Biophys. & Biochem. Cytol., **2:** 777–784.

McCOMAS, A. J. 1963. Responses of the rat dorsal column system to mechanical stimulation of the hind paw. J. Physiol., **166:** 435–445.

McCulloch, W. S. 1949. Cortico-cortical connections. In P. C. Bucy (Editor), *The Precentral Motor Cortex*, Ed. 2. University of Illinois Press, Urbana, Ill. Ch. 8, pp. 214–242.

McCulloch, W. S., and Garol, H. W. 1941. Cortical origin and distribution of corpus callosum and anterior commissure in the monkey (*Macaca mulatta*). J. Neurophysiol., **4:** 555–563.

Machne, X., Calma, I., and Magoun, H. W. 1955. Unit activity of central cephalic brain stem in EEG arousal. J. Neurophysiol., **18:** 547–558.

Machne, X., and Segundo, J. P. 1956. Unitary responses to afferent volleys in amygdaloid complex. J. Neurophysiol., **19:** 232–240.

McManus, J. F. A., and Mowry, R. W. 1960. *Staining Methods. Histologic and Histochemical.* Paul B. Hoeber Inc., New York, pp. 324–357.

McMasters, R. E., Weiss, A. H., and Carpenter, M. B. 1966. Vestibular projections to the nuclei of the extraocular muscles. Degeneration resulting from discrete partial lesions of the vestibular nuclei in the monkey. Am. J. Anat., **118:** 163–194.

McKinley, W. A., and Magoun, H. W. 1942. The bulbar projection of the trigeminal nerve. Am. J. Physiol., **137:** 217–224.

McLardy, T. 1948. Projection of the centromedian nucleus of the human thalamus. Brain, **71:** 290–303.

McLardy, T. 1950. The thalamic projection to frontal cortex in man. J. Neurol. Neurosurg. & Psychiat., **13:** 198–202.

MacLean, P. D. 1952. Some psychiatric implications of physiological studies on frontotemporal portions of limbic system (visceral brain). Electroencephalog. & Clin. Neurophysiol., **4:** 407–418.

MacLean, P. D. 1954. The limbic system and its hippocampal formation: Studies in animals and their possible application to man. J. Neurosurg., **11:** 29–44.

MacLean, P. D. 1957. Chemical and electrical stimulation of the hippocampus in unrestrained animals. I. Methods and electroencephalographic findings. A. M. A. Arch. Neurol. & Psychiat., **78:** 113–127.

MacLean, P. D. 1957a. Chemical and electrical stimulation of the hippocampus in unrestrained animals. II. Behavioral findings. A. M. A. Arch. Neurol. & Psychiat., **78:** 128–142.

MacLean, P. D. 1958. Contrasting functions of limbic and neocortical systems of the brain and their relevance to psycho-physiological aspects of medicine. Am. J. Med., **25:** 611–626.

MacLean, P. D., and Delgado, J. M. R. 1953. Electrical and chemical stimulation of frontotemporal portion of limbic system in the waking animal. Electroencephalog. & Clin. Neurophysiol., **5:** 91–100.

McLennan, H. 1963. *Synaptic Transmission.* W. B. Saunders Company, Philadelphia, pp. 3–15.

Madonick, M. J. 1957. Statistical control studies in neurology. 8. The cutaneous abdominal reflex. Neurology, **7:** 459–465.

Maffei, L., and Pompeiano, O. 1962. Cerebellar control of flexor motoneurons. Arch. ital. Biol., **100:** 476–509.

Magoun, H. W. 1952. An ascending reticular activating system in the brain stem. A. M. A. Arch. Neurol. & Psychiat., **67:** 145–154.

Magoun, H. W. 1954. The ascending reticular system and wakefulness. In J. B. Delafresnaye (Editor), *Brain Mechanisms and Consciousness.* Blackwell Scientific Publications, Oxford, pp. 1–20.

Magoun, H. W. 1963. *The Waking Brain*, Ed. 2. Charles C Thomas, Publisher, Springfield, Ill., 188 pp.

Magoun, H. W., Atlas, D., Ingersoll, E. H., and Ranson, S. W. 1937. Associated facial, vocal and respiratory components of emotional expression. J. Neurol. & Psychopath., **17:** 241–255.

Magoun, H. W., and Rhines, R. 1946. An inhibitory mechanism in the bulbar reticular formation. J. Neurophysiol., **9:** 165–171.

Magoun, H. W., and Rhines, R. 1947. *Spasticity: The Stretch-reflex and Extrapyramidal Systems.* Charles C Thomas, Publisher, Springfield, Ill.

Malmo, R. B. 1948. Psychological aspects of frontal gyrectomy and frontal lobotomy in mental patients. A. Res. Nerv. & Ment. Dis. Proc., **27:** 537–564.

Malone, E. F. 1910. Über die Kerne des menschlichen Diencephalon. Aus dem Anhang zu den Abhandlungen der königl. preuss. Akademie der Wissenschaften, p. 92.

Manni, E., Bortolami, R., and Desole, C. 1966. Eye muscle proprioception in the semilunar ganglion. Exp. Neurol., **16:** 226–236.

Marburg, O. 1942. Primary endings of the optic nerve in man and in animals. Arch. Ophth., **28:** 61–78.

Marburg, O., and Warner, F. J. 1947. The pathways of the tectum (anterior colliculus) of the midbrain in cats. J. Nerv. & Ment. Dis., **106:** 415–446.

Marie, P. 1906. Revision de la question de l'aphasie: La troisième circonvolution frontale gauche ne joue aucun rôle special dans la fonction du langage. Semana Méd., **26:** 241–247.

Markee, J. E., Sawyer, C. H., and Hollinshead, W. H. 1946. Activation of the anterior hypophysis by electrical stimulation in the rabbit. Endocrinology, **38:** 345–357.

MARSDEN, C. D. 1961. Pigmentation in the nucleus substantiae nigrae of mammals. J. Anat.,
95: 256–261.

MARSHALL, W. H. 1950. The relation of dehydration of the brain to the spreading depression
of Leão. Electroencephalog. & Clin. Neurophysiol., 2: 177–186.

MARSHALL, W. H. 1959. Spreading cortical depression of Leão. Physiol. Rev., 39: Suppl. 3,
239–279.

MARSHALL, W. H., AND ESSIG, C. F. 1951. Relation of air exposure of cortex to spreading depression of Leão. J. Neurophysiol., 14: 265–
273.

MARSHALL, W. H., ESSIG, C. F., AND DUBROFF, S. J.
1951. Relation of temperature of cerebral cortex to spreading depression of Leão. J. Neurophysiol., 14: 153–156.

MARSHALL, W. R., WOOLSEY, C. N., AND BARD, P.
1941. Observations on cortical somatic sensory mechanisms of the cat and monkey. J.
Neurophysiol., 4: 1–24.

MARTIN, J. P. 1927. Hemichorea resulting from
a local lesion of the brain. (The syndrome
of the body of Luys.) Brain, 50: 637–651.

MARTIN, J. P. 1959. Remarks on the functions of
the basal ganglia. Lancet, 1: 999–1005.

MARTIN, J. P. 1960. Further remarks on the functions of the basal ganglia. Lancet, 1: 1362–
1365.

MARTIN, J. P. 1967. The Basal Ganglia and Posture. Pitman Medical Publishing Company,
Ltd., London, 152 pp.

MARTIN, J. P., AND ALCOCK, N. S. 1934. Hemichorea associated with lesions of the corpus
Luysii. Brain, 57: 504–516.

MARTIN, J. P., AND HURWITZ, L. J. 1962. Locomotion and the basal ganglia. Brain, 85: 261–276.

MARTIN, J. P., HURWITZ, L. J., AND FINLAYSON, M. H.
1962. The negative symptoms of basal gangliar
disease. A survey of 130 postencephalitic cases.
Lancet, 2: 1–6 and 62–66.

MARTIN, J. P., AND McCAUL, I. R. 1959. Acute
hemiballismus treated by ventrolateral thalamo-
lysis. Brain, 82: 104–108.

MASSAZZA, A. 1923. La citoarchitettonica del
midollo spinale umano. Riv. patol. nerv., 28:
22–43.

MASSERMAN, J. H. 1943. Behavior and Neurosis.
University of Chicago Press, Chicago.

MASSION, J. 1967. The mammalian red nucleus.
Physiol. Rev., 47: 383–436.

MASUCCI, E. F. 1965. Bilateral ophthalmoplegia in
basilar-vertebral artery disease. Brain, 88: 97–
106.

MASUROVSKY, E. B., BUNGE, M. B., AND BUNGE, R. P.
1967. Cytological studies of organotypic cultures of rat dorsal root ganglia following X-ir-

radiation in vitro. I. Changes in neurons and
satellite cells. J. Cell Biol., 32: 467–496.

MATTHEWS, P. B. C. 1964. Muscle spindles and
their motor control. Physiol. Rev., 44: 219–
288.

MATZKE, H. A. 1951. The course of fibers arising
from the nucleus gracilis and cuneatus of the
cat. J. Comp. Neurol., 94: 439–452.

MAXWELL, D. S., AND KRUGER, L. 1965. The fine
structure of astrocytes in the cerebral cortex
and their response to focal injury produced by
heavy ionizing particles. J. Cell Biol., 25: 141–
157.

MAXWELL, D. S., AND KRUGER, L. 1965a. Small
blood vessels and the origin of phagocytes in the
rat cerebral cortex following heavy particle
irradiation. Exper. Neurol., 12: 33–54.

MAXWELL, D. S., AND KRUGER, L. 1966. The reactive oligodendrocyte. An electron microscopic
study of cerebral cortex following Alpha particle irradiation. Am. J. Anat., 118: 437–460.

MAYNARD, E. A., SCHULTZ, R. L., AND PEASE, D. C.
1957. Electron microscopy of the vascular bed
of rat cerebral cortex. Am. J. Anat., 100: 409–
434.

MEESEN, H., AND OLSZEWSKI, J. 1949. A Cytoarchitectonic Atlas of the Rhombencephalon
of the Rabbit. S. Karger, Basel.

MEHLER, W. R. 1966. Further notes on the center
median nucleus of Luys. In D. P. PURPURA AND
M. D. YAHR (Editors), The Thalamus. Columbia University Press, New York, pp. 109–127.

MEHLER, W. R. 1966a. The posterior thalamic
region. Confinia neurol., 27: 18–29.

MEHLER, W. R., FEFERMAN, M. E., AND NAUTA,
W. J. H. 1956. Ascending axon degeneration
following anterolateral chordotomy in the monkey. Anat. Rec., 124: 332–333.

MEHLER, W. R., FEFERMAN, M. E., AND NAUTA,
W. J. H. 1960. Ascending axon degeneration
following anterolateral cordotomy. An experimental study in the monkey. Brain, 83: 718–
750.

MEHLER, W. R., VERNIER, V. G., AND NAUTA, W. J. H.
1958. Efferent projections from the dentate and
interpositus nuclei in primates. Anat. Rec.,
130: 430–431.

MELTZER, S. J. 1906–07. The factors of safety in
animal structure and animal economy. Harvey
Lect. pp. 139–169.

MERKEL, F. 1875. Tastzellen und Tastkörperchen
bei den Hausthieren und beim Menschen.
Arch. mikr. Anat., 11: 636–652.

MERRILLEES, N. C. R. 1962. Some observations on
the fine structure of a Golgi tendon organ of a
rat. In D. BARKER (Editor), Symposium on
Muscle Receptors. Hong Kong University
Press, Hong Kong, pp. 199–206.

MERRILLEES, N., SUNDERLAND, S., AND HAYHOW, W. 1950. Neuromuscular spindles in the extraocular muscles in man. Anat. Rec., **108:** 23–30.

MERTON, P. A. 1953. Speculations on the servo-control of movement. In G. E. W. WOLSTEN-HOLME (Editor), *The Spinal Cord*. Churchill, London, pp. 247–255.

METTLER, F. A. 1932. Connections of the auditory cortex of the cat. J. Comp. Neurol., **55:** 139–183.

METTLER, F. A. 1935. Corticifugal fiber connections of the cortex of *Macaca mulatta*. The frontal region. J. Comp. Neurol., **61:** 509–542.

METTLER, F. A. 1942. Relation between pyramidal and extrapyramidal function. A. Res. Nerv. & Ment. Dis., Proc., **21:** 150–227.

METTLER, F. A. 1943. Extensive unilateral cerebral removals in the primate. Physiologic effects and resultant degeneration. J. Comp. Neurol., **79:** 185–243.

METTLER, F. A. 1944. The tegmento-olivary and central tegmental fasciculi. J. Comp. Neurol., **80:** 149–175.

METTLER, F. A. 1944a. On the origin of the fibers in the pyramid of the primate brain. Proc. Soc. Exper. Biol. & Med., **57:** 111–113.

METTLER, F. A. 1947. The non-pyramidal motor projections from the frontal cerebral cortex. A. Res. Nerv. & Ment. Dis., Proc., **26:** 162–199.

METTLER, F. A. 1947a. Extracortical connections of the primate frontal cerebral cortex. I. Thalamo-cortical connections. J. Comp. Neurol., **86:** 95–117.

METTLER, F. A. 1947b. Extracortical connections of the primate frontal cerebral cortex. II. Corticofugal connections. J. Comp. Neurol., **86:** 119–154.

METTLER, F. A. 1948. *Neuroanatomy*. C. V. Mosby Company, St. Louis, 536 pp.

METTLER, F. A. 1949. *Selective Partial Ablation of the Frontal Cortex: A Correlative Study of the Effects on Human Psychotic Subjects*. Paul B. Hoeber, Inc., New York, 527 pp.

METTLER, F. A. 1955. The experimental anatomo-physiologic approach to the study of diseases of the basal ganglia. J. Neuropath. & Exper. Neurol., **14:** 115–141.

METTLER, F. A., COOPER, I. S., LISS, H., CARPENTER, M. B., AND NOBACK, C. R. 1954. Patterns of vascular failure in the central nervous system. J. Neuropath. & Exper. Neurol., **13:** 528–539.

METTLER, F. A., LISS, H. R., AND STEVENS, G. H. 1956. Blood supply of the primate striopallidum. J. Neuropath. & Exper. Neurol., **15:** 377–383.

METTLER, F. A., AND LUBIN, A. J. 1942. Termination of the brachium pontis. J. Comp. Neurol., **77:** 391–397.

METUZALS, J. 1965. Ultrastructure of the nodes of Ranvier and their surrounding structures in the central nervous system. Ztschr. Zellforsch. Mikrosk. Anat., **65:** 719–759.

MEYER, A., BECK, E., AND McLARDY, T. 1947. Prefrontal leucotomy: A neuroanatomical report. Brain, **70:** 18–49.

MEYER, D. R., AND WOOLSEY, C. N. 1952. Effects of localized cortical destruction upon auditory discriminative conditioning in the cat. J. Neurophysiol., **15:** 149–162.

MEYER, M. 1949. Study of efferent connections of the frontal lobe in the human brain after leucotomy. Brain, **72:** 265–296.

MEYERS, R. E. 1956. Function of corpus callosum in interocular transfer. Brain, **79:** 358–363.

MICKLE, W. A., AND ADES, H. W. 1952. A composite sensory projection area in the cerebral cortex of the cat. Am. J. Physiol., **170:** 682–689.

MILLEN, J. W., AND WOOLLAM, D. H. M. 1961. Observations on the nature of the pia mater. Brain, **84:** 514–520.

MILLEN, J. W., AND WOOLLAM, D. H. M. 1962. *The Anatomy of the Cerebrospinal Fluid*. Oxford University Press, New York, pp. 90–102.

MILLER, M. R., RALSTON, H. J., AND KASAHARA, M. 1958. The pattern of cutaneous innervation of the human hand. Am. J. Anat., **102:** 183–218.

MILLER, M. R., RALSTON, H. J., AND KASAHARA, M. 1960. The pattern of cutaneous innervation of the human hand, foot, and breast. In W. MONTAGNA (Editor), *Advances in Biology of Skin. Cutaneous Innervation*. Vol. 1. Pergamon Press, New York, pp. 1–47.

MINCKLER, J. R., AND KLEMME, R. M. AND MINCKLER, D. 1944. The course of efferent fibers from the human premotor cortex. J. Comp. Neurol., **81:** 259–267.

MINKOWSKI, M. 1913. Experimentelle Untersuchungen über die Beziehungen der Grosshirnrinde und der Netzhaut zu den primären optischen Zentren, besonders zum Corpus geniculatum externum. Arb. Hirnanat. Inst. Zürich, **7:** 255–362.

MINKOWSKI, M. 1923-24. Etude sur les connections anatomiques des circonvolutions rolandiques, parietales et frontales. Schweiz. Arch. Neurol. u. Psychiat., **12:** 71–104 and 227–268; **14:** 255–278; **15:** 97–132.

MISCOLCZY, D. 1931. Über die Endigungsweise der spinocerebellaren Bahnen. Ztschr. Anat., **96:** 537–542.

MISCOLCZY, D. 1934. Die Endigungsweise der olivocerebellaren Faserung. Arch. Psychiat. **102:** 197–201.

VON MONAKOW, C. 1895. Experimentelle und

pathologisch-anatomische Untersuchungen über die Haubenregion, den Sehhugel und die Regio subthalamica. Arch. Psychiat., **27**: 1–129.

VON MONAKOW, C. 1905. *Gehirnpathologie*, Ed. 2. Holder, Wien, 1319 pp.

VON MONAKOW, C. 1909. Der rote Kern, die Haube und die Regio subthalamica bei einigen Säugetieren und beim Menschen. I. Anatomisches und Experimentelles. Arb. Hirnanat. Inst. Zürich, **4**: 103–226.

VON MONAKOW, C. 1914. Die Lokalisation im Grosshirn und der Abbau der Funktion durch korticale Herde. J. F. Bergmann, Wiesbaden. Ch. 12, p. 1033.

MONIZ, E. 1931. *Diagnostic des tumeurs cérébrales et e préuve de l'encéphalographie artérielle.* Masson et Cie., Paris, 512 pp.

MONIZ, E. 1934. *L'Angiographie cérébrale, ses applications et resultats en anatomie, physiologie et clinique.* Masson et Cie., Paris, 327 pp.

MONIZ, E. 1936. *Tentatives opératoire dans le traitement de certaines psychoses.* Masson et Cie., Paris, 248 pp.

MONRAD-KROHN, G. H. 1924. On the dissociation of voluntary and emotional innervation in facial paresis of central origin. Brain, **47**: 22–35.

MONRAD-KROHN, G. H. 1939. On facial dissociation. Acta psychiat. et neurol. scandinav., **14**: 557–566.

MOREL, F. 1947. La massa intermedia ou commissure grise. Acta anat., **4**: 203–207.

MOREST, D. K. 1960. A study of the structure of the area postrema with Golgi methods. Am. J. Anat., **107**: 291–303.

MOREST, D. K. 1967. Experimental study of the projections of the nucleus of the tractus solitarius and the area postrema in the cat. J. Comp. Neurol., **130**: 277–299.

MORGAN, L. R. 1927. The corpus striatum. Arch. Neurol. & Psychiat., **18**: 495–549.

MORIN, F. 1955. A new spinal pathway for cutaneous impulses. Am. J. Physiol., **183**: 245–252.

MORIN, F., AND CATALANO, J. V. 1955. Central connections of a cervical nucleus (nucleus cervicalis lateralis of the cat). J. Comp. Neurol., **103**: 17–32.

MORIN, F., AND GARDNER, E. D. 1953. Spinal pathways for cerebellar projections in the monkey (*Macaca mulatta*). Am. J. Physiol., **174**: 155–161.

MORIN, F., SCHWARTZ, H. G., AND O'LEARY, J. L. 1951. Experimental study of the spinothalamic and related tract. Acta psychiat. et neurol. scandinav., **26**: 371–396.

MORISON, R. S., AND DEMPSEY, E. W. 1942. A study of thalamocortical relations. Am. J. Physiol., **135**: 281–292.

MORISON, R. S., AND DEMPSEY, E. W. 1942a. Mechanisms of thalamocortical augmentation and repetition. Am. J. Physiol., **138**: 297–308.

MORRISON, L. R. 1929. *Anatomical Studies of the Central Nervous Systems of Dogs without Forebrain or Cerebellum.* De Erven F. Bohn, Haarlem. (Reviewed in Arch. Neurol. & Psychiat., 1930, **24**: 218–220.)

MORUZZI, G., AND MAGOUN, H. W. 1949. Brain stem reticular formation and activation of the EEG. Electroencephalog. & Clin. Neurophysiol., **1**: 455–473.

MORUZZI, G., AND POMPEIANO, O. 1956. Crossed fastigial influence on decerebrate rigidity. J. Comp. Neurol., **106**: 371–392.

MOTT, F. W., AND SHERRINGTON, C. S. 1895. Experiments upon the influence of sensory nerves upon movement and nutrition of the limbs. Proc. Roy. Soc., **57**: 481–488.

MOULTON, D. G., AND BEIDLER, L. M. 1967. Structure and function in the peripheral olfactory system. Physiol. Rev., **47**: 1–52.

MOUNTCASTLE, V. B. 1957. Modality and topographic properties of single neurons of cat's somatic sensory cortex. J. Neurophysiol., **20**: 408–434.

MOUNTCASTLE, V. B. (Editor). 1962. *Interhemispheric Relations and Cerebral Dominance.* Johns Hopkins Press, Baltimore, 294 pp.

MOUNTCASTLE, V. B., AND HENNEMAN, E. 1949. Pattern of tactile representation in thalamus of cat. J. Neurophysiol., **12**: 85–100.

MOUNTCASTLE, V. B., AND HENNEMAN, E. 1952. The representation of tactile sensibility in the thalamus of the monkey. J. Comp. Neurol., **97**: 409–440.

MOUNTCASTLE, V. B., AND POWELL, T. P. S. 1959. Central nervous mechanisms subserving position sense and kinesthesis. Bull. Johns Hopkins Hosp., **105**: 173–200.

MOUNTCASTLE, V. B., AND POWELL, T. P. S. 1959a. Neural mechanisms subserving cutaneous sensibility with special reference to the role of afferent inhibition in sensory perception and discrimination. Bull. Johns Hopkins Hosp., **105**: 201–232.

MOZELL, M. M. 1964. Olfactory discrimination; electrophysiological spatio-temporal basis. Science, **143**: 1336–1337.

MUGNAINI, E., AND WALBERG, F. 1964. Ultrastructure of neuroglia. Ergebn. Anat. u. Entwicklungsgesch., **37**: 194–236.

MUNGER, B. L. 1965. The intraepidermal innervation of the snout skin of the opossum. A light and electron microscope study, with observations of the nature of Merkel's Tastzellen. J. Cell Biol., **26**: 79–97.

MUNGER, B. L. 1966. In A. V. S. DE REUCK AND

J. Knight (Editors), *Touch, Heat, and Pain.* Ciba Foundation Symposium. Little, Brown and Company, Boston, pp. 129–130.

Muralt, A. V. 1946. *Die Signalübermittlung im Nerven.* Verlag Birkhäuser, Basel.

Murray, M. R. 1957. Tissue culture studies of neural tissue. In W. F. Windle (Editor), *New Research Techniques of Neuroanatomy.* Charles C Thomas, Publisher, Springfield, Ill. Ch. 5, pp. 40–50.

Murray, M. R. 1965. Nervous tissue *in vitro.* In E. N. Wilmer (Editor), *Cells and Tissues in Culture. Methods, Biology and Physiology,* Vol. 2. Academic Press, New York, pp. 373–455.

Murray, M. R. and Stout, A. P. 1947. Adult human sympathetic ganglion cells cultivated *in vitro.* Am. J. Anat., 80: 225–273.

Mussen, A. T. 1927. Experimental investigations on the cerebellum. Brain, 50: 313–349.

Mytilineou, C., Issidorides, M., and Shanklin, W. M. 1963. Histochemical reactions of human autonomic ganglia. J. Anat., 97: 533–542.

Nageotte, J. 1906. The pars intermedia or nervus intermedius of Wrisberg, and the bulbo-pontine gustatory nucleus in man. Rev. Neurol. Psychiat. Edinb., 4: 473–488.

Nakao, H. 1958. Emotional behavior produced by hypothalamic stimulation. Am. J. Physiol., 194: 411–418.

Namba, T., Nakamura, T., and Grob, D. 1968. Motor nerve endings in human extraocular muscle. Neurology, 18: 403–407.

Nandy, K. 1968. Histochemical study of chromatolytic neurons. Arch. Neurol., 18: 425–434.

Naquin, H. A. 1954. Argyll-Robertson pupil following herpes zoster ophthalmicus, with remarks on the efferent pupillary pathways. Am. J. Ophth., 38: 23–33.

Narabayashi, H., Nagao, T., Saito, Y., Yoshida, M., and Nagahata, M. 1963. Stereotaxic amygdalotomy for behavior disorders. Arch. Neurol., 9: 1–16.

Narabayashi, H., Okuma, T., and Shikiba, S. 1956. Procaine oil blocking of the globus pallidus. A.M.A. Arch. Neurol. & Psychiat., 75: 36–48.

Nathan, P. W., and Smith, M. C. 1951. The centripetal pathway from the bladder and urethra within the spinal cord. J. Neurol. Neurosurg. & Psychiat., 14: 262–280.

Nathan, P. W., and Smith, M. C. 1955. Long descending tracts in man. I. Review of present knowledge. Brain, 78: 248–303.

Nathan, P. W., and Smith, M. C. 1955a. Spino-cortical fibers in man. J. Neurol. Neurosurg. & Psychiat., 18: 181–190.

Nathaniel, E. J. H., and Nathaniel, D. R. 1966. The ultrastructural features of the synapses in the posterior horn of the spinal cord in the rat. J. Ultrastruct. Res., 14: 540–555.

Nathaniel, E. J. H., and Pease, D. C. 1963. Degenerative changes in rat dorsal roots during Wallerian degeneration. J. Ultrastruct. Res., 9: 511–532.

Nathaniel, E. J. H., and Pease, D. C. 1963a. Regenerative changes in rat dorsal roots following Wallerian degeneration. J. Ultrastruct. Res., 9: 533–549.

Nauta, W. J. H. 1956. An experimental study of the fornix in the rat. J. Comp. Neurol., 104: 247–272.

Nauta, W. J. H. 1958. Hippocampal projections and related neural pathways to the midbrain in the cat. Brain, 81: 319–340.

Nauta, W. J. H. 1961. Fibre degeneration following lesions of the amygdaloid complex in the monkey. J. Anat., 95: 515–531.

Nauta, W. J. H. 1962. Neural associations of the amygdaloid complex in the monkey. Brain, 85: 505–520.

Nauta, W. J. H., and Bucher, V. M. 1954. Efferent connections of the striate cortex in the albino rat. J. Comp. Neurol., 100: 257–285.

Nauta, W. J. H., and Gygax, P. A. 1951. Silver impregnation of degenerating axon terminals in the central nervous system: (1) technic; (2) chemical notes. Stain Technol., 26: 5–11.

Nauta, W. J. H., and Gygax, P. A. 1954. Silver impregnation of degenerating axons in the central nervous system: A modified technic. Stain Technol., 29: 91–93.

Nauta, W. J. H., and Kuypers, H. G. J. M. 1958. Some ascending pathways in the brain stem reticular formation. In H. H. Jasper *et al.* (Editors), *Reticular Formation of the Brain.* Henry Ford Hospital International Symposium. Little, Brown and Company, Boston. Ch. 1, pp. 3–30.

Nauta, W. J. H., and Mehler, W. R. 1966. Projections of the lentiform nucleus in the monkey. Brain Res., 1: 3–42.

Nauta, W. J. H. and Whitlock, D. G. 1954. An anatomical analysis of the non-specific thalamic projection system. In J. F. Delafresnaye (Editor), *Brain Mechanisms and Consciousness* (Symposium). Blackwell Scientific Publications, Oxford, pp. 81–98.

Neff, W. D., and Diamond, I. T. 1958. The neural basis of auditory discrimination. In H. F. Harlow and C. N. Woolsey (Editors), *Biological and Biochemical Bases of Behavior.* University of Wisconsin Press, Madison, Wisc., pp. 101–126.

Neff, W. D., Fisher, J. F., Diamond, I. T., and Yela, M. 1956. Role of auditory cortex in discrimination requiring localization of sound in space. J. Neurophysiol., 19: 500–512.

Ngai, S. H., and Wang, S. C. 1957. Organization

of central respiratory mechanisms in the brain stem of the cat: Localization by stimulation and destruction. Am. J. Physiol., **190:** 343–349.

NIEMER, W. T., AND MAGOUN, H. W. 1947. Reticulospinal tracts influencing motor activity. J. Comp. Neurol., **87:** 367–379.

NOVAK, J., AND SALAFSKY, B. 1967. Early electrophysiological changes after denervation of slow skeletal muscle. Exper. Neurol., **19:** 388–400.

NYBERG-HANSEN, R. 1964. Origin and termination of fibers from the vestibular nuclei descending in the medial longitudinal fasciculus. An experimental study with silver impregnation methods in the cat. J. Comp. Neurol., **122:** 355–368.

NYBERG-HANSEN, R. 1965. Sites and mode of termination of reticulospinal fibers in the cat. An experimental study with silver impregnation methods. J. Comp. Neurol., **124:** 71–99.

NYBERG-HANSEN, R. 1966. Functional organization of descending supraspinal fibre systems to the spinal cord. Anatomical observations and physiological correlations. Ergebn. Anat. u. Entwicklungsgesch., **39:** (no. 2) 1–48.

NYBERG-HANSEN R., AND BRODAL, A. 1963. Sites of termination of corticospinal fibers in the cat. An experimental study with silver impregnation methods. J. Comp. Neurol., **120:** 369–392.

NYBERG-HANSEN, R., AND BRODAL, A. 1964. Sites and mode of termination of rubrospinal fibers in the cat. An experimental study with silver impregnation methods. J. Anat., **98:** 235–253.

NYBERG-HANSEN, R., AND MASCITTI, T. A. 1964. Sites and mode of termination of fibers of the vestibulospinal tract in the cat. An experimental study with silver impregnation methods. J. Comp. Neurol., **122:** 369–387.

NYBY, O., AND JANSEN, J. 1951. An experimental investigation of the corticopontine projection in *Macaca mulatta*. Norske Vid.-Akad. Avh. Mat.-Naturv., **3:** 1–47.

OLDS, J. 1960 Differentiation of reward systems in the brain by self-stimulation technics. S. R. RAMEY AND D. S. O'DOHERTY (Editors), In *Electrical Studies on the Unanesthetized Brain*. Paul B. Hoeber, Inc., New York. Ch. 2, pp. 17–51.

OLDS, J., AND MILNER, P. 1954. Positive reinforcement produced by electrical stimulation of septal area and other regions of the rat brain. J. Comp. & Physiol. Psychol., **47:** 419–427.

O'LEARY, J. L., KERR, F. W. L., AND GOLDRING, S. 1958. The relation between spinoreticular and ascending cephalic systems. In H. H. JASPERS *ET AL*. (Editors), *Reticular Formation of the Brain*. Henry Ford Hospital International

Symposium. Little, Brown and Company, Boston. Ch. 8, pp. 187–201.

OLSZEWSKI, J. 1950. On the anatomical and functional organization of the spinal trigeminal nucleus. J. Comp. Neurol., **92:** 401–413.

OLSZEWSKI, J. 1952. *The Thalamus of the Macaca Mulatta*. S. Karger AG, Basel, 93 pp.

OLSZEWSKI, J. 1954. Cytoarchitecture of the human reticular formation. In J. F. DELAFRESNAYE (Editor), *Brain Mechanisms and Consciousness* (Symposium). Blackwell Scientific Publications, Oxford, pp. 54–80.

OLSZEWSKI, J., AND BAXTER, D. 1954. *Cytoarchitecture of the Human Brain Stem*. J. B. Lippincott Company, Philadelphia.

OPPENHEIMER, D. R., PALMER, E., AND WEDDELL, G. 1958. Nerve endings in the conjunctiva. J. Anat., **92:** 321–352.

ORBACH, J., AND CHOW, K. L. 1959. Differential effects of resection of somatic areas I and II in monkeys. J. Neurophysiol., **22:** 195–203.

ORBACH, J., MILNER, B., AND RASMUSSEN, T. 1960. Learning and retention in monkeys after amygdalahippocampus resection. Arch. Neurol., **3:** 230–251.

ORKLAND, R. K., NICHOLS, J. G., AND KUFFLER, S. W. 1966. Effect of nerve impulses on the membrane potential of glial cells in the central nervous system of Amphibia. J. Neurophysiol. **29:** 788–806.

ORTMANN, R. 1960. Neurosecretion. In J. FIELD (Editor) *Handbook of Physiology, Neurophysiology*. II. American Physiological Society, Washington, D.C., Ch. 40, pp. 1039–1065.

OSCARSSON, O. 1964. Three ascending tracts activated from group I afferents in forelimb nerves of the cat. In J. C. ECCLES AND J. P. SCHADÉ (Editors), *Physiology of Spinal Neurons*, Vol. 12, *Progress in Brain Research*, Elsevier Publishing Company, Amsterdam, pp. 179–196.

OSCARSSON, O. 1964a. Integrative organization of the rostral spinocerebellar tract in the cat. Acta physiol. scandinav., **64:** 154–166.

OSCARSSON, O. 1965. Functional organization of the spino- and cuneocerebellar tracts. Physiol. Rev., **45:** 495–522.

OSCARSSON, O. 1967. Functional significance of information channels from the spinal cord to the cerebellum. In M. D. YAHR AND D. P. PURPURA (Editors), *Neurophysiological Basis of Normal and Abnormal Motor Activities*. Raven Press, New York, pp. 93–113.

OSCARSSON, O., AND UDDENBERG, N. 1964. Identification of a spinocerebellar tract activated from forelimb afferents in the cat. Acta physiol. scandinav., **62:** 125–136.

OZEKI, M., AND SATO, J. 1964. Initiation of impulses at the non-myelinated terminal in Pacinian corpuscles. J. Physiol. (Lond.), **170:** 167–185.

OZEKI, M., AND SATO, M. 1965. Changes in the membrane potential and the membrane conductance associated with a sustained compression of the non-myelinated nerve terminal in Pacinian corpuscles. J. Physiol. (Lond.), **180:** 186–208.

PALAY, S. L. 1945. Neurosecretion. VII. The preoptico-hypophysial pathway in fishes. J. Comp. Neurol., **82:** 129–143.

PALAY, S. L. 1956. Synapses in the central nervous system. J. Biophys. Biochem. Cytol., Suppl. **2:** 193–201.

PALAY, S. L. 1958. An electron microscopical study of neuroglia. In W. F. WINDLE (Editor), *Biology of Neuroglia.* Charles C Thomas, Publisher, Springfield, Ill., pp. 24–38.

PALAY, S. L. 1966. The role of neuroglia in the organization of the central nervous system. In K. RODAHL AND B. ISSEKUTZ, JR. (Editors), *Nerve as A Tissue.* Hoeber Med. Div., Harper and Row, New York, pp. 3–10.

PALAY, S. L., MCGEE-RUSSELL, S. M., GORDON, S., AND GRILLO, M. A. 1962. Fixation of neural tissues for electron microscopy by perfusion with solutions of osmium tetroxide. J. Cell Biol., **12:** 385–410.

PALAY, S. L., AND PALADE, G. E. 1955. The fine structure of neurons. J. Biophys. & Biochem. Cytol., **1:** 69–88.

PAPEZ, J. W. 1927. Subdivisions of the facial nucleus. J. Comp. Neurol., **43:** 159–191.

PAPEZ, J. W. 1936. Evolution of the medial geniculate body. J. Comp. Neurol., **64:** 41–61.

PAPEZ, J. W. 1937. A proposed mechanism of emotion. Arch. Neurol. & Psychiat., **38:** 725–743.

PAPEZ, J. W. 1938. Thalamic connections in a hemidecorticate dog. J. Comp. Neurol., **69:** 103–119.

PAPEZ, J. W. 1942. A summary of fiber connections of the basal ganglia with each other and with other portions of the brain. A. Res. Nerv. & Ment. Dis. Proc., **21:** 21–68.

PAPEZ, J. W. 1956. Central reticular path to intralaminar and reticular nuclei of thalamus for activating EEG related to consciousness. Electroencephalog. & Clin. Neurophysiol., **8:** 117–128.

PAPEZ, J. W. 1956a. Path for projection of nonspecific diffuse impulses to cortex for EEG, related to consciousness. Dis. Nerv. System, **17:** 3–8.

PAPEZ, J. W., BENNETT, A. E., AND CASH, P. T. 1942. Hemichorea (Hemiballismus): Association with a pallidal lesion involving afferent and efferent connections of the subthalamic nucleus; curare

therapy. Arch. Neurol. & Psychiat., **47:** 667–676.

PAPEZ, J. W., AND FREEMAN, G. L. 1930. Superior colliculi and their fiber connections in the rat. J. Comp. Neurol., **51:** 409–439.

PAPEZ, J. W., AND RUNDLES, W. 1937. The dorsal trigeminal tract and the centre median nucleus of Luys. J. Nerv. & Ment. Dis., **85:** 509–519.

PAPPAS, G. D. 1966. Electron microscopy of neuronal junctions involved in transmission in the central nervous system. In K. RODAHL AND B. ISSEKUTZ, JR. (Editors), *Nerve as A Tissue.* Hoeber Med. Div., Harper and Row, New York, pp. 49–87.

PARMELEE, A. H., JR., WENNER, W. H., AKIYAMA, V. A., STERN E., AND FLESCHER, J. 1967. Electroencephalography and brain maturation. In A. MINKOWSKI (Editor), *Regional Development of the Brain in Early Life.* F. A. Davis, Company Philadelphia, pp. 459–480.

PARTRIDGE, M. 1950. *Prefrontal Leucotomy: A Survey of 300 Cases Personally Followed over 1½–3 Years.* Blackwell Scientific Publications, Oxford, 496 pp.

PASS, I. J. 1933. Anatomic and functional relationship of nuc. dorsalis (Clarke's column). Arch. Neurol. & Psychiat., **30:** 1025–1045.

PATTEN, B. M. 1953. *Human Embryology*, Ed. 2. The Blakiston Company, New York.

PATTON, H. D. 1961. Reflex regulation of movement and posture. In T. C. RUCH ET AL. (Editors), *Neurophysiology.* W. B. Saunders Company, Philadelphia. Ch. 6, pp. 167–198.

PATTON, H. D. 1961a. Special properties of nerve trunks and tracts. In T. C. RUCH ET AL. (Editor), *Neurophysiology.* W. B. Saunders Company, Philadelphia. Ch. 3, pp. 66–95.

PATTON, H. D., AND RUCH, T. C. 1946. The relation of the foot of the pre- and postcentral gyrus to taste in the monkey and chimpanzee. Fed. Proc., **5:** 79.

PATTON, H. D., RUCH, T. C., AND WALKER, A. E. 1944. Experimental hypogeusia from Horsley-Clarke lesions of the thalamus in Macaca mulatta. J. Neurophysiol., **7:** 171–184.

PAYNE, F. 1924. General description of a 7-somite human embryo. Contrib. Embryol., **16:** 115–124.

PEARSON, A. A. 1944. The oculomotor nucleus in the human fetus. J. Comp. Neurol., **80:** 47–63.

PEARSON, A. A. 1949. The development and connections of the mesencephalic root of the trigeminal nerve in man. J. Comp. Neurol., **90:** 1–46.

PEARSON, A. A. 1949a. Further observations on the mesencephalic root of the trigeminal nerve. J. Comp. Neurol., **91:** 147–194.

PEARSON, A. A. 1952. Role of gelatinous substance

of spinal cord in conduction of pain. A. M. A. Arch. Neurol. & Psychiat., **68:** 515–529.

PEARSON, A. A., SAUTER, R. W., AND BUCKLEY, T. E. 1966. Further observations on the cutaneous branches of the dorsal primary rami of the spinal nerves. Am. J. Anat., **118:** 891–904.

PEELE, T. L. 1942. Cytoarchitecture of individual parietal areas in the monkey (*Macaca mulatta*) and the distribution of the efferent fibers. J. Comp. Neurol., **77:** 693–737.

PEELE, T. L. 1961. *The Neuroanatomical Basis for Clinical Neurology*. McGraw Hill Book Company, New York.

PENFIELD, W. 1920. Alterations of the Golgi apparatus in nerve cells. Brain, **43:** 290–305.

PENFIELD, W. 1932. Neuroglia, normal and pathological. In W. G. PENFIELD (Editor), *Cytology and Cellular Pathology of the Nervous System*, Vol. II. Paul B. Hoeber, Inc., New York, pp. 423–479.

PENFIELD, W. 1957. Vestibular sensation and the cerebral cortex. Ann. Otol. Rhin. & Laryng., **66:** 691–698.

PENFIELD, W., AND BOLDREY, E. 1937. Somatic motor and sensory representation in the cerebral cortex of man as studied by electrical stimulation. Brain, **60:** 389–443.

PENFIELD, W., AND EVANS, J. 1932. Functional defects produced by cerebral lobectomies. A. Res. Nerv. & Ment. Dis., Proc., **13:** 352–377.

PENFIELD, W., AND JASPER, H. H. 1954. *Epilepsy and the Functional Anatomy of the Human Brain*. Little, Brown and Company, Boston, 896 pp.

PENFIELD, W. G., AND McNAUGHTON, F. 1940. Dural headache and innervation of the dura mater. Arch. Neurol. & Psychiat., **44:** 43–75.

PENFIELD, W., AND MILNER, B. 1958. Memory deficit produced by bilateral lesions in the hippocampal zone. A. M. A. Arch. Neurol. & Psychiat., **79:** 475–497.

PENFIELD, W., AND RASMUSSEN, T. 1950. *The Cerebral Cortex of Man. A Clinical Study of Localization of Function*. Macmillan Company, New York. 248 pp.

PENFIELD, W., AND ROBERTS, L. 1959. *Speech and Brain Mechanisms*. Princeton University Press, Princeton, N. J., 279 pp.

PENFIELD, W., AND WELCH, K. 1951. The supplementary motor area of the cerebral cortex. A clinical and experimental study. A. M. A. Arch. Neurol. & Psychiat., **66:** 289–317.

PERL, E. R., AND WHITLOCK, D. G. 1961. Somatic stimuli exciting spinothalamic projections in thalamic neurons in the cat and monkey. Exper. Neurol., **3:** 256–296.

PERL, E. R., WHITLOCK, D. G., AND GENTRY, J. R. 1962. Cutaneous projection to second-order neurons of the dorsal column system. J. Neurophysiol., **25:** 337–353.

PETERS, A. 1960. The formation and structure of myelin sheaths in the central nervous system. J. Biophys. Biochem. Cytol., **8:** 431–446.

PETERS, A. 1966. The node of Ranvier in the central nervous system. Quart. J. Exper. Physiol., **51:** 229–236.

PETERS, A. 1968. An introduction to neuronal fine structure. M. & Biol. Illust., **18:** 103–109.

PETERS, A., AND VAUGHN, J. E. 1967. Microtubules and filaments in the axons and astrocytes of early postnatal rat optic nerve. J. Cell Biol., **32:** 113–119.

PETERSON, E. R., AND MURRAY, M. R. 1955. Myelin sheath formation in cultures of avian spinal ganglia. Am. J. Anat., **96:** 319–355.

PETRAS, J. M. 1967. Cortical, tectal and tegmental fiber connections in the spinal cord of the cat. Brain Res., **6:** 275–324.

PETRAS, J. M. 1964. Some fiber connections of the precentral cortex (areas 4 and 6) with the diencephalon in the monkey (Macaca mulatta). Anat. Rec., **148:** 322.

PETRAS, J. M. 1965. Some fiber connections of the precentral and postcentral cortex with the basal ganglia, thalamus and subthalamus. Tr. Am. Neurol. A., **90:** 274–275.

PFAFFMANN, C. 1939. Afferent impulses from the teeth resulting from a vibratory stimulus. J. Physiol., **97:** 220–232.

PHALEN, G. S., AND DAVENPORT, H. A. 1937. Pericellular end-bulbs in the central nervous system of vertebrates. J. Comp. Neurol., **68:** 67–81.

PICK, J., AND SHEEHAN, D. 1946. Sympathetic rami in man. J. Anat., **80:** 12–20.

PINEDA, A., MAXWELL, D. S., AND KRUGER, L. 1967. The fine structure of neurons and satellite cells in the trigeminal ganglion of cat and monkey. Am. J. Anat., **121:** 461–488.

PINES, I. L. 1925. Über die Innervation der Hypophysis cerebri. II. Mitteilung: Über die Innervation des Mittel- und Hinterlappens der Hypophyse. Ztschr. ges. Neurol. u. Psychiat., **100:** 123–138.

PITTS, R. F. 1940. The respiratory center and its descending pathways. J. Comp. Neurol., **72:** 605–625.

PITTS, R. F. 1946. Organization of the respiratory center. Physiol. Rev., **26:** 609–630.

PITTS, R. F., MAGOUN, H. W., AND RANSON, S. W. 1939. Localization of the medullary respiratory centers in the cat. Am. J. Physiol., **126:** 673–688.

POGGIO, G. F., AND MOUNTCASTLE, V. B. 1960. A study of the functional contributions of the lemniscal and spinothalamic systems to somatic sensibility. Bull. Johns Hopkins Hosp., **106:** 266–316.

POIRIER, L. J. 1952. Anatomical and experimental studies on the temporal pole of the macaque. J. Comp. Neurol., **96:** 209–248.

POIRIER, L. J., AND BERTRAND, C. 1955. Experimental and anatomical investigation of the lateral spinothalamic and spinotectal tracts. J. Comp. Neurol., **102**: 745–757.

POIRIER, L. J., AND BOUVIER, G. 1966. The red nucleus and its efferent nervous pathways in the monkey. J. Comp. Neurol., **128**: 233–244.

POIRIER, L. J., AND SOURKES, T. L. 1965. Influences of the substantia nigra on catecholamine content of the striatum. Brain, **88**: 181–192.

POMERAT, C. M. 1951. Pulsatile activity of cell from the human brain in tissue culture. J. Nerv. & Ment. Dis., **114**: 430–449.

POMERAT, C. M. 1952. Dynamic neurogliology. Texas Rep. Biol. & Med., **10**: 885–913.

POMERAT, C. M. 1954. The use of cinematographic records for the analysis of cell activity. Excerpta Med., **8**: Sect. I, 422.

POMPEIANO, O. 1956. Sulle risposte posturali alla stimolazione elettrica del nucleo rosso nel gatto decerebrato. Boll. soc. ital. biol. sper., **32**: 1450–1451.

POMPEIANO, O. 1957. Analisi degli effetti della stimolazione elettrica del nucleo rosso nel gatto decerebrato. Rend. Accad. naz. Lincei, cl. sci. fis. mat. nat., **22**: 100–103.

POMPEIANO, O. 1958. Responses to electrical stimulation of the intermediate part of the cerebellar anterior lobe in the decerebrate cat. Arch. ital. biol., **96**: 330–360.

POMPEIANO, O. 1959. Organizzazione somatotopica delle risposte flessorie alla stimolazione elettrica del nucleo interposito nel gatto decerebrato. Arch. sc. biol., **43**: 163–176.

POMPEIANO, O. 1960. Organizzazione somatotopica delle risposte posturali alla stimolazione elettrica del nucleo di Deiters nel gatto cerebrato. Arch. sc. biol., **44**: 497–511.

POMPEIANO, O. 1960a. Localizzazione delle risposte estensorie alla stimolazione elettrica del nucleo interposito nel gatto decerebrato. Arch. sc. biol., **44**; 473–496.

POMPEIANO, O., AND BRODAL, A. 1957. Experimental demonstration of a somatotopical origin of rubrospinal fibers in the cat. J. Comp. Neurol., **108**: 225–251.

POMPEIANO, O., AND BRODAL, A. 1957. The origin of the vestibulospinal fibres in the cat. An experimental-anatomical study, with comments on the descending medial longitudinal fasciculus. Arch. ital. biol., **95**: 166–195.

POMPEIANO, O., AND BRODAL, A. 1957b. Spinovestibular fibers in the cat. An experimental study. J. Comp. Neurol., **108**: 353–382.

POMPEIANO, O., AND MORRISON, A. R. 1965. Vestibular influences during sleep. I. Abolition of rapid eye movements of desynchronized sleep following vestibular lesions. Arch. ital. biol., **103**: 569–595.

POMPEIANO, O., AND WALBERG, F. 1957. Descending connections to the vestibular nuclei. An experimental study in the cat. J. Comp. Neurol., **108**: 465–502.

POOL, J. L. 1954. Neurophysiological symposium; visceral brain of man. J. Neurosurg., **11**: 45–63.

POTTS, T. K. 1924. The main peripheral connections of the human sympathetic nervous system. J. Anat., **59**: 129–135.

POWELL, T. P. S. 1952. Residual neurons in the human thalamus following hemidecortication. Brain, **75**: 571–584.

POWELL, T. P. S., AND COWAN, W. M. 1956. A study of thalamo-striate relations in the monkey. Brain, **79**: 364–391.

POWELL, T. P. S., AND COWAN, W. M. 1962. An experimental study of the projection of the cochlea. J. Anat., **96**: 269–284.

POWELL, T. P. S., AND COWAN, W. M. 1963. Centrifugal fibers in the lateral olfactory tract. Nature, **199**: 1296–1297.

POWELL, T. P. S., AND COWAN, W. M. 1967. The interpretation of the degenerative changes in the intralaminar nuclei of the thalamus. J. Neurol. Neurosurg. & Psychiat., **30**: 140–153.

POWELL, T. P. S., COWAN, W. M., AND RAISMAN, G. 1965. The central olfactory connexions. J. Anat., **99**: 791–813.

POWELL, T. P. S., AND ERULKAR, S. D. 1962. Transneuronal cell degeneration in the auditory relay nuclei of the cat. J. Anat., **96**: 249–268.

POWELL, T. P. S., GUILLERY, R. W., AND COWAN, W. M. 1957. A quantitative study of the fornix-mammillo-thalamic system. J. Anat., **91**: 419–432.

POWELL, T. P. S., AND MOUNTCASTLE, V. B. 1959. The cytoarchitecture of the postcentral gyrus of the monkey macaca mulatta. Bull. Johns Hopkins Hosp., **105**: 108–131.

POWELL, T. P. S., AND MOUNTCASTLE, V. B. 1959a. Some aspects of the functional organization of the cortex of the postcentral gyrus of the monkey: A correlation of findings obtained in a single unit analysis with cytoarchitecture. Bull. Johns Hopkins Hosp., **105**: 133–162.

PREISIG, H. 1904. Le noyau rouge et le pédoncule cérébelleux supérieur. J. Psychol. u. Neurol. (Leipzig), **3**: 215–230.

PRENTISS, C. W., AND AREY, L. B. 1920. *A Laboratory Manual and Textbook of Embryology.* W. B. Saunders Company, Philadelphia. Ch. 12, pp. 321–352.

PRESTON, J. B., AND WHITLOCK, D. G. 1960. Precentral facilitation and inhibition of spinal motoneurons. J. Neurophysiol., **23**: 154–170.

PRESTON, J. B., AND WHITLOCK, D. G. 1961. Intracellular potentials recorded from motoneurons following precentral gyrus stimulation in primate. J. Neurophysiol., **24**: 91–100.

PRIBRAM, K. H., AND BAGSHAW, M. 1953. Further analysis of the temporal lobe syndrome utilizing fronto-temporal ablations. J. Comp. Neurol., **99**: 347–375.

PRIBRAM, K. H., AND FULTON, J. F. 1954. An experimental critique of the effects of anterior cingulate ablation in monkey. Brain, **77**: 34–44.

PRIBRAM, K. H., ROSNER, B. S., AND ROSENBLITH, W. A. 1954. Electrical response to acoustic clicks in monkey: Extent of neocortex activated. J. Neurophysiol., **17**: 336–344.

PURPURA, D. P. 1959. Nature of electrocortical potentials and synaptic organizations in cerebral and cerebellar cortex. In C. C. PFEIFFER AND J. R. SMYTHIES (Editors), *International Review of Neurobiology*, Vol. I. Academic Press, New York, pp. 47–163.

PURPURA, D. P., AND COHEN, B. 1962. Intracellular synaptic activities of thalamic neurons during evoked recruiting responses. In *22nd International Congress of Physiological Sciences*. Excerpta Medica International Congress Series 48. Leiden.

PURPURA, D. P., FRIGYESI, T. L., McMURTRY, J. G., AND SCARFF, T. 1966. Synaptic mechanisms in thalamic regulation of cerebellocortical projection activity. In D. P. PURPURA AND M. D. YAHR (Editors), *The Thalamus*. Columbia University Press, New York, pp. 153–170.

PURPURA, D. P., AND GRUNDFEST, H. 1956. Nature of dendritic potentials and synaptic mechanisms in cerebral cortex of cat. J. Neurophysiol., **19**: 573–595.

QUENSEL, F. 1910. Über den Stabkranz des menschlichen Stirnhirns. Folia neuro-biol. (Leipzig), **4**: 319–334.

QUENSEL, W. 1944. Über die Faserspezifität in sensiblen Hautnerven. Pflügers Arch. ges. Physiol., **248**: 1–20.

QUILLIAM, T. A. 1966. Unit design and array patterns in receptor organs. In A. V. S. DE REUCK AND J. KNIGHT (Editors), *Touch, Heat and Pain*. Ciba Foundation Symposium. Little, Brown and Company, Boston, pp. 86–112.

RADEMAKER, G. G. T. 1926. *Die Bedeutung der roten Kerne und des übrigen Mittelhirns für Muskeltonus, Körperstellung, und Labyrinthreflexe*. Julius Springer, Berlin, pp. 64–222.

RAISMAN, G., COWAN, W. M., AND POWELL, T. P. S. 1965. The extrinsic afferent, commissural and association fibres of the hippocampus. Brain, **88**: 963–996.

RAISMAN, G., COWAN, W. M., AND POWELL, T. P. S. 1966. An experimental analysis of the efferent projections of the hippocampus. Brain, **89**: 83–108.

RALSTON, H. J., III 1965. The organization of the substantia gelatinosa Rolandi in the cat lumbosacral spinal cord. Ztschr. Zellforsch. **67**: 1–23.

RALSTON, H. J., III 1968. The fine structure of neurons in the dorsal horn of the cat spinal cord. J. Comp. Neurol., **132**: 275–302.

RALSTON, H. J., III 1968a. Dorsal root projections to the dorsal horn neurons in the cat spinal cord. J. Comp. Neurol., **132**: 303–330.

RALSTON, H. R., III, MILLER, M. R., AND KASAHARA, M. 1960. Nerve endings in human fasciae, tendons, ligaments, periosteum, and joint synovial membrane. Anat. Rec., **136**: 137–148.

RAMON-MOLINER, E. 1958. A tungstate modification of the Golgi-Cox method. Stain Technol., **33**: 19–29.

RANSON, S. W. 1912. The structure of the spinal ganglia and of the spinal nerves. J. Comp. Neurol., **22**: 159–175.

RANSON, S. W. 1913. The course within the spinal cord of the non-medullated fibers of the dorsal roots: a study of Lissauer's tract in the cat. J. Comp. Neurol., **23**: 259–281.

RANSON, S. W. 1914. The tract of Lissauer and the substantia gelatinosa Rolandi. Am. J. Anat., **16**: 97–126.

RANSON, S. W. 1936. *The Anatomy of the Nervous System*. W. B. Saunders Company, Philadelphia.

RANSON, S. W., AND BILLINGSLEY, P. R. 1918. The superior cervical ganglion and the cervical portion of the sympathetic trunk. J. Comp. Neurol., **29**: 313–358.

RANSON, S. W., AND INGRAM, W. R. 1932. The diencephalic course and termination of the medial lemniscus and brachium conjunctivum. J. Comp. Neurol., **56**: 257–275.

RANSON, S. W., AND MAGOUN, H. W. 1933. The central path of the pupillo-constrictor reflex in response to light. Arch. Neurol. & Psychiat., **30**: 1193–1204.

RANSON, S. W., AND RANSON, S. W., JR. 1942. Efferent fibers of the corpus striatum. A. Res. Nerv. & Ment. Dis. Proc., **21**: 69–76.

RASMUSSEN, A. T. 1936. Tractus tecto-spinalis in the cat. J. Comp. Neurol., **63**: 501–525.

RASMUSSEN, A. T., AND PEYTON, W. T. 1948. The course and termination of the medial lemniscus in man. J. Comp. Neurol., **88**: 411–424.

RASMUSSEN, G. L. 1946. The olivary peduncle and other fiber projections of the superior olivary complex. J. Comp. Neurol., **84**: 141–219.

RASMUSSEN, G. L. 1957. Selective silver impregnation of synaptic endings. In W. F. WINDLE (Editor), *New Research Techniques in Neuroanatomy*. Charles C Thomas, Publisher, Springfield, Ill., pp. 27–39.

RASMUSSEN, G. L. 1960. Efferent fibers of the cochlear nerve and cochlear nucleus. In G. L. RASMUSSEN AND W. F. WINDLE (Editors), *Neural Mechanisms of the Auditory and Vestibular Systems.* Charles C Thomas, Publisher, Springfield, Ill. Ch. 8, pp. 105–115.

RASMUSSEN, G. L. 1964. Anatomical relationships of the ascending and descending auditory systems. In W. S. FIELDS AND B. R. ALFORD (Editors), *Neurological Aspects of Auditory and Vestibular Disorders* (Houston Symposium). Charles C Thomas, Publisher, Springfield, Ill., Ch. 1, pp. 1–14.

RAUBER-KOPSCH. 1943. In F. KOPSCH (Editor), *Lehrbuch und Atlas der Anatomie des Menschen,* Vol. III. *Nervensystem-Sinnesorgane.* Georg Thieme, Leipzig, p. 97.

RAVIC, P., AND YAKOVLEV, P. I. 1968. Development of the corpus callosum and cavum septi in man. J. Comp. Neurol., **132:** 45–72.

REGER, J. F. 1955. Electron microscopy of the motor end plate in rat intercostal muscle. Anat. Rec., **122:** 1–10.

REGER, J. F. 1957. The ultrastructure of normal and denervated neuromuscular synapses in mouse gastrocnemius muscle. Exper. Cell Res., **12:** 661–665.

RENSHAW, B. 1940. Activity in the simplest spinal reflex pathways. J. Neurophysiol., **3:** 370–387.

RENSHAW, B. 1941. Influence of discharge of motoneurons upon excitation of neighboring motoneurons. J. Neurophysiol., **4:** 167–183.

RENSHAW, B. 1946. Central effects of centripetal impulses in axons of spinal ventral roots. J. Neurophysiol., **9:** 191–204.

REXED, B. 1952. The cytoarchitectonic organization of the spinal cord in the cat. J. Comp. Neurol., **96:** 415–495.

REXED, B. 1954. A cytoarchitectonic atlas of the spinal cord in the cat. J. Comp. Neurol., **100:** 297–379.

REXED, B. 1964. Some aspects of the cytoarchitectonics and synaptology of the spinal cord. In J. C. ECCLES AND J. P. SCHADE (Editors), *Progress in Brain Research,* Vol. II. *Organization of the Spinal Cord.* Elsevier Publishing Company, Amsterdam, pp. 58–92.

REXED, B., AND BRODAL, A. 1951. The nucleus cervicalis lateralis: a spinocerebellar relay nucleus. J. Neurophysiol., **14:** 399–407.

RHODIN, J. A. G. 1963. *An Atlas of Ultrastructure.* W. B. Saunders Company, Philadelphia, pp. 37–49.

RHOTON, A. L., O'LEARY, J. L., AND FERGUSON, J. P. 1966. The trigeminal, facial, vagal and glossopharyngeal nerves in the monkey. Arch. Neurol., **14:** 530–540.

RICHTER, C. P., AND HINES, M. 1932. Experimental production of the grasp reflex in adult monkeys by lesions of the frontal lobe. Am. J. Physiol., **101:** 87–88.

RICHTER, C. P., AND HINES, M. 1934. The production of the "grasp reflex" in adult macaques by experimental frontal lobe lesions. A. Res. Nerv. & Ment. Dis., Proc., **13:** 211–224.

RICHTER, C. P., AND WOODRUFF, B. G. 1945. Lumbar sympathetic dermatomes in man determined by the electrical skin resistance method. J. Neurophysiol., **8:** 323–338.

RICHTER, D. 1957. Editor, *Metabolism of the Nervous System.* Second International Neurochemical Symposium, Åarhus, Denmark, 1956. Pergamon Press, New York, 599 pp.

RIES, E. A., AND LANGWORTHY, O. R. 1937. A study of the surface structure of the brain of the whale (*Balaenoptera physolus* and *Physeter catadon*). J. Comp. Neurol., **68:** 1–47.

RIESE, W. 1925. Beiträge zur Faseranatomie der Stammganglien. J. Psychol. u. Neurol., **31:** 81–122.

VAN RIJNBERK, G. 1926. Les dernières recherches relatives à la question de la localisation dans le cervelet: anatomie, physiologie, clinique. Arch. néerl. physiol., **10:** 183–301.

RILEY, C. M. 1952. Familial autonomic dysfunction. J. A. M. A., **149:** 1532–1535.

RILEY, C. M. 1957. Familial dysautonomia. Advances Pediat., **9:** 157–190.

RILEY, C. M., DAY, R. L., GREELEY, D. M., AND LANGFORD, 1949. Central autonomic dysfunction with defective lacrimation. Pediatrics, **3:** 468–481.

RILEY, C. M., AND MOORE, R. H. 1966. Familial dysautonomia differentiated from related disorders. Pediatrics, **37:** 435–446.

RILEY, H. A. 1930. The central nervous system control of the ocular movements and the disturbances of this mechanism. Arch Ophth., **4:** 640–661 and 885–910.

RILEY, H. A. 1943. *An Atlas of the Basal Ganglia, Brain Stem and Spinal Cord.* Williams & Wilkins Company, Baltimore, 708 pp.

RINVIK, E. 1966. The cortico-nigral projection in the cat. An experimental study with silver impregnation methods. J. Comp. Neurol., **126:** 241–254.

RINVIK, E., AND WALBERG, F. 1963. Demonstration of a somatotopically arranged cortico-rubral projection in the cat. An experimental study with silver methods. J. Comp. Neurol., **120:** 393–407.

DEL RIO-HORTEGA, P. 1932. Microglia. In W. G. PENFIELD (Editor), *Cytology and Cellular Pathology of the Nervous System,* Vol. II. Paul B. Hoeber, Inc., New York, pp. 483–534.

DE ROBERTIS, E. 1959. Submicroscopic morphology of the synapse. Internat. Rev. Cytol., **8:** 61–96.

DE ROBERTIS, E. 1966. Synaptic complexes and synaptic vesicles as structural and biochemical units of the central nervous system. In K. RODAHL AND B. ISSEKUTZ, JR. (Editors), *Nerve as A Tissue*, Hoeber Med. Div., Harper and Row, New York, pp. 88–115.

DE ROBERTIS, E., AND BENNETT, H. S. 1954. Submicroscopic vesicular component in the synapse. Fed. Proc., **13:** 35.

DE ROBERTIS, E., DE IRALDI, A. P., DE LORES, R., ARNAIZ, G., AND SALGANICOFF, L. 1962. Cholinergic and non-cholinergic nerve endings in rat brain. I. Isolation and subcellular distribution of acetylcholine and acetylcholinesterase. J. Neurochem., **9:** 23–35.

DE ROBERTIS, E. D. P., NOWINSKI, W. W., AND SAEZ, F. A. 1965. The plasma membrane. In E. D. P. DE ROBERTIS *ET AL.* (Editors), *Cell Biology.* W. B. Saunders Company, Philadelphia, pp. 109–128.

ROBERTSON, D. M., AND VOGEL, F. S. 1962. Concentric lamination of glial processes in oligodendrogliomas. J. Cell Biol., **15:** 313–334.

ROBERTSON, J. D. 1955. Ultrastructure of adult vertebrate peripheral myelinated nerve fibers in relation to myelinogenesis. J. Biophys. & Biochem. Cytol., **1:** 271–278.

ROBERTSON, J. D. 1956. The ultrastructure of a reptilian myoneural junction. J. Biophys. & Biochem. Cytol., **2:** 381–394.

ROBERTSON, J. D. 1958. The ultrastructure of Schmidt-Lantermann clefts and related shearing defects of the myelin sheath. J. Biophys. & Biochem. Cytol., **4:** 39–46.

ROBERTSON, J. D. 1959. Preliminary observations on the ultrastructure of nodes of Ranvier. Ztschr. Zellforsch. u. mikroskop. Anat., **50:** 553–560.

ROBERTSON, J. D. 1960. Electron microscopy of the motor end-plate and the neuromuscular spindle. Am. J. Phys. Med., **39:** 1–43.

ROBERTSON, J. D. 1966. Current problems of unit membrane structure and contact relationships. In K. RODAHL AND B. ISSEKUTZ, JR. (Editors), *Nerve as A Tissue.* Hoeber Med. Div., Harper and Row, New York, pp. 11–48.

RODRIGUEZ-ECHANDIA, E. L., PIEZZI, R. S., AND RODRIGUEZ, E. M. 1968. Dense-core microtubules in neurons and gliocytes of the toad Bufo arenarum Hensel. Am. J. Anat., **122:** 157–168.

RODRIGUEZ, L. A. 1955. Experiments on the histologic locus of the hemato-encephalic barrier. J. Comp. Neurol., **102:** 27–46.

RODRIGUEZ, L. A. 1957. The role of the meningeal tissues in the hemato-encephalic barrier. J. Comp. Neurol., **107:** 455–474.

ROEDER, F., AND ORTHNER, H. 1956. Erfahrungen mit stereotaktischen Eingriffen. I. Mitteilung: Zur Pathogenese und Therapie extrapyramidalmotorischer Bewegungsstörungen. Erfolgreiche Behandlung eines Falles schwerem Hemiballismus mit gezielter Electrokoagulation des Globus pallidus. Deutsche Ztschr. Nervenh., **175:** 419–434.

ROGER, A., ROSSI, G. F., AND ZIRONDOLI, A. 1956. Le rôle des nerfs craniens dans le maintien de l'état vigile de la preparation "encéphale isolé." Electroencephalog. & Clin. Neurophysiol., **8:** 1–13.

ROGERS, D. C., AND BURNSTOCK, G. 1966. Multiaxonal autonomic junctions in smooth muscle of the toad. (Bufo Marinus). J. Comp. Neurol., **126:** 625–652.

ROGERS, F. T. 1922. Studies of the brain stem. VI. An experimental study of the corpus striatum of the pigeon as related to various instinctive types of behavior. J. Comp. Neurol., **35:** 21–59.

ROSE, J. E. 1952. The cortical connections of the reticular complex of the thalamus. A. Res. Nerv. & Ment. Dis. Proc., **30:** 454–479.

ROSE, J. E. 1960. Organization of frequency sensitive neurons in the cochlear complex of the cat. In G. L. RASMUSSEN AND W. F. WINDLE (Editors), *Neural Mechanisms of the Auditory and Vestibular Systems.* Charles C Thomas, Publisher, Springfield, Ill. Ch. 9, pp. 116–136.

ROSE, J. E., AND GALAMBOS, R. 1952. Microelectrode studies on the medial geniculate body of the cat. I. The thalamic region activated by click stimuli. J. Neurophysiol., **15:** 343–357.

ROSE, J. E., GALAMBOS, R., AND HUGHES, J. R. 1959. Microelectrode studies of the cochlear nuclei of the cat. Bull. Johns Hopkins Hosp., **104:** 211–251.

ROSE, J. E., GREENWOOD, D. B., GOLDBERG, J. M., AND HIND, J. E. 1963. Some discharge characteristics of single neurons in the inferior colliculus of the cat. I. Tonotopical organization, relation of spike-counts to tone intensity, and firing patterns of single elements. J. Neurophysiol., **26:** 294–320.

ROSE, J. E., GROSS, N. B., GEISLER, C. D., AND HIND, J. E. 1966. Some neural mechanisms in the inferior colliculus of the cat which may be relevant to localization of a sound source. J. Neurophysiol., **29:** 288–314.

ROSE, J. E., AND MOUNTCASTLE, V. B. 1952. The thalamic tactile region in rabbit and cat. J. Comp. Neurol., **97:** 441–490.

ROSE, J. E., AND MOUNTCASTLE, V. B. 1959. Touch and kinesthesis. In J. FIELDS (Editor), *Handbook of Physiology*, Section I, Vol. I. American Physiological Society, Washington, D. C., Ch. 17, pp. 387–429.

Rose, J. E., and Woolsey, C. N. 1943. A study of thalamocortical relations in the rabbit. Bull. Johns Hopkins Hosp., **72:** 65–128.

Rose, J. E., and Woolsey, C. N. 1943a. Potential changes in the olfactory brain produced by electrical stimulation of the olfactory bulb. Fed. Proc., **2:** 42.

Rose, J. E., and Woolsey, C. N. 1949. The relation of thalamic connections, cellular structure and evocable electrical activity in the auditory region of the cat. J. Comp. Neurol., **91:** 441–466.

Rose, J. E., and Woolsey, C. N. 1958. Cortical connections and functional organization of the thalamic auditory system of the cat. In H. F. Harlow and C. N. Woolsey (Editors), *Biological and Biochemical Bases of Behavior.* University of Wisconsin Press, Madison, Wisc., pp. 127–150.

Rose, M. 1935. Cytoarchitektonik und Myeloarchitektonik der Grosshirnrinde. In O. Bumke and O. Foerster (Editors), *Handbuch der Neurologie,* Vol. I. Springer, Berlin, pp. 588–778.

Rosegay, H. 1944. An experimental investigation of the connections between the corpus striatum and the substantia nigra in the cat. J. Comp. Neurol., **80:** 293–310.

Rosenbluth, J. 1962. Subsurface cisterns and their relationships to the neuronal plasma membrane. J. Cell Biol., **13:** 405–421.

Rosenzweig, M. R. 1954. Cortical correlates of auditory localization and of related perceptual phenomena. J. Comp. & Physiol. Psychol., **47:** 269–276.

Rosett, J. 1933. *Intercortical Systems of the Human Cerebrum, Mapped by Means of New Anatomic Methods.* Columbia University Press, New York.

Ross, L. L., Bornstein, M. B., and Lehrer, G. 1962. Electron microscope observations of rat and mouse cerebellum in tissue culture. J. Cell Biol., **14:** 19–30.

Rossi, G. F. 1963. Sleep-inducing mechanisms in the brain stem. Electroencephalog. & Clin. Neurophysiol., Suppl. **24:** 113–132.

Rossi, G. F., and Brodal, A. 1956. Corticofugal fibers to the brain stem reticular formation. An experimental study in the cat. J. Anat., **90:** 42–62.

Rossi, G. F., and Brodal, A. 1956a. Spinal afferents to the trigeminal sensory nuclei and the nucleus of the solitary tract. Confinia neurol., **16:** 321–332.

Rossi, G. F., and Brodal, A. 1957. Terminal distribution of spinoreticular fibers in the cat. A. M. A. Arch. Neurol. & Psychiat., **78:** 439–453.

Rossi, G. F., Minobe, K., and Candia, O. 1963. An experimental study of the hypnogenic mechanisms of the brain stem. Arch. ital. biol., **101:** 470–492.

Rossi, G. F., and Zanchetti, A. 1957. The brain stem reticular formation. Anatomy and physiology. Arch. ital. biol., **95:** 199–435.

Rossi, G. F., and Zirondoli, A. 1955. On the mechanism of the cortical desynchronization elicited by volatile anesthetics. Electroencephalog. & Clin. Neurophysiol., **7:** 383–390.

Rubinstein, L. J., Klatzo, I., and Miquel, J. 1962. Histochemical observations on oxidative enzyme activity of glial cells in a local brain injury. J. Neuropath. & Exper. Neurol., **21:** 116–136.

Ruffini, A. 1894. Sur un nouvel Organe nerveux terminal et sur la présence des corpuscles Golgi-Mazzoni dans le conjunctif sous-cutane de la pulpe des doigts de l'homme. Arch. ital. biol., **21:** 249–265.

Rundles, R. W., and Papez, J. W. 1937. Connections between the striatum and the substantia nigra in a human brain. Arch. Neurol. & Psychiat., **38:** 550–563.

Russell, G. V. 1954. The dorsal trigemino-thalamic tract in the cat. Reconsidered as a lateral reticulo-thalamic system of connections. J. Comp. Neurol., **101:** 237–264.

Russell, G. V. 1955. A schematic presentation of thalamic morphology and connections. Texas Rep. Biol. & Med., **13:** 989–992.

Russell, J. R., and DeMyer, W. 1961. The quantitative cortical origin of pyramidal axons of Macaca rhesus. Neurology, **11:** 96–108.

Russell, W. R. 1948. Functions of the frontal lobes. Lancet, **254:** 356–360.

Rylander, G. 1948. Personality analysis before and after frontal lobotomy. A. Res. Nerv. & Ment. Dis. Proc., **27:** 691–705.

Sachs, E., Jr., Brendler, S. J., and Fulton, J. F. 1949. The orbital gyri. Brain, **72:** 227–240.

Salafsky, B., and Jasinski, D. 1967. Early electrophysiological changes after denervation of fast skeletal muscle. Exper. Neurol., **19:** 375–387.

von Santha, K. 1928. Zur Klinik und Anatomie des Hemiballismus. Arch. Psychiat., **84:** 664–678.

Sasaki, K., Namikawa, A., and Hashiramoto, S. 1960. The effect of midbrain stimulation upon alpha motoneurones in lumbar spinal cord. Nippon Seirigaku Zassi, **3:** 303–316.

Sasaki, K., Tanaka, T., and Mori, K. 1962. Effects of stimulation of pontine and bulbar reticular formation upon spinal motoneurons of the cat. Jap. J. Physiol., **12:** 45–62.

Scarff, J. E. 1940. Primary cortical centers for movement of upper and lower limbs in man. Arch. Neurol. & Psychiat., **44:** 243–299.

Scarff, J. E. 1949. Unilateral prefrontal lobotomy for relief of intractable pain and termination of narcotic addiction. Surg. Gynec. & Obst., **89:** 385–392.

SCHAEFFER, J. P. 1953. *Morris' Human Anatomy,* Sect. 8. Blakiston Company, New York, p. 1189.

SCHALTENBRAND, G. 1955. Plexus und Meningen. Saccus vasculosus. In W. VON MÖLLENDORFF (Editor), *Handbuch der mikroskopisch. Anatomie des Menschen,* Vol. IV, Part 2, pp. 94–98.

SCHARRER, B. 1965. Recent progress in the study of neuroendocrine mechanisms in insects. Arch. Anat. Microscop. Morph. Exper., **54:** 331–342.

SCHARRER, E. 1944. The blood vessels of the nervous tissue. Quart. Rev. Biol., **19:** 308–318.

SCHARRER, E., AND SCHARRER, B. 1940. Secretory cells within the hypothalamus. A. Res. Nerv. & Ment. Dis. Proc., **20:** 170–194.

SCHARRER, E., AND SCHARRER, B. 1945. Neurosecretion. Physiol. Rev., **25:** 171–181.

SCHEIBEL, M. E., AND SCHEIBEL, A. B. 1954. Observations on the intracortical relations of the climbing fibers of the cerebellum. A Golgi study. J. Comp. Neurol., **101:** 733–764.

SCHEIBEL, M. E., AND SCHEIBEL, A. B. 1958. Structural substrates for integrative patterns in the brain stem reticular core. In H. H. JASPERS *ET AL.* (Editors), *Reticular Formation of the Brain.* Little, Brown & Company, Boston. Ch. 2, pp. 31–55.

SCHEIBEL, M. E., AND SCHEIBEL, A. B. 1958a. Neurons and neuroglial cells as seen with the light microscope. In W. F. WINDLE (Editor), *Biology of Neuroglia.* Charles C Thomas, Publisher, Springfield, Ill., pp. 5–23.

SCHEIBEL, M. E., AND SCHEIBEL, A. B. 1966. The organization of the nucleus reticularis thalami: A Golgi study. Brain Res., **1:** 43–62.

SCHEIBEL, M. E., AND SCHEIBEL, A. B. 1966a. The organization of the ventral anterior nucleus of the thalamus. A Golgi study. Brain Res., **1:** 250–268.

SCHERRER, H., AND HERNÁNDEZ-PÉON, R. 1955. Inhibitory influence of reticular formation upon synaptic transmission in gracilis nucleus. Fed. Proc., **14:** 132.

SCHLAG, J., AND FAIDLERBE, J. 1961. Recruiting responses in the brain stem reticular formation. Arch. ital. biol., **99:** 135–162.

SCHLESINGER, B. 1939. Venous drainage of the brain, with special reference to Galenic system. Brain, **62:** 274–291.

SCHMIDT, C. F. 1960. Central nervous system circulation, fluids and barriers—introduction. In J. FIELD (Editor), *Handbook of Physiology,* Section I, Vol. III. American Physiological Society, Washington, D. C., Ch. 70, 1745–1760.

SCHMITT, F. O., BEAR, R. S., AND PALMER, K. J. 1941. X-ray diffraction studies on the structure of the nerve myelin sheath. J. Cell. & Comp. Physiol., **18:** 31–42.

SCHNITZLEIN, H. N., HOFFMAN, H. H., HAMLETT, D. M., AND HOWELL, E. M. 1963. A study of the sacral parasympathetic nucleus. J. Comp. Neurol., **120:** 477–493.

SCHREINER, L. H., AND KLING, A. 1953. Behavior changes following rhinencephalic injury in cat. J. Neurophysiol., **16:** 643–659.

SCHREINER, L. H., AND KLING, A. 1954. Effects of castration on hypersexual behavior induced by rhinencephalic injury in cat. Arch. Neurol. & Psychiat., **72:** 180–186.

SCHÜTZ, H. 1891. Anatomische Untersuchungen über den Faserverlauf im zentralen Höhlengrau und den Nervenfaserschwund in demselben bei der progressiven Paralyse der Irren. Arch. Psychiat., **22:** 527–587.

SCHULTZ, R. L., MAYNARD, E. A., AND PEASE, D. C. 1957. Electron microscopy of neurons and neuroglia of cerebral cortex and corpus callosum. Am. J. Anat., **100:** 369–407.

SCHULTZ, R. L., MAYNARD, E. A., AND PEASE, D. C. 1957. Electron microscopy of neurons and neuroglia of cerebral cortex and corpus callosum. Am. J. Anat., **100:** 369–408.

SCHULTZ, R. L., AND PEASE, D. C. 1959. Cicatrix formation in rat cerebral cortex as revealed by electron microscopy. Am. J. Path., **35:** 1017–1041.

SCHWARTZ, P., AND FINK, L. 1926. Morphologie und Entstehung der geburtstraumatischen Blutungen im Gehirn und Schädel des Neugeborenen. Ztschr. Kinder., **40:** 427–474.

SCHWYN, R. C. 1967. An autoradiographic study of satellite cells in autonomic ganglia. Am. J. Anat., **121:** 727–740.

SCOTT, D., AND CLEMENTE, C. D. 1952. Mechanism of spinal cord regeneration in the cat. Fed. Proc., **11:** 143–144.

SCOTT, D., JR. 1963. Influence of nerve growth factor on spinal regeneration in kittens. Anat. Rec., **145:** 283.

SCOVILLE, W. B. 1954. Neurophysiological symposium; limbic lobe in man. J. Neurosurg., **11:** 64–66.

SCOVILLE, W. B., AND MILNER, B. 1957. Loss of recent memory after bilateral hippocampal lesions. J. Neurol. Neurosurg. & Psychiat., **20:** 11–21.

SEDDON, H. J. 1943. Three types of nerve injury. Brain, **66:** 237–288.

SHANTHAVEERAPPA, T. R., AND BOURNE, G. H. 1962. The 'perineural epithelium', a metabolically active, continuous, protoplasmic cell barrier surrounding peripheral nerve fasciculi. J. Anat., **96:** 527–537.

SHANTHAVEERAPPA, T. R., AND BOURNE, G. H. 1964. Arachnoid villi in the optic nerve of man and the monkey. Exper. Eye Res., **3:** 31–35.

SHANTHAVEERAPPA, T. R., AND BOURNE, G. H. 1966.

Perineural epithelium: A new concept of its role in the integrity of the peripheral nervous system. Science, **154:** 1464–1467.

SHANZER, S., WAGMAN, I. H., AND BENDER, M. B. 1959. Further observations on the median longitudinal fasciculus. Tr. Am. Neurol. A., 14–17.

SHEALY, C. N., AND PEELE, T. L. 1957. Studies on amygdaloid nucleus of cat. J. Neurophysiol., **20:** 125–139.

SHEEHAN, D. 1941. Spinal autonomic outflows in man and monkey. J. Comp. Neurol., **75:** 341–370.

SHEEHAN, D. 1941a. The autonomic nervous system. Ann. Rev. Physiol., **3:** 399–448.

SHENKIN, H. A., AND LEWEY, F. H. 1944. Taste aura preceding convulsions in a lesion of the parietal operculum. J. Nerv. & Ment. Dis., **100:** 352–354.

SHEPS, J. G. 1945. The nuclear configuration and cortical connections of the human thalamus. J. Comp. Neurol., **83:** 1–56.

SHERRINGTON, C. S. 1893. Experiments in examination of the peripheral distribution of the fibers of the posterior roots of some spinal nerves. Phil. Tr. Roy. Soc. London, ser. B, **184b:** 641–763.

SHERRINGTON, C. S. 1893a. Note on the spinal portion of some ascending degenerations. J. Physiol., **14:** 255–302.

SHERRINGTON, C. S. 1898. Decerebrate rigidity, and reflex coordination of movements. J. Physiol., **22:** 319–332.

SHERRINGTON, C. S. 1906. *The Integrative Action of the Nervous System.* Charles Scribner's Sons, New York. (Reprinted, Yale University Press, New Haven, 1947.)

SHIMAMOTO, T., AND VERZEANO, M. 1954. Relations between caudate and diffusely projecting thalamic nuclei. J. Neurophysiol., **17:** 278–288.

SHOWERS, M. J. C. 1958. Correlation of medial thalamic nuclear activity with cortical and subcortical neuronal arc. J. Comp. Neurol., **109:** 261–315.

SHOWERS, M. J. C. 1959. The cingulate gyrus: additional motor area and cortical autonomic regulator. J. Comp. Neurol., **112:** 231–301.

SHOWERS, M. J. C., AND CROSBY, E. C. 1958. Somatic and visceral responses from cingulate gyrus. Neurology, **8:** 561–565.

SHRIVER, J. E., FRASER, R. A. R., AND CARPENTER, M. B. 1968. The organization of pallidosubthalamic projections in the rhesus monkey. Anat. Rec., **160:** 428.

SHRIVER, J. E., STEIN, B. M., AND CARPENTER, M. B. 1968. Central projections of spinal dorsal roots in the monkey. I. Cervical and upper thoracic dorsal roots. Am. J. Anat., **123:** 27–74.

SHUANGSHOTI, S., AND NETSKY, M. G. 1966. Histo-

genesis of choroid plexus in man. J. Comp. Neurol., **118:** 283–316.

SIMPSON, D. A. 1952. The projection of the pulvinar to the temporal lobe. J. Anat., **86:** 20–28.

SINCLAIR, D. C. 1967. *Cutaneous Sensation.* Oxford University Press, New York, pp. 35–80.

SINCLAIR, D. C., WEDDELL, G., AND FEINDEL, W. H. 1948. Referred pain and associated phenomena. Brain, **71:** 184–211.

SJÖQVIST, O. 1938. Studies on pain conduction in the trigeminal nerve. A contribution to surgical treatment of facial pain. Acta psychiat. neurol., Scandinav. **17:** (suppl.) 1–139.

SLOAN, N., AND JASPER, H. 1950. The identity of spreading depression and "suppression." Electroencephalog. & Clin. Neurophysiol., **2:** 59–78.

SMIRNOW, A. 1895. Über die sensiblen Nervenendigungen im Herzen bei Amphibien und Säugetieren. Anat. Anz., **10:** 737–749.

SMITH, C. A., RASMUSSEN, G. L. 1963. Recent observations on the olivo-cochlear bundle. Ann. Otol., Rhin. & Laryng., **72:** 489–507.

SMITH, M. C. 1951. The use of Marchi staining in the later stages of human tract degeneration. J. Neurol. Neurosurg. & Psychiat., **14:** 222–225.

SMITH, M. C. 1956. The recognition and prevention of artefacts of the Marchi method. J. Neurol. Neurosurg. & Psychiat., **19:** 74–83.

SMITH, M. C. 1957. The anatomy of the spino-cerebellar fibers in man. I. The course of the fibers in the spinal cord and brain stem. J. Comp. Neurol., **108:** 285–352.

SMITH, M. C. 1961. The anatomy of the spino-cerebellar fibers in man. II. The distribution of the fibers in the cerebellum. J. Comp. Neurol., **117:** 329–354.

SMITH, O. A., JR., AND CLARKE, N. P. 1964. Central autonomic pathways. A study in functional neuroanatomy. J. Comp. Neurol., **122:** 399–406.

SMITH, W. K. 1945. The functional significance of the rostral cingular cortex as revealed by its responses to electrical excitation. J. Neurophysiol., **8:** 241–255.

SMYTH, G. E. 1939. The systemization and central connections of the spinal tract and nucleus of the trigeminal nerve. Brain, **62:** 41–87.

SNIDER, R. S. 1936. Alterations which occur in mossy terminals of the cerebellum following transection of the brachium pontis. J. Comp. Neurol., **64:** 417–435.

SNIDER, R. S. 1950. Recent contributions to the anatomy and physiology of the cerebellum. Arch. Neurol. & Psychiat., **64:** 196–219.

SNIDER, R. S., AND ELDRED, E. 1952. Cerebro-cerebellar relationships in the monkey. J. Neurophysiol., **15:** 27–40.

SNIDER, R. S., STOWELL, A. 1944. Receiving areas

of the tactile, auditory, and visual systems in the cerebellum. J. Neurophysiol., **7:** 331–357.

SNYDER, M., HALL, W. C., AND DIAMOND, I. T. 1966. Vision in tree shrews after removal of striate cortex. Psychoneurol. Sc., **6:** 243–244.

SOKOLOFF, L. 1960. Metabolism in the central nervous system in vivo. In J. FIELD (Editor), *Handbook of Physiology*, Section I, Vol. III. American Physiological Society, Washington, D. C., Ch. 77, pp. 1845–1864.

SOSA, J. M., AND DEZORRILLA, N. B. 1966. Spinal ganglion cytological responses to axon and to dendrite sectioning. Acta anat., **65:** 236–255.

SOTELO, C. 1967. Cerebellar neuroglia: morphological and histochemical aspects. In C. A. FOX AND R. S. SNIDER (Editors), *The Cerebellum*. *Progress in Brain Research*, Vol. 25. Elsevier Publishing Company, Amsterdam, pp. 226–250.

SPEIDEL, C. G. 1919. Gland cells of internal secretion in the spinal cord of the skates. Carnegie Inst. Wash. Publ., **13:** 1–31.

SPERRY, R. W. 1961. Cerebral organization and behavior. Science, **133:** 1749–1757.

SPERRY, R. W. 1962. Some general aspects of interhemispheric integration. In V. B. MOUNTCASTLE (Editor), *Interhemispheric Relations and Cerebral Dominance*. Johns Hopkins Press, Baltimore. Ch. 3, pp. 43–49.

SPIEGEL, E. A. 1929. Experimentalstudien am Nervensystem: XV. Der Mechanismus des labyrinthären Nystagmus. Ztschr. Hals- Nasen- u. Ohrenh., **25:** 200–217.

SPIEGEL, E. A., AND SOMMER, I. 1944. *Neurology of the Eye, Ear, Nose and Throat*. Grune and Stratton, Inc., New York, 667 pp.

SPIEGEL, E. A., KLETZKIN, M., AND SZEKELY, E. G. 1954. Pain reactions upon stimulation of the tectum mesencephali. J. Neuropath. & Exper. Neurol., **13:** 212–220.

SPIEGEL, E. A., SZEKELY, E. G., AND BAKER, W. W. 1957. Electrographic study of thalamic impulses to the striatum and pallidum. Electroencephalog. & Clin. Neurophysiol., **9:** 291–299.

SPIEGEL, E. A., AND WYCIS, H. T. 1950. Pallido-thalamotomy in chorea. Arch. Neurol. & Psychiat., **64:** 295–296.

SPIEGEL, E. A., AND WYCIS, H. T. 1954. Ansotomy in paralysis agitans. Arch. Neurol. & Psychiat., **71:** 598–614.

SPIEGEL, E. A., AND WYCIS, H. T. 1958. Pallido-ansotomy: anatomic-physiologic foundation and histopathologic control. In W. S. FIELDS (Editor), *Pathogenesis and Treatment of Parkinsonism*. Charles C Thomas, Publisher, Springfield, Ill. Ch. 3, pp. 86–105.

SPILLER, W. G. 1924. Ophthalmoplegia internuclearis anterior; a case with necropsy. Brain, **47:** 345–357.

SPRAGUE, J. M. 1951. Motor and propriospinal cells in the thoracic and lumbar ventral horn of the Rhesus monkey. J. Comp. Neurol., **95:** 103–124.

SPRAGUE, J. M. 1958. The distribution of dorsal root fibers on motor cells in the lumbosacral spinal cord of the cat, and the site of excitatory and inhibitory terminals in monosynaptic pathways. Proc. Roy. Soc., London, ser. B, **149:** 534–556.

SPRAGUE, J. M., AND CHAMBERS, W. W. 1953. Regulation of posture in intact and decerebrate cat. I. Cerebellum, reticular formation, vestibular nuclei. J. Neurophysiol., **16:** 451–463.

SPRAGUE, J. M., AND CHAMBERS, W. W. 1954. Control of posture by reticular formation and cerebellum in the intact, anesthetized, unanesthetized and in the decerebrated cat. Am. J. Physiol., **176:** 52–64.

SPRAGUE, J. M., AND HA, H. 1964. The terminal fields of dorsal root fibers in the lumbosacral spinal cord of the cat, and the dendritic organization of the motor nuclei. In J. C. ECCLES AND J. P. SCHADÉ (Editors), *Organization of the Spinal Cord, Progress in Brain Research*, Vol. 2. Elsevier Publishing Company, Amsterdam, pp. 120–152.

SPRAGUE, J. M., LEVITT, M., ROBSON, K., LIU, C. N., STELLER, E., AND CHAMBERS, W. W. 1963. A neuroanatomical and behavioral analysis of the syndromes resulting from midbrain lemniscal and reticular lesions in the cat. Arch. ital. biol., **101:** 225–295.

SPRAGUE, J. M., AND MEIKLE, T. H., JR. 1965. The role of the superior colliculus in visually guided behavior. Exper. Neurol., **11:** 115–146.

STAAL, A. 1961. *Subcortical Projections on the Spinal Gray Matter of the Cat*. Koninkl. Druk., Lankhout-Immig N. V., The Hague, 164 pp.

STARZL, T. E., AND MAGOUN, H. W. 1951. Organization of the diffuse thalamic projection system. J. Neurophysiol., **14:** 133–146.

STARZL, T. E., TAYLOR, C. W., AND MAGOUN, H. W. 1951. Ascending conduction in reticular activating system, with special reference to the diencephalon. J. Neurophysiol., **14:** 461–477.

STARZL, T. E., TAYLOR, C. W., AND MAGOUN, H. W. 1951a. Collateral afferent excitation of the reticular formation of the brain stem. J. Neurophysiol., **14:** 479–496.

STARZL, T. E., AND WHITLOCK, D. G. 1952. Diffuse thalamic projection system in monkey. J. Neurophysiol., **15:** 449–468.

STEIN, B. M., AND CARPENTER, M. B. 1965. Effects of dorsal rhizotomy upon subthalamic dyskinesia in the monkey. Arch. Neurol., **13:** 567–583.

STEIN, B. M., AND CARPENTER, M. B. 1967. Central projections of portions of the vestibular ganglia innervating specific parts of the labyrinth in the rhesus monkey. Am. J. Anat., **120:** 281–318.

STENGEL, E. 1926. Über den Ursprung der Nervenfasern der Neurohypophyse im Zwischenhirn. Arb. Neurol. Inst. Wiener Univ., **28**: 25–37.

STENSAAS, L. J. 1968. The development of hippocampal and dorsolateral pallial regions of the cerebral hemisphere in fetal rabbits. J. Comp. Neurol., **132**: 93–108.

STEPIEN, L. S., CORDEAU, J. P., AND RASMUSSEN, T. 1960. The effect of temporal lobe and hippocampal lesions on auditory and visual recent memory in monkeys. Brain, **83**: 470–489.

STERN, G. 1966. The effects of lesions in the substantia nigra. Brain, **89**: 449–478.

STERN, K. 1938. Note on the nucleus ruber magnocellularis and its efferent pathway in man. Brain, **61**: 284–289.

STEVENSON, J. A. F. 1949. Effects of hypothalamic lesions on water and energy metabolism in the rat. Recent Progr. Hormone Res., **4**: 363–394.

STOOKEY, B., AND SCARFF, J. 1943. Injuries of peripheral nerves. In *Neurosurgery and Thoracic Surgery*, National Research Council, Committee on Surgery. W. B. Saunders Company, Philadelphia. pp. 81–184.

STOPFORD, J. S. B. 1915. The arteries of the pons and medulla oblongata. Part I. J. Anat. & Physiol., **50**: 131–164.

STOPFORD, J. S. B. 1916. The arteries of the pons and medulla oblongata. Part II. J. Anat. & Physiol., **51**: 255–280.

STOTLER, W. A. 1953. An experimental study of the cells and connections of the superior olivary complex of the cat. J. Comp. Neurol., **98**: 401–423.

STRATFORD, J. 1954. Cortico-thalamic connections from gyrus proreus and first and second somatic sensory areas of the cat. J. Comp. Neurol., **100**: 1–14.

STRONG, O. S. 1915. A case of unilateral cerebellar agenesia. J. Comp. Neurol., **25**: 361–391.

SUGAR, O., AMADOR, L. V., AND GRIPONISSIOTES, B. 1950. Corticocortical connections of the walls of the superior temporal sulcus in the monkey (*Macaca mulatta*). J. Neuropath. & Exper. Neurol., **9**: 179–185.

SUGAR, O., FRENCH, J. D., AND CHUSID, J. G. 1948. Corticocortical connections of the superior surface of the temporal operculum in the monkey (*Macaca mulatta*). J. Neurophysiol., **11**: 175–184.

SUGAR, O., AND GERARD, R. W. 1940. Spinal cord regeneration in the rat. J. Neurophysiol., **3**: 1–19.

SUH, T. H., AND ALEXANDER, L. 1939. Vascular system of the human spinal cord. Arch. Neurol. & Psychiat., **41**: 659–677.

SULKIN, N. M. 1953. Histochemical studies of the pigments in the human autonomic ganglion cells. J. Gerontol., **8**: 435–445.

SULKIN, N. M., AND SRIVANIJ, P. 1960. The experimental production of senile pigments in the nerve cells of young rats. J. Gerontol., **15**: 2–9.

SUNDERLAND, S. 1950. Capacity of reinnervated muscles to function efficiently after prolonged denervation. Arch. Neurol. & Psychiat., **64**: 755–771.

SUNDERLAND, S. 1952. Factors influencing the course of regeneration and the quality of the recovery after nerve suture. Brain, **75**: 19–54.

SUNDERLAND, S., AND BRADLEY, K. C. 1950. Endoneurial tube shrinkage in the distal segment of a severed nerve. J. Comp. Neurol., **93**: 411–420.

SWANN, H. G. 1934. The function of the brain in olfaction. II. The results of destruction of olfactory and other nervous structures upon the discrimination of odors. J. Comp. Neurol., **59**: 175–201.

SWANN, H. G. 1935. The function of the brain in olfaction. III. The effects of large cortical lesions on olfactory discrimination. Am. J. Physiol., **111**: 257–262.

SWEET, W. H., TALLAND, G. A., AND ERVIN, F. R. 1959. Loss of recent memory following section of the fornix. Tr. Am. Neurol., **84**: 76–82.

SYMONDS, C. 1966. Disorders of memory. Brain, **89**: 625–644.

SZABO, J. 1962. Topical distribution of the striatal efferents in the monkey. Exper. Neurol., **5**: 21–36.

SZABO, J. 1967. The efferent projections of the putamen in the monkey. Exper. Neurol. **19**: 463–476.

SZEKELY, E. G. 1957. Cortical recruiting on thalamic stimulation after elimination of the pallidum. Confinia neurol., **17**: 243–249.

SZENTÁGOTHAI, J. 1950. The elementary vestibuloocular reflex arc. J. Neurophysiol., **13**: 395–407.

SZENTÁGOTHAI, J. 1950a. Recherches experimentales sur les voies oculogyres. Semaine hôp. Paris, **26**: 2989–2995.

SZENTÁGOTHAI, J. 1964. Neuronal and synaptic arrangement in the substantia gelatinosa Rolandi. J. Comp. Neurol., **122**: 219–239.

SZENTÁGOTHAI-SCHIMERT, J. 1941. Die Endigungsweise der absteigenden Rückenmarksbahnen. Ztschr. Anat., **111**: 322–330.

SZENTÁGOTHAI, J., AND ALBERT, A. 1955. The synaptology of Clarke's column. Acta morphol. hungaricae, **5**: 43–51.

SZENTÁGOTHAI, J., AND RAJKOVITS, K. 1959. Über den Ursprung der Kletterfasern des Kleinhirn. Ztschr. Anat. Entwicklungsgesch., **121**: 130–141.

TABER, E. 1961. The cytoarchitecture of the brain stem of the cat. I. Brain stem nuclei of cat. J. Comp. Neurol., **116**: 27–70.

TAIT, J., AND McNALLY, W. J. 1925. Rotation and

acceleration experiments, mainly on frogs. Am. J. Physiol., **75:** 140–154.

TALAIRACH, J., PAILLAS, J. E., AND DAVID, M. 1950. Dyskinésie de type hémiballique traitée par cortectomie frontale limitée, puis par coagulation de l'anse lenticulaire et de la portion interne du globus pallidus. Rev. neurol., **83:** 440–451.

TALBOT, S. A., AND MARSHALL, W. H. 1941. Physiological studies on neuronal mechanisms of visual localization and discrimination. Am. J. Ophth., **24:** 1255–1263.

TALBOT, S. A. 1942. A lateral localization in the cat's visual cortex. Fed. Proc., **1:** 84.

TARKHAN, A. A., AND ABD-EL-MALEK, S. 1950. On the presence of sensory nerve cells on the hypoglossal nerve. J. Comp. Neurol., **93:** 219–228.

TASAKI, I. 1954. Nerve impulses in individual auditory nerve fibers of guinea pig. J. Neurophysiol., **17:** 97–122.

TASAKI, I., AND CHANG, J. J. 1958. Electric response of glia cell in cat brain. Science, **128:** 1209–1210.

TAUB, A. 1964. Local, segmental and supraspinal interaction with a dorsolateral spinal cutaneous afferent system. Exper. Neurol., **10:** 357–374.

TAUB, A., AND BISHOP, P. O. 1965. The spinocervical tract: Dorsal column linkage, conduction velocity, primary afferent spectrum. Exper. Neurol., **13:** 1–21.

TAVERAS, J. 1961. Angiographic observation in occlusive cerebrovascular disease. Neurology, **11:** 86–90.

TAVERAS, J. M., AND WOOD, E. H. 1964. *Diagnostic Neuroradiology.* Williams and Wilkins Company, Baltimore, 960 pp.

TAYLOR, J., GREENFIELD, J. G., AND MARTIN, J. P. 1922. Two cases of syringomyelia and syringobulbia, observed clinically over many years and examined pathologically. Brain, **45:** 323–356.

TELLO, J. F. 1922. Die Entstehungen der motorischen und sensiblen Nervenendigungen. Ztschr. ges. Anat., **64:** 348–440.

TENNYSON, V. M. 1962. Electron microscopic observations of the development of the neuroblast in the rabbit embryo. In S. S. BREESE (Editor), *Fifth International Congress for Electron Microscopy,* Vol. II. (Philadelphia), Academic Press, Inc., New York, N8.

TENNYSON, V. M. 1965. Electron microscopic study of the developing neuroblast of the dorsal root ganglion of the rabbit embryo. J. Comp. Neurol., **124:** 267–318.

TENNYSON, V. M., AND PAPPAS, G. D. 1961. Electron microscope studies of the developing telencephalic choroid plexus in normal and hydrocephalic rabbits. In W. FIELDS AND M. DESMOND (Editors), *Disorders of the Developing Nervous System.* Charles C Thomas, Publisher, Springfield, Ill., Ch. 12, pp. 267–318.

TENNYSON, V. M., AND PAPPAS, G. D. 1964. Fine structure of the developing telencephalic and myelencephalic choroid plexus of the rabbit. J. Comp. Neurol., **123:** 379–412.

TENNYSON, V. M., AND PAPPAS, G. B. 1965. Some aspects of the fine structure of the ependymal lining. In J. MINCKLER (Editor) *Neuropathology.* McGraw-Hill Book Company, New York.

TENNYSON, V. M., AND PAPPAS, G. D. 1968. The fine structure of the choroid plexus: adult and developmental stages. In A. LAJTHA AND D. H. FORD (Editors), *Brain Barrier Systems. Progress in Brain Research.* Vol. 29. Elsevier Publishing Company, Amsterdam, pp. 63–86.

TERZIAN, H. 1958. Observations on the clinical symptomatology of bilateral partial or total removal of the temporal lobe in man. In M. BALDWIN AND P. BAILEY (Editors). *Temporal Lobe Epilepsy.* Charles C Thomas, Publisher, Springfield, Ill., pp. 510–529.

TERZIAN, H., AND ORE, G. D. 1955. Syndrome of Klüver and Bucy reproduced in man by bilateral removal of the temporal lobes. Neurology, **5:** 373–380.

TERZUOLO, C., AND TERZIAN, H. 1953. Cerebellar increase of postural tonus after deafferentation and labyrinthectomy. J. Neurophysiol., **16:** 551–561.

THAEMERT, J. C. 1963. The ultrastructure and disposition of vesiculated nerve processes in smooth muscle. J. Cell Biol., **16:** 361–377.

THAEMERT, J. C. 1966. Ultrastructural interrelationships of nerve processes and smooth muscle cells in three dimensions. J. Cell Biol., **28:** 37–49.

THAEMERT, J. C. 1966a. Ultrastructure of cardiac muscle and nerve contiguities. J. Cell Biol., **29:** 156–162.

THIÉBLOT, L. 1965. Physiology of the pineal body. In J. ARIENS KAPPERS AND J. P. SCHADÉ (Editors), *Structure and Function of the Epiphysis Cerebri, Progress in Brain Research* Vol. 10. Elsevier Publishing Company, Amsterdam, pp. 479–488.

THOMAS, C. E., AND COMBS, C. M. 1962. Spinal cord segments. A. Gross structure in the adult cat. Am. J. Anat., **110:** 37–48.

THOMAS, C. E., AND COMBS, G. M. 1965. Spinal cord segments. B. Gross structure in the adult monkey. Am. J. Anat., **116:** 205–216.

THOMAS, D. M., KAUFMAN, R. P., SPRAGUE, J. M. AND CHAMBERS, W. W. 1956. Experimental studies of the vermal cerebellar projections in the brain stem of the cat (fastigiobulbar tract). J. Anat., **90:** 371–385.

THOMAS, P. K. 1963. The connective tissue of peripheral nerve: an electron microscope study. J. Anat., **97:** 35–44.

THOMPSON, J. M., WOOLSEY, C. N., AND TALBOT, S. A. 1950. Visual areas I and II of cerebral cortex of rabbit. J. Neurophysiol., **13:** 277–288.

THOMPSON, R., AND HAWKINS, W. F. 1961. Memory unaffected by mammillary body lesions in the rat. Exper. Neurol., **3**: 189–196.

THOMSON, A. F., AND WALKER, A. E. 1951. Behavioral alterations following lesions of the medial surface of the temporal lobe. A. M. A. Arch. Neurol. & Psychiat., **65**: 251–252.

TONCRAY, J. E., AND KRIEG, W. J. S. 1946. The nuclei of the human thalamus. A comparative approach. J. Comp. Neurol., **85**: 421–459.

TORVIK, A. 1956. Afferent connections to the sensory trigeminal nuclei, the nucleus of the solitary tract and adjacent structures. An experimental study in the rat. J. Comp. Neurol., **106**: 51–142.

TORVIK, A. 1957. The ascending fibers from the main trigeminal sensory nucleus. An experimental study in the cat. Am. J. Anat., **100**: 1–15.

TORVIK, A., AND BRODAL, A. 1957. The origin of reticulospinal fibers in the cat. An experimental study. Anat. Rec., **128**: 113–137.

TOWER, D. B. 1960. Chemical architecture of the central nervous system. In J. FIELD (Editor), *Handbook of Physiology*, Section I, Vol. III. American Physiological Society, Washington, D. C., pp. 1793–1813.

TOWER, S. S. 1936. Extrapyramidal action from the cat's cerebral cortex: motor and inhibitory. Brain, **59**: 408–444.

TOWER, S. S. 1940. Pyramidal lesion in the monkey. Brain, **63**: 36–90.

TOWER, S. S. 1949. The pyramidal tract. In P. C. BUCY (Editor), *The Precentral Motor Cortex*, Ed. 2. University of Illinois Press, Urbana, Ill. Ch. 6, pp. 149–172.

TOZER, F. M., AND SHERRINGTON, C. S. 1910. Receptors and afferents of the third, fourth and sixth cranial nerves. Proc. Roy. Soc. London, ser. B, **82**: 450–457.

TRAVIS, A. M. 1955. Neurological deficiencies after ablation of the precentral motor area in *Macaca mulatta*. Brain, **78**: 155–173.

TRAVIS, A. M. 1955a. Neurological deficiencies following supplementary motor area lesions in *Macaca mulatta*. Brain, **78**: 174–198.

TRETIAKOFF, C. 1919. Contribution à l'étude de l'anatomopathologie du locus niger de Sommering. Thèse, Université de Paris, Number 293. Jouve et Cie, Paris.

TRUEX, R. C. 1939. Observations on the chicken Gasserian ganglion with special reference to the bipolar neurons. J. Comp. Neurol., **71**: 473–486.

TRUEX, R. C. 1940. Morphological alterations in the Gasserian ganglion cells and their association with senescence in man. Am. J. Path., **16**: 255–268.

TRUEX, R. C. 1941. Degenerate versus multipolar neurons in sensory ganglia. Am. J. Path., **17**: 211–218.

TRUEX, R. C. 1951. The sympathetic ganglions of hypertensive patients. Arch. Path., **51**: 186–191.

TRUEX, R. C., AND KELLNER, C. E. 1948. *Detailed Atlas of the Head and Neck*. Oxford University Press, New York.

TRUEX, R. C., SCOTT, J. C., LONG, D. M., AND SMYTHE, M. Q. 1955. Effect of vagus nerves on heart rate of young dogs. An anatomic-physiologic study. Anat. Rec., **123**: 201–226.

TRUEX, R. C., AND TAYLOR, M. 1968. Gray matter lamination of the human spinal cord. Anat. Rec., **160**: 502.

TSCHIRGI, R. D. 1960. Chemical environment of the central nervous system. In J. FIELD (Editor), *Handbook of Physiology*, Section I, Vol. III. American Physiological Society, Washington, D. C., Ch. 78, pp. 1865–1890.

TSUKAHARA, N., TOYAMA, K., AND KOSAKA, K. 1964. Intracellular recorded responses of the red nucleus neurons during antidromic and orthodromic activation. Experientia, **20**: 632–637.

TWITCHELL, T. E. 1954. Sensory factors in purposive movement. J. Neurophysiol., **17**: 239–252.

TYLER, D. B., AND BARD, P. 1949. Motion sickness. Physiol. Rev., **29**: 311–369.

UZMAN, B. G., AND NOGUEIRA-GRAF, G. 1957. Electron microscope studies of the formation of nodes of Ranvier in mouse sciatic nerves. J. Biophys. & Biochem. Cytol., **3**: 589–598.

VALENSTEIN, E. S., AND NAUTA, W. J. H. 1959. A comparison of the distribution of the fornix system in the rat, guinea pig, cat and monkey. J. Comp. Neurol., **113**: 337–363.

VALVERDE, F. 1965. *Studies on the Piriform Lobe*. Harvard University Press, Cambridge, 138 pp.

VERHAART, W. J. C. 1935. Die aberrierenden Pyramidenfasern bei Menschen und Affen. Schweiz. Arch. Neurol. u. Psychiat. **36**: 170–190.

VERHAART, W. J. C. 1950. Fiber analysis of the basal ganglia. J. Comp. Neurol., **93**: 425–440.

VERHAART, W. J. C. 1954. The tractus trigeminalis of Wallenberg. Acta psychiat. et. neurol. scandinav., **29**: 269–279.

VERHAART, W. J. C., AND KENNARD, M. A. 1940. Corticofugal degeneration following thermocoagulation of areas 4, 6, and 4S in *Macaca mulatta*. J. Anat., **74**: 239–254.

VERHAART, W. J. C., AND KRAMER, W. 1952. The uncrossed pyramidal tract. Acta psychiat. et neurol. scandinav., **27**: 181–200.

VERSTEEGH, C. 1927. Ergebnisse partieller Labyrinthexstirpation bei Kaninchen. Acta otolaryng., **11**: 393–408.

VERZEANO, M., LINDSLEY, D. B., AND MAGOUN, H. W.
1953. Nature of recruiting response. J. Neurophysiol., 16: 183–195.

VICTOR, M. 1964. Functions of memory and learning in man and their relationship to lesions in the
temporal lobe and diencephalon. In M. A. B.
BRAZIER (Editor), Brain Function. RNA in Brain
Function; Memory and Learning, Vol. III. Amer-
can Institute of Biological Sciences, Washington,
D. C.

VICTOR, M., ANGEVINE, J. B., MANCALL, E. L., AND
FISHER, C. M. 1961. Memory loss with lesions
of hippocampal formation. Arch. Neurol.,
5: 244–263.

VIZOSO, A. D., AND YOUNG, J. Z. 1948. Internode
length and fibre diameter in developing and regenerating nerves. J. Anat., 82: 110–134.

VOGT, C., AND VOGT, O. 1919. Allgemeine Ergebnisse unserer Hirnforschung. Vierte Mitteilung: Die physiologische Bedeutung der archi-
tektonischen Rindenreizungen. J. Psychol. u.
Neurol., 25: 279–462.

VONEIDA, T. J. 1960. An experimental study of the
course and destination of fibers arising in the
head of caudate nucleus in the cat and monkey.
J. Comp. Neurol., 115: 75–87.

VOSS, H. 1956. Zahl und Anordnung der Muskel-
spindeln in den oberen Zungenbeinmuskeln,
im M. trapezius und M. latissimus dorsi. Anat.
Anz., 103: 443–446.

VRAA-JENSEN, G. F. 1942. The Major Nucleus of
the Facial Nerve, with a Survey of the Efferent
Innervation of the Facial Muscles. Ejnar
Munksgaard, Copenhagen. Thesis, 157 pp.

WAELSCH, H. 1957. Editor, Ultrastructure and
Cellular Chemistry of Neural Tissue. Sym-
posium, American Neurological Society and
Medical School, Western Reserve University.
Paul B. Hoeber, Inc., New York, 249 pp.

WAKSMAN, B. H. 1961. Experimental study of
diphtheritic polyneuritis in the rabbit and guinea
pig. III. The blood nerve barrier in the rabbit. J. Neuropath & Exp. Neurol., 20: 35–77.

WALBERG, F. 1952. Lateral reticular nucleus in
medulla oblongata in mammals; comparative-
anatomical study. J. Comp. Neurol., 96: 283–
343.

WALBERG, F. 1956. Descending connections to the
inferior olive. An experimental study in the cat.
J. Comp. Neurol., 104: 77–173.

WALBERG, F. 1957. Corticofugal fibres to the nuclei of the dorsal columns. An experimental
study in the cat. Brain, 80: 273–287.

WALBERG, F. 1957a. Do the motor nuclei of the
cranial nerves receive corticofugal fibres? An
experimental study in the cat. Brain, 80:
597–605.

WALBERG, F. 1958. On the termination of rubrobulbar fibers. Experimental observations in the
cat. J. Comp. Neurol., 110: 65–73.

WALBERG, F. 1958a. Descending connections to the
lateral reticular nucleus. An experimental study
in the cat. J. Comp. Neurol., 109: 465–504.

WALBERG, F. 1961. Fastigiofugal fibers to the perihypoglossal nuclei in the cat. Exper. Neurol.,
3: 525–541.

WALBERG, F., BOWSHER, D., AND BRODAL, A. 1958.
The termination of primary vestibular fibers
in the vestibular nuclei in the cat. An experimental study with silver methods. J. Comp.
Neurol., 110: 391–419.

WALBERG, F., AND JANSEN, J. 1961. Cerebellar cor-
ticovestibular fibers in the cat. Exper. Neurol.,
3: 32–52.

WALBERG, F., AND POMPEIANO, O. 1960. Fastigiofugal fibers to the lateral reticular nucleus. An
experimental study in the cat. Exper. Neurol.,
2: 40–53.

WALBERG, F., POMPEIANO, O., BRODAL, A., AND JAN-
SEN, J. 1962. The fastigiovestibular projection
in the cat. An experimental study with silver
impregnation methods. J. Comp. Neurol., 118:
49–75.

WALKER, A. E. 1936. An experimental study of the
thalamocortical projection of the macaque monkey. J. Comp. Neurol., 64: 1–39.

WALKER, A. E. 1938. The thalamus of the chimpanzee. IV. Thalamic projections to the cerebral cortex. J. Anat., 73: 37–93.

WALKER, A. E. 1938a. The Primate Thalamus.
University of Chicago Press, Chicago.

WALKER, A. E. 1939. The origin, course and terminations of the secondary pathways of the trigeminal nerve. J. Comp. Neurol.,
71: 59–89.

WALKER, A. E. 1939a. Anatomy, physiology and
surgical considerations of the spinal tract of the
trigeminal nerve. J. Neurophysiol., 2: 234–248.

WALKER, A. E. 1942. Somatotopic localization of
spinothalamic and secondary trigeminal tracts
in mesencephalon. Arch. Neurol. & Psychiat.,
48: 884–889.

WALKER, A. E. 1949. Afferent connections. In P. C.
BUCY (Editor), The Precentral Motor Cortex,
Ed. 2. University of Illinois, Urbana, Ch. 4,
pp. 112–132.

WALKER, A. E. 1959. Normal and pathological
physiology of the thalamus. In G. SCHALTEN-
BRAND AND P. BAILEY (Editors), Introduction to
Stereotaxis with an Atlas of the Human Brain,
Vol. I. Georg Thieme, Stuttgart, pp. 291–330.

WALKER, A. E. 1966. Internal structure and afferent relations of the thalamus. In D. P. PUR-
PURA AND M. D. YAHR (Editors), The Thalamus.
Columbia University Press, New York, pp. 1–
12.

WALKER, A. E., AND FULTON, J. F. 1938. Hemidecortication in chimpanzee, baboon, macaque, potto, cat and coati: A study in encephalization. J. Nerv. & Ment. Dis., **87**: 677–700.

WALKER, A. E., AND WEAVER, T. A., JR. 1942. The topical organization and termination of fibers of the posterior columns in *Macaca mulatta*. J. Comp. Neurol., **76**: 145–158.

WALL, P. D., AND TAUB, A. 1962. Four aspects of the trigeminal nucleus and a paradox. J. Neurophysiol., **25**: 110–126.

WALLENBERG, A. 1905. Die secondären Bahnen aus dem frontalen sensiblen Trigeminus Kerne des Kaninchens. Anat. Anz., **26**: 145–155.

WALLS, G. L. 1942. *The Vertebrate Eye and Its Adaptive Radiation*. Hafner Publishing Company, New York (reprinted 1963).

WALTHER, J. B., AND RASMUSSEN, G. L. 1960. Descending connections of auditory cortex and thalamus of the cat. Fed. Proc., **19**: 291.

WANG, S. C. 1955. Bulbar regulation of cardiovascular activity. In *Proceedings of the Annual Meeting of the Council for High Blood Pressure Research*. American Heart Association, pp. 145–158.

WARD, A. A., JR. 1948. The cingular gyrus: Area 24. J. Neurophysiol., **11**: 13–24.

WARD, A. A., JR., AND MCCULLOCH, W. S. 1947. The projection of the frontal lobe on the hypothalamus. J. Neurophysiol., **10**: 309–314.

WARRINGTON, W. B., AND GRIFFITH, F. 1904. On the cells of the spinal ganglia and on the relationship of their histological structure to axonal distribution. Brain, **27**: 297–326.

WARWICK, R. 1953. Representation of the extraocular muscles in the oculomotor nuclei of the monkey. J. Comp. Neurol., **98**: 449–504.

WARWICK, R. 1954. The ocular parasympathetic nerve supply and its mesencephalic sources. J. Anat., **88**: 71–93.

WARWICK, R. 1955. The so-called nucleus of convergence. Brain, **78**: 92–114.

WATERSTON, D. 1933. Observations on sensation. The sensory functions of the skin for touch and pain. J. Physiol., **77**: 251–275.

WEBSTER, H. D. 1962. Transient, focal accumulation of axonal mitochondria during the early stages of Wallerian degeneration. J. Cell Biol., **12**: 361–384.

WEBSTER, K. E. 1961. Cortico-striate interrelations in the albino rat. J. Anat., **95**: 532–544.

WEBSTER, K. E. 1965. The cortico-striatal projection in the cat. J. Anat., **99**: 329–338.

WEDDELL, G. 1941. The pattern of cutaneous innervation in relation to cutaneous sensibility. J. Anat., **75**: 346–367.

WEDDELL, G., TAYLOR, D. A., AND WILLIAMS, C. M. 1955. Studies on the innervation of skin. III. The patterned arrangement of the spinal sensory nerves to the rabbit ear. J. Anat., **89**: 317–342.

WEED, L. H. 1922. The cerebrospinal fluid. Physiol. Rev., **2**: 171–203.

WEIL, A., AND LASSEK, A. 1929. A quantitative distribution of the pyramidal tract in man. Arch. Neurol. & Psychiat., **22**: 495–510.

WEINBERGER, L. M., AND GRANT, F. C. 1942. Experiences with intramedullary tractotomy. III. Studies in sensation. Arch. Neurol. & Psychiat., **48**: 355–381.

WEISS, P., AND HISCOE, H. B. 1948. Experiments on the mechanism of nerve growth. J. Exper. Zool., **107**: 315–396.

WEISS, P., AND WANG, H. 1936. Neurofibrils in living ganglion cells of the chick, cultivated *in vitro*. Anat. Rec., **67**: 105–117.

WELCH, W. K., AND KENNARD, M. A. 1944. Relation of cerebral cortex to spasticity and flaccidity. J. Neurophysiol., **7**: 255–268.

WELKER, W. I., BENJAMIN, R. M., MILES, R. C., AND WOOLSEY, D. N. 1957. Motor effects of cortical stimulation in squirrel monkey (*Saimiri sciureus*). J. Neurophysiol., **20**: 347–364.

WHEATLEY, M. D. 1944. Hypothalamus and affective behavior in cats. Arch. Neurol. & Psychiat., **52**: 296–316.

WHITE, J. C., OKELBERRY, A. M., AND WHITELAW, G. P. 1936. Vasomotor tonus of the denervated artery. Arch. Neurol. & Psychiat., **36**: 1251–1276.

WHITE, L. E. 1965. Olfactory bulb projections of the rat. Anat. Rec., **152**: 465–480.

WHITFIELD, I. C. 1967. *The Auditory Pathway*. The Williams & Wilkins Company, Baltimore.

WHITLOCK, D. G. 1952. A neurohistological and neurophysiological investigation of the afferent fiber tracts and the receptive areas of the avian cerebellum. J. Comp. Neurol., **97**: 567–636.

WHITLOCK, D. G., AND NAUTA, W. J. H. 1956. Subcortical projections from the temporal neocortex in the *Macaca mulatta*. J. Comp. Neurol., **106**: 183–212.

WHITLOCK, D. G., AND PERL, E. R. 1961. Thalamic projections of spinothalamic pathways in monkey. Exper. Neurol., **3**: 240–255.

WHITTIER, J. R. 1947. Ballism and the subthalamic nucleus (nucleus hypothalamicus; Corpus Luysi). Arch. Neurol. & Psychiat., **58**: 672–692.

WHITTIER, J. R., AND METTLER, F. A. 1949. Studies on the subthalamus of the rhesus monkey. I. Anatomy and fiber connections of the subthalamic nucleus of Luys. J. Comp. Neurol., **90**: 281–317.

WHITTIER, J. R., AND METTLER, F. A. 1949a. Studies on the subthalamus of the rhesus monkey. II. Hyperkinesia and other physiologic effects of subthalamic lesions with special reference to the subthalamic nucleus of Luys. J. Comp. Neurol., **90**: 319–372.

WICHMANN, R. 1900. *Die Rückenmarksnerven und ihre Segmentbezüge*, part 2, Viotto Salle, Berlin, pp. 151–279.

WILSON, S. A. K. 1912. Progressive lenticular degeneration; a familial nervous disease associated with cirrhosis of the liver. Brain, **34**: 295–509.

WILSON, S. A. K. 1914. An experimental research into the anatomy and physiology of the corpus striatum. Brain, **36**: 427–492.

WILSON, S. A. K. 1925. Disorders of motility and muscle tone with special reference to the corpus striatum (Croonian Lectures). Lancet, **2**: 215–291.

WILSON, S. A. K. 1928. *Modern Problems in Neurology*. Edward Arnold and Company, London.

WINDLE, W. F. 1926. Non-bifurcating nerve fibers of the trigeminal nerve. J. Comp. Neurol., **40**: 229–240.

WINDLE, W. F. (Editor), 1955. *Regeneration in the Central Nervous System*. Charles C Thomas, Publisher, Springfield, Ill., 311 pp.

WINDLE, W. F. (Editor). 1957. *New Research Techniques of Neuroanatomy*. Charles C Thomas, Publisher, Springfield, Ill.

WINDLE, W. F. (Editor), 1958. *Biology of Neuroglia*. Charles C Thomas, Publisher, Springfield, Ill., 340 pp.

WINDLE, W. F., AND CHAMBERS, W. W. 1950. Regeneration in the spinal cord of the cat and dog. J. Comp. Neurol., **93**: 241–257.

WINKLER, C. 1918–1933. *Opera omnia*, Vols. 1 to 10. E. F. Bohn, Haarlem.

WINTER, D. L., 1965. N. Gracilis of cat. Functional organization and corticofugal effects. J. Neurophysiol., **28**: 48–70.

WISCHNITZER, S. 1960. The ultrastructure of the nucleus and nucleocytoplasmic relations. Internat. Rev. Cytol., **10**: 137–162.

WISLOCKI, G. B., AND LEDUC, E. 1953. The cytology and histochemistry of the subcommissural organ and Reissner's fibers in rodents. J. Comp. Neurol., **97**: 515–543.

WOLF, G. A., JR. 1941. The ratio of preganglionic neurons to postganglionic neurons in the visceral nervous system. J. Comp. Neurol., **75**: 235–243.

WOLF, G., AND SUTIN, J. 1966. Fiber degeneration after lateral hypothalamic lesions in the rat. J. Comp. Neurol., **127**: 137–156.

WOODBURNE, R. T. 1936. A phylogenetic consideration of the primary and secondary centers and connections of the trigeminal complex in a series of vertebrates. J. Comp. Neurol., **65**: 403–501.

WOODBURNE, R. T., CROSBY, E. C., AND McCOTTER, R. E. 1946. The mammalian midbrain and isthmus regions. Part II. The fiber connections. A. The relations of the tegmentum of the midbrain with the basal ganglia in the macaca mulatta. J. Comp. Neurol., **85**: 67–92.

WOODBURY, D. M. 1958. Symposium discussion. In W. F. WINDLE, (Editor), *Biology of Neuroglia*. Charles C Thomas, Publisher, Springfield, Ill., pp. 120–127.

WOODBURY, D. M. 1965. Blood-cerebrospinal fluid-brain fluid relations. In T. C. RUCH AND H. D. PATTON (Editors), *Physiology and Biophysics*. W. B. Saunders, Company, Philadelphia, pp. 942–950.

WOOLLARD, H. H. 1935. Observations on the terminations of cutaneous nerves. Brain, **58**: 352–367.

WOOLLARD, H. H., AND HARPMAN, J. A. 1940. The connections of the inferior colliculus and dorsal nucleus of the lateral lemniscus. J. Anat., **74**: 441–458.

WOOLSEY, C. N. 1947. Patterns of sensory representation in the cerebral cortex. Fed. Proc., **6**: 437–441.

WOOLSEY, C. N. 1958. Organization of somatic sensory and motor areas of the cerebral cortex. In H. F. HARLOW AND C. N. WOOLSEY (Editors), *Biological and Biochemical Bases of Behavior*. University of Wisconsin, Madison, Wisc., pp. 63–81.

WOOLSEY, C. N., AND FAIRMAN, D. 1946. Contralateral, ipsilateral and bilateral representation of cutaneous receptors in somatic areas I and II of the cerebral cortex of pigs, sheep and other mammals. Surgery, **19**: 684–702.

WOOLSEY, C. N., SETTLAGE, P. H., MEYER, D. R., SENCER, W., HAMUY, T. P., AND TRAVIS, A. M. 1951. Patterns of localization in precentral and "supplementary" motor area and their relation to the concept of a premotor area. A. Res. Nerv. & Ment. Dis. Proc., **30**: 238–264.

WOOLSEY, C. N., AND WALZL, E. M. 1942. Topical projection of nerve fibers from local regions of the cochlea to the cerebral cortex of the cat. Bull. Johns Hopkins Hosp., **71**: 315–344.

WOOLSEY, C. N., AND WANG, G. H. 1945. Somatic areas I and II of the cerebral cortex of the rabbit. Fed. Proc., **4**: 79.

WYBURN, G. M. 1958. The capsule of spinal ganglion cells. J. Anat., **92**: 528–533.

WYCIS, H. T., AND SPIEGEL, E. A. 1952. Ansotomy in paralysis agitans. Confinia neurol., **12**: 245–246.

YNTEMA, C., AND HAMMOND, W. S. 1954. The origin of intrinsic ganglia of trunk viscera from vagal neural crest in the chick embryo. J. Comp. Neurol., **101**: 515–542.

YAKOVLEV, P. I., AND LECOURS, A. R. 1967. The myelogenetic cycles of regional maturation of the brain. In A. MINKOWSKI (Editor), *Regional Development of the Brain in Early Life.* F. A. Davis Company, Philadelphia, pp. 3–70.

YAKOVLEV, P. I., LOCKE, S., AND ANGEVINE, J. B. 1966. The limbus of the cerebral hemisphere, limbic nuclei of the thalamus, and the cingulate bundle. In D. P. PURPURA AND M. C. YAHR (Editors), *The Thalamus.* Columbia University Press, New York, pp. 77–91.

YOUNG, J. Z. 1949. Factors influencing the regeneration of nerves. Advances Surg., 1: 165–220.

ZACKS, S. I. 1964. *The Motor Endplate.* W. B. Saunders, Philadelphia, pp. 1–83.

ZANGWILL, O. L. 1960. *Cerebral Dominance and Its Relation to Psychological Function.* Charles C Thomas, Publisher, Springfield, Ill., 31 pp.

ZIMMERMAN, E. A., CHAMBERS, W. W., AND LIU, C. N. 1964. An experimental study of the anatomical organization of the cortico-bulbar system in the albino rat. J. Comp. Neurol., 123: 301–324.

ZÜLCH, K. J. 1954. Mangeldurchblutung an der Grenzzone zweier Gefässgebiete als Ursache bisher ungeklärter Rückenmarksschädigungen. Deutsche Ztschr. Nervenh., 172: 81–101.

SECTION I

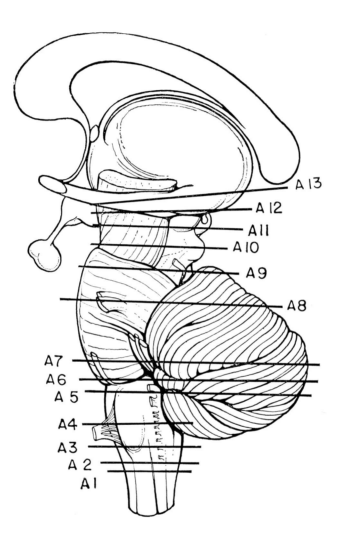

Brain Stem Atlas

Drawing of the brain stem indicating the level and plane of sections A-1 through A-13.

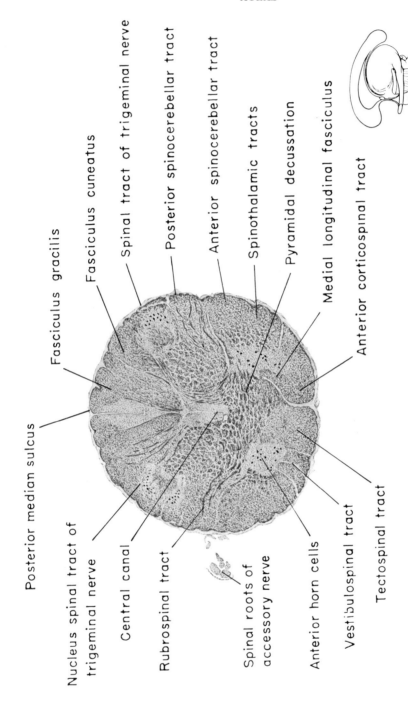

Posterior median sulcus

Fasciculus gracilis

Fasciculus cuneatus

Spinal tract of trigeminal nerve

Posterior spinocerebellar tract

Anterior spinocerebellar tract

Spinothalamic tracts

Pyramidal decussation

Medial longitudinal fasciculus

Anterior corticospinal tract

Nucleus spinal tract of trigeminal nerve

Central canal

Rubrospinal tract

Spinal roots of accessory nerve

Anterior horn cells

Vestibulospinal tract

Tectospinal tract

A-1. Transverse section of the caudal medulla near its junction with the cervical spinal cord. ×8.

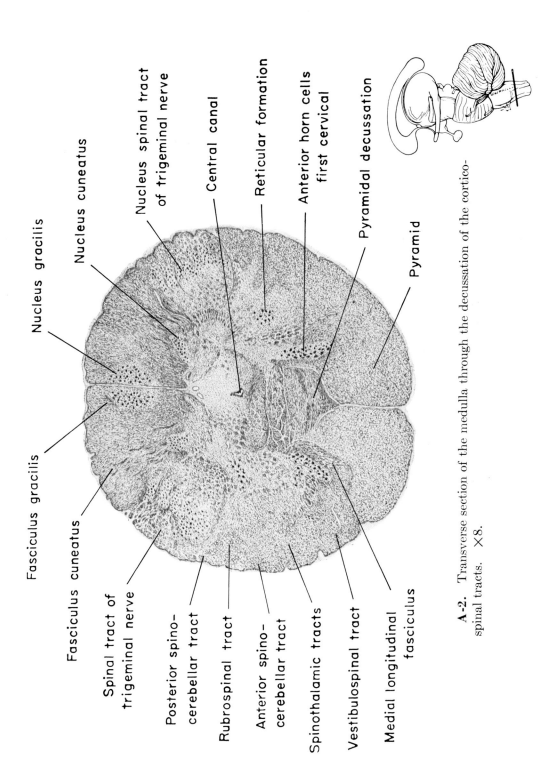

A-2. Transverse section of the medulla through the decussation of the cortico-spinal tracts. ×8.

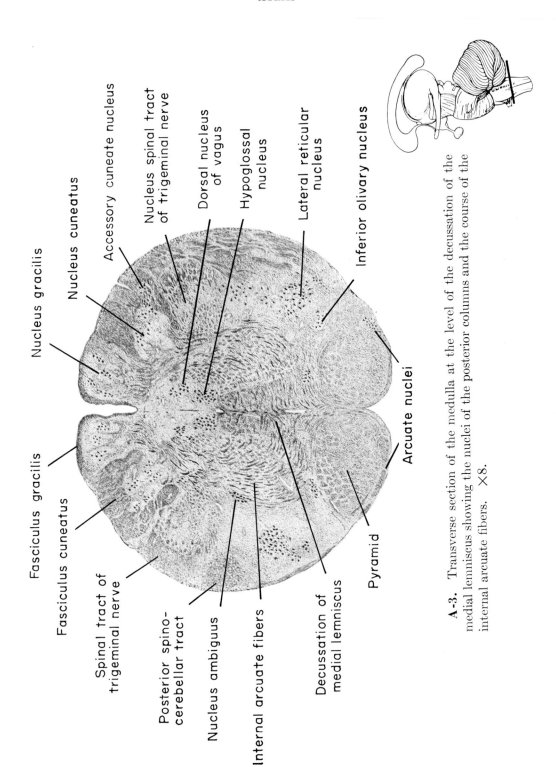

Fasciculus gracilis

Nucleus gracilis

Fasciculus cuneatus

Nucleus cuneatus

Accessory cuneate nucleus

Nucleus spinal tract of trigeminal nerve

Dorsal nucleus of vagus

Hypoglossal nucleus

Lateral reticular nucleus

Inferior olivary nucleus

Spinal tract of trigeminal nerve

Posterior spino-cerebellar tract

Nucleus ambiguus

Internal arcuate fibers

Decussation of medial lemniscus

Pyramid

Arcuate nuclei

A-3. Transverse section of the medulla at the level of the decussation of the medial lemniscus showing the nuclei of the posterior columns and the course of the internal arcuate fibers. ×8.

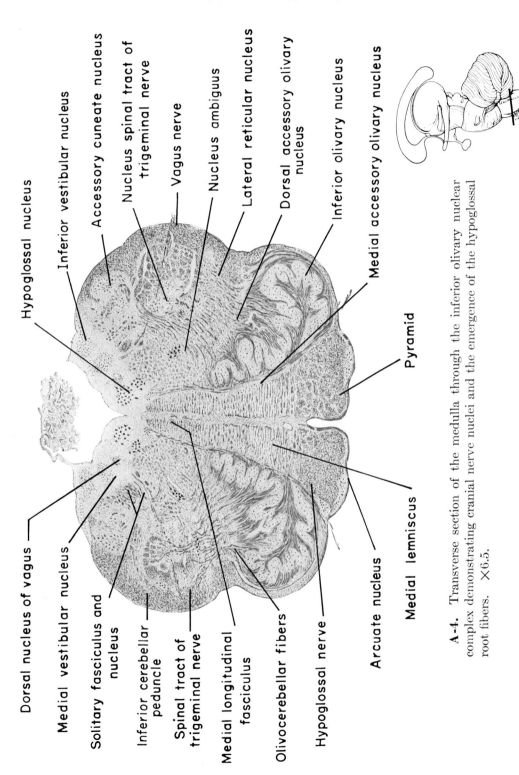

Hypoglossal nucleus

Inferior vestibular nucleus

Accessory cuneate nucleus

Nucleus spinal tract of trigeminal nerve

Vagus nerve

Nucleus ambiguus

Lateral reticular nucleus

Dorsal accessory olivary nucleus

Inferior olivary nucleus

Medial accessory olivary nucleus

Dorsal nucleus of vagus

Medial vestibular nucleus

Solitary fasciculus and nucleus

Inferior cerebellar peduncle

Spinal tract of trigeminal nerve

Medial longitudinal fasciculus

Olivocerebellar fibers

Hypoglossal nerve

Arcuate nucleus

Medial lemniscus

Pyramid

A-4. Transverse section of the medulla through the inferior olivary nuclear complex demonstrating cranial nerve nuclei and the emergence of the hypoglossal root fibers. ×6.5.

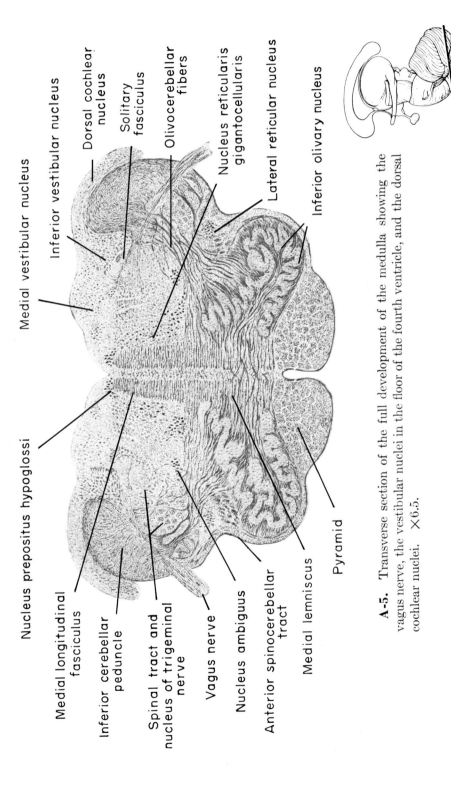

Medial vestibular nucleus

Nucleus prepositus hypoglossi

Inferior vestibular nucleus

Dorsal cochlear nucleus

Solitary fasciculus

Olivocerebellar fibers

Nucleus reticularis gigantocellularis

Lateral reticular nucleus

Inferior olivary nucleus

Medial longitudinal fasciculus

Inferior cerebellar peduncle

Spinal tract and nucleus of trigeminal nerve

Vagus nerve

Nucleus ambiguus

Anterior spinocerebellar tract

Medial lemniscus

Pyramid

A-5. Transverse section of the full development of the medulla showing the vagus nerve, the vestibular nuclei in the floor of the fourth ventricle, and the dorsal cochlear nuclei. ×6.5.

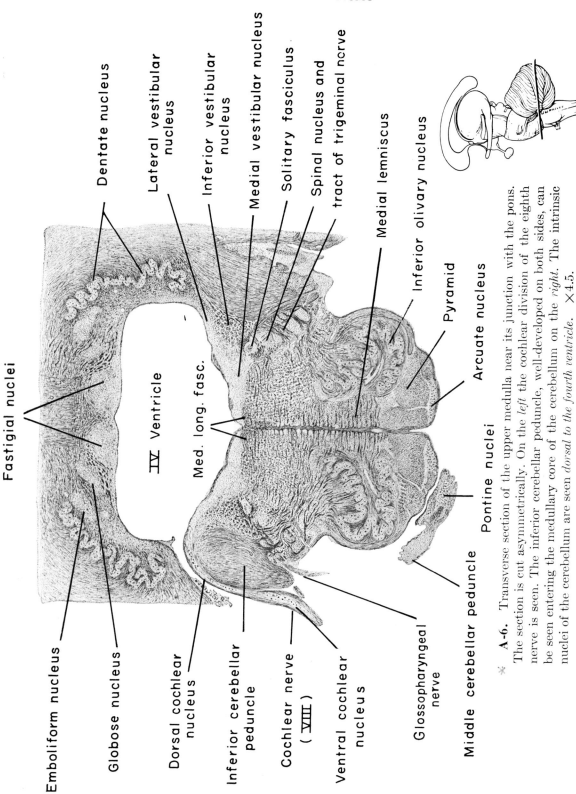

Fastigial nuclei

Emboliform nucleus

Globose nucleus

Dorsal cochlear nucleus

Inferior cerebellar peduncle

Cochlear nerve (VIII)

Ventral cochlear nucleus

Glossopharyngeal nerve

Middle cerebellar peduncle

Pontine nuclei

Arcuate nucleus

Pyramid

Inferior olivary nucleus

Medial lemniscus

Spinal nucleus and tract of trigeminal nerve

Solitary fasciculus

Medial vestibular nucleus

Inferior vestibular nucleus

Lateral vestibular nucleus

Dentate nucleus

Med. long. fasc.

IV Ventricle

A-6.   Transverse section of the upper medulla near its junction with the pons. The section is cut asymmetrically. On the *left* the cochlear division of the eighth nerve is seen. The inferior cerebellar peduncle, well-developed on both sides, can be seen entering the medullary core of the cerebellum on the *right*. The intrinsic nuclei of the cerebellum are seen *dorsal to the fourth ventricle.* ×4.5.

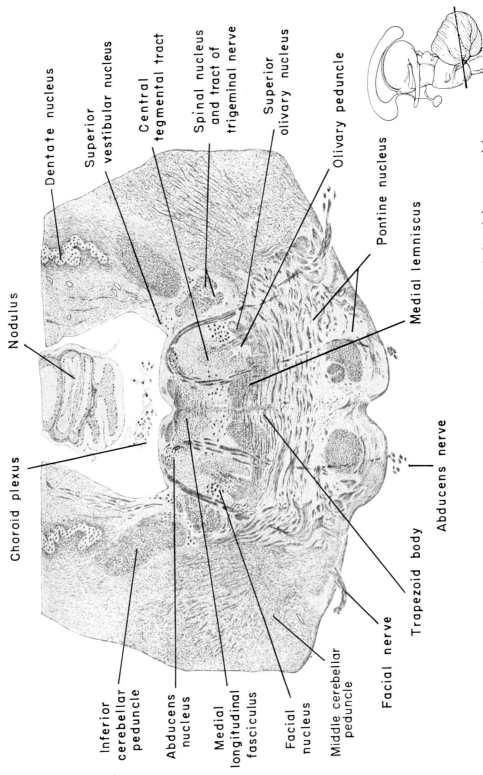

Dentate nucleus

Superior vestibular nucleus

Central tegmental tract

Spinal nucleus and tract of trigeminal nerve

Superior olivary nucleus

Olivary peduncle

Pontine nucleus

Medial lemniscus

Nodulus

Choroid plexus

Inferior cerebellar peduncle

Abducens nucleus

Medial longitudinal fasciculus

Facial nucleus

Middle cerebellar peduncle

Facial nerve

Trapezoid body

Abducens nerve

✳ **A-7.** Transverse section through the pons at the level of the abducens nuclei showing part of the course of the root fibers of N. VI and VII. The middle cerebellar peduncle, massive at this level, is seen entering the cerebellum. ×4.5.

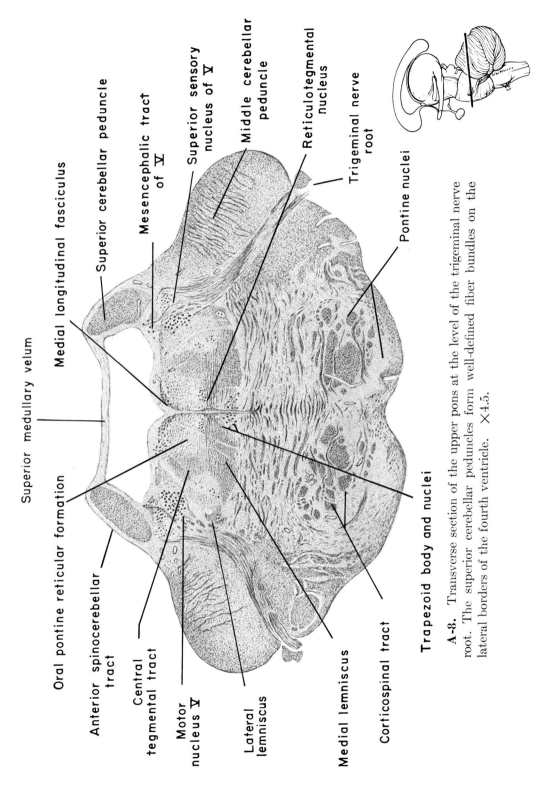

Superior medullary velum

Medial longitudinal fasciculus

Superior cerebellar peduncle

Mesencephalic tract of Ⅴ

Superior sensory nucleus of Ⅴ

Middle cerebellar peduncle

Reticulotegmental nucleus

Trigeminal nerve root

Pontine nuclei

Oral pontine reticular formation

Anterior spinocerebellar tract

Central tegmental tract

Motor nucleus Ⅴ

Lateral lemniscus

Medial lemniscus

Corticospinal tract

Trapezoid body and nuclei

A-8.   Transverse section of the upper pons at the level of the trigeminal nerve root. The superior cerebellar peduncles form well-defined fiber bundles on the lateral borders of the fourth ventricle.   ×4.5.

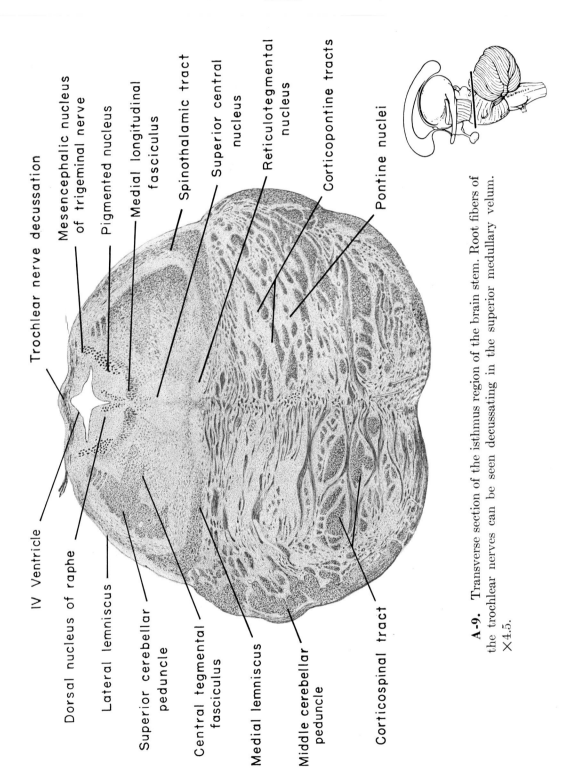

Trochlear nerve decussation

Mesencephalic nucleus
of trigeminal nerve

Pigmented nucleus

Medial longitudinal
fasciculus

Spinothalamic tract

Superior central
nucleus

Reticulotegmental
nucleus

Corticopontine tracts

Pontine nuclei

IV Ventricle

Dorsal nucleus of raphe

Lateral lemniscus

Superior cerebellar
peduncle

Central tegmental
fasciculus

Medial lemniscus

Middle cerebellar
peduncle

Corticospinal tract

A-9. Transverse section of the isthmus region of the brain stem. Root fibers of the trochlear nerves can be seen decussating in the superior medullary velum. ×4.5.

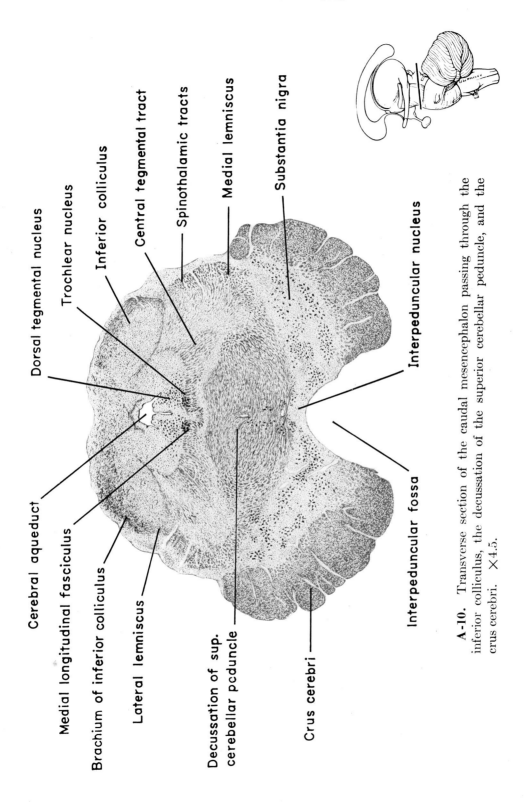

Cerebral aqueduct

Medial longitudinal fasciculus

Brachium of inferior colliculus

Lateral lemniscus

Decussation of sup. cerebellar peduncle

Crus cerebri

Dorsal tegmental nucleus

Trochlear nucleus

Inferior colliculus

Central tegmental tract

Spinothalamic tracts

Medial lemniscus

Substantia nigra

Interpeduncular nucleus

Interpeduncular fossa

A-10. Transverse section of the caudal mesencephalon passing through the inferior colliculus, the decussation of the superior cerebellar peduncle, and the crus cerebri. ×4.5.

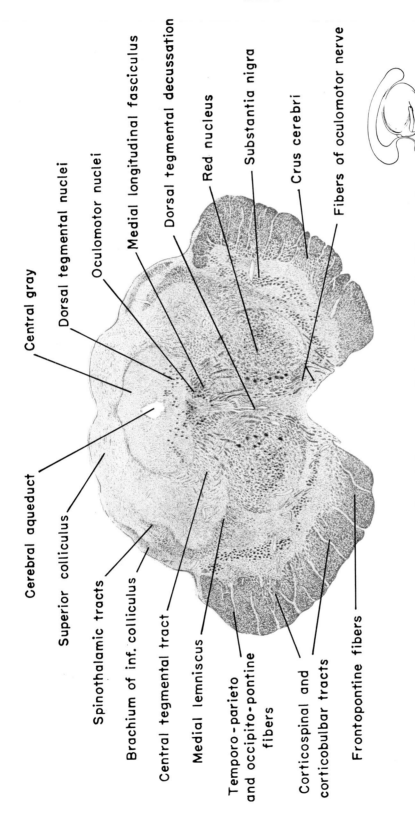

Central gray

Dorsal tegmental nuclei

Oculomotor nuclei

Medial longitudinal fasciculus

Dorsal tegmental decussation

Red nucleus

Substantia nigra

Crus cerebri

Fibers of oculomotor nerve

Cerebral aqueduct

Superior colliculus

Spinothalamic tracts

Brachium of inf. colliculus

Central tegmental tract

Medial lemniscus

Temporo-parieto and occipito-pontine fibers

Corticospinal and corticobulbar tracts

Frontopontine fibers

A-11. Transverse section of the mesencephalon at the level of the superior colliculus. ×4.5.

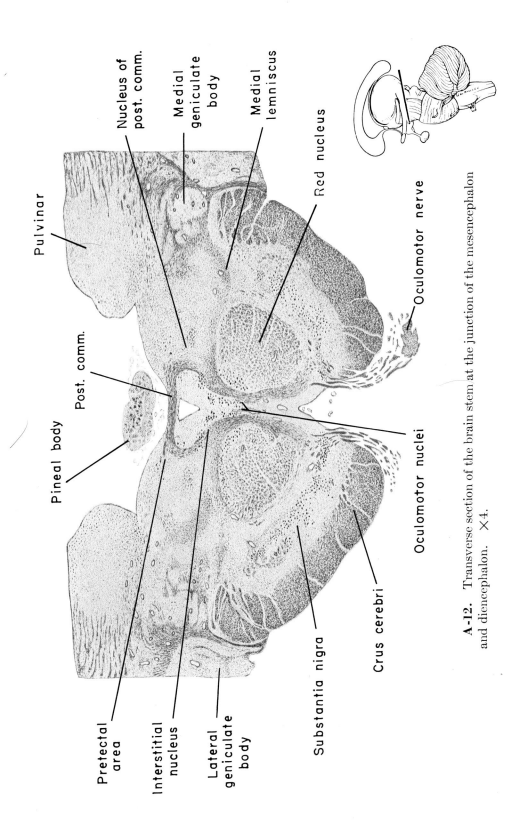

Pulvinar

Nucleus of post. comm.

Medial geniculate body

Medial lemniscus

Red nucleus

Oculomotor nerve

Pineal body

Post. comm.

Oculomotor nuclei

Pretectal area

Interstitial nucleus

Lateral geniculate body

Substantia nigra

Crus cerebri

A-12. Transverse section of the brain stem at the junction of the mesencephalon and diencephalon. ×4.

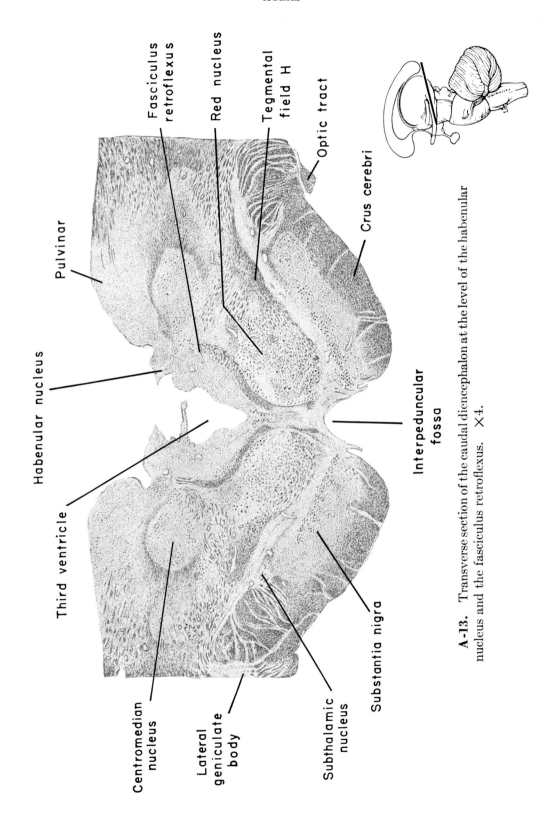

A-13. Transverse section of the caudal diencephalon at the level of the habenular nucleus and the fasciculus retroflexus. ×4.

SECTION II

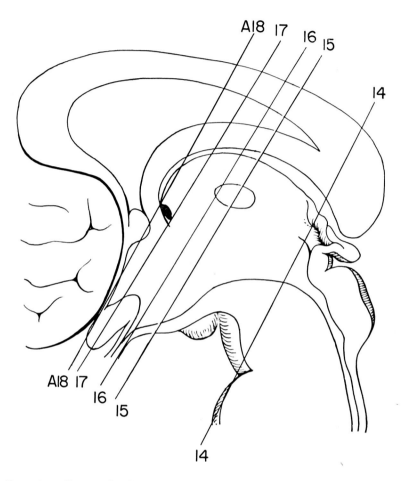

Outline of median sagittal surface of brain indicating level and plane of frontal sections A–14 to A–18.

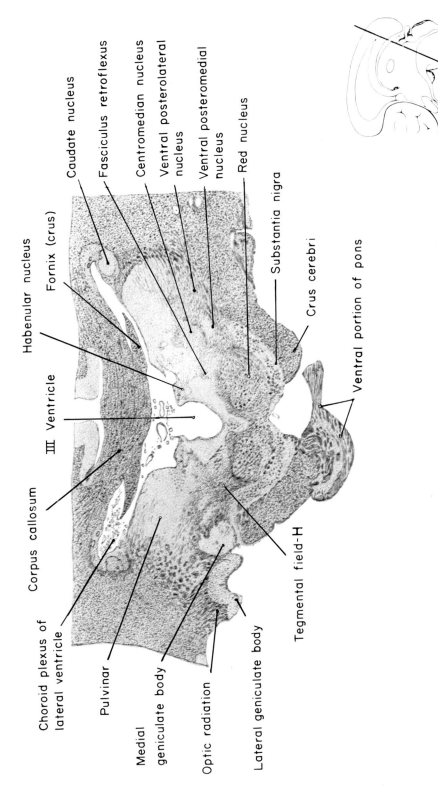

A-14. Frontal section through the junction of the midbrain and the diencephalon at the level of the habenular nucleus. ×2.5.

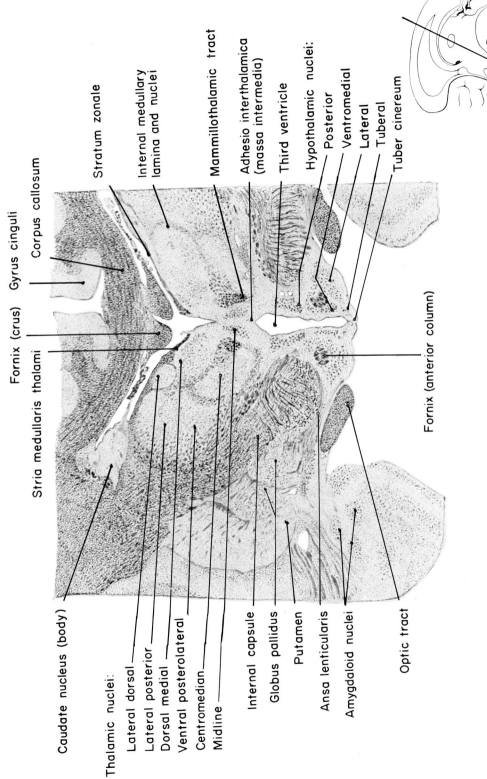

Gyrus cinguli

Corpus callosum

Stratum zonale

Internal medullary lamina and nuclei

Mammillothalamic tract

Adhesio interthalamica (massa intermedia)

Third ventricle

Hypothalamic nuclei:

Posterior

Ventromedial

Lateral

Tuberal

Tuber cinereum

Fornix (crus)

Stria medullaris thalami

Caudate nucleus (body)

Thalamic nuclei:

Lateral dorsal

Lateral posterior

Dorsal medial

Ventral posterolateral

Centromedian

Midline

Internal capsule

Globus pallidus

Putamen

Ansa lenticularis

Amygdaloid nuclei

Optic tract

Fornix (anterior column)

A–15. Frontal section through the diencephalon and lenticular nucleus at the level of the tuber cinereum and interthalamic adhesion. ×3.

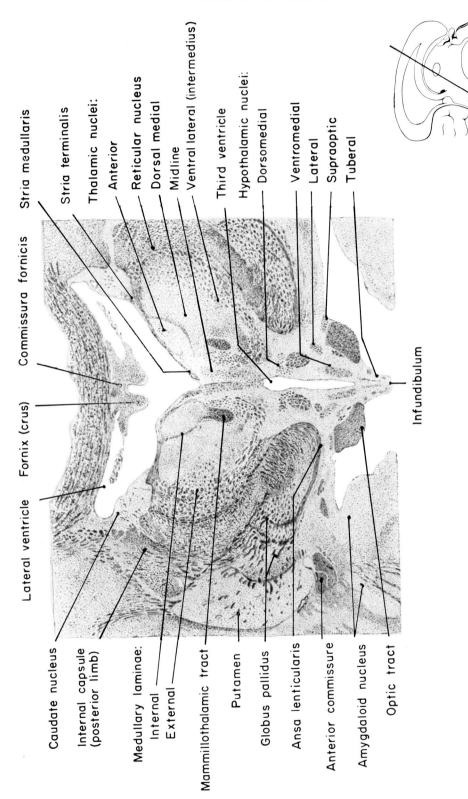

Caudate nucleus

Internal capsule (posterior limb)

Medullary laminae:
Internal
External

Mammillothalamic tract

Putamen

Globus pallidus

Ansa lenticularis

Anterior commissure

Amygdaloid nucleus

Optic tract

Lateral ventricle

Fornix (crus)

Commissura fornicis

Stria medullaris

Stria terminalis

Thalamic nuclei:
Anterior

Reticular nucleus

Dorsal medial

Midline

Ventral lateral (intermedius)

Third ventricle

Hypothalamic nuclei:
Dorsomedial

Ventromedial

Lateral

Supraoptic

Tuberal

Infundibulum

A–16. Frontal section through the diencephalon and lenticular nucleus at the level of the infundibulum and interthalamic adhesion. ×3.

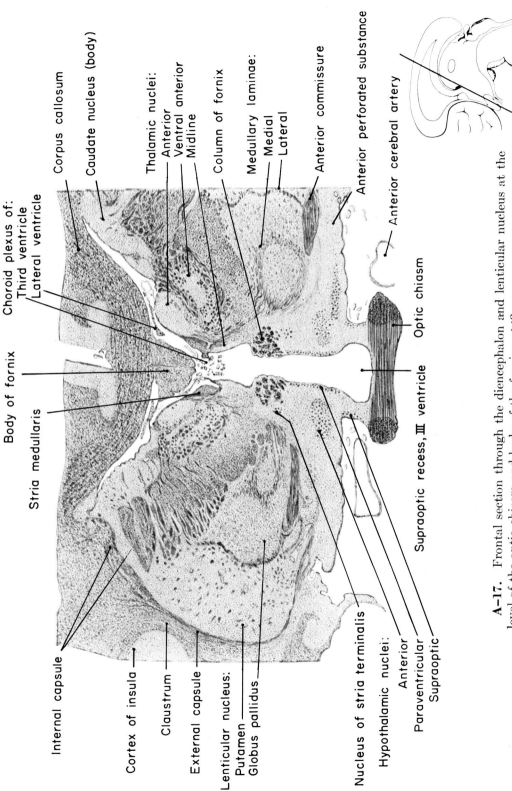

Corpus callosum

Caudate nucleus (body)

Thalamic nuclei:
Anterior
Ventral anterior
Midline

Column of fornix

Medullary laminae:
Medial
Lateral

Anterior commissure

Anterior perforated substance

Anterior cerebral artery

Choroid plexus of:
Third ventricle
Lateral ventricle

Body of fornix

Stria medullaris

Internal capsule

Cortex of insula

Claustrum

External capsule

Lenticular nucleus:
Putamen
Globus pallidus

Nucleus of stria terminalis

Hypothalamic nuclei:
Anterior
Paraventricular
Supraoptic

Supraoptic recess, III ventricle

Optic chiasm

A–17. Frontal section through the diencephalon and lenticular nucleus at the level of the optic chiasm and body of the fornix. ×3.

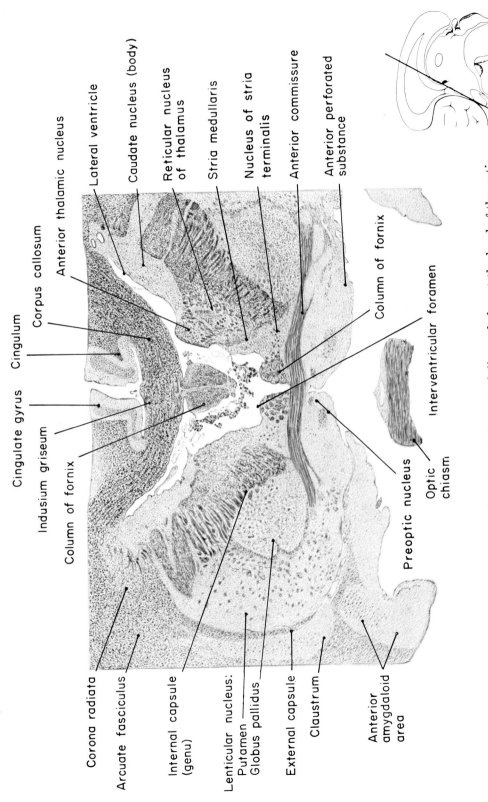

A–18. Frontal section through the rostral diencephalon at the level of the optic chiasm and interventricular foramen. ×3.

SECTION III

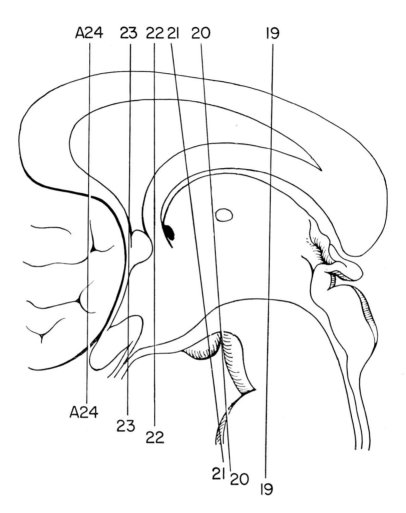

Outline of median sagittal surface of brain indicating level and plane of frontal sections A–19 to A–24.

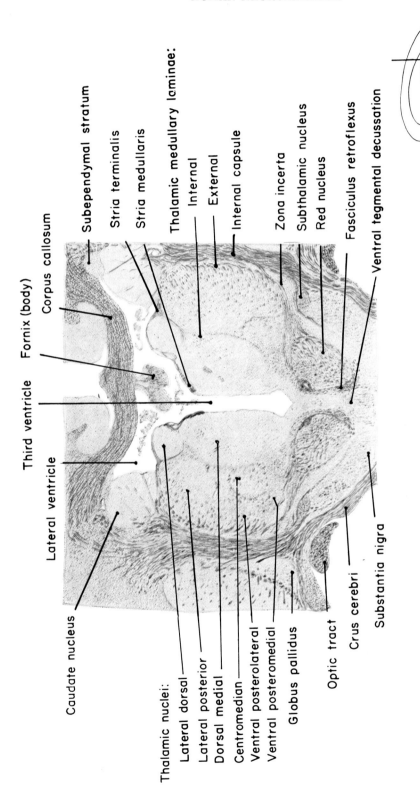

Thalamic nuclei:
Lateral dorsal
Lateral posterior
Dorsal medial
Centromedian
Ventral posterolateral
Ventral posteromedial
Globus pallidus

Optic tract
Crus cerebri
Substantia nigra

Caudate nucleus

Lateral ventricle

Third ventricle

Fornix (body)
Corpus callosum

Subependymal stratum
Stria terminalis
Stria medullaris
Thalamic medullary laminae:
Internal
External
Internal capsule
Zona incerta
Subthalamic nucleus
Red nucleus
Fasciculus retroflexus
Ventral tegmental decussation

A–19. Frontal section through midbrain and diencephalon at the level of red nucleus and posterior thalamic nuclei. ×2.5.

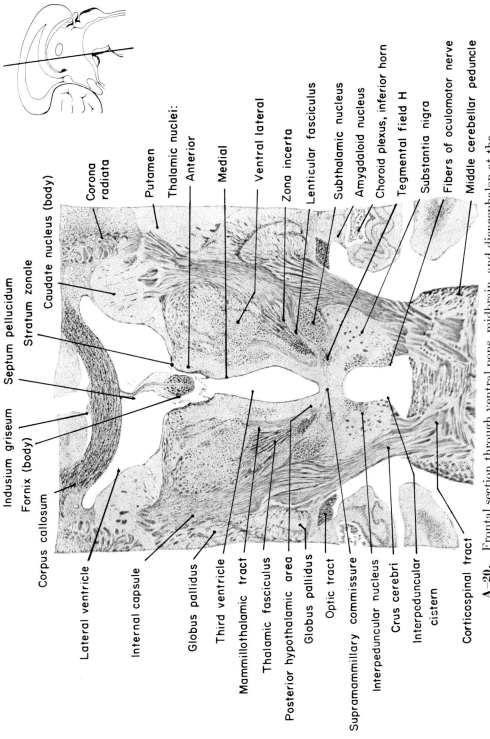

Indusium griseum
Fornix (body)
Corpus callosum
Lateral ventricle
Internal capsule
Globus pallidus
Third ventricle
Mammillothalamic tract
Thalamic fasciculus
Posterior hypothalamic area
Globus pallidus
Optic tract
Supramammillary commissure
Interpeduncular nucleus
Crus cerebri
Interpeduncular cistern
Corticospinal tract

Septum pellucidum
Stratum zonale
Caudate nucleus (body)
Corona radiata
Putamen
Thalamic nuclei:
Anterior
Medial
Ventral lateral
Zona incerta
Lenticular fasciculus
Subthalamic nucleus
Amygdaloid nucleus
Choroid plexus, inferior horn
Tegmental field H
Substantia nigra
Fibers of oculomotor nerve
Middle cerebellar peduncle

A–20. Frontal section through ventral pons, midbrain, and diencephalon at the level of the interpeduncular fossa and posterior hypothalamus. ×3.

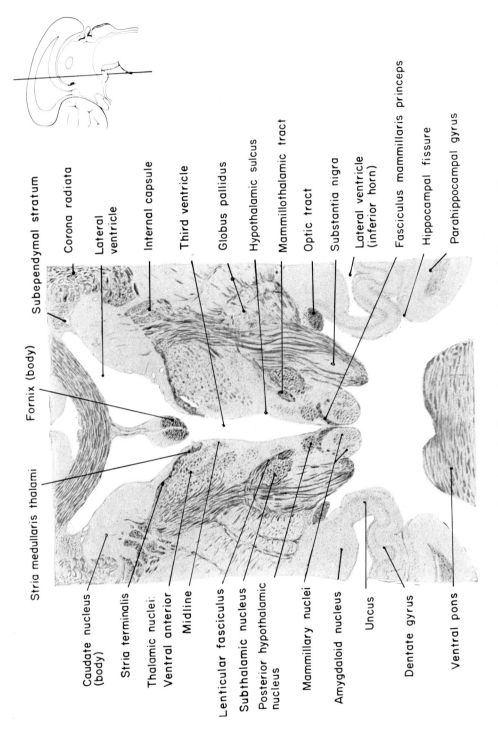

A–21. Frontal section through diencephalon at the level of the mammillary body. ×3.

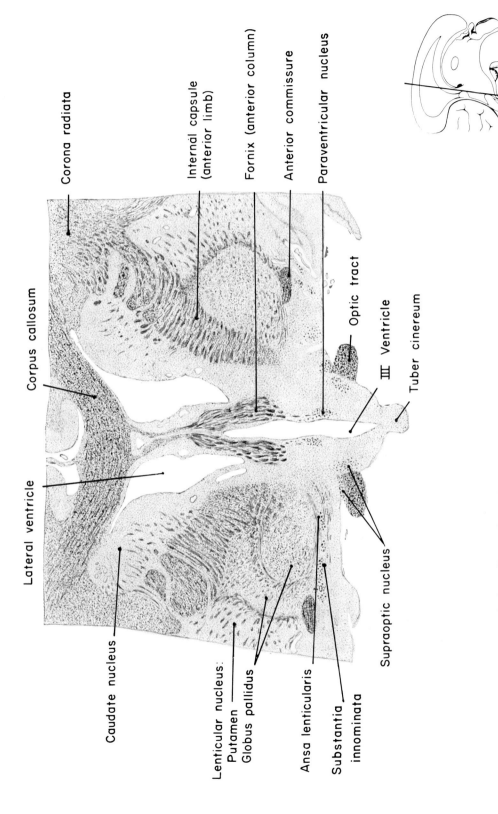

A–22. Frontal section through rostral hypothalamus and lenticular nucleus at the level of the tuber cinereum and column of the fornix. ×3.

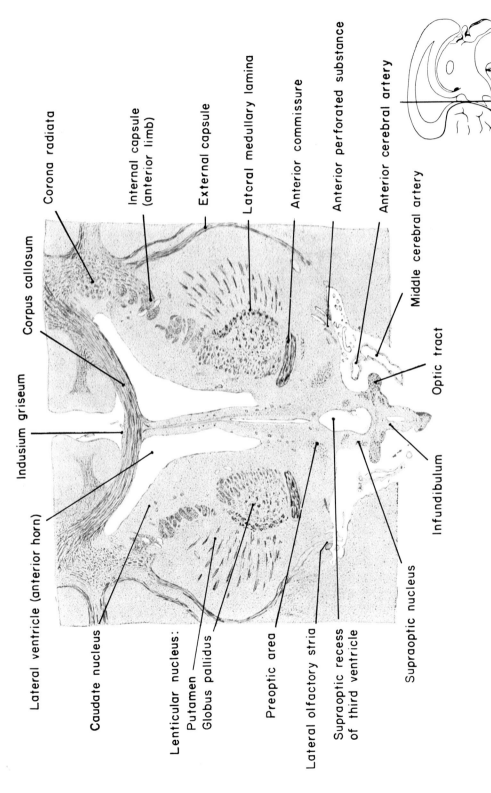

Lateral ventricle (anterior horn)

Caudate nucleus

Lenticular nucleus:
Putamen
Globus pallidus

Preoptic area

Lateral olfactory stria

Supraoptic recess
of third ventricle

Supraoptic nucleus

Indusium griseum

Corpus callosum

Corona radiata

Internal capsule
(anterior limb)

External capsule

Lateral medullary lamina

Anterior commissure

Anterior perforated substance

Anterior cerebral artery

Middle cerebral artery

Optic tract

Infundibulum

A–23. Frontal section through basal ganglia and anterior hypothalamus at the level of the infundibulum and anterior limb of the internal capsule. ×3.

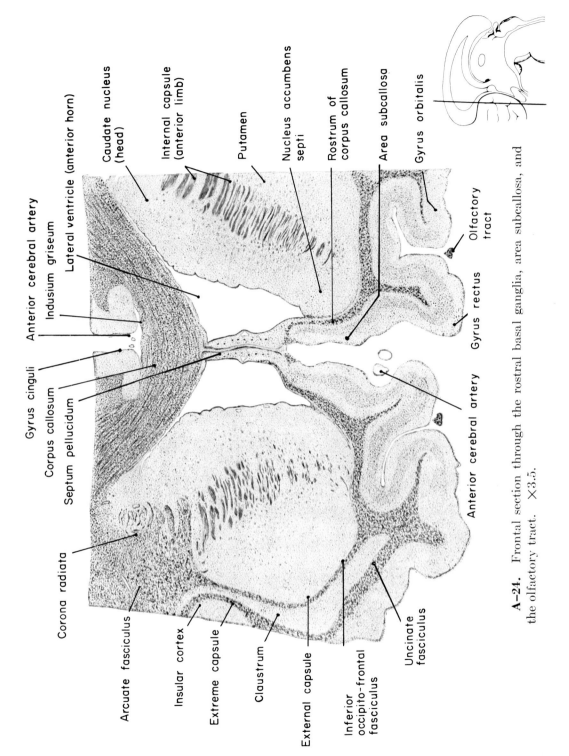

A-24. Frontal section through the rostral basal ganglia, area subcallosa, and the olfactory tract. ×3.5.

Caudate nucleus (head)

Internal capsule (anterior limb)

Putamen

Nucleus accumbens septi

Rostrum of corpus callosum

Area subcallosa

Gyrus orbitalis

Lateral ventricle (anterior horn)

Indusium griseum

Anterior cerebral artery

Gyrus cinguli

Corpus callosum

Septum pellucidum

Olfactory tract

Gyrus rectus

Anterior cerebral artery

Corona radiata

Arcuate fasciculus

Insular cortex

Extreme capsule

Claustrum

External capsule

Inferior occipito-frontal fasciculus

Uncinate fasciculus

SECTION IV

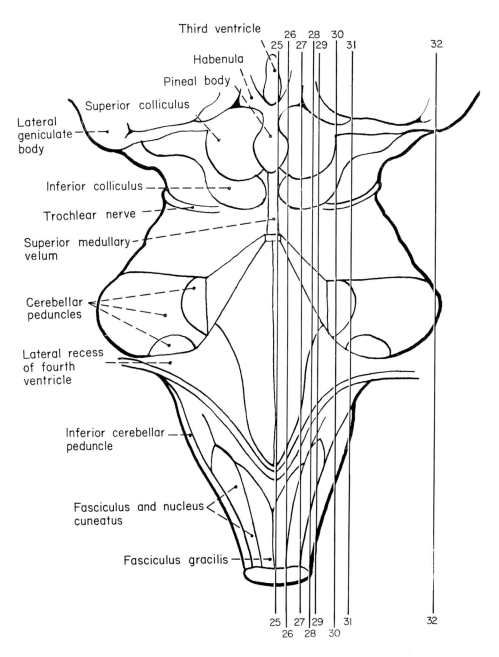

Outline of dorsal surface of brain indicating level and plane of parasagittal sections A–25 to A–32.

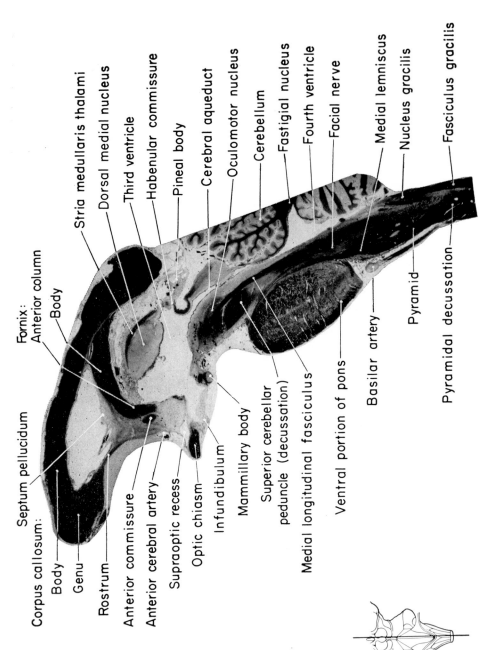

Corpus callosum:
Body
Genu
Rostrum
Septum pellucidum
Fornix:
Anterior column
Body
Stria medullaris thalami
Dorsal medial nucleus
Third ventricle
Habenular commissure
Pineal body
Cerebral aqueduct
Oculomotor nucleus
Cerebellum
Fastigial nucleus
Fourth ventricle
Facial nerve
Medial lemniscus
Nucleus gracilis
Fasciculus gracilis

Anterior commissure
Anterior cerebral artery
Supraoptic recess
Optic chiasm
Infundibulum
Mammillary body
Superior cerebellar peduncle (decussation)
Medial longitudinal fasciculus
Ventral portion of pons
Basilar artery
Pyramid
Pyramidal decussation

A–25. Parasagittal section through the ventricular system and brain stem at the level of the pineal body. × 1.5

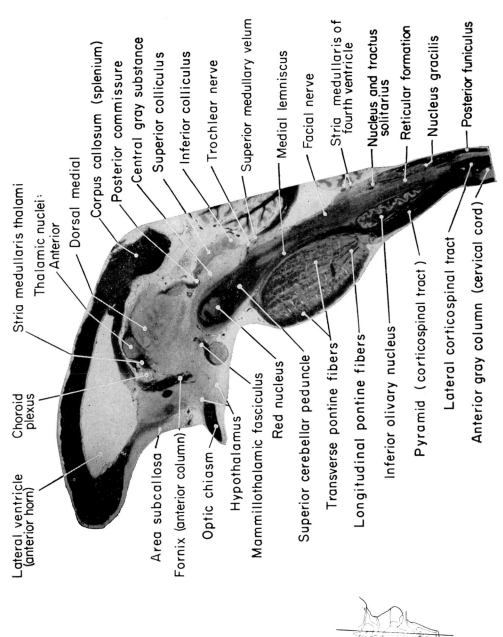

Lateral ventricle (anterior horn)

Choroid plexus

Stria medullaris thalami

Thalamic nuclei: Anterior

Dorsal medial

Corpus callosum (splenium)

Posterior commissure

Central gray substance

Superior colliculus

Inferior colliculus

Trochlear nerve

Superior medullary velum

Medial lemniscus

Facial nerve

Stria medullaris of fourth ventricle

Nucleus and tractus solitarius

Reticular formation

Nucleus gracilis

Posterior funiculus

Area subcallosa

Fornix (anterior column)

Optic chiasm

Hypothalamus

Mammillothalamic fasciculus

Red nucleus

Superior cerebellar peduncle

Transverse pontine fibers

Longitudinal pontine fibers

Inferior olivary nucleus

Pyramid (corticospinal tract)

Lateral corticospinal tract

Anterior gray column (cervical cord)

A–26. Parasagittal section through brain stem at the level of the nucleus gracilis and emergence of the trochlear nerve. × 1.3

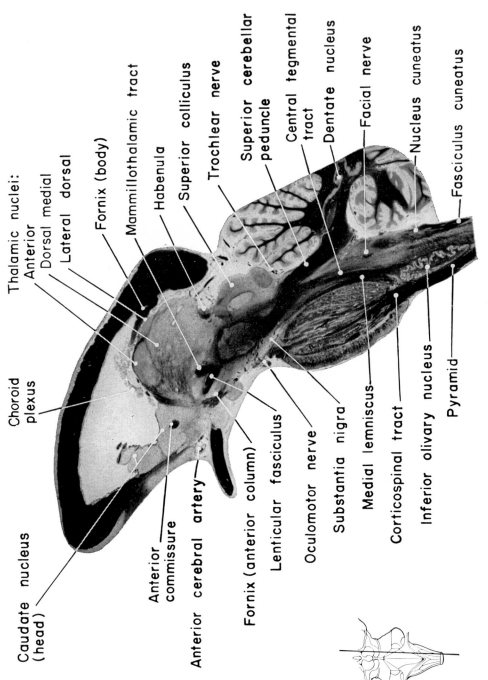

Caudate nucleus (head)

Choroid plexus

Thalamic nuclei:
Anterior
Dorsal medial
Lateral dorsal

Fornix (body)

Mammillothalamic tract

Habenula

Superior colliculus

Trochlear nerve

Superior cerebellar peduncle

Central tegmental tract

Dentate nucleus

Facial nerve

Nucleus cuneatus

Fasciculus cuneatus

Anterior commissure

Anterior cerebral artery

Fornix (anterior column)

Lenticular fasciculus

Oculomotor nerve

Substantia nigra

Medial lemniscus

Corticospinal tract

Inferior olivary nucleus

Pyramid

A–27. Parasagittal section through the brain stem at the level of the nucleus cuneatus and habenula. × 1.3

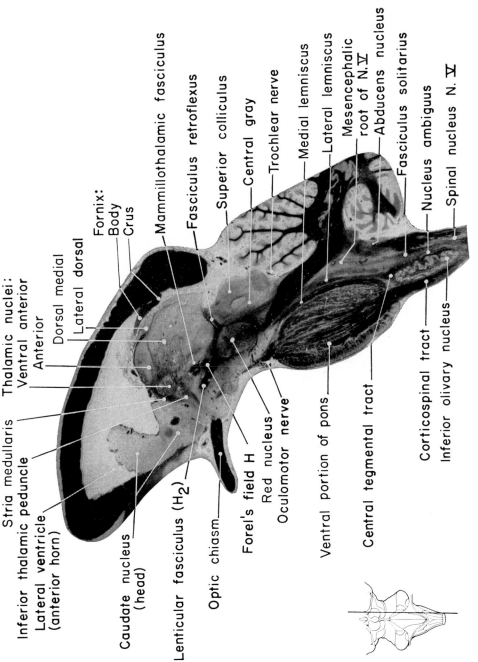

Stria medullaris

Thalamic nuclei:
Ventral anterior

Inferior thalamic peduncle
Anterior

Lateral ventricle
(anterior horn)
Dorsal medial

Lateral dorsal

Fornix:
Body
Crus

Mammillothalamic fasciculus

Fasciculus retroflexus

Superior colliculus

Central gray

Trochlear nerve

Medial lemniscus

Lateral lemniscus

Mesencephalic
root of N.Ⅴ

Abducens nucleus

Fasciculus solitarius

Nucleus ambiguus

Spinal nucleus N. Ⅴ

Caudate nucleus
(head)

Lenticular fasciculus (H₂)

Optic chiasm

Forel's field H

Red nucleus

Oculomotor nerve

Ventral portion of pons

Central tegmental tract

Corticospinal tract

Inferior olivary nucleus

A–28.   Parasagittal section through the brain stem at the level of the nucleus ambiguus, lateral lemniscus, and fasciculus retroflexus. × 1.3

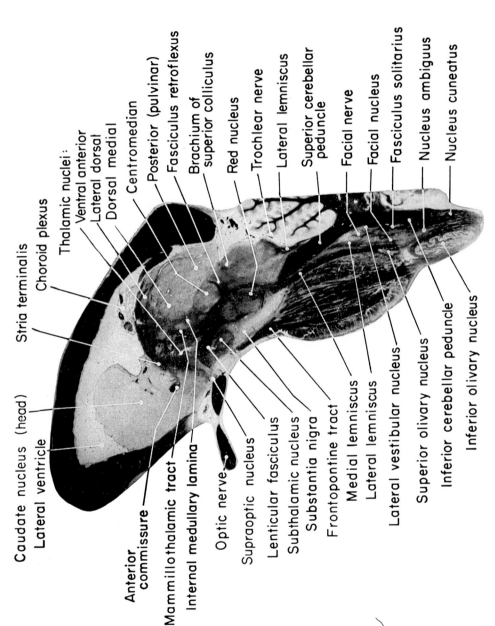

Caudate nucleus (head)
Lateral ventricle
Stria terminalis
Choroid plexus
Thalamic nuclei:
Ventral anterior
Lateral dorsal
Dorsal medial
Centromedian
Posterior (pulvinar)
Fasciculus retroflexus
Brachium of superior colliculus
Red nucleus
Trochlear nerve
Lateral lemniscus
Superior cerebellar peduncle
Facial nerve
Facial nucleus
Fasciculus solitarius
Nucleus ambiguus
Nucleus cuneatus

Anterior commissure
Mammillothalamic tract
Internal medullary lamina
Optic nerve
Supraoptic nucleus
Lenticular fasciculus
Subthalamic nucleus
Substantia nigra
Frontopontine tract
Medial lemniscus
Lateral lemniscus
Lateral vestibular nucleus
Superior olivary nucleus
Inferior cerebellar peduncle
Inferior olivary nucleus

A–29. Parasagittal section through the brain stem at the level of the facial nucleus, subthalamic and centromedian nuclei. × 1.3

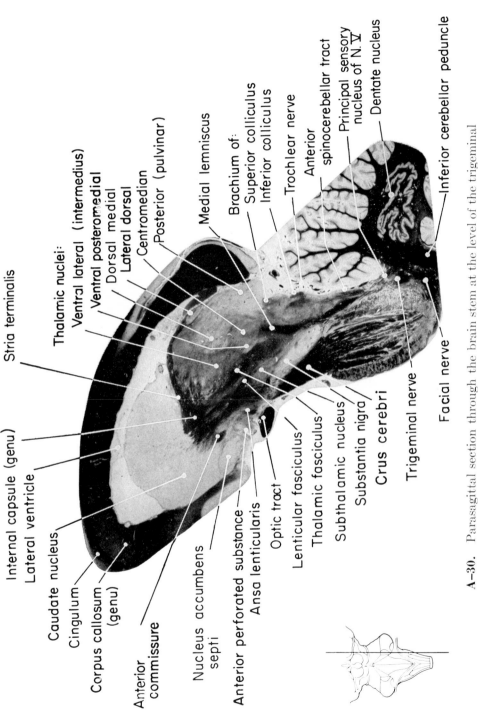

A-30. Parasagittal section through the brain stem at the level of the trigeminal nerve, brachia of the colliculi, and thalamic nuclei. × 1.5

Stria terminalis

Internal capsule (genu)
Lateral ventricle

Caudate nucleus

Cingulum

Corpus callosum (genu)

Anterior commissure

Nucleus accumbens septi

Anterior perforated substance
Ansa lenticularis

Optic tract

Lenticular fasciculus

Thalamic fasciculus

Subthalamic nucleus

Substantia nigra

Crus cerebri

Trigeminal nerve

Facial nerve

Thalamic nuclei:
Ventral lateral (intermedius)
Ventral posteromedial
Dorsal medial
Lateral dorsal
Centromedian
Posterior (pulvinar)

Medial lemniscus

Brachium of:
Superior colliculus
Inferior colliculus

Trochlear nerve

Anterior spinocerebellar tract

Principal sensory nucleus of N. V

Dentate nucleus

Inferior cerebellar peduncle

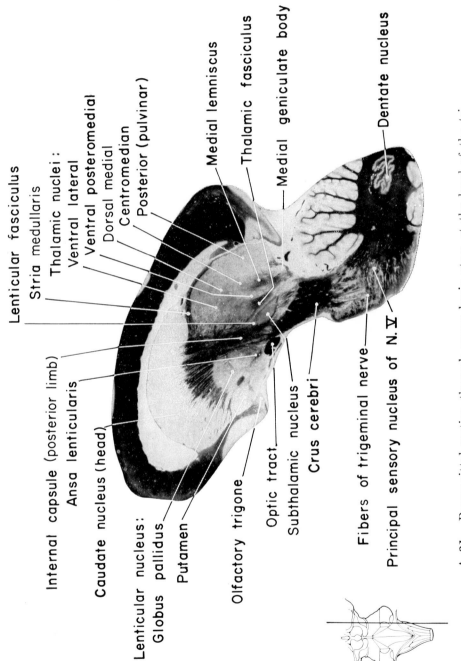

Lenticular fasciculus
Stria medullaris
Thalamic nuclei :
Ventral lateral
Ventral posteromedial
Dorsal medial
Centromedian
Posterior (pulvinar)
Medial lemniscus
Thalamic fasciculus
Medial geniculate body
Dentate nucleus

Internal capsule (posterior limb)
Ansa lenticularis

Caudate nucleus (head)

Lenticular nucleus:
Globus pallidus
Putamen

Olfactory trigone

Optic tract
Subthalamic nucleus
Crus cerebri

Fibers of trigeminal nerve
Principal sensory nucleus of N. V

A–31. Parasagittal section through upper brain stem at the level of the trigeminal nerve and the medial geniculate body. × 1.3

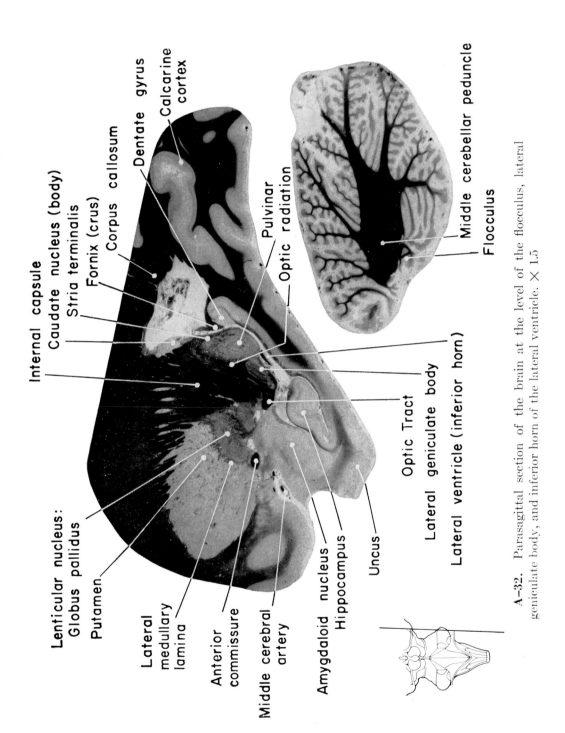

Internal capsule
Caudate nucleus (body)
Stria terminalis
Fornix (crus)
Corpus callosum
Dentate gyrus
Calcarine cortex

Pulvinar
Optic radiation

Middle cerebellar peduncle
Flocculus

Lenticular nucleus:
Globus pallidus
Putamen

Lateral medullary lamina
Anterior commissure
Middle cerebral artery
Amygdaloid nucleus
Hippocampus
Uncus

Optic Tract
Lateral geniculate body
Lateral ventricle (inferior horn)

A–32. Parasagittal section of the brain at the level of the flocculus, lateral geniculate body, and inferior horn of the lateral ventricle. × 1.5

Index

Boldface numbers indicate principal references. *Italic* numbers refer to illustrations.

Boldface numbers indicate principal references. *Italic* numbers refer to illustrations.

Boldface numbers indicate principal references. *Italic* numbers refer to illustrations.

Boldface numbers indicate principal references. *Italic* numbers refer to illustrations.

Boldface numbers indicate principal references. *Italic* numbers refer to illustrations.

Boldface numbers indicate principal references. *Italic* numbers refer to illustrations.

Boldface numbers indicate principal references. *Italic* numbers refer to illustrations.

Boldface numbers indicate principal references. *Italic* numbers refer to illustrations.

Boldface numbers indicate principal references. *Italic* numbers refer to illustrations.

Boldface numbers indicate principal references. *Italic* numbers refer to illustrations.

Boldface numbers indicate principal references. *Italic* numbers refer to illustrations.

Boldface numbers indicate principal references. *Italic* numbers refer to illustrations.

Boldface numbers indicate principal references. *Italic* numbers refer to illustrations.

Boldface numbers indicate principal references. *Italic* numbers refer to illustrations.

Boldface numbers indicate principal references. *Italic* numbers refer to illustrations.

Boldface numbers indicate principal references. *Italic* numbers refer to illustrations.

Boldface numbers indicate principal references. *Italic* numbers refer to illustrations.

Boldface numbers indicate principal references. *Italic* numbers refer to illustrations.

Boldface numbers indicate principal references. *Italic* numbers refer to illustrations.

Boldface numbers indicate principal references. *Italic* numbers refer to illustrations.

Nigral efferent fibers, **402–404,** *16-14*
 nigrostriatal, **402, 505**
 nigrothalamic, 402, *16-14*
Ninth cranial nerve, **324–326,** *14-19, 14-22*
Nissl bodies, **117–119, 119–121,** *6-1E*
 chromatolysis, **142–144,** *6-26*
 electron microscopic study, **141**
 granules, **121**
 material, **121**
Node of Hensen, 90, *5-1*
Node of Ranvier, **129,** *6-15, 6-16*
 electron microscopy of, **129**
 internodal length, **129**
Nodosal ganglion (*see* Ganglion, vagus, inferior)
Nodulus, 38, **405,** *17-1,* 420, 435
Nonspecific thalamocortical relationships, **485–488,**
 582–583
 association cortex, 555, **584–587**
 cortical electrical activity, **485–488,** 582–583
 local, 485
 recruiting response, **486–487, 583**
 microelectrical analysis, 583
 dendritic activity, **583**
 sleep, **583–584**
Noradrenalin, 138, 225
Notochord, 4, 90
 notochordal process, 90
Nucleolar satellite, **119,** *6-7*
Nucleolus, **119,** *6-7*
Nucleus (nuclei), abducens nerve, 299, **360–361,** *15-4*
 accessory nerve, **320–321,** *14-18, 14-19*
 accumbens septi, *A-24*
 ambiguus, 322, *14-18*
 amygdaloid (nuclear complex), 42, *5-12,* **498–500,**
  20-2, 20-4, 21-4, 523, 525, **539–541**
 ansa lenticularis, 452, **507,** *20-6*
 anterior horn, **247–248,** *12-4, 12-6*
 anterior median, **387**
 anterior, of thalamus, 448, *18-6,* 451, **454, 460,**
  19-4, 474, 484, **494**
 anterior olfactory, 519, **524,** *21-3*
 arcuate, 314, *14-16*
 association, of thalamus, **485–488**
 basal magnocellular, 249
 Bechterew (superior vestibular nucleus), **349,**
  15-11
 branchiomotor, of facial nerve, **357–358,** *15-2*
 caudal central, **385,** *16-9*
 caudate, 42, *3-13,* 66, 72, 452, *18-12,* **457,** *19-1,*
  19-9, **501,** *20-4,* 503, 504
 central, magnocellular, 249
 of thalamus (*see* centromedian)
 centrodorsal, 249
 centromedian, 448, *18-5,* **463–467,** *19-3, 19-4,* **485–**
  488, 579, **582**
 cochlear, dorsal, 330, *14-25,* **341–342**
  ventral, 330, *14-25,* **341–342**
 commissural, of vagus nerve, **323,** *14-12*
 cornucommissural, 249
 cuneate, 34, 259, *13-6,* 302, **306–307,** *14-8, 14-14*
  accessory, 273, **310,** *14-11, 14-15,* 421
 Dankschewitsch, **394–395,** *16-11*
 Deiters' (lateral vestibular), 282, *13-21,* 349, *15-12,*
  427–428, *17-17*
 dentate, **416–418,** *17-11, 17-14,* 434

dorsal, of Clarke, **249, 256,** *13-4,* **269–271,** *13-15,*
 273
 motor, of vagus nerve, **322,** *14-18*
 paramedian reticular, 317, *14-18*
 raphe, 337, 363, *15-21*
 sensory, of vagus nerve, **323–324,** *14-20*
 tegmental, **379–380,** 448, *18-6*
dorsomedial, 450
 of thalamus, 450, *18-8,* **461–462,** *19-2, 19-4,* **485,**
  493
Edinger-Westphal, *11-3,* **387,** 389, *16-9*
emboliform, 390, **418,** *17-11,* 426, *17-15*
eminentiae teretis, *see* medial eminence
facial nerve, **357–358,** *15-4*
fasciculus solitarius, **323–324,** *14-20*
fastigial, 416, **427–428,** *17-11, 17-16, 17-17,* **436–437**
Forel's field (prerubral), 446, 447, *18-8,* 497, **507,**
 20-5, 20-8
gelatinous substance, **249,** *12-15,* **255–256**
geniculate, lateral, 41, 441, *18-4,* **472–473,** *19-6,*
 19-11
 medial, 41, 441, *18-4,* **472,** *19-9*
globose, **418,** *17-11*
gracilis, 259, *13-6,* **302–306,** *14-8*
gustatory, 324
habenular, 39, *3-13,* **446,** *18-6*
hypoglossal nerve, **319–320,** *14-1, 14-3*
intercalatus, 320
intermediolateral, *11-3,* **248,** *12-8*
intermediomedial, 249
interpeduncular, 39, *16-4,* **380**
interstitial (of Cajal), 287, 353, 354, **394,** *16-11, 16-*
 12, 16-13, 446
intralaminar, 268, 318, 363, **398–401,** 426, 448,
 463–467, 485–488
lateral cervical, **268–269,** *13-14*
lateral lemniscus, **345,** *15-9, 15-21*
lateral reticular medulla, **314,** *14-18*
lateral, of thalamus, 461, **467–468,** *19-4*
 dorsal, 461, **467,** *19-4*
 posterior, 445, 461, **467–468,** *19-4*
lenticular, 42, *3-13,* **452,** *18-10,* **501–502,** *20-3*
hypothalamic, anterior, **491,** *19-14*
 dorsomedial, **491,** *19-14*
 lateral, 488, *19-14,* **491,** *19-15*
 paraventricular, **489,** *19-15,* **494**
 posterior, 489, *19-14,* **491**
 supraoptic, **489,** *19-14,* **494**
 ventromedial, **491,** *19-14*
inferior central (of raphe), 333
inferior colliculus, 39, *14-2,* **376, 378–379,** *16-2,*
 16-3
magnocellularis, 248
mammillary, 41, **448, 491,** *19-14,* **525–526,** 536
 intercalatus, 448, **491**
 lateral, 448, **491**
 medial, 448, **491,** *19-15*
mammilloinfundibular, 491
medial eminence, *14-2,* **338,** *15-4*
median central, 463
mesencephalic, of V, **368,** *15-18, 15-19*
midline, of thalamus, **462–463,** *19-2*
motor, of facial nerve, **357,** *15-4, 15-13*
 accessory, 357, *15-4*
 of spinal cord, **247–248**

Boldface numbers indicate principal references. *Italic* numbers refer to illustrations.

Boldface numbers indicate principal references. *Italic* numbers refer to illustrations.

Boldface numbers indicate principal references. *Italic* numbers refer to illustrations.

Boldface numbers indicate principal references. *Italic* numbers refer to illustrations.

Boldface numbers indicate principal references. *Italic* numbers refer to illustrations.

Boldface numbers indicate principal references. *Italic* numbers refer to illustrations.

Boldface numbers indicate principal references. *Italic* numbers refer to illustrations.

Boldface numbers indicate principal references. *Italic* numbers refer to illustrations.

Boldface numbers indicate principal references. *Italic* numbers refer to illustrations.

Boldface numbers indicate principal references. *Italic* numbers refer to illustrations.

Boldface numbers indicate principal references. *Italic* numbers refer to illustrations.

Boldface numbers indicate principal references. *Italic* numbers refer to illustrations.

Boldface numbers indicate principal references. *Italic* numbers refer to illustrations.